# THE SHORTER PEPYS

# THE SHORTER PEPYS

SELECTED AND EDITED
BY
ROBERT LATHAM

from
*The Diary of Samuel Pepys, a new and complete transcription,*
edited by Robert Latham and William Matthews

UNIVERSITY OF CALIFORNIA PRESS
BERKELEY, LOS ANGELES

Published in the United States by
the University of California Press, 1985.
Published in Great Britain by Bell & Hyman Ltd, London

The selection in this volume is taken from
*The Diary of Samuel Pepys, a new and complete transcription*
edited by Robert Latham and William Matthews,
Volumes I–XI, 1970–83, published by
the University of California Press.

ISBN: 0-520-03426-0
Library of Congress Catalog Number 85-040210

Designed by Malcolm Harvey Young

Produced in Great Britain

# CONTENTS

# CONTENTS

# -✤LIST OF ILLUSTRATIONS✤-

# —❧LIST OF MAPS❧—

# —❧GENEALOGICAL TABLES❧—

xi

# ⟡ PREFACE ⟡

The manuscript of the diary survives in the Pepys Library at
Magdalene College, Cambridge, and consists of six leather-bound
volumes neatly written in ink on unruled paper.[1] The writing is in
shorthand, with occasional words (mostly personal and place
names) in longhand. The shorthand Pepys used was a system of
'tachygraphy' invented by Thomas Shelton (1601–?50) whose
manual of instruction on the subject Pepys bought – in the 1642
edition – as a young man.[2] Isaac Newton occasionally employed
the same system. The art of abbreviating words by means of
letters or symbols is an old one – we owe to it the records of some
of St Paul's Epistles and some of Cicero's Orations – and although
it did not become a widespread accomplishment in its more
sophisticated forms until its use in business in the late nineteenth
century, it was in demand in England from Elizabethan times
onwards – among lawyers and their clerks, for instance, as a
means of recording evidence and case-reports, and among the
general public for a variety of purposes, but particularly (with the
growth of Puritanism in the seventeenth century) as a method of
taking notes of sermons. Pepys, who appears to have learned it as
an undergraduate, used it throughout the rest of his life both for
private and official business.

The presence of the diary volumes in the Pepys Library was
hardly noticed until the diary of his friend John Evelyn was
published in 1818. The Master of Magdalene then arranged for a
few pages to be transcribed by his uncle, the statesman Lord
Grenville, who had used shorthand as a law student. With this to
help him, John Smith, an undergraduate of St John's College, was
employed on the gigantic task of transcribing the whole diary. A
small bowdlerised selection from his fifty-four notebooks was
published in 1825 by the 3rd Lord Braybrooke, the Master's
brother, under the imprint of Henry Colburn. It had an immediate
success, and Braybrooke was encouraged to bring out a re-issue in

1828 and further editions in 1848–9 and 1854, adding to each new edition a few more notes and a few more words of the text. After his death in 1858 a second transcription was made by the Rev. Mynors Bright, a classical scholar and Fellow of Magdalene, and was published in 1875–9 in six volumes, by a different publisher, Bickers. Bright provided a more generous selection of the original (some four-fifths) than Braybrooke in any of his versions, but, discouraged by its reception from the reviewers, who were scathing about its lack of annotation, he insisted on having no more than one thousand copies printed. The way was thus open for another editor. Bright died in 1883, bequeathing to Magdalene the manuscript of his transcription (which, like Smith's, was complete except for certain passages considered unprintable), and expressing the wish that if it were ever to be published, it should be brought out by George Bell & Son, who had acquired the rights in the Braybrooke editions. Bell and Magdalene then arranged for the production of a new edition. It was an expanded and slightly revised version of Bright's six volumes and was edited by H. B. Wheatley, a London bibliographer and antiquarian, who had already declared an interest in Pepys by constructing the index to Bright's edition and by publishing *Samuel Pepys and the World he lived in* (1880). Wheatley's edition came out between 1893 and 1899 in ten volumes. About nine-tenths of the diary were now made public: the only omissions (apart from five days' entries overlooked by accident) were about a hundred brief passages which could hardly have been published in Victorian England without offence. More regrettable from a broader point of view was the fact that the text Wheatley used (almost entirely the work[3] of Bright) was peppered with inaccuracies, and that he saw fit to smooth out the occasional rough edges of Pepys's prose. His commentary, while an improvement on those of his predecessors, was patchy and thin, and fell short of the best standards of his day.

The text from which the present selection has been made is that of the edition of 1970–83, edited by myself and the late Professor Matthews, and is principally the work of Professor Matthews, who was an expert on seventeenth-century English shorthand and on the history of the language. For my part, I, as a historian, played a minor role in its construction, checking the readings and making suggestions wherever textual difficulties could be solved from a knowledge of historical fact or of Pepys's orthography and linguistic usages elsewhere than in the diary. The commentary, in which I had the help of several colleagues, was principally my responsibility. This edition, occupying eleven volumes, was the first in which the diary had been printed without excisions of any sort and in which the text had been equipped with a large-scale editorial apparatus. The present volume is a recension of that work, reproducing in reduced form its text and (to a less extent) its editorial commentary. It is designed for the reader who requires a version which can be contained within one volume but which at the same time gives a substantial proportion of what Pepys wrote.

The selection amounts to about one-third of the original million-and-a-quarter words. Something is lost in any selection – perhaps in this case the loss is principally the impression given by the full diary of the author's prodigious mental energy – but I have tried to make the abridgement as representative of the whole work as I can. There is no attempt to offer 'The Best of Pepys'. It is designed to reflect as clearly as its parent text Pepys's concern to write both autobiography and history, and his habit of reporting the usual as well as the unusual.

A variety of methods has been employed in making cuts in the text. The biggest reductions have been made by omitting entire entries – sometimes a whole succession of them. At other points sentences or paragraphs are sacrificed, and, on a few rare occasions, phrases are telescoped where this can be done without damage to the sense. For instance, at 27 May 1663, where Pepys reports parliamentary news from his cousin Roger Pepys, the words here given in italics are omitted: 'He tells me that the King hath sent to them [the Commons] to hasten to make an end by Midsummer, *because of his going into the country*; so they have set upon four bills to despatch'. (Neither at this point nor elsewhere are marks of omission inserted.) On the other hand, as often as possible, whole entries have been reproduced without abbreviation so that the reader may appreciate the virtues of Pepys's habit of recounting the full tale of each day's happenings and observations. Similarly, where he tells the story of a critically important episode – the Fire or the Dutch raid on the Medway or his affair with Deb Willet – there are virtually no excisions of any sort.

No alterations have been made in the original manuscript except for these reductions and a few (very rare) editorial intrusions (in square brackets) made in the interests of clarity, principally where Pepys's meaning has been made obscure by editorial compression. His accidental repetitions and omissions ('wife' for 'my wife' and so on) are left uncorrected where they do not impede understanding. They are very few and have a certain significance in that they reflect the fact that he was writing informally and not for publication.

The spelling follows that of the text in the eleven-volume edition and is as far as possible Pepys's own. He wrote plainly and only a handful of passages where the ink has faded or the writing is cramped are difficult to read. The problems of transcription arise rather from other causes. One is that the shorthand is inefficient in that it fails to represent diphthongs and to distinguish between long and short vowels (e.g. between 'bit' and 'bite', 'ris' and 'rise', 'down' and 'done'). It also makes it easy to confuse certain vowels when they occur between consonants.[4] A second source of difficulty is that Pepys often uses abbreviations in both the shorthand and the longhand, making the initial letter or syllable do service for the whole word. The longhand 'h', for instance, stands for all forms of the verb 'to have', and the choice between 'has' and 'hath' has to be made by the editor. Pepys's own longhand spellings in his letters of the period have provided the means of determining many of these doubtful points. Where names in longhand are abbreviated, the context usually gives the clue to the answer – as to whether 'WH' represents Will Hewer or Will Howe, or whether 'Exch' is the Exchange or the Exchequer.

In the case of certain shorthand words, the spelling is made clear by the shorthand itself – 'then' for the modern 'than', 'themselfs' for 'themselves', 'fallow' for 'follow' etc. In other cases, we can sometimes reconstruct a probable spelling from Pepys's longhand usages. (Certainty is impossible because his usages were far from consistent.) But in those cases where we have no guidance from the shorthand and no evidence from his longhand habits, shorthand words are spelt out in modern style. To this there is no alternative, since there was no standard seventeenth-century orthography.

Pepys's eccentric ways with capital and lower-case letters have

been followed faithfully in the belief that this gives an idiosyncra-
tic look to the page without presenting any serious difficulty to the
reader. His habit of writing headings to certain entries and titles of
books etc. in a longhand larger than usual is represented in the text
by the use of italics. His abbreviations of titles of rank ('Captain'
etc.) have been regularised in a modern style. As for punctuation,
the manuscript has very little because of the danger of confusion
with the symbols of the shorthand. Pepys uses full stops (representing them by a triangle of dots or a tick) to mark off phrases as
well as sentences. They have been printed as full points or as
dashes, according to their use. His brackets (always round) have
been retained; his colons (used as marks of abbreviation) have in
nearly all cases been replaced by full points. The hyphens are
mostly editorial though in a few cases they stand for Pepys's own
(which he represented by double lines). Pepys had no strict rules in
his longhand for apostrophes used to denote possession. He might
or might not insert them; and very occasionally he wrote out the
pronoun: e.g. 'Mr Pepys his meaning' (p. 679). Here they are
printed in all instances where Pepys employs them, and in the
shorthand they are inserted editorially in modern style. The
paragraphing is necessarily editorial since the reduction of the text
has altered the design of Pepys's own paragraphs.

At certain points short passages of editorial explanation are
added. For the rest the commentary has been kept to a minimum
in order to make room for a maximum of Pepys. The Index has
been designed to serve not only the normal purposes of an index
but also to a limited extent as a substitute for footnotes. There the
reader will find at selected points such items of information (taken
from the full edition) as can be conveyed in brief headnotes to the
entries. A few footnotes are appended to the text where there are
difficulties for the reader which cannot be resolved by this
method. A Glossary is provided at p. 1029, and asterisks within
the text direct the reader's attention to it at points where changes
in the meanings of words since Pepys's day might lead to
misunderstanding.[5]

*Notes*

1. See illustr., nos 22, 23, 24, 25.

2. *A Tutor to Tachygraphy, or Short-writing* (1642), which Pepys retained in his Library. Mynors Bright was the first of the transcribers of the diary to be aware of the fact that Pepys used the Shelton system. He himself learned it from this copy. It has been reprinted in facsimile, with an introduction by Professor William Matthews, by the Augustan Reprint Society (William Andrews Clark Memorial Library, University of California at Los Angeles, 1970).

3. The 'unprintable' passages omitted in Bright's transcription were supplied to Wheatley by Hugh Callendar, Fellow of Trinity College, a physicist interested also in stenography.

4. The vowel, when occurring between consonants, is indicated by their relative position, with 'a' in the top position, 'u' in the bottom, and the rest in between. It is thus easy to confuse adjacent vowels – 'a' and 'e', 'e' and 'i', 'i' and 'o', and 'o' and 'u'.

5. In 17th-century usage, for instance, 'Navy' meant Navy Office and 'officers of the Navy' its officials; 'amused' could mean bemused; 'family' often meant the whole household, including servants; 'of course' meant as usual and 'call' served for call on and call for.

# -ᴥ ACKNOWLEDGEMENTS ᴥ-

Since this volume is a reduction of the complete edition I must here renew my thanks – though I cannot for reasons of space particularise them – to the scholars who contributed to it. Greatest of all is my debt to my co-editor, the late Professor William Matthews, for his work on the text.

In the production of the present edition I have incurred other debts. Dr C. S. Knighton has constructed the Index and helped with the proof reading; Sir Oliver Millar, Surveyor of the Queen's Pictures, and Sarah Wimbush of the National Portrait Gallery have given me advice about illustrations; Hilary Evans has worked on the maps. I am grateful to them all. Finally I must extend my thanks for their invaluable help to Peter Cochrane, Mary Butler, and Elizabeth Brooke-Smith, my publisher's editors, to Mary Coleman and Aude Fitzsimons of the Pepys Library, and – as always – to my wife.

# -✣INTRODUCTION✣-

In his own lifetime Pepys was best known as a great naval administrator. To a select public he was also known as one of the leading amateurs of learning of his day and the owner of a remarkable library. It was not until the nineteenth century that he earned his widest fame – as a diarist. His diary was first published (in a heavily abbreviated form) in 1825. He had written it as a young man without any thought of publication, for diaries, though commonly enough written, were not thought suitable material for the printing press. In the Civil War a few military journals had been printed, and extracts from Archbishop Laud's diary had been published by his enemy William Prynne, but these were publicity exercises and quite exceptional. Diaries were, of their nature, private: Pepys kept his entirely for his own enjoyment. Hence its unselfconscious charm; hence too its frankness. More vividly and more completely than any other diary in the language it reveals both the writer and the world he lived in.

He was born in London on 23 February 1633 in Salisbury Court, off Fleet Street. His mother was a Londoner of simple birth, once a washmaid; his father, John, a tailor. But the Pepyses of earlier generations (mostly Cambridgeshire farmers) had included men of ability. In the fifteenth century they were bailiffs to the abbey of Crowland, and in John Pepys's generation there were several of his cousins who rose to eminence as lawyers – one of them, Richard Pepys, a Lord Chief Justice of Ireland under the Commonwealth. Of John's sons the diarist was the only one to show promise. Tom, a year younger, succeeded to his father's business, and died at 30. Another son, John, eight years Pepys's junior, made his way to St Paul's School and Cambridge, then drifted into Holy Orders out of want of ambition, but failing to obtain preferment was found a place by his brother in the public service as Clerk to Trinity House and later Joint-Clerk to the Navy Board. He made no mark in either post and died unmarried at the age of 36, burdened by debts which Pepys had to pay off.

Pepys himself was sent for a while during the Civil War to the grammar school at Huntingdon, and then lived, in all probability, with his uncle Robert Pepys of Brampton, who was steward to the Mountagus of Hinchingbrooke nearby. Edward Mountagu, the young squire of Hinchingbrooke – eight years older than Pepys and later his patron – was related to the Pepyses through his mother, a great-aunt of the diarist, and it is likely that it was at this time that he and the young Pepys became acquainted. Soon after the end of the war Pepys returned to London and was put to school at St Paul's, which he left in 1651 with an exhibition to Cambridge. He was probably meant for the law, and was at first entered at Trinity Hall, a lawyers' college, but before going up was transferred to Magdalene. What little we know about Pepys during his college days seems to be recognisably characteristic of him. He was awarded scholarships, he made friends, some of them close and dear ones, like Dick Cumberland (later a bishop) whom he later hoped his sister Paulina might marry; he was reprimanded for drunken misbehaviour; he knew at least one lady of the town; and he wrote an unfinished romance (later torn up) entitled 'Love a Cheate'.

Soon after taking his degree in 1654 Pepys entered the service of Edward Mountagu as his secretary and agent in London. Mountagu, one of Cromwell's young colonels in the Civil War, had broken with the army extremists and retired to his estates in 1648, but in the spring of 1653 had been returned as M.P. and at the end of the year had been made a Councillor of State in Cromwell's Protectorate. He now needed a man of business to look after his official lodgings in Whitehall Palace, and Pepys for his part needed a career. By December 1655 he was able to marry Elizabeth St Michel, a pretty fifteen-year-old daughter of a Huguenot refugee. His responsibilities mounted: in 1656 his patron was made a General-at-Sea, and, being away in the summers on naval service, and in the winters often away at Hinchingbrooke, he came to depend a great deal on Pepys's assistance. Pepys proved a faithful steward – prompt in the execution of orders, punctual and systematic in his accounts. Sometime in or after 1656 he was introduced to a post in the public service as clerk to George Downing in the Exchequer. He had, in a modest way, arrived.

But he had his setbacks. At some unknown date he and his wife had what he refers to in his diary as their 'old differences', and separated for a time; in March 1658 he underwent a dangerous operation for the removal of a kidney stone. By the following August, however, he had recovered and had settled with his wife and a maid in Axe Yard, Westminster.

Shortly afterwards, in September 1658, Oliver Cromwell died, and the republic which Mountagu and Pepys served lost the only leader capable of holding it together. Mountagu had supported, in vain, every proposal to make the Protectorate hereditary, as well as the more radical proposal to make Cromwell King. After Oliver's death he transferred his allegiance to Richard, his son and successor, but Richard was too diffident a politician to survive in the jungle rivalries which now broke loose. With his overthrow in April 1659, Mountagu distanced himself, in common with many other moderates, from the revolutionary cause. Despatched with a fleet to the Baltic in March 1659 to mediate in the war between Sweden and Denmark, he found himself increasingly at logger-heads with the government, in which unyielding republicans were now in the ascendant. He made contact with agents of the exiled Charles II, and in August brought home his fleet in circumstances which suggested that he was eager to take part in the royalist risings of that month. Arriving after their collapse, he found himself in disgrace, and retired to Hinchingbrooke for the winter. Pepys, who at the end of May had paid him a brief visit in the Baltic carrying letters from the government, remained in charge of his affairs in London. His letters to Mountagu on public as well as private affairs were one of the means whereby his master kept in touch with events.

In October the general officers of the army took over the government, dismissing the Rump parliament (i.e. what remained of the parliament of the Civil War) which had been in session since Richard's fall in April. But they no longer commanded a revolutionary army worth the name, and their men, unpaid for months, deserted in droves. The public, tired of political experiments, gradually set their hopes on a return to the old scheme of government, or something like it – a monarchy and a parliament. The most powerful section of the army, under General Monck in Scotland, had declared its opposition to the October *putsch* and

had moved south towards the border, giving silent encouragement to the belief that it would support the cause of a free
parliament – a parliament, that is, whose members would be
untrammelled by an oath to the republic. December saw the
collapse of the army's rule. On the 5th the London apprentices
mobbed the soldiers. On the 13th the fleet declared for a free
parliament, its example being followed soon afterwards by the
Dublin garrison and most of the army in Ireland. On the 19th the
Common Council of the City of London, already in touch with
Monck, secured a promise of a free parliament from Fleetwood,
Commander-in-Chief of the army, to whom this represented the
only hope of pay for his men. On Christmas Eve the rank and file
of some of the London regiments demonstrated in favour of a
parliament, and on Boxing Day the Rump was allowed to
reassemble. Finally on 1 January Monck moved his leading troops
over the Tweed, and on the following day began to march south.

On that same New Year's Day Pepys began to keep his diary.
For the first few months its entries are full of political news – the
establishment in February of a new government, effectively under
Monck, the elections to a free parliament in March and April, and
on 1 May the parliamentary vote for the restoration of monarchy –
'the happiest May-day', as Pepys wrote, 'that hath been many a
year'. Mountagu, made General-at-Sea with Monck, was ordered
to bring Charles II home from exile in Holland, and on 11 May set
sail from the Downs. He took Pepys with him as Admiral's
Secretary and Treasurer to the Fleet – a considerable promotion
for one who until then had not been much more than a domestic
steward. He was now addressed in correspondence as 'Samuel
Pepys, Esquire', dined with captains, and at The Hague was
presented to the King and his brother the Duke of York. His
standing with Mountagu was now higher than ever. On the fleet's
return Mountagu was showered with titles and offices, becoming
a Knight of the Garter, Earl of Sandwich, Vice-Admiral of the
Kingdom, Master of the Great Wardrobe, and Clerk of the Privy
Seal. At the same time he promised Pepys that they would 'rise
together'. In June he acquired for him a government post of some
importance – that of Clerk of the Acts to the Navy Board – as well
as making him one of his deputies at the Privy Seal. Alone among
Mountagu's entourage to be so highly favoured, Pepys now

moved house to the Clerk's official lodgings in the Navy Office building in Seething Lane in the City.

With this appointment Pepys's apprentice days were over. He was now one of the Principal Officers of the Navy, with two clerks at his beck and call, a handsome salary of £350 and the prospect of making even handsomer 'profits'. The Navy Board, under the direction of the Lord High Admiral of the Kingdom (from 1660–73 the Duke of York) dealt with the civil administration of the navy in much the same way as it continued to do until its abolition in 1832. It was responsible for designing, building and repairing the ships, managing the dockyards, victualling the fleets and providing most of their stores and equipment (apart from guns and ammunition, which were provided by the Ordnance Board). Reconstituted in 1660 after the Interregnum, when it had been replaced by committee rule, the Board now consisted, apart from Pepys, of: the Treasurer (Sir George Carteret, head of the office); the Comptroller (Col. Robert Slingsby in 1660, Sir John Mennes from 1661); the Surveyor (Sir William Batten); two Commissioners with general duties (Sir William Penn and Lord Berkeley of Stratton), and a resident Commissioner at Chatham, the largest of the dockyards, Peter Pett, the shipbuilder. Except for Berkeley, a soldier and courtier, all had seen service at sea or in naval administration. Pepys was not only young, but in naval affairs a tyro with only a few weeks of pen-pushing to his credit. But he had what was to prove of greater worth than either the rank or the experience of his colleagues – the mental powers, the physical vitality and the love of order which go to the making of a great administrator.

The diary tells the story of his developing skill and reputation. Within a few days of beginning his new work, he had resigned his Exchequer clerkship and, characteristically, was making an inventory of the Navy Board's papers; within a few months, he had familiarised himself with much of its routine and had asserted his rights as Clerk against the claims of his colleagues. By his capacity for hard work – starting at 4 a.m. in summer when necessary – he was setting a pace which no rival on the Board could match. Not that he was ever in danger of becoming a drudge: he was much too lively. His life was often a round of conviviality, music, theatre-going and philandering.

The year beginning in January 1662 with the issue of the Duke of York's Instructions to the Navy Board saw a marked advance in Pepys's progress as Clerk. He gave up his part-time work as Sandwich's deputy at the Privy Seal, redoubled his attendance at the office and took vows to protect himself against wine, women and plays. The diary for the spring and summer of 1662 speaks a new note: it chronicles the life of a single-minded official, learning a new pleasure – that of following his business. He remodelled many of the office books, he began to take frequent lessons from experts in shipbuilding, he learnt about the measuring of timber, and the stoving of hemp. From being a secretary registering the Board's decisions, he had become a leader: able to sway the Board, even against the arguments of Mennes and Batten, the Comptroller and the Surveyor, in the award of contracts; more knowledgeable than his colleagues on most matters, and the only one among them with a synoptic view of the office business. His growth in confidence and maturity is shown by his deliberately risking the loss of Sandwich's goodwill in November 1663. Sandwich had been openly conducting a love affair in Chelsea which threatened his family honour and had led to his neglecting attendance at court. Pepys, after much hesitation, wrote him a 'great letter of reproof'. His intervention earned him Sandwich's displeasure for a time, but the love affair was broken off.

'Chance without merit' had brought him into the navy, he told a friend on 1 November 1665; only diligence, he added, could keep him there. The test came in 1664–7 during the Second Dutch War, when the national effort turned on the navy, and when the scrutiny of parliament was fastened on the conduct of naval officials. At every turn the Board was hamstrung by lack of money. Generous though parliament was, it was not generous enough. Seeing so much at stake and so much going wrong, Pepys drove hard on colleagues, clerks and contractors. He roused the dockyards by surprise inspections, and rooted out some of the worst effects of corruption. Troubles mounted and multiplied; disaster and disgrace often seemed close. The war proved indecisive. The summer campaign of 1665 was fought to the accompaniment of the Plague; that of 1666 was followed in September by the Great Fire of London. 1666 saw also the loss of Pepys's patron: Sandwich was sent to Spain as ambassador in disgrace, having permitted irregularities in the disposal of prize goods. In June 1667, while peace negotiations were under way, the Dutch made a spoiling raid on the river approaches to the capital, carrying off from Chatham the *Royal Charles*, the pride of the English fleet.

Through all these difficulties Pepys kept his head, though not without fears for the outcome. He throve on work. In 1664 he was appointed a member of the Fishery Corporation. In 1665 he undertook the Treasurership of the Tangier Committee in addition to his other duties – an arduous appointment, but lucrative, gained in competition with a well-placed and high-born rival, Henry Brouncker. To live in the company of crisis stimulated him. Friendships and love affairs multiplied; theatre visits became more frequent; diary entries longer. In February 1665 he was elected a Fellow of the Royal Society, where he took his place as one of the amateurs of miscellaneous learning who constituted most of the Society's membership, and attended discourses and demonstrations on all manner of subjects – from comets and hydrostatics to French methods of baking bread – watching the experiments with a delight that was occasionally tinged with incomprehension.

But work for the navy remained his first concern. It was, of course, impossible for the Navy Board, under the spur of war – and of Pepys – to become, of a sudden, quite united and thoroughly efficient. It remained a prey to delays and corruption – its accounts improperly kept and in arrear, its meetings irregular. But it had its successes. It handled greater sums of money than had ever been granted for war purposes before; it made larger contracts; at Pepys's initiative it achieved reforms in the victualling system and the methods of checking pursers' and storekeepers' accounts. It was Pepys who defended the office before Parliament – his three-hour speech on pay tickets on 5 March 1668 was clearly a notable performance – and who in November 1669 drew up an eighteen-point memorandum replying with crushing effect to the report of the Brooke House committee which had criticised the office's conduct of its responsibilities during the war.[1]

By the time the diary ended in the spring of 1669, Pepys's professional and social success was well established. He was, in Albemarle's phrase, 'the right hand of the Navy'; master of an elegant household; owner of a coach and pair; rich enough to retire if parliamentary critics should oust him, as they had ousted Pett and almost ousted Penn. But although prosperous and successful, he was by no means free from care. He was just recovering from the effects of his wife's discovery in October 1668 of his affair with her companion, Deborah Willet. He was worried to distraction at times about his eyes, which since 1664 had been causing him such discomfort that at times they would 'ake, ready to drop out'. The trouble – which persisted to the end of his life – appears to have been a combination of long sight and astigmatism, for the latter of which there was no remedy available until the invention of cylindrical lenses in 1825. The eye-strain imposed by the hard work of the war years had not been eased by any of the remedies recommended by advisers and friends. Spectacles, paper tubes, bleedings, pills – all of them proved useless. Strong light now hurt his eyes acutely; the writing of the diary became so difficult that he convinced himself that he was going blind, 'which [is] almost as much', he wrote in his last entry, 'as to see myself go into my grave'. Sadly he drew the entries to a close at the end of May 1669. In the following autumn he took a long holiday in Holland, Flanders and France with his wife. A bare fortnight or so after their return Elizabeth died, at the age of 29, from a fever caught on the journey.

Pepys's marriage had survived the strains created by his infidelities, but principally because only one of them – the affair with Deb – had been brought to light. He had lavished attention on Elizabeth when she was unwell, but at other times had often been domineering and selfish. If she complained of loneliness and neglect, he would usually assume that it was enough to pity her, or to buy her a present, or to arrange for her to take lessons in music and drawing. Yet of his genuine affection for her there can be no doubt. Perhaps one of the reasons for his selfishness was that they had no children. At first, he had felt the lack of them; by September 1664 he seems to have become almost reconciled to childlessness, even glad of it.

As for the other members of his family, his mother had died in March 1667 at Brampton, the Huntingdonshire property left to Pepys and his father by Robert Pepys in 1661. Old John Pepys lived on there until 1680, made comfortable by an annuity paid him by Samuel. Paulina, Pepys's only surviving sister, seven years younger than himself – 'full of freckles and not handsome in face' – for long seemed unmarriageable, hard as he tried to find a suitable match. In February 1668, however, she was married off to a country neighbour, John Jackson of Ellington, with a dowry of £600 provided by Pepys. It was their second son John who ultimately became Pepys's heir.

The diary, once ended, was never resumed. The urge to record did not die in him, but his fear of going blind was even stronger, and he contented himself after 1669 with keeping occasional short journals.[2] His life at the conclusion of the diary had reached only its mid-point, and the major part of his career still lay ahead. In June 1673 he left the Navy Board for the Admiralty, where he became Secretary to the commission which took over most of the Lord High Admiral's duties when the Duke of York was extruded from office by the Test Act against Papists. In the following year he went to live in his new official lodgings at Derby House, in Cannon Row, by the Thames, south of the Strand. The problems of the Third Dutch War (1672–4) occupied his first few months of office. Afterwards he directed an epoch-making programme of recovery and reform, in the course of which not only were thirty new ships built – an unprecedented number – but also some of the basic elements of a professional naval service laid down. The practice of half-pay and superannuation-pay for sea-officers was extended; the duties of lieutenants defined for the first time, and an establishment introduced for naval chaplains. By 1678 the navy was a sizeable, disciplined force, and the Lord High Admiral's office (though still small) a government department equipped with a systematic body of records. For all this, Pepys himself – typical of a new school of civil servants who were transforming several parts of the public service at this time – was mainly responsible. He had been elected to Parliament (for Castle Rising, Norfolk, in 1673–8, and later for Harwich) and there he now spoke (a shade too portentously, his opponents thought)[3] for the navy. But he could be forgiven his pride. Not only was he, more than any other person of his day, the architect of a new fighting force, and of the administrative machine supporting it, but he was among the first to see that executive efficiency could never be achieved without an understanding with the parliament which provided the money.

In 1678–9 his career was checked by sudden disaster. His old master the Duke of York was accused by the authors of the absurd 'Popish Plot' of being involved in a French-inspired Catholic conspiracy to assassinate the King, poison the Queen and take over England by force for the benefit of the Antichrist of Rome. Pepys himself was accused in the Commons of being a secret Papist and of having plotted with his colleague Sir Anthony Deane, the shipbuilder, to sell naval secrets to France. He was forced to resign in May 1679 and along with Deane spent six weeks in the Tower. On being released he responded by throwing himself into the preparation of a vast armoury of papers in their defence, some of them collected by agents he sent to Paris for the purpose.[4] In the end no charges were preferred.

He now took up residence with his friend the wealthy bachelor Will Hewer, once his clerk, in a newly-built house in York Buildings, off the Strand. Occasional weekends he would spend with his old friend James Houblon, one of the greatest London merchants of his day, at a cottage in Parson's Green, near Hammersmith. Though no longer employed by the government, he was still a welcome visitor at court and was occasionally consulted informally on naval affairs. In October 1680 he was at Newmarket with the King and took down, at Charles's dictation, the story of his escape after the Battle of Worcester in 1651, during which he had hidden in the Boscobel oak.[5] Two years later he accompanied the Duke of York to Edinburgh. For a few months in 1683–4 he served as secretary to the expedition sent to Tangier to supervise its abandonment. He then kept once again a short-hand diary, but its affinities with the great diary are few and slight.[6] On his return, he was rewarded with employment. In June 1684 the King ended the inept rule of the Admiralty Committee appointed in 1679 and made Pepys his Secretary for Admiralty Affairs, a new post which he continued to hold after the Duke of York succeeded to the throne as James II in 1685. In modern terms, he now combined the duties of a permanent secretary of a department with those of a Secretary of State. At Pepys's suggestion James in 1686 temporarily suppressed the Navy Office and set up a Special Commission to perform most of its work. With its help Pepys set about restoring the navy to its former level of efficiency. In the only book he ever published, *Memoires*

*Relating to the State of the Royal Navy* (1690), he wrote a business-like account of his achievements. It remains a mystery why a public servant so eminent and so successful – and above all so close to the court throughout two reigns – was never knighted. It would have been out of character for him to have refused the honour if it was ever offered to him. But he had to be content with other honours – the Mastership of Trinity House (1676–7, 1685–6), the Mastership of the Clothworkers' Company (1677–8) and the Presidency of the Royal Society (1684–6).

He was in particularly close touch with James during his last days on the throne, one of his final services being to provide a yacht in which the infant Prince of Wales, whose birth had precipitated the crisis, was conveyed to France. Shortly after James's fall, Pepys fell too. He stayed in office for a few weeks in the Interregnum which followed James's flight, but resigned in February 1689, after William and Mary had accepted the throne. He never took the oaths to the new rulers. Apart from two abortive attempts in 1689 and 1690 to re-enter parliament, he now steered clear of politics. There were two brief periods in the same years when he was detained on suspicion of being a Jacobite plotter, but he fought off the charges without difficulty and settled down to enjoy the consolations of private life. He had moved house again in the spring of 1688 and was living next door to the house he had shared with Hewer. (Hewer himself moved to a splendid country villa he had acquired in Clapham.) Here he lived the life of an amateur of learning and a patron of the arts: conducting a large correspondence with the leading virtuosi of the time – Evelyn, Newton and Wallis among them – entertaining his friends with music and conversation, and above all attending to what was now his principal business – the improvement of his library. His collection, which included books, manuscripts, music, maps and prints, was vastly extended (he bought perhaps one-half of the total in these years of retirement), and with the help of his nephew Jackson and a clerk, Paul Lorrain, he put it all in order. Under his direction catalogues, tables of contents, and indexes were made, and written out in Lorrain's beautiful calligraphy; prints were sorted and pasted into albums; binders set to work, additional bookcases ordered. The climax came in 1699 when Jackson was sent off for two years on a Grand Tour of the

continent during which he was to make many invaluable pur-
chases. At times Pepys had not stirred out of doors for weeks and
months on end, being now frail in health and anxious to put the
finishing touches to his collection before it was too late. Last touch
of all was the provision he made a fortnight before his death, in a
codicil to his will, that the library after Jackson's death should pass
into the possession of his old college at Cambridge, there to be
preserved entire and unaltered 'for the benefit of posterity'.[7] Few
collectors have been so wise in their dispositions for the future.

In his last years he emerged only occasionally from these private
concernments to give service to a few public causes. He took the
lead, for example, as a Governor of Christ's Hospital, in reorga-
nising its constitution, and in reforming the teaching at its
mathematical school for the training of navigators which he had
played a large part in founding in 1673. For this work he was
given the freedom of the City in 1699. He was now content to
enjoy a quiet and well-regulated domesticity, his household being
presided over by Mary Skynner, with whom he had had a long
and affectionate association, never consecrated by marriage but
accepted as respectable by all his friends. Why he never married
her is a puzzle that has never been solved. He refreshed himself,
particularly after his health began to break down in 1697, by
prolonged visits to Hewer's large and imposing residence in
Clapham, and retired there finally in the summer of 1701. It was at
Clapham, on 26 May 1703, at the age of 70, that he died after a
long and painful illness, in the presence of Mary Skynner, Jackson
and Hewer and a group of household servants. Since the Revolution of 1688 his ecclesiastical association had been with the High
Churchmen who like himself refused to take the oaths to the
monarchs who had supplanted the King to whom they had
pledged their lifelong loyalty, and it was one of the most
distinguished of them, the scholarly George Hickes, nonjuring
Bishop of Thetford, whom he chose to attend him at his deathbed.
Hickes administered communion and gave him the absolution of
the church. He was buried beside his wife in the chancel of St
Olave's, Hart Street. Among those who attended the funeral –
apart from friends like John Evelyn – were the Archbishop of
Canterbury, the Bishop of London, members of the Board of
Admiralty, the Vice-President and several Fellows of the Royal

Society, Aldrich, Dean of Christ Church, Oxford, and Bentley, Master of Trinity College, Cambridge. The occasion was an impressive tribute to Pepys the Secretary to the Admiralty and Pepys the virtuoso – a man 'unexcelled', in Evelyn's words, 'in the Knowledge of the Navy ... universaly beloved, Hospitable, Generous, Learned in many things, skill'd in Musick, a very great Cherisher of Learned men'.[8] It has been left to later generations to recognise their debt to a Pepys even more universally beloved – the Pepys of the diary.

The practice of keeping diaries seems to have become increasingly common in England from Elizabethan times, and had several specific origins, apart from the growth of literacy in general. In many cases it was a development from the keeping of household accounts. In other cases it reflected an interest in travel – a favourite subject. But perhaps it was the habit of self-examination encouraged by Protestantism, and the growing interest in public affairs, that more than anything else stimulated the practice.

Pepys nowhere states why he kept one. He occasionally mentions his diary's usefulness (for example, in storing information that might help to protect him against parliamentary criticism of his official work, or to remind him of what tip to give to the parish sexton at New Year), but these were incidental benefits and could not have been in his mind when he started it. His reasons, like those of most diarists, are to be inferred from the diary itself. It is plain enough from the opening passages that he has clearly in mind what sort of diary he means to write. It is not to be a series of casual jottings about day-to-day events, or a baring of the soul in confession – two types of diary common enough at the time. It is to be a systematic account of his own affairs and also of what he calls the 'state of the nation'. As the diary continues, the two themes run in counterpoint, as it were, now one, now the other, taking over as the main subject. At each of the summaries he writes at the end of the year or volume, the narrative is halted so that he may sum up the private and public events in turn, in much the same way as he makes up his monthly and annual accounts of expenses and savings. As a result his diary has a firm and clear structure. One of its origins, therefore, must be the love of order and neatness that was so marked a feature of his temperament, and which shows itself in many forms – in his handwriting, his dress, his carefully arranged library and his taste for formality in the design of buildings and gardens. 'No man in England', Clarendon was once moved to say of him, 'was of more method'. The diary, fully and regularly kept, had the effect of imposing a factitious order on the succession of often random events that made up each day's experience. Besides the diary he kept other personal records, which already by the 1660s included letter-books, memorandum books, account books, a tale book and a book of vows. All were methods of canalising the stream of experience – the diary best of all because it was the most comprehensive and the most intimate.

His decision to start it seems to have been a response to the political excitements of December 1659. He began it immediately afterwards – with an entry for Sunday 1 January 1660: the start of a new week, a new month, a new year and (as he hoped) of a new political era. He bought a notebook bound in simple but rich brown calf, of the sort that stationers sold to customers who wanted something better than an everyday memorandum book, as a commonplace book of some kind. Its pages were ruled in red at the upper and outer margins. On loose sheets, or possibly in a separate book (he later refers to a 'by-book'), he began to make the notes and drafts which often preceded the composition of the diary itself.[9] All this almost entirely in shorthand, in the Shelton system he appears to have learnt at Cambridge. His writing habits were not regular, but he continued to compose it in much the same way, making entries every day or every few days, while his memory of events was still clear and their impact still fresh. Although he had plenty of opportunity to alter his entries if he had chosen to, he refrained, not even filling the rare blank where at the moment of composition he had been unable to recall a name. Being a man of system, he left virtually not a single day without a substantial entry,[10] so that he reveals his daily life from rising to dinner, from dinner to supper and from supper to bed throughout the whole diary period. Moreover, he took the trouble to write in continuous prose. Even when hard pressed for time, he was never content in the final version to make do with mnemonic words and phrases.[11] In the sheer technique of diary keeping – quite apart from the value of what he wrote – he has no equal.

Since he had an exact mind and an unflagging interest in everything that happened (as well as the means of writing quickly), it came naturally and easily to him to write in great detail, whether the subject was a coronation or a country walk or a quarrel with his wife. Evelyn has a graphic description of the Fire, but it is Pepys who notices the pigeons trapped on the window ledges and the cat that took refuge in a chimney-hole. It is this richness of detail that gives the diary its astonishing vividness.

The concern for detail follows from the thoroughness of his technique. Not everything is written down of course, but there is no important aspect of his experience (including his dreams) that is left without some record. No other diarist of his day attempted anything so comprehensive. Evelyn's diary (from 1620 to 1706) covers a lifetime, but is highly selective, being meant to be read by his descendants, and being rewritten to a large extent with that in view. The diary of Robert Hooke, the scientist and architect (1672–83), was regularly kept and covers a wide sweep of ground, but is thin, and often nothing more than disconnected notes. Other diarists, now deservedly forgotten, write irregularly and in the form of brief jottings, often using the printed almanacks whose increasing availability encouraged this sort of diary keeping. Others again might write voluminously, but on only one aspect of their experience – John Ray, John Locke or Celia Fiennes on their travels, Anthony Wood on university events, John Milward and Anchitel Grey on parliamentary debates, Ralph Josselin on village events as seen by a Puritan parson.[12] None of Pepys's contemporaries, as far as we know, attempted a diary in the all-inclusive Pepysian sense and on the Pepysian scale.[13] But thoroughness was second nature to Pepys, and he was as thorough in the writing of his diary as in his work as a public servant or his achievements as a bibliophile.

The small and passing everyday events are set down with great regularity – almost always what he ate and drank, and often what he wore. Although there are no extended passages of introspection, he rarely fails, when the matter warrants it, to record his thoughts. He keeps careful notes on his health, enters the more important of his occasional disbursements and at appropriate intervals summaries of his financial balances, and rarely lets many days go by without an account of his music-making, his reading, and his theatre-going. Little or nothing seems to be left for the Recording Angel to cover. Perhaps the extraordinary frankness and honesty for which the diary is famous is in a way a reflection of this thoroughness. He does not hesitate to admit to the record his fits of bad temper and jealousy, and the occasions when he was guilty of physical (and even moral) cowardice, of dishonesty in the office and of infidelity to his wife. These were facts and the record would be incomplete without them. There was little danger of prying eyes discovering them since they were all concealed in the shorthand, and some (the philandering episodes) concealed still further in a macaronic mixture mainly of English, French and Spanish. Moreover, to confess was also to remind himself of the need to reform. He often, after a lapse, renews his vows against self-indulgence. There was more than a trace of the Puritan in Pepys.

His history of public affairs is marked by similar thoroughness. There is no better contemporary account of the 1660s. His first-hand reports of the Restoration, the Dutch War, the Plague and the Fire have become classical. In addition he recounts the course of political events in close, almost daily, detail. He had had a passionate interest in politics from the days when he had raised a schoolboy's cheer at the execution of Charles I. Now he had the entrée to the court, rubbed shoulders with royalty and knew a wide range of courtiers, ministers and members of parliament. As a result, his diary contains an extremely well-informed though discontinuous history of ministries, parliament and public opinion. His own part in public affairs is naturally in the forefront of the story. He reveals how business was managed in the Navy Office – how he and his colleagues cooperated and quarrelled; how they worked with other departments and with members of the mercantile and shipping community of the City; how they prepared estimates for parliament. It is the only insider's history of the work of the civil service that we have for this period.

A diary so packed with matter, however interesting, might well be unreadable were it not for its manner. But Pepys had a gift for happiness that amounts to genius, and it lights up almost every page. Whenever he pauses to reflect on his condition, it is usually to thank God, despite his troubles, for his good health and his good fortune. Moreover, he had a natural flair for writing, as is clear from his letters and memoranda as well as from his diary.[14] In the diary his method of presentation will often vary with his subject. When recalling the voluminous views of Sir Philip Warwick on public finance, he writes as he would write an office memorandum. When he makes observations on the ordinary events of an ordinary day, his language can be fresh and flexible, so that one can almost catch the inflexions of his voice. 'I to church', he writes at 31 January 1669 (obviously here using no notes) 'and there did hear the Doctor that is lately turned Divine, I have forgot his name – I met him a while since at Sir D. Gawden's at dinner – Dr. Waterhouse'. On other occasions his words are more artfully composed – to describe a scene, such as the Fire, or to express a mood, as in the moving passage with which the diary ends. If he tells a story he tells it well – unhurriedly, giving full value to every significant turn in the story, and holding the reader in delighted suspense. At 29 November 1667 there is for example the tale of his mistaking the chimney sweep for burglars; and in October of the same year the long account of his search for his buried gold in the Brampton garden, when he and Hewer dug around for hours and panned the earth in the summer-house 'just as they do for Dyamonds in other parts of the world'. Best of all in narrative power, his story of those agonising weeks in the autumn of 1668 when Elizabeth discovered his affair with her companion, Deb Willet, drove the young girl from her service and put Pepys under orders as strict as she could make them never to see Deb again. A novelist might envy the sensitivity and understanding with which it is told.

Pepys as a writer has in fact some of the characteristics of a novelist. He is notably observant, often catching his characters in an informal pose – the King weighing himself after tennis, Lord Clarendon nodding off at a meeting. Some of the figures who appear only casually are made unforgettable – the waterman who carried pins in his mouth, the 'mighty fat woman' who sang with 'so much pleasure to herself . . . relishing it to her very heart', and (most memorable of all perhaps) the shepherd on Epsom Downs, with his iron-shod boots and his woollen stockings and his little boy reading the Bible to him – 'the most like one of the old Patriarchs that ever I saw in my life'.

A good case could be made for Pepys as the most evocative of

English diarists; and an equally good case for his being the most informative. It is the combination of the two qualities which makes him unique.

## Notes

1. Pepys Lib. 2554.

2. Except for the Tangier diary of 1683–4 (q.v. below, n.6), they have not been published. Again with that exception, they were not so much diaries as memoranda arranged in diurnal form, and were in some cases written out by clerks from his notes or at his dictation. There was a journal of 1670 recording his examination by the Privy Council about the report of the Brooke House Committee (Pepys Lib. 2874, pp. 385–403); his pencilled notes of the Commons' debates on the 1677 shipbuilding programme (Bodleian Lib., Rawlinson MSS c 859); two journals of 1679–80 concerning his defence against the accusations brought against him in the Popish Plot (Pepys Lib. 2881, pp. 45–85; 2882, pp. 1189–1235), and a journal of 1686 relating to the work of the Special Commission appointed in that year (Pepys Lib. 1490, pp. 7–79).

3. Anchitel Grey, *Debates of the House of Commons* (1763), v. 388.

4. The papers are mostly in Bodleian Lib., Rawlinson MSS A 173, 175, 176, 181, 188, 190, 193 and 194. They were extensively used by Sir Arthur Bryant in *Samuel Pepys: the Years of Peril* (1935), pp. 202–413, where extracts may be found. Fair copies are in Pepys Lib. 2881–2.

5. First published by Sir David Dalrymple in 1766, and several times republished. The most accurate version is that by William Matthews (1966).

6. First transcribed and published by John Smith in 1841 in *The Life, Journals and Correspondence of Samuel Pepys*; reprinted by R. G. Howarth, *Letters and the Second Diary of Samuel Pepys* (1933). The best edition is by Edwin Chappell: *The Tangier Papers of Samuel Pepys* (Navy Records Soc. 1935).

7. The will and codicil are printed in H. B. Wheatley, *Pepysiana* (1899), App. I.

8. Diary, 26 May 1703.

9. But it is clear that he sometimes made his entry in the diary without first composing a complete draft or even any draft at all: cf. p. 983 (31 January).

10. There is a gap between 29 September 1668 and the following 11 October when he was away in Hampshire and in East Anglia.

11. Two passages describing journeys in April and June 1668 during which he was away from home were left in note form, entered on loose sheets of paper which were later inserted into the volume. The second of them is printed below, pp. 921–8. Another similar, but shorter, passage in June 1660 was written in abbreviated form: see p. 55.

12. Editions of Evelyn, Hooke, Locke, Fiennes and Josselin are listed below, p. 1028. The other diaries mentioned are John Ray, *Observations . . . made in a Journey through the Low Countries . . .* (1673); *The Diary of John Milward . . . 1666–8*, ed. C. Robbins (Cambridge 1938); and Anchitel Grey, *Debates of the House of Commons . . . 1667–94* (10 vols, 1763). It should be added that the author of the religious diary – concerned mainly to record spiritual experience – often gives valuable information about everyday life, since to him daily happenings were evidence of the workings of Providence. Josselin is a particularly good example: so, too, on a smaller scale, is the delightful Presbyterian shopkeeper, Roger Lowe, of Ashton-in-Makerfield, Lancs. – a sort of primitive artist among diarists. His diary covers 1663–74.

13. Bulstrode Whitelocke, the Puritan lawyer and politician (1605–75), kept a remarkable diary which is reminiscent of Pepys's in its life-like detail. Extracts were published in *The Improbable Puritan, A Life of Bulstrode Whitelocke* (1975) by Ruth Spalding, who is preparing an edition.

14. See, for example, his tactful letter to Sandwich (below, pp. 322–4), and the elaborate memorandum printed in the appendix to Richard Ollard's *Samuel Pepys* (Oxford Paperbacks, 1984).

# ❧CHRONOLOGICAL SUMMARY❧

1633    23 February: Born in Salisbury Court, Fleet Street
3 March: Baptised in St Bride's, Fleet Street

c. 1644    At the grammar school, Huntingdon

c. 1646–50  At St Paul's School, London

1649    Saw Charles I beheaded

1650    Awarded leaving exhibition

1651–4    At Magdalene College, Cambridge
1651, 1653  Awarded scholarships

1654    Takes his B.A.

c. 1654    Appointed secretary and domestic steward (in Whitehall Palace) to Edward Mountagu

1655    10 October/1 December: Married to Elizabeth St Michel

?1656    Appointed clerk to George Downing, Teller of the Receipt in the Exchequer

1658    26 March: Operated on for the stone
c. August: Moves to Axe Yard

1659    May: Carries letters to Mountagu in the Baltic

1660    1 January: Begins diary
9 March: Appointed Admiral's secretary by Mountagu
*25 April: Convention Parliament meets*
May: Accompanies Mountagu's fleet to Holland to bring over Charles II
*29 May: Charles II enters London*

28 June: Resigns clerkship in Exchequer

29 June: Appointed Clerk of the Acts to the Navy Board

12 July: Mountagu created Earl of Sandwich

17 July: Moves to lodgings in Navy Office, Seething Lane

18 July: Will Hewer engaged as servant and clerk

23 July: Sworn in as Sandwich's deputy as clerk in Privy Seal Office

24 September: Sworn in as J.P.

1661     *23 April: Coronation of Charles II*

*8 May: Cavalier Parliament meets*

5 July: His uncle Robert Pepys dies; he and his father inherit Brampton property

August–September: His parents and sister Paulina move from London to Brampton

1662     15 February: Admitted as Younger Brother of Trinity House

*21 May: King marries Catherine of Braganza*

17 August: Resigns deputy-clerkship in Privy Seal

20 November: Appointed to Tangier Committee

1663     17 November: Writes 'great letter of reproof' to Sandwich

1664     15 March: His brother Tom dies

8 April: Appointed to Corporation for the Royal Fishery

1665     15 February: Elected Fellow of the Royal Society

*22 February: Second Dutch War begins*

20 March: Appointed Treasurer of Tangier Committee

*Spring: Great Plague begins in London*

*3 June: Battle of Lowestoft*

5 July: Elizabeth moves to Woolwich

*2 August: Attack on Dutch fleet in Bergen harbour*

21 August: Navy Office moves to Greenwich

*September: Sandwich captures Dutch E. Indiamen*

October: Takes lodgings at Greenwich

4 December: Appointed Surveyor-General of the Victualling

6 December: Composes 'Beauty Retire'

1666     January: Navy Office and Pepys household move back to London
*March: Sandwich arrives in Spain as Ambassador*
March–May: Portrait painted by Hayls
*1–4 June: Four Days Fight*
*25 July: St James's Day Fight*
*9–10 August: Attack on Dutch ships in Vlie*
*2–5 September: The Great Fire of London*

1667     25 March: His mother dies at Brampton
*10–13 June: Dutch raid on Thames and Medway*
13 June: Sends his gold to Brampton
28 July: Resigns Surveyorship of Victualling
*31 July: Treaty of Breda ends Second Dutch War*
30 September: Deb Willet joins household
7–12 October: Visits Brampton to recover his gold
22 October: Defends Navy Board before parliamentary Committee on Miscarriages

1668     27 February: His sister Paulina marries John Jackson
5 March: Defends Navy Board before House of Commons
5–17 June: His holiday tour to West Country
*September: Sandwich returns*
25 October: Elizabeth discovers him *in flagrante* with Deb

1669     31 May: Discontinues his diary
June–October: Travels to Low Countries and France
10 November: Elizabeth dies

1670     January–February: Examined before Privy Council on report of Brooke House Committee
30 March: His brother John appointed Clerk to Trinity House

1672     24 January: Admitted as Elder Brother of Trinity House
*17 March: Third Dutch War begins*
*28 May: Death of Sandwich in Battle of Sole Bay*

1673     29 January: Navy Office destroyed by fire; he moves to Winchester Street

15 *June: Duke of York resigns as Lord High Admiral under terms of Test Act excluding Roman Catholics; office put in commission*

18 June: Appointed Secretary to Admiralty Commission; is succeeded at Navy Board by his brother John and Thomas Hayter as Joint Clerks

19 August: King establishes mathematical school at Christ's Hospital

4 November: Elected M.P. for Castle Rising, Norfolk

| | |
|---|---|
| 1674 | Moves to Derby House, new headquarters of Admiralty |
| | 19 *February: Treaty of Westminster ends Third Dutch War* |
| 1676 | 1 February: Appointed a Governor of Christ's Hospital |
| | 22 May: Elected Master of Trinity House |
| 1677 | 23 February: Speech in House of Commons urging grant for 30 new ships |
| | 15 March: His brother John buried |
| | 8 August: Elected Master of Clothworkers' Company |
| 1679 | 5 February: Elected M.P. for Harwich |
| | 21 May: Resigns as Secretary to Admiralty and Treasurer for Tangier |
| | 22 May–9 July: In Tower on suspicion of treasonable correspondence with France |
| | c. July: Moves to Will Hewer's house in York Buildings, Buckingham Street |
| 1680 | 30 June: Proceedings against him abandoned |
| | c. September: His brother-in-law John Jackson dies |
| | 3, 5 October: Takes down at King's dictation story of his escape after Battle of Worcester |
| | 4 October: His father buried at Brampton |
| 1682 | May: Accompanies Duke of York to Edinburgh |
| 1683 | 30 July: Sets out for Tangier as secretary to expedition under Lord Dartmouth to evacuate colony |
| 1683–4 | December–February: Visits Cadiz and Seville |

1684      30 March: Returns to England

10 June: Appointed King's Secretary for Naval Affairs

1 December: Elected President of Royal Society

1685      *6 February: Death of Charles II; accession of Duke of York as James II*

19 May: Takes seat as M.P. for Harwich, having been elected for both Harwich and Sandwich

20 July: Nominated Master of Trinity House by King under new charter

1686      March: Special Commission for the Recovery of the Navy begins to sit

30 November: Resigns Presidency of Royal Society

1688      c. March: Moves to house next door in York Buildings

29 June: Called as witness in Trial of Seven Bishops

12 October: Special Commission dissolved

*5 November: William of Orange lands*

*23 December: James II takes flight to France*

1689      16 January: Defeated in parliamentary election at Harwich

*13 February: William and Mary become joint sovereigns*

20 February: Resigns his post as Secretary for Naval Affairs

May–July: Detained on suspicion of Jacobitism

26 August: Resigns Mastership of Trinity House

1690      25–30 June: Imprisoned on suspicion of Jacobitism

Publishes his *Memoires Relating to the State of the Royal Navy* [*1679–88*]

1699      27 April: Made freeman of City of London for services to Christ's Hospital

1701      c. June: Retires to Hewer's house at Clapham

2 August: Makes will

1703      26 May: Dies at Clapham

4 June: Buried at St Olave's, Hart Street

1715    Will Hewer, his executor, dies

1723    John Jackson, his nephew and heir, dies

1724    July: His library moved from Clapham to Magdalene College, Cambridge

1766    His account of the King's escape after the Battle of Worcester first published by Sir David Dalrymple

1825    His diary first published (in heavily abbreviated form) by Lord Braybrooke from the transcription by John Smith

1841    His Tangier Journal first published by John Smith

1884    His monument erected in St Olave's

1983    His statue erected in Seething Lane

# PRINCIPAL PERSONS

## I *Family and Household*

Elizabeth Pepys, wife; John and Margaret Pepys, parents; Tom and John Pepys, younger brothers; Paulina ('Pall') Pepys (m. John Jackson), sister; Robert Pepys (of Brampton), uncle; Thomas Pepys, uncle; Roger Pepys (of Impington), cousin

Uncle Fenner, brother-in-law of Pepys's mother; Anthony and Will Joyce, his sons-in-law; Jane Turner, cousin; Theophila ('The[oph].') Turner, her daughter; Uncle Wight, half-brother of Pepys's father; Tom Trice, stepson of Uncle Robert

Alexander and Dorothea St Michel, Elizabeth's parents; Balthasar St Michel ('Balty'), her brother

Servants: Jane Birch; Mary Ashwell; Mary Mercer; Deb Willet; Tom Edwards

## II *Colleagues and Clerks*

Principal Officers of the Navy Board: Sir George Carteret, Treasurer; Sir John Mennes, Comptroller; Sir William Batten, Surveyor; Sir William Penn, Peter Pett, Viscount Brouncker, Commissioners

Sir William Coventry, Secretary to the Lord High Admiral; Sir Denis Gauden, Victualler of the Navy; Anthony Deane (kt 1675), shipbuilder; Thomas Povey, Treasurer of Tangier Committee

Clerks: Will Hewer and Tom Hayter (clerks to Pepys); Thomas Turner (Clerk-General of the Navy Board)

## III *The Royal Family*

The King, Charles II; The Queen, Catherine of Braganza; The Queen-Mother, Henrietta Maria; James, Duke of York, Lord High Admiral, the

King's brother; James, Duke of Monmouth, the King's bastard; Prince
Rupert, the King's cousin

## IV

George (Monck), Duke of Albemarle, Captain-General of the Kingdom
Edward Backwell, goldsmith-banker
Mrs Bagwell, Pepys's mistress
Will and Mary Batelier, friends
Thomas Betterton, actor
The Earl of Bristol, politician
The Duke of Buckingham, politician
Lady Castlemaine, the King's mistress
The Earl of Clarendon, Lord Chancellor
George Cocke, timber merchant
Capt. Henry Cooke, court musician
John Creed, servant to Sandwich
Lord Crew, Sandwich's father-in-law
Sir George Downing, Exchequer official, ambassador to the Netherlands
    and Secretary to the Treasury
John Evelyn, virtuoso and friend
Capt. Robert Ferrer, servant to Sandwich
Sir Richard Ford, merchant and neighbour
Nell Gwyn, actress
Thomas Hill, merchant
Thomas Hollier, surgeon
Will Howe, servant to Sandwich
Elizabeth Knepp, actress
Betty Martin (b. Lane), Pepys's mistress
Daniel Milles, Rector of St Olave's
Betty Mitchell (b. Howlett), friend
Monck: *see* George (Monck), Duke of Albemarle
Henry Moore, Sandwich's man of business
Mountagu: *see* Edward Mountagu, Earl of Sandwich
James Pearse, naval and court surgeon
Doll Powell (b. Lane), Pepys's mistress
Edward Mountagu, Earl of Sandwich, Pepys's patron ('my Lord')
Jemima Mountagu, Countess of Sandwich ('my Lady')
The Earl of Southampton, Lord Treasurer
Frances Teresa Stuart (Duchess of Richmond), court beauty
Sir William Warren, timber merchant

When he begins his diary Pepys is close on 27, and married. He has not long since recovered from an operation for the stone (in March 1658) and is still nervous of a recurrence of the trouble. He is employed by his patron Edward Mountagu ('my Lord') as his man of business, and also has a minor clerkship in the Exchequer.

In public affairs great changes are clearly impending – though what changes no-one is sure. The military government established by Lambert in October 1659 has collapsed and on Boxing Day the Rump Parliament – 'interrupted' by Lambert's coup – has resumed its sessions. It is now, in early January, to elect a Council of State. The Rump, consisting of only 50 M.P.s, is the remnant of the parliament elected in the autumn of 1640 two years before the Civil War broke out. It symbolises therefore the return of civilian government and represents to all except the republican and puritan extremists the best available hope of returning to some form of political stability. It has the support of Monck, commander of the republic's best troops, the regiments stationed in Scotland (who is a strong believer in civilian government, but whose views are otherwise mysterious), of Lawson, the commander of the fleet, and of the Common Council of London, newly elected on 21 December. All support it in the expectation that it will accept that its rôle is that of a provisional government, whose function is to arrange for the election of a 'full and free' parliament – one, that is, in which all constituencies are represented and whose members are not bound by an oath to preserve the republic. This however is not likely to happen unless the Rump is expanded by the admission of the 154 'secluded members' – the moderates excluded in Pride's Purge just before the execution of the King in 1649. Parliament thus reinforced would be able to pass the legislation necessary for its own dissolution.

The Rump is soon persuaded – by addresses from every part of the country and even more powerfully by Monck's army, which begins to move south at the turn of the year and arrives in London on 3 February – to admit the secluded members on 21 February. Writs for elections are issued on 16 March, and the new parliament (or Convention) meets on 25 April. Members of the House of Lords join it, though not officially summoned, and the two Houses receive on 1 May a conciliatory message from Charles II (the Declaration of Breda). They vote on the same day for government 'by King, Lords and Commons'. The King is proclaimed on 8 May, and a fleet commanded by Mountagu, with Pepys as his secretary, already on station in the Channel, sails to Holland to bring him home.

Pepys's account of these crucial months which led to the Restoration is the best to survive. His own wishes appear plainly enough in the diary's narrative, but at the same time he makes it clear how long the issue hung doubtful.

# 1660

Blessed be God, at the end of the last year I was in very good health, without any sense of my old pain but upon taking of cold. I lived in Axe yard, having my wife and servant Jane, and no more in family then us three. My wife, after the absence of her terms for seven weeks, gave me hopes of her being with child, but on the last day of the year she hath them again.

The condition of the State was thus. *Viz.* the Rump, after being disturbed by my Lord Lambert, was lately returned to sit again. The officers of the army all forced to yield. Lawson lie[s] still in the River and Monke is with his army in Scotland. Only my Lord Lambert is not yet come in to the Parliament; nor is it expected that he will, without being forced to it. The new Common Council of the City doth speak very high; and hath sent to Monke their sword-bearer, to acquaint him with their desires for a free and full Parliament, which is at present the desires and the hopes and expectation of all – 22 of the old secluded members having been at the House door the last week to demand entrance; but it was denied them, and it is believed that they nor the people will not be satisfied till the House be filled.

My own private condition very handsome; and esteemed rich, but endeed very poor, besides my goods of my house and my office, which at present is somewhat uncertain. Mr. Downing master of my office.

## ⭐ JANUARY ⭐

1. *Lords day.* This morning (we lying lately in the garret) I rose, put on my suit with great skirts, having not lately worn any other clothes but them. Went to Mr. Gunnings church at Exeter house, where he made a very good sermon upon these words: That in the

1

fullness of time God sent his Son, made of a woman, &c., shewing that by "made under the law," is meant his circumcision, which is solemnised this day. Dined at home in the garret, where my wife dressed the remains of a turkey, and in the doing of it she burned her hand. I stayed at home all the afternoon, looking over my accounts. Then went with my wife to my father's; and in going, observed the great posts which the City hath set up at the Conduit in Fleet street. Supped at my father's, where in came Mrs. The[oph]. Turner and Madam Morris and supped with us. After that, my wife and I went home with them, and so to our own home.

2.  In the morning, before I went forth, old East brought me a dozen of bottles of sack and I gave him a shilling for his pains. Then I went to Mr. Sheply, who was drawing of sack in the wine-cellar to send to other places as a gift from my Lord,[1] and told me that my Lord hath given him order to give me the dozen of bottles. Then I went to Mr. Crew's and borrowed 10*l*: of Mr. Andrewes for my own use; and so went to my office, where there was nothing to do. Then I walked a great while in Westminster hall, where I heard that Lambert was coming up to London. Great talk that many places have declared for a free Parliament; and it is believed that they will be forced to fill up the House with the old members. From the Hall I called at home, and so went to Mr. Crew's (my wife, she was to go to her father's), thinking to have dined; but I came too late. So Mr. Moore and I and another Gentleman went out and drank a cup of ale together in the new market, and there I eat some bread and cheese for my dinner. After that, Mr. Moore and I went as far as Fleet street together and parted. Then I went home, and finding my wife gone to see Mrs. Hunt, I went to Will's and there sat with Mr. Ashwell talking and singing till 9 a-clock, and so home. There, having not eat anything but bread and cheese, my wife cut me a slice of brawn which I received from my Lady,[2] which proves as good as ever I had any. So to bed, and my [wife] had a very bad night of it through wind and cold.

3.  Mr. Sheply, Hawly and Moore dined with me on a piece of beef and cabbage, and a collar of brawn. We then fell to cards till dark, and then I went home with Mrs. Jem. Thence back to Whitehall, where I understood that the Parliament have passed the

1. Edward Mountagu, his patron.
2. Jemima, wife of Edward Mountagu.

Act for Indemnity to the soldiers and officers that would come in in so many days, and that my Lord Lambert should have benefit of the said Act. They have also voted that all vacancy in the House by the death of any of the old members shall be filled up; but those that are living shall not be called in. Thence I went home; and there found Mr. Hunt and his wife and Mr. Hawly, who sat with me till 10 at night at cards, and so broke up. And to bed.

4.   Early came Mr. Vanly to me for his half-year's rent, which I had not in the house, but took his man to my office and there paid him. Then I went down into the Hall and to Will's, where Hawly brought a piece of his Cheshire cheese, and we were merry with it. Then into the Hall again, where I met with the Clerk and quartermaster of my Lord's troop, and took them to the Swan and gave them their morning's draught, they being just come to town. Mr. Jenkings showed me two bills of exchange for money to receive upon my Lord's and my pay. It snowed hard all this morning and was very cold, and my nose was much swelled with cold. Strange, the difference of men's talk: some say that Lambert must of necessity yield up; others, that he is very strong, and that the Fifth-monarchy men will stick to him if he declares for a free Parliament. I heard that the Parliament spent this day in fast and prayer; and that my Lord Lambert his forces were all forsaking him and that he was left with only 50 horse and that he did now declare for the Parliament himself. Home and so to bed; but much troubled with my nose, which was much swelled.

5.   I dined with Mr. Sheply at my Lord's lodgings upon his turkey pie; and so to my office again, where the Excise money was brought and some of it told to soldiers till it was dark. Then I went home, and after writing a letter to my Lord, and told him the news that the Parliament hath this night voted that the members that was discharged from setting in the years 1648 and 49 was duly discharged, and that there should be writs issued presently for the calling of others in their places. And that Monke and Fairfax were commanded up to town, and that the Prince's lodgings were to be provided for Monke at Whitehall. Then I went with my lanthorn to Mr. Fage to consult concerning my nose, who told me that it was nothing but cold; and after that, we did discourse concerning public business, and he told me that it is true the City hath not time enough to do much, but they are resolved to shake off the soldier[s]; and

that unless there be a free Parliament chosen, he doth believe there are half the Common Council will not levy any money by order of this Parliament. From thence I went to my father's, where I found Mrs. Ramsey and her grandchild, a pretty girl, and stayed a while and talked with them and my mother and then took my leave; only, heard of an invitation to go to dinner tomorrow to my Cosen Tho. Pepys.

6. This morning Mr. Sheply and I did eat our breakfasts at Mrs. Harpers, my brother John being with me, upon a cold turkey pie and a goose; from whence I went to my office, where we paid money to the soldiers till one of the clock, at which time we made an end; and I went home and took my wife and went to my Cosen Tho. Pepys's and found them just sat down to dinner, which was very good; only the venison pasty was palpable beef, which was not handsome. After dinner I took my leave, leaving my wife with my cousin Stradwick, and went to Westminster to Mr. Vines, where George and I fiddled a good while, Dick and his wife (who was lately brought to bed) and her sister being there; but Mr. Hudson not coming according to his promise, I went away; and calling at my house on the wench, I took her and the lanthorn with me to my cousin Stradwick. Where, after a good supper, there being there my father, mother, brothers, and sister, my cousin Scot and his wife, Mr. Drawwater and his wife and her brother, Mr. Stradwick, we had a brave cake brought us, and in the choosing, Pall was queen and Mr. Stradwick was king. After that, my wife and I bid Adieu and came home, it being still a great frost.

8. *Sunday*. In the morning I went to Mr. Gunings, where a good sermon, wherein he showed the life of Christ and told us good authority for us to believe that Christ did fallow his father's trade, and was a carpenter till 30 years of age. From thence to my father's to dinner; where I found my wife, who was forced to dine there, we not having one coal of fire in the house and it being very hard frosty weather.

9. For these two or three days, I have been much troubled with thoughts how to get money to pay them that I have borrowed money of, by reason of my money being in my Uncles hands. I rose early this morning, and looked over and corrected my brother John's speech which he is to make the next Apposition; and after

that I went towards my office and in my way met with W. Simons, Muddiman, and Jack Price and went with them to Harpers, and in many sorts of talk I stayed till 2 of the clock in the afternoon. Thence I went with Muddiman to the Coffee-house, and gave 18*d*. to be entered of the Club.[1] Thence into the Hall, where I heard for certain that Monke was coming to London. Thence to Mrs. Jem and found her in bed, and some was afraid that it would prove the smallpox. Thence back to Westminster hall, where I heard how Sir H. Vane was this day voted out of the House and to sit ño more there. Here I met with [the] Quarter Maister of my Lord's troop and his clerk Mr. Jenings, and took them home and gave [them] a bottle of wine and the remainder of my collar of brawn, and so good-night. After that, came in Mr. Hawly, who told me that I was missed this day at my office and that tomorrow I must pay all the money that I have, at which I was put to a great loss how I should get money to make up my cash, and so went to bed in great trouble.

10.   Went out early, and in my way met with Greatorex, and at an alehouse he showed me the first sphere of wire that ever he made, and indeed it was very pleasant. Whence to Mr. Crews and borrowed 10*l*; and so to my office and was able to pay my money. Thence into the Hall; and meeting the Quarter Maister, Jenings and Capt. Rider, we four went to a cook's to dinner. Thence Jenings and I into London, it being through heat of the sun a great thaw and dirty, to show our bills of return; and coming back, drank a pint of wine at the Star in Cheapside. So to Westminster, overtaking Capt. Okeshott in his silk cloak, whose sword got hold of many people in walking. Thence to the Coffee-house, where were a great confluence of gentlemen; *viz*. Mr. Harrington, Poultny cheareman, Gold, Dr. Petty, &[c]., where admirable discourse till 9 at night.

12.   I drink my morning [draught] at Harpers with Mr. Sheply and a seaman; and so to my office, where Capt. Holland came to see me and appointed a meeting in the afternoon. Then I wrote letters to Hinchingbrooke and sealed them at Wills, and after that went home; and thence to the Half Moon, where I found the Captain and Mr. Billingsly and Newman, a barber; where we were very merry and had the young man that plays so well on the Welch harp. Billingsly paid for all. Thence home, and finding my letters this day

1. The Rota Club, established for political debate.

not gone by the carrier, I new-sealed them; but my Brother Tom coming, we fell into discourse about my intention to feast the Joyces: I sent for a bit of meat for him from the cook's, and forgot to send my letters this night. So I went to bed and in discourse broke to my wife what my thoughts were concerning my design of getting money by, &c.

13. To my office, where nothing to do. So to Will's with Mr. Pinkny, who invited me to their feast at his Hall the next Monday. Thence I went home and took my wife and dined at Mr. Wade's. And after that we went and visited Catau.[1] From thence home again, and my wife was very unwilling to let me go forth; but with some discontent, would go out if I did; and I going forth towards Whitehall, I saw she fallowed me, and so I stayed and took her round through Whitehall, and so carried her home angry.

14. Nothing to do at our office. I went with my wife and left her at market, and went myself to the Coffee-house and heard exceeding good argument against Mr. Harrington's assertion that over-balance of propriety* was the foundation of government. Home and wrote to Hinchingbrooke, and sent that and my other letters that missed of going on Thursday last. So to bed.

15. Having been exceedingly disturbed in the night with the barking of a dog of one of our neighbours, that I could not sleep for an hour or two, I slept late; and then in the morning took physic, and so stayed within all day. At noon my Brother John came to me, and I corrected as well as I could his Greek speech against the Apposition, though I believe he himself was as well able to do it as myself. After that, we went to read in the great *Officiale* about the blessing of bells in the Church of Rome. After that, my wife and I in pleasant discourse till night that I went to supper, and after that to make an end of this week's notes in this book, and so to bed. It being a cold day and a great snow, my physic did not work so well as it should have done.

16. At noon Harry Ethell came to me and went along with Mr. Maylard by coach as far as Salsbury Court; and there we set him down and we went to the Clerkes,[2] where we came a little too late;

1. Kate Sterpin.
2. The Parish Clerks' Hall.

but in a closet we had a very good dinner by Mr. Pinkny's courtesy. And after dinner we had pretty good singing and one Hazard sung alone after the old fashion, which was very much cried up; but I did not like it. Thence we went to the Greene Dragon on Lambeth hill, both the Mr. Pinknys, Smith, Harrison, Morrice that sang the bass, Sheply and I, and there we sang of all sorts of things and I ventured with good success upon things at first sight and after that played on my flagelette; and stayed there till 9 a-clock, very merry and drawn on with one song after another till it came to be so late. After that, Sheply, Harrison and myself, we went towards Westminster on foot, and at the Golden Lion, near Charing cross, we went in and drank a pint of wine, and so parted; and thence home, where I found my wife and maid a-washing. I sat up till the bell-man came by with his bell, just under my window as I was writing of this very line, and cried, "Past one of the clock, and a cold, frosty, windy morning." I then went to bed and left my wife and the maid a-washing still.

17. To the Coffee club and heard very good discourse; it was in answer to Mr. Harrington's answer, who said that the state of the Roman government was not a settled government, and so it was no wonder that the balance of propriety was in one hand and the command in another, it being therefore always in a posture of war; but it was carried by Ballat that it was a steady government; though, it is true by the voices, it had been carried before that it was an unsteady government. So tomorrow it is to be proved by the opponents that the balance lie in one hand and the government in another.

18. All the world is now at a loss to think what Monke will do: the City saying that he will be for them, and the Parliament saying he will be for them.

19. This morning I was sent for to Mr. Downing, and at his bedside he told me that he hath a kindness for me, and that he thought that he hath done me one; and that was, that he hath got me to be one of the Clerks of the Council; at which I was a little stumbled and could not tell what to do, whether to thank him or no; but I by and by did, but not very heartily, for I feared that his doing of it was but only to ease himself of the salary which he give me. Thence to my office, and so with Mr. Sheply and Moore to dine

upon a turkey with Mrs. Jem; and after that, Mr. Moore and I went to the French ordinary, where Mr. Downing this day feasted Sir Arth. Haslerig and a great many more of the Parliament; and did stay to put him in mind of me. Here he gave me a note to go and invite some other members to dinner tomorrow. So I went to Whitehall, and did stay at Marshes with Simons, Luellin and all the rest of the Clerks of the Council, who I hear are all turned out, only the two Leighs; and they do all tell me that my name was mentioned the last night, but that nothing was done in it. Hence I went and did leave some of my notes at the lodgings of the members, and so home. To bed.

20. To my office. At noon went by water with Mr. Maylard and Hales to the Swan in Fishstreete at our colly-feast, where we were very merry at our Jole of ling. And from thence, after a great and good dinner of fish, Mr. Fauconbridge would go drink a cup of ale at a place where I had like to have shit in a skimmer that lay over the house of office. Thence, calling on Mr. Stephens and Wooton (with whom I drank) about business of my Lord's, I went to the Coffee club, where there was nothing done but choosing of a committee for orders. Thence to Westminster hall, where Mrs. Lane and the rest of the maids have their white scarfs, all having been at the burial of a young bookseller in the Hall. Thence to Mr. Sheply and took him to my house and drank with him, in order to his going tomorrow.[1] So parted, and I sat up late making up my accounts before he go.

21. Up early in finishing my accounts and writing to my Lord; and from thence to my Lord's and took leave of Mr. Sheply and possession of all the keys and the house. Thence to my office for some money to pay Mr. Sheply, and sent it him by the old man.[2]

22. I went in the morning to Mr. Messum's, where I met with W. Thurburne and sat with him in his pew. A very eloquent sermon about the duty of all to give good example in our lives and conversation, which I fear he himself was most guilty of not doing. After sermon, at the door by appointment my wife met me; and so to my father's to dinner, where we have not been, to my shame, in a fortnight before. After dinner my father showed me a letter from

1. To Hinchingbrooke.
2. East, a servant of Mountagu's.

Mr. Widdrington of Christ's College in Cambrige, wherein he doth express very great kindness for my brother, and my father entends that my brother shall go to him. This day I began to put on buckles to my shoes, which I had bought yesterday of Mr. Wotton.

23.   To my office and there did nothing but make up my balance. Came home and found my wife dressing of the girl's head, by which she was made to look very pretty. I went out and paid Wilkinson what I did owe him, and brought a piece of beef home for dinner. Thence I went out and paid Waters the Vintner, and went to see Mrs. Jem, where I found my Lady Wright; but Scott was so drunk that he would not be seen. Here I stayed and made up Mrs. Anns bills and played a game or two at cards; and thence to Westminster hall, it being very dark. I pay Mrs. Michell my bookseller, and back to Whitehall, and in the garden, going through to the Stone Gallery, I fell in a ditch, it being very dark. At the Clerks' chamber I met with Simons and Luellin and went with them to Mr. Mounts chamber at the Cockpit, where we had some rare pot venison and Ale to abundance till almost 12 at night; and after a song round, we went home.

24.   In the morning to my office; where after I had drank my morning draught at Will's with Ethell and Mr. Stevens, I went and told part of the excise money till 12 a-clock. And then called on my wife and took her to Mr. Pierce's, she in the way being exceedingly troubled with a pair of new pattens, and I vexed to go so slow, it being late. There when we came, we found Mrs. Carrick very fine, and one Mr. Lucy, who called one another husband and wife; and after dinner, a great deal of mad stir; there was pulling off Mrs. Bride's and Mr. Bridegroom's ribbons, with a great deal of fooling among them that I and my wife did not like; Mr. Lucy and several other gentlemen coming in after dinner, swearing and singing as if they were mad; only, he singing very handsomely.

25.   Called up early to Mr. Downing; he gave me a Character,* such a one as my Lord's, to make perfect. And likewise gave me his order for 500*l*: to carry to Mr. Frost; which I did, and so to my office. Where I did do something about the character till 12 a-clock. Then home and found my wife and the maid at my Lord's, getting things ready against tomorrow.

26. Home from my office to my Lord's lodgings, where my wife had got ready a very fine dinner: *viz*. a dish of marrow-bones. A leg of mutton. A loin of veal. A dish of fowl, three pullets, and two dozen of larks, all in a dish. A great tart. A neat's tongue. A dish of anchoves. A dish of prawns, and cheese. My company was my father, my uncle Fenner, his two sons, Mr. Pierce, and all their wifes, and my brother Tom. We were as merry as I could frame myself to be in that company. W. Joyce, talking after the old rate and drinking hard, vexed his father and mother and wife. And I did perceive that Mrs. Pierce her coming so gallant, that it put the two young women quite out of courage. When it became dark, they all went away but Mr. Pierce and W. Joyce and their wifes and Tom, and drank a bottle of wine afterwards, so that Will did heartily anger his father and mother by staying. At which I and my wife were very much pleased. Then they all went and I fell to writing of two Characters for Mr. Downing, and carried them to him at 9 a-clock at night; and he did not like them but corrected them, so that tomorrow I am to do them anew. To my Lord's lodging again and sat by the great log, it being now a very good fire, with my wife; and eat a bit and so home.

28. To Heaven;[1] where Luellin and I dined on a breast of mutton all alone, discoursing of the changes that we have seen and the happiness of them that have estates of their own.

29. In the morning I went to Mr. Guning's, where he made an excellent sermon upon the 2 of the *Galatians*, about the difference that fell between St. Paul and Peter (the feast-day of St. Paul being but a day or two ago); whereby he did prove that contrary to the doctrine of the Roman Church, St. Paul did never own any dependence or that he was inferior to St. Peter, but that they were equal; only, one a perticular charge of preaching to the Jews and the other to the Gentiles. Here I met with Mr. Moore and went home with him to dinner to Mr. Crews, where Mr. Spurrier being in town did dine with us. From thence I went home and spent the afternoon in casting up of my accounts; and do find myself to be worth 40*l* and more, which I did not think, but am afraid that I have forgot something.

1. An eating-house.

30.   This morning, before I was up, I fell a-singing of my song *Great, good, and just, &c.* and put myself thereby in mind that this was the fatal day, now ten year since, his Majesty died. There seems now to be a general cease of talk, it being taken for granted that Monke doth resolve to stand to the Parliament and nothing else. I spent a little time this night in knocking up nails for my hats and cloaks in my chamber.

# ─✣FEBRUARY✣─

1.   To Mrs. Jem: and spoke with Madam Scott and her husband, who did promise to have her thing for her neck done this week.[1] Thence home and took Gammer East and James the porter, a soldier, to my Lord's lodgings – who told me how they were drawn into the field today, and that they were ordered to march away tomorrow to make room for Gen. Monke. But they did shout their Collonell (Coll. Fich) and the rest of the officers out of the field, and swore they would not go without their money; and that if they would not give it them, they would go where they might have it, and that was the City. Here I took some bedding to send to Mrs. Ann for her to lie in now she hath her fits of the ague. Thence I went to Wills, and stayed like a fool there and played at cards till 9 a-clock and so came home – where I found Mr. Hunt and his wife, who stayed and sat with me till 10; and so good-night.

2.   Our waterman, White, told us how the watermen have lately been abused by some that have a desire to get in to be watermen to the State, and have lately presented an address of 9 or 10000 hands to stand by this Parliament; when it was only told them that it was to a petition against Hackny coaches. And that today they have put out another to undeceive the world and to clear themselfs; and that among the rest, Cropp, my waterman and one of great practice, was one that did cheat them thus. James, the soldier, came; who told us how they had been all day and night upon their guard at St. James's and that through the whole town they did resolve to stand to what they had began, and that tomorrow he did believe they would go into the City and be received there.

1. Jemima Mountagu, daughter of 'my Lord', suffered from a malformation of the neck which was being treated by Scott.

3.   Drank my morning draught at Harpers and was told there that the soldiers were all quiet, upon promise of pay. Thence into St. James's Park, and walked there to my place for my Flagelette and there played a little, it being a most pleasant morning and sunshine. Thence to my office, where I paid a little more money to some of the soldiers under Lieut.-Coll. Miller. About noon Mrs. Turner came to speak with me and Joyce, and I took them and showed them the manner of the House's sitting, the doorkeeper very civilly opening the door for us. Thence with my Cosen Roger Pepys; it being term time, we took him out of the Hall to Priors, the Renish winehouse, and there had a pint or two of wine and a dish of Anchoves, and bespake three or four dozen of bottles of wine for him against his Wedding. So we called for nothing more there, but went and bespoke a shoulder of mutton at Wilkinsons, to be dressed as well as it could be done, and sent a bottle of wine home to my house. In the meantime, she and I and Joyce went walking all over Whitehall, whither Gen. Monke was newly come and we saw all his forces march by in very good plight and stout officers. Thence to my house, where we dined; but with a great deal of patience, for the mutton came in raw and so we were fain to stay the stewing of it. In the meantime, we sat studying of a posy for a ring for her, which she is to have at Rog. Pepys his wedding. After dinner I left them and went to hear news; but only found that the Parliament house was most of them with [Monck] at Whitehall, and that in his passage through the town he had many cry to him for a free Parliament; but little other welcome. I saw in the Palace yard how unwilling some of the old soldiers were yet to go out of town without their money; and swore, if they had it not in three days as they were promised, they would do them more mischief in the country then if they had stayed here; and that is very likely, the country being all discontented. The town and guard are already full of Monkes soldiers. I returned, and it growing dark, I and they went to take a turn in the park, where Theoph. (who was sent for to us to dinner) outrun my wife and another poor woman, that laid a pot of ale with me that she would outrun her. After that, I set them as far as Charing cross and there left them and my wife; and I went to see Mrs. Ann, who begun very high about a flock bed I sent her, but I took her down. Here I played at cards till 9 a-clock. So home and to bed.

4.   All the news today is that the Parliament this morning voted

the House to be made up 400 forthwith. This day my wife killed her turkey that Mr. Sheply gave her, that came out of Zeeland with my Lord; and could not get her maid Jane by no means at any time to kill anything.

5. *Lord's day.* In the morning before church time, Mr. Hawly, who hath for this day or two looked something sadly, which methought did speak something in his breast concerning me, came to me, telling me that he was out 24*l*, which he could not tell what was become of, and that he doth remember that he had such a sum in a bag the other day, and could not tell what he did with it; at which I was very sorry but could not help him. In the morning to Mr. Guning, where a stranger, an old man, preached a good honest sermon upon "What manner of love is this that we should be called the sons of God." After sermon I could not find my wife, who promised to be at the gate against my coming out, and waited there a great while; then went to my house and finding her gone, I returned and called at the Chequer, thinking to dine at the ordinary with Mr. Chetwind or Mr. Thomas; but they not being there, I went to my father and found her there, and there I dined. To their church in the afternoon, and in Mrs. Turners pew my wife took up a good black hood and kept it. A stranger preached a poor sermon, and so I read over the whole book of the story of Tobit. After sermon, we to my father's – where I writ some notes for my Brother John to give to the Mercers tomorrow, it being the day of their Apposition. After supper, home; and before going to bed, I stood writing of this day its passages – while a drum came by, beating of a strange manner of beat, now and then a single stroke; which my wife and I wondered at, what the meaning of it should be.

6. To Westminster and overtook Mr. Squibb and walked with him thither; where we found the soldiers all set in the Palace yard to make way for Gen. Monke to come to the House. At the Hall we parted; and meeting Swan, he and I to the Swan and drank our morning draught; so back again to the Hall, where I stood upon the steps and saw Monke go by, he making observance to the judges as he went along.

7. In the morning, I went early to give Mr. Hawly notice of my being forced to go into London; but he having also business, we left

our office business to Mr. Spicer and he and I walked as far as the Temple, where I halted a little and then went to Pauls schoole; but it being too soon, I went and drank my morning draught with my Cosen Tom. Pepys the turner, and saw his house and shop. Thence to school, where he that made the speech for the seventh form, in praise of the Founder,[1] did show a book that Mr. Crumlum had lately got, which is believed to be of the Founder's own writing. After all the speeches, in which my Brother John came off as well as any of the rest, I went straight home and dined. Mr. Moore told me of a picture hung up at the Exchange, of a great pair of buttocks shitting of a turd into Lawsons mouth, and over it was writ "The thanks of the House." Boys do now cry "Kiss my Parliament" instead of "Kiss my arse," so great and general a contempt is the Rump come to among all men, good and bad.

9.    As soon as out of my bed, I wrote letters into the country to go by the carrier today. Before I was out of my bed, I heard the soldiers very busy in the morning, getting their horses ready where they lay at Hiltons, but I knew not then their meaning in so doing. After I had writ my letters, I went to Westminster. In the Hall, I understand how Monke is this morning gone into London with his army; and met with Mr. Fage, who told me that he doth believe that Monke is gone to secure some of the Common Council of the City, who were very high yesterday there and did vote that they would not pay any taxes till the House was filled up. I called at Mr. Harpers, who told me how Monke had this day clapped up many of the Common Council, and that the Parliament had voted that he should pull down their gates and portcullisses, their posts and their chains, which he doth entend to do, and doth lie in the City all night. I went home and got some Allum to my mouth, where I have the beginnings of a Cancre, and have also a plaster to my boyle underneath my chin.

11.    This morning I lay long abed; and then to my office where I read all the morning my Spanish book of Rome. At noon I walked in the Hall, where I heard the news of a letter from Monke, who was now gone into the City again and did resolve to stand for the sudden filling up of the House; and it was very strange how the countenance of men in the Hall was all changed with joy in half an

1. Dean Colet (d. 1519).

hour's time. So I went up to the Lobby, where I saw the Speaker reading of the letter; and after it was read, Sir A. Haslerig came out very angry. The House presently after rose, and appointed to meet again at 3 a-clock. I went then down into the Hall, where I met with Mr. Chetwind, who had not dined no more then myself; and so we went towards London, in our way calling at two or three shops, and could have no dinner; at last, within Temple bar, we found a pullet ready-roasted, and there we dined. After that, he went to his office in Chancery lane, calling at the Rolles, where I saw the lawyers pleading; then to his office, where I sat in his study singing while he was with his man (Mr. Powells son) looking after his business. Thence we took coach for the City to Guildhall, where the hall was full of people expecting Monke and Lord Mayor to come thither, and all very joyful. Here we stayed a great while; and at last, meeting with a friend of his, we went to the Three Tun tavern and drank half a pint of wine; and not liking the wine, we went to an alehouse, where we met with company of this third man's acquaintance and there we drank a little: hence I went alone to Guildhall to see whether Monke was come yet or no, and met him coming out of the chamber where he had been with the Mayor and Aldermen; but such a shout I never heard in all my life, crying out "God bless your Excellence!" Here I met with Mr. Lock, and took him to an alehouse and left him there to fetch Chetwind; when we were come together, Lock told us the substance of the letter that went from Monke to the Parliament: that he and his officers were put upon such offices against the City as they could not do with any content or honour. That there are many members now in the House that were of the late tyrannical Committee of Safety. That Lambert and Vane are now in town, contrary to the vote of Parliament. That therefore he doth desire that all writts for filling up of the House be issued by Friday next, and that in the meantime he would retire into the City, only leave them guards for the security of the House and Council. The occasion of this was the order that he had last night to go into the City and disarm them and take away their charter; whereby he and his officers see that the House had a mind to put them on things that should make them odious; and so it would be in their power to do what they would with them. He told us that the Mayor and Aldermen had offered him their own houses for himself and his officers, and that his soldiers would lack for nothing. And endeed I saw many people give the soldiers drink and money, and all along in the streets cried, "God bless them!" and extraordinary good words. In Cheapside there was a great many bonefires, and Bow bells and all the bells in all the churches as we went home were a-ringing. Hence we went homewards, it being about 10 a-clock. But the common joy that was everywhere to be seen! The number of bonefires – there being fourteen between St. Dunstan's and Temple bar. And at Strand bridge I could at one view tell 31 fires. In King streete, seven or eight; and all along burning and roasting and drinking for rumps – there being rumps tied upon sticks and carried up and down. The buchers at the maypole in the Strand rang a peal with their knifes when they were going to sacrifice their rump. On Ludgate hill there was one turning of the spit, that had a rump tied upon it, and another basting of it. Indeed, it was past imagination, both the greatness and the suddenness of it. At one end of the street, you would think there was a whole lane of fire, and so hot that we were fain to keep still on the further side merely for heat. Thence home, and my wife and I went out again to show her the fires; and after walking as far as the Exchange, we returned and to bed.

12.    In the morning, it being Lords day, Mr. Pierce came to me to enquire how things go. We drank our morning draught together and thence to Whitehall, where Dr. Homes preached; but I stayed not to hear; but walking in the court, I heard that Sir Arth. Haslerig was newly gone into the City to Monke and that Monkes wife removed from Whitehall last night. Home again, where at noon came according to my invitation my Cosen Tho. Pepys and his partener, came and dined with me; but before dinner we went and took a walk round the parke, it being a most pleasant day as ever I saw. After dinner we three went into London together, where I heard that Monke had been at Paul's in the morning and the people had shouted much at his coming out of the church. In the afternoon he was at a church in Broad street, whereabout he doth lodge. But not knowing how to see him, we went and walked half an hour in Moorefields, which was full of people, it being so fine a day. Hence home where my wife and I had some high words upon my telling her that I would fling the dog which her brother gave her out at the window if he pissed the house any more.

16.    In the morning at my lute. Then came Shaw and Hawly, and I gave them their morning draught at my house. So to my office, where I writ by the carrier to my Lord; and sealed my letter at Wills and gave it old East to carry it to the carrier's – and to take up a box

of China oranges and two little barrels of Scallops at my house, which Capt. Cuttance sent to me for my Lord. Here I met with Osborne and with Shaw and Spicer, and then we went to the Sun tavern in expectation of a dinner, where we had sent us only two trencherfuls of meat, at which we were very merry, while in came Mr. Wade and his friend Capt. Moyse, and here we stayed till 7 at night, I winning a Quart of sack of Shaw that one trencherful that was sent us was all lamb, and he that it was veale. I, by having but 3*d.* in my pocket, made shift to spend no more; whereas if I had had more I had spent more, as the rest did. So that I see it is an advantage to a man to carry little in his pocket. Home; and after supper and a little at my lute, I went to bed.

17. In the morning, Tom, that was my Lord's foot-boy, came to see me and had 10*s.* of me of the money of his which I have to keep of his. So that now I have but 35*s.* more of his. Then came Mr. Hill the instrument maker, and I consulted with him about the altering of my lute and my viall. After him, I went into my study and made up my accounts, and find that I am about 40*l* beforehand in the world. And that is all. So to my office and from thence brought Mr. Hawly home with me to dinner; and after dinner wrote a letter to Mr. Downing about his business – and gave it Hawly; and so I went to Mr. Gunings to his weekly fast; and after sermon, meeting there with Mr. L'impertinent, we went and walked in the park till it was dark. I played on my pipe at the Echo, and then drank a cup of ale at Jacob's. So to Westminster hall, and he with me; where I heard that some of the members of the House was gone to meet with some of the secluded members and Gen. Monke in the City. Hence we went to Whitehall, thinking to hear more news. Where I met with Mr. Hunt, who told me how Monke had sent for all his goods that he had here into the City. And yet again, he told me that some of the members of the House had this day laid in firing into their lodgings at Whitehall for a good while. So that we are at a great stand to think what will become of things, whether Monke will stand to the Parliament or no. Hence, Monsieur Limpertinent and I to Harpers and there drank a cup or two to the King, and to his fair sister Frances good health, of whom we had much discourse of her not being much the worse for the smallpox which she had this last summer. So home and to bed. (This day we were invited to my uncle Fenners wedding feast, but went not, this being the 27th year.)

18.    A great while at my Viall and voice, learning to sing *Fly boy*, *fly boy* without book. So to my office, where little to do. In the Hall I met with Mr. Eglin and one Looker, a famous gardiner, servant to my Lord Salsbury; and among other things, the gardiner told a strange passage in good earnest: how formerly Mr. Eglin did in his company put his finger, which being sore had a black case over it, into a woman's belly, he named her Nan (which I guess who it is), and left his case within her; which Mr. Eglin blushed but did not deny it. Which truly I was sorry to hear and did think of it a good while afterward. Home to dinner; and then went to my Lord's lodgings to my turret there, and took away most of my books and sent them home by my maid. Hither came Capt. Holland to me, who took me to the Half Moone tavern and Mr. Southorne, Blackburnes clerk. Thence he took me to the Mitre in Fleet street, where we heard (in a room over the music-room) very plainly through the ceiling. Here we parted, and I to Mr. Wottons and with him to an alehouse and drank; where he told me a great many stories of comedies which he had formerly seen acted and the names of the principal actors, and gave me a very good account of it. Hence to Whitehall, where I met with Luellin and at the Clerkes chamber wrote a letter to my Lord. So home and to bed. This day, two soldiers were hanged in the Strand for their late mutiny at Somerset house.

19.    *Lords day*. Early in the morning, I set my books that I brought home yesterday up in order in my study. Thence, forth to Mr. Harpers to drink a draught of purle; whither by appointment Monsieur L'impertinent who did intend too, upon my desire, to go along with me to St. Bartholomew's to hear one Mr. Sparkes; but it raining very hard, we went to Mr. Gunings and heard an excellent sermon. And speaking of the character that the Scripture gave of Ann the mother of the Blessed Virgin, he did there speak largely in commendation of Widowhood, and not as we do to marry two or three wifes or husbands, one after another. Here I met with Mr. Moore and went home with him to dinner, where he told me the discourse that happened between the secluded members and the members of the House before Monke last Friday. How the secluded said that they did not entend by coming in to express revenge upon these men, but only to meet and dissolve themselfs, and only to issue writs for a free Parliament. He told me that there is great likelihood that the secluded members will come in, and so Mr.

Crew and my Lord are likely to be great men, at which I was very glad. After dinner there was many secluded members come in to Mr. Crew; which, it being the Lord's day, did make Mr. Moore believe that there was something extraordinary in the business. Hence home and brought my wife to Mr. Messums to hear him. And indeed he made a very good sermon; but only, too eloquent for a pulpit. After sermon, to my father's and fell in discourse concerning our going to Cambrige the next week with my Brother John.

20.   In the morning at my lute. Then to my office, where my partener and I made even our balance. Took him home to dinner with me, where my Brother John came to dine with me. After dinner I took him to my study at home and at my Lord's, and gave him some books and other things against his going to Cambrige. After he was gone, I went forth to Westminster hall, where I met with Chetwind, Simons and Gregory; and with them to Marshes at Whitehall to drink, and stayed there a pretty while reading a pamphlet, well-writ and directed to Gen. Monke in praise of the form of Monarchy which was settled here before the Warrs. In the evening Simons and I to the Coffee Clubb, where nothing to do. After a small debate upon the Question whether learned or unlearned subjects are the best, the club broke off very poorly, and I do not think they will meet any more. Hence with Vines &c to Wills; and after a pot or two, home; and so to bed.

21.   In the morning, going out, I saw many soldiers going toward Westminster; and was tol[d] that they were going to admit the secluded members again. So I to Westminster hall, and in Chancery row I saw about 20 of them, who had been at Whitehall with gen. Monke, who came thither this morning and made a speech to them and recommended to them a commonwealth, and against Ch. Stuart. They came to the House and went in one after another, and at last the Speaker came. But it is very strange that this could be carried so private, that the other members of the House heard nothing of all this till they found them in the House, insomuch that the soldiers that stood there to let in the secluded members, they took for such as they had ordered to stand there to hinder their coming in. Mr. Prin came with an old basket-hilt sword on, and had a great many great shouts upon his going into the hall. They sat till noon, and at their coming out Mr. Crew saw me and bid me

come to his house; which I did, and he would have me dine with him, which I did, and he very joyful; told me that the House had made Gen. Monke generall of all the forces in England, Scotland, and Ireland. He advised me to send for my Lord forthwith, and told me that there is no Question but, if he will, he may now be imployed again; and that the House doth entend to do nothing more then to issue writs and to settle a foundation for a free parliament. After dinner I back to Westminster hall with him in his coach. Here I met with Mr. Lock and Pursell, Maisters of Musique; and with them to the Coffee-house into a room next the Water by ourselfs. Here we had variety of brave Italian and Spanish songs and a Canon for 8 *Voc:*, which Mr. Lock had newly made on these words: *Domine salvum fac Regem*, an admirable thing. Here, out of the window it was a most pleasant sight to see the City from [one] end to the other with a glory about it, so high was the light of the Bonefires and so thick round the City, and the bells rang everywhere.

22. In the morning, entended to have gone to Mr. Crews to borrow some money; but it raining, I forebore and went to my Lord's lodging and look that all things were well there. Then home and sang a song to my vial; so to my office and to Wills, where Mr. Pierce found me out and told me that he would go with me to Cambrige, where Coll. Ayres's Regiment, to which he is surgeon, lieth. To my father's to dinner, where nothing but a small dish of powdered beef and a dish of carrots, they being all busy to get things ready for my Brother John to go tomorrow. Hence home to my study, where I only writ thus much of this day's passages to this
and so out again. To Whitehall, where I met with Will Simons and Mr. Mabbott at marshes, who told me how the House had this day voted that the gates of the City should be set up at the cost of the State. Home for my lantern and so to my father's, where I directed John what books to put [up] for Cambrige.

24–25. I rose very early; and taking horse at Scotland yard at Mr. Garthwayts stable, I rode to Mr. Pierces – who rose; and in a Quarter of an hour, leaving his wife in bed (with whom Mr. Lucy methought was very free as she lay in bed), we both mounted and so set forth about 7 of the clock, the day and the way very foul. About Ware we overtook Mr. Blayton, brother-in-law to Dick Vines, who went thenceforward with us; and at Puckrige we baited. Where we had a loin of mutton fried and were very merry; but the way exceeding bad from Ware thither. Then up again and as far as Foulmer, within six mile of Cambrige, my mare being almost tired: here we lay at the Chequer. Playing at cards till supper, which was a breast of veal roasted. I lay with Mr. Pierce, who we left here the next morning upon his going to Hinchingbrooke to speak with my Lord before his going to London; and we two came to Cambrige by 8 a-clock in the morning, to the Faulcon in the Petty Cury. Where we found my father and brother very well. After dressing myself, about 10 a-clock, my father, brother and I to Mr. Widdrington at Christ's College, who received us very civilly and caused my brother to be admitted, while my father, he and I sat talking. After that done, we take leave. My father and brother went to visit some friends, Pepys's, scholars in Cambrige, while I went to Magdalen College to Mr. Hill, with whom I found Mr. Zanchy, Burton, and Hollins, and was exceeding civilly received by them; I took leave, on promise to sup with them, and to my Inn again, where I dined with some others that were there at an ordinary. After dinner, my brother to the college and my father and I to my Cosen Angiers to see them; where Mr. Fairbrother came to us. Here we sat a while talking. My father, he went to look after his things at the Carriers and my brother's chamber, while Mr. Fairbrother, my Cosen Angier and Mr. Zanchy, who I met at Mr. Morton's shop (where I bought *Elenchus Motuum*, having given my former to Mr. Downing when he was here), to the Three tuns, where we drank pretty hard and many healths to the King &c till it begin to be darkish; then we broke up and I and Mr. Zanchy went to Magdalen College, where a very handsome supper at Mr. Hills chamber, I suppose upon a club among them; where in their discourse I could find that there was nothing at all left of the old preciseness in their discourse, specially on Saturday nights. And Mr. Zanch[y] told me that there was no such thing nowadays among them at any time. After supper and some discourse, then to my Inn, where I found my father in his Chamber; and after some discourse and he well satisfied with this day's work, we went to bed, my brother lying with me, his things not being come by the carrier that he could not lie in the college.

26. *Sunday*. My brother went to the college to Chappell. My father and I went out in the morning and walk out in the fields behind King's College and in King's College chapel yard; and there

we met with Mr. Fayrbrother. Who took us to Butolphes Church, where we heard Mr. Nicolas of Queen's College (who I knew in my time to be Tripos with great applause) upon this text: "For thy commandments are broad." Thence my father and I to Mr. Widdrington's chamber to dinner, where he used us very courteously again and had two fellow-commoners at table with him, and Mr. Pepper, a fellow of the college. After that we broke up; and my father, Mr. Zanch[y] and I to my Cosen Angiers to supper, where I caused two bottles of wine to be carried from the Rose tavern; but was drank up, and I had not the wit to let them know at table that it was I that paid for them, and so I lost my thanks for them. So to my Inn, where, after I had wrote a note and enclosed the certificate to Mr. Widdrington, I bade good-night to my father; and John went to bed but I stayed up a little while, playing the fool with the lass of the house at the door of the chamber; and so to bed.

27.  Up by 4 a-clock, and after I was ready, took my leave of my father, whom I left in bed; and the same of my Brother John, to whom I gave 10s. Mr. Blayton and I took horse and straight to Saffron Walden, where at the White Hart we set up our horses and told the maister of the house to shew us Audly end house; who took us on foot through the park and so to the house, where the housekeeper showed us all the house; in which the stateliness of the ceilings, chimney-pieces, and form of the whole was exceedingly worth seeing. He took us into the cellar, where we drank most admirable drink, a health to the King. Here I played on my Flagelette, there being an excellent Echo. He showed us excellent pictures; two especially, those of the four Evangelistes and Henry 8th. After that, I gave the man 2s. for his trouble and went back again. In our going, my landlord carried us through a very old Hospital or Almeshouse, where 40 poor people was maintained; a very old foundation, and over the chimney in the mantelpiece was an Inscripcion in brass: *Orate pro animâ Thomæ Bird* &c.; and the poor's box also was in the same chimney-piece, with an Iron door and locks to it, into which I put sixpens: they brought me a draught of their drink in a brown bowl, tipped with silver, which I drank of; and at the bottom was a picture of the Virgen and the Child in her arms, done in silver. So we went to our Inn, and after eating of something and kissed the daughter of the house, she being very pretty, we took leave; and so that night, the road pretty good but the weather rainy, to Eping. Where we sat and played a game at

draughts; and after supper and some merry talk with a plain bold maid of the house, we went to bed.

28.   Up in the morning, and had some red Herrings to our breakfast while my boot-heel was a-mending; by the same token, the boy left the hole as big as it was before. Then to horse and for London through the Forrest, where we found the way good, but only in one path; which we kept as if we had rode through a kennel all the way.

29.   To my office, and drank at Wills with Mr. Moore, who told me how my Lord is chosen generall-at-sea by the Council and that it is thought that Monke will be joined with him therein.

## –✯MARCH✯–

1.   To my office, where little to do; but Mr. Sheply comes to me, so at dinner time he and I went to Mr. Crews, it being the day that John, Mr. John Crew's coachman, was to be buried in the afternoon, he being a day or two before killed with a blow of one of his horses that struck his skull into his brains. From thence Mr. Sheply and I went into London to Mr. Laxton's, my Lord's Apothecary; and so by water to Westminster, where at the Sun he and I spent two or three hours at a pint or two of wine, discoursing of matters in the country; among other things, telling me that my Uncle[1] did to him make a very kind mention of me and what he would do for me. Thence I went home, and went to bed betimes.

2.   This morning I went early to my Lord at Mr. Crew's, where I spoke to him. Here were a great many too, come to see him, as Secretary Thurlow who is now by this Parliament chosen again Secretary of State. There was also gen. Monkes trumpeters to give my Lord a sound of their trumpets this morning. Great is the talk of a single person, and that it would now be Charles, George, or Richard again.[2] Great also is the dispute now in the House in whose name the writs shall run for the next Parliament – and it is

1. Robert Pepys of Brampton.
2. i.e. Charles Stuart, George Monck, or Richard, son of Oliver Cromwell.

said that Mr. Prin in open House said, "In King Charles's." From Westminster hall, home. Spent the evening in my study; and so after talk with my wife, then to bed.

3.   To Westminster hall, where I found my Lord was last night voted one of the generalls-at-sea, and Monke the other. I met my Lord in the Hall, who bade me come to him at noon. I met with Mr. Pierce the purser, Lieut. Lambert, Mr. Creed, and Will Howe, and went with them to the Sun Taverne. Up to my office, but did nothing. At noon home to dinner to a sheep's head; my Brother Tom came and dined with me, and told me that my mother was not very well and that my Aunt Fenner was very ill too. After dinner, I to Warwick house in Holborne to my Lord, where he dined with my Lord of Manchester, Sir Dudly North, my Lord Fiennes, and my Lord Barkly. I stayed in the great hall, talking with some gentlemen there till they all came out. Then I by coach with my Lord to Mr. Crews, in our way talking of public things and how I should look after getting of his Comission's despatch. He told me he feared there was new design hatching, as if Monke had a mind to get into the saddle. Returning, met with Mr. Gifford, who took me and gave me half a pint of wine and told me, as I this day hear from many, that things are in a very doubtful posture, some of the Parliament being willing to keep the power in their hands. After I had left him, I met with Tom Harper, who took me to a place in Drury lane, where we drank a great deal of strong water, more then ever I did in [my] life at one time before. He talked hog-high that my Lord Protector would come in place again, which endeed is much discoursed of again, though I do not see it possible. Hence home and writ to my father at Brampton by the post; so to bed.

4.   *Lords day*. Before I went to church I sang *Orpheus Hymne* to my Viall. After that to Mr. Guning's; an excellent sermon upon Charity. Then to my mother to dinner, where my wife and the maid was come. After dinner, we three to Mr. Messum's, where we met Monsieur Limpertinent, who got us a seat and told me a ridiculous story; how that last week he had caused a simple citizen to spend 8*ol* in entertainments of him and some friends of his, upon pretence of some service that he would do him in his suit after a widow. Then to my mother again; and after supper, she and I talked very high about Religion, I in defence of the Religion I

was born in.[1] Then home.

5.   Early in the morning, Mr. Hill comes to string my Theorbo, which we were about till past 10 a-clock, with a great deal of pleasure. To Westminster by water, only seeing Mr. Pinkny at his own house, where he showed me how he hath alway kept the Lion and Unicorne in the back of his chimney bright, in expectation of the King's coming again. Great hopes of the King's coming again. To bed.

6.   *Shrove-tuesday*. I called Mr. Sheply and we both went up to my Lord's lodgings at Mr. Crew's, where he bade us to go home again and get a fire against an hour after – which we did at Whitehall, whither he came; and after talking with him and I about his going to sea, he called me by myself to go along with him into the garden, where he asked me how things were with me and what he hath endeavoured to do with my uncle to get him to do something for me; but that he would say nothing to. He likewise bade me look out now, at this turn, some good place; and he would use all his own and all the interest of his friends that he hath in England to do me good. And asked me whether I could without too much incon-venience go to sea as his Secretary, and bade me think of it. He also begin to talk of things of state, and told me that he should now want one in that capacity at sea that he might trust in. And therefore he would have me to go. He told me also that he did believe the King would come in, and did discourse with me about it and about the affection of the people and City – at which I was full glad. After he was gone, I waiting upon him through the garden till he came to the Hall, I left him and went up to my office, where Mr. Hawly brought one to me, a seaman that had promised 10*l* to him if he gat him a purser's place, which I think to endeavour to do. While we were drinking, in comes Mr. Day, a Carpenter in Westminster, to tell me that it was Shrove-tuesday and that I must go with him to their yearly club upon this day, which I confess I had quite forgot. So I went to the Bell, where was Mr.'s Eglin, Veezy, Vincent a butcher, one more, and Mr. Tanner, with whom I played upon a viall and he the viallin after dinner, and were very merry, with a special good dinner – a leg of veal and bacon, two capons and sausages and fritters, with abundance of wine. This day I hear that

1. Orthodox Anglicanism: his mother appears to have inclined towards Puritanism.

the Lords do entend to sit, and great store of them are now in town and I see in the Hall today. My Lord told me that there was great endeavours to bring in the Protector[1] again; but he told me too, that he did believe it would not last long if he were brought in; no, nor the King neither (though he seems to think that he will come in), unless he carry himself very soberly and well. Everybody now drink the King's health without any fear, whereas before it was very private that a man dare do it. My mind, I must needs remember, hath been very much eased and joyed in my Lord's great expression of kindness this day; and in discourse thereupon, my wife and I lay awake an hour or two in our bed.

7. *Ash wednesday*. My father newly come home from Brampton very well; who left my Uncle with his leg very dangerous, and he doth believe he cannot continue in that condition long. He tells me that my Uncle did acquaint him very largely what he did intend to do with his estate; to make me his Heire and to give my Brother Tom some things, and that my father and mother should have something likewise for to raise portions for Joh. and Pall: I pray God he may be as good as his word.

8. This noon I met with Capt. Holland at the Dog Taverne, with whom I advised how to make some advantage of my Lord's going to sea, which he told me might be by having of five or six servants entered on board, and I to give them what wages I pleased, and so their pay to be mine.

9. To my Lord at his lodging and came to Westminster with him in the coach, and he in the Painted chamber walked a good while; and I telling him that I was willing and ready to go with him to sea, he agreed that I should, and advised me what to write to Mr. Downing about it. All night troubled in my thoughts how to order my business upon this great change with me, that I could not sleep; and being overheated with drink, I made a promise the next morning to drink no strong drink this week, for I find that it makes me sweat in bed and puts me quite out of order.

10. In the morning went to my father, whom I took in his cutting-house; and there I told him my resolution to go to sea with my Lord

1. Richard Cromwell.

and consulted with him how to dispose of my wife; and at last resolved of letting her be at Mr. Bowyers. Thence to the Treasurer of the Navy, where I received 500*l* for my Lord; and having left 200 of it with Mr. Rawlinson at his house for Sheply, I went with the rest to the Sun taverne on Fish street hill, where Mr. Hill, Stevens and Mr. Hater of the Navy Office had invited me; where we had good discourse and a fine breakfast of Mr. Hater. Then by coach home, where I took occasion to tell my wife of my going to sea, who was much troubled thereat and was with some dispute at last willing to continue at Mr. Bowyers in my absence.

11.   *Sunday*. All the day busy without my band on, putting up my books and things in order to my going to sea. At night my wife and I went to my father's to supper, where J. Norton and Ch. Glascocke supped with us; and after supper home, where the wench had provided all things against tomorrow to wash. And so to bed, where I much troubled with my cold and coughing.

12.   This day the wench ris at 2 in the morning to wash, and my wife and I lay talking a great while; I, by reason of my cold, could not tell how to sleep. My wife and I to the Exchange,[1] where we bought a great many things, where I left her and went into London to do a great many things, in order to my going. So came back and at Wilkinson's found Mr. Sheply and some sea people, as the cook of the *Nazeby* and others, at dinner. Then to the White horse in Kings street, where I got Mr. Biddles horse to ride to Huntsmore to Mr. Bowyers; where I found him and all well and willing to have my wife come and board with them while I was at sea, which was the business I went about. Here I lay and took a thing for my cold by Mrs. Bowyers direction, *viz*. a spoonful of honey and a nutmeg scraped into it and so take it into the mouth, which I found did do me much good.

13.   It rained hard and I got up early and got to London by 8 a-clock. At my Lord's lodgings I spoke with him, who told me that I was to be Secretary and Creed to be Deputy-Treasurer for the Fleet, at which I was troubled but I could not help it. After that to my father's to look after things, and so at my shoemaker and others. At night to Whitehall, where I met with Simons and Luellin; drank

---

1. The New Exchange in the Strand.

with them at Roberts's at Whitehall. Things seem very doubtful what will be the end of all; for the Parliament seems to be strong for the King, which the soldiers do all talk against.

14.   To my Lord, where infinite of applications to him and to me, to my great trouble; my Lord he gave me all the papers that was given to him, to put in order and give him an account of them. Here I got half-a-piece of a person of Mr. Wrights recommending to my Lord to be preacher in the *Speaker* frigate. I went hence to St. James, and Mr. Pierce the surgeon with me, to speak with Mr. Clerke, Monkes secretary, about getting some soldiers removed out of Huntington to Oundle; which my Lord told me he did to do a courtesy to the town, that he might have the greater interest in them in the choice of the next Parliament. This done (where I saw Gen. Monke and methought he seemed a dull, heavy man), he and I to Whitehall, where with Luellin we dined at Marshes. Coming home, telling my wife what we had to dinner, she had a mind to some Cabbage, and I sent for some and she had it. Went to the Admiralty, where a strange thing how I was already courted by the people. This morning, among others that came to me, I hired a boy of Jenkins of Westminster, and Burr to be my clerk. So home and late at night put up my things in a sea-chest that Mr. Sheply lent me – and so to bed.

16.   No sooner out of bed but troubled with abundance of Clients, seamen. My landlords, Vanly's, man came to me and I paid him rent for my house for this Quarter ending at Ladyday, and took an acquittance that he brought me from his master. Then to Mr. Sheply to the Rhenish winehouse; where Mr. Pim the tailor was, and gave us a morning draught and a neat's tongue. Home, and with my wife to London. We dined at my father's, where Joyce Norton and Mr. Armiger dined also; after dinner my wife took leave of them in order to her going tomorrow to Huntsmore. In my way home I went to the Chappell in Chancery lane to bespeak paper of all sorts and other things belonging to writing, against my voiage. So home, where I spent an hour or two about my business in my study. Then to Westminster hall, where I heard how the Parliament had this day dissolved themselfs and did pass very cheerfully through the Hall and the Speaker without his Mace. The whole Hall was joyful thereat, as well as themselfs; and now they begin to talk loud of the King. Tonight I am told that yesterday,

about 5 a-clock in the afternoon, one came with a ladder to the great Exchange and wiped with a brush the Inscripcion that was upon King Charles, and that there was a great bonefire made in the Exchange and people cried out "God bless King Charles the Second!" From the Hall I went home to bed, very sad in mind to part with my wife tomorrow, but God's will be done.

17. This morning bade Adieu in bed to the company of my wife. We rose and I gave my wife some money to serve her for a time, and what papers of consequence I had. Then I left her to get her ready and went to my Lord's with my boy Eliezer to my Lord's lodging at Mr. Crews. Here I had much business with my Lord; and papers, great store, given me by my Lord to dispose of as of the rest. After that, with Mr. Moore home to my house and took my wife by coach to the Chequer in Holborne; where after we had drunk &c., she took coach and so farewell. Thence with Mr. Hawly to dinner at Mr. Crews. After dinner, to my own house, where all things were put up into the dining-room and locked up, and my wife took the key along with her. This day, in the presence of Mr. Moore (who made it) and Mr. Hawly, I did (before I went out with my wife) seal my will to her, whereby I did give her all that I have in the world but my books, which I gave to my Brother John, excepting only French books, which my wife is to have. In the evening at the Admiralty: met my Lord there and got a Comission for Williamson to be Captain of the *Harp* frigate.

18. This day was very rainy all day. I rose early and went to the Barber's (Jervas) in the Palace yard and was trimmed* by him; and afterward drank with him a cup or two of ale, and did begin to hire his man to go with me to sea. Then to my Lord's lodging, where I found Capt. Williamson and gave him his commission to be Captain of the *Harpe* and he gave me a piece of gold and 20*s*. in silver. So to my own house, where I stayed a while and then to dinner with Mr. Sheply at my Lord's lodgings. After that to Mr. Messum's, where he made a very gallant sermon upon "Pray for the life of the King, and the King's son" (*Esra* 6. 10).

19. Early to my Lord, where infinite of business to do, which makes my head full; and indeed, for these two or three days I have not been without a great many cares and thoughts concerning them. After that to the Admiralty, where a good while with Mr.

Blackborne, who told me that it was much to be feared that the King would come in, for all good men and good things were now discouraged. All the discourse nowaday is that the King will come again; and for all I see, it is the wishes of all and all do believe that it will be so. My mind is still much troubled for my poor wife, but I hope that this undertaking will be worth my pains.

20.    The weather still very rainy. By coach to London, and took a short melancholly leave of my father and mother, without having time to drink or say anything of business one to another; and endeed, I had a fear upon me that I should scarce ever see my mother again, she having a great cold then upon her. Then to Westminster, where by reason of rain and an Easterly wind, the water was so high that there was boats rowed in King streete and all our yard was drownded, that one could not go to my house, so as no man hath seen the like almost. Most houses full of water.

22.    I went forth about my own business to buy a pair of riding gray serge Stockings, a sword and belt and shoes. And after that took Wotton and Brigden to the Popes head tavern in Chancery lane, where Gilb. Holland and Shelston was; and we dined and drank a great deal of wine, and they paid all. Strange how these people do now promise me anything; one a Rapier, the other a vessel of wine or a gown, and offered me his silver hatband to [do] him a courtesy. I pray God keep me from being proud or too much lifted up hereby.

23.    Up early. Carried my Lord's Will in a black box to Mr. Wm. Mountagu for him to keep for him. Then to the Barbers and put on my Cravatt there. So to my Lord again, who was almost ready to be gone and had stayed for me. Hither came Gill. Holland, and brought me a Stick-rapier, and Shelston a sugar-loaf; and had brought his wife, which he said was a very pretty woman, to the Ship tavern hard by for me to see, but I could not go. Young Reeve also brought me a little Perspective glasse which I bought for my Lord; it cost me 8s. So after that my Lord in Sir H. Wrights coach with Capt. Isham, and Mr. Tho. and John Crew with him. And I and W. Howe in a Hackny to the Towre, where the barges stayed for us. My Lord and the Captain in one, and W. How and I and Mr. Ibbott and Mr. Burr in the other, to the Long Reach, where the *Swiftsure* lay at Anchor (in our way we saw the great breach which

the late high water had made, to the loss of many 1000*l* to the people about Limehouse). As soon as my Lord on board, the guns went off bravely from the Ships; and a little while after comes the Vice-admirall Lawson and seemed very respectful to my Lord, and so did the rest of the Comanders of the frigates that were thereabouts. I to the Cabbin allotted for me, which was the best that any had that belonged to my Lord. I got out some things out of my chests for writing, and to work presently, Mr. Burr and I both. I supped at the Deck table with Mr. Sheply. We were late, writing of orders for the getting of ships ready, &c. After that to bed in my cabin, which was but short; however, I made shift with it and slept very well; and the weather being good, I was not sick at all; yet I know not when I shall be.

24.   I despatch many letters today abroad – and it was late before we could get to bed. Mr. Sheply and How supped with me in my Cabbin, and the boy Eliezr. flung down a can of beer upon my papers which made me give him a box of the eare, it having all spoiled my papers and cost me a great deal of work. So to bed.

25.   About 2 a-clock in the morning, letters came from London by our Coxon; so they waked me, but I would not rise but bid him stay till morning, which he did; and then I rose and carried them in to my Lord, who read them a-bed. Among the rest, there was the Writt and Mandate for him to dispose to the Cinque Ports for choice of Parliament men. There was also one for me from Mr. Blackburne, who with his own hand superscribes it to *S.P. Esqr.*, of which, God knows, I was not a little proud. About 10 a-clock Mr. Ibbotts at the end of the long table begin to pray and preach and endeed made a very good sermon, upon the duty of a Christian to be steadfast in the faith. After that, the Captain, Cuttance, and I have oysters, my Lord being in his Cabbin, not entending to stir out today. After that, up into the great Cabbin above to dinner with the Captain, where was Capt. Isham and all the officers of the ship. I took place of all but the Captain. After dinner I writ a great many letters to my friends at London; and after that, the sermon begin again, all which time I slept, God forgive me. After that, it being a fair day, I walked with the Captain upon the Deck talking. At night I supped with him and after that had orders from my Lord about some business to be done against tomorrow, which I sat up late and did; and then to bed.

26.   This day it is two years since it pleased God that I was cut of the stone at Mrs. Turner's in Salisbury court. And did resolve while I live to keep it a festival, as I did the last year at my house, and for ever to have Mrs. Turner and her company with me. But now it pleases God that I am where I am and so am prevented to do it openly; only, within my soul I can and do rejoice and bless God, being at this time, blessed be His holy name, in as good health as ever I was in my life. This morning I ris early and went about making of an establishment of the whole fleet and a list of all the ships, with the number of men [and] guns: about an hour after that, we had a meeting of the principal commanders and seamen to proportion out the number of these things. After that to dinner, there being very many commanders on board. All the afternoon very many orders were made, till I was very weary. At night Mr. Sheply and W. Howe came and brought some bottles of wine and something to eat at my Cabbin, where we were very merry, remembering the day of being cut of the stone. The Captain, Cuttance, came afterwards and sat drinking a bottle of wine till 11 a-clock at night, which is a kindness he doth not usually do to the greatest officer in the ship. After that to bed.

29.   We lie still a little below Gravesend. At night Mr. Sheply returned from London and told us of several elections for the next Parliament. That the King's Effigies was new-making, to be set up in the Exchange again.

30.   I was saluted in the morning with two letters from some that I had done a favour to, which brought me in each a piece of gold. This day, while my Lord and we were at dinner, the *Nazeby* came in sight toward us, and at last came to Anchor close by us. After dinner my Lord and many others went on board her, where everything was out of order; and a new chimney made for my Lord in his bedchamber, which he was much pleased with.

# ⚯APRILL⚯

1.   *Lords day*. Mr. Ibbott preached very well. After dinner my Lord did give me a private list of all the ships that were to be set out this summer, wherein I do discern that he hath made it his care to

put by as much of the Anabaptists as he can. By reason of my Lord and my being busy to send away the Packet by Mr. Cooke of the *Nazeby*, it was 4 a-clock before we could begin sermon again. This day Capt. Guy came on board from Dunkirke, who tells me that the King will come in and that the soldiers at Dunkirke do drink the King's health in the streets. At night the Captain, Sir R. Stayner, Mr. Sheply, and I did sup together in the Captain's cabin. I made a commission tonight to Capt. Wilgress of the *Beare*, which got me 30s. So after writing a while, I went to bed.

2.    Up very early, and to get all my things and my boy's packed up. Great concourse of commanders here this morning to take leave of my Lord upon his going into the *Naseby*, so that the table was full; so there dined below many commanders and Mr. Creed, who was much troubled to hear that he could not go along with my Lord, for he had already got all his things thither, thinking to stay there. After dinner I went in one of the boats with my boy before my Lord, and made shift before night to get my cabin in pretty good order. It is but little; but very convenient, having one window to the sea and another to the Deck – and a good bed.

3.    Late to bed. About 3 in the morning there was great knocking at my cabin, which with much difficulty (as they say) waked me and I rise; but it was only for a packet, so I went to my bed again. And in the morning gave it my Lord. This morning Capt. Isham comes on board to see my Lord and drink his wine before he went into the Downes; there likewise came many merchants to get convoy to the Baltique, which a course was taken for. They dined with my Lord, and one of them, by name Ald. Wood, talked much to my Lord of the hopes that we have now to be settled (under the King he meant); but my Lord took no notice of it. At night busy a-writing, and so to bed. My heart exceeding heavy for not hearing of my dear wife; and indeed, I do not remember that ever my heart was so apprehensive of her absence as at this very time.

5.    Infinite of business all the morning of orders to make, that I was very much perplexed that Mr. Burr had failed me of coming back last night, and we ready to set sail. Which we did about noon, and came in the evening to Lee road and anchored.

6.    This morning came my brother-in-law Balty to see me and to

desire to be here with me as Reformado, which did much trouble me. But after dinner (my Lord using him very civilly at table), I spoke to my Lord and he promised me a letter to Capt. Stokes for him, that he should be there. All the day with him, walking and talking; we under sail as far as the Spitts. In the afternoon, W. How and I to our Viallins, the first time since we came on board. In the evening, it being fine moonshine, I stayed late, walking upon the Quarter-deck talking with Mr. Cuttance, learning of some sea terms; and so down to supper and to bed – having an hour before put Balty into Bur's cabin, he being out of the ship.

7.   This day, about 9 a-clock in the morning, the wind grew high; and we being among the sands, lay at anchor. I begin to be dizzy and squeamish. Before dinner, my Lord sent for me down to eat some oysters, the best my Lord said that ever he eat in his life, though I have eat as good at Bardsey. After dinner and all the afternoon I walked upon the deck to keep myself from being sick; and at last, about 5 a-clock, went to bed and got a caudle made me, and sleep upon it very well.

8.   *Lords day*. Very calm again and I pretty well, but my head ached all day. About noon set sail; in our way I saw many wracks and masts, which are now the greatest guides for ships. We had a brave wind all the afternoon. And overtook two good merchantmen that overtook us yesterday, going to the East Indys, and the lieutenant and I lay out of his window with his glass, looking at the women that were on board them, being pretty handsome. I and Will Howe, the surgeon, parson, and Balty supped in the Lieutenant's cabin and afterward sat disputing, the parson for and I against extemporary prayer very hot.

9.   We having sailed all night, were come in sight of the North and South forelands in the morning, and so sailed all day. In the afternoon we had a very fresh gale, which I brooked better than I thought I should be able to do. About 5 a-clock we came to the Goodwin; so to the castles about Deale, where our fleet lay, among whom we anchored. Great was the shot of guns from the castles and ships and our answers, that I never heard yet so great rattling of guns. Nor could we see one another on board for the smoke that was among us, nor one ship from another.

11.   The wind all this day was very high – so that a gentleman that was at dinner with my Lord that came along with Sir John Bloys (who seemed a fine man) was forced to rise from table. This afternoon came a great paquet of letters from London directed to me; among the rest, two from my dear wife, the first that I have since my coming away from London. All the news from London is that things go ever further toward a King. That the Skinners Company the other day at their entertaining of Gen. Monke had took down the Parliament arms in their Hall and set up the Kings. In the evening my Lord and I had a great deal of discourse about the several Captaines of the fleet and his interest among them, and had his mind clear to bring in the King. He confessed to me that he was not sure of his own Captain to be true to him, and that he did not like Capt. Stokes. At night W. Howe and I at our viallins in my cabin, where Mr. Ibbott and the Lieutenant were late. I stayed the Lieutenant late, showing him my manner of keeping a Journall. After that, to bed. It comes now in my mind to observe that I am sensible that I have been a little too free to make mirth with the Minister of our ship, he being a very sober and an upright man.

14.   I slept till almost 10 a-clock – and then rise and drank a good morning draught there with Mr. Sheply, which occasioned my thinking upon the happy life that I live now, had I nothing to care for but myself. The sea was this morning very high; and looking out of the window, I saw our boat come with Mr. Pierce the purser in it, in great danger; who endeavouring to come on board us, had like to have been drowned had it not been for a rope.

18.   At night sent a packet to London. And Mr. Cooke returned thence, bringing me this news: that the Sectarys do talk high what they will do; but I believe all to no purpose. That the Cavaliers are something unwise to talk so high on the other side as they do. That it is evident now that the Generall and the Council do resolve to make way for the King's coming. And it is now clear that either the Fanatiques must now be undone, or the Gentry and citizens throughout England and clergy must fall, in spite of their Militia and army, which is not at all possible I think. At night I supped with W. Howe and Mr. Luellin (being the first time that I have been so long with him) in the great cabin below. After that to bed; and W. Howe sat by my bedside and he and I sang a psalm or two; and so I to sleep.

19.   A great deal of business all this day; and Burr being gone to shore without my leave did vex me much. This day it hath rained much, so that when I came to go to bed I found it wet through; so I was fain to wrap myself up in a dry sheet and so lie all night.

20.   All the morning I was busy to get my window altered and to have my table set as I would have it; which after it was done, I was infinitely pleased with it, and also to see what a command I have to have everyone ready to come and go at my command. This day one told me how that at the Eleccion at Cambrige for Knight of the shire, Wendby and Thornton, by declaring to stand for the Parliament and a King and the settlement of the Church, did carry it against all expectation against Sir Dudl. North and Sir Thom. Willis. I supped tonight with Mr. Sheply below at the half-deck table; and after that saw Mr. Pickering, whom my Lord brought down to his cabin; and so to bed.

21.   This day dined Sir John Boys and some other gentlemen, formerly great Cavaliers; and among the rest, one Mr. Norwood, for whom my Lord gave a convoy to carry him to the Brill; but he is certainly going to the King – for my Lord commanded me that I should not enter his name in my book. My Lord doth show them and that sort of people great civility. All their discourse and others' are of the King's coming, and we begin to speak of it very freely. And heard how in many churches in London and upon many signs there and upon merchants' ships in the river they have set up the King's arms. In the afternoon the Captain would by all means have me up to his cabin; and there treated me huge nobly, giving me a barrel of pickled oysters, and opened another for me, and a bottle of wine, which was a very great favour. At night late singing with W. Howe, and under the barber's hands in the coach. This night there came one with a letter from Mr. Edwd. Mountagu to my Lord, with command to deliver it to his own hand. I do believe that he doth carry some close business on for the King.

23.   In the evening, the first time that we have had any sport among the seamen; and indeed, there was extraordinary good sport, after my Lord had done playing, at ninepins. After that, W. Howe and I went to play two Trebles in the great Cabbin below; which my Lord hearing, after supper he called for our instruments and played a set of Lock's, two trebles and a bass. And that being

done, he fell to singing of a song made upon the Rump, with which he pleased himself well – to the tune of *The Blacksmith*. After all that done, then to bed.

26. This day came Mr. Donne back from London, who brought letters with him that signify the meeting of the Parliament yesterday. And in the afternoon, by other letters I hear that about twelve of the Lords met and have chosen my Lord of Manchester Speaker of the House of Lords (the young Lords that never sot yet, do forbear to sit for the present); and Sir Harbottle Grimstone Speaker of the House of Commons. Dr. Renalds preached before the Commons before they sat. My Lord told me how Sir H. Yelverton (formerly my schoolfellow) was chosen in the first place for Northamptonshire and Mr. Crew in the second. And told me how he did believe that the Cavaliers have now the upper hand clear of the Presbyterians. All the afternoon I was writing of letters; among the rest, one to W. Simons, Peter Luellin and Tom Doling; which because it is somewhat merry, I keep a copy of. After that done, Mr. Sheply, W. Howe and I down with Jo. Goods into my Lord's Storeroome of wine and other drink, where it was very pleasant to observe the massy timbers that the ship is made of. We in the room were wholly under water and yet a deck below that. After that to supper, where Tom Guy supped with us and we had very good laughing; and after that some Musique, where Mr. Pickering, beginning to play a bass part upon my viall, did it so like a fool that I was ashamed of him. After that to bed.

29. *Sunday*. This day I put on first my fine cloth suit, made of a cloak that had like to have been beshit behind a year ago the very day that I put it on. After sermon in the morning, Mr. Cooke came from London with a packet, bringing news how all the young lords that were not in arms against the Parliament do now sit. That a letter is come from the King to the House; which is locked up by the Council till next Tuesday, that it may be read in the open House when they meet again, they having adjourned till then to keep a fast tomorrow – and so the contents is not yet known.

30. After dinner to ninepins, W. Howe and I against Mr. Creed and the Captain; we lost 5s. apiece to them. After that, W. How, Mr. Sheply and I, we got my Lord's leave to go to see Capt. Sparling: so we took boat and first went on shore, it being very

pleasant in the fields. But a very pitiful town Deale is. We went to Fullers (the famous place for ale); but they had none but what was in the fat. After that to Pooles, a tavern in the town, where we drank; and so to boat again and went to the *Assistance*, where we were treated very civilly by the Captain; and he did give us such musique upon the harp by a fellow that he keeps on board, that I never expect to hear the like again – yet he a drunken simple fellow to look on as any I ever saw. After that on board the *Nazeby*, where we found my Lord at supper; so I sat down and very pleasant my Lord was with Mr. Creed and Sheply, who he puzled about finding out the meaning of the three holes which my Lord hath cut over the Chrystall of his watch. After supper, some musique. Then Mr. Sheply, W. Howe and I up to the Lieutenants Cabbin, where we drank, and I and Will Howe were very merry; and among other froliques, he pulls out the spiket of the little vessel of ale that was there in the Cabbin and drew some into his Mounteere; and after he had drunk, I endeavouring to dash it in his face, he got my velvett studying-cap and drew some into mine too, that we made ourselfs a great deal of mirth, but spoiled my clothes with the ale that we dash up and down; after that, to bed very late – with drink enough in my head.

# –⚜MAY⚜–

1.   This morning I was told how the people of Deale have set up two or three Maypooles and have hung up their flags upon the top of them, and so resolve to be very merry today, it being a very pleasant day. I wished myself in Hide parke. After dinner to nine-pins, and won something. The rest of the afternoon at my cabin, writing and piping. While we were at supper, we heard a great noise upon the Quarter Deck; so we all rise instantly, and found that it was to save the Coxon of the *Cheritons* boate; who dropping overboard, could not be saved, but was drowned. Today I put on my suit that was altered from the great skirts to little ones.

2.   In the morning at a breakfast of Radyshes at the Pursers cabin. After that to writing – till dinner – at which time comes Dunne from London with letters that tell us the wellcome Newes of the Parliaments votes yesterday, which will be remembered for the

happiest May day that hath been many a year to England. The King's letter was read in the House, wherein he submits himself and all things to them – as to an act of Oblivion to all, unless they shall please to except any; – as to the confirming of the Sales of the King's and Church lands, if they see good. The House, upon reading the letter, order 50000*l* to be forthwith provided to send to His Maiesty for his present supply. And a committee chosen to return an answer of thank[s] to His Majesty for his gracious Letter. And that the letter be kept among the Records of the Parliament. And in all this, not so much as one Noe. Upon notice made from the Lords to the Commons of their desire that the Commons would join with them in their vote for King, Lords, and Commons, the Commons did concur and voted that all books whatever that are out against the government of King, Lords, and Commons should be brought into the House and burned. Great joy all yesterday at London; and at night more bonefires then ever and ringing of bells and drinking of the King's health upon their knees in the streets, which methinks is a little too much. But everybody seems to be very joyful in the business – insomuch that our sea-commanders now begin to say so too, which a week ago they would not do. And our seamen, as many as have money or credit for drink, did do nothing else this evening.

3.   This morning my Lord showed me the King's declaration and his letter to the two Generalls to be communicated to the fleet. The contents of the letter are his offer of grace to all that will come in within 40 days, only excepting them that the Parliament shall hereafter except. That the sales of lands during these troubles, and all other things, shall be left to the Parliament, by which he will stand. The letter dated at Breda, April$\frac{4}{14}$ 1660, in the 12th year of his Raigne. Upon the receipt of it this morning by an express, Mr. Phillips, one of the messengers of the Council from Gen. Monke, my Lord summoned a council of war, and in the meantime did dictate to me how he would have the vote ordered which he would have pass this council. Which done, the commanders all came on board, and the council set in the coach (the first council of war that hath been in my time), where I read the letter and declaration; and while they were discoursing upon it, I seemed* to draw up a vote; which being offered, they passed. Not one man seemed to say no to it, though I am confident many in their hearts were against it. After this was done, I went up to the Quarter-deck with my Lord and the

commanders, and there read both the papers and the vote; which done, and demanding their opinion, the seamen did all of them cry out "God bless King Charles!" with the greatest joy imaginable. That being done, Sir R. Stayner, who had invited us yesterday, took all the commanders and myself on board him to dinner; where dinner not being ready, I went with Capt. Hayward to the *Plimouth* and *Essex*, and did what I had to do there and returned, where very merry at dinner. After dinner, to the rest of the ships (I stayed at the *Assistance* to hear the harper a good while) quite through the fleet. Which was a very brave sight, to visit all the ships and to be received with the respect and Honour that I was on board them all. And much more to see the great joy that I brought to all men; not one through the whole fleet showing the least dislike of the business. In the evening, as I was going on board the Vice-Admirall, the Generall begun to fire his guns, which he did all that he had in the ship; and so did all the rest of the commanders, which was very gallant, and to hear the bullets go hissing over our heads as we were in the boat. This done and finished my Proclamation, I returned to the *Nazeby*, where my Lord was much pleased to hear how all the fleet took it; and in a transport of joy showed me a private letter of the King's to him and another from the Duke of Yorke in such familiar style as to their common friend, with all kindness imaginable. And I found by the letters, and so my Lord told me too, that there hath been many letters sped between them for a great while, and I perceive unknown to Monke. The King speaks of his being courted to come to The Hague, but doth desire my Lord's advice whether to come to take ship. And the Duke offers to learn the seaman's trade of him, in such familiar words as if Jack Cole and I had writ them. This was very strange to me, that my Lord should carry all things so wisely and prudently as he doth, and I was over-joyful to see him in so good condition; and he did not a little please himself to tell me how he had provided for himself so great a hold in the King.

4. After this to supper, and then to writing of letters till 12 at night and so up again at 3 in the morning. My Lord seemed to put great confidence in me and would take my advice in many things. I perceive his being willing to do all the Honour in the world to Monke and to let him have all the Honour of doing the business, though he will many times express his thoughts of him to be but a thick-skulled fellow; so that I do believe there is some agreement

more then ordinary between the King and my Lord to let Monke carry on the business, for it is he that must do the business, or at least that can hinder the business if he be not flattered and observed. This my Lord will hint himself sometimes. I wrote this morning many letters, and to all the copies of the vote of the council of Warr I put my name; that if it should come in print, my name may be at it. I sent a copy of the vote to Doling, inclosed in this letter:

"Sir,

He that can fancy a fleet (like ours) in her pride, with pendants loose, guns roaring, caps flying, and the loud *Vive le Roy's* echoed from one ship's company to another, he and he only can apprehend the joy this enclosed vote was received with, or the blessing he thought himself possessed of that bore it, and is

Your humble servant."

About 9 a-clock I got all my letters done, and sent them by the messenger that came yesterday. The rest of the afternoon at ninepins. In the evening came a packet from London; among the rest, a letter from my wife which tells me that she hath not been well, which did exceedingly trouble me; but my Lord sending Mr. Cooke this night, I wrote to her and sent a piece of gold inclosed to her, and writ also to Mrs. Bowyer and enclosed a half-piece to her for a token. After supper at the table in the coach, my Lord talking concerning the uncertainty of the places of the Exchequer to them that have them now, he did at last think of an office which doth belong to him in case the King doth restore every man to his places that ever have been patent, which is to be one of the clerks of the Signett,[1] which will be a fine imployment for one of his sons. After all this discourse, we broke up and to bed.

6. *Lords day.* This morning, while we were at sermon, comes in Dr. Clarges and a Dozen gentlemen with him to see my Lord – who after sermon dined with him. I remember that last night, upon discourse concerning Clarges, my Lord told me that he was a man of small *entendimiento*. It fell very well today; a stranger preached here today for Mr. Ibbott, one Mr. Stanly, who prayed for King Charles, by the Grace of God, &c., which gave great contentment to the gentlemen that were on board here, and said they would talk of it when they came to Breda, as not having it done yet in London so publicly. After they were gone from on board, my Lord writ a

1. Correctly, Privy Seal.

letter to the King and gave it me [to] carry privately to Sir W. Compton on board the *Assistance*, which I did; and after a health to his Majesty on board there, I left them under sail for Breda: back again and found them at sermon; I went up to my cabin and looked over my accounts, and found that all my debts paid and my preparation to sea paid for, I have above 40*l* clear in my purse. After supper to bed.

7.  This morning Capt. Cuttance sent me a dozen of bottles of Margett ale – three of which I drank presently with some friends in the Coach: my Lord went this morning about the flag-ships in a boat, to see what alterations there must be as to the armes and flags. He did give me order also to write for silk flags and Scarlett wastecloaths. For a rich barge. For a noise of Trumpetts; and a set of Fidlers. In the afternoon I lost 5*s*. at ninepins. After supper, Musique and to bed – having also among us at the coach-table wrote a letter to the French Embassador in French – about the release of a ship that we have taken. After I was in bed, Mr. Sheply and W. Howe came and sat in my cabin, where I gave them three bottles of Marget ale, and sat laughing and very merry till almost one a-clock in the morning; and so good-night.

8.  All the morning busy. After dinner my Lord and we at ninepins: I lost nine shillings. My letters today tell me how it was entended that the King should be proclaimed today in London with a great deal of pomp. I have also news who they are that are chosen of the Lords and Commons to attend the King. And also the whole story of what we did the other day in the fleet at reading the King's declaration; and my name at the bottom of it. After supper, some music and to bed – I resolving to rise betimes tomorrow to write letters to London.

9.  Up very early, writing a letter to the King as from the two Generalls of the fleet in answer to his letter to them, wherein my Lord doth give most humble thanks for his gracious letter and declaration. And promises all duty and obedience to him.

10.  My Lord called me into his cabin and told me how he was commanded to set sail presently for the King, and was very glad thereof; and so put me to writing of letters and other work that night till it was very late, he going to bed. I got him afterwards to

sign things in bed. After I had done some more work, I to bed also.

11. Up very early in the morning. And so about a great deal of business, in order to our going hence today. This morning we begun to pull down all the State's arms in the fleet – having first sent to Dover for painters and others to come to set up the King's. After dinner we set sail from the Downes, I leaving my boy to go to Deale for my linen. It blew very hard all this night, that I was afeared of my boy. About 11 at night came the boats from Deale with great store of provisions; by the same token John Goods told me that above 20 of the fowle are smothered. But my boy was put on board the *Northwich*. To bed.

13. *Lords day*. Trimmed in the morning; after that to the Cooke-room with Mr. Sheply, the first time that I was there this voyage. Then to the Quarter-Deck, upon which the taylors and painters were at work cutting out of some pieces of yellow cloth into the fashion of a crown and *C.R.* and put it upon a fine sheet, and that into the flag instead of the State's arms; which, after dinner, was finished and set up – after it had been showed to my Lord, who took physic today and was in his chamber; and liked it so well as to bid me give the tailors 20s. among them for doing it. Mr Cooke came after us in the *Yarmouth*, bringing me a letter from my wife and a Latin letter from my brother Jo:, with both which I was exceedingly pleased. No sermon all day, we being under sail; only at night, prayers, wherein Mr. Ibbott prayed for all that were related to us in a spiritual and fleshly way.

14–15. In the morning, when I waked and rose, I saw myself out of the Scuttle close by the shore, which afterwards I was told to be the Duch shore. The Hague was clearly to be seen by us. My Lord went up in his night gowne into the Cuddy to see how to dispose thereof for himself and us that belong to him, to give order for our removall today. Some masty Duchmen came on board to proffer their boats to carry things from us on shore &c., to get money by us. Before noon, some gentlemen came on board from the shore to kiss my Lords hands. And by and by Mr. North and Dr. Clerke went to kiss the Queen of Bohemia's hands from my Lord, with a dozen of attendants from on board to wait on them; among which I sent my boy – who, like myself, is with child to see any strange thing. After noon they came back again, having kissed the Queen of

Bohemia's hand, and was sent again by my Lord to do the same to the Prince of Orange. So I got the Captain to ask leave for me to go, which my Lord did give; and I, taking my boy and Judge-Advocate [Fowler] with me, went in company with them. The weather bad; we were soundly washed when we came near the shore, it being very hard to land there. The shore is, as all the country between that and The Hague, all sand. The rest of the company got a coach by themselfs. Mr. Creed and I went in the fore-part of a coach, wherein there was two very pretty ladies, very fashionable and with black paches, who very merrily sang all the way and that very well. And were very free to kiss the two blades that were with them. I took out my Flagelette and piped, but in piping I dropped my rapier stick; but when I came to The Hague, I sent my boy back again for it and he found it, for which I gave him *6d.*, but some horse had gone over it and broke the scabbard. The Hague is a most neat place in all respects. Here we walked up and down a great while, the town being now very full of Englishmen.

But going to see the Prince, he was gone forth with his Governor; and so we walked up and down the town and Court to see the place; and by the help of a stranger, an Englishman, we saw a great many places and were made to understand many things, as the intention of the Maypoles which we saw there standing at every great man's door, of different greatness according to the Quality of the person. About 10 at night the Prince comes home, and we found an easy admission. His attendance very inconsiderable as for a prince. But yet handsome, and his tutor a fine man and himself a very pretty boy. It was bright Mooneshine tonight. This done, we went to a place we had taken up to sup in – where a sallet and two or three bones of mutton were provided for a matter of ten of us, which was very strange. After supper the Judge and I to another house to bed, leaving them there; and he and I lying together in one of their press-beds, there being two more in the same room, but all very neat and handsome; and my boy sleeping upon a bench by me, we lay till past 3 a-clock; and then rise and up and down the town to see it by daylight. Where we saw soldiers of the Prince's guard, all very fine, and the Burgers of the town with their arms and musquets as bright as silver; I meeting this morning a Schoole-Master that spoke good English and French, he went along with us and showed us the whole town. And indeed, I cannot speak enough of the gallantry of the town. Everybody of fashion speak French or Latin, or both. The women, many of them very pretty and in good habitt, fashionable, and black spots. He went with me to buy a couple of basketts, one of them for Mrs. Pierce, the other for my wife. After he was gone (we having first drank with him at our lodging), the Judge and I go the *grand Salle*, where we were showed the place where the States-generall sit in council. The hall is a great place, where the flags that they take from their enemies are all hung up. And things to be sold, as in Westminster hall, and not much unlike it but that not being so big – but much neater. After this to a bookseller's and bought, for the love of the binding, three books – the French Psalms in four parts, Bacon's *organon* and Farnaby's *Rhetoric.*

Coming on board, we found all the Commissioners of the House of Lords at dinner with my Lord; who after dinner went away for shore. In the afternoon my Lord called me on purpose to show me his fine clothes which are now come hither; and indeed, are very rich – as gold and silver can make them. Only his sword he and I do not like. In the afternoon my Lord and I walked together in the Coach two houres, talking together upon all sorts of discourse – as Religion, wherein he is I perceive wholly Scepticall, as well as I, saying that indeed the Protestants as to the Church of Rome are wholly fanatiques. He likes uniformity and form of prayer.

16.   This afternoon Mr. Ed. Pickering told me in what a sad, poor condition for clothes and money the King was, and all his attendants, when he came to him first from my Lord – their clothes not being worth 40*s.*, the best of them. And how overjoyed the King was when Sir J. Greenville brought him some money; so joyful, that he called the Princesse Royall and Duke of Yorke to look upon it as it lay in the Portmanteau before it was taken out. My Lord told me too, that the Duke of Yorke is made High Admirall of England.

17.   Up early to write down my last two days observations. Before dinner, Mr. Edward[1] and I, W. Howe, Pim and my boy, to Skeveling, where we took coach, and so to The Hague, where walking, intending to find one that might show us the King incognito, I met with Capt. Whittington and Dr. Cade, a merry mad parson of the King's. And they two after dinner got the child and me (the others not being able to crowd in) to see the King, who

---

1. 'My Lord's' eldest son, Edward Mountagu, later Viscount Hinchingbrooke.

kissed the child very affectionately. There we kissed his and the Duke of Yorkes and the Princesse Royalls hands. The King seems to be a very sober man; and a very splendid Court he hath in the number of persons of Quality that are about him; English, very rich in habit. From the King to the Lord Chancellor who did lie bed-rid of the goute: he spoke very merrily to the child and me. After that, to see the Queen of Bohemia, who used us very respectfully. Her hand we all kissed. She seems a very debonaire, but plain lady. After that, we went to see a house of the Princesse Dowagers in a parke about half a mile or a mile from The Hague, where there is one the most beautiful room[s] for pictures in the whole world. She had her own picture upon the top, with this word, dedicating it to the memory of her husband:

*Incomparabili marito inconsolabilis vidua.*

Here I met with Mr. Woodcock of Cambrige, Mr Hardye and another. And Mr. Woodcock beginning, we had two or three fine songs, he and I and W. Howe, to the Echo, which was very pleasant, and the more because in a haven of pleasure and in a strange country – that I never was taken up more with a sense of pleasure in my life. After that we parted and back to The Hague and took a tour or two about the Forehault, where the ladies in the evening do as our ladies do in Hideparke. But for my life I could not find one handsome; but their coaches very rich and themselfs so too.

18. To Delfe to see the town, where when we were come, we got a smith's boy to go along with us (but could speak nothing but Duch), and he showed us the church where Van Trump lies intombed with a very fine Monument: his epitaph concludes thus (*Tandem Bello Anglico tantum non victor certé invictus vivere et vincere desijt*). There is a sea-fight the best cut in Marble, with the Smoake the best expressed that ever I saw in my life. From thence to the great church that stands in a fine great Merket-place over against the Stathouse; and there I saw a stately tomb of the old Prince of Orange, of Marble and brass. Wherein, among other rarities, there is the angels with their trumpets, expressed as it were calling. Here were very fine organs in both the churches. It is a most sweet town, with bridges and a river in every street. Observing that in every

house of entertainment there hangs in every room a poor-man's box and desirous to know the reason thereof, it was told me that it is their custom to confirm all bargains by putting something into the poor people's box, and that that binds as fast as anything. We saw likewise the Guesthouse, where it was very pleasant to see what neat preparation there is for the poor. We saw one poor man a-dying there. Back by water, where a pretty sober Duch lass sat reading all the way, and I could not fasten any discourse upon her.

19.   I and the child to walk up and down the town – where I met my old chamber-fellow Mr. Ch. Anderson and a friend of his (both Physicians), Mr. Wright, who took me to a Duch house where there was an exceeding pretty lass and right for the sport; but it being Saturday, we could not have much of her company; but however, I stayed with them (having left the child with his uncle Pickering, who I met in the streets) till 12 at night; by that time Charles was almost drunk; and then broke up, he resolving to go thither again (after he had seen me at my lodging) and lie with the girl, which he told me he had done in the morning. Going to my lodging, we met with the bellman, who strikes upon a clapper, which I took in my hand and it is just like the clapper that our boys fright the birds away from the corn with in summer time in England. To bed.

20.   Up early; and with Mr. Pickering and the child by waggon to Scheveling, where it not being yet fit to go off, I went to lie down in a chamber in the house, where in another bed there was a pretty Duch woman in bed alone; but though I had a month's-mind to her, I had not the boldness to go to her. So there I sleep an hour or two. At last she rise; and then I rise and walked up and down the chamber and saw her dress herself after the Duch dress, and talked to her as much as I could; and took occasion, from her ring which she wore on her first finger, to kiss her hand; but had not the face to offer anything more. So at last I left her there and went to my company. Commissioner Pett at last comes to our lodging, and caused the boats to go off; so some in one boat, some in another, we all bid Adieu to the shore. But through badness of weather we were in great danger, and a great while before we could get the ship; so that of all the company not one but myself that was not sick – I keeping myself in the open ayre, though I was soundly wet for it. I having

spoke a word or two with my Lord, being not very well settled, partly through last night's drinking and want of sleep, I lay down in my gown upon my bed and sleep till the 4 a-clock gun the next morning waked me, which I took for 8 at night that night; and rising to piss, mistook the sun-rising for the sun-setting on Sunday night. So into my naked bed and sleep till 9 a-clock.

21. Then John Goods waken[ed] me and by the Captaines boy brought me four barrels of Mallows oysters which Capt. Tatnell had sent me from Murlace. The weather foul all this day also. By letter that came hither in my absence, I understand that the Parliament hath ordered all persons to be secured, in order to a trial, that did sit as judges in the late King's death; and all the officers, too, attending the court. At Court I find that all things grow high. The old Clergy talk as being sure of their lands again, and laugh at the presbitery; and it is believed that the Sales of the King and Bishops' lands will never be confirmed by Parliament, there being nothing now in any man's power to hinder them and the King from doing what they have a mind; but everybody willing to submit to anything. We expect every day to have the King and Duke on board so soon as it is fair. My Lord doth nothing now; but offers all things to the pleasure of the Duke as Lord High Admirall – so that I am at a loss what to do.

22. News brought that the two Dukes are coming on board, which, by and by they did in a Duch boat, the Duke of Yorke in yellow trimming, the Duke of Gloucester in gray and red. My Lord went in a boat to meet them, the Captain, myself, and others standing at the entering Port. So soon as they were entered we shot the guns off round the fleet. After that, they went to view the ship all over and were most exceedingly pleased with it. They seem to be both very fine Gentlemen. After that done, upon the Quarter-Deck table under the awning, the Duke of Yorke and my Lord, Mr. Coventree and I spent an houre at allotting to every ship their service in their return to England; which having done, they went to dinner, where the table was very full – the two Dukes at the upper end, my Lord Opdam next on one side, and my Lord on the other. After dinner, the Dukes and my Lord to see the Vice- and Rere-Admirall; and I in a boat after them. After that done, they made to the shore in the Duch boat that brought them, and I got into the boat with them. But the shore was so full of people to expect their

48

coming as that it was black (which otherwise is white sand) as everyone would stand by another. When we came near the shore, my Lord left them and came into his own boat, and Gen. Pen and I with him – my Lord being very well pleased with this day's work. By the time we came on board again, news is sent us that the King is on shore; so my Lord fired all his guns round twice, and all the fleet after him; which in the end fell into disorder, which seemed very handsome. The gun over against my Cabbin I fired myself to the King, which was the first time that he hath been saluted by his own ships since this change. But holding my head too much over the gun, I have almost spoiled my right eye. Nothing in the world but going of guns almost all this day. In the evening we begun to remove Cabbins; I to the Carpenters Cabbin and Dr. Clerke with me.

23. In the morning came infinite of people on board from the King, to go along with him. My Lord, Mr. Crew, and others go on shore to meet the King as he comes off from shore. Where (Sir R. Stayner bringing His Majesty into the boat) I hear that His Majesty did with a great deal of affection kiss my Lord upon his first meeting. The King, with the two Dukes, the Queen of Bohemia, Princesse Royalle, and Prince of Orange, came on board; where I in their coming in kissed the Kings, Queen and Princesses hands, having done the other before. Infinite shooting off of the guns, and that in a disorder on purpose, which was better then if it had been otherwise. Dined in a great deal of state, the Royall company by themselfs in the coach, which was a blessed sight to see. After dinner, the King and Duke altered the name of some of the Shipps, *viz.* the *Nazeby* into *Charles* [etc.]. That done, the Queen, Princess Royall, and Prince of Orange took leave of the King, and the Duke of Yorke went on board the *London*, and the Duke of Glocester the *Swiftsure* – which done, we weighed Ancre, and with a fresh gale and most happy weather we set sail for England – all the afternoon the King walking here and there, up and down – (quite contrary to what I thought him to have been), very active and stirring. Upon the Quarter-deck he fell in discourse of his escape from Worcester. Where it made me ready to weep to hear the stories that he told of his difficulties that he had passed through. As his travelling four days and three nights on foot, every step up to the knees in dirt, with nothing but a green coat and a pair of country breeches on and a pair of country shoes, that made him so sore all over his feet that

he could scarce stir. His sitting at table at one place, where the master of the house, that had not seen him in eight years, did know him but kept it private; when at the same table there was one that had been of his own Regiment at Worcester, could not know him but made him drink the Kings health and said that the King was at least four fingers higher then he. In another place, at his Inn, the master of the house, as the King was standing with his hands upon the back of a chair by the fireside, he kneeled down and kissed his hand privately, saying that he would not ask him who he was, but bid God bless him whither that he was going.

24.   Up, and made myself as fine as I could with the Linning stockings and wide Canons that I bought the other day at Hague. Extraordinary press of Noble company and great mirth all the day. At supper three Doctors of Physique at my Cabbin – where I put Dr. Scarborough in mind of what I heard him say about the use of the eyes. Which he owned, that children do in every day's experience look several ways with both their eyes, till custom teaches them otherwise. And that we do now see with one eye – our eyes looking in Paralell lynes.

25.   By the morning we were come close to the land and everybody made ready to get on shore. The King and the two Dukes did eat their breakfast before they went, and there being set some Shipps diet before them, only to show them the manner of the Shipps diet, they eat of nothing else but pease and pork and boiled beef. I spoke with the Duke of York about business, who called me Pepys by name, and upon my desire did promise me his future favour. Great expectation of the King's making some Knights, but there was none. About noon (though the Brigantine that Beale made was there ready to carry him), yet he would go in my Lord's barge with the two Dukes; our captain steered, and my Lord went along bare with him. I went, and Mr. Mansell and one of the King's footmen, with a dog that the King loved (which shit in the boat, which made us laugh and me think that a King and all that belong to him are but just as others are) went in a boat by ourselfs; and so got on shore when the King did, who was received by Gen. Monke with all imaginable love and respect at his entrance upon the land at Dover. Infinite the Croud of people and the gallantry of the Horsmen, Citizens, and Noblemen of all sorts. The Mayor of the town came and gave him his white staffe, the badge of his place,

which the King did give him again. The Mayor also presented him from the town a very rich Bible, which he took and said it was the thing that he loved above all things in the world. A Canopy was provided for him to stand under, which he did; and talked awhile with Gen. Monke and others; and so into a stately coach there set for him; and so away straight through the towne toward Canterbury without making any stay at Dover. The Shouting and joy expressed by all is past imagination.

27. *Lords day.* Called up by John Goods to see the Garter and Heralds coate which lay in the coach, brought by Sir Edwd. Walker, King-at-armes, this morning for my Lord. My Lord hath summoned all the commanders on board him to see the ceremony. Which was thus: Sir Edw., putting on his Coate and having laid the George and Garter and the King's letter to my Lord upon a Crimson Cushion (in the coach, all the commanders standing by), makes three congees to him, holding the Cushion in his arms. Then laying it down with the things upon it upon a chair – he takes the letter and delivers it to my Lord, which my Lord breaks open and gives him to read. It was directed to "Our trusty and well beloved Sir Edw. Montagu, Knight, one of our Generalls-at-sea, and our Companion-elect of our Noble Order of the Garter." The contents of the letter is to show that the Kings of England have for many years made use of this Honour as a special mark of favour to persons of good extraction and virtue (and that many Emperors, Kings and Princes of other countries have borne this honour) and that whereas my Lord is of a noble family and hath now done the King such service by sea at this time as he hath done, he doth send him this George and Garter to wear as Knight of that Order, with a dispensation for the other ceremony of the Habitt of the Order and other things till hereafter when it can be done. So the Herald, putting the ribbon about his neck and the garter about his left leg – he salutes him with joy as Knight of the Garter, and that was all. My Lord and the ship's company down to Sermon. I stayed above to write, and look over my new song-book, which came last night to me from London in lieu of that that my Lord had of me. The officers being all on board, there was not room for me at table, so I dined in my Cabbin; where among other things, Mr. Dunn brought me a Lobster and a bottle of oyle instead of a bottle of Vinegar, whereby I spoiled my dinner. Many orders in the ordering of ships this afternoon. Late to a sermon. After that up to the

Lieutenant's Cabbin, where Mr. Sheply, I, and the Minister supped. And after that I went down to W. Howe's Cabbin and there with a great deal of pleasure sang till it was late. After that to bed.

28. Called up at 2 in the morning for letters for my Lord from the Duke of Yorke – but I went to bed again till 5. Trimmed early this morning. This morning the Captain did call over all the men in the ship (not the boys) and gave every one of them a Duckett of the King's money that he gave the ship – and the officers according to their Quality. For my share, I received in the Captain's Cabbin 60 Ducketts. The rest of the morning busy writing letters. Supped with my Lord, and after that to bed. This night I had a strange dream of bepissing myself, which I really did; and having kicked the clothes off, I got cold and found myself all muck-wet in the morning and had a great deal of pain in making water, which made me very melancholy.

30. About 8 a-clock in the morning, the Lieutenant came to me to know whether I would eat a dish of Mackrell, newly-ketched this morning, for my breakfast – which the Captain and we did in the coach. All yesterday and today I have a great deal of pain in making water and in my back, which made me afeared. But it proved nothing but cold which I took yesterday night. All this morning making up my accounts, in which I counted that I have made myself now worth about 80*l*, at which my heart was glad and blessed God. In the afternoon, Mr. Sheply told me how my Lord had put me down for 70 Gilders among the money which was given to my Lord's servants, which my heart did much rejoice at.

31. This day my Lord took Phisique – and came not out of his chamber. All the morning making orders. After dinner, a great while below in the great Cabbin, trying with W. Howe some of Mr. Lawes's songs, perticularly that of *What is a kisse*, with which we had a great deal of pleasure. After that to making of orders again. The captain of the *Assistance*, Capt. Sparling, brought me this afternoon a pair of silk stockings, of a light blue, which I was much pleased with. The Captain and I to supper. And after that, a most pleasant walk till 10 at night with him upon the Deck, it being a fine evening. My pain was gone again that I had yesterday, blessed be God.

This day, the Month end, I in very good health. And all the world in a merry mood because of the King's coming. I expect every minute to hear by Mr. Cooke how my poor wife doth. This day I begun to teach Mr. Edwd., who I find to have a very good Foundation laid for his Latin by Mr. Fuller. I find myself in all things well as to body and mind, but only for the absence of my wife.

# ❧ JUNE ❧

1. At night Mr. Cooke comes from London with letters – leaving all things there very gallant and joyful. And brought us word that the Parliament had ordered the 29 of May, the King's birthday, to be for ever kept as a day of thanksgiving for our redemption from tyranny and the King's return to his Government, he entering London that day. My wife was in London when he came thither, and hath been there a week with Mr. Bowyer and his wife. My poor wife hath not been well a week before; but thanks be to God, is well again. She would fain see me and be at her house again, but we must be content. She writes me word how the Joyces go very rich and grow very Proud; but it is no matter. And that there was a talk that I should be knighted by the King; which they laugh at, but I think myself happier in my wife and estate then they are in theirs. To bed.

2. Being with my Lord in the morning about business in his Cabbin, I took occasion to give him thanks for his love to me in the share that he had given me of his Majestys money and the Dukes. He told me that he hoped to do me a more lasting kindness, if all things stand as they are now between him and the King – but says "We must have a little patience and we will rise together. In the meantime I will do you all the good Jobbs I can." Which was great content for me to hear from my Lord. All the morning with the Captain, computing how much the 30 ships that came with the King from Scheveling their pay comes to for a month (because the King promised to give them all a month's pay) and it comes to 6538*l*: and the *Charles* perticularly, 777*l*. I wish we had the money. All the afternoon with two or three captains in the Captain's cabin, drinking of white wine and sugar and eating pickled oysters – where Capt. Sparling told us the best Story that ever I heard; about

a gentleman that persuaded a country fellow to let him gut his oysters or else they would stink.

3.    At sermon in the morning. After dinner into my cabin to cast my accounts up; and find myself to be worth near 100*l*, for which I bless Almighty God – it being more then I hoped for so soon; being, I believe, not clearly worth 25*l* when I came to sea, besides my house and goods. Then to set my papers in order, they being increased much upon my hand through want of time to put them in order.

5.    After supper my Lord called for the Lieutenant's Gitterne, and with two Candlesticks with money in them for Symballs we made some barber's Musique, with which my Lord was much pleased. So to bed.

6.    In the morning I had letters come that told me, among other things, that my Lord's place of Clerke of the Signett[1] was fallen to him. Which he most lovingly did tell me that I should execute, in case he could not get a better imployment for me at the end of the year – because he thought that the Duke of Yorke would command all, but he hoped that the Duke would not remove me but to my advantage. I had a great deal of talk about my uncle Robt:, and he told me that he could not tell how his mind stood as to his estate. But he would do all that lay in his power for me. After dinner came Mr. Cooke from London, who told me that my wife he left well at Huntsmore, though her health not altogether so constant as it used to be, which my heart is troubled for. My letters tell me that my Lord hath some great place conferred on him, and they say Master of the Wardrobe. I wrote to my father for a coat to be made me against I come to London, which I think will not be long.

7.    About 3 in the morning the people begun to wash the deck and the water came pouring into my mouth, which wakened me; and I was fain to rise and get on my gown, and sleep leaning upon my table. After dinner came Mr. John Wright and Mr. Moore, with the sight of whom my heart was very glad. They brought an order for my Lord's coming up to London – which my Lord resolved to do tomorrow.

1. Correctly, Privy Seal.

8.   Out early. Took horse at Deale. I troubled much with the King's Gittar and Fairebrother, the rogue that I entrusted with the carrying of it on foot, whom I thought I had lost. Came to Canterbury; dined there. I saw the Minster and the remains of Beckett's tombe. Came to Gravesend. A good handsome wench I kissed, the first that I have seen a great while. Supped with my Lord.

9.   Up betimes. 25s. the reckoning for very beer. Paid the house and by boats to London, six boats. Landed at the Temple. To Mr. Crews. To my father's and put myself into a handsome posture to wait upon my Lord. Dined there. To Whitehall with my Lord and Mr. Edw. Mountagu. Found the King in the parke. There walked. Gallantry great. To Will How till 10 at night. Back and to my fathers.

10.   *Whitsunday*. Up and to my Lord's. To Mr. Merstons, where Monsieur Impertinent. At my father's found my wife. After dinner, my wife and I to walk in Lincolnes Inne walks. After prayers she home and I to my Lord. Stayed there: and so to my father's, where I met Mr. Fairebrother. To bed with my wife.

17.   *Lords day*. Lay long abed. To Mr. Messums; a good sermon. This day the Organs did begin to play at Whitehall before the King. Dined at my father's. After dinner to Mr. Messums again, and so in the garden and heard Chappells father preach, that was page to the protector. And just by the window that I stood at, there sat Mrs. Butler the great beauty. After sermon to my Lord and then into grays Inne walks, where Mr. Edwd. and I saw many beauties. So to my father's, where Mr. Cooke, W. Bowyer, and my Cozen Joyce Norton supped. To bed.

18.   To my Lord, where much business and some hopes of getting some money thereby. With him to the parliament house, where he did entend to have gone to have made his appearance today, but he met Mr. Crew upon the stairs and would not go in. To the Admiralty and so to my Lord's lodgings, where he told me that he did look after the place of the Clerk of the Acts for me. So to Mr. Crews and my father's and to bed. My wife went this day to Huntsmoore for her things, and I was very lonely all night. This evening my wife's brother Balty came to me to let me know his bad

condition and to get a place for him, but I perceive he stands upon a place for a gentleman that may not stain his family; when, God help him, he wants bread.

19. Much business at my Lord's. This morning my Lord went into the House of Commons and there had the thanks of the House, in the name of the parliament and the Commons of England, for his late service to his King and Country. My wife and the girl and dog came home today. We were [told] of W. Howe being sick today; but he was well at night. When I came home I found a Quantity of Chocolatte left for me, but I know not from whom.

20. Up by 4 in the morning to write letters to sea and a Comission for him that Murford solicits for. Called on by Capt. Sparling, who did give me my Duch money again, and so much as he had changed into English money, by which my mind was eased of a great deal of trouble – and some other sea-Captains. I did give them a good morning draught. And so to my Lord, who lay long in bed this day, because he came home late from supper with the King. With my Lord to the Parliament house; and after that, with him to Gen. Monkes, where he dined at the Cockepitt. I home and dined with my wife, now making all things ready there again.

22. My dear friend Mr. Fuller of Twickenham and I dined alone at the Sun taverne, where he told me how he hath the grant of being Deane of St. Patrickes in Ireland, and I him my condition; and both rejoiced one for another. My Lord abroad, and I to my house and set things in a little order there. To bed, the first time since my coming from sea, in my own house, for which God be praised.

23. To my Lord's lodgings, and there stayed to see the King touch people of the King's evil. But he did not come at all, it rayned so. And the poor people were forced to stand all the morning in the rain in the garden. Afterwards, he touched them in the banquetting-house. With my Lord to my Lord Frezendorfes, where he dined today – where he told me that he had obtained a promise of the Clerk of the Acts place for me, at which I was glad.

25. With my Lord to Whitehall all the morning. I spoke with Mr. Coventry about my business, who promised me all the assistance I could expect. At the Leg in King street. Thence to the Admiralty,

where I met with Mr. Turner of the Navy Office, who did look after the place of Clerk of the Acts. He was very civil to me and I to him, and shall be so. There came a letter from my Lady Monke to my Lord about it this evening. But he refused to come to her; but meeting in Whitehall with Sir Tho. Clerges, her brother, my Lord returned answer that he would not desist in my business. And that he believed that Gen. Monke would take it ill if my Lord should name the officers in his army. And therefore he desired to have the naming of one officer in the fleet. At Dorsett house I met with Mr. Kipps my old friend, with whom the world is well changed, he being now seal-bearer to the Lord Chancellor, at which my wife and I are very well pleased, he being a very good-natured man. Home, and late writing letters. Then to my Lord's lodgings, this being the first night of his coming to Whitehall to lie since his coming from sea.

27.    With my Lord to the Duke, where he spoke to Mr. Coventry to despatch my business of the Acts, in which place everybody gives me joy, as if I were in it; which God send. Dined with my Lord and all his officers of his Regiment, who invited my Lord and his friends, as many as he would bring, to dinner at the Swan at Dowgate, a poor house and ill dressed but very good fish and plenty. To Westminster and with W. Howe by coach to the Speaker's, where my Lord supped with the King; but we could not get in. So back again; and after a song or two in my chamber in the dark, which doth (now that the bed is out) sound very well, I went home and to bed.

28.    My brother Tom came to me with Patternes to choose for a suit. I paid him all to this day, and did give him 10l upon account. To Mr. Coventry, who told me that he would do me all right in my business. To Sir G. Downing, the first visit I have made him since he came. He is so stingy a fellow, I care not to see him. I quite cleared myself of his office, and did give him liberty to take anybody in. I went also this morning to see Mrs. Pierce the Chyrurgeon. I found her in bed in her house in Margaret churchyard – her husband returned to sea. I did invite her to go to dinner with me and my wife today. After all this to my Lord, who lay a-bed till 11 a-clock, it being almost 5 before he went to bed, they supped so late last night with the King. After my Lord was awake, I went up to him to the Nursery, where he doth lie; and

having talked with him a little, I took leave and carried my wife and Mrs. Pierce to Cloathworkers hall to dinner, where Mr. Pierce the purser met us. We were invited by Mr. Chaplin the victualler, where Nich. Osborne was. Our entertainment very good. A brave hall. Good company and very good Musique. Where among other things, I was pleased that I could find out a man by his voice, whom I had never seen before, to be one that sung behind the Curtaine formerly at Sir W. Davenants opera. Here Dr. Gauden and Mr. Gauden the victualler dined with us. After dinner to Mr. Rawlinson's to see him and his wife. And would have gone to my aunt Wight, but that her only child, a daughter, died last night. Home and to my Lord, who supped within; and Mr. Edwd. Mountagu, Mr. Tho. Crew and others with him sat up late. I home and to bed.

29.   This day or two my maid Jane hath been lame, that we cannot tell what to do for want of her. Up and to Whitehall, where I got my warrant from the Duke to be Clerk of the Acts. Meeting Mr. Townsend in the palace [yard] – he and I and another or two went and dined at the Leg there. Then to Whitehall, where I was told by Mr. Huchinson at the Admiralty that Mr. Barlow my Predecessor, Clerk of the Acts, is yet alive and coming up to town to look after his place – which made my heart sad a little. At night told my Lord thereof and he bade me to get possession of my patent; and he would do all that could be done to keep him out. This night my Lord and I looked over the list of the Captains, and marked some that my Lord hath a mind to have put out. Home and to bed. Our wench very lame, abed these two days.

30.   To my Lord and with him to Whitehall, where I saw a great many fine Antique heads of marble that my Lord Northumberland hath given the King. Here meeting with Mr. De Cretz, he looked over many of the pieces in the gallery with me and told me whose hands they were, with great pleasure. Dined at home and Mr. Hawly with me upon six of my pigeons which my wife is resolved to kill here. This day came Will my boy to me, the wench continuing lame so that my wife could not be longer without somebody to help her. To Mr. Crews, and there took money and paid Mrs. Anne, Mrs. Jemimahs maid, off quite. And so she went away and another came to her. To Whitehall with Mr. Moore, where I met with a letter from Mr. Turner of the Navy office, offering me 150l to be joined with me in my patent, and to advise

me how to improve the advantage of my place and to keep off Barlow. To my Lord's till late at night, and so home.

## –❧JULY❧–

1. This morning came home my fine Camlott cloak with gold buttons – and a silk suit; which cost me much money and I pray God to make me be able to pay for it. I went to the cook's and got a good joint of meat, and my wife and I dined at home alone. In the afternoon to the Abbey, where a good sermon by a stranger, but no Common Prayer yet.

2. Infinite of business, that my heart and head and all was full. Met with Purser Washington, with whom and a lady, a friend of his, I dined at the Bell Taverne in King's street; but the rogue had no more manners then to invite me thither and to let me pay my club. All the afternoon with my Lord, going up and down the town. At 7 at night he went home, and there the Principall officers of the Navy;[1] among the rest, myself was reckoned one. We had order to meet tomorrow to draw up such an order of the Council as would put us in action before our patents were passed – at which my heart was glad. At night supped with my Lord, he and I together in the great dining-room alone by ourselfs, the first time that ever I did it in London. Home to bed. My maid pretty well again.

3. All the morning, the officers and commissioners of the Navy, we met at Sir G. Carteret's chamber and agreed upon orders for the Council to supersede the old and impower us to act. In the afternoon my heart was quite pulled down by being told that Mr. Barlow was to enquire today for Mr. Coventry. But at night I met with my Lord, who told me that I need not fear, for he would get me the place against the world. And when I came to W. Howe, he told me that Dr. Petty hath been with my Lord and did tell him that Barlow was a sickly man and did not entend to execute the place for himself; which put me in great comfort again. Till 2 in the morning writing letters and things for my Lord to send to sea. So home to my wife to bed.

1. The Principal Officers of the Navy Board (at this time the Treasurer, Comptroller, Surveyor, Clerk of the Acts and three Commissioners).

4. Up very early in the morning; and landing my wife at White Friars stairs, I went to the bridge and so to the Treasurer's of the Navy, with whom I spoke about the business of my office; who put me into very good hopes of my business. At his house comes Commissioner Pett; and I and he went to view the houses in Seething lane belonging to the Navy, where I find the worst very good; and had great fears in my mind that they will shuffle me out of them, which troubles me. So to Westminster hall; where meeting with Monsieur L'impertinent and W. Bowyer, I took them to the Sun tavern and gave them a lobster and some wine, and sat talking like a fool with them till 4 a-clock. So to my Lord's and walking all the afternoon in Whitehall Court, in expectation of what shall be done in the Council as to our business. It was strange to see how all the people flocked together bare to see the King looking out of the Council window. At night my Lord told me how my orders that I drow last night, about giving us power to act, are granted by the Council – at which he and I were very glad. Home and to bed, my boy lying in my house this night the first time.

5. This morning my brother Tom brought me my Jackanapes coat with silver buttons. It rained this morning, which makes us fear the glory of this great day will be lost, the King and Parliament being to be intertained by the City today with great pomp. Mr. Hater was with me today, and I agreed with him to be my clerk. Being at Whitehall, I saw the King, the Dukes and all their attendants go forth in the rain to the City and bedaggled many a fine suit of clothes. I was forced to walk all the morning in Whitehall, not knowing how to get out because of the rain. Met with Mr. Cooling, my Lord Chamberlins secretary, who took me to dinner among the gentlemen wayters – and after dinner into the wine-cellar. He told me how he hath a project for all us Secretaries to join together and get money by bringing all business into our hands. Thence to the Admirallty, where Mr. Blackburne, and I (it beginning to hold up) went and walked an hour or two in the park, he giving of me light in many things in my way in this office that I go about. At my Lord's at night comes Dr. Petty to me to tell me that Barlow was come to town and other things, which put me into a despair and I went to bed very sad.

6. In the morning with my Lord at Whitehall, got the order of the Council for us to act. Sir G. Carteret and I to the Treasurer's Office,

where he set some things in order there. And so home, calling upon Sir Geffery Palmer, who did give me advice about my patent which put me to some doubt to know what to do – Barlow being alife. Homeward called at Mr. Pims about getting me a coat of velvett, and he took me to the Half Moone, and there the house so full that we stayed above half an hour before we could get anything. So to my Lord's, where in the dark W. Howe and I did sing Extemporys, and I find by use that we are able to sing a bass and a treble pretty well. So home and to bed.

7. To my Lord. One with me to buy a clerk's place with me, and I did demand 100*l*. To the Council chamber, where I took out an order for the advance of the salaries of the officers of the Navy, and I find mine to be raised to 350*l* per annum. Thence to the Change, where I bought two fine prints of Ragotts from Rubens; and afterward dined with my uncle and Aunt Wight, where her sister Con and her husband was. After that to Mr. Rawlinsons with my uncle; and thence to the Navy Office, where I begin to take an inventory of the papers and goods and books of the office. To my Lord's. Late writing letters. So home to bed.

8. *Lords day*. To Whitehall to chapel, where I got in with ease by going before the Lord Chancellor with Mr. Kipps. Here I heard very good Musique, the first time that I remember ever to have heard the Organs and singing-men in Surplices in my life. The Bishop of Chichester preached before the King and made a great flattering sermon, which I did not like that clergy should meddle with matters of state. Dined with Mr. Luellin and Salsbury at a cook's shop. Home, and stayed all the afternoon with my wife till after sermon; there till Mr. Fairebrother came to call us out to my father's to supper. He told me how he had perfectly procured me to be made Maister in arts by proxy – which did somewhat please me, though I remember my Cosen Rogr. Pepys was the other day dissuading me from it. While we were at supper came W. Howe to supper to us. And after supper went home to bed.

9. To the Navy Office, where in the afternoon we met and sat; and there I begun to sign bills in the office the first time. From thence Capt. Holland and Mr. Browne of Harwich took me to a tavern and did give me a collacion.

10.   This day I put on first my new silk suit, the first that ever I wore in my life. This morning came Nan Pepys's husband Mr. Hall to see me, being lately come to town – I had never saw him before. I took him to the Swan tavern with Mr. Eglin and there drank our morning draught. Home, and called my wife and took her to Dr. Clodius's to a great wedding of Nan Hartlib to mynheer Roder, which was kept at Goring house with very great state, cost, and noble company. But among all the beauties there, my wife was thought the greatest.

11.   With Sir Wm. Pen by water to the Navy Office, where we met and despatched business. And that being done, we went all to dinner to the Dolphin upon Maj. Bournes invitation. After that to the Office again, where I was vexed, and so was Commissioner Pett, to see a busy fellow come to look out the best lodgings for my Lord Barkely, and the combining between him and Sir W. Pen; and endeed, was troubled much at it.

12.   Up early, and by coach to Whitehall, with Commissioner Pett; where after we had talked with my Lord, I went to the Privy Seal and got my bill[1] perfected there and at the Signett: and then to the House of Lords and met with Mr. Kipps, who directed me to Mr. Beale to get my patent ingrossed. But he not having time to get it done in Chancery hand, I was forced to run all up and down Chancery lane and the Six Clerks' Office, but could find none that could write that hand that were at leisure: and so in a despair went to the Admiralty, where we met the first time there – my Lord Mountagu, my Lord Barkely, Mr. Coventry, and all the rest of the Principall Officers and Commissioners, only the Controller who is not yet chosen. At night to Mr. Spong's and there I got him to come to me to my Lord's lodgings at 11 a-clock of night, where I got him to take my bill to write it himself (which was a great providence that he could do it) against tomorrow morning. I late writing letters to sea by the post. And so went home to bed, in great trouble because I heard at Mr. Beales today that Barlow hath been there and said that he would make a stop in that business.

13.   Up early, the first day that I put on my black Camlott coat with silver buttons. To Mr. Spong, whom I found in his night-

---

1. The warrant for the issue of the patent appointing him Clerk of the Acts.

gown writing of my patent; and he had done as far as he could by 8 a-clock. It being done, we carried it to Worcester house to the Chancellors, where Mr. Kipps got me the Chancellors *Recepi* to my Bill. And so carried it to Mr. Beale for a Dockett; but he was very angry, and unwilling to do it, because he said it was ill-writ (because I had got it writ by another hand and not by him); but by much importunity I got Mr. Spong to go to his office and make an end of my patent, and in the meantime Mr. Beale to be preparing my Dockett; which being done, I did give him two pieces, after which it was strange how civil and tractable he was to me. From thence I went to the Navy Office, where we despatched much business and resolved of the houses for the Officers and Comissioners, which I was glad of, and I got leave to have a door made me into the leads. To my Lord's, late writing letters. And great doings of Musique at the next house, which was Whallys; the King and Dukes there with Madam Palmer[1], a pretty woman that they have a fancy to to make her husband a cuckold. Here, at the old door that did go into those lodgings, my Lord and I and W. Howe did stand listening a great while to the Musique. After that, home to bed with the greatest quiet of mind that I have had a great while, having eat nothing but a bit of bread and cheese today, and a bit of bread and butter after I was a-bed.

14.   Up early and advised with my wife for the putting of all our things in a readiness to be sent to our new house. To Westminster hall, where I paid all my debts in order to my going away from thence. Here I met with Mr. Eglin, who would needs take me to the Leg in King's street and give me a dish of meat to dinner; and so I sent for Monsieur Limpertinent, where we sat long and were merry. After that, parted; and I took Mr. Butler with me into London by coach and showed him my house at the Navy Office. And did give order for the laying in coals. So into Fanchurch street and there did give him a glass of wine at Rawlinson's, and was trimmed in the street. So to my Lord's late writing letters; and so home, where I find my wife hath packed up all her goods in the house, fit for a removal. So to bed.

15.   *Lords day.* Lay long in bed to recover my rest. Going forth, met with Mr. Sheply and went and drank my morning draught

---

1. Later Lady Castlemaine.

with him at Wilkinsons, and my Brother Spicer. After that to Westminster Abbey, and in Henry the 7ths chapel heard part of a sermon, the first that ever I heard there. To my Lord's and dined all alone at the table with him. My wife at home all this day, she having no clothes out, all being packed up yesterday. For this month I have wholly neglected anything of news, and so have beyond belief been ignorant how things go. And now, by my patent, my mind is in some quiet; which God keep. I was not at my father's tonight, I being afeared to go for fear he should still solicit me to speak to my Lord for a place in the Wardrobe, which I dare not do because of my own business yet. My wife and I mightily pleased with our new house that we hope to have.

17.    This morning (as endeed all the mornings nowadays) much business at my Lord's. There came to my house before I went out, Mr. Barlow, an old consumptive* man and fair-conditioned – with whom I did discourse a great while; and after much talk, I did grant him what he asked – *viz.,* 50*l* per annum if my salary be not encreased and 100*l* per annum in case it be to 350*l*; at which he was very well pleased to be paid as I received my money, and not otherwise. That done and the day proving fair, I went home and got all my goods packed up and sent away. And my wife and I and Mrs. Hunt went by coach, overtaking the carts a-drinking in the Strand – being come to my house and set in the goods; and at night sent my wife and Mrs. Hunt to buy something for supper; they bought a Quarter of lamb; and so we eat it but it was not half roasted. To bed, the first night that I ever lay here with my wife.

18.    This morning the carpenter made an end of my door out of my chamber upon the leads. This morning we met at the office. I dined at my house in Seething lane. Thence to my Lord about business; and being in talk, in comes one with half a Bucke from Hinchingbrooke, and it smelling a little strong, my Lord did give it me, though it was as good as any could be. I did carry it to my mother to dispose of as she pleased. After that home; where Wll. Ewre[1] now was and did lie this night with us, the first night.

19.    I did lie late a-bed. I and my wife by water. Landed her at Whitefriars with her boy, with an Iron of our new range which is

---

1. Will Hewer, Pepys's new clerk.

already broke and my wife will have changed, and many other things she hath to buy with the help of my father today. I to my Lord and find him in bed. After talk with my Lord I went to Westminster hall, where I took Mr. Michell and his wife (and Mrs. Murford we sent for afterward) to the Dogg tavern, where I did give them a dish of anchoves and olives and paid for all. And did talk of our old discourse when we did use to talk of the King, in the time of the Rump, privately. After that to the Admiralty Office in Whitehall, where I stayed and writ my last observations for these four days last past. Great talk of the difference between the Episcopall and Presbyterian clergy, but I believe it will come to nothing. So home and to bed.

20. We sat at the office this morning (Sir W. Batten and Mr. Pett being upon a Survey to Chatham): this morning I sent my wife to my father's and with him to go buy 5*l*-worth of pewter. After we rose at the office, I went to my father's, where my uncle Fenner and all his crew and Capt. Holland and his wife and my wife were at dinner at a venison pasty, of the venison that I did give my mother the other night. I did this time show so much coldness to W. Joyce that I believe all the table took notice of it. Home and to bed.

21. To my Lord and spoke to him about the business of the Privy Seale for me to be sworn. Went to the Six Clerks' Office to Mr. Spong for the writings, and dined with him at a club at the next door, where we had three voices to sing catches. So to my house to write letters and so to Whitehall about business of my Lord's concerning his creation, and so home and to bed.

22. *Lords day.* All the last night it had rained hard. I went out and looked into several churches; and so to my uncle Fenners, whither my wife was got before me; and we, my father and mother and all the Joyces and my aunt Bell, whom I had not seen many a year before. After dinner, I to Whitehall (my wife to church with K. Joyce), where I found my Lord at home and walked in the garden with him, he showing me all the respect that can be. I left him – and went to walk in the park, where great endeavouring to get into the Inward park, but could not. And one man was basted by the keeper for carrying some people over on his back through the water. Afterward to my Lord's, where I stayed and drank with Mr. Sheply; and having first sent to get a pair of oares, it was the first

time that ever I went by water on the Lord's day. Home, and at night had a chapter read; and I read prayers out of the Common Prayer book, the first time that ever I read prayers in this house. So to bed.

23. After dinner to my Lord, who took me to Secretary Nicholas; and there, before him and Secretary Morris, my Lord and I, upon our knees, together took our oaths of Allegiance and Supremacy and the oath of the Privy Seale – of which I was much glad, though I am not likely to get anything by it at present; but I do desire it, for fear of a turn-out of our office. That done and my Lord gone from me, I went with Mr. Cooling and his Brother and Sam Hartlibb, little Jenings and some others to the King's head tavern at Charing cross; where after drinking, I took boat and so home. Where we supped merrily among ourselfs (our little boy proving a droll); and so after prayers, to bed.

25. This morning my Lord took leave of the House of Commons – and had the thanks of the House for his great services to his country. In the afternoon (but this is a mistake, for it was yesterday in the afternoon) Monsieur Limpertinent and I met, and I took him to the Sun and drank with him; and in the evening going away, we met his mother and sisters and father coming downstairs from the Gatehouse, where they lodge. Where I did the first time salute them all; and very pretty Madam Frances is endeed. Home and to bed.

26. Early to Whitehall, thinking to have a meeting of my Lord and the Principal Officers; but my Lord could not, it being the day that he was to go and be admitted in the House of Lords, his patent being done, which he presented upon his knee to the Speaker; and so it was read in the House and he took his place. I at the Privy Seal Office with Mr. Hooker, who brought me acquainted with Mr. Crofts of the Signet, and I invited them to a dish of meat at the Leg in King street; and so we dined there and I paid for all and had very good light given me as to my imployment there. In the evening met with T. Doling, who carried me to St. James's fair; and there meeting with W. Symons and his wife and Luellin and D. Scobells wife and cousin, we went to Woods at the Pell-mell (our old house for clubbing) and there we spent till 10 at night. At which time I sent to my Lord's for my clerk Will to come to me, and so by link home to bed. Where I find Comissioner Willoughby had sent for all his

things away out of my bedchamber; which is a little disappointment, but it is better then pay too dear for them.

27. The last night Sir W. Batten and Sir W. Penn came to their
houses at the office. Met this morning and did business till noon.
Dined at home and from thence to my Lord's, where Will, my
clerk, and I were all the afternoon making up my accounts; which
we had done by night, and I find myself worth about 100*l* after all
my expenses.

28. To the Sun tavern and sent for Mr. Butler, who was now all
full of his high discourse in praise of Ireland, whither he and his
whole family is going by Coll. Dillons persuasion – but so many
lies I never heard in praise of anything as he told of Ireland. So home
late at night and to bed.

29. *Lords day*. I and my boy Will to Whitehall; and I with my Lord
to Whitehall chapel, where I heard a cold sermon of the Bishop of
Salsbury, Duppa, and the ceremonies did not please me, they do so
overdo them. In the afternoon, with Dick Vines and his Brother
Payton, we walked to Lisson greene and Marybone – and back
again. And finding my Lord at home, I got him to look over my
accounts, which he did approve of and signed them; and so we are
even to this day. Of this I was glad; and do think myself worth in
good clear money about 120*l*. Home late, calling in at my father's
without stay. To bed.

31. To Whitehall, where my Lord and the Principal Officers met
and had great discourse about raising of money for the Navy; which
is in very sad condition, and money must be raised for it. Mr.
Blackeburne, Dr. Clerke, and I to the Quakers and dined there. I
back to the Admiralty and there was doing things in order to the
calculating of the debts of the Navy and other business all the
afternoon.

# ⸙AUGUST⸙

1. Up very early, and by water to Whitehall to my Lord's; and
there up to my Lord's lodging and there talked with him about the

affairs of the Navy and how I was now to wait today at the Privy Seale. Comissioner Pett was with me, whom I desired to make my excuse at the office for my absence this day. Thence to the Privy Seale Office, where I got (by Mr. Mathews means) possession of the books and table. In the afternoon at the office again, where we had many things to sign; and I went to the Council chamber and there got my Lord to sign the first bill, and the rest all myself – but received no money today. After I had signed all, I went with Dicke Scobell and Luellin to drink at a bottle-beer house in the Strand; and after staying there a while (having sent W. Ewre home before), I took boat and homewards went, and in Fish street bought a lobster; and as I had bought it I met with Winter and Mr. Delabarr and there, with a piece of Sturgeon of theirs, we went to the Sun tavern in that street and eat them. Late home and to bed.

2. To Westminster by water with Sir W. Batten and Sir W. Penn (our servants in another boat) to the Admiralty; and from thence I went to my Lord's to fetch him thither. Where we stayed all the morning about ordering of money for the victuallers and advising how to get a sum of money to carry on the business of the Navy. From thence, dined with Mr. Blackburne at his house with his friends, where we were very well treated and merry. From thence, W. Ewre and I to the office of Privy Seale, where I stayed all the afternoon and received about 40*l* for yesterday and today, at which my heart rejoiced for God's blessing to me, to give me this advantage by chance – there being of this 40*l* about 10*l* due to me for this day's work. So great is the present profit of this office above what it was in the King's time; there being the last month about 300 bills, whereas in the last King's time it was much to have 40. With my money, home by coach. It being the first time that I could get home before our gates were shut since I came to the Navy Office. When I came home, I find my wife not very well of her old pain in the lip of her *chose*, which she had when we were first married.

3. Up betimes this morning; and after the Barber had done with me, then to the office, where I and Sir W. Penn only did meet and despatch business. At noon my wife and I by coach to Dr Clerkes to dinner. I was very much taken with his lady, a comely, proper woman (though not handsome); but a woman of the best language

that ever I heard any in my life. Here dined Mrs. Pierce and her husband.

5.   *Lords day*. My wife being much in pain, I went this morning to Dr. Williams (who had cured her once of this business) in Holborne, and he did give me an oyntment which I sent home by my boy and a plaster, which I took with me to Westminster, where I dined with Mr. Sheply (my Lord dining at Kensington).

6.   This morning at the office; and that being done, home to dinner all alone, my wife being ill in pain a-bed – which I was troubled at, and not a little impatient. After dinner to Whitehall at the Privy Seale all the afternoon; and at night with Mr. Man to Mr. Rawlinson's in Fanchurch street, where we stayed till 11 a-clock at night; so home and to bed – my wife being all this day in great pain. This night Mr. Man offered me 1000*l* for my office of Clerk of the Acts, which made my mouth water; but yet I dare not take it till I speak with my Lord to have his consent.

9.   With Judge-Advocate Fowler, Mr. Creed and Mr. Sheply to the Rhenish winehouse, and Capt. Hayward of the *Plymouth*, who is now ordered to carry my Lord Winchelsea Embassador to Constantinople. We were very merry, and Judge-Advocate did give Capt. Hayward his oath of Allegiance and Supremacy. Thence to my office of Privy Seale; and having signed some things there, with Mr. Moore and Deane Fuller to the Leg in King street; and sending for my wife, we dined there – very merry, and after dinner parted. After dinner, with my wife to Mrs. Blackburne to visit her. She being within, I left my wife there; and I to the Privy Seal, where I despatch some business; and from thence to Mrs. Blackburne again, who did treat my wife and I with a great deal of civility and did give us a fine collation of collar of beef, &c. Thence, I having my head full of drink through having drunk so much Rhenish wine in the morning and more in the afternoon at Mrs. Blackburne. Came home and so to bed, not well; and very ill all night.

10.   I had a great deal of pain all night and a great looseness upon me, so that I could not sleep. In the morning I rose with much pain and to the office I went and dined at home; and after dinner, with great pain in my back, I went by water to Whitehall to the Privy Seale; and that done, with Mr. Moore and Creed to Hideparke by

coach and saw a fine foot-race, three times round the park, between an Irishman and Crow that was once my Lord Claypooles footman. Crow beat the other above two miles. Returned from Hide parke; I went to my Lord's and took Will (who waited for me there) by coach and went home taking my lute home with me [which] hath been all this while since I came from sea at my Lord's for him to play on. To bed, in some pain still. For this month or two, it is not imaginable how busy my head hath been, so that I have neglected to write letters to my Uncle Robt. in answer to many of his, and to other friends; nor endeed have I done anything as to my own family; and especially this month, my waiting at the Privy Seale makes me much more unable to think of anything, because of my constant attendance there after I have done at the Navy Office. But blessed be God for my good chance of the Privy Seale; where I get every day, I believe, about 3*l* per diem. This place I got by chance and my Lord did give it me by chance, neither he nor I thinking it to be of the worth that he and I find it to be. Never since I was a man in the world was I ever so great a stranger to public affairs as now I am, having not read a newsbook or anything like it, or enquired after any news, or what the Parliament doth or in any wise how things go. Many people look after my house in axe yard to hire it of me, so that I am troubled with them; and I have a mind to get the money to buy goods for my house at the Navy Office, and yet I am loath to put it off, because that Mr. Man bids me 1000*l* for my office, which is so great a sum that I am loath to settle myself at my new house, lest I should take Mr. Man's offer in case I find my Lord willing to it.

11. I rose today without any pain, which makes me think that my pain yesterday was nothing but from my drinking too much the day before.

12. *Lordsday*. To my Lord; and with him to Whitehall chapel, where Mr. Calamy preached and made a good sermon up[on] these words: "To whom much is given, of him much is required." He was very officious with his three reverences to the King, as others do. After sermon a brave Anthem of Capt. Cookes, which he himself sung, and the King was well pleased with it. My Lord dined at my Lord Chamberlins and I at his house with Mr. Sheply. After that I went to walk; and meeting Mrs. Lane of Westminster hall, I took her to my Lord's and did give her a bottle of wine in the garden, where Mr. Fairebrother of Cambrige did come and find us

and drank with us. After that I took her to my house,[1] where I was exceeding free in dallying with her, and she not unfree to take it. At night home and called at my father's, where I found Mr. Fairebrother; but I did not stay but went homewards and called in at Mr. Rawlinsons, whither my uncle Wight was coming; and did come, but was exceeding angry (he being a little fuddled, and I think it was that I should see him in that case) as I never saw him in all my life – which I was somewhat troubled at. Home and to bed.

15. To the office; and after dinner by water to Whitehall, where I find the King gone this morning by 5 of the clock to see a Duch pleasure-boat[2] below bridge, where he dines, and my Lord with him. The King doth tire all his people that are about him with early rising since he came. To the office. All the afternoon I stayed there. And in the evening went to Westminster hall, where I stayed at Mrs. Michells; and with her and her husband sent for some drink and drunk with them: by the same token, she and Mrs. Murford and another old woman of the Hall were going a-gossiping* tonight. From thence to my Lord's, where I found him within and he did give me direction about his business in his absence, he entending to go into the country tomorrow morning.

16. This morning my Lord (all things being ready) carried me by coach to Mr. Crews, in the way talking how good he did hope my place would be to me and, in general, speaking that it was not the salary of any place that did make a man rich, but the opportunities of getting money while he is in the place: where he took leave and went into the coach, and so for Hinchingbrooke: my Lady Jem and Mr. Thomas Crew in the coach with him. Thence to Whitehall about noon, where I met with Mr. Madge, who took me along with him and Capt. Cooke (the famous singer) and other Maisters of Musique to dinner at an ordinary above Charing cross, where we dined, all paying their club. Thence to the Privy Seal, where there hath been but little work these two days. In the evening, home.

19. *Lords day.* In the morning my wife tells me that [her little] bich hath whelp[ed] four young ones and is very well after it, my wife having had a great fear that she would die thereof, the dog that got them being very big. This morning Sir W. Batten, Pen and myself

1. In Axe Yard.
2. Presented to the King by the city of Amsterdam.

71

went to church to the churchwardens to demand a pew, which at present could not be given us, but we are resolved to have one built. So we stayed and heard Mr. Mills, a very good Minister. Home to dinner, where my wife had on her new petticoat that she bought yesterday, which endeed is a very fine cloth and a fine lace; but that being of a light colour and the lace all silver, it makes no great show. Mr. Creed and my Brother Tom dined with me. After dinner my wife went and fetched the little puppys to us, which are very pretty ones. After they were gone, I went up to put my papers in order; and finding my wife's clothes lie carelessly laid up, I was angry with her, which I was troubled for. After that, my wife and I went and walked in the garden; and so home to bed.

20. Office day. As Sir W. Pen and I were walking in the garden, a messenger came to me from the Duke of Yorke to fetch me to the Lord Chancellor, but my Lord Chancellor being gone to the House of Lords, I went thither and (there being a law case tried before them this day) got in; and there stayed all the morning, seeing their manner of sitting on Woolpacks, &c., which I never did before. After the House was up, I spoke to my Lord and had order from him to come to him at night. The afternoon at the Privy Seale; where reckoning with Mr. Moore,[1] he had got 100*l* for me together, which I was glad of, guessing that the profits of this month to me would come to 100*l*. In the evening I went all alone to drink at Mrs. Harpers, where I found Mrs. Crisps daughter, with whom and her friends I stayed and drank. And so with W. Ewre by coach to Worcester house, where I light, sending him home with the 100*l* that I received today. Here I stayed and saw my Lord Chancellor come into his Great Hall, where wonderful how much company there was to expect him at a Seale. Before he would begin any business, he took my papers of the state of the debts of the fleet and there viewed them before all the people and did give me his advice privately how to order things to get as much money as we can of the parliament. That being done, I went home, where I find all my things come home from sea, of which I was glad, though many of my things are quite spoiled with mould, by reason of lying so long a-shipboard and my cabin being not tight. I spent much time to dispose of them tonight, and so to bed.

1. His deputy.

22. Office. Which done, Sir W. Penn took me into the garden and there told me how Mr. Turner doth entend to petition the Duke for an Allowance Extra as one of the Clerks of the Navy, which he desired me to join with him in the furthering of. Which I promised to do, so that it did not reflect upon me or to my damage to have any other added, as if I was not able to perform my place; which he did wholly disown to be any of his intention, but far from it. I took Mr. Hater home with me to dinner, with whom I did advise, who did give me the same counsel.

23. To the Admiralty chamber, where we and Mr. Coventry have a meeting about several businesses. Among others, it was moved that Phin. Pett (kinsman to the Commissioner) of Chatham should be suspended his imployment till he had answered to some articles put in against him; as, that he should formerly say that the King was a bastard and his mother a whore. Thence to Westminster hall, where I met with my father Bowyer[1] and Mr. Spicer, and them I took to the Leg in King's street and did give them a dish or two of meat; and so away to the Privy Seale, where the King being out of Towne, we have had nothing to do these two days. To Westminster hall, where I met with W. Symons, T. Doling and Mr. Booth, and with them to the Dogg, where we eat a Muske millon (the first that I have eat this year) and were very merry with W. Symons, calling him Mr. Deane, because of the Deanes lands that his uncle had left him, which are like to be lost all. Thence home by water; and very late at night writing letters to my Lord to Hinchingbrooke and also to the Vice-Admirall in the Downes; and so to bed.

24. Office; and then with Sir W. Batten and Sir W. Penn to the parish church to find out a place where to build a seat or a gallery to sit in; and did find one, which is to be done speedily. Thence with them to dinner at a tavern in Thames street, where they were invited to a roasted haunch of venison and other very good victuals and company. Thence to Whitehall to the Privy Seale, but nothing to do. At night by land to my father's, where I found my mother not very well. I did give her a pint of sack. My father came in and Dr. T. Pepys, who talked with me in French a great while about looking out of a place for him. But I find him a weak man and

1. Robert Bowyer had been Pepys's 'father' in the Exchequer – i.e. the senior official under whom Pepys and his brother clerks worked.

speaks the worst French that ever I heard of one that hath been so long beyond sea. Thence into Paul's churchyard and bought Barkley's *Argenis* in Latin; and so home and to bed. I find at home that Capt. Bun hath sent me four dozen bottles of wine to me today. The King came back to Whitehall tonight.

26. *Lords day*. With Sir W. Penn to the parish church, where we are placed in the highest pew of all, where a stranger preached a dry and tedious long sermon. Dined at home, and with my wife to church again in the afternoon. Home again and walked in the garden and on the leads till night; and so to supper and to bed.

27. This morning comes one with a vessel of Northdowne ale from Mr. Pierce the purser to me. And after him, another with a brave Turkey carpet and a Jarre of Olives from Capt. Cuttance and a pair of fine Turtle-doves from John Burr to my wife. These things came up today in our smack; and my boy Ely came along with them and came after office was done to see me. I did give him half a crowne because I saw that he was ready to cry to see that he could not be entertained by me here. In the afternoon to the Privy Seale, where good stir of work now toward the end of the month. From thence with Mr. Mount, Luellin and others to the Bullhead till late, and so home. Where about 10 a-clock Maj. Hart came to me – whom I did receive with wine and a dish of Anchoves, which made me so dry that I was ill with them all night and was fain to have the girl rise to fetch me some drink.

28. At home looking over my papers and books and house as to the fitting of it to my mind till 2 in the afternoon. Some time I spent this morning beginning to teach my wife some skill in Musique, and find her apt beyond imagination. This day I heard my poor mother hath these two days been very ill, and I fear she will not last long. To bed – a little troubled that I fear my boy Will is a thief and hath stole some money of mine – perticularly a letter that Mr. Jenkins did leave the last week with me with half a crown in to send to his son.

29. Office day. Before I went to the office, my wife and I examined my boy Will about his stealing of things, as we doubted yesterday; but he denied all with the greatest subtility and confidence in the world. To the office; and after office, then to the

church, where we took another view of the place where we had
resolved to build a gallery; and have set men about doing it. Home
to dinner; and there I find that my wife hath discovered my boy's
theft and a great deal more then we imagined. At which I was vexed
and entend to put him away. To my office at Privy Seale in the
afternoon; and from thence at night to the Bull head with Mount,
Luellin and others; and thence to my father's; and he being at my
uncle Fenner's, I went thither to him, and there sent for my boy's
father and talked with him about his son and had his promise that if
I will send home his boy, he will take him notwithstanding his
indentures. Home at night; and find that my wife hath found out
more, of the boy's stealing 6s. out of W. Ewres closet and hid it in
the house of office – at which my heart was troubled. To bed and
caused the boy's clothes to be brought up to my chamber. But after
we were all a-bed, the wench (which lies in our chamber) called us
to listen of a sudden; which put my wife into such a fright that she
shook, every joynt of her, and a long time that I could not get her
out of it. That noise was the boy, we did believe, was got in a
desperate mood out of his bed to do himself or Wm.[1] some
mischief. But the wench went down and got a candle lighted; and
finding the boy in bed and locking the doors fast, with a candle
burning all night, we slept well, but with a great deal of fear.

31.    Early to wait upon my Lord at Whitehall; and with him to the
Duke's chamber. So to my office in Seething lane. Dined at home;
and after dinner to my Lord again; who told me that he is ordered to
go suddenly to sea,[2] and did give me some orders to be drawing
upon against his going. This afternoon I agreed to let my house
quite out of my hands to Mr. Dalton (of the wine-cellar to the King,
with whom I have drunk in the old wine-cellar two or three times)
for 41l. At night, made up even at Privy Seale for this month against
tomorrow to give up possession, and so home and to bed. Blessed
be God all things continue well with and for me; I pray God fit me
for a change of my fortune.

> 1. Will Hewer.
> 2. To bring over the Princess Royal from Holland.

## —❧SEPTEMBER❧—

1. *Saturday*. Mr. Moore and I and several others being invited today by Mr. Goodman, a friend of his, we dined at the Bull head upon the best venison pasty that ever I eat of in my life; and with one dish more, it was the best dinner I ever was at. Here ris in discourse at table a dispute between Mr. Moore and Dr. Clerke, the former affirming that it was essentiall to a Tragedy to have the argument of it true, which the Doctor denyed and left to me to be judge – and the cause to be determind next Tuesday morning at the same place upon the eating of the remains of the pasty, and the loser to spend 10s. All this afternoon sending express to the fleet to order things against my Lord's coming – and taking direction of my Lord about some rich furniture to take along with him for the Princesse.

3. About noone, my Lord having taken leave of the King in the Shield Gallery (where I saw with what kindnesse the King did hugg my Lord at his parting), I went over with him and saw him in his Coach at Lambeth and there took leave of him, going to the Downes. In the afternoon with Mr. Moore to my house to cast up our Privy Seale accounts, where I find that my Lord's comes to 400 and odd pounds, and mine to 132*l* – out of which I do give him as good as 25*l* for his pains, with which I doubt he is not Satisfyed – but my heart is full glad. Thence with him to Mr. Crews and did fetch as much money as did make even our accounts between him and I. Home; and there found Mr. Cooke come back from my Lord for me to get him some things bought for him to be brought after him – a toilette Capp and Combe-case of Silke to make use of in Holland (for he is to go himself to The Hague) which I am to do tomorrow morning. This day my father and my uncle Fenner and both his sons have been at my house to see it; and my wife did treat them nobly with wine and Anchoves. By reason of my Lord's going today I could not get to the office to meet today.

4. I did many things this morning at home before I went out – as looking over the Joyners, who are flooring my dining-roome – and

doing business with Sir Wms both[1] at the office. And so to Whitehall and so to the bull head where we had the remaynes of our pasty, where I did give my verdict against Mr. Moore upon last Saturdays wager. Where Dr. Fuller coming in doth confirme me in my verdict. From thence to my Lord's and dispatcht Mr. Cooke away with the things to my Lord. From thence to Axeyard to my house; where standing at the door, Mrs. Diana comes by, whom I took into my house upstairs and there did dally with her a great while, and find that in Latin *"nulla puella negat."* So home by water; and there sat up late, putting my papers in order and my money also, and teaching my wife her Musique lesson, in which I take great pleasure. So to bed.

5.    In the evening, my wife being a little impatient, I went along with her to buy her a necklace of pearle which will cost 4*l* 10*s.* – which I am willing to comply with her in, for her incouragement and because I have lately got money, having now above 200*l* in Cash beforehand in the world. Home; and having in our way bought a rabbett and two little lobsters, my wife and I did supp late; and so to bed. Great newes nowaday of the Duc D'Anjou's desire to marry the Princesse Henriette. Hugh Peters is said to be taken. And the Duke of Glocester is fallen ill and is said will prove the smallpox.

6.    To my house and sent all my books to my Lord's, in order to send them to my house that I now dwell in. Home and to bed.

7.    An office day; and in the afternoon at home all the day, it being the first that I have been at home all day since I came hither. Putting my papers, books and other things in order, and writing of letters. This day my Lord set sail from the Downes for Holland.

8.    All day also at home. At night sent for by Sir W. Penn, with whom I sat late, drinking a glass of wine – and discoursing; and I find him to be a very Sociable man, and an able man and very Cunning*.

9.    *Sunday.* In the morning with Sir W. Pen to church; and a very good sermon of Mr. Mills. Home to dinner, and Sir W. Pen with me to such as I had; and it was very handsome, it being the first time

---

1. Batten and Penn.

that he ever saw my wife or house since we came hither.

10.   *office day.* news brought us of the Dukes intention to go tomorrow to the fleet for a day or two to meet his sister. Coll. Slingsby and I to Whitehall, thinking to proffer our service to the Duke to wait upon him; but meeting with Sir G. Carteret, he sent us in all haste back again to hire two Catches for the present use of the Duke. So we returned and landed at the Beare at the bridge-foot, where we saw Suthwark faire (I having not at all seen Bartlmew fayre); and so to the towre wharfe, where we did hire two Catches. So to the office and found Sir W. Batten at dinner with some friends upon a good Chine of beef, on which I eat heartily, I being very hungry.

11.   At Sir W. Battens with Sir W. Pen we drank our morning draught, and from thence for an houre in the office and despatch a little business. Dined at Sir W. Battens; and by this time I see that we are like to have a very good correspondency and neighbour-hood, but chargeable. All the afternoon at home looking over my Carpenters. At night I called Tho. Hater out of the office to my house to sit and talk with me. After he was gone, I caused the Girle to wash the wainscote of our parler, which she did very well; which caused my wife and I good sport. Up to my chamber to read a little, and write my Diary for three or four days past. The Duke of Yorke did go today by break-of-day to the Downes. The Duke of Glocester ill. To bed.

12.   *office day.* My Brother Tom came to my house with a letter from my Brother John, wherein he desires some books – Barthol. *Anatomy*; Rosinus *Roman antiquities*, and Gassendus *astronomy*. The last of which I did give him, and an angell toward my father's buying of the others. At home all the afternoon looking after my workmen in my house, whose lazinesse doth much trouble me.

13.   old East comes to me in the morning with letters and I did give hima bottle of Northdown ale, which made the poor man almost drunk. This day the Duke of Glocester dyed of the smallpox – by the great negligence of the Doctors.

16.   *Sunday.* To Dr. Hardys church and sat with Mr. Rawlinson and heard a good sermon upon the occasion of the Dukes death. His

text was – "And is there any evil in the city and the Lord hath not done it?" Home to dinner – having some sport with Wm: who never hath been at Common prayer before. After dinner, I alone to Westminster, where I spent my time walking up and down in Westminster Abbey all sermon time. From thence to the parke, where I saw how far they have proceeded in the pellmell and in making of a river through the parke, which I have never seen before since it was begun. Thence to Whitehall garden, where I saw the King in purple mourning for his brother. So home; and in my way met with Dinah, who spoke to me and told me she hath a desire to speak to [me] about some business when I come to Westminster again – which she spoke in such a manner that I was afeared she might tell me something that I would not hear of our last meeting at my house at Westminster. Home, it being very dark. There was a gentleman in the poultry had a great and dirty fall over a water-pipe that lay along the Channell.

18. At home all the morning looking over my workmen in my house. After dinner, Sir W. Batten, Pen, and myself by Coach to Westminster hall, where we met Mr. Wayte that belongs to the Treasurer; and so we went up to the Committee of Parliament which are to consider of the debts of the army and navy, and did give in our account of the 25 shipps.[1] Coll. Birch was very impertinent* and troublesome. But at last we did agree to fit the accounts of one ship more perfectly for their view within a few days, that they might see what a trouble it is to do what they desire. From thence, Sir Williams both going by water home, I took Mr. Wayte to the Rhenish winehouse and drank with him and so parted.

21. *office day*. There all the morning and afternoon till 4 a-clock. Then to Whitehall, thinking to have put up my books at my Lord's, but am disappointed for want of a chest which I have at Mr. Bowyers. Back by water about 8 a-clock; and upon the water saw [the] corps of the Duke of Gloucester brought down Somersett house stairs to go by water to Westminster to be buried tonight. I landed at the old Swan and went to the Hoope taverne and (by former agreement) sent for Mr. Chaplin, who with Nich. Osborne and one Daniel came to us and there we drank off two or three quarts of wine, which was very good (the drawing of our wine causing a

---

1. i.e. those that were to be paid off.

great quarrell in the house between the two drawers which should draw us the best). Home, where I find my boy (my mayd's brother)[1] come out of the country today; but was gone to bed and so I could not see him tonight. I to bed.

22. This morning I called up the boy to me and find him a pretty well-looked boy, and one that I think will please me. I went this morning to Westminster by land along with Luellin. We walked on to Fleetstreete, where at Mr. Standings in Salsbury court we drank our morning draught and had a pickled herring. Among other discourse here, he told me how the pretty woman that I always loved at the beginning of Cheapeside that sells children's coates was served by the Lady Bennett (a famous Strumpet), who by counterfeiting to fall into a swoune upon the sight of her in her shop, became acquainted with her and at last got her ends of her to lie with a gallant that had hired her to Procure this poor soul for him. To Westminster to my Lord's; and there in the house of office vomited up all my breakfast, my stomach being ill all this day by reason of the last night's debauch. And stayed here all day in my Lord's chamber and upon the leads gazing upon Diana, who looked out at a window upon me. At last I went out to Mr. Harpers, and she standing over the way at the gate, I went over to her and appointed to meet tomorrow in the afternoon at my Lord's. Here I bought a hanging jack. From thence by coach home (by the way at the New Exchange I bought a pair of Short black stockings to wear over a pair of silk ones for mourning; and here I met with The[oph]. Turner and Joyce buying of things to go into mourning too for the Duke, which is now the mode of all the ladies in towne), where I writ some letters by the post to Hinchingbrooke to let them know that this day Mr. Edwd. Pickering is come from my Lord and says that he left him well in Holland and that he will be here within three or four days. To bed, not well of my last night's drinking yet. I had the boy up tonight for his sister to teach him to put me to bed, and I heard him read, which he doth pretty well.

23. *Lords day.* My wife got up to put on her mourning today and to go church this morning. I up and set down my Journall for these five days past. This morning came one from my father's with a black cloth coate, made of my short cloak, to walk up and down in.

1. Wayneman Birch.

To church, my wife and I with Sir W. Battin, where we heard of Mr. Mills a very good sermon upon these words: "So run that you may obtaine." After sermon, with Mr. Pierce to Whitehall and from thence to my Lord, but Diana did not come according to our agreement. So calling at my father's (where my wife had been this afternoon but was gone home), I went home. This afternoon, the King having news of the Princesses being come to Margetts, he and the Duke of Yorke went down thither in Barges to her.

24. *office day*. From thence to dinner by Coach with my wife to my Cozen Scotts – and the company not being come, I went over the way to the Barbers. So thither again to dinner, where was my uncle Fenner and my aunt, my father and mother and others. Among the rest, my Cozen Rich. Pepys, their elder brother, whom I have not seen these fourteen years, ever since he came from New England. I rose from table and went to the Temple church, where I had appointed Sir W. Batten to meet him; and there at Sir Henige Finch, Sollicitor-Generall's Chamber, before him and Sir W. Wilde, Recorder of London (whom we sent for from his chamber), we were sworn Justices of Peace for Middlesex, Essex, Kent, and Southampton,[1] with which Honour I did find my mind mightily pleased, though I am wholly ignorant in the duty of a Justice of Peace. From thence to my Lord's to enquire whether they have had anything from my Lord or no. Knocking at the door, there passed by Monsieur L'impertinent, for whom I took a Coach and went with him to a dancing-meeting in Broadstreete, at the house that was formerly the Glasse house (Luke Channell Maister of the Schoole) where I saw good dancing. But it growing late and the room very full of people, and so very hott, I went home.

25. To the office, where Sir W. Batten, Coll. Slingsby, and I sat a while; and Sir R. Ford coming to us about some business, we talked together of the interest of this kingdom to have a peace with Spain and a war with France and Holland – where Sir R. Ford talked like a man of great reason and experience. And afterwards did send for a Cupp of Tee (a China drink of which I never had drank before) and went away. Then came Coll. Birch and Sir R. Browne (by a former appointment) and with them from Towre wharf in the barge belonging to our office we went to Deptford to pay off the ship

1. The counties in which the royal dockyards were situated.

*Successe*. At the globe we had a very good dinner, and after that to the pay again; which being finished, we returned by water again. And I from our office by Coach to Westminster to enquire for my Lord's coming thither (the King and the Princesse coming up the River this afternoon as we were at our pay); and I find him gone to Mr. Crews, where I find him well; only, had got some brush upon his foot which was not well yet. My Lord told me how the ship that brought the Princesse and him (the *Tredagh*) did knock six times upon the Kentish Knock, which put them in great fear for the ship; but got off well. From him late, and by Coach home – where the playsterers being at work in all the rooms in my house, my wife was fain to make a bed upon the ground for her and I; and so there we lay all night.

28. *office day*. All the afternoon at home among my workmen; work till 10 or 11 at night; and did give them drink and were very merry with them – it being my luck to meet with a sort of Drolling workmen upon all occasions. To bed.

29. All day at home to make an end of our dirty work of the playsterers; and indeed, my Kitchin is now so handsome that I did not repent of all the trouble that I have been put to to have it done. This day or yesterday I hear Prince Robt.[1] is come to Court; but welcome to nobody.

# –❊OCTOBER❊–

1. Early to my Lord to Whitehall; and there he did give me some work to do for him and so with all haste to the office. Dined at home, and my father by chance with me. After dinner he and I advised about hangings for my rooms, which are now almost fit to be hung, the painters beginning to do their work today. My layings out upon my house in Furniture are so great that I fear I shall not be able to go through them without breaking one of my bags of 100*l*, I having but 200*l* yet in the world.

2. With Sir W. Pen by water to Whitehall – being this morning

1. Rupert.

visited before I went out by my brother Tom, who told me that for
his lying out-of-doors a day and a night my father hath forbid him
to come any more into his house – at which I was troubled and did
soundly chide him for doing so; and upon confessing his fault, I told
him I would speak to my father. At Whitehall I met with Capt.
Clerke and took him to the Legg in King streete and did give him a
dish or two of meat, and his purser that was with him, for his old
kindness to me on board. After that at Wills I met with Mr. Spicer;
and with him to the abby to see them at vespers there, where I find
but a thin congregacion allready. So that I see religion, be it what it
will, is but a humour, and so the esteem of it passeth as other things
do. From thence by Coach to my father's and discoursed with him
about Tom and did give my advice to take him home again, which I
think he will do in prudence rather then put him upon learning the
way of being worse.

3. With Sir W. Batten and Pen by water to Whitehall, where a
meeting of the Dukes of Yorke and Albermarle, my Lord Sandwich
and all the Principal Officers, about the Winter gard; but we
determined of nothing. From thence to my Lord's, who sent a great
iron chest to Whitehall; and I saw it carried into the King's closet,
where I saw most incomparable pictures. Among the rest, a book
open upon a deske which I durst have sworn was a reall book, &c.
Back again to my Lord and dined all alone with him, who doth treat
me with a great deal of respect. And after dinner did discourse an
houre with me and advise about getting of some way to get himself
some money to make up for all his great expenses – saying that he
believed he might have anything that he would ask of the King.
This day I heard the Duke[1] speak of a great design that he and my
Lord of Pembrooke have, and a great many others, of sending a
venture to some parts of affrica to dig for gold ore there. They
entend to admit as many as will venture their money, and so make
themselfs a company. 250*l* is the lowest share for every man. But I
do not find that my Lord doth much like it.

4. *Thursday.* This morning I was busy looking over papers at the
office all alone. And being visited by Lieut. Lambert of the *Charles*
(to whom I was formerly much beholden to), I took him along with
me to a little alehouse hard by our office. From thence I and Lieut.

---

1. The Duke of York.

Lambert to Westminster Abbey, where we saw Dr. Fruen translated to the Archbishopric of Yorke. Here I saw the Bishops of Winchester, Bangor, Rochester, Bath and Wells, and Salisbury, all in their habitts, in King Henry the 7ths chappell. But Lord, at their going out, how people did most of them look upon them as strange Creatures, and few with any kind of love or Respect. From thence we two to my Lord's, where we took Mr. Sheply and W. Howe to the Rayne Deare and had some oysters, which were very good, the first I have eat this year. So back to my Lord's to dinner; and after dinner Lieut. Lambert and I did look upon my Lord's Modell,[1] and he told me many things in a ship that I desired to understand.

6. To Whitehall, where I was to give my Lord an account of the Stacions and Victualls of the fleet in order to the choosing of a fleet fit for him to take to sea to bring over the Queene.[2] But my Lord not coming in before 9 at night, I stayed no longer for him, but went back again home and so to bed.

7. *Lordsday.* To Whitehall on foot, calling at my father's to change my long black Cloake for a short one (long cloaks being now quite out); but he being gone to church, I could not get one, and therefore I proceeded on and came to my Lord before he went to Chappell; and so went with him, where I heard Dr. Spurstow preach before the King a poor dry sermon; but a very good Anthemne of Capt. Cookes afterwards. To my Lord's and dined with him; he all dinner time talking French to me and telling me the story how the Duke of Yorke hath got my Lord Chancellors daughter with child, and that she doth lay it to him. Discoursing concerning what if the Duke should marry her,[3] my Lord told me that among his father's many old sayings that he had writ in a book of his, this is one: that he that doth get a wench with child and marries her afterward it is as if a man should shit in his hat and then clap it upon his head. I perceive my Lord is grown a man very indifferent in all matters of Religion, and so makes nothing of these things. After dinner to the Abby, where I heard them read the church service, but very Ridiculously, that endeed I do not in my mind like it at all. A poor cold sermon of Dr. Lambs, one of the Prebends, in his habitt, came afterwards; and

1. Ship-model.
2. Until the King's marriage in 1662, Pepys's references to the 'Queen' are to Henrietta-Maria, the Queen Mother.
3. They had been secretly married on 8 September.

so all ended. And by my troth a pitiful sorry devocion it is that these men pay. So walked home by land. And before supper I read part of the Maryan persecution in Mr. Fuller. So to supper, prayer, and to bed.

9.   This morning, Sir W. Batten with Coll. Birch to Deptford to pay off two ships. Sir W. Pen and I stayed to do business, and afterward together to Whitehall, where I went to my Lord and found him in bed not well. And saw in his chamber his picture, very well done; and am with child till I get it copyed out, which I hope to do when he is gone to sea. To Whitehall again, where at Mr. Coventrys chamber I met with Sir W. Pen again, and so with him to Redriffe by water and from thence walked over the fields to Deptford (the first pleasant walk I have had a great while); and in our way had a great deal of merry discourse, and find him to be a merry fellow and pretty good-natured and sings very bawdy songs. About noon we dined together and were very merry at table, telling of tales. After dinner to the pay of another ship till 10 at night. And so home in our barge, a clear Mooneshine night and it was 12 a-clock before we got home – where I find my wife in bed and part of our chambers hung today by the Upholster; but not being well done, I was fretted, and so in a discontent to bed.

10.   *office day* all the morning. At night comes Mr. Moore and stayed late with me to tell me how Sir Hards: Waller (who only pleads guilty), Scott, Cooke, Peters, Harrison, &c. were this day arraigned at the bar at the Sessions house,[1] there being upon the bench the Lord Mayor, Gen. Monke, my Lord of Sandwich, &c.; such a bench of noblemen as hath not been ever seen in England. They all seem to be dismayed and will all be condemned without Question. In Sir Orland. Brigeman's charge, he did wholly rip up the unjustnesse of the war against the King from the beginning, and so it much reflects upon all the Long Parliament; though the King hath pardoned them, yet they must hereby confess that the King doth look upon them as traytors.

11.   In the morning to my Lord's, where I met with Mr. Creed, and with him and Mr. Blackburne to the Rhenish winehouse – where we sat drinking of healths a great while, a thing which Mr

---

1. At the trial of the regicides.

Blackburne formerly would not upon any terms have done. After
we had done there, Mr. Creed and I to the Leg in King street to
dinner, where he and I and my Will had a good udder to dinner; and
from thence to walk in St. James's Park – where we observed the
several engines at work to draw up water, with which sight I was
very much pleased. Here in the park we met with Mr. Salsbury,
who took Mr. Creed and me to the Cockpitt to see *The Moore of
Venice*, which was well done. Burt acted the Moore; by the same
token, a very pretty lady that sot by me cried to see Desdimona
smothered.

12.   *office day* all the morning. After dinner I went home, where I
found Mr. Cooke, who told me that my Lady Sandwich is come to
town today, whereupon I went to Westminster to see her; and
found her at supper, so she made me sit down all alone with her; and
after supper stayed and talked with her – she showing most
extraordinary love and kindness and did give me good assurance of
my Uncles resolution to make me his heire. From thence home and
to bed.

13.   To my Lord's in the morning, where I met with Capt.
Cuttance. But my Lord not being up, I went out to Charing cross to
see Maj.-Gen. Harrison hanged, drawn, and quartered – which was
done there – he looking as cheerfully as any man could do in that
condition. He was presently cut down and his head and his heart
shown to the people, at which there was great shouts of joy. It is
said that he said that he was sure to come shortly at the right hand of
Christ to judge them that now have judged him. And that his wife
doth expect his coming again. Thus it was my chance to see the
King beheaded at Whitehall and to see the first blood shed in
revenge for the blood of the King at Charing cross. From thence to
my Lord's and took Capt. Cuttance and Mr. Sheply to the Sun
taverne and did give them some oysters. After that I went by water
home, where I was angry with my wife for her things lying about,
and in my passion kicked the little fine Baskett which I bought her
in Holland and broke it, which troubled me after I had done it.
Within all the afternoon, setting up shelfes in my study. At night to
bed.

15.   office all the morning. My wife and I by water; I landed her at

Whitefriers, who went to my father's to dinner, it being my father's wedding day, there being a very great dinner and only the Fenners and Joyces there. I was forced to go to my Lord's to get him to meet the officers of the Navy this afternoon, and so could not go along with her. But I missed my Lord, who was this day upon the bench at the Sessions house. So I dined there and went to Whitehall, where I met with Sir W. Batten and Pen, who with the Comptroller, Treasurer, and Mr. Coventry (at his Chamber) made up a list of such ships as are fit to be kept out for the Winter guard – and the rest to be paid off by the Parliament when they can get money, which I doubt will not be a great while. That done, I took Coach and called my wife at my father's, and so home where I fell to read *The fruitlesse precaution* (a book formerly recommended by Dr. Clerke at sea to me), which I read in bed till I had made an end of it and do find it the best-writ tale that ever I read in my life. After that done, to sleep, which I did not very well do because that my wife, having a stopping in her nose, she snored much, which I never did hear her do before.

17. *office day*. At noon comes Mr. Creede to me, whom I took along with me to the feathers in Fishstreete, where I was invited by Capt. Cuttance to dinner – a dinner made by Mr. Dawes and his brother. We have two or three dishes of meat well done. Their great designe was to get me concerned in a business of theirs about a vessel of theirs that is in the service, hired by the King, in which I promise to do them all the service I can.

19. office in the morning. This morning my Dining-room was finished with greene Serge hanging and gilt leather, which is very handsome. This morning Hacker and Axtell were hanged and Quarterd, as the rest are. This night I sat up late to make up my accounts ready against tomorrow for my Lord; and I find him to be above 80*l* in my debt, which is a good sight and I bless God for it.

20. This morning one came to me to advise with me where to make me a window into my cellar in lieu of one that Sir W. Batten had stopped up; and going down into my cellar to look, I put my foot into a great heap of turds, by which I find that Mr. Turners house of office is full and comes into my cellar, which doth trouble me; but I will have it helped. To my Lord's by land, calling at

several places about business. Where I dined with my Lord and Lady; where he was very merry and did talk very high how he would have a French Cooke and a Master of his Horse, and his lady and child to wear black paches; which methought was strange, but he is become a perfect Courtier; and among other things, my Lady saying that she would have a good Merchant for her daughter Jem, he answered that he would rather see her with a pedlar's pack at her back, so she married a Gentleman, rather then that she should marry a Citizen. This afternoon, going through London and calling at Crowes the upholster in Saint Bartholmew – I saw the limbs of some of our new Traytors set upon Aldersgate, which was a sad sight to see; and a bloody week this and the last have been, there being ten hanged, drawn, and Quarterd. Home; and after writing a letter to my Uncle by the post, I went to bed.

21. *Lords day*. To the Parish church in the morning, where a good sermon by Mr. Mills. Today at noon (God forgive me), I strung my Lute, which I have not touched a great while before.

22. *office day*. After that to dinner at home upon some ribbs of roast beef from the Cookes (which of late we have been forced to do because of our house being alway under the painters' and other people's hands, that we could not dress it ourselfs): after dinner to my Lord's, where I find all preparing for my Lord's going to sea to fetch the Queene tomorrow. At night my Lord came home, with whom I stayed long and talked of many things. Among others, I got leave of him to have his picture, that was done by Lilly, coppyed. And talking of religion, I find him to be a perfect Sceptique, and said that all things would not be well while there was so much preaching, and that it would be better if nothing but Homilys were to be read in churches. This afternoon (he told me), there hath been a meeting before the King and my Lord Chancellor of some Episcopalian and Presbyterian Divines; but what hath passed he could not tell me. After I had done talk with him, I went to bed with Mr. Sheply in his Chamber, but could hardly get any sleep all night, the bed being ill-made and he a bad bedfellow.

24. I lay and slept long today. *Office day*. I took occasion to be angry with my wife before I ris about her putting up of half-a-crowne of mine in a pepper box, which she hath forgot where she hath lain it. But we were friends again, as we are always. Then I rise

to Jack Cole, who came to see me. Then to the office. So home to dinner – where I find Capt. Murford, who did put 3*l* in my hands for a friendship I have done him; but I would not take it, but bid him keep it till he hath enough to buy my wife a necklace. This afternoon I went to Mr. Greatorex, where I met [Mr. Spong]; and so to an alehouse, where I bought of him a drawing pen and he did show me the manner of the Lamp glasses, which carry the light a great way. Good to read in bed by and I intend to have one of them. So to Mr. Lillys[1] with Mr. Spong; where well received, there being a Clubb there tonight among his friends[2] – among the rest, Esquire Ashmole, who I find a very ingenious Gentleman; with him we two sang afterward in Mr. Lillys study. That done, we all parted and I home by Coach, taking Mr. Booker with me – who did tell me a great many fooleries what may be done by Nativitys; and blaming Mr. Lilly for writing to please his friends and to keep in with the times (as he did formerly to his owne dishonour) and not according to the rules of Art, by which he could not well erre, as he hath done. I set him downe at Limestreete end; and so home, where I found a box of Carpenters tooles sent by my Cozen Tho. Pepys, which I have bespoake of him for to imploy myself with sometimes. To bed.

29. I up earely, it being my Lord Mayors day (Sir Rich. Browne); and neglecting my office, I went to the Wardrobe, where I met my Lady Sandwich and all the Children. Where after drinking of some strang and incomparable good Clarett of Mr. Rumballs, he and Mr. Townsend did take us and set the young Lords at one Mr. Nevills, a draper in Pauls churchyard; and my Lady and my Lady Pickering and I to one Mr. Isackson's, a linendraper at the Key in Cheapside – where there was a company of fine ladies and we were very civilly treated and had a very good place to see the pageants; which were many and I believe good for such kind of things but in themselfs but poor and absurd. After the ladies were placed, I took Mr. Townsend and Isackson to the next door, a tavern, and did spend 5*s.* upon them. The show being done, with much ado we got as far as Pauls, where I left my Lady in the coach and went on foot with my Lady Pickering to her lodging, which was a poor one in Blackfryers, where she never invited me to go in at all with her –

1. William Lilly the astrologer; not to be confused with Lely the painter, whose name Pepys often spells in the same way.
2. Apparently all astrologers.

which methought was very strange for her to do. So home, where I was told how my lady Davis[1] was now come to our next lodgings and hath locked up the leads doore from me, which put me into so great a disquiet that I went to bed and could not sleep till morning at it.

30. Within all the morning and dined at home, my mind being so troubled that I could not mind nor do anything till I speak with the Comptroller to whom the lodgings belong. In the afternoon, to ease my mind, I went to the Cockpitt all alone and there saw a very fine play called *The Tamer tamed*, very well acted.

31. *office day*. Much troubled all this morning in my mind about the business of my walk in the leades. I speak of it to the Comptroller and the rest of the principall officers, who are all unwilling to meddle in anything that may anger my Lady Davis; and so I am fain to give over for the time that she doth continue therein. Dined at home, and there I have news that Sir W. Pen is resolved to ride to Sir W. Batten's country house tomorrow and would have me to go with him. So I sat up late, getting together my things to ride in, and was fain to cut a pair of old bootes to make leathers for those that I was to wear. To bed.

This month I conclude with my mind very heavy for the loss of the leades – as also for the greatnesse of my late expenses. Insomuch that I do not think that I have above 150*l* clear money in the world. But I have, I bless God, a great deal of good Household stuffe. I hear today that the Queen is landed at Dover and will be here on Friday next the 2 of November. My wife hath been so ill of late of her old pain that I have not known her this fortnight almost, which is a pain to me.

## -❧NOVEMBER❧-

1. This morning Sir W. Pen and I were mounted earely. And have very merry discourse all the way, he being very good company. We came to Sir Wm. Battens, where he lives like a prince, and we were made very welcome. Among other things, he showed us my Lady's

1. Wife of John Davis, Navy Office clerk: 'my lady' is ironical.

closet, where there was great store of rarities. As also a chaire which he calls King Harrys chair, where he that sits down is catched with two irons that come round about him, which makes good sport. Here dined with us two or three more country gentlemen; among the rest, Mr. Christmas my old Schoolfellow, with whom I had much talk. He did remember that I was a great roundhead when I was a boy, and I was much afeared that he would have remembered the words that I said the day that the King was beheaded (that were I to preach upon him, my text should be: "The memory of the wicked shall rot"); but I found afterward that he did go away from schoole before that time. He did make us good sport in imitating Mr. Case, Ash, and Nye, the ministers – which he did very well. But a deadly drinker he is, and grown exceeding fat.

2. office. In the afternoon I went to Whitehall, where when I came I saw the boats going very thick to Lambeth and all the stairs to be full of people: I was told the Queene was a-coming, so I got a sculler for sixpence to carry me thither and back again; but I could not get to see the Queen. So came back and to my Lord's, where he was come and I Supt with him, he being very merry, telling merry stories of the country Mayors how they entertained the King all the way as he came along and how the country gentlewomen did hold up their heads to be kissed by the King, not taking his hand to kiss as they should do. I observed this night very few bonfires in the City, not above three in all London for the Queenes coming; whereby I guess that (as I believed before) her coming doth please but very few.

4. *Lords day*. In the morn to our own church, where Mr. Mills did begin to nibble at the Common Prayer by saying "Glory be to the Father," &c after he had read the two psalms. But the people have beene so little used to it that they could not tell what to answer. After dinner to Westminster, where I went to my Lord; and having spoke with him, I went to the abby, where the first time that ever I heard the organs in a Cathedrall. My wife seemed very pretty today, it being the first time that I have given her leave to weare a black patch.

5. *Office day*. Being disappointed of money, we failed of going to Deptford to pay off the *Henriette* today. Dined at home; and at home all the day and at the office at night, to make up an account of

what the debts of 19 of the 25 ships that should have been paid off is encreased since the adjournment of the Parliament – they being to sit again tomorrow. This 5 of November is observed exceeding well in the City; and at night great bonefires and fireworks. At night Mr. Moore came and sat with me, and there I took a book and he did instruct me in many law-notions, in which I took great pleasure. To bed.

6. To the Sun and did give [Mr. Creed and Mr. Chetwind] a barrel of oysters and have good discourse; among other things, Mr. Chetwind told me how he did fear that this late business of the Duke of Yorke's[1] will prove fatal to my Lord Chancellor. From thence Mr. Creed and I to Wilkinsons and dined together; and in great haste thence to our office, where we met all commonly, for the sale of two ships by an inch of candle (the first time that ever I saw any of this kind), where I observed how they do invite one another and at last how they all do cry; and we have much to do to tell who did cry last. The ships were the *Indian* sold for 1300*l*, and the *Halfe moone* sold for 830*l*. Home and fell a-reading of the tryalls of the late men that were hanged for the King's death; and found good satisfaccion in reading thereof. At night to bed; and my wife and I did fall out about the dog's being put down into the Sellar, which I have a mind to have done because of his fouling the house; and I would have my will. And so we went to bed and lay all night in a Quarrell. This night I was troubled all night with a dream that my wife was dead, which made me that I slept ill all night.

7. *office day*. Being sent for in the morning, I went by water to my Lord; where I dined with him. After dinner he bade all go out of the room, and did tell me how the King hath promised him 4000*l* per annum for ever and hath already given him a bill under his hand (which he showed me) for 4000*l* that Mr. Fox is to pay him. My Lord did advise with me how to get this received and to put out 3000*l* into safe hands at use, and the other he will make use of for this present occasion. This he did advise with me about with much Secresy. After all this he called for the Fiddles and books, and we two and W. Howe and Mr. Childe did sing and play some psalmes of Will. Lawes and some songs. And so I went away.

1. See above, p. 84 (7 October) & n. 3.

8.   This morning Sir Wm. and the Treasurer and I went by barge with Sir Wm. Doyly and Mr. Prin to Deptford to pay off the *Henrietta*, and have a good dinner. In the afternoon Comissioner Pett and I went on board the [Dutch] Yaght;[1] which endeed is one of the finest things that ever I saw for neatness and room in so small a vessel. Mr. Pett is to make one to out-do this for the Honour of his country, which I fear he will scarce better.

11.   *Lords day.* This morning I went to Sir W. Batten's about going to Deptford tomorrow. And so, eating some hog's pudding of my Lady's making, of the hog that I saw a-fattening the other day at her house, he and I went to church into our new Gallery (the first time that ever it was used and it not being yet quite finished ); there came after us Sir W. Pen, Mr. Davis, and his eldest son. There being no women this day, we sat in the foremost pew and behind us our servants; but I hope it will not be always so, it not being handsome for our servants to sit so equal with us. This day also did Mr. Mills begin to read all the Common prayer, which I was glad of. Home to dinner. And then walked to Whitehall, it being very cold and foule and rainy weather. I found my Lord at home; and after giving him an account of some business, I returned and went to my father's, where I found my wife. And there we supped and Dr. Tho. Pepys (who my wife told me after I was come home that he hath told my Brother Tho. that he loved my wife so well that if she have a childe he would never marry, but leave all that he hath to my childe); and after supper we walked home, my little boy carrying a link and Will leading my wife. So home and to prayers and to bed.

12.   To my father's, where I found my wife (who hath been with my father today buying of a tablecloth and a dozen of napkins of Diaper, the first that ever I bought in my life). My father and I took occasion to go forth; and went and drank at Mr. Standings, and there discoursed seriously concerning my sister's coming to live with me – which I have much mind for her good to have, and yet I am much afeared of her ill-nature. Coming home again, he and I and my wife, my mother and Pall, went all together into the little Roome, and there I told her plainly what my mind was: to have her come not as a sister in any respect but as a servant – which she promised me that she would, and with many thanks did weep for

---

1. See above, p. 71 (15 August) & n. 2.

joy. Which did give me and my wife some content and satisfaccion. So by coach home and to bed.

13.    earely going to my Lord's, I met with Mr. Moore (who was going to my house; and endeed I find to be a most careful, painful, and able man in business) and took him by water to the Wardrobe and showed him all the house; and endeed there is a great deal of roome in it – but very ugly till my Lord hath bestowed great cost upon it. So to the Exchequer and there took Spicer and his fellow Clarke to the Dogg taverne and did give them a peck of oysters; and so home to dinner. Where I find my wife making of pyes and tarts to try her oven with (which she hath never yet done); but not knowing the nature of it, did heat it too hot and so did a little overbake her things, but knows how to do better another time. At home all the afternoon. At night made up my accounts of my Sea expences in order to my clearing of my imprest bill of 30*l* which I had in my hands at the beginning of my voyage – which I entend to show to my Lord tomorrow. To bed.

14.    *Office day*. To the office till late at night; and so Sir W. Pen, the Comptroller and I to the Dolphin, where we found Sir W. Batten (who is seldom a night from hence); and there we did drink a great Quantity of Sack. And did tell many merry stories, and in good humours we were all. So home and to bed.

15.    To Westminster, and it being very cold upon the Water, I went all alone to the Sun and drank a draught of mulled White wine. To my Lord's – where I found my Lord within and stayed hearing him and Mr. Childe playing upon my Lord's new Organ – the first time I ever heard it. My Lord did this day show me the Kings picture which was done in Flanders, that the King did promise my Lord before he ever saw him and that we did expect to have had at sea before the King came to us. But it came but today. And endeed it is the most pleasant and the most like him that ever I saw picture in my life.[1] As dinner was coming to table, my wife came hither and I got her carried into my Lady (who took phisique today and was just now hiring of a French maid that was with her, and could not understand one another till my wife came to interpret): here I did leave my wife to dine with my Lord (the first time that ever he

_____

1. Reproduced below, plate 10.

did take notice of her as my wife, and did seem to have a great esteem for her); and did myself walk homewards (hearing that Sir W. Pen was gone before in a coach) to overtake him. To Sir W. Batten's to dinner, he having a couple of servants married today; and so there was a great number of Merchants and others of good Quality, on purpose after dinner to make an offering, which when dinner was done, we did; and I did give 10s. and no more, though I believe most of the rest did give more and did believe that I did so too.

16.   Up earely to my father's, where by appointment Mr. Moore came to me; and he and I to the Temple, and thence to Westminster hall to speak with Mr. Wm. Mountagu about his looking upon the title of those lands which I do take as Security for 3000l of my Lord's money.[1] That being done, Mr. Moore and I parted; and in the Hall I met with Mr. Fontleroy (my old acquaintance, whom I have not seen in a long time) and he and I to the Swan; and in discourse he seems to be wise and say little, though I know things are changed against his mind. Thence home by water, where my father, Mr. Snow and Mr. Moore did dine with me. After dinner Mr. Snow and I went up together to discourse about the putting out of 80l to a man which lacks the money and would give me 15l per annum for eight years for it – which I did not think profit enough; and so he seemed to be disappointed by my refusal of it. But I would not now part with my money easily.

18.   Lords day. In the morning to our own church, where Mr. Powell (a crooke legged man that went formerly with me to Pauls schoole) preached a good sermon. In the afternoon too to our own church and my wife with me (the first time that she and my Lady Battin came to sit in our new pew); and after sermon my Lady took us home and there we supped with her and Sir W. Batten and Pen and were much made of – the first time that ever my wife was there. So home and to bed.

19.   office day. After we have done a little at the office this morning, I went along with the Treasurer in his Coach to Whitehall. And in our way, in discourse do find him a very good-natured man. And talking of those men who now stand condemned for murdering the

1. See above, p. 92 (7 November).

King, he says that he believes that if the law would give leave, the King is a man of so great compassion that he would wholly acquit them. After dinner to the office, where we sat all the afternoon till night. So home, and to my Musique and sat up late at it. And so to bed, leaving my wife to sit up till 2 a-clock that she might call the wench up to wash.

20.    About 2 a-clock my wife wakes me and comes to bed; and so both to sleep and the wench to wash. I rise and with Will to my Lord's by land, it being a very hard frost and the first we have had this year. There I stayed with my Lord and Mr. Sheply, looking over my Lord's accounts and to set matters straight between him and Sheply. And he did commit the viewing of those accounts to me – which was a great joy to me to see that my Lord doth look upon me as one to put trust in. Then to the Organ, where Mr. Childe and one Mr. Mackworth (who plays finely upon the viallin) were playing, and so we played till dinner. After dinner Mr. Sheply and I to the new Playhouse near Lincolnes Inn fields (which was formerly Gibbons's tennis-court), where the play of *Beggars' bush* was newly begun. And so we went in and saw it. It was well acted (and here I saw the first time one Moone, who is said to be the best actor in the world, lately come over with the King); and endeed it is the finest playhouse, I believe, that ever was in England. From thence, after a pot of ale with Mr. Sheply at a house hard by, I went by link home, calling a little by the way at my father's and my uncle Fenner's, where all pretty well. And so home, where I found the house in a washing pickle; and my wife in a very joyful condition when I told her that she is to see the Queene next Thursday. Which puts me in mind to say that this morning I found my Lord in bed late, he having been with the King, Queene, and Princesse at the Cockpitt all night, where Gen. Monke treated them; and after supper, a play – where the King did put a great affront upon Singleton's Musique, he bidding them stop and bade the French Musique play – which my Lord says doth much out-do all ours.

21.    Lay long in bed. This morning my wife and I went to Paternoster Rowe and there we bought some greene watered Moyre for a morning wastcoate. And after that we went to Mr. Cades to choose some pictures for our house. After that my wife went home and I to Popes head [Alley] and bought me an aggat heafted knife which cost me 5s. So home to dinner; and so to the

office all the afternoon. And at night to my viallin (the first time that I have played on it since I came to this house) in my dining-roome; and afterwards to my Lute there – and I took much pleasure to have the neighbours come forth into the yard to hear me. So downe to supper and sent for the barber, who stayed so long with me that he was locked into the house and we were fain to call up Griffith to let him out. So up to bed, leaving my wife to wash herself and to do other things against tomorrow to go to Court.

22.    This morning came the Carpenters to make me a door at the other side of my house, going into the Entry – which I was much pleased with. At noon my wife and I walked to the old Exchange; and there she bought her a white whiske and put it on, and I a pair of gloves; and so we took coach for Whitehall to Mr. Foxes – where we found [Mrs. Foxe] within, and an alderman of London paying a 1000*l* or 1400*l* in gold upon the table for the King, which was the most gold that ever I saw together in my life. Mr. Fox came in presently and did receive us with a great deal of respect. And then did take my wife and I to the Queenes presence-Chamber. Where he got my wife placed behind the Queenes chaire and I got into the Crowd; and by and by the Queen and the two princesses came to dinner. The Queen, a very little plain old woman and nothing more in her presence in any respect nor garbe then any ordinary woman. The Princesse of Orange I have often seen before. The Princess Henriettee is very pretty, but much below my expectation – and her dressing of herself with her haire frized short up to her eares did make her seem so much the less to me. But my wife, standing near her with two or three black paches on and well dressed, did seem to me much handsomer then she. I took Coach for my wife and I homewards; and I light at the Maypoole in the Strand and sent my wife home. I to the new playhouse and saw part of *The Traytor* (a very good Tragedy); where Moone did act the Traytor very well.

24.    At home I have a fire made in my Closett and put my papers and books and things in order. And that being done, I fell to entering those two good songs of Mr. Lawes, *Helpe, helpe, O helpe* &c. and *O God of heaven and Hell* in my song book – to which I have got Mr. Childe to set the base to the Theorbo. And that done, to bed.

25.    *Lords day*. In the forenoon I alone to our church. And after

dinner I went and ranged about to many churches. Among the rest, to the Temple, where I heard Dr. Wilkins a little (late maister of Trinity in Cambrige); and that being done, to my father's to see my mother, who is troubled much with the Stone. And that being done, I went home. So to supper and to bed.

26. *Office day.* To it all the morning. And dined at home, where my father came and dined with me – who seems to take much pleasure to have a son that is neat in his house, I being now making my new door into the entry, which he doth please himself much with. After dinner to the office again and there till night. And that being done, the Comptroller and I to the Miter to a glass of wine – where we fell in discourse of poetry, and he did repeat some verses of his own making, which were very good. Home; there hear that my Lady Batten hath given my wife a visitt (the first that ever she made her), which pleased me exceedingly. So after supper to bed.

27. To Whitehall – where I find my Lord gone abroad to the Wardrobe, whither he doth now go every other morning, and doth seem to resolve to understand and look after that business himself. From thence to Westminster hall; and in King streete, there being a great stop of coaches, there was a falling-out between a drayman and my Lord Chesterfield's coachman, and one of his footmen killed. At the Hall I met with Mr. Creed; and he and I to Hell[1] to drink our morning draught. And so I to my Lord's again, where I find my wife. And she and I dined with him and my Lady and great company of my Lord's friends, and my Lord did show us great respect.

28.   I find that Mr. Creed hath sent me the 11*l* 05*s*. 00 that is due to me upon the remaynes of account for my sea business – which is also so much clear money to me; and my bill of impresse for 30*l* is also cleared. So that I am wholly clear as to the Sea in all respects. To the office and was there till late at night – and among the officers do hear that we may have our Salaryes allowed by the Treasurer,[2] which doth make me very glad and praise God for it. Home to supper; and Mr. Hater supped with me, whom I did give order to take up my money of the Treasurer[3] tomorrow if it can be had. So to bed.

1. A rival establishment to Heaven: cf. above, p. 10 (28 January) & n.
2. The Lord Treasurer.
3. The Navy Treasurer.

29.   My heart is much rejoiced and do bless Almighty God that he is pleased to send me so sudden and unexpected a payment of my salary so soon after my great disbursements – so that now I hope I am worth 200*l* again. In a great ease of mind and spirit, I fell about the auditing of Mr. Sheplys last accounts with my Lord, by my Lord's desire. And about that I sat till 12 a-clock at night, till I begun to doate; and so to bed – with my heart praising God for his mercy to us.

30.   *Office day*. To the office in the morning, where Sir G. Carter[e]t did give us an account how Mr. Holland doth entend to prevail with the parliament that his project of discharging the seamen all at present by tickett and so to promise interest to all men that will lend money upon them at 8 per cent for so long as they are unpaid – whereby he doth think to take away the growing debt, which doth now lie upon the kingdom for lack of present money to discharge the seamen. But this we are troubled at, as some diminucion to us. I having two barrells of Oysters at home, I caused one of them and some wine to be brought to the inner room in the office, and there the Principal Officers did go and eat them. So we sat till noon; and then to dinner. And to it again in the afternoon till night. At home I sent for Mr. Hater and broke the other barrell with him. And did afterward sit down, discoursing of sea tearmes to learn of him. And he being gone, I went up and sat till 12 at night again to make an end of my Lord's accounts – as I did the last night. Which at last I made a good end of; and so to bed.

# –❧DECEMBER❧–

1.   *Saturday*. This morning, observing some things to be laid up not as they should be by the girl, I took a broom and basted her till she cried extremely, which made me vexed, but before I went out I left her appeased: and so to Whitehall, where I found Mr. Moore attending for me at the Privy Seale. But nothing to do today.

3.   This morning I took a resolucion to Rise early in the morning; and so I rose by candle, which I have not done all this winter. And

spent my morning in fidling till time to go to the office. Where Sir
G. Carteret did begin again discourse concerning Mr. Hollands
proposition, which the King doth take very ill. And so Sir George,
in lieu of that, doth propose that seamen shall have half in present
money and tickets for the other half, to be paid in three months
after. Which we judge to be very practicable. After office, home to
dinner – where came in my Cosen Snow by chance, and I have a
very good Capon to dinner.

4.   To Whitehall to Sir G. Carteret's Chamber, where all the
officers met; and so we went up to the Duke of Yorke and he took
us into his Closet and we did open to him our project of stopping
the growing charge of the fleet, by paying them in hand one moyety
and the other four months hence. This he doth like; and we returned
by his order to Sir G. Carteret's chamber, and there we did draw up
this design in order to be presented to the parliament. From thence I
to my Lord's and dined with him and told him what we have done
today. I home by water; and with Mr. Hater in my chamber all
alone, he and I did put this morning's design into words. This day
the parliament voted that the bodies of Oliver, Ireton, Bradshaw,
and [Pride] should be taken up out of their graves in the abby and
drawn to the gallows and there hanged and buried under it. Which
(methinks) doth trouble me, that a man of so great courage as he
was should have that dishonour, though otherwise he might
deserve it enough.

5.   I dined at home; and after dinner went to the new Theatre and
there I saw *The Merry Wifes of Windsor* acted. The humours of the
Country gentleman and the French Doctor very well done; but the
rest but very poorly, and Sir J. Falstaffe as bad as any. From thence I
went to my father's and there found my mother still ill of the stone
and hath just newly voided one, which she hath let drop into the
Chimny; and could not find it to show it me. From thence home
and to bed.

6.   To Whitehall to the Privy Seale, where abundance of Pardons
to seal; but I was much troubled for it, because that there is no fees
coming for them to me. Thence Mr. Moore and I alone to the Legg
in King Street and dined together on a Neats tongue and udder.

7.   To the office – and there stayed till past 12 a-clock; and so I left

the Comptroller and Surveyor and went to Whitehall to my Lord's. Where I find my Lord gone this morning to Huntington – as he told me yesterday he would. I stayed and dined with my Lady, there being Loud the Page's mother there and dined also with us, and seemed to have been a very pretty woman and of good discourse. Before dinner I examined Loud in his Latin and find him a very pretty boy and gone a great way in Latin. So to the Privy Seale, where signed a deadly number of Pardons, which doth trouble me to get nothing by. Home by water; and there was much pleased to see that my little room is likely to come to be finished soon. I fell a-reading in Fuller's *history of Abbys* and my wife in *Grand Cyrus* till 12 at night; and so to bed.

8. I went to dinner with my wife and Mr. and Mrs. Pierce the Chyrurgeon to Mr. Pierce the Purser (the first time that ever I was at his house), who doth live very plentifully and finely. We have a lovely Chine of beef and other good things, very complete – and drank a great deal of wine. And her daughter played after dinner upon the virginalls, and at night by lanthorne home again; and Mr. Pierce and his wife being gone home – I went to bed, having drank so much wine that my head was troubled – and was not very well all night. And the Winde, I observed, was ris exceedingly this night before I went to bed.

9. *Lords day.* Being called up earely by Sir W. Batten, I rose and went to his house and he told me the ill news that he hath this morning from Woolwich: that the *Assurance* (formerly Capt. Hollands ship, and now Capt. Stoakes, designed for Guiny and manned and victualled), was by a gust of wind sunk down to the bottom. Twenty men drowned. Sir Wms both went by barge thither to see how things are – and I am sent to the Duke of Yorke to tell him. And by boat, with some other company going to Whitehall from the old Swan, I went to the Duke. And first calling upon Mr. Coventry at his Chamber, I went to the Duke's bedside (who hath sat up late last night and lay long this morning), who was much surprized therewith. This being done, I went to Chappell and sat in Mr. Blagraves pew and there did sing my part along with another before the King – and with much ease. From thence going to my Lady, I met with a letter from my Lord (which Andrew hath been at my house to bring me, but missed me) commanding me to go to Mr. Denham to get a man to go to him tomorrow to

Hinchingbrooke to Contrive with him about some alteracions in his house; which I did, and got Mr. Kennard. Dined with my Lady and stayed all afternoon with her; and had infinite of talk of all kinds of things, especially of beauty of men and women, with which she seems to be much pleased to talk of.

10.   Up exceeding early to go to the Comptroller, thinking to have gone with him to Whitehall. But he not being up and it being a very fine bright Moonshine morning, I went and walked all alone twenty turns in Cornhill, from gracious streete corner to the Stockes and back again – from 6 a-clock till past 7 – so long that I was weary: and going to the Controller's, thinking to find him ready, I find him gone. At which I was troubled, and being weary, went home. And from thence with my wife by water to Westminster. I to the hall and there met with Coll. Slingsby: so hearing that the Duke of Yorke is gone down this morning to see the ship sunk yesterday at Woolwich, he and I returned by his Coach to the office. And after that to dinner. After dinner he came to me again and sat with me at my house. And among other discourse, he told me that it is expected that the Duke will marry the Lord Chancellor's daughter at last. Which is likely to be the ruine of Mr. Davis and my Lord Barkely, who have carried themselfs so high against the Chancellor – Sir Ch. Barkely swearing that he and others have lain with her often, which all believe to be a lie. He and I in the evening to the Coffee-house in Cornhill, the first time that ever I was there. And I find much pleasure in it through the diversity of company – and discourse. Home and find my wife at my Lady Battens, and have made a bargain to go see the ship sunk at Woolwich, where both the Sir Wms are still, since yesterday. And I do resolve to go along with them. From thence home and up to bed – having first been in my study; and to ease my mind did go to cast up how my cash stands, and I do find, as near as I can, that I am worth in money clear 240*l* – for which God be praised. This afternoon there was a Couple of men with me, with a book in each of their hands, demanding money for polemony[1]; and I over-looked the book and saw myself set down *Samuel Pepys, gent.*, 10*s.* for himself and for his servants 2*s.* Which I did presently pay without any dispute; but I fear I shall not escape so, and therefore I have long ago laid by 10*l*: for them; but I think

1. The poll tax.

I am not bound to discover myself.

11. My wife and I up very early this day. And though the weather was bad and the wind high, yet my Lady Batten and her mayde and we two did go by our barge to Woolwich (my Lady being very fearful), where we found both Sir Wms: and much other company, expecting the weather to be better that they might go about weighing up the *Assurance*, which lies there under water; only the upper deck may be seen, and the masts. Capt. Stoakes is very melancholly; and being in search for some clothes and money of his, which he says he hath lost out of his Cabbin, I did the first office of a Justice of Peace to examine a seaman thereupon. But could find no reason to commit him. After dinner, my Lady being very fearefull, she stayed and kept my wife there; and I and another gentleman, a friend of Sir W. Pen's, went back in the barge; very merry by the way, and I went as far as Whitehall in her. To the Privy Seale, where I signed many pardons and some few things else. From thence, Mr. Moore and I into London to a taverne near my house and there we drank and discoursed of ways how to put out a little money to the best advantage. And at present he hath persuaded me to put out 250*l* for 50*l* per annum for eight years – and I think I shall do it. Thence home – where I find the wench washing: and I up to my study, and there did make up an even 100*l* and sealed it to lie by. After that to bed.

12. Troubled for the absence of my wife. After dinner to the Privy Seale and sealed abundance of pardons, and little else. From thence to the Exchequer and up with J. Spicer to his office and took 100*l*; and by Coach with it as far as my father's, where I called to see them, and my father did offer me six pieces of gold in lieu of six pounds that he borrowed of me the other day; but it went against me to take of him, and therefore did not, though I was afterward a little troubled that I did not. Thence home and told out this 100*l* and sealed it up with the other last night, it being the first 200*l* that ever I saw together of my own in my life – for which God be praised. So to my Lady Battens and sat an hour or two and talked with her daughter and people, in the absence of her father and mother and my wife, to pass away the time. After that home and to bed – reading myself asleep while the wench sat mending my breeches by my bedside.

13.  All the day long looking upon my workmen, who this day begin to paint my Parlour. Only at noon my Lady Batten and my wife came home, and so I step to my Lady's, where was Sir John Lawson and Capt. Holmes; and there we dined and had very good red wine of my Lady's own making in England.

14.  With the Comptroller at the office a little both forenoon and afternoon; and at night step a little with him to the Coffee-house, where we light upon very good company and have very good discourse concerning insects and their having a generative faculty as well as other Creatures. This night in discourse the Comptroller told me, among other persons that were heretofore the principall officers of the Navy, there was one Sir Peter Bucke a Clerk of the acts, of which to myself I was not a little proud.

17.  This day my parlour is gilded, which doth please me well.

21.  To my Lady and dined with her. She told me how dangerously ill the Princess Royall is: and that this morning she was said to be dead. That she hears that she hath married herself to young Jermin, which is worse then the Duke of Yorkes marrying the Chancellor's daughter – which is now publicly owned. After dinner to the office all the afternoon. At seven at night I walked through the dirt to Whitehall to see whether my Lord be come to town; and I find him come – and at supper; and I supped with him. He tells me that my aunt at Brampton hath voided a great Stone (the first time that ever I heard she was troubled therewith) and cannot possibly live long. That my uncle is pretty well, but full of pain still. After supper home and to bed.

22.  All the morning with my paynters – who will make an end of all this day, I hope. At noon I went to the Sun tavern on Fish streete hill to a dinner of Capt. Teddimans, where was my Lord Inchiquin (who seems to be a very fine person), Sir W. Pen, Capt. Cuttance, and one Mr. Lawrence (a fine gentleman now going to Algier) and other good company; where we have a very fine dinner, good Musique and a great deal of Wine. We stayed here very late; at last, Sir W. Pen and I home together, he so overgone with wine that he could hardly go; I was forced to lead him through the street and he was in a very merry and kind moode. I home (found my house clear

of the workmen and their work ended), my head troubled with wine; and I, very merry, went to bed – my head akeing all night.

25. *Christmas day*. In the morning to church; where Mr. Mills made a very good sermon. After that home to dinner, where my wife and I and my brother Tom (who this morning came to see my wife's new mantle put on, which doth please me very well) – to a good shoulder of Mutton and a Chicken. After dinner to church again, my wife and I, where we have a dull sermon of a stranger which made me sleep; and so home; and I, before and after supper, to my Lute and Fullers *History*, at which I stayed all alone in my Chamber till 12 at night; and so to bed.

27. With my wife to Sir W. Batten's to dinner, where much and good company. Good and much entertainment. My wife, not very well, went home. I stayed late there, seeing them play at cards; and so home and to bed. This afternoon there came in a strange lord to Sir W. Batten's by a mistake and enters discourse with him, so that we could not be rid of him till Sir Arn. Brames and Mr. Bens and Sir Wm. fell a-drinking to him till he was drunk, and so sent him away. About the middle of the night I was very ill, I think with eating and drinking too much; and so I was forced to call the mayde (who pleased my wife and I in her running up and down so inocently in her smock) and vomited in the bason; and so to sleep, and in the morning was pretty well – only got cold and so have pain in pissing, as I used to have.

28. *office day*. There all the morning. Dined at home alone with my wife; and so stayed within all the afternoon and evening at my lute, with great pleasure; and so to bed with great content.

31. At the office all the morning. And after that home; and not staying to dine, I went out and in Paul's churchyard I bought the play of *Henery the fourth*. And so went to the new Theatre (only calling at Mr. Crews and eat a bit with the people there at dinner) and there saw it acted; but my expectation being too great, it did not please me as otherwise I believe it would; and my having a book I believe did spoil it a little. That being done, I went to my Lord's, where I found him private at cards with my Lord Lauderdale and some persons of Honour; so Mr. Sheply and I over to Harpers and

there drank a pot or two, and so parted – my boy taking a catt home with him from my Lord's, which Sarah hath given him for my wife, we being much troubled with mice.

# 1661

At the end of the last and the beginning of this year I do live in one of the houses belonging to the Navy office as one of the principall officers – and have done now about half a year. After much trouble with workmen, I am now almost settled – my family being, myself, my wife, Jane, Will Ewre, and Wayneman, my girl's brother. Myself in a constant good health – and in a most handsome and thriving condition. Blessed be Almighty God for it. I am now taking of my sister Paulina to come and live with me.

As to things of State – the King settled and loved of all. The Duke of Yorke lately matched to my Lord Chancellor's daughter, which doth not please many. The Queene upon her return to France. The Princesse of Orange lately dead, and we into new mourning for her. The parliament, which hath done all this great good to the King, beginning to grow factious, the King did dissolve it December 29 last – and another likely to be chosen speedily.

I take myself now to be worth 300*l* clear in money. And all my goods and all manner of debts paid, which are none at all.

## ⚜JANUARY⚜

1.   Comes in my Brother Tho., and after him my father, Dr. Tho. Pepys, my uncle Fenner and his two sons (Anthonys only child dying this morning, yet he was so civil to come and was pretty merry) to breakfast. And I have for them a barrel of oysters, a dish of neat's tongues, and a dish of Anchoves – wine of all sorts, and Northdown ale. We were very merry till about 11 a-clock, and then they went away. At noon I carried my wife by Coach to my Cosen Tho. Pepys; where we, with my father, Dr. Tho., Cozen

Stradwick, Scott, and their wifes dined. Here I saw first his Second wife, which is a very respectful* woman. But his dinner a sorry, poor dinner for a man of his estate – there being nothing but ordinary meat in it.

2.   To my office, and there all the morning; and so home to dinner – where I found Pall (my sister) was come; but I do not let her sit down at table with me; which I do at first, that she may not expect it hereafter from me. After dinner I to Westminster by water – and there found my Brother Spicer at the Legg with all the rest of the Exchequer men (most of whom I now do not know) at dinner. I took a turne in the hall, and bought the King and Chancellors speeches at the dissolving the parliament last Saturday. This day I lent Sir W. Batten and Capt. Rider my chine of beef for to serve at dinner tomorrow at Trinity house, the Duke of Albemarle being to be there and all the rest of the Bretheren, it being a great day for the reading over of their new Charter which the King hath newly given them.

3.   Early in the morning to the Exchequer, where I told over what money I have of my Lord's and my own there, which I find to be 970*l*: thence to Will's, where Spicer and I eat our dinner of a roasted leg of porke which Will did give us. And after that, I to the Theatre, where was acted *Beggars bush* – it being very well done; and here the first time that ever I saw Women come upon the stage. From thence to my father's, where I find my mother gone by Bird the carrier to Brampton, upon my uncles great desire, my aunt being now in despair of life. So home.

4.   Office all the morning; dined at home, and Mr. Moore with me – with whom I had been early this morning at Whitehall at the Jewell Office, to choose of a piece of gilt plate for my Lord in returne of his offering to the King (which it seems is usuall at this time of the year, and an Earle gives 20 pieces in gold in a purse to the King). I chose a gilt tankard weighing 31 ounces and a half, and he is allowed 30; so I paid 12*s*. for the ounce and a half over what he is to have. But strange it was to me to see what a company of small Fees I was called upon by a great many to pay there; which I perceive is the manner that courtiers do get their estates. After dinner Mr. Moore and I to the Theatre, where was *The Scornefull Lady* acted very well

– it being the first play that ever he saw.[1] Thence with him to drink a cup of ale at Hercules pillars, and so parted. I called to see my father, who told me by the way how Will and Mary Joyce do live a strange life together, nothing but fighting, &c., so that sometimes her father hath a mind to have them divorced. Thence home.

6. *Lords day and Twelfeday.* My wife and I to church this morning; and so home to dinner to a boiled leg of mutton – all alone. To church again; where before Sermon, a long Psalm was set that lasted an houre while the Sexton gathered his year's contribucion through the whole church.

7. This morning news was brought to me to my bedside that there hath been a great stirr in the City this night by the Fanatiques, who have been up and killed six or seven men, but all are fled.[2] My Lord Mayor and the whole City have been in armes, above 40000.[3] To the office; and after that to dinner, where my brother Tom came and dined with me; and after dinner (leaveing 12*d*. with my servants to buy a cake with at night, this day being kept as Twelfeday), Tom and I and my wife to the Theatre and there saw *The Silent Woman*, the first time that ever I did see it and it is an excellent play. Among other things here, Kinaston the boy hath the good turn to appear in three shapes: 1, as a poor woman in ordinary clothes to please Morose; then in fine clothes as a gallant, and in them was clearly the prettiest woman in the whole house – and lastly, as a man; and then likewise did appear the handsomest man in the house. From thence by link to my Cosen Stradwickes, where my father and we and Dr. Pepys, Scott and his wife, and one Mr. Ward and his. And after a good supper we have an excellent cake, where the mark for the Queene was cut; and so there was two queenes, my wife and Mrs. Ward; and the King being lost, they chose the Doctor to be King, so we made him send for some wine; and then home: and in our way were in many places strictly examined, more then in the worst of times, there being great fears of these fanatiques rising again. For the present I do not hear that any of them are taken.

9. waked in the morning about 6 a-clock by people running up

1. Public performances of plays had been forbidden under the Puritans.
2. The Fifth-Monarchists', or Venner's, rising.
3. ? a slip for 4000.

and down in Mr. Davis's house, talking that the Fanatiques were up in armes in the City, and so I rise and went forth, where in the street I find everybody in arms at the doors; so I returned (though with no good courage at all, but that I might not seem to be afeared) and got my sword and pistol, which however I have no powder to charge, and went to the door, where I found Sir R. Ford; and with him I walked up and down as far as the Exchange, and there I left him. In our way, the streets full of trainebands, and great stories what mischief these rogues have done; and I think near a dozen have been killed this morning on both sides. Seeing the city in this condition, the shops shut and all things in trouble, I went home and sat, it being office day, till noon. So home and dined at home, my father with me. And after dinner he would needs have me go to my uncle Wights (where I have been so long absent that I am ashamed to go): I found him at home and his wife; I can see they have taken my absence ill, but all things are past and we good friends; and here I sat with my aunt till it was late, my uncle going forth about business – my aunt being very fearful to be alone. So home to my lute till late, and then to bed – there being strict guards all night in the City, though most of the enemy they say are killed or taken.

10. Mr. Davies told us the perticular examinations of these Fanatiques that are taken. And in short it is this: Of all these Fanatiques that have done all this, *viz.*, routed all the train-bands that they met with – put the King's lifeguard to the run – killed about 20 men – broke through the City gates twice – and all this in the daytime, when all the City was in armes – are not in all above 31. Whereas we did believe them (because they were seen up and down in every place almost in the City, and have been about Highgate two or three dayes, and in several other places) to be at least 500. A thing that never was heard of, that so few men should dare and do so much mischief. Their word was "King Jesus, and the heads[1] upon the gates!" Few of them would receive any Quarter but such as were taken by force and kept alive, expecting Jesus to come and reign here in the world presently,* and will not believe yet but their work will be carried on, though they do die.

12. *Saturday.* With Coll. Slingsby and a friend of his, Maj. Waters (a deafe and most amorous melancholy gentleman, who is under a

---

1. Of the regicides.

despayre in love as the Collonell told me, which makes him bad company, though a most good-natured man), by water to Redriffe; and so on foot to Deptford – our servants by water. Where we fell to choosing four Captains to command the guards, and choosing the places where to keep them and other things in order thereunto. We dined at the globe, having our messenger with us to take care for us. Never till now did I see the great authority of my place, all the Captains of the fleet coming cap in hand to us. Having stayed very late there talking with the Collonell, I went home with Mr. Davis, storekeeper (whose wife is ill and so I could not see her), and was there most princlike lodged, with so much respect and honour that I was almost at a loss how to behave myself.

13. In the morning we all went to church and sat in the pew belonging to us. Where a cold sermon of a young [man] that never hath preached before. Here Comissioner Pett came with his wife and daughters – the eldest, being his wife's daughter, is a very comely black woman. So to the globe to dinner. By Coach to Greenwich church, where a good sermon, a fine church, and a great company of handsome women. After sermon to Deptford again; where at the Comissioners and the globe we stayed long. And so I to Mr. Davis's to bed again. But no sooner in bed but we have an alarme and so we rise. And the Comptroller comes into the yard to us – and seamen of all the ships present repair to us; and there we armed, with everyone a handspike, with which they were as fierce as could be. At last we hear that it was only five or six men that did ride through the guard in the towne without stopping to the guard that was there and some say shot at them. But all being quiett there, we caused the seamen to go on board again; and so we all to bed (after I had sat awhile with Mr. Davis in his study, which is filled with good books and some very good song bookes): I likewise to bed.

15. Up and down the yard all the morning, and seeing the seamen exercize, which they do already very handsomely. Taking our leaves of the officers of the yard, we walked to the waterside and in our way walked into the Ropeyard, where I do look into the tarrhouses and other places, and took great notice of all the several works belonging to the making of a Cable. So after a cup of burnt wine at the taverne there, we took barge and went to blackwall and viewed the dock and the new wett dock which is newly made

there, and a brave new merchantman which is to be launched shortly, and they say to be called the *Royall oake*. Hence we walked to dick shoare, and thence to the towre, and so home – where I found my wife and pall abroad; so I went to see Sir Wm. Pen, and there found Mr. Coventry come to see him. I sat a great while with Sir Wm. after he was gone, and have much talk with him. I perceive none of our officers care much for one another, but I do keep in with them all as much as I can. Home, where my wife not yet come home. So I went up to put my papers in order. And then was much troubled my wife was not come, it being ten a-clock just now striking as I write this last line.

18. In the afternoon we met at the office and sat till night. And then I to see my father, who I found well, and took him to Standings to drink a cup of ale. He told me my aunt at Brampton is yet alive, and my mother well there. In comes Will. Joyce to us, drunk and in a talking vapouring humour, of his state and I know not what – which did vex me cruelly. After him Mr. Hollier[1] [who] had learned at my father's that I was here (where I had appointed to meet him); and so he did give me something to take for prevention. Will. Joyce not letting us talk as I would, I left my father and him and took Mr. Hollier to the Greyhound – where he did advise me above all things both as to the Stone and the decay of my memory (of which I now complain to him), to avoyd drinking often; which I am resolved, if I can, to leave off. Hence home; and took home with me from the bookesellers Ogilbys *Æsop*, which he hath bound for me; and endeed, I am very much pleased with the book. Home and to bed.

19. After dinner I went to the Theatre, where I saw *The Lost lady*, which doth not please me much. Here I was troubled to be seen by four of our office Clerkes, which sat in the half-Crowne box and I in the 1s. 6d. From hence by Linke, and bought two mousetrapps of Tho. Pepys the Turner; and so went and drank a cup of ale with him; and so home and wrote by post to Portsmouth to my Lord, and so to bed.

21. It is strange what weather we have had all this winter; no cold

1. Pepys's surgeon: it was almost certainly he who operated on him for the stone in 1658.

at all, but the ways are dusty and the flyes fly up and down, and the rosebushes are full of leaves; such a time of the year as never was known in this world before here. This day, many more of the fith monarchy men were hanged.

22.   To the Controller's house, where I read over his proposalls to the Lord Admirall for the regulating of the officers of the navy* – in which he hath taken much pains – only, he doth seem to have too good an opinion of them himself. From thence in his coach to Mercer's Chappell. And so up to the great hall, where we met with the King's Councell for trade upon some proposalls of theirs for settling convoys for the whole English trade – and that by having 33 ships (4 fourth-rates, 19 fifth, 10 sixth) settled by the King for that purpose – which endeed was argued very finely by many persons of Honour and merchants that were there. It pleased me much now to come in this condition to this place, where I was once a peticioner for my exhibicion in Pauls school. And also where Sir G. Downing (my late master) was chaireman, and so but equally concerned with me. From thence home; and after a little dinner by coach to Whitehall, and I met with Dr. Tho. Fuller and took him to the Dogg, where he tells me of his last and great book that is coming out: that is, his history of all the families of England – and could tell me more of my owne then I knew myself. And also to what perfection he hath now brought the art of memory; that he did lately to four eminently great Schollars dictate together in Latin upon different Subjects of their proposing, faster then they were able to write, till they were tired. And by the way, in discourse tells me that the best way of beginning a sentence, if a man should be out and forget his last sentence (which he never was), that then his last refuge is to begin with an *Utcunque*.

23.   I to the office all the morning. My wife and people at home busy, to get things ready for tomorrow dinner. At noon, without dinner, went into the City; and there meeting with Greatorex, we went and drank a pot of ale. He told me that he was upon a design to go to Tenariffe to try experiments there. With him to Gresham Colledge (where I never was before) and saw the manner of the house, and find great company of persons of Honour there.[1] Thence to my bookseller's and for books; and to Stevens the

---

1. A meeting of the Society known after 1662 as the Royal Society.

silversmith to make clean some plate against tomorrow. And so home, by the way paying many little debts for wine and pictures, &c., which is my great pleasure. I in my chamber all the evening, looking over my Osborns works and new Emanuel Thesaurus's *Patriarchae*. So late to bed – having eat nothing today but a piece of bread and cheese at the alehouse with Greatrex – and some bread and butter at home.

24. At home all day. There dined with me Sir Wm. Batten and his Lady and daughter – Sir W. Pen – Mr. Fox (his lady being ill could not come) and Capt. Cuttance. The first dinner I have made since I came hither. This cost me above 5*l*. And merry we were – only, my chimny smokes. The company all go away. And by and by Sir Wms both, and my Lady Batten and his daughter came again and supped with me and talked till late; and so to bed, being glad that that trouble is over.

27. *Lords day*. Before I rose, letters came to me from Portsmouth, telling me that my Lord Sandwich set sail with the Queene yesterday from thence for France. To church, leaving my wife now sick of her *menses* at home. A poor dull sermon, of a stranger. Home; and at dinner was very angry at my people's eating a fine pudding (made me by Slater the Cooke last Thursday) without my wife's leave. To church again; and a good sermon of Mr. Mills. This day the parson read a proclamacion at church for the keeping of Wednesday next, the 30th of January, a fast for the murther of the late King.

28. At the office all the morning. Dined at home. And after dinner to Mr. Crews and thence to the Theatre, where I saw again *The Lost Lady*, which doth now please me better then before. And here, I sitting behind in a dark place, a lady spat backward upon me by a mistake, not seeing me. But after seeing her to be a very pretty lady, I was not troubled at it at all. This noon I had my presse set up in my chamber for papers to be put in.

29. Mr. Moore making up accounts with me all this morning till Lieut. Lambert came; and so with them over the water to Southwark and so over the fields to Lambeth, and there drank – it being a most glorious and warm day, even to amazement, for this time of the year. Thence to my Lord's, where we find my Lady

gone with some company to see Hampton Court; so we three went to [Whitefriars] (the first time that ever I was there since plays begun);[1] and there, after great patience and little expectacions from so poor beginnings, I saw three acts of *The Mayd in the Mill* acted, to my great content. But it being late, I left the play and them, and by water through bridge home. And so to Mr. Turner's house, where the Comptroller, Sir Wm. Baten, and Mr. Davis and their ladies; and here we have a most neat little, but costly and genteele supper. And after that, a great deal of impertinent mirth by Mr. Davis and some catches, and so broke up. And going away, Mr. Davis's eldest son took up my old Lady Slingsby in his armes and carried her to the Coach, and is said to be able to carry three [of] the biggest men that were in the company – which I wonder at. So home and to bed.

30th. *Fast day*. The first time that this day hath been yet observed. And Mr. Mills made a most excellent sermon – upon "Lord, forgive us our former iniquitys." Speaking excellently of the justice of God in punishing man for the sins of his ancesters. Home, and John Goods comes; and after dinner Sir Wm. Pen and I into Moore-fields and have a rare walk, it being a most pleasant day. And besides much discourse, did please ourselfs to see young Davis and Whitton, two of our clerks, going by us in the field – who we observe to take much pleasure together; and I did most often see them at plays together. I went away home, and there understand that my mother is come home well from Brampton. And have a letter from my brother John – a very ingenious one; and he therein begs to have leave to come to town at the Coronacion. Then to my Lady Batten's, where my wife and she are lately come back again from being abroad and seeing of Cromwell, Ireton, and Bradshaw hanged and buried at Tiburne. Then I home.

# ❧FEBRUARY❧

1. *Friday*. A full office all this morning; and busy about answering the Comissioners of Parliament[2] to their letter, wherein they desire to borrow two Clerkes of ours – which we will not grant them.

---

1. Cf. above, p. 109, n. 1.
2. Appointed to pay off ships.

2.    There dined here my Uncle Wight and my aunt – my father and mother and my brother Tom – Dr. Fairebrother and Mr. Mills the parson and his wife, who is a neighbour's daughter of my uncle Robts. and knows my aunt Wight and all her and my friends there. And so we have excellent company today. After dinner I was sent for to Sir G. Carterets, where he was and I find the Comptroller; who are upon writing a letter to the Comissioners of parliament; in some things a rougher style then our last, because they seem to speak high to us. So the Comptroller and I thence to a tavern hard by, and there did agree upon drawing up some letters to be sent to all the pursers and clerks of the Cheques to make up their accounts. Then home, where I find the parson and his wife gone – and by and by the rest of the company, very well pleased, and I too – it being the last dinner I entend to make a great while. It having now cost me almost 15*l* in three dinners within this fortnight.

3.    *Lordsday.* This day I first begun to go forth in my coate and sword, as the manner now among gentlemen is. To Whitehall. In my way heard Mr. Tho. Fuller preach at the Savoy upon our forgiving of other men's trespasses – showing, among [other] things, that we are to go to law never to Revenge, but only to repayre – which I think a good distinction. So to Whitehall, where I stayed to hear the trumpets and kettle-drums – and then the other drums; which is much cried up, though I think it dull, vulgar music.

4.    earely up to Court with Sir Wm. Pen; where at Mr. Coventry's chamber we met with all our fellow officers; and there a hot debate about the business of paying off the fleet and how we should joyne with the Commissioners of Parliament. That being done, I to the tavern, where Sir Wm. Pen and the Comptroller and several others were, men and women; and we had a very great and merry dinner. And after dinner the Comptroller begun some sports; among others, the Nameing of people round, and afterward demanding Questions of them that they are forced to answer their names to; which doth make very good sport. And here I took pleasure to take the forfeits of the ladies who could not do their duty, by kissing of them – among others, a pretty lady who I found afterward to be wife to Sir W. Battens son.

5.    *washing day.* My wife and I by water to Westminster. She to her

mother's and I to Westminster hall, where I find a full terme; and here I went to Will's and there found Shaw and Ashwell and another, Brograve (who knew my mother washmaid to my Lady Veere); who by cursing and swearing made me weary of his company, and so I went away. Into the Hall and there saw my Lord Treasurer (who was sworn today at the Exchequer, with a very great company of Lords and persons of Honour to attend him) go up to the Treasury Offices and take possession thereof. And also saw the heads of Cromwell, Bradshaw, and Ireton set up upon the further end of the hall.

6.   Called up by my Cosen Snow, who sat by me while I was trimmed, and then I drank with him – he desiring a courtesy for a friend, which I have done for him. Then to the office and there sat long; then to dinner – Capt. Murford with me. I had a dish of fish and a good Hare, which was sent me the other day by Goodenough the plaisterer. So to the office again, where Sir W. Pen and I sat all alone answering of peticions and nothing else. And so to Sir W. Batten's, where comes Mr. Jessop (one whom I could not formerly have looked upon; and now he comes cap in hand to us from the Commissioners of the Navy, though endeed he is a man of a great estate and of good report) about some business from them to us, which we answered by letter. Here I sat long with Sir W., who is not well. And then home and to my chamber and some little Musique; and so to bed.

7.   With Sir Wm. Batten and Pen to Whitehall to Mr. Coventry's chamber to debate upon the business we were upon the other morning; and thence to Westminster hall and after a walk or two, to my Lord's; where, while I and my Lady was in her chamber in talk, in comes my Lord from Sea, to our great wonder. He had dined at Havre de Grace on Monday last and came to the Downe[s] the next day and lay at Canterbury that night; and so to Dartford, and thence this morning to Whitehall. All my friends, his servants, well. Among other, Mr. Creed and Capt. Ferrers tell me the story of my Lord Duke of Buckingam's and my Lords falling out at Havre de Grace at Cards – they two, and my Lord St. Albans, playing. My Lord sent the next morning to the Duke to know whether he did remember what he said last night and whether he would owne them with his sword and a second; which he said he would, and so both sides agreed. But my Lord St. Albans and the Queene and Abbot

Mountagu did waylay them at their lodgings till the difference was made up, much to my Lord's honour, who hath got great reputation thereby.

8. At the office all the morning. At noon to the Exchange. Here I met with many sea-commanders; and among others, Capt. Cuttle, and Curtis and Mootham; and I went to the Fleece tavern to drink and there we spent till 4 a-clock telling stories of Algier and the manner of the life of Slaves[1] there; and truly, Capt. Mootham and Mr. Dawes (who have been both slaves there) did make me full acquainted with their condition there. As, how they eat nothing but bread and water. At their redempcion, they pay so much for the water that they drink at the public fountaynes during their being slaves. How they are beat upon the soles of the feet and bellies at the Liberty of their *Padron*. How they are all at night called into their master's Bagnard, and there they lie. How the poorest men do use their slaves best. How some rogues do live well, if they do endent to bring their masters in so much a week by their industry or theft; and then they are put to no other work at all. And theft there is counted no great crime at all. Thence to Mr. Rawlinsons, having met my old friend Dick Scobell, and there I drank a great deal with him; and so home and to bed betimes, my head akeing.

10. *Lord's day*. Took Phisique all day. And God forgive me, did spend it in reading of some little French Romances. At night my wife and I did please ourselfs talking of our going into France, which I hope to effect this summer.

13. At the office all the morning. Dined at home; and poor Mr. Wood with me – who after dinner would have borrowed money of me, but I would lend none. Then to Whitehall by coach with Sir W. Pen, where we did very little business; and so back to Mr. Rawlinson's, where I took him in and gave him a cup of wine – he having formerly known Mr. Rawlinson. And here I met my uncle Wight and he drank with us. Then with him to Sir W. Batten's; whither I sent for my wife and we chose Valentines against tomorrow. My wife chose me, which did much please me. My Lady Batten, Sir W. Pen &c. Here we sat late; and so home to bed – having got my Lady Batten to give me a spoonful

---

1. Taken by the pirates of Algiers.

of hony for my cold.

14.   *Valentine's day.* Up earely and to Sir W. Battens. But would not go in till I had asked whether they that opened the doore was a man or a woman. And Mingo, who was there, answered "a Woman;" which, with his tone, made me laugh. So up I went and took Mrs. Martha for my Valentine (which I do only for complacency), and Sir W. Batten, he go[es] in the same manner to my wife. And so we were very merry. About 10 a-clock we with a great deal of company went down by our barge to Deptford; and there only went to see how forward Mr. Pett's yacht is. And so all into the barge again, and so to Woolwich on board the *Rosebush*, Capt. Brown's ship, that is brother-in-law to Sir W. Batten – where we had a very fine dinner dressed on shoare. And great mirth and all things sucessefull – the first time I ever carried my wife a-shipboard – as also my boy Waineman, who hath all this day been called "young Pepys", as Sir W. Pen's boy "young Pen". The talk of the towne now is, who the King is like to have for his Queene – and whether Lent shall be kept with the strictnesse of the King's proclamacion; which it is thought cannot be, because of the poor, who cannot buy fish – and also the great preparacion for the King's crowning is now much thought upon and talked of.

15.   At the office all the morning. And in the afternoon at making up my accounts for my Lord. And that being done, I find myself to be clear (as I think) 350*l* in the world, besides my goods in my house, and all things paid for.

17.   *Lords day.* A most tedious, unseasonable, and impertinent sermon by an Irish Doctor. His text was "Scatter them, O Lord, that delight in warr." Sir Wm. Batten and I very much angry with the parson. And so I to Westminster as soon as I came home. To my Lord's – where I dined with Mr. Sheply and Howe. After dinner (without speaking to my Lord), Mr. Sheply and I into the City. And so I home and took my wife to my Uncle Wights and there did Supp with them; and so home again – and to bed.

18.   At the office all the morning. Dined at home with a very good dinner; only my wife and I, which is not yet very usuall. In the afternoon my wife and I and Mrs. Martha Batten, my Valentine, to the Exchange; and there, upon a payre of embroydered and six

payre of plain white gloves, I laid out 40s. upon her. It is much talked that the King is already marryed to the neece of the Prince de Ligne and that he hath two sons already by her – which I am sorry to hear, but yet am gladder that it should be so then that the Duke of Yorke and his family should come to the Crowne – he being a professed friend to the Catholiques.

19.    By coach to Whitehall with Coll. Slingsby (carrying Mrs. Turner with us); and there he and I into the House, where we met with Sir G. Cartret – who afterward, with the Duke of Yorke, my Lord Sandwich, and others, went into a private room to consult. And we were a little troubled that we were not called in with the rest. But I do believe it was upon something very private. We stayed walking in the galery, where we met with Mr. Slingsby, that was formerly a great friend of Monsieur Blondeau's – who showed me the stamps of the King's new coyne; which is strange to see how good they are in the stamp and bad in the mony, for lack of skill to make them. But he says Blondeau will shortly come over and then we shall have it better, and the best in the world. The Controller and I to the Comissioners of Parliament; and after some talk, away again – and to drink a cup of ale. He tells me he is sure that the King is not yet married, as it is said; nor that it is known who he will have. To my Lord's and found him dined; and so I lost my dinner. But I stayed and played with him and Mr. Childe &c., some things of four partes; and so it raining hard and bitter cold (the first winter day we have yet had this winter), I took coach home and spent the evening in reading of a Latin play, the *Naufragium joculare*. And so to bed.

23.    This my *Birth day, 28 yeeres*. This morning Sir W. Batten, Pen, and I did some business. Then after dinner by water to Whitefryers to the playhouse, and there saw *The Changeling*, the first time it hath been acted these 20 yeeres – and it takes exceedingly. Besides, I see the gallants do begin to be tyred with the Vanity and pride of the Theatre actors, who are endeed grown very proud and rich. Then by linke home – and there to my book awhile and to bed. I met today with Mr. Townsend, who tells me that the old man is yet alive in whose place in the Wardrobe he hopes to get my father – which I do resolve to put for. I also met with the Comptroller, who told me how it was easy for us all, the principall officers, and proper for us, to labour to get into the next parliament

– and would have me to aske the Dukes letter.[1] But I shall not endeavour it – because it will spend much money, though I am sure I could well obtaine it. This is now 28 years that I am born. And blessed be God, and a state of full content and great hopes to be a happy man in all respects, both to myself and friends.

24. *Sunday.* Mr. Mills made an excellent sermon in the morning against Drunkennesse that ever I heard in my life. I dined at home. Another good one of his in the afternoon. My Valentine had her fine gloves on at church today that I did give her. After sermon my wife and I into Sir W. Batten's and sat awhile. Then home – I to read. Then to supper and to bed.

26. *Shrovetuesday.* I left my wife in bed, being indisposed by reason of *ceux-là* – and I to Mrs. Turners, who I find busy with The[oph]. and Joyce making of things ready for Fritters. So I to Mr. Crews and there delivered Cottgraves dictionary – to my Lady Jemimah. And then with Mr. Moore to my Cozen Tom Pepys's; but he being out of town, I spoke with his lady – though not of the business I went about, which was to borrow 1000*l* for my Lord. Back to Mrs. Turners, where several friends, all strangers to me but Mr. Armiger, din'd. Very merry, and the best fritters that ever I eat in my life. After that look out at Window; saw the flinging at Cocks.[2]

27. At the office all the morning. Then came into the garden to me young Mr. Powell and Mr. Hooke, that I once knew at Cambrige, and I took them in and gave them a bottle of wine and so parted. Then I called for a dish of fish, which we had for dinner – this being the first day of Lent; and I do entend to try whether I can keep it or no. This day the Comissioners of Parliament begin to pay off the Fleet, beginning with the *Hampshire* – and do it at Guildhall for fear of going out of the town into the power of the seamen, who are highly incensed against them.

28. This month ends with two great Secrets under dispute, but yet known to very few. First, who the King will marry. And what the meaning of this fleet is which we are now sheathing to set out for

1. Of recommendation.
2. The Shrove-Tuesday custom of throwing sticks at a bird tethered by its leg.

the Southward. Most think against Argier against the Turke, or to the East Indys against the Dutch – who we hear are setting out a great fleet thither.[1]

# ⁓❧MARCH❧⁓

1.   To Whitefryers and saw *The Bondman* acted – an excellent play and well done – but above all that ever I saw, Baterton doth the Bondman the best. Then to my father's and find my mother ill. After staying a while with them, then I went home – and sat up late, spending my thoughts how to get money to bear me out in my great expense at the Coronacion, against which all provide – and Scaffolds setting up in every street. I have many designs in my head to get some, but know not which will take. To bed.

4.   My Lord went this morning on his journy to Hinchingbrooke, Mr. Packer with him; the chief business being to look over and determine how and in what manner his great work of building[2] shall be done.

7.   This morning Sir Wms both went to Woolwich to sell some old provisions there. I to Whitehall and up and down about many businesses. Dined at my Lord's. Then to Mr. Crew to Mr. Moore and he and I to London to Guildhall to see the seamen paid off; but could not without trouble. And so I took him to the Fleece tavern, where the pretty woman that Luellin lately told me the story of dwells; but I could not see her. Then towards home; and met Spicer, D. Vines, Ruddiard and a company more of my old acquaintances and went into a place to drink some ale; and there we stayed playing the fools till late; and so I home.

8.   All the morning at the office. At noon Sir W. Batten, Coll. Slingsby and I by coach to the tower, to Sir John Robinsons, to dinner. Where great good cheer. High company; among others, the Duchess of Albemerle, who is even a plain, homely dowdy. I was much contented to ride in such state into the towre and be received

1. The English fleet in fact went in June to Algiers and Portugal.
2. Hinchingbrooke was now partially rebuilt and the garden redesigned.

among such high company – while Mr. Mount, my Lady Duchesses gentleman-usher, stood waiting at table, whom I ever thought a man so much above me in all respects. Also, to hear the discourse of so many high Cavaleers of things past – it was of great content and joy to me.

9. To my Lord's, where we find him newly come from Hinchingbrooke, where he left my uncle very well, but my aunt not likely to live. I stayed and dined with him. He took me asside and asked me what the world spoke of the King's marriage. Which I answering as one that knew nothing, he enquired no further of me. But I do perceive by it that there is something in it that is ready to come out, that the world knows not of yet.

10. *Lords day*. Heard Mr. Mills in the morning, a good sermon. Dined at home on a poor Lenten dinner of Coleworts and bacon. In the afternoon again to church and there heard one Castle, whom I knew of my year in Cambrige: he made a dull sermon.

14. With Sir W. Batten and Pen to Mr. Coventry's and there had a dispute about my claime to the place of Pourveyor for Petty provisions. And at last, to my content did conclude to have my hand to all the bills for those provisions and Mr. Turner to purvey them, because I would not have him to lose the place. Then to my Lord's; and so with Mr. Creed to an alehouse, where he told me a long story of his amours at Portsmouth to one of one Mrs. Boates daughters – which was very pleasant. Dined with my Lord and Lady; and so with Mr. Creed to the Theatre, and there saw *King and no King*, well acted. Thence with him to the Cock-ale house at Temple barr, where he did aske my advice about his amours and I did give it him; which was to enquire into the condition of his competitor, which is a son of Mr. Gawdens; and that I promised to do for him – and he to make [what] use he can of it to his advantage. Home and to bed.

19. We met at the office this morning about some perticular business. And then I to Whitehall and there dined with my Lord; and after dinner Mr. Creed and I to Whitefriers, where we saw *The Bondman* acted most excellently; and though I have seen it often, yet I am every time more and more pleased with Batterton's action.

20.   The great talk of the towne is the strange eleccion that the City
of London made yesterday for Parliament men – *viz*., Fowke,
Love, Jones, and [Thompson], men that are so far from being
episcopall that they are thought to be anabaptistes; and chosen with
a great deal of zeale, in spite of the other party that thought
themselfs very strong – crying out in the hall, "noe bishops! noe
Lord Bishops!". It doth make people to fear it may come to worse,
by being an example to the countries to do the same. And endeed,
the bishops are so high, that very few do love them.

21.   Up very earely and to work and study in my chamber. And
then to Whitehall to my Lord, and there did stay with him a good
while discoursing upon his accounts. Here I stayed with Mr. Creed
all the morning. And at noon dined with my Lord, who was very
merry; and after dinner we sang and fiddled a great while. Then I by
water (Mr. sheply, pinkny, and others going part of the way) home
and there hard at work setting my papers in order and writing
letters till night. And so to bed.

23.   All the morning at home putting papers in order. Dined at
home. And then out to the Red bull (where I have not been since
plays came up again), where I was led by a seaman that knew me,
that is here as a servant, up to the tireing-room; where strange the
confusion and disorder that there is among them in fitting
themselfs; especially here, where the clothes are very poore and the
actors but common fellows. At last into the pitt, where I think there
was not above ten more then myself, and not 100 in the whole
house – and the play (which is called *All's lost by Lust*) poorly done –
and with so much disorder; among others, that in the Musique-
room, the boy that was to sing a song not singing it right, his master
fell about his eares and beat him so, that put the whole house into an
uprore. Thence homewards and at the Miter met my uncle Wight,
and with him Lieut.-Coll. Baron, who told us how Crofton, the
great presbyterian minister that hath lately preached so highly
against Bishops, is clapped up this day into the tower – which doth
please some and displease others exceedingly. Home and to bed.

25.   *Lady-day*. This morning came workmen to begin the making
of me a new pair of stairs up out of my parlour, which, with other
work that I have to do, I doubt will keep me this two months; and
so long I shall be all in dirt – but the work doth please me very well.

To the office then. And there all the morning. [At night] to my father's and there stayed talking with my mother and him late about my dinner tomorrow. So homewards and took up a boy that had a lanthorn, that was picking up of rags, and got him to light me home. And had great discourse with him how he could get sometimes three or four bushels of rags in a day, and gat 3*d*. a bushel for them. And many other discourses, what and how many ways there are for poor children to get their livings honestly. So home to bed – at 12 a-clock at night, being pleased well with the work that my workmen have begun today.

26.   Up early to do business in my study. This is my great day, that three year ago I was cut of the stone – and blessed be God, I do yet find myself very free from pain again. All this morning I stayed at home looking after my workmen, to my great content, about my stairs. And at noon by coach to my father's, where Mrs. Turner, The[oph]., Joyce, Mr. Morrice, Mr. Armiger, Mr. Pierce the surgeon and his wife – my father and mother and myself and my wife. Very merry at dinner. Among other things, because Mrs. Turner and her company eate no flesh at all this Lent and I had a great deal of good flesh, which made their mouths water.

27.   Up earely – to see my workmen at work. My brother Tom comes to me, and among other things, I looked over my old clothes and did give him a suit of black stuff clothes and a hat and some shooes. At the office all the morning – where Sir G. Carteret comes. At noon I find my stairs quite broke down, that I could not get up but by a lather. And my wife not being well, she kept her chamber all this day. Then to the Dolphin to a dinner of Mr. Harris's, where Sir Wms both and my Lady Batten and her two daughters and other company – where a great deal of mirth. And there stayed till 11 a-clock at night. And in our mirth, I sang and sometimes fiddled (there being a noise of fiddlers there) and at last we fell to dancing – the first time that ever I did in my life – which I did wonder to see myself to do. At last we made Mingo, Sir W. Battens black, and Jack, Sir W. Pens, dance; and it was strange how the first did dance with a great deal of seeming skill. Home, where I find my wife all day in her chamber, and so to bed.

## —❧ APRILL ❧—

6. Up among my workmen. Then to Whitehall; and there at Privy Seale and elsewhere did business. And among other things, met with Mr. Townsend, who told of his mistake the other day to put both his legs through one of his Knees of his breeches and went so all day. Then with Mr. Creed and Moore to the Legg in the Palace [Yard] to dinner – which I gave them. And after dinner I saw the girl of the house, being very pretty, go into a chamber, and I went in after her and kissed her. Then by water, Creed and I, to Salsbury Court and there saw *Loves Quarrell* acted the first time; but I do not like the designe nor words. So calling at my father's, where they and my wife well; and so home and to bed.

8–9. Up early, my Lady Batten knocking at her door that comes into one of my chambers – I did give directions to my people and workmen; and so about 8 a-clock we took barge at the Tower – Sir Wm. Batten and his Lady, Mrs. Turner, Mr. Fowler and I. A very pleasant passage. And so to Gravesend, where we dined; and from thence a coach took them and I and Fowler, with some others come from Rochester to meet us, on horseback – at Rochester, where light at Mr. Alcocks and there drank and had good sport with his bringing out so many sorts of cheese. Then to the hill house at Chatham,[1] where I never was before. And I find a pretty pleasant house – and am pleased with the armes that hang up there. Here we supped very merry, and late to bed; Sir Wm. telling me that old Edgeborow, his predecessor, did die and walk in my chamber – did make me somewhat afeared, but not so much as for mirth sake I did seem. So to bed in the Treasurer's chamber and lay and sleep well – till 3 in the morning, and then waking; and by the light of the moon I saw my pillow (which overnight I flung from me) stand upright, but not bethinking myself what it might be, I was a little afeared. But sleep overcame all, and so lay till high morning – at which time I had a caudle brought me and a good fire made. Sir Wm. and I by coach to the dock and there viewd all the storehouses and the old goods that are this day to be sold, which was great pleasure to me; and so back again by coach home – where we had a good dinner. And among other strangers that came, there was Mr. Hempson and his wife, a pretty woman and speaks Latin. Mr. Allen and two

---

1. Used as the pay-house of the yard.

daughters of his, both very tall and the youngest very handsome, so much as that I could not forbear to love her exceedingly – having, among other things, the best hand that ever I saw. After dinner we went to fit books and things (Tom Hater being this morning come to us) for the Sale by an inch of candle. And very good sport we and the ladies that stood by had to see the people bid. Among other things sold, there was all the State's armes; which Sir W. Batten bought, entending to set up some of the images in his gardens and the rest to burn on the Coronacion night. The sale being done, the ladies and I and Capt. Pett and Mr. Castle took barge; and down we went to see the *Sovereigne*; which we did, taking great pleasure therein – singing all the way; and among other pleasures, I put my Lady, Mrs. Turner, Mrs. Hempson, and two Mrs. Allen's into the lantern and I went in to them and kissed them, demanding it as a fee due to a Principall officer. With all which we were exceeding merry, and drank some bottles of wine and neat's tongue, &c. Then back again home and so supped; and after much mirth, to bed.

10.    In the morning to see the Dock houses. First, Mr. Pett's the builder, and there was very kindly received. And among other things, he did offer my Lady Batten a parrot, the best ever I saw – that knew Mingo as soon as it saw him, having bred formerly in the house with them. But for talking and singing, I never heard the like. My Lady did accept of it. At night, to Hempson's: here we had, for my sake, two fiddles, the one a bass viall; on which he that played, played well some Lyra lessons,* but both together made the worst musique that ever I heard. We had a fine collacion, but I took little pleasure in that, for the illnesse of the Musique and for the intentnesse of my mind upon Mrs. Rebecca Allen. After we had done eating, the ladies went to dance; and among the men we had, I was forced to dance too – and did make an ugly shift. Mrs. R. Allen danced very well, and seems the best-humourd woman that ever I saw. Among other things, Capt. Pett was saying that he thought that he had got his wife with Childe since I came thither.[1] Which I tooke hold of and was merrily asking him what he would take to have it said for my honour that it was of my getting? He merrily answered that he would, if I would promise to be godfather to it if it did come within the time just; and I said that I would. So that I must remember to compute it when the time comes.

---

1. In January 1661.

11. At 2 a-clock, with very great mirth, we went to our lodging and to bed. And lay till 7; and then called up by Sir W. Batten – so I rise. And we did some business; and at about 9 a-clock, after we had breakfasted, we Sett forth for London; and endeed, I was a little troubled to part with Mrs. Rebecca – for which God forgive me. But of all the journys that ever I made, this was the merriest, and I was in a strange moode for mirth. I met two little schooleboys, going with pichers of ale to their schoolmaster to break up against Easter; and I did drink of some of one of them and give him two pence. By and by we came to two little girls keeping cowes; and I saw one of them very pretty, so I had a minde to make her aske my blessing. And telling that I was her godfather, she asked me innocently whether I was not Ned Wooding, and I said that I was; so she kneeled down and very simply cried, "Pray, godfather, pray to God to bless me" – which made us very merry and I gave her twopence. In several places I asked women whether they would Sell me their children; that they denied me all, but said they would give me one to keep for them if I would.

14. *Easter. Lords day.* In the morning towards my father's. And by the way heard Mr. Jacomb at Ludgate, upon these words, "Christ loved you and therefore let us love one another." And made a lazy sermon, like a presbyterian. Then to my father's and dined there, and Dr. Fairbrother (lately come to town) with us. After dinner I went to the Temple and there heard Dr. Griffith; a good sermon for the day. So with Mr. Moore (whom I met there) to my Lord's – and there he showed me a Copy of my Lord Chancellor's patent for Earle, and I read the preamble, which is very short, modest, and good. Here my Lord saw us and spoke to me about getting Mr. Moore to come and governe his house while he goes to sea, which I promised him to do. And did afterward speak to Mr. Moore and he is willing. Then hearing that Mr. Barnwell was come with some of my Lord's children yesterday to town to see the Coronacion, I went and found them at the Goate at Charing cross; and there I went and drank with them a good while – whom I find in very good health and very merry.

16. So soon as word was brought me that Mr. Coventry was come with the barge to the Tower, I went to him and find him reading of the psalmes in shorthand (which he is now busy about); and had good sport about the long marks that are made there for

sentences in Divinity, which he is never like to make use of. Here he and I sat till the Comptroller came; and then we put off for Deptford – where we went on board the Kings pleasure-boat that Comissioner Pett is making; and endeed, it will be a most pretty thing. From thence to Comissioner Petts lodging and there had a good breakefast; and in come the two Sir Wms from Walthamstow. And so we sat down and did a great deal of public business about the fitting of the fleet that is now going out.

20.   Here comes my boy to tell me that the Duke of Yorke hath sent for all the Principall officers &c to come to him today. So I went by water to Mr. Coventrys and there stayed and talked a good while with him till all the rest came. We went up and saw the Duke dress himself, and in his night habitt he is a very plain man. Then he sent us to his closet, where we saw, among other things, two very fine chests covered with gold and Indian varnish, given him by the East India Company of Holland. The Duke comes; and after he had told us that the fleet was designed for Algier (which was kept from us till now), we did advise about many things as to the fitting of the fleet and so went away. And from thence to the Privy Seale, where little to do. So to the Cockpitt; and there, by favour of one Mr. Bowman, got in and saw *The Humorsome Lieutenant* acted before the King, but not very well done. But my pleasure was great to see the manner of it; and so many great beauties, but above all Mrs. Palmer, with whom the King doth discover a great deal of Familiarity.

21.   In the morning we were troubled to hear it rain as it did, because of the great show tomorrow. After I was ready, I walked to my father's. Then I went home; and all the way is so thronged with people to see the Triumphall Arches that I could hardly pass for them.

22.       *King's going from the Tower to Whitehall*[1]

Up earely and made myself as fine as I could, and put on my velvet coat, the first day that I put it on though made half a year ago: and being ready, Sir W. Batten, my Lady, and his two daughters and his

1. The last occasion on which this part of the coronation ceremonies was performed.

son and wife, and Sir W. Penn and his son and I went to Mr. Young's the Flagg-maker in Cornhill; and there we had a good room to ourselfs, with wine and good cake, and saw the Shew very well – in which it is impossible to relate the glory of that this day – expressed in the clothes of them that rid – and their horses and horse-cloths. Among others, my Lord Sandwich. My Lord Monke rode bare after the King, and led in his hand a spare horse, as being Maister of the Horse. The King, in a most rich imbrodered suit and cloak, looked most nobly. Wadlow, the vintner at the Devil in Fleetstreet, did lead a fine company of Souldiers, all young comely men, in white doublets. There fallowed the Vice-Chamberlin, Sir G. Carteret, a company of men all like turkes; but I know not yet what they are for. The Streets all gravelled; and the houses, hung with Carpets before them, made brave show, and the ladies out of the windows. One of which, over against us, I took much notice of and spoke of her, which made good sport among us. So glorious was the show with gold and silver, that we were not able to look at it – our eyes at last being so much overcome with it. Both the King and the Duke of Yorke took notice of us as he saw us at the window.

23.   I lay with Mr. Sheply, and about 4 in the morning I rose.

### *Coronacion day.*

And got to the abby, where I fallowed Sir J. Denham the surveyour with some company that he was leading in. And with much ado, by the favour of Mr. Cooper his man, did get up into a great scaffold across the north end of the abby – where with a great deal of patience I sat from past 4 till 11 before the King came in. And a pleasure it was to see the Abbey raised in the middle, all covered with red and a throne (that is a chaire) and footstoole on the top of it. And all the officers of all kinds, so much as the very fidlers, in red vests. At last comes in the Deane and prebends of Westminster with the Bishops (many of them in cloth-of-gold Copes); and after them the nobility all in their parliament robes, which was a most magnificent sight. Then the Duke and the King with a scepter (carried by my Lord of Sandwich) and Sword and mond before him, and the crowne too. The King in his robes, bare-headed, which was very fine. And after all had placed themselfs – there was a sermon and the service. And then in the Quire at the high altar he passed all the ceremonies of the Coronacion – which, to my very great grief, I and most in the Abbey could not see. The crowne being put upon his head, a great shout begun. And he came forth to the Throne and there passed more ceremonies: as, taking the oath and having things read to him by the Bishopp, and his lords (who put on their capps as soon as the King put on his Crowne) and Bishopps came and kneeled before him. And three times the King-at-armes went to the three open places on the scaffold and proclaimed that if any one could show any reason why Ch. Steward should not be King of England, that now he should come and speak. And a Generall pardon was also read by the Lord Chancellor; and meddalls flung up and down by my Lord Cornwallis – of silver; but I could not come by any. But so great a noise, that I could make but little of the Musique; and endeed, it was lost to everybody. But I had so great a list to pisse, that I went out a little while before the King had done all his ceremonies and went round the abby to Westminster hall, all the way within rayles, and 10000 people, with the ground coverd with blue cloth – and Scaffolds all the way. Into the hall I got – where it was very fine with hangings and scaffolds, one upon another, full of brave ladies. And my wife in one little one on the right hand.

Here I stayed walking up and down; and at last, upon one of the side-stalls, I stood and saw the King come in with all the persons (but the Souldiers) that were yesterday in the cavalcade; and a most pleasant sight it was to see them in their several robes. And the King came in with his Crowne on and his sceptre in his hand – under a Canopy borne up by six silver staves, carried by Barons of the Cinqueports – and little bells at every end. And after a long time he got up to the farther end, and all set themselfs down at their several tables – and that was also a rare sight. And the King's first Course carried up by the Knights of the bath. And many fine ceremonies there was of the Heralds leading up people before him and bowing; and my Lord of Albimarles going to the Kitchin and eat a bit of the first dish that was to go to the King's table. But above all was these three Lords, Northumberland and Suffolke and Duke of Ormond, coming before the Courses on horseback and staying so all dinner-time; and at last, to bring up (Dymock) the King's Champion, all in armor on horseback, with his Speare and targett carried before him. And a herald proclaim that if any dare deny Ch. Steward to be lawful King of England, here was a Champion that would fight with him; and with those words the Champion flings down his gantlet; and all this he doth three times in his going up toward the King's table. At last, when he is come, the King Drinkes to him and then sends him the Cup, which is of gold; and he drinks it off and then rides back again with the cup in his hand. I went from table to table to see the Bishops and all others at their dinner, and was infinite pleased with it. And at the Lords' table I met with Wll. Howe and he spoke to my Lord for me and he did give him four rabbits and a pullet; and so I got it, and Mr. Creed and I got Mr. Michell to give us some bread and so we at a Stall eat it, as everybody else did what they could get. I took a great deal of pleasure to go up and down and look upon the ladies – and to hear the Musique of all sorts; but above all, the 24 viollins. And strange it is, to think that these two days have held up fair till now that all is done and the King gone out of the hall; and then it fell a-raining and thundering and lightening as I have not seen it do some years – which people did take great notice of God's blessing of the work of these two days – which is a foolery, to take too much notice of such things.

[To] Mr. Bowyers, [where] a great deal of company; some I knew, others I did not. Here we stayed upon the leads and below till it was late, expecting to see the Fireworkes; but they were not performd tonight. Only, the City had a light like a glory round about it, with bonefyres. To Axe yard, in which, at the further end, there was three great bonefyres and a great many great gallants, men and women; and they laid hold of us and would have us drink the King's health upon our knee, kneeling upon a fagott; which we all did, they drinking to us one after another – which we thought a strange Frolique. But these gallants continued thus a great while, and I wondered to see how the ladies did tiple. At last I sent my wife and her bedfellow to bed, and Mr. Hunt and I went in with Mr. Thornbury (who did give the company all their wines, he being yeoman of the wine-cellar to the King) to his house; and there we drank the King's health and nothing else, till one of the genlemen fell down stark drunk and there lay speweing. And I went to my Lord's pretty well. But no sooner a-bed with Mr. Sheply but my head begun to turne and I to vomitt, and if ever I was foxed it was now – which I cannot say yet, because I fell asleep and sleep till morning – only, when I waked I found myself wet with my spewing. Thus did the day end, with joy everywhere.

Now after all this, I can say that besides the pleasure of the sight of these glorious things, I may now shut my eyes against any other objects, or for the future trouble myself to see things of state and shewe, as being sure never to see the like again in this world.

24. Waked in the morning with my head in a sad taking through the last night's drink, which I am very sorry for. So rise and went out with Mr. Creed to drink our morning draught, which he did give me in Chocolate to settle my stomach.

## —❧MAY❧—

12. I stayed at home all this morning, being the Lords day – making up my private accounts and setting papers in order. After dinner I went awhile to my chamber to set my papers right. Then I walked forth toward Westminster; and at the Savoy heard Dr. Fuller preach upon Davids words ("I will wait with patience all the days of my appointed time until my change comes"); but methought it was a poor dry sermon. And I am afeared my former high esteem of his preaching was more out of opinion then judgement. From thence homeward; but met with Mr. Creed, with whom I went and walked in Grayes Inn walks; and from thence to Islington and there eate and drank at the house my father and we were wont of old to go to. And after that walked homeward, and parted in Smithfield; and so I home – much wondering to see how things are altered with Mr. Creed, who twelve months ago might have been got to hang himself almost, as soon as to go to a drinking-house on a Sunday.

14. In the evening Mr. Sheply came to me for some money; and so he and I to the Mitre and there we had good wine and a gammon of bacon. My Uncle Wight, Mr. Talbott, and others were with us, and we were pretty merry. So at night home and to bed – finding my head grow weak nowadays if I come to drink wine; and therefore hope that I shall leave it off of myself, which I pray God I could do.

17. All the morning at home; at noon Lieut. Lambert came to me, and he and I to the Exchange and thence to an ordinary over against it – where to our dinner we had a fellow play well upon the bagpipes and whistle like a bird exceeding well. And I had a fancy to learn to whistle as he doth, and did promise to come some other day and

give him an Angell to teach me. To the office and sat there all the afternoon till 9 at night. So home to my musique; and my wife and I sat singing in my chamber a good while together. And then to bed.

18. Toward Westminster from the towre by water; and was fain to stand upon one of the peeres about the bridge before the men could drag their boat through the lock, and which they could not do till another was called to help them. Being through bridge, I find the Thames full of boats and gallys; and upon enquiry find that there was a wager to be run this morning. So spying of Payne in a galley, I went into him and there stayed, thinking to have gone to Chelsy with them; but upon the start, the wager-boats fell foul one of another, till at last one of them goes over, pretending foule play; and so the other rew away alone – and all our sport lost. So I went ashore at Westminster; and to the hall I went, where it was very pleasant to see the hall in the condition it is now, with the judges in the benches at the further end of it – which I had not seen all this tearme till now. Thence with Mr. Spicer, Creed and some others to drink; and so away homewards by water with Mr. Creed, whom I left in London going about business; and I home – where I stayed all the afternoon. And in the garden reading *Faber fortunae* with great pleasure. So home to bed.

19. *Lords day*. To my Lord's, where we went and sat talking and laughing in the drawing-room a great while. All our talk about their going to sea this voyage,[1] which Capt. Ferrers is in some doubt whether he shall go or no. But swears that he would go if he were sure never to come back again. And I giving him some hopes, he grew so mad with joy that he fell a-dancing and leaping like a madman. Now it fell out so that the balcone windows were open; and he went to the rayle and made an offer to leap over and asked what if he should leap over there. I told him I would give him 40*l* if he did not go to sea. With that, though I shut the door and W. Howe hindered him all we could, yet he opened them again and with a vault leaps down into the garden – the greatest and most desperate frolic that ever I saw in my life. I run to see what was become of him, and we find him crawled upon his knees – but could not rise. So we went down into the garden and dragged him to the bench, where he looked like a dead man – but could not stir. And though he

---

1. See above, p. 122, n. 1.

had broke nothing, yet his pain in his back was such as he could not endure. With this, my Lord (who was in the little new room) came to us in an amaze and bid us carry him up; which by our strength we did and so laid him in Easts bed by the doore – where he lay in great pain. We sent for Doctor and Chyrurgeon, but none to be found; till by and by, by chance comes in Dr. Clerke – who is afeared of him. So we sent to get a lodgeing for him; and I went up to my Lord, where Capt. Cooke, Mr. Gibbons, and others of the King's Musique were come to present my Lord with some songs and Symphonys, which were performed very finely; which being done, I took leave and supped at my father's – where was my Cozen Beck, come lately out of the country. I am troubled to see my father so much decay of a suddaine as he doth, both in his seeing and hearing – and as much, to hear of him how my Brother Tom doth grow disrespectfull to him and my mother. I took leave and went home. Where to prayers (which I have not had in my house a good while), and so to bed.

20.   At noon Mr. Creed came to me; and he and I to the Exchange, and so to an ordinary to dinner; and after dinner to the Miter and there sat drinking while it rained very much. Then to the office, where I find Sir Wms both, choosing of Maisters for the new fleet of ships that is ordered to be set forth. And Pen seeming to be in an ugly humour, not willing to gratify one that I mentioned to be put in, did vex me. We sat late, and so home. Mr. Moore came to me when I was going to bed, and sat with me a good while, talking about my Lord's business and our own. And so good-night.

22.   At night, before I went to bed, the barber came to trim me and wash me, and so to bed, in order to my being clean tomorrow.

23.   This day I went to my Lord, and about many other things at Whitehall – and there made even my accounts with Mr. Sheply at my Lord's. And then with him and Mr. Moore and John Bowles to the Renish winehouse, and there came Jonas Moore the Mathematician to us. And there he did by discourse make us fully believe that England and France were once the same continent, by very good arguments. And spoke very many things, not so much to prove the Scripture false, as that the time therein is not well computed nor understood. From thence home by water and there shifted myself into my black silke sute (the first day I have put it on this year); and

so to my Lord Mayors by coach, where a great deal of Honourable company – and great entertainment. At table I had very good discourse with Mr. Ashmole, wherein he did assure me that froggs and many other insects do often fall from the Sky ready-formed. Dr. Bates's singularity, in not rising up nor drink the King's nor other healths at the table, was very much observed. From thence we all took coach and to our office. And there sat till it was late. And so I home and to bed by day light. This day was kept a Holyday through the towne. And it pleased me to see the little boys go up and down in procession with their broomestaffes in their hands, as I have myself long ago gone.[1]

24.   At home all the morning making up my private accounts; and this is the first time that I do find myself to be clearly worth 500*l* in money, besides all my goods in my house, &c. In the afternoon at the office late. And then I went to the Wardrobe, where I find my Lord at supper and therefore I walked a good while till he had done; and then I went in to him, and there looked over my accounts and they were committed to Mr. Moore to see me paid what remained due to me. Then down to the Kitchin to eat a bit of bread and butter, which I did. And there I took one of the maids by the chin, thinking her to be Susan; but it proved to be her sister, which is very like her. From thence home.

25.   All the morning at home about business. At noon to the Temple; where I stayed and looked over a book or two at Playfords and then to the Theatre, where I saw a piece of *The Silent woman*, which pleased me. So homewards, and in my way bought *The Bondman* in Pauls churchyard. And so home – where I find all clean and the harth and range, as it is now enlarged, set up; which pleases me very much.

29.   *Kings birth day.* Rose earely; and having made myself fine and put six spoons and a porringer of Silver in my pocket to give away today, Sir W. Pen and I took Coach and (the weather and ways being foule) went to Waltamstowe. And being come thither, heard Mr. Ratcliffe (my former schoolefellow at Pauls, who is yet a mere boy) preach upon "Nay, lett him take all, since my Lord the King is

---

1. The customary procession of boys perambulating the parish bounds on Ascension Day.

returned," &c: he reads all, and his sermon very simple* – but I looked for no better. Back to dinner to Sir Wms; and then after a walk in the fine gardens, we went to Mrs. Brown's,[1] where Sir W. Pen and I were godfathers and Mrs. Jordan and Shipman god-mothers to her boy. And there, before and after the Christening, we were with the women above in her chamber; but whether we carried ourselfs well or ill, I know not – but I was directed by young Mrs. Batten. One passage, of a lady that eate wafers with her dog, did a little displease me. I did give the midwife 10s. and the nurse 5s. and the maid of the house 2: but for as much as I expected to give the name to the Childe, but did not, it being called John, I forbore then to give my plate – till another time, after a little more advice. All being done, we went to Mrs. Shipmans, who is a great butter-woman; and I did see there the most of milke and cream, and the cleanest, that ever I saw in my life. After we had filled our bellies with cream, we took our leaves and away. In our way we had great sport to try who should drive fastest, Sir W. Batten's coach or Sir W. Pen's charriot, they having four and we two horses, and we beat them. But it cost me the spoiling of my clothes and velvet coate with dirt. Being come home, I to bed; and gave my breeches to be dried by the fire against tomorrow.

30. This day I hear the parliament hath ordered a bill to be brought in for the restoring the Bishops to the House of Lords – which they had not done so soon but to spite Mr. Prynne, who is every day so bitter against them in his discourse in the House.

## ✤JUNE✤

1. *Saturday*. Having taken our leaves of Sir W. Batten and my Lady, who are gone this morning to Chatham to keep their Whitsuntide, Sir W. Penn and I and Mr. Gauden by water to Woolwich; and there went from ship to ship to give order for and take notice of their forwardness to go forth. And then to Deptford and did the like – having dined at Woolwich with Capt. Poole at the taverne there. From Deptford we walked to Redriffe, calling at the Halfway house; and there came into a room where there was

1. Batten's sister.

infinite of new cakes placed, that are made against Whitsuntide; and there we were very merry. By water home and there did businesses of the office. Among others, got my Lord's imprest of 1000*l* and Mr. Creeds of 10000*l* against this voyage, their bills signed. Having writ letters into the country and read something, I went to bed.

2. *Sunday. Whitsunday.* The barber having done with me, I went to church and there heard a good sermon of Mr. Mills, fit for the day. Then home to dinner. And then to church again. And going home, I find Gratorex (whom I expected today at dinner) come to see me. And so he and I in my chamber, drinking of wine and eating of anchoves an hour or two – discoursing of many things in Mathematiques; and among other, he showed me how it comes to pass the strength that Levers have; and he showed me that what is got as to matter of strength is lost by them as to matter of time. It rained very hard (as it hath done of late, so much that we begin to doubt a famine); and so he was forced to stay longer then I desired.

3. To the Wardrobe – where, discoursing with my Lord, he did instruct me as to the business of the wardrobe, in case in his absence Mr. Townsend should die; and told me that he doth intend to joyne me and Mr. Moore with him as to that business, now he is going to sea. And spoke to me many other things, as to one that he doth put the greatest confidence in – of which I am proud. Here I have a good occasion to tell him (what I have had long in my mind) that since it hath pleased God to bless me with something, I am desirous to lay out something for my father, and so have pitched upon Mr. Yong's place in the wardrobe – which I desired he would give order in his absence if the place should fall, that I might have the refusal of – which my Lord did freely promise me. At which I was very glad – he saying that he would do that at the least. So I saw my Lord in the barge going to Whitehall; and I and Mr. Creed home to my house, whither my father and my Cosen Scott came to dine with me. And so we dined together very well, and before we had done, in comes my father Bowyer and my mother[1] and four daughters, and there stayed all the afternoon – which cost me great store of wine and were very merry. By and by I am called to the office, and there stayed a little. So home again and took Mr. Creed and left them; and so he and I to the Tower to speak for some ammunicion for ships for

---

1. Wife of 'father' Bowyer: cf. above, p. 73 (23 August) & n.

my Lord. And so he and I with much pleasure walked quite round the tower, which I never did before. So home; and after a walk with my wife upon the leads, I and she went to bed.

4. To my Lord Crew's to dinner with him. And had very good discourse about having of young noblemen and gentlemen to think of going to sea, as being as honourable service as the land war. And among other things, told us how in Queen Elisabeth's times, young noblemen would wait with a trencher at the back of another till he is come to age himself. And witnessed in my Lord, young Lord of Kent that then was, who waited upon my Lord Bedford at table, when a letter came to my Lord Bedford that the Earldome of Kent was fallen to his servant, the young Lord; and so rose from table and made him sit down in his place, and took a lower for himself – for so he was by place to sit. From thence to the theatre and saw *Harry the Fourth*, a good play. That done, I went over the water and walked over the fields to Southworke; and so home and to my lute. At night to bed.

5. This morning, did give my wife 4*l* to lay out upon lace and other things for herself. I to Wardrobe and so to Whitehall and Westminster; where I dined with my Lord and Ned Pickering – alone at his lodgings. After dinner to the office, where we sat and did business; and then Sir W. Penn and I went home with Sir R. Slingsby to bowles in his ally and there had good sport; and afterward went in and drank and talked. So home, Sir William and I; and it being very hot weather, I took my flagilette and played upon the leads in the garden, where Sir W. Penn came out in his shirt into his leads and there we stayed talking and singing and drinking of great draughts of Clarret and eating botargo and bread and butter till 12 at night, it being moonshine. And so to bed – very near fuddled.

6. My head hath aked all night and all this morning with my last night's debauch. Called up this morning by Lieut. Lambert, who is now made Captain of the *Norwich*; and he and I went down by water to Greenwich, in our way observing and discoursing upon the things of a ship; he telling me all I asked him – which was of good use to me. There we went and eat and drank and hear musique at the Globe; and saw the simple motion that is there, of a woman with a rod in her hand, keeping time to the music while it plays –

which is simple methinks.[1] Back again by water, calling at Capt. Lamberts house, which is very handsome and neat, and a fine prospect at top. So to the office, where we sat a little. And then the Captain and I again to Bridewell, to Mr. Holland; where his wife also (a plain dowdy) and his mother was. Here came two young gentlewomen to see Mrs. Holland and one of them could play pretty well upon the viallin; but good God, how these ignorant people did cry her up for it. We were very merry. I stayed and supped here; and so home and to bed. The weather very hot; this night I left off my wastecoate.

10. earely to my Lord – who privately told me how the King hath made him embassador in the bringing over the Queen.[2] That he is to go to Algier &c. to settle that business and to put the fleet in order there; and so to come back to Lisbone with three ships, and there to meet the fleet that is to fallow him. He sent for me to tell me that he doth intrust me with the seeing of all things done in his absence as to this great preparation, as I shall receive orders from my Lord Chancellor and Mr. Edw. Mountagu. At all which, my heart is above measure glad – for my Lord's honour, and some profit to myself I hope. I stayed and dined with my Lady; but after we were sat, comes in some persons of condition; and so the children and I rise and dined by ourselfs, all the children and I, and were very merry – and they mighty fond of me. Then I to the office, and there sat a while. So home; and at night to bed – where we lay in Sir R. Slingsby's lodgings – in the dining-room there, in our green bed – my house being now in its last work of painting and whiting.

11. At the office this morning, Sir G. Carteret with us. And we agreed upon a letter to the Duke of Yorke, to tell him the sad condition of this office for want of money. How men are not able to serve us more without some money. And that now, the credit of the office is brought so low, that none will sell us anything without our personal security given for the same. All the afternoon abroad about several businesses; and at night home and to bed.

13. I went up and down to Ald. Backwells, but his servants not

---

1. This was an automaton attached to a mechanical organ.
2. Charles's betrothal to the Infanta Catherine had been anounced to Parliament on 8 May.

being up, I went home and put on my gray cloth suit and faced white coate, made of one of my wife's pettycoates – the first time that I have had it on. And so, in a riding garbe, back again and spoke with Mr. Shaw at the Aldermans; who offers me 300*l*, if my Lord pleases, to buy cloth with[1] – which pleased me well. So to the Wardrobe and got my Lord to order Mr. Creed to imprest so much upon me, to be paid by Ald. Backwell. So with my Lord to Whitehall by water. And he having taken leave of the King, comes to us at his lodgeings and from thence goes to the garden Staires and there takes barge. And at the stairs was met by Sir R. Slingsby, who there took his leave of my Lord; and I heard my Lord thank him for his kindness to me, which Sir Robert answered much to my advantage. I went down with my Lord in the barge to Deptford; and there went on board the Duch yacht and stayed there a good while, W. Howe not being come with my Lord's things, which made my Lord angry. By and by he comes and so we set sayle; and anon went to dinner. My Lord and we very merry. And after dinner I went down below and there sang and took leave of W. Howe, Capt. Rolt, and the rest of my friends; then went up and took leave of my Lord, who gave me his hand and parted with great respect. So went, and Capt. Ferrers with me, into our wherry. And my Lord did give five guns, all they had charged, which was the greatest respect my Lord could do me and of which I was not a little proud. So with a sad and merry heart I left them, sailing pleasantly from Erith, hoping to be in the Downes tomorrow earely. We toward London in our boat. Pulled off our Stockings and bathed our legs a great while in the River – which I had not done some years before.

14.   To Whitehall to my Lord's. Where I find Mr. Edwd. Mountagu and his family come to lie during my Lord's absence. I sent to my house, by my Lord's order, his shipp[-model] and Triangle virginall. So to my father's and did give him order about the buying of this cloth to send to my Lord. But I could not stay with him myself; for having got a great cold by my playing the foole in the water yesterday, I was in great pain and so went home by coach to bed, and went not to the office at all. And by keeping myself warme, I broke wind and so came to some ease. Rise and eat some supper and so to bed again.

1. A gift from the King to the Bey of Algiers.

19.   All the morning almost at home, seeing my stairs finished by the painter, which please me well. So with Mr. Moore to Westminster hall, it being terme, and then by water to the Wardrobe – where very merry. So home to the office all the afternoon. Thanks be to God, I am very well again of my late payne. And tomorrow hope to be out of my pain of dirt and trouble in my house, of which I am now become very weary. One thing I must observe here, while I think of it; that I am now become the most negligent man in the world as to matter of newes. Insomuch, that nowadays I neither can tell any nor aske any of others.

25.   Up this morning to put my papers in order that are come from my Lord's, so that now I have nothing there remaining that is mine, which I have had till now. This morning came Mr. Goodgroome to me, recommended by Mr. Mage. With whom I agreed presently to give him 20s. entrance; which I then did, and 20s. a month more to teach me to sing. And so we begun and I hope I shall come to something in it. His first song is *La cruda la bella*. He gone, my Brother Tom comes; with whom I made even with my father and the two drapers for the cloths I sent to sea lately. At home all day. In the afternoon came Capt. Allen and his daughter Rebecca and Mr. Hempson; and by and by both Sir Wms, who sat with me till it was late. And I had a very gallant collacion for them. At night to bed.

26.   To Westminster about several businesses. Then to dine with my Lady at the Wardrobe – taking Deane Fuller along with me. Then home, where I heard that my father had been to find me out about special business; so I took coach and went to him; and find by a letter to him from my aunt that my uncle Robert is taken with a dizzinesse in his head. So that they desire my father to come downe to look after his business – by which we guess that he is very ill; and so my father doth think to go tomorrow. And so God's will be done. Back by water to the office. There till night; and so home to my musique and then to bed.

28.   At home all the morning, practising to sing, which is now my great trade. And at noon to my Lady and dined with her. So back and to the office. And there sat till 7 at night; and then Sir W. Penn in his coach and I, we went to Moorefields and there walked; and stood and saw the wrestling, which I never saw so much of before – between the North and West countrymen. So home; and this night

had our bed set up in our room that we called the Nursery, where we lay; and I am very much pleased with the room.

30. *Lords day*. After dinner, Sir Wms both and I by water to Whitehall; where having walked up and down, at last met with the Duke of Yorke according to an order sent us yesterday from him, to give him an account where the fault lay in the not sending out of the ships. Which we find to be only the wind hath been against them, and so they could not get out of the River. Hence I to Grayes Inn walk all alone; and with great pleasure seeing the fine ladies walk there – myself humming to myself (which nowadays is my constant practice since I begun to learn to sing) the *trillo*; and find by use that it doth come upon me. Home, very weary, and to bed – finding my wife not sick but yet out of order, that I fear she will come to be sick. This day the Portuguese Embassador came to Whitehall to take leave of the King, he being now going to end all with the Queene and to send her over.

The weather now very fair and pleasant, but very hot. My father gone to Brampton to see my Uncle Robt., not knowing whether to find him dead or alive. Myself, lately under a great expense of money upon myself in clothes and other things; but I hope to make it up this summer, by my having to do in getting things ready to send with the next fleet for the Queene. Myself in good health; but mighty apt to take cold, so that this hot weather I am fain to wear a cloth before my belly.

## –❧JULY❧–

2. To Westminster hall and there walked up and down, it being term-time. Spoke with several; among others, my Cosen Rogr. Pepys, who was going up to the parliament-house and enquired whether I had heard from my father since he went to Brampton – which I had done yesterday, who writes that my uncle is by fits stupid and like a man that is drunk, and sometimes speechless. Home; and after my singing master had done and took Coach and went to Sir Wm. Davenant's opera – this being the fourth day that it hath begun, and the first that I have seen it. Today was acted the second part of *The Siege of Rhodes*. The King being come, the Scene opened; which endeed is very fine and magnificent, and well acted,

all but the Eunuches, who was so much out that he was hissed off the stage. Home and wrote letters to my Lord to Sea; and so to bed.

6. Waked this morning with news, brought me by a messenger on purpose, that my Uncle Robert is dead – and died yesterday. So I rose, sorry in some respect; glad in my expectations in another respect. So I made myself ready. Went and told my Uncle Wight – my Lady – and some others thereof. And bought me a pair of boots in St. Martins and got myself ready; and then to the post-house and set out about 11 or 12 a-clock, taking the messenger with me that came to me; and so we rode and got well by 9 a-clock to Brampton, where I find my father well. My Uncles corps in a coffin, standing upon joynt-stooles in the chimny in the hall; but it begun to smell, and so I caused it to be set forth in the yard all night and wached by two men. My aunt I find in bedd in a most nasty ugly pickle, made me sick to see it. My father and I lay together tonight, I greedy to see the Will but did not aske to see it till tomorrow.

7. *Lords day*. In the morning my father and I walked in the garden and read the Will; where though he gives me nothing at present till my father's death, or at least very little, yet I am glad to see that he hath done so well for us all – and well to the rest of his kindred. After that done, we went about getting things, as ribbands and gloves, ready for the burial. Which in the afternoon was done; where it being Sonday, all people far and near came in and in the greatest disorder that ever I saw; we made shift to serve them what we had of wine and other things; and then to carry him to the church, where Mr. Taylor buried him and Mr. Turner preached a funerall Sermon – where he spoke not perticularly of him anything, but that he was one so well-known for his honesty, that it spoke for itself above all that he could say for it. And so made a very good sermon. Home with some of the company who supped there; and things being quiet, at night to bed.

8–13. I fell to work, and my father, to look over his papers and clothes. And continued all this week upon that business – much troubled with my aunts base ugly humours. We had new of Tom Trices[1] putting in a caveat against us in behalfe of his mother, to whom my Uncle hath not given anything, and for good reason

---

1. Stepson of Robert Pepys.

therein expressed; which troubled us also. But above all, our trouble is to find that his estate appears nothing as we expected and all the world believes. Nor his papers so well sorted as I would have had them, but all in confusion, that break my brains to understand them. We missed also the Surrenders of his Coppyhold land, without which the land could not come to us but to the heire-at-law.[1] So that what with this and the badness of the drink and the ill opinion I have of the meat, and the biting of the gnatts by night – and my disappointment in getting home this week – and the trouble of sorting all the papers, I am almost out of my wits with trouble. Only, I appear the more contented, because I would not have my father troubled.

15.    Up by 3 a-clock this morning and rode to Cambrige, and was there by 7 a-clock. Where after I was trimmed, I went to Christ College and find my brother John at 8 a-clock in bed, which vexed me. Then to Kings College chappell, where I find the schollers in their surplices at the service with the organs – which is a strange sight to what it used in my time to be here. Rode to Impington – where I find my old Uncle[2] setting all alone, like a man out of the world. He can hardly see; but all things else he doth pretty livelyly. Then with Dr. John Pepys and him, I read over the Will and had their advice therein; who, as to the sufficiency thereof, confirmed me, and advised me as to the other parts thereof.

16–19.    These four days we spent in putting things in order – letting of the cropp upon the ground – agreeing with Stankes to have a care of our business in our absence, and we think ourselfs in nothing happy but in lighting upon him to be our bayly – in riding to Offord and Sturtlow, and up and down all our lands; and in the evening walking, my father and I, about the fields talking. To supper and to bed – my aunt continuing in her base hypocriticall tricks.

21.    *Lords day.* At home all the morning, putting my papers in order against my going tomorrow and doing many things else to that end. Had a good dinner, and Stankes and his wife with us. To my business again in the afternoon; and in the evening came the two

1. The deceased's brother Thomas.
2. Talbot Pepys.

Trices, Mr. Greene, and Mr. Philips, and so we begun to argue; at last it came to some agreement, that for our giving of my aunt 10*l*, she is to quit the house; and for the other matters, they are to be left to the law, which doth please us all; and so we broke up pretty well satisfyed.

22.   Up by 3 and going by 4 on my way to London. But the day proves very cold; so that having put on noe stockings but thread ones under my boots, I was fain at Bigglesworth to buy a pair of coarse woollen ones and put them on. So by degrees, till I came to Hatfield before 12 a-clock – where I had a very good dinner with my hostesse at my Lord of Salsburys Inn; and after dinner, though weary, I walked all alone to the Vineyard, which is now a very beautiful place again; and coming back, I met with Mr. Looker my Lord's gardener (a friend of Mr. Eglins), who showed me the house, the chappell with rare pictures, and above all the gardens, such as I never saw in all my life; nor so good flowers nor so great goosburys, as big as nutmegs. Back to the Inne and drank with him; and so to horse again, and with much ado got to London and set him up in Smithfield.

23.   Put on my mourning. Made visits to Sir W. Pen and Batten. Then to Westminster and at the hall stayed talking with Mrs. Michell a good while; and in the afternoon, finding myself unfit for business, I went to the Theatre and saw *Breneralt*; I never saw before. It seemed a good play, but ill acted; only, I sat before Mrs. Palmer, the King's mistress, and filled my eyes with her, which much pleased me.

24.   This morning in bed my wife tells me of our being robbed of our silver tankard; which vexed me all day for the negligence of my people to leave the door open. To the office all the afternoon; which is a great pleasure to me again – to talk with persons of Quality and to be in command; and I gave it out among them that the estate left me is 200*l* a year in land, besides money – because I would put an esteem upon myself. At night home and to bed, after I had set down my Journall ever since my going from London this journy, to this houre. This afternoon I hear that my man Will hath lost his cloak with my tankard, at which I am very glad.

26.   At home all the morning; and walking, met with Mr. Hill of

Cambrige in Popes head ally with some women with him; whom he took and me into the taverne there and did give us wine. And would fain seem to be very knowing in the affairs of state, and tells me that the King would be forced to favour Presbytery, or the City would leave him; but I heed not what he says, though upon enquiry I do find that things in the Parliament are at a great disorder. Home at noon, and there find Mr. Moore and with him to an ordinary alone and dined; and there he and I read my Uncles Will and I had his opinion on it, and still find more and more trouble like to attend it. Back to the office all the afternoon. And that done, home for all night. Having the beginning of this week made a vowe to myself to drink no wine this week (finding it to unfit me to look after business), and this day breaking of it against my will, I am much troubled for it – but I hope God will forgive me.

27.   To Westminster; where at Mr. Mountagu's chamber I heard a Frenchman play upon the Gittar most extreme well; though, at the best, methinks it is but a bawble. From thence to Westminster hall. In the Lobby I spoke with Mr. George Mountagu. He told me in discourse that my Lord Chancellor is much envyed and that many great men, such as the Duke of Buckingham and my Lord of Bristoll, do endeavour to undermine him. And that he believes it will not be done, for that the King (though he loves him not in the way of a companion, as he doth these young gallants that can answer him in his pleasures), yet cannot be without him for his policy and service. From thence to the Wardrobe, where my wife met me, it being my Lord of Sandwiches Birthday. And so we had many friends here, Mr. Townsend and his wife and Capt. Ferrers' lady and Capt. Isham, and were very merry and had a good venison pasty. After dinner Mr. Townsend was called upon by Capt. Cooke; so we three went to a taverne hard by and there he did give us a song or two; and without doubt, he hath the best manner of singing in the world.

29.   Did business in the office. So home to dinner – and my brother Tom dined with me; and after dinner he and I alone in my chamber had a great deal of talk, and I find that unless my father can forbear to make profit of his house in London and leave it to Tom, he hath no mind to set up the trade anywhere else. And so I know not what to do with him. After this I went with him to my mother and there told her how things do fall out short of our expectacions;

which I did (though it be true) to make her leave off her spending,
which I find she is nowadays very free in, building upon what is left
us by my uncle to bear her out in it – which troubles me much.

# –⁂AUGUST⁂–

12.   At the office this morning. At home in the afternoon, and had
notice that my Lord Hinchingbrooke is fallen ill – which I fear is
with the fruits that I did give them on Saturday last at my house. So
in the evening I went thither and there find him very ill, and in great
fear of the smallpox. And so I went home with my heart full of
trouble for my Lord Hinchingbrooke's sickness, and more for my
Lord Sandwich's himself; whom we are now confirmed is sick
ashore at Alicante – who if he should miscarry, God knows in what
a condition would his family be.

13.   To the privy Seale in the morning. Then to the Wardrobe to
dinner, where I met my wife and find my young Lord very ill. So
my Lady intends to send her other three Sons, Sidney, Oliver, and
John, to my house, for fear of the smallpox. After dinner I went to
my father's, where I find him within and went up to him; and there
find him settling his papers against his removall,[1] and I took some
old papers of difference between me and my wife[2] and took them
away. After that, Pall being there, I spoke to my father about my
intention not to keep her longer for such and such reasons; which
troubled him and me also, and had like to have come to some high
words between my mother and me, who is become a very simple
woman. [Thence] home and there find my Lady's three sons come,
of which I am glad that I am in condition to do her and my Lord any
service in this kind.

14.   This morning Sir W. Batten and Sir W. Penn and I waited
upon the Duke of Yorke in his Chamber, to give him an account of
the condition of the Navy for lack of money and how our own very
bills are offered upon the Exchange to be sold at 20 in the 100 loss.

---

1. To Brampton.
2. Nothing is known of this quarrel, except that they separated for a short while,
and that Elizabeth went to live at Charing Cross.

He is much troubled at it, and will speak to the King and Council of it this morning. And so I went to my Lady's and dined with her, and find my Lord Hinchingbrooke somewhat better. At home I find a letter from Mr. Creed of the 15 of July last, that tells me that my Lord is rid of his pain (which was Wind got into the Muscles of his right side) and his feaver, and is now in hopes to go aboard in a day or two; which doth give me mighty great comfort.

16.    At the office all the morning, though little to be done because all our Clerkes are gone to the buriall of Tom. Whitton, one of the Controllers Clerkes, a very ingenious and a likely young man to live as any in the office. But it is such a sickly time, both in City and country everywhere (of a sort of fever) that never was heard of almost, unless it was in a plague time. Among others, the famous Tom. Fuller is dead of it – and Dr. Nichols, Deane of Pauls; and my Lord Generall Monke is very dangerous ill. Dined at home with the Children and were merry, and my father with me.

19.    At the office all the morning. At noon the children are sent for by their mother, my Lady Sandwich, to dinner, and my wife goes along with them by coach; and she to my father's and dines there and from thence with them to see Mrs. Cordery, who doth invite them before my father goes into the country; and thither I should have gone too, but that I am sent for to the Privy Seale: and there I find a thing of my Lord Chancellors to be sealed this afternoon and so I am forced to go to Worcester house, where several Lords are met in council this afternoon. And while I am waiting there, in comes the King in a plain common riding-suit and velvet capp, in which he seemed a very ordinary man to one that had not known him. So walked home; and there I find that my Lady doth keep the children at home and lets them not come any more hither at present – which a little troubles me, to lose their company. This day my aunt Fenner dyed.

24.    At the office in the morning and did business. By and by we are called to Sir W. Battens to see the strange creature that Capt. Holmes hath brought with him from Guiny; it is a great baboone, but so much like a man in most things, that (though they say there is a Species of them) yet I cannot believe but that it is a monster got of a man and she-baboone. I do believe it already understands much english; and I am of the mind it might be tought to speak or make

signs. To the Opera and there saw *Hamlet Prince of Denmarke*, done with Scenes very well. But above all, Batterton did the Prince's part beyond imagination.

26. This morning before I went out I made even with my mayd Jane, who hath this day been my maid three yeares and is this day to go into the country to her mother. The poor girl cried, and I could hardly forbear weeping to think of her going; for though she be grown lazy and spoiled by Palls coming, yet I shall never have one to please us better in all things, and so harmlesse, while I live. So I paid her her wages and gave her 2*s*.-6*d*. over, and bade her Adieu – with my mind full of trouble for her going.

27. My wife and I to the Theatre and there saw *The Joviall Crew*, where the King, Duke and Duchesse, and Madam Palmer were; and my wife, to her great content, had her full sight of them all, all the while. The play full of mirth. Thence to my father's and there stayed to talk a while; and so by foot home by mooneshine. In my way and at home, my wife making a sad story to me of her brother Balty's condition, and would have me to do something for him; which I shall endeavour to do, but am afeared to meddle therein for fear I shall not be able to wipe my hands of him again when I once concern myself for him. I went to bed, my wife all the while telling me his case with teares, which troubled me.

31. At home and the office all the morning; and at noon comes Luellin to me and he and I to the taverne, and after that to Bartlemew faire; and there, upon his motion, to a pitiful alehouse, where we had a dirty slut or two come up that were whores; but my very heart went against them, so that I took no pleasure but a great deal of trouble at being there and getting from thence, for fear of being seen. From thence he and I walked toward Ludgate and parted. I back again to the fair all alone and there met with my ladies Jemimah and Paulina, with Mr. Pickering and Madamoiselle,[1] at seeing the Monkys dance, which was much to see what they could be brought to do; but it troubled me to sit among such nasty company. After that, with them into Christs: Hospitall, and there Mr. Pickering bought them some fairings, and I did give every of them a bauble, which was the little globes of glass with things

---

1. Mlle le Blanc, the young ladies' governess.

hanging in them, which pleased the ladies very well.

Thus ends the month. My mayde Jane newly gone, and Pall left now to do all the work till another mayde comes; which shall not be till she goes away into the country with my mother. Myself and wife in good health. My Lord Sandwich in the Straits and newly recovered of a great sickness at Alicante. My father gone to settle at Brampton. And myself under much business and trouble for to settle things in the estate to our content. But which is worst, I find myself lately too much given to seeing of plays and expense and pleasure, which makes me forget my business, which I must labour to amend. No money comes in, so that I have been forced to borrow a great deal of money for my own expenses and to furnish my father, to leave things in order. I have some trouble about my Brother Tom, who is now left to keep my father's trade, in which I have great fears that he will miscarry – for want of brains and care.

at Court things are in very ill condition, there being so much æmulacion, poverty, and the vices of swearing, drinking, and whoring, that I know not what will be the end of it but confusion. And the Clergy so high, that all people that I meet with, all do protest against their practice. In short, I see no content or satisfaccion anywhere in any one sort of people. The season very sickly everywhere of strange and fatall feavers.

# –✤SEPTEMBER✤–

5. To the Privy Seale this morning about business – in my way taking leave of my mother, who goes to Brampton today. But doing my business at the Privy Seale pretty soon, I took boat and went to my uncle Fenners; and there I find my mother and my wife and Pall (of whom I had this morning at my own house taken leave, and given her 20s. and good counsel how to carry herself to my father and mother); and so I took them, it being late, to Beards, where they were stayed for; and so I put them into the Waggon and saw them going presently – Pall crying exceedingly. My wife and I to the fair, and I showed her the Italian dancing the ropes and the women that do strange tumbling tricks. And so by foot home.

8. *Lords day*. To church, it being a very wet night last night and today. Dined at home. And so to church again with my wife in the

afternoon. And coming home again, find our new mayde Doll asleep that she could not hear to let us in, so that we were fain to send the boy in at a window to open the door to us. So up to my chamber all alone. And troubled in mind to think how much of late I have addicted myself to expense and pleasure, that now I can hardly reclaime myself to look after my great business of settling Gravely business,[1] till it is now almost too late. I pray God give me grace to begin now to look after my business; but it always was, and I fear will ever be, my foible, that after I am once got behindhand with business, I am hard to set to it again to recover it. In the evening I begun to look over my accounts; and upon the whole, I do find myself, by what I can yet see, worth near 600*l*; for which God be blessed – which put me into great comfort. So to supper and bed.

9. To the Privy Seale in the morning, but my Lord[2] did not come. So I went with Capt. Morrice at his desire into the King's Privy Kitchin to Mr. Sayres the Master-Cooke, and there we had a good slice of beef or two to our breakfast. And from thence he took us into the wine-cellar; where by my troth we were very merry, and I drank too much wine – and all along had great and perticular kindness from Mr. Sayre. But I drank so much wine that I was not fit for business; and therefore, at noon I went and walked in Westminster hall a while; and thence to Salsbury Court playhouse, where was acted the first time *Tis pitty shee's a Whore* – a simple play and ill acted; only, it was my fortune to sit by a most pretty and most ingenious lady, which pleased me much.

11. To Dr. Williams, who did carry me into his garden, where he hath abundance of grapes. And did show me how a dog that he hath doth kill all the Cattes that come thither to kill his pigeons, and doth afterwards bury them. And doth it with so much care that they shall be quite covered, that if but the tip of the tail hangs out, he will take up the cat again and dig the hole deeper – which is very strange. And he tells me he doth believe that he hath killed above 100 cats. To dinner, where I find my wife's brother Balty, as fine as hands could make him, and his servant, a Frenchman, to wait on him; and came to have my wife to visit a young lady which he is a servant to and

---

1. See below, p. 155 (20 September).
2. Lord Robartes, Lord Privy Seal.

hath hope to trapan and get for his wife. I did give way for my wife to go with him, and so after dinner they went. And Mr. Moore and I out again, he about his business and I to Dr. Williams to talk with him again; and he and I walking through Lincolne's Inn fields, observed at the Opera a new play, *Twelfth night*, was acted there, and the King there. So I, against my own mind and resolution, could not forbear to go in, which did make the play seem a burthen to me, and I took no pleasure at all in it. And so after it was done, went home with my mind troubled for my going thither, after my swearing to my wife that I would never go to a play without her. So that what with this and things going so crosse to me as to matters of my uncles estate, makes me very much troubled in my mind. And so to bed. My wife was with her brother to see his mistress today, and says she is young, rich, and handsome, but not likely for him to get.

12. Though it was an office day, yet I was forced to go to the Privy Seale; at which I was all the morning. And from thence to my Lady's to dinner at the Wardrobe. And in my way, upon the Thames I saw the King's new pleasure-boat, that is come now for the King to take pleasure in above bridge – and also two fine Gundalo's[1] that are lately brought, which are very rich and fine.

15. *Lords day.* To my aunt Kites in the morning – to help my uncle Fenner to put things in order against anon, for the burial. And at noon home again; and after dinner to church, my wife and I. And after sermon with my wife to the buriall of my aunt Kite – where besides us and my uncle Fenners family, there was none of any Quality, but poor rasckally people. So we went to church with the Corps and there had service read at the grave; and back again with Pegg Kite – who will be, I doubt, a troublesome carrion to us Executors. But if she will not be ruled, I shall fling up my Executorship. After that home – and Will. Joyce along with me – where we sat and talked and drunk and eat an hour or two; and so he went away. And I up to my chamber, and then to prayers and to bed.

16. In the afternoon, by appointment to meet Dr. Williams and his atturny, and they and I to Tom. Trice. Here we were at high

1. Gondolas; a gift from the Doge and Senate of Venice.

153

words – and then parted; and we to Standings in Fleetstreete, where we sat and drunk and talked a great while – about my going down to Gravely Court,[1] which will be this week. At night I went home and there find letters from my father informing me of the Court, and that I must come down and meet him at Impington – which I presently resolved to do. And the next morning got up, telling my wife of my journy; and she with a few words got me to hire her a horse to go along with me.

17. So I went to my Lady's and elsewhere to take leave. And of Mr. Townsend did borrow a very fine side-saddle for my wife; and so after all things were ready, she and I took coach to the end of the towne toward Kingsland; and there got upon my horse and she upon her pretty mare that I hired her. And she rides very well; by the mare at one time falling, she got a fall but no harm. So we got to ware and there supped and to bed, very merry and pleasant.

18. The next morning, up early and begun our march. The way about Puckrige very bad; and my wife in the very last dirty place of all got a fall but no hurt, though some dirt. At last she begun, poor wretch, to be tired, and I to be angry at it; but I was to blame, for she is a very good companion as long as she is well. In the afternoon we got to Cambrige, where I left my wife at my Cosen Angiers, while I went to Christ College and there find my brother in his chamber – and talked with him; and so to the barbers and then to my wife again and remounted for Impington. Where my Uncle received me and my wife very kindly. And by and by, in comes my father. And we supped and talked and were merry; but being weary and sleepy, my wife and I to bed without talking with my father about our business.

19. Up early; and my father and I alone into the garden and there talked about our business and what to do therein. So after I had talked and advised with my uncle by his bedside, we all horsed away and to Cambrige, where my father and I, having left my wife at the Beare with my brother, went to Mr. Sedgewicke the steward of Gravely. And there talked with him, but could get little hopes from anything that he would tell us; but at last I did give him a fee, and then he was free to tell me what I asked; which was something,

1. The court of the manor in which some of the disputed copyholds were situated.

though not much comfort. From thence to our horses and with my wife went down and rode through Sturbrige fayre; but the fair was almost done, so we did not light there at all, but went back to Cambrige and there at the beare had some herings, we and my brother; and after dinner set out for Brampton, where we come in very good time and find all things well; and being somewhat weary, after some talk about tomorrow's business with my father, we went to bed.

20.   Will Stankes and I set out in the morning betimes for Gravely, where to an alehouse and drank; and then to the Court – which was a simple meeting of a company of country rogues, with the Steward and two Fellows of Jesus College, that are lords of the towne. Where the Jury were sworne; and I producing no surrender (though I told them I was sure there is and must be one somewhere), they find my Uncle Tho. heire-at-law, as he is; and so though I did advise them to forbear being admitted this Court, my uncle was admitted; and his son also, in reversion after his father, which he did well in to secure his money. The father paid a year and half for his fine, and the son half a year; in all 48*l*, besides about 3*l* fees. So that I do believe the charges of his journys and other expenses herein, cannot be less then 70*l* – which will be a sad thing for them if a surrender be found. After all was done, I openly wished them joy in it. And so rode to Offord with them and there parted fairly, without any words. So with Stankes home and supped; and after telling my father how things went, I went to bed with my mind in good temper, because I saw the matter and manner of the Court and the bottom of my business, wherein I was before and should always have been ignorant.

21.   All the morning pleasing myself with my father; going up and down the house and garden with my father and my wife, contriving some alterations.

23.   We took horse and got early to Baldwick; where there was a fair, and we put in and eat a mouthful of porke, which they made us pay 14*d*. for, which vexed us much. And so away to Stevenage and stayed till a showre was over; and so rode easily to Welling – where we supped well and had two beds in the room and so lay single; and must remember it that, of all the nights that ever I slept in my life, I never did pass a night with more epicurisme of sleep – there being

now and then a noise of people stirring that waked me; and then it was a very rainy night; and then I was a little weary, that what between waking and then sleeping again, one after another, I never had so much content in all my life. And so my wife says it was with her.

24. We rose and set forth; but find a most sad alteration in the roade by reason of last night's rains, they being now all dirty and washy, though not deep. So we rode easily through and only drinking at Halloway at the sign of a woman with Cakes in one hand and a pot of ale in the other, which did give good occasion of mirth, resembling her to the mayd that served us; we got home very timely and well. And finding there all well, and letters from Sea that speak of my Lord's being well and his accion, though not considerable of any side, at Argier, I went straight to my Lady and there sat and talked with her; and so home again; and after supper, we to bed somewhat weary.

25. The Queene of England (as she is now owned and called) I hear, doth keep open Court and distinct at Lisbone. Thence, much against my nature and will (yet such is the power of the Devil over me I could not refuse it) to the Theatre and saw *The Merry Wifes of Windsor*, ill done. And that ended, with Sir W. Pen and Sir G. Ascue to the Taverne and so home with him by coach. And after supper to prayers and to bed – in full quiet of mind as to thought, though full of business, blessed be God.

27. At noon met my wife at the Wardrobe – and there dined, where we find Capt. Country (my little Captain that I loved, who carried me to the Sound)[1] come with some Grapes and Millons from my Lord at Lisbone – the first that ever I saw any. And my wife and I eat some, and took some home. But the grapes are rare things. Here we stayed; and in the afternoon comes Mr. Edw. Mountagu to talk with my Lady and me about the provisions fit to be bought and sent to my Lord along with him. And told us that we need not trouble ourselfs how to buy them, for the King would pay for all, and that he would take care to get them – which put my Lady and me into a great deal of ease of mind. Here we stayed and supped too; and after my wife had put up some of the grapes in a basket for

1. In 1659 Pepys had sailed with letters to Mountagu's fleet in the Baltic.

to be sent to the King, we took coach and home – where we find a hampire of Millons sent to me also.

29. *Lords day*. At dinner and supper, I drank, I know not how, of my owne accord, so much wine, that I was even almost foxed and my head aked all night. So home, and to bed without prayers, which I never did yet since I came to the house of a Sunday night: I being now so out of order that I durst not read prayers, for fear of being perceived by my servants in what case I was. So to bed.

30. This morning up by mooneshine; at 5 a-clock to Whitehall to meet Mr. Moore at the Privy Seale; but he not being come as appointed, I went into King Streete to the Red Lyon to drink my morning draught and there I heard of a fray between the two Embassadors of Spaine and France; and that this day being the day of the entrance of an Embassador from Sweden, they were entended to fight for the precedence. In Cheapeside hear that the Spaniard hath got the best of it and killed three of the French coach-horses and several men and is gone through the City next to our King's coach. At which it is strange to see how all the City did rejoice. And endeed, we do naturally all love the Spanish and hate the French. But I, as I am in all things curious, presently got to the waterside and there took oares to Westminster palace, thinking to have seen them come in thither with all the coaches; but they being come and returned, I run after them with my boy after me, through all the dirt and the streets full of people; till at last at the mewes I saw the Spanish coach go, with 50 drawne swords at least to guard it and our soldiers shouting for joy. And so I fallowed the coach, and then met it at Yorke house, where the Embassador lies; and there it went in with great state. So then I went to the French [ambassador's] house, where I observe still that there is no men in the world of a more insolent spirit where they do well or before they begin a matter, and more abject if they do miscarry, then these people are. For they all look like dead men and not a word among them, but shake their heads. So having been very much dawbed with dirt, I got a coach and home – where I vexed my wife in telling of her this story and pleading for the Spaniard against the French.

So ends this month. Myself and family in good condition of health. But my head full of my Lord's and my own and the office business – where we are now very busy about the business of sending forces to Tanger.[1] And the fleet to my Lord of Sandwich, who is now at Lisbone to bring over the Queene – who doth now keep a Court as Queen of England. The want of money puts all things, and above all things the Navy, out of order; and yet I do not see that the King takes care to bring in any money, but thinks of new designs to lay out money.

## –⚜OCTOBER⚜–

1.   This morning my wife and I lay long in bed; and among other things, fell in talk of Musique and desired that I would let her learn to sing – which I did consider and promised her she should: so before I rose, word was brought me that my singing master Mr. GoodGroome was come to teach me; and so she rise and this morning begun to learn also. To the office, where busy all day. So to dinner and then to the office again till night; and then to my study at home to set matters and papers in order – which, though I can hardly bring myself to do, yet doth please me much when it is done. So eat a bit of bread and cheese and to bed.

5.   At the office all the morning; then dined at home, and so stayed at home all the afternoon, putting up my Lord's Modell of the *Royall James*, which I borrowed of him long ago to hang up in my room. And at night Sir W. Pen and I alone to the Dolphin and there eat some bloat-herrings and drank good sack. Then came in Sir W. Warren and another and stayed a while with us; and then Sir Arnld. Brames, with whom we stayed late and till we had drank too much wine; so home and I to bed, pleased at my afternoon's work in hanging up the Shipp. So to bed.

6.   *Lords day*. The winter coming on, many of parish ladies are come home and appear at church again; among others, the three sisters of the Thornburys, very fine, and the most zealous people that ever I saw in my life; even to admiration★, if it were true zeal. There was also my pretty black girl, Mrs. Dekins. And Mrs. Margaret Pen this day came to church in a new flowered satin suit that my wife helped to buy her the other day.

1. Acquired as part of Catherine of Braganza's dowry.

10.    At the office all the morning. Dined at home; and after dinner, Sir W. Pen and my wife and I to the theatre, where the King came today; and there was *The Traytor* most admirably acted – and a most excellent play it is. So home and entended to be merry, it being my sixth wedding night;[1] but by a late bruise in one of my testicles I am in so much pain that I eat my supper and in pain to bed; yet my wife and I pretty merry.

11.    All day in bed with a cataplasme to my Codd; and at night rise a little and to bed again, in more ease then last night. This noon there came my brother and Dr. Tom. and Snow to dinner, and by themselfs were merry.

16.    In bed till 12 a-clock. This morning came several maids to my wife to be hired; and at last she pitched upon one Nell, whose mother, an old woman, came along with her; but would not be hired under half a year, which I am pleased at their drolenesse. This day dined by appointment with me Dr. Tho. Pepys and my Cosen Snow and my brother Tom, upon a Fin of Ling and some Sounds, neither of which did I ever know before, but most excellent meat they are both, that in all my life I never eat the like fish. So after dinner came in W. Joyce and eat and drank and were merry. So up to my chamber and put all my papers at rights. And in the evening our maid Mary (who was with us upon triall for a month) did take her leave of us, going as we suppose to be married, for the maid liked us and we her; but all she said was that she had a mind to live in a tradesmans house where there was but one maid. So to supper and to bed.

17.    To the cook's, and there dined with Capt. Lambert and had much talk of Portugall from whence he is lately come, and he tells me that it is a very poor dirty place – I mean the City and Court of Lisbone. That the King is a very rude and simple fellow; and for reviling of somebody a little while ago and calling of him cuckold, was run into the cods with a sword, and had been killed had he not told them that he was their king. That there is there no glass

1. Under a Commonwealth ordinance of 1653 all marriages were to be solemnised by a magistrate in a civil ceremony; no others were to be valid in law. Pepys and his wife were married in this way on 1 December 1655. But it seems from the evidence of this entry and others that they had also been married in church on the previous 10 October.

windows, nor will have any. That the King hath his meat sent up by a dozen of lazy guards, and in pipkins sometimes, to his own table – and sometimes nothing but fruits, and now and then half a hen. And that now the Infanta is becoming our Queene, she is come to have a whole hen or goose to her table – which is not ordinary.

19.    At the office all morning; and at noon Mr. Coventry, who sat with us all this morning, and Sir G. Carteret, Sir W. Penn and myself by coach to Capt. Marshes at Limehouse, to a house that hath been their ancestors for this 250 years – close by the Limehouse which gives the name to the place. Here they have a design to get the King to hire a docke for the herring busses (which is now the great design on foote) to lie up in. We had a very good and handsome dinner, and excellent wine. I not being neat in clothes, which I find a great fault in me, could not be so merry as otherwise and at all times I am and can be, when I am in good habitt; which makes me remember my father Osborne's[1] rule for a gentleman, to spare in all things rather then in that. So by coach home; and so to write letters by post, and so to bed.

20.    *Lordsday*. At home in bed all the morning to ease my late tumour; but up to dinner, and much offended in mind at a proud trick my man Will: hath got, to keep his hatt on in the house; but I will not speak of it to him today, but I fear I shall be troubled with his pride and lazinesse, though in other things he is good enough. To church in the afternoon, where a sleepy presbyter preached. And then to Sir W. Batten, who is to go to Portsmouth tomorrow too, to wait upon the Duke of Yorke, who goes to take possession and to set in order the Garrison there. Supped at home and to bed.

22.    At the office all the morning, where we had a Deputacion* from the Duke in his absence (he being gone to Portsmouth) for us to have the whole dispose and ordering of the fleet.[2] In the afternoon, about business up and down; and at night to visit Sir R. Slingsby, who is fallen sick of this new disease, an ague and fever. So home after visiting my aunt Wight and Mrs. Norbury (who continues still a very pleasant lady); and to supper and so to bed.

1. Author of *Advice to a Son* (1658).
2. Now fitting out for the Mediterranean.

25. To Whitehall; and so to dinner at the Wardrobe, where my wife met me; and there we met with a venison pasty, and my Lady very merry and very handsome methought. After dinner, my wife and I to the Opera and there saw again *Love and Honour*, a play so good that it hath been acted but three times and I have seen them all, and all in this week; which is too much, and more then I will do again a good while. Coming out of the house, we met Mrs. Pierce and her comrade, Mrs. Clifford; and I seeming willing to stay with them to talk, my wife grew angry; and whether she be jealous or no I know not, but she loves not that I should speak of Mrs. Pierce. Home on foot, very discontentedly. In my way, I calling at the Instrument-maker's, Hunts, and there saw my Lute, which is now almost done, it being to have a new neck to it and to be made to double Strings. So home and to bed. This day I did give my man Will a sound lesson about his forbearing to give us the respect due to a master and mistress.

26. In the evening news was brought that Sir R. Slingsby our Comptroller (who hath this day been sick a week) is dead; which put me into so great a trouble of mind, that all the night I could not sleep, he being a man that loved me and had many Qualitys that made me to love him above all the officers and Comissioners in the Navy. Coming home, we called at Dan. Rawlinson's and there drank good sack; and so home.

27. *Lords day*. At church in the morning; where in the pew, both Sir Wms and I had much talk about the death of Sir Rbert. which troubles me much, and them in appearance; though I do not believe it, because I know that he was a Cheque to their ingrossing the whole trade of the navy office.

30. All the morning at the office. At noon played on my Theorbo and much pleased therewith – as it is now altered with a new neck. In the afternoon Capt. Lambert called me out by appointment and we walked together to Deptford; and there in his ship the *Norwich* I got him to show me every hole and corner of the ship, much to my informacion and the purpose of my going. At my coming home, I am sorry to find my wife displeased with her maid Doll:, whose fault is that she cannot keep her peace, but will alway be talking in an angry manner, though it be without any reason and to no purpose. Which I am sorry for – and do see the inconvenience that

doth attend the increase of a man's fortune, by being forced to keep more servants, which brings trouble.

# ❧NOVEMBER❧

2. At the office all the morning; where Sir John Minnes our new Comptroller was fetched by Sir Wm. Pen and myself from Sir W. Battens and led to his place in the office – the first time that he hath come hither. And he seems a good fair-condition[ed] man and one that I am glad hath the office. This night my boy Wainman, as I was in my chamber, [I] overheard him let off some Gunpouder; and hearing my wife chide him below for it, and a noise made, I call him up and find that it was powder that he had put in his pocket, and a mach carelessely with it, thinking that it was out; and so the match did give fire to the powder and had burned his side and his hand, that he put into his pocket to put out the fire. But upon examination, and finding him in a lie about the time and place that he bought it, I did extremely beat him. And though it did trouble me to do it, yet I thought it necessary to do it. So to write by the post, and to bed.

3. *Lords day*. This day I stirred not out, but took physique and it did work very well; and all the day, as I was at leisure, I did read in Fuller's *Holy Warr* (which I have of late bought) and did try to make a Song in the prayse of a Liberall genius (as I take my own to be) to all studies and pleasures; but it not proving to my mind, I did reject it and so proceeded not in it. At night my wife and I had a good supper by ourselfs, of a pullet hashed; which pleased me much to see my condition come to allow ourselfs a dish like that. And so at night to bed.

4. In the morning, being very rainy, by Coach with Sir W. Penn and my wife to Whitehall; and sent her to Mrs. Hunts, and he and I to Mr. Coventry about business; and so sent for her again, and all three home again; only, I to the Miter (Mr. Rawlinson's), where Mr. Pierce the purser had got us a most rare Chine of beef and a dish of marrow bones. Our Company, my Uncle Wight, Capt. Lambert, one Capt. Doves, and purser Barber, Mr. Rawlinson, and ourselfs – and very merry. After dinner I took Coach and called

my wife at my brother's, where I left her; and to the Opera, where we saw *The Bondman*, which of old we both did so doate on, and do so still; though, to both our thinking, not so well acted here (having too great expectacions) as formerly at Salsbury Court – but for Baterton; he is called by us both the best actor in the world. So home by coach, I lighting by the way at my uncle Wights and stayed there a little, and so home after my wife. And to bed.

9. At the office all the morning. At noon Mr. Davenport, Phillips and Mr. Wm. Bernard and Furbisher came by appointment and dined with me, and we were very merry. After dinner, I to the Wardrobe and there stayed talking with my Lady all the afternoon, till late at night. Among other things, my Lady did mightily urge me to lay out money upon my wife, which I perceived was a little more earnest then ordinary; and so I seemed to be pleased with it and do resolve to bestow a lace upon her – and what with this and other talk, we were exceeding merry. So home at night.

13. By appointment, we all went this morning to wait upon the Duke of Yorke, which we did in his chamber as he was dressing himself in his riding-suit to go this day by sea to the Downes. After we had given him our letter relating the bad condition of the Navy for want of mony, he referred it to his coming back and so parted. And I to Westminster hall and to see *La belle* Pearce; and so on foot to my Lord Crews, where I find him come to his new house, which is next to that he lived in last. Here I was well received by my Lord and Sir Thomas – with whom I had great talk; and he tells me in good earnest that he doth believe the parliament (which comes to sit again the next week) will be troublesome to the Court and Clergy, which God forbid. But they see things carried so by my Lord Chancellor and some others, that get money themselfs, that they will not endure it. From thence to the Theatre and there saw *Father's owne Sonn* again. And so it raining very hard, I went home by Coach, with my mind very heavy for this my expenseful life; which will undo me I fear, after all my hopes, if I do not take up – for now I am coming to lay out a great deal of money in clothes upon my wife, I must forbear other expenses.

15. At home all the morning. And at noon with my wife to the Wardrobe to dinner; and there did show herself to my Lady in the hankercher that she bought the lace for the other day; and endeed, it

is very handsome. Here I left my wife, and went to my Lord Privy Seale to Whitehall and there did give him a copy of the fees of the office as I have received them, and he was well pleased with it. So to the Opera, where I met my wife and Capt. Ferrers and Madamoiselle la Blanc, and there did see the second part of *The Siege of Rhodes* very well done. And so by coach set her home; and the coach driving down the hill through Thames street (which I think never any coach did before from that place to the bridge-foot); but going up Fish street hill, his horses were so tired that they could not be got to go up the hill, though all the street boys and men did beat and whip them. At last I was fain to send my boy for a link, and so light out of the coach till we got another at the corner of Fanchurch street; and so home. And to bed.

17.   *Lords day*. To our own church. And at noon by invitation Sir W. Penn dined with me and I took Mrs. Hester (my Lady Batten's kinswoman) to dinner from church with me – and we were very merry. So to church again and heard a simple fellow upon the praise of church musique, and exclaiming against men's wearing their hats on in the church. But I slept part of the sermon, till later prayer and blessing; and all was done without waking, which I never did in my life. So home; and by and by comes my Uncle Wight and my aunt and Mr. Norbury and his lady. And we drank hard and were very merry till supper time; and then we parted, my wife and I being invited to Sir Pen's where we also were very merry; and so home to prayers and to bed.

19.   At the office all the morning; and coming home, find Mr. Hunt with my wife in the chamber alone; which God forgive me, did trouble my head; but remembering that it was washing-day and that there was no place else with a fire for him to be in, it being also cold weather, I was at ease again. He dined with us; and after dinner took coach and carried him with us as far as my Cosen Scotts (where we set him down and parted) and my wife and I stayed there at the christening of my Cosens boy – where my Cosen Sam. Pepys of Ireland and I were godfathers. And I did name the child Samuell. There was a company of pretty women there in the chamber; but we stayed not, but went with the Minister into another room and eat and drank. And at last, when most of the women were gone, Sam and I went into my Cosen Scott, who was got off her bed; and so we stayed and talked and were very merry (my she-Cosen

Stradwick being godmother); and then I left my wife to go home by coach. (It cost me 20*s*. between the midwife and the two nurses today.)

23.   To Westminster with my wife (she to her father's); and about 10 a-clock, back again home; and there I to the office a little and thence by coach with Comissioner Pett to Cheapeside to one Savill a painter, who I entend shall do my picture and my wife's.[1] Thence I to dinner to the Wardrobe, and so home to the office and there all the afternoon till night; and then both Sir Wms to my house; and in comes Capt. Cock, and they to Cards. By and by Sir Wm. Batten and Cock, after drinking a good deal of wine, went away; and Sir W. Penn stayed with my wife and I to supper, very pleasant; and so good-night. This day I had a Chine of beefe sent home, which I bespoke to send and did send it, as a present to my uncle Wight.

25.   To Westminster hall in the morning with Capt. Lambert – and there he did at the Dogg give me, and some other friends of his, his foy, he being to set sail today toward the Streights. Here we had oysters and good wine. Having this morning met in the hall with Mr. Sanchy, we appointed to meet at the play this afternoon. At noon, at the rising of the House, I met with Sir W. Pen, and with him and Maj.-Gen. Massy (who I find by discourse to be a very ingenious man, and among other things, a great master in the Secresys of powder and fireworkes) and another Knight to dinner at the Swan in the Palace yard, and our meat brought from the Legg. And after dinner Sir W. Pen and I to the Theatre and there saw *The Country Captain*, a dull play; and that being done, I left him with his Torys and went to the Opera and saw the last act of *The Bondman*; and there find Mr. Sanchy and Mrs. Mary Archer, sister to the fair Betty, whom I did admire at Cambrige. And thence took them to the fleece in Covent Garden, there to bid good-night to Sir W. Penn, who stayed for me. But Mr. Sanchy could not by any argument get his lady to trust herself with him into the taverne, which he was much troubled at; and so we returned immediately into the city by Coach, and at the Miter in Cheapside there light and drank, and then set her at her uncles in the Old Jury. And so he and I back again thither and drank till past 12 at night, till I had drank

1. Both are untraced.

something too much – he all the while telling me his intentions to get this girle, who is worth 1000*l*. And many times we had her sister Betty's health, whose memory I love. At last parted, and I well home; only, have got cold and was hoarse, and so to bed.

26.   Not well in the morning and lay long in bed. At last rise and at noon with my wife to my Uncle Wights, where we met Mr. Cole, Mr. Rawlinson, Norbury and his wife and her daughter, and other friends to the Chine of beef that I sent them the other day, and eat and were merry. By and by I am called to the office, whither I went and there we sat late; and after the office done, Sir Wms both and I and Capt. Cock and Mr. Bence (who being drunk, showed himself by his talk a bold foole, and so we were fain to put him off and get him away) we sat till 9 a-clock by ourselfs in the office, talking and drinking three or four bottles of wine. And so home and to bed. My wife and her mayde Dorothé falling out, I was troubled at it.

28.   At home all the morning. At noon Will brought me from Whitehall, whither I had sent him, some letters from my Lord Sandwich from Tanger – where he continues still, and hath done some execution upon the Turks – and retaken an Englishman from them, of one Mr. Parker's, a merchant in Markelane.

30.   I am this day in very good health, only got a little cold. The Parliament hath sat a pretty while. The old condemned Judges of the late King have been brought before the Parliament, and like to be hanged. I am deep in Chancery against Tom Trice; God give me a good issue. And my mind under great trouble for my late great expending of money vainly, which God stop for the future. This is the last day for the old State's Coyne to pass in common payments, but they say it is to pass in public payments to the King three months still.

# –✤DECEMBER✤–

1.   *Lords day.* We have this day cut a brave Coller of Brawne from Winchcombe, which proves very good. And also opened the glass of Girkins which Capt. Cock did give my wife the other day, which are rare things. So at night to bed. There hath lately been great

Clapping up of some statesmen,* such as Ireton, Moyer and others; and they say upon a great plot, but I believe no such thing;[1] but it is but justice that they should be served as they served the poor Cavaliers and I believe it will oftentimes be so as long as I live, whether there be cause or no.

3. To my Lady, where my Lady Wright was at dinner with her. And all our talk about the great happiness that my Lady Wright says there is in being in the fashion and in variety of fashions, in scorn of others that are not so, as citizens wifes and country-gentlewomen – which though it did displease me enough, yet I said nothing to it.

14. All the morning at home, lying abed with my wife till 11 a-clock – such a habitt we have got this winter, of lying long abed. Dined at home. And in the afternoon to the office. There sat late; and so home and to bed.

16. Up by 5 a-clock this morning by candlelight (which I have not been of many a day), being called up by one Mr. Bollen by appointment, who hath business to be done with my Lord Privy Seale this morning. And so by Coach, calling Mr. Moore at the Wardrobe, to Chelsy, and there did get my Lord to seal it. And so back again to Westminster hall, and thence to my Lord Sandwiches lodgings, where I met my wife (who had been to see Mrs. Hunt, who was brought to bed the other day of a boy); and got a Joynt of meat thither from the Cookes and she and I and Sarah dined together; and after dinner to the Opera, where there was a new play (*Cutter of Colemanstreete*) made in the year 1658, with reflection much upon the late times. And it being the first time, the pay was doubled; and so to save money, my wife and I went up into the gallery and there sat and saw very well; and a very good play it is – it seems of Cowly's making. From thence by coach home. And to bed.

22. *Lords day.* To church in the morning, where the Reader made a boyish young sermon. Home to dinner; and there I took occasion, from the blackness of the meat as it came out of the pot, to fall out with my wife and the maids for their sluttery; and so left the table and went up to read in Mr. Selden till church time; and then my

1. He appears to have been right.

wife and I to church and there in the pew, with the rest of the company, was Capt. Holmes in his gold-laced suit; at which I was troubled, because of the old business which he attempted upon my wife. So with my mind troubled, I sat still; but by and by I took occasion from the rain now holding up (it raining when we came into the church) to put my wife in mind of going to the christening (which she was invited to) of N. Osbornes child. Which she did; and so went out of the pew and my mind was eased. So home after sermon, and there came by appointment Dr. T. Pepys, Will Joyce, and my brother Tom and supped with me; and very merry they were and I seemed to be, but I was not pleased at all with their company. So they being gone, we went to bed.

23.    early up and by Coach (before daylight) to the Wardrobe and took up Mr. Moore; and he and I to Chelsy to my Lord Privy Seale and there sealed some things, he being to go out of town for all Christmas tomorrow. So back again to Westminster; and from thence by water to the Treasury Office, where I find Sir W. Penn paying off the *Sophia* and *Griffen* and there I stayed with him till noon; and having sent for some Coller of beef and a minced-pie, we eat and drank, and so I left him there. So I took Coach; and lighting at my bookseller's in Pauls churchyard, I met there with Mr. Cromlom and the Second Master of Pauls school; and thence I took them to the Starr and there we sat and talked; and I had great pleasure in their company, and very glad I was of meeting him so accidentally, I having omitted too long to go to see him. Here, in discourse of books, I did offer to give the Schoole what book he would choose of 5*l*. So we parted; and I home and to Mr. Selden and then to bed.

25.    *Christmas day.* In the morning to church; where at the door of our pew I was fain to stay, because that the Sexton had not opened the door. A good sermon of Mr. Mills. Dined at home all alone. And taking occasion, from some fault in the meat, to complain of my maid's Sluttery, my wife and I fell out, and I up to my Chamber in a discontent. After dinner my wife comes up to me and all friends again; and she and I to walk upon the Leads; and there Sir W. Pen called us and we went to his house and supped with him. But before supper, Capt. Cock came to us half-drunck and begun to talk; but Sir W. Pen, knowing his humour and that there was no end of his talking, drinks four great glasses of wine to him one after another,

healths to the King &c., and by that means made him drunk, and so he went away; and so we sat down to supper and were merry; and so after supper home and to bed.

26.    This morning Sir W. Pen and I to the Treasury office; and there we paid off the *Amity* and another ship, and so home; and after dinner Sir Wm. came to me, and he and his son and daughter and I and my wife by Coach to Moorefields to walk (but it was most foule weather); and so we went into an alehouse and there eat some cakes and ale; and a Washeall-bowle woman and girl came to us and sung to us; and after all was done, I called my boy (Waynman) to us to eat some cake that was left, and the woman of the house told us that he had called for two Cakes and a pot of ale for himself, at which I was angry and am resolved to correct him for it. So home; and Sir W. Penn and his son and daughter to supper to me to a good Turkey, and were merry at Cards; and so to bed.

28.    At home all the morning; and in the afternoon, all of us at the office upon a letter from the Duke for the making up of a speedy estimate of all the debts of the Navy – which put into good forwardness, I home and Sir W. Penn to my house, who with his children stayed playing at Cards late. And so to bed.

29.    *Lords day*. Long in bed with my wife. And though I had determined to go to dine with my wife at my Lady's (chiefly to put off dining with Sir W. Penn today, because Holmes dined there), yet I could not get a coach time enough to go thither; and so I dined at home and my brother Tom with me. And then a coach came and I carried my wife to Westminster and she went to see Mrs. Hunt; and I to the Abby and there meeting with Mr. Hooper, he took me in among the Quire and there I sang with them their service.

30.    At the office about this Estimate. And so with my wife and Sir. W. Penn to see our pictures[1] – which do not much displease us. And so back again; and I stayed at the Miter, whither I had invited all my old acquaintance of the Exchequer to a good Chine of beefe – which with three barrels of oysters and three pullets and plenty of wine and mirth, was our dinner. There was about twelve of us. Among others, Mr. Bowyer the old man, and Mr.

1. See above, p. 165 (23 November) & n.

Faulconberge, Shadwell, Taylor, Spicer, Woodruffe, Servington, &c.; and here I made them a foolish promise to give them one this day twelvemonth, and so for ever while I live. But I do not entend it.

31.   My wife and I this morning to the paynters; and there she sat the last time and I stood by and did tell him some little things to do, that now her picture I think will please me very well. And after her, her little black dogg sat in her lap and was drawn, which made us very merry. So home to dinner, and so to the office and there late, finishing our estimate of the debts of the Navy to this day; and it comes to near 37400o*l*.

So home; and after supper and my barber had trimmed me, I sat down to end my Journall for this year; and my condition at this time, by God's blessing, is thus: My health (only upon ketching cold, which brings great pain in my back and making of water, as it use to be when I had the stone) very good, and so my wife's in all respects. My servants, W. Hewer, Sarah, Nell, and Waynman. My house at the Navy Office. I suppose myself to be worth about 500*l* clear in the world, and my goods of my house my owne, and what is coming to me from Brampton when my father dies – which God defere. But by my uncles death, the whole care and trouble of all and settling of all lies upon me; which is very great because of law-suits, especially that with T. Trice about the inter[e]st of 200*l* – which will I hope be ended soon. My chiefest thoughts is now to get a good wife for Tom – there being one offered by the Joyces, a cousin of theirs, worth 200*l* in ready money. I am also upon writing a little treatise to present to the Duke, about our privilege in the seas as to other nations striking their flags to us. But my greatest trouble is that I have for this last half-year been a very great spendthrift in all manner of respects, that I am afeared to cast up my accounts, though I hope I am worth what I say above. But I will cast them up very shortly. I have newly taken a solemne oath about abstaining from plays and wine, which I am resolved to keep according to the letter of the oath, which I keepe by me. The fleete hath been ready to sail for Portugall, but hath lack[ed] wind this fortnight. And by that means my Lord is forced to keep at sea all this winter till he brings home the Queen – which is the expectacion of all now – and the greatest matter of public talk.

# ❧JANUARY❧

1. Waking this morning out of my sleep on a sudden, I did with my elbow hit my wife a great blow over her face and nose, which waked her with pain – at which I was sorry. And to sleep again. Up, and went forth with Sir Wm. Pen by coach toward Westminster; and in my way, seeing that *The Spanish Curate* was acted today, I light and let him go alone; and I home again and sent to young Mr. Pen and his sister to go anon with my wife and I to the Theatre. That done, Mr. W. Pen came to me and he and I walked out, and to the Stacioners and looked over some pictures and maps for my house. And so home again to dinner. And by and by came the two young Pens, and after we had eat a barrel of oysters, we went by coach to the play and there saw it well acted, and a good play it is. Only, Diego the Sexton did overdo his part too much.

3. Lay long in bed. And so up and abroad to several places about petty businesses. Among other, to Tom's, who I find great hopes of that he will do well, which I am glad of and am not now so hasty to get a wife for him as I was before. So to dinner to my Lord Crew's, with him and his Lady. And after dinner to Faithornes and there bought some pictures of him; and while I was there, comes by the Kings lifeguard, he being gone to Lincolns Inne this afternoon to see the Revells there; there being according to an old Custome, a Prince and all his nobles, and other matters of sport and charge. So home and up to my chamber – to look over papers and other things, my mind being much troubled for these four or five days because of my present great expense, and will be so till I cast up and see how my estate stands. And that I am loath to do, for fear I have spent too much – and delay it, the rather that I may pay for my pictures and my wife's and the book that I am buying for Paul's Schoole before I do cast up my accompts.

5. *Lords day*. To church; and before sermon there was a long

psalm and half another sung out while the Sexton gathered what the church would give him for this last year (I gave him 3*s*., and have the last week given the Clerke 2*s*., which I set down that I may know what to do the next year, if it please the Lord that I live so long); but the jest was, the Clerke begins the 25 psalm, which hath a proper tune to it, and then the 116, which cannot be sung with that tune, which seemed very ridiculous.

6. *Twelfe day*. This morning I sent my lute to the painter's; and there I stayed with him all the morning, to see him paint the neck of my lute in my picture – which I was not much pleased with after it was done. Thence to dinner to Sir Wm. Pens (it being a solemn feast-day with him, his wedding day; and we have, besides a good chine of beef and other good cheer, eighteen mince-pies in a dish, the number of the years that he hath been married); where Sir W. Batten and his Lady and daughter was, and Coll. Treswell and Maj. Holmes, who I perceive would fain get to be free and friends with my wife; but I shall prevent it, and she herself hath also a defyance against him.

8. I rose and went to Westminster hall, and there walked up and down upon several businesses; and among others, I met with Sir W. Pen, who told me that he had this morning heard Sir G. Carteret extreme angry against my man Will; that he was every other day with the Comissioners of Parliament at Westminster and that his uncle[1] was a rogue and that he did tell his uncle everything that passes at the office.

10. To Whitehall and there spoke with Sir Paul Neale about a Mathematicall request of my Lord's to him; which I did deliver to him, and he promised to imploy somebody to answer it – something about observation of the Moone and stars; but what, I did not mind.

11. To Sir Wm. Battens, where in discourse I heard the Custome of the Eleccion of the Dukes of Genoa, who for two years are every day attended in the greatest state and 4 or 500 men always waiting upon him as a king. And when the two years are out and another is chose, a messenger is sent to him, who stands at the bottom of the

1. Robert Blackborne, a leading naval official under the Commonwealth.

stairs, and he at the top, and says, *Vostra Illustrissima Serenidad sta finita et puede andar en casa* – "Your serenity is now ended; and now you may be going home;" and so claps on his hat and the old Duke (having by custome sent his goods home before) walks away, it may be but with one man at his heels, and the new one brought immediately in his room, in the greatest state in the world. Another account was told us, how in the Dukedome of Regusa in the Adriatique (a State that is little, but more ancient they say then Venice, and is called the mother of Venice) and the Turkes lie round about it – that they change all the officers of their guard, for fear of conspiracy, every 24 houres, so that nobody knows who shall be Captain of the guard tonight; but two men come to a man, and lay hold of him as a prisoner and carry him to the place; and there he hath the keys of the garrison given him, and he presently issues his orders for that night's Watch; and so always, from night to night. Sir Wm. Rider told the first of his own knowledge; and both he and Sir Wm. Batten confirm the last.

13.   All the morning at home, and Mr. Berchenshaw (whom I have not seen a great while, came to see me), who stayed with me a great while talking of Musique; and I am resolved to begin to learne of him to compose and to begin tomorrow, he giving of me so great hopes that I shall soon do it. Before 12 a-clock comes by appointment Mr. Peter and the Deane and Coll. Honiwood, brothers, to dine with me. But so soon that I was troubled at it. But however, I entertained them with talk and oysters till one a-clock; and then we sat down to dinner. Mr. Peter after dinner did show us the experiment (which I have heard talk of) of the Chymicall glasses, which break all to dust by breaking off the little small end – which is a great mystery to me.

14.   All the morning at home – Mr. Berchenshaw, by appointment yesterday, coming to me, and begun composition of Musique. And he being gone, I to settle my papers and things in my chamber; and so after dinner, in the afternoon to the office and thence to my chamber about several businesses of the office and my own; and then to supper and to bed. This day my brave vellum covers to keep pictures in came in, which pleases me very much.

15.   This morning Mr. Berchenshaw came again; and after he had examined me and taught me something in my work, he and I went

to breakfast in my chamber, upon a Coller of brawne. And after we had eaten, he asked me whether we have not committed a fault in eating today, telling me that it is a fast-day, ordered by the parliament to pray for more seasonable weather – it having hitherto been some summer weather, that it is, both as to warmth and every other thing, just as if it were the middle of May or June, which doth threaten a plague (as all men think) to fallow; for so it was almost the last winter and the whole year after hath been a very sickly time, to this day. I did not stir out of my house all day, but con'd my Musique; and at night, after supper to bed.

16. At night to Sir W. Batten and there saw him and Capt. Cock and Stokes play at Cards, and afterwards supped with them. Stokes told us that notwithstanding the country of Gambo is so unhealthy, yet the people of that place live very long, so as the present King there is 150 years old, which they count by Raynes because every year it rains continually four months together. He also told us that the kings there have above 100 wives apiece, and offered him the choice of any of his wifes to lie with, and so he did Capt. Holmes. So home and to bed.

19. *Lords day.* To church in the morning, where Mr. Mills preached upon Christ's being offered up for our sins. And there, proveing the æquity with what Justice God could lay our sins upon his Son, he did make such a sermon (among other things, pleading from God's universall Soverainty over all his Creatures, the power he hath of commanding what he would of his Son, by the same rule as that he might have made us all and the whole world from the beginning to have been in hell, arguing from the power the potter hath over his clay), that I could have wished he had let it alone. And speaking again, that God the Father is now so satisfyd by our Security for our debt that we might say at the last day, as many of us as have interest in Christ's death – Lord, we owe thee nothing – our debt is paid – we are not beholden to thee for anything, for thy debt is paid thee to the full – which methinks were very bold words.

20. This morning Sir Wm. Batten and Penn and [I] did begin the examining the Treasurers accounts – the first that ever he hath passed in the office. Which is very long – and we were all at it till noon. Then to dinner, he providing a fine dinner for us; and we eate it at Sir Wm. Batten's, where we were very merry, there being at

table the Treasurer and we three – Mr. Wayth, Fenn, Smith, Turner, and Mr Morrice the Wine Cooper (who this day did divide the two butts, which we four did send for, of Sherry from Cales, and mine was put into a hogshead and the vessell filled up with four gallons of Malago wine; but what it will stand us in I know not, but it is the first great Quantity of wine that I ever bought). And after dinner to the office all the afternoon, till late at night. And then home, where my aunt and uncle Wight and Mrs. Anne Wight came to play at Cards (at gleeke, which she taught me and my wife the last week); and so to supper and then to Cards, and so good-night. Then I to my practice of Musique and then at 12 a-clock to bed. This day the workmen begin to make me a sellar door out of the back yard – which will much please me.

23. All the morning with Mr. Berchenshaw and after him Mr. Moore, in discourse of business; and at noon by Coach by invitacion to my Uncle Fenners, where I find his new wife, a pitiful, old, ugly, illbread woman in a hatt, a midwife. Here were many of his and as many of her relations, sorry mean people. And after choosing our gloves, we all went over to the Three Crane taverne, and (though the best room of the house) in such a narrow dogghole we were crammed (and I believe we were near 40) that it made me loathe my company and victuals; and a sorry poor dinner it was too.

25. At home and the office all the morning. Walking in the garden to give the gardener directions what to do this year (for I entend to have the garden handsome), Sir Wm. Pen came to me. Thence with him to the Trinity house to dinner, where Sir Richard Brown (one of the clerks of the Council, and who is much concerned against Sir N. Crisp's project of making a great sasse in the King's Lands about Deptford, to be a wett dock to hold 200 sail of ships – but the ground, it seems, was long since given by the King to Sir Richd.) was; and after the Trinity house men had done their business, the maister, Sir Wm. Rider, came to bid us welcome; and so to dinner – where good cheer and discourse, but I eat a little too much beef, which made me sick; and so after dinner we went to the office, and there in the garden I went in the darke and vomited, whereby I did much ease my stomach. Thence to supper with my wife to Sir Wm. Pens. And so while we were at supper, comes Mr. Moore with letters from my Lord Sandwich, speaking of his lying still at Tanger, looking for the fleet – which we hope is now in a good way thither.

26.   *Lords day*. To church in the morning and then home to dinner alone with my wife; and so both to church in the afternoon and home again; and so to read and talk with my wife, and to supper and bed. It having been a very fine clear frosty day – God send us more of them, for the warm weather all this winter makes us fear a sick summer. But thanks be to God, since my leaving drinking of wine, I do find myself much better and to mind my business better and to spend less money, and less time lost in idle company.

27.   This morning, both Sir Wms and I by barge to Deptford yard to give order in businesses there; and called on several ships also to give orders.

28.   This morning (after my musique practice with Mr. Berchensha) with my wife to the paynters,[1] where we stayed very late to have her picture mended; which at last is come to be very like her, and I think well done. But the paynter, though a very honest man, I find to be very silly as to matter of skill in shadowes – for we were long in discourse, till I was almost angry to hear him talk so simply. So home to dinner and then to the office, and so home for all night.

## –❧FEBRUARY ❧–

3.   After musique practice I went to the office, and there with the two Sir Wms all the morning about business. At noon I dined with Sir W. Batten with many friends more, it being his Wedding-day. And among other Froliques, it being their third year, they had three pyes, whereof the middlemost was made of an ovall form in an Ovall hole within the other two which made much mirth and was called the middle peace; and above all the rest, we had great striving to steal a spoonefull out of it; and I remember Mrs. Mills the minister's wife did steal one for me and did give it me; and to end all, Mrs. Shippman did fill the pie full of White wine (it holding at least a pint and a half) and did drink it off for a health to Sir Wm. and my Lady, it being the greatest draught that ever I did see a woman drink in my life. Before we had dined came Sir G. Carteret, and we went all three to the office and did business there till night. And then

1. See above, p. 165 (23 November) & n.

to Sir Wm. Batten again, and I went along with my Lady and the rest of the gentlewomen to Maj. Holmes's, and there we had a fine supper; among others, excellent lobsters, which I never eat at this time of the year before. The Major hath good lodgings at the Trinity house. Here we stayed late, and at last home. And being in my chamber, we do hear great noise of mirth at Sir Wm. Battens, tearing the ribbands from my Lady and him. So I to bed.

4.   To Westminster hall, where it was full terme. Here all the morning; and at noon to my Lord Crewes – where one Mr. Templer (an ingenious [man] and a person of honour he seems to be) dined; and discoursing of the nature of Serpents, he told us of some that in the waste places of Lancashire do grow to a great bigness, and that do feed upon larkes, which they take thus – they observe when the lark is soared to the highest, and do crawle till they come to be just underneath them; and there they place themselfs with their mouths uppermost, and there (as is conceived) they do eject poyson up to the bird; for the bird doth suddenly come down again in its course of a circle, and falls directly into the mouth of the serpent – which is very strange. He is a great traveller; and speaking of the Tarantula, he says that all the harvest long (about which time they are most busy) there are fidlers go up and down in the fields everywhere, [in] expectation of being hired by those that are stung.

5.   earely at the office; Sir G. Carteret, the two Sir Wms and myself all alone, reading over the Duke's Institucions for the Settlement of our office. Whereof we read as much as concerns our owne duties, and left the other officers for another time. I did move several things for my purpose, and did ease my mind. At noon Sir W. Pen dined with me; and after dinner, he and I and my wife to the Theater and went in; but being there very earely, we went out again to the next door and drank some Renish wine and Sugar; and so to the House again and there saw *Rule a Wife and have a Wife* – very well done; and here also I did look long upon my Lady Castlemayne, who, notwithstanding her late sickness, continues a great beauty. Home, and supped with Sir W. Pen and played at Cards with him; and so home and to bed – putting some cataplasme to my testicle, which begins to swell again.

6.   After dinner the Barber trimmed me; and so to the office,

where I do begin to be exact in my duty there and exacting my
privileges – and shall continue to do so.

8.    All morning in the sellar with the Colliers, removing the Coles
out of the old coal-hole into the new one, which cost me 8s. the
doing; but now the cellar is done and made clean, it doth please me
exceedingly, as much as anything that was ever yet done to my
house. I pray God keep me from setting my mind too much upon it.
About 3 a-clock, the Colliers having done, I went up to dinner (my
wife having often urged me to come, but my mind is so set upon
these things that I cannot but be with the workmen to see things
done to my mind; which if I am not there is seldom done); and so to
the office, and thence to talk with Sir W. Penn, walking in the dark
in the garden some turns, he telling me of the ill management of our
office and how Wood the Timber merchant and others were very
Knaves, which I am apt to believe. Home, and wrote letters to my
father and my brother John, and so to bed – being a little chillish –
entending to take physique tomorrow morning.

9.    *Lordsday*. I took physic this day, and was all day in my chamber
– talking with my wife about her laying out of 20l:, which I had
long since promised her to lay out in clothes against Easter for
herself. And composing some ayres (God forgive mee). At night,
to prayers and to bed.

10.    Musique practice a good while. Then to Pauls churchyard,
and there I met with Dr: Fullers *Englands worthys* – the first time that
I ever saw it; and so I sat down reading in it, till it was 2 a-clock
before I thought of the time's going. And so I rose and went home
to dinner, being much troubled that (though he had some discourse
with me about my family and armes) he says nothing at all, nor
mentions us either in Cambrige or Norfolke. But I believe endeed,
our family were never considerable. At home all the afternoon; and
at night to bed.

11.    Dined at home, and at the office in the afternoon. So home to
Musique, my mind being full of our alteracions in the garden and
my getting of things in the office settled to the advantage of my
Clerkes, which I find Mr. Turner much troubled at. And myself am
not quiet in mind – but I hope by degrees to bring it to it. At night

begun to compose songs, and begin with *Gaze not on Swans*. So to bed.

13. After Musique comes my Cosen Tom. Pepys the Executor; and he did stay with me above two houres, discoursing about the difference between my uncle Thomas and me,[1] and what way there may be to make it up, and I have hopes we may do good of it for all this.

14. *Valentine's day*. I did this day purposely shun to be seen at Sir W. Battens – because I would not have his daughter to be my Valentine,[2] as she was the last year, there being no great friendship between us now as formerly. This morning in comes W. Bowyer, who was my wife's Valentine, she having (at which I made good sport to myself) held her hands all the morning, that she might not see the paynters that were at work in gilding my chimny-piece and pictures in my dining-room.

15. With the two Sir Wms to the Trinity house; and there in their society had the business debated of Sir Nicholas Crisps Sasse at Deptford. Then to dinner; and after dinner I was sworne a younger Brother, Sir W. Rider being Deputy-Maister for my Lord of Sandwich; and after I was sworn, all the elder Brothers shake me by the hand; it is their Custome it seems. Thence to the office, and so to Sir Wm. Battens all three; and there we stayed till late, talking together in complaint of the Treasurers instruments – above all, Mr. Waith – at whose child's christening our wifes and we should have been today, but none of them went and I am glad of it – for he is a very rogue. So home and drew up our report for Sir N. Crisp's Sasse, and so to bed.

17. This morning, both Sir Wms, myself, and Capt. Cock and Capt. Tinker (of the *Convertine*, which we are going to look upon, being entended [to go] with these ships fitting for the East Indys) down to Deptford; and thence, after being on ship-board, to Woolwich – and there eat something. The Sir Wms being unwilling to eat flesh, Capt. Cock and I had a breast of veale roasted. And here I drank wine upon necessity, being ill for want of it. And I find reason to fear that by my too sudden leaving off wine, I do contract

---

1. Over the Brampton inheritance: see above, pp. 144–5 (8–13 July).
2. Custom required her to choose the first person she saw.

many evils upon myself. Going and coming, we played at Gleeke, and I won 9s.-6d. clear, the most that ever I won in my life. I pray God it may not tempt me to play again.

18. Lay long in bed. Then up to the office (we having changed our days to Tuseday and Saturday in the morning and Thursday at night); and by and by, with Sir Wm. Pen, Mr. Kenard and others to Survey his house again and to contrive for the alterations there – which will be handsome I think. Having agreed with Sir Wm. Pen and my wife to meet them at the Opera, and finding by my walking in the streets, which were everywhere full of brickbattes and tyeles flung down by the extraordinary Winde the last night (such as hath not been in memory before, unless at the death of the late Protector), that it was dangerous to go out of doors; and hearing how several persons have been killed today by the fall of things in the streets and that the pageant in Fleetstreete is most of it blown down, and hath broke down part of several houses, among others Dick Brigdens, and that one Lady Sanderson, a person of Quality in Covent garden, was killed by the fall of the house in her bed last night, I sent my boy home to forbid them to go forth.

20. This morning came Mr. Childe to see me, and set me something to my Theorbo. And by and by comes letters from Tanger from my Lord, telling me how, upon a great defeate given to the Portugeses there by the Moores, he had put in 300 men into the Towne, and so hee is in possession; of which we are very glad, because now the Spaniards designes of hindering our getting that place are frustrated. I went with the letters inclosed to my Lord Chancellor to the House of Lords, and did give it him in the House.

22. Having got a very great cold, I got something warm tonight, and so to bed.

23. *Lords day*. My cold being increased, I stayed at home all day, pleasing myself with my dining-room, now graced with pictures, and reading of Dr. Fullers *worthys*. So I spent the day; and at night comes Sir W. Pen and supped and talked with me. This day, by God's mercy I am 29 years of age, and in very good health and like to live and get an estate; and if I have a heart to be contented, I think I may reckon myself as happy a man as any is in the world – for which God be praised. So to prayers and bed.

24.   Long with Mr. Berchenshaw in the morning at my Musique practice, finishing my song of *Gaze not on swans* in two parts, which pleases me well. And I did give him 5*l* for this month or five weeks that he hath taught me, which is a great deal of money and troubled me to part with it. After supper, called Will up and chid him before my wife for refusing to go to church with the maids yesterday, and telling his mistress that he would not be made a slave of – which vexes me. So to bed.

25.   All the morning at the office. At noon with Mr. Moore to the Coffee-house – where among other things, the great talk was of the effects of this late great wind; and I heard one say that he hath five great trees standing together blown down, and going to lop them – one of them, as soon as the lops were cut off, did by the weight of the root rise again and fasten. We have letters from the Forrest of Deane, that above 1000 oakes and as many beeches are blown down in one walke there. And letters from my father tells me of 20 hurt to us down at Brampton.

26.   Mr. Berchensha with me all the morning, composing of musique to *This cursed Jeaulousy, what is it?*, a song of Sir W. Davenants. After dinner I went to my Bookesellers, W. Joyces and several other places, to pay my debts and do business – I being resolved to cast up my accounts within a day or two, for I fear I have run out too far.

27.   This morning came Mr Berchensha to me; and in our discourse, I finding that he cries up his rules for most perfect (though I do grant them to be very good, and the best I believe that ever yet were made) and that I could not persuade him to grant wherein they were somewhat lame, we fell to angry words, so that in a pet he flung out of my chamber and I never stopped him, being entended to have put him off today whether this had happened or no, because I think I have all the rules that he hath to give, and so there remains nothing but practice now to do me good – and it is not for me to continue with him at 5*l* per mensem. So I settled to put his rules all in fair order in a book, which was my work all the morning till dinner. After dinner to the office till late at night; and so home to write by the post, and so to bed.

28.   The boy failing to call us up as I commanded, I was angry and

resolved to whip him for that and many other faults today. I bid Will get me a rod, and he and I called the boy up to one of the upper rooms of the Controllers house toward the garden, and there I reckoned all his faults and whipped him soundly; but the rods were so small that I fear they did not much to hurt him, but only to my arme, which I am already, within a Quarter of an houre, not able to stir almost. After supper, to bed.

# –⁕MARCH⁕–

1.   My wife and I by coach, first to see my little picture that is a-drawing, and thence to the Opera and there saw *Romeo and Julett*, the first time it was ever acted. But it is the play of itself the worst that ever I heard in my life, and the worst acted that ever I saw these people do; and I am resolved to go no more to see the first time of acting, for they were all of them out more or less. Thence home, and after supper and wrote by the post – I settled to what I have long entended, to cast up my accounts with myself; and after much pains to do it and great fear, I do find that I am 500*l* in money beforehand in the world, which I was afeared I was not. But I find that I have spent above 250*l* this last half year, which troubles me much. But by God's blessing, I am now resolved to take up, having furnished myself with all things for a great while, and tomorrow to think upon some rules and obligacions upon myself to walk by.

2.   *Lords day*. With my mind much eased, talking long in bed with my wife about our frugall life for the time to come, proposing to her what I could and would do if I were worth 2000*l*; that is, be a Knight and keep my coach – which pleased her; and so I do hope we shall hereafter live to save something, for I am resolved to keep myself by rules from expences. To church in the morning; none in the pew but myself. So home to dinner. And after dinner came Sir Wm. and talked with me till church time; and then to church, where at our going out I was at a loss by Sir W. Pen's putting me upon it whether to take my wife or Mrs. Martha (who alone was there); and I begun to take my wife, but he jogged me and so I took Martha and led her down before him and my wife.

3d.   All morning at home about business with my brother Tom and then with Mr. Moore; and then I set to make some strict rules for my future practice in my expenses, which I did bind myself in the presence of God by oath to observe, upon penaltys therein set down. And I do not doubt but hereafter to give a good account of my time and to grow rich – for I do find a great deal more of content in those few days that I do spend well about my business then in all the pleasures of a whole week, besides the trouble which I remember I always have after them for the expense of my money. Dined at home and then up to my chamber again about business; and so to the office – about despatching of the East India ships,[1] where we stayed till 8 at night; and then after I had been at Sir Wm. Pens awhile, discoursing with him and Mr. Kenard the Joyner about the new building in his house, I went home, where I find a vessel of oysters sent me from Chatham. And I fell to eat some and then to supper; and so after the barber had done, to bed. I am told that this day the Parliament hath voted 2s. per annum for every chimney in England, as a constant Revenue for ever to the Crowne.

4th. At the office all the morning. Dined at home at noon. And then to the office again in the afternoon to put things in order there, my mind being very busy in settling the office to ourselfs,[2] I having now got distinct offices for the other two. By and by, Sir W. Penn and I and my wife in his Coach to Moorefields, where we walked a great while, though it was no fair weather and cold; and after our walk we went to the Popeshead and eat cakes and other fine things, and so home. I up to my chamber to read and write, and so to bed.

5. In the morning to the paynters about my little picture. Thence to Toms about business; and so to the pewterers to buy a poore's box to put my forfeites in, upon breach of my late vowes. So to the Wardrobe and dined, and thence home and to my office and there sat looking over my papers of my voyage when we fetched over the King, and tore so many of those that were worth nothing, as filled my closet as high as my knees. I stayed doing this till 10 at night; and so home and to bed.

6. Up earely, my mind full of business. Then to the office, where

---

1. Sent to Bombay to take possession of Bombay as part of Catherine of Braganza's dowry.
2. Pepys and his clerks.

the two Sir Wms and I spent the morning passing the Victuallers accounts – the first I have had to do withal.

7.    early to Whitehall to the Chappell; where by Mr. Blagrave's means, I got into his pew and heard Dr. Creeton, the great Scochman, preach – before the King and Duke and Duchesse – upon the words of Michah: "Roule yourselves in dust." He made a most learned sermon upon the words; but in his applicacion, the most Comicall man that ever I heard in my life – just such a man as Hugh peters. Saying that it had been better for the poor Cavalier never to have come in with the King into England again; for he that hath the impudence to deny obedience to the lawful magistrate and to swear to the oath of allegeance &c, were better treated nowadays in newgate then a poor Royalist that hath suffered all his life for the King is at Whitehall among his friends. He discoursed much against a man's lying with his wife in Lent, saying that he might be as incontinent during that time with his own wife as at another time in another man's bed.

10.    At the office, doing business all the morning. And my wife being gone to buy some things in the City, I dined with Sir W. Batten; and in the afternoon met Sir W. Pen at the Treasury Office and there paid off the *Guift* – where late at night, and so called in and eat a bit at Sir W. Battens again; and so home and to bed, tomorrow being washing-day.

12.    At the office from morning till night, putting of papers in order, that so I may have my office in an orderly condition. I took much pains in sorting and folding of papers.

13.    All day either at the office or at home, busy about business till late at night – I having lately fallowed my business much. And I find great pleasure in it, and a growing content.

14.    At the office all the morning. At noon Sir W. Penn and I making a bargaine with the workmen about his house. In which I did see things not so well contracted for as I would have, and I was vexed and made him so too, to see me so criticall in the agreement. Home to dinner. In the afternoon came the German, Dr Kuffler, to discourse with us about his Engine to blow up ships. We doubted not [the] matter of fact, it being tried in Cromwells time, but the

safety of carrying them in ships. We concluded nothing, but shall discourse with the Duke of Yorke tomorrow about it. Then to my lute, upon which I have not played a week or two; and trying over the two songs of *Nulla nulla*, &c and *Gaze not on Swans*, which Mr. Berchinsha set for me a little while ago, I find them most incomparable songs as he hath set them – of which I am not a little proud, because I am sure none in the world hath them but myself, not so much as he himself that set them. So to bed.

15. With Sir G. Carteret and both the Sir Wms at Whitehall to wait on the Duke in his chamber, which we did, about getting money for the navy – and other things. So back again to the office all the morning. Then to the Exchange to hire a ship for the Maderas, but could get none. Then home to dinner, and Sir G. Carteret and I all the afternoon by ourselfs upon business in the office, till late at night: so to write letters and home to bed.

18. All the morning at the office with Sir W. Pen. Dined at home, and Luellin and Blurton with me. After dinner to the office again, where Sir George Carteret and we stayed awhile, and then Sir W. Pen and I on board some of the ships now fitting for East Indys and Portugall, to see in what forwardness they are. And so back home again.

19. All the morning and afternoon at my office, putting things in order. And in the evening I do begin to digest my uncle the Captain's papers into one book, which I call my *Brampton booke*, for my clearer understanding things how they are with us.

21. With Sir W. Batten by water to Whitehall, and he to Westminster. I went to see Sarah and my Lord's Lodgeings, which are now all in dirt, to be repaired against my Lord's coming from sea with the Queene. Thence to Westminster hall and there walked up and down and heard the great difference that hath been between my Lord Chancellor and my Lord of Bristoll, about a proviso that my Lord Chancellor would have brought into the bill for Conformity, that it shall be in the power of the King, when he sees fit, to dispence with the act of Conformity. And though it be carried in the House of Lords, yet it is believed it will hardly pass in the Commons.

22.   At the office all the morning. At noon, Sir Wms both and I by water down to the *Lewes*, Capt. Dekins his ship, a merchantman – where we met the owners, Sir John Lewes and Ald. Lewes and several other great merchants; among others, one Jefferys, a merry man that is a fumbler; and he and I called brothers, and he made all the mirth in the company. We had a very fine dinner, and all our wifes' healths with seven or nine guns apiece.

23.   *Lords day.* This morning was brought me my boyes fine livery, which is very handsome, and I do think to keep to black and gold lace upon gray, being the colour of my armes, for ever. To church in the morning. And so home with Sir W. Batten and there eat some boiled great oysters; and so home, and while I was at dinner with my wife, I was sick and was forced to vomitt up my oysters again and then I was well. To Whitehall and there met with Capt. Isham, this day come from Lisbone with letters from the Queene to the King. And did give me letters which speak that our fleet is all at Lisbon; and that the Queene doth not entend to embarque sooner then tomorrow come fortnight.

24.   earely, Sir G. Carteret, both Sir Wms, and I on board the *Experiment* to dispatch her away, she being to carry things to the Maderas with the East India fleet. Here (Sir W. Penn going to Deptford to send more hands), we stayed till noon, talking and eating and drinking a good ham of English bacon; and having put things in good order, home – where I find Jane, my old maid, come out of the country; and I have a mind to have her again. By and by comes *la Belle* Perce to see my wife and to bring her a pair of peruques of hair, as the fashion now is for ladies to wear – which are pretty and are of my wife's own hair, or else I should not endure them. After a good while stay, I went to see if any play was acted, and I find none upon the post, it being passion weeke. To Westminster hall and there bought Mr. Grant's book of observations upon the weekely bills of Mortality – which appear to me, upon first sight, to be very pretty. So back again and took my wife, calling at my brother Tom's, whom I find full of work, which I am glad of; and thence at the New Exchange and so home. And I to Sir W. Battens and supped there, out of pure hunger to save getting anything ready at home, which is a thing I do not nor shall not use to do. So home and to bed.

25. *Lady day*. All the morning at the office. Dined with my wife at home. Then to the office, where (while Sir Wms both did examine the Victuallers account) I sat in my closet drawing letters and other businesses – being much troubled for want of an order of the Councells lately sent us, about making of boates for some ships now going to Jamaica. At last, late at night, I had a Copy sent me of it by Sir G. Lane from the Council Chamber. With my mind well at ease, home and to supper and bed.

26. Up earely – this being, by God's great blessing, the fourth solemne day of my cutting for the stone this day four year. And am by God's mercy in very good health, and like to do well, the Lord's name be praised for it. To the office and Sir G. Carterets all the morning, about business. At noon came my good guest Madame Turner, The[oph]. and Cosen Norton, and a gentleman, one Mr. Lewin of the King's life-guard; by the same token he told us of one of his fellows, killed this morning in the dewell. I had a pretty dinner for them – *viz*: a brace of stewed Carps, six roasted chicken, and a Jowle of salmon hot, for the first course – a Tanzy and two neats' tongues and cheese the second. And were very merry all the afternoon, talking and singing and piping on the Flagelette. In the evening they went with great pleasure away; and I with great content, and my wife, walked half an houre in the garden; and so home to supper and to bed. We had a man-cook to dress dinner today, and sent for Jane to help us. And my wife and she agreed 3*l* a year (she would not serve under) till both could be better provided; and so she stays with us.

27. earely, Sir G. Carteret, both Sir Wms and I by Coach to Deptford, it being very windy and rainy weather – taking a Codd and some prawnes in Fishstreete with us. We settled to pay the *Guernsy* – a small ship, but came to a great deal of money, it having been unpaid ever since before the King came in – by which means, not only the King pays wages while the ship hath lain still, but the poor men have most of them been forced to borrow all the money due for their wages before they receive it, and that at a dear rate, God knows. So that many of them had very little to receive at the table – which grieved me to see it.

30. *Easterday*. Having my old black suit new-furbished, I was pretty neat in clothes today – and my boy, his old suit new-

trimmed, very handsome. To church in the morning. And so home, leaving the two Sir Wms to take the Sacrament – which I blame myself that I have hitherto neglected all my life, but once or twice at Cambrige. Dined with my wife, a good shoulder of veal, well dressed by Jane and handsomely served to table – which pleased us much and made us hope that she will serve our turns well enough. My wife and I to church in the afternoon and seated ourselfs, she below me; and by that means the precedence of the pew which my Lady Batten and her daughter takes, is confounded. And after sermon she and I did stay behind them in the pew and went out by ourselfs a good while after them – which we judge a very fine project hereafter, to avoyd contention. So my wife and I to walk an hour or two on the leads; which begins to be very pleasant, the garden being in good condition. So to supper, which is also well served in. We had a lobster to supper with a crab Pegg Pen sent my wife this afternoon; the reason of which we cannot think, but something there is of plot or design in it – for we have a little while carried ourselfs pretty strange to them. After supper, to bed.

## ⸙APRILL⸙

1. After dinner I and the two young ladies and my wife to the playhouse, the Opera, and saw *The Mayd in the mill*, a pretty good play. In the middle of the play, my Lady Paulina, who had taken physique this morning, had need to go forth; and so I took the poor lady out and carried her to the Grange, and there sent the mayde of the house into a room to her, and she did what she had a mind to. And so back again to the play. And that being done, in their coach I took them to Islington; and there, after a walk in the fields, I took them to the great Chescake house and entertained them, and so home; and after an hour stay with my Lady, their coach carried us home; and so, weary to bed.

4. By barge, Sir George, Sir Wms both, and I, to Deptford; and there fell to pay off the *Drake* and *Hampshire*. I was much troubled today to see a dead man lie floating upon the waters; and had done (they say) these four days and nobody takes him up to bury him, which is very barbarous.

5.   At the office till almost noon; and then broke up. Then came Sir
G. Carteret, and he and I walked together alone in the garden,
taking notice of some faults in the office, perticularly of Sir Wm.
Batten's. And he seemed to be much pleased with me, and I hope
will be the ground of a future interest of mine in him, which I shall
be glad of.

6.   *Lords day*. By water to Whitehall to Sir G. Carteret, to give him
an account of the backwardnesse of the ships we have hired to
Portugall. At which he is much troubled. Thence to the Chappell
and there, though crowded, heard a very honest sermon before the
King by a Canon of Christ Church – upon these words: "Having a
forme of godliness but denying," &c. Among other things, did
much insist upon the sin of adultery – which methought might
touch the King and the more because he forced it into his sermon,
methought besides his text. So up and saw the King at dinner; and
thence with Sir G. Carteret to his lodgings, to dinner with him and
his Lady – where I saluted her – she seems a good lady. And all their
discourse, which was very much, was upon their sufferings and
services for the King.

9.   Sir G. Carteret, Sir Wms both, and myself all the morning at
the office, passing the Victualler's accounts; and at noon to dinner at
the Dolphin – where a good Chine of beef and other good cheer. At
dinner Sir George showed me an account in french of the great
Famine, which is to the greatest extremity in some part of France at
this day – which is very strange.

10.   To Westminster with the two Sir Wms by water – and did
several businesses. And so to the Wardrobe with Mr. Moore to
dinner. Yesterday came Coll. Talbot with letters from Portugall –
that the Queene is resolved to embarque for England this week.

11.   Up early to my lute and a song. Then about 6 a-clock with Sir
W. Pen by water to Deptford and among the ships now going to
Portugall with men and horse, to see them dispatched. So to
Greenwich; and had a fine pleasant walk to Woolwich, having in
our company Capt. Minnes, with whom, I was much pleased to
hear him talk, in fine language but pretty well for all that. Among
other things, he and the other Captains that were with us tell me
that Negros drownded look white and lose their blacknesse – which

I never heard before. At Woolwich, up and down to do the same business and so back to Greenwich by water; and there, while something is dressing for our dinner, Sir Wm. and I walked into the Parke, where the King hath planted trees and made steps in the hill up to the Castle, which is very magnificent. So to dinner at the Globe, and Capt. Lambert of the Dukes pleasure-boat came to us and dined with us. And were merry and so home. And I in the evening to the Exchange and spoke with Uncle Wight; and so home and walked with my wife on the leads late; and so the barber came to me; and so to bed very weary, which I seldom am.

13. *Lords day*. Sir W. [Batten] comes to me to bring me a paper of Fieldes (with whom we have lately had a great deal of trouble at the office), being a bitter petition to the King against our office, for not doing Justice upon his complaint to us of embezzlement of the King's stores by one Turpin.[1] I took Sir Wm. to Sir W. Pens (who was newly come from Walthamstowe), and there we read it and discoursed; but we do not much fear it, the King referring it to the Duke of Yorke. So we drank a glass or two of wine; and so home and I to bed – my wife being in bed already.

16. Up earely and took my physique; it wrought all the morning well. At noon dined; and all the afternoon, Mr. Hater to that end coming to me, he and I did go about my abstracting all the Contracts made in the office since we came into it. So at night to bed.

18. This morning, sending the boy down into the cellar for some beer, I fallowed him with a cane, and did there beat him for his staying of arrands and other faults, and his sister came to me down and begged for him: so I forebore. And afterwards in my wife's chamber did there talk to Jane how much I did love the boy for her sake and how much it doth concern to correct the boy for his faults, or else he would be undone. So at last she was well pleased. This morning Sir G. Carteret, Sir W. Batten and I met at the office and did conclude of our going to Portsmouth next week. In which, my

---

1. Field had been imprisoned for slandering the Navy Board. He now brought actions for wrongful arrest against the Board collectively and Pepys and Batten individually, on the ground that the Board had no powers of magistracy in the City. He won the cases but was awarded only small damages. In 1664 an act was passed giving the Board the required powers.

mind is at a great loss what to do with my wife, for I cannot persuade her to go to Brampton and I am loath to leave her at home. All the afternoon in several places to put things in order for my going. At night home and to bed.

22.　After taking leave of my wife, which we could hardly do kindly, because of her mind to go along with me – Sir W. Penn and I took coach and so over the bridge to Lambeth – W. Bodham and Tom Hewet going as clerks to Sir W. Penn, and my Will for me. Here we got a dish of buttered eggs, and there stayed till Sir G. Carteret came to us from Whitehall, who brought Dr. Clerke with him, at which I was very glad. And so we set out. And I was very much pleased with his company, and were very merry all the way.

23.　Up earely and to Petersfield, and there dined well; and thence got a contry-man to guide us by Havan, to avoid going through the forrest;[1] but he carried us much out of the way. The Doctor and I lay together at Wiards the Chyrurgeons in Portsmouth – his wife a very pretty woman. We lay very well and merrily. In the morning, concluding him to be of the eldest blood and house of the Clerkes, because that all the fleas came to him and not to me.

25.　All the morning at Portsmouth at the pay; and then to dinner and again to the pay; and at night got the Doctor to go lie with me, and much pleased with his company; but I was much troubled in my eyes, by reason of the healths I have this day been forced to drink.

26.　Sir G. and I and his clerk, Mr. Stephens, and Mr. Holt our guide, over to Gosport, and so rode to Southampton. In our way, besides my Lord Southamptons parks and lands, which in one viewe we could see 6000*l* per annum, we observed a little churchyard, where the graves are accustomed to be all Sowed with Sage. At Southampton we went to the Mayors and there dined, and had Sturgeon of their own catching the last week. The towne is one most gallant street – and is walled round with stone. Many old walls of religious houses, and the Keye well worth seeing.

28.　The Doctor and I begun Philosophy discourse, exceeding

1. The Forest of Bere.

pleasant. He offers to bring me into the college of the Virtuosoes and my Lord Brunkard's acquaintance. And to show me some anatomy, which makes me very glad. And I shall endeavour it when I come to London.

30. This morning Sir G. came down to the yard, and there we mustered over all the men and determined of some regulacions in the yard. And then to dinner, all the officers of the yard with us; and after dinner walk to Portsmouth – there to pay off the *Successe*. This afternoon, after dinner, comes Mr. Stephenton, one of the Burgeses of the towne, to tell me that the Mayor and burgesses did desire my acceptance of a Burgessshipp and were ready at the Mayor['s] to make me one. So I went and there they were all ready and did with much civility give me my oath; and after the oath, did by custom shake me all by the hand. So I took them to a taverne and made them drink; and paying the reckoning, went away. It cost me a piece in gold to the Towne Clerk and 10*s*. to the bayliffes, and spent 6*s*.

## MAY

1. Sir G. Carteret, Sir W. Pen, and myself, with our clerks, set out this morning from Portsmouth very early and got by noon to Petersfield, several of the officers of the yard accompanying us so far. Here we dined and were merry. To horse again after dinner, and got to Gilford – where after supper I to bed, having this day been offended by Sir Wm. Pens foolish talk, and I offending him with my answers; among others, he in discourse complaining of want of Confidence, did ask me to lend him a grain or two, which I told him I thought he was better stored with then myself, before Sir George. So that I see I must keep a greater distance then I have done. And I hope I may do it, because of the interest which I am making with Sir George. To bed all alone, and my Will in the truckle-bed.

2. earely to coach again and to Kingston, where we baited a little; and presently to coach again and got earely to London; and I find all well at home, and Mr. Hunt and his wife had dined with my wife today – and been very kind to my wife in my absence. After I had washed myself, it having been the hottest day that hath been this

year, I took them all by coach to Mrs. Hunts; and I to Dr. Clerkes lady and give her her [husband's] letter and token. She is a very fine woman, and what with her person and the number of fine ladies that were with her, I was much out of countenance and could hardly carry myself like a man among them. But however, I stayed till my courage was up again; and talked to them and viewed her house, which is most pleasant; and so drank and goodbye.

3. Sir W. Penn and I by coach to St. James's, and there to the Dukes chamber, who hath been a-hunting this morning and is come back again. To dinner to my Lady Sandwich; and Sir Tho. Crewes children coming thither, I took them and all my Lady's to the Tower and showed them the lions and all that was to be shown, and so took them to my house and there made much of them; and so saw them back to my Lady's – Sir Th. Crewes children being as pretty and the best behaved that ever I saw of their age.

4. *Lords day*. Lay long, talking with my wife. Then up and Mr. Holliard came to me and let me blood, about 16 ounces, I being exceeding full of blood, and very good. I begun to be sick; but lying upon my back, I was presently well again and did give him 5s. for his pains; and so we parted. And I to my chamber to write down my Journall from the beginning of my late Journy to this houre. Dined well. And after dinner, my arm tied up with a black ribbon, I walked with my wife to my Brother Toms, our boy waiting on us with his sword, which this day he begins to wear to out-do Sir W. Pens boy, who this day, and Sir W. Batten['s] too, begin to wear new liverys. But I do take mine to be the neatest of them all.

7. Walked to Westminster; where I understand the news that Mr. Mountagu is this last night come to the King, with news that he left the Queene and fleet in the bay of Biscay, coming this way-ward, and that he believes she is now at the Isle of Scilly. So at noon to my Lord Crewes and there dined; and after dinner Sir Tho. Crew and I talked together; and among other instances of the simple light discourse that sometimes is in the Parliament house, he told me how in the late business of Chymny-money, when all occupyers were to pay, it was questioned whether women were under that name to pay, and somebody rose and said that they were not occupiers, but occupied.

8.   At the office all the morning, doing business alone. And then to the Wardrobe, where my Lady going out with the children to dinner, I stayed not but returned home; and was overtaken in St Paul's churchyard by Sir G. Carteret in his coach, and so he carried me to the Exchange, where I stayed awhile. He told me that the Queene and the fleet were in Mounts bay on monday last – and that the Queene endures her sickness pretty well. He also told me how Sir John Lawson hath done some execution upon the Turkes in the Straight, of which I am glad and told the news the first on the Exchange. And was much fallowed by merchants to tell it. So home and to dinner. And by and by to the office, and after the rest gone (my Lady Albemarle being this day at dinner at Sir W. Batten), Sir G. Carteret comes and he and I walked in the garden; and among other discourse, he tells me that it is Mr. Coventry that is to come to us as a Comissioner of the Navy. At which he is much vexed, and cries out upon Sir W. Penn and threatens him highly; and looking upon his lodgings, which are new enlarging, he in passion cried "*guarda mi spada!* for by God, I may chance to keep him in Ireland when he is there" – for Sir W. Penn is going thither with my Lord Lieutenant, but it is my design to keep much in with Sir G. and I think I have begun very well towards it. So to the office, and was there late doing business; and so, with my head full of business, I to bed.

10.   By myself at the office all the morning, drawing up instruccions for Portsmouth yard in those things wherein we at our late being there did think fit to reforme. And got them signed this morning to send away tonight, the Duke being now there. At the office all afternoon; and in the evening comes Sir G. Carteret, and he and I did hire a ship for Tanger, and other things together; and I find that he doth single me out to join with him apart from the rest; which I am much glad of. So home; and after being trimmed, to bed.

11.   *Lordsday*. To our own church in the morning; where our Minister being out of town, a dull, flat Presbiter preached. Dined at home, and my wife's brother with us, we having a good dish of stewed beef of Janes own dressing, which was well done, and a piece of Sturgeon, of a barrel lately sent me by Capt. Cocke. In the afternoon to Whitehall and there walked an hour or two in the

parke, where I saw the King now out of mourning[1] – in a suit laced with gold and silver, which it was said was out of fashion. Thence to the Wardrobe and there consulted with the ladies[2] about our going to Hampton court tomorrow; and thence home and after settled business there, my wife and I to the Wardrobe; and there we lay all night in Capt. Ferrers chamber, but the bed so saft that I could not sleep that hot night.

12. Mr. Townsend called us up by 4 a-clock. And by 5 the three ladies, my wife and I, and Mr. Townsend, his son and daughter, were got to the barge and set out. We walked from Moreclacke to Richmond, and so to boat again; and from Teddington to Hampton Court, Mr. Townsend and I walked again – and there met the ladies and were showed the whole house by Mr. Marriot – which endeed is nobly furnished – perticularly the Queenes bed, given her by the States of Holland. A Lookeing glase, sent by the Queene-Mother from France, hanging in the Queens chamber. And many brave pictures. So to Mr. Marriots, and there we rested ourselfs and drank. And so to barge again, and there we had good victuals and wine and were very merry. And got home about 8 at night, very well. So my wife and I took leave of my Lady and home by a hackny-coach, the easiest that ever I met with. And so to bed.

15. To Westminster; and at the Privy Seale I saw Mr. Coventrys seal for his being Comissioner with us – at which I know not yet whether to be glad or otherwise. So, doing several things by the way, I walked home; and after dinner to the office all the afternoon. At night all the bells in the towne rung, and bonefires made for the joy of the Queenes arrivall; who came and landed at Portsmouth last night. But I do not see much thorough joy, but only an indifferent one, in the hearts of people, who are much discontented at the pride and luxury of the Court, and running in debt. So to bed.

18. *Whitsunday*. By water to Whitehall and there to Chappell in my pew, belonging me as Clerk of the Privy Seale. And there I heard a most excellent sermon of Dr. Hacke[t], Bishop of Lichfield and Coventry – upon these words: "Hee that drinketh this water shall never thirst." We had an excellent Anthemne sung by Capt.

1. For his aunt, Elizabeth, Queen of Bohemia (d. 13 February).
2. Lady Mountagu's daughters, Jemima, Paulina and Anne.

Cooke and another, and brave Musique; and then the King Come down and offered, and took the Sacrament upon his Knees – a sight very well worth seeing. Thence with Sir G. Carteret to his lodgeing to dinner, with his Lady. We were very merry, and good discourse, and I had much talk with my Lady – after dinner; and so to Chappell again and there had another good Anthemne of Capt. Cookes. Thence to the Councell Chamber; where the King and Council sat till almost 11 a-clock at night, and I forced to walk up and down the gallerys till that time of night. They were reading all the bills over that are to pass tomorrow at the House, before the King's going out of towne – and progueing the House.

20.    Sir W. Penn and I did a little business at the office, and so home again. Then comes Deane Fuller after we had dined, but I got something for him; and very merry we were for an houre or two, and I am most pleased with his company and goodness. At last parted, and my wife and I by coach to the Opera and there saw the second part of *Seige of Rhodes*, but it is not so well done as when Roxalana was there – who, it is said, is now owned by my Lord of Oxford. Thence to tower wharfe and there took boat; and we all walked to halfeway house and there eat and drunk – and were pleasant; and so finally home again in the evening, and so good-night – this being a very pleasant life that we now lead, and have long done; the Lord be blessed and make us thankful. But though I am much against too much spending, yet I do think it best to enjoy some degree of pleasure, now that we have health, money and opportunities, rather then to leave pleasures to old age or poverty, when we cannot have them so properly.

21.    My wife and I by water to Westminster; and after she had seen her father (of whom lately I have heard nothing at all what he does, or her mother), she came to me to my Lord's Lodgeings, where she and I stayed, walking into Whitehall garden; and in the privy Garden saw the finest smocks and linen petticoats of my Lady Castlemaynes, laced with rich lace at the bottomes, that ever I saw; and did me good to look upon them. So to Wilkinsons, she and I and Sarah, to dinner, where I had a good Quarter of Lamb and a salat. Here Sarah told me how the King dined at my Lady Castlemayne, and supped, every day and night the last week. And that the night that the bonefires were made for joy of the Queenes arrivall, the King was there; but there was no fire at her door,

though at all the rest of the doors almost in the street; which was much observed. And that the King and she did send for a pair of scales and weighed one another; and she, being with child, was said to be heavyest. But she is now a most disconsolate creature, and comes not out of doors – since the King's going.

23. At the office good part of the morning. And then about noon with my wife on foot to the Wardrobe. My wife went up to the dining-roome to my Lady Paulina and I stayed below, talking with Mr. Moore in the parler, reading of the King and Chancellors late speeches at the prorogueing of the Houses of Parliament. And while I was reading, news is brought me that my Lord Sandwich is come and gone up to my Lady – which put me into great suspence of joy. So I went up, waiting my Lord's coming out of my Lady's chamber – which by and by he did, and looks very well and my soul is glad to see him. He very merry. And hath left the King and Queene at Portsmouth, and is come up to stay here till next Wednesday, and then to meet the King and Queen at Hampton Court.

24. Abroad with Mr. Creede, of whom I informed myself of all I have a mind to know. Among other things – the great difficulty my Lord hath been in all this summer for lack of good and full orders from the King – and I doubt our Lords of the Council do not mind things as the late powers did, but their pleasures or profit more. That the *Huego de Toros* is a simple sport, yet the greatest in Spaine. That the Queene hath given no rewards to any of the Captaines or Officers, but only to my Lord Sandwich; and that was a bag of gold (which was no honourable present) of about 1400*l* Sterling. How recluse the Queene hath ever been and all the voyage never came upon the deck, or put her head out of her Cabin – but did love my Lord's musique; and would send for it down to the stateroom, and she set in her Cabin within hearing of it. That my Lord was forced to have some clashing with the Council of Portugall about payment of the porcion before he could get it – which was, besides Tanger and a free trade in the Indys, two millions of crownes – half now, and the other half in twelve months. But they have brought but little money; but the rest in Sugars and other Commoditys, and bills of Exchange. That the King of Portugall is a very foole almost, and his mother doth all.

25.  *Lords day*. To trimming myself, which I have this week done every morning, with a pumice stone, which I learnt of Mr. Marsh when I was last at Portsmouth; and I find it very easy, speedy and cleanly, and shall continue the practice of it. To church and heard a good sermon of Mr. Woodcockes at our church. Dined at home, and Mr. Creede with me. This day I had the first dish of pease I have had this year. After discourse, he and I abroad; and walked up and down and look into many churches – among other, Mr. Baxters at Blackefryers. Then to the Wardrobe, where I find my Lord takes physic, so I did not see him. But with Capt. Ferrers to Charing cross; and there at the Triumph taverne he showed me some portugall Ladys which are come to towne before the Queene. They are not handsome, and their farthingales a strange dress. Many ladies and persons of Quality come to see them. I find nothing in them that is pleasing. And I see they have learnt to kiss and look freely up and downe already, and I do believe will soon forget the recluse practice of their own country. They complain much for lack of good water to drink. So to the Wardrobe back on foot, and supped with my Lady; and so home, and after a walk upon the leads with my wife, to prayer and bed.

26.  Up by 4 a-clock in the morning and fell to the preparing of some accounts for my Lord of Sandwich. By and by, by appointment comes Mr. Moore; and by what appears to us at present, we find that my Lord is above 7000*l* in debt and that he hath money coming into him that will clear all; and so we think him clear – but very little money in his purse. Thence home and to the Trinity house, where the Bretheren (who have been at Deptford today choosing a new Maister; which is Sir J. Minnes, notwithstanding Sir W. Batten did contend highly for it; at which I am not a little pleased, because of his proud Lady) about 3 a-clock came hither, and so to dinner. I seated myself close by Mr. Prin; who, in discourse with me, fell upon what records he hath of the lust and wicked lives of the Nuns heretofore in England, and showed me out of his pocket one wherein 30 Nuns for their lust were ejected of their house, being not fit to live there, and by the Popes command to be put, however, into other Nunnerys. I could not stay to end dinner with them; but rise and privately went out, and by water to my brother's; and thence to take my wife to the Redd bull, where we saw *Dr. Faustus*; but so wretchedly and poorly done, that we were sick of it – and the worse because by a former resolution it is to

be the last play we are to see till Michaelmas. Thence homewards by
coach through Moorefields, where we stood a while and saw the
Wrestling. At home, got my lute upon the Leades and there played;
and so to bed.

29.    With my wife and the two maids and the boy took boat and to
Foxhall – where I have not been a great while – to the Old Spring
garden. And there walked long and the wenches gathered pinks.
Here we stayed; and seeing that we could not have anything to eat
but very dear and with long stay, we went forth again without any
notice taken of us; and so we might have done if we had had
anything. Thence to the New one, where I never was before, which
much exceeds the other. And here we also walked, and the boy
creeps through the hedge and gather[s] abundance of roses. And
after long walk, passed out of doors as we did in the other place.
And so to another house that was an ordinary house, and here we
have cakes and powdered beef and ale; and so home again by water,
with much pleasure. This day, being the Kings birthday, was very
solemnely observed; and the more for that the Queene this day
comes to Hampton Court. In the evening bonefires were made, but
nothing to the great number that was heretofore at the burning of
the Rump. So to bed.

31.    By and by to Whitehall, hearing that Sir G. Carteret was come
to towne; but I could not find him, and so back to Tom's; and
thence I took my father to my house and there he dined with me –
discoursing of our business with uncle Thomas and T. Trice. After
dinner he departed, and I to the office, where we met. And that
being done, I walked to my Brother – and the Wardrobe and other
places about business, and so home. And had Sarah to comb my
head clean, which I find so foul with poudering and other troubles,
that I am resolved to try how I can keep my head dry without
pouder. And I did also in a sudden fit cut off all my beard,* which I
have been a great while bringing up, only that I may with my
pumice-stone do my whole face, as I now do my chin, and so save
time – which I find a very easy way and gentile. So she also washed
my feet in a bath of hearbes; and so to bed.
    This month ends with very fair weather for a great while
together. My health pretty well, but only wind doth now and then
torment me about the fundament extremely. The Queene is
brought a few days since to Hampton Court; and all people say of

her to be a very fine and handsome lady and very discreet, and that the King is pleased enough with her: which I fear will put Madam Castlemaines nose out of Joynt. The Court is wholly now at Hampton. A peace with Argiers is lately made; which is also good news. My father is lately come to towne to see us, and though it hath cost and will cost more money, yet I am pleased with the alteracions on my house at Brampton. My Lord Sandwich is lately come with the Queene from Sea, very well and good repute. Upon an audit of my estate I find myself worth about 530*l de Claro*. [The] Act for Uniformity is lately printed, which it is thought will make mad work among the presbyterian ministers. Spirits of all sides are very much discontented; some thinking themselfs used, contrary to promise, too hardly; and the other, that they are not rewarded so much as they expected by the King. God keep us all. I have by a late oath obliged myself from wine and playes, of which I find good effect.

# –❧JUNE❧–

2.    Up earely about business. And then to the Wardrobe with Mr. Moore and spoke to my Lord about exchange of the Crusados into Sterling money – and other matters. So to my father at Toms; and after some talk with him, away home; and by and by comes my father to dinner with me. And then by coach, setting him down in cheapside, my wife and I to Mrs. Clarkes at Westminster, the first visit that ever we both made her yet. We find her in a *dishabillée* – entending to go to Hampton Court tomorrow. We had much pretty discourse, and a very fine lady she is. Thence by water to Salsbury Court, and Mrs. Turner not being at home, home by Coach. And so after walking on the leads and supper, to bed. This day my wife put on her slashed wastecoate, which is very pretty.

3.    Up by 4 a-clock. And to my business in my chamber – to even accounts with my Lord and myself; and very fain I would become master of 1000*l*, but I have not above 530*l* towards it yet. At the office all the morning, and Mr. Coventry brought his patent and took his place with us this morning. Upon our making a Contract, I went, as I use to do, to draw the heads thereof; but Sir W. Pen most basely told me that the Controller is [to] do it, and so begun to

imploy Mr. Turner about it, at which I was much vexed and begun to dispute; and what with the letter of the Dukes orders, and the practice of our predecessors, which Sir G. Carteret knew best when he was Comptroller, it was ruled for me. What Sir J. Minnes will do when he comes I know not, but Sir W. Penn did it like a base raskall, and so I shall remember him while I live. After office done, I went down to the Tower wharfe, where Mr. Creed and Sheply was ready with three chests of Crusados, being about 6000*l*, ready to bring on shore to my house; which they did, and put it in my further cellar – and Mr Sheply took the key. Thence to the Wardrobe, where I find my Lady come from Hampton Court, where the Queene hath used her very civilly; and my Lady tells me is a most pretty woman – at which I am glad. Yesterday (Sir R. Ford told me) the Aldermen of the City did attend her in their habitts, and did present her with a gold Cupp, and 1000*l* in gold therein. Home and to the office; where, about 8 at night, comes Sir G. Carteret and Sir W. Batten. And so we did some business. And then home and to bed, my mind troubled about Sir W. Penn – his playing the rogue with me today. As also about the charge of money that is in my house, which I had forgot. But I made the maids to rise and light a candle and set it in the dining room to scare away thiefs. And so to sleep.

4.   Sir W. Batten and I by water down to Woolwich and there saw an experiment made of Sir R. Ford's holland's yarne (about which we have lately had so much stir; and I have much concerned myself for our Ropemaker, Mr. Hughes, who hath represented it as bad); and we found it to be very bad, and broke sooner then, upon a fair triall, five threades of that against four of Riga yarn; and also that some of it hath old Stuffe that hath been tarred, coverd over with new hempe, which is such a cheat as hath not been heard of. I was glad of this discovery, because I would not have the King's workmen discouraged (as Sir W. Batten doth most basely do) from representing the faults of merchants goods, when there is any.

5.   To the Wardrobe; and there my Lord did enquire my opinion of Mr. Moore, which I did give to the best advantage I could, and by that means shall get him joyned with Mr. Townesend in the Wardrobe business. He did also give me all Mr. Sheplys and Mr. Moores accounts to view – which I am glad of, as being his great trust in me, and I would willingly keep up a good interest with him.

To dinner, and find Dr. Tho. Pepys at my house. But I was called from dinner, by a note from Mr. Moore, to Ald. Backwells to see some thousands of my Lord's Crusados weighed. And we find that 3000 come to about 530 or 40*l* generally.

7. To the office, where all the morning. And I find Mr. Coventry is resolved to do much good and to inquire into all the miscarriages of the office. At noon with him and Sir W. Batten to dinner at Trinity house – where among others, Sir J. Robinson, Lieutenant of the Tower, was. My mind in great trouble whether I should go as I entended to Hampton Court tomorrow or no. At last, resolved the contrary because of the charge thereof and I am afeared now to bring in any accounts for journys; and so will others I suppose be, because of Mr. Coventry's prying into them. Thence sent for to Sir G. Carterets, and there talked with him a good while. I perceive, as he told me, were it not that Mr. Coventry hath already feathered his nest in selling of places, he doth like him very well and hopes great good from him. But he complains so of lack of money, that my heart is very sad, under the apprehension of the fall of the office.

9. earely up and at the office with Mr. Hater, making my Alphabet of Contracts, upon the dispatch of which I am now very intent, for that I am resolved much to inquire into the price of commodities. Dined at home; and after dinner to my brother's and several other places; among the rest, to Gratorex's and with him and another stranger to the Taverne, but I drunk no wine. He commended Bond, of our end of the towne, to teach me to measure Timber – and some other things that I would learn in order to my office. So home to supper and to bed.

10. At the office all the morning. Much business and great hopes of bringing things, by Mr. Coventry's means, to a good condition in the office. Dined at home, Mr. Hunt with us. To the office again in the afternoon; but not meeting as was intended, I went to my brother's and booksellers and other places about business, and paid off all for books to this day and do not entend to buy any more of any kind a good while – though I had a great mind to have bought the King's *works*, as they are new-printed in folio, and present it to my Lord. But I think it will be best to save the money. So home and to bed.

11. At the office all the morning, Sir W. Batten, Sir W. Penn and I, about the Victuallers accounts. Then home to dinner, and to the office again all the afternoon, Mr. Hater and I writing over my Alphabet faire, in which I took great pleasure to rule the lines and to have the Capitall words writ with red inke.

12. This morning I tried on my riding-cloth suit with close knees, the first that ever I made, and I think they will be very convenient – if not too hot to wear any other open-knees after them. At the office all the morning – where we have a full Board, *viz.*, Sir G. Carteret, Sir John Mennes, Sir W. Batten, Mr. Coventry, Sir W. Pen, Mr. Pett and myself. Among many other businesses, I did get a vote signed by all concerning my issuing of warrants, which they did not smell the use I entend to make of it; but it is to plead for my clerks to have their right of giving out all warrants, in which I am not a little pleased. But a great difference happened between Sir G. Carteret and Mr. Coventry about passing the victuallers account, and whether Sir George is to pay the Victualler his money, or the Exchequer; Sir George claiming it to be his place to save his threepences.[1] It ended in anger, and I believe will come to be a Question before the King and Council. I did what I could to keep myself unconcerned in it, having some things of my own to do before I would appear high in anything.

13. Up by 4 a-clock in the morning and read Cicero's *Second Oracion against Cataline*, which pleased me exceedingly; and more I discern therein then ever I thought was to be found in him. But I perceive it was my ignorance, and that he is as good a writer as ever I read in my life. By and by to Sir G. Carterets to talk with him about yesterday's difference at the office; and offered my service to look into any old books or papers that I have that may make for him. He was well pleased therewith – and did much inveigh against Mr. Coventry. Upon the whole, I do find that he doth much esteem of me and is my friend. And I may make good use of him. Thence to several places about businesses; among others, to my Brother and there Tom Beneere the barber trimmed me. Thence to my Lady's and there dined with her – Mr. Loxton, Gibbons, and Goodgroone with us, and after dinner some Musique, and so home to my business; and in the evening, my wife and I and Sarah and the boy, a

1. His 'poundage' (commission) of 3*d*. in the pound.

most pleasant walk to Halfway house; and so home and to bed.

14. Up by 4 a-clock in the morning and upon business at my office. Then we sat down to business; and about 11 a-clock, having a room got ready for us, we all went out to the Tower hill; and there, over against the Scaffold made on purpose this day, saw Sir Henry Vane[1] brought. A very great press of people. He made a long speech, many times interrupted by the Sheriffe and others there; and they would have taken his paper out of his hand, but he would not let it go. But they caused all the books of those that writ after him[2] to be given the Sheriffe; and the Trumpets were brought under the scaffold, that he might not be heard. Then he prayed, and so fitted himself and received the blow. But the Scaffold was so crowded that we could not see it done. But Boreman, who had been upon the Scaffold, came to us and told us that first he begun to speak of the irregular proceeding against him; that he was, against Magna Charta, denied to have his excepcions against the Endictment allowed. And that there he was stopped by the Sheriffe. Then he drow out his paper of Notes and begun to tell them; first, his life, that he was born a Gentleman, that he was bred up and had the Qualitys of a Gentleman, and to make him in the opinion of the world more a Gentleman, he had been, till he was seventeen year old, a Goodfellow. But then it pleased God to lay a foundacion of Grace in his heart, by which he was persuaded against his worldly interest to leave all preferment and go abroad, where he might serve God with more freedom. Then he was called home and made a member of the Long parliament; where he never did, to this day, anything against his conscience, but all for the glory of God. Here he would have given them an account of the proceedings of the Long parliament, but they so often interrupted him, that at last he was forced to give over; and so fell into prayer for England in Generall, then for the churches in England, and then for the City of London. And so fitted himself for the block and received the blow. He had a blister or Issue upon his neck, which he desired them not to hurt. He changed not his colour or speech to the last, but died justifying himself and the cause he had stood for; and spoke very confidently of his being presently at the right hand of Christ. And in all things appeared the most resolved man that ever died in that

1. The republican politician; condemned for High Treason.
2. sc. wrote notes of his speech.

manner, and showed more of heate then cowardize, but yet with all humility and gravity. One asked him why he did not pray for the King: he answered, "Nay," says he, "you shall see I can pray for the King; I pray, God bless him."

16. Up before 4 a-clock; and after some business, took Will forth and he and I walked over the Tower hill through St. Catharines and Ratcliffe (I think it is) by the waterside above a mile before we could get a boat; and so over the water in a Scull (which I have not done a great while) and walked finally to Deptford, where I saw in what forwardness the work is for Sir W. Battens house and mine, [1] and it is almost ready. I also, with Mr. Davis, did view my Cosen Joyces tallow and compared it with the Irish tallow we bought lately; and find ours much more white, but as soft as it; now what is the fault, or whether it be or no a fault, I know not. So walked home again as far as over against the tower, and so over and home – where I find Sir W. Penn and Sir John Minnes discoursing about Sir J. Mennes house and his coming to live with us; and I think he entends to have Mr. Turners house and he to come to his lodgings, which I shall be very glad of. We three did go to Mr. Turners to view his house, which I think was to the end that Sir J. Mennes might see it. Then by water with my wife to the Wardrobe and dined there; and in the afternoon with all the children by water to Greenwich, where I showed them the King's Yacht, the house and the parke, all very pleasant; and so to the taverne and had the Musique of the house, and so merrily home again; Will and I walked home from the Wardrobe, having left my wife at the tower wharf coming by – whom I find gone to bed not very well, she having her month's upon her. So to bed.

19. Up by 5 a-clock; and while my man Will was getting himself ready to come up to me, I took and played on my lute a little. So to dress myself and to my office to prepare things against we meet this morning. We sat long today and had a great private business before us about contracting with Sir W. Rider, Mr. Cutler, and Capt. Cocke for 500 ton of hempe, which we went through and I am to draw up the conditions. Home to dinner, where I find Mr. Moore. And he and I did cast up our accounts together and even them. And

1. The houses were being raised by a storey, and the timber frames for the new roof were being made in the dockyard.

then with the last chest of Crusados to Ald. Backwells; by the same token, his lady, going to take coach, stood in the shop and having a gilded glassful of perfumed comfits given her by Don Duarte de Silva, the Portugall merchant that is come over with the Queene, I did offer at a taste, and so she poured some out into my hand; and though good, yet pleased me the better coming from a pretty lady. So home and at the office, preparing papers and things; and endeed, my head hath not been so full of business a great while and with so much pleasure, for I begin to see the pleasure of it. God give me health. So to bed.

21. Having from my wife and the maids complaints made of the boy, I called him up and with my whip did whip him till I was not able to stir, and yet I could not make him confess any of the lies that they tax him with. At last, not willing to let him go away a conqueror, I took him in task again and pulled off his frock to his shirt, and whipped him till he did confess that he did drink the Whay, which he hath denied. And pulled a pinke, and above all, did lay the candlesticke upon the ground in his chamber, which he hath denied this Quarter of this year. I confess it is one of the greatest wonders that ever I met with, that such a little boy as he could possibly be able to suffer half so much as he did to maintain a lie. But I think I must be forced to put him away. So to bed, with my arme very weary.

22. *Lords day*. This day I first put on my slasht doublet, which I like very well. Coming home tonight, I met with Will Swan, who doth talk as high for the fanatiques as ever he did in his life; and doth pity my Lord Sandwich and me that we should be given up to the wickedness of the world, and that a fall is coming upon us all. For he finds that he and his company are the true spirit of the nation, and the greater part of the nation, too – who will have liberty of conscience in spite of this act of uniformity, or they will die; and if they may not preach abroad, they will preach in their own houses. He told me that certainly Sir H. Vane must be gone to Heaven, for he died as much a martyr and saint as ever any man died. And that the King hath lost more by that man's death then he will get again a good while. At all which, I know not what to think; but I confess I do think that the Bishops will never be able to carry it so high as they do.

23. Up earely this morning; and my people are taking down the

hangings and things in my house because of the great dust that is already made by the pulling down of Sir W. Batten's house, and will be by my own when I come to it. To my office, and there hard at work all the morning. After a little dinner, to my office again. And in the evening Sir W. Warren came to me about business; and that being done, discoursing of Deales, I did offer to go along with him among his deal ships, which we did, to half a scoare; where he showed me the difference between Dram, Swinsound, Christiana and others, and told me many pleasant notions concerning their manner of cutting and sawing them by watermills, and the reason how deals become dearer and cheaper; among others, when the snow is not so great as to fill up the vallys, that they pass from hill to hill over the snow, then it is dear carriage. From on board he took me to his yard, where vast and many piles of deals, sparres, and balkes and Euphroes – the difference between which I never knew before. And endeed, am very proud of this evening's work. He had me into his house, which is most pretty and neat and well furnished. After a glass, not of wine, for I could not be tempted to drink any, but a glass of mum, I well home by water; but it being late, was forced to land at the custome house, and so home – and to bed. And after I was abed, letters came from the Duke for the fitting out of four ships forthwith from Portsmouth (I know not yet for what), so I was forced to make Will get them writ, and signed them in bed and sent them away by expresse. And so to sleep.

24.   *Midsummer day*.   Up earely and to my office, putting things in order against we sit. Sit all the morning, and I bless God I find that by my diligence of late and still, I do get ground in the office every day. At noon to the change, where I begin to be known also. And so home to dinner and then to the office, all the afternoon dispatching business. At night news is brought me that Field, the rogue,[1] hath this day cast me at Guildhall in 30*l* for his imprisonment, to which I signed his commitment with the rest of the officers. But they having been parliament-men, he hath begun the law with me and threatens more. But I hope the Duke of Yorke will bear me out.

25.   Up by 4 a-clock and put my accounts with my Lord into a very good order, and so to my office – where having put many things in order, I went to the Wardrobe but find my Lord gone to

1. See above, p. 190 (13 April) & n.

Hampton Court. After discourse with Mr. Sheply, we parted and I into Thames street beyond the bridge and there enquired among the shops the price of tarr and oyle; and do find great content in it and hope to save the King money by this practice. So home to dinner and then to the Change; and so home again and at the office, preparing business against tomorrow all the afternoon. At night walked with my wife upon the leads; and so to supper and to bed. My [wife] having lately a great paine in her eare, for which this night she begins to take phisique; and I have got cold and so have a great deal of my old pain.

26. Up and took phisique, but such as to go abroad with, only to loosen me, for I am bound. So to the office – and there all the morning, setting till noon; and then took Comissioner Pett home with me to dinner, where my stomach was turned when my sturgeon came to table, upon which I saw very many little worms creeping, which I suppose was through the staleness of the pickle. He being gone, comes Mr. Nicholson, my old fellow-student at Magdalen, and we played three or four things upon violin and Basse; and so parted, and I to my office till night; and then came Mr. Sheply and Creede in order to setting some accounts of my Lord right; and so to bed.

27. Up earely, not quite rid of my pain. I took more phisique, and so made myself ready to go forth. So to my Lord, who ris as soon as he heard I was there and in his nightgown and shirt stood talking with me alone two houres, I believe – concerning his greatest matters of state and interest. Among other things that the Duke at Portsmouth did thank my Lord for all his pains and care; and that he perceived it must be the old Captains[1] that must do the business, and that the new ones would spoil all. And that my Lord did very discreetly tell the Duke (though quite against his judgment and inclinacion) that, however, the King's new Captaines ought to be borne with a little and encouraged. By which he will oblige that party and prevent, as much as may be, their envy; but he says that certainly things will go to wrack if ever the old Captains should be wholly out, and the new ones only command. Mr. Holliard hath been with my wife today and cured her of her pain in her eare, by taking out a most prodigious quantity of hard wax that had

1. Those commissioned in the Commonwealth navy.

hardened itself at the bottom of the eare, of which I am very glad.

28.  Great talk there is of a fear of a war with the Duch;[1] and we have order to pitch upon 20 ships to be forthwith set out; but I hope it is but a scarecrow to the world, to let them see that we can be ready for them; though God knows, the King is not able to set out five ships at this present without great difficulty, we neither having money, credit, nor stores. My mind is now in a wonderful condition of quiet and content, more then ever in all my life – since my minding the business of my office, which I have done most constantly; and I find it to be the very effect of my late oaths against wine and plays; which, if God please, I will keep constant in. For now my business is a delight to me and brings me great credit, and my purse encreases too.

29.  *Lords day*. Up by 4 a-clock, and to the settling of my own accounts, and I do find upon my monthly ballance (which I have undertaken to keep from month to month) that I am worth 650*l*, the greatest sum that ever I was yet master of. I pray God give me a thankful spirit, and care to improve and increase it.

30.  Up betimes and to my office, where I find Griffens girl making it clean; but God forgive me, what a mind I have to her, but did not meddle with her. She being gone, I fell upon boring holes for me to see from my closet into the great office without going forth, wherein I please myself much. So settled to business; and at noon with my wife to the Wardrobe and there dined and stayed talking all the afternoon with my Lord. And about 4 a-clock took coach with my wife and Lady and went toward my house, calling at my Lady Carteret's, who was within by chance (she keeping altogether at Deptford for a month or two) and so we sat with her a little. Thence to my house, where I took great pride to lead her through the Court[2] by the hand, she being very fine and her page carrying up her train. She stayed a little at my house, and then walked through the garden and took water; and went first on board the King's pleasure-boat – which pleased her much; then to Greenwich parke, and with much ado, she was able to walk up to the top of the hill. And so down again and took boat, and so

---

1. Hostilities did not break out until 1664.
2. The main courtyard of Whitehall Palace.

through bridge to Blackfriars and home – she being much pleased with the ramble – in every perticular of it. So we supped with her and then walked home, and to bed.

## *Observations*

This I take to be as bad a Juncture as ever I observed. The King and his new Queene minding their pleasures at Hampton Court. All people discontented; some that the King doth not gratify them enough; and the others, Fanatiques of all sorts, that the King doth take away their liberty of conscience; and the heighth of the Bishops, who I fear will ruin all again. They do much cry up the manner of Sir H. Vanes death, and he deserves it. They clamour against the Chimny-money and say they will not pay it without force. And in the meantime, like to have wars abroad – and Portugall to assist, when we have not money to pay for any ordinary layings-out at home. Myself all in dirt about building of my house and Sir W. Batten's a storey higher. Into a good way; fallen on minding my business and saving money, which God encrease; and I do take great delight in it and see the benefit of it. In a longing mind of going to see Brampton, but cannot get three days time, do what I can. In very good health, my wife and myself.

## –❊ JULY ❊–

1.   To the office. And there we sat till past noon; and then Capt. Cuttance and I by water to Deptford, where the *Royall James* was paying-off by Sir W. Batten and Sir W. Penn. To the pay again after dinner; and seeing of Cooper the Mate of the ship, whom I knew in the *Charles*, I spoke to him about teaching the Mathematiques, and do please myself in my thoughts of learning of him. And bid him come to me in a day or two. Towards evening I left them and to Redriffe by land. Mr. Cowly the Clerk of the Cheque with me, discoursing concerning the abuses of the yard, in which he did give me much light. So by water home.

2.   Up while the chimes went 4 – and put down my Journall; and

so to my office to read over such instruccions as concern the officers of the yards; for I am much upon seeing into the miscarriages there. By and by, by appointment comes Comissioner Pett and then a messenger from Mr. Coventry, who sits in his boat expecting us; and so we down to him at the Tower and there took water all, and to Deptford (he in our passage taking notice how much difference there is between the old Captains for obedience and order, and the King's new Captains, which I am very glad to hear him confess); and there we went into the Storehouse and viewd, first the provisions there and then his books (but Mr. Davis himself was not there, he having a kinswoman in the house dead; for which, when by and by I saw him, he doth trouble himself most ridiculously, as if there was never another woman in the world); in which so much lazinesse, as also in the Clerkes of the Cheque and Survey (which after one another we did examine), as that I do not perceive that there is one-third of their duties performed. But I perceive, to my great content, Mr. Coventry will have things reformed.

3.   Up by 4 a-clock and to my office till 8 o'clock, writing over two Copys of our contract with Sir Wm. Rider &c. for 500 ton of Hempe; which, because it is a secret, I have the trouble of writing over, as well as drawing. Then home to dress myself and so to the office – where another fray between Sir Rich: Ford and myself about his yarne. At noon, we all by invitation dined at the Dolphin with the Officers of the Ordinance; where Sir W. Compton and Mr. Oneale and other great persons were, and a very great dinner. But I drank, as I still do, but my allowance of wine. Then to my office all the afternoon, as long as I could see – about setting many businesses in order. In the evening came Mr. Lewes to me, and very ingeniously did inquire whether I did ever look into the business of the Chest at Chatham; and after my readiness to be informed did appear to him, he did produce a paper wherein he stated the government of the Chest to me; and upon the whole did tell me how it hath ever been abused, and to this day is, and what a meritorious act it would be to look after it; which I am resolved to do, if God bless me – and do thank him very much for it. So home; and after a turn or two upon the leads with my wife, who hath lately had but little of my company since I begun to fallow my business; but is contented therewith since she sees how I spend my time. And so to bed.

4. Up by 5 a-clock; and after my Journall put in order, to my office about my business, which I am resolved to fallow, for every day [I] see what ground I get by it. By and by comes Mr. Cooper, Mate of the *Royall Charles*, of whom I entend to learn Mathematiques; and so begin with him today, he being a very able man and no great matter, I suppose, will content him. After an hour's being with him at Arithmetique, my first attempt being to learn the Multiplicacion table, then we parted till tomorrow: and so to my business at my office again – till noon; about which time Sir W. Warren did come to me about business and did begin to instruct me in the nature of Firre, timber and deals, telling me the nature of every sort; and from that, we fall to discourse of Sir W. Batten's corruption and the people that he imploys, and from one discourse to another of that kind; I was much pleased with his company and so stayed talking with him alone at my office till 4 in the afternoon, without eating or drinking all day; and then parted and I home to eat a bit, and so back again to my office.

6. *Lords day*. Lay long in bed today with my wife, merry and pleasant. And then rose and settled my accounts with my wife for housekeeping, and do see that my kitchen, besides wine, fire, candle, soap, and many other things, comes to about 30s. a week or a little over. To church, where Mr. Mills made a lazy sermon; so home to dinner, where my brother Tom dined with me. And so my wife and I to church again in the afternoon. And that done, I walked to the Wardrobe and spent my time with Mr. Creede and Mr. Moore, talking about business; so up to supper with my Lady – who tells me with much trouble that my Lady Castlemayne is still as great with the King and that the King comes often to her as ever he did. At which, God forgive me, I am well pleased. It begun to rain, and so I borrowed a hat and cloak of Mr. Moore and walked home, where I found Capt. Ferrer with my wife; and after spending a matter of an hour with him, he went home and we all to bed.

7. My morning's work at the office was to put the new books of my office into order and writing on the backsides what books they be and transferring out of some old books some things into them.

9. To my business till night; then Mr. Cooper and I to our business, and then came Mr. Mills the Minister to see me – which he

hath but rarely done to me, though every day almost to others of us; but he is a cunning fellow and knows where the good victualls is and the good drink, at Sir W. Batten. However, I used him civilly, though I love him as I do the rest of his coat. So to supper and to bed.

11.    Up by 4 a-clock, and hard at my multiplicacion table, which I am now almost maister of. And so made me ready and to my office – where by and by comes Mr. Pett and then a messenger from Mr. Coventry, who stays in his boat at the Tower for us; so we to him and down to Deptford first and there viewed some Deales, lately served in at a low price; which our officers, like knaves, would undervalue in their worth – but we find them good. Then to Woolwich and viewed well all the houses and stores there, which lie in very great confusion for want of storehouses. And then to Mr. Ackworths and Sheldens to view their books – which we find not to answer the King's service and security at all, as to the stores. Then to the Ropeyard and there viewed the hemp, wherein we find great corruption. And then saw a trial between Sir R. Fords yarn and our own, and find great oddes. So by water back again, about 5 in the afternoon, to Whitehall, and so to St. James's and at Mr. Coventrys chamber, which is very neat and fine, we had a pretty neat dinner; and after dinner fell to discourse of business and regulation and do think of many things that will put matters into better order.

12.    Up by 5 a-clock – and put things in my house in order, to be laid up against my workmen come on Monday to take down the top of my house – which trouble I must go through now, but it troubles me much to think of it. So to my office – where till noon we sat; and then I to dinner and to the office all the afternoon, with much business. At night with Cooper at Arithmetique; and then came Mr. Creede about my Lord's accounts, to even them; and he gone, I to supper and to bed.

16.    This day I was told that my Lady Castlemayne (being quite fallen out with her husband) did yesterday go away from him with all her plate, Jewells and other best things; and is gone to Richmond to a brother of hers; which I am apt to think was a design to get out of town, that the King might come at her the better. But strange it is, how for her beauty I am willing to conster all this to the best and

to pity her wherein it is to her hurt, though I know well enough she is a whore.

17.  To my office; and by and by to our sitting – where much business. Mr. Coventry took his leave, being to go with the Duke over for the Queene-Mother. I dined at home and so to my Lord's, where I presented him with a true state of all his accounts to last Monday, being the 14 of July – which did please him; and to my great joy, I continue in his great esteem and opinion. I this day took a general acquittance from my Lord to the same day – so that now I have but very few persons to deal withal for money in the world. Home, and find much business to lie upon my hand; and was late at the office, writing letters by candlelight, which is rare at this time of the year. But I do it with much content and joy, and then I do please me to see that I begin to have people direct themselfs to me in all businesses.

18.  Up very early and got a-top of my house, seeing the design of my work; and like it very well, and it comes into my head to have my dining-[room] wainscoated, which will be very pretty. By and by, by water to Deptford to put several things in order, being myself now only left in town; and so back again to the office and there doing business all the morning and the afternoon also, till night, and then came Cooper for my Mathematiques; but in good earnest, my head is so full of business that I cannot understand it as otherwise I should do. At night to bed, being much troubled at the rain coming into my house, the top being open.

20.  *Lords day.* My wife and I went into the office and there measured a silk flag that I have found there, and hope to get it to myself, for it hath not been demanded since I came to the office. But my wife is not hasty to have it, but rather to stay a while longer and see the event, whether it will be missed or no.

21.  To Woolwich to the Ropeyard; and there looked over the several sorts of hemp, and did fall upon my great survey of seeing the working and experiments of the strength and the charge in the dressing of every sort; and I do think have brought it to so great a certainty as I have done the King great service in it. And do purpose to get it ready against the Dukes coming to towne, to present to him. I breakfasted at Mr. Falconer's well, and much pleased with

my inquiries. Thence to the Dock, where we walked in Mr. Sheldens garden, eating more fruit and drinking and eating figs, which were very good, and talking, while the *Royall James* was bringing towards the docke; and then we went out and saw the manner and trouble of dockeing such a ship; which yet they could not do, but only brought her head into the docke and so shored her up till next tide. But, good God, what a deal of company was there from both yards to help to do it, when half the company would have done it as well; but I see it is impossible for the King to have things done as cheap as other men.

25.    At my office all the morning, reading Mr. Holland's discourse of the Navy, lent me by Mr. Turner; and am much pleased with them, they hitting the very diseases of the Navy which we are troubled with nowadays. I shall bestow writing of them over and much reading thereof. This morning Sir W. Batten came in to the office and desired to speak with me. He begun with telling me that he observed a strangeness between him and me of late, and would know the reason of it – telling me that he heard I was offended with merchants coming to his house and making contracts there. I did tell him that as a friend I have spoke of it to Sir W. Pen and desired him to take a time to tell him of it, and not as a backbiter; with which he was satisfied. at last, he desired the difference between our wifes might not make a difference between us; which I was exceeding glad to hear, and do see every day the fruits of looking after my business, which I pray God continue me in – for I do begin to be very happy.

27.    *Lords day*. At church, alone in the pew, in the morning. In the afternoon, by water I carried my wife to Westminster; where she went to take leave of her father and I to walk in the parke, which is now every day more and more pleasant, by the new works upon it. Here meeting with Laud Crispe, I took him to the further end and sot under a tree in the corner and there sung some songs; he singing well, but no skill and so would sing false sometimes.

28.    Up early; and by 6 a-clock after my wife was ready, I walked with her to the George and at Holborne conduict, where the Coach stood to carry her and her maid to Bugden; but that not being ready, my brother Tom stayed with them to see them gone; and so I took a troubled, though willing, godbwy, because of the bad

condition of my house to have a family in it. So home all alone to dinner, and then to the office again, and in the evening Cooper comes; and he being gone, to my chamber a little troubled and melancholy; to my lute late, and so to bed – Will lying there at my feet, and the wench in my house in Will's bed.

30. Up early and to my office; where Cooper came to me and begun his lecture upon the body of a ship – which my having of a modell in the office is of great use to me, and very pleasant and useful it is.

31. Up early and among my workmen and ordering my roomes above – which will please me very well. So to my office. And then we sat all the morning, where I begin more and more to grow considerable there. At noon, Mr. Coventry and I by his coach to the Exchange together and in Lumbard streete met Capt. Browne of the *Rosebush*; at which he was cruel angry and did threaten to go today to the Duke at Hampton Court and get him turned out because he was not sailed. But at the Exchange we resolved of eating a bit together, which we did at the Shipp, behind the exchange; and so took boat at Billingsgate, and went down on board the *Rosebush* at Woolwich and find all things out of order; but after frighting the officers there, we left them, to make more haste; and so on shore to the yard and did the same to the officers of the yard, that the ship was not despatched. Here we find Sir W. Batten going about his Survey; but so poorly and unlike a survey of the Navy, that I am ashamed of it and so is Mr. Coventry. We found fault with many things; and among others, the measure of some timber now serving in, which Mr. Day the assistant told us of. And so by water home again, all the way talking of the office business and other very pleasant discourse, and much proud I am of getting thus far into his books – which I think I am very much in. So home late; and it being the last day of the month, I did make up my accounts before I went to bed, and find myself worth about 650*l*, for which the Lord God be praised. And so to bed. I drank but two glasses of wine this day, and yet it makes my head ake all night, and indisposed me all the next day – of which I am glad.

I am now in town only with my man Will and Jane; and because my house is in building, I do lie at Sir W. Pen's house, he being gone to Ireland. My wife, her maid and boy gone to Brampton. I am very well entered into the business and esteem of the office, and do ply it close and find benefit by it.

# ✤AUGUST✤

1. God forgive me, I was sorry to hear that Sir W. Pens maid Betty was gone away yesterday, for I was in hopes to have had a bout with her before she had gone, she being very pretty. I have also a mind to my own wench, but I dare not, for fear she should prove honest and refuse and then tell my wife.

6. At night, writing in my Study, a mouse run over my table, which I shut up fast under my shelfe's upon my table till tomorrow. And so home and to bed.

7. Up by 4 a-clock and to my office; and by and by Mr. Cooper comes and to our modell – which pleases me more and more. At this till 8 a-clock, and so we sat in the office and stayed all the morning, my interest still growing, for which God be praised. This morning I got unexpectedly the *Reserve* for Mr. Cooper to be Maister of, which was only by taking an opportune time to motion, which is one good effect of my being constant at the office; that nothing passes without me, and I have the choice of my own times to propose anything I would have. Dined at home and to the office again at my business all the afternoon till night, and so to supper and to bed – it being become a pleasure to me nowadays to fallow my business, and the greatest part of it may be imputed to my drinking no wine and going to no plays.

8. Up by 4 a-clock in the morning and at 5 by water to Woolwich, there to see the manner of Tarring; and all the morning looking to see the several proceedings in making of Cordage and other things relating to that sort of works, much to my satisfaccion. At noon came Mr. Coventree on purpose from Hampton Court to see the same. And dined with Mr. Falconer; and after dinner, to several experiments of Hempe and perticularly some Millan hemp that is brought over ready-dressed. Thence we walked, talking, very good discourse all the way to Greenwich; and I do find most excellent discourse from him. Among other things, his rule of

suspecting every man that proposes anything to him to be a knave, or at least to have some ends of his own in it. Another rule is a proverb that he that cannot say no (that is, that is of so good a nature that he hath, cannot deny anything or cross another in doing anything) is not fit for business. The last of which is a very great fault of mine, which I must amend in. Thence by boat. And it being rough, he told me the passage of a Frenchman through London bridge; where when he saw the great fall, he begun to cross himself and say his prayers in the greatest fear in the world; and as soon as he was over, he swore *"Morbleu c'est le plus grand plaisir du mond"* – being the most like a French humour in the world. To Deptford and there surprized the yard and called them to a muster, and discovered many abuses, which we shall be able to understand hereafter and amend. Thence walked to Redriffe and so to London bridge, where I parted with him. And walked home. And did a little business, and to supper and to bed.

13.    Up earely and to my office – where people came to me about business, and by and by we met on purpose to inquire into the business of the Flaggmakers, where I am the person that doth chiefly manage the business against them on the King's part; and I do find it the greatest cheat that I have yet found – they having 8*d*. per yard allowed them by pretence of a contract, when no such thing appears; and it is 3*d*. more then was formerly paid and then I now offer the Board to have them done.

14.    Up early and to look over my works, and find my house to go on apace. So to my office to prepare business; and then we met and sat till noon. And then Comissioner Pett and I being invited, went by Sir John Winter's coach, sent for us, to the Miter in Fanchurch street – to a venison-pasty; where I find him a very worthy man and good discourse – most of which was concerning the Forrest of Deane and the timber there and Iron workes, with their great antiquity and the vast heaps of cinders which they find, and are now of great value, being necessary for the making of Iron at this day and without which they cannot work. Thence to my office about business till late, and so home and to bed.

17.    *Lords day.* Up very earely, this being the last Sunday that the Presbyterians are to preach, unless they read the new Comon

Prayer and renounce the Covenant,[1] and so I had a mind to hear Dr. Bates's farewell sermon, and walked to St. Dunstans, where, it being not 7 a-clock yet, the doors were not open; and so I went and walked an hour in the Temple garden, reading my vows; which it is a great content to me to see how I am a changed man, in all respects for the better, since I took them – which the God of Heaven continue to me and make me thankful for. At 8 a-clock I went and crowded in at a back door among others, and the church being half-full almost before any doors were open publicly. And so got into the Gallry besides the pulpit and heard very well. His text was, "Now the god of peace" – the last *Hebrews* and the 20 verse – he making a very good sermon and very little reflections in it to anything of the times. Besides the sermon, I was very well pleased with the sight of a fine lady that I have often seen walk in Grayes Inn walks. After dinner to St. Dunstan's again, and the church quite crouded before I came, which was just at one a-clock; but I got into the gallery again, but stood in a crowd and did exceedingly sweat all the while. He pursued his text again very well, and only at the conclusion told us after this manner – "I do believe that many of you do expect that I should say something to you in reference to the time, this being the last time that possibly I may appear here. You know it is not my manner to speak anything in the pulpit that is extraneous to my text and business. Yet this I shall say, that it is not my opinion, faction, or humour that keeps me from complying with what is required of us, but something which after much prayer, discourse and study yet remains unsatisfied and commands me herein. Wherefore, if it is my unhappinesse not to receive such an illuminacion as should direct me to do otherwise, I know no reason why men should not pardon me in this world, and am confident that God will pardon me for it in the next." And so he concluded. I hear most of the Presbyters took their leaves today. And the City is much dissatisfied with it. I pray God keep peace among us and make the Bishops careful of bringing in good men in their room, or else all will fly a-pieces; for bad ones will not down with the City.

1. According to the terms of the Act of Uniformity passed in May. As a result about a thousand parsons were extruded from their livings, fifty or so in London and Westminster alone. The Covenant (1643) was an attempt to impose Presbyterianism on the Church of England as the price of Scottish help to Parliament in the Civil War.

20. Up earely and to my office. And thence to my Lord Sandwich, who I find in bed and he sent for me in; and among other talk, doth tell me that he hath put me into commission with a great many great persons in the business of Tanger,[1] which is a very great Honour to me and may be of good concernment to me. By and by comes in Mr. Coventry to us, who my Lord tells that he is also put into the commission, and that I am there; of which he said he was glad and did tell my Lord that I was endeed the life of this office, and much more to my commendation, beyond measure. And that whereas before he did bear me respect for his sake, he doth do it now much more for my own – which is a great blessing to me – Sir G. Carteret having told me what he did yesterday concerning his speaking to my Lord Chancellor about me. So that on all hands, by God's blessing, I find myself a very rising man. By and by comes my Lord Peterborow in, with whom we talked a good while, and he is going tomorrow towards Tanger again. I perceive there is yet little hopes of peace with Guyland, which is of great concernment to Tanger. And many other things I heard which yet I understand not, and so cannot remember. In the evening Mr. Hayward came to me to advise with him about the business of the Chest, which I have now a mind to put in practice, though I know it will vex Sir Wm. Batten – which is one of the ends, God forgive me, that I have in it. So home and eat a bit, and to bed.

22. About 3 a-clock this morning I waked with the noise of the rayne, having never in my life heard a more violent shower. And then the Catt was locked in the chamber and keeped a great mewing, and leapt upon the bed, which made me I could not sleep a great while. Then to sleep, and about 5 a-clock rose and up to my office. And about 8 a-clock went down to Deptford and there with Mr. Davis did look over most of his stores; by the same token, in the great storehouse, while Capt. Badily was talking to us, one from a trap-doore above let fall unawares a coyle of cable, that it was 10000 to one it had not broke Capt. Bodily's neck, it came so near him – but did him no hurt. I went on with looking and informing myself of the Stores, with great delight; and having done there, I took boat home again and dined. And after dinner sent for some of my workmen and did scold at them, so as I hope my work will be hastened.

1. See above, p. 158 (30 September) & n.

23. Up earely and about my works in my house to see what is done and design more. Then to my office; and by and by we sat till noon at the office. Mr. Creede by appointment being come, he and I went out together, and at an ordinary in Lumbardstreete dined together; and so walked down to the Styllyard and so all along Thames streete, but could not get a boat: I offered 8*s.* for a boat to attend me this afternoon and they would not, it being the day of the Queenes coming to town from Hampton Court. So we fairly walked it to Whitehall; and through my Lord's lodgings we got into Whitehall garden, and so to the bowling-greene and up to the top of the new banqueting-house* there over the Thames, which was a most pleasant place as any I could have got. And all the show consisted chiefly in the number of boats and barges – and two Pageants, one of a King and another of a Queene, with her maydes of honour sitting at her feet very prettily. Anon came the King and and Queene in a barge under a Canopy, with 10000 barges and boats I think, for we could see no water for them – nor discern the King nor Queen. And so they landed at Whitehall bridge, and the great guns on the other side went off. But that which pleased me best was that my Lady Castlemayne stood over against us upon a piece of Whitehall – where I glutted myself with looking on her. But methought it was strange to see her Lord and her upon the same place, walking up and down without taking notice one of another; only, at first entry, he put off his hat and she made him a very civil salute – but afterwards took no notice one of another. But both of them now and then would take their child, which the nurse held in her armes, and dandle it. One thing more; there happend a scaffold below to fall, and we feared some hurt but there was none; but she, of all the great ladies only, run down among the common rabble to see what hurt was done, and did take care of a child that received some little hurt; which methought was so noble. Anon there came one there, booted and spurred, that she talked long with. And by and by, she being in her haire, she put on his hat, which was but an ordinary one, to keep the wind off. But methought it became her mightily, as everything else do.

29. To my office, and among other businesses, did begin with Mr. Lewes to look into the nature of a pursers account and the business of victualling; in which there is great variety, but I find I shall understand it and be able to do service there also.

31. *Lords day.* To my office and there made my monthly [balance], and find myself worth in money about 686*l* 19*s*. 02½*d*. for which God be praised. And endeed, greatly I ought to thank Almighty God, who doth most manifestly bless me in my endeavours to do the duty of my office – I now saving money and my expenses being very little. My wife is still in the country. My house all in dirt, but my work in a good forwardness and will be much to my mind at last.

## –❧SEPTEMBER❧–

3. Up betimes; but now the days begin to shorten and so whereas I used to rise by 4 a-clock, it is not broad daylight now till after 5 a-clock, so that it is 5 before I do rise. To my office; and about 8 a-clock I went over to Redriffe and walked to Deptford, where I find Mr. Coventry and Sir W. Pen beginning the pay – it being my desire to be there today, because it is the first pay that Mr. Coventry hath been at and I would be thought to be as much with Mr. Coventry as I can. Here we stayed till noon, and by the time paid off the *Breda*; and then to dinner at the Taverne, where I have obtained that our commons is not so large as they used to be, which I am glad to see. After dinner, by water to the office; and there we met and sold the *Weymouth*, *Successe*, and *Fellowship* Hulke. Where pleasant to see how backward men are at first to bid; and yet when the candle is going out, how they bawl and dispute afterward who bid the most first. And here I observed one man cunninger then the rest, that was sure to bid the last man and to carry it; and enquiring the reason, he told me that just as the flame goes out the smoke descends, which is a thing I never observed before, and by that he doth know the instant to bid last – which is very pretty. In our discourse in the boat, Mr. Coventry told us how the Fanatiques and the Presbyters that did entend to rise about this times did choose this day as the most auspicious to them in their endeavours against monarchy – it being fatal twice to the King,[1] and the day of Olivers death. But blessed be God, all is likely to be quiet I hope.

5. To Mr. Bland's the merchant, by invitation (I alone of all our

1. At the battles of Dunbar (1650) and Worcester (1651).

company of this office), where I find all the officers of the Customes; very grave fine gentlemen, and I am very glad to know them; *viz*. Sir Job Harvy, Sir John Wostenham, Sir John Jacob, Sir Nicho. Crisp, Sir John Harrison and Sir John Shaw – very good company. And among other pretty discourse, some was of Sir Jerom Bowes, Embassador from Queene Elizabeth to the Emperor of Russia – who, because some of the noblemen there would go up the stairs to the Emperor before him, he would not go up till the Emperor had ordered those two men to be dragged downstair, with their heads knocking upon every stair till they were killed. And when he was come up, they demanded his sword of him before he entered the room; he told them, if they would have his sword, they should have his boots too; and so caused his boots to be pulled off and his night-gown and night-cap and slippers to be sent for, and made the Emperor stay till he could go in his night-dress, since he might not go as a soldier. And lastly, when the Emperor in contempt, to show his command over his subjects, did command one to leap from the window down and broke his neck in the sight of our Embassador, he replied that his mistress did set more by and did make better use of the necks of her subjects: but said that to show what her subjects would do for her, he would, and did, fling down his gantlett before the Emperor and challenged all the nobility there to take it up in defence of the Emperor against his Queene. For which, at this very day, the name of Sir Jer. Bowes is famous and honoured there.

7. *Lords day*. To Whitehall Chappell, where I heard a good sermon of the Deane of Elys upon Returning to the old wayes – and a most excellent Anthem (with Symphony's between) sung by Capt. Cooke. Then home with Mr. Fox and his lady and there dined with them, where much company came to them. Most of our discourse was what Ministers are flung out that will not conform. And the care of the Bishop of London that we are here supplied with very good men. Meeting Mr. Pierce the Chyrurgeon, he took me into Somersett house and there carried me into the Queene-Mother's presence-chamber, where she was, with our own Queene sitting on her left hand (whom I did never see before; and though she be not very charming, yet she hath a good modest and innocent look which is pleasing): here I also saw Madam Castlemayne and, which pleased me most, Mr.

Crofts[1] the King's bastard, a most pretty sparke of about 15 year old; who I perceive doth hang much upon my Lady Castlemayne and is alway with her. And I hear the Queenes, both of them, are mighty kind to him. By and by, in comes the King, and anon the Duke and his Duchesse; so that, they being all together, was such a sight as I could never almost have happened to see with so much ease and leisure.

8. Up betimes and to my office, preparing an account to give the Duke this morning of what we have of late done at the office. About 7 a-clock I went forth, thinking to go along with Sir John Minnes and the rest, and I find them gone, which did vex me; so I went directly to the old Swan and took boat before them and to Sir G. Carteret's lodgings at Whitehall; and there staying till he was dressed, talking with him, he and I to St. James's, where Sir Wms both and Sir John were come; and so up with Mr. Coventry to the Duke, who after he was out of his bed, did send for us in; and when he was quite ready, took us into his closet and there told us that he doth entend to renew the old custom for the Admiralls* to have their principal officers to meet them once a week to give them an account what they have done that week, which I am glad of; and so the rest did tell his Royal Highness that I could do it best for the time past, and so I produced my short notes and did give him an account of all that we have of late done and proposed to him several things for his commands; which he did give us and so dismiss us.

12. At my office all the morning – Mr. Lewes teaching me to understand the method of making up pursers accounts, which is very needful for me and very hard. Dined at home, all in dirt and my mind weary of being thus out of order; but I hope in God it will away, but for the present I am very melancholy, as I have been a great while. All the afternoon, till 9 at night, at my office; and then home and eat an egge or two, and so to my lodgings. And to bed.

14. *Lords day.* Sir George told me of a Chest of Drawers that was given Sir W. Batten by Hughes the Ropemaker, whom he hath since put out of his employment, and now the fellow doth cry out upon Sir Wm. for his Cabinet.

1. Created Duke of Monmouth, 14 February 1663, but known by that title for some months before.

19. Up betimes and to my office; and at 9 a-clock (none of the rest going) I went alone to Deptford and there went on to pay Woolwich yard; and so at noon dined well, being chief at the table, and do not see but everybody begins to give me as much respect and honour as any of the rest. After dinner to pay again and so till 9 at night – my great trouble being that I was forced to begin an ill practice of bringing down the wages of servants, for which people did curse me; which I do not love. At night, after I had eaten a cold pullet, I walked by brave Mooneshine, with three or four armed [men] to guard me, to Redriffe – it being a joy to my heart to think of the condition that I am now in, that people should of themselfs provide this for me, unspoke to. I hear this walk is dangerous to walk alone by night, and much robbery committed here. So from thence by water home. And so to my lodgings to bed.

21. *Lords day.* Got up betimes and walked [towards] St. James's. The Queene coming by in her coach, going to her chapel at St. James's (the first time it hath been ready for her), I crowded after her; and got up to the room where her closet is and there stood and saw – the fine Alter, ornaments, and the fryers in their habits and the priests come in with their fine Copes. And many other very fine things. I heard their Musique too; which may be good, but it did not appear so to me, neither as to their manner of singing nor was it good Concord to my eares, whatever the matter was. The Queene very devoute. But what pleased me best was to see my dear Lady Castlemayne; who though a protestant, did wait upon the Queene to chapel. By and by, after masse was done, a Fryer with his Coole did rise up and preach a sermon in Portuges; which I not understanding, did go away.

23. Sir G. Carteret told me how in most *Cabaretts* in France they have writ upon the walls, in fair letters to be read, *Dieu te regarde*, as a good lesson to be in every man's mind. And have also, as in Holland, their poor's box; in both which places, at the making all contracts and bargains they give so much, which they call God's penny.

27. Up betimes and among my workmen, and with great pleasure see the posts in my entry taken down, beyond expectation; so that now, the boy's room being laid into the entry doth make my coming in very handsome, which was the only fault remaining

almost in my house. We sat all the morning. And in the afternoon I got many jobbs done to my mind, and my wife's chamber put into a good readiness against her coming – which she did at night, for Will did, by my leave to go, meet her upon the road and at night did bring me word she was come to my brother's by my order. So I made myself ready and put things at home in order, and so went thither to her. Being come, I find her and her maid and dog very well – and herself grown a little fatter then she was. I was very well pleased to see her; and after supper, to bed and had her company with great content – and much mutual love. Only, I do perceive that there hath been fallings-out between my mother and she, and a little between my father and she; but I hope all is well again. And I perceive she likes Brampton house and seat better then ever I did myself. And tells me how my Lord hath drawn a plot of some alterations to be made there, and hath brought it up, which I saw and like well. I perceive my Lord and Lady have been very kind to her. And Capt. Ferrers, so kind that I perceive [I] have some jealousy of him; but I know what is the Captain's manner of carriage, and therefore it is nothing to me.

29. *Michaelmas day*. This day my oaths for drinking of wine and going to plays are out, and so I do resolve to take a liberty today and then to fall to them again. Up and by coach to Whitehall, in my way taking up Mr. Moore and walked with him, talking a good while about business in St. James's parke. And there left him and to Mr. Coventry's, and so with him and Sir W. Penn up to the Duke; where the King came also and stayed till the Duke was ready. To Toms, and there taking up my wife, maid, dog and him, did carry them home – where my wife is much pleased with my house, and so am I fully. I sent for some dinner and there dined (Mrs. Margt Pen being by, to whom I had spoke to go along with us to a play this afternoon) and then to the King's Theatre, where we saw *Midsummers nights dreame*, which I have never seen before, nor shall ever again, for it is the most insipid ridiculous play that ever I saw in my life. I saw, I confess, some good dancing and some handsome women, which was all my pleasure.

30. Strange to see how easily my mind doth revert to its former practice of loving plays and wine, having given myself a liberty to them both these two days; but this night I have again bound myself to Christmas next, in which I desire God to bless me and preserve

me, for under God I find it to be the best course that ever I could take to bring myself to mind my business. I have also made up this evening my monthly ballance; and find that notwithstanding the loss of 30*l* to be paid to the Loyall and necessitous Cavaliers by act of Parliament, yet I am worth about 680*l* – for which the Lord God be praised. My condition at present is this. I have long been building; and my house, to my great content, is now almost done; but yet not so but that I shall have dirt, which troubles me too – for my wife hath been in the country at Brampton these two months, and is now come home a week or two before the house is ready for her. My mind is somewhat troubled about my best chamber, which I Question whether I shall be able to keep or no. I am also troubled for my journy which I must needs take suddenly to the Court at Brampton, but most of all for that I am not provided to understand my business, having not minded it a great while; and at the best shall be able but to make a bad matter of it. But God, I hope, will guide all to the best, and I am resolved tomorrow to fall hard to it: I pray God bless me therein, for my father and mother and all our well-doings do depend upon my care therein.

Things are all quiet, but the King poor and no hopes almost of his being otherwise, by which things will go to wrack, especially in the Navy. The late outing of the presbyter Clergy, by their not renouncing the Covenant as the act [of] Parliament commands, is the greatest piece of state now in discourse. But for aught I see, they are gone out very peaceably and the people not so much concerned therein as was expected. My brother Tom is gone out of town this day to make a second journey to his mistress at Banbury – of which I have good expectations – and pray God to bless him therein. My mind, I hope, is settled to fallow my business again, for I find that two days' neglect of business doth give me more discontent in mind then ten times the pleasure thereof can repair again, be it what it will.

# –❧OCTOBER❧–

4. To my office in the morning after I was up (my wife beginning to make me lie long a-mornings), where we sat till noon. And then dined at home; and after a little with my workmen, to my office till 9 at night. Among other things, examining the perticulars of the

miscarriage of the *Satisfaccion*, sunk the other day on the Duch coast through the negligence of the pilott.

5. *Lords day*. Lay long in bed, talking with my wife; and among other things, fell out about my mayde Sarah, which my wife would fain put away, when I think her as good a servant as ever came into a house, but it seems my wife would have one that could dress a head well. But we were friends at last. I to church; and this day the parson hath got one to read with a surplice on; I suppose himself will take it up hereafter – for a cunning fellow he is as any of his coate. Dined with my wife; and then to talk again above, chiefly about her learning to dance, against her going next year into the country; which I am willing she shall do.

17. To my Lord Sandwich by water and told him how well things did go in the country with me,[1] of which he was very glad, and seems to concern himself much for me. Thence with Mr. Creede to Westminster hall, and by and by thither comes Capt. Ferrer, upon my sending for him; and we three to Creedes chamber and there sat a good while and drank Chocolate. Here I am told how things go at Court; that the young men get uppermost, and the old serious lords are out of favour. That Sir H. Bennet being brought into Sir Edwd. Nicholas place, Sir Ch. Barkely is made Privy purse – a most vicious person, and one whom Mr. Pierce the surgeon today (at which I laugh to myself) did tell me that he offered his wife 300*l* per annum to be his whore. He also told me that none in Court hath more the King's eare now then Sir Ch. Barkely and Sir H. Bennet and my Lady Castlemayne, whose interest is now as great as ever. And that Mrs. Haslerigge, the great beauty, is got with child and now brought to bed, and lays it to the King or the Duke of York. He tells me too, that my Lord St Albans is like to be Lord Treasurer; all which things do trouble me much.

19. *Lords day*. I am sorry to hear that the news of the selling of Dunkirke[2] is taken so generally ill, as I find it is among the merchants; and other things, as removal of officers at Court, good

---

1. Pepys had recently visited Brampton where the court of the manor rejected his Uncle Thomas's claim to the Brampton part of Robert Pepys's estate. Cf. above, pp. 144–5 (8–13 July).
2. Acquired from Spain in 1658 and now sold to France.

for worse; and all things else made much worse in their report among people then they are. And this night, I know not upon what ground, the gates of the City ordered to be kept shut and double guards everywhere. So home; and after preparing things against tomorrow for the Duke, to bed. Endeed, I do find everybody's spirit very full of trouble and the things of the Court and Council very ill taken – so as to be apt to appear in bad colours if there should ever be a beginning of trouble – which God forbid.

20. With Comissioner Pett to Mr. Lillys the great painter, who came forth to us; but believing that I came to bespeak a picture, he prevented us by telling us that he should not be at leisure these three weeks, which methinks is a rare thing; and then to see in what pomp his table was laid for himself to go to dinner. And here among other pictures, I saw the so much by me desired picture of my Lady Castlemayne, which is a most blessed picture and that that I must have a copy of.

24. After with great pleasure lying a great while, talking and sporting in bed with my wife (for we have [been] for some years now, and at present more and more, a very happy couple, blessed be God), I got up and to my office; and having done there some business, and by water and then walked to Deptford to discourse with Mr. Cowly and Davis about my late conceptions about keeping books of the distinct works done in the yards, against which I find no objection but their ignorance and unwillingness to do anything of pains and what is out of their old dull road. But I like it well, and will proceed in it. So home and dined there with my wife upon a most excellent dish of tripes of my own directing, covered with mustard, as I have heretofore seen them done at my Lord Crews; of which I made a very great meal and sent for a glass of wine for myself. This noon came to see me and sit with me a little after dinner, Mr. Pierce the Chyrurgeon – who tells me how ill things go at Court; that the King doth show no countenance to any [that] belong to the Queene, nor above all to such english as she brought over with her or hath here since, for fear they should tell her how he carries himself to Mrs. Palmer.

26. *Lords day.* Up, and put on my new Scallop, and is very fine. To church and there saw, the first time, Mr. Mills in a Surplice; but it seemed absurd for him to pull it over his eares in the reading-pew

after he had done before all the church, to go up to the pulpitt to preach without it. Home and dined; and Mr. Sympson, my Joyner that doth my dining-room, and my brother Tom with me to a delicate fat pig. Then to church again and heard a simple Scott preach most tediously. So home and then to see Sir W. Batten, who is pretty well again; and then to my uncle Wights to show my fine band and to see Mrs. Margtt Wight, but she was not there. All this day, soldiers going up and down the towne, there being an alarme and many Quakers and others clapped up; but I believe without any reason. Only, they say in Dorsettshire there hath been some rising discovered. So after supper home and then to my study; and making up my monthly account to myself, I find myself, by my expense in bands and clothes this month, abated a little of my last, and that I am worth 679*l* still; for which God be praised. So home and to bed, with quiet mind, blessed be God, but afeared of my candle's going out, which makes me write thus slubberingly.

27. To my Lord Sandwich, who nowadays calls me into his chamber, and alone did discourse with me about the jealousys that the Court hath of people's rising; wherein he doth much dislike my Lord Monkes being so eagre against a company of poor wretches, dragging them up and down the street: but would have him rather to take some of the greatest ringleaders of them and punish them; whereas this doth but tell the world the King's fears and doubts. Thence to Westminster hall and walked there long with Mr. Creede; and then to the great half-Crowne ordinary at the King's head near Charing Crosse, where we had a most excellent neat dinner and very high company, and in a noble manner. After dinner he and I into another room over a pot of ale and talked. He showed me[1] our commission, wherein the Duke of Yorke – Prince Robt., Duke of Albemarle, Lord Peterburgh, Lord Sandwich, Sir G. Carteret, Sir Wm. Compton, Mr. Coventry, Sir R. Ford, Sir Wm. Rider, Mr. Cholmly, Mr. Povy, myself, and Capt. Cuttance, in this order, are joyned for the carrying on the service of Tanger – which I take for a great honour to me. He told me what great faction there is at Court. And above all, what is whispered, that young Crofts is lawful son to the King, the King being married to his mother. How true this is, God knows. But I believe the Duke of Yorke will not be fooled in this of three crowns. Thence to

1. Pepys remained a member of the committee until 1679 and served as its Treasurer from March 1665.

Whitehall and walked long in the galleries till (as they are commanded to all strange persons) one came to tell us, we not being known and being observed to walk there four or five houres (which was not true), he was commanded to ask who we were; which being told, he excused his Question and was satisfied. These things speak great fear and jealousys. So walk to the Exchange and there took many turnes with him. Among other things, observing one very pretty Exchange lass with her face full of black patches, which was a strange sight. So bid him good-night.

29.  *Lord Mayors day.* Entended to have made me fine and by invitation to have dined with my Lord Mayor today; but going to see Sir Wm. Batten this morning, I find Sir G. Carteret and Sir J. Mennes going with Sir W. Batten and myself to examine Sir G. Carteret's accounts for the last year; whereupon I settled to it with them all the day long, only dinner time (which Sir George gave us); and by night did as good as finish them.

30.   This morning, walking with Mr. Coventry in the garden, he did tell me how Sir G. Carteret hath carried the business of the Victuallers money to be paid by himself, contrary to old practice; at which he is angry I perceive. And yet he did not deny Sir G. Carteret his due, in saying that he is a man that doth take the most pains and gives himself the most to do business of any man about the Court, without any desire of pleasure or divertisements – which is very true. But, which pleased me mightily, he said, in these words, that he was resolved, whatever it cost him, to make an experiment and see whether it was possible for a man to keep himself up in Court by dealing plainly and walking uprightly without any private game a-playing. In the doing whereof, if his ground doth slip from under him, he will be contented; but he is resolved to try and never to baulke taking notice of anything that is to the King's prejudice, let it fall where it will – which is a most brave resolution. I would not forget two passages of Sir J. Mennes at yesterday's dinner. The one, that to the Question how it comes to pass that there are no boars seen in London, but many Sowes and pigs, it was answered that the Constable gets them a-nights. The other, Tho. Killegrew's way of getting to see plays when he was a boy. He would go to the Red bull, and when the man cried to the boys, "Who will go and be a divell, and he shall see the play for nothing?" – then would he go in and be a devil upon the stage, and so got to see [the] play.

31.   Lay pretty long in bed; and then up and among my workmen – the Carpenters being this day laying of my floor in my dining-room, with whom I stayed a good while; and so to my office and did a little business, and so home to dinner; and after dinner, all the afternoon with my carpenters, making them lay all my boards but one in my dining-room this day, which I am confident they would have made two good days' work of if I had not been there. Thus ends this month. I and my family in good health, but weary heartily of dirt; but now in hopes within two or three weeks to be out of it. My head troubled with much business – my law businesses for Brampton make me mad almost, for that I want time to fallow them; but I must by no means neglect them. I thank God I do save money, though it be but a little; but I hope to find out some jobb or other that I may get a sum by to set me up. I thank God I have no crosses, but only much business to trouble my mind with. In all other things, as happy a man as any in the world, for the whole world seems to smile upon me; and if my house were done, that I could diligently fallow my business, I would not doubt to do God and the King, and myself, good service. And all I do impute almost wholly to my late temperance, since my making of my vowes against wine and plays, which keeps me most happily and contentfully to my business – which God continue. Public matters are full of discontent – what with the sale of Dunkirke – and my Lady Castlemayne and her faction at Court; though I know not what they would have, more then to debauch the King, whom God preserve from it.

## –❧NOVEMBER❧–

1.   Up, and after a little while with my workmen, I went to my office and then to our sitting all the morning. At noon with Mr. Creede, whom I find at my house, to the Trinity house to a great dinner there by invitation, and much company. It seem[s] one Capt. Evans makes his Elder Brother's dinner today. Among other discourses, one Mr. Oudant, Secretary to the late Princesse of Orange, did discourse of the convenience as to keeping the highways from being deep, by their horses in Holland (and Flanders, where the ground is as miry as ours is) going in their carts

and waggons, as ours in coaches.[1] Wishing the same here, as an expedient to make the ways better; and I think there is something in it, where there is breadth enough.

2. Lay long with pleasure, talking with my wife – in whom I never had greater content, blessed be God, then now; she continuing with the same care and thrift and innocence (so long as I keep her from occasions of being otherwise) as ever she was in her life, and keeps the house as well. To church, where Mills (after he had read the service and shifted himself as he did the last day) preached a very ordinary sermon. So home to dinner with my wife. Then up into my new rooms, which are almost finished, and there walked with great content, talking with my wife till church time, and then to church; and there being a lazy preacher, I sleep out the sermon and so home.

3. Pierce the Chyrurgeon tells me that my Lady Castlemayne is with child; but though it be the King's, yet her Lord being still in towne and sometime seeing of her, though never to eat or lie together, it will be laid to him. He tells me also how the Duke of York is smitten in love with my Lady Chesterfield (a virtuous lady, daughter of my Lord of Ormond); and so much, that the Duchesse of Yorke hath complained to the King and her father about it, and my Lady Chesterfield is gone into the country for it. At all which I am sorry; but it is the effect of idlenesse and having nothing else to imploy their great spirits upon.

5. Up and with my painters, painting my dining-room all day long till night, not stirring out at all. Only in the morning my Lady Batten did send to speak with me and told me very civilly that she did not desire, nor hoped I did, that anything should pass between us but what was civill, though there was not the neighbourliness between her and my wife that was fit to be; and so complained of my maid's mocking of her when she called "Nan" to her maid within her own house; my maid Jane in my yard overheard her and mocked her. And some other such-like things she told me, and of my wife's speaking unhandsomely of her; to all which I did give her a very respectful answer, such as did please her, and am sorry endeed that this should be, though I do not desire there should be

1. sc. abreast instead of in tandem.

any acquaintance between my wife and her. But I promised to avoid such words and passages for the future; so home. At night I called up my maids and schooled Jane; who did answer me so humbly and drolly about it, that though I seemed angry, I was much pleased with her, and wife also. So at night to bed.

10. To my Lord Crews. By and by came in great Mr. Swinfen, the parliament-man – who, among other discourse of the rise and fall of familys, told us of Bishop Bridgeman (brother of Sir Orlando) who lately hath bought a seat anciently of the Lever and then the Ashtons; and so he hath in his great hall window (having repaired and beautified the house) hath caused four great places to be left for Coates of armes. In one he hath put the Lever's, with this motto, *Olim*. In another the Ashton's, with this, *Heri*. In the next, his own, with this, *Hodie*. In the fourth, nothing but this motto, *Cras nescio cujus*. Thence towards my brother's; met with Jacke Cole in Fleete streete and he and I went into his Cosen Mary Coles (whom I never saw since she was married) and drank a pint of wine, and much good discourse. I find him a little conceited, but he hath good things in him and a man may know the temper of the City by him, he being of a general conversation and can tell how matters go; and upon that score, I will encourage his acquaintance.

12. At noon dined at home with my wife. And by and by, by my wife's appointment comes two young ladies, sisters, acquaintance of my wife's brother's, who are desirous to wait upon some ladies – and proffer their service to my wife. The youngest, endeed, hath a good voice and sings very well, besides other good Qualitys; but I fear hath been bred up with too great liberty for my family, and I fear great inconveniences of expenses and my wife's liberty will fallow, which I must study to avoide till I have a better purse – though I confess the gentlewoman being pretty handsome and singing makes me have a good mind to her. Anon I took them by coach and carried them to a friend's of theirs in Lincolnes Inne fields, and there I left them. Thence I walked home, calling a little in Paul's Churchyard; and I thank God, can read and never buy a book, though I have a great mind to it. From hence home to my office and there made an end, though late, of my colleccion of the prices of Masts for these twelve years to this day, in order to the buying of some of [Mr.] Wood. And I bound it up in painted paper, to lie by as a book for future use. So home and to supper and bed.

And a little before and after we were in bed, we had much talk and difference between us about my wife's having a woman; which I seemed much angry at that she should go so far in it without consideration and my being consulted with. So to sleep.

13.   Up – and begun our discontent again and sorely angered my wife; who endeed doth live very lonely. But I do perceive that it is want of work that doth make her and all other people think of ways of spending their time worse; and this I owe to my building, that doth not admit of her undertaking anything of work, because the house hath been and is still so dirty. To my office late. And this afternoon my wife in her discontent sent me a letter, which I am in a quandary what to do, whether to read it or not; but I purpose not, but to burn it before her face, that I may put a stop to more of this nature. But I must think of some way, either to find her somebody to keep her company, or to set her to work and by imployment to take up her thoughts and time. After doing what I had to do, I went home to supper. And there was very sullen to my wife, and so went to bed and to sleep (though with much ado, my mind being troubled) without speaking one word to her.

14.   She begun to talk in the morning and to be friends, believing all this while that I had read her letter, which I perceive by her discourse was full of good counsel and relating the reason of her desiring a Woman and how little charge she did entend it to be to me. So I begun and argued it so full and plain to her, and she to reason it highly to me to put her away and take one of the Bowyers if I did dislike her, that I did resolve, when the house is ready, she shall try her for a while.

22.   *Saturday.* This morning, from some difference between my wife and Sarah her maid, my wife and I fell out cruelly, to my great discontent. But I do see her set so against the wench, which I take to be a most extraordinary good servant, that I was forced for the wench's sake to bid her get her another place – which shall cost some trouble to my wife, however, before I suffer to be. This day I bought the book of country-dances against my wife's woman Gosnell comes, who dances finely. And meeting Mr. Playford, he did give me his Latin Songs of Mr. Deerings, which he lately printed. This day Mr. Moore told me that for certain the Queene Mother is married to my Lord St. Albans, and he is like to be made

Lord Treasurer.[1] News that Sir J. Lawson hath made up a peace now with Tunis and Tripoli as well as Argiers; by which he will come home very highly honoured.

24. Sir J. Mennes, Sir W. Batten and I going forth toward Whitehall, we hear that the King and the Duke are come this morning to the Tower to see the Dunkirke money. So we by coach to them and there went up and down all the Magazins with them. But methought it was but poor discourse and frothy that the King's companions (young Killigrew among the rest, about the codpieces on some of the men in armer there to be seen) had with him. We saw none of the money; but Mr. Slingsby did show the King and I did see the stamps of the new money that is now to be made by Blondeau's fashion, which are very neat and like the King. Thence the King to Woolwich, though a very cold day; and the Duke to Whitehall, commanding us to come after him, which we did by coach; and in his closet, my Lord Sandwich being there, did discourse with us about getting some of this money to pay off the Fleets and other matters.

25. Great talk among people how some of the fanatiques do say that the end of the world is at hand and that next Tuesday is to be the day – against which, whenever it shall be, good God fit us all.

27. At my waking, I find the tops of the houses covered with snow, which is a rare sight, that I have not seen these three years. Up, and put my people to perfect the cleaning of my house, and so to the office – where we sat all the morning till noon; and then we all went to the next house upon Tower hill to see the coming by of the Russia Embassador – for whose reception all the City trained bands do attend in the streets, and the King's Lifeguard, and most of the wealthy citizens in their black velvet coats and gold chains (which remain of their gallantry at the King's coming in); but they stayed so long that we went down again home to dinner. And after I had dined, I heard that they were coming, and so I walked to the Conduict in the *quarrefour* at the end of gracious street and cornhill; and there (the spouts thereof running, very near me, upon all the people that were under it) I saw them pretty well go by. I could not see the Embassador in his coach – but his attendants in their habitts

---

1. Neither rumour was true.

and fur caps very handsome comely men, and most of them with Hawkes upon their fists to present to the King. But Lord, to see the absurd nature of Englishmen, that cannot forbear laughing and jeering at everything that looks strange. So back and to the office; and there we met and sat till 7 a-clock, making a bargain with Mr. Wood for his Masts of New England.

30. *Lords day.* To church in the morning, and Mr. Mills made a pretty good sermon. It is a bitter cold frost today. Dined alone with my wife today with good content, my house being quite clean from Top to bottom. In the afternoon, I to the French church here in the City, and stood in the Isle all the sermon – with great delight hearing a very admirable sermon from a very young man, upon the Article in our creed (in order of Catechisme) upon the Resurreccion. Thence home and to visit Sir W. Pen. Here was Sir W. Batten and his Lady and Mrs. Turner; and I very merry, talking of the confidence of Sir Rd. Ford's new-married daughter; though she married so strangely lately, yet appears at church as briscke as can be and takes place of her elder sister, a maid. Thence home and to supper; and then, cold as it is, to my office to make up my monthly account; and I do find that through the fitting of my house this month, I have spent in that and Kitchin 50*l* this month. So that now I am worth but 660*l* or thereabouts. This being done I went home and to prayers and to bed. (This day I first did wear a muffe, being my wife's last year's muff; and now I have bought her a new one, this serves me very well.)

Thus ends this month, in great frost. Myself and family all well, but my mind much disordered about my Uncles law business,[1] being now in an order of being arbitrated between us, which I wish to God it were done. I am also somewhat uncertain what to think of my going about to take a woman-servant into my house in the Quality of a Woman for my wife. My wife promises it shall cost me nothing but her meat and wages, and that it shall not be attended with any other expenses; upon which termes I admit of it, for that it will I hope save me money in having my wife go abroad on visitts and other delights. So that I hope the best, but am resolved to alter it if matters prove otherwise then I would have them.

Public matters in an ill condition of discontent against the heighth and vanity of the Court and their bad payments; but that which

1. See above, p. 228 (17 October) & n. 1.

troubles most is the Clergy, which will never content the City, which is not to be reconciled to Bishopps; the more the pity that differences must still be. Dunkirke newly sold and the money brought over – of which we hope to get some to pay the Navy – which, by Sir J. Lawson's having dispatched the business in the Straights by making peace with Argier, Tunis and Tripoly, and so his fleet will also shortly come home, will now every day grow less, and so the King's charge be abated – which God send.

## –❧DECEMBER❧–

1. Up and by coach with Sir J. Mennes and Sir W. Batten to Whitehall to the Duke's chamber; where, as is usual, my Lord Sandwich and all us, after his being ready, to his closet and there discoursed of matters of the Navy. And here Mr. Coventry did do me the great kindness to take notice to the Duke of my pains in making a collection of all Contracts about Masts, which hath been of good use to us. Thence I to my Lord Sandwiches to Mr. Moore to talk a little about business; and then over the parke (where I first in my life, it being a great frost, did see people sliding with their Sckeates, which is a very pretty art) to Mr. Coventry's chamber to St. James's, where we all met to a venison pasty; and were here very merry. Here we stayed till 3 or 4 a-clock, and so to the Council chamber, where there met – the Duke of Yorke, Prince Robert, Duke of Albermarle, my Lord Sandwich, Sir Wm. Compton, Mr. Coventry, Sir J. Minnes, Sir R. Ford, Sir W. Rider, myselfe, and Capt. Cuttance, as Commissioners for Tanger. And after our Comission was read by Mr. Creede, who I perceive is to be our Secretary, we did fall to discourse of matters. As first, the supplying of them forthwith with victualls; then the Reducing it to make way for the money which upon their reduction is to go to the building of the molde. And so to other matters ordered against next meeting. This done, we broke up and I to the Cockepitt, with much crouding and waiting, where I saw *The Valiant Cidd* acted – a play I have read with great delight, but is a most dull thing acted (which I never understood before), there being no pleasure in it, though done by Baterton and my Ianthe and another fine wench that is come in the room of Roxalana. Nor did the King or Queene once smile all the whole play, nor any of the company seem to take any pleasure but

what was in the greatness and gallantry of the company. Thence to my Lord's; and Mr. Moore being in bed, I stayed not, but with a link walked home and got thither by 12 a-clock. Knocked up my boy and put myself to bed.

2. To the office, where we sat as Comissioners for the Chest, and so examined most of the old accomptants to the Chest about it; and so we broke up and I to my office till late, preparing business; and so home, being cold. And this night first put on a wastecoate. So to bed.

3. Called up by Comissioner Pett, and with him (by water much against my will) to Deptford; and after drinking a warm morning draught, with Mr. Wood and our officers measuring all the morning his New England Masts, with which sight I was much pleased for my information, though I perceive great neglect and indifference in all the King's officers in what they do for the King. That done, to the globe and there dined with Mr. Woode; and so by water with Mr. Pett home again, all the way reading his Chest accompts, in which I did see things did not please me; as, his allowing himself 300*l* for one year's looking to the business of the Chest and 150*l* per annum for the rest of the years. But I found no fault to him himself, but shall when they come to be read at the board. Home and did a little business; and so, taking Mr. Pett by the way, we walked to the Temple, in our way seeing one of the Russia Embassadors coaches go along, with his footmen not in liverys but their country habits; one of one colour and another of another, which was very strange.

5. I find Gosnell come, who my wife tells me is like to prove a pretty companion, of which I am glad. So to my office for a little business and then home in the evening, to entertain myself a little with my wife and her – who sings exceeding well, and I shall take great delight in her. And so merrily to bed.

6. Up, and to the office and there sat all the morning. Dined at home with my wife and Gosnell, my mind much pleased with her; and after dinner sat with them a good while, till my wife seemed to take notice of my being at home now more then at other times; I went to the office and there I sat till late.

7. *Lords day*. A great snow; and so to church this morning with my wife (which is the first time she hath been at church since her going to Brampton) and Gosnell attending her – which was very gracefull. So home, and we dined above in our dining-room, the first time since it was new done.

8. Up; and carrying Gosnell by coach, set her down at Temple barr, she going about business of hers today. By the way she was telling me how Balty did tell her that my wife did go every day in the week to Court and plays, and that she should have liberty of going abroad as often as she pleased, and many other lies; which I am vexed at, and I doubt the wench did come in some expectation of – which troubles me. So to the Duke and Mr. Coventry, I alone, the rest being at a pay and elsewhere. Then to my Lord Sandwiches and there spent the rest of the morning in making up my Lord's accounts with Mr. Moore; and then dined with Mr. Moore and Battersby his friend – very well, and merry and good discourse. Then into the parke to see them slide with their Scates, which is very pretty, and so to the Dukes, where the Comittee for Tanger met; and here we sat down all with him at a table and had much good discourse about that business – and is to my great content. That done, and hearing what play it was that is to be acted before the King tonight, I would not stay; but home by coach – where I find my wife troubled about Gosnell, who brings word that her uncle, Justice Jiggins, requires her to come three times a week to him to fallow some business that her mother intrusts her withal, and that unless she may have that leisure given her, he will not have her to take any place – for which we are both troubled, but there is no help for it; and believing it to be a good providence of God to prevent my running behind-hand in the world, I am somewhat contented therewith and shall make my wife so; who, poor wretch, I know will consider of things, though in good earnest, the privacy of her life must need be irkesome to her. So I made Gosnell [sing] and we sat up, looking over the book of Dances till 12 at night, not observing how the time went; and so to prayers and to bed.

9. Lay long with my wife, contenting her about the business of Gosnells going, and I perceive she will be contented as well as myself. After dinner stayed within all the afternoon, being vexed in

my mind about the going away of Sarah this afternoon, who cried mightily, and so was I ready to do, and Jane did also. And then anon went Gosnell away, which did trouble me too, though upon many considerations it is better that I am rid of that charge. Altogether makes my house appear to me very lonely, which troubles me much.

11. Up, it being a great frost upon the snow; and we sat all the morning upon Mr. Creedes accounts, wherein I did him some service and some disservice. At noon he dined with me and we sat all the afternoon together, discoursing of ways to get money, which I am now giving myself wholly up to; and in the evening he went away and I to my office, concluding all matters concerning our great letter, so long in doing, to my Lord Treasurer, till almost one in the morning; and then home with my mind much eased, and so to bed.

14. *Lords day*. Lay with great content talking with my wife in bed; and so up and to church. And then home and had a neat dinner by ourselfs; and after dinner I walked to Whitehall and my Lord's, and up and down till Chappell time and then to the King's chappell, where I heard the service; and so to my Lord's, and there Mr. Howe and Pagett (the counsellor, an old lover of Musique); we sang some psalms of Mr. Lawes and played some Symphonys between till night.

15. To my Lord's and there with Mr. Creed, Moore and Howe to the Crowne and dined; and thence to Whitehall, where I walked up and down the Gallerys, spending my time upon the pictures till the Duke and the Comittee for Tanger met (the Duke not staying with us); where the only matter was to discourse with my Lord Rutherford, who is this day made Governor of Tanger for I know not what reasons, and my Lord of Peterbrough to be called home; which though it is said is done with kindness, yet all the world may see it is done otherwise; and I am sorry to see a Catholicke Governor sent to command there, where all the rest of the officers almost are such already. But God knows what the reason is, and all may see how slippery places all Courtiers stand in. Thence by coach home, and so driving through the backside of the Shambles in Newgate Market, my coach plucked down two pieces of beef into the Dirt; upon which the butchers stopped the horses, and a great rout of

people in the street – crying that he had done him 40s. and 5l worth of hurt; but going down, I saw that he had done little or none; and so I gave them a Shilling for it and they were well contented, and so home. And there to my Lady Batten to see her, who tells me she hath just now a letter from Sir Wm., how that he and Sir J. Mennes did very narrowly escape drowning on the roade, the waters are so high, but is well. But Lord, what a Hypocrite-like face she made to tell it me.

16. I went by coach to my brother's, where I met Sarah, my late mayd, who told me out of good-will to me, for she loves me dearly, that I would beware of my wife's brother, for he is begging and borrowing of her[1] often; and told me of her Scallop-whisk and her borrowing of 50s. from Will, which she believes for him and her father. I do observe so much goodness and seriousness in the maid, that I am again and again sorry that I have parted with her, though it was full against my will then. And if she had anything in the world, I would commend her for a wife for my brother Tom.

20. To Whitehall where we met upon the Tanger Commission – and discoursed many things thereon. But little will be done before my Lord Rutherford comes there as to the Fortificacions or Molle. That done, my Lord Sandwich and I walked together a good while in the Matted Gallery, he acquainting me with his late enquiries into the Wardrobe business, to his content; and tells me how things stand – and that the first year was worth about 3000l to him and the next about as much; so that at this day, if he were paid, it will be worth about 7000l to him.

23. At noon home to dinner with my wife alone. And after dinner sat by the fire and then up to make up my accounts with her, and find that my ordinary housekeeping comes to 7l a month – which is a great deal. By and by comes Dr. Pierce; who among other things, tells me that my Lady Castlemaynes interest at Court encreases and is more and greater then the Queenes. That she hath brought in Sir H. Bennet and Sir Ch. Barkeley; but that the Queene is a most good lady and takes all with the greatest meekness that may be. He tells me too, that the King is much concerned in the Chancellors sickness; and that the Chancellor is as

1. Pepys's wife.

great, he thinks, as ever he was with the King.

24. To my Lord Crew's and dined alone with him; and after dinner, much discourse about matters. Upon the whole, I understand there are great factions at Court; and something he said that did imply a difference like to be between the King and the Duke in case the Queene should not be with child – I understand, about this bastard.[1] He says also that some great man will be aimed at when the Parliament comes to sit again; I understand, the Chancellor. And that there is a bill will be brought in, that none that have been in armes for the Parliament shall be capable of office. And that the Court are weary of my Lord Albemarle and Chamberlin.[2] He wishes that my Lord Sandwich had some good occasion to be abroad this summer which is coming on. And that my Lord Hinchingbrooke were well married, and Sydny[3] had some place at Court. He pities the poor Ministers that are put out, to whom he says the King is beholden for his coming in; and that if any such thing had been foreseen, he had never come in. After this, and much other discourse of the sea and breeding young gentlemen to the sea, I went away. This evening Mr. Gauden sent me, against Christmas, a great Chine of beefe and three dozen of Toungs. I did give 5s. to the man that brought it and half-crown to the porters. This day also, the parish Clerke brought the general bill of Mortality, which cost me half-Crowne more.

25. *Christmas day*. Up pretty early, leaving my wife not well in bed. And with my boy walked, it being a most brave cold and dry frosty morning, and had a pleasant walk to Whitehall; where I entended to have received the Comunion with the family, but I came a little too late. So I walked up into the house and spent my time looking over pictures, perticularly the ships in King H the 8ths voyage to Bullen – marking the great difference between their build then and now. By and by down to the Chappell again, where Bishop Morly preached upon the Song of the Angels – "Glory to God on high – on earth peace, and good will towards men." Methought he made but a poor sermon, but long and reprehending the mistaken jollity of the Court for the true joy that shall and ought

1. Monmouth.
2. The Lord Chamberlain, the Earl of Manchester.
3. Sandwich's second son.

to be on these days. Perticularized concerning their excess in playes and gameing, saying that he whose office it is to keep the Gamesters in order and within bounds serves but for a second rather in a Duell, meaning the Groome porter. Upon which, it was worth observing how far they are come from taking the Reprehensions of a Bishop seriously, that they all laugh in the chapel when he reflected on their ill actions and courses. The sermon done, a good Anthemne fallowed, with vialls; and then the King came down to receive the Sacrament, but I stayed not; but calling my boy from my Lord's lodging and giving Sarah some good advice, by my Lord's order, to be Sober and look after the house, I walked home again with great pleasure; and there dined by my wife's bedside with great content, having a mess of brave plum-porridge and a roasted Pullett for dinner; and I sent for a mince-pie abroad, my wife not being well to make any herself yet. After dinner sat talking a good while with her, her [pain] being become less, and then to see Sir W. Penn a little; and so to my office, practising arithmetique alone with great content, till 11 at night; and so home to supper and to bed.

26.   Up. My wife to the making of Christmas-pies all day, being now pretty well again. And I abroad to several places about small businesses; among others, bought a bake pan in Newgate market and sent it home; it cost me 16s. Then to [Mr. Moore at] the Wardrobe, who is not yet well. Hither came Mr. Battersby; and we falling into a discourse of a new book of Drollery in verse called *Hudebras*, I would needs go find it out; and met with it at the Temple, cost me 2s.- 6d. But when I came to read it, it is so silly an abuse of the Presbyter-Knight going to the warrs, that I am ashamed of it; and by and by meeting at Mr. Townsends at dinner, I sold it to him for 18d.

29.   To Whitehall and got up to the top gallery in the banquetting-house to see the Audience of the Russia Embassador; which after long waiting and fear of the falling of [the] gallery, it being so full and part of it being parted from the rest for nobody to come upon, merely from the weakenesse thereof. And very handsome it was. After they were come in, I went down and got through the croude almost as high as the King and the Embassadors, where I saw all the presents, being rich furs, hawkes, carpets, cloths of tissue, and sea-horse teeth. The King took two or three hawkes upon his fist, having a glove on, wrought with gold, given him for that purpose.

The son of one of the Embassadors was in the richest suit, for pearl and tissue, that ever I did see, or shall, I believe. After they and all the company had kissed the King's hand, then the three Embassadors and the son, and no more, did kiss the Queenes. One thing more I did observe, that the chief Embassador did carry up his master's Letters in state before him, on high; and as soon as he had delivered them, he did fall down to the ground and lay there a great while. So with Mr. Creede to the Harp and ball; and there meeting with Mr. How, Goodgroome and young Coleman, did drink and talk with them; and I have almost found out a young gentlewoman for my turn to wait on my wife, of a good family and that can sing. Thence I went away; and getting a coach, went home and sat late talking with my wife about our entertaining Dr. Clarkes lady and Mrs. Pierce shortly, being in great pain that my wife hath never a winter gowne; being almost ashamed of it that she should be seen in a taffata one when all the world wears Moyre. So to prayers and to bed.

30.    To the Change-ward to see what play there was, but I liked none of them; and so homeward and calling in at Mr. Rawlinsons, where he stopped me to dine with him and two East India officers of ships and Howell our Turner. With the officers I had good discourse, perticularly of the people at the Cape of Good Hope – of whom they of their own knowledge do tell me these one or two things. *viz.*, that when they come to age, the men do cut off one of the stones of each other, which they hold doth help them to get children the better and to grow fat. That they never sleep lying, but always sitting upon the ground. That their speech is not so articulate as ours, but yet understand one another well. That they paint themselfs all over with the grease the Duch sell them (who have a fort there) and Sutt. After dinner, drinking five or six glasses of wine (which liberty I now take till I begin my oath again), I went home.

31.    Mr. Povy and I to Whitehall, he carrying me thither on purpose to carry me into the Ball this night before the King. All the way, he talking very ingenuously; and I find him a fine gentleman and one that loves to live nobly and neatly, as I perceive by his discourse of his house, pictures, and horses. He brought me first to the Duke's chamber, where I saw him and the Duchesse at supper, and thence into the room where the Ball was to be, crammed with

fine ladies, the greatest of the Court. By and by comes the King and Queen, the Duke and Duchesse, and all the great ones; and after seating themselfs, the King takes out the Duchess of Yorke, and the Duke the Duchesse of Buckingham, the Duke of Monmouth my Lady Castlemayne, and so other lords other ladies; and they danced the Bransle. After that, the King led a lady a single Coranto; and then the rest of the lords, one after another, other ladies. Very noble it was, and great pleasure to see. Then to Country dances; the King leading the first which he called for; which was – says he, *Cuckolds all a-row*, the old dance of England. Of the ladies that danced, the Duke of Monmouth's mistress and my Lady Castlemayne and a daughter of Sir Harry De Vickes were the best. The manner was, when the King dances, all the ladies in the room, and the Queen herself, stands up; and endeed he dances rarely and much better then the Duke of Yorke. Having stayed here as long as I thought fit, to my infinite content, it being the greatest pleasure I could wish now to see at Court, I went out, leaving them dancing.

Thus ended this year, with great mirth to me and my wife. Our condition being thus – we are at present spending a night or two at my Lord's lodgings at Whitehall. Our home at the Navy office – which is and hath a pretty while been in good condition, finished and made very convenient. My purse is worth about 650*l* – besides my goods of all sorts – which yet might have been more but for my late layings-out upon my house and public assessment, and yet would not have been so much if I had not lived a very orderly life all this year, by virtue of the oaths that God put into my heart to take against wine, plays, and other expenses, and to observe for these last twelve months – and which I am now going to renew, I under God oweing my present content therunto. My family* is myself and wife – Wm. my clerk – Jane, my wife's upper-maid; but I think growing proud and negligent upon it, we must part; which troubles me – Susan our cook-maid, a pretty willing wench but no good cook – and Waynman my boy, who I am now turning away for his naughty tricks. We have had from the beginning our healths to this day, very well, blessed be God. Our late mayde Sarah going from us (though put away by us) to live with Sir W. Penn doth trouble me, though I love the wench – so that we do make ourselfs a little strange to him and his family for it, and resolve to do so. We have lately had it in our thoughts, and I can hardly bring myself off of it since Mrs. Gosnell cannot be with us, to find out another to be in the quality of a Woman to my wife, that can sing or dance. And yet finding it hard to save anything at the year's end as I now live, I think I shall not be such a fool – till I am more warm in my purse; besides my oath of entering into no such expenses till I am worth 1000*l*. By my last year's diligence in my office, blessed be God, I am come to a good degree of knowledge therein; and am acknowledged so by all the world, even the Duke himself, to whom I have a good accesse, and by that and my being Comissioner with him for Tanger, he takes much notice of me, and I doubt not but by the continuance of the same endeavours I shall in a little time come to be a man much taken notice of in the world – especially, being come to so great an esteem with Mr. Coventry. The only weight that lies heavy upon my mind is the ending the business with my uncle Thomas about my dead uncles estate, which is very ill on our side; and I fear, when all is done, I must be forced to maintain my father myself, or spare a good deal towards it out of my own purse – which will be a very great pull-backe to me in my fortune. But I must be contented and bring it to an issue one way or other.

Public matters stand thus. The King is bringing, as is said, his family and Navy and all other his charges to a less expense. In the meantime, himself fallowing his pleasures more then with good advice he would do – at least, to be seen to all the world to do so – his dalliance with my Lady Castlemayne being public every day, to his great reproach. And his favouring of none at Court so much as those that are the confidants of his pleasure as Sir H. Bennet and Sir Ch. Barkely – which good God put it into his heart to mend – before he makes himself too much contemned by his people for it. The Duke of Monmouth is in so great splendour at Court and so dandled by the King, that some doubt, if the King should have no child by the Queene (which there is yet no appearance of), whether he would not be acknowledged for a lawful son. And that there will a difference fallow upon it between the Duke of York – and him – which God prevent. My Lord Chancellor is threatened by people to be Questioned, the next sitting of the parliament, by some spirits that do not love to see him so great. But certainly he is a good servant to the King. The Queene Mother is said to keep too great a Court now; and her being married to my Lord St. Albans is commonly talked of, and that they had a daughter between them in France. How true, God knows.[1] The Bishopps are high and go on without any diffidence in pressing uniformity; and the Presbyters

---

1. See above, pp. 235–6 (22 November) & n.

seem silent in it and either conform or lay down, though without doubt they expect a turn and would be glad these endeavours of the other Fanatiques would take effect – there having been a plot lately found, for which four have been publicly tried at the old Bayly and hanged. My Lord Sandwich is still in good esteem, and now keeping his Christmas in the country. And I in good esteem, I think, as any man can be with him. In fine, for the good condition of myself, wife, family and estate, in the great degree that it is, and for the public state of the nation, so quiet as it is, the Lord God be praised.

# 1663

## JANUARY

1. Lay with my wife at my Lord's lodgings, where I have been these two nights, till 10 a-clock with great pleasure talking; and then I rose. And to Whitehall, where I spent a little time walking among the Courtiers, which I perceive I shall be able to do with great confidence, being now beginning to be pretty well-known among them. Then to my wife again and dined, Mrs. Sarah with us, in the chamber we lay in. Among other discourse, Mrs. Sarah tells us how the King sups at least four or [five] times every week with my Lady Castlemayne; and most often stays till the morning with her and goes home through the garden all alone privately, and that so as the very Centry's take notice of it and speak of it. She tells me that about a month ago she quickened at my Lord Gerrards at dinner and cried out that she was undone; and all the lords and men were fain to quit the room, and women called to help her. In fine, I find that there is nothing almost but bawdry at Court from top to bottom, as if it were fit I could instance, but it is not necessary. Only, they say my Lord Chesterfield, Groom of the Stole to the Queene, is either gone or put away from Court upon the score of his lady's having smitten the Duke of York, so as that he is watched by the Duchesse of Yorke and the lady is retired into the country upon it. How much of this is true, God knows, but it is common talk. After dinner I did reckon with Mrs. Sarah for what we have eat and drank here, and gave her a crowne; and so took coach and to the Duke's house, where we saw *The Villaine* again; and the more I see it, the more I am offended at my first undervaluing the play, it being very good and pleasant and yet a true and allowable Tragedy. The house was full of Citizens and so the less pleasant, but that I was willing to make an end of my gaddings and to set to my business for all the year again tomorrow.

4. *Lords day*. Up and to church, where a lazy sermon. And so home to dinner to a good piece of powdered beef, but a little too

salt. At dinner my wife did propound my having of my sister Pall at my house again to be her Woman, since one we must have – hoping that in that quality possibly she may prove better than she did before. Which I take very well of her, and will consider of it – it being a very great trouble to me that I should have a sister of so ill a nature that I must be forced to spend money upon a stranger, when it might better be upon her if she were good for anything.

6. *Twelfth day.* After dinner to the Dukes house and there saw *Twelfth night* acted well, though it be but a silly play and not relating at all to the name or day. Thence Mr. Battersby (the apothecary), his wife and I and mine by coach together, and setting him down at his house, he paying his share, my wife and I home and find all well. Only, myself somewhat vexed at my wife's neglect in leaving of her scarfe, waistcoat, and night-dressings in the coach today that brought us from Westminster, though I confess she did give them to me to look after – yet it was her fault not to see that I did take them out of the coach. I believe it might be as good as 25*s.* loss or thereabouts. So to my office, however, to set down my last three days' Journall, and writing to my father about my sending him some wine and things this week for his making an entertainment of some friends in the country, and so home. This night making an end wholly of Christmas, with a mind fully satisfyed with the great pleasures we have had by being abroad from home. And I do find my mind so apt to run to its old wont of pleasures, that it is high time to betake myself to my late vows, which I will tomorrow, God willing, perfect and bind myself to, that so I may for a great while do my duty, as I have well begun, and encrease my good name and esteem in the world and get money, which sweetens all things and whereof I have much need.

7. Up pretty earely; that is, by 7 a-clock, it being not yet light before or then. So to my office all the morning, signing the Treasurers ledger, part of it where I have not put my hand. And then eat a mouthful of pie at home to stay my stomach; and so with Mr. Waith by water to Deptford and there, among other things, viewed old pay-books and find that the Comanders did never heretofore receive any pay for the Rigging-time but only for Sea time, contrary to what Sir J. Minnes and Sir W. Batten told the Duke the other day. I also searched all the ships in the Wett docke for fire and found all in good order – it being very dangerous for the

King that so many ships lie together there. I was among the Canvas in stores also with Mr. Harris the Saylmaker, and learnt the difference between one sort and another to my great content. And so by water home again – where my wife tells me stories how she hears that by Sarahs going to live at Sir W. Penn's, all our affairs of my family are made known and discoursed of there, and theirs by my people – which doth trouble me much, and I shall take a time to let Sir W. Penn know how he hath dealt in taking her without our full consent. So to my office, and by and by home to supper. And so to prayers and bed.

8.    Dined at home; and there being the famous new play acted the first time today, which is call[ed] *The Adventures of five houres*, at the Duke's house, being they say made or translated by Coll. Tuke, I did long to see it and so made my wife to get her ready, though we were forced to send for a smith to break open her Trunke, her maid Jane being gone forth with the keyes. And so we went; and though earely, were forced to sit almost out of sight at the end of one of the lower formes, so full was the house. And the play, in one word, is the best, for the variety and the most excellent continuance of the plot to the very end, that ever I saw or think ever shall. And all possible, not only to be done in that time, but in most other respects very admittible and without one word of ribaldry. And the house, by its frequent plaudites, did show their sufficient approbacion. So home, with much ado in an hour getting a coach home; and after writing letters at my office, I went home to supper and to bed – now resolving to set up my rest as to plays till Easter, if not Whitsuntide next, excepting plays at Court.

9.    My wife begun to speak again of the necessity of her keeping somebody to bear her company; for her familiarity with her other servants is it that spoils them all, and other company she hath none (which is too true); and called for Jane to reach her out of her trunk, giving her the keys to that purpose, a bundle of papers; and pulls out a paper, a copy of what, a pretty while since, she had writ in a discontent to me, which I would not read but burned.[1] She now read it, and was so picquant, and wrote in English and most of it true, of the retirednesse of her life and how unpleasant it was, that being writ in English and so in danger of being met with and read

1. See above, p. 235 (13 November).

by others, I was vexed at it and desired her and then commanded her to teare it – which she desired to be excused it; I forced it from her and tore it, and withal took her other bundle of papers from her and leapt out of the bed and in my shirt clapped them into the pockets of my breeches, that she might not get them from me; and having got on my stockings and breeches and gown, I pulled them out one by one and tore them all before her face, though it went against my heart to do it, she crying and desiring me not to do it. But such was my passion and trouble to see the letters of my love to her, and my Will, wherein I had given her all I have in the world when I went to sea with my Lord Sandwich, to be joyned with a paper of so much disgrace to me and dishonour if it should have been found by anybody. Having tore them all, saving a bond of my uncle Robts. which she hath long had in her hands, and our Marriage licence and the first letter that ever I sent her when I was her servant, I took up the pieces and carried them into my chamber, and there, after many disputes with myself whether I should burn them or no, and having picked up the pieces of paper she read today and of my Will which I tore, I burnt all the rest. And so went out to my office – troubled in mind. Mr. Bland came in the evening to me hither, and sat talking to me about many things of Merchandize; and I should be very happy in his discourse, durst I confess my ignorance to him, which is not so fit for me to do.

12. With Mr. Creede to the Kings head ordinary; but people being sat down, we went to two or three places; at last found some meat at a welch cook's at Charing cross and there dined, and our boys. After dinner to the Change to buy some linen for my wife; and going back, met our two boys; mine had struck down Creedes boy in the dirt, with his new suit on in the dirt, all over dirty, and the boy taken by a gentlewoman into a house to make clean, but the poor boy was in a pitiful taking and pickle; but I basted my rogue soundly. So I went to the [Tangier] Comittee, where we spent all this night attending to Sir J. Lawsons description of Tanger and the place for the molde, of which he brought a very pretty draught. Concerning the making of the molle, Mr. Cholmely did also discourse very well, having had some experience in it. So home, and find my wife's new gowne come home and she mightily pleased with it. But I appeared very angry that there was no more things got ready against tomorrow's feast, and in that passion sat up long and went discontented to bed.

13.    So my poor wife rose by 5 a-clock in the morning, before day, and went to market and bought fowle and many other things for dinner – with which I was highly pleased. And the chine of beef was done also before 6 a-clock, and my own Jacke, of which I was doubtful, doth carry it very well. Things being put in order and the Cooke come, I went to the office, where we sat till noon; and then broke up and I home – whither by and by comes Dr. Clerke and his lady – his sister and a she-Cosen, and Mr. Pierce and his wife, which was all my guest[s]. I had for them, after oysters – at first course, a hash of rabbits and lamb, and a rare chine of beef – next, a great dish of roasted fowl, cost me about 30s., and a tart; and then fruit and cheese. My dinner was noble and enough. I had my house mighty clean and neat, my room below with a good fire in it – my dining-room above, and my chamber being made a withdrawing-chamber, and my wife's a good fire also. I find my new table very proper, and will hold nine or ten people well, but eight with great room. After dinner, the women to Cards in my wife's chamber and the Doctor [and] Mr. Pierce in mine, because the dining-room smokes unless I keep a good charcole fire, which I was not then provided with. At night to supper; had a good sack-posset and cold meat and sent my guests away about 10 a-clock at night – both them and myself highly pleased with our management of this day. And indeed, their company was very fine and Mrs. Clerke a very witty, fine lady, though a little conceited and proud. So weary to bed. I believe this day's feast will cost me near 5l.

15.    Up, and to my office preparing things. By and by we met and sat, Mr. Coventry and I, till noon. Then I took him in to dine with me, I having a wild goose roasted and a cold chine of beef and a barrel of oysters. We dined alone in my chamber, and then he and I to fit ourselfs for horseback, he having brought me a horse; and so to Debtford, the ways being very dirty. There we walked up and down the yard and wet-dock and did our main business, which was to examine the proof of our new way of the Call-bookes, which we think will be of great use. And so to horse again and I home with his horse, leaving him to go over the fields to Lambeth – his boy at my house taking home his horse. I vexed, having left my key in my other pocket in my chamber and my door is shut, so that I was forced to set my boy in at the window; which done, I shifted myself, and so to my office till late.

19.   By coach to Mr. Povys, being invited thither by a messenger this morning from him – where really, he made a most excellent and large dinner, even to admiration; he bidding us in a frolique to call for what we had a mind and he would undertake to give it us – and we did, for prawns – Swan – venison after I had thought the dinner was quite done, and he did immediately produce it, which I thought great plenty. And he seems to set off his rest in this plenty and the neatness of his house; which he after dinner showed me from room to room, so beset with delicate pictures, and above all, a piece of per[s]pective in his closet in the low parler. His stable, where was some most delicate horses, and the very racks painted, and mangers, with a neat leaden painted cistern and the walls done with Dutch tiles like my chimnies. But still, above all things, he bid me go down into his wine-cellar, where upon several shelves there stood bottles of all sorts of wine, new and old, with labells pasted upon each bottle, and in that order and plenty as I never saw books in a bookseller's shop. And herein, I observe, he puts his highest content and will accordingly commend all that he hath, but still they deserve to be so.

24.   By coach to Mr. Povys, where Sir W. Compton, Mr. Bland, Gawden, Sir J. Lawson and myself met to settle the victualling of Tanger for the time past (which with much ado we did) and for a six month supply more.

27.   Up and to the office, where sat till 2 a-clock; and then home to dinner, whither by and by comes in Creede and he and I talked of our Tanger business and do find that there is nothing in the world done with true integrity but there is design along with it; as in my Lord Rutherford, who designs to have the profit of victualling of the garrison himself, and others to have the benefit of making the molle. So that I am almost discouraged from coming any more to the Committee, were it not that it will possibly hereafter bring me to some acquaintance of the great men. Then to the office again, where very busy till past 10 at night; and so home to supper and bed.

28.   Up, and all the morning at my office doing business – and at home seeing my painters' work measured. So to dinner and abroad with my wife, carrying her to Unthankes, where she lights and I to my Lord Sandwiches, whom I find missing his ague fit today and is

pretty well, playing at dice (and by this I see how time and example may alter a man; he being now acquainted with all sorts of pleasures and vanities which heretofore he never thought of nor loved, or it may be, hath allowed) with Ned Pickering and his page Loud. Thence to Wottons the shoemaker and there bought another pair of new boots for the other I bought my last journey, that would not fit me. And here I drank with him and his wife, a pretty woman, they broaching a vessel of Cyder a-purpose for me. So home, and there find my wife come home and seeming to cry; for bringing home in a coach her new Ferradin waistcoat, in Cheapside a man asked her whether that was the way to the tower, and while she was answering him, another on the other side snatched away her bundle out of her lap, and could not be recovered – but ran away with it – which vexes me cruelly, but it cannot be helped. So to my office and there till almost 12 at night with Mr. Lewes, learning to understand the manner of a pursers account – which is very hard and little understood by my fellow-officers, and yet mighty necessary. So at last with great content broke up, and home to supper and bed.

30. *A solemne Fast for the King's murther.* And we were forced to keep it more then we would have done, having forgot to take any victuals into the house. I to church in the forenoon, and Mr. Mills made a good sermon upon David's heart smiting him for cutting off the garment of Saule. Home and whiled away some of the afternoon at home, talking with my wife. So to my office, and all alone making up my month's accounts; which to my great trouble I find that I am got no further then 640*l* – but I have had great expenses this month. I pray God the next may be a little better, as I hope it will. In the evening my [Navy] manuscript is brought home, handsomely bound to my full content; and now I think I have a better collection in reference to the Navy, and shall have by the time I have filled it, then any of my predecessors. So home to eat something, such as we have, bread and butter and milk; and so to bed.

31. In the evening examining my wife's letter entended to my Lady and another to Madamoiselle; they were so false-spelt that I was ashamed of them and took occasion to fall out about them with my wife, and so she writ none; at which, however, I was sorry, because it was in answer to a letter of Madamoiselle – about business. Late home to supper and to bed.

# ⊹FEBRUARY⊹

4.   Up earely and to Mr. Moore, and thence to Mr. Lovell about
my law businesses, and from him to Pauls schoole, it being
opposicion-day there. I heard some of their speeches, and they were
just as schoolboys used to be, of the seven Liberall Sciences; but I
think not so good as ours were in our time. Mr. Crumlum did me
much honour by telling many what a present I had made to the
school, showing my *Stephanus* in four volumes, cost me 4*l* 10*s*.
Thence with Mr. Elborough (he being all of my old acquaintance
that I could meet with here) to a Cookes shop to dinner, but I find
him a fool as he ever was, or worse. Thence to my Cosen Roger
Pepys and Mr. Phillips about my law businesses, which stand very
bad. And so home to the office; where after doing some business, I
went home, where I find our new mayd Mary, that is come in Janes
place.

6.   To a bookseller's in the Strand and there bought *Hudibras*
again, it being certainly some ill humour to be so set against that
which all the world cries up to be the example of wit – for which I
am resolved once again to read him and see whether I can find it or
no. So to Mr. Povys and there find them at dinner and dined there –
there being, among others, Mr. Williamson, Latin Secretary, who I
perceive is a pretty knowing man and a scholar, but it may be thinks
himself to be too much so. Thence after dinner to the Temple to my
Cosen Roger Pepys, where met us my uncle Tho. and his son; and
after many high demands, we at last came to a kind of agreement
upon very hard terms, which are to be prepared in writing. My
Cosen Roger was so sensible of our coming to agreement that he
could not forbear weeping; and endeed, though it be very hard, yet
I am glad to my heart that we are like to end our trouble.[1] And I to
my Lord Sandwich and there stayed, there being a Comittee to sit
upon the Contract for the Molle, which I dare say none of us that
were there understood; but yet they agreed of things as Mr.
Cholmly and Sir J. Lawson demanded, who are the undertakers;
and so I left them to go on to agree, for I understood it not. So
home; and being called by a coachman who had a fare in him, he
carried me beyond the Old Exchange and there set down his fare,
who would not pay him what was his due because he carried a

---

1. For this dispute, see above, pp. 144–5 (8–13 July).

stranger with him; and so after wrangling, he was fain to be content with 6*d*.; and being vexed, the coachman would not carry me home a great while, but set me down here for the other 6*d*. But with fair words he was willing to it; and so I came home and to my office, setting business in order; and so home to supper and to bed – my mind being in disorder as to the greatness of this day's business that I have done, but yet glad that my trouble therein is like to be over.

7. Up and to my office, whither by agreement Mr. Coventry came before the time of setting to confer about preparing an account of the extraordinary charge of the Navy since the King's coming. So by and by we sat, and so till noon. Then home to dinner; and in the afternoon some of us met again upon something relating to the Victualling; and thence to my writing of letters late, and making my Alphabet to my new Navy-booke, very pretty. And so after writing to my father by the post about the endeavour to come to a composition with my uncle, though a very bad one, desiring him to be contented therewith – I went home to supper and bed.

8. *Lords day*. Up; and it being a very great frost, I walked to Whitehall and to my Lord Sandwiches; by the fireside till chapel time and so to chapel, where there preached little Dr. Duport of Cambrige upon Josiahs words, "But I and my house, we will serve the Lord." But though a great scholar, he made the most flat, dead sermon, both for matter and manner of delivery, that ever I heard; and very long beyond his hour, which made it worse. And then Creede and I and Capt. Ferrers to the parke – and there walked finely, seeing people slide – we talking all the while and Capt. Ferrers telling me, among other Court passages – how about a month ago, at a Ball at Court, a child was dropped by one of the ladies in dancing; but nobody knew who, it being taken up by somebody in their handkercher. The next morning all the Ladies of Honour appeared early at Court for their vindication, so that nobody could tell whose this mischance should be. But it seems Mrs. Wells fell sick that afternoon and hath disappeared ever since, so that it is concluded it was her. Another story was how my Lady Castlemayne, a few days since, had Mrs. Stuart to an entertainment, and at night begun a frolique that they two must be married; and married they were, with ring and all other ceremonies of

church service, and ribbands and a sack-posset in bed and flinging the stocking. But in the close, it is said that my Lady Castlemayne, who was the bridegroom, rose, and the King came and took her place with pretty Mrs. Stuart. This is said to be very true. Whether the wind and the cold did cause it or no, I know not; but having been this day or two mightily troubled with an iching all over my body, which I took to be a louse or two that might bite me – I find this afternoon that all my body is inflamed and my face in a sad redness and swelling and pimpled; so that I was, before we had done walking, not only sick but ashamed of myself to see myself so changed in my countenance; so that after we had thus talked, we parted and I walked home with much ado, the ways being so full of ice and water by people's trampling. At last got home and to bed presently and had a very bad night of it, in great pain in my stomach and great fever.

10. In the morning visited by Mr. Coventry and others, and very glad I am to see that was so much enquired after and my sickness taken notice of as I did. I keep my bed all day and sweat again at night, by which I expect to be very well tomorrow.

11. Took a glister in the morning and rise in the afternoon. My wife and I dined on a pullet and I eat heartily – having eat nothing since Sonday but water-gruel and posset-drink. But must needs say that our new maid Mary hath played her part very well, in her readiness and discretion in attending me, of which I am very glad.

12. Up, and find myself pretty well; and so to the office and there all the morning. Rise at noon and home to dinner – in my green chamber, having a good fire – whither there came my wife's brother and brought Mary Ashwell with him, whom we find a very likely person to please us both for person, discourse, and other qualities. She dined with us, and after dinner went away again, being agreed to come to us about three weeks or a month hence. My wife and I well pleased with our choice, only I pray God I may be able to maintain it.

15. *Lords day.* Sending Will to church, myself stayed at home, hanging up in my green chamber my picture of the *Soveraigne* and putting some things in order there. So to dinner to three Duckes and two Teales, my wife and I. Then to church, where a dull

sermon; and so home and after walking about the house a while, discoursing with my wife, I to my office, there to set down something and prepare businesses for tomorrow – having in the morning read over my vowes, which through sickness I could not do the last Lord's day, and not through forgetfulness or negligence; so that I hope it is no breach of my vowe not to pay my forfeiture. So home, and after prayers to bed – talking long with my wife and teaching her things in Astronomy.

21.    Up and to the office, where Sir John Minnes (most of the rest being at the Parliament-house); all the morning [an]swering petitions and other business. Towards noon there comes a man in, as if upon ordinary business, and shows me a Writt from the Exchequer, called a Comission of Rebellion,[1] and tells me that I am his prisoner – in Fields business. Which methought did strike me to the heart, to think that we could not sit safe in the middle of the King's business. I told him how and where we were imployed and bid him have a care; and perceiving that we were busy, he said he would and did withdraw for an houre – in which time Sir J. Minnes took coach and to Court to see what he could do from thence; and our Sollicitor against Field came by chance and told me that he would go and satisfy the fees of the Court and would end the business. So he went away about that, and I stayed in my closet, till by and by the man and four more of his fellows came to know what I would do; I told them stay till I heard from the King or my Lord Chief Baron, to both whom I had now sent. With that they consulted and told me that if I would promise to stay in the house they would go and refresh themselfs, and come again and know what answer I had. So they away and I home to dinner – whither by chance in comes Mr. Hawly and dined with me. Before I had dined, the Baylys came back again with the Constable, and at the office knock for me but found me not there; and I hearing in what manner they were come, did forbear letting them know where I was. So they stood knocking and enquiring for me. By and by at my parlour-window comes Sir W. Batten's Mingo to tell me that his Maister and Lady would have me come to their house through Sir J. Mennes's lodgings, which I could not do; but however, by lathers did get over the pale between our yards and so to their house, where

1. A writ used to secure the appearance of defendant. For the case, see above, p. 190 (13 April) & n.

I find them (as they have reason) to be much concerned for me – my Lady especially.

The fellows stayed in the yard swearing with one or two constables; and some time we locked them into the yard and by and by let them out again, and so keeped them all the afternoon, not letting them see me or know where I was. One time, I went up to the top of Sir W. Batten's house and out of one of their windows spoke to my wife out of one of ours – which methought, though I did it in mirth, yet I was sad to think what a sad thing it would be for me to be really in that condition. By and by comes Sir J. Mennes, who (like himself and all that he doth) tells us that he can do no good, but that my Lord Chancellor wonders that we did not cause the seamen to fall about their eares – which we wished we could have done without our being seen in it; and Capt. Grove being there, he did give them some affront and would have got some seamen to have drubbed them, but he had not time nor did we think it fit to have it done, they having executed their commission. But there was occasion given that he did draw his sword upon one of them and he did complain that Grove had pricked him in the breast – but no hurt done; but I saw that Grove would have done our business to them if we had bid him. By and by comes Mr. Clerke our Sollicitor, who brings us a release from our adverse atturny, we paying the fees of the Comission, which comes to five markes, and pay the charges of these fellows, which are called the Comissioners (but are the most rake-shamed rogues that ever I saw in my life); so he showed them his release and [they] seemed satisfied and went away with him to their atturny to be paid by him. But before they went, Sir W. Batten and my Lady did begin to taunt them; but the rogues answered them as high as themselfs and swore they would come again, and called me rogue and Rebell and they would bring the Sheriffe and untile his house before he should harbour a Rebell in his house – and that they would be here again shortly. Well, at last they went away; and I by advice took occasion to go abroad, and walked through the street to show myself among the neighbours, that they might not think worse then the business is.

25.　　The Commons in parliament, I hear, are very high to stand to the act of uniformity, and will not indulge the papists (which is endeavoured by the court party) nor the Presbyters.

27. Up and to my office, whither several persons came to me about office business. About 11 a-clock Comissioner Pett and I walked to Chyrurgeons hall (we being all invited thither and promised to dine there), where we were led into the Theatre; and by and by came the Reader, Dr. Tearne, with the Maister and Company, in a very handsome manner; and all being settled, he begun his lecture, this being the second upon the Kidnys, Ureters, and yard, which was very fine; and his discourse being ended, we walked into the hall; and there being great store of company we had a fine dinner and good learned company, many Doctors of Physique, and we used with extraordinary great respect. After dinner Dr. Scarborough took some of his friends, and I went along with them, to see the body alone; which we did; he was a lusty fellow, a seaman that was hanged for a robbery. I did touch the dead body with my bare hand; it felt cold, but methought it was a very unpleasant sight. But all the Doctors at table conclude that there is no pain at all in hanging, for that it doth stop the circulacion of the blood and so stops all sense and motion in an instant. Thence we went into a private room, where I perceive they prepare the bodies, and there was the Kidnys, Ureters, yard, stones and semenary vessels upon which he read today. And Dr. Scarborough, upon my desire and the company's, did show very clearly the manner of the disease of the stone and the cutting and all other Questions that I could think of.

## MARCH

9. Up betimes to my office, where all the morning. About noon Sir J. Robinson, Lord Mayor, desiring way through the garden from the Tower, called in at the office and there invited me (and Sir W. Penn, who happened to be in the way) to dinner, which we did. And there had a great Lent dinner of fish, little flesh. And thence he and I in his coach, against my will (for I am resolved to shun too great fellowship with him) to Whitehall; but came too late, the Duke having been with our fellow-officers before we came, for which I was sorry. Thence he and I to walk one turn in the parke and so home by coach, and I to my office, where late; and so home to supper and bed. There dined with us today Mr. Slingsby of the Mint, who showed us all the new pieces, both gold and silver

(examples of them all), that are made for the King by Blondeaus way, and compared them with those made for Oliver – the pictures of the latter made by Symons, and of the King by one Rotyr, a German I think, that dined with us also. He extolls these of Rotyrs above the others; and endeed, I think they are the better, because the sweeter of the two; but upon my word, those of the Protectors are more like in my mind then the King's – but both very well worth seeing.

10. Dined upon a poor Lenten dinner at home, my wife being vexed at a fray this morning with my Lady Batten about my boy's going thither to turn the water-cock, with their maids leave, but my Lady was mighty high upon it, and she would teach his mistress better manners; which my wife answered aloud, that she might hear, that she could learn little manners of her. After dinner to my office, and then we sat all the afternoon till 8 at night; and so wrote my letters by the post, and so before 9 home, which is rare with me of late, I staying longer; but with multitude of business, my head akes and so I can stay no longer, but home to supper and to bed.

12. Up betimes and to my office all the morning with Capt. Cocke, ending their account of their Riga Contract for Hemp. So home to dinner, my head full of business against the office. After dinner comes my uncle Thomas with a letter to my father, wherein, as we desire, he and his son do order their Tenants to pay their rents to us; which pleases me well. In discourse he tells me my uncle Wight thinks much that I do never see them, and they have reason; but I do apprehend their hav[ing] been too far concerned with my uncle Tho. against us, so that I have had no mind hitherto; but now I will go see them. He being gone, I to the office; where at the choice of Maisters and Chyrurgeons for the fleet now going out, I did my business as I could wish, both for the persons I have a mind to serve and in getting the warrants signed drawn by my clerks, which I was afeared of. Sat late; and having done, I went home; where I find Mary Ashwell come to live with us, of whom I hope well and pray God she may please us – which though it cost me something, yet will give me much content. So to supper and to bed. And find by her discourse and carriage tonight, that she is not proud but will do what she is bid; but for want of being abroad, knows not how to give that respect to her mistress as she will do when she is told it – she having been used only to little children, and there was a kind of a

mistress over them. Troubled all night with my cold, I being quite hoarse with it, that I could not speak to be heard at all almost.

15. *Lords day*. Up and with my wife and her woman Ashwell, the first time, to church; where our pew so full with Sir J. Mennes's sister and her daughter, that I perceive when we come all together some of us must be shut out – but I suppose we shall come to some order what to do therein. Dined at home, and to church again in the afternoon; and so home and I to my office till the evening, doing one thing or other and reading my vowes as I am bound every Lord's day, and so home to supper and talk; and Ashwell is such good company that I think we shall be very lucky in her. So to prayers and to bed. This day, the weather, which of late hath been very hot and fair, turns very wet and cold, and all the church-time this afternoon it thundered mightily, which I have not heard a great while.

17. Up betimes and to my office a while, and then home and to Sir Wm. Batten; with whom by coach to St. Margaretts hill in Southworke, where the Judge of the Admiralty came and the rest of the Doctors of the Civill law and some other Comissioners; whose Commission of Oyer and Terminer was read, and then the charge given by Dr. Exton – which methought was somewhat dull, though he would seem to entend it to be very Rhetoricall, saying that Justice had two wings, one of which spread itself over the land and the other over the water, which was this Admiralty court. That being done and the Jury called, they broke up and to dinner to a Taverne hard by, where a great dinner, and I with them; but I perceive that their design and consultation was, I could overhear them, how to proceed with the most solemnity and spend time, there being only two businesses to do, which of themselfs would not spend much time. So home, with my mind at very great ease, over the water to the Tower; and thence, there being nobody at the office, we being absent and so no office could be kept – Sir W. Batten and I to my Lord Mayors, where we found my Lord with Coll. Strangways and Sir Rd. Floyd, Parliament men, in the cellar drinking; where we sat with them and then up, and by and by comes in Sir Rd. Ford. In our drinking, which was alway going, we had many discourses; but from all of them, I do find Sir R. Ford a very able man of his brains and tongue, and a Scholler. But my Lord Mayor I find to be a talking, bragging Bufflehead, a fellow that

would be thought to have led all the City in the great business of bringing in the King; and that nobody understood his plots and the dark lanthorn he walked by, but led them and plowed with them as oxen and Asses (his own words) to do what he had a mind – when in every discourse, I observe him to be as very a coxcomb as I could have thought had been in the City.

18. Wake betimes and talked a while with my wife about a wench that she had hired yesterday, which I would have enquired after before she comes, she having lived in great families, and so up to my office – where all the morning; and at noon home to dinner and after dinner by water to Redriffe, my wife and Ashwell with me, and so walked; I left them at Halfway house and I to Deptford, where up and down the storehouses and on board two or three ships now getting ready to go to sea; and so back and finde my wife walking in the way, so home again, merry with our Ashwell, who is a merry jade; and so a while to my office and then home to supper and to bed. This day, my Tryangle (which was put in tune yesterday) did please me very well, Ashwell playing upon it pretty well.

19. Up betimes and to Woolwich all alone by water, where took the officers most a-bed. I walked and enquired how all matters and businesses go. And by and by to the Clerk of the Cheques house and there eat some of his good Jamaica brawne, and so walked to Greenwich – part of the way Deane walking with me, talking of the pride and corruption of most of his fellow officers of the yard (and which I believe to be true). So to Deptford, where I did the same to great content. At noon Mr. Wayth took me to his house, where I dined and saw his wife, a pretty woman, and had a good fish dinner; and after dinner he and I walked to Redriffe, talking of several errors in the Navy; by which I learned a great deal and was glad of his company. So by water home, and by and by to the office, where we sat till almost 9 at night. So after doing my own business in my office, writing letters &c., home to supper and to bed, being weary and vexed that I do not find other people so willing to do business as myself when I have taken pains to find out what in the yards is wanting and fitting to be done.

21. Up betimes and to my office, where busy all the morning. And at noon, after a little dinner, to it again; and by and by, by

appointment, our full board met, and Sir Phillip Warwicke and Sir Robt. Long came from my Lord Treasurer to speak with us about the state of the debts of the Navy and how to settle it, so as to begin upon the new Foundacion of 200000*l* per annum which the King is now resolved not to exceed.

25. *Lady day*. This evening came Capt. Grove about hiring ships for Tanger. I did hint to him my desire that I could make some lawfull profit thereof – which he promises, that he will tell me of all that he gets and that I shall have a share – which I did not demand, but did silently consent to it – and money, I perceive something will be got thereby. At night Mr. Bland came and sat with me at my office till late, and so I home and to bed. This day being washing-day and my maid Susan ill, or would be thought so, puts my house so out of order that we have no pleasure almost in anything, my wife being troubled thereat for want of a good cook-maid.

26. Up betimes and to my office – leaving my wife in bed to take her physique; myself also not being out of some pain today, by some cold that I have got by the sudden change of the weather from hot to cold. This day is five years since it pleased God to preserve me at my being cut of the Stone; of which, I bless God, I am in all respects well – only, now and then upon taking cold I have some pain, but otherwise in very good health alway. But I could not get my feast to be keeped today as it used to be, because of my wife's being ill and other disorders by my servants being out of order. This morning came a new Cooke-maid at 4*l* per annum, the first time I ever did give so much – but we do hope it will be nothing lost by keeping a good cook. She did live last at my Lord Monkes house. And endeed, at dinner did get what there was very prettily ready and neat for me, which did please me much.

# –✴APRILL✴–

3. Going out of Whitehall, I met Capt. Grove, who did give me a letter directed to myself from himself; I discerned money to be in it and took it, knowing, as I found it to be, the proceed of the place I have got him, to have the taking up of vessells for Tanger. But I did not open it till I came home to my office; and there I broke it open,

not looking into it till all the money was out, that I might say I saw no money in the paper if ever I should be Questioned about it. There was a piece in gold and 4*l* in silver. So home to dinner with my father and wife. And after dinner up to my Tryangle, where I find that above my expectation Ashwell hath very good principles of Musique and can take out a lesson herself with very little pains – at which I am very glad. Thence away back again by water to Whitehall and there to the Tanger Committee, where we find ourselfs at a great stand – the establishment being but 70000*l* per annum – and the forces to be kept in the town, at the least estimate that my Lord Rutherford can be got to bring it, is 53000*l*. The charge of this year's work of the Molle will be 13000*l* – besides 1000*l* a year to my Lord Peterburgh as a pension, and the fortificacions and contingencys – which puts us to a great stand.

4. Up betimes and to my office. Home to dinner whither by and by comes Roger Pepys, Mrs. Turner, her daughter, Joyce Norton and a young lady, a daughter of Coll. Cockes – my uncle Wight – his wife and Mrs. Anne Wight – this being my feast, in lieu of what I should have had a few days ago, for my cutting of the Stone, for which the Lord make me truly thankful. Very merry before, at, and after dinner, and the more for that my dinner was great and most neatly dressed by our own only mayde. We had a Fricasse of rabbets and chicken – a leg of mutton boiled – three carps in a dish – a great dish of a side of lamb – a dish roasted pigeons – a dish of four lobsters – three tarts – a Lampry pie, a most rare pie – a dish of anchoves – good wine of several sorts; and all things mighty noble and to my great content. After dinner to Hide parke. At the parke was the King, and in another coach my Lady Castlemayne, they greeting one another at every Tour. Here about an hour; and so leaving all by the way, we home and find the house as clean as if nothing had been done there today from top to bottom – which made us give the Cooke 12*d*. a piece, each of us.

5. *Lords day.* Up and spent the morning till the Barber came in reading in my chamber part of Osborne's *Advice to his Son* (which I shall not never enough admire for sense and language); and being by and by trimmed – to church, myself, wife, Ashwell, &c; and home to dinner, it raining. While that was prepared, to my office to read over my vowes, with great affection* and to very good purpose. So to dinner, and very well pleased with it. Then to

church again, where a simple bawling young Scott preached. So home to my office alone till dark, reading some part of my old *Navy precedents*, and so home to supper. And after some pleasant talk, my wife, Ashwell and I – to prayers and to bed.

7.    Up very betimes; and angry with Will that he made no more haste to rise after I called him. So to my office and all the morning there. At noon to the Exchange and so home to dinner, where I find my wife hath been with Ashwell at La Roches to have her tooth drawn, which it seems akes much. But my wife could not get her to be contented to have it drawn after the first twich, but would let it alone; and so they came home with it undone, which made my wife and me good sport. After dinner to the office, where Sir J. Mennes did make a great complaint to me alone, how my clerk Mr. Hater had entered in one of the Seabookes a ticket to have been signed by him before it had been examined; which makes the old foole mad almost, though there was upon enquiry the greatest reason in the world for it – which though it vexes me, yet it is most [plain] to see from day to day what a coxcomb he is, and that so great a trust should lie in the hands of such a foole. We sat all the afternoon; and I late at my office, it being post night; and so home to supper. And after supper to bed; and after some talk, to sleep.

14.    Up betimes to my office, where busy till 8 a-clock, that Sir W. Batten, Sir J. Mennes, Sir W. Penn and I down by barge to Woolwich to see the *Royall James* lanched, where she hath been under repair a great while. We stayed in the yard till almost noon, and then to Mr. Falconer's to a dinner of fish of our own sending. And when it was just ready to come upon the table, word is brought that the King and Duke are come, so they all went away to show themselfs, while I stayed and had a little dish or two by myself, resolving to go home; and by the time I had dined, they came again, having gone to little purpose, the King I believe taking little notice of them. So they to dinner, and I stayed a little with them and so good-bye. I walked to Greenwich, studying my slide-rule for measuring of timber, which is very fine. Thence to Deptford by water and walked through the yard, and so walked to Redriffe and so home, pretty weary, and to my office; where anon they all came home, the ship well lanched, and so sat at the office till 9 at night – and I longer, doing business at my office; and so home to supper, my father being come, and to bed.

16. Up betimes and to my office. Anon met to pass Mr. Pitts (Sir J. Lawson's Secretary and Deputy Treasurer) accounts for the voyage last to the Streights – wherein the demands are strangely irregular; and I dare not oppose it alone, for making an enemy, and both no good but only bring a review upon my Lord Sandwiches; but God knows, it troubles my heart to see it and to see the Comptroller, whose duty it is, to make no more matter of it. At noon home for an hour to dinner, and so to the office, public and private, till late at night; so home to supper and bed with my father.

17. Up by 5 a-clock, as I have long done, and to my office all the morning; at noon home to dinner with my father with us. Our dinner, it being Goodfriday, was only sugar sopps and fish; the only time that we have had a Lenten dinner all this Lent. This morning Mr. Hunt the instrument-maker brought me home a Basse viall to see whether I like it, which I do not very well; besides, I am under a doubt whether I had best buy one yet or no – because of spoiling my present mind and love to business. After dinner my father and I walked into the City a little and parted; and I to Pauls churchyard to cause the title of my English *Mare Clausum* to be changed and the new title, dedicated to the King, to be put to it, because I am ashamed to have the other seen dedicate[d] to the Commonwealth. So home and to my office till night; and so home to talk with my father, and sup and to bed – I having not had yet one Quarter of an hour's leisure to sit down and talk with him since he came to towne. Nor do I know till the holidays when I shall.

19. *Easterday*. Up, and this day put on my close-kneed colourd suit; which, with new stockings of that colour, with belt and new gilt-handle sword, is very handsome. To church alone. And so to dinner, where my father and brother Tom dined with us. And after dinner to church again, my father sitting below in the chancel. After church done (where the young scotchman preaching, I slept all the while) my father and I see my uncle and aunt Wight; and after a stay of an hour there, my father to my brothers and I home to supper. And after supper fell in discourse of dancing, and I find that Ashwell hath a very fine carriage, which makes my wife almost ashamed of herself to see herself so outdonne; but tomorrow she begins to learn to dance for a month or two. So to prayers and to bed – my Will being gone with my leave to his father's this day for a day or two, to take physique these holidays.

20. Up betimes as I use to do, and in my chambers begun to look over my father's accounts, which he brought out of the country with him by my desire, whereby I may see what he hath received and spent. And I find that he is not anything extravagant, and yet it doth so far outdo his estate that he must either think of lessening his charge or I must be forced to spare money out of my purse to help him through; which I would willing do, as far as 20*l* goes. Somewhat troubled at Ashwell's desiring and insisting over-eaguerly upon her going to a ball to meet some of her old companions at a dancing school here in town next Friday; but I am resolved she shall not go.

26. *Lords day.* All the afternoon upon my accounts, and find myself worth full 700*l*, for which I bless God, it being the most I was ever yet worth in money. In the evening (my father being gone to my brother's to lie tonight) my wife, Ashwell, and the boy and I, and the dog, over the water and walked to Halfway house and beyond, into the fields gathering of Cowslipps; and so to Halfway house with some cold lamb we carried with us, and there supped; and had a most pleasant walk back again – Ashwell all along telling us some parts of their maske at Chelsy school, which was very pretty; and I find she hath a most prodigious memory, remembering so much of things acted six or seven years ago. So home; and after reading my vowes, being sleepy, without prayers to bed; for which God forgive me.

27. At home with my wife and Ashwell, talking of her going into the country this year; wherein we had like to have fallen out, she thinking that I have a design to have her go, which I have not; and to let her stay here I perceive will not be convenient, for she expects more pleasure then I can give her here, and I fear I have done very ill in letting her begin to learn to dance.

30. Up; and after drinking my morning draught with my father and W. Stankes,[1] I went forth to Sir W. Batten, who is going (to no purpose, as he uses to do) to Chatham upon a Survey. So to my office, where till towards noon; and then to the Exchange and back home to dinner, where Mr. Hunt, my father, and W. Stankes; but Lord, what a stir Stankes makes with his being crowded in the

1. Their bailiff at Brampton.

streets and wearied in walking in London, and would not be woo'd by my wife and Ashwell to go to a play nor to Whitehall or to see the Lyons, though he was carried in a coach. I never could have thought there had been upon earth a man so little curious in the world as he is. At the office all the afternoon till 9 at night; so home – to cards with my father, wife and Ashwell, and so to bed.

## –❧MAY❧–

1. Up betimes and my father with me, and he and I all the morning and Will Stankes private in my wife's Closet above, settling our matters concerning our Brampton estate &c.; and I find that there will be, after all debts paid within 100*l*, 50*l* per annum clear coming towards my father's maintenance. I advised my father to good husbandry and to living within the compass of 50*l* a year; and all in such kind words as made not only both them but myself to weep – and I hope it will have a good effect. So toward Hide parke, whither all the world I think are going; and in my going (almost thither) met W. How coming, galloping upon a little crop black nag (it seems one that was taken in some ground of my Lord's, by some mischance being left by his maister, a Thiefe; this horse being found with black cloth eares on and a false mayne, having none of his own); and I back again with him to the Chequer at Charing cross, and by his advice saddled a delicate stone-horse of Capt. Ferrers. And with that rid in state to the park – where none better mounted then I almost; but being in a throng of horses, seeing the King's Riders showing tricks with their managed-horses, which were very strange, my stone-horse was very troublesome and begun to fight with other horses, to the endangering him and myself; and with much ado I got out and kept myself out of harm's way. By and by, about 7 or 8 a-clock, homeward. In my way in Leadenhall street there was morris dancing, which I have not seen a great while. So home to see Sir J. Minnes, who is well again; and after staying talking with him a while, I took leave and went to hear Mrs. Turner's daughter play on the Harpsicon, but Lord, it was enough to make any man sick to hear her; yet was I forced to commend her highly. So home to supper and to bed, Ashwell playing upon the Tryangle very well before I went to bed. This day Capt. Grove sent me a side of porke, which was the oddest present, sure, that was

ever made to any man; and the next, I remember I told my wife, I
believe would be a pound of candles or a shoulder of mutton. But
the fellow doth it in kindness and is one I am beholding to.

3. *Lords day*. Up before 5 a-clock, and alone at setting my
Brampton papers to rights according to my father's and my
computation and resolution the other day, to my good content. To
dinner with my wife, who not being very well, did not dress herself
but stayed at home all day; and so I to church in the afternoon; and
so home again and up to teach Ashwell the grounds of time and
other things on the Tryangle, and made her take out a psalm very
well, she having a good eare and hand. And so a while to my office
and then home to supper – and prayers, to bed – my wife and I
having a little falling-out because I would not leave my discourse
below with her and Ashwell to go up and talk with her alone upon
something she hath to say. She reproached me that I rather talk with
anybody then her – by which I find I think she is jealous of my
freedom with Ashwell – which I must avoid giving occasion of.

4. The Dancing Maister came; whom standing by seeing him
instructing my wife, when he had done with her he would needs
have me try the steps of a *Coranto*; and what with his desire and my
wife's importunity, I did begin, and then was obliged to give him
entry-money, 10*s*. – and am become his Scholler. The truth is, I
think it is a thing very useful for any gentleman and sometimes I
may have occasion of using it; and though it cost me, which I am
heartily sorry it should, besides that I must by my oath give half as
much more to the poor, yet I am resolved to get it up some other
way; and then it will not be above a month or two in a year. So
though it be against my stomach, yet I will try it a little while; if I see
it comes to any great inconvenience or charge, I will fling it off.
After I had begun with the steps of half a *coranto*, which I think I
shall learn well enough, he went away and we to dinner.

5. To my office, busy late, writing letters; and then came Sir W.
Warren, staying for a letter in his business by the post, and while
that was writing, he and I talk about merchandise, trade and getting
of money. I made it my business to enquire what way there is for a
man bred like me to come to understand anything of trade. He did
most discretely answer me in all things, showing me the danger for
me to meddle either in ships or merchandise of any sort, or

common Stockes, but what I have, to keep at interest, which is a good, quiet and easy profit and once in a little while something offers that with ready money you may make use of money to good profit – wherein I concur much with him, and parted late with great pleasure and content in his discourse; and so home to supper and to bed.

6.   Up betimes and to my office; a good while at my new rulers, then to business. And towards noon to the exchange with Creede, where we met with Sir J. Minnes coming in his coach from Westminster; who tells us in great heat that, by God, the parliament will make mad work; that they will render all men incapable of any military or Civill imployment that have borne arms in the late troubles against the King, excepting some persons – which if it be so, as I hope it is not, will give great cause of discontent, and I doubt will have but bad effects. I left them at the Exchange and I walked to Pauls churchyard to look upon a book or two, and so back and thence to the Trinity house and there dined – where, among other discourse worth hearing among the old Seamen, they tell us that they have ketched often in Greenland in fishing Whales, with the Iron grapnells that had formerly been struck into their bodies covered over with fat – that they have had eleven hogsheadds of Oyle out of the Tongue of a Whale.

8.   Up very ealely and to my office, there preparing letters to my father, of great import in the settling of our affairs and putting him upon a way [of] good husbandry – I promising him to make out of my own purse him up 50*l* per annum, till either by my Uncle Thomas's death or the fall of the Wardrobe place he be otherwise provided. That done, I by water to the Strand and there viewed the Queene-Mother's works at Somerset house; and thence to the new playhouse, the second day of its being opened. The play was *The Humorous Lieutenant* – a play that hath little good in it. In the dance, the Tall Devil's actions was very pretty. The play being done, we home by water, and to my office to set down this day's passage. And though my oath against going to plays doth not oblige me against this house, because it was not then in being, yet believing that at that time my meaning was against all public houses, I am resolved to deny myself the liberty of two plays at Court which are in arreare to me for the months of March and Aprill; which will more then countervail this excess. So home to supper. And at

supper comes Pembleton; and afterwards we all up to dancing till late, and so broke up and to bed; and they say that I am like to make a dancer.

9.   Up betimes and to my office; whither sooner then ordinary comes Mr. Hater, desiring to speak a word to me alone, which I was from the disorder of his countenance amused* at; and so the poor man begun telling me that by Providence being the last Lord's day at a meeting of some Friends upon doing of their duties, they were surprized and he carried to the Counter, but afterward released; however, hearing that Sir W. Batten doth hear of [it], he thought it good to give me an account of it, lest it might tend to any prejudice to me. I was extraordinary surprized with it and troubled for him, knowing that now it is out, it is impossible for me to conceal it, or keep him in imployment under me without danger to myself. I cast about all I could and did give him the best advice I could; desiring to know if I should promise that he would not for the time to come commit the same, he told me he desired that I would rather forbear to promise that; for he durst not do it, what[ever] God in His providence shall do with him; and that for my part, he did bless God and thank me for all the love and kindness I have showed him hitherto. I could not, without tears in my eyes, discourse with him further, but at last did pitch upon telling the truth of the whole to Mr. Coventry as soon as I could; and to that end did use means to prevent Sir W. Batten (who came to town last night) from going to that end today, lest he might doe it to Sir G. Carteret or Mr. Coventry before me – which I did prevail, and kept him at the office all the morning. At noon dined at home with a heavy heart for the poor man.

10.   *Lords day.* Up betimes and put on a black cloth suit with white Lynings under all, as the fashion is to wear, to appear under the breeches. So being ready, walked to St. James – where I sat talking with Mr. Coventry while he made himself ready, about several businesses of the Navy. And after the Duke being gone out, he and I walked to Whitehall together over the parke, I telling him what had happened about Tom Hater; at which he seems very sorry, but tells me that if it is not made very public it will not be necessary to put him away at present, but give him a good caucion for the time to come. However, he will speak to the Duke about it and know his pleasure. Parted with him there; and I walked back to St. James's

and was there at Masse, and was forced in the croud to kneel down; and Masse being done, to the King's head ordinary, whither I sent for Mr. Creed and there we dined; where many parliament-men and most of their talk was about the news from Scotland that the Bishop of Galloway was besieged in his house by some women and had like to have been outraged, but, I know not how, he was secured – which is bad news and looks just as it did in the beginning of the late troubles. From thence they talked of rebellion; and I perceive they make it their great maxime to be sure to Maister the City of London, whatever comes of it or from it. After that, to some other discourse; and among other things, talking of the way of ordinaries, that it is very convenient because a man knows what he hath to pay, one did wish that among many bad, we could learn two good things of France – which were that we would not think it below the gentleman or person of honour at a taverne to bargain for his meat before he eats it; and next, to take no servants without Certificate from some friend or gentleman of his good behaviour and abilities.

12.   Up between 4 and 5; and after dressed myself, then to my office to prepare business against the afternoon – where all the morning and dined at noon at home, where a little angry with my wife for minding nothing now but the dancing-maister, having him come twice a day, which is a folly.

15.   Up betimes and walked to St. James's; where Mr Coventry being in bed, I walked in the park, discoursing with the keeper of the Pell Mell who was sweeping of it – who told me of what the earth is mixed that doth floor the Mall, and that over all there is Cockle-shells powdered and spread, to keep it fast; which however, in dry weather turns to dust and deads the ball. Thence to Mr. Coventry ; and sitting by his bedside, he did tell me that he sent for me to discourse upon my Lord Sandwiches allowances for his several pays, and what his thoughts are concerning his demands; which he could not take the freedom to do face to face, it being not so proper as by me; and did give me a most friendly and ingenious account of all. After done with him about those things, he told me that for Mr. Hater, the Dukes word was, in short, that he found he had a good servant, an Anabaptist; and unless he did carry himself more to the scandall of the office, he would bear with his opinion till he heard further – which doth please me very much. To dinner with

[my Lord], there dining there my Lord Mountagu of Boughton, Mr Wm. Mountague his brother, the Queen's Sollicitor, &c.; and a fine dinner. Their talk about a ridiculous falling-out two days ago at my Lord of Oxfords house at an entertainment of his, there being there my Lord of Albemarle, Lynsey, two of the Porters, my Lord Bellasse[s], and others; where there was high words and some blows and pulling off of perriwiggs – till my Lord Monke took away some of their swords and sent for some soldiers to guard the house till the fray was ended. To such a degree of madness the nobility of this age is come.

After dinner I went up to Sir Tho. Crew, who lies there not very well in his head, being troubled with vapours and fits of dizzinesse; and there I sat talking with him all the afternoon, from one discourse to another. The most was upon the unhappy posture of things at this time; that the King doth mind nothing but pleasures and hates the very sight or thoughts of business. That my Lady Castlemayne rules him; who he says hath all the tricks of Aretin that are to be practised to give pleasure. It seems the present favourites now are my Lord Bristoll, Duke of Buckingham, Sir H. Bennet, my Lord Ashley, and Sir Ch. Berkely; who among them have cast my Lord Chancellor upon his back, past ever getting up again; there being now little for him to do, and waits at court attending to speak to the King as others do. My Lord Albemarle, I hear, doth bear through and bustle among them and will not be removed from the King's good opinion and favour, though none of the Cabinett; but yet he is envied enough. It is made very doubtful whether the King doth not entend the making of the Duke of Monmouth legitimate; but surely the Commons of England will never do it nor the Duke of Yorke suffer it – whose lady I am told is very troublesome to him by her jealousy. Having thus freely talked with him and of many more things, I took leave; and by coach to St. James's and there told Mr. Coventry what I had done with my Lord, with great satisfaction; and so, well pleased, home – where I find it almost night and my wife and the Dancing Maister alone above, not dancing but walking. Now, so deadly full of jealousy I am, that my heart and head did so cast about and fret, that I could not do any business possibly, but went out to my office; and anon late home again, and ready to chide at everything; and then suddenly to bed and could hardly sleep, yet durst not say anything.

16. Up, with my mind disturbed and with my last night's doubts

upon me. For which I deserve to be beaten, if not really served as I am fearful of being; especially since, God knows, that I do not find honesty enough in my own mind but that upon a small temptation I could be false to her, and therefore ought not to expect more justice from her – but God pardon both my sin and my folly herein. To my office and there setting all the morning; and at noon dined at home. After dinner comes Pembleton again; and I being out of humour, would not see him, pretending business; but Lord, with what jealousy did I walk up and down my chamber, listening to hear whether they danced or no or what they did; notwithstanding I afterwards knew, and did then believe, that Ashwell was with them. So to my office awhile; and my jealousy still reigning, I went in and, not out of any pleasure but from that only reason, did go up to them to practise; and did make an end of *La Duchesse*, which I think [I] should with a little pains do very well. So broke up and saw him gone.

21.    Being at supper, my wife did say something that caused me to oppose her in; she used the word "Devil," which vexed me; and among other things, I said I would not have her to use that word, upon which she took me up most scornfully; which before Ashwell and the rest of the world, I know not nowadays how to check as I would heretofore, for less then that would have made me strike her. So that I fear, without great discretion, I shall go near to lose too my command over her; and nothing doth it more then giving her this occasion of dancing and other pleasure, whereby her mind is taken up from her business and finds other sweets besides pleasing of me, and so makes her that she begins not at all to take pleasure in me or study to please me as heretofore. But if this month of her dancing were but out (as my first was this night, and I paid off Pembleton for myself), I shall hope with a little pains to bring her to her old wont. This day, Susan that lived with me lately, being out of service, and I doubt a simple wench, my wife doth take her for a little time to try her, at least till she goes into the country; which I am yet doubtful whether it will be best for me to send her or no, for fear of her running on in her liberty before I have brought her to her right temper again.

22.    Up pretty betimes; and shall I hope come to myself and business again after a small playing the truant, for I find that my interest and profit do grow daily, for which God be praised and

keep me to my duty. To my office. And anon one tells me that Rundall the house-carpenter of Deptford hath sent me a fine Blackebird – which I went to see. He tells me he was offered 20s. for him as he came along, he doth so whistle. So to my office, and busy all the morning. Among other things, learning to understand the course of the tides, and I think I do now do it. At noon Mr. Creede comes to me, and he and I to the Exchange, where I had much discourse with several merchants; and so home with him to dinner and then by water to Greenwich; and calling at the little alehouse at the end of the town to wrap a rag about my little left toe, being new-sore with walking, we walked pleasantly to Woolwich, in our way hearing the Nightingales sing. So to Woolwich yard; and after doing many things there, among others preparing myself for a dispute against Sir W. Penn in the business of Bewpers, wherein he is guilty of some corruption to the King's wrong, we walked back again without drinking there; which I never do, because I would not make my coming troublesome to any, nor would become obliged too much to any. Going back, took boat at Greenwich and to Deptford, where I did the same thing and find Davis, the Storekeeper, a knave and shuffling in the business of Bewpers, being of the party with Young and Whistler to abuse the King; but I hope I shall be even with them. So walked to Redriffe, drinking at the Halfway house; and so walk and by water to Whitehall, all our way by water, both coming and going, reading a little book said to be writ by a person of Quality concerning English Gentry to be preferred before Titular honours; but the most silly nonsense, no sense nor grammar, yet in as good words that ever I saw in all my life, that from beginning to end you meet not with one entire and regular sentence.

23. Waked this morning between 4 and 5 by my black-Bird, which whistles as well as ever I heard any; only it is the beginning of many tunes very well, but there leaves them and goes no further. So up and to my office, where we sat. Home to dinner; and after dinner by water to the temple and there took my Lyra viall book, bound up with blank paper for new lessons. Thence to Greatorex's; and there, seeing Sir J. Mennes and Sir W. Penn go by by coach, I went in to them and to Whitehall, where, in the matted gallery, Mr. Coventry was; who told us how the parliament hath required of Sir G. Carteret and him an account what money shall be necessary to be settled upon the Navy for the ordinary charge, which they intend to

report 200000*l* per annum; and how to allot this, we met this afternoon and took their papers for our perusal, and so we parted. Thence back by water to Greatorex's, and there he showed me his Varnish which he hath invented, which appears every whit as good, upon a stick which he hath done, as the Indian, though it did not do very well upon my paper rules with Musique lines, for it sunk and did not shine.

24. *Lords day*. Having taken one of Mr. Holliards pills last night, it brought a stool or two this morning; and so I forebore going to church this morning, but stayed at home, looking over my papers about T. Trices business;[1] and so at noon dined, and my wife telling me that there was a pretty lady come to church with Pegg Pen today, I against my intention had a mind to go to church to see her, and did so – and she is pretty handsome. But over against our gallery I espied Pembleton and saw him leer upon my wife all the sermon, I taking no notice of him, and my wife upon him; and I observed she made a curtsey to him at coming out, without taking notice to me at all of it; which, with the consideration of her being desirous these two last Lord's-days to go to church both forenoon and afternoon, doth really make me suspect something more then ordinary. But I must have patience and get her into the country, or at least to make an end of her learning to dance as soon as I can.

25. Up; and my pill working a little, I stayed within most of the morning. Ashwell did by and by come to me with an errand from her mistress, to desire money to buy a country suit for her against she goes as we talked last night; and so I did give her 4*l* and believe it will cost me the best part of 4 more to fit her out; but with peace and honour, I am willing to spare anything so as to be able to keep all ends together and my power over her undisturbed. Mr. Alsopp the King's Brewer tells me of a horse of his that lately, after four days' pain, voided at his fundament four stones, bigger then that I was cut of, very heavy and in the middle of each of them either a piece of Iron or wood. The King hath two of them in his closet, and a third, the College of Physicians to keep for rarities; and by the King's command he causes the turd of the horse to be every day searched to find more.

1. See above, pp. 144–5 (8–13 July).

26.   Lay long in bed, talking and pleasing myself with my wife. So up and to my office a while and then home, where I find Pembleton; and I am led to conclude that there is something more then ordinary between my wife and him. There dined with me Mr. Creed and Capt. Grove; but nothing could get the business out of my head, I fearing that this afternoon, by my wife's sending every[one] abroad and knowing that I must be at the office, she hath appointed him to come. This is my devilish jealousy; which I pray God may be false, but it makes a very hell in my mind; which the God of heaven remove, or I shall be very unhappy. So to the office, where we sat a while. By and by, my mind being in great trouble, I went home to see how things were; and there I find as I doubted, Mr. Pembleton with my wife and nobody else in the house, which made me almost mad; and going up to my chamber, after a turn or two I went out again and to the office; and Mr. Coventry nor Sir G. Carteret being there, I made a quick end of our business and desired leave to be gone, pretending to go to the Temple, but it was home; and so up to my chamber and, as I think, if they had any intentions of hurt, I did prevent doing anything at that time; but I continued in my chamber vexed and angry till he went away, pretending aloud, that I might hear, that he could not stay, and Mrs. Ashwell not being within they would not dance. And Lord, to see how my jealousy wrought so far, that I went saftly up to see whether any of the beds were out of order or no, which I found not; but that did not content me, but I stayed all the evening walking, and though anon my wife came up to me and would have spoke of business to me, yet I construed it to be but impudence; and though my heart was full, yet I did say nothing, being in a great doubt what to do. So at night suffered them to go all to bed, and late put myself to bed in great discontent, and so to sleep.

27.   So I waked by 3 a-clock, my mind being troubled; and so took occasion by making water to wake my wife, and after having lain till past 4 a-clock, seemed going to rise, though I did it only to see what she would do; and so going out of the bed, she took hold of me and would know what ayled me; and after many kind and some cross words, I begun to tax her discretion in yesterday's business, but she quickly told me my owne, knowing well enough that it was my old disease of Jealousy; which I disowned, but to no purpose. After an hour's discourse, sometimes high and sometimes kind, I find very good reason to think that her freedom with him was very

great and more then was convenient, but with no evil intent. And
so after a while I caressed her and parted seeming friends, but she
crying and in a great discontent. So I up and by water to the
Temple. Here I met with my Cosen Roger Pepys and walked a
good while with him; and among other discourse, as a secret he
hath committed to nobody yet but myself, he tells me that his sister
Claxton now resolving to give over the keeping of his house at
Impington, he thinks it fit to marry again; and would have me, by
the help of my uncle Wight or others, to look him out a widow
between 30 and 40 year old, without children and with a fortune,
which he will answer in any degree with a Joynture fit for her
fortune. A woman sober and no high flyer as he calls it. I demanded
his estate; he tells me (which he says also he hath not done to any)
that his estate is not full 800*l* per annum, but it is 780*l* per annum – of
which 200*l* is by the death of his last wife; which he will allot for a
Joynture for a wife, but the rest, which lies in Cambrigeshire, he is
resolved to leave entire for his eldest son. I undertook to do what I
can in it, and so I shall. He tells me that the King hath sent to them[1]
to hasten to make an end by Midsummer; so they have set upon
four bills to despatch – the first of which is, he says, too devilish a
severe act against conventicles; so beyond all moderation, that he is
afeared it will ruin all. Telling me that it is matter of the greatest
grief to him in the world that he should be put upon this trust of
being a parliament-man, because he says nothing is done, that he
can see, out of any truth and sincerity, but mere envy and design.
Thence by water to Chelsy, all the way reading a little book I
bought of Improvement of trade, a pretty book and many things
useful in it. So walked to Little Chelsy, where I find my Lord
Sandwich with Mr. Becke, the maister of the house, and Mr. Creed
at dinner. And I sat down with them, and very merry. After dinner
(Mr. Gibbons being come in also before dinner done) to Musique;
they played a good Fancy, to which my Lord is fallen again and says
he cannot endure a merry tune – which is a strange turn of his
humour, after he hath for two or three years flung off the practice of
Fancies and played only fiddlers tunes. Then into the great garden
up to the banquetting-house; and there by his glass we drow in the
Species very pretty. Afterwards to ninepins, where I won a shilling
– Creed and I playing against My Lord and Cooke. This day there
was great thronging to Bansted downes, upon a great horse-race

---

1. The House of Commons.

and foot-race; I am sorry I could not go thither.

So home, back as I came, to London bridge and so home – where I find my wife in a musty humour, and tells me before Ashwell that Pembleton had been there and she would not have him come in unless I was there, which I was ashamed of; but however, I had rather it should be so then the other way. So to my office to put things in order there. And by and by comes Pembleton and word is brought me from my wife thereof, that I might come home; so I sent word that I would have her go dance, and I would come presently. So being at a great loss whether I should appear to Pembleton or no, and which would most proclaim my jealousy to him, I at last resolved to go home; and took Tom Hater with me and stayed a good while in my chamber, and there took occasion to tell him how I hear that parliament is putting an act out against all sorts of Conventicles and did give him good counsel, not only in his own behalfe but my own, that if he did hear or know anything that could be said to my prejudice, that he would tell me; for in this wicked age (especially Sir W. Batten being so open to my reproches and Sir J. Mennes, for the neglect of their duty, and so will think themselfs obliged to scandalize me all they can to right themselfs if there shall be any enquiry into the matters of the Navy, as no doubt there will) a man ought to be prepared to answer for himself in all things that can be enquired concerning him. After much discourse of this nature to him, I sent him away and then went up; and there we danced country dances and single, my wife and I, and my wife paid him off for this month also, and so he is cleared. After dancing, we took him down to supper and were very merry; and I made myself so and kind to him as much as I could, to prevent his discourse; though I perceive to my trouble that he knows all, and my doty doth me the disgrace to publish it as much as she can. Which I take very ill, and if too much provoked shall witness it to her. After supper and he gone, we to bed.

28. To the Dukes house and there saw *Hamlett* done, giving us fresh reason never to think enough of Baterton. Who should we see come upon the Stage but Gosnell, my wife's maid, but neither spoke, danced nor sung; which I was sorry for. But she becomes the stage very well.

29. This day is kept strictly as a holyday, being the King's Coronacion. We lay long in bed. And it rained very hard, rain and

hail almost all the morning. By and by Creed and I abroad and called at several churches; and it is a wonder to see, and by that to guess, the ill temper of the City at this time, either to religion in general or to the King, that in some churches there was hardly ten people in the whole church, and those poor people.

30.　　Up betimes and Creed and I by water to Fleetestreete; and my brother not being ready, he and I walked to the New Exchange and there dranke our morning draught of Whay, the first I have done this year. But I perceive the lawyers come all in as they go to the hall, and I believe it is very good. So to my brother's and there I find my aunt James, a poor, religious, well-meaning, good humble soul, talking of nothing but God Almighty, and that with so much innocence that mightily pleased me. Here was a fellow that said grace so long, like a prayer; I believe the fellow is a cunning fellow, and yet I by my brother's desire did give him a crowne, he being in great want and it seems a parson among the fanatiques and a cousin of my poor aunts – whose prayers, she told me, did do me good among the many good souls that did by my father's desires pray for me when I was cut of the stone, and which God did hear; which I also in complaisance did owne, but God forgive me, my mind was otherwise. So home; and after supper did wash my feet, and so to bed.

31.　　This month, the greatest news is the heighth and heat that the Parliament is in enquiring into the Revenue, which displeases the Court, and their backwardness to give the King any money. Their enquiring into the selling of places doth trouble a great many; among the chief, my Lord Chancellor (against whom perticularly it is carried) and Mr. Coventry, for which I am sorry. The King of France was given out to be poisoned and dead; but it proves to be the meazles and is well, or likely to be soon well again. I find myself growing in the esteem and credit that I have in the office, and I hope falling to my business again will confirm me in it, and the saving of money – which God grant.

　　My whole family lying longer this morning then was fit, and besides, Will having neglected to brush my cloak as he ought to do till I was ready to go to church, and not then till I bid him, I was very angry; and seeing him make little matter of it, but seeming to make a matter indifferent whether he did it or no, I did give him [a] box on the eare, and had it been another day had done more.

This is the second time I ever struck him.

# ⚜ JUNE ⚜

2.   Up and by water to Whitehall; and so to St. James to Mr. Coventry, where I had an hour's private talk with him. Most of it was discourse concerning his own condition, at present being under the censure of the House, being concerned with others in the Bill for selling of offices. He undertakes to prove that he did never take a token of any Captain to get him imployed in his life beforehand, or demanded anything. And for the other accusacion, that the Cavaliers are not imployed, he looked over the list of them now in the service, and of the 27 that are imployed, 13 have been heretofore alway under the King. Two, Neutralls; and the other 12 men of great courage and such as had either the King's perticular command or great recomendacion to put them in, and none by himself. Besides that, he says it is not the King's nor Dukes opinion that the whole party of the late officers should be rendered desperate; and lastly, he confesses that the more of the Cavaliers are put in, the less of discipline hath fallowed in the fleet; and that whenever there comes occasion, it must be the old ones that must do any good – there being none, he says, but Capt. Allen good for anything of them all.

3.   To the Exchange and thence home to dinner, taking Deane of Woolwich along with me; and he dined alone with me, [my] wife being undressed, and he and I spent all the afternoon finely, learning of him the method of drawing the lines of a ship, to my great satisfaction; and which is well worth my spending some time in, as I shall do when my wife is gone into the country. In the evening to the office and did some business. Then home and, God forgive me, did from my wife's unwillingness to tell me whither she had sent the boy, presently suspect that he was gone to Pembleton's, and from that occasion grew so discontented that I could hardly speak or sleep all night.

4.   I did by a wile get out of my boy that he did not yesterday go to Pembleton's or thereabouts, but only was sent at that time for some starch; and I did see him bring home some – and yet all this cannot

make my mind quiet. In [Westminster] hall today, Dr. Pierce tells me that the Queene begins to be briske and play like other ladies, and is quite another woman from what she was, of which I am glad – it may be it may make the King like her the better and forsake his two mistresses, my Lady Castlemaine and Steward.

5. Up and to read a little; and by and by, the Carver coming, I directed him how to make me a neat head for my viall that is making. About 10 a-clock my wife and I, not without some discontent, abroad by coach, and I set her at her father's; but their condition is such that she will not let me see where they live – but goes by herself when I am out of sight. Thence I to my brother's, taking care for a passage for my wife the next week in a coach to my father's. Thence to Pauls churchyard, where I find several books ready bound for me; among others, the new *Concordance* of the Bible, which pleases me much and is a book I hope to make good use of.

6. Lay in bed till 7 a-clock, yet rise with an opinion that it was not 5; and so continued, though I heard the clock strike, till noon and could not believe that it was so late as it truly was. I was hardly ever so mistaken in my life before. Up and to Sir G. Carteret at his house and spoke to him about business; but he being in a bad humour, I had no mind to stay with him, but walked (drinking my morning draught of Whey by the way) to Yorke house, where the Russia Embassador doth lie; and there I saw his people go up and down louseing themselfs; they are all in a great hurry, being to be gone the beginning of next week. By and by comes Sir John Hebden the Russia Resident to me, and he and I in his coach to Whitehall to Secretary Morrices, to see the orders about the Russia Hemp that is to be fetched from Archangell for our King; and that being done, to coach again and he brought me into the City; and so I home, and after dinner abroad by water and met by appointment Mr. Deane in the Temple church; and he and I over to Mr. Blackburys yard and thence to other places; and after that, to a drinking house; in all which places I did so practise and improve my measuring of timber, that I can now do it with great ease and perfection, which doth please me mightily. This fellow Deane is a conceited fellow and one that means the King a great deal of service, more of disservice to other people that go away with profits which he cannot make; but however, I learn much of him and he is, I perceive, of great use to

the King in his place, and so I shall give him all the encouragement I can. Hebden did today in the coach tell me how he is vexed to see things at Court ordered as they are; by nobody that attends business, but every man himself or his pleasures. He cries up my Lord Ashley to be almost the only man that he sees to look after business; and with that ease and mastery that he wonders at him. He cries out against the King's dealing so much with goldsmiths, and suffering himself to have his purse kept and commanded by them. He tells me also with what exact care and order the States of Hollands stores are kept in their Yards, and everything managed there by their builders with such husbandry as is not imaginable – which I will endeavour to understand further, if I can by any means learn.

7.   *Whitsunday. Lords day.* Lay long, talking with my wife, sometimes angry; and ended pleased and hope to bring our matters to a better posture in a little time, which God send. So up and to church, where Mr. Mills preached; but I know not how, I slept most of the sermon. Thence home and dined with my wife and Ashwell and after dinner discoursed very pleasantly; and so I to church again in the afternoon. And the Scott preaching again, slept all the afternoon.

9.   We met at the office, Mr. Coventry, Sir J. Mennes and I; and so in the evening, business done, I went home. Spent my time till night with my wife. Presently after my coming home comes Pembleton, whether by appointment or no I know not, or whether by a former promise that he would come once before my wife's going into the country. But I took no notice, but let them go up and Ashwell with them to dance; which they did, and I stayed below in my chamber; but Lord, how I listened and laid my eare to the door, and how I was troubled when I heard them stand still and not dance. Anon they made an end and had done, and so I suffered him to go away and spoke not to him, though troubled in my mind; but showed no discontent to my wife, believing that this is the last time I shall be troubled with him. So my wife and I to walk in the garden, and so home and to supper and to bed.

11.   Dined at home and then to the office, where we sat all the afternoon. And at night home and spent the evening with my wife, and she and I did jangle mightily about her cushions that she

wrought with worsteds the last year, which are too little for any use; but were good friends by and by again. But one thing I must confess I do observe, which I did not before; which is, that I cannot blame my wife to be now in a worse humour then she used to be, for I am taken up in my talk with Ashwell, who is a very witty girle, that I am not so fond of her as I used and ought to be; which now I do perceive, I will remedy.

12. Up and my office, there conning my measuring-Ruler, which I shall grow a master of in a very little time. At noon to the Exchange, and so home to dinner and abroad with my wife by water to the Royall Theatre and there saw *The Comittee*, a merry but an indifferent play; only Lacy's part, an Irish footman, is beyond imagination. Here I saw my Lord Falconbrige and his Lady, my Lady Mary Cromwell, who looks as well as I have known her and well-clad; but when the House begun to fill, she put on her vizard and so kept it on all the play – which is of late become a great fashion among the ladies, which hides their whole face.

13. To the office and there had a difference with Sir W. Batten about Mr. Bowyers tarr; which I am resolved to cross, though he sent me last night, as a bribe, a barrell of Sturgeon; which it may be I shall send back, for I will not have the King abused so abominably in the price of what we buy by Sir W. Batten's corruption and underhand dealing. So from the office by water, Mr. Wayth with me, to the Parliament-house; and there I spoke and told Sir G. Carteret all, with which he is well pleased and doth recall his willingness, yesterday it seems, to Sir W. Batten, that we should buy a great Quantity of tarr, being abused by him. Thence with Mr. Wayth, after drinking a cup of ale at the Swan, talking of the corruptions of the Navy, by water; I landed him at Whitefryers, and I to the Exchange and so home to dinner, where I find my wife's brother; and thence after dinner by water to the Royall Theatre, where I am resolved to bid farewell, as shall appear by my oaths tomorrow, against all plays, either at public houses or Court, till Christmas be over.

15. Up betimes; and anon my wife rose and did give me her keys and put other things in order, and herself, against her going this morning into the country. I was forced to go to Thames street and strike up a bargaine for some tarr, to prevent being abused therein

by Hill, who was with me this morning and is mightily surprized
that I should tell him what I can have the same tarr with his for.
Thence home; but finding my wife gone, I took coach and after her
to her Inne; where I am troubled to see her forced to sit in the back of
the coach, though pleased to see her company, none but women
and one parson. And so kissing her often and Ashwell once, I bid
them Adieu; and so home by coach and thence by water to
Deptford to the Trinity house, where I came a little late but I found
them reading their charter; which they did like fools, only reading
here and there a bit, whereas they ought to do it all, every word; and
then proceeded to the Eleccion of a Maister, which was Sir W.
Batten, who made a heavy, short speech to them, moving them to
give thanks to the late Maister for his pains, which he said was very
great, and giving them thanks for their choice of him, wherein he
would serve them to the best of his power. Then to the choice of
their Assistants and Wardens, and so rose. Thence to church, where
Dr. Britton preached a sermon full of words against the Nonconformists; but no great matter in it, nor proper for the day at all. His
text was, "With one minde and one mouth give glory to God, the
father of our Lord Jesus Christ."

That done, by water, I in the barge with the Maister, to the
Trinity house at London, where, among others, I find my Lord
Sandwich and Craven and my Cosen Rogr. Pepys and Sir Wm.
Wheeler. Anon we sat down to dinner; which was very great, as
they always have. Great variety of talk. Both at and after dinner we
had great discourses of the nature and power of Spirits and whether
they can animate dead bodies; in all which, as of the general
appearing of spirits, my Lord Sandwich is very scepticall. He says
the greatest warrants that ever he had to believe any, is the present
appearing of the Devil in Wiltshire, much of late talked of, who
beats a drum up and down; there is books of it, and they say very
true. But my Lord observes that though he doth answer to any tune
that you will play to him upon another drum, yet one tune he tried
to play and could not; which makes him suspect the whole, and I
think it is a good argument. Sometimes they talked of handsome
women; and Sir J. Mennes saying that there was no beauty like
what he sees in the country-markets, and especially at Bury, in
which I will agree with him that there is a prettiest woman I ever
saw – my Lord replied: "Why, Sir John, what do you think of your
neighbour's wife?" looking upon me, "do not you think that he
hath a great beauty to his wife? Upon my word he hath!" – which I

was not a little proud of. Thence by Barge along with my Lord to Blackefryers, where he landed; and I thence walked home, where vexed to find my boy (whom I boxed at his coming for it) and Will abroad, though he was but upon tower hill a very little while. My head akeing with the healths I was forced to drink today, I sent for the barber; and he having done, I up to my wife's closet and there played on my viallin a good while; and without supper, anon to bed – sad for want of my wife, whom I love with all my heart, though of late she hath given me some troubled thoughts.

21. *Lords day*. Up betimes and fell to reading my Latin grammer, which I perceive I have great need of, having lately found it by my calling Will to the reading of a Chapter in Latin; and I am resolved to go through it. After being trimmed, I by water to Whitehall and so over the parke, it raining hard, to Mr. Coventrys chamber – where I spent two hours, talking with him about businesses of the Navy and how by his absence things are like to go with us; and with good content from my being with him, he carried me by coach and set me down at Whitehall, and thence to rights home by water. He showed me a list which he hath prepared for the parliament's viewe if the business of his selling of offices should be brought to further hearing, wherein he reckons up, as I remember, 236 offices of ships which have been disposed of without his taking one farthing. This, of his own accord, he opened his Cabinett on purpose to show me; meaning, I suppose, that I should discourse abroad of it and vindicate him therein; which I shall with all my power do. At home, being wet, shifting my band and things and then to dinner; and after dinner went up and tried a little upon my Tryangle, which I understand fully and with a little use I believe could bring myself to do something. So to church and slept all the sermon, the Scott, to whose voice I am not to be reconciled, preaching.

22. Up betimes and to my office, reading over all our letters of the office that we have writ since I came into the Navy – whereby to bring the whole series of matters into my memory and to enter in my manuscript some of them that are needful and of general influence. By and by with Sir Wm. Batten by coach to Westminster, where I walked in the hall from one man to another. Hear that the House is still divided about the manner of levying the Subsidys which they entend to give the King, both as to the manner, the time, and the number. Thence with Creed and bought a Lobster,

and then to an alehouse; where the maid of the house is a confident merry lass and, if modest, is very pleasant to the customers that come thither. Here we eat it, and thence to walk in the parke a good while – the Duke being gone a-hunting; and by and by came in and shifted himself, he having in his hunting, rather then go about, light and led his horse through a River up to his breast, and came so home; and when we were come, which was by and by, we went into to him; and being ready, he retired with us and we had a long discourse with him; but Mr. Creeds accounts stick still, through the perverse ignorance of Sir G. Carteret, which I can[not] safely control as I would. Thence to the park again and there walked up and down an hour or two till night with Creede, talking; who is so knowing and a man of that reason, that I cannot but love his company, though I do not love the man, because he is too wise to be made a friend of and acts all by interest and policy.

23.  Up by 4 a-clock and so to my office. But before I went out, calling, as I have of late done, for my boy's Copybook, I find that he hath not done his taske, and so I beat him and then went up to fetch my ropes end; but before I got down the boy was gone; I searched the cellar with a Candle, and from top to bottom could not find him high nor low. So to the office; and after an hour or two, by water to the Temple to my Cosen Roger, who I perceive is a deadly high man in the parliament business, and against the Court – showing me how they have computed that the King hath spent, at least hath received, about four Millions of money since he came in. So home to dinner alone; and there I find that my boy had got out of doors, and came in for his hat and band and so is gone away to his brother. But I do resolve even to let him go for good and all.

24.  Up before 4 a-clock, and so to my lute an hour and more and then by water, drinking my morning draught alone in an alehouse in Thames streete, to the Temple; and there, after a little discourse with my cousin Roger about some business, away by water to St. James and there an hour's private discourse with Mr. Coventry. We did talk highly of Sir W. Batten's corruption, which Mr. Coventry did very kindly say that it might be only his heaviness and unaptness for business that he doth things without advice and rashly and to gratify people that do eat and drink and play with him. And that now and then he observes that he signs bills only in anger and fury, to be rid of them. From that, we discoursed of the evil of

putting out men of experience in business, as the Chancellor; and from that, to speak of the condition of the King's party at present; who, as the papists, though otherwise fine persons, yet being by law kept for these four score years out of imployment, they are now wholly uncapable of business; and so the Cavalers for 20 years – who, says he, for the most part have either given themselfs over to look after country and family business, and those the best of them, and the rest to debauchery &c.

26.   Sir W. Batten, Sir J. Mennes, my Lady Batten and I by coach to Bednall green to Sir W. Riders to dinner – where a fine place, good lady, and their daughter Mrs. Middleton, a fine woman. A noble dinner and a fine merry walk with the ladies alone after dinner in the garden, which is very pleasant. The greatest Quantity of Strawberrys I ever saw, and good. At table, discoursing of thunder and lightning, they told many stories of their own knowledge at table; of their masts being shivered from top to bottom, and sometimes only within and the outside whole. But among the rest, Sir Wm. Rider did tell a story of his own knowledge, that a Genoese Gally in Legorne roade was struck by thunder so as the mast was broke a-pieces and the shackle upon one of the slaves was melted clear off of his leg, without hurting his leg. Sir Wm. went on board the vessel and would have contributed toward the release of the slave whom Heaven had thus set free, but he could not compass it and so he was brought to his fetters again. In the evening home; and I a little to my Tryangle and so to bed.

28.   *Lords day*. I went to cast up my monthly accounts; and to my great trouble, I find myself 7*l* worse then I was the last month, but I confess it is by my reckoning beforehand a great many things; yet however, I am troubled to see that I can hardly promise myself to lay up much from month's end to month's end, about 4 or 5*l* at most, one month with another, without some extraordinary gettings. But I must and I hope I shall continue to have a care of my own expenses. So to the reading my vowes seriously, and then to supper. This evening there came my boy's Brother to see for him; and tells me he knows not where he is, himself being out of towne this week, and is very sorry that he is gone; and so am I, but he shall come no more. So to prayers and to bed.

29.   Up betimes and to my office; and by and by to the Temple and

there appointed to meet in the evening about my business. And thence I walked home; and up and down the streets is cried mightily the great victory got by the Portugalls against the Spaniards,[1] where 10000 slain, 3 or 4000 taken prisoners, with all the artillery, baggage, money, &c., and Don John of Austria forced to fly with a man or two with him – which is very great news. Thence home and at my office all the morning, and so dined at home; and then by water to St. James, but no meeting, today being holyday; but met Mr. Creed in the park, and after a walk or two, discoursing his business, I took leave of him in Westminster hall, whither we walked; and then came again to the hall and fell in talk with Mrs. Lane and after great talk that she never went abroad with any man as she used heretofore to do, I with one word got her to go with me and to meet me at the further Rhenish winehouse – where I did give her a Lobster and do so towse her and feel her all over, making her believe how fair and good a skin she had; and endeed, she hath a very white thigh and leg, but monstrous fat. When weary, I did give over, and somebody having seen some of our dalliance, called aloud in the street, "Sir! why do you kiss the gentlewoman so?" and flung a stone at the window – which vexed me – but I believe they could not see my towsing her; and so we broke up and went out the back way, without being observed I think.

30. Thus, by God's blessing, end this book of two years. Being in all points in good health, and a good way to thrive and do well. Some money I do and can lay up, but not much; being worth now above 700*l*, besides goods of all Sorts. My wife in the country with Ashwell her woman, with my father. Myself at home with W. Hewre and my cook-maid Hannah, my boy Waynman being lately run away from me. In my office, my repute and understanding good, especially with the Duke, and Mr. Coventry. Only, the rest of the officers do rather envy then love me, I standing in most of their lights, especially Sir W. Batten, whose cheats I do daily oppose, to his great trouble, though he appears mighty kind and willing to keep friendship with mee, while Sir J. Mennes, like a dotard, is led by the nose by him. My wife and I (by my late jealousy, for which I am truly to be blamed) have not that fondness between us which we used and ought to have, and I fear will be lost hereafter if I do not take some course to oblige her and yet preserve

1. At the battle of Ameixial (29 May, by the English calendar).

my authority. Public matters are in an ill condition – parliament sitting and raising four subsidys for the King, which is but a little, considering his wants; and yet that parted withal with great hardness – they being offended to see so much money go, and no debts of the public paid, but all swallowed by a luxurious Court – which the King, it is believed and hoped, will retrench in a little time, when he comes to see the utmost of the Revenue which shall be settled on him.

My differences with my uncle Tho. at a good quiett, blessed be God, and other matters. The weather wett for two or three months together, beyond belief; almost not one fair day coming between till this day, which hath been a very pleasant, and the first pleasant this summer.

## JULY

4. With Creede to the King's head ordinary; but coming late, dined at the second table very well for 12*d.*; and a pretty gentleman in our company who confirms my Lady Castlemaynes being gone from Court, but knows not the reason. He told us of one wipe the Queene a little while ago did give her, when she came in and found the Queene under the dresser's hands and had been so long – "I wonder your Majesty," says she, "can have the patience to sit so long a-dressing:" "Oh," says the Queene, "I have so much reason to use patience, that I can very well bear with it." He thinks that it may be the Queene hath commanded her to retire, though that is not likely. Thence with Creede to hire a coach to carry us to Hide parke, today there being a general muster of the King's Guards, horse and foot, yet methought all these gay men are not the soldiers that must do the King's business, it being such as these that lost the old King all he had and were beat by the most ordinary fellows that could be. This day in the Dukes chamber, there being a Roman story in the hangings and upon the standards written these four letters, S P Q R, Sir G. Carteret came to me to know what the meaning of those four letters were – which ignorance is not to be borne in a Privy Counsellor methinks, that a schoolboy should be whipt for not knowing.

8. Being weary and going to bed late last night, I slept till 7 a-

clock, it raining mighty hard, and so did every minute of the day after, sadly – that I know not what will become of the corn this year, we having had but two fair days these many months. Up and to my office, where all the morning busy. And then at noon home to dinner alone, upon a good dish of eeles given me by Michell the Bewpers-man. And then to my viall a little. And then down into the cellar, and up and down with Mr. Turner to see where his vault for turds may be made bigger, or another made him; which I think may well be. And so to my office, where very busy all day setting things in order, my contract books, and preparing things against the next sitting. In the evening I received letters out of the country; among others, from my wife, who methinks writes so coldly that I am much troubled at it and I fear shall have much ado to bring her to her old good temper. So home to supper and music, which is all the pleasure I have of late given myself or is fit I should others, spending too much time and money. Going in, I stepped to Sir W. Batten and there stayed and talked with him, my Lady being in the country, and sent for some lobsters; and Mrs. Turner came in and did bring us an Umble-pie hot out of her oven, extraordinary good, and afterward some spirits of her making (in which she hath great judgment), very good; and so home, merry with this night's refreshment.

9.  Up; making water this morning (which I do every morning as soon as I am awake) with greater plenty and freedom then I used to do, which I think I may impute to last night drinking of Elder spiritts. Sir W. Batten and I sot a little this afternoon at the office; and then I by water to Deptford and there mustered the yard, purposely (God forgive me) to find out Bagwell, a carpenter whose wife is a pretty woman, that I might have some occasion of knowing him and forcing her to come to the office again – which I did so luckily, that going thence, he and his wife did of themselfs meet me in the way, to thank me for my old kindness; but I spoke little to her, but shall give occasion for her coming to me.

16.  Up and despatched things into the country – to my father's – and two Keggs of Sturgeon and a dozen bottles of wine to Cambrige for my Cosen Rogr. Pepys, which I gave him. By and by down by water on several Deale ships and stayed upon a Stage in one place, seeing Calkers sheathing of a ship. Then at Wapping to my carvers about my viall head. So home, and thence to my viall–

maker's in Bishopsgate street; his name is Wise, who is a pretty fellow at it. Thence to the Exchange and so home to dinner. And then to my office, where a full board and busy all the afternoon; and among other things, made a great contract with Sir W. Warren for 40000 deales Swinsound, at 3*l* 17*s*. per cent. In the morning, before I went on the water, I was at Thamestreet about some pitch; and there meeting Anthony Joyce, I took him and Mr. Stacy the Tarr merchant to the tavern – where Stacy told me many old stories of my Lady Battens former poor condition, and how her former husband broke, and how she came to her estate. At night, after office done, I went to Sir W. Batten, where my Lady and I [had] some high words about emptying our houses of office; where I did tell her my mind and at last agreed that it should be done through my office, and so all well. So home and to bed.

18. Up and to my office, where all the morning. And Sir J. Mennes and I did a little, and but a little, business at the office. So I eate a bit of victuals at home and so abroad to several places, as my booksellers; and lastly to Westminster hall – where I expected some bands made me by Mrs. Lane. By and by Mrs. Lane comes; and my bands not being done, she and I parted and met at the Crowne in the palace yard, where we eat (a chicken I sent for) and drank and were mighty merry, and I had my full liberty of towsing her and doing what I would but the last thing of all.

22. Abroad, calling at several places upon small errands; among others, to my brother Toms barbers and had my hair cut while his boy played on the vyallin; a plain boy, but hath a very good genius and understands the book very well. Thence to my Lord Crews; my Lord not being come home, I met and stayed below with Capt. Ferrer, who was come to wait upon my Lady Jemimah to St. James's, she being one of the four ladies that holds up the mantle at the christening this afternoon of the Dukes child, a boy. In discourse of the ladies at Court, Capt. Ferrer tells me that my Lady Castlemayne is now as great again as ever she was, and that her going away was only a fit of her own, upon some slighting words of the King's, so that she called for her coach at a Quarter of an hour's warning and went to Richmond; and the King the next morning, under pretence of going a-hunting, went to see her and make friends, and never was a-hunting at all – after which she came back to Court and commands the King as much as ever, and hath

and doth what she will. This day I hear that the Moores have made some attaques upon the outworkes of Tanger; but my Lord Tiviott, with the loss of about 200 men, did beat them off, and killed many of them.

24. To Mr. Blands, where Mr. Povey, Gauden and I were invited to dinner – which we had very finely, and great plenty but for drink, though many and good; I drunk nothing but small beer and water, which I drunk so much that I wish it may not do me hurt. They have a kinswoman they call daughter in the house, a short, ugly, red-haired slut that plays upon the virginalls and sings, but after such a country manner, I was weary of it but yet could not but commend it. So by and by after dinner comes Monsieur Gotier, who is beginning to teach her; but Lord, what a drolle fellow it is, to make her hold open her mouth and telling this and that so drolly, would make a man burst; but himself I perceive sings very well.

25. To Clapham to Mr. Gaudens, who had sent his coach for me. When I came [thither], our first thing was to show me his house which is almost built, wherein he and his family lives. I find the house very regular and finely contrived, and the gardens and offices about it as convenient and as full of good variety as ever I saw in my life. It is true he hath been censured for laying out so much money; but he tells me that he built it for his brother, who is since dead (the Bishopp); who, when he should come to be Bishop of Winchester, which he was promised, to which Bishopricke at present there is no house, he did entend to dwell here. Besides, with the good husbandry in making his bricks and other things, I do not think it costs him so much money as people think and discourse. I saluted his lady and the young ladies, he having many pretty children, and his sister, the Bishop's widow, who was, it seems, Sir W. Russells daughter, the Treasurer of the Navy – who, by her discourse at dinner, I find to be a very well-bred and a woman of excellent discourse – even so much as to have my attention all dinner with much more pleasure then I did give to Creede, whose discourse was mighty merry in inveighing against Mr. Gaudens victuals that they had at sea the last voyage; which he prosecuted till methought the women begun to take it seriously. After dinner, by Mr. Gaudens motion, we got Mrs. Gauden and her sister to sing to a viall, on which Mr. Gaudens eldest son (a pretty man, but a simple one methinks) played – but very poorly and the Musique bad, but yet I

commended it. I took the viall and played some things from one of
their books, Lyra lessons, which they seemed to like well. Thus we
passed an hour or two after dinner, and towards the evening we
bade them Adieu and took horse, being resolved that we would go
to Epsum; so we set out; and being gone a little way, I sent home
Will to look to the house, and Creed and I rid forward – the road
being full of citizens going and coming towards Epsum – where,
when we came, we could hear of no lodging, the town so full. But
which was better, I went towards Ashted, my old place of pleasure,
and there (by direction of one goodman Arthur, whom we met on
the way) we went to Farmer Page's, and there we got a lodging in a
little hole we could not stand upright in, upon a low truckle-bed.
But rather then go further to look, we stayed there. And while
supper was getting ready, I took him to walk up and down behind
my Cosen Pepys's house that was, which I find comes [a] little short
of what I took it to be when I was a little boy (as things use
commonly to appear greater then then when one comes to be a man
and know more); and so up and down in the Closes which I know
so well methinks, and account it good fortune that I lie here, that I
may have opportunity to renew my old walks. So to our lodging to
supper; and among other meat, had a brave dish of creame, the best
I ever eat in my life – and with which we pleased ourselfs much.
And by and by to bed, where with much ado, yet good sport, we
made shift to lie, but with little ease.

26.    *Lords day*. Up and to the Wells, where great store of Citizens;
which was the greatest part of the company, though there were
some others of better Quality. I met many that I knew; and we
drunk each of us two pots and so walked away – it being very
pleasant to see how everybody turns up his tail, here one and there
another, in a bush, and the women in their Quarters the like.
Thence I walked Creede to Mr. Minnes's house, which hath now a
good way made to it, and finely walled round; and thence to
Durdans and walked round it and within the Courtyard and to the
bowling-green, where I have seen so much mirth in my time; but
now no family in it (my Lord Barkely, whose it is, being with his
family at London); and so up and down by Minnes's wood, with
great pleasure viewing my old walks and where Mrs. Hely and I did
use to walk and talk, with whom I had the first sentiments of love
and pleasure in woman's company, discourse and taking her by the
hand – she being a pretty woman. So I led him to Ashted church (by

the place where Peter, my cosens man, went blindfold and found a certain place we chose for him upon a wager) where we had a dull Doctor, one Downe, worse then I think ever Parson King was (of whom we made so much scorn); and after sermon home and stayed while our dinner, a couple of large Chickens, were dressed and a good mess of Creame – which anon we had with good content. And after dinner he and I to walk; and I led him to the pretty little wood behind my Cosen's house, into which we got at last by clambering and our little dog with us; but when we were in among the Hazletrees and bushes, Lord, what a course did we run for an hour together, losing ourselfs; and endeed, I despaired I should ever come to any path, but still from thicket to thicket – a thing I could hardly have believed a man could have been lost so long in so small a room. At last, I found out a delicate walk in the middle that goes quite through the wood; and then went out of the wood and hallowed Mr. Creede and made him hunt me from place to place; and at last went in and called him into my fine walk – the little dog still hunting with us through the wood. In this walk, being all bewildred and weary and sweating, Creed, he lay down upon the ground; which I did a little but durst not long, but walked from him in the fine green walk, which is half a mile long, there reading my vowes as I used to on Sundays. To Yowel and there set up our horses and selfs for all night.

27. Up in the morning about 7 a-clock; and resolved of riding to the Wells. But it being much a warmer day then yesterday, there was great store of gallant company, more then then to my greater pleasure. There was at a distance, under one of the trees on the common, a company got together that sung; I, at that distance, and so all the rest, being a quarter of a mile off, took them for the waytes; so I rid up to them and find them only voices – some Citizens, met by chance, that sing four or five parts excellently. I have not been more pleased with a snapp of Musique, considering the circumstances of the time and place, in all my life anything so pleasant. We drank each of us three cups; and so after riding up to the horsemen upon the Hill where they were making of matches to run – we went away and to Yowell, where we find our Breakefast, the remains of our supper last night hasht. And by and by, after the smith had set on two new shoos to Creedes horse – we mounted; and with little discourse, I being intent upon getting home in time, we rode hard home. Set up horse at Foxhall, and I by water

(observing the King's barge attending his going to the House this day) home, it being about one a-clock.

So got myself ready and shifting myself; and so by water to Westminster and there came, most luckily, to the Lords House as the House of Comons were going into the Lords' House, and there I crowded in along with the Speaker – and got to stand close behind him – where he made his speech to the King (who sat with his crown on and robes, and so all the Lords in their robes, a fine sight); wherein he told his Majesty what they have done this parliment, and now offered for his Royall consent. The Speakers speech was far from any Oratory, but was as plain (though good matter) as anything could be and void of elocution. After the bills passed, the King, sitting in his throne with his speech writ in a paper which he held in his lap and scarce looked off of it, I thought, all the time he made his speech to them – giving them thanks for their subsidys. He desired that nothing of old faults should be remembred, or severity for the same used to any in the country, it being his desire to have all forgot as well as forgiven. But however, to use all care in suppressing any tumults, &c.; assuring them that the restless spirits of his and their adversarys have great expectations of something to be done this summer. So to Whitehall and by water to the Bridge; and so home to bed – weary and well pleased with my Journy in all respects. Only, it cost me about 20s.; but it was for my health and I hope will prove so. Only, I do find by my riding a little swelling to arise just by my Anus. I had the same the last time I rode, and then it fell again; and now it is up again about the bigness of the bagg of a Silkeworme. Makes me fearful of a Rupture, but I will speak to Mr. Hollyard about it, and I am glad to find it now, that I may prevent it before it goes too far.

28. Up, after sleeping very well; and so to my office, setting down the Journall of this last three days. And so settled to business again – I hope with greater chearefullnesse and successe by this refreshment.

31. Up earely to my accounts this month; and I find myself worth clear 730*l* – the most I ever had yet; which contents me, though I encrease but very little. To the Exchange, where I met Dr. Pierce, who tells me as a friend, the great Injury that he thinks I do myself by being so Severe in the yards, and contracting the ill will of the whole Navy for those offices singly upon myself. Now I discharge

a good conscience therein, and I tell him that no man can (nor doth he say any say it) charge me with doing wrong; but rather do as many good offices as any man. However, I will make use of his counsel and take some Course to prevent having the single ill will of the office. Before I went to the office, I went to the Coffee-house where Sir J. Cutler and Mr. Grant came. And there Mr. Grant showed me letters of Sir Wm. Pettys, wherein he says that his vessel which he hath built upon two Keeles (a modell whereof, built for the King, he showed me) hath this month won a wager of 50*l* in sailing between Dublin and Holyhead with the pacquett-boat, the best ship or vessel the King hath there. In their coming back from Holyhead, they started together; and this vessel came to Dublin by 5 at night and the pacquet-boat not before 8 the next morning; and when they came they did believe that this vessel had been drownded or at least behind, not thinking she could have lived in that sea. To bed – ending the month with pretty good content of mind. My wife in the country – and myself in good esteem and likely by pains to become considerable I think, with God's blessing upon my diligence.

## ⸙AUGUST⸙

4.   To Westminster hall; and not finding Mrs. Lane, with whom I purposed to be merry, I went to Jervas's and took him and his wife over the water to their mother Palmers (the woman that speaks in the belly and with whom I had two or three years ago so good sport with Mr. Mallard), thinking, because I had heard that she is a woman of that sort, that I might there have light upon some lady of pleasure (for which God forgive me); but blessed be God, there was none nor anything that pleased me – but a poor little house which she hath set out as fine as she can. And for her singing which she pretends to, is only some old bawdy songs, and those sung abominably; only, she pretends to be able to sing both bass and treble; which she doth, something like but not like what I thought formerly and expected now. Nor doth her speaking in her belly take me now as it did then, but it may be that is because I know it and see her mouth when she speaks, which should not be.

5.   All the morning at the office; whither Deane of Woolwich

came to me and discoursed of the body of ships, which I am now going about to understand. And then I took him to the Coffee-house, where he was very earnest against Mr. Grant's report in favour of Sir W. Petty's vessel, even to some passion on both sides almost. So to the Exchange, and thence home to dinner with my brother. And in the afternoon to Westminster hall and there found Mrs. Lane; and by and by, by agreement, we met at the parliament-stairs (in my [way] down to the boat, who should meet us but my Lady Jemimah, who saw me lead her but said nothing to me of her, though I stayed to speak to her to see whether she would take notice of it or no) and off to Stangate; and so to the Kingshead at Lambeth marsh and had variety of meats and drink; come to *xs*. But I did so towse her and handled her; but could get nothing more from her, though I was very near it. But as wanton and bucksome as she is, she dares not adventure upon that business – in which I very much commend and like her. Stayed pretty late, and so over with her by water; and being in a great sweat with my towsing of her, I durst not go home by water, but took coach. And at home, my brother and I fell upon Des Cartes, and I perceive he hath studied him well and I cannot find but he hath minded his book and doth love it. This evening came a letter about business from Mr. Coventry, and with it a Silver pen he promised me, to carry inke in; which is very necessary. So to prayers and to bed.

6. At noon I to the Change; and meeting with Sir W. Warren, to a Coffee-house and there finished a contract with him for the office, and so parted. And I to my Cosen Mary Joyces at a Gossiping, where much company and good Cheere. There was the King's falconer that lives by Pauls and his wife, a ugly pusse but brought him money. He speaking of the strength of hawkes, which will strike a fowle to the ground with that force that shall make the fowl rebound a great way from [the] ground, which no force of man or art can do. But it was very pleasant to hear what reasons he and another, one Ballard, a rich man of the same company of Leathersellers of which the Joyces are, did give for this. Ballards wife, a pretty and a very well-bred woman, I took occasion to kiss several times, and she to carve, drink and show me great respect. After dinner, to talk and laugh. I drank no wine, but sent for some water, the beer not being good. A fidler was sent for; and there one Mrs. Lurkin, a neighbour, a good and merry poor woman, but a very tall woman, did dance and show such tricks that made us all

merry. But above all, a daughter of Mr. Brumfield's, black but well-shaped and modest, did dance very well, which pleased me mightily; and I begun the *Duchesse* with her, but could not do it; but however, I came off well enough and made mighty much of her, kissing and leading her home with her Cosen Anthony and Kate Joyce (Kate being very handsome and well, that is, handsomely dressed today, and I grew mighty kind and familiar with her and kissed her soundly, which she takes very well). To their house and there I left them – having on our way, though 9 a-clock at night, carried them into a puppet-play in Lincolnes Inn fields; where there was the Story of Holofernes and other clockwork, well done. So I walked home, very well contented with this afternoon's work, I thinking it convenient to keep in with the Joyces against a bad day, if I should have occasion to make use of them.

7.   Up and to my office a little, and then to Browns for my Measuring Rule, which is made, and is certainly the best and the most commodious for carrying in one's pocket and most useful that ever was made, and myself have the honour of being as it were the inventor of this form of it. After dinner I walked to Deptford and there found Sir W. Penn; and I fell to measuring of some plank that was serving into the yard; which the people took notice of and the measurer himself was amuzed* at, for I did it much more ready then he. And I believe Sir W. Penn would be glad I could have done less, or he more. By and by he went away, and I stayed walking up and down, discoursing with the officers of the yard of several things; and so walked back again, and on my way young Bagwell and his wife waylayd me to desire my favour about getting him a better ship; which I shall pretend to be willing to do for them, but my mind is to know his wife a little better. So home; and my brother John and I up, and I to my Musique and then to discourse with him; and I find him not so thorough a philosopher, at least in Aristotle, as I took him for, he not being able to tell me the definicion of fire nor which of the four Qualitys belonged to each of the four elements. So to prayers and to bed. Among other things, being much satisfyed in my new Rule.

9.   *Lords day.* Up; and leaving my brother John to go somewhither else, I to church and heard Mr. Mills (who is lately returned out of the country, and it seems was fetched in by many of the parishioners with great state) preach upon the Authority of the

Ministers, upon these words: "Wee are therefore Embassadors of Christ." Wherein, among other high expressions, he said that such a learned man used to say that if a minister of the word and an Angell should meet him together, he would salute the Minister first – which methought was a little too high. This day I begun to make use of the Silver pen (Mr. Coventry did give mee) in writing of this sermon, taking only the heads of it in Latin; which I shall I think continue to do. So home and at my office, reading my vowes; and so to Sir W. Batten to dinner. Thence in the afternon with my Lady Batten, leading her through the streets by the hand to St. Dunstans church, hard by us (where by Mrs. Russells means we were set well); and heard an excellent sermon of one Mr. Gifford, the parson there – upon "Remember Lot's wife." Home and stayed up a good while, examining Will in his Latin bible and my brother along with him in his Greeke. And so to prayers and to bed. This afternoon I was amuzed at the tune set to the psalm by the clerke of the parish; and thought at first that he was out, but I find him to be a good songster, and the parish could sing it very well and was a good tune. But I wonder that there should be a tune in the psalms that I never heard of.

10.   After dinner I went to Greatorex's, whom I found in his garden and set him to work upon my Ruler, to ingrave an Almanacke and other things upon the brasses of it – which a little before night he did, but the latter part he slubberd over, that I must get him to do it over better or else I shall not fancy my Rule. Which is such a folly that I am come to now, that whereas before my delight was in multitude of books and spending money in that and buying alway of other things, now that I am become a better husband and have left off buying, now my delight is in the neatness of everything, and so cannot be pleased with anything unless it be very neat; which is a strange folly. Hither came W. Howe about business; and he and I had a great deal of discourse about my Lord Sandwich, and I find by him that my Lord doth dote upon one of the daughters of Mrs. [Becke] where he lies, so that he spends his time and money upon her. He tells me she is a woman of a very bad fame and very impudent, and hath told my Lord so. Yet for all that, my Lord doth spend all his evenings with her, though he be at Court in the daytime – in fine, I perceive my Lord is dabling with this wench, for which I am sorry; though I do not wonder at it, being a man amorous enough and now begins to allow himself the

liberty that he sees everybody else at Court takes.

11.   We met and sat at the office all the morning. And at noon, I to the Change, where I met Dr. Pierce; who tells me that the King comes to town this day from Tunbrige to stay a day or two, and then fetch the Queen from thence – who he says is grown a very debonnaire lady and now hugs him and meets him galloping upon the road, and all the actions of a fond and pleasant lady that can be.

12.   By water to my brother's and there I hear my wife is come and gone home, and my father is come to town also. I walked with him a little while and left him to lie at that end of the town, and I home – where methinks I find my wife strange, not knowing, I believe, in what temper she could expect me to be in; but I fell to kind words and so we were very kind; only, she could not forbear telling me how she had been used by them and her maid Ashwell in the country; but I find it will be best not to examine it, for I doubt she's in fault too, and therefore I seek to put it off from my hearing; and so to bed and there enjoyed her with great content. And so to sleep.

13.   Lay long in bed with my wife, talking of family matters. And so up and to the office, where we sat all the morning. And then home to dinner; and after dinner my wife and I to talk again about getting of a couple of good maids and to part with Ashwell; which troubles me for her father's sake, though I shall be glad to have that charge taken away of keeping a woman.

17.   Up; and then fell into discourse, my wife and I, to Ashwell; and much against my Will, I am fain to express a willingness to Ashwell that she should go from us; and yet in my mind I am glad of it, to ease me of the charge. So she is to go to her father this day. And leaving my wife and her talking highly, I went away by coach with Sir J. Mennes and Sir W. Batten to St. James and there attended of course* the Duke. And so to Whitehall, where I met Mr. Moore and he tells me with great sorrow of my Lord's being debauched, he fears, by this woman at Chelsy; which I am troubled at and resolve to speak to him of it if I can seasonably.

22.   Up by 4 a-clock to go with Sir W. Batten to Woolwich, and Sir J. Mennes; which we did, though not before 6 or 7 by their lying a-bed. Our business was to survey the new wharfe building there,

in order to the giving more to him that doth it, Mr. Randall, then contracted for; but I see no reason for it, though it be well done, yet not better then contracted to be. Here we eat and drunk at the Clerk of the Cheques; and in taking water at the Tower gate, we drank a cup of strong water, which I did out of pure conscience to my health; and I think is not excepted by my oaths, but it is a thing I shall not do again, hoping to have no such occasion. After breakfast there, Mr. Castle and I walked to Greenwich, and in our way met some Gypsys who would needs tell me my fortune, and I suffered one of them – who told me many things common, as others do, but bid me beware of a John and a Thomas, for they did seek to do me hurt. And that somebody should be with me this day sennit to borrow money of me, but I should lend them none. She got ninepence of me; and so I left them.

27.    Up, after much pleasant talk with my wife and a little that vexes me, for I see that she is confirmed in it that all that I do is by design, and that my very keeping of the house in dirt,[1] and the doing of this and anything else in the house, is but to find her imployment to keep her within and from minding of her pleasure. In which, though I am sorry to see she minds it, is true enough in a great degree.

28.    At the office betimes (it being cold all night and this morning, and a very great frost they say abroad; which is much, having had no summer at all almost); where we sat, and in the afternoon also, about settling the Establishment of the number of men borne on ships, &c., till the evening; and after that, in my closet till late, and quite tired with business, home to supper and to bed.

29.    To Jervas the barbers and there was trimmed and did deliver back a periwigg which he brought me by my desire the other day to show me, having some thoughts, though no great desire or resolution yet to wear one. And so I put it off for a while. Thence to my wife, and calling at both the Exchanges, buying stockings for her and myself; and also at Leadenhall, where she and I, it being candlelight, bought meat for tomorrow, having ne'er a maid to do it; and I myself bought, while my wife was gone to another shop, a leg of beef, a good one, for sixpence, and my wife says is worth my

---

1. New floors had just been laid in the dining-room and elsewhere.

money. So walked home, with a woman carrying our things, and had a very pleasant walk from Whitehall home. So to my office and there despatched some business; and so home to supper and to bed. We called at Toms as we came by, and there saw his new building, which will be very convenient. But I am mightily displeased at a letter he sent me last night to borrow 20*l* more of me; and yet gives me no account, as I have long desired, how matters stand with him in the world. I am troubled also to see how, contrary to my expectation, my brother John neither is the schollar nor minds his studies as I thought he would have done – but loiters away his time, so that I must send him soon to Cambrige again.

30. *Lords day*. Lay long, then up; and Will being ill of the toothake, I stayed at home and made up my accounts; which to my great content arise to 750*l* clear Creditor, the most I have had yet. Dined alone with my wife, my brother dining abroad at my uncle Wights I think. To church, I alone, in the afternoon; and there saw Pembleton come in and look up, which put me into a sweat, and seeing not my wife there, went out again. But Lord – how I was afeared that he might, seeing me at church, go home to my wife; so much it is out of my power to preserve myself from jealousy – and so sot impatient all the sermon. Home and find all well and no sign of anybody being there, and so with great content playing and dallying with my wife; and so to my office, doing a little business there among my papers, and home to my wife to talk – supper and bed.

31. This noon came Jane Gentleman to serve my wife as her chambermaid; I wish she may prove well; she is only thick of hearing, which may be a trouble, but we know not yet, nor is it always so much as at other times. So ends this month, with my mind pretty well in quiet, and in good disposition of health since my drinking at home of a little wine with my beer; but nowhere else do I drink any wine at all. My house in a way to be clean again, the Joyners and all having done; but only we lack a Cooke-maid and Jane our chambermaid is but new come to us this day. The King and Queene and the Court at the Bath. My Lord Sandwich in the country, newly gone, with my doubts concerning him having been debauched by a slut at his lodgings at Chelsy. My brother John with me, but not to my great content, because I do not see him mind his study or give me so good account thereof as I expected. My Brother

Tom embarqued in building, and I fear in no good condition for it, for he sent to me to borrow more money, which I shall not lend him. Myself in good condition in the office, and I hope in a good way of saving of money at home.

## SEPTEMBER

1. In the evening, my brother John coming to me to complain that my wife seems to be discontented at his being here and shows him great disrespect; so I took and walked with him in the garden and discoursed long with him about my affairs, and how imprudent it is for my father and mother and him to take exceptions without great cause at my wife, considering how much it concerns them to keep her their friend, and for my peace; not that I would ever be led by her to forget or desert them in the main, but yet she deserves to be pleased and complied with a little, considering the manner of life that I keep her to and how convenient it were for me to have Brampton for her to be sent to when I have a mind or occasion to go abroad to Portsmouth or elsewhere about pleasure or business, when it will not be safe for me to leave her alone. So directed him how to behave himself to her, and gave him other counsel; and so to my office, where late, and then home to supper and to bed.

3. To Deptford; and after a word or two with Sir J. Mennes, walked to Redriffe and so home. In my way, it coming into my head, overtaking of a beggar or two on the way that looked like Gypsys, it came into my head what the Gypsys eight or nine days ago had foretold, that somebody that day sennit should be with me to borrow money, but I should lend none; and looking, when I came to my office, upon my Journall, that my Brother John had brought me a letter that day from my Brother Tom to borrow 20*l* more of me, which had vexed me so, that I had sent the letter to my father into the country, to acquaint him of it. But it pleased me mightily to see how, contrary to my expectation, having so lately lent him 20*l*, and believe that he had money by him to spare, and that after some days not thinking of it, I should look back and find what the Gypsy had told me to be so true.

4. Made my wife get herself presently ready, and so carried her by

coach to [Bartholomew] fair and showed her the Munkys dancing on the ropes; which was strange, but such dirty sport that I was not pleased with it. There was also a horse with hoofes like Rams hornes – a goose with four feet – and a cock with three. Thence to another place and saw some German clockeworks, the Salutacion of the Virgin Mary and several Scripture stories; but above all, there was at last represented the Sea, with Neptune, Venus, mermaids, and Cupid on a Dolphin, the sea rolling. Thence home by coach with my wife, and I a while to the office; and so to supper and to bed.

8.   Up and to my vyall a while; and then to my office, one Phillips having brought me a draught of the *Katharin* Yacht, prettily well done for the common way of doing it. At the office all the morning, making up our last half-year's account to my Lord Treasurer, which comes to 160000*l* or thereabouts, the proper expense of this half-year; only, with an addition of 13000*l* for the threepences[1] due of the last account to the Treasurer for his disbursements and 1100*l* for this half-year's; so that in three years and half, his threepences come to 14100*l*. Dined at home with my wife, it being washing day; we had a good pie, baked of a leg of mutton. And then to my office and then abroad; and among other places, to Moxon's and there bought a payre of Globes, cost me 3*l* 10*s*. – with which I am well pleased, I buying them principally for my wife, who hath a mind to understand them – and I shall take pleasure to teach her. But here I saw his great Window in his dining-room, where there is the two Terrestriell Hemispheres, so painted as I never saw in my life, and nobly done and to good purpose – done by his own hand. Thence home to my office and there at business late. And then to supper, home and to bed – my people sitting up longer then ordinary before they had done their washing.

9.   To Whitehall to Sir G. Carterets, but did not speak with him; and so to Westminster hall, God forgive me, thinking to meet Mrs. Lane, but she was not there; but here I met with Ned Pickering, with whom I walked three or four hours till evening, he telling me the whole business of my Lord's folly with this Mrs. Becke at Chelsy, of all which I am ashamed to see my Lord so grossly play the beast and fool, to the flinging off of all Honour, friends, servants

1. See above, p. 203, n.

and every thing and person that is good, and only will have his private lust undisturbed with this common whore – his sitting up, night after night alone, suffering nobody to come to them, and all the day too.

10. Up betimes and to my office. And then sat all the morning, making a great contract with Sir W. Warren for 3000*l* worth of Masts; but good God, to see what a man might do were I a knave – the whole business, from beginning to the end, being done by me out of the office, and signed to by them upon but once reading of it to them, without the least care or consultation either of quality, price, number, or need of them, only in general that it was good to have a store. But I hope my pains was such as the King hath the best bargain of Masts hath been bought these 27 years in this office. Dined at home and then to my office again, many people about business with me. And then stepped a little abroad about business to the Wardrobe, but missed Mr. Moore, and elsewhere. And in my way met Mr. Moore, who tells me of the good peace that is made at Tanger with the Moores, but to continue from six months to six months. And that the Molle is laid out and likely to be done with great ease and successe.

11. This morning, about 2 or 3 a-clock, knocked up in our backyard; and rising to the window, being moonshine, I find it was the Constable and his watch, who had found our backyard door open and so came in to see what the matter was. So I desired them to shut the door and bid them good-night. And so to bed again. And at 6 a-clock up and a while to my vyall, and then to the office, where all the morning upon the victuallers account and then with him to dinner to the Dolphin, where I eat well but drunk no wine neither, which keeps me in such good order that I am mightily pleased with myself for it. Hither Mr. Moore came to me, and he and I home and advised about business; and so after an hour's examining the state of the Navy debts lately cast up, I took coach to Sir Ph. Warwickes; but finding Sir G. Carteret there, I did not go in, but directly home again, it raining hard – having first of all been with Creed and Mrs. Harper about a cook-maid, and am like to have one from Creede's lodging. In my way home visited my Lord Crew and Sir Tho., thinking they might have enquired by the by of me, touching my Lord's matters at Chelsey, but they said nothing; and so after some slight common talk, I bid them good-night. At home to my office;

and after a while doing business, home to supper – and bed.

12.   Up betimes; and by water to Whitehall and thence to Sir Ph.
Warwickes; and there had half an hour's private discourse with him
and did give him some good satisfaccion in our Navy matters, and
he also me, as to the money paid and due to the Navy – so as he
makes me assured, by perticulars, that Sir G. Carteret is paid within
80000*l*, every farthing, that we to this day, nay to Michaelmas day
next, have demanded; and that I am sure is above 50000*l* more then
truly our expense hath been – whatever is become of the money.
Home, with great content that I have thus begun an acquaintance
with him, who is a great man and a man of as much business as any
man in England – which I will endeavour to deserve and keep.

*Pepys is now at Brampton, having ridden there with his wife on the 14th–
15th to attend the manorial court in connection with the dispute with his
uncle Thomas Pepys about Robert Pepys's estate (see above, pp. 144–5).
He now rides to Wisbech to investigate the chances of gaining something
from the estate of another relative, John Day, who had died in 1649.*

17.   Up; and my father being gone to bed ill last night, and
continuing so this morning, I was forced to come to a new
consideration, whether it was fit for to let my uncle [Thomas] and
his son go to Wisbeech about my uncle Days estate alone or no, and
concluded it unfit and so resolved to go with them myself; and so
leaving my wife there, I begun a journy with them; and with much
ado through the Fens, along Dikes, where sometimes we were
ready to have our horses sink to the belly, we got by night, with
great deal of stir and hard riding, to Parsons drove, a heathen place –
where I found my uncle and aunt Perkins and their daughters, poor
wretches, in a sad poor thatched cottage, like a poor barne or stable,
peeling of Hemp (in which I did give myself good content to see
their manner of preparing of hemp) and in a poor condition of
habitt; took them to our miserable Inne and there, after long stay
and hearing of Franke their son, the miller, play upon his Treble (as
he calls it), with which he earnes part of his living, and singing of a
country bawdy song, we set down to supper: the whole Crew and
Frankes wife and children (a sad company, of which I was ashamed)
supped with us. And after supper, I talking with my aunt about her
report concerning my uncle Days Will and surrender, I find her in
such different reports from what she writes and says to other

people, and short of what I expected, that I fear little will be done of good in it. By and by news is brought us that one of our horses is stole out of the Stable; which proves my uncles, at which I was inwardly glad; I mean, that it was not mine. And at this we were at a great loss; and they doubting a person that lay at next door, a Londoner, some lawyer's clerk, we caused him to be secured in his bed and made care to be taken to seize the horse; and so, about 12 at night or more, to bed in a sad, cold, nasty chamber; only, the maid was indifferent handsome, and so I had a kiss or two of her, and I to bed. And a little after I was asleep, they waked me to tell me that the horse was found, which was good news; and so to sleep till the morning – but was bit cruelly (and nobody else of our company, which I wonder at) by the gnatts.

18.  Up, and got our people together as soon as we could; and after eating a dish of cold Creame, which was my supper last night too, we took leave of our beggarly company, though they seem good people too, and over most sad Fenns (all the way observing the sad life that the people of that place (which if they be born there, they call the "Breedlings" of the place) do live, sometimes rowing from one spot to another, and then wadeing) to Wisbeech, a pretty town and a fine church and library, where sundry very old Abbee manuscripts – and a fine house, built on the church ground by Secretary Thurlow, and a fine gallery built for him in the church, but now all in the Bishop of Elys hands. After visiting the church &c., we out of town by the help of a stranger, to find out one Blinkehorne a miller, of whom we might inquire something of old Days disposal of his estate and in whose hands it now is; and by great chance we met him and brought him to our Inne to dinner; and instead of being informed in his estate by this fellow, we find that he is the next heire to the estate, which was matter of great sport to my Cosen Tho. and me, to see such a fellow prevent us in our hopes.

*Pepys and his wife have ridden back to London on the 20th–21st.*

24.  In the afternoon, telling my wife that I go to Deptford, I went by water to Westminster hall; and there finding Mrs. Lane, took her over to Lambeth where we were lately, and there did what I would with her but only the main thing, which she would not consent to, for which God be praised; and yet I came so near, that I was

provoked to spend. But trust in the Lord I shall never do so again while I live. After being tired with her company, I landed her at Whitehall and so home and at my office writing letters, till 12 at night almost; and then home to supper and bed and there find my poor wife hard at work, which grieved my heart to see that I should abuse so good a wretch,* and that it is just with God to make her bad to me for my wronging of her; but I do resolve never to do the like again. So to bed.

27. Spend the evening with my poor wife – consulting about her closet, clothes, and other things. At night to supper, though with little comfort, I finding myself, both head and breast, in great pain; and which troubles me most, my right eare is almost deaf. It is a cold, which God Almighty in justice did give me while I sat lewdly sporting with Mrs. Lane the other day with the broken window in my neck. I went to bed with a posset, being very melancholy in consideration of the loss of my hearing.

28. The Comissioners for Tanger met, and there my Lord Tiviott, together with Capt. Cuttance, Capt. Evans, and Jonas Moore, sent to that purpose, did bring us a brave draught of the Molle to be built there, and report that it is likely to be the most considerable place the King of England hath in the world; and so I am apt to think it will. After discourse of this and of supplying the Guarrison with some more horse, we rise; and Sir J. Mennes and I home again, finding the street about our house full, Sir R. Ford beginning his Shrevalty today. And what with his and our houses being new-painted, the street begins to look a great deal better then it did – and more gracefull.

30. In the afternoon by water to Whitehall to the Tanger Committee, where my Lord Tiviott brought his accounts; which grieves me to see, that his accounts being to be examined by us, there is none of the great men at the Board that in compliment will except against anything in his accounts, and so none of the little persons dare do it: so the King is abused.

# –✧OCTOBER✧–

2.   At the Change met with Mr. Cutler, and he and I to a Coffee-house and there discoursed; and he doth assure me that there is great likelihood of a war with Holland – but I hope we shall be in good condition before it comes to break out. I like his company and will make much of his acquaintance.

6.   Slept pretty well, and my wife waked to ring the bell to call up our maids to the washing about 4 a-clock and I was, and she, angry that our bell did not wake them sooner; but I will get a bigger bell. So we to sleep again till 8 a-clock. At noon, Lewellin coming to me, I took him and Deane, and there met my uncle Thomas and we dined together. But was vexed that it being washing-day, we had no meat dressed; but sent to the cook's and my people had so little wit to send in our meat from abroad in the cook's dishes, which were marked with the name of the Cooke upon them; by which, if they observed anything, they might know it was not my own dinner. Finding myself beginning to be troubled with wind, as I used to be, and with pain in making water, [at night] I took a couple of pills that I had by me of Mr. Hollyards.

7.   They wrought in the morning and I did keep my bed; and my pain continued on me mightily, that I keeped within all day in great pain, and could break no wind nor have any stool after my physic had done working. So in the evening I took coach and to Mr. Hollyards, but he was not at home; and so home again. And whether the coach did me good or no I know not, but having a good fire in my chamber, I begun to break six or seven small and great farts; and so to bed and lay in good ease all night, and pissed pretty well in the morning, but no more wind came as it used to do plentifully, after it once begun, nor any inclination to stool.

13.   *Rules for my health.* 1. To begin to keep myself warm as I can. 2. Strain as little as ever I can backwards, remembering that my pain will come by and by, though in the very straining I do not feel it. 3. Either by physic forward or by clyster backward, or both ways, to get an easy and plentiful going to stool and breaking of wind. 4. To begin to suspect my health immediately when I begin to become costive and bound, and by all means to keep my body loose, and that to obtain presently after I find myself going to the contrary.

Creede with me to dinner; and after dinner John Cole my old friend came to see and speak with me about a friend. I find him ingenious, but do more and more discern his City pedantry; but however, I will endeavour to have his company now and then, for that he knows much of the temper of the City and is able to acquaint therein as much as most young men – being of large acquaintance, and himself I think somewhat unsatisfied with the present state of things at Court and in the Church.

14.   After dinner my wife and I, by Mr. Rawlinsons conduct, to the Jewish Synagogue – where the men and boys in their Vayles, and the women behind a lettice out of sight; and some things stand up, which I believe is their Law, in a press, to which all coming in do bow; and at the putting on their veils do say something, to which others that hear him do cry Amen, and the party doth kiss his veil. Their service all in a singing way, and in Hebrew. And anon their Laws, that they take out of the press, is carried by several men, four or five, several burthens in all, and they do relieve one another, or whether it is that everyone desires to have the carrying of it, I cannot tell. Thus they carried [it] round, round about the room while such a service is singing. And in the end they had a prayer for the King, which they pronounced his name in Portugall; but the prayer, like the rest, in Hebrew. But Lord, to see the disorder, laughing, sporting, and no attention, but confusion in all their service, more like Brutes then people knowing the true God, would make a man forswear ever seeing them more; and endeed, I never did see so much, or could have imagined there had been any religion in the whole world so absurdly performed as this.

20.   Up and to the office, where we sat; and at noon Sir G. Carteret, Sir J. Mennes and I to dinner to my Lord Mayors, being invited; where was the Farmers of the Customes, my Lord Chancellors three Sons, and other great and much company, and a very great noble dinner, as this Mayor is good for nothing else. No extraordinary discourse of anything, every man being intent upon his dinner, and myself willing to have drunk some wine to have warmed my belly; but I did for my oath sake willingly refrain it, but am so well pleased and satisfied afterwards thereby, for it doth keep me always in so good a frame of mind that I hope I shall not ever leave this practice. Thence home and took my wife by coach to Whitehall; and she set down at my Lord's lodgings, I to a Comittee

of Tanger, and thence with her homeward; called at several places by the way – among others, at Paul's churchyard; and while I was in Kirtons shop, a fellow came to offer kindness or force to my wife in the coach. But she refusing, he went away, after the coachman had struck him and he the coachman. So I being called, went thither; and the fellow coming out again of a shop, I did give him a good cuff or two on the chops; and seeing him not oppose me, I did give him another; at last, found him drunk, of which I was glad and so left him and home; and so to my office a while and so home to supper and to bed.

21.   This evening after I came home, I begun to enter my wife in Arithmetique, in order to her studying of the globes, and she takes it very well – and I hope with great pleasure I shall bring her to understand many fine things.

26.   Creed and I to the Kings head Ordinary, where much and very good company; among others, one very talking man, but a Scholler, that would needs put in his discourse and philosophy upon every occasion; and though he did well enough, yet his readiness to speak spoilt all. Thence Creed and I to one or two Periwegg shops about the Temple (having been very much displeased with one that we saw, a head of greasy and old woman's haire, at Jervas's in the morning); and there I think I shall fit myself of one very handsomely made.

28.   Up and at my office all the morning; and at noon Mr. Creed came to me and dined with me; and after dinner Capt. Murford came to me and he and I discoursed highly upon his breach of contract with us. After that, Mr. Creed and I abroad, I doing several errands; and with him at last to the great Coffee-house and there, after some common discourse, we parted and I home, paying what I owed at the Miter in my way; and at home, Sympson the Joyner coming, he set up my press for my cloaks and other small things; and so to my office a little, and to supper and to bed.

29.   Up, it being *my Lord Mayors Day*, Sir Anthony Bateman. This morning was brought home my new velvet cloak; that is, lined with velvet, a good cloth the outside – the first that ever I had in my life, and I pray God it may not be too soon now that I begin to wear it. I had it this day brought home, thinking to have worn it to

dinner; but I thought it would be better to go without it because of
the Crowde, and so I did not wear it. In dressing myself and
wanting a band, I found all my bands that were newly made clean,
so ill-smoothed that I crumpled them and flung them all on the
ground and was angry with Jane, which made the poor girl mighty
sad, so that I were troubled for it afterwards. At noon I went forth,
and by coach to Guild Hall (by the way calling to shit at Mr.
Rawlinsons) and there was admitted; and meeting with Mr. Proby
(Sir R. Ford's son) and Lieut.- Coll. Baron, a City commander, we
went up and down to see the tables; where under every salt there
was a Bill of fare, and at the end of the table the persons proper for
that table. Many were the tables, but none in the Hall but the
Mayors and the Lords of the privy Councell that had napkins or
knives – which was very strange. We went into the Buttry and there
stayed and talked, and then into the hall again; and there wine was
offered and they drunk, I only drinking some Hypocras, which
doth not break my vowe, it being, to the best of my present
judgment, only a mixed compound drink, and not any wine – if I
am mistaken, God forgive me; but I hope and do think I am not. By
and by met with Creed; and we with the others went within the
several Courts and there saw the tables prepared for the ladies and
Judges and Bishops – all great sign of a great dinner to come. By and
by, about one a-clock, before the Lord Mayor came, came into the
hall, from the room where they were first led into, the Lord
Chancellor (Archbishopp before him), with the Lords of the
Council and other Bishopps, and they to dinner. Anon comes the
Lord Mayor, who went up to the Lords and then to the other tables
to bid wellcome; and so all to dinner. I set near Proby, Baron, and
Creed at the Merchant Strangers table – where ten good dishes to a
messe, with plenty of wine of all sorts, of which I drunk none; but it
was very unpleasing that we had no napkins nor change of
trenchers, and drunk out of earthen pitchers and wooden dishes. It
happened that, after the Lords had half dined, came the French
Ambassador up to the Lords' table, where he was to have sat; but
finding the table set, he would not sit down nor dine with the Lord
Mayor, who was not yet come, nor have a table to himself, which
was offered; but in a discontent went away again. After I had dined,
I and Creed rose and went up and down the house, and up to the
ladies room and there stayed gazing upon them. But though there
were many and fine, both young and old, yet I could not discern
one handsome face there, which was very strange. I expected

Musique, but there was none; but only trumpets and drums, which displeased me. The dinner, it seems, is made by the Mayor and two Sheriffs for the time being, the Lord Mayor paying one half and they the other – and the whole, Proby says, is reckoned to come to about 7 or 800*l* at most. Being wearied with looking upon a company of ugly women, Creed and I went away; and took coach and through Cheapside and there saw the pageants, which were very silly. And thence to the Temple; where meeting Greatorex, he and we to the Hercules pillers, there to show me the manner of his going about a great work of drayning of Fenns, which I desired much to know; but it did not appear very satisfactory to me as he discoursed it, and I doubt he will fail in it.

31. To the office, where busy till night; and then to prepare my monthly account, about which I stayed till 10 or 11 a-clock at night; and to my great sorrow, find myself 43*l* worse then I was the last month; which was then 760*l* and now is but 717*l*. But it hath chiefly arisen from my layings-out in clothes for myself and wife – *viz.*, for her, about 12*l*; and for myself, 55*l* or thereabouts – having made myself a velvet cloak, two new cloth-suits, black, plain both – a new shag-gown, trimmed with gold buttons and twist; with a new hat, and silk top[s] for my legs, and many other things, being resolved henceforward to go like myself. And also two periwigs, one whereof costs me 3*l* and the other 40*s*. I have wore neither yet, but will begin next week, God willing. So that I hope I shall not now need to lay out more money a great while, I having laid out in clothes for myself and wife, and for her closet and other things without, these two months (this and the last), besides household expenses of victuals &c., above 110*l*. But I hope I shall with more comfort labour to get more, and with better successe then when, for want of clothes, I was forced to sneak like a beggar. Having done this, I went home; and after supper to bed.

## NOVEMBER

1. *Lords day*. This morning my brother's man brought me a new black bays waistcoat faced with silk, which I put on – from this day laying by half-shirts for this winter. He brought me also my new gowne of purple Shagg, trimmed with gold, very handsome. He

also brought me, as a gift from my brother, a velvet hat, very fine to ride in and the fashion, which pleases me very well; to which end I believe he sent it me, for he knew I had lately been angry with him. Up and to church with my wife; and at noon dined at home alone – a good calf's head boiled and dumplings, an excellent dinner methought it was.

2.   Up and by coach to Whitehall; and there in the long matted gallery I find Sir G. Carteret, Sir J. Mennes, and Sir W. Batten; and by and by comes the King to walk there, with three or four with him; and as soon as he saw us, "Oh," says he, "here is the Navy Office," and there walked twenty turns the length of the gallery – talking methought but ordinary talk. By and by came the Duke, and he walked and at last went into the Duke's lodgings. The King stayed so long that we could not discourse with the Duke, and so we parted. I heard the Duke say that he was going to wear a perriwigg; and they say the King also will. I never till this day observed that the King is mighty gray.

3.   Up and to the office, where busy all the morning; and at noon to the Coffee-house and there heard a long and most passionate discourse between two Doctors of Physique (of which one was Dr. Allen, whom I knew at Cambridge) and a Couple of Apothecarys; these maintaining Chymistry against their Galenicall physic; and the truth is, one of the Apothecaries, whom they charged most, did speak very prettily; that is, his language and sense good, though perhaps he might not be so knowing a physician as to offer to contest with them. I home; and by and by comes Chapman the periwig-maker, and [upon] my liking it, without more ado I went up and there he cut off my haire; which went a little to my heart at present to part with it, but it being over and my periwig on, I paid him 3*l* for it; and away went he with my own hair to make up another of; and I by and by, after I had caused all my maids to look upon it and they conclude it to become me, though Jane was mightily troubled for my parting with my own hair and so was Besse – I went abroad to the Coffee-house; and coming back, went to Sir W. Penn and there sat with him and Capt. Cocke till late at night, Cocke talking of some of the Roman history very well, he having a good memory. To supper and then a little to my viall, and afterward with my wife to her Arithmetique, and so to bed.

4. Up and to my office, showing myself to Sir W. Batten and Sir J. Mennes, and no great matter made of my periwig, as I was afeared there would. Among other things, there came to me this morning Shales of Portsmouth by my order, and I begun to discourse with him about the arreares of stores belonging to the Victualling Office there; and by his discourse, I am in some hopes that if I can get a grant from the King of such a part of all I discover, I may chance to find a way to get something by the by, which doth greatly please me the very thoughts of. Home to dinner and very pleasant with my wife, who is this day also herself making of Marmalett of Quince, which she now doth very well herself. I left her at it, and by coach I to the New Exchange and several places to buy and bring home things; among others, a case I bought of the Trunke-makers for my periwigg; and so home and to my office late.

6. This morning, waking, my wife was mighty earnest with me to persuade me that she should prove with child – which if it be, let it come and welcome. Up to my office, whither Comissioner Pett came, newly come out of the country, and he and I walked together in the garden, talking of business a great while. Thence, he being gone, to my office and there despatched many people. And at noon to the Change to the Coffee-house; and among other things, heard Sir John Cutler say that of his own experience in time of thunder, so many barrels of beer as have a piece of Iron laid upon them will not be stirred, and the others will.

8. *Lords day.* Up; and it being late, to church. I found that my coming in a perriwigg did not prove so strange to the world as I was afeared it would, for I thought that all the church would presently have cast their eye all upon me – but I found no such thing. Here an ordinary lazy sermon of Mr. Mills, and then home to dinner and there Tom came and dined with us; and after dinner, to talk about a new black cloth-suit that I have a-making; and so at church time I to church again – where the Scott preached, and I slept most of the time. Thence home and I spent most of the evening upon Fullers *Church History* and Barcklys *Argenis*; and so after supper to prayers and to bed.

9. To Westminster hall, where I met with Mr. Pierce the surgeon; and among other things, he asked me seriously whether I knew

anything of my Lord's being out of Favour with the King. And told me that for certain the King doth take mighty notice of my Lord's living obscurely in a corner, not like himself and becoming the honour that he is come to. He told me also how loose the Court is, nobody looking after business but every man his lust and gain; and how the King is now become besotted upon Mrs. Steward, that he gets into corners and will be with her half an hour together, kissing her to the observation of all the world; and she now stays by herself and expects it, as my Lady Castlemayne did use to do; to whom the King, he says, is still kind, so as now and then he goes to have a chat with her as he believes, but with no such fondness as he used to do. But yet it is thought that this new wench is so subtle, that she lets him not do anything more then is safe to her. But yet his doting is so great that Pierce tells me it is verily thought, that if the Queen had died, he would have married her. The Duke of Monmouth is to have part of the Cockepitt new built for lodgings for him; and they say to be made Captain of the Guards in the room of my Lord Gerard. In the evening to the Coffee-house and there sat, till by and by, by appointment, Will brought me word that his uncle Blackeburne was ready to speak with me. So I went down to him, and he and I to a taverne hard by. Mr. Blackeburne and I fell to talk of many things; wherein I did speak so freely to him in many things agreeing with his sense, that he was very open to me in all things. First, in that of Religion, he makes it great matter of prudence for the King and Council to suffer liberty of conscience. And imputes the loss of Hungary to the Turke from the Emperors denying them this liberty of their religion. He says that many pious Ministers of the word of God – some thousands of them, do now beg their bread. And told me how highly the present Clergy carry themselfs everywhere, so as that they are hated and laughed at by everybody. He tells me that the King, by name, with all his dignities, is prayed for by them that they call Fanatiques, as heartily and powerfully as in any of the other churches that are thought better. And that let the King think what he will, it is them that must help him in the day of Warr – for, as they are the most, so generally they are the most substantiall sort of people, and the soberest. And did desire me to observe it to my Lord Sandwich, among other things, that of all the old army now, you cannot see a man begging about the street. But what? You shall have this Captain turned a shoemaker; the lieutenant, a Baker; this, a brewer; that, a haberdasher; this common soldier, a porter; and every man in his apron and frock,

&c., as if they never had done anything else – whereas the [Cavaliers] go with their belts and swords, swearing and cursing and stealing – running into people's houses, by force oftentimes, to carry away something. And this is the difference between the temper of one and the other; and concludes (and I think with some reason) that the spirits of the old Parliament-soldier[s] are so quiet and contented with God's providences, that the King is safer from any evil meant him by them, a thousand times more then from his own discontented Cavalier[s]. And then to the public management of business: it is done, as he observes, so loosely and so carelessly, that the kingdom can never be happy with it, every man looking after himself and his own lust and luxury; among other things, he instanced in the business of mony; he doth believe that half of what the Parliament gives the King is not so much as gathered.

From thence we begun to talk of the Navy, and perticularly of Sir W. Pen – of whose rise to be a general I had a mind to be informed. He told me he was always a conceited man and one that would put the best side outward, but that it was his pretence of sanctity that brought him into play. Lawson and Portman and the Fifth-monarchy men, among whom he was a great brother, importuned that he might be general; and it was pleasant to see how Blackburn himself did act it; how when the Comissioners of the Admiralty would enquire of the Captains and Admiralls of such and such men, how they would with a sithe and casting up the eye say, "Such a man fears the Lord" – or, "I hope such a man hath the Spirit of God," and such things as that. But he tells me that there was a cruel Articling against Pen after one fight, for cowardice in putting himself within a Coyle of Cables, of which he had much ado to acquit himself. Thus far, and upon many more things, we had discoursed, when some persons in a room hard by begun to sing in three parts very finely, and to play upon a Flagilette so pleasantly, that my discourse afterward was but troublesome and I could not attend it; and so anon considering of a sudden the time a-night, we find it 11 a-clock, which I thought it had not been by two hours, but we were close in talk; and so we rise, he having drunk some wine and I some beer and sugar, and so by a fair moonshine home and to bed. My wife troubled with toothake.

11. Up and to my office all the morning; and at noon to the Coffee-house, where with Dr. Allen some good discourse about physic and Chymistry. And among other things, I telling him what

Dribble the German Doctor do offer, of an Instrument to sink ships, he tells me that which is more strange: that something made of gold, which they call in Chymistry *Aurum Fulminans*; a grain, I think he said, of it put into a silver spoon and fired, will give a blow like a musquett and strike a hole through the spoon downward, without the least force upward.

12. To [my Lord's] lodgings. Anon my Lord doth come in and I begun to fall in discourse with him; but my heart did misgive me that my Lord would not take it well, and then found him not in a humour to talk; and so after a few ordinary words, my Lord not talking in that manner as he uses to do, I took leave and spent some time with W. Howe; and told him how I could not do what I had so great a mind and resolution to do, but that I thought it would be as well to do it in writing; which he approves of, and so I took leave of him and by coach home, my mind being full of it and in pain concerning it. So to my office, busy very late, the nights running on faster then one thinks. And so home to supper and to bed.

13. To dinner, where I expected Comissioner Pett; and had a good dinner, but he came not. After dinner came my Perriwigg-maker and brings me a second perriwigg, made of my own hair; which comes to 21*s*. and 6*d*. more then the worth of my own hair – so that they both come to 4*l* 1*s*. 6*d*., which he sayth will serve me two years – but I fear it. He being gone, I to my office and put on my new Shagg purple gown with gold buttons and loop lace – I being a little fearful of taking cold and of pain coming upon me. Here I stayed, making an end of a troublesome letter, but to my advantage against Sir W. Batten, giving Sir G. Carteret an account of our late great contract with Sir W. Warren for masts; wherein I am sure I did the King 600*l* service. After that, about 9 or 10 a-clock, to supper in my wife's chamber, and then about 12 to bed.

14. By the way, I hear today that my boy Waynman hath behaved himself so with Mr. Davis, that they have got him put into a Berbados ship to be sent away; and though he sends to me to get a release for him, I will not, out of love to the boy; for I doubt to keep him here were to bring him to the gallows.

15. *Lords day*. I dined by myself; and in the afternoon to my office again and there drew up a letter to my Lord, stating to him what the

world talks concerning him, and leaving it to him; and myself to be thought of by him as he pleases, but I have done but my duty in it. I wait Mr. Moores coming for his advice about sending it. So home to supper to my wife, myself finding myself, by cold got last night, beginning to have some pain; which grieves me much in my mind, to see to what a weakness I am come. This day being our Queenes birthday, the guns of the tower went all off. And in the evening the Lord Mayor sent from church to church to order the constables to cause bonefires to be made in every street – which methinks is a poor thing to be forced to be commanded. After a good supper with my wife, and hearing on the maids read in the Bible, we to prayers and to bed.

17.  With Mr. Moore to my office and there I read to him the letter I have writ to send to my Lord, to give him an account how the world, both City and Court, doth talk of him and his living as he doth there, in such a poor and bad house, so much to his disgrace – which Mr. Moore doth conclude so well drawn, that he would not have me by any means to neglect sending it; assuring me, in the best of his judgment, that it cannot but endear me to my Lord, instead of what I fear, of getting his offence; and did offer to take the same words and send them, as from him with his hand, to him – which I am not unwilling should come (if they are at all fit to go) from anybody but myself. And so he being gone, I did take a copy of it to keep by me in shorthand, and sealed them up to send tomorrow by my Will. So home, Mr. Hollyard being come. I had great discourse with him about my disease. He tells me again that I must eat in a morning some loosening grewell; and at night, roasted apples. That I must drink now and then ale with my wine, and eat bread and butter and honey – and rye bread if I can endure it, it being loosening. I must also take once a week a glister of his past prescription; only, honey now and then instead of butter – which things I am now resolved to apply myself to. He being gone, I to my office again to a little business; and then home to supper and to bed – being in a little pain by drinking of cold small beer today, and being in a cold room at the Taverne I believe.

18.  This morning I sent Will with my great letter of reproof to my Lord Sandwich, who did give it into his own hand.
*My Lord.*
    I do verily hope that neither the manner nor matter of this advice

will be condemned by your Lordshipp, when for my defence in the first I shall allege my double attempt (since your return from Hinchingbrooke) of doing it personally, in both of which your Lordships occasions, no doubtfulness of mine prevented me. And that being now fearful of a sudden summons to Portsmouth for the discharge of some ships there, I judge it very unbecoming the duty which (every bit of bread I eat tells me) I owe to your Lordshipp to expose the safety of your Honour to the uncertainty of my return. For the matter (my Lord), it is such as could I in any measure think safe to conceal from, or likely to be discovered to you by any other hand, I should not have dared so far to own what from my heart I believe is false, as to make myself but the relater of others discourse. But, Sir, your Lordships honour being such as I ought to value it to be, and finding both in City and Court that discourses pass to your prejudice, too generally for mine or any man's controlling but your Lordships, I shall (my Lord), without the least greatening or lessening the matter, do my duty in laying it shortly before you. People of all conditions (my Lord) raise matter of wonder from your Lordships so little appearance at Court – some concluding thence your disfavour there. To which purpose I have had Questions asked me; and endeavouring to put off such insinuacions by asserting the contrary, they have replied that your Lordships living so beneath your Quality, out of the way and declining of Court attendance, hath been more then once discoursed about the King. Others (my Lord), when the chief Ministers of State, and those most active of the Council have been reckoned up (wherein your Lordship never use to want an eminent place), have said, touching your Lordshipp, that now your turn was served and the King had given you a good estate, you left him to stand or fall as he would. And, perticularly in that of the Navy, have enlarged upon your letting fall all service there. Another sort (and those the most) insist upon the bad report of the house wherein your Lordship (now observed in perfect health again) continues to sojourne. And by name have charged one of the daughters for a common Courtizan, alleging both places and persons where and with whom she hath been too well known. And how much her wantonness occasions (though unjustly) scandal to your Lordship; and that as well to gratifying of some enemies as to the wounding of more friends, I am not able to tell. Lastly (my Lord), I find a general coldness in all persons towards your Lordship; such as, from my first dependence on you, I never yet knew. Wherein I shall not offer to interpose any thoughts or advice of mine, well knowing your Lordship needs not any. But, with a most faithful assurance that no person nor papers under Heaven is privy to what I here write, besides myself and this, which I shall be careful to have put into your own hands, I rest confident of your Lordships just construction of my dutiful intents herein, and in all humility take leave.

May it please your Lordship, Your Lordships most obedient servant,

S.P. Nov. 17. 1663.

*Memorandum.* The letter beforegoing was sent sealed up, and enclosed in this that fallows.

*My Lord.*

If this finds your Lordshipp either not alone or not at leisure, I beg the suspending your opening of the enclosed till you shall be both – (the matter very well bearing such a delay) and in all humility remain.

May it please your Lordshipp, Your Lordshipps most obedient servant,

S.P. Nov. 17.1663.

My servant hath my directions to put this into your Lordships own hand, but not to stay for any answer.

19.  With Sir G. Carteret by coach to my Lord Treasurer, to discourse with him about Mr. Gauden's having of money and to offer to him whether it would not be necessary, Mr. Gaudens credit being so low as it is, to take security of him if he demands any great sum, such as 20000*l*, which now ought to be paid him. My Lord Treasurer we found in his bed-chamber, being laid up of the goute; I find him a very ready man and certainly a brave servant to the King, he spoke so quick and sensibly of the King's charge. Nothing displeased me in him but his long nails, which he lets grow upon a pretty thick white short hand, that it troubled me to see them. Thence with Sir G. Carteret by coach, and he set me down at the New Exchange. In our way he told me there is no such thing likely yet as a Dutch war, neither they nor we being in condition for it, though it will come certainly to that in some time, our interests lying the same way, that is to say in trade. But not yet.

20.  My wife tells me that she and her brother have had a great falling-out tonight, he taking upon him to challenge great obligation upon her, and taxing her for not being so as she ought to her

friends,* and that she can do more with me then she pretends, and I know not what; but God be thanked, she cannot.

21. At the office all the morning; and at noon I receive a letter from Mr. Creed with a token, *viz.*, a very noble parti-coloured Indian gowne for my wife. The letter is oddly writ, over-prizing his present and little owning any past service of mine, but that this was his genuine respects and I know not what. I confess I had expectations of a better account from him of my service about his accounts, and so gave his boy 12*d.* and sent it back again. And after having been at the pay of a ship this afternoon at the Treasury, I went by coach to Ludgate; and by pricing several there, I guess this gowne may be worth about 12 or 15*l.* But however, I expect at least 50*l* of him. So in the evening I wrote him a letter telling him clearly my mind, a copy of which I keep, and his letter; and so I resolve to have no more such correspondence as I used to have, but will have satisfaction of him as I do expect. So to write my letters; and after all done, I went home to supper and to bed – my mind being pretty well at ease from my letter to Creed, and more for my receipt this afternoon of 17*l* at the Treasury, for the 17*l* paid a year since to the Carver for his work at my house, which I did entend to have paid myself; but finding others to do it, I thought it not amisse to gett it too – but I am afeared that we may hear of it to our greater prejudices hereafter.

22. *Lords day.* Up pretty early; and having last night bespoke a coach, which failed me this morning, I walked as far as the Temple and there took coach and to my Lord's lodgings; whom I find ready to go to chappell. But coming, he begin with a very serious countenance to tell me that he had received my late letter; wherein, first he took notice of my care of him and his honour and did give me thanks for that part of it where I say that from my heart I believe the contrary of what I do there relate to be the discourse of others. But since I entended it not a reproach, but matter of information and for him to make a judgment of it for his practice, it was necessary for me to tell him the persons of whom I have gathered the several perticulars which I there insist on. I would have made excuses in it; but seeing him so earnest in it, I found myself forced to it; and so did tell him Mr. Pierce the surgeon in that of his low living being discoursed of at Court – a maid-servant that I kept that lived at Chelsy school, and also Mr. Pickering, about the report touching

the young woman; and also Mr. Hunt in axe yard, near whom she lodged. I told him the whole City doth discourse concerning his neglect of business; and so I many times asserting my dutiful intention in all this, and he owning his accepting of it as such. That that troubled me most in perticular is that he did there assert the civility of the people of the house and the young gentlewoman, for whose reproach he was sorry. I could not forbear weeping before him at the latter end; which since I am ashamed of, though I cannot see what he can take it to proceed from but my tenderness and good will to him. After this discourse was ended, he begun to talk very cheerfully of other things, and I walked with him to Whitehall and we discoursed of the pictures in the gallery; which, it may be, he might do out of policy, that the boy might not see any strangeness in him; but I rather think that his mind was somewhat eased, and hope that he will be to me as he was before. At Chappell I had room in the Privy Seale pew with other gentlemen, and there heard Dr. Killigrew preach; but my mind was so, I know not whether troubled or only full of thoughts of what had passed between my Lord and me, that I could not mind it nor can at this hour remember three words; the Anthemne was good after sermon, being the 51 psalme – made for five voices by one of Capt. Cookes boys, a pretty boy – and they say there are four or five of them that can do as much. And here I first perceived that the King is a little Musicall, and kept good time with his hand all along the Anthem. Thence I to the Kings head ordinary and there dined; good and much company and a good dinner; most of their discourse was about hunting, in a dialect I understood very little. Thence by coach to our own church; and there, my mind being yet unsettled, I could mind nothing; and after sermon home and there told my wife what had passed; and thence to my office, where doing business only to keep my mind imployed till late; and so home to supper, to prayers and to bed.

26. Up and to the office, where we sat all the morning; and at noon I to the Change and there met with Mr. Cutler the merchant, who would needs have me home to his house by the Dutch church; and there in an old but good house with his wife and mother, a couple of plain old women, I dined; a good plain dinner, and his discourse after dinner with me upon matters of the navy victuall-ing, very good and worth my hearing. And so home to my office in the afternoon, with my mind full of business; and there at it late, and so home to supper to my poor wife and to bed – myself being in

a little pain in one of my testicles, by a stroke I did give it in pulling up my breeches yesterday over-eagerly. The plague, it seems, grows more and more at Amsterdam. And we are going upon making of all ships coming from thence and Hambrough, or any other infected places, to perform their Quarantine (for 30 days as Sir Rd. Browne expressed it in the order of the Council, contrary to the import of the word; though in the general acceptation, it signifies now the thing, not the time spent in doing it) in Holehaven – a thing never done by us before.

28. Up and at the office; sat all the morning and at noon by Mr. Coventrys coach to the Change; and after a little while there, where I met with Mr. Pierce the surgeon, who tells me for good news that my Lord Sandwich is resolved to go no more to Chelsy, and told me he believed that I had been giving my Lord some counsel, which I neither denied nor affirmed but seemed glad with him that he went thither no more. And so I home to dinner, and thence abroad to Pauls churchyard and there looked upon the second part of *Hudibras*; which I buy not but borrow to read, to see if it be as good as the first, which the world cries so mightily up; though it hath not a good liking in me, though I had tried by twice or three times reading to bring myself to think it witty. Back again home; and to my office and there late doing businesses, and so home to supper and to bed. I have been told it two or three times, but today for certain I am told how in Holland publicly they have pictured our King with reproach. One way is with his pockets turned the wrong side outward, hanging out empty – another, with two courtiers picking of his pocket – and a third, leading of two ladies, while others abuse him – which amounts to great contempt.

29. *Lords day*. This morning I put on my best black cloth-suit trimmed with Scarlett ribbon, very neat, with my cloak lined with Velvett and a new Beaver, which altogether is very noble, with my black silk knit canons I bought a month ago. I to church alone, my wife not going; and there I find my Lady Batten in a velvet gowne, which vexed me that she should be in it before my wife, or that I am able to put her into one; but what cannot be, cannot be. However, when I came home I told my wife of it; and to see my weakness, I could on the sudden have found my heart to have offered her one, but second thoughts put it by; and endeed, it would undo me to think of doing as Sir W. Batten and his Lady do, who hath a good

estate besides his office. A good dinner we had of *bœuf a la mode*, but not dressed so well as my wife used to do it. So after dinner I to the French church; but that being too far begun, I came back to St. Dunstans by us, and heard a good sermon and so home.

# ⥽DECEMBER⥼

2. My wife troubled all last night with the toothake, and this morning. I up and to my office, where busy; and so home to dinner with my wife, who is better of her teeth then she was. And in the afternoon by agreement called on by Mr. Bland, and with him to the Ship, a neighbour tavern and there met his Antagonist Mr. Custos and his referee Mr. Clerke, a merchant also, and begun the dispute about the freight of a ship hired by Mr. Bland to carry provisions to Tanger, and the freight is now demanded; whereas, he says that the goods were some spoiled, some not delivered; and upon the whole, demands 1300*l* of the other. And their minds are both so high, their demands so distant, and their words so many and hot against one another, that I fear we shall bring it to nothing. But however, I am glad to see myself so capable of understanding the business as I find I do, and shall endeavour to do Mr. Bland all the just service I can therein. Here we were in a bad room, which vexed me most; but we meet at another house next. So at noon I home and to my office till 9 a-clock; and so home to my wife to keep her company; Arithmetique; then to supper and to bed – she being well of her teeth again.

4th.    Up pretty betimes; that is, about 7 a-clock, it being now dark then. And so got me ready with my clothes, breeches and warm stockings, and by water with Henry Russell, cold and wet and windy, to Woolwich to a hemp ship there; and stayed looking upon it and giving direction as to the getting it ashore, and so back again, very cold; and at home, without going on shore anywhere, about 12 a-clock, being fearful of taking cold. And so dined at home – and shifted myself, and so all the afternoon at my office till night, and then home to keep my poor wife company; and so to supper and to bed.

6.    *Lords day*. Lay long in bed; and then up and to church alone

(which is the greatest trouble that I have, by not having a man or boy to wait on me) and so home to dinner; my wife, it being a cold day and it begin to snow (the first snow we have seen this year), kept her bed till after dinner. And I below by myself looking over my arithmetique books and Timber Rule. So my wife rise anon, and she and I all the afternoon at Arithmetique; and she is come to do Addicion, Substraccion and Multiplicacion very well – and so I purpose not to trouble her yet with Division, but to begin with the globes to her now. At night I to my office and spent an hour or two reading Rushworth; and so to supper home, and to prayers and bed – finding myself by cold to have some pain begin with me, which God defend should encrease.

7.   Up betimes; and it being a frosty morning, walked on foot to Whitehall, but not without some fears of my pain coming. At Whitehall I hear and find that there was the last night the greatest Tide that ever was remembered in England to have been in this River – all Whitehall having been drowned – of which there was great discourse. Anon we all met, and up with the Duke and did our business; and by and by my Lord of Sandwich came in, but whether it be my doubt or no I cannot tell, but I do not find that he made any sign of kindness or respect to me, which troubles me more then anything in the world.

9.   This day Mrs. Russell did give my wife a very fine St. George in Alabaster, which will set out my wife's closet mightily.

10.   Up, pretty well, the weather being become pretty warm again. And to the office, where we sat all the morning; and I confess, having received so lately a token from Mrs. Russell, I did find myself concerned for our not buying some tallow of her (which she bought on purpose yesterday most unadvisedly, to her great loss, upon confidence of putting it off to us); so hard it is for a man not to be warped against his duty and maister's interest that receives any bribe or present, though not as a bribe, from anybody else. But she must be contented and I, to do her a good turn when I can without wrong to the King's service. Thence to St. Paul's churchyard to my booksellers; and having gained this day in the office, by my stationer's bill to the King, about 40s. or 3l, I did here sit two or three hours, calling for twenty books to lay this money out upon; and found myself at a great loss where to choose, and do

see how my nature would gladly returne to the laying out of money in this trade. I could not tell whether to lay out my money for books of pleasure, as plays, which my nature was most earnest in; but at last, after seeing Chaucer – Dugdales *History of Pauls*, Stow's *London*, Gesner, *History of Trent*, besides Shakespeare, Johnson, and Beaumonts plays, I at last chose Dr. Fuller's *worthys, the Cabbala or collections of Letters of State* – and a little book, *Delices de Hollande*, with another little book or two, all of good use or serious pleasure; and *Hudibras*, both parts, the book now in greatest Fashion for drollery, though I cannot, I confess, see enough where the wit lies. My mind being thus settled, I went by link home; and so to my office and to read in Rushworth; and so home to supper and to bed.

11. To the Coffee-house and there, among others, had good discourse with an Iron-merchant, who tells me the great evil of discouraging our natural manufacture of England in that commodity by suffering the Swede to bring in three times more then ever they did, and our own Ironworkes be lost – as almost half of them, he says, are already. Then I went and sat by Mr. Harrington and some East Country merchants; and talking of the country about Quinsborough[1] and thereabouts – he told us himself that for fish, none there, the poorest body, will buy a dead fish; but must be alive, unless it be in winter; and then they told us the manner of putting their nets into the water through holes made in the thicke Ice; they will spread a net of half a mile long, and he hath known 130 and 170 barrells of fish taken at one draught. And then the people comes with Sledges upon the Ice, with snow at the Bottome, and lay the fish in and cover them with snow, and so carry them to market. And he hath seen when the said fish have been frozen in the sled, so as that he hath taken a fish and broke a-pieces, so hard it hath been; and yet the same fishes, taken out of the snow and brought into a hot room, will be alive and leap up and down. Swallow often are brought up in their nets out of the mudd from under water, hanging together to some twigg or other, dead in ropes; and brought to the fire, will come to life. Fowl killed in December (Ald. Barker said) he did buy; and putting into the box under his sled, did forget to take them out to eate till Aprill next, and they then were found there and were, through the frost, as sweet and fresh and eat as well as at first killed. Young Beares are there; their flesh sold in

1. Königsberg, East Prussia.

market as ordinarily as beef here, and is excellent sweet meat. They tell us that Beares there do never hurt anybody, but fly away from you unless you pursue and set upon them – but Wolves do much mischief. Mr. Harrington told us how they do to get so much honey as they send abroad. They make hallow a great Firr tree, leaving only a small slitt down straight in one place; and this they close up again, only leave a little hole and there the Bees go in and fill the bodies of these trees as full of wax and honey as they can hold; and the inhabitants at their times go and open that slit and take what they please, without killing the bees, and so let them live there still and make more. Firr trees are always planted close together, because of keeping one another from the violence of the windes; and when a fellet is made, they leave here and there a grown tree to preserve the young ones coming up. The great entertainment and sport of the Duke of Corland and the princes thereabouts is hunting; which is not with dogs as we, but he appoints such a day and summons all the country people as to a *Campagnia*; and by several companies gives every one their circuit, and they agree upon a place where the Toyle is to be set; and so, making fires every company as they go, they drive all the wild beast – whether bears – wolfe, foxes, Swine, and stags and rowes, into the Toyle; and there the great men have their stands in such and such places and shoot at what they have a mind to, and that is their hunting. They are not very populous there, by reason that people marry women seldom till they are towards or above 30; and men 30 or 40, or more oftentimes, year old. Against a public hunting, the Duke sends that no wolfes be killed by the people; and whatever harm they do, the Duke makes it good to the person that suffers it – as Mr. Harrington instanced in a house where he lodged, where a wolfe broke into a hog-stye and bit three or four great pieces off of the back of the hog before the house could come to help it (it crying, and that did give notice to the people of the house); and the man of the house told him that there was three or four wolfs thereabouts that did them great hurt; but it was no matter, for the Duke was to make it good to him, otherwise he could kill them.

12.  We had this morning a great dispute between Mr. Gauden, victualler of the Navy, and Sir J. Lawson and the rest of the Commanders going out againt Argier, about their fish and keeping of Lent; which Mr. Gauden so much insists upon to have it observed, as being the only thing that makes up the loss of his dear

bargain all the rest of the year. At noon went home; and there I find that one Abrahall, who strikes in for the serving of the King with Ship-chandlery ware, hath sent my wife a Japan gowne; which pleases her very well and me also, it coming very opportune – but I know not how to carry myself to him, I being already obliged so far to Mrs. Russell – so that I am in both their pays.

14.   W. Howe tells me that my Lord, it is true, for a while after my letter was displeased, and did show many slightings of me when he had occasion of mentioning me to his Lordshipp, but that now my Lord is in good temper, and he doth believe will show me as much respect as ever – and would have me not to refrain to come to him. This news, I confess, did much trouble me; but when I did hear how he is come to himself and hath wholly left Chelsy and that slut, and that I see he doth fallow his business and becomes in better repute then before, I am rejoiced to see it, though it doth cost me some disfavour for a time; for if not his good nature and ingenuity, yet I believe his memory will not bear it alway in his mind. But it is my comfort that this is the thing, after so many years good service, that hath made him my enemy.

15.   To my office, and there very late with Sir W. Warren upon very serious discourse. And in the close, he and I did fall to talk very openly of the business of this office, and (if I was not a little too open to tell him my interest, which is my fault) he did give me most admirable advice, and such as doth speak him a most able and worthy man, and understanding seven times more then ever I thought to be in him. He did perticularly run over every one of the officers and Comanders, and showed me how I had reason to mistrust every one of them, either for their falseness or their over-great power, being too high to fasten a real friendship in. And did give me a common but a most excellent [saying] to observe in all my life; he did give it in rhyme, but the sense was this: that a man should treat every friend in his discourse and opening of his mind to him as of one that may hereafter be his foe. He did also advise me how I should take occasion to make known to the world my care and the pains that I take in my business; and above all, to be sure to get a thorough knowledge in my imployment, and to that add all the Interest at Court that I can – which I hope I shall do. He stayed talking with me till almost 12 at night, and so goodnight, being sorry to part with him and more sorry that he should have as far as

Wapping to walk tonight. So I to my Journall and so home – to supper and to bed.

20.  *Lords day*. After a dull sermon of the Scotchman, home; and there I find my brother Tom and my two Cosens Scotts, he and she – the first time they were ever here, And by and by in comes my uncle Wight and Mr. Norbury, and they sat with us a while drinking of wine, of which I did give them plenty. But they two would not stay supper, but the other two did; and we were as merry as I could be with people that I do wish well to but know not what discourse either to give them or find from them. We showed them our house from top to bottom, and had a good turkey roasted for our supper, and store of wine. And after supper sent them home on foot; and so we to prayers and to bed.

21.  Being directed by sight of bills upon the walls, did go to Shooe lane to see a Cocke-fighting at a new pit there – a sport I was never at in my life. But Lord, to see the strange variety of people, from Parliament-man (by name Wildes, that was Deputy-governor of the Tower when Robinson was Lord Mayor) to the poorest prentices, bakers, brewers, butchers, draymen, and what not; and all these fellows one with another in swearing, cursing, and betting. I soon had enough of it; and yet I would not but have seen it once, it being strange to observe the nature of those poor creatures, how they will fight till they drop down dead upon the table and strike after they are ready to give up the ghost – not offering to run away when they are weary or wounded past doing further. Whereas, where a Dunghill brood comes, he will, after a sharp stroke that pricks him, run off the stage, and then they wring off his neck without more ado. Whereas the other they preserve, though their eyes be both out, for breed only of a true cock of the game. One thing more it is strange to see, how people of this poor rank, that look as if they had not bread to put in their mouths, shall bet 3 or 4*l* at one bet and lose it, and yet bet as much the next battell, as they call every make of two cocks – so that one of them will lose 10 or 20*l* at a meeting. Thence, having enough of it, by coach to my Lord Sandwiches; where I find him within with Capt. Cooke and his boys, Dr. Childe, Mr. Mage, and Mallard, playing and singing over my Lord's Anthemne which he hath made to sing in the King's Chappell. My Lord saluted me kindly and took me into the withdrawing-room to hear it at a distance; and endeed, it sounds

very finely and is a good thing, I believe, to be made by him – and they all commend it. And after that was done, Capt. Cooke and his two boys did sing some Italian songs, which I must in a word say I think was fully the best Musique that I ever yet heard in all my life.

24. Up betimes; and though it was a most foggy morning and cold, yet with a gally down to Eriffe, several times being at a loss whither we went. There I mustered two ships of the King's, lent by him to the Guiny Company, which are manned better then ours at far less wages. Thence on board two of the King's; one of them the *Leopard*, Capt. Beech, who I find an able and serious man. He received me civilly, and his wife was there, a very well-bred and knowing woman – born at Antwerp, but speaks as good English as myself, and an ingenious woman. Here was also Sir G. Carteret's son, who I find a pretty, but very talking man; but good humour. Thence back again, entertaining myself upon my sliding-rule with great content; and called at Woolwich, where Mr. Chr. Pett, having an opportunity of being alone, did tell me his mind about several things he thought I was offended with him in, and told me of my kindness to his Assistant; I did give him such an answer as I thought was fit, and left him well satisfied – he offering to do me all the service, either by draughts or modells, that I should desire. Thence straight home, being very cold but yet well, I thank God. And at home find my wife making mince-pies; and by and by comes in Capt. Ferrers to see us and among other talk, tells us of the goodness of the new play of *Henry the 8th*, which makes me think long till my time is out; but I hope before I go, I shall set myself such a stint as I may not forget myself, as I have hitherto done till I was forced for these [six] months last past wholly to forbid myself the seeing of one. He gone, I to my office and there late, writing and reading; and so home to bed.

25. *Christmas.* Lay long, talking pleasantly with my wife; but among other things, she begin, I know not whether by design or chance, to enquire what she should do if I should by an accident die; to which I did give her some slight answer, but shall make good use of it to bring myself to some settlement for her sake, by making a Will as soon as I can. Up, and to church, where Mr. Mills made an ordinary sermon; and so home and dined with great pleasure with my wife; and all the afternoon, first looking out at window and seeing the boys playing at many several sports in our back-yard by

Sir W. Pens, which minded me of my own former times; and then I begin to read to my wife upon the globes, with great pleasure and to good purpose, for it will be pleasant to her and to me to have her understand those things. In the evening to the office, where I stayed late reading Rushworth, which is a most excellent collection of the beginning of the late quarrels in this kingdom. And so home to supper and to bed with good content of mind.

26.    Up; and walked forth first to the Minerys to Brown's, and there with great pleasure saw and bespoke several Instruments – and so to Cornhill to Mr. Cades, and there went up into his warehouse to look for a map or two; and there finding great plenty of good pictures, God forgive me how my mind run upon them. And bought a little one for my wife's closet presently, and concluded presently of buying 10*l* worth, upon condition he would give me the buying of them. Now, it is true I did still within me resolve to make the King one way or other pay for them, though I saved it to him another way. Thence to the Coffee-house; and sat long in good discourse with some gentlemen concerning the Roman Empire. So home and find Mr. Hollyard there; and he stayed and dined with us, we having a pheasant to dinner. He gone, I all the afternoon with my wife to Cards. And God forgive me, to see how the very discourse of plays, which I shall be at liberty to see after New Year's day next, doth set my mind upon them, that I must be forced to stint myself very strictly before I begin, or else I fear I shall spoil all. So to my office, writing letters, and then to read and make an end of Rushworth; which I did, and do say that it is a book the best worth reading for a man of my condition, or any man that hopes to come to any public condition in the world, that I do know. So home to supper and to bed.

31.    We had to dinner, my wife and I, a fine Turkey and a mince-pie, and dined in state, poor wretch, she and I; and have thus kept our Christmas together, all alone almost – having not once been out. But tomorrow my vowes are all out as to plays and wine; but I hope I shall not be long before I come to new ones, so much good, and God's blessing, I find to have attended them. Thence to the office and did several businesses and answered several people; but my head akeing and it being my great night of accounts, I went forth, took coach, and to my brother's, but he was not within; and so I back again and sat an hour or two at the Coffee[-house], hearing

some simple discourse about Quakers being charmed by a string about their wrists. And so home; and after a little while at my office, I home and supped; and so had a good fire in my chamber and there sat till 4 a-clock in the morning, making up my accounts and writing this last Journall of the year.

And first, I bless God I do find that I am worth in money, besides all my household stuff or anything of Brampton, above 800*l* – for which the good God be pleased to give me a thankful heart and a mind careful to preserve this and encrease it. I do live at my lodgings in the Navy Office – my family being, besides my wife and I, Jane Gentleman, Besse our excellent good-natured cook-maid, and Susan, a little girl – having neither man nor boy, nor like to have again a good while – living now in most perfect content and quiet and very frugally also. My health pretty good, but only that I have been much troubled with a costivenesse which I am labouring to get away, and have hopes of doing it. At the office I am well, though envied to the devil by Sir W. Batten, who hates me to death but cannot hurt me. The rest either love, or at least do not show otherwise, though I know Sir W. Penn to be a false knave touching me, though he seems fair. My father and mother well in the country; and at this time, the young ladies of Hinchingbrooke with them, their house having the smallpox in it. The Queene, after a long and sore sickness, is become well again. And the King minds his mistress a little too much. But I hope all things will go well, and in the Navy perticularly; wherein I shall do my duty, whatever comes of it. The great talk is the designs of the King of France; whether against the Pope or King of Spain nobody knows; but a great and a most promising prince he is, and all the princes of Europe have their eye upon him. My wife's brother come to great unhappiness by the ill-disposition, my wife says, of his wife, and her poverty; which she now professes, after all her husband's pretence of a great portion. But I see none of them; at least, they come not to trouble me. My brother Tom I know not what to think of, for I cannot hear whether he minds his business or no. And my brother John, at Cambrige with as little hopes of doing good there; for when he was here, he did give me great cause of dissatisfaction with his manner of life. Pall with my father, and God knows what she doth there or what will become of her, for I have not anything yet to spare her, and she grows now old and must be disposed of one way or other. The Turkes very fur entered into Germany, and all that part of the world at a loss what to expect from his proceedings.

Myself, blessed be God, in a good way and design and resolution by sticking to my business to get a little money, with doing the best service I can to the King also – which God continue. So ends the old year.

# 1664

## ⊹ JANUARY ⊹

1.   Went to bed between 4 and 5 in the morning with my mind in good temper of satisfaction – and slept till about 8, that many people came to speak with me. And then, being to dine at my uncle Wights, I went to the Coffee-house (sending my wife by Will) and there stayed talking an hour with Coll. Middleton and others; and among other things, about a very rich widow, young and handsome, of one Sir Nich. Golds, a merchant lately fallen, and of great Courtiers that already look after her. Her husband not dead a week yet. She is reckoned worth 80000*l*. Thence to my Uncle Wights, where Dr. [Burnet] among others dined, and his wife a seeming proud conceited woman; I know not what to make of her. But the Doctors discourse did please me very well about the disease of the Stone; above all things extolling Turpentine, which he told me how it may be taken in pills with great ease. There was brought to table a hot pie made of swan I sent them yesterday, given me by Mr. Howe; but we did not eat any of it. But my wife and I rise from table pretending business, and went to the Dukes house, the first play I have been at these six months, according to my last vowe; and here saw the so much cried-up play of *Henry the 8th* – which, though I went with resolution to like it, is so simple a thing, made up of a great many patches, that, besides the shows and processions in it, there is nothing in the world good or well done. Thence, mightily dissatisfied, back at night to my uncle Wights and supped with them; but against my stomach out of the offence the sight of my aunts hands gives me; and ending supper with a mighty laugh (the greatest I have had these many months) at my uncles being out in his grace after meat, we rise and broke up and my wife and I home and to bed – being sleepy since last night.

2.   I do find that I am not able to conquer myself as to going to plays till I do come to some new vow concerning it and that I am now come: that is to say, that I will not see above one in a month at

any of the public theatres till the sum of 50s. be spent, and then none before New Year's Day next, unless that I do become worth 1000*l* sooner then then – and then I am free to come to some other terms. And so I took my wife to the King's house and there met with Mr. Nicholson my old colleague – and saw *The Usurper*, which is no good play, though better then what I saw yesterday. However, we ris unsatisfied and took coach and home. And I to the office late, writing letters; and so home to supper and to bed.

3.    *Lords day*. Lay long in bed; and then rose and with a fire in my chamber stayed within all day, looking over and settling my accounts in good order – by examining all my books and the kitchen books; and I find that though the proper profit of my last year was but 305*l*, yet I did by other gain make it up 444*l* – which in every part of it was unforeseen of me; and therefore it was a strange oversight for lack of examining my expenses that I should spend 690*l* this year. But for the time to come, I have so distinctly settled all my accounts in writing and the perticulars of all my several layings-out, that I do hope I shall hereafter make a better judgment of my spendings then ever. I dined with my wife in her chamber, she in bed. And then down again and till 11 at night; and broke up and to bed with great content, but could not make an end of writing over my vows as I purposed, but I am agreed in everything how to order myself for the year to come, which I trust in God will be much for my good. So up to prayers and to bed. This noon Sir W. Pen came to invite me and my wife against next Wednesday, being Twelfth-day, to his usual feast, his wedding day.

4.    Up betimes, and my wife being ready and her maid Besse and the girl, I carried them by coach and set them all down in Covent garden and there left them, and I to my Lord Sandwich[es] lodgings, but he not being up, I to the Dukes chamber, and there by and by to his closet; where, since his lady was ill, a little red bed of velvet is brought for him to lie alone, which is a very pretty one. After doing business here, I to my Lord's again and there spoke with him, and he seems now almost friends again as he used to be. Here meeting Mr. Pierce the surgeon, he told me, among other Court news, how the Queene is very well again and the King lay with her on Saturday night last. And that she speaks now very pretty English and makes her sense out now and then with pretty phrases – as among others, this is mightily cried up – that meaning

339

to say that she did not like such a horse so well as the rest, he being too prancing and full of tricks, she said he did "make too much vanity." Thence to the Tennice Court (after I had spent a little time in Westminster hall, thinking to have met with Mrs. Lane, but I could not and am glad of it) and there saw the King play at Tennis and others. But to see how the King's play was extolled without any cause at all, was a loathsome sight, though sometimes endeed he did play very well and deserved to be commended; but such open flattery is beastly. Afterward to St. James's park, being unwilling to go to spend money at the ordinary, and there spent an hour or two, it being a pleasant day, seeing people play at Pell Mell – where it pleased me mightily to hear a gallant, lately come from France, swear at one of his companions for suffering his man (a spruce blade) to be so saucy as to strike a ball while his master was playing on the Mall. Home – and at my office till 12 at night, making my solemn vowes for the next year, which I trust in the Lord I shall keep. But I fear I have a little too severely bound myself in some things and in too many, for I fear I may forget some. But however, I know the worst, and shall by the blessing of God observe to perform or pay my forfeits punctually. So home and to bed – with my mind at rest.

6.   *Twelfth day*. Up and to my office, where very busy all the morning; being endeed over-loaded with it through my own desire of doing all I can. At noon to the Change but did little, and so home to dinner with my poor wife; and after dinner read a lecture to her in Geography, which she takes very prettily, and with great pleasure to her and me to teach her. And so to the office again, where as busy as ever in my life, one thing after another and answering people's business. Perticularly, drawing up things about Mr. Woods masts, which I expect to have a quarrel about with Sir W. Batten before it be ended – but I care not. At night home to my wife to supper, discourse, prayers, and to bed. This morning I begun a practice which I find, by the ease I do it with, that I shall continue, it saving me money and time – that is, to Trimme myself with a Razer – which pleases me mightily.

7.   Up, putting on my best clothes, and to the office, where all the morning we sat busy; among other things, upon Mr. Wood's performance of his contract for Masts, wherein I was mightily concerned, but I think was found all along in the right and shall have

my desire in it, to the King's advantage. At noon all of us to dinner to Sir W. Pens, where a very handsome dinner. Sir J. Lawson among others, and his lady and his daughter, a very pretty lady and of good deportment – with looking upon whom I was greatly pleased. The rest of the company of the women were all of our own house, of no satisfaction or pleasure at all. My wife was not there, being not well enough nor had any great mind. But to see how Sir W. Penn imitates me in everything, even in his having of his chimney piece in his dining-room the same with that in my wife's closet – and in everything else, I perceive, wherein he can. But to see again how he was out in one compliment: he lets alone drinking any of the ladies' healths that were there (my Lady Batten and Lawson) till he had begun with my Lady Carteret, who was absent (and that was well enough), and then Mr. Coventry's mistress, at which he[1] was ashamed and would not have had him have drunk it, at least before the ladies present; but his policy, as he thought, was such that he would do it. After dinner, by coach with Sir G. Carteret and Sir J. Mennes by appointment to Auditor Beale's in Salsbury court, and there we did with great content look over some old Leigers to see in what manner they were kept; and endeed it was in an extraordinary good method, and such as (at least out of design to keep them imployed) I do persuade Sir J. Mennes to go upon; which will at least do so much good, it may be, to keep them for want of something to do from envying those that do something.

8.    Up and all the morning at my office and with Sir J. Mennes, directing him and Mr. Turner about keeping of their books according to yesterday's work – wherein I shall make them work enough. At noon to the Change and there long; and from thence by appointment took Luellin, Mount, and W. Symons and Mr. Pierce the surgeon home to dinner with me, and were merry. But Lord, to hear how W. Symons doth commend [her] and look sadly, and then talk bawdily and merrily, though his wife was dead but the other day, would make a dog laugh. We had great pleasure this afternoon, among other things, to talk of our old passages together in Cromwells time. And how W. Symons did make me laugh and wonder today, when he told me how he had made shift to keep in, in good esteem and imployment, through eight governements in one year (the year 1659, which were endeed, and he did name them

1. Coventry.

all) and then failed unhappy in the ninth, *viz*, that of the King's coming in. Upon the Change, a great talk there was one Mr. Tryan, an old man, a merchant in Lymestreete, robbed last night (his man and maid being gone out after he was a-bed) and gagged and robbed of 1050*l* in money and about 4000*l* in Jewells which he had in the house as security for money. It is believed that his man, by many circumstances, is guilty of confederacy, by their ready going to his secret Till in his desk wherein the key of his cash chest lay.

11. Waked this morning by 4 a-clock by my wife, to call the maids to their wash. And what through my sleeping so long last night and vexation for the lazy sluts lying so long against their great wash, neither my wife nor I could sleep one winke after that time till day; and then I rose and by coach (taking Capt. Grove with me and three bottles of Tent, which I sent to Mrs. Lane by my promise on Saturday night last) to Whitehall and there with the rest of our company to the Duke and did our business; and thence I to the Tennis Court till noon and there saw several great matches played; and so by invitation to St. James's, where at Mr. Coventry's chamber I dined with my Lord Barkely, Sir G. Carteret, Sir Edwd. Turner, Sir Ellis Layton, and one Mr. Seymour, a fine gentleman; where admirable good discourse of all sorts, pleasant and serious. Thence after dinner to Whitehall; where the Duke being busy at the Guinny business – the Duke of Albemarle, Sir W. Rider, Povy, Sir J. Lawson and I to the Duke of Albemarle's lodgings and there did some business; and so to the Court again and I to the Duke of Yorkes lodgings, where the Guinny Company are choosing their Assistants for the next year by balletting. Thence by coach with Sir J. Robinson, Lieutenant of the Tower; he set me down at Cornhill; but Lord, the simple discourse that all the way we had, he magnifying his great undertakings and cares that have been upon him for these last two years, and how he commanded the City to the content of all parties, when the loggerhead knows nothing almost that is sense. Thence to the Coffee-house, whither comes Sir W. Petty and Capt. Grant, and we fell in talk (besides a young gentleman I suppose a merchant, his name Mr. Hill, that hath travelled and I perceive is a master in most sorts of Musique and other things) of Musique, the Universall Character – art of Memory – Granger's counterfeiting of hands – and other most excellent discourses, to my great content, having not been in so good company a great while. And had I time I should covett the

acquaintance of that Mr. Hill. This morning I stood by the King, arguing with a pretty Quaker woman that delivered to him a desire of hers in writing. The King showed her Sir J. Minnes, as a man the fittest for her quaking religion, saying that his beard was the stiffest thing about him. And again merrily said, looking upon the length of her paper, that if all she desired was of that length, she might lose her desires. She modestly saying nothing till he begun seriously to discourse with her, arguing the truth of his spirit against hers. She replying still with these words, "O King!", and thou'd him all along.

12. Up and to the office, where we sat all the morning; and at noon to the Change awhile and so home – getting things against dinner ready. And anon comes my uncle Wight and my aunt with their Cozen Mary and Robert, and by chance my Uncle Tho. Pepys. We had a good dinner, the chief dish a swan roasted, and that excellent meat. At dinner and all day very merry. After dinner to Cards, where till evening; then to the office a little and to cards again with them – and lost half-a-Crowne. They being gone, my wife did tell me how my Uncle did this day accost her alone and spoke of his hopings she was with child; and kissing her earnestly, told her he should be very glad of it; and from all circumstances, methinks he doth seem to have some intention of good to us, which I shall endeavour to continue more then ever I did yet. So to my office till late and then home to bed – after being at prayers, which is the first time after my late vow to say prayers in my family twice in every week.

13. Up and to my office a little, and then abroad to many several places about business; among others, to the Geometrical Instrument makers, and then through Bedlam (calling by the way at a old bookseller's, and there fell into looking over Spanish books and pitched upon some, till I thought of my oath when I was going to agree for them and so with much ado got myself out of the shop, glad at my heart, and so away) to the Affrican house to look upon their book of contracts for several commodities for my information in the prize* we give in the Navy. So to the Coffee[-house] where extraordinary good discourse of Dr. Whist[l]ers upon my Question concerning the keeping of Masts, he arguing against keeping them dry, by showing the nature of Corrupcion in bodies and the several ways thereof.

21. Up; and after sending my wife to my aunt Wight's to get a place to see Turner[1] hanged, I to the office, where we sat all the morning. And at noon, going to the Change and seeing people flock in that, I enquired and found that Turner was not yet hanged; and so I went among them to Leadenhall street at the end of Lyme street, near where the robbery was done, and to St. Mary Axe, where he lived; and there I got for a shilling to stand upon the wheel of a Cart, in great pain, above an hour before the execution was done – he delaying the time by long discourses and prayers one after another, in hopes of a reprieve; but none came, and at last was flung off the lather in his cloak. A comely-looked man he was, and kept his countenance to the end – I was sorry to see him. It was believed there was at least 12 or 14000 people in the street.

22. Up; and it being a brave morning, by water with a galley to Woolwich and there, both at the ropeyard and the other yard, did much business; and thence to Greenwich to see Mr. Pett and others value the Carved work of the *Henrietta* (God knows in an ill manner for the King); and so to Deptford and there viewed Sir W. Petty's vessel, which hath an odd appearance but not such as people do make of it, for I am of the opinion that he would never have discoursed so much of it if it were not better then other vessels, and so I believe that he was abused the other day, as he is now, by tongues that I am sure speak before they know anything good or bad of her. I am sorry to find his ingenuity discouraged so. So home, reading all the way a good book; and so home to dinner, and after dinner a lesson on the globes to my wife; and so to my office, where till 10 or 11 a-clock at night; and so home to supper and to bed.

23. Up and to the office, where we sat all the morning. At noon home to dinner, where Hawly came to see us and dined with us. And after we had dined came Mr. Mallard; and after he had eat something, I brought down my vyall, which he played on – the first Maister that ever touched her yet, and she proves very well and will be, I think, an admirable instrument. He played some very fine things of his own, but I was afeared to enter too far in their commendation for fear he should offer to copy them for me out, and so I be forced to give or lend him something. So to the office in

1. Convicted of the robbery described above, p. 342 (8 January).

the evening, whither Mr. Comander came to me and we discoursed about my Will, which I am resolved to perfect the next week by the grace of God. He being gone, I to write letters and other business late. And so home to supper and to bed.

24.   *Lords day*. Lay long in bed. And then up; and being desirous to perform my vows that I lately made, among others to be performed this month, I did go to my office and there fell on entering out of a by-book part of my second Journall book, which hath lay these two years and more unentered. Upon this work till dinner; and after dinner, to it again till night and then home to supper; and after supper, to read a lecture to my wife upon the globes, and so to prayers and to bed. This evening also, I drow up a rough draught of my last Will – to my mind.

27.   Up and to the office; and at noon to the Coffee-house, where I sat with Sir G. Asckue and Sir Wm. Petty, who in discourse is methinks one of the most rational men that ever I heard speak with a tongue, having all his notions the most distinct and clear; among other things saying that in all his life these three books were the most esteemed and generally cried up for wit in the world – *Religio Medici,* Osborne's *Advice to a Son,* and *Hudibras.* Thence to the Change; and after doing much business, home, taking Comissioner Pett thence with me, and all alone dined together. He was mighty serious with me in discourse about the consequence of Sir W. Petty's boat[1] as the most dangerous thing in the world if it should be practised in the world, by endangering our loss of the command of the seas and the trade while the Turkes and others shall get the use of them, which, without doubt, by bearing more sail will go faster then any other ships; and not being of burden, our Merchants cannot have the use of them and so will be at the mercy of their enemies – so that I perceive he is afeared that the Honour of his trade will down, though (which is a truth) he pretends this consideration to hinder the growth of this invention. He being gone, my wife and I took coach and to Covent garden to buy a mask at the French house, Madam Charett's, for my wife – in the way observing the street full of coaches at the new play, *The Indian Queene*; which for show, they say, exceeds *Henry the 8th.* Thence back to Mrs. Turners and sat a while with them, talking of plays and I know not what;

1. See above, p. 299 (31 July).

and so called to see Tom, but not at home, though they say he is in a deep consumption, and Mrs. Turner and Dike and they say he will not live two months to an end. So home and to the office, and then to supper and to bed.

30. Up, and a sorry sermon of a young fellow I knew at Cambrige. But the day kept solemnly for the King's murther, and I all day within doors making up my Brampton papers; and in the evening Mr. Comander came and we made perfect and signed and sealed my last Will and Testament, which is so to my mind, and I hope to the liking of God Almighty, that I take great joy in myself that it is done, and by that means my mind in a good condition of quiet. At night, to supper and to bed. This evening, being in an humour of making all things even and clear in the world, I tore some old papers; among others, a Romance which (under the title of *Love a Cheate*) I begun ten year ago at Cambridge; and at this time, reading it over tonight, I liked it very well and wondered a little at myself at my vein at that time when I wrote it, doubting that I cannot do so well now if I would try.

31. *Lords day*. Up, and in my chamber all day long (but a little at dinner) settling all my Brampton Accounts to this day in very good order, I having obliged myself by oath to do that and some other things within this month. I did also perfectly prepare a state of my Estate and annexed it to my last Will and Testament, which now is perfect. And lastly, I did make up my month's accounts and find that I have gained above 50*l* this month clear, and so am worth 858*l* clear, which is the greatest sum I ever yet was maister of. And also read over my usual vowes, as I do every Lord's day, but with greater seriousness then ordinary, and I do hope that every day I shall see more and more the pleasure of looking after my business and laying up of money. And blessed be God for what I have already been enabled by his Grace to do.

# –❖FEBRUARY❖–

1. To Whitehall, where in the Dukes chamber the King came and stayed an hour or two, laughing at Sir W. Petty, who was there about his boat, and at Gresham College in general. At which poor

Petty was I perceive at some loss, but did argue discreetly and bear the unreasonable follies of the King's objections and other bystanders with great discretion – and offered to take oddes against the King's best boats; but the King would not lay, but cried him down with words only. Gresham College he mightily laughed at for spending time only in weighing of ayre, and doing nothing else since they sat. Thence to Westminster hall and there met with diverse people, it being term-time. Here I met with Mr. Pierce, who tells me of several passages at Court; among others, how the King, coming the other day to his Theatre to see *The Indian Queene* (which he commends for a very fine thing), my Lady Castlemaine was in the next box before he came; and leaning over other ladies a while to whisper with the King, she ris out of that box and went into the King's and sat herself on the King's right hand between the King and the Duke of Yorke – which he swears put the King himself, as well as everybody else, out of countenance, and believes that she did it only to show the world that she is not out of favour yet – as was believed. Thence with Ald. Maynell by his coach to the Change, and there with several people busy; and so home to dinner and took my wife out immediately to the King's Theatre, it being a new month (and once a month I may go) and there saw *The Indian Queen* acted, which endeed is a most pleasant show and beyond my expectation; the play good but spoiled with the Ryme, which breaks the sense. But above my expectation most, the eldest Marshall did do her part most excellently well as ever I heard woman in my life, but her voice not so sweet as Ianthes – but however, we came home mightily contented. Here we met Mr. Pickering and his mistress, Mrs Doll. Wilde. He tells me that the business runs high between the Chancellor and my Lord Bristoll against the Parliament. And that my Lord Lauderdale and Cooper open high against the Chancellor – which I am sorry for. In my way home I light and to the Coffee-house, where I heard Lieut.-Coll. Baron tell very good stories of his travels over the high hills in Asia above the Cloudes. How clear the heaven is above them. How thick, like a mist, the way is through the cloud, that wets like a sponge one's clothes. The ground above the clouds all dry and parched, nothing in the world growing, it being only a dry earth. Yet not so hot above as below the clouds. The stars at night most delicate bright and a fine clear blue sky. But cannot see the earth at any time through the clouds, but the clouds look like a world below you.

347

2. Up and to the office; where, though Candlemass day, Mr. Coventry, Sir W. Penn and I are all the morning, the others being at a Survey at Deptford; at noon by coach to the Change with Mr. Coventry. Thence to the Coffee-house with Capt. Cocke, who discoursed well of the good effects in some kind of a Duch war and conquest (which I did not consider before but the contrary); that is, that the trade of the world is too little for us two, therefore one must down. Secondly, that though our merchants will not be the better husbands by all this, yet our Wool will bear a better prize by vaunting of our cloths, and by that our tenants will be better able to pay rents and our lands will be more worth, and all our own manufactures – which now the Dutch out-vie us in. That he thinks the Duch are not in so good a condition as heretofore, because of want of men always, and now from the wars against the Turke more then ever. Thence to the Change again, and thence off to the Sun taverne with Sir W. Warren and with him discoursed long and had good advice and hints from him; and among [other] things, he did give me a pair of gloves for my wife, wrapped up in paper; which I would not open, feeling it hard, but did tell him my wife should thank him, and so went on in discourse. When I came home, Lord, in what pain I was to get my wife out of the room without bidding her go, that I might see what these gloves were; and by and by, she being gone, it proves a pair of white gloves for her and 40 pieces in good gold: which did so cheer my heart that I could eat no victuals almost for dinner for joy to think how God doth bless us every day more and more – and more yet I hope he will upon the encrease of my duty and endeavours. I was at great loss what to do, whether tell my wife of it or no; which I could hardly forbear, but yet I did and will think of it first before I do, for fear of making her think me to be in a better condition or in a better way of getting money then yet I am. After dinner to the office, where doing infinite of business till past 10 at night to the comfort of my mind; and so home with joy to supper and to bed.

3. In Covent garden tonight, going to fetch home my wife, I stopped at the great Coffee-house there, where I never was before – where Draydon the poet (I knew at Cambrige) and all the wits of the town, and Harris the player and Mr. Hoole of our college; and had I had time then, or could at other times, it will be good coming thither, for there I perceive is very witty and pleasant discourse. But I could not tarry and it was late; they were all ready to go away.

4.   Up and to the office, where after a while setting, I left the board upon pretence of serious business and by coach to Paul's schoole, where I heard some good speeches of the boys that were to be elected this year. Thence by and by with Mr. Pullen and Banes (a great nonconformist) with several other of my old acquaintance to the Nags head tavern and there did give them a bottle of sack; and away again and I to the school and up to hear the upper form examined; and there was kept by very many of the Mercers, Clutterbucke, Barker, Harrington, and others, and with great respect used by them all and had a noble dinner. Here they tell me that in Dr. Colett's Will he says that he would have a master found for the school that hath good skill in Latin and (if it could be) one that had some knowledge of the Greeke; so little was Greek known here at that time. Dr. Wilkins and one Mr. Smallwood, posers. After great pleasure there, and especially to [hear] Mr. Crumlum so often to tell of my being a benefactor to the school – I to my booksellers and there spent an hour looking over *Theatrum Urbium* and *Flandria illustrata*, with excellent cuts, with great content. So homewards and called at my little Millener's, where I chatted with her, her husband out of the way, and a mad merry soul she is. So home to the office; and by and by comes my wife home from the burial of Capt. Groves wife at Wapping (she telling me a story how her maid Jane, going into the boat, did fall down and show her arse in the boat) and all; and comes my Uncle Wight and Mr. Maes with the state of their case, which he told me very discreetly and I believe is a very hard one. And so after drinking a bottle of ale or two, they gone and I a little more to the office; and so home to prayers and to bed.

5.   Up; and down by water, a brave morning, to Woolwich and there spent an hour or two to good purpose; and so walked to Greenwich and thence to Deptford, where I find (with Sir W. Batten upon the survey) Sir J. Mennes, Sir W. Penn and my Lady Batten come down and going to dinner. I dined with them, and so after dinner by water home, all the way going and coming reading *Faber fortunæ*, which I can never read too often. At home a while with my wife; and so to my office, where till 8 a-clock, and then home to look after some Brampton papers and perticularly those of my uncles accounts as Generall-Receiver of the county for the year 1647 of our Monthly Assessement; which, contrary to my expectation, I found in such good order and so thoroughly that I did

not expect nor could have thought; and that being done, having seen discharges for every farthing of money he received, I went to bed late with great quiet.

8.   Up, and by coach called upon Mr. Phillips and after a little talk with him, away to my Lord Sandwiches; but he being gone abroad, I stayed a little and talked with W. Howe; and so to Westminster in term-time. And there met Mr. Pierce, who told me largely how the King still doth dote upon his women, even beyond all shame. And that the good Queen will of herself stop before she goes sometimes into her dressing-room, till she know whether the King be there, for fear he should be, as she hath sometimes taken him, with Mrs. Stuart. And that some of the best parts of the Queenes Joynture is, contrary to faith and against the opinion of my Lord Treasurer and his Council, bestowed or rented, I know not how, to my Lord Fitzharding and Mrs. Stuart and others of that crew. That the King doth dote infinitely upon the Duke of Monmouth, apparently as one that he entends to have succeed him. God knows what will be the end of it.

9.   Up and to the office, where sat all the morning. At noon by coach with Mr. Coventry to the Change, where busy with several people. Great talk of the Duch proclaiming themselfs in India lords of the Southern Seas and deny traffique there to all ships but their own, upon pain of confiscation – which makes our merchants mad. Great doubt of two ships of ours, the *Greyhound* and another very rich, coming from the Streights, for fear of the Turkes. By and by comes Mr. Moore, with whom much good discourse of my Lord; and among other things, told me that my Lord is mightily altered, that is, grown very high and stately and doth not admit of any to come into his chamber to him as heretofore; and that I must not think much of his strangeness to me, for it was the same he doth to everybody. And that he would not have me to be solicitous in the matter, but keep off and give him now and then a visit and no more, for he says he himself doth not go to him nowadays but when he sends for him, nor then doth not stay for him if he be not there at the hour appointed. "For," says he, "I do find that I can stand upon my own legs and I will not by an over-submission make myself cheap to anybody and contemptible" – which was the doctrine of the world that I lacked most – and shall fallow it. I discoursed with him about my money that my Lord hath and the 1000*l* that I stand

bound with him in to my Cosen Tho. Pepys, in both which I will get myself at liberty as soon as I can – for I do not like his being angry and in debt both together to me; and besides, I do not perceive he looks after paying his debts, but runs farther and farther in.

11. Up, and after much pleasant discourse with my wife, and to the office, where we sat all the morning and did much business, and some much to my content, by prevailing against Sir W. Batten for the King's profit. At noon home to dinner my wife and I, hand-to-fist to a very fine pig. This noon Mr. Falconer came and visited my wife and brought her a present, a silver state-cup and cover, value about 3 or 4*l*. He did not stay dinner with me. I am almost sorry for this present, because I would have reserved him for a place to go in summer a-visiting at Woolwich with my wife.

15. Up; and carrying my wife to my Lord's lodgings, left her and I to Whitehall to the Duke; where he first put on a periwigg today but methought his hair, cut short in order thereto, did look very prettily of itself before he put on his periwig. Thence to his closet and did our business. And thence Mr. Coventry and I down to his chamber and spent a little time; and so parted and I took my wife homeward, I stopping at the Coffee-house and thence a while to the Change (where great news of the arrivall of two rich ships, the *Greyhound* and another, which they were mightily afeared of and great insurance given); and so home to dinner and after an hour with my wife at her globes, I to the office, where very busy till 11 at night; and so home to supper and to bed. This afternoon Sir Tho. Chamberlin came to the office to me and showed me several letters from the East Indys, showing the heighth that the Dutch are come to there; showing scorn to all the English even in our only Factory there of Surratt, beating several men and hanging the English Standard St. George under the Duch flag in scorn; saying that whatever their masters do or say at home, they will do what they list and will be masters of all the world there, and have so proclaimed themselfs Soveraigne of all the South Seas – which certainly our King cannot endure, if the parliament will give him money. But I doubt and yet do hope they will not yet, till we are more ready for it.

17. Up, and with my wife, setting her down by her father's in

Long acre, in so ill-looked a place, among all the bawdy-houses, that I was troubled at it to see her go thither. Thence I to Whitehall and there walked up and down, talking with Mr. Pierce, who tells me of the King's giving of my Lord Fitzharding two leases, which belongs endeed to the Queene, worth 20000*l* to him, and how people do talk of it – and other things of that nature, which I am sorry to hear. He and I walked round the parke with great pleasure and back again; and finding no time to speak with my Lord of Albemarle, I walked to the Change and there met my wife at our pretty Dolls and so took her home, and Creed also, whom I met there, and sent her home while Creed and I stayed on the Change; and by and by home and dined – where I found an excellent Mastiffe, his name Towzer, sent me by a surgeon. After dinner I took my wife again by coach (leaving Creed by the way, going to Gresham College, of which he is now become one of the Virtuosos) and to Whitehall, where I delivered a paper about Tanger to my Lord Duke of Albemarle in the council chamber; and so to Mrs. Hunts to call my wife, and so by coach straight home and at my office till 3 a-clock in the morning – having spent much time this evening in discourse with Mr. Cutler, who tells me how the Dutch deal with us abroad and do not value us anywhere. And how he and Sir W. Rider have found reason to lay aside Capt. Cocke in their company, he having played some indiscreet and unfair tricks with them, and hath lost himself everywhere by his imposing upon all the world with the conceit he hath of his own wit. And so hath, he tells me, Sir Rd. Ford also, both of whom are very witty men. He being gone, Sir W. Rider come and stayed with me till about 12 at night, having found ourselfs work till that time about understanding the measuring of Mr. Woods masts; which though I did so well before as to be thought to deal very hardly against Wood, yet I am ashamed I understood it no better and do hope yet, whatever be thought of me, to save the King some more money. And out of an impatience to break up with my head full of confused confounded notions but nothing brought to a clear comprehension, I was resolved to set up, and did, till now it is ready to strike 4 a-clock, all alone, cold, and my candle not enough left to light me to my own house; and so, with my business however brought to some good understanding and set it down pretty clear, I went home to bed, with my mind at good quiet and the girle setting up for me (the rest all a-bed); I eat and drank a little and to bed, weary, sleepy, cold, and my head akeing.

18–19.   Called up to the office; and much against my will, I rose, my head akeing mightily – and to the office, where I did argue to good purpose for the King what I have been fitting myself for the last night against Mr. Wood, about his masts; but brought it to no issue. Very full of business till noon, and then with Mr. Coventry to the Affrican house and there fell to my Lord Peterborough's accounts; and by and by to dinner, where excellent discourse – Sir G. Carteret and other of the Affrican Company with us. And then up to the accounts again, which were by and by done; and then I straight home, my head in great pain and drowzy; so after doing a little business at the office and wrote to my father about sending him the mastiffe was given me yesterday, I home and by daylight to bed, about 6 a-clock, and fell to sleep. Wakened about 12 when my wife came to bed, and then to sleep again and so till morning, and then up in good order in my head again; and shaved myself and then to the office, whither Mr. Cutler came and walked and talked with me a great while, and then to the Change together; and it being early, did tell me several excellent examples of men raised upon the Change by their great diligence and saving – as also his own fortune and how Credit grew upon him; that when he was not really worth 1100*l*, he had credit for 100000*l* – of Sir W. Rider, how he ris – and others.

22.   This evening came Mr. Alsopp the King's Brewer, with whom I spent an hour talking and bewailing the posture of things at present. The King led away by half a dozen men, that none of his serious servants and friends can come at him. These are Lodderdale, Buckingham, Hamilton, Fitzharding, to whom he hath it seems given 12000*l* per annum too, in the best part of the King's estate and that that the old Duke of Buckingham could never get of the King. Projers is another, and Sir H. Bennett. He loves not the Queen at all, but is rather sullen to her; and she by all reports incapable of children. He is fond of the Duke of Monmouth that everybody admires* it; and he says the Duke hath said that he would be the death of any man that says the King was not married to her[1] – though Alsopp says it is well known that she was a common whore when the King lay with her. But it seems, he says, that the King is mighty kind to these his bastard children and at this day will go at midnight to my Lady Castlemaynes nurses and take

1. Monmouth's mother, Lucy Walter.

the child and dance it in his arms. That he is not likely to have his
tables up again in his house,[1] for the crew that are about him will
not have him come to common view again, but keep him obscurely
among themselfs. He hath this night, it seems, ordered that the hall
(which there is a ball to be in tonight before the King) be guarded, as
the Queen-mother's is, by his Horse Guards; whereas heretofore
they were by the Lord Chamberlin or Steward and their people.
But it is feared they will reduce all to the soldiery, and all other
places taken away. And which is worst of all, that he will alter the
present militia and bring all to a flying army. That my Lord
Lodderdale, being middleton's enemy and one that scores the
Chancellor, even to open affronts before the King, hath got the
whole power of Scottland into his hand; whereas the other day he
was in a fair way to have had his whole estate and honour and life
voted away from him. That all the Court are mad for a Dutch war;
but both he and I did concur that it was a thing rather to be dreaded
then hoped for – unless, by the French King's falling upon Flanders,
they and the Dutch should be divided. That the talk which these
people about our King that I named before have, is to tell him how
neither privileges of Parliament nor City is anything; but his will is
all and ought to be so; and their discourse, it seems, when they are
alone, is so base and sordid that it makes the eares of the very
gentlemen of back-staires, I think he called them, to tingle to hear it
spoke in the King's hearing – and that must be very bad endeed.
That my Lord Digby did send to Lisbon a couple of priests to search
out what they could against the Chancellor concerning the match,
as to the point of his knowing beforehand that she was not capable
of bearing children[2] and that something was given her to make her
so. Ireland in a very distracted condition about the hard usage
which the protestants meet with, and the too good which the
catholiques. And from all together, God knows my heart, I expect
nothing but ruin can fallow, unless things are better ordered in a
little time.

He being gone, my wife came and told me how kind my uncle
Wight hath been to her today also; and that though she sees that all
his kindness to us comes from respect to her, she discovers nothing
but great civility from him; yet by what she says, he otherwise will

---

1. sc. will not dine in public in the palace.
2. Clarendon was said to have planned the King's marriage to a barren Princess in
the dynastic interest of his daughter, the Duchess of York.

tell me. But today he told her plainly that had she a child it should be his heire; and that should I or she want, he would be a good friend to us, and did give my wife instructions to consent to all his wife says at any time, she being a pettish woman; which argues a design he hath I think of keeping us in with his wife, in order to our good, sure – and he declaring her jealousy of him, that so he dares not come to see my wife as otherwise he would do and will endeavour to do. It looks strange, putting all together; but yet I am in hopes he means well. After all this discourse with my wife at my office alone, she home to see how the wash goes on and I to make an end of my work; and so home to supper and to bed.

23. Up, it being *Shrove Tuseday*, and at the office sat all the morning. At noon to the Change and there met with Sir W. Rider; and of a sudden, knowing what I had at home, brought him and Mr. Cutler and Mr. Cooke, clerk to Mr. Secretary Morrice, a sober and learned man and one I knew heretofore when he was my Lord [Lockhart's] secretary at Dunkirke. I made much of them and had a pretty dinner for a sudden; we talked very pleasantly, and they many good discourses of their travels abroad. After dinner, they gone and I to my office, where doing many businesses very late; but to my good content, to see how I grow in estimation every day more and more, and have things given more oftener then I used to have formerly; as, to have a case of very pretty knifes with agate hafts by Mrs. Russell. So home and to bed. This day, by the blessing of God, I have lived 31 years in the world; and by the grace of God I find myself not only in good health in everything, and perticularly [as] to the stone, but only pain upon taking cold; and also in a fair way of coming to a better esteem and estate in the world then ever I expected; but I pray God give me a heart to fear a fall and to prepare for it.

24. *Ashwendesday*. Up and by water, it being a very fine morning, to Whitehall and there to speak with Sir Ph. Warrwicke, but he was gone out to Chappell. So I spent much of the morning walking in the park and going to the Queen's chapel, where I stayed and saw their masse till a man came and bid me go out or kneel down; so I did go out. And thence to Somersett house and there into the chapel, where Monsieur Despagne used to preach. But now it is made very fine and was ten times more crowded then the Queen's chapel at St. James's – which I wonder at. Thence down to the

garden of Somersett house and up and down the new building, which in every respect will be mighty magnificent and costly. I stayed a great while talking with a man in the garden that was sawing a piece of marble – and did give him 6d. to drink. He told me much of the nature and labour of that work; how he could not saw above 4 inch. of the stone in a day; and of a greater, not above one or two. And after it is sawed, then it is rubbed with coarse and then with finer and finer sand till they come to putty, and so polish it as smooth as glass. Their saws have no teeth, but it is the sand only which the saw rubs up and down that doth the thing. Thence by water to the Coffee-house and there sat long with Ald. Barker, talking of Hemp and that trade. And thence to the Change a little; and so home and dined with my wife, and then to the office till the evening, and then walked a while merrily with my wife in the garden; and so she gone, I to work again till late; and so home to supper and to bed.

25.    Up and to the office, where we sat, and thence with Mr. Coventry by coach to the Glasshouse and there dined, and both before and after did my Lord Peterborough's accounts. Thence home to the office and there did business till called by Creed; and with him by coach (setting my wife at my brother's) to my Lord's and saw the young ladies and talked a little with them; and thence to Whitehall a while, talking but doing no business; but resolved of going to meet my Lord tomorrow, having got a horse of Mr. Coventry today. So home, taking up my wife. And after doing something at my office, home, God forgive me, disturbed in mind out of my jealousy of my wife tomorrow when I am out of town, which is a hell to my mind and yet without all reason. God forgive me for it and mend me. So home, and getting my things ready for my journey, to bed.

26.    Up; and after dressing myself handsomely for riding, I out and by water to Westminster to Mr. Creeds chamber; and after drinking some Chocolatte and playing on the vyall, Mr. Mallard being there, upon Creeds new vyall, which proves methinks much worse then mine, and looking upon his new contrivance of a desk and shelves for books, we set out from an Inne hard by, whither Mr. Coventrys horse was carried – and around about the bush through bad ways to Highgate; good discourse in the way had between us and it being all day a most admirable pleasant day. We,

upon consultation, had stopped at the Cocke, a mile a-this-side Barnett, being unwilling to put ourselfs to the charge or doubtful acceptance of any provision against my Lord's coming by, and there got something and dined, setting a boy to look towards Barnett hill against their coming. And after two or three false alarms they came, and we met the coach very gracefully, and I had a kind receipt from both Lord and Lady as I could wish and some kind discourse; and then rode by the coach a good way and so fell to discoursing with several of the people there, being a dozen attending the coach and another coach for the maids and parson. Among others, talking with W. Howe, he told me how my Lord in his hearing the other day did largely tell my Lord Peterburgh and Povy (who went with them down to Hinchingbrooke) how and when he discarded Creed and took me to him; and that since, the Duke of Yorke hath several times thanked him for me – which did not a little please me. And anon, I desiring Mr. Howe to tell me upon [what] occasion this discourse happened, he desired me to say nothing of it now, for he would not have my Lord to take notice of our being together, but he would tell me another time – which put me into some trouble to think what he meant by it; but when we came to my Lord's house, I went in; and whether it was my Lord's neglect or general indifference I know not, but he made me no kind of compliment there and methinks the young ladies look somewhat highly upon me. So I went away without bidding adieu to anybody, being desirous not to be thought too servile; but I do hope and believe that my Lord doth yet value me as high as ever, though he dares not admit me to the freedom he once did – and that my Lady is still the same woman. So rode home and there found my uncle Wight. Tis an odd thing, as my wife tells me, his caressing* her and coming on purpose to give her visitts; but I do not trouble myself for him at all, but hope the best and very good effects of it. He being gone, I eat something and my wife – I told all this day's passages, and she to give me very good and rationall advice how to behave myself to my Lord and his family, by slighting everybody but my Lord and Lady and not to seem to have the least society or fellowship with them; which I am resolved to do, knowing that it is my high carriage that must do me good there, and to appear in good clothes and garbe. To the office a little; and being weary, early home and to bed.

27.  Up, but weary, and to the office, where we sat all the

morning. Before I went to the office there came Bagwell's wife to me to speak for her husband. I liked the woman very well and stroked her under the chin, but could not find in my heart to offer anything uncivil to her, she being I believe a very modest woman. At noon with Mr. Coventry to the affrican house, and to my Lord Peterborough's business again; and then to dinner, where before dinner we had the best oysters I have seen this year, and I think as good in all respects as ever I eat in my life. I eat a great many.

28. *Lords day.* Up and walked to Pauls; and by chance it was an extraordinary day for the Readers of the Inns of Court and all the students to come to church, it being an old ceremony not used these 25 years – upon the first Sunday in Lent. Abundance there was of students, more then there was room to seat but upon forms, and the Church mighty full. One Hawkins preached, an Oxford man – a good sermon upon these words: "But the wisdom from above is first pure, then peaceable." Both before and after sermon I was most impatiently troubled at the Quire, the worst that ever I heard. But what was extraordinary, the Bishop of London, who sat there in a pew made a-purpose for him by the pulpitt, doth give the last blessing to the congregation – which was, he being a comely old man, a very decent thing methought. The Lieutenant of the Tower, Sir J. Robinson, would needs have me by coach home with him; and sending word home to my house, I did go and dine with him, his ordinary table being very good – and his Lady a very high-carriaged but comely big woman; I was mightily pleased with her. His officers of his Regiment dined with him. No discourse at table to any purpose. Only, after dinner my Lady would needs see a boy which was represented to her to be an innocent country boy, brought up to town a day or two ago and left here to the wide world, and he losing his way, fell into the Tower; and which my Lady believes and takes pity of him and will keep him; but though a little boy and but young, yet he tells his tale so readily and answers all Que[s]tions so wittily, that for certain he is an arch rogue and bred in this town. But my Lady will not believe it, but ordered victuals to be given him – and I think will keep him as a footboy for their eldest son. After dinner to Chappell in the Tower with the Lieutenant, with the Keyes carried before us and the Warders and gentleman Porter going before us. And I sat with the Lieutenant in his pew in great state, but slept all the sermon. None, it seems, of the prisoners in the Tower that are there now, though they may,

will come to prayers there. Church being done, I back to Sir Johns house, and there left him and home; and by and by to Sir Wm. Pen and stayed a while talking with him about Sir J. Mennes his folly in his office, of which I am sick and weary to speak of it; and how the King is abused in it – though Pen, I know, offers the discourse only like a rogue to get it out of me; but I am very free to tell my mind to him in the case, being not unwilling he should tell him again if he will, or anybody else. Thence home and walked in the garden by brave Mooneshine with my wife above two hours, till past 8 a'-clock; then to supper, and after prayers to bed.

29.  Up and by coach with Sir W. Pen to Charing cross, and there I light and to Sir Ph. Warwicke to visit him and discourse with him about navy business, which I did at large – and he most largely with me, not only about the navy but about the general Revenue of England, above two hours I think, many staying all the while without; but he seemed to take pains to let me either understand the affairs of the Revenue or else to be a wittnesse of his pains and care in stating of it. He showed me endeed many excellent collections of the state of the Revenue in former Kings and the late times and the present. He showed me how the very Assessements between 1643 and 1659, which was taxes (besides Excize, Customes, Sequestra- cions, Decimacions, King and Queenes and Church lands, or anything else but just the assessements) come to above 15 Millions. He showed me a discourse of his concerning the Revenues of this and foreign States. How that of Spayne was great, but divided with his kingdoms and so came to little. How that of France did and doth much exceed ours before for quantity; and that it is at the will of the Prince to tax what he will upon his people; which is not here. That the Hollanders have the best manner of tax, which is only upon the expense of provisions, by an excize; and doth conclude that no other tax is proper for England but a pound rate or excize upon the expense of provisions. He showed me every perticular sort of payment away of money since the King's coming in to this day; and told me, from one to one, how little he hath received of profit from most of them, and I believe him truly. That the 1200000*l* which the parliament with so much ado did first vote to give the King, and since hath been re-examined by several committees of the present parliament, is yet above 300000*l* short of making up really to the King the 1200000*l* – as by perticulars he showed me. And in my Lord Treasurer's excellent letter to the King upon this subject, he

tells the King how it was the spending more then the revenue that did give the first occasion of his father's ruine, and did since to the Rebells; who he says, just like Henry the 8, had great and sudden encrease of wealth, but yet by over-spending both died poor. And further tells the King how much of this 1200000*l* depends upon the life of the Prince and so must be renewed by parliament again to his Successor; which is seldom done without parting with some of the prerogatives of the Crown; or, if denied and he persists to take it of the people, it gives occasion to a Civill war, which may, as it did in the late business of Tonnage and Poundage, prove fatal to the Crowne. He showed me how many ways the Lord Treasurer did take before he moved the King to Farme the Customes in the manner he doth, and the reasons that moved him to do it. He showed me a very excellent argument to prove that our Importing lesse then we export doth not impoverish the kingdom, according to the received opinion – which though it be a paradox and that I do not remember the argument, yet methought there was a great deal in what he said; and upon the whole, I find him a most exact and methodicall man and of great industry. And very glad that he thought fit to show me all this, though I cannot easily guess the reason why he should do it to me – unless from the plainness that he sees I use to him in telling him how much the King may suffer for our want of understanding the case of our Treasury.

## MARCH

2. To the office till dinner; and after dinner, my wife to cut my hair short, which is grown pretty long again. And then to the office and there till 9 at night doing business. This afternoon we had a good present of tongues and Bacon from Mr. Shales of Portsmouth. So at night home to supper; and being troubled with my eye, to bed. This morning Mr. Burgby, one of the writing clerks belonging to the Council, was with me about business, a knowing man. He complains how most of the Lords of the Council do look after themselfs and their own ends and none the public, unless Sir Edw. Nicholas. Sir G. Carteret is diligent, but all for his own ends and profit. My Lord Privy Seale, a destroyer of everybody's business and doth no good at all to the public. The Archbishop of

Canterbury speaks very little nor doth much, being now come to the highest pitch that he can expect. He tells me he believes that things will go very high against the Chancellor by Digby, and that bad things will be proved. Talks much of his neglecting the King and making the King to trot every day to him, when he is well enough to go to visit his Cosen, Chief Justice Hide, but not to the Council or King. He commends my Lord of Ormond mightily in Ireland; but cries out cruelly of Sir G. Lane for his corruption and that he hath done my Lord great dishonour by selling of places here, which are now all taken away and the poor wretches ready to starve. That nobody almost understands or judges of business better then the King, if he would not be guilty of his father's fault, to be doubtful of himself and easily be removed from his own opinion. That my Lord Lauderdale is never from the King's eare nor counsel and that he is a most cunning fellow. Upon the whole, that he finds things go very bad everywhere; and even in the Council, nobody minds the public.

8.   Up, with some little discontent with my wife upon her saying that she had got and used some puppy-dog water, being put upon it by a desire of my aunt Wight to get some for her; who hath a mind, unknown to her husband, to get some for her ugly face. I to the office, where we sat all the morning. Thence home, whither Luellin came and dined with me; but we made no long stay at dinner, for *Heraclius* being acted, which my wife and I have a mighty mind to see, we do resolve, though not exactly agreeing with the letter of my vowe, yet altogether with the sense, to see another this month – by going hither instead of that at Court, there having been none conveniently since I made my vow for us to see there, nor like to be this Lent; and besides, we did walk home on purpose to make this going as cheap as that would have been to have seen one at Court; and my conscience knows that it is only the saving of money and the time also that I entend by my oaths, and this hath cost no more of either – so that my conscience before God doth, after good consultation and resolution of paying my forfeit did my conscience accuse me of breaking my vow, I do not find myself in the least apprehensive that I have done any vyolence to my oaths. The play hath one very good passage well managed in it; about two persons pretending and yet denying themselfs to be son to the Tyrant Phocas and yet heire of Mauricius to the Crowne. The guarments like Romans very well. The little

guirle[1] is come to act very prettily and spoke the epilogue most admirably. But at the beginning, at the drawing up of the Curtaine, there was the finest Scene of the Emperor and his people about him, standing in their fixed and different postures in their Roman habits, above all that ever I yet saw at any of the Theatres. Walked home, calling to see my brother Tom, who is in bed and I doubt very ill – of a consumption. To my office a while; and so home to supper and to bed.

9.   Up pretty betimes to my office, where all day long, but a little at home at dinner, at my office finishing all things about Mr. Wood's contract for Masts; wherein I am sure I shall save the King 400*l* before I have done. At night home to supper and to bed.

10.   Up and to the office, where all the morning doing business. And at noon to the Change and there very busy; and so home to dinner with my wife to a good hog's harslet, a piece of meat I love but have not eat of I think this seven year. And after dinner abroad by coach, set her at Mrs. Hunts and I to Whitehall; and at the Privy Seale office enquired and found the Bill come for the Corporation of the Royall Fishery; whereof the Duke of Yorke is made present Governor and several other very great persons, to the number of 32, made his assistants for their lives: whereof, by my Lord Sandwichs favour, I am one and take it not only as a matter of honour but that that may come to be of profit to me. And so with great content went and called my wife; and so home and to the office, where busy late; and so home to supper and to bed.

12.   Lay long, pleasantly entertaining myself with my wife; and then up and to the office – where busy till noon, vexed to see how Sir J. Mennes deserves rather to be pitied for his dotage and folly then imployed at a great salary to ruin the King's business. At noon to the Change and thence home to dinner; and then down to Deptford, where busy a while; and then walking home, it fell hard a-raining. So at Halfway house put in; and there meeting Mr. Stacy with some company of pretty women – I took him aside to a room by ourselfs and there talked with him about the several sorts of Tarrs; and so by and by parted and I walked home, and there late at the office; and so home to supper and to bed.

1. ? Ann Gibbs.

13.   *Lords day.* I lay long in bed, talking with my wife; and then up, in great doubt whether I should not go see Mr. Coventry or no, who hath not been well these two or three days; but it being foul weather, I stayed within; and so to my office and there all the morning reading some Common law, to which I will allot a little time now and then, for I much want it. At noon home to dinner; and then after some discourse with my wife, to the office again; and by and by Sir W. Pen came to me after sermon and walked with me in the garden, and then one comes to tell me that Anth. and Will Joyce were come to see me; so I in to them and made mighty much of them, and very pleasant we were. And most of their business I find to be to advise about getting some woman to attend my Brother Tom, whom they say is very ill and seems much to want one – to which I agreed, and desired them to get their wifes to enquire out one. By and by they bid me good-night; but immediately as they were gone out of doors comes Mrs. Turner's boy with a note to me, to tell me that my brother Tom was so ill as they feared he could not long live and that it would be fit I should come and see him. So I sent for them back, and they came; and Will Joyce desiring to speak with me alone, I took him up and there he did plainly tell me, to my great astonishment, that my brother is deadly ill and that their chief business of coming was to tell me so; and which is worse, that his disease is the pox, which he hath heretofore got and hath not been cured, but is come to this; and that this is certain, though a secret told his father Fenner by the Doctor which he helped my brother to. This troubled me mightily; but however, I thought fit to go see him for speech of people's sake, and so walked along with them, and in our way called on my Uncle Fenner (where I have not been this 12 months and more) and advised with him; and then to my brother, who lies in bed talking idle. He could only say that he knew me and then fell to other discourse, and his face like a dying man – which Mrs. Turner, who was here, and others conclude he is. The company being gone, I took the mayde, which seems a very grave and serious woman, and in W. Joyces company did enquire how things are with her master. She told me many things very discreetly and said she had all his papers and books and key of his cutting-house. And showed me a bag which I and Wm: Joyce told, coming to 5*l* 14*s*. – which we left with her again. After giving her good counsel, and the boys, and seeing a nurse there of Mrs. Holden's choosing, I left them and so walked home, greatly troubled to think of my brother's condition

and the trouble that would arise to me by his death or continuing sick. So at home, my mind troubled, to bed.

14. Up, and walked to my brother's, where I find he hath continued talking idle all night and now knows me not – which troubles me mightily. So I walked down and discoursed a great while alone with the mayde, who tells me many passages of her master's practices and how she concludes that he hath run behindhand a great while and owes money and hath been dunned by several people; among others, by one Cave, both husband and wife, but whether it was for money or something worse she knows not. But there is one Cranburne, I think she called him, in Fleete lane with whom he hath many times been mighty private, but what their dealings have been she knows not, but believes they were naught.* And then his sitting up two Saturday nights, one after another, when all were a-bed, doing something to himself; which she now suspects what it was but did not before. But tells me that he hath been a very bad husband as to spending his time, and hath often told him of it. So that upon the whole, I do find he is, whether he lives or dies, a ruined man. And what trouble will befall me by it, I know not. The Doctors give him over and so do all that see him. He talks no sense two words together now. And I confess it made me weep to see that he should not be able when I asked him, to say who I was. [My uncle Fenner] tells me his thoughts long of my brother's bad husbandry; and from that, to say that he believes he owes a great deal of money – as, to my Cozen Scott, I know not how much – and Dr. Tho. Pepys, 30*l*; but that the Doctor confesses that he is paid 20*l* of it. And what with that and what he owes my father and me, I doubt he is in a very sad condition; that if he lives, he will not be able to show his head – which will be a very great shame to me.

15–16. Up and to the office, where we sat all the morning; and at noon comes Madam Turner and her daughter The[oph]. – her chief errand to tell me that she had got Dr. Wiverly her Doctor to search my brother's mouth, where Mr. Powell says there is an Ulcer; from whence he concludes that he hath had the pox. But the Doctor swears there is not, nor ever was any. And my brother being very sensible, which I was glad to hear, he did talk with him about it; and he did wholly disclaim that ever he had that disease or that ever he said to Powell that he had it – all which did put me into great comfort as to that reproach which was spread against him. So I sent for a barrel of oysters and they dined, and we were very merry, I being willing to be so upon this news. After dinner we took coach and to my brother's; where, contrary to my expectation, he continues as bad or worse, talking idle and now not at all knowing any of us as before. Here we stayed a great while, I going up and down the house looking after things. In the evening Dr. Wiverley came again and I sent for Mr. Powell (the Doctor and I having first by ourselfs searched my brother again at his privities; where he was as clear as ever he was born, and in the Doctor's opinion had been ever so). And we three alone discoursed that business, where the Coxcomb did give us his simple reasons for what he had said; which the Doctor fully confuted and left the fellow, only saying that he should cease to report any such thing and that what he had said was the best of his judgment, from my brother's words and ulcer, as he supposed, in his mouth. I threatened him that I would have satisfaction if I heard any more such discourse. And so good night to them two, giving the Doctor a piece for his fee but the other nothing.

I to my brother again, where Madam Turner and her company, and Mrs. Croxton, my wife, and Mrs. Holding. About 8 a-clock my brother begun to fetch his spittle with more pain and to speak as much, but not so distinctly; till at last, the phlegm getting the maistery of him and he beginning as we thought to rattle, I had no mind to see him die, as we thought he presently would, and so withdrew and led Mrs. Turner home. But before I came back, which was in a quarter of an hour, my brother was dead. I went up and found the nurse holding his eyes shut; and he, poor wretch, lying with his chops fallen, a most sad sight and that which put me into a present very great transport of grief and cries. And endeed, it was a most sad sight to see the poor wretch lie now still and dead and pale like a stone. I stayed till he was almost cold, while Mrs. Croxton, Holden, and the rest did strip and lay him out – they observing his corps, as they told me afterwards, to be as clear as any they ever saw. And so this was the end of my poor brother, continuing talking idle and his lips working even to his last, that his phlegm hindered his breathing; and at last his breath broke out, bringing a flood of phlegm and stuff out with it, and so he died. This evening he talked among other talk a great deal of French, very plain and good; as among others – "*quand un homme boit quand il n'a poynt d'inclinacion a boire il ne luy fait jamais de bien.*" I once begun to

tell him something of his condition and asked him whither he
thought he should go. He in distracted manner answered me –
"Why, whither should I go? there are but two ways. If I go to the
bad way, I must give God thanks for it. And if I go the other way, I
must give God the more thanks for it; and I hope I have not been so
undutiful and unthankful in my life but I hope I shall go that way."
This was all the sense, good or bad, I could get of him this day.

I left my wife to see him laid out, and I by coach home, carrying
my brother's papers, all I could find, with me. And having wrote a
letter to my father, telling him what hath been said, I returned by
coach, it being very late and dark, to my brother's. But all being
gone, the Corps laid out and my wife at Mrs. Turners, I thither; and
there, after an hour's talk, we up to bed – my wife and I in the little
blue chamber. And I lay close to my wife, being full of disorder and
grief for my brother, that I could not sleep nor wake with
satisfaction; at last I slept till 5 or 6 a-clock. And then I rose and up,
leaving my wife in bed, and to my brother's, where I set them on
cleaning the house. And my wife coming anon to look after things,
I up and down to my Cosen Stradwickes and uncle Fenners about
discoursing for the funeral, which I am resolved to put off till Friday
next. Thence home and trimmed myself; and then to the Change
and told my uncle Wight of my brother's death; and so by coach to
my Cosen Turners and there dined very well. But my wife having
those upon her today and in great pain, we were forced to rise in
some disorder and in Mrs. Turners coach carried her home and put
her to bed. Then back again with my Cosen Norton to Mrs.
Turners and there stayed a while talking with Dr. Pepys, that
puppy, whom I had no patience to hear. So I left them, and to my
brother's to look after things – and saw the Coffin brought; and by
and by Mrs. Holden came and saw him nailed up. Then came W.
Joyce to me half-drunk, and much ado I had to tell him the story of
my brother's being found clear of what was said, but he would
interrupt me by some idle discourse or other, of his crying what a
good man and a good speaker my brother was and God knows
what. At last, weary of him, I got him away and I to Mrs. Turner's;
and there, though my heart is still heavy to think of my poor
brother, yet I could give way to my fancy to hear Mrs. The[oph].
play upon the Harpsicon – though the Musique did not please me
neither. Thence to my brother's and found them with my maid
Elizabeth, taking an Inventory of the goods of the house; which I
was well pleased at, and am much beholding to Mr. Honywoods

man in doing of it. His name is Herbert, one that says he knew me
when he lived with Sir Samuel Morland – but I have forgot him. So
I left them at it and by coach home and to my office, there to do a
little business; but God knows, my heart and head is so full of my
brother's death and the consequences of it, that I can do very little or
understand it. So home to supper; and after looking over some
business in my chamber, to bed to my wife, who continues in bed in
some pain still. This day I have a great barrel of Oysters given me
by Mr. Barrow, as big as 16 of others, and I took it in the coach with
me to Mrs. Turner's and gave them her. This day the Parliament
met again after a long prorogation – but what they have done I have
not been in the way to hear.

17.    After office I to my brother's again, and thence to Madam
Turners, in both places preparing things against tomorrow. And
this night I have altered my resolution of burying him in the
churchyard among my young brothers and sisters; and bury him in
the church in the middle Isle, as near as I can to my mother's pew –
this costs me 20s. more. This being all, home by coach, bringing
my brother's silver tankard for safety along with me; and so to
supper after writing to my father, and so to bed.

18.    Up betimes and walked to my brother's, where a great while
putting things in order against anon. Then to Madam Turners and
eat a breakfast there. And so to Wotton my shoemaker and there
got a pair of shoes blacked on the soles, against anon for me. So to
my brother's, and to the church and with the grave-maker chose a
place for my brother to lie in, just under my mother's pew. But to
see how a man's tombes are at the mercy of such a fellow, that for
6d. he would (as his own words were) "I will justle them together
but I will make room for him" – speaking of the fullness of the
middle Isle where he was to lie. And that he would for my father's
sake do my brother that is dead all the civility he can; which was to
disturb other corps that are not quite rotten to make room for him.
And methought his manner of speaking it was very remarkable – as
of a thing that now was in his power to do a man a courtesy or not.
At noon my wife, though in pain, comes; but I being forced to go
home, she went back with me – where I dressed myself and so did
Besse; and so to my brother's again – whither, though invited as the
custom is at 1 or 2 a-clock, they came not till 4 or 5. But at last, one
after another they came – many more then I bid; and my reckoning

that I bid was 120, but I believe there was nearer 150. Their service was six biscuits a-piece and what they pleased of burnt claret – my Cosen Joyce Norton kept the wine and cakes above – and did give out to them that served, who had white gloves given them. But above all, I am beholden to Mrs. Holding, who was most kind and did take mighty pains, not only in getting the house and everything else ready, but this day in going up and down to see the house filled and served, in order to mine and their great content I think – the men setting by themselfs in some rooms, and women by themselfs in others – very close, but yet room enough. Anon to church, walking out into the street to the Conduict and so across the street, and had a very good company along with the Corps. And being come to the grave as above, Dr. Pierson, the minister of the parish, did read the service for buriall and so I saw my poor brother laid into the grave; and so all broke up and I and my wife and Madam Turner and her family to my brother's, and by and by fell to a barrell of oysters, Cake, and cheese of Mr. Honiwoods, with him in his chamber and below – being too merry for so late a sad work; but Lord, to see how the world makes nothing of the memory of a man an hour after he is dead. And endeed, I must blame myself; for though at the sight of him, dead and dying, I had real grief for a while, while he was in my sight, yet presently after and ever since, I have had very little grief endeed for him. By and by, it beginning to be late, I put things in some order in the house and so took my wife and Besse (who hath done me very good service in cleaning and getting ready everything and serving the wine and things today, and is endeed a most excellent good-natured and faithful wench and I love her mightily) by coach home; and so after being at the office to set down this day's work, home to supper and to bed.

19.    Up and to the office, where all the morning; and at noon my wife and I alone, having a good hen with eggs to dinner, with great content. Then by coach to my brother's, where I spent the afternoon in paying some of the charges of the buriall and in looking over his papers; among which I find several letters of my brother John's to him, speaking very foul words of me and my deportment to him here, and very crafty designs about Sturtlow land and God knows what – which I am very glad to know and shall make him repent them. Anon my father and my brother John came to town by coach. I sat till night with him, giving him an account of things. He, poor man, very sad and sickly. I in great pain through a

simple squeezing of my cods today, by putting one leg over another as I have formerly done, which made me hasten home; and after a little at the office, in great disorder home to bed.

20. *Lords day.* Kept my bed all the morning, having laid a poultice to my cods last night to take down the tumour there which I got yesterday; which it did do, being applied pretty warm and soon after the beginning of the swelling – and the pain was gone also. We lay talking all the while; among other things, of religion, wherein I am sorry so often to hear my wife talk of her being and resolving to die a Catholique; and endeed, a small matter I believe would absolutely turn her, which I am sorry for.

21. Up; and it snowing this morning a little, which from the mildness of the winter and the weather beginning to be hot and the summer to come on apace is a little strange to us – I did not go abroad, because of my tumour, for fear it shall rise again; but stayed within and by and by my father came, poor man, to me, and my brother John; after much talk and taking them up to my chamber, I did there after some discourse bring in my business of anger with John and did before my father read all his roguish letters; which troubled my father mightily, especially to hear me say what I did, against my allowing anything for the time to come to him out of my own purse, and other words very severe – while he, like a simple rogue, made very silly and churlish answers to me, not like a man of any goodness or wit – at which I was as much disturbed as the other. This day the House of Parliament met and the King met them, with the Queene with him – and he made a speech to them; among other things, discoursing largely of the plots abroad against him and the peace of the kingdom. And among other things, that the dissatisfied party had great hopes upon the effect of the act for a Trienniall parliament granted by his father – which he desired them to peruse, and I think repeal. So the House did retire to their own House and did order that act to be read tomorrow before them. And I suppose will be repealed, though I believe much against the will of a good many that sit there.

23. To the office, where very busy all the morning; and so to the Change and off thence with Sir W. Ryder to the Trinity house and there dined very well. And good discourse among the old men – of Islands now and then rising and falling again in the sea; and that

there is many dangers of grounds and rocks that come just up to the edge almost of the sea, that is never discovered and ships perish without the world's knowing the reason of it. Among other things, they observed that there are but two seamen in the Parliament house, *viz.*, Sir W. Batten and Sir W. Pen – and not above 20 or 30 merchants; which is a strange thing in an Island, and no wonder that things of trade go no better nor are better understood. Thence home and all the afternoon at the office; only, for an hour in the evening my Lady Jemimah, Paulina, and Madam Pickering came to see us; but my wife would not be seen, being unready. Very merry with them, they mightily talking of their thrifty living for a fortnight before their mother came to town and other such simple talk, and of their merry life at Brampton at my father's this winter. So they being gone, to the office again till late; and so home and to supper and bed.

25. *Lady day.* Up and by water to Whitehall, and there to Chappell, where it was most infinite full to hear Dr. Critton. He said the greatest part of the Lay Magistrates in England were puritans and would not do justice;[1] and the Bishops, their powers were so taken away and lessened, that they could not exercise the power they ought. He told the King and the ladies, plainly speaking of death and of the skulls and bones of dead men and women, how there is no difference – that nobody could tell that of the great Marius or Alexander from a pyoneer; nor, for all the pains the ladies take with their faces, he that should look in a Charnell-house could not distinguish which was Cleopatras or fair Rosamonds or Jane Shoares. Thence by water home. After dinner to the office. Thence with my wife to see my father and discourse how he finds Tom's matters, which he doth very ill, and that he finds him to have been so negligent that he used to trust his servants with cutting out of clothes, never hardly cutting out anything himself. And by the abstract of his accounts, we find him to [owe] about above 290*l* and to be coming to him under 200*l*. Thence home with my wife, it being very durty on foot, and bought some fowl in Gracious street and some oysters against our feast tomorrow. So home; and after at the office a while, home to supper and to bed.

26. Up very betimes, and to my office and there read over some

1. Against the nonconformists.

papers against a meeting by and by at this office of Mr. Povy, Sir W. Rider, Creed, Vernat[y] and Mr. Gauden about my Lord Peterborough's accounts for Tanger – wherein we proceeded a good way; but Lord, to see how ridiculous Mr. Povy is in all he says or doth; not like a man nor fit for to be in such imployments as he is, and perticularly that of a Treasurer (paying many and very great sums without the least written order), as he is to be King of England. And seems but this day, after much discourse of mine, to be sensible of that part of his folly, besides a great deal more in other things. That being done – Sir J. Mennes and I sat all the morning; and then I to the Change and there got a way, by pretence of business with my Uncle Wight, to put off Creed, whom I had invited to dinner; and so home and there find Madam Turner, her Daughter The[oph]., Joyce Norton, my father and Mr. Honywood, and by and by comes my uncle Wight and aunt – this being my solemn feast for my cutting of the stone, it being now, blessed be God, this day six yeares since that time. And I bless God I do in all respects find myself free from that disease or any signs of it, more then that upon the least cold I continue to have pain in making water, by gathering of wind and growing costive – till which be removed I am at no ease; but without that, I am very well. Dinner not being presently ready, I spent some time myself and showed them a map of Tanger, left this morning at my house by Creed, cut by our order, the Comissioners, new drawn by Jonas Moore – which is very pleasant and I purpose to have it finely set out and hung up. After dinner Sir W. Batten sent to speak with me and told me that he had proffered our bill[1] today in the House; and that it was read without any dissenters and he fears not but will pass very well – which I shall be glad of. He tells me also how, upon occasion of some prentices being put in the pillory today for beating of their master, or some suchlike thing, in Cheapeside – a company of prentices came and rescued them and pulled down the Pillory; and they being set up again, did the like again. So that the Lord Mayor and Maj.-Gen. Browne was fain to come and stay there to keep the peace; and drums all up and down the City was beat to raise the train-bands for to quiet the town. And by and by going out with my Uncle and Aunt Wight by coach with my wife through Cheapside (the rest of the company, after much content and mirth, being broke up), we saw a trained-band stand in Cheapside upon their guard. We went

1. Empowering the officers of the Navy Board to act as magistrates in the City.

much against my uncles will as far almost as Hyde park, he and my aunt falling out all the way about it, which vexed me. But all was peace again presently. And so it raining very fast, we met many brave coaches coming from the park, and so we turned and set them down at home; and so home ourselfs and ended the day with great content – to think how it hath pleased the Lord in six years time to raise me from a condition of constant and dangerous and most painful sickness and low condition and poverty to a state of constant health almost – great honour and plenty, for which the Lord God of Heaven make me truly thankful. My wife found her gown come home laced; which is indeed very handsome but will cost me a great deal of money, more than ever I intended – but it is but for once. So to the office and did business; and then home and to bed.

31. My head of late mighty full of business, and with good content to myself in it; though sometimes it troubles me that nobody else but I should bend themselfs to serve the King with that diligence, whereby much of my pains proves ineffectual.

# –❧APRILL❧–

1. Up and to my office, where busy till noon; and then to the Change – where I find all the merchants concerned with the presenting their complaints to the committee of Parliament appointed to receive them this afternoon against the Dutch. So home to dinner and thence by coach, setting my wife down at the New Exchange; I to Whitehall and coming too soon for the Tanger Committee, walked to Mr. Blagrave for a song I left long ago there. Back to Whitehall and in the Gallery met the Duke of Yorke (I also saw the Queene going to the parke and her maids of honour; she herself look ill, and methinks Mrs. Stewart is grown fatter and not so fair as she was) and he called me to him and discourse a good while with me; and after he was gone twice or thrice, stayed and called me again to him the whole length of the Howse. And at last talked of the Dutch; and I perceive doth much wish that the Parliament will find reason to fall out with them. He gone, I by and by find that the Comissioners of Tanger met at the Duke of Albemarles, and so I have lost my labour. So with Creed to the Change and there took up my wife and left him, and we two home,

and I to walk in the garden with W. Howe, whom we took up, he having been to see us. He tells me how Creede hath been questioned before the Council about a letter that hath been met with, wherein he is mentioned by some fanatiques as a serviceable friend to them; but he says he acquitted himself well in it. But however, something sticks against him, he says, with my Lord; at which I am not very sorry, for I believe he is a false fellow. I walked with him to Pauls, he telling me how my Lord is little at home – minds his carding and little else – takes little notice of anybody; but that he doth not think that he is displeased, as I fear, with me; but is strange to all – which makes me the less troubled. So walked back home, and late at the office; so home and to bed. This day Mr. Turner did lend me, as a rarity, a manuscript of one Mr. Wells, writ long ago, teaching the method of building a ship; which pleases me mightily. I was at it tonight but durst not stay long at it, I being come to have a great pain and water in my eyes after candlelight.

2. Up and to my office, and afterwards sat – where great contest with Sir W. Batten and Mr. Wood and that doting fool Sir J. Mennes, that says whatever Sir W. Batten says, though never minding whether to the King's profit or not. At noon to the Coffee-house, where excellent discourse with Sir W. Petty; who proposed it, as a thing that is truly questionable, whether there really be any difference between waking and dreaming – that it is hard not only to tell how we know when we do a thing really or in a dream, but also to know what the difference between one and the other. Thence to the Change; but hearing at this discourse and afterward with Sir Tho. Chamberlin, who tells me what I heard from others, that the complaints of most Companies were yesterday presented to the committee of Parliament against the Dutch, excepting that of the East India, which he tells me was because they would not be said to be the first and only cause of a war with Holland, and that it is very probable as well as most necessary that we fall out with that people – I went to the Change and there found most people gone; and so home to dinner, and thence to Sir W. Warren's and with him passed the whole afternoon; first looking over two ships of Capt. Taylors and Phin. Pett's now in building, and am resolved to learn something of that art, for I find it is not hard, and very useful. And thence to Woolwich; and after seeing Mr. Falconer, who is very ill, I to the yard and there heard Mr. Pett tell me several things of Sir W. Batten's ill managements; and so with Sir W. Warren walked to

Greenwich, having good discourse; and thence by water, it being now moonshine and 9 or 10 a-clock at night, and landed at Wapping and by him and his man safely brought to my door; and so he home – having spent the day with him very well. So home and eat something and then to my office a while; and so home to prayers and to bed.

6. Up and to my office – whither by and by came John Noble, my father's old servant, to speak with me. I smelling the business, took him home; and there all alone he told me how he had been serviceable to my brother Tom in the business of his getting his servant, an ugly jade, Margeret, with child. She was brought to bed in St. Sepulchers parish of two children. One is dead, the other is alive; her name Elizabeth and goes by the name of Taylor, daughter to John Taylor. It seems Tom did a great while trust one Crawly with the business, who daily got money of him; and at last, finding himself abused, he broke the matter to J. Noble – upon a vow of secrecy. Toms first plot was to go on the other side the water and give a beggar-woman something to take the child. They did once go, but did nothing, J. Noble saying that seven year hence the mother might come to demand the child and force him to produce it, or to be suspected of murther. Then, I think it was, that they consulted and got one Cave, a poor pensioner in St. Brides parish, to take it, giving him 5*l*; he thereby promising to keep it for ever, without more charge to them. The parish hereupon indite the man Cave for bringing this child upon the parish, and by Sir Rd. Browne is sent to the Counter.

7. Up and to my office, where busy; and by and by comes Sir W. Warren and old Mr. Bond in order to the resolving me some questions about masts and their proportions but he could say little to me to my satisfaction and so I held him not long but parted. So to my office, busy till noon, and then to the Change, where high talk of the Duch's protest against our Royall Company in Guinny and their granting letters of Marke against us there. And everybody expects a war, but I hope it will not yet be so nor that this is true. Thence to dinner, where my wife got me a pleasant French Fricasse of veale for dinner. And thence to the office, where vexed to see how Sir W. Batten ordered things this afternoon (*vide* my office book; for about this time I have begun, my notions and informations increasing now greatly every day, to enter all occurrences

extraordinary in my office in a book by themselfs);[1] and so in the evening, after long discourse and eased my mind by discourse with Sir W. Warren, I to my business late; and so home to supper and to bed.

8.    Up betimes and to the office; and anon it begin to be fair, after a great shower this morning; Sir W. Batten and I by water (calling his son Castle by the way, between whom and I no notice at all of his letter the other day to me) to Deptford; and after a turn in the yard, I went with him to the Almeshouse to see the new building which he with some ambition is building of there, during his being Maister of Trinity house. And a good work it is; but to see how simply he answered somebody concerning setting up the arms of the corporation upon the door, that and anything else; he did not deny it but said he would leave that to the Maister that comes after him. There I left him and to the King's yard again and there made good enquiry into the business of the poop lanterns; wherein I find occasion to correct myself mightily for what I have done in the contract with the platerer and am resolved, though I know not how, to make them to alter it, though they signed it last night. And so I took Stanes home with me by boat and discoursed it; and he will come to reason when I can make him to understand it. No sooner landed but it fell a mighty storm of rain and hayle; so I put into a Cane shop and bought one to walk with, cost me 4s.-6d. – all of one Joynt. So home to dinner, and had an excellent Good friday dinner of pease porridge – and apple pie. So to the office all the afternoon, preparing a new book for my contracts. And this afternoon came home the office globes, done to my great content. In the evening, a little to visit Sir W. Pen, who hath a feeling this day or two of his old pain. Then to walk in the garden with my wife, and so to my office a while, and then home to the only Lenten supper I have had of wiggs and ale. And so to bed. This morning betimes came to my office to me Boatswain Smith of Woolwich, telling me a notable piece of knavery of the officers of that yard and Mr. Gold, in behalf of a contract made for some old ropes by Mr. Wood. And I believe I shall find Sir W. Batten of the plot.

9.    The last night, whether it was from cold I got today upon the water I know not – or whether it was from my mind being over-

1. Probably his 'Navy White Book', now in the Pepys Library.

concerned with Stanes's business of the platery of the navy, for my minde was mighty troubled with that business all night long – I did wake about one a-clock in the morning, a thing I most rarely do – and pissed a little with great pain. Continued sleepy, but in a high fever all night, fiery hot and in some pain. Toward morning I slept a little. And waking, found myself better – but pissed with some pain. And rose, I confess, with my clothes sweating, and it was somewhat cold too; which I believe might do me more hurt – for I continued cold and apt to shake all the morning, but that some trouble with Sir J. Mennes and Sir W. Batten kept me warm. At noon home to dinner upon tripes. And so though not well, abroad with my wife by coach to her tailor's and the New Exchange; and thence to my father's and spoke one word with him; and thence home, where I find myself sick in my stomach and vomited, which I do not use to do. Then I drank a glass or two of Hypocras, and to the office to despatch some business necessary. And so home and to bed – and by the help of Mithrydate slept very well.

12.    Up; and after my wife had dressed herself very fine in her new laced gown, and very handsome endeed – W. Howe also coming to see us – I carried her by coach to my uncle Wights and set her down there; and W. Howe and I to the Coffee-house, where we sat talking about getting of him some place under my Lord of advantage, if he should go to sea. And I would be glad to get him secretary and to out Creed if I can – for he is a crafty and false rogue. Thence a little to the Change, and thence took him to my Uncle Wight – where dined my father, poor melancholy man, that used to be as full of life as anybody – and also my aunts brother Mr. Sutton, a merchant in Flanders, a very sober, fine man – and Mr. Cole and his lady. And after dinner got a coach, very dear, it being Easter time and very foul weather, to my Lord's and there visited my Lady. And leaving my wife there, I and W. Howe to Mr. Pagets and there heard some musique, not very good – but only one Dr. Walgrave, an Englishman bred at Rome, who plays the best upon the lute that I ever heard man. Here I also met Mr. Hill, the little merchant. And after all was done, we sung. I did well enough a psalm or two of Lawes; he, I perceive, hath good skill and sings well – and a friend of his sings a good bass. Thence late; walked with them two as far as my Lord's, thinking to take up my wife and carry them home. But there being no coach to be got, away they went. And I stayed a great while, it being very late, about 10 a-clock, before a coach could be

got. I found my Lord and ladies and my wife at supper. My Lord seems very kind. But I am apt to think still the worst, and that it is only in show, my wife and Lady being there. So home and find my father come to lie at our house; and so supped and saw him, poor man, to bed – my heart never being fuller of love to him, nor admiration of his prudence and pains heretofore in the world then now, to see how Tom hath carried himself in his trade – and how the poor man hath his thoughts going to provide for his younger children and my mother. But I hope they shall never want. So myself and wife to bed.

13. To St. James – where I found Mr. Coventry (the Duke being now come thither for the summer) with a goldsmith, sorting out his old plate to change for new; but Lord, what a deal he hath. I stayed and had two or three hours discourse with him – talking about the disorders of our office, and I largely to tell how things are carried by Sir W. Batten and Sir J. Mennes to my great grief. He seems much concerned also, and for all the King's matters that are done after the same rate everywhere else, and even the Dukes household matters too – generally with corruption, but most endeed with neglect and indifference. I spoke very loud and clear to him my thoughts of Sir J. Mennes and the other, and trust him with the using of them. Then to talk of our business with the Dutch; he tells me fully that he believes it will not come to a warr. For first he showed me a letter from Sir George Downing[1] his own hand, where he assures him that the Dutch themselfs do not desire but above all things fear it. And that they neither have given letters of Mart against our ships in Guinny, nor doth De Ruyter stay at home with his fleet with an eye to any such thing, but for want of a wind, and is now come out and is going to the Streights. He tells me also that the most he expects is that upon the merchants' complaints, the parliament will represent them to the King, desiring his securing of his subjects against them. And though perhaps they may not directly see fit, yet even this will be enough to let the Dutch know that the Parliament do not oppose the King; and by that means take away their hopes, which was that the King of England could not get money or do anything towards a war with them. He tells me also that the Dutch States are in no good order themselfs, differing one with another. And that for certain none but the States of Holland

---

1. Ambassador to the United Provinces.

and Zealand will contribute towards a war, the other reckoning themselfs, being inland, not concerned in the profits of war or peace. But it is pretty to see what he says. That those here that are forward for a war at Court, they are reported in the world to be only designers of getting money into the King's hands. They that elsewhere are for it have a design to trouble the kingdom and to give the fanatics an opportunity of doing hurt. And lastly, those that are against it (as he himself for one is very cold therein) are said to be bribed by the Dutch.

14. Up betimes. And after my father's eating something, I walked out with him as far as Milk street, he turning down to Cripplegate to take coach. And at the end of the street I took leave, being much afeared I shall not see him here any more, he doth decay so much every day. And so I walked on, there being never a coach to be had till I came to Charing cross; and there Coll. Froud took me up and carried me to St. James's – where with Mr. Coventry and Povy &c. about my Lord Peterborough's accounts; but Lord, to see still what a puppy that Povy is with all his show is very strange. Thence to Whitehall and W. Coventry and I and Sir W. Rider resolved upon a day to meet and make an end of all that business. Thence walked with Creed to the Coffee-house in Covent garden, where no company. But he told me many fine experiments at Gresham College, and some demonstrating that the heat and cold of the weather doth rarify and condense the very body of glasse; as, in a Bolt head with cold water in it, put into hot water, shall first, by rarifying the glass, make the water sink, and then when the heat comes to the water, makes that rise again. And then put into cold water, makes the water, by condensing the glass, to rise; and then when the Cold comes to the water, makes it sink – which is very pretty, and true; he saw it tried.

17. *Lords day.* Up; and I put on my best cloth black suit and my velvet cloak, and with my wife, in her best laced suit, to church – where we have not been these nine or ten weeks. The truth is, my jealousy hath hindered it, for fear she should see Pembleton. He was here today, but I think sat so as he could not see her; which did please me, God help me, mightily – though I know well enough that in reason this is nothing but my ridiculous folly. Home to dinner; and in the afternoon, after long consulting whether to go to Woolwich or no to see Mr. Falconer, but endeed to prevent my

wife going to church, I did however go to church with her, where a young simple fellow did preach – I slept soundly all the sermon; and thence to Sir W. Pens, my wife and I, and there sat talking with him and his daughter; and thence with my wife walked to my Uncle Wights and there supped; where very merry, but I vexed to see what charges the vanity of my aunt puts her husband to among her friends,* and nothing at all among ours. Home and to bed.

19.   Up and to St. James's, where long with Mr. Coventry, Povy &c. in their Tanger accounts; but such the folly of that coxcomb Povy that we could do little in it. And so parted for that time, and I to walk with Creed and Vernaty in the physique garden in St. James park, where I first saw Orange trees – and other fine trees. So to Westminster hall and thence by water to the Temple; and so walked to the Change and there find the Change full of news from Guiny; some say the Dutch have sunk our ships and taken our fort and others say we have done the same to them. But I find by our merchants that something is done, but is yet a secret among them. So home to dinner and then to the office; and at night with Capt. Taylor, consulting how to get a little money by letting him the *Elias* to fetch masts from New England. So home to supper and to bed.

22.   Having directed it last night, I was called up this morning before 4 a-clock. It was full light, enough to dress myself; and so by water against tide, it being a little coole, to Greenewich and thence (only that it was somewhat foggy till the sun got to some heighth) walked with great pleasure to Woolwich, in my way staying several times to listen to the nightingales. I did much business [and] discovered a plain cheat, which in time I shall publish, of Mr. Ackeworths. Thence, having visited Mr. Falconer also, who lies still sick but hopes to be better, I walked to Greenwich, Mr. Deane with me. Much good discourse, and I think him a very just man; only, a little conceited, but yet very able in his way. And so he by water with me also to town. I home, and immediately dressing myself, by coach with my wife to my Lord Sandwiches; but they having dined, we would not light but went to Mrs. Turners and there got something to eat; and thence, after reading part of a good play, Mrs. The[oph]., my wife and I in their coach to Hide parke, where great plenty of gallants. And pleasant it was, only for the dust. Here I saw Mrs. Bendy, my Lady Spillman's fair daughter that was, who continues yet very handsome. Many others I saw,

379

with great content. And so back again to Mrs. Turners, and then took a coach and home. I did also carry them into St. James's park and showed them the garden. To my office awhile while supper was making ready, and so home to supper and to bed.

**23.** *Coronacion day.* Up; and after doing something at my office, and it being a holiday, no sitting likely to be, I down by water to Sir W. Warren's, who hath been ill, and there talked long with him; good discourse, especially about Sir W. Batten's knaveries and his son Castle['s] ill language of me behind my back, saying that I favour my fellow Traytours – but I shall be even with him. So home and to the Change, where I met with Mr. Coventry – who himself is now full of talk of a Dutch war, for it seems the Lords have concurred in the Commons' vote about it and so the next week it will be presented to the King. Insomuch that he doth desire we would look about to see what stores we lack, and buy what we can. Home to dinner, where I and my wife much troubled about my money that is in my Lord Sandwiches hand, for fear of his going to sea and be killed. But I will get what of it out I can. All the afternoon, not being well, at my office and there did much business, my thoughts still running upon a warr and my money. At night home to supper and to bed.

**24.** *Lords day.* Up; and all the morning in my chamber setting some of my private papers in order – for I perceive that now public business takes up so much of my time that I must get time a-Sundays or a-nights to look after my own matters. Dined and spent all the afternoon talking with my wife. At night, a little to the office and so home to supper and to bed.

**25.** Up; and with Sir W. Pen by coach to St. James's; and there up to the Duke, and after he was ready, to his closet – where most of our talk about a Dutch war, and discoursing of things endeed now for it. The Duke (which gives me great good hope) doth talk of setting up a good discipline in the fleet. In the Duke's chamber there is a bird, given him by Mr. Pierce the surgeon, comes from the East Indys – black the greatest part, with the finest coller of white about the neck.[1] But talks many things, and neyes like the horse and other things, the best almost that ever I heard bird in my life. Thence I

1. Probably a mina from Bengal.

walked to my Lord Sandwiches, where by agreement I met my wife and there dined with the young ladies; my Lady being not well, kept her chamber. Much simple discourse at table among the young ladies. After dinner walked in the garden, talking with Mr. Moore about my Lord's business. He told me my Lord runs in debt every day more and more, and takes little care how to come out of it. He counted to me how my Lord pays use now for above 9000*l* – which is a sad thing, especially considering the probability of his going to sea in great danger of his life – and his children, many of them, to provide for. Thence, the young ladies going out to visit, I took my wife by coach out through the City, discoursing how to spend the afternoon – and conquered, with much ado, a desire of going to a play. But took her out at Whitechapel and to Bednell green; so to Hackny, where I have not been many a year, since a little child I boarded there. Thence to Kingsland by my nurse's house, Goody Lawrence, where my brother Tom and I was kept when young. Then to Newington green and saw the outside of Mrs. Herberts house where she lived, and my aunt Ellen with her. But Lord, how in every point I find myself to over-value things when a child. Thence to Islington, and so to St. John's to the Red bull and there saw the latter part of a rude Prize fight – but with good pleasure enough. And thence back to Islington and at the Kings head, where Pitts lived, we light and eat and drunk for remembrance of the old house sake. And so through Kingsland again and so to Bishopsgate, and so home with great pleasure – the country mighty pleasant; and we with great content home, and after supper to bed.

30. Up, and all the morning at the office. At noon to the Change; where after business done, Sir W. Rider and Cutler took me to the Old James and there did give me a good dish of Mackrell, the first I have seen this year, very good – and good discourse. After dinner we fell to business about their contract for Tarr, in which and in another business of Sir W. Rider's Canvas, wherein I got him to contract with me, I hold them to some terms, against their Wills, to the King's advantage, which I believe they will take notice of to my credit.

All the news now is what will become of the Dutch business, whether war or peace. We all seem to desire it, as thinking ourselfs to have advantages at present over them; but for my part I dread it. The Parliament promises to assist the King with lives and fortunes.

And he receives it with thanks, and promises to demand satisfaction of the Dutch. My poor Lady Sandwich is fallen sick three days since of the Mezles. Never more quiet in my family all days of my life then now, there being only my wife and I and Besse and the little girl Susan; the best wenches, to our content, that we can ever expect.

## –✳MAY✳–

1. *Lords day*. Lay long in bed. Went not to church, but stayed at home to examine my last night's accounts, which I find right – and that I am 908*l* Creditor in the world – the same I was last month. Dined; and after dinner – down by water with my wife and Besse with great pleasure, as low as Greenwich, and so back again, playing as it were leisurely upon the water to Deptford, where I landed and sent my wife up higher, to land below Halfway house. I to the King's yard and there spoke about several businesses with the officers; and so with Mr. Wayth, consulting about Canvas, to Halfway house where my wife was; and after eating there we broke and walked home before quite dark. So to supper, prayers, and to bed.

3. Up; and being ready, went by agreement to Mr. Blands and there drank my morning draught in good Chocolatte, and slabbering my band sent home for another. And so he and I by water to Whitehall and walked to St. James, where met Creed and Vernatty and by and by Sir W. Rider; and so to Mr. Coventry's chamber and there upon my Lord Peterburgh's accounts, where I endeavoured to show the folly and punish it as much as I could of Mr. Povy, for of all the men in the world, I never knew any man of his degree so great a coxcomb in such imployments. I see I have lost him for ever, but I value it not; for he is a coxcomb and I doubt not over-honest by some things which I see. And yet for all his folly, he hath the good luck now and then to speak his follies in so good words and with as good a show as if it were reason and to the purpose – which is really one of the wonders of my life. In the evening to my Uncle Wight's; and not finding them come home, they being gone to the parke and the Mullbury garden, I went to the Change, and there meeting with Mr. Hempson, whom Sir W.

Batten hath lately turned out of his place, merely because of his coming to me when he came to town before he went to him. And there he told me many rogueries of Sir W. Batten. How he knows and is able to prove that Capt. Cox of Chatham did give him 10*l* in gold to get him to certify for him at the King's coming in. And that Tom Newborne did make poor men give him 3*l* to get Sir W. Batten to cause them to be entered in the yard; and that Sir W. Batten hath oftentimes said – "By God, Tom, you shall get something and I will have some on't." His present Clerke that is come in Norman's room hath given him something for his place. That they live high and (as Sir Frances Clerkes Lady told his wife) do lack money as well as other people, and have bribes of a piece of Sattin and cabinetts and other things from people that deal with him; and that hardly anybody goes to sea or hath anything done by Sir W. Batten but it comes with a bribe; and that this is publicly true – that his wife was a whore and that he had Libells flung within his doors for a cuckold as soon as he was married. That he received 100*l* in money and in other things, to the value of 50 more of Hempson and that he entends to give him back but 50*l*. That he hath abused the Chest and hath now some 1000*l* by him of it.

4. Up; and my new Taylor, Langford, comes and takes measure of me for a new black cloth suit and cloak. And I think he will prove a very careful fellow and will please me well. Thence to attend my Lord Peterborough in bed and give him an account of yesterday's proceeding with Povey. I perceive I labour in a business will bring me little pleasure; but no matter, I shall do the King some service. Thence to the Coffee-house and to the Change a while. News uncertain how the Dutch proceed; some say for, some say against a warr. The plague encreases at Amsterdam. So home to dinner; and after dinner to my office, where very late, till my eyes (which begin to fail me nowadays by candlelight) begin to trouble me. Home at night to supper and to bed.

6. This morning up and to my office, where Sympson my Joyner came to work upon altering my closet, which I alter by setting the door in another place, and several other things to my great content. Busy at it all day; only, in the afternoon home and there, my books at the office being out of order, wrote letters and other businesses. So at night, with my head full of the business of my closet, home to bed. And strange it is to think how building doth fill my mind and

put out all other things out of my thoughts.

11.   Up; and all day, both forenoon and afternoon, at my office, to
see it finished by the Joyner and washed and everything in order;
and endeed, now my closet is very convenient and pleasant for me.
My uncle Wight came to me to my office this afternoon and from
me went to my house to see my wife; and strange to think that my
wife should by and by send for me after he was gone, to tell me that
he should begin discourse of her want of children and his also, and
how he thought it would be best for him and her to have one
between them, and he would give her 500*l* either in money or jewell
beforehand and make the child his heyre. He commended her body
and discoursed that for all he knew the thing was lawful. She says
she did give him a very warm answer, such as he did not excuse
himself by saying that he said this in jest but told her that since he
saw what her mind was, he would say no more to her of it, and
desired her to make no words of it. It seemed he did say all this in a
kind of counterfeit laugh; but by all words that passed, which I
cannot now so well set down, it is plain to me that he was in good
earnest, and that I fear all his kindness is but only his lust to her.
What to think of it of a sudden I know not, but I think not to take
notice yet of it to him till I have thought better of it. So, with my
mind and head a little troubled, I received a letter from Mr.
Coventry about a mast for the Dukes Yacht; which, with other
business, makes me resolve to go betimes to Woolwich tomorrow.
So to supper and to bed.

13.   Up before 3 a-clock; and a little after upon the water, it being
very light as at noon and a bright sun rising; but by and by a
rainbow appeared, the first that ever in a morning I saw, and then it
fell a-raining a little but held up again; and I to Woolwich, where
before all the men came to work, I with Mr. Deane spent two hours
upon the new ship,[1] informing myself in the names and natures of
many parts of her, to my great content, and so back again without
doing anything else; and after shifting myself, away to Westminster. In the painted chamber I heard a fine conference between
the sum of the two Houses upon the bill for conventicles. The Lords
would be freed from having their houses searched by any but the
Lord-Lieutenant of the county. And upon being found guilty, to be

---

1. The *Royal Catherine*, a 2nd-rate.

tried only by their peers; and thirdly, would have it added that whereas the Bill says that "that (among other things) shall be a conventicle wherein any such meeting is found doing anything contrary to the Liturgy of the Church of England," they would have it added "or practice." The Commons to the Lords said that they knew not what might hereafter be found out which might be called the practice of the Church of England, for there are many things may be said to be the practice of the Church which were never established by any law, either common, Statute, or Cannon – as, singing of psalms – binding up prayers at the end of the Bible – and prayings extempore before and after sermon. And though these are things indifferent, yet things, for aught they at present know, may be started which may be said to be the practice of the Church which would not be fit to allow.

14.   Up, full of pain, I believe by cold got yesterday. To the office, where we sat; and after office, home to dinner, being in extraordinary pain. After dinner, my pain increasing, I was forced to go to bed; and by and by my pain ris to be as great for an hour or two as ever I remember it was in any fit of the stone, both in the lower part of my belly and in my back also. No wind could I break. I took a glister, but it brought away but a little and my heighth of pain fallowed it. At last, after two hours lying thus in most extraordinary anguish, crying and roaring, I know not whether it was my great sweating that [made] me do it, but upon getting by chance among my other tumblings, upon my knees in bed, my pain begin to grow less and so continued less and less, till in an hour after I was in very little pain, but could break no wind nor make any water; and so continued and slept well all night.

15.   *Lords day*. Rose, and as I had intended without reference to this pain, took physic and it wrought well with me. My wife lying from me tonight, the first time she did in the same house ever since we were married I think (unless while my father was in town that he lay with me); she took physic also today, and both of our physics wrought well; so we passed our time today, our physic having done working, with some pleasure talking; but I was not well, for I could make no water yet but a drop or two with great pain, nor break any wind. In the evening came Mr. Vernatty to see me and discourse about my Lord Peterborough's business. And also my Uncle Wight and Norbury; but I took no notice nor showed any different

countenance to my Uncle Wight or he to me, for all that he carried himself so basely to my wife the last week – but will take time to make my use of it. So being exceeding hot, to bed and slept well.

16. Forced to rise because of going to the Duke to St. James, where we did our usual business; and thence by invitation to Mr. Pierce's the surgeon, where I saw his wife, whom I had not seen in many months before. She holds her complexion still; but in everything else, even in this her new house and the best rooms in it and her closet, which her husband with some vainglory took me to show me, she continues the veriest slattern that ever I knew in my life. By and by we to see an experiment of killing a dog by letting opium into his hind leg. He and Dr. Clerke did fail mightily in hitting the vein, and in effect did not do the business after many trials; but with the little they got in, the dog did presently fall asleep and so lay till [h]e cut him up. And a little dog also, which they put it down his throate; he also staggered first, and then fell asleep and so continued; whether he recovered or no after I was gone, I know not – but it is a strange and sudden effect.

18. Up and within all the morning, being willing to keep as much as I could within doors. But receiving a very wakening letter from Mr. Coventry about fitting of ships, which speaks something like to be done, I went forth to the office, there to take order in things. And after dinner to Whitehall to a Committee of Tanger, but did little. So home again and to Sir W. Pen – who, among other things of haste in this new order for ships, is ordered to be gone presently to Portsmouth to look after the work there. I stayed to discourse with him; and so home to supper, where upon a fine couple of pigeons, a good supper. And here I met a pretty Cabinet sent me by Mr. Shales, which I gave my wife – the first of that sort of goods I ever had yet – and very conveniently it comes for her closet. Stayed up late finding out the private boxes, but could not do some of them; and so to bed, afeared that I have been too bold today in venturing in the cold. This day I begin to drink Buttermilke and whey – and I hope to find great good by it.

22. *Lords day.* Up and by water to Whitehall to my Lord's lodgings; and with him walked to Whitehall without any great discourse, nor do I find that he doth mind business at all. Here the Duke of Yorke called me to him to ask me whether I did intend to

go with him to Chatham or no; I told him, if he commanded, but I
did believe there would be business here for me; and so he told me,
then it would be better to stay – which I suppose he will take better
then if I had been forward to go. Thence, after staying and seeing
the throng of people to attend the King to chapel; but Lord, what a
company of sad idle people they are – I walked to St. James with
Coll. Remes; where stayed a good while and then walked to
Whitehall with Mr. Coventry, talking about business. So meeting
Creed, took him with me home and to dinner, a good dinner; and
thence by water to Woolwich, where mighty kindly received by
Mrs. Falconer and her husband, who is now pretty well again – this
being the first time I ever carried my wife thither. I walked to the
Docke, where I met Mrs. Ackworth alone at home; and God
forgive me, what thoughts I had; but I had not the courage to stay,
but went to Mr. Pett's and walked up and down the yard with him
and Deane, talking about the despatch of the ships now in haste; and
by and by Creed and my wife and a friend of Mr. Falconers came
with the boat and called me; and so by water to Deptford, where I
landed; and after talking with others, walked to Halfway house
with Mr. Wayth, talking about the business of his supplying us
with Canvas, and he told me in discourse several instances of Sir W.
Batten's cheats. So to Halfway house, whither my wife and them
were gone before; and after drinking there, we walked and by water
home, sending Creed and the other with the boat home. Then I
wrote a letter to Mr. Coventry; and so a good supper of pease, the
first I eat this year, and so to bed.

29.   *Sunday. Whitsunday. Kings Birth and Restauracion day*. Up; and
having received a letter last night, desiring it from Mr. Coventry, I
walked to St. James; and there he and I did long discourse together
of the business of the office and the war with the Dutch and he
seemed to argue mightily with the little reason that there is for all
this. He doth, as to the effect of the war, tell me clearly that it is not
any skill of the Dutch that can hinder our trade if we will, we having
so many advantages over them, of Windes, good ports, and men.
But it is our pride and the laziness of the merchant. He seems to
think that there may be some Negotiacion which may hinder a war
this year; but that he speaks doubtfully, as unwilling, I perceive, to
be thought to discourse any such thing. The main thing he desired
to speak with me about was to know whether I do understand my
Lord Sandwiches intentions as to going to sea with this fleet; saying

that the Duke, if he desires it, is most willing to it; but thinking that twelve ships is not a fleet fit for my Lord to be troubled to go out with, he is not willing to offer it him till he hath some intimations of his mind to go or not. He spoke this with very great respect as to my Lord, though methinks it is strange they should not understand one another better at this time then to need another's mediacion. Thence walked over the park to Whitehall, Mr. Povy with me, and was taken in a very great showre in the middle of the park, that we were very wet. So up into the House and with him to the King's closet, whither by and by the King came, my Lord Sandwich carrying the sword. A Bishop preached; but he speaking too low for me to hear behind the King's closet, I went forth and walked and discoursed with Coll. Reames, who seems a very willing man to be informed in his business of Canvas, which he is undertaking to strike in with us to serve the Navy. By and by my Lord Sandwich came forth and called me to him; and we fell into discourse a great while about his business, wherein he seems to be very open with me and to receive my opinion as he used to do; and I hope I shall become necessary to him again. He desired me to think of the fitness or not for him to offer himself to go to sea, and to give him my thoughts in a day or two. Thence, after sermon, among the ladies on the Queenes side; where I saw Mrs. Stuart, very fine and pretty but far beneath my Lady Castlemaine. Thence with Mr. Povy home to dinner, where extraordinary cheer. And after dinner, up and down to see his house. And in a word, methinks for his perspective upon his wall in his garden and the springs rising up – with the perspective in the little closet – his room floored above with woods of several colours, like, but above the best Cabinet work I ever saw – his grotto and vault, with his bottles of wine and a well therein to keep them cool – his furniture of all sorts – his bath at the top of his house – good pictures and his manner of eating and drinking, doth surpass all that ever I did see of one man in all my life.

31. Up, and called upon Mr. Hollyard, with whom I advised and shall fall upon some course of doing something for my disease of the wind, which grows upon me every day more and more. Thence to my Lord Sandwiches; and while he was dressing, I below discoursed with Capt. Cooke and I think, if I do find it fit to keep a boy at all, I had as good be supplied from him with one as anybody. By and by up to my Lord – and to discourse about his going to sea

and the message I had from Mr. Coventry to him. He wonders, as he well may, that this course should be taken, and he every day with the Duke (who nevertheless seems most friendly to him), who hath not yet spoke one word to my Lord of his desire to have him go to sea. My Lord doth tell me clearly that were it not that he, as all other men that were of the parliaments side, are obnoxious to reproach, and so is forced to bear what otherwise he would not, he would never suffer everything to be done in the Navy and he never be consulted; and it seems, in the naming of all these commanders for this fleet, he hath never been asked one Question. But we concluded it wholly inconsistent with his Honour not to go [with] this fleet, nor with the reputation which the world hath of his interest at Court; and so he did give me commission to tell Mr. Coventry that he is most willing to receive any commands from the Duke in this fleet, were it less then it is, and that perticularly in this service. With this message I parted; and by coach to the office, where I found Mr. Coventry and told him this. Dined at home; and so to the office, where a great while alone in my office, nobody near, with Bagwell's wife of Deptford; but the woman seems so modest that I durst not offer any courtship to her, though I had it in my mind when I brought her in to me. But am resolved to do her husband a courtesy, for I think he is a man that deserves very well. I was told today that upon Sunday night last, being the King's birthday – the King was at my Lady Castlemaine's lodgings (over the hither-gate at Lambert's lodgings) dancing with fiddlers all night almost, and all the world coming by taking notice of it – which I am sorry to hear.

The discourse of the town is only whether a war with Holland or no. And we are preparing for it all we can, which is but little. Myself subject more then ordinary to pain by winde, which makes me very sad – together with the trouble which at present lies upon me in my father's behalf, rising from the death of my brother – which are many and great. Would to God they were over.

─✤JUNE✤─

1. Up, having lain long, going to bed very late after the ending my accounts. Being up, Mr. Hollyard came to me; and to my great sorrow, after his great assuring me that I could not possibly have

the stone again, he tells me that he doth verily fear that I have it again and hath brought me something to dissolve it – which doth make me very much troubled and pray to God to ease me. He gone, I down by water to Woolwich and Deptford to look after the despatch of the ships, all the way reading Mr. Spencers book of Prodigys, which is most ingeniously writ, both for matter and style. Home at noon and my little girl got me my dinner; and I presently out by water and landed at Somerset stairs and thence through Coventgarden, where I met with Mr. Southwell (Sir W. Pen's friend), who tells me the very sad newes of my Lord Tiviott's and 19 more commission officers being killed at Tanger by the Moores, by an ambush of the enemy's upon them while they were surveying their lines; which is very sad, and he says afflicts the King much. Thence to W. Joyces, where by appointment I met my wife (but neither of them at home); and she and I to the King's house and saw *The Silent Woman*; but methought not so well done or so good [a] play as I formerly thought it to be, or else I am nowadays out of humour. Before the play was done, it fell such a storm of Hayle that we in the middle of the pit[1] were fain to rise, and all the house in a disorder; and so my wife and I out and got into a little alehouse and stayed there an hour after the play was done before we could get a coach; which at last we did (and by chance took up Joyce Norton and Mrs. Bowles and set them at home); and so home ourselfs and I a little to my office and so home to supper and to bed.

2. Up and to the office, where we sat all the morning; and then to the Change, where after some stay, by coach with Sir J. Mennes and Mr. Coventry to St. James and there dined with Mr. Coventry very finely; and so over the park to Whitehall to a Committee of Tanger about providing provisions, money, and men for Tanger. At it all the afternoon; but it is strange to see how poorly and brokenly things are done of the greatest consequence – and how soon the memory of this great man is gone, or at least out of mind, by the thoughts of who goes next, which is not yet known. My Lord of Oxford, Muskerry, and several others are discoursed of. It seems my Lord Tiviotts design was to go out a mile and a half out of the town to cut down a wood in which the enemy did use to lie in ambush. He had sent several spyes; but all brought word that the way was clear, and so might be for anybody's discovery of an

---

1. There was a glazed cupola immediately overhead.

enemy before you are upon them. There they were all snapped, he and all his oficers, and about 200 men as they say – there being left now in the garrison but four Captains. This happened the 3rd of May last, being not before the day twelvemonth of his entering into his government there; but at his going out in the morning, he said to some of his officers, "Gentlemen, let us look to ourselfs, for it was this day three years that so many brave Englishmen were knocked on the head by the Moores, when Fines made his sally out." Here till almost night; and then home with Sir J. Mennes by coach, and so to my office a while and home to supper and bed – being now in constant pain in my back; but whether it be only wind or what it is, the Lord knows; but I fear the worst.

3. Up, still in a constant pain in my back, which much afflicts me with fear of the consequence of it. All the morning at the office; we sat at the office extraordinary, upon the business of our stores; but Lord, what a pitiful account the Surveyor makes of it grieves my heart. This morning before I came out, I made a bargain with Capt. Taylor for a ship for the Commissioners for Tanger, wherein I hope to get 40 or 50l. To the Change and thence home and dined; and then by coach to Whitehall, sending my wife to Mr. Hunts. At the Committee for Tanger all the afternoon; where a sad consideration to see things of so great weight managed in so confused a manner as it is, so as I would not have the buying of an acre of land bought by – the Duke of Yorke and Mr. Coventry, for aught I see, being the only two that do anything like men. Prince Robert doth nothing but swear and laugh a little, with an oath or two, and that's all he doth. Thence called my wife and home; and I late at my office and so home to supper and bed, pleased at my hopes of gains by today's work, but very sad to think of the state of my health.

4. This noon Mr. Coventry discoursed largely and bravely to me concerning the different sort of valours, the active and passive valour. For the latter, he brought as an instance General Blacke, who in the defending of Taunton and Lime for the Parliament did through his stubborn sort of valour defend it the most *opiniastrement* that ever any man did anything – and yet never was the man that ever made any attaque by land or sea, but rather avoyded it on all, even fair occasions. On the other side, Prince Rupert the boldest attaquer in the world for personal courage; and yet in the defending of Bristoll, no man did ever anything worse, he wanting the

patience and seasoned head to consult and advise for defence and to bear with the evils of a Siege. The like he says is said of my Lord Tiviott, who was the boldest adventurer of his person in the world, and from a mean man in few years was come to this greatness of command and repute only by the death of all his officers, he many times having the luck of being the only survivor of them all, by venturing upon services for the King of France that nobody else would. And yet no man upon a defence – he being all fury and no judgment in a fight. He tells me above all of the Duke of Yorke, that he is more himself, and more of judgment is at hand in him, in the middle of a desperate service then at other times – as appeared in the business of Dunkirke, wherein no man ever did braver things or was in hotter service in the close of that day, being surrounded with enemies; and then, contrary to the advice of all about him, his counsel carried himself and the rest through them safe – by advising that he might make his passage with but a dozen with him; "For," says he, "the enemy cannot move after me so fast with a great body, and with a small one we shall be enough to deal with them." And though he is a man naturally Martiall to the highest degree, yet a man that never in his life talks one word of himself or service of his own; but only that he saw such or such a thing, and lays it down for a maxime that a Hector can have no courage. He told me also, as a great instance of some men, that the Prince of Conde's excellence is that there not being a more furious man in the world, danger in fight never disturbs him, more then just to make him Civill and to command in words of great obligation to his officers and men but without any the least disturbance in his judgment or spirit.

8.    All day before dinner with Creed, talking of many things; among others, of my Lord's going so often to Chelsy; and he, without my speaking much, doth tell me that his daughters do perceive all and do hate the place and the young woman there, Mrs. Betty Becke – for my Lord, who sent them thither only for a disguise for his going thither, will come under pretence to see them, and pack them out of doors to the park and stay behind with her. But now the young ladies are gone to their mother to Kensington. To dinner. And after dinner, till 10 at night in my study, writing of my old broken office-notes in shorthand all in one book, till my eyes did ake, ready to drop out. So home to supper and to bed.

10.    Up, and by water to Whitehall and there to a Committee of

Tanger. And had occasion to see how my Lord Ashwith[1] deports himself; which is very fine endeed, and it joys my heart to see that there is anybody looks so near into the King's business as I perceive he doth in this business of my Lord Peterborough's accounts. Thence into the parke and met and walked with Capt. Sylas Taylor, my old acquaintance while I was of the Exchequer, and Dr. Whore – talking of music and perticularly of Mr. Berchenshaw's way,[2] which Taylor magnifies mightily, and perhaps but what it deserves – but not so easily to be understood as he and others make of it. Thence home by water; and after dinner abroad to buy several things: as, a map and powder and other small things; and so home to my office, and in the evening with Capt. Taylor by water to our Tanger ship; and so home well pleased, having received 26*l* profit today of my bargain for this ship – which comforts me mightily, though I confess my heart, what with my being out of order as to my health and the fear I have of the money my Lord oweth me and I stand endebted to him in, is much cast down of late. In the evening home to supper and to bed.

11. Up and to the office, where we sat all the morning – where some discourse aris from Sir G. Carteret and Mr. Coventry which gives me occasion to think that something like a war is expected now indeed. Mr. Creed dined with me; and thence after dinner by coach with my wife, only to take the ayre, it being very warm and pleasant, to Bowe and old Ford and thence to Hackny; there light and played at shuffleboard, eat cream and good cherries; and so with good refreshment home. There to my office, vexed with Capt. Taylor about the delay of carrying down the ship hired by me for Tanger. And late, about that and other things, at the office. So home to supper and to bed.

12. *Lords day.* All the morning in my chamber, consulting my lesson of shipbuilding. And at noon Mr. Creed by appointment came and dined with us and sat talking all the afternoon, till about church time my wife and I begin our great dispute about going to Griffins child's christening, where I was to have been godfather; but Sir J. Mennes refusing, he wanted an equal for me and my Lady Batten and so sought for others. Then the question was whether my

---

1. Lord Ashley, later Earl of Shaftesbury.
2. His rules of composition.

wife should go; and she having dressed herself on purpose, was very angry and begin to talk openly of my keeping her within doors before Creed; which vexed me to the guts, but I had the discretion to keep myself without passion; and so resolved at last not to go, but to go down by water. Which we did, by H. Russell, to the Halfway house and there eat and drank; and upon a very small occasion had a difference again broke out, where without any the least cause she had the cunning to cry a great while and talk and blubber; which made me mighty angry in mind but said nothing to provoke her, because Creed was there. But walked home, being troubled in my mind also about the knavery and neglect of Capt. Fudge and Taylor, who were to have had their ship for Tanger ready by Thursday last, and now the men by a mistake are come on board, and not any Maister or man or boy of the ship's company on board with them when we came by her side this afternoon. And also, I received a letter from Mr. Coventry this day in complaint of it.

13.  So up at 5 a-clock, and with Capt. Taylor on board her at Deptford and found all out of order, only the soldiers civil and Sir Arth. Bassett a civil person. I rated at Capt. Taylor, whom contrary to my expectation I found a lying and a very stupid blundering fellow, good for nothing; and yet we talk of him in the Navy as if he had been a excellent officer, but I find him a lying knave – and of no judgment or despatch at all. After finding the condition of the ship, no master, not above four men, and many ships provisions, sails and other things wanting, I went back and called upon Fudge; whom I found, like a lying rogue, unready to go on board; but I did so hare him that I made him get everything ready and left Taylor and H. Russell to quicken him; and so away and I by water on to Whitehall, where I met his Royal Highness at a Tanger Committee about this very thing and did there satisfy him how things are; at which all was pacified without any trouble – and I hope may end well yet; but I confess I am at a vile trouble for fear the rogue should not do his work and I come to shame and loss of the money I did hope justly to have got by it. Thence walked with Mr. Coventry to St. James's. After dinner, we did talk of a History of the Navy of England, how fit it were to be writ; and he did say that it hath been in his mind to propose to me the writing of the history of the late Dutch warr[1] – which I am glad to hear, it being a thing I much

1. Of 1652–4.

desire and sorts mightily with my genius – and if done well, may recommend me much. So he says he will get me an order for making of searches to all records &c. in order thereto, and I shall take great delight in doing of it. Thence by water down to the Tower, and thither sent for Mr. Creed to my house, where he promised to be; and he and I down to the ship and find all things in pretty good order. And I hope will end to my mind. Thence, having a gally, down to Greenwich and there saw the King's works,[1] which are great a-doing there. And so to the Cherry garden and so carried some cherries home; and after supper to bed – my wife lying with me; which from my not being thoroughly well, nor she, we have not done above once these two or three weeks.

14. Up and to the office, where we sat all the morning and had great conflict about the flags again. So home to dinner; and after dinner by coach to Kensington, in the way overtaking Mr. Laxton the Apothecary with his wife and daughters, very fine young lasses, in a coach. And so both of us to my Lady Sandwich, who had lain this fortnight here at Deane Hodges. Much company came hither today, my Lady Carteret &c., Sir Wm. Wheeler and his Lady, and above all Mr. Becke of Chelsy and wife and daughter, my Lord's Mistress – one that hath not one good feature in her face and yet is a fine lady, of a fine Talle and very well carriaged and mighty discreet. I took all the occasion I could to discourse with the young ladies in her company, to give occasion to her to talk; which now and then she did and that mighty finely, and is I perceive a woman of such an ayre, as I wonder the less at my Lord's favour to her, and I dare warrant him she hath brains enough to entangle him. Two or three hours we were in her company, going into Sir H. Finch's garden and seeing the fountayne and singing there with the ladies; and a mighty fine cool place it is, with a great laver of water in the middle, and the bravest place for music I ever heard. After much mirth, discoursing to the ladies in defence of the city against the country or court, and giving them occasion to invite themselfs tomorrow to me to dinner to my venison pasty, I got their mother's leave and so good-night – very well pleased with my day's work; and above all, that I have seen my Lord's Mistress. So home to supper. A little at my office and to bed.

1. At Greenwich Palace.

15–16.   Up and by appointment with Capt. Witham (the Captain that brought the news of the disaster at Tanger where my Lord Tiviott was slain) and Mr. Tooker to Beares Quay and there saw, and more afterward at the several Granarys, several parcels of Oates. And strange it is to hear how it will heat itself if laid up green and not often turned. We came not to any agreement, but did cheapen several parcels; and thence away, promising to send again to them. And anon at noon comes Mr. Creed by chance, and by and by the three young ladies, and very merry we were with our pasty, very well baked – and a good dish of roasted chickens – pease – lobsters – strawberries. And after dinner to cards; and about 5 a-clock by water down to Greenwich and up to the top of the hill and there played upon the ground at Cards; and so to the Cherry garden and then by water, singing finely, to the Bridge and there landed; and so took boat again and to Somersett house. And by this time, the tide being against us, it was past 10 of the clock; and such a troublesome passage in regard of my Lady Paulina's fearfulness, that in all my life I never did see any poor wretch in that condition. Being come hither, there waited for them their coach; but it being so late, I doubted what to do how to get them home. After half an hour's stay in the street, I sent my wife home by coach with Mr. Creed's boy – and myself and Creed in the coach home with them; but Lord, the fear that my Lady Paulina was in every step of the way; and endeed, at this time of the night it was no safe thing to go that road,[1] so that I was even afeared myself, though I appeared otherwise. We came safe, however, to their house, where all were abed. We knocked them up, my Lady and all the family being in bed. So put them into doors; and leaving them with the maids, bade them goodnight and then into the town, he and I, it being about 12 a-clock and past; and to several houses, Inns, but could get no lodging, all being in bed; at the last house, at last we found some people drinking and roaring, and there got in; and after drinking, got an ill bed, where I lay in my drawers and stockings and waistcoat.

19.   *Lords day.* Up, and all the morning and afternoon (only at dinner at home) at my office, doing many businesses for want of time on the weekdays. In the afternoon the greatest shower of rain

1. To Kensington.

of a sudden and the greatest and most continued Thunder that ever I heard I think in my life. In the evening home to my wife – and there talked seriously of several of our family concernments; and among others, of bringing Pall out of the country to us here, to try to put her off;[1] which I am very desirous, and my wife also, of. So to supper – prayers, which I have of late too much omitted. So to bed.

20.   It having been a very cold night last night, I had got some cold, and so in pain by wind; and a sure præcursor of pain, I find, is sudden letting off some farts; and when that stops, then my passages stop and my pain begins. Up, and did several businesses; and so with my wife by water to Whitehall – she to her father's, I to the Duke, where we did our usual business. And among other discourse of the Dutch, he was merrily saying how they print that Prince Robt., Duke of Albemarle, and my Lord Sandwich are to be Generalls; and soon after is to fallow them "*Vieux Pen*", and so the Duke called him in mirth Old Pen. They have, it seems, lately wrote to the King to assure him that their setting-out ships were only to defend their fishing trade and to stay near home, not to annoy the King's subjects; and to desire that he would do the like with his ships – which the King laughs at, but yet is troubled they should think him such a child, to suffer them to bring home their fish and east India Company's ships, and then they will not care a fart for us. Thence to Westminster hall, it being term-time. And meeting Pickering, he tells me how my Lady last week went to see Mrs. Becke the mother. And by and by the daughter came in. But that my Lady doth say herself (as he says) that, she knew not for what reason, for she never knew they had a daughter (which I do not believe), she was troubled and her heart did rise as soon as she appeared, and seems the most ugly woman that ever she saw. This, if true, were strange; but I believe it is not. Thence to my Lord's lodgings and were merry with the young ladies; who make a great story of their appearing before their mother the morning after we carried them, the last week, home so late. And that their mother took it very well, at least without any anger. Here I heard how the rich widow, my Lady Gold, is married to one Neale, after he had received a box on the eare by her brother (who was there a sentinel

1. To marry her off.

in behalf of some Courtier) at the door; but made him draw, and wounded him. She called Neale up to her and sent for a priest, married presently, and went to bed. The brother sent to the Court and had a Serjeant sent for Neale; but Neale sent for him up to be seen in bed, and she owned him for her husband. And so all is past. It seems Sir H. Bennett did look after her.

22. Up, and I find Mr. Creed below, who stayed with me a while; and then I to business all the morning. At noon to the Change and Coffee-house, where great talk of the Dutch preparing of 60 sail of ships. The plague grows mightily among them, both at sea and land.

24. Up, and out with Capt. Witham in several places again to look for Oates for Tanger. And among other places, to the City Granarys, where it seems every company have their granary, and obliged to keep such a quantity of Corne alway there, or at a time of scarcity to issue so much at so much a bushell. And a fine thing it is to see their stores of all sorts for piles for the bridge and for pipes – a thing I never saw before. Thence to the office and there busy all the morning. At noon to my uncle Wights and there dined, my wife being there all the morning. After dinner to Whitehall and there met with Mr. Pierce and he showed me the Queen's bedchamber and her closet, where she had nothing but some pretty pious pictures and books of devotion. And her holy water at her head as she sleeps, with a clock by her bedside wherein a lamp burns that tells her the time of the night at any time. Thence with him to the park and there met the Queen coming from chappell, with her Maids of honour all in Silver lace gowns. Thence he carried me to the King's closet; where such variety of pictures and other things of value and rarity, that I was properly confounded and enjoyed no pleasure in the sight of them – which is the only time in my life that ever I was so at a loss for pleasure in the greatest plenty of objects to give it me.

26. *Lords day.* Up, and Sir J. Minnes set me down at my Lord Sandwiches, where I waited till his coming down. When he came too, could find little to say to me; but only a general question or two and so goodbye. Here his little daughter, my Lady Katharin, was brought, who is lately come from my father's at Brampton to have her cheeke looked after, which is and hath long been sore. But my Lord will rather have it be as it is, with a scarr in her face, then

endanger its being worse by tampering. He being gone, I went home, a little troubled to see he minds me no more; and with Creed with me, called at several churches – which, God knows, are supplied with very young men,[1] and the churches very empty.

28.   Up; and this day put on a half-shirt first this summer, it being very hot; and yet so ill-tempered I am grown, that I am afeared I shall ketch cold while all the world is ready to melt away. To the office all the morning. At noon to dinner at home. Then to my office till the evening. Then out about several businesses; and then by appointment to the Change and thence with my uncle Wight to the Mum house; and there drinking, he doth complain of his wife most cruelly, as the most troublesome woman in the world; and how she will have her will, saying she brought him a portion and God knows what – by which, with many instances more, I perceive they do live a sad life together. Thence to the Miter, and there came Dr. Burnett to us and Mr. Maes. But the meeting was chiefly to bring the Doctor and me together, and there I begin to have his advice about my disease and then invited him to my house; and I am resolved to put myself into his hands. Here very late, but I drank nothing, nor will – though he doth advise me to take care of cold drinks. So home and to bed.

30.   Up, and to the office, where we sat all the morning. At noon home to dinner, Mr. Wayth with me; and by and by comes in Mr. Falconer and his wife and dined with us – the first time she was ever here. We had a pretty good dinner – very merry in discourse. Sat after dinner an hour or two. Then down by water to Deptford and Woolwich about getting of some business done, which I was bound to by my oath this month. Walked back from Woolwich to Greenwich all alone, save a man that had a cudgell in his hand; and though he told me he laboured in the King's yards and many other good arguments that he is an honest man, yet God forgive me, I did doubt he might knock me on the head behind with his club – but I got safe home. Then to the making-up my month's accounts; and find myself still a gainer and rose to 951*l*, for which God be blessed. I end the month with my mind full of business and some sorrow that I have not exactly performed all my vowes, though my not

1. As a consequence of the expulsions which followed the Act of Uniformity: see above, p. 219 & n.

doing is not my fault and shall be made good out of my first leisure.

Great doubts yet whether the Dutch war go on or no. The fleet ready in the Hope, of twelve sail – the King and Queenes go on board, they say, on Saturday next. Young children of my Lord Sandwich gone with their maids from my mother's; which troubles me, it being, I hear from Mr. Sheply, with great discontent – saying that though they buy good meate, yet can never have it before it stinks – which I am ashamed of.

# –✥JULY✥–

1.  Up, and within all the morning – first bringing down my Tryangle to my chamber below, having a new frame made proper for it to stand on. By and by comes Dr. Burnett – who assures me that I have an Ulcer either in the Kidnys or Blather; for my water, which he saw yesterday, he is sure the Sediment is not slime gathered by heat, but is a direct pusse. He did write me down some direction what to do for it – but not with the satisfaction I expected. I did give him a piece; with good hopes, however, that his advice will be of use to me – though it is strange Mr. Hollyard should never say one word of this ulcer in all his life to me. He being gone, I to the Change and thence home to dinner; and so to my office, busy till the evening; and then by agreement came Mr. Hill and Andrew and one Cheswicke, a maister who plays very well upon the Spinette, and we sat singing Psalms till 9 at night, and so broke up with great pleasure; and very good company it is, and I hope I shall now and then have their company. They being gone, I to my office till toward 12 a-clock, and then home and to bed. Upon the Change this day I saw how uncertain the Temper of the people is – that from our discharging of about 200 that lay idle, having nothing to do upon some of our ships which were ordered to be fitted for service and their works are now done – the town doth talk that the King discharges all his men, 200 yesterday and 800 today, and that now he hath got 100000*l* in his hand, he values not a Dutch warr. But I undeceived a great many, telling them how it is.

2.  Up and to the office, where all the morning. At noon to the Change; and there (which is strange) I could meet with nobody that I could invite home to my venison pasty, but only Mr. Alsop and

Mr. Lanyon, whom I invited last night, and a friend they brought along with them. So home; and with our venison pasty we had other good meat and good discourse. After dinner sat close to discourse about our business of the victualling of the garrison of Tanger – taking their prices of all provisions; and I do hope to order it so that they, and I also, may get something by it – which doth much please me, for I hope I may get nobly and honestly, with profit to the King. They being gone, came Sir W. Warren and he and I discoursed long about the business of masts; and then in the evening to the office, where late writing letters, and then home to look over some Brampton papers, which I am under an oath to despatch before I spend one half-hour in any pleasure or go to bed before 12 a-clock; to which, by the grace of God I will be true. Then to bed. When I came home, I found that tomorrow being Sunday, I should gain nothing by doing it tonight, and tomorrow I can do it very well and better then tonight: I went to bed before my time, but with a resolution of doing the thing to better purpose tomorrow.

3.   *Lords day*. Up and ready, and all the morning in my chamber looking over and settling some Brampton businesses. At noon to dinner, where the remains of yesterday's venison and a couple of brave green geese; which we are fain to eat alone, because they will not keep – which troubled us. After dinner, I close to my business; and before the evening, did end it with great content and my mind eased by it. Then up and spent the evening walking with my wife, talking; and it thundering and lightening mightily all the evening – and this year have had the most thunder and lightening, they say, of any in man's memory; and so it is it seems in France and everywhere else. So to prayers and to bed.

4.   Up, and many people with me about business; and then out to several places, and so at noon to my Lord Crews and there dined, and very much made on there by him. He offered me the selling of some land of his in Cambrigeshire, a purchase of about 1000*l* – and if I can compass it, I will. After dinner I walked homeward, still doing business by the way, and at home find my wife this day of her own accord to have lain out 25*s*. upon a pair of pendances for her eares; which did vex me and brought both me and her to very high, and very foul words from her to me, such as trouble me to think she should have in her mouth, and reflecting upon our old

differences,[1] which I hate to have remembered. I vowed to break them, or that she should go and get what she could for them again. I went with that resolution out of doors. The poor wretch afterward, in a little while, did send out to change them for her money again. I fallowed Besse her messenger at the Change and there did consult and sent her back; I would not have them changed, being satisfied that she yielded. So went home, and friends again as to that business; but the words I could not get out of my mind, and so went to bed at night discontented; and she came to bed to me, but all would not make me friends, but sleep and rise in the morning angry. This day the King and the Queenes went to visit my Lord Sandwich and the fleet going forth, in the Hope.

6. Up very betimes, and my wife also, and got us ready; and about 8 a-clock, having got some bottles of wine and beer and neat's tongues, we went to our barge at the Towre, where Mr. Pierce and his wife and a kinswoman and his sister, and Mrs. Clerke and her sister and cousin were to expect us. And so set out for the Hope, all the way down playing at Cards and other sports, spending our time pretty merry. Came to the Hope about one, and there showed them all the ship[s] and had a collacion of anchoves, Gammon &c.; and after an hour's stay or more imbarked again for home, and so to cards and other sports till we came to Greenwich; and there Mrs. Clerke and my wife and I on shore to an alehouse for them to do their business, and so to the barge again, having shown them the King's pleasure-boat. And so home to the Bridge, bringing night home with us and it raining hard, but we got them on foot to the Beare and there put them into a boat; and I back to my wife in the barge and so to the Tower wharf and home – being very well pleased today with the company, especially Mrs. Pierce, who continues her complexion as well as ever, and hath at this day, I think, the best complexion that ever I saw on any woman, young or old, or child either, all days of my life. Also, Mrs. Clerkes kinswoman sings very prettily, but is very confident in it. Mrs. Clerke herself witty, but spoils all in being so conceited and making so great a flutter with a few fine clothes and some bad tawdry things worn with them. But the charge of the barge lies heavy upon me, which troubles me; but it is but once, and I may make Pierce do me some courtesy as great. Being come home, I weary to bed with

1. See above, p. 148 (13 August) & n. 2.

sitting. The reason of Dr. Clerkes not being here was the King's being sick last night and let blood, and so he durst not come away today.

8.   To Paul's churchyard about books – and to the binders and directed the doing of my Chaucer, though they were not full neat enough for me, but pretty well it is – and thence to the clasp-makers to have it clasped and bossed. So to the Change and home to dinner, and so to my office till 5 a-clock; and then came Mr. Hill and Andrews and we sung an hour or two. Then broke up and Mr. Alsop and his company came and consulted about our Tanger victualling, and brought it to a good head. So they parted and I to supper and to bed.

9.   Up, and at the office all the morning; in the afternoon by coach with Sir J. Mennes to Whitehall and there to a Committee for Fishing; but the first thing was swearing to be true to the Company, and we were all sworn. But a great dispute we had (which methought is very Ominous to the Company); some, that we should swear to be true to the best of our power; and other, to the best of our understanding; and carried in the last (though in that we are the least able to serve the Company) because we would not be obliged to attend the business when we can, but when we list. This consideration did displease me, but it was voted and so went.

10.   *Lords day*. Up, and by water towards noon to Somersett house; and walked to my Lord Sandwiches and there dined with my Lady and the children. And after some ordinary discourse with my Lady, after dinner took our leaves and [my] wife hers, in order to her going to the country tomorrow. Here my Lady showed us my Lady Castlemaynes picture, finely done – given my Lord, and a most beautiful picture it is. Thence with my Lady Jem and Mr. Sidny to St. Gyles church, and there heard a long poor sermon. Thence set them down and in their coach to Kate Joyces christening – where much company – good service of sweetmeats. And after an hour's stay left them and in my Lord's coach, his noble rich coach, home; and there my wife fell to putting things in order against her going tomorrow. And I to read and so to bed – where I not well, and so had no pleasure at all this night with my poor wife.

11.   But betimes up this morning; and getting ready, we by coach

to Holborne, where at 9 a-clock they set out, and I and my man Will on horse by her to Barnett, a very pleasant day, and there dined with her company, which was very good – a pretty gentlewoman with her that goes but to Huntington, and a neighbour to us in town. Here we stayed two hours and then parted for altogether – and my poor wife I shall soon want, I am sure. Thence I and Will to see the Wells, half a mile off; and there I drunk three glasses and went and walked, and came back and drunk two more. The woman would have had me drunk three more; but I could not, my belly being full – but this wrought very well; and so we rode home round by Kingsland, Hackney, and Mile end, till we were quite weary – and my water working at least seven or eight times upon the road, which pleased me well. And so home, weary; and not being very well, I betimes to bed. And there fell into a most mighty sweat in the night, about 11 a-clock; and there, knowing what money I have in the house and hearing a noise, I begin to sweat worse and worse, till I melted almost to water. I rung, and could not in half an hour make either of the wenches hear me; and this made me fear the more, lest they might be gag'd; and then I begin to think that there was some design in a stone being flung at the window over our stairs this evening, by which the thiefes meant to try what looking there would [be] after them and know our company. These thoughts and fears I had, and do hence apprehend the fears of all rich men that are covetous and have much money by them. At last Jane rose and then I understand it was only the dog wants a lodging and so made a noyse. So to bed, but hardly slept; at last did, and so till morning.

15.    Up, and to my Lord Sandwiches; where he sent for me up. He begun to tell me that he had now pitched upon his day of going to sea, upon Monday next; and that he would now give me an account how matters are with him. He told me that his work now in the world is only to keep up his interest at Court, having little hopes to get more considerably; he saying that he hath now about 8000*l* per annum. It is true, he says, he oweth about 10000*l*. But he hath been at great charges in getting things to this pass in his estate – besides his building and goods that he hath bought. He says he hath now evened his reckonings at the Wardrobe till Michaelmas last, and hopes to finish it to Lady-day before he goes. He says, now there is due too, 7000*l* to him there, if he knew how to get it paid. He says he is as great with the Chancellor, or greater, then ever in his life.

That with the King he is the like; and told me an instance, that whereas he formerly was of the private council to the King before he was last sick, and that by that sickness an interruption was made in his attendance upon him, the King did not constantly call him, as he used to do, to his private council, only in businesses of the sea and the like; but of late, the King did send a message to him by Sir Hary Bennet, to excuse the King to my Lord that he had not of late sent for him as he used to do to his private council, for it was not out of any distaste, but to avoid giving offence to some others, whom he did not name but my Lord supposes it might be Prince Rupert, or it may be only that the King would rather pass it by an excuse then be thought unkind. But that now he did desire him to attend him constantly; which he hath of late done, and the King never more kind to him in his life then now. The Duke of Yorke, as much as is possible; and in the business of late, when I was to speak to my Lord about his going to sea, he says that he finds the Duke did it with the greatest ingenuity and love in the world; and hath caused in his commission that he be made Admirall of this and what other ships or fleets shall hereafter be put out after these – which is very noble. He tells me, in these cases and all others, he finds that bearing of them patiently is his best way, without noise or trouble; and things wear out of themselfs and come fair again. "But," says he, "take it from me never to trust too much to any man in the world, for you put yourself into his power; and the best-seeming friend and real friend as to the present may have or take occasion to fall out with you; and then out comes all. This," says he, "is the whole condition of my estate and interest; which I tell you because I know not whether I shall see you again or no." Then as to the voyage, he thinks it will be of charge to him, and no profit; but that he must not now look after nor think to encrease, but study to make good what he hath, that what is due to him from the Wardrobe or elsewhere may be paid; which otherwise would fail, and all a man hath be but small content to him. So we seemed to take leave one of another; my Lord of me, desiring me that I would write to him and give him information upon all occasions in matters that concern him – which, put together with what he preambled with yesterday, makes me think that my Lord doth truly esteem me still, and desires to preserve my service to him – which I do bless God for. In the middle of our discourse my Lady Crew came in to bring my Lord Word that he hath another son, my Lady being brought to bed just now. I did not think her time had been so nigh; but she is well brought to bed, for which God be praised – and send my Lord to study the laying up of something the more.

16. To Whitehall to the Tanger Comittee; and there above my expectation got the business of our contract for the Victualling carried for my people – *viz.*, Alsop, Lanyon and Yeabsly. And by their promise I do thereby get 300*l* per annum to myself – which doth overjoy me; and the matter is left to me to draw up. Mr. Lewes was in the gallery, and is mightily amused at it; and I believe Mr. Gauden will make some stir about it, for he wrote to Mr. Coventry today about it, to argue why he should for the King's convenience have it; but Mr. Coventry most justly did argue freely for them that served the cheapest.

17. *Lords day*. All the morning at my office doing business there, it raining hard. So dined at home alone. After dinner walked to my Lord's – and there found him and much other guest[s] at table at dinner, and it seems they have christened his young son today, called him James; I got a piece of cake. I got my Lord to sign and seal my business about my selling of Brampton land; which though not so full as I would, yet is as full as I can at present. Walked home again, and there fell to read; and by and by comes my Uncle Wight, Dr. Burnett and another gentleman, and talked and drank – and the Doctor showed me the manner of eating Turpentine; which pleases me well, for it is with great ease. So they being gone, I to supper and to bed.

18. Up, and walked to my Lord's and there took my leave of him, he seeming very friendly to me, in as serious a manner as ever in his life – and I believe he is very confident of me. He sets out this morning for Deale. Thence to St. James to the Duke and there did our usual business. He discourses very freely of a war with Holland, to begin about winter; so that I believe we shall come to it.

20. This evening being moonshine, I played a little late upon my flagelette in the garden. But being at Westminster hall, I met with great news: that Mrs. Lane is married to one Martin, one that serves Capt. Marsh. She is gone abroad with him today, very fine. I must have a bout with her very shortly, to see how she finds marriage.

21. Up, and to the office, where we sat all the morning; among

other things, making a contract with Sir W. Warren for almost 1000 Gottenburg masts, the biggest that ever was made in the Navy and wholly of my composing, and a good one I hope it is for the King. Dined at Sir W. Batten, where I have not eat these many months. Sir G. Carteret, Mr. Coventry, Sir J. Mennes and myself there only, and my Lady. A good venison pasty, and very merry and pleasant I made myself with my Lady, and she as much to me. This morning to the office comes Nich. Osborne, Mr. Gauden's clerk, to desire of me what piece of plate I would choose to have, a 100*l* or thereabouts, bestowed upon me in – he having order to lay out so much, and out of his freedom with me doth of himself come to make this question: I a great while urged my unwillingness to take any, not knowing how I could serve Mr. Gauden; but left it wholly to himself. So at noon I find brought home in fine leather cases a pair of the noblest Flaggons that ever I saw all days of my life. Whether I shall keep them or no, I cannot tell; for it is to oblige me to him in that business of the Tanger victualing, wherein I doubt I shall not; but glad I am to see that I shall be sure to get something on one side or other, have it which will. So with a merry heart, I looked upon them and locked them up. Thence to Westminster and to Mrs. Lane's lodging to give her joy. And there suffered me to deal with her as I used to do; and by and by her husband comes, a sorry simple fellow, and his letter to her, which she proudly showed me, a simple, silly, nonsensical thing. A man of no discourse, and I fear married her to make a prize of; which he is mistaken in. And a sad wife I believe she will prove to him, for she urged me to appoint a time, as soon as he is gone out of town, to give her a meeting next week.

22. Up and to my office, where busy all the morning. At noon to the Change, and so home to dinner and then down by water to Deptford; where coming too soon, I spent an hour in looking round the yard and putting Mr. Shish to measure a piece or two of timber; which he did most cruelly wrong and to the King's loss, 12 or 13*s*. in a piece of 28f[oot] in contents. Thence to the Clerke of the Cheques, from whose house Mr. Falconer was buried today – Sir J. Mennes and I the only principall officers that were there. We walked to church with him; and then I left them without staying the sermon, and straight home by water and there find as I expected, Mr. Hill and Andrews and one slovenly and ugly fellow, Seignor Pedro, who sings Italian songs to the Theorbo most neatly;

and they spent the whole evening in singing the best piece of musique, counted of all hands in the world, made by Seignor Charissimi the famous master in Rome. Fine it was endeed, and too fine for me to judge of. They have spoke to Pedro to meet us every week, and I fear it will grow a trouble to me if we once come to bid guests to meet us, especially idle masters – which doth a little displease me to consider. They gone, comes Mr. Lanyon, who tells me Mr. Alsop is now become dangerously ill and fears his recovery, which shakes my expectation of 300*l* per annum by that business. And therefore bless God for what Mr. Gauden hath sent me; which from some discourse today with Mr. Osborne, swearing that he knows not anything of this business of the victualling but the contrary, that it is not that that moves Mr. Gauden to send it me, for he hath had order for it any time these two months. Whether this be true or no, I know not; but I shall hence with the more confidence keep it. To supper and to the office a little and to walk in the garden, the moon shining bright and fine warm fair weather. And so home to bed.

23.   Walked toward Westminster; and being in an idle and wanton humour, walked through Fleet alley, and there stood a most pretty wench at one of the doors. So I took a turn or two; but what by sense of honour and conscience, I would not go in. But much against my will, took coach and away to Westminster hall, and there light of Mrs. Lane and plotted with her to go over the water; so met at Whites stairs in Channel row, and over to the old house at Lambeth marsh and there eat and drank and had my pleasure of her twice – she being the strangest woman in talk, of love to her husband sometimes, and sometimes again she doth care not for him – and yet willing enough to allow me a liberty of doing what I would with her. So spending 5 or 6*s.* upon her, I could do what I would; and after an hour's stay and more, back again and set her ashore there again, and I forward to Fleetstreete and called at Fleet alley, not knowing how to command myself; and went in and there saw what formerly I have been acquainted with, the wickedness of those houses and the forcing a man to present expense. The woman, endeed, is a most lovely woman; but I had no courage to meddle with her, for fear of her not being wholesome, and so counterfeited that I had not money enough. It was pretty to see how cunning that Jade was; would not suffer me to have to do in any manner with her after she saw I had no money; but told me then I

would not come again, but she now was sure I would come again – though I hope in God I shall not, for though she be one of the prettiest women I ever saw, yet I fear her abusing me. So desiring God to forgive me for this vanity, I went home, taking some books home from my bookseller and taking his lad home with me, to whom I paid 10*l* for books I have laid up money for and laid out within these three weeks – and shall do no more a great while I hope. So to my office, writing letters; and then home and to bed, weary of the pleasure I have had today and ashamed to think of it.

26.    All the morning at the office. At noon to Anth. Joyces to our gossips dinner;[1] I had sent a dozen and a half bottles of wine thither and paid my double share besides, which is 18*s*. Very merry we were, and when the women were merry and ris from table, I above with them, ne'er a man but I; I begin discourse of my not getting of children and prayed them to give me their opinions and advice; and they freely and merrily did give me these ten among them. 1. Do not hug my wife too hard nor too much. 2. Eat no late suppers. 3. Drink Juyce of sage. 4. Tent and toast. 5. Wear cool Holland-drawers. 6. Keep stomach warm and back cool. 7. Upon my query whether it was best to do at night or morn, they answered me neither one nor other, but when we have most mind to it. 8. Wife not to go too strait-laced. 9. Myself to drink Mum and sugar. 10. Mrs Ward did give me to change my plat. The 3rd, 4th, 6th, 7th, and 10th they all did seriously declare and lay much stress upon them, as rules fit to be observed indeed, and especially the last: to lie with our heads where our heels do, or at least to make the bed high at feet and low at head. Very merry all, as much as I could be in such sorry company. Great discourse of the fray yesterday[2] in Moore-fields, how the Butchers at first did beat the Weavers (between whom there hath been ever an old competition for mastery), but at last the weavers rallied and beat them. At first the butchers knock down all for weavers that had green or blue aprons, till they were fain to pull them off and put them in their breeches. At last, the butchers were fain to pull off their sleeves, that they might not be known, and were soundly beaten out of the field, and some deeply wounded and bruised – till at last the weavers went out tryumph-ing, calling, "A hundred pound for a Butcher!" Toward [evening] I

---

1. To celebrate the christening of his daughter: see above, p. 403 (10 July).
2. St James's Day, a holiday.

to Mr. Reeves to see a Microscope, he having been with me today morning, and there chose one which I will have. Thence back and took up young Mrs. Harman, a pretty-bred and pretty-humored woman, whom I could love well, though not handsome, yet for her person and carriage and black eye. By the way met her husband going for her, and set them both down at home; and so home to my office a while, and so to supper and bed.

27. Up; and after some discourse with Mr. Duke, who is to be Secretary to the Fishery and is now Secretary to the Committee for Trade, who I find a very ingenious man, I went to Mr. Povys and there heard a little of his empty discourse; and fain he would have Mr. Gauden been the victualler for Tanger, which none but a fool would say to me, when he knows he hath made it his request to me to get him something of these men that now do it. Thence to St. James's; but Mr. Coventry being ill and in bed, I did not stay, but to Whitehall a little, walked up and down, and so home to fit papers against the afternoon. And after dinner to the Change a little and then to Whitehall, where anon the Duke of Yorke came and a Committee we had of Tanger; where I read over my rough draft of the contract for Tanger Victualling and acquainted them with the death of Mr. Alsopp, which Mr. Lanyon had told me this morning – which is a sad consideration, to see how uncertain a thing our lives are and how little to be presumed of in our greatest undertakings. The words of the contract approved of, and I home; and there came Mr. Lanyon to me and brought my neighbour Mr. Andrews to me, whom he proposes for his partener in the room of Mr. Alsopp; and I like well enough of it. We read over the contract together and discoursed it well over, and so parted; and I am glad to see it once over in this condition again, for Mr. Lanyon and I had some discourse today about my share in it; and I hope, if it goes on, to have my first hopes of 300*l* per annum. They gone, I to supper and to bed. This afternoon came my great store of Coles in, being ten Chaldron, so that I may see how long they will last me.

28. At the office all the morning. Dined, after Change, at home, and then abroad and seeing *The Bondman* upon the posts, I consulted my oaths and find I may go safely this time without breaking it; I went thither, notwithstanding my great desire to have gone to Fleete ally, God forgive me, again. There I saw it acted; it is true, for want of practice they had many of them forgot their parts a

little, but Baterton and my poor Ianthe out-do all the world. There is nothing more taking in the world with me then that play.

My present posture is this. My wife in the country and my maid Besse with her, and all quiet there. I am endeavouring to find a Woman for her to my mind; and above all, one that understands musique, especially singing. I am the willinger to keep one because I am in good hopes to get 2 or 300*l* per annum extraordinary by the business of the victualing of Tanger. I am pretty well in health; only, subject to wind upon any cold, and then immediate and great pains. All our discourse is of a Dutch war; and I find it is likely to come to it, for they are very high and desire not to compliment us at all as far as I hear, but to send a good fleet to Guinny to oppose us there. My Lord Sandwich newly gone to sea, and I, I think, fallen into his very good opinion again; at least, he did before his going, and by his letter since, show me all manner of respect and confidence. I am over-Joyed in hopes that upon this month's account I shall find myself worth 1000*l*, besides the rich present of two silver and gilt flagons which Mr. Gauden did give me the other day. I do now live very prettily at home, being most seriously, quietly, and neatly served by my two maids, Jane and the girl Su – with both of whom I am mightily well pleased. My greatest trouble is the settling of Brampton estate, that I may know what to expect and how to be able to leave it when I die, so as to be just to my promise to my Uncle Tho. and his son. The next thing is this cursed trouble my Brother Tom is likely to put us to by his death, forcing us to law with his Creditors, among others Dr. Tom Pepys, and that with some shame, as trouble. And the last, how to know in what manner, as to saving or spending, my father lives, lest they should run me in debt as one of my uncles executors, and I never the wiser nor better for it. But in all this I hope shortly to be at leisure to consider and inform myself well.

## –⚜AUGUST⚜–

2. To the King's playhouse and there saw *Bartholomew fayre*, which doth still please me and is, as it is acted, the best comedy in the world I believe. I chanced to sit by Tom Killigrew – who tells me that he is setting up a Nursery; that is, is going to build a house in Moorefields wherein he will have common plays acted. But four

operas* it shall have in the year, to act six weeks at a time – where we shall have the best Scenes and Machines, the best Musique, and everything as Magnificent as is in Christendome; and to that end hath sent for voices and painters and other persons from Italy.

3. Up betimes and set some Joyners on work to new lay my floor in our Wardrobe, which I intend to make a room for Musique. Thence abroad to Westminster; among other things, to Mr. Blagrave's and there have his consent for his kinswoman to come to be with my wife for her woman; at which I am well pleased – and hope she may do well.

4. Up betimes and to the office, fitting myself against a great dispute about the East India Company, which spent afterward with us all the morning. At noon dined with Sir W. Pen, a piece of beef only, and I counterfeited a friendship and mirth which I cannot have with him. Yet out with him by his coach, and he did carry me to a play and pay for me at the King's house, which is *The Rivall Ladys*, a very innocent and most pretty witty play – I was much pleased with it; and it being given me, I look upon it as no breach to my oath. Here we hear that Clun, one of their best actors, was the last night, going out of towne (after he had acted *The Alchymist*, wherein was one of his best parts that he acts) to his country house, was set upon and murdered; one of the rogues taken, an Irish fellow. It seems, most cruelly butchered and bound – the house will have a great miss of him.

5–6. Up very betimes and set my plasterer to work about whiting and colouring my Musique roome; which having with great pleasure seen done, about 10 a-clock I dressed myself, and so mounted upon a very pretty Mare, sent me by Sir W. Warren according to his promise yesterday – and so through the City, not a little proud, God knows, to be seen upon so pretty a beast; and to my Cosen W. Joyces, who presently mounted too, and he and I out of town toward Highgate, in the way, at Kentish towne, showing me the place and manner of Cluns being killed and laid in a ditch; and yet was not killed by any wounds, having only one in his arm, but bled to death through his strugling. He told me also the manner of it – of his going home so late, drinking with his whore – and manner of having it found out. Thence forward to Barnett and there drank, and so by night to Stevenige, it raining a little but not much; and there to my great trouble find that my wife was not come, nor any Stamford coach gone down this week, so that she cannot come. So, vexed and weary and not thoroughly out of pain neither in my old parts – I after supper to bed. And after a little sleep, W. Joyce comes in his shirt to my chamber, with a note and a messenger from my wife that she was come by Yorke coach to Bigglesworth, and would be with us tomorrow morning. So, I mightily pleased at her discreet action in this business, I with peace to sleep again till next morning. So up; and W. Joyce and I to a game at Bowles on the green there – till 8 a-clock; and then comes my wife in the coach, and a coach full of women. So, very joyful, drank there, not lighting; and we mounted and away with them to Welling, and there light and dined very well, and merry and glad to see my poor wife.

7. *Lords day*. Lay long, caressing my wife and talking – she telling me sad stories of the ill, improvident, disquiet, and sluttish manner that my father and mother and Pall live in the country; which troubles me mightily and I must seek to remedy it. So up and ready – and my wife also; and then down and I showed my wife, to her great admiration and joy, Mr. Gaudens present of plate, the two Flaggons; which endeed are so noble that I hardly can think that they are yet mine. So blessing God for it, we down to dinner, mighty pleasant; and so up after dinner for a while and I then to Whitehall; walked thither – having at home met with a letter of Capt. Cooke's, with which he had sent a boy for me to see, whom he did intend to recommend to me. I therefore went, and there met and spoke with him. He gives me great hopes of the boy, which pleases me; and at Chappell I there met Mr. Blagrave, who gives a report of the boy; and he showed me him and I spoke to him, and the boy seems a good willing boy to come to me, and I hope will do well.[1] So I walked homeward and met with Mr. Spong; and he with me as far as the Old Exchange, talking of many ingenuous things, Musique, and at last of Glasses, and I find him still the same ingenuous man that ever he was; and doth, among other fine things, tell me that by his Microscope of his own making he doth discover that the wings of a Moth is made just as the feathers of the wing of a bird, and that most plainly and certainly. While we were talking, came by several poor creatures, carried by by Constables

1. This was Tom Edwards, who became a favourite servant and married the Pepyses' beloved maid Jane Birch.

for being at a conventicle. They go like lambs, without any resistance. I would to God they would either conform, or be more wise and not be ketched. Thence parted with him, mightily pleased with his company, and away homeward, calling at Dan Rawlinson and supped there with my Uncle Wight; and then home and eat again for form sake with her, and then to prayers and to bed.

10. Up; and being ready, abroad to do several small businesses; among others, to find out one to engrave my tables upon my new sliding-Rule with silver plates, it being so small that Browne that made it cannot get one to do it. So I found out Cocker, the famous writing master, and got him to do it; and I sat an hour by him to see him design it all, and strange it is to see him with his natural eyes to cut so small at his first designing it, and read it all over without any missing, when for my life I could not with my best skill read one word or letter of it – but it is use; but he says that the best light, for his life, to do a very small thing by (contrary to Chaucer's words to the sun: that he should lend his light to them that small seals grave), it should be by an artificiall light of a candle, set to advantage as he could do it. I find the fellow, by his discourse, very ingenuous; and among other things, a great admirer and well read in all our English poets and undertakes to judge of them all, and that not impertinently. Well pleased with his company and better with his beginning upon my Rule, I left him and home; whither Mr. Deane by agreement came to me and dined with me, and by chance Gunner Batters's wife. Thence I to Cockers again and sat by him, with good discourse again for an hour or two; and then left him and by agreement with Capt. Sylas Taylor (my old acquaintance at the Exchequer) to the post-office to hear some Instrument Musique of Mr. Berchenshaws before my Lord Brunkard and Sir Rob. Murrey. I must confess, whether it be that I hear it but seldom, or that really voices is better, but so it is, that I found no pleasure at all in it, and methought two voyces were worth twenty of it. So home to my office a while, and then to supper and to bed.

12. Up, and all the morning busy at the office with Sir W. Warren about a great contract for New England Masts; wherein I was very hard with him, even to the making him angry. But I thought it fit to do it, as well as just for me on the King's behalf. At noon to the Change a little; and so to dinner and then out by coach, setting my wife and maid down, going to Stevens the Silversmith's to change

some old silver lace and to go buy new silk lace for a petticoat. I to Whitehall and did much business at a Tanger committee – where among other things, speaking about propriety of the houses there and how we ought to let the portugeses have right done them, as many of them as continue or did sell the houses while they were in possession – and something further in their favour – the Duke (in an anger I never observed in him before) did cry, says he, "All the world rides us, and I think we shall never ride anybody." Thence home; and though late, yet Pedro being there he sang a song and parted; I did give him 5s., but find it burdensome and so will break up the meeting.

13. Up; and before I went to the office comes my Taylor with a coat I have made to wear within doors, purposely to come no lower then my knees; for by my wearing a gown within doors comes all my tenderness about my legs. There comes also Mr. Reeve with a Microscope and Scotoscope; for the first I did give him 5l 10s., a great price; but a most curious bauble it is, and he says as good, nay, the best he knows in England, and he makes the best in the world. The other he gives me, and is of value; and a curious curiosity it is to [see] objects in a dark room with. Mightily pleased with this, I to the office, where all the morning. There, offered by Sir W. Penn his coach to go to Epsum and carry my wife, I stepped out and bade my wife make her ready; but being not very well, and other things advising me to the contrary, I did forbear going; and so Mr. Creed dining with me, I got him to give my wife and me a play this afternoon, lending him money to do it – which is a fallacy that I have found now once to avoid my vowe with, but never to be more practised I swear. And to the new play at the Dukes house, of *Henery the 5th* – a most noble play, writ by my Lord Orery; wherein Baterton, Harris, and Ianthes parts are most incomparably wrote and done, and the whole play the most full of heighth and raptures of wit and sense that ever I heard. Thence home and to my office; wrote by the post, and then to read a little in Dr. Powre's booke of discovery by the Microscope, to enable me a little how to use and what to expect from my glasse. So to supper and to bed.

15. Up, and with Sir J. Mennes by coach to St. James and there did our business with the Duke; who tells us more and more signs of a Dutch warr and how we must presently set out a fleet for Guinny – for the Dutch are doing so, and there I believe the war will

begin. Thence home with him again, in our way he talking of his cures abroad while he was with the King as a Doctor; and above all men, the pox. And among others, Sir J. Denham he told me he had cured after it was come to an ulcer all over his face to a miracle. By coach home, calling by the way at Charing cross and there saw the great Dutchman that is come over, under whose arm I went with my hat on and could not reach higher then his eyebrows with the tip of my fingers, reaching as high as I could. He is a comely and well-made man, and his wife a very little but pretty comely Dutch woman. It is true he wears pretty high-heeled shoes, but not very high, and doth generally wear a Turbant, which makes him show yet taller then he really is, though he is very tall as I have said before. Home to my office, and then to supper, and then to my office again late, and so home to bed.

16. Wakened about 2 a-clock this morning with the noise of Thunder, which lasted for an hour; with such continued Lightenings, not flashes but flames, that all the sky and ayre was light; and that for a great while, not a minute's space between new flames all the time; such a thing as I never did see, nor could have believed had ever been in nature. And being put into a great sweat with it, could not sleep till all was over – and that accompanied with such a storm of rain as I never heard in my life. I expected to find my house in the morning overflowed with the rain breaking in, and that much hurt must needs have been done in the City with this lightening; but I find not one drop of rain in my house, nor any news of hurt done. But it seems it hath been here and all up and down the counties hereabouts, the like tempest – Sir W. Batten saying much of the greatness thereof at Epsum.

17. To my Lord Crews and there with him a good while; before dinner talked of the Duch war and find that he doth much doubt that we shall fall into it without the money or consent of Parliament that is expected, or the reason for it that is fit to have for every war. So to Capt. Cookes but he was not at home; but I there spoke with my boy Tom Edwards and directed him to go to Mr. Townsend (with whom I was in the morning) to have measure taken of his clothes to be made him there out of the Wardrobe – which will be so done, and then I think he will come to me. Thence to Whitehall; and after long staying, there was no committee of the Fishery as was expected. Here I walked long with Mr. Pierce, who tells me the

King doth still sup every night with my Lady Castlemayne, who he believes hath lately slunk a great belly away, for from very big she is come to be down again. Thence to Mrs. Pierces and with her and my wife to see Mrs. Clarke; where with him and her very merry, discoursing of the late play of *Henery the 5th* – which they conclude the best that ever was made. I am mightily pleased with [Dr. Clarke] for he is the only man I know that I would learn to pronounce by, which he doth the best that ever I heard any man. Thence home and to the office late; and so to supper and to bed.

19.   At noon dined at home; and after dinner my wife and I to Sir W. Penn's to see his Lady the first time – who is a well-looked, fat, short, old Dutchwoman, but one that hath been heretofore pretty handsome; and is now very discreet and I believe hath more wit then her husband. Here we stayed talking a good while. And very well pleased I was with the old woman at first visit. So away home, and I to my office; my wife to go see my aunt Wight, newly come to town. Creed came to me and he and I out; among other things, to look out a man to make a case for to keep my Stone that I was cut of in. And he to buy Daniels *History*; which he did, but I missed of my end. So parted upon Ludgate hill and I home and to the office, where busy till supper; and home to supper to a good dish of fritters, which I bespoke and were done much to my mind; then to the office a while again, and so home to bed.

23.   Lay long, talking with my wife and angry a while about her desiring to have a French maid all of a sudden; which I took to arise from yesterday's being with her mother. But that went over, and friends again; and so she be well qualitied, I care not much whether she be French or no, so a protestant. Thence to the office; and at noon to the Change, where very busy getting ships for Guiny and for Tanger. So home to dinner; and then abroad all the afternoon, doing several errands to comply with my oath of ending many businesses before Bartholomew day, which is two days hence. Among others, I went into New Bridewell in my way to Mr. Cole, and is very handsome, several at work. And among others, one pretty whore brought in last night, which works very lazily. I did give them 6*d.* to drink, and so away – to Grayes Inn, but missed Mr. Cole and so homeward; called at Harman's and there bespoke some chairs for a room. And so home and busy late; and then to supper and to bed. The Dutch East India fleet are now come home safe,

which we are sorry for. Our fleets on both sides are hastening out to Guinny.

26. This day my wife tells me Mr. Pen, Sir Wms son, is come back from France and came to visit her – a most modish person, grown, she says, a fine gentleman.[1]

27. Up and to the office, where all the morning. At noon to the Change and there almost made my bargain about a ship for Tanger, which will bring me in a little profit with Capt. Taylor. Off the Change with Mr Cutler and Sir W. Rider to Cutlers house; and there had a very good dinner, and two or three pretty young ladies of their relations there. Thence to my Case-maker for my Stone case; and had it to my mind, and cost me 24s. – which is a great deal of money, but it is well done and pleases me. So doing some other small errands, I home and there find my boy Tom Edwards come – sent me by Capt. Cooke, having [been] bred in the King's chapel these four years. I purpose to make a clerk of him; and if he deserves well, to do well by him. Spent much of the afternoon to set his chamber in order; and then to the office, leaving him at home. And late at night, after all business was done, I called Will and told him my reason of taking a boy, and that it is of necessity, not out of any unkindness to him, nor should be to his injury. And then talked about his landlord's daughter[2] to come to my wife, and I think it will be. So home and find my boy a very schooleboy that talks inocently and impertinently; but at present it is a sport to us, and in a little time he will leave it. So sent him to bed, he saying that he used to go to bed at 8 a-clock. And then all of us to bed, myself pretty well pleased with my choice of a boy. All the news this day is that the Dutch are with 22 sail of ships of warr crewsing up and down about Ostend; at which we are alarmed. My Lord Sandwich is come back into the Downes with only eight sail, which is or may be a prey to the Dutch, if they knew our weakness and inability to set out any more speedily.

28. *Lords day.* Up, and with my boy alone to church – the first time I have had anybody to attend me to church a great while. Home to dinner and there met Creed; who dined, and we merry

1. This was William Penn, later the famous Quaker.
2. Mary Mercer.

together, as his learning is such and judgment that I cannot but be pleased with it. After dinner I took him to church into our gallery with me, but slept the best part of the sermon, which was a most silly one. So he and I to walk to the Change a while, talking from one pleasant discourse to another; and so home, and thither came my Uncle Wight and aunt and supped with us, mighty merry. And Creed lay with us all night. So to bed – very merry to think how Mr. Holliard (who came in this evening to see me) makes nothing but proving as a most clear thing that Rome is antichrist.

29. Up betimes, intending to do business at my office, by 5 a-clock. After dinner I to Westminster to Jervas's a while; and so doing many errands by the way, and necessary ones, I home. And thither came the woman, with her mother, which our Will recommends to my wife. I like her well, and I think will please us. My wife and they agreed, and she is to come the next week – at which I am very well contented, for then I hope we shall be settled; but I must remember that never since I was housekeeper I ever lived so quietly, without any noise or one angry word almost, as I have done since my present maids, Besse, Jane and Susan, came and were together. Now I have taken a boy and am taking a woman, I pray God we may not be worse; but I will observe it. After being at my office a while – home to supper and to bed.

30. Up and to the office, where sat long; and at noon to dinner at home. After dinner comes Mr. Pen to visit me, and stayed an hour talking with me. I perceive something of learning he hath got, but a great deal, if not too much, of the vanity of the French garbe and affected manner of speech and gait – I fear all real profit he hath made of his travel will signify little. So he gone, I to my office and there very busy till late at night; and so home to supper and to bed.

31. Up by 5 a-clock and to my office, where T. Hater and Will met me; and so we despatch a great deal of my business as to the ordering my papers and books, which were behindhand. All the morning very busy at my office. At noon home to dinner and there my wife hath got me some pretty good oysters, which is very soon, and the soonest I think I ever eat any. After dinner I up to hear my boy play upon a lute which I have this day borrowed of Mr. Hunt; and endeed, the boy would with little practice play very well upon the Lute – which pleases me well. So by coach to the Tanger

Committee, and there have another small business, by which I may get a little small matter of money. Stayed but little there; and so home and to my office very late, casting up my month's accounts; and blessed be God, find myself worth 1020*l* – which is still the most I ever was worth. So home and to bed.

## SEPTEMBER

2. Up very betimes and walked (my boy with me) to Mr. Coles, and after long waiting below, he being under the barber's hands, I spoke with him and he did give me much hopes of getting my debt that my brother owed me, and also that things would go well with my father. Walked home, doing very many errands by the way, to my great content. And at the Change met and spoke with several persons about serving us with pieces-of-eight at Tanger. So home to dinner above stairs, my wife not being well of those in bed – I dined by her bedside. But I got her to rise, and abroad with me by coach to Bartholomew Fayre, and our boy with us, and there showed them and myself the dancing on the ropes and several other the best shows. But pretty it is, to see how our boy carries himself, so innocently clownish as would make one laugh. Here till late and dark. Then up and down to buy combes for my wife to give her maids; and then by coach home and there at the office set down my day's work; and then home to bed.

3. I have had a bad night's rest tonight, not sleeping well, as my wife observed, and once or twice she did wake me; and I thought myself to be mightily bit with fleas, and in the morning she chid her maids for not looking the fleas a-days. But when I rise, I find that it is only the change of the weather from hot to cold, which (as I was two winters ago) doth stop my pores, and so my blood tingles and iches all day all over my body and so continued to do, all the day long just as I was then; and if it continues to be so cold, I fear I must come to the same pass. But sweating cured me then, and I hope and am told will this also. At the office; sat all the morning. Dined at home; and after dinner to Whitehall to the Fishing Committee, but not above four of us met, which could do nothing; and a sad thing it is to see so great a work so ill fallowed – for at this pace it can come to nothing but disgrace to us all. Broke up and did nothing. So I

walked to Westminster, and there at my barber's had good luck to find Jane alone; and there I talked with her and got the poor wretch to promise to meet me in the abbey on tomorrow come sennit, telling me that her maister and mistress have a mind to get her a husband, and so will not let her go abroad without them – but only in sermon time a-Sundays she doth go out. I would I could get a good husband for her, for she is one I alway thought a good-natured as well as a well-looked girl.

4. *Lords day*. Lay long in bed; then up and took physique, Mr. Hollyard['s]. But it being cold weather and myself negligent of myself, I fear I took cold and stopped the working of it. But I feel myself pretty well. All the morning looking over my old wardrobe and laying by things for my brother John and my father, by which I shall leave myself very bare in clothes, but yet as much as I need and the rest would but spoil in the keeping. Dined, my wife and I, very well. All the afternoon my wife and I above, and then the boy and I to singing of psalms, and then came in Mr. Hill and he sung with us a while; and he being gone, the boy and I again to the singing of Mr. Porter's mottets, and it is a great joy to me that I am come to this condition, to maintain a person in the house able to give me such pleasure as this boy doth by his thorough understand of music, as he sing anything at first sight. Mr. Hill came to tell me that he had got a gentlewoman for my wife, one Mrs. Ferrabosco, that sings most admirably. I seemed glad of it; but I hear she is too gallant for me and am not sorry that I misse her. Then I to the office, setting some papers right; and so home to supper and to bed – after prayers.

5. Up and to St. James and there did our business with the Duke – where all our discourse of war, in the highest measure. Prince Robt. was with us – who is fitting himself to go to sea in the *Heneretta*. And afterward in Whitehall, I met him and Mr. Gray and he spoke to me; and in other discourse, says he, "God damn me, I can answer but for one ship, and in that I will do my part; for it is not in that as in [an] army, where a man can command everything." By and by to a committee for the Fishery, the Duke of Yorke there – where after Duke was made Secretary, we fell to name a committee; whereof I was willing to be one because I would have my hand in that business, to understand it and be known in doing something in it. And so after cutting out work for that committee, we ris; and I to my wife to Unthankes, and with her from shop to shop, laying out

near 10*l* this morning in clothes for her. And so I to the Change, where a while, and so home and to dinner, and thither came W. Bowyer and dined with us; but strange to see how he could not endure onyons in sauce to lamb, but was overcome with the sight of it and so was forced to make his dinner of an egg or two. He tells us how Mrs. Lane is undone by her marrying so bad, and desires to speak with me; which I know is wholly to get me to do something for her to get her husband a place which he is in no wise fit for. After dinner I down to Woolwich with a galley, and then to Deptford and so home – all the way reading Sir J. Suck[l]ings *Aglaura*, which methinks is but a mean play – nothing of design in it.

6.    Up and to the office, where we sat all the morning. At noon home to dinner. Then to my office and there waited, thinking to have had Baggwell's wife come to me about business, that I might have talked with her; but she came not. So I to Whitehall by coach with Mr. Andrews; and there I got his contract for the victualling of Tanger signed and sealed by us there. So that all that business is well over, and I hope to have made a good business of it – and to receive 100*l* by it the next week – for which God be praised. Thence to W. Joyces and Anthonys to invite them to dinner to meet my aunt James at my house. So home, having called upon Doll, our pretty Change woman, for a pair of gloves trimmed with yellow ribbon (to [the] petticoat she bought yesterday), which costs me 20*s*. But she is so pretty, that, God forgive me, I could not think it too much; which is a strange slavery that I stand in to beauty, that I value nothing near it. So going home and my coach stopping in Newgate market over against a poulterer's shop, I took occasion to buy a rabbit; but it proved a deadly old one when I came to eat it – as I did do after an hour's being at my office; and after supper, again there till past 11 at night. And so home and to bed. This day, Mr. Coventry did tell us how the Duke did receive the Dutch Embassador the other day – by telling him that whereas they think us in Jest, he believes that the Prince (Rupert), which goes in this fleet to guinny, will soon tell them that we are in earnest; and that he himself will do the like here in the head of fleet here at home. And that for the *Meschants*,[1] which he told the Duke there were in England which did hope to do themselfs good by the King's being at war, says he, "the English have ever united all this private

1. Miscreants, sc. Puritan fanatics.

differences to attend Forraigne," and that Cromwell, notwith-standing the *Meschants* in his time (which were the Cavaliers), he did never find them interrupt him in his foreign businesses. And that he did not doubt but to live to see the Dutch as fearful of provoking the English under the government of a King, as he remembers them to have been under that of a Coquin. I writ all this story to my Lord Sandwich tonight into the Downes, it being very good and true, word for word from Mr. Coventry today.

7. Lay long today, pleasantly discoursing with my wife about the dinner we are to have for the Joyces a day or two hence. Then up and with Mr. Margetts to Limehouse to see his ground and ropeyard there; which is very fine, and I believe we shall imploy it for the Navy – for the King's grounds are not sufficient to supply our dispense if a warr comes. Thence back to the Change – where great talk of the forwardness of the Dutch; which puts us all to a stand, and perticularly myself for my Lord Sandwich, to think him to lie where he is for a Sacrifice if they should begin with us. So home and Creed with me, and to dinner; and after dinner, I out to my office, taking in Bagwells wife, who I knew waited for me; but company came to me so soon, that I could have no discourse with her as I intended, of pleasure. So anon abroad with Creed; walked to Bartholomew fayre, this being the last day, and there saw the best dancing on the ropes that I think I ever saw in my life – and so all say. And so by coach home – where I find my wife hath had her head dressed by her woman Mercer, which is to come to her tomorrow; but my wife being to go to a christening tomorrow, she came to do her head up tonight. So a while to my office, and then to supper and to bed.

9. Up, and to put things in order against dinner, I out and bought some things; among others, a dozen of Silver Salts. Home and to the office, where some of us met a little; and then home and at noon comes my company – *viz.*, Anth. and Will Joyce and their wifes – my aunt James newly come out of Wales, and my Cosen Sarah Gyles – her husband did not come, and by her I did understand afterward that it was because he was not yet able to pay me the 40s. she had borrowed a year ago of me. I was as merry as I could, giving them a good dinner; but W. Joyce did so talk, that he made everybody else Dumb, but only laugh at him. I forgot, there was Mr. Harman and his wife. My aunt a very good harmelesse

woman. All their talk is of her and my two she-Cosen Joyces and Will's little boy Will (who was also here today) [going] down to Brampton to my father's next week – which will be trouble and charge to them; but however, my father and mother desire to see them, and so let them. They eyed mightily my great Cupboard of plate, I this day putting my two Flaggons upon my table; and endeed, it is a fine sight and better then ever I did hope to see of my own. Mercer dined with us at table, this being her first dinner in my house. After dinner left them and to Whitehall, where a small Tanger committee; and so back again home and there my wife and Mercer and Tom and I sat till 11 at night, singing and fiddling; and a great joy it is to see me maister of so much pleasure in my house, that it is, and will be still I hope, a constant pleasure to me to be at home. The girle plays pretty well upon the Harpsicon, but only ordinary tunes; but hath a good hand. Sings a little, but hath a good voyce and eare. My boy, a brave boy, sings finely and is the most pleasant boy at present, while his ignorant boy's tricks last, that ever I saw. So to supper, and with great pleasure to bed.

10.   Up and to my office, where we sat all the morning. And I much troubled to think what the end of our great sluggishness will be, for we do nothing in this office like people able to carry on a warr. We must be put out, or other people put in. Dined at home. And then my wife and I and Mercer to the Dukes house and there saw *The Rivalls*, which is no excellent play, but good action in it – especially, Gosnell comes and sings and dances finely; but for all that, fell out of the Key, so that the Musique could not play to her afterward; and so did Harris also, go out of the tune to agree with her. Thence home, and late writing letters; and this night I received by Will 105*l* – the first fruits of my endeavours in the late Contract for victualling of Tanger – for which God be praised. For I can with a safe conscience say that I have therein saved the King 5000*l* per annum, and yet got myself a hope of 300*l* per annum without the least wrong to the King. So to supper and to bed.

11.   *Lords day*. Up, and to church in the best manner I have gone a good while; that is to say, with my wife and her woman Mercer along with us and Thom my boy waiting on us. A dull sermon. Home; dined. Left my wife to go to church alone; and I walked in haste, being late, to the Abby at Westminster according to promise to meet Jane Welsh; and there wearily walked, expecting her till 6 a-

clock from 3. But no Jane came, which vexed me. Only, part of it I
spent with Mr. Blagrave walking in the Abbey, he telling me the
whole government and discipline of Whitehall chapel and the
caution now used against admitting any debauched persons – which
I was glad to hear, though he tells me there are persons bad enough.
Thence, going home, went by Gervas's; and there stood Jane at the
door, and so I took her in and drank with her, her maister and
mistress being out of door. She told me how she could not come to
me this afternoon, but promised another time. So I walked home,
contented with my speaking with her, and walked to my uncle
Wights, where they were all at supper; and among others, fair Mrs.
Margtt Wight, who endeed is very pretty. So after supper home to
prayers and to bed. This afternoon, it seems, Sir J. Minnes fell sick
at church; and going down the gallery stairs, fell down dead; but
came to himself again and is pretty well.

12.    Up, and to my Cosen Anth. Joyce's and there took leave of
my aunt James and both Cosens their wifes, who are this day going
down to my father's by coach. I did give my aunt xxs. to carry as a
token to my mother, and xs. to Pall. Thence by coach to St. James
and there did our business as usual with the Duke. And saw him
with great pleasure play with his little girle – like an ordinary
private father of a child.

16.    Up betimes and to my office, where all the morning very busy
putting papers to rights. And among other things, Mr. Gauden
coming to me, I had a good opportunity to speak to him about his
present, which hitherto hath been a burden to me, that I could not
do it, because I was doubtful that he meant it as a temptation to me
to stand by him in the business of Tangier victualling. But he clears
me it was not, and that he values me and my proceedings therein
very highly – being but what became me; and that what he did was
for my old kindnesses to him in despatching of his business – which
I was glad to hear; and with my heart in good rest and great joy,
parted and to my business again. At noon to the Change, where by
appointment I met Sir W. Warren; and afterward to the Sun tavern,
where he brought to me, being all alone, a 100l in a bag; which I
offered him to give him my receipt for, but he told me no, it was my
owne, which he had a little while since promised me and was glad
that (as I had told him two days since) it would now do me
courtesy. And so most kindly he did give it me, and I as joyfully,

even out of myself, carried it home in a coach – he himself expressly taking care that nobody might see this business done, though I was willing enough to have carried a servant with me to have received it; but he advised me to do it myself. So home with it and to dinner. After dinner, I forth with my boy to buy several things, Stooles and Andirons and candlesticks, &c., household stuff. And walked to the Mathematical instrument-maker in Moorefields and bought a large pair of compasses. And there met Mr. Pargiter, and he would needs have me to drink a cup of Horseredish ale, which he and a friend of his, troubled with the stone, have been drinking of – which we did, and then walked into the fields as far almost as Sir G. Whitmores, all the way talking of Russia – which he says is a sad place; and though Mosco is a very great city, yet it is, from the distance between house and house, and few people compared with this – and poor sorry houses, the Emperor himself living in a wooden house – his exercise only flying a hawke at pigeons and carrying pigeons ten or twelve mile off and then laying wagers which pigeon shall come soonest home to her house. All the winter within doors, some few playing at Chesse but most drinking their time away. Women live very slavishly there. And it seems, in the Emperor's Court no room hath above two or three windows, and those the greatest not a yard wide or high – for warmth in winter time. And that the general cure for all diseases there is their sweating-houses – or people that are poor, they get into their ovens, being heated, and there lie. Little learning among things of any sort – not a man that speaks Latin, unless the Secretary of State by chance. Mr. Pargiter and I walked to the Change together and there parted; and so I to buy more things and then home; and after a little at my office – home to supper and to bed.

18.   Last night it seems my aunt Wight did send my wife a new scarfe, laced, as a token for her many givings to her. It is true, now and then we give them small toys, as oranges, &c. – but my aime is to get myself something more from my uncles favour then this.

19.   I met with Dr. Pierce today; who speaking of Dr. Fraizer's being so earnest to have such a one (one Collins) go Chyrurgeon to the Princes person, and will have him go in his terms and with so much money put into his hands, he tells me (when I was wondering that Fraizer should order things with the Prince in that confident manner) that Fraizer is so great with my Lady Castlemayne and

Steward and all the ladies at Court, in helping to slip their calfes when there is occasion, and with the great men in curing of their claps, that he can do what he please with the King in spite of any man, and upon the same score with the Prince – they all having more or less occasion to make use of him. Sir G. Carteret tells me this afternoon that the Dutch are not yet ready to set out; and by that means do lose a good wind, which would carry them out and keep us in. And moreover, he says that they begin to bogle in the business, and he thinks may offer terms of peace for all this; and seems to argue that it will be well for the King too – and I pray God send it.

29. *Michaelmas day.* Up, and to the office, where all the morning. Dined at home and Creed with me. After dinner I to Sir G. Carteret, and with him to his new house he is taking in Broadstreete; and there surveyed all the rooms and bounds in order to the drawing up a lease thereof. And that done, Mr Cutler (his landlord) took me up and down and showed me all his ground and houses, which is extraordinary great, he having bought all the Augustin fryers; and many many a 1000*l* he hath and will bury there. So home to my business, clearing my papers and preparing my accounts against tomorrow for a monthly and a great Auditt. So to supper and to bed. Fresh newes came of our beating the Dutch at Guiny quite out of all their castles almost, which will make them quite mad here at home, sure. And Sir G. Carteret did tell me that the King doth joy mightily at it; but asked him, laughing, "But," says he, "how shall I do to answer this to the Embassador, when he comes?" Nay, they say that we have beat them out of the New Netherlands too – so that we have been doing them mischiefe a great while in several parts of the world, without public knowledge or reason. Their Fleete for Guinny is now, they say, ready and abroad, and will be going this week. Coming home tonight, I did go to examine my wife's house-accounts; and finding things that seemed somewhat doubtful, I was angry, though she did make it pretty plain; but confessed that when she doth misse a sum, she doth add something to other things to make it. And upon my being very angry, she doth protest she will here lay up something for herself to buy her a neckelace with – which madded me and doth still trouble me, for I fear she will forget by degrees the way of living cheap and under a sense of want.

30. Up, and all day, both morning and afternoon, at my accounts, it being a great month both for profit and layings-out – the last being 89*l* – for kitchen, and clothes for myself and wife, and a few extraordinaries for the house. And my profits, besides salary, 239*l*. So that I have this week, notwithstanding great layings-out (and preparations for laying-out, which I make as paid this month), my balance doth come to 1203*l* – for which the Lord's name be praised.

# –✣OCTOBER✣–

1. Up and at the office both forenoon and afternoon, very busy, and with great pleasure in being so. This morning, Mrs. Lane (now Martin) like a foolish woman came to the Hors shoo hard by, and sent for me while I was at the office to come to speak with her, by a note sealed up – I know, to get me to do something for her husband; but I sent her an answer that I would see her at Westminster. And so I did not go, and she went away, poor soul. At night home to supper, weary and my eyes sore with writing and reading – and to bed. We go now on with great Vigour in preparing against the Dutch, who they say will now fall upon us without doubt, upon this high news come of our beating them so wholly in Guiny.

2. *Lords day.* My wife not being well to go to church, I walked with my boy through the City, putting in at several churches; among others, at Bishopsgate, and there saw the picture usually put before the King's book, put up in the church; but very ill painted, though it were a pretty piece to set up in a church. I entended to have seen the Quakers, who they say do meet every Lord's day at the Mouth at Bishopsgate; but I could see none stirring, nor was it fit to ask for the place. So I walked over Moorefields, and thence to Clerkenwell church and there (as I wished) sat next pew to the fair Butler, who endeed is a most perfect beauty still. And one I do very much admire myself for my choice of her for a beauty – she having the best lower part of her face that ever I saw all days of my life. After church I walked to my Lady Sandwiches through my Lord Southamptons new buildings in the fields behind Grays Inn; and endeed they are very great and a noble work. So I dined with my Lady; and the same innocent discourse that we used to have. Only, after dinner, being alone, she asked me my opinion about Creed,

whether he would have a wife or no and what he was worth, and proposed Mrs. Wright for him; which she says she heard he was once enquiring after. She desired I would take a good time and manner of proposing it; and I said I would, though I believed he would love nothing but money, and much was not to be expected there she said. So away back to Clerkenwell church, thinking to have got sight of la belle Boteler again, but failed; and so after church walked all over the fields home; and there my wife was angry with me for not coming home and for gadding abroad to look after beauties, she told me plainly; so I made all peace, and to supper. This evening came Mrs. Lane (now Martin) with her husband to desire my help about a place for him; it seems poor Mr. Daniel is dead, of the Victualling Office – a place too good for this puppy to fallow him in – but I did give him the best words I could; and so after drinking a glass of wine, sent them going, but with great kindness. So to supper, prayers, and to bed.

3.   Up. With Sir J. Mennes by coach to St. James's, and there all the news now of very hot preparations for the Dutch; and being with the Duke, he told us he was resolved to make a Tripp himself, and that Sir W. Pen should go in the same ship – which honour, God forgive me, I could grudge him for his knavery and dissimulation, though I do not envy much the having the same place myself. Talk also of great haste in the getting out another fleet and building some ships; and now it is likely we have put one another, by each other's dalliance, past a retreat. Thence, with our heads full of business, we broke up, and I to my barbers and there only saw Jane and stroked her under the chin; and away to the Exchange and there long about several businesses, hoping to get money by them. And thence home to dinner and there found Hawly. But meeting Bagwell's wife at the office before I went home, I took her into the office and there kissed her only. She rebuked me for doing it; saying, that did I do so much to many bodies else, it would be a stain to me. But I do not see but she takes it well enough; though in the main, I believe she is very honest. So after some kind discourse, we parted, and I home to dinner; and after dinner down to Deptford, where I found Mr. Coventry; and there we made an experiment of Hollands and our Cordage and ours out-did it a great deal, as my book of observations tells perticularly. Here we were late. And so home together by water; and I to my office, where late putting things in order.

4. Up, and to the office, where we sat all the morning. And this morning Sir W. Pen went to Chatham to look after the ships now going out thence – and perticularly that wherein the Duke and himself goes. He took Sir G. Ascue with him, whom I believe he hath brought into play. At noon to the Change; and thence home, where I find my aunt James and the two she-Joyces. They dined and were merry with us. Thence after dinner to a play, to see *The Generall*; which is so dull and so ill acted, that I think it is the worst I ever saw or heard in all my days. I happened to sit next to Sir Ch. Sidly; who I find a very witty man, and did at every line take notice of the dullness of the poet and badness of the action, and that most pertinently; which I was mightily taken with – and among others, where by Altemira's command Clarimont the Generall is commanded to rescue his Rivall whom she loved, Lucidor, he after a great deal of demurre breaks out – "Well – Ile save my Rivall and make her confess. That I deserve, while he doth but possesse." "Why, what! Pox!" says Sir Ch. Sydly, "would he have him have more, or what is there more to be had of a woman then the possessing her?" Thence, setting all them at home, I home with my wife and Mercer, vexed at my losing my time and above 20*s*. in money and neglecting my business to see so bad a play. Tomorrow, they told us, should be acted, or the day after, a new play called *The Parsons Dreame*, acted all by women. So to my office and there did business; and so home to supper and to bed.

5. Up betimes and to my office. And thence by coach to New Bridewell to meet with Mr. Poyntz to discourse with him (being master of the workhouse there) about making of Bewpers for us – but he was not within. However, his clerk did lead me up and down through all the houses. And there I did with great pleasure see the many pretty works and the little children imployed, everyone to do something; which was a very fine sight and worthy incouragement. I cast away a Crowne among them, and so to the Change – and among the Linnen wholesale Drapers to enquire about Callicos, to see what can be done with them for the supplying our want of Bewpers for flags. And I think I shall do something therein to good purpose for the King. So to the Coffee-house and there fell in discourse with the Secretary of the Virtuosi of Gresham College, and had very fine discourse with him. He tells me of a new-invented Instrument to be tried before the College anon, and I intend to see it. So to Trinity house, and there I dined among the old dull fellows.

And so home – and to my office a while; and then comes Mr. Cocker to see me and I discoursed with him about his writing and ability of sight, and how I shall do to get some glass or other to help my eyes by Candlelight; and he tells me he will bring me the helps he hath within a day or two, and show me what he doth. Thence to the Musique-meeting at the post office, where I was once before. And thither anon come all the Gresham College and a great deal of noble company. And the new instrument was brought, called the Arched Viall – where, being tuned with Lutestrings and played on with Kees like an Organ – a piece of Parchment is always kept moving; and the strings, which by the keys are pressed down upon it, are grated, in imitation of a bow, by the parchment; and so it is intended to resemble several vyalls played on with one bow – but so basely and harshly, that it will never do. But after three hours' stay, it could not be Fixt in tune; and so they were fain to go to some other Musique of instruments, which I am grown quite out of love with; and so I, after some good discourse with Mr. Spong, Hill, Grant, Dr. Whisler, and others by turns, I home to my office and there late; and so home – where I understand my wife hath spoke to Jane and ended matters of difference between her and her, and she stays with us; which I am glad of, for her fault is nothing but sleepiness and forgetfulness; otherwise, a good-natured, quiet, well-meaning, honest servant, and one that will do as she is bid, so one called upon her and will see her do it. This morning by 3 a-clock, the Prince and King, and Duke with him, went down the River; and the Prince under sail the next tide after, and so is gone from the Hope. God give him better success then he used to have.

7. Lay pretty while, with some discontent, abed, even to the having bad words with my wife, and blows too, about the ill serving-up of our victuals yesterday; but all ended in love. And so I rose and to my office, busy all the morning. At noon dined at home, and then to my office again; and then abroad to look after Callicos for Flaggs, and hope to get a small matter by my pains therein and yet save the King a great deal of money. And so home to my office; and there came Mr. Cocker and brought me a Globe of glasse and a frame of oyled paper (as I desired), to show me the manner of his gaining light to grave by and to lessen the glaringnesse of it at pleasure, by an oyled paper. This I bought of him, giving him a Crowne for it; and so, well satisfied, he went away and I to my business again; and so home to supper, prayers, and to bed.

9.  *Lords day*. Lay pretty long; but however, up time enough with my wife to go to church. Then home to dinner; and Mr. Fuller (my Cambridge acquaintance) coming to me about what he was with me lately, to release a waterman, he told me he was to preach at Barking church; and so I to hear him, and he preached well and neatly. Thence, it being time enough, to our own church; and there stood privately at the great doore to gaze upon a pretty lady and from church dogged her home, whither she went to a house near Tower hill; and I think her to be one of the prettiest women I ever saw. So home and at my office a while, busy; then to my Uncle Wights, whither it seems my wife went after sermon, and there supped; but my aunt and uncle in a very ill humour one with another, but I made shift with much ado to keep them from scolding; and so after supper, home – and to bed without prayers, it being cold and tomorrow washing-day.

10.  This day by the blessing of God, my wife and I have been married nine years[1] – but my head being full of business, I did not think of it, to keep it in any extraordinary manner. But bless God for our long lives and loves and health together, which the same God long continue, I wish from my very heart.

13.  After being at the office all the morning, I home and dined; and taking leave of my wife, with my mind not a little troubled how she would look after herself or house in my absence, especially too, leaving a considerable sum of money in the office, I by coach to the Red Lyon in Aldersgate Streete and there by agreement met W. Joyce and Tom Trice, and mounted – I upon a very fine mare that Sir W. Warren helps me to. And so very merrily rode till it was very dark, I leading the way through the dark to Welling; and there, not being very weary, to supper and to bed – but very bad accomoda-tion at the Swan. In this day's Journy I met with Mr. White, Cromwells Chaplin that was, and had a great deal of discourse with him. Among others, he tells me that Richard [Cromwell] is and hath long been in France, and is now going into Italy – he owns publicly that he doth correspond and return him all his money. That Richard hath been in some straits at the beginning, but relieved by his friends. That he goes by another name, but doth not disguise himself nor deny himself to any man that challenges him.

1. See above, p. 159 (10 October) & n.

432

He tells me for certain, that offers had been made to the old man[1] of marriage between the King and his daughter, to have obliged him; but he would not. He thinks (with me) that it never was in his power to bring in the King with the consent of any of his officers about him. And that he scorned to bring him in as Monke did, to secure himself and deliver everybody else. When I told him of what I found writ in a French book of one Monsieur Sorbiere, that gives an account of his observations here in England – among other things, he says that it is reported that Cromwell did in his life-time transpose many of the bodies of the kings of England from one grave to another, and that by that means it is not known certainly whether the head that is now set up upon a post be that of Cromwell or of one of the kings – Mr. White tells me that he believes he never had so poor a low thought in him to trouble himself about. He says the hand of God is much to be seen; that all his children are in good condition enough as to estate, and that their relations that betrayed their family are all now either hanged or very miserable.

14. Up by break of day and got to Brampton by 3 [*sic.*] a-clock – where my father and mother overjoyed to see me – my mother ready to weep every time she looked upon me. After dinner my father and I to the Court and there did all our business to my mind, as I have set down in a paper perticularly expressing our proceedings at this Court. So home, where W. Joyce full of talk and pleased with his journey. And after supper, I to bed and left my father, mother and him laughing.

15. My father and I up and walked alone to Hinchingbrooke; and among the other late chargeable works that my Lord hath done there, we saw his waterworks and the *Ora*, which is very fine – and so is the house all over. But I am sorry to think of the money at this time spent therein. Back to my father's (Mr. Sheply being out of town) and there breakfasted, after making an end with Barton about his businesses. And then my mother called me into the garden and there, but all to no purpose, desiring me to be friends with John; but I told her I cannot, nor endeed easily shall; which afflicted the poor woman, but I cannot help it. Then taking leave, W. Joyce and I set out, calling T. Trice at Bugden; and thence got by night to Stevenage and there mighty merry, though I in bed more

1. Oliver Cromwell.

weary then the other two days, which I think proceeded from our galloping so much – my other weariness being almost all over. But I find that a coney-skin in my breeches preserves me perfectly from galling – and that eating after I come to my Inne, without drinking, doth keep me from being stomach-sick; which drink doth presently make me. We lay all in several beds in the same room; and W. Joyce full of his impertinent tricks and talk, which then made us merry, as any other fool would have done. So to sleep.

16.   *Lords day.* It raining, we set out; and about 9 a-clock got to Hatfield in church-time, and I light and saw my simple Lord Salsbury sit there in his gallery. Stayed not in the church; but thence mounted again, and to Barnett by the end of sermon and there dined at the Red Lyon. Very weary again, but all my weariness yesterday night and today in my thighs only, the rest of my weariness in my shoulders and arms being quite gone. Thence home, parting company at my Cosen Anth. Joyces by 4 a-clock. Weary, but very well, to bed at home, where I find all well. Anon my wife came to bed; but for my ease rose again and lay with her woman.

18.   Up and to the office; where among other things, we made a very great contract with Sir W. Warren for 3000 load of Timber. At noon dined at home. In the afternoon to the Fishery. Thence I with Mr. Gray in his coach to Whitehall; but the King and Duke being abroad, we returned to Somersett house. In discourse, I find him a very worthy and studious gentleman in the business of Trade; and among other things, he observed well to me how it is not the greatest wits but the steady man that is a good merchant: he instanced in Ford and Cocke, the last of whom he values above all men as his oracle, as Mr. Coventry doth Mr. Jolliffe. He says that it is concluded among merchants, that where a Trade hath once been and doth decay, it never recovers again; and therefore, that the manufacture of Cloath of England will never come to esteem again. That among other faults, Sir Rd. Ford cannot keep a secret; and that it is so much the part of a merchant to be guilty of that fault, that the Duke of Yorke is resolved to commit no more secrets to the merchants of the Royall Company. That Sir Ellis Layton is, for a speech of forty words, the wittiest man that ever he knew in his life; but longer, he is nothing; his judgment being nothing at all, but his wit most absolute. At Somersett house he carried me in and there I

saw the Queenes new rooms, which are most stately and nobly furnished; and there I saw her, and the Duke of Yorke and Duchesse were there.

20.    Up and to the office, where all the morning. At noon my uncle Tho. came; dined with me and received some money of me. Then I to my office, where I took in with me Bagwells wife; and there I caressed her, and find her every day more and more coming, with good words and promise of getting her husband a place, which I will do. So we parted, and I to my Lord Sandwich at his lodgings; and after a little stay, away with Mr. Cholmely to Fleet street, in the way he telling me that Tanger is like to be in a bad condition with this Fitzgerald, he being a man of no honour nor presence, nor little honesty, and endeavours to raise the Irish and suppress the English interest there, and offends everybody – and doth nothing that I hear of well – which I am sorry for.

23.    *Lords day*. Up and to church. At noon comes unexpected Mr. Fuller the Minister, and dines with me – and also I had invited Mr. Cooper, with one I judge came from sea. And he and I spent the whole afternoon together, he teaching me some things in understanding of plats. At night to the office doing business, and then home to supper; then a psalm, to prayers, and to bed.

25.    Up and to the office, where we sat all the morning and finished Sir W. Warren's great contract for timber; with great content to me, because just in the terms I wrote last night to Sir W. Warren, and against the terms proposed by Sir W. Batten. At noon home to dinner and there find Creed and Hawly. After dinner comes in Mrs. Ingram, the first time, to make a visit to my wife. After a little stay I left them, and to the committee of the Fishery, and there did make my report of the late public Collections for the Fishery, much to the satisfaction of the Comittee, and I think much to my reputation, for good notice was taken of it and much it was commended. So home (in my way taking care of a piece of plate for Mr. Chr. Pett, against the lanching of his new great ship tomorrow at Woolwich, which I singly did move to His Royall Highness yesterday, and did obtain it for him, to the value of 20 peeces). And he, under his hand, doth acknowledge to me that he did never receive so great a kindness from any man in the world as from me herein. So to my office and then to supper; and then to my office

again, where busy late, being very full nowadays of business, to my great content I thank God; and so home to bed – my house being full of a design to go tomorrow, my wife and all her servants, to see the new ship lanched.

26. Up – my people rising mighty betimes to fit themselfs to go by water; and my boy, he could not sleep, but wakes about 4 a-clock and in bed lay playing on his lute till daylight, and it seems did the like last night till 12 a-clock. About 8 a-clock, my wife, she and her woman and Besse and Jane and W. Hewers and the boy, to the waterside and there took boat. And by and by, I out of doors to look after the Flagon, to get it ready to carry to Woolwich. That being not ready, I stepped aside and found out Nellson, he that Whistler buys his Bewpers of, and did there buy five pieces at their price. And am in hopes thereby to bring them down, or buy ourselfs all we spend of Nellson at the first hand. This jobb was greatly to my content. And by and by, the Flaggon being finished at the Burnishers, I home; and there fitted myself and took a hackney coach I hired (it being a very cold and fowle day) to Woolwich, all the way reading in a good book touching the Fishery; and that being done, in the book upon the statutes of Charitable uses, mightily to my satisfaction. At Woolwich, I there up to the King and Duke and they liked the plate well. Here I stayed above with them while the ship was lanched; which was done with great success, and the King did very much like the ship, saying she had the best bow that ever he saw. But Lord, the sorry talk and discourse among the great courtiers round about him, without any reverence in the world, but with so much disorder. By and by the Queen comes and her maids of honour; one whereof, Mrs. Boynton, and the Duchesse of Buckeingham, had been very sick coming by water in the barge (the water being very rough); but what silly sport they made with them, in very common terms methought, was very poor, and below what people think these great people say and do. The launching being done, the King and company went down to take barge; and I sent for Mr. Pett and put the Flaggon into the Dukes hand, and he, in the presence of the King, did give it, Mr. Pett taking it upon his knee. This, Mr. Pett is wholly beholding to me for, and he doth know and I believe will acknowledge it.

27. Up, and to the office, where all the morning busy. At noon Sir G. Carteret, Sir J. Mennes, Sir W. Batten, Sir W. Penn and myself

were treated at the Dolphin by Mr. Foly the Ironmonger, where a good plain dinner; but I expected Musique, the missing of which spoiled my dinner. Only, very good merry discourse at dinner. Thence with Sir G. Carteret by coach to Whitehall to a committee of Tanger: and thence back to London, and light in Cheapside and I to Nellsons; and there met with a rub at first, but took him out to drink and there discoursed, to my great content, so far with him that I think I shall agree with him for Bewpers, to serve the Navy with. So with great content home and to my office, where late. And having got a great cold in my head yesterday, home to supper and to bed.

28.    Slept ill all night, having got a very great cold the other day at Woolwich in head, which makes me full of snot. Up in the morning, and my tailor brings me home my fine new coloured cloth suit, my cloak lined with plush, as good a suit as ever I wore in my life and mighty neat, to my great content. To my office, and there all the morning. At noon to Nellsons and there bought 20 pieces more of Bewpers, and hope to go on with him to a contract. Thence to the Change a little; and thence home with Luellin to dinner, where Mr. Deane met me by appointment; and after dinner he and I up to my chamber and there hard at discourse, and advising him what to do in his business at Harwich; and then to discourse of our old business of Ships, and taking new rules of him to my great pleasure; and he being gone, I to my office a little and then to see Sir W. Batten, who is sick of a greater cold then I; and thither comes to me Mr. Holliard, and into the chamber to me; and poor man (beyond all I ever saw of him), was a little drunk, and there sat talking and finding acquaintance with Sir W. Batten and my Lady by relations on both sides, that there we stayed very long. At last broke up and he home, much overcome with drink – but well enough to get well home. So I home to supper and to bed.

29.    Up; and it being my Lord Mayor's show, my boy and three maids went out; but it being a very foul rainy day from morning to night, I was sorry my wife let them go out. All the morning at the office. At dinner at home. In the afternoon to the office again; and about 4 a–clock by appointment to the Kings head tavern upon Fishstreete hill, whither Mr. Wolfe (and Parham by his means) met me to discourse about the Fishery; and a great light I had by Parham, who is a little conceited but a very knowing man in his

way, and in the general fishing trade of England. Here I stayed three hours and eat a barrel of very fine oysters of Wolfes giving me; and so it raining hard – home and to my office, and then home to bed.

30.   *Lords day*. Up; and this morning put on my new fine coloured cloth suit, with my cloak lined with plush – which is a dear and noble suit, costing me about 17*l*. To church and then home to dinner; and after dinner, to a little musique with my boy, and so to church with my wife; and so home and with her all the evening, reading and at musique with my boy with great pleasure; and so to supper, prayers, and to bed.

## –✣NOVEMBER✣–

1.   Up and to the office, where busy all the morning. At noon (my wife being invited to my Lady Sandwiches) all alone dined at home upon a good goose with Mr. Wayth – discoursing of business. Thence I to the committee of the Fishery and there we sat, with several good discourses and some bad and simple ones and with great disorder, and yet by the men of business of the town. But my report in the business of the collections[1] is mightily commended and will get me some reputation; and endeed is the only thing looks like a thing well done since we sat. Thence with Mr. Parham to the tavern, but I drank no wine; only, he did give me another barrel of oysters. And he brought one Maj. Greene, an able fishmonger, and good discourse to my information. So home and late at business at my office. Then to supper and to bed.

2.   Up betimes, and down with Mr. Castle to Redriffe, and there walked to Deptford to view a parcel of brave Knees of his, which endeed are very good. And so back again – home – I seeming very friendly to him, though I know him to be a rogue and one that hates me with his heart. Home and to dinner, and so to my office all the afternoon, where in some pain in my backe, which troubled me; but I think it comes only with stooping and from no other matter.

3.   Up, and to the office – where strange to see how Sir W. Penn is

---

1. See above, p. 435 (25 October).

flocked to by people of all sorts against his going to sea. At the office did much business; among other, an end of that that hath troubled me long, the business of Bewpers and Flaggs. At noon to the Change; and thence by appointment was met with Bagwells wife, and she fallowed me into Moorefields and there into a drinking-house – and all alone eat and drank together. I did there caress her; but though I did make some offer, did not receive any compliance from her in what was bad, but very modestly she denied me; which I was glad to see and shall value her the better for it – and I hope never tempt her to any evil more.

4.   Waked very betimes and lay long awake, my mind being so full of business. Then up and to St. James, where I find Mr. Coventry full of business, packing up for his going to sea with the Duke. Walked with him, talking, to Whitehall; where to the Duke's lodgings, who is gone thither to lodge lately. I appeared to the Duke; and thence Mr. Coventry and I an hour in the long gallery, talking about the management of our office. He tells me the weight of despatch will lie most upon me. And told me freely his mind touching Sir W. Batten and Sir J. Mennes – the latter of whom, he most aptly said, was like a lapwing; that all he did was to keep a flutter, to keep others from the nest that they would find. He told me an odd story of the former, about the Lighthouses: how just before, he had certified to the Duke against the use of them, and what a burden they are to trade – and presently after, at his being at Harwich, comes to desire that he might have the setting one up there – and gets the usefulness of it certified also by the Trinity house. After long discoursing and considering all our stores and other things – as, how the King hath resolved upon Capt. Taylor and Coll. Middleton, the first to be commissioner for Harwich and the latter for Portsmouth – I away to the Change and there did very much business. So home to dinner, and Mr. Duke, our Secretary for the Fishery, dined with me. After dinner, to discourse of our business – much to my content. And then he away and I by water among the smiths on the other side; and to the alehouse with one and was near buying four or five anchors, and learned something worth my knowing of them. And so home and to my office, where late, with my head very full of business; and so away home to supper and to bed.

5.   Up, and to the office, where all the morning. At noon to the

Change and thence home to dinner; and so with my wife to the Duke's house to a play, *Macbeth*; a pretty good play, but admirably acted. Thence home, the coach being forced to go round by London wall home because of the Bonefires – the day being mightily observed in the City. To my office late at business; and then home to supper and to bed.

6. *Lords day*. Up, and with my wife to church. Dined at home. And I all the afternoon close at my office, drawing up some proposals to present to the committee for the Fishery tomorrow – having a great good intention to be serviceable in that business if I can. At night to supper with my uncle Wight, where very merry; and so home – to prayers and to bed.

7. Up, and with Sir W. Batten to Whitehall, where mighty thrusting about the Duke, now upon his going. We were with him long; he advised us to fallow our business close and to be directed in his absence by the committee of the Councell for the Navy. By and by a meeting of the Fishery, where the Duke was; but in such haste, and things looked so superficially over, that I had not a fit opportunity to propose my paper that I wrote yesterday; but I had showed it to Mr. Gray and Wren before, who did like it most highly as they said, and I think they would not dissemble in that manner in a business of this nature. But I see the greatest businesses are done so superficially, that I wonder anything succeeds at all among us that is public.

8. Up, and to the office – where by and by Mr. Coventry came; and after doing a little business, took his leave of us, being to go to sea with the Duke tomorrow. At noon I and Sir J. Mennes and Lord Berkely (who with Sir J. Duncum and Mr. Chichly are made Maisters of the Ordnance) to the Office of the Ordnance to discourse about Wadding for guns. Thence to dinner, all of us, to the Lieutenant of the Towers – where a good dinner, but disturbed in the middle of it by the King's coming into the Tower; and so we broke up, and to him and went up and down the storehouses and magazines; which are, with the addition of the new great Storehouse, a noble sight. He gone, I to my office, where Bagwell's wife stayed for me; and together with her a good while, to meet again shortly. So all the afternoon at my office – till late; and then to bed – joyed in my love and ability to fallow my business. This day Mr.

Lever sent my wife a pair of silver candlesticks, very pretty ones – the first man that ever presented me to whom I have not only done little service, but apparently did him the greatest disservice in his business of accounts, as Purser generall, of any man at the board.

9.   Called up, as I had appointed, by H. Russell, between 2 and 3 a-clock: and I and my boy Tom by water with a galley down to the Hope, it being a fine starry night. Got thither by 8 a-clock and there, as expected, found the *Charles*, her mainmast setting. Comissioner Pett aboard. I up and down to see the ship I was so well acquainted with[1] – and a great work it is, the setting so great a mast. Thence the Comissioner and I on board Sir G. Ascue in the *Henery* – who lacks men mightily. Thence, not staying, the wind blowing hard, I made use of the *Jemmy* Yacht and returned to the Tower in her – my boy being a very droll boy and good company. Home and eat something, and then shifted myself and to Whitehall; and there, the King being in his Cabinet council (I desiring to speak with Sir G. Carteret), I was called in and demanded by the King himself many Questions, to which I did give him full answers. There was at this council my Lord Chancellor, Archbishop of Canterbury, Lord Treasurer, the two Secretarys, and Sir G. Carteret. Not a little contented at this chance of being made known to these persons, and called often by my name by the King – I to Mr. Pierce's to take leave of him, but he not within but saw her; and made very little stay but straight home to my office, where I did business, and then to supper and to bed.

11.   Up, and with Sir J. Mennes and Sir W. Batten to the council chamber at Whitehall, to the committee of the Lords for the Navy – where we were made to wait an hour or two before called in. Sir Edw. Walker coming in, in discourse did say that there was none of the families of princes in Christendom that do derive themselfs so high as Julius Cæsar, nor so far by a thousand years, that can directly prove their rise. Only, some in Germany do derive themselfs from the patrician familys of Rome, but that uncertainly. And among other things, did much enveigh against the writing of Romances; that five hundred years hence, being wrote of matters in general true, as the Romance of *Cleopatra*, the world will not know which is the true and which the false. Here was a gentleman

1. On the Dutch voyage, 1660.

attending here that told us he saw the other day, and did bring the draft of it to Sir Fr. Prigeon, of a monster born of an hostlers wife at Salsbury; two women-children perfectly made, joyned at the lower part of their bellies, and every part perfect as two bodies, and only one payre of legs, coming forth on one side from the middle where they were joined. It was alive 24 hours, and cried and did as all hopeful children do; but being showed too much to people, was killed. By and by we were called in, where a great many lords – Annesly in the chair. But Lord, to see what work they will make us, and what trouble we shall have to inform men in a business they are to begin to know when the greatest of our hurry is, is a thing to be lamented – and I fear the consequence will be bad to us.

13. *Lords day*. The morning to church, where mighty sport to hear our Clerk sing out of tune, though his master sits by him that begins and keeps the tune aloud for the parish. Dined at home very well. And spent all the afternoon with my wife within doors – and getting a speech out of *Hamlett*, "To bee or not to bee," without book. In the evening, to sing psalms; and in came Mr. Hill to see me, and then he and I and the boy finely to sing; and so anon broke up after much pleasure. He gone, I to supper and so to prayers and to bed.

14. Up, and with Sir W. Batten to Whitehall to the Lords of the Admiralty and there did our business betimes. Thence to Sir Ph. Warwicke about Navy business – and my Lord Ashly; and afterward to my Lord Chancellor, who is very well pleased with me and my carrying of his business. And so to the Change, where mighty busy; and so home to dinner, where Mr. Creed and Moore; and after dinner I to my Lord Treasurers, to Sir Ph. Warwicke there, and then to Whitehall to the Duke of Albimarle about Tanger; and then homeward to the Coffee-house to hear news: and it seems the Dutch, as I afterward find by Mr. Coventrys letters, have stopped a ship of masts of Sir W. Warrens, coming for us in a Swedes ship; which they will not release upon Sir G. Downings claiming her – which appears as the first act of hostility – and is looked upon as so by Mr. Coventry.

15. That I might not be too fine for the business I intend this day, I did leave off my fine new cloth suit lined with plush and put on my poor black suit; and after office done (where much business but

little done), I to the Change; and thence Bagwell's wife with much ado fallowed me through Moorfields to a blind alehouse, and there I did caress her and eat and drank, and many hard looks and sithes the poor wretch did give me, and I think verily was troubled at what I did; but at last, after many protestings, by degrees I did arrive at what I would, with great pleasure. Then in the evening, it raining, walked to the town to where she knew where she was; and then I took coach and to Whitehall to a Committee of Tanger, where, and everywhere else I thank God, I find myself growing in repute; and so home and late, very late, at business, nobody minding it but myself; and so home to bed – weary and full of thoughts. Businesses grow high between the Dutch and us on every side.

16. My wife not being well, waked in the night; and strange to see how dead sleep our people sleeps, that she was fain to ring an hour before anybody would wake. At last one rose and helped my wife; and so to sleep again. Up, and to my business; and then to Whitehall, there to attend the Lords Commissioners; and so directly home and dined with Sir W. Batten and my Lady, and after dinner had much discourse tending to profit with Sir W. Batten, how to get ourselfs into the prize office, or some other fair way of obliging the King to consider us in our extraordinary pains. Then to the office, and there all the afternoon very busy, and so till past 12 at night; and so home to bed. This day my wife went to the burial of a little boy of W. Joyces.

17. Up, and to my office and there all the morning mighty busy, and taking upon me to tell the Comtroller how ill his matters were done. And I think, endeed, if I continue thus, all the business of the office will come upon me, whether I will or no.

18. This day I had a letter from Mr. Coventry that tells me that my Lord Brunkard is to be one of our Comissioners, of which I am very glad, if any more must be.

21. Up; and to the Lords at Whitehall, where they do single me out to speak to and to hear – much to my content. And received their commands perticularly in several businesses. Thence by their order to the Atturny Generall's about a new warrant for Capt. Taylor, which I shall carry for him to be Comissioner, in spite of Sir W. Batten; and yet endeed, it is not I, but the ability of the man,

that makes the Duke and Mr. Coventry stand by their choice. I to Change and there stayed long, doing business. And this day for certain, news is come that Teddiman hath brought in 18 or 20 Duchmen, merchants, their Burdeaux fleet, and two men of war to Portsmouth. And I had letters this afternoon that three are brought into the Downes and Dover – so that the war is begun: God give a good end to it. After dinner at home all the afternoon, busy; and at night with Sir W. Batten and Sir J. Mennes looking over the business of stating the accounts of the Navy charge to my Lord Treasurer, where Sir J. Mennes's paper served us in no stead almost, but was all false; and after I had done it with great pains, he being by, I am confident he understands not one word in it. At it till 10 at night almost. Thence by coach to Sir Ph. Warwickes by his desire, to have conferred with him; but he being in bed, I to Whitehall to the Secretary's and there wrote to Mr. Coventry; and so home by coach again. A fine clear moonshine night, but very cold. Home to my office a while, it being past 12 at night; and so to supper and to bed.

22. At the office all the morning. Sir G. Carteret, upon a motion of Sir W. Batten's, did promise, if we would write a letter to him, to show it to the King on our behalf, touching our desire of being Commissioners of the Prize office. I wrote a letter to my mind; and after eating a bit at home (Mr. Sheply dining and taking his leave of me), abroad and to Sir G. Carteret with the letter; and thence to my Lord Treasurer's, where with Sir Ph. Warwicke long studying all we could to make the last year swell as high as we could. And it is much to see how he doth study for the King to do it, to get all the money from the Parliament, all he can – and I shall be serviceable to him therein, to help him to heads upon which to enlarge the report of the expense. He did observe to me how obedient this Parliament was for a while; and the last sitting, how they begun to differ and to carp at the King's officers; and what they will do now, he says, is to make agreement for the money, for there is no guess to be made of it. He told me he was prepared to convince the parliament that the Subsidys are a most ridiculous tax (the four last not rising to 40000*l*)[1] and unæquall. He talks of a tax of assessement of 70000*l* for five years, the people to be secured that it shall continue no longer then there is really a warr – and the charges thereof to be

---

1. sc. £40,000 each.

paid. He told me that one year of the late Dutch war cost 1623000*l*. Thence to my Lord Chancellors, and there stayed long with Sir W. Batten and Sir J. Mennes to speak with my Lord about our Prize Office business; but being sick and full of visitants, we could not speak with him, and so away home. Where Sir Rd. Ford did meet us, with letters from Holland this day that it is likely the Duch fleet will not come out this year; they have not victuals to keep them out, and it is likely they will be frozen before they can get back. So home to supper, where troubled to hear my poor boy Tom hath a fit of the stone, or some other pain like it. I must consult Mr. Holliard for him. So at one in the morning, home to bed.

24.    Up and to the office, where all the morning busy answering of people. About noon out with Comissioner Pett, and he and I to a Coffee-house to drink Jocolatte, very good; and so by coach to Westminster, being the first day of the Parliaments meeting. After the House had received the King's speech and what more he had to say, delivered in writing (the Chancellor being sick), it rose; and I with Sir Ph. Warwicke home and conferred our matters about the charge of the Navy, and am more to give him in the excessive charge of this year's expense. I dined with him, and Mr. Povy with us and Sir Edmd. Pooly, a fine gentleman, and Mr. Chichly; and fine discourse we had and fine talk – being proud to see myself accepted in such company and thought better then I am. After dinner Sir Phillip and I to talk again; and then away home to the office, where sat late, beginning our sittings now in the afternoon because of the parliament; and they being rose, I to my office, where late, till almost one a-clock and then home to bed.

25.    Up, and at my office all the morning to prepare an account of the charge we have been put to extraordinary by the Dutch already; and I have brought it to appear 852700*l*; but God knows, this is only a scare to the Parliament, to make them give the more money. Thence to the Parliament-house and there did give it to Sir Ph. Warwicke, the House being hot upon giving the King a supply of money. And I by coach to the Change and took up Mr. Jenings along with me (my old acquaintance), he telling me the mean manner that Sir Samuel Morland lives near him, in a house he hath bought and laid out money upon; in all, to the value of 1200*l* – but is believed to be a beggar. And so I ever thought he would be. From the Change, with Mr. Deering and Luellin to the Whitehorse tavern

in Lombard street – and there dined with them, he giving me a dish of meat, to discourse in order to my serving Deering; which I am already obliged to do, and shall do it – and would be glad he were a man trusty, that I might venture something along with him. Thence home; and by and by, in the evening, took my wife out by coach, leaving her at Unthankes, while I to Whitehall and to Westminster hall, where I have not been to talk a great while; and there hear that Mrs. Lane and her husband live a sad life together, and he is gone to be a paymaster to a company to Portsmouth to serve at sea. She big with child. Thence I home, calling my wife – and at Sir W. Batten's hear that the House hath given the King 2500000*l* to be paid for this war, only for the Navy, in three years time; which is a joyful thing to all the King's party I see – but was much opposed by Mr. Vaughan and others, that it should be so much. So home and to supper and to bed.

27.   *Lords day.* To church in the morning. Then dined at home, and to my office and there all the afternoon setting right my business of Flaggs; and after all my pains, find reason not to be sorry, because I think it will bring me considerable profit. In the evening came Mr. Andrews and Hill, and we sung with my boy Ravenscrofts four-part psalms, most admirable music. Then (Andrews not staying) we to supper; and after supper fell into the rarest discourse with Mr. Hill about Rome and Italy, the most pleasant that I ever had in my life. At it very late, and then to bed.

30.   Up, and with Sir W. Batten and Sir J. Mennes to the committee of the Lords and there did our business; but Lord, what a sorry despatch those great persons give to business. Thence to the Change and there hear the certainty and circumstances of the Duch having called in their fleet and paid their men half-pay, the other to be paid them upon their being ready upon beat-of-drum to come to serve them again – and in the meantime to have half-pay. This is said. Thence home to dinner, and so to my office all the afternoon. In the evening my wife and Sir W. Warren with me to Whitehall, sending her with the coach to see her father and mother. He and I up to Sir G. Carteret and first I alone, and then both, had discourse with him about things of the Navy; and so I and he calling my wife at Unthankes, home again and long together, talking how to order things in a new contract for Norway goods, as well to the King's as to his advantage. He gone, I to my monthly accounts; and bless

God, I find I have encreased my last balance, though but little – but I hope ere long to get more. In the meantime, praise God for what I have, which is 1209*l*. So, with my heart glad to see my accounts fall so right in this time of mixing of monies and confusion, I home to bed.

## DECEMBER

2. Lay long in bed. Then up and to the office, where busy all the morning. At home dined. After dinner, with my wife and Mercer to the Dukes house and there saw *The Rivalls*, which I had seen before. But the play not good, nor anything but the good actings of Baterton and his wife and Harris. Thence homeward, and the coach broke with us in Lincoln's Inn Fields; and so walked to Fleet street and there took coach and home and to my office – whither by and by comes Capt. Cocke and then Sir W. Batten; and we all to Sir J. Minnes and I did give them a barrel of oysters I had given me, and so there sat and talked; where good discourse of the late troubles, they knowing things, all of them very well – and Cocke from the King's own mouth, being then intrusted himself much, doth know perticularly that the Kings credulity to Cromwells promises private to him – against the advice of his friends and the certain discovery of the practices and discourses of Cromwell in council (by Maj. Huntington) – did take away his life, and nothing else. Then to some loose atheisticall discourse of Cockes, when he was almost drunk; and then about 11 a-clock broke up, and I to my office to fit up an account for Povey, wherein I hope to get something. At it till almost 2 a-clock; then home to supper and to bed.

3. The Duke of Yorke being expected tonight with great joy from Portsmouth, after his having been abroad at sea three or four days with the fleet; and the Dutch are all drawn into their harbours – but it seems like a victory. And a matter of some reputation to us it is, and blemish to them; but in no degree like what it is esteemed at – the weather requiring them to do so.

10. Lay long; at which I am ashamed, because of so many people's observing it that know not how late I sit up, and for fear of Sir W. Batten's speaking of it to others – he having stayed for me a good

while. At the office all the morning, where comes my Lord Brunkard with his patent in his hand and delivered it to Sir J. Mennes and myself, we alone being there – all the day. And at noon I in his coach with him to the Change, where he set me down. A modest civil person he seems to be, but wholly ignorant in the business of the Navy as possible, but I hope to make a friend of him, being a worthy man. Thence, after hearing the great news of so many Duchmen being brought in to Portsmouth and elsewhere, which it is expected shall either put them upon present revenge or despair, I with Sir W. Rider and Cutler to dinner all alone to the Great James – where good discourse, and I hope occasion of getting something hereafter. After dinner to Whitehall to the Fishery, where the Duke was with us. So home and late at my office, writing many letters; then home to supper and to bed. Yesterday came home, and this night I visited, Sir W. Pen, who dissembles great respect and love to me, but I understand him very well. Maj. Holmes is come from Guiny and is now at Plymouth, with great wealth they say.

11. *Lords day*. Up and to church alone in the morning. Dined at home mighty pleasantly; in the afternoon I to the French church – where much pleased with the three sisters of the parson, very handsome; especially in their noses – and sing prettily. I hear a good sermon of the old man, touching duty to parents. Here was Sir Samll. Morland and his Lady, very fine, with two footmen in new liverys – the church taking much notice of them – and going into their coach after sermon with great gazeing. So I home, and my Cousin Mary Pepys's husband came after me and told me that out of the money he received some months since,[1] he did receive 18*d*. too much, and did now come and give it me, which was very pretty. So home, and there found Mr. Andrews and his lady, a well-bred and a tolerable pretty woman, and by and by Mr. Hill; and to singing and then to supper. Then to sing again, and so good-night. To prayers and to bed. It is a little strange how these psalms of Ravenscroft, after two or three times singing, prove but the same again, though good – no diversity appearing at all almost.

12. Up and with Sir W. Batten by coach to Whitehall, where all of us with the Duke. Mr. Coventry privately did tell me the reason of

1. Part of a legacy from Robert Pepys.

his advice against our pretences to the Priz[e] office (in his letter from Portsmouth); because he knew that the King and the Duke had resolved to put in some parliament-men that have deserved well and that would need be obliged by putting them in. Thence homeward; called at my booksellers and bespoke some books against the year out. And then to the Change; and so home to dinner and then to the office, where my Lord Brunkard comes and reads over part of our instructions in the Navy; and I expounded it to him, so he is become my disciple. He gone, comes Cutler to tell us that the King of France hath forbid any Canvas to be carried out of his kingdom. And I, to examine, went with him to the East India house to see a letter, but came too late. So home again and there late, till 12 at night, at my office; and then home to supper and to bed. This day (to see how things are ordered in the world), I had a command from the Earle of Sandwich (at Portsmouth) not to be forward with Mr. Cholmly and Sir J. Lawson about the Molle at Tanger, because that what I do therein will (because of his friendship to me known) redound against him, as if I had done it upon his scoare. So I wrote to my Lord my mistake, and am contented to promise never to pursue it more – which goes against my mind with all my heart.

14. Up; and after a while at the office, I abroad in several places; among other, to my booksellers and there spoke for several books against New Year's day, I resolving to lay out about 7 or 8*l*, God having given me some profit extraordinary of late. And bespoke also some plate, spoons, and forks. I pray God keep me from too great expenses, though these will still be pretty good money. Then to the Change; and I home to dinner, where Creed (and Mr. Cæsare, my boy's lute master, who plays endeed mighty finely); and after dinner I abroad, parting from Creed, and away to and fro, laying-out or preparing for laying-out more money, but I hope and resolve not to exceed therein. And tonight spoke for some fruit for the country for my father against Christmas; and where should I do it but at the pretty woman's that use to stand at the door in Fanchurch street – I having a mind to know her. So home and late at my office, evening reckonings with Shergoll and so away home to supper and to bed, not being very well through my taking cold of late and so troubled with some wind.

15. Called up very betimes by Mr. Cholmly, and with him a good

while about some of his Tanger accounts. And discoursing of the condition of Tanger, he did give me the whole account of the difference between FitzGerald and Norwood; which were very high on both sides, but most imperious and base on Fitz.Gerald's. And yet, through my Lord Fitzharding's means, the Duke of Yorke is led rather to blame Norwood and to speak that he should be called home, then be sensible of the other. It seems, of all mankind there is no man so led by another as the Duke is by my Lord Muskerry and this FitzHarding. Insomuch, as when the King would have him to be Privy purse, the Duke wept and said, "But, Sir, I must have your promise, if you will have my dear Charles from me, that if ever you have occasion for an army again, I may have him with me" – believing him to be the best commander of an army in the world. But Mr. Cholmly thinks, as all other men I meet with do, that he is a very ordinary fellow. It is strange how the Duke also doth love naturally and affect the Irish above the English. He, of the company he carried with him to sea, took above two-thirds Irish and French. He tells me the King doth hate my Lord Chancellor. And that they, that is the King and my Lord Fitzharding, do laugh at him for a dull fellow; and in all this business of the Duch war doth nothing by his advice, hardly consulting him. Only, he is a good minister in other respects, and the King cannot be without him; but above all, being the Dukes father-in-law, he is kept in; otherwise, Fitzharding were able to fling down two of him. This all the wise and grave lords see, and cannot help it but yield to it. He being gone, I abroad to the carriers to see some things sent away to my father against Christmas; and I thence to Moorefields, and there up and down to several houses to drink, to look for a place pour rancontrer la femme de je sais quoy against next Monday, but could meet none; but so to the Coffee-house, where great talk of the Comett seen in several places and among our men at sea and by my Lord Sandwich, to whom I intend to write about it tonight. Thence home to dinner; and then to the office, where all the afternoon; and in the evening home to supper, and then to the office late, and so to bed. This night I begun to burn wax candles in my closet at the office, to try the charge and to see whether the smoke offends like that of tallow candles.

16. Up and by water to Deptford, thinking to have met la femme de Bagwell, but failed; and having done some business at the yard, I back again, it being a fine fresh morning to walk. Back again, Mr.

Wayth walking with me to Halfway house, talking about Mr. Castles fine knees lately delivered in – in which I am well informed that they are not as they should be to make them knees. And I hope shall make good use of it to the King's service. Thence home; and having dressed myself, to the Change and thence home to dinner. And so abroad by coach with my wife, and bought a looking-glass by the Old Exchange which costs me 5*l* 5*s*. – and 6*s*. for the hooks. A very fair glass.

17. Up and to the office, where we sat all the morning. At noon, I to the Change and there, among others, had my first meeting with Mr. Lestrange,[1] who hath endeavoured several times to speak with me – it is to get now and then some news of me, which I shall as I see cause give him. He is a man of fine conversation I think; but I am sure, most courtly and full of compliment. Thence home to dinner; and then came the looking-glass man to set up the looking-glass I bought yesterday in my dining-room, and very handsome it is.

18. *Lords day*. To church; where God forgive me, I spent most of my time in looking my new Morena at the other side of the church, an acquaintance of Pegg Pen's. So home to dinner and then to my chamber to read Ben. Johnsons *Cateline*, a very excellent piece. And so to church again; and thence we met at the office to hire ships, being in great haste and having sent for several maisters of Shipps to come to us. Then home, and there Mr. Andrews and Hill came and we sung finely. And by and by, Mr. Fuller the parson, and supped with me, he and a friend of his; but my music friends would not stay supper. At and after supper, Mr. Fuller and I [told] many stories of apparitions and delusions thereby. He gone, I a little to my office and then to prayers and to bed.

19. Going to bed betimes last night, we waked betimes. And from our people's being forced to take the key to go out to light a candle, I was very angry and begun to find fault with my wife for not commanding her servants as she ought. Thereupon, she giving me some cross answer, I did strike her over her left eye such a blow, as the poor wretch did cry out and was in great pain; but yet her spirit was such as to endeavour to bite and scratch me. But I cogging with her, made her leave crying, and sent for butter and

1. Roger L'Estrange, editor of the government newspapers.

parsley, and friends presently one with another; and I up, vexed at my heart to think what I had done, for she was forced to lay a poultice or something to her eye all day, and is black – and the people of the house observed it. But I was forced to rise; and up and with Sir J. Mennes to Whitehall, and there we waited on the Duke. And among other things, Mr. Coventry took occasion to vindicate himself before the Duke and us, being all there, about the choosing of Taylor for Harwich. Upon which the Duke did clear him, and did tell us that he did expect that after he had named a man, none of us shall then oppose or find fault with that man. But if we had anything to say, we ought to say it before he had chose him. Sir G. Carteret thought himself concerned, and endeavoured to clear himself. And by and by Sir W. Batten did speak, knowing himself guilty; and did confess that being pressed by the Council, he did say what he did, that he was accounted a fanatique; but did not know that at that time he had been appointed by his Royal Highness – to which the Duke [replied] that it was impossible but he must know that he had appointed him; and so it did appear that the Duke did mean all this while Sir W. Batten. So by and by we parted; and Mr. Coventry did privately tell me that he did this day take this occasion to mention the business, to give the Duke an opportunity of speaking his mind to Sir W. Batten in this business – of which I was heartily glad. Thence home; and not finding Bagwell's wife as I expected, I to the Change and there walked up and down, and then home; and she being come, I bid her go and stay at Mooregate for me; and after going up to my wife (whose eye is very bad, but she in very good temper to me); and after dinner, I to the place and walked round the fields again and again; but not finding her, I to the Change and there found her waiting for me and took her away and to an alehouse, and there I made much of her; and then away thence and to another, and endeavoured to caress her; but elle ne vouloit pas, which did vex me but I think it was chiefly not having a good easy place to do it upon. So we broke up and parted; and I to the office, where we sat hiring of ships an hour or two; and then to my office and thence (with Capt. Taylor home to my house) to give him instructions and some notice of what, to his great satisfaction, had happened today – which I do because I hope his coming into this office will a little cross Sir W. Batten and may do me good. He gone, I to supper with my wife, very pleasant; and then a little to my office and to bed – my mind, God forgive me, too much running upon what I can faire avec la femme de Bagwell demain –

having promised to go to Deptford and à aller à sa maison avec son mari when I come thither.

20.    Up and walked to Deptford, where after doing something at the yard, I walked, without being observed, with Bagwell home to his house and there was very kindly used, and the poor people did get a dinner for me in their fashion – of which I also eat very well. After dinner I found occasion of sending him abroad; and then alone avec elle je tentoy à faire ce que je voudrais, et contre sa force je le faisoy, bien que pas à mon contentment. By and by, he coming back again, I took leave and walked home; and then there to dinner, where Dr. Fayrbrother came to see me, and Luellin; we dined, and I to the office, leaving them – where we sat all the afternoon, and I late at the office. To supper and to the office again very late; then home to bed.

22.    Up and betimes to my office and then out to several places. Among others, to Holborne to have spoke with one Mr. Under-wood about some English Hemp – he lies against grays Inn. Thereabouts, I to a barbers shop to have my hair cut. And there met with a copy of verses, mightily commended by some gentleman there, of my Lord Mordants in excuse of his going to sea – this late expedition, with the Duke of York. But Lord, they are but sorry things; only, a Lord made them. Thence to the Change; and there among the merchants, I hear fully the news of our being beaten to dirt at Guiny by De Ruyter with his fleet.

23.    Up and to my office. Then came by appointment Cosen Tom Trice to me, and I paid him the 20*l* remaining due to him upon the bond of 100*l* given him by agreement, November 1663, to end the difference between us about my aunts, his mother's, money.[1] And here, being willing to know the worst, I told him, "I hope now there is nothing remaining between you and I of future disputes;" "No," says he, "nothing at all that I know of, but only a small matter of about 20 or 30*s.* that my father Pepys received for me, of rent due to me in the country – which I will in a day or two bring you an account of;" and so we parted. This day Sir W. Batten sent, and afterward spoke to me, to have me and my wife come and dine with them on Monday next – which is a mighty condescension in

1. See above, pp. 144–5 (8–13 July).

them, and for some great reason I am sure; or else it pleases God, by my late care of business, to make me more considerable even with them then I am sure they would willingly own me to be. God make me thankful and careful to preserve myself so – for I am sure they hate me, and it is hope or fear that makes them flatter me. It being a bright night, which it hath not been a great while, I purpose to endeavour to be called in the morning to see the Comett; though I fear we shall not see it, because it rises at the highest but 16 degrees, and then the houses will hinder us.

24.    Having sat up all night, to past 2 a-clock this morning, our porter, being appointed, comes and tells us that the Bellman tells him that the star is seen upon Tower hill. So I, that had been all night setting in order all my old papers in my chamber, did leave off all; and my boy and I to Tower hill, it being a most fine bright moonshine night and a great frost, but no Comett to be seen; so after running once round the Hill, I and Tom, we home and then to bed. Rose about 9 a-clock; and then to the office, where sitting all the morning. At noon to the Change to the Coffee-house, and there heard Sir Rd. Ford tell the whole story of our defeat at Guinny – wherein our men are guilty of the most horrid cowardize and perfidiousness, as he says and tells it, that ever Englishmen were. Capt. Raynolds, that was the only commander of any of the King's ships there, was shot at by De Ruyter, with a bloody flag flying. He, instead of opposing (which endeed had been to no purpose, but only to maintain honour), did poorly go on board himself to ask what DeRuter would have; and so yielded to whatever Ruyter would desire. The King and Duke are highly vexed at it, it seems, and the business deserves it. Thence home to dinner and then abroad to buy some things; and among others, to my bookseller's and there saw several books I spoke for, which are finely bound and good books, to my great content. So home and to my office, where late. This evening, I being informed, did look and saw the Comett, which is now, whether worn away or no I know not, but appears not with a tail; but only is larger and duller then any other star, and is come to rise betimes and to make a great arch, and is gone quite to a new place in the heavens then it was before – but I hope, in a clearer night something more will be seen. So home to bed.

25.    *Lords day and Christmas Day.* Up (my wife's eye being ill still of the blow I did in a passion give her on Monday last) to church alone

– where Mr. Mills, a good sermon. To dinner at home, where very pleasant with my wife and family. After dinner, I to Sir W. Batten's and there received so much good usage (as I have of late done) from him and my Lady, obliging me and my wife, according to promise, to come and dine with them tomorrow with our neighbours, that I was in pain all the day, and night too after, to know how to order the business of my wife's not going. Thence to the French church; but coming too late, I returned and to Mr. Rawlinson's church, where I heard a good sermon of one that I remember was at Pauls with me, his name Maggett. And very great store of fine women there is in this church, more then I know anywhere else about us. So home and to my chamber, looking over and setting in order my papers and books; and so to supper, and then to prayers and to bed.

26. Up and with Sir W. Penn to Whitehall, and there with the rest did our usual business before the Duke; and then with Sir W. Batten back and to his house, where I by sickness excused my wife's coming to them today. Thence I to the Coffee-house, where much good discourse; and all the opinion now is that the Duch will avoid fighting with us at home but do all the hurt they can to us abroad – which it may be they may for a while; but that I think cannot support them long. Thence to Sir W. Batten, where Mr. Coventry and all our families here, women and all, and Sir R. Ford and his. And a great feast – and good discourse and merry. I here all the afternoon and evening till late; only stepped in to see my wife. Then to my office to enter my day's work; and so home to bed, where my people and wife innocently at cards, very merry. And I to bed, leaving them to their sport and blindman's buff.

27–28. My people came to bed after their sporting, at 4 a-clock in the morning. I up at 7, and to Deptford and Woolwich in a galley, the Duke calling to me out of the barge, in which the King was with him going down the River, to know whither I was going; I told him to Woolwich. But was troubled afterward I should say no farther, being in a galley, lest he think me too profuse in my journys. Did several businesses; and then back again by 2 a-clock to Sir J. Mennes to dinner by appointment, where all yesterday's company but Mr. Coventry, who could not come. Here merry; and after an hour's chat, I down to the office, where busy late, and then home to supper and to bed. The Comett appeared again tonight, but duskishly. I went to bed, leaving my wife and all her folks, and Will also, to come to make Christmas gamballs tonight. I waked in the morning about 6 a-clock, and my wife not come to bed. I lacked a pot but there was none, and bitter cold, so was forced to rise and piss in the chimny, and to bed again. Slept a little longer, and then hear my people coming up and so I rose; and my wife to bed at 8 a-clock in the morning, which vexed me a little, but I believe there was no hurt in it all, but only mirth – therefore took no notice. I abroad with Sir W. Batten to the Council Chamber, where all of us to discourse about the way of measuring ships and the freight fit to give for them by the Tun – where it was strange methought, to hear so poor discourses among the Lords themselfs: and most of all, to see how a little empty matter, delivered gravely by Sir W. Penn, was taken mighty well, though nothing in the earth to the purpose. But clothes, I perceive more and more every day, is a great matter. Thence home with Sir W. Batten by coach; and I home to dinner, finding my wife still in bed. After dinner, abroad; and among other things, visited my Lady Sandwich and was there with her and the young ladies playing at Cards till night; then home and to my office late; then home to bed – leaving my wife and people up to more sports, but without any great satisfaction to myself therein.

30. Lay very long in bed with wife, it being very cold and my wife very full of a resolution to keep within doors, not so much as to go to church or see my Lady Sandwich before Easter next – which I am willing enough to, though I seem the contrary. This and other talk kept me a-bed till almost 10 a-clock. Then up and made an end of looking over all my papers and books and taking everything out of my chamber to have all made clean. At noon dined; and after dinner, forth to several places to pay away money to clear myself in all the world; and among other, paid my bookseller 6*l* for books I had from him this day, and the silversmiths 22*l* 18*s*. 00*d*. for spoons, forks, and sugar box. And being well pleased with seeing my business done to my mind, as to my meeting with people and having my books ready for me – I home and to my office and there did business late; and then home to supper, prayers, and to bed.

31. At the office all the morning, and after dinner there again; despatched first my letters, and then to my accounts, not of the month but of the whole year also, and was at it till past 12 at night – it being bitter cold; but yet I was well satisfied with my work and, above all, to find myself, by the great blessing of God, worth 1349*l*

– by which, as I have spent very largely, so I have laid up above 500*l* this year above what I was worth this day twelvemonth. The Lord make me for ever thankful to his holy name for it. Thence home to eat a little, and so to bed. As soon as ever the clock struck one, I kissed my wife in the kitchen by the fireside, wishing her a merry New year, observing that I believe I was the first proper wisher of it this year, for I did it as soon as ever the clock struck one. So ends the old year, I bless God with great joy to me; not only from my having made so good a year of profit, as having spent 420*l* and laid up 540*l* and upward. But I bless God, I never have been in so good plight as to my health in so very cold weather as this is, nor indeed in any hot weather these ten years, as I am at this day and have been these four or five months. But am at a great loss to know whether it be my Hare's foote,[1] or taking every morning of a pill of Turpentine, or my having left off the wearing of a gowne. My family is my wife, in good health, and happy with her – her woman Mercer, a pretty modest quiet maid – her chambermaid Besse – her cook-maid Jane – the little girle Susan, and my boy which I have had about half a year, Tom Edwards, which I took from the King's Chappell. And a pretty and loving quiet family I have as any man in England. My credit in the world and my office grows daily, and I am in good esteem with everybody I think. My troubles of my uncles estate pretty well over. But it comes to be but of little profit to us, my father being much supported by my purse. But great vexations remain upon my father and me from my Brother Tom's death and ill condition, both to our disgrace and discontent – though no great reason for either. Public matters are all in a hurry about a Duch warr. Our preparations great. Our provocations against them great; and after all our presumption, we are now afeared as much of them as we lately contemned them. Everything else in the State quiet, blessed be God. My Lord Sandwich at sea with the fleet at Portsmouth – sending some about to cruise for taking of ships, which we have done to a great number. This Christmas I judged it fit to look over all my papers and books, and to tear all that I found either boyish or not to be worth keeping, or fit to be seen if it should please God to take me away suddenly.

---

1. Worn as a charm.

# ⚜ 1665 ⚜

## ⚜ JANUARY ⚜

1. *Lords day.* Lay long in bed, having been busy late last night. Then up and to my office, where upon ordering my accounts and papers with respect to my understanding my last year's gains and expense. Now this day, I am dividing my expense, to see what my clothes and every perticular hath stood me in; I mean, all the branches of my expense. At noon, a good venison pasty and a turkey to ourselfs, without anybody so much as invited by us – a thing unusual for so small a family of my condition – but we did it and were very merry. After dinner to my office again, where very late alone upon my accounts, but have not brought them to order yet; and very intricate I find it, notwithstanding my care all the year to keep things in as good method as any man can do. Past 11 a-clock, home to supper and to bed.

2. Up, and it being a most fine hard frost, I walked a good way toward Whitehall; and then being overtaken with Sir W. Penn's coach, went into it, and with him thither and there did our usual business with the Duke. Thence, being forced to pay a great deal of money away in boxes (that is, basons at Whitehall), I to my barbers, Gervas's, and there had a little opportunity of speaking with my Jane alone, and did give her something. Thence to the Swan, and there did sport a good while with Herbert's young kinswoman without hurt though, they being abroad, the old people. Then to the hall, and there agreed with Mrs. Martin, and to her lodgings which she hath now taken to lie in, in Bowe streete – pitiful poor things, yet she thinks them pretty; and so they are for her condition I believe, good enough. Here I did ce que je voudrais avec her most freely; and it having cost me 2s. in wine and cake upon her, I away, sick of her impudence – and by coach to my Lord Brunkers by appointment, in the piazza in Covent Guarding – where I occasioned much mirth with a ballet I brought with me, made from the seamen at sea to their ladies in town – saying Sir W. Penn, Sir G.

Ascue, and Sir J. Lawson made them. Here a most noble French dinner and banquet, the best I have seen these many a day, and good discourse. Thence to my bookseller's and at his binders saw Hookes book of the Microscope, which is so pretty that I presently bespoke it; and away home to the office, where we met to do something; and then, though very late, by coach to Sir Ph. Warwickes; but having company with him, could not speak with him. So back again home, where, thinking to be merry, was vexed with my wife's having looked out a letter in Sir Ph. Sidny about jealousy for me to read, which she industriously and maliciously caused me to do; and the truth is, my conscience told me it was most proper for me, and therefore was touched at it; but took no notice of it, but read it out most frankly. But it stuck in my stomach; and moreover, I was vexed to have a dog brought to my house to lime our little bitch, which they make him do in all their sights; which God forgive me, doth stir my Jealousy again, though of itself the thing is a very immodest sight. However, to Cards with my wife a good while, and then to bed.

3.  Up, and by coach to Sir Ph. Warwickes, the street being full of footballs, it being a great frost. And find him and Mr. Coventry walking in St. James park. I did my errand to him about the felling of the King's timber in the forests, and then to my Lord of Oxford, Justice in Eyre, for his consent thereto, for want whereof my Lord Privy Seale stops the whole business. I found him in his lodgings, in but an ordinary furnished house and room where he was, but I find him to be a man of good discreet replies. Thence to the Coffee-house, where certain news that the Dutch have taken some of our Colliers to the north – some say four, some say seven. Thence to the Change a while, and so home to dinner and to the office, where we sat late, and then I to write my letters. Then to Sir W. Batten's, who is going out of town to Harwich tomorrow, to set up a Lighthouse there which he hath lately got a patent from the King to set up, that will turn much to his profit. Here very merry, and so to my office again, where very late, and then home to supper and to bed – but sat up with my wife at cards till past 2 in the morning.

6.  Lay long in bed, but most of it angry and scolding with my wife about her warning Jane our cook-maid to be gone – and upon that, she desires to go abroad today to look a place. A very good maid she is and fully to my mind, being neat – only, they say a little

apt to scold; but I hear her not. To my office all the morning, busy. Dined at home. To my office again, being pretty well reconciled to my wife; which I did desire to be, because she had designed much mirth today to end Christmas with among her servants. At night home, being Twelfenight, and there chose my piece of cake, but went up to my vial and then to bed, leaving my wife and people up at their sports, which they continue till morning, not coming to bed at all.

9.  Up, and walked to Whitehall, it being still a brave frost and I in perfect good health, blessed be God. In my way saw a woman that broke her thigh, in her heels slipping up upon the frosty street. To the Duke, and there we did our usual work. Here I saw the Royall Society bring their new book, wherein is nobly writ their Charter and laws, and comes to be signed by the Duke as a Fellow; and all the Fellows' hands are to be entered there and lie as a monument, and the King hath put his, with the word "Founder". Thence I to Westminster to the Swan to Herberts girl, and lost time a little with her. And so took coach, and to my Lord Crews and dined with him; who receives me with the greatest respect that could be – telling me that he doth much doubt of the success of this war with Holland; we going about it, he doubts, by the instigation of persons that do not enough apprehend the consequences of the danger of it – and therein I do think with him. Thence to Whitehall to a Tanger Comittee; where I was accosted and most highly complimented by my Lord Bellasses our new Governor, beyond my expectation or measure I could imagine he would have given any man, as if I were the only person of business that he intended to rely on, and desires my correspondence with him. This I was not only surprized at, but am well pleased with and may make good use of it. Our patent is renewed, and he and my Lord Barkely and Sir Tho. Ingram put in as commissioners. Here some business happened which may bring me some profit. Thence took coach; and calling my wife at her tailor's (she being come this afternoon to bring her mother some apples, neats tongues and brain) I home, and there at my office late with Sir W. Warren and had a great deal of good discourse and counsel from him – which I hope I shall take, being all for my good in my deportment in my office, yet with all honesty. He gone, I home to supper and to bed.

11.  Up, and very angry with my boy for lying long a-bed and

forgetting his Lute. To my office all the morning. At noon to the Change, and so home to dinner. After dinner to Gresham College to my Lord Brunker and Comissioner Pett, taking Mr. Castle with me, there to discourse over his draught of a ship he is to build for us – where I first find reason to apprehend Comissioner Pett to be a man of any ability extraordinary in anything, for I found he did turn and wind Castle like a chicken in his business, and that most pertinently and master-like. And great pleasure it was to me to hear them discourse, I of late having studied something thereon, and my Lord Brunker is a very able person also himself in this sort of business, as owning himself to be a master in the business of all lines and Conicall Sections. Thence home, where very late at my office, doing business to my content; though [God] knows with what a do it was that when I was out I could get myself to come home to my business, or when I was there, though late, could stay there from going abroad again. To supper and to bed. This night when I came home, I was much troubled to hear my poor Canary-bird that I have kept these three or four years is dead.

14.   With my wife to the King's house, there to see *Vulpone*, a most excellent play – the best I think I ever saw, and well acted. So with Sir W. Penn home in his coach, and then to the office; so home [to] supper and bed – resolving, by the grace of God, from this day to fall hard to my business again, after some, a week or fortnight's, neglect.

15.   *Lords day*. Up; and after a little at my office to prepare a fresh draft of my vows for the next year, I to church, where a most insipid young coxcomb preached. Then home to dinner; and after dinner to read in Rusworths *Collections* about the charge against the late Duke of Buckingham, in order to the fitting me to speak and understand the discourse anon before the King, about the suffering the Turkey merchants to send out their fleet at this dangerous time, when we can neither spare them ships to go, nor men nor King's ships to convoy them. At 4 a-clock with Sir W. Penn in his coach to my Lord Chancellors, where by and by Mr. Coventry, Sir W. Penn, Sir J. Lawson, Sir G. Ascue, and myself were called in to the King, there being several of the Privy Council, and my Lord Chancellor lying at length upon a couch (of the goute I suppose); and there Sir W. Penn begun, and he had prepared heads in a paper and spoke pretty well to purpose, but with so much leisure and

gravity as was tiresome – besides, the things he said was but very poor to a man in his trade after a great consideration. But it was to purpose endeed, to dissuade the King from letting these Turkey ships to go out – saying (in short), the King having resolved to have 130 ships out by the spring, he must have above 20 of them merchantmen – towards which, he in the whole river could find but 12 or 14; and of them, the five ships taken up by these merchants were a part, and so could not be spared. That we should need 30000 to man these 130 ships; and of them in service we have not above 16000, so we shall need 14000 more. That these ships will with their convoys carry above 2000 men, and those the best men that could be got, it being the men used to the southward that are the best men for war, though those bred in the north among the Colliers are good for labour. That it will not be safe for the merchants, nor honourable for the King, to expose these rich ships with his convoy of six ships to go, it not being enough to secure them against the Dutch, who without doubt will have a great fleet in the Straights. This, Sir J. Lawson enlarged upon. Sir G. Ascu, he chiefly spoke that the warr and trade could not be supported together – and therefore, that trade must stand still to give way to that. This Mr. Coventry seconded, and showed how the medium of the men the King hath, one year with another, imployed in his Navy since his coming, hath not been above 3000 men, or at most 4000 men; and now having occasion of 30000, the remaining 26000 must be found out of the trade of the nation. He showed how the Cloaths sending by these merchants to Turkey are already bought and paid for to the workmen, and are as many as they would send these twelve months or more; so the poor do not suffer by their not going, but only the merchant, upon whose hands they lie dead – and so the inconvenience is the less. All ended with a conviction (unless future discourse with the merchants should alter it) that it was not fit for them to go out, though the ships be loaded. Staying without, my Lord Fitzharding came thither and fell to discourse of Prince Rupert, and made nothing to say that his disease was the pox and that he must be Fluxed, telling the horrible degree of the disease upon him, with its breaking out on his head. But above all, I observed how he observed from the Prince that Courage is not what men take it to be, a contempt of death; "For," says he, "how Chagrin the Prince was the other day when he thought he should die – having no more mind to it then another man; but," says he, "some men are more apt to think they shall escape then another

1. Samuel Pepys, by John Hayls, 1666. He holds the manuscript of his song, 'Beauty Retire'.

2. Elizabeth Pepys, from an engraving by James Thomson after the portrait by
John Hayls, 1666

man in fight, while another is doubtful he shall be hit. But when the first man is sure he shall die, as now the Prince is, he is as much troubled and apprehensive of it as any man else. For," says he, "sence we told him that we believe he would overcome his disease, he is as merry, and swears and laughs and curses and doth all the things of a [man] in health, as ever he did in his life" – which methought was a most extraordinary saying, before a great many persons there of quality. So by and by with Sir W. Penn home again; and after supper to the office to finish my vows, and so to bed.

18.    Up, and by and by to my bookseller's and there did give thorough direction for the new binding of a great many of my old books, to make my whole study of the same binding, within very few. Thence to my Lady Sandwiches, who sent for me this morning. Dined with her – and it was to get a letter of hers conveyed by a safe hand to my Lord's own hand at Portsmouth; which I did undertake. Here my Lady did begin to talk of what she hath heard concerning Creed; of his being suspected to be a fanatic and a false fellow. I told her I thought he was as shrewd and cunning a man as any in England, and one that I would fear first should outwit me in everything – to which she readily concurred. Thence to Mr. Povy's by agreement; and there, with Mr. Sherwin, Auditor Beale, and Creede and I, hard at it very late about Mr. Povys accounts; but such accounts I never did see, or hope again to see in my days. At night late, they gone, I did get him to put out of this account our sums that are *in posse* only yet – which he approved of when told, but would never have stayed it if I had been gone. Thence at 9 at night home; and so to supper, vexed and head akeing, and to bed.

20.    To the Swan at noon, and there sent for a bit of meat and dined and had my baiser of the fille of the house there – but nothing plus. So took coach and to my Lady Sandwiches; and so to my booksellers and there took home Hookes book of Microscopy, a most excellent piece, and of which I am very proud. So home, and by and by again abroad with my wife about several businesses; and met at the New Exchange, and there to our trouble find our pretty Doll is gone away to live, they say with her father in the country – but I doubt something worse. So homeward, in my way buying a hare and taking it home – which arose upon my discourse today

with Mr. Batten in Westminster hall – who showed me my mistake, that my hares-foot[1] hath not the joyne to it, and assures me he never had his cholique since he carried it about him. And it is a strange thing how fancy works, for I no sooner almost handled his foot but my belly begin to be loose and to break wind; and whereas I was in some pain yesterday and t'other day, and in fear of more today, I became very well, and so continue. At home to my office a while, and so to supper – read, and to cards and to bed.

21. At the office all the morning. Thence my Lord Brunker carried me as far as Mr. Povy's and there I light and dined, meeting Mr. Sherwin, Creed, &c. there upon his accounts. After dinner they parted, and Mr. Povy carried me to Somersett house and there showed me the Queen-mother's chamber and closet, most beautiful places for furniture and pictures; and so down the great stone stairs to the garden and tried the brave Eccho upon the stairs – which continues a voice so long as the singing three notes, concords, one after another, they all three shall sound in consort together a good while most pleasantly. Thence to a Tanger Comittee at Whitehall, where I saw nothing ordered by judgment, but great heat and passion and faction now, in behalf of my Lord Bellasses and to the reproach of my Lord Tiviott, and dislike as it were of former proceedings. So away with Mr. Povey, he carrying me homeward to Mark lane in his coach. A simple fellow I now find him, to his utter shame, in his business of accounts, as none but a sorry fool would have discovered himself – and yet in little light sorry things, very cunning; yet in the principal, the most ignorant man I ever met with in so great trust as he is. To my office till past 12, and then home to supper and to bed – being now mighty well; and truly, I cannot but impute it to my fresh Hares Foote. Before I went to bed, I sat up till 2 a-clock in my chamber, reading of Mr. Hookes Microscopical Observations, the most ingenious book that ever I read in my life.

22. *Lords day*. Up, leaving my wife in bed, being sick of her months, and to church. Thence home, and in my wife's chamber dined very merry, discoursing among other things of a design I have come in my head this morning at church, of making a match between Mrs. Betty Pickering and Mr. Hill my friend, the

1. See above, p. 457 & n.

merchant that loves musique and comes to me a-Sundays, a most ingenious and sweet-natured and highly accomplished person. I know not how their fortunes may agree, but their disposition and merits are much of a sort, and persons, though different, yet equally I think acceptable.

23. Up, and with Sir W. Batten and Sir W. Penn to Whitehall; but there finding the Duke gone to his lodgings at St. James's for altogether, his Duchesse being ready to lie in, we to him and there did our usual business. And here I met the great news, confirmed by the Dukes own relation, by a letter from Capt. Allen – first, of our loss of two ships, the *Phœnix* and *Nonesuch*, in the Bay of Gibraltar – then, of his and his seven ships with him, in the Bay of Cales or thereabouts, fight with the 34 Duch Smirna fleet – sinking the *King Salamon*, a ship worth 150000*l* or more, some say 200000*l*, and another, and taking three merchant-ships. Thence to Jervas's, my mind, God forgive me, running too much after sa fille, but elle not being within, I away by coach to the Change – and thence home to dinner; and finding Mrs. Bagwell waiting at the office after dinner, away elle and I to a cabaret where elle and I have été before; and there I had her company toute l'après-dîner and had mon plein plaisir of elle – but strange, to see how a woman, notwithstanding her greatest pretences of love à son mari and religion, may be vaincue. Thence to the Court of the Turky Company at Sir Andr. Rickard's, to treat about carrying some men of ours to Tanger, and had there a very civil reception, though a denial of the thing, as not practicable with them, and I think so too. So to my office a little; but being minded to make an end of my pleasure today, that I might fallow my business, I did take coach and to Jervas's again, thinking to avoir rencontré Jane; mais elle n'était pas dedans. So I back again to my office, where I did with great content faire a vow to mind my business and laisser aller les femmes for a month; and am with all my heart glad to find myself able to come to so good a resolution, that thereby I may fallow my business, which, and my honour thereby, lies a-bleeding. So home to supper and to bed.

24. Up, and by coach to Westminster hall and the Parliament-house, and there spoke with Mr. Coventry and others about business; and so back to the Change, where no news more then that the Dutch have, by consent of all the Provinces, voted no trade to be suffered for 18 months, but that they apply themselfs wholly to the

war. And they say it is very true but very strange, for we use to believe they cannot support themselfs without trade. Thence home to dinner and then to the office, where all the afternoon and at night till very late; and then home to supper and bed, having a great cold, got on Sunday last by sitting too long with my head bare for Mercer to comb me and wash my eares.

25.   Up, and busy all the morning. Dined at home upon a Hare py, very good meat; and so to my office again, and in the afternoon by coach to attend the Council at Whitehall, but come too late; so back with Mr. Gifford, a merchant, and he and I to the Coffee-house, where I met Mr. Hill and there he tells me that he is to bee Assistant to the Secretary of the Prize Office (Sir Ellis Layton), which is to be held at Sir Rd. Fords – which methinks is but something low, but perhaps may bring him something considerable. But it makes me alter my opinion of his being so rich as to make a fortune for Mrs. Pickering. Thence home and visited Sir J. Mennes, who continues ill but is something better. There he told me what a mad freaking fellow Sir Ellis Layton hath been and is – and once at Antwerp, was really mad. Thence to my office late, my cold troubling me and having, by squeezing myself in a coach, hurt my testicles; but I hope I will cease its pain without swelling. So home, out of order, to supper and so to bed.

30.   This is solemnly kept as a Fast[1] all over the City; but I kept my house, putting my closett to rights again, having lately put it out of order in removing my books and things in order to being made clean. At this all day, and at night to my office, there to do some business. And being late at it, comes Mercer to me to tell me that my wife was in bed and desired me to come home, for they hear, and have night after night lately heard, noises over their head upon the leads. Now, it is strange to think how, knowing that I have a great sum of money in my house, this puts me into a most mighty affright, that for more then two hours I could not almost tell what to do or say, but feared this and that – and remembered that this evening I saw a woman and two men stand suspiciously in the Entry in the dark; I calling to them, they made me only this answer: the woman said that the men came to see her. But who she was I could not tell. The truth is, my house is mighty dangerous, having

---

1. In commemoration of the execution of Charles I.

so many ways to be come to, and at my windows over the stairs, to see who goes up and down – but if I escape tonight, I will remedy it. God preserve us this night safe. So at almost 2 a-clock, I home to my house and in great fear to bed, thinking every running of a mouse really a thief – and so to sleep, very brokenly all night long – and found all safe in the morning.

# –✤FEBRUARY✤–

4. To my office, and there all the morning. At noon, being invited, I to the Sun behind the Change to dinner to my Lord Bellasses – where a great deal of discourse with him – and some good. Among other at table, he told us a very handsome passage of the King's sending him his message about holding out the town of Newarke, of which he was then governor for the King. This message he sent in a Slugg bullet, being writ in Cypher and wrapped up in lead and swallowed. So the messenger came to my Lord and told him he had a mesage from the King, but it was yet in his belly; so they did give him some physic, and out it came.

7. Up, and to my office, where busy all the morning. And at home, at dinner, it being Shrove Tuseday, had some very good fritters. All the afternoon and evening at the office. And at night home to supper and to bed. This day Sir W. Batten, who hath been sick four or five days, is now very bad, so as that people begin to fear his death – and I at a loss whether it will be better for me to have him die, because he is a bad man, or live, for fear a worse should come.

9. Up, and to my office, where all the morning very busy. At noon home to dinner, and then to my office again – where Sir Wm. Petty came, among other things, to tell me that Mr. Barlow is dead; for which, God knows my heart, I could be as sorry as is possible for one to be for a stranger by whose death he gets 100*l* per annum[1] – he being a very honest man. But after having considered that when I come to consider the providence of God, by this means unexpectedly to give me 100*l* a year more in my estate, I have cause

1. See above, p. 64 (17 July).

to bless God, and do it from the bottom of my heart. So home late at night, after 12 a-clock, and so to bed.

12. *Lords day*. Up, and to church to St. Lawrence to hear Dr. Wilkins the great scholar, for curiosity, I having never heard him. But was not satisfied with him at all. Only, a gentleman sat in the pew I by chance sat in, that sang most excellently, and afterward I found by his face that he hath been a paul's scholler, but know not his name – and I was also well pleased with the church, it being a very fine church. So home to dinner, and then to my office all the afternoon, doing of business; and in the evening comes Mr. Hill (but no Andrews) and we spent the evening very finely, singing, supping, and discoursing. Then to prayers and to bed.

13. Up, and to St. James's; did our usual business before the Duke. Thence I to Westminster and by water (taking Mr. Stapely the rope-maker by the way) to his rope-ground and to Limehouse, there to see the manner of Stoves, and did excellently inform myself therein. And coming home, did go on board Sir W. Petty's *experiment* – which is a brave roomy vessel – and I hope may do well. So went on shore to a Dutch [house] to drink some Mum, and there light upon some Dutchmen, with whom we had good discourse touching Stoveing and making of cables. But to see how despicably they speak of us for our using so many hands more to do anything then they do, they closing a cable with 20 that we use 60 men upon. Thence home and eat something; and then to my office, where very late; and then to supper and to bed.

14. *St. Valentine*. This morning comes betimes Dicke Pen to be my wife's valentine, and came to our bedside. By the same token, I had him brought to my side, thinking to have made him kiss me; but he perceived me, and would not. So went to his Valentine – a notable, stout, witty boy. I up, about business; and opening the doore, there was Bagwell's wife, with whom I talked afterwards and she had the confidence to say she came with a hope to be time enough to be my Valentine, and so endeed she did – but my oath preserved me from losing any time with her. And so I and my boy abroad by coach to Westminster, where did two or three businesses; and then home to the Change, and did much business there. My Lord Sandwich is, it seems, with his fleet at Alborough bay. So home to dinner, and then to the office, where till 12 almost at night,

and then home to supper and to bed.

15. Up, and to my office, where busy all the morning. At noon with Creed to dinner to Trinity house to dinner, where a very good dinner among the old Sokers – where and extraordinary discourse of the manner of the loss of the *Royall Oake*, coming home from Bantam, upon the rocks of Scilly; many passages therein being very extraordinary – and if I can, I will get it in writing. Thence with Creed to Gresham College – where I had been by Mr. Povy the last week proposed to be admitted a member; and was this day admitted, by signing a book and being taken by the hand by the Præsident, my Lord Brunkard, and some words of admittance said to me. But it is a most acceptable thing to hear their discourses and see their experiments; which was this day upon the nature of fire, and how it goes out in a place where the ayre is not free, and sooner out where the ayre is exhausted; which they showed by an engine on purpose. After this being done, they to the Crowne tavern behind the Change, and there my Lord and most of the company to a club supper – Sir P. Neale, Sir R. Murrey, Dr. Clerke, Dr. Whistler, Dr. Goddard, and others of most eminent worth. Above all, Mr. Boyle today was at the meeting, and above him Mr. Hooke, who is the most, and promises the least, of any man in the world that ever I saw. Here, excellent discourses till 10 at night, and then home.

18. Up, and to the office, where sat all the morning. At noon to the Change, and thence to the Royall Oake taverne in Lumbard Streete, where Sir Wm. Petty and the owners of the Double-bottomed boat (the *Experiment*) did entertain my Lord Brunkard, Sir R. Murry, myself and others with marrow-bones and a chine of beefe of the victuals they have made for this ship – and excellent company and good discourse; but above all, I do value Sir Wm. Petty. Thence home, and took my Lord Sandwiches Draught of the Harbour of Portsmouth down to Ratcliffe to one Burston, to make a plat for the King and another for the Duke and another for himself – which will be very neat. So home, and till almost one a-clock in the morning at my office; and then home to supper and to bed. My Lord Sandwich and his fleet of 25 ships in the Downes, returned from crucing; but could not meet with any Dutchmen.

19. Lay in bed, being Lords day, all the morning talking with my

wife, sometimes pleased, sometimes displeased; and then up and to dinner. All the afternoon also at home and Sir W. Batten's, and in the evening comes Mr. Andrews and we sung together; and then to supper (he not staying) and at supper, hearing by accident of my mayds their letting in a rogueing Scotch woman that haunts the office, to help them to wash and scour in our house, and that very lately, I fell mightily out, and made my wife, to the disturbance of the house and neighbours, to beat our little girle; and then we shut her down into the cellar and there she lay all night. So we to bed.

20.    Up, and with Sir J. Mennes to attend the Duke; and then we back again and rode into the beginnings of my Lord Chancellors new house near St. James's, which common people have already called Dunkirke house, from their opinion of his having a good bribe for the selling of that town.[1] And very noble I believe it will be. Near that is my Lord Berkely beginning another on one side, and Sir J. Denham on the other. Thence I to the House of Lords and spoke with my Lord Bellases; and so to the Change and there did business; and so to the Sun Taverne – having in the morning had some high words with Sir J. Lawson about his sending of some bayled goods to Tanger; wherein the truth is, I did not favour him. But being conscious that some of my profit may come out, by some words that fell from him; and to be quiet, I have accommodated it. Here we dined, merry; but my club and the rest come to 7s. 6d., which was too much. Thence to the office and there found Bagwells wife, whom I directed to go home and I would do her business; which was to write a letter to my Lord Sandwich for her husband's advance into a better ship as there should be occasion – which I did; and by and by did go down by water to Deptford yard, and then down further and so landed at the lower end of the town; and it being dark, did privately entrer en la maison de la femme de Bagwell, and there I had sa compagnie, though with a great deal of difficulty; néanmoins, enfin je avais ma volonté d'elle. And being sated therewith, I walked home to Redriffe, it being now near 9 a-clock; and there I did drink some strong waters and eat some bread and cheese, and so home – where at my office, my wife comes and tells me that she hath hired a chambermaid, one of the prettiest maids that ever she saw in her life, and that she is really jealous of me for her – but hath ventured to hire her from month to month. But I

---

1. See above, p. 228 (19 October) & n. 2.

think she means merrily. So to supper and to bed.

21.   Up, and to the office (having a mighty pain in my forefinger
of my left hand, from a strain that it received last night in struggling
avec la femme que je mentioned yesterday), where busy till noon;
and then, my wife being busy in going with her woman to a hot-
house to bath herself, after her long being within doors in the dirt,
so that she now pretends to a resolution of being hereafter very
clean – how long it will hold, I can guess – I dined with Sir W.
Batten and my Lady, they being nowadays very fond of me. So to
the Change, and off of the Change with Mr. Wayth to a cook's shop
and there dined again, for discourse with him about Hamaccos and
the abuse now practised in tickets, and more like every day to be –
also, of the great profit Mr. Fen makes of his place – he being
(though he demands but ½ per cent of all he pays, and that is easily
computed) but very little pleased with any man that gives him no
more. So to the office; and after office my Lord Brunkerd carried
me to Lincoln's Inn fields, and there I with my Lady Sandwich
(good lady), talking of innocent discourse of good housewifery and
husbands for her daughters, and the luxury and looseness of the
times and other such things, till past 10 a-clock at night; and so by
coach home, where a little at my office, and so to supper and to bed.
My Lady tells me what mad freaks the mayds of Honour at Court
have – that Mrs. Jennings, one of the Duchess's maids, the other
day dressed herself like an orange-wench and went up and down
and cried oranges – till falling down, or by such accident (though in
the evening), her fine shoes were discerned and she put to a great
deal of shame.

23.   This day, by the blessing of Almighty God, I have lived 32
years in the world – and am in the best degree of health at this
minute that I have been almost in my life-time, and at this time in
the best condition of estate that ever I was in; the Lord make me
thankful. Up, and to the office, where busy all the morning. At
noon to the Change, where I hear the most horrid and astonishing
news that ever was yet told in my memory – that De Ruiter, with
his fleet in guinny, hath proceeded to the taking of whatever we
have – forts, goods, ships, and men – and tied our men back to back
and thrown them all into the sea – even women and children also.
This a Swede or Hamburger is come into the River and tells that he
saw the thing done. Home to dinner, and then to the office, where

sat all the afternoon; and then at night to take my finall leave of Mrs. Bland, who sets out tomorrow for Tanger. And then I back to my office till past 12, and so home to supper and to bed.

24. Up, and to my office, where all the morning – upon advising again with some Fishermen and the Waterbayliffe of the City, by Mr. Coventry's direction, touching the protections[1] which are desired for the fishermen upon the River; and I am glad of the occasion to make me understand something of it. At noon home to dinner, and all the afternoon, till 9 at night, in my chamber, and Mr. Hater with me (to prevent being disturbed at the office), to perfect my contract-book, which for want of time hath a long time lain without being entered in, as I used to do, from month to month.

25. Up, and to the office, where all the morning. At noon to the Change; where just before I came, the Swede that had told the King and the Duke so boldly this great lie, of the Dutch flinging our men back to back into the sea at Guinny, so perticularly and readily and confidently, was whipped round the Change – he confessing it a lie, and that he did it in hopes to get something. Thence to the Sun Taverne, and there dined with Sir W. Warren and Mr. Gifford the merchant; and I hear how Nich. Colborne, that lately lived and got a great estate there, is gone to live like a prince in the country; and that this Wadlow, that did the like at the Devil by St. Dunstanes, did go into the country, and there spent almost all he had got, and hath now choused this Colborne out of his house, that he might come to his old trade again. Thence home to the office, where despatch much business; at night late home and to clean myself with warm water; my wife will have me, because she doth herself; and so to bed.

27. Up, and to St. James's, where we attend the Duke as usual. At home to dinner; and then in Sir J. Mennes's coach, my wife and I with him, and also Mercer, abroad; he and I to Whitehall, and he would have his coach to wait upon my wife on her visits – it being the first time my wife hath been out of doors (but the other day to bath her) several weeks. We to a committee of the Council to discourse concerning pressing of men; but Lord, how they meet; never sit down – one comes, now another goes, then comes another

1. From the press-gang.

– one complaining that nothing is done, another swearing that he hath been there these two hours and nobody came. At last it came to this: my Lord Annesly, says he, "I think we must be forced to get the King to come to every committee, for I do not see that we do anything at any time but when he is here." And I believe he said the truth. And very constant he is at the council table on council days; which his predecessors, it seems, very rarely did. But thus, I perceive, the greatest affair in the world at this day is likely to be managed by us. But to hear how my Lord Berkely and others of them do cry up the discipline of the late times here, and in the former Dutch warr, is strange – wishing with all their hearts that the business of religion were not so severely carried on as to discourage the sober people to come among us, and wishing that the same law and severity were used against drunkenness as there was then – saying that our evil-living will call the hand of God upon us again. Thence to walk alone a good while in St. James park with Mr. Coventry, who I perceive is grown a little melancholy, and displeased to see things go as they do – so carelessly.

28.   At the office all the morning. At noon dined at home. After dinner my wife and I to my Lady Batten's, it being the first time my wife hath been there, I think, these two years; but I have a mind in part to take away that strangeness, and so we did, and all very quiet and kind. Came home; I to the taking my wife's kitchen account at the latter end of the month, and there find 7s. wanting – which did occasion a very high falling out between us; I endeed too eagerly insisting upon so poor a thing, and did give her very provoking words, calling her "beggar" and reproaching her friends;* which she took very stomachfully, and reproached me justly with mine; and I confess, being myself, I cannot see what she could have done less. I find she is very cunning, and when she least shows it, hath her wit at work; but it is an ill one, though I think not so bad but with good usage I might well bear with it; and the truth is, I do find that my being over-solicitous and jealous and froward, and ready to reproach her, doth make her worse. However, I find that now and then a little difference doth do not hurt – but too much of it will make her know her force too much. We parted, after many high words, very angry; and I to my office to my month's accounts, and find myself worth 1270*l* – for which the Lord God be praised. So, at almost 2 a-clock in the morning, I home to supper and to bed.

   And so ends this month, with great expectation of the Hollanders coming forth; who are, it seems, very high and rather more ready then we. God give a good issue to it.

# –✣MARCH✣–

1.  Up – and this day being the day that, by a promise a great while ago made to my wife, I was to give her 20*l* to lay out in clothes against Easter, she did, notwithstanding last night's falling-out, come to peace with me and I with her, but did boggle mightily at the parting with my money, but at last did give it her; and then she abroad to buy her things, and I to my office, where busy all the morning. At noon I to dinner at Trinity house – and thence to Gresham College, where, first Mr. Hooke read a second very curious* Lecture about the late Comett, among other things, proving very probably that this is the very same Comett that appeared before in the year 1618, and that in such a time probably it will appear again – which is a very new opinion – but all will be in print. Then to the meeting, where Sir G. Carterets two sons, his own and Sir N. Slany, were admitted of the Society. And this day I did pay my admission money – 40*s*. – to the Society. Here was very fine discourses – and experiments; but I do lack philosophy enough to understand them, and so cannot remember them. Among others, a very perticular account of the making of the several sorts of bread in France, which is accounted the best place for bread in the world.

4.  Up very betimes; and walked, it being bitter cold, to Ratcliffe to the plat-maker's and back again. To the office, where we sat all the morning. I, with being empty and full of ayre and wind, had some pain today. Dined alone at home, my wife being gone abroad to buy some more things. All the afternoon at the office. At night home to supper and to bed. This day was proclaimed at the Change the war with Holland.

7–8.  Up, and was pretty well; but going to the office, and I think it was sitting with my back to the fire, it set me in a great rage again that I could not continue till past noon at the office, but was forced to go home; nor could sit down to dine, but betook myself to my bed; and being there a while, my pain begun to abate and grow less and less. Anon I went to make water, not dreaming of anything but my testicle, that by some accident I might have bruised as I used to do – but in pissing, there came from me two stones; I could feel them, and caused my water to be looked into, but without any pain to me in going out – which makes me think that it was not a fit of the stone at all; for my pain was asswaged upon my lying down a great while before I went to make water. Anon I made water again very freely and plentifully. I kept my bed in good ease all the evening; then rose and sat up an hour or two; and then to bed and lay till 8 a-clock; and then, though a bitter cold day, yet I rose, and though my pain and tenderness in my testicle remains a little, yet I do verily think that my pain yesterday was nothing else, and therefore I hope my disease of the stone may not return to me, but void itself in pissing; which God grant – but I will consult my physitian. This morning is brought me to the office the sad news of the *London*, in which Sir J. Lawsons men were all bringing her from Chatham to the Hope, and thence he was to go to sea in her – but a little a-this-side the buoy of the Nower, she suddenly blew up. About 24 and a woman that were in the round-house and coach saved; the rest, being above 300, drowned – the ship breaking all in pieces – with 80 pieces of brass ordinance. She lies sunk, with her round-house above water. Sir J. Lawson hath a great loss in this, of so many good chosen men, and many relations among them. I went to the Change, where the news taken very much to heart. So home to dinner, and Mr. Moore with me; then I to Gresham College and there saw several pretty experiments; and so home and to my office – and at night, about 11, home to supper and to bed.

9. Up and to the office, where we sat all the morning. At noon to dinner at home and then abroad with my wife. Left her at the New Exchange, and I to Westminster, where I hear Mrs. Martin is brought to bed of a boy and christened Charles – which I am very glad of, for I was fearful of being called to be a godfather to it. But it seems it was to be done suddenly, and so I escaped. It is strange, to see how a liberty, and going abroad without purpose of doing anything, doth lead a man to what is bad; for I was just upon going to her, where I must of necessity have broken my oath or made a forfeit. But I did not, company being (I heard by my porter) with her; and so I home again, taking up my wife, and was set down by her at Paules schoole, where I visited Mr. Crumlum at his house. And Lord, to see how ridiculous a conceited pædagogue is, though

a learned man – he is being so dogmaticall in all he doth and says. But among other discourse, we fall to the old discourse of Pauls Schoole; and he did, upon my declaring my value of it, give me one of Lillys grammer of a very old impression, as it was in the Catholique times; which I shall much set by. And so after some small discourse, away and called upon my wife at a linen-draper's shop buying linen; and so home and to my office, where late, and home to supper and to bed. This night my wife had a new suit of Flowerd ash-Coloured silk, very noble.

17.   Up, and to my office; and then with Sir W. Batten to St. James, where many came to take leave, as was expected, of the Duke; but he doth not go till Monday. The Duke did give us some commands, and so broke up, not taking leave of him. But the best piece of newes is that instead of a great many troublesome Lords, the whole business is to be left with the Duke of Albemarle, to act as Admirall[1] in his stead; which is a thing that doth cheer my heart – for the other would have vexed us with attendance, and never done the business. Thence to the Committee of Tanger, where the Duke a little, and then left us and we stayed – a very great Committee – the Lords Albemarle, Sandwich, Barkely, Fitzharding, Peterborough, Ashley, Sir Tho. Ingram, Sir G. Carteret, and others. The whole business was the stating of Povys accounts; of whom, to say no more, never could man say worse himself nor have worse said of him then was by that company to his face – I mean as to his folly, and very reflecting words to his honesty. So broke up. Then he took occasion to desire me to step aside, and he and I by water to London together: in the way, of his own accord, proposed to me that he would surrender his place of Treasurer to me, to have half the profit. The thing is new to me; but the more I think, the more I like it, and do put him upon getting it done by the Duke: whether it takes or no, I care not, but I think at present it may have some convenience in it.

19.   *Lords day.* Mr. Povy and I in his coach to Hide parke, being the first day of the Tour there – where many brave ladies. Among others, Castlemayne lay impudently upon her back in her coach asleep with her mouth open. There was also my Lady Kerneeguy once my Lady Anne Hambleton, that is said to have given the Duke

1. sc. Lord High Admiral of the Kingdom.

a clap upon his first coming over. Here I saw Sir J. Lawson's daughter and husband, a fine couple – and also Mr. Southwell and his new lady, very pretty. Thence back, putting in at Dr. Whore's, where I saw his lady, a very fine woman. So home, and thither by my desire comes by and by Creed and lay with me, very merry – and full of discourse what to do tomorrow, and the conveniences that will attend my having of this place; and I do think they may be very great.

20. Up, Creed and I, and had Mr. Povy's coach sent for us, and we to his house – where we did some business, in order to the work of this day. Povy and I to my Lord Sandwich, who tells me that the Duke is not only a friend to the business, but to me, in terms of the greatest love and respect and value of me that can be thought; which overjoys me. The Duke did direct Secretary Bennet, who was there, to declare his mind to the Committee that he approves of me for Treasurer, and with a character of me to be a man whose industry and discretion he would trust as soon as any man's in England – and did the like to my Lord Sandwich. So to Whitehall to the Committee of Tanger and there I received their constitution under all hands presently, so that I am already confirmed their Treasurer, and put into a condition of striking of Tallys. And all without one harsh word or word of dislike; but quite the contrary – which is a good fortune beyond all imagination. Here we rose, and Povy and Creed and I, all full of joy, thence to dinner – they setting me down at Sir J. Winter's by promise; and dined with him, and a worthy fine man he seems to be, and of good discourse. Our business was to discourse of supplying the King with Iron for Ancors, if it can be judged good enough. And a fine thing it is, to see myself come to the condition of being received by persons of this rank – he being, and having long been, Secretary to the Queene-mother.

22. To Mr. Povys, and with Creed to the Change and to my house; but it being washing-day, dined not at home, but took him (I being invited) to Mr. Hublands the merchant, where Sir W. Petty and abundance of most ingenious men, owners and freighters of the *Experiment*, now going with her two bodies to sea. Most excellent discourse. Among others, Sir Wm. Petty did tell me that in good earnest, he hath in his will left such parts of his estate to him that could invent such and such things – as among others, that could

discover truly the way of milk coming into the breasts of a woman – and he that could invent proper Characters to express to another the mixture of relishes and tastes. And says that to him that invents gold, he gives nothing for the Philosopher's stone; "for," says he, "they that find out that will be able to pay themselfs – but," says he, "by this means it is better then to give to a lecture. For here my executors, that must part with this, will be sure to be well convinced of the invention before they do part with their money." Then to Gresham College and there did see a kitlin killed almost quite (but that we could not quite kill her) with sucking away the Ayre out of a Receiver wherein she was put – and then the ayre being let in upon her, revives her immediately. Nay, and this ayre is to be made by putting together a Liquor and some body that firments – the steam of that doth do the work. Thence home, and thence to Whitehall, where the House full of the Dukes going tomorrow; and thence to St. James, wherein these things fell out:

1 I saw the Duke. Kissed his hand. And had his most kind expressions of his value and opinion of me, which comforted me above all things in the world.

2 The like from Mr. Coventry, most heartily and affectionately.

3 Saw, among other fine ladies, Mrs. Middleton, a very great beauty I never knew or heard of before;

4 I saw Waller the Poet, whom I never saw before.

So, very late, by coach home with W. Pen, who was there. To supper and to bed – with my heart at rest and my head very busy, thinking of my several matters now on foot – the new comfort of my old Navy business, and the new one of my imployment on Tanger.

23. Up, and to my Lord Sandwich, who fallows the Duke this day by water down to the Hope, where the *Prince* lies. He received me, busy as he was, with mighty kindness and joy at my promotions, telling me most largely how the Duke hath expressed on all occasions his good opinion of my service and love for me. I paid my thanks and acknowledgment to him; and so back home.

27. Up betimes to Mr. Povy's, and there did sign and seal my agreement with him about my place of being Treasurer for Tanger – it being, the greatest part of it, drawn out of a draft of his own drawing up; only, I have added something here and there in favour of myself. Thence to the Duke of Albemarle, the first time that we

officers of the Navy have waited upon him since the Duke of York's going, who hath deputed him to be Admirall in his absence. And I find him a quiet, heavy man, that will help business when he can and hinder nothing – and am very well pleased with our attendance on him.

# –❧APRILL❧–

1. With Sir G. Carteret to my Lord Treasurers, and by and by comes Sir W. Batten and Sir J. Mennes and anon we come to my Lord and there did lay open the expense for the six months past, and an estimate of the seven months to come, to November next – the first arising to above 500000*l*; and the latter will, as we judge, come to above a Million. But to see how my Lord Treasurer did bless himself, crying he could do no more then he could, nor give more money then he had, if the occasion and expense were never so great, which is but a sad story; and then to hear how like a passionate and ignorant asse Sir G. Carteret did harangue upon the abuse of Tickets, did make me mad almost, and yet was fain to hold my tongue. Thence home, vexed mightily to see how simply our greatest ministers do content themselfs to understand and do things, while the King's service in the meantime lies a-bleeding. At my office late, writing letters, till ready to drop down asleep with my late sitting up late and running up and down a-days. So to bed.

2. *Lords day.* At my office all the morning, renewing my vowes in writing. And then home to dinner. All the afternoon Mr. Tasborough, one of Mr. Povy's clerks, with me about his maister's accounts; in the evening Mr. Andrews and Hill sung – but supped not with me. Then after supper to bed.

3. Up, and to the Duke of Albemarle and Whitehall, where much business; thence home and to dinner; and then with Creed, my wife, and Mercer to a play at the Dukes of my Lord Orerey's, called *Mustapha* – which being not good, made Baterton's part and Ianthes but ordinary too, so that we were not contented with it at all. Thence home and to the office a while; and then home to supper and to bed. All the pleasure of the play was, the King and my Lady

Castlemaine was there – and pretty witty Nell[1] at the King's house, and the younger Marshall, sat next us; which pleased me mightily.

4. All the morning at the office busy. At noon to the Change, and then went up to the Change to buy a pair of cotton stockings, which I did at the husband's shop of the most pretty woman there, who did also invite me to buy some linen of her; and I was glad of the occasion and bespoke some bands of her, entending to make her my seamstress – she being one of the prettiest and most modest-looked women that ever I did see. Dined at home; and to the office, where very late, till I was ready to fall down asleep, and did several times nod in the middle of my letters.

5. This day was kept publicly, by the King's command, as a Fast day against the Duch war. And I betimes with Mr. Tooker, whom I have brought into the Navy to serve us as a husband to see goods timely shipped off from hence to the fleet and other places, and took him with me to Woolwich and Deptford, where by business I have been hindered a great while of going. Did a very great deal of business. And then home, and there by promise find Creed, and he and my wife, Mercer and I, by coach to take the ayre; and where we have formerly been, at Hackny, did there eat some pullets we carried with us and some other things of the house; and after a game or two at shuffleboard, home; and Creed lay with me but being sleepy, he had no mind to talk about business, which endeed I intended by inviting him to lie with me. But I would not force it on him, and so to bed, he and I, and to sleep – being the first time I have been so much at my ease and taken so much fresh ayre these many weeks or months.

7. Up betimes to the Duke of Albemarle about money to be got for the Navy, or else we must shut up shop. Thence to Westminster hall and up and down, doing not much; then to London, but to prevent Povys dining with me (who I see is at the Change) I went back again and to Herberts at Westminster; there sent for a bit of meat and dined, and then to my Lord Treasurers and there with Sir Ph. Warwicke; and thence to Whitehall, in my Lord Treasurer's chamber with Sir Philip till dark night, about four hours talking of the business of Navy charge and how Sir G. Carteret doth order

1. Nell Gwyn.

business, keeping us in ignorance what he doth with his money. And also, Sir Philip did show me nakedly the King's condition for money for the Navy; and he doth assure me, unless the King can get some noblemen or rich money-gentlemen to lend him money – or to get the City to do it – it is impossible to find money. We having already, as he says, spent one year's share of the three-years' tax, which comes to 2500000*l*. Being very glad of this day's discourse, in all but that I fear I shall quite lose Sir G. Carteret, who knows that I have been privately here all this day with Sir Ph. Warwicke. However, I will order it so as to give him as little offence as I can. So home to my office, and then to supper and to bed.

8.    The French Embassadors are come incognito before their train, which will hereafter be very pompous. It is thought they come to get our King to joyne with the King of France in helping him against Flanders, and they to do the like to us against Holland. We have lain a good while with a good fleet at Harwich. The Dutch not said yet to be out. We, as high as we make our show, I am sure are unable to set out another small fleet, if this should be worsted. Wherefore, God send us peace I cry.

11.    Up, and betimes to Ald. Cheverton to treat with him about hemp, and so back to the office. At noon dined at the Sun behind the Change, with Sir Edw. Deering and his brother and Comissioner Pett, we having made a contract with Sir Edw. this day about Timber. Thence to the office, where late very busy; but with some trouble, have also some hopes of profit too. So home to supper and to bed.

12.    Dined at home; and thence to Whitehall again (where I lose most of my time nowadays, to my great trouble, charge, and loss of time and benefit) and there, after the Council rose, Sir G. Carteret, my Lord Brunkard, Sir Tho. Harvy, and myself down to my Lord Treasurer's chamber to him and the Chancellor and the Duke of Albemarle. And there I did give them a large account of the charge of the Navy, and want of money. But strange, to see how they held up their hands, crying, "What shall we do?" Says my Lord Treasurer, "Why, what means all this, Mr. Pepys? This is true, you say, but what would you have me to do? I have given all I can for my life. Why will not people lend their money? Why will they not trust the King as well as Oliver? Why do our prizes come to

nothing, that yielded so much heretofore?" And this was all we could get, and went away without other answer. Which is one of the saddest things, that at such a time as this, with the greatest action on foot that ever was in England, nothing should be minded, but let things go on of themselfs – do as well as they can. So home, vexed. And going to my Lady Battens, there found a great many women with her in her chamber, merry – my Lady Pen and her daughter, among others; where my Lady Pen flung me down upon the bed, and herself and others, one after another, upon me, and very merry we were; and thence I home and called my wife with my Lady Pen to supper, and very merry as I could be, being vexed as I was. So home to bed.

13.   Lay long in bed, troubled a little with wind, but not much. So to the office and there all the morning. At noon to Sheriffe Watermans to dinner, all of us men of the office in town – and our wifes, my Lady Carteret and daughters, and Lady Batten, Pen, and my wife, &c.; and very good cheer we had and merry. Musique at and after dinner, and a fellow danced a jigg; but when the company begin to dance, I came away, lest I should be taken out; and God knows how my wife carried herself, but I left her to try her fortune. So home, and late at the office; then home to supper and to bed.

16.   *Lords day*. Lay long in bed. Then up and to my chamber and my office, looking over some plats, which I find necessary for me to understand pretty well, because of the Duch warr. Then home to dinner, where Creed dined with us. And so after dinner he and I walked to the Rolls chapel, expecting to hear the great Stillingfleete preach; but he did not, but a very sorry fellow, which vexed me. The sermon done, we parted, and I home – where I find Mr. Andrews; and by and by comes Capt. Taylor, my old acquaintance at Westminster that understands Musique very well and composes mighty bravely; he brought us some things of two parts to sing, very hard. But that that is the worst, he is very conceited of them; and that, though they are good, makes them troublesome to one, to see him every note commend and admire them. He supped with me, and a good understanding man he is and a good Scholler – and among other things, a great Antiquary. And among other things, he can, as he says, show the very Originall Charter to Worcester of King Edgars, wherein he styles himself *Rex Marium Brittaniæ* &c.; which is the great text that Mr. Selden and others do quote, but

imperfectly and upon trust. But he hath the very originall, which he says he will show me. He gone, we to bed. This night I am told the news is come of our taking of three Duch men-of-war, with the loss of one of our Captains.

17. Up, and to the Duke of Albemarles, where he showed me Mr. Coventry's letters; how three Dutch privateers are taken, in one whereof Everson's son is Captaine. But they have killed poor Capt. Golding in the *Diamond*. Two of them, one of 32 and the other of 20 odd guns, did stand stoutly up against her, which hath 46, and the *Yarmouth*, that hath 52 guns, and as many more men as they – so that they did more then we could expect, not yielding till many of their men were killed. And Everson, when he was brought before the Duke of Yorke and was observed to be shot through the hat, answered that he wished it had gone through his head, rather then been taken. One thing more is written: that two of our ships the other day appearing upon the coast of Holland, they presently fired their Beacons round the country, to give notice. And news is brought the King that the Dutch Smirna fleet is seen upon the back of Scottland; and thereupon, the King hath wrote to the Duke that he doth appoint a fleet to go to the Northward to try to meet them coming home round – which God send. Thence to Whitehall; where the King seeing me, did come to me, and calling me by name, did discourse with me about the ships in the River; and this is the first time that ever I knew the King did know me personally, so that hereafter I must not go thither but with expectation to be Questioned, and to be ready to give good answers. This day was left at my house a very neat Silver watch, by one Briggs, a Scrivener and Sollicitor; at which I was angry with my wife for receiving, or at least opening the box wherein it was, and so far witnessing our receipt of it as to give the messenger 5s. for bringing it. But it can't be helped, and I will endeavour to do the man a kindness – he being a friend of my uncle Wights.

22. Up, and Mr. Cæsar, my boy's lute Maister, being come betimes to teach him, I did speak with him seriously about the boy, what my mind was if he did not look after his lute and singing, that I would turn him away – which I hope will do some good upon the boy. All the morning busy at the office. At noon dined at home; and then to the office again, very busy till very late; and so home to supper and to bed – my wife making great preparation to go to

Court to chapel to-morrow. This day I have news from Mr. Coventry that the fleet is sailed yesterday from Harwich to the coast of Holland, to see what the Duch will do. God go along with them.

23. *Lords day.* Mr. Povy, according to promise, sent his coach betimes, and I carried my wife and her woman to Whitehall chapel and set them in the Organ loft. And I, having list to untruss, went to the Harp and ball, and there drank also, and entertained myself in talk with the maid of the house, a pretty maid and very modest. Thence to the chapel and heard the famous young Stillingfleete, who I knew at Cambridge and is now newly admitted one of the King's chaplains – and was presented, they say, to my Lord Treasurer for St. Andrews Holborne, where he is now minister, with these words: that they (the Bishops of Canterbury, London, and another) believed he is the ablest young man to preach the gospel of any since the Apostles. He did make the most plain, honest, good, grave sermon, in the most unconcerned and easy yet substantial manner, that ever I heard in my life – upon the words of Samuell to the people – "Fear the Lord in truth with all your heart, and remember the great things that he hath done for you" – it being proper to this day, the day of the King's Coronation. Thence to Mr. Povy's, where mightily treated, and Creed with us. But Lord, to see how Povy overdoes everything in commending it doth make it nauseous to me, and was not (by reason of my large praise of his house) over-acceptable to my wife. Thence after dinner Creed and we by coach; took the ayre in the fields beyond St. Pancras, it raining now and then; which it seems is most welcome weather. And then all to my house – where comes Mr. Hill, Andrews, and Capt. Taylor, and good Musique; but at supper, to hear the arguments we had against Taylor concerning a Corant – he saying that the law of a dancing Corant is to have every barr to end in a pricked Crochet and quaver – which I did deny, was very strange. It proceeded till I vexed him; but all parted friends, for Creed and I to laugh at when he was gone. After supper Creed and I together to bed in Mercer's bed – and so to sleep.

24. To the Cockepitt, and there walked an hour with my Lord Duke of Albemarle alone in his garden, where he expressed in great words his opinion of me: that I was the right hand of the Navy here, nobody but I taking any care of anything therein – so that he should not know what could be done without me – at which I was (from

him) not a little proud. Thence to a Committee of Tanger – where, because not a Quorum, little was done. And so away to my wife (Creed with me) to my wife at Mrs. Pierces; who continues very pretty and is now great with child. I had not seen her a great while. Thence by coach to my Lord Treasurer's, but could not speak with Sir Ph. Warwicke. So by coach with my wife and Mercer to the park; but the King being there, and I nowadays being doubtful of being seen in any pleasure, did part from the Tour, and away out of the park to Knightsbridge and there eat and drank in the coach, and so home; and I, after a while at my office, home to supper and to bed – having got a great Cold, I think by my pulling off my periwigg so often.

28.　Down the River to visit the victualling ships, where I find all out of order. And come home to dinner, and then to write a letter to the Duke of Albemarle about the victualling ships; and carried it myself to the council chamber, where it was read; and when they rise, my Lord Chancellor, passing by, stroked me on the head, and told me that the Board had read my letter and taken order for the punishing of the watermen for not appearing on board the ships. And so did the King afterward, who doth now know me so well, that he never sees me but he speaks to me about our Navy business.

29.　All the morning busy at the office. In the afternoon to my Lord Treasurers and there got my Lord Treasurer to sign the warrant for my striking of tallies.[1] And so doing many Jobbs in my way. Home, and there late writing letters – being troubled in my mind to hear that Sir W. Batten and Sir J. Mennes do take notice that I am nowadays much from the office, upon no office business – which vexes me, and will make me mind my business the better, I hope in God. But what troubles me more, is that I do omit to write, as I should do, to Mr. Coventry; which I must not do, though this night I minded it so little as to sleep in the middle of my letter to him, and committed forty blotts and blurrs in my letter to him. But of this I hope never more to be guilty – if I have not already given him sufficient offence. So late home, and to bed.

30.　*Lords day*. Up, and to my office alone all the morning, making up my monthly accounts; which though it hath been very intricate,

---

1. As Treasurer for Tangier.

and very great disbursements and receipts and odd reckonings, yet I differed not from the truth – *viz.*, between my first computing what my profit ought to be, and then what my cash and debts do really make me worth, not above 10*s.* – which is very much, and I do much value myself upon that account. And herein, I with great joy find myself to have gained this month above 100*l* clear; and in the whole, to be worth above 1400*l* – the greatest sum I ever yet was worth. Thence home to dinner and there find poor Mr. Spong walking at my door; where he had knocked, and being told I was at the office, stood modestly there walking, because of disturbing me; which methinks was one of the most modest acts (of a man that hath no need of being so to me) that ever I knew in my life. He dined with me; and then after dinner, to my closet, where abundance of mighty pretty discourse; wherein, in a word, I find him the man of the world that hath of his own ingenuity obtained the most in most things, being withal no scholler. He gone, I took boat and down to Woolwich and Deptford; and made it late home, and so to supper and to bed.

Thus I end this month: in great content as to my estate and gettings. In much trouble as to the pains I have taken and the rubs I expect yet to meet with about the business of Tanger. The fleet, with about 106 ships, upon the coast of Holland, in sight of the Dutch within the Texell. Great fears of the Sickenesse[1] here in the City, it being said that two or three houses are already shut up. God preserve us all.

## MAY

1. Up, and to Mr. Povy's, and by his bedside talked a good while. Thence to the Duke of Albemarle, where I sorry to find myself to come a little late. And so home, and at noon, going to the Change, met my Lord Brunkerd, Sir Robert Murry, Deane Wilkins, and Mr. Hooke, going by coach to Coll. Blunt's to dinner. So they stopped and took me with them. Landed at the Tower wharf and thence by water to Greenwich, and there coaches met us and to his house, a very stately seat for situation and brave plantations; and among others, a Vineyard. No extraordinary dinner, nor any other

1. The Great Plague.

entertainment good – but only, after dinner to the tryall of some experiments about making of coaches easy. And several we tried, but one did prove mighty easy (not here for me to describe, but the whole body of that coach lies upon one long spring) and we all, one after another, rid in it; and it is very fine and likely to take. These experiments were the intent of their coming, and pretty they are. Thence back by coach to Greenwich and in his pleasure-boat to Deptford; and there stopped, and in to Mr. Evelings, which is a most beautiful place,[1] but it being dark and late, I stayed not; but Dean Wilkins and Mr. Hooke and I walked to Redriffe, and noble discourse all day long did please me. And it being late, did take them to my house to drink, and did give them some sweetmeats – and thence sent them with a lanthorn home – two worthy persons as are in England, I think, or the world. So to my Lady Batten, where my wife is tonight; and so after some merry talk, home to bed.

3. Up betimes, and walked to Sir Ph. Warwickes, where a long time with him in his chamber alone, talking of Sir G. Carteret's business and the abuses he puts on the nation by his bad payments – to both our vexations; but no hope of remedy for aught I see. So to the Change and thence home to dinner; and so out to Gresham College and saw a cat killed with the Duke of Florence's poison. And saw it proved that the oyle of Tobacco, drawn by one of the Society, doth the same effect, and is judged to be the same thing with the poison, both in colour and smell and effect. (I saw also an abortive child, preserved fresh in spirit of salt). Thence parted, and to Whitehall to the council chamber about an order touching the Navy (our being impowered to commit seamen or maisters that do not, being hired or pressed, fallow their work), but they could give us none. So, a little vexed at that, because I put in the memorial to the Duke of Albemarle alone, under my own hand – home; and after some time at the office, home to bed.

5. Up betimes, and by water to Westminster, there to speak the first time with Sir Robt. Long, to give him my privy seal and my Lord Treasurers order for Tanger Tallys. He received me kindly enough. Thence home by water; and presently down to Woolwige and back to Blackewall, and there viewed the Breach, in order to a

1. Sayes Court, Deptford.

mast-Docke; and so to Deptford to the Globe, where my Lord Brunkard, Sir J. Mennes, Sir W. Batten, and Comissioner Pett were at dinner, having been at the Breach also – but they find it will be of too great charge to make use of it. After dinner to Mr. Evelings; he being abroad, we walked in his garden, and a lovely noble ground he hath endeed. And among other rarities, a hive of Bees; so, as being hived in glass, you may see the Bees making their honey and Combs mighty pleasantly. Thence home, and I by and by to Mr. Povy's to see him, who is yet in his chamber, not well. And thence by his advice to one Lovetts, a Varnisher, to see his manner of new varnish, but found not him at home; but his wife a very beautiful woman, who showed me much variety of admirable work; and is in order to my having of some papers fitted with lines, for my use for Tables and the like. I know not whether I was more pleased with the thing, or that I was showed it by her. But resolved I am to have some made. So home to my office late, and then to supper and to bed. My wife tells me that she hears that my poor aunt James hath had her breast cut off here in town – her breast having long been out of order. This day, after I had suffered my own hayre to grow long, in order to wearing it, I find the convenience of Perrywiggs is so great, that I have cut off all short again, and will keep to periwigs.

7.   *Lords day*.   Up, and to church with my wife. Home and dined. After dinner came Mr. Andrews, and spent the afternoon with me about our Tanger business of the victuals and then parted. And after sermon comes Mr. Hill and a gentleman, a friend of his, one Mr. Scott, that sings well also; and then comes Mr. Andrews, and we all sung and supped; and then to sing again, and passed the Sunday very pleasantly and soberly; and so I to my office a little, and then home to prayers and to bed. Yesterday begun my wife to learn to Limb of one Browne, which Mr. Hill helps her to. And by her beginning, upon some eyes, I think she will [do] very fine things – and I shall take great delight in it.

9.   Up betimes, and to my business at the office, where all the morning. At noon comes Mrs. The[oph]. Turner and dines with us. And my wife's painting-maister stayed and dined, and I take great pleasure in thinking that my wife will really come to something in that business. Here dined also Luellin. So after dinner to the office and there very busy till almost midnight, and so home

) supper and to bed. This day we have news of eight ships being
ιken by some of ours, going into the Texell, their two men of war
ιat convoyed [them] running in. They came from about Ireland,
ɔund to the North.

ɔ.    Up betimes, and abroad to the Cockepitt, where the Duke[1]
id give Sir W. Batten and me an account of the late taking of eight
ιips and of his[2] intent to come back to the Gunfleete with the fleet
resently – which creates us much work and haste therein, against
ιe fleet comes. So to Mr. Povy; and after discourse with him,
ome and thence to the Guard in Southworke, there to get some
ɔldiers, by the Duke's order, to go keep press-men on board our
ιips. So to the Change and did much business; and then home to
inner and there find my poor mother come out of the country
ɔday, in good health; and I am glad to see her, but my business,
ʌhich I am sorry for, keeps me from paying the respect I ought to
ɛr at her first coming – she being grown very weak in her
ιdgment, and doting again in her discourse, through age and some
-ouble in her family. Left her and my wife to go abroad to buy
ɔmething, and then I to my office. In the evening, by appointment
ɔ Sir W. Warren and Mr. Dering at a tavern hard by, with intent to
ɔ some good upon their agreement in a great bargain of plank. So
ome to my office again, and then to supper and to bed, my mother
ɛing in bed already.

2.    By water to the Exchequer, and there up and down through
ιl the offices to strike my tallies for 17500l – which methinks is so
reat a testimony of the goodness of God to me; that I, from a mean
lerk there, should come to strike tallies myself for that sum, and in
ιe authority that I do now, is a very stupendous mercy to me. I
hall have them struck tomorrow. But to see how every little fellow
ɔoks after his fees, and to get what he can for everything, is a
trange consideration – the King's Fees, that he must pay himself
ɔr this 17500l, coming to above 100l. Thence, called my wife at
Jnthankes, to the New Exchange and elsewhere to buy a lace band
ɔr me, but we did not buy. But I find it so necessary to have some
andsome clothes, that I cannot but lay out some money there-
pon.

1. Albemarle.
2. The Duke of York's.

489

13. Up, and all day in some little grutchings of pain, as I use to have – from Winde – arising, I think, from my fasting so long and want of exercise – and I think, going so hot in clothes, the weather being hot and I in the same clothes I wore all winter. To the Change after office, and received my Wach from the watchmaker; and a very fine [one] it is – given me by Briggs the Scrivener. But Lord, to see how much of my old folly and childishnesse hangs upon me still, that I cannot forbear carrying my watch in my hand in the coach all this afternoon, and seeing what a-clock it is 100 times. And am apt to think with myself: how could I be so long without one – though I remember since, I had one and found it a trouble, and resolved to carry one no more about me while I lived.

14. *Lords day.* Up, and with my wife to church, it being Whitsunday. My wife very fine in a new yellow birds-eye Hood, as the fashion is now. We had a most sorry sermon. So home to dinner, my mother having her new suit brought home, which makes her very fine. After dinner my wife and she and Mercer to Tho. Pepys's wife's christening of his first child. And I took a coach and to Wanstead, the house where Sir H. Mildmay did [live] and now Sir Rob. Brookes lives, having bought it of the Duke of Yorke, it being forfeited to him. A fine seat, but an old-fashion house and being not full of people, looks desolately. Thence to Walthamstow, where Sir W. Batten by and by came home, walking up and down the house and garden with my Lady, very pleasant. Then to supper, very merry; and then back by coach by dark night – I, all the afternoon in the coach, reading the treasonous book of the Court of King James, printed a great while ago and worth reading, though ill intended. As soon as came home, upon a letter from Duke of Albemarle, I took boat, at about 12 at night and down the River in a galley, my boy and I, down to the Hope and so up again, sleeping and waking with great pleasure; my business, to call upon every one of our victualling ships to set them a-going.

15. And so home; and after dinner, to the King's playhouse all alone, and saw *Loves Maistresse*. Some pretty things and good variety in it, but no or little fancy in it. Thence to the Duke of Albemarle to give him account of my day's works – where he showed me letters from Sir G. Downing, of four days' date, that the Duch are come out and joyned – well-manned and resolved to

board our best ships; and fight for certain they will. Thence to the Swan at Herberts, and there the company of Sarah a little while; and so away and called at the Harp and Ball, where the maid, Mary, is very formosa; but Lord, to see in what readiness I am, upon the expiring of my vowes this day, to begin to run into all my pleasures and neglect of business. Thence home; and being sleepy, to bed.

22. Up, and down to the ships, which now are hindered from going to the fleet (to our great sorrow and shame) with the provisions, the wind being against them. So to the Duke of Albemarle – and thence down by water to Deptford, it being Trinity Monday and so the day of choosing the Master of Trinity house for the next year – where, to my great content, I find that contrary to the practice and design of Sir W. Batten to break the rule and custom of the Company in choosing their Masters by succession, he would have brought in Sir W. Rider or Sir W. Pen over the head of Hurleston (who is a knave too besides, I believe): the Younger Brothers did all oppose it against the Elder, and with great heat did carry it for Hurleston – which I know will vex him to the heart. Thence, the election being over, to church; where an idle sermon from that conceited fellow Dr. Britton, saving that his advice to unity and laying aside all envy and enmity among them was very apposite. Thence walked to Redriffe, and so to the Trinity house; and a great dinner, as is usual. And so to my office, where busy all the afternoon till late; and then home to bed – being much troubled in mind for several things. First, for the condition of the fleet for lack of provisions. The blame this office lies under, and the shame that they deserve to have brought upon them for the ships not being gone out of the River. And then for my business of Tanger, which is not settled; and lastly, for fear that I am not observed to have attended the office business of late as much as I ought to do, though there hath been nothing but my attendance on Tanger that hath occasioned my absence, and that of late not much.

24. Up by 4 a-clock in the morning; and with W. Hewer there till 12 without intermission, putting some papers in order. Thence to the coffee-house with Creed, where I have not been a great while – where all the news is of the Dutch being gone out – and of the plague growing upon us in this town and of remedies against it; some saying one thing, some another.

28.   *Lords day*. Went to chapel and heard a little Musique and there
met with Creed, and with him a little while walking and to
Wilkinsons for me to drink, being troubled with Winde; and at
noon to Sir Ph. Warwicke's to dinner, where abundance of
company came in unexpectedly. And here I saw one pretty piece of
household stuff; as the company encreaseth, to put a larger leaf
upon an Ovall table. After dinner much good discourse with Sir
Phillip, who I find, I think, a most pious good man, and a professor
of a philosiphicall manner of life and principles like Epictetus
whom he cites in many things. Thence to my Lady Sandwiches,
where to my shame I had not been a great while before. Here, upon
my telling her a story of my Lord of Rochester's running away on
Friday night last with Mrs. Mallet, the great beauty and fortune of
the [West], who had supped at Whitehall with Mrs. Stewart and
was going home to her lodgings with her grandfather, my Lord
Haly, by coach, and was at Charing cross seized on by both horse
and foot-men and forcibly taken from him, and put into a coach
with six horses and two women provided to receive her, and carried
away. Upon immediate pursuit, my Lord of Rochester (for whom
the King had spoke to the lady often, but with no success) was taken
at Uxbridge; but the lady is not yet heard of, and the King mighty
angry and the Lord sent to the Tower. Hereupon, my Lady did
confess to me, as a great secret, her being concerned in this story –
for if this match breaks between my Lord Rochester and her, then
by the consent of all her friends, my Lord Hinchingbrooke stand
fair, and is invited for her. She is worth, and will be at her mother's
death (who keeps but a little from her), 2500*l* per annum. Pray God
give a good success to it. But my poor Lady, who is afeared of the
sickness and resolved to be gone into the country, is forced to stay
in town a day or two or three about it, to see the event of it. Thence
home, and to see my Lady Pen – where my wife and I were shown a
fine rarity: of fishes kept in a glass of water, that will live so for ever
and finely marked they are, being foreign. So to supper at home and
to bed.

29.   Lay long in bed, being in some little pain of the wind
Collique. Then up and to the Duke of Albemarle, and so to the
Swan and there drank at Herberts; and so by coach home, it being
kept a great holiday through the City, for the birth and restoration
of the King. To my office, where I stood by and saw Symson the
Joyner do several things, little Jobbs, to the rendering of my closet

handsome and the setting up of some neat plats that Burston hath for my money made me. And so home to dinner; and then, with my wife, mother, and Mercer in one boat, and I in another, down to Woolwich, I walking from Greenwich, the others going to and fro upon the water till my coming back, having done but little business. So home and to supper, and weary to bed. We have everywhere taken some prizes. Our merchants have good luck to come home safe: Colliers from the North, and some Streights-men just now – and our Hambrough ships, of whom we were so much afeared, are safe in Hambrough. Our Fleete resolved to sail out again from Harwich in a day or two.

## –❊JUNE❊–

1. Up, and to the office, where sat all the morning. At noon to the Change and there did some business and home to dinner, whither Creed comes. And after dinner I put on my new silk Camelott Sute, the best that ever I wore in my life, the suit costing me above 24*l*. In this I went with him to Goldsmiths hall to the burial of Sir Tho. Viner; which hall, and Haberdashers also, was so full of people, that we were fain for ease and coolness to go forth to Paternoster row to choose a silk to make me a plain ordinary suit. That done, we walked to Cornehill, and there at Mr. Cades stood in the Balcon and saw all the funerals, which was with the Bluecoat boys and old men – all the Aldermen, and Lord Mayor, &c., and the number of the company very great – the greatest I ever did see for a Taverne. Hither came up to us Dr. Allen – and then Mr. Povy and Mr. Fox. The show being over, and my discourse with Mr. Povy – I took coach and to Westminster hall, where I took the fairest flower and by coach to Tothill fields for the ayre, till it was dark. I light, and in with the fairest flower to eat a cake, and there did do as much as was safe with my flower, and that was enough on my part. Broke up, and away without any notice; and after delivering the rose where it should be, I to the Temple and light; and came to the middle door and there took another coach, and so home – to write letters; but very few, God knows, being (by my pleasure) made to forget everything that is. The coachman that carried [us] cannot know me again, nor the people at the house where we were. Home to bed, certain news being come that our fleet is in sight of the Dutch ships.

2.   Met an express from Sir W. Batten at Harwich, that the fleet is all sailed from Solebay, having spied the Dutch Fleete at sea – and that if the Calmes hinder not, they must needs be now engaged with them.

3.   All this day, by all people upon the River and almost everywhere else hereabout, were heard the Guns, our two fleets for certain being engaged; which was confirmed by letters from Harwich, but nothing perticular; and all our hearts full of concernment for the Duke, and I perticularly for my Lord Sandwich and Mr. Coventry after his Royal Highness.

7.   This day, much against my Will, I did in Drury lane see two or three houses marked with a red cross upon the doors, and "Lord have mercy upon us" writ there – which was a sad sight to me, being the first of that kind that to my remembrance I ever saw. It put me into an ill conception of myself and my smell, so that I was forced to buy some roll tobacco to smell to and chaw – which took away the apprehension.

8.   About 5 a-clock my wife came home, it having lightened all night hard, and one great shower of rain. She came and lay upon the bed. I up, and to the office, where all the morning. I alone at home to dinner, my wife, mother, and Mercer dining at W. Joyces, I giving her a caution to go round by the Half Moone to his house, because of the plague. I to my Lord Treasurer's, by appointment of Sir Tho. Ingram's, to meet the goldsmiths – where I met with the great news, at last newly come, brought by Bab May from the Duke of Yorke, that we have totally routed the Dutch.[1] That the Duke himself, the Prince, my Lord Sandwich, and Mr. Coventry are all well. Which did put me into such a joy, that I forgot almost all other thoughts. The sum of the news is:

*Victory over the Dutch. June. 3. 1665.*

This day they engaged – the Dutch neglecting greatly the opportunity of the wind they had of us – by which they lost the benefit of their fireships. The Earl of Falmouth, Muskery, and Mr. Rd. Boyle killed on board the Dukes ship, the *Royall Charles*, with one shot. Their blood and brains flying in the Duke's face – and the

---

1. At the Battle of Lowestoft.

d J. E. of Sandwich.

3. Edward Mountagu, 1st Earl of Sandwich, by Sir Peter Lely, c. 1659–60

4. James, Duke of York, by Samuel Cooper, ?c.1660

5. Sir George Carteret,
by Sir Peter Lely, ?c.1660

6. Sir William Coventry,
by John Riley

7. Sir William Penn,
by Sir Peter Lely

8. Sir John Mennes,
painted in the studio of
Sir Anthony van Dyck,
c.1640
(early nineteenth-
century copy)

9. William Hewer, by Sir Godfrey Kneller, c.1686

head of Mr. Boyle striking down the Duke, as some say. Earle of Marlbrough, Portland, Rere-[A]dm. Sansum (to Prince Rupert) killed, and Capt. Kirby and Ableson. Sir Jo. Lawson wounded on the knee – hath had some bones taken out, and is likely to be well again. Upon receiving the hurt, he sent to the Duke for another to command the *Royall Oake*. The Duke sent Jordan out of the *St. George*, who did brave things in her. Capt. Jer. Smith of the *Mary* was second to the Duke, and stepped between him and Capt. Seaton of the *Urania* (76 guns and 400 men), who had sworn to board the Duke. Killed him, 200 men, and took the ship. Himself losing 99 men, and never an officer saved but himself and Lieutenant. His maister endeed is saved, with his leg cut off. Adm. Opdam blown up. Trump killed, and said by Holmes. All the rest of their Admiralls, as they say, but Everson (whom they dare not trust for his affection to the prince of Orange) are killed. We have taken and sunk, as is believed, about 24 of their best ships. Killed and taken near 8 or 10000 men; and lost, we think, not above 700. A great victory, never known in the world. They are all fled; some 43 got into the Texell and others elsewhere, and we in pursuit of the rest.

Thence, with my heart full of Joy, home, and to my office a little; then to my Lady Pen's, where they are all joyed and not a little puffed up at the good success of their father; and good service endeed is said to have been done by him. Had a great bonefire at the gate; and I with my Lady Pens people and others to Mrs. Turner's great room, and then down into the street. I did give the boys 4*s.* among them – and mighty merry; so home to bed – with my heart at great rest and quiet, saving that the consideration of the victory is too great for me presently to comprehend.

10.    Lay long in bed; and then up and at the office all the morning. At noon dined at home, and then to the office, busy all the afternoon. In the evening home to supper, and there to my great trouble hear that the plague is come into the City (though it hath these three or four weeks since its beginning been wholly out of the City); but where should it begin but in my good friend and neighbour's, Dr. Burnett in Fanchurch street – which in both points troubles me mightily.

11.    *Lords day*. Up, and expected long a new suit; but coming not, dressed myself in my late new black silk camelot suit; and when full

ready, comes my new one of Colour'd Farrinden, which my wife puts me out of love with; which vexes [me], but I think it is only my not being used to wear Colours, which makes it look a little unusual upon me. To my chamber, and there spent the morning reading. At noon by invitation comes my two cousin Joyces and their wifes – my aunt James, and he-cousin Harman – his wife being ill. I had a good dinner for them, and as merry as I could be in such company. They being gone, I out of doors a little to show forsooth my new suit, and back again; and in going, saw poor Dr. Burnets door shut. But he hath, I hear, gained great goodwill among his neighbours; for he discovered it himself first, and caused himself to be shut up of his own accord – which was very handsome. In the evening comes Mr. Andrews and his wife and Mr. Hill, and stayed and played and sung and supped – most excellent pretty company; so pleasant, ingenious, and harmless, I cannot desire better. They gone, we to bed – my mind in great present ease.

13. Up, and to the office, where all the morning doing business. At noon with Sir G. Carteret to my Lord Mayors to dinner, where much company in a little room – and though a good, yet no extraordinary Table. His name, Sir John Lawrence – whose father, a very ordinary old man, sat there at table – but it seems a very rich man. [Ald. Sir Richard Browne] did here openly tell in boasting, how he had, only upon suspicion of disturbances (if there had been any bad news from sea), clapped up several persons that he was afeared of. And that he had several times done the like and would do, and take no bail where he saw it unsafe for the King.

14. I met with Mr. Cowling, who observed to me how he finds everybody silent in the praise of my Lord of Sandwich, to set up the Duke and the Prince. But that the Duke did, both to the King and my Lord Chancellor, write abundantly of my Lord's courage and service. And I this day met with a letter of Capt. Ferrers, where he tells us my Lord was with his ship in all the heat of the day, and did most worthily. Met with Creed, and he and I to Westminster and there saw my Lord Marlborough brought to be buried – several Lords of the Council carrying him, and with the Heralds in some state. Thence, vexed in my mind to think that I do so little in my Tanger business, and so home, and after supper to bed.

15. Up, and put on my new stuff suit with close knees, which

becomes me most nobly as my wife says. At the office all day. At noon put on my first laced band, all lace, and to Kate Joyce's to dinner; where my mother, wife, and abundance of their friends, and good usage. Thence wife and Mercer and I to the Old Exchange and there bought two lace bands more, one of my Semstresse, whom my wife concurs with me to be a pretty woman. So down to Deptford and Woolwich, my boy and I. At Woolwich discoursed with Mr. Shelden about my bringing my wife down for a month or two to his house; which he approves of, and I think will be very convenient. So late back and to the office, wrote letters, and so home to supper and to bed. This day the Newsbook (upon Mr Moores showing Lestrange Capt. Ferrers letter) did do my Lord Sandwich great right as to the late victory. The Duke of Yorke not yet come to town.

The town grows very sickly, and people to be afeared of it – there dying this last week of the plague 112, from 43 the week before – whereof, one in Fanchurch street and one in Broadstreete by the Treasurer's office.

16. Up, and to the office, where I set hard to business – but was informed that the Duke of Yorke is come, and hath appointed us to attend him this afternoon. So after dinner and doing some business at the office, I to Whitehall, where the Court is full of the Duke and his Courtiers, returned from sea – all fat and lusty, and ruddy by being in the sun. I kissed his hands, and we waited all the afternoon. By and by saw Mr. Coventry, which rejoiced my very heart. Anon he and I from all the rest of the company walked into the matted gallery – where after many expressions of love, we fell to talk of business. Among other things, how my Lord Sandwich, both in his counsels and personal service, hath done most honorably and serviceably. Sir J. Lawson is come to Greenwich, but his wound in his knee yet very bad. Jonas Poole in the *Vantguard* did basely, so as to be, or will be, turned out of his ship. Capt. Holmes, expecting upon Sansums death to be made Rere-admirall to the Prince (but Harman is put in), hath delivered up to the Duke his commission, which the Duke took and tore. He, it seems, had bid the Prince, who first told him of Holmes's intention, that he should dissuade him from it, for that he was resolved to take it if he offered it. Yet Holmes would do it, like a rash, proud coxcomb – but he is rich, and hath it seems sought an occasion of leaving the service. Several of our Captains have done ill. The great Shipps are the ships do the

business, they quite deadening the enemy – they run away upon sight of the *Prince*. It is strange, to see how people do already slight Sir Wm. Berkely, my Lord Fitzharding's brother, who three months since was the delight of the Court. Capt. Smith of the *Mary*, the Duke talks mightily of, and some great thing will be done for him. Strange, to hear how the Dutch do relate, as the Duke says, that they are the conquerors – and bonefires are made in Dunkirke in their behalf – though a clearer victory can never be expected. Mr. Coventry thinks they cannot have lost less then 6000 men; and we not dead above 200, and wounded about 400; in all, about 600. Thence home, and to my office till past 12 and then home to supper and to bed – my wife and mother not being yet come home from W. Hewres chamber, who treats my mother tonight. Capt. Grove, the Duke told us this day, hath done the basest thing at Lastoffe, in hearing of the guns and could not (as others) be got out, but stayed there – for which he will be tried; and is reckoned a prating coxcombe, and of no courage.

17.    It stroke me very deep this afternoon, going with a Hackny-coach from my Lord Treasurer's down Holborne – the coachman I found to drive easily and easily; at last stood still, and came down hardly able to stand; and told me that he was suddenly stroke very sick and almost blind, he could not see. So I light and went into another coach, with a sad heart for the poor man and trouble for myself, lest he should have been stroke with the plague – being at that end of the town that I took him up. But God have mercy upon us all. Sir Jo. Lawson, I hear, is worse then yesterday – the King went to see him today, most kindly. It seems his wound is not very bad, but he hath a fever – a thrush and a Hickup, all three together; which are, it seems, very bad symptoms.

20.   *Thanksgiving day for Victory over the Dutch.* Up, and to the office, where very busy alone all the morning till church time; and there heard a mean sorry sermon of Mr. Mills. Then to the Dolphin Taverne, where all we officers of the Navy met with the Comissioners of the Ordnance by agreement and dined – where good Musique, at my direction. Our club came to 34*s*. a man – nine of us. Thence after dinner I to Whitehall with Sir W. Berkely in his coach. And so I walked to Herberts and there spent a little time avec la mosa, sin hazer algo con ella que kiss and tocar ses mamelles, que

me haza hazer la cosa a mi mismo con gran plaisir. Thence by water to Foxhall, and there walked an hour alone, observing the several humours of the citizens that were there this holiday, pulling of cherries and God knows what. And so home to my office, where late, my wife not being come home with my mother, who have been this day all abroad upon the water, my mother being to go out of town speedily. So I home and to supper and to bed. This day I informed myself that there died four or five at Westminster of the plague, in one alley in several houses upon Sunday last – Bell Alley, over against the Palace gate. Yet people do think that the number will be fewer in the town then it was the last week.

24. *Midsummer Day*. Up very betimes, by 6, and at Dr. Clerkes at Westminster by 7 of the clock, having overnight by a note acquainted him with my intention of coming. And there I, in the best manner I could, broke my errand about a match between Sir G. Carterts eldest son and my Lord Sandwiches eldest daughter – which he (as I knew he would) took with great content; and we both agreed that my Lord and he, being both men relating to the sea – under a kind aspect of His Majesty – already good friends, and both virtuous and good families, their allyance might be of good use to us. And he did undertake to find out Sir George this morning, and put the business in execution. So being both well pleased with the proposition, I saw his neece there and made her sing me two or three songs, very prettily; and so home to the office – where to my great trouble, I found Mr. Coventry and the board met before I came. I excused my late coming, by having been upon the River about office business. So to business all the morning. [After dinner] to Dr. Clerke, and there find that he hath broke the business to Sir G. Carteret and that he takes the thing mighty well. Thence I to Sir G. Carteret at his Chamber, and in the best manner I could, and most obligingly, moved that business; he received it with great respect and content and thanks to me, and promised that he would do what he could possibly for his son, to render him fit for my Lord's daughter. And showed great kindness to me, and sense of my kindness to him herein. Sir Wm. Pen told me this day that Mr. Coventry is to be sworn a Privy Counsellor – at which my soul is glad. So home and to my letters by the post, and so home – to supper and bed.

25.  *Lords day*. Up, and several people about business came to me
by appointment, relating to the office; thence I to my closet about
my Tanger papers. At noon dined. And then I abroad by water, it
raining hard, thinking to have gone down to Woolwich; but I did
not, but back through bridge to Whitehall – where after I had
again visited Sir G. Carteret and received his (and now his Lady's)
full content in my proposal, I went to my Lord Sandwich; and
having told him how Sir G. Carteret received it, he did direct me
to return to Sir G. Carteret and give him thanks for his kind
reception of this offer, and that he would the next day be willing
to enter discourse with him about that business. Which message I
did presently do, and so left the business, with great joy to both
sides. My Lord, I perceive, entends to give 5000*l* with her, and
expects about 800*l* per annum joynture. So by water home and to
supper and bed, being weary with long walking at Court. But had
a psalm or two with my boy and Mercer before bed, which
pleased me mightily.

26.  The plague encreases mightily – I this day seeing a house, at a
bittmakers over against St. Clements church in the open street, shut
up; which is a sad sight.

29.  Up, and by water to Whitehall, where the Court full of
waggons and people ready to go out of town. The Mortality bill is
come to 267 – which is about 90 more then the last; and of these,
but 4 in the City – which is a great blessing to us. So home, calling
at Somersett house, where all are packing up too; the Queene-
mother setting out for France this day to drink Bourbon waters
this year, she being in a consumption – and entends not to come till
winter come twelvemonths. To the office, where busy a while,
putting some things in my office in order, and then to letters till
night. About 10 a-clock home – the days being sensibly shorter:
before, I have once kept a summer's day by shutting up office by
daylight, but my life hath been still as it was in winter almost. But I
will for a month try what I can do by daylight. So home to supper
and to bed.

30.  Thus this book of two years ends. Myself and family in good
health, consisting of myself and wife – Mercer, her woman – Mary,
Alce and Su, our maids; and Tom, my boy. In a sickly time, of the
plague growing on. Having upon my hands the troublesome care

of the Treasury of Tanger, with great sums drawn upon me and nothing to pay them with. Also, the business of the office great. Consideration of removing my wife to Woolwich. She lately busy in learning to paint, with great pleasure and successe. All other things well; especially a new interest I am making, by a match in hand between the eldest son of Sir G. Carteret and my Lady Jemimah Mountagu. The Duke of York gone down to the fleet; but, all suppose, not with intent to stay there – as it is not fit, all men conceive, he should.[1]

# ❧ JULY ❧

1. Called up betimes, though weary and sleepy, by appointment by Mr. Povy and Coll. Norwood, to discourse about some payments of Tanger. They gone, I to the office and there sat all the morning. At noon dined at home, and then to the Duke of Albemarles by appointment to give him an account of some disorder in the yard at Portsmouth, by workmen's going away of their own accord for lack of money, to get work of hay-making or anything else to earn themselfs bread. Thence I to Westminster, where I hear the sickness encreases greatly. And to the Harp and Ball with Mary, talking, who tells me simply her losing of her first love in the country in Wales and coming up hither unknown to her friends. And it seems Dr. Williams doth pretend love to her, and I have found him there several times. Thence by coach, and late at the office and so to bed – sad at the news that seven or eight houses in Bazing hall street are shut up of the plague.

6. Up, and forth to give order at my pretty grocer's wife's house, who, her husband tells me, is going this day for the summer into the country. I bespoke some sugar &c. for my father, and so home to the office, where all the morning. At noon dined at home, and then by water to Whitehall to Sir G. Carteret about money for the office; a sad thought, for in a little time all must go to wrack, winter coming on apace, when a great sum must be ready to pay part of the

---

1. sc. as heir presumptive to the King.

fleet. And so far we are from it, that we have not enough to stop the mouths of poor people and their hands from falling about our eares here, almost in the office. God give a good end to it. Sir G. Carteret told me one considerable thing. Ald. Backewell is ordered abroad upon some private score with a great sum of money – wherein I was instrumental the other day in shipping him away. It seems some of his Creditors have taken notice of it, and he was like to be broke yesterday in his absence – Sir G. Carteret telling me that the King and the Kingdom must as good as fall with that man at this time; and that he was forced to get 4000*l* himself to answer Backewells people's occasions, or he must have broke; but committed this to me as a great secret – and which I am heartily sorry to hear. Thence, after a little merry discourse of our marrying business, I parted; and by coach to several places, among others to see my Lord Brunkerd, who is not well but was at rest when I came. I could not see him, nor had much mind, one of the great houses within two doors of him being shut up; and Lord, the number of houses visited which this day I observed through the town, quite round in my way by Long Lane and London Wall.

7.   Up, and having set my neighbour Mr. Hudson, wine cooper, at work drawing out a tierce of wine for the sending of some of it to my wife – I abroad, only taking notice to what a condition it hath pleased God to bring me, that at this time I have two tierces of claret – two quarter-cask of canary, and a smaller vessel of sack – a vessel of tent, another of Malaga, and another of white wine, all in my wine-cellar together – which I believe none of my friends of my name now alive ever had of his own at one time.

13.   Lay long, being sleepy; and then up to the office, my Lord Brunker (after his sickness) being come to the office, and did what business there was; and so I by water, at night late, to Sir G. Carterets. But there being no oares to carry me, I was fain to call a Sculler that had a gentleman already in it; and he proved a man of love to Musique and he and I sung together the way down – with great pleasure, and an accident extraordinary to be met with. There came to Dinner, they having dined, but my Lady caused something to be brought for me and I dined well, and mighty merry, especially my Lady Slany and I about eating of Creame and brown bread – which she loves as much as I. Thence, after long discourse with them and my Lady alone, I and wife, who by agreement met me

here, took leave; and I saw my wife a little way down[1] (it troubling me that this absence makes us a little strange instead of more fond) and so parted, and I home to some letters and then home to bed. Above 700 dead of the plague this week.

14. My Lady Jem is beyond expectation come to Dagenhams, where Mr. Carteret is to go to visit her tomorrow; and my proposal of waiting on him, he being to go alone to all persons strangers to him, was well accepted and so I go with him. But Lord, to see how kind my Lady Carteret is to her – sends her most rich Jewells, and provides bedding and things of all sorts most richly for her – which makes my Lady and me out of our wits almost, to see the kindness she treats us all with – as if they would buy the young lady. Thence away home; and foreseeing my being abroad two days, did sit up late, making of letters ready against tomorrow and other things; and so to bed – to be up betimes by the help of a larum-wach, which by chance I borrowed of my watchmaker today while my own is mending.

15. Up, and after all business done at the office, though late, I to Deptford. But before I went out of the office, saw there young Bagwells wife returned; but could not stay to speak to her, though I had a great mind to it. And also another great lady, as to fine clothes, did attend there to have a ticket signed; which I did do, taking her through the garden to my office, where I signed it and had a salute of her; and so I away by boat to Redriffe, and thence walked; and after dinner, at Sir G. Carteret, where they stayed till almost 3 a-clock for me; and anon took boat, Mr. Carteret and I, to the ferry-place at Greenwich and there stayed an hour, after crossing the water to and again to get our coach and horses over, and by and by set out and so toward Dagenham. But Lord, what silly discourse we had by the way as to matter of love-matters, he

---

1. The Carterets were staying at the Navy Treasurer's official house at Deptford. Because of the Plague, Elizabeth Pepys had been staying since 5 July at Woolwich at the house of the Clerk of the Cheque, William Sheldon. Pepys joined her there occasionally during the next few weeks, but continued to base himself on Seething Lane. In mid-August the Navy Board moved to rooms in the royal palace at Greenwich, and at the end of the month Pepys found it convenient to settle at Woolwich. He had to spend occasional nights in lodgings at Greenwich, however, and by 11 October had established himself there at Mrs Clarke's. On 7 January 1666 he moved back to London where the Navy Board resumed its meetings on the 9th. Elizabeth had returned to Seething Lane on 2 December.

being the most awkerd man I ever I met withal in my life as to that business. Thither we came by time to begin to be dark, and were kindly received by my Lady Wright and my Lord Crew; and to discourse they went, my Lord discoursing with him, asking of him questions of Travell, which he answered well enough in a few words. But nothing to the lady from him at all. To supper, and after supper to talk again, he yet taking no notice of the lady. My Lord would have had me have consented to leaving the young people together tonight to begin their amours, his staying being but to be little. But I advised against it, lest the lady might be too much surprized. So they led him up to his chamber, where I stayed a little to know how he liked the lady; which he told me he did mightily, but Lord, in the dullest insipid manner that ever lover did. So I bid him good-night, and down to prayers with my Lord Crew's family. And after prayers, my Lord and Lady Wright and I to consult what to do; and it was agreed at last to have them go to church together as the family used to do, though his lameness was a great objection against it; but at last my Lady Jem sent me word by my Lady Wright that it would be better to do just as they used to do before his coming, and therefore she desired to go to church – which was yielded then to.

16. *Lords day*. I up, having lain with Mr. Moore in the Chaplins chamber. And having trimmed myself, down to Mr. Carteret; and he being ready, we down and walked in the gallery an hour or two, it being a most noble and pretty house that ever for the bigness I saw. Here I taught him what to do; to take the lady alway by the hand to lead her; and telling him that I would find opportunity to leave them two together, he should make these and these compliments, and also take a time to do the like to my Lord Crew and Lady Wright. After I had instructed him, which he thanked me for, owning that he needed my teaching him, my Lord Crew came down and family, the young lady among the rest; and so by coaches to church, four mile off – where a pretty good sermon – and a declaration of penitence of a man that had undergone the Church censure for his wicked life. Thence back again by coach – Mr. Carteret having not had the confidence to take his lady once by the hand, coming or going; which I told him of when we came home, and he will hereafter do it. So to dinner. My Lord excellent discourse. Then to walk in the gallery and to sit down. By and by my Lady Wright and I go out (and then my Lord Crew, he not by

design); and lastly my Lady Crew came out and left the young people together. And a little pretty daughter of my Lady Wright's most innocently came out afterward, and shut the door to, as if she had done it, poor child, by inspiration – which made us without have good sport to laugh at. They together an hour; and by and by church time, whither he led her into the coach and into the church; and so at church all the afternoon. Several handsome ladies at church – but it was most extraordinary hot that ever I knew it. So home again and to walk in the gardens, where we left the young couple a second time; and my Lady Wright and I to walk together, who to my trouble tells me that my Lady Jem must have something done to her body by Scott before she can be married, and therefore care must be had to send him – also, that some more new clothes must of necessity be made her, which and other things, I took care of. Anon to supper, and excellent discourse and dispute between my Lord Crew and the Chaplin, who is a good Scholler but a nonconformist. Here this evening I spoke with Mrs. Carter, my old acquaintance that hath lived with my Lady these twelve or thirteen years, the sum of all whose discourse, and others for her, is that I would get her [a] good husband; which I have promised, but know not when I shall perform. After Mr. Carteret carried to his chamber, we to prayers again and then to bed.

17.　Up, all of us, and to Billiards – my lady Wright, Mr. Cartert, myself and everybody. By and by the young couple left together. Anon to dinner, and after dinner Mr. Carteret took my advice about giving to the servants, and I led him to give 10*l* among them, which he did by leaving it to the chief manservant, Mr. Medows, to do for him. Before we went, I took my Lady Jem apart and would know how she liked this gentleman and whether she was under any difficulty concerning him. She blushed and hid her face awhile, but at last I forced her to tell me; she answered that she could readily obey what her father and mother had done – which was all she could say or I expect. So anon took leave and for London. But Lord, to see, among other things, how all these great people here are afeared of London, being doubtful of anything that comes from thence or that hath lately been there, that I was forced to say that I lived wholly at Woolwich. In our way Mr. Carteret did give me mighty thanks for my care and pains for him, and is mightily pleased – though the truth is, my Lady Jem hath carried herself with mighty discretion and gravity, not being forward at all in any degree but mighty serious in her answers to him.

18. Up, and to the office, where all the morning. And so to my house and eat a bit of victuals; and so to the Change, where a little business, and a very thin Exchange; and so walked through London to the Temple, where I took water for Westminster to the Duke of Albemarle to wait on him; and so to Westminster hall and there paid for my newsbooks and did give Mrs. Michell (who is going out of town because of the sickness) and her husband a pint of wine. And so Sir W. Warren coming to me by appointment, we away by water home, by the way discoursing about the project I have of getting some money, and doing the King good service too, about the mast-dock at Woolwich, which I fear will never be done if I do not go about it. After despatching letters at the office, I by water down to Deptford, where I stayed a little while; and by water to my wife, whom I have not seen six or five days. And there supped with her and mighty pleasant, and saw with content her drawings and so to bed mighty merry. I was much troubled this day to hear at Westminster how the officers do bury the dead in the open Tuttle fields, pretending want of room elsewhere; whereas the New Chapel churchyard was walled in at the public charge in the last plague-time[1] merely for want of room, and now none but such as are able to pay dear for it can be buried there.

20. Up in a boat, among other people, to the Tower, and there to the office, where we sat all the morning. So down to Deptford and there dined; and after dinner saw my Lady Sandwich and Mr. Carteret and his two sisters over the water, going to Dagenhams, and my Lady Carteret toward Cranburne. So all the company broke up in most extraordinary joy – wherein I am mighty contented that I have had the good fortune to be so instrumental, and I think it will be of good use to me. So walked to Redriffe, where I hear the sickness is, and endeed is scattered almost everywhere – there dying 1089 of the plague this week. My Lady Carteret did this day give me a bottle of plague-water [to take] home with me. So home to write letters late, and then home to bed, where I have not lain these three or four nights. I received yesterday a letter from my Lord Sandwich, giving me thanks for my care about their marriage business and desiring it to be despatched, that

---

1. In 1647.

no disappointment may happen therein – which I will help on all I can. This afternoon I waited on the Duke of Albemarle; and so to Mrs. Crofts, where I found and saluted Mrs. Burrows, who is a very pretty woman for a mother of so many children. But Lord, to see how the plague spreads; it being now all over Kings street, at the Axe and the next door to it, and in other places.

26. Up; and after doing a little business, down to Deptford with Sir W. Batten – and there left him, and I to Greenwich to the park, where I hear the King and Duke are come by water this morn from Hampton Court. They asked me several Questions. The King mightily pleased with his new buildings there.[1] Great variety of talk – and was often led to speak to the King and Duke. By and by they to dinner; and all to dinner and sat down to the King saving myself, which though I could not in modesty expect, yet God forgive my pride, I was sorry I was there, that Sir W. Batten should say that he could sit down where I could not – though he had twenty times more reason then I. But this was my pride and folly. The King having dined, he came down, and I went in the barge with him, I sitting at the door hearing him and the Duke talk and seeing and observing their manner of discourse; and God forgive me, though I adore them with all the duty possible, yet the more a man considers and observes them, the less he finds of difference between them and other men, though (blessed be God) they are both princes of great nobleness and spirits. The Barge put me into another boat that came to our side, Mr. Holder with a bag of gold to the Duke; and so they away, and I home to the office. The Duke of Monmouth is the most skittish, leaping gallant that ever I saw, alway in action, vaulting or leaping or clambering. I home to set my Journall for these four days in order, they being four days of as great content and honour and pleasure to me as ever I hope to live or desire or think anybody else can live. For methinks if a man could but reflect upon this, and think that all these things are ordered by God Almighty to make me contented, and even this very marriage now on foot is one of the things entended to find me content in in my life and matter of mirth, methinks it should make one mightily more satisfied in the world then he is. This day poor Robin Shaw at Backewells died – and Backewell himself now in Flanders. The King himself asked about Shaw; and being told he was dead, said he

1. At Greenwich Palace.

was very sorry for it. The Sickenessse is got into our parish this week; and is got endeed everywhere, so that I begin to think of setting things in order, which I pray God enable me to put, both as to soul and body.

27.   Called up at 4 a-clock. Up, and to my preparing some papers for Hampton Court; and so by water to Foxhall, and there Mr. Gaudens coach took me up; and by and by I took up him, and so both thither – a brave morning to ride in, and good discourse with him. So despatched all my business, having assurance of continuance of all hearty love from Sir W. Coventry; and so we stayed and saw the King and Queene set out toward Salsbury – and after them, the Duke and Duchesse – whose hands I did kiss. And it was the first time I did ever or did see anybody else kiss her hand; and it was a most fine white and fat hand. But it was pretty to see the young pretty ladies dressed like men; in velvet coats, caps with ribbands, and with laced bands just like men – only, the Duchesse herself it did not become. They gone, we with great content took coach again. At home met the weekly Bill, where above 1000 encreased in the Bill; and of them, in all, about 1700 of the plague – which hath made the officers this day resolve of sitting at Deptford, which puts me to some consideration what to do. Therefore, home to think and consider of everything about it; and without determining anything, eat a little supper and to bed, full of the pleasure of these six or seven last days.

28.   Up betimes, and down to Deptford – where after a little discourse with Sir G. Carteret, who is much displeased with the order of our officers yesterday to remove the office to Deptford; pretending other things, but to be sure it is with regard to his own house (which is much because his family is going away). I am glad I was not at the order-making, and so I will endeavour to alter it. Set out with my Lady all alone with her with six horses to Dagenhams, going by water to the Ferry. And a pleasant going and good discourse – and when there, very merry and the young couple now well acquainted. But Lord, to see in what fear all the people here do live would make one mad. They are afeared of us that come to them, insomuch that I am troubled at it and wish myself away. But some cause they have, for the Chaplain, with whom but a week or two ago we were here mighty high disputing, is since fallen into a fever and dead, being gone hence to a friend's a good way off – a

sober and healthful man. These considerations make us all hasten
the marriage; and resolve it upon Monday next, which is three days
before we entended it. Mighty merry all of us; and in the evening,
with full content took coach again, and home by daylight with
great pleasure. And thence I down to Woolwich, where find my
wife well; and after drinking and talking a little, we to bed.

29. Up betimes. And after viewing some of wife's pictures,
which now she is come to do very finely, to my great satisfaction,
beyond what I could ever look for – I went away; and by water to
the office, where nobody to meet me, but busy all the morning. At
noon to dinner, where I hear that my Will is come in thither and laid
down upon my bed, ill of the headake; which put me into
extraordinary fear, and I studied all I could to get him out of the
house, and set my people to work to do it without discouraging
him. Writing of letters hard; and then at night home and fell to my
Tanger Papers – till late; and then to bed – in some ease of mind that
Will is gone to his lodging and that he is likely to do well, it being
only the the headake.

30. *Lord's day*. Up, and in my nightgown, cap, and neckcloth,
undressed all day long; lost not a minute, but in my chamber setting
my Tanger accounts to rights, which I did by night, to my very
heart's content; not only that it is done, but I find everything right
and even beyond what, after so long neglecting them, I did hope
for. The Lord of Heaven be praised for it. Will was with me today
and is very well again. It was a sad noise to hear our Bell to toll and
ring so often today, either for deaths or burials; I think five or six
times. At night, weary with the day's work but full of joy at my
having done it – I to bed, being to rise betimes tomorrow to go to
the wedding at Dagenhams. So to bed – fearing I have got some
cold sitting in my loose garment all this day.

31. Up, and very betimes, by 6 a-clock, at Deptford; and there
find Sir G. Carteret and my Lady ready to go – I being in my new
coloured-silk suit and coat, trimmed with gold buttons and gold
braid lace round my hands, very rich and fine. By water to the
Ferry, where, when we came, no coach there – and tide of ebb so far
spent as the horse-boat could not get off on the other side the river
to bring away the coach. So we were fain to stay there in the
unlucky Isle of Doggs – in a chill place, the morning cool and wind

fresh, above two if not three hours, to our great discontent. Yet being upon a pleasant errand, and seeing that could not be helped, we did bear it very patiently; and it was worth my observing, I thought as ever anything, to see how upon these two scores, Sir G. Carteret, the most passionate man in the world and that was in greatest haste to be gone, did bear with it, and very pleasant all the while, at least not troubled much so as to fret and storm at it. Anon the coach comes – in the meantime there coming a citizen thither with his horse to go over, that told us he did come from Islington this morning, and that Proctor the vintener of the Miter in Woodstreet, and his son, is dead this morning there – of the plague. He having laid out abundance of money there – and was the greatest vintener for some time in London for great entertainments. We fearing the canonicall hour would be past before we got thither, did with a great deal of unwillingness send away the Licence and wedding-ring. So that when we came, though we drove hard with six horses, yet we found them gone from home; and going toward the church, met them coming from church – which troubled us. But however, that trouble was soon over – hearing it was well done – they being both in their old Cloaths. My Lord Crew giving her – there being three coach-fulls of them. The young lady mighty sad, which troubled me; but yet I think it was only her gravity, in a little greater degree then usual. All saluted her, but I did not till my Lady Sandwich did ask me whether I had not saluted her or no. So to dinner, and very merry we were; but yet in such a Sober way as never almost any wedding was in so great families – but it was much better. After dinner, company divided, some to cards – others to talk. My Lady Sandwich and I up to settle accounts and pay her some money – and mighty kind she is to me, and would fain have had me gone down for company with her to Hinchingbrooke – but for my life I cannot. At night to supper, and so to talk and, which methought was the most extraordinary thing, all of us to prayers as usual, and the young Bride and bridegroom too. And so after prayers, Soberly to bed; only, I got into the bridegroom's chamber while he undressed himself, and there was very merry – till he was called to the bride's chamber and into bed they went. I kissed the bride in bed, and so the curtaines drawne with the greatest gravity that could be, and so good-night. But the modesty and gravity of this business was so decent, that it was to me, endeed, ten times more delightful then if it had been twenty times more merry and Joviall. Whereas I feared I must have sat up all night, we did here all get good beds – and I lay in the same I did before, with Mr. Brisband, who is a good scholar and sober man; and we lay in bed, getting him to give me an account of Rome, which is the most delightful talk a man can have of any traveller. And so to sleep – my eyes much troubled already with the change of my drink.

Thus I ended this month with the greatest joy that ever I did any in my life, because I have spent the greatest part of it with abundance of joy and honour, and pleasant Journys and brave entertainments, and without cost of money. And at last live to see that business ended with great content on all sides. This evening with Mr. Brisband speaking of inchantments and spells, I telling him some of my Charmes, he told me this of his own knowledge at Bourdeaux in France. The words these –

> *Voicy un Corps mort*
> *Royde comme un Baston*
> *Froid comme Marbre*
> *Leger comme un Esprit,*
> *Levons te au nom de Jesus Christ.*

He saw four little Girles, very young ones, all kneeling, each of them upon one knee; and one begin the first line, whispering in the eare of the next, and the second to the third, and the third to the fourth, and she to the first. Then the first begun the second line, and so round quite through. And putting each one finger only to a boy that lay flat upon his back on the ground, as if he was dead. At the end of the words, they did with their four fingers raise this boy as high as they could reach. And he being there and wondering at it (as also being afeared to see it – for they would have had him to have bore a part in saying the words in the room of one of the little girls, that was so young that they could hardly make her learn to repeat the words), did, for fear there might be some sleight used in it by the boy, or that the boy might be light, called the cook of the house, a very lusty fellow, as Sir G. Carteret's Cooke, who is very big, and they did raise him just in the same manner. This is one of the strangest things I ever heard, but he tells it me of his own knowledge and I do heartily believe it to be true. I enquired of him whether they were Protestant or Catholique girls, and he told me they were Protestant – which made it the more strange to me.

Thus we end this month, as I said, after the greatest glut of content that ever I had; only, under some difficulty because of the plague, which grows mightily upon us, the last week being about 1700 or 1800 of the plague. My Lord Sandwich, at sea with a fleet of about 100 sail to the Norward, expect De Ruyter or the Duch East India fleet. Myself having obliged both these families in this business very much, as both my Lady and Sir G. Carteret and his Lady do confess exceedingly; and the latter two also now call me Cosen, which I am glad of. So God preserve us all friends long, and continue health among us.

# –✤AUGUST✤–

1. Slept and lay long, then up; and my Lord and Sir G. Carteret being gone abroad, I first to see the bridegroom and bride, and found them both up, and he gone to dress himself. Both red in the face and well enough pleased this morning with their night's lodging. Thence down, and Mr. Brisband and I to Billiards. Anon came my Lord and Sir G. Carteret in, who had been looking abroad and visiting some farms that Sir G. Carteret hath thereabouts – and among other things, report the greatest stories of the bigness of the Calfes they find there ready to sell to the butchers; as big, as they say, as little Cowes. And that they do give them a piece of Chalke to lick, which they hold makes them white in the flesh within. Very merry at Dinner, and so to talk and laugh after dinner, and up and down, some to [one] place, some to another – full of content on all sides. Anon, about 5 a-clock, Sir G. Carteret and his lady and I took coach, with the greatest joy and kindness that could be from the two families – or that ever I saw with so much appearance, and I believe reality, in all my life. Drove hard home, and it was night ere we got to Deptford – where, with much kindness from them to me, I left them; and home to the office, where I find all well. And being weary and sleepy, it being very late, I to bed.

6. *Lords day.* Dressed and had my head combed by my little girle, to whom I confess que je sum demasiado kind, nuper ponendo sæpe mes mains in su dos choses de son breast. Mais il faut que je leave it, lest it bring me to alguno major inconvenience. So to my business in my chamber – look[ing] over and settling more of my papers then I could do the two last days I have spent about them. In the

evening, it raining hard, down to Woolwich, where after some little talk, to bed.

8. Up, and to the office, where all the morning we sat. At noon I home to dinner alone. And after dinner Bagwell's wife waited at the door, and went with me to my office, en lequel jo haze todo which I had a corasón a hazer con ella. So parted, and I to Sir W. Batten's and there sat the most of the afternoon, talking and drinking too much with my Lord Bruncker, Sir G. Smith, G. Cocke, and others, very merry. I drunk a little, mixed, but yet more then I should do. So to my office a little, and then to the Duke of Albemarle's about some business. The streets mighty empty all the way now, even in London, which is a sad sight. And to Westminster hall, where talking, hearing very sad stories from Mrs. Mumford among others, of Mrs. Michell's son's family. And poor Will that used to sell us ale at the Hall door – his wife and three children dead, all I think in a day. So home through the City again, wishing I may have taken no ill in going; but I will go, I think, no more thither. Late at the office and then home to supper, having taken a pullet home with me. And then to bed. The News of De Ruter's coming home is certain – and told to the great disadvantage of our fleet and the praise of De Ruyter; but it cannot be helped – nor do I know what to say to it.

11. Up, and all day long finishing and writing over my will twice, for my father and my wife. Only in the morning a pleasant rancontre happened, in having a young married woman brought me by her father, old Delkes, that carries pins alway in his mouth, to get her husband off, that he should not go to sea. Uno ombre pouvait avoir done any cosa cum ella, but I did natha sino besar her. After they were gone, my mind run upon having them called back again; and I sent a messenger to Blackewall but he failed, so I lost my expectation. I to the Exchequer about striking new tallies; and I find the Exchequer, by Proclamacion, removing to Nonesuch. Back again and at my papers, and putting up my books into chests, and settling my house and all things in the best and speediest order I can, lest it should please God to take me away or force me to leave my house. Late up at it, and weary and full of wind, finding perfectly that so long as I keep myself in company at meals and do there eat lustily, which I cannot do alone, having no love to eateing, but my mind runs upon my business, I am as well as can be; but

when I come to be alone, I do not eat in time, nor enough, nor with any good heart, and I immediately begin to be full of wind, which brings me pain, till I come to fill my belly a-days again; then am presently well.

12.   The people die so, that now it seems they are fain to carry the dead to be buried by daylight, the nights not sufficing to do it in. And my Lord Mayor commands people to be within at 9 at night, all (as they say) that the sick may have liberty to go abroad for ayre. There is one also dead out of one of our ships at Deptford, which troubles us mightily – the *Providence* fireship, which was just fitted to go to sea. But they tell me today, no more sick on board. And this day W. Bodham tells me that one is dead at Woolwich, not far from the Ropeyard. I am told too, that a wife of one of the groomes at Court is dead at Salsbury, so that the King and Queene are speedily to be all gone to [Wilton]. God preserve us.

13.   *Lords day*. Up betimes, and to my chamber (it being a very wet day all day, and glad I am that we did not go by water to see the *Soveraigne* today as I entended), clearing all matters in packing up my papers and books – and giving instructions in writing to my Executors, thereby perfecting the whole business of my Will, to my very great joy. So that I shall be in much better state of soul, I hope, if it should please the Lord to call me away this sickly time. At night to read, being weary with this day's great work. And then after supper to bed, to rise betimes tomorrow. And to bed with a mind as free as to the business of the world as if I were not worth 100*l* in the whole world, everything being evened under my hand in my books and papers; and upon the whole, I find myself worth (besides Brampton estate) the sum of 2164*l* – for which the Lord be praised.

14.   Up; and my mind being at mighty ease from the despatch of my business so much yesterday, I down to Deptford to Sir G. Carteret; where with him a great while, and a great deal of private talk concerning my Lord Sandwich's and his matters – and chiefly of the latter, I giving him great deal of advice about the necessity of his having caution concerning Fenn, and the many ways there are of his being abused by any man in his place. And why he should not bring his son in to look after his business, and more, to be a Comissioner of the Navy; which he listened to and liked, and told me how much the King was his good maister, and was sure would

not deny him that or anything else greater then that. And I find him a very cunning man, whatever at other times he seems to be. And among other things, he told me he was not for the Fanfarroons, to make a show with a great Title, as he might have had long since, but the main thing to get an estate; and another thing, speaking of minding of business, "By God," says he, "I will, and have already almost brought it to that pass, that the King shall not be able to whip a cat but I must be at the tayle of it" – meaning, so necessary he is, and the King and my Lord Treasurer and all do confess it. Which, while I mind my business, is my own case in this office of the Navy; and I hope shall be more, if God give me life and health. Thence by agreement to Sir J. Minnes's lodgings, where I find my Lord Bruncker; and so by water to the Ferry, and there took Sir W. Batten's coach that was sent for us and to Sir W. Battens, where very merry, good cheer, and up and down the garden, with great content to me. And after dinner beat Capt. Cocke at Billiards; won about 8s. of him and my Lord Bruncker. So in the evening, after much pleasure, back again – and I by water to Woolwich, where supped with my wife; and then to bed betimes, because of rising tomorrow at 4 of the clock, in order to the going out with Sir G. Carteret toward Cranborne to meet my Lord Hinchingbrooke in his way to Court. This night I did present my wife with the Dyamond ring a while since given me by Mr. [?Blayton], Dicke Vines's brother, for helping him to be a purser – valued at about 10l – the first thing of that nature I did ever give her. Great fears we have that the plague will be a great Bill this week.

15.   Up by 4 a-clock and walked to Greenwich, where called at Capt. Cockes and to his chamber, he being in bed – where something put my last night's dream into my head, which I think is the best that ever was dreamed – which was, that I had my Lady Castlemayne in my armes and was admitted to use all the dalliance I desired with her, and then dreamed that this could not be awake but that it was only a dream. But that since it was a dream and that I took so much real pleasure in it, what a happy thing it would be, if when we are in our graves (as Shakespeere resembles it), we could dream, and dream but such dreams as this – that then we should not need to be so fearful of death as we are this plague-time.

16.   To the Exchange, which I have not been a great while. But Lord, how sad a sight it is to see the streets empty of people, and

very few upon the Change – jealous of every door that one sees shut up, lest it should be the plague – and about us, two shops in three, if not more, generally shut up. Mighty merry with Capt. Cocke and Fenn at Sir G. Smiths, and a brave dinner. But I think Cocke is the greatest Epicure that is; eats and drinks with the greatest pleasure and Liberty that ever man did.

17. Up, and to the office,[1] where we sat all the morning; and at noon dined together upon some victuals I had prepared at Sir W. Batten's upon the King's charge. And after dinner, I having despatched some business and set things in order at home, we down to the water and by boat to Greenwich to the *Bezan* Yacht, where Sir W. Batten, Sir J. Mennes, my Lord Bruncker and myself, with some servants (among others, Mr. Carcasse, my Lord's Clerke, a very civil Gentleman) imbarked in the Yacht, and down we went most pleasantly – and noble discourse I had with my Lord Bruncker, who is a most excellent person. Short of Gravesend, it grew calme, and so we came to an Anchor – and to supper mighty merry. And after, it being moonshine, we out of the Cabbin to laugh and talk; and then, as we grew sleepy, went in, and upon ve[l]vet cushions of the King's that belong to the Yacht fell to sleep – which we all did pretty well till 3 or 4 of the clock – having risen in the night to look for a new Comet which is said to have lately shone. But we could see no such thing.

18. Up about 5 a-clock and dressed ourselfs; and to sail again down to the *Soveraigne* at the buoy of the Noure – a noble ship, now rigged and fitted and manned. We did not stay long, but to enquire after her readiness; and thence to Sheerenesse, where we walked up and down, laying out the ground to be taken in for a yard to lay provisions for cleaning and repairing of ships; and a most proper place it is for that purpose. Thence with great pleasure up the Meadeway, our yacht contending with Comissioner Pett's, wherein he met us from Chatham; and he had the best of it. Here I came by, but had not tide enough to stop at Quinbrough. With mighty pleasure spent the day in doing all and seeing these places, which I had never done before. So to the Hill house at Chatham, and there dined; and after dinner spent some time discoursing of business – among others, arguing with the Comissioner about his proposing

1. He is now back in London.

the laying out so much money upon Sheerenesse, unless it be to the slighting of Chatham yard, for it is much a better place then Chatham; which, however, the King is not at present in purse to do, though it were to be wished he were. Thence in Comissioner Pett's coach (leaving them there), I late in the dark to Gravesend, where great is the plague, and I troubled to stay there so long for the tide. At 10 at night, having supped, I took boat alone, and slept well all the way to the Tower docke, about 3 a-clock in the morning. So knocked up my people and to bed.

19.    Slept till 8 a-clock; and then up, and met with letters from the King and Lord Arlington for the removal of our office to Greenwich. I also wrote letters and made myself ready to go to Sir G. Carteret at Windsor; and having borrowed a horse of Mr. Blackbrough, did send him to wait for me at the Duke of Albemarle's door – when on a sudden, a letter comes to us from the Duke of Albemarle, to tell us that the fleet is all come back to Solebay and are presently to be despatched back again. Whereupon I presently by water to the Duke of Albemarle to know what news – and there I saw a letter from my Lord Sandwich to the Duke of Albemarle, and also from Sir W. Coventry and Capt. Teddiman, how my Lord, having commanded Teddiman with 22 ships (of which but 15 could get thither, and of those 15 but eight or nine could come up to play) to go to Bergen,[1] where after several messages to and fro from the Governor of the Castle, urging that Teddiman ought not to come thither with more then five ships, and desiring time to think of it, all the while he suffering the Dutch ships to land their guns to their best advantage – Teddiman, on the second present, begun to play at the Dutch ships (whereof ten East Indiamen) and in three hours' time ( the town and Castle without any provocation playing on our ships) they did cut all our cables, so as the wind being off the land, did force us to go out – and rendered our fireships useless – without doing anything but what hurt, of course, our guns must have done them. We having lost five commanders – besides Mr. Edwd. Mountagu and Mr. Windham. Our fleet is come home, to our great grief with not above five weeks dry and six days wet provision. However, must out again;

---

1. In Norway, which was then under the rule of Denmark. Sandwich had been led to believe that the governor had agreed to connive with him in this attack on the Dutch E. India fleet which had taken refuge in the harbour.

and the Duke hath ordered the *Souveraigne* and all other ships ready to go out to go to the fleet to strengthen them. This news troubles us all, but cannot be helped. Having read all this news, and received commands of the Duke with great content, he giving me the words which to my great joy he hath several times said to me, that his greatest reliance is upon me – and my Lord Craven also did come out to talk with me, and told me that I am in mighty esteem with the Duke, for which I bless God.

25. Up betimes to the office, and there, as well as all the afternoon (saving a little dinner time, all alone) till late at night, writing letters and doing business, that I may get beforehand with my business again, which hath run behind a great while; and then home to supper and to bed. This day I am told that Dr. Burnett my physician is this morning dead of the plague – which is strange, his man dying so long ago, and his house this month open again. Now himself dead – poor unfortunate man.

26. Up betimes, and prepared to my great Satisfaction an account for the Board of my office disbursements, which I had suffered to run on to almost 120*l*. That done, I down by water to Greenwich, where we met the first day, my Lord Brouncker, Sir J. Mennes, and I, and I think we shall do well there. And begun very auspiciously to me, by having my account abovesaid passed and put into a way of having it presently paid. We parted at my Lord Brunckers door – where I went in (having never been there before) – and there he made a noble entertainment for Sir J. Mennes, myself, and Capt. Cocke; none else – saving some painted lady that dined there, I know not who she is.[1] But very merry we were. Thence I by water home, in my way seeing a man taken up dead out of the Hold of a small ketch that lay at Deptford; I doubt it might be the plague, which, with the thought of Dr. Burnett, did something disturb me, so that I did not what I entended and should have done at the office as to business. But home sooner then ordinary; and after supper to read melancholy alone, and then to bed.

28. Up; and being ready, I out to Mr. Colvill the goldsmith's, having not for some days been in the streets. But now, how few people I see, and those walking like people that had taken leave of

1. She was Abigail Williams, Brouncker's mistress.

the world. I there, and made even all accounts in the world between him and I in very good condition. And would have done the like with Sir Rob. Viner, but he is out of town – the sickness being everywhere thereabouts. I to the Exchange, and I think there was not 50 people upon it and but few more like to be, as they told me, Sir G. Smith and others. Thus, I think to take Adieu today of London streets, unless it be to go again to Viners. Home to dinner, and there W. Hewer brings me 119*l* he hath received for my office disbursements, so that I think I have 1800*l* and more in the house; and blessed be God, no money out but what I can very well command, and that but very little – which is much the best posture I ever was in in my life, both as to the quantity and the certainty I have of the money I am worth, having most of it in my own hand. But then this is a trouble to me, what to do with it, being myself this day going to be wholly at Woolwich.[1] But for the present I am resolved to venture it in an Iron Chest – at least, for a while. In the afternoon I sent down my boy to Woolwich with some things before me, in order to my lying there for good and all, and so I fallowed him. Just now comes news that the Fleete is gone, or going this day, out again – for which God be praised; and my Lord Sandwich hath done himself great right in it in getting so soon out again. Pray God he may meet the Enemy.

31. Thus this month ends, with great sadness upon the public through the greatness of the plague, everywhere through the Kingdom almost. Every day sadder and sadder news of its encrease. In the City died this week 7496; and of them 6102 of the plague. But it is feared that the true number of the dead this week is near 10000 – partly from the poor that cannot be taken notice of through the greatness of the number, and partly from the Quakers and others that will not have any bell ring for them. Our fleet gone out to find the Dutch, we having about 100 sail in our fleet, and in them, the *Soveraigne* one; so that it is a better fleet then the former with the Duke was. All our fear is that the Dutch should be got in before them – which would be a very great sorrow to the public, and to me perticularly, for my Lord Sandwichs sake. A great deal of money being spent, and the Kingdom not in a condition to spare, nor a parliament, without much difficulty, to meet to give more. And to that, to have it said "What hath been done by our late fleets?" As to

1. For his movements, see above, p. 503, n.

myself, I am very well; only, in fear of the plague, and as much of an Ague, by being forced to go early and late to Woolwich, and my family to lie there continually. My late gettings have been very great, to my great content, and am likely to have yet a few more profitable jobbs in a little while – for which, Tanger and Sir W. Warren I am wholly obliged to.

## –❄SEPTEMBER❄–

3. *Lords day.* Up, and put on my colourd silk suit, very fine, and my new periwigg, bought a good while since, but darst not wear it because the plague was in Westminster when I bought it. And it is a wonder what will be the fashion after the plague is done as to periwigs, for nobody will dare to buy any haire for fear of the infection – that it had been cut off of the heads of people dead of the plague. Before church time comes Mr. Hill (Mr. Andrews failing because he was to receive the sacrament), and to church, where a sorry dull parson; and so home and most excellent company with Mr. Hill, and discourse of Musique. I took my Lady Pen home and her daughter Peg, and merry we were, and after dinner I made my wife show them her pictures, which did mad pegg Pen who learns of the same man – and cannot do so well. After dinner left them, and I by water to Greenwich, where much ado to be suffered to come into the town because of the sickness, for fear I should come from London – till I told them who I was. So up to the church, where at the door I find Capt. Cocke in my Lord Brunkers coach, and he came out and walked with me in the churchyard till the church was done. Talking of the ill-government of our Kingdom, nobody setting to heart the business of the Kingdom, but everybody minding their perticular profit or pleasures, the King himself minding nothing but his ease – and so we let things go to wrack. This arose upon considering what we shall do for money when the fleet comes in, and more if the fleet should not meet with the Dutch, which will put a disgrace upon the King's actions, so as the Parliament and Kingdom will have the less mind to give more money. Besides, so bad an account of the last money, we fear, will be given; not half of it being spent, as it ought to be, upon the Navy. Besides, it is said that at this day our Lord Treasurer cannot tell what the profits of Chimny money is; what it comes to per annum –

nor looks whether that or any other part of the Revenue be duly gathered as it ought – the very money that should pay the City the 200000*l* they lent the King being all gathered and in the hands of the Receiver, and hath been long, and yet not brought up to pay the City, whereas we are coming to borrow 4 or 500000*l* more of the City – which will never be lent as is to be feared. Church being done, my Lord Brouncker, Sir J. Mennes, and I up to the Vestry at the desire of the Justices of the Peace, Sir Th. Bidolph and Sir W. Boreman and Ald. Hooker – in order to the doing something for the keeping of the plague from growing; but Lord, to consider the madness of people of the town, who will (because they are forbid) come in Crowds along with the dead Corps to see them buried. But we agreed on some orders for the prevention thereof. Among other stories, one was very passionate methought – of a complaint brought against a man in the town for taking a child from London from an infected house. Ald. Hooker told us it was the child of a very able citizen in Gracious street, a sadler, who had buried all the rest of his children of the plague; and himself and wife now being shut up, and in despair of escaping, did desire only to save the life of this little child; and so prevailed to have it received stark naked into the arms of a friend, who brought it (having put it into new fresh clothes) to Grenwich; where, upon hearing the story, we did agree it should be permitted to be received and kept in the town. Thence with my Lord Brouncker to Capt. Cockes, where we mighty merry, and supped; and very late, I by water to Woolwich, in great apprehensions of an Ague. Here was my Lord Brouncker's lady of pleasure, who I perceive goes everywhere with him, and he I find is obliged to carry her and make all the Courtship to her that can be.

5.    Up, and walked, with some Captains and others talking to me, to Greenwich – they crying out upon Capt. Teddiman's management of the business of Bergen; that he stayed treating too long while he saw the Dutch fitting themselfs. And that at first he might have taken every ship and done what he would with them. How true I cannot tell. Here we sat very late, and for want of money (which lies heavy upon us) did nothing of business almost. Thence home with my Lord Brouncker to dinner, where very merry with him and his Doxy. After dinner comes Coll. Blunt in his new Charriott made with Springs, as that was of Wicker wherein a while since we rode at his house. And he hath rode, he says, now this Journy, many mile in it with one horse, and outdrives any coach

and out-goes any horse, and so easy he says. So for Curiosity I went into it to try it; and up the hill to the Heath and over the Cartrutts went to try it, and found it pretty well, but not so easy as he pretends; and so back again and took leave of my Lord and drove myself in the chariot to the office – and there ended my letters; and home pretty betimes, and there find W. Pen, and he stayed supper with us, and mighty merry talking of his Travells and the French humours, &c; and so parted and to bed.

6.   Busy all the morning writing letters to several. So to dinner – to London to pack up more things thence; and there I looked into the street and saw Fires burning in the street, as it is through the whole City by the Lord Mayors order. Thence by water to the Duke of Albemarle. All the way fires on each side the Thames; and strange to see in broad daylight two or three Burialls upon the Bankeside, one at the very heels of another – doubtless all of the plague – and yet at least 40 or 50 people going along with every one of them.

7.   Up by 5 of the clock, mighty full of fear of an Ague, but was obliged to go; and so by water, wrapping myself up warm, to the Tower; and there sent for the Weekely Bill and find 8252 dead in all, and of them, 6978 of the plague – which is a most dreadfull Number – and shows reason to fear that the plague hath got that hold that it will yet continue among us. Thence to Brainford, reading *The Villaine* (a pretty good play) all the way. There a coach of Mr. Povy's stood ready for me, and he at his house ready to come in; and so we together merrily to Swakely, Sir R. Viner's – a very pleasant place, bought by him of Sir James Harringtons lady. He took us up and down with great respect and showed us all his house and grounds; and is a place not very moderne in the gardens nor house, but the most uniforme in all that ever I saw – and some things to excess. Pretty to see over the Screene of the Hall (put up by Sir J. Harrington, a Long Parliament-man) the King's head, and my Lord of Essex on one side and Fairfax on the other – and upon the other side of the Screene, the parson of the parish and the lord of the manor and his sisters. The window-cases, door-cases, and Chimnys of all the house are Marble. He showed me a black boy that he had that died of a consumption; and being dead, he caused him to be dried in a Oven, and lies there entire in a box. By and by to dinner, where his lady I find yet handsome, but hath been a very handsome woman – now is old – hath brought him near 100000*l*. And now he

lives no man in England in greater plenty, and commands both King and Council with his Creditt he gives them. Here was a fine lady, a merchant's wife, at dinner with us; and who should be here in the quality of a Woman but Mrs. Worships daughter, Dr. Clerke's niece. And after dinner Sir Rob. led us up to his long gallery, very fine, above stairs (and better or such furniture I never did see), and there Mrs. Worship did give us three or four very good songs, and sings very neatly – to my great delight. After all this, and ending the chief business to my content, about getting a promise of some money of him – we took leave, being exceeding well treated here. And a most pleasant Journy we had back, Povy and I; his company most excellent in anything but business – he here giving me an account of as many persons at Court as I had a mind or thought of enquiring after. He tells me, by a letter he showed me, that the King is nor hath been of late very well, but quite out of humour and, as some think, in a consumption and weary of everything. He showed me my Lord Arlingtons house that he was born in, in a Towne called Harlington. And so carried me through a most pleasant country to Brainford, and there put me into my boat and good-night. So I wrapped myself warm, and by water got to Woolwich about one in the morning. My wife and all in bed.

8. Up, and several with me about business. Anon comes my Lord Brouncker, as I expected, and we to the enquiring into the business of the late desertion of the Shipwrights from work, who had left us for three days together for want of money. And upon this all morning and brought it to a pretty good issue, that they, we believe, will come tomorrow to work.

9. Up, and walked to Greenwich; and there we sat and despatched a good deal of business I had a mind to. At noon by invitation to my Lord Brouncker's, all of us, to dinner, where a good venison pasty and mighty merry. Here was Sir W. Doyly, lately come from Ipswich about the sick and wounded – and Mr. Eveling and Capt. Cocke. My wife also was sent for by my Lord Brouncker, by Cocke, and was here. After dinner my Lord and his mistress would see her home again, it being a most cursed rainy afternoon, having had none a great while before. And I, forced to go to the office on foot through all the rain, was almost wet to the skin, and spoiled my silk breeches almost. Rained all the afternoon and evening, so as my letters being done, I was forced to get a bed at Capt. Cockes – where

I find Sir W. Doyly and he and Eveling at supper; and I with them, full of discourse of the neglect of our masters, the great officers of State, about all businesses, and especially that of money – having now some thousand prisoners kept to no purpose, at a great charge, and no money provided almost for the doing of it. We fell to talk largely of the want of some persons understanding to look after businesses, but all goes to wrack. "For," says Capt. Cocke, "My Lord Treasurer, he minds his ease and lets things go how they will; if he can have his 8000*l* per annum and a game at Lombre, he is well. My Lord Chancellor, he minds getting of money and nothing else; and my Lord Ashly will rob the devil and the Alter but he will get money if it be to be got." But that that puts us into this great melancholy was news brought today, which Capt. Cocke reports as a certain truth, that all the Dutch fleet, men-of-war and merchant East India ships, are got every one in from Bergen the 3rd of this month, Sunday last – which will make us all ridiculous. The fleet came home with shame to require great deal of money, which is not to be had – to discharge many men, that must get the plague then or continue at greater charge on shipboard. Nothing done by them to encourage the Parliament to give money – nor the Kingdom able to spare any money if they would, at this time of the plague. So that as things look at present, the whole state must come to Ruine. Full of these melancholy thoughts, to bed – where though I lay the saftest I ever did in my life, with a down bed (after the Danish manner, upon me), yet I slept very ill, chiefly through the thoughts of my Lord Sandwiches concernment in all this ill-success at sea.

10. *Lords day.* News come to me by an express from Mr. Coventry, telling me the most happy news of my Lord Sandwiches meeting with part of the Dutch; his taking two of their East India ships and six or seven others, and very good prize – and that he is in search of the rest of the fleet, which he hopes to find upon the Well bancke – with the loss only of the *Hector*, poor Capt. Cuttle. This news doth so overjoy me, that I know not what to say enough to express it; but the better to do it, I did walk to Greenwich; and there sending away Mr. Andrews, I to Capt. Cocke's where I find my Lord Brouncker and his mistress and Sir J. Mennes – where we supped (there was also Sir W. Doyly and Mr. Eveling); but the receipt of this news did put us all into such an extasy of joy, that it inspired into Sir J. Mennes and Mr. Eveling such a spirit of mirth, that in all my life I never met with so merry a two hours as our

company this night was. Among other humours, Mr. Eveling's repeating of some verses made up of nothing but the various acceptations of May and Can, and doing it so aptly, upon occasion of something of that nature, and so fast, did make us all die almost with laughing, and did so stop the mouth of Sir J. Mennes in the middle of all his mirth (and in a thing agreeing with his own manner of Genius) that I never saw any man so out-done in all my life; and Sir J. Mennes's mirth too, to see himself out-done, was the crown of all our mirth. In this humour we sat till about 10 at night; and so my Lord and his mistress home, and we to bed – it being one of the times of my life wherein I was the fullest of true sense of joy.

13. Up, and walked to Greenwich, taking pleasure to walk with my minute wach in my hand, by which I am now come to see the distances of my way from Woolwich to Greenwich. And do find myself to come within two minutes constantly to the same place at the end of each quarter of an hour. Here we Rendezvoused at Capt. Cocke's and there eat oysters; and so my Lord Brouncker, Sir J. Mennes and I took the boat; and in my Lord's coach to Sir W. Hickes's, whither by and by my Lady Batten and Sir Wm. comes. It is a good seat – with a fair grove of trees by it, and the remains of a good garden. But so let to run to ruine, both house and everything in and about it – so ill furnished and miserably looked after, I never did see in all my life. Not so much as a latch to his dining-room door – which saved him nothing, for the wind blowing into the room for want thereof, flung down a great Bowpott that stood upon the side-table, and that fell upon some Venice glasses and did him a crown's worth of hurt. He did give us the meanest dinner – of beef – shoulder and umbles of venison which he takes away from the keeper of the Forest – and a few pigeons; and all in the meanest manner that ever I did see – to the basest degree. After dinner we officers of the Navy stepped aside to read some letters and consider some business, and so in again. I was only pleased at a very fine picture of the Queene Mother – when she was young, by Van Dike; a very good picture and a lovely sweet face.

14. Up, and walked to Greenwich and there fitted myself in several businesses to go to London, where I have not been now a pretty while. But before I went from the office, news is brought by word of mouth that letters are now just now brought from the Fleete of our taking a great many more of the Dutch fleet – in which

I did never more plainly see my command of my temper, in my not admitting myself to receive any kind of joy from it till I had heard the certainty of it. And therefore went by water directly to the Duke of Albemarle, where I find a letter of the 12th from Soldbay, from my Lord Sandwich, of the fleet's meeting with about 18 more of the Dutch fleet and his taking of most of them; and the messenger says they had taken three after the letter was wrote and sealed; which being 21, and the 14 took the other day, is [35] sail – some of which are good, and others rich ships – which is so great a cause of joy in us all, that my Lord and everybody is highly joyed thereat. And having taken a copy of my Lord's letter, I away back again to the Bear at the Bridge foot, being full of wind and out of order, and there called for a biscuit and a piece of cheese and gill of sack – being forced to walk over the Bridge toward the Change, and the plague being all thereabouts. Here my news was highly welcome, and I did wonder to see the Change so full, I believe 200 people; but not a man or merchant of any fashion, but plain men all. And Lord, to see how I did endeavour all I could to talk with as few as I could, there being now no observation of shutting up of houses infected, that to be sure we do converse and meet with people that have the plague upon them. I to Sir Rob. Viners, where my main business was about settling the business of Debusty's 5000*l* tallies – which I did for the present to enable me to have some money. And so home, buying some things for my wife in the way. So home and put up several things to carry to Woolwich – and upon serious thoughts, I am advised by W. Griffin to let my money and plate rest there, as being as safe as any place, nobody imagining that people would leave money in their houses now, when all their families are gone. So for the present, that being my opinion, I did leave them there still. But Lord, to see the trouble that it puts a man to to keep safe what with pain a man hath been getting together; and there is good reason for it. Down to the office, and there wrote letters to and again about this good news of our victory, and so by water home late –

Where when I came home, I spent some thoughts upon the occurrences of this day, giving matter for as much content on one hand and melancholy on another as any day in all my life – for the first, the finding of my money and plate and all safe at London, and speeding in my business of money this day – the hearing of this good news, to such excess after so great a despair of my Lord's doing anything this year – adding to that, the decrease of 500 and

10. Charles II on the eve of the Restoration. Attributed to Simon Luttichuys.

11. Barbara Villiers, Countess of Castlemaine, painted in the studio of Sir Peter Lely, c.1664

12. Nell Gwyn, by Simon Verelst, c.1670

13. George Monck, 1st Duke of Albemarle, by Sir Peter Lely

more, which is the first decrease we have yet had in the sickness since it begun – and great hopes that the next week it will be greater. Then on the other side – my finding that though the Bill in general is abated, yet the City within the walls is encreased and likely to continue so, and is close to our house there – my meeting dead corps's of the plague, carried to be buried close to me at noonday through the City in Fanchurch street – to see a person sick of the sores carried close by me by Grace church in a hackney-coach – my finding the Angell tavern at the lower end of Tower hill shut up; and more then that, the alehouse at the Tower stairs; and more then that, that the person was then dying of the plague when I was last there, a little while ago at night, to write a short letter there, and I overheard the mistress of the house sadly saying to her husband somebody was very ill, but did not think it was of the plague – to hear that poor Payne my water[man] hath buried a child and is dying himself – to hear that a labourer I sent but the other day to Dagenhams to know how they did there is dead of the plague; and that one of my own watermen, that carried me daily, fell sick as soon as he had landed me on Friday morning last, when I had been all night upon the water (and I believed he did get his infection that day at Brainford) is now dead of the plague – to hear that Capt. Lambert and Cuttle are killed in the taking these ships and that Mr. Sidny Mountague is sick of a desperate fever at my Lady Carteret's at Scott's hall – to hear that Mr. Lewes hath another daughter sick – and lastly, that both my servants, W. Hewers and Tom Edwards, have lost their fathers, both in St. Sepulcher's parish, of the plague this week – doth put me into great apprehensions of melancholy, and with good reason. But I put off the thoughts of sadness as much as I can; and the rather to keep my wife in good heart, and family also. After supper (having eat nothing all day) upon a fine Tench of Mr. Sheldens taking, we to bed.

15. Up, it being a cold misling morning, and so by water to the office, where very busy upon several businesses. At noon got the messenger, Marlow, to get me a piece of bread and butter and cheese and a bottle of beer and ale, and so I went not out of the office but dined off that, and my boy Tom, but the rest of my clarks went home to dinner. Then to my business again, and by and by sent my waterman to see how Sir W. Warren doth, who is sick, and for which I have reason to be very sorry, he being the friend I have got most by of most friends in England but the King. Who returns me

that he is pretty well again, his disease being an ague. I by water to Deptford, thinking to have seen my valentine, but I could not and so come back again – and to the office, where a little business; and thence with Capt. Cocke and there drank a cup of good drink (which I am fain to allow myself during this plague time, by advice of all and not contrary to my oath, my physician being dead and Chyrurgeon out of the way whose advice I am obliged to take); and so by water home and eat my supper, and so to bed – being in much pain to think what I shall do this winter time; for, go every day to Woolwich I cannot, without endangering my life, and staying from my wife at Greenwich is not handsome.

16. Up, and walked to Greenwich, reading a play, and to the office, where I find Sir J. Mennes gone to the fleet like a doting fool, to do no good but proclaim himself an asse – for no service he can do there, nor inform my Lord (who is come in thither to the Buoy of the Nore) in anything worth his knowledge. At noon to dinner to my Lord Bruncker, where Sir W. Batten and his Lady came by invitation, and very merry we are – only, that the discourse of the likelihood of the increase of the plague this week makes us a little sad. But then again, the thoughts of the late prizes make us glad. At night to Capt. Cockes, meaning to lie there, it being late; and he not being home, I walked to him to my Lord Bruncker's and there stayed a while, they being at tables; and so by and by parted, and walked to his house, and after a mess of good broth, to bed in great pleasure, his company being most excellent.

17. *Lords day*. Up, and before I went out of my chamber, did draw a Musique Scale, in order to my having it at any time ready in my hand to turn to for exercise, for I have a great mind in this vacation to perfect myself in my Scale, in order to my practising of composition. And so that being done, I downstairs and there find Capt. Cocke under the barber's hands – the barber that did heretofore trim Comissioner Pett, and with whom I have been. He offered to come this day after dinner with his violin, to play me a set of Lyra ayres upon it, which I was glad of, hoping to be merry thereby. Being ready, we to church, where a company of fine people to church, and a fine church and very good sermon (Mr. Plume being a very excellent scholler and preacher); coming out of the church, I met Mrs. Pierce, whom I was shamed to see, having not been with her since my coming to town – but promised to visit

her. Thence with Capt. Cocke (in his coach) home to dinner, whither comes by invitation My Lord Bruncker and his mistress, and very good company we were. But in dinner-time comes Sir Jo. Minnes from the fleet like a simple weak man, having nothing to say of what he hath done there, but tells us of what value he imagines the prizes to be, and that my Lord Sandwich is well and mightily concerned to hear that I was well. But this did put me upon a desire of going thither; and moving of it to my Lord, we presently agreed upon it to go this very Tide, we two and Capt. Cocke. So everybody prepared to fit himself for his Journy, and I walked to Woolwich to trim and shift myself; and by the time I was ready they came down in the *Bezan* Yacht, and so I aboard and my boy Tom. And there very merrily we sailed to below Gravesend, and there came to Anchor for all night and supped and talked, and with much pleasure at last settled ourselfs to sleep – having very good lodging upon Cushions in the Cabbin.

18.    By break of day we came to within sight of the fleet, which was a very fine thing to behold, being above 100 ships, great and small – with the flag-ships of each squadron distinguished by their several flags on their main, fore, or mizzen masts. Among others, the *Soveraigne, Charles*, and *Prince*, in the last of which my Lord Sandwich was. When we called by her side, his Lordship was not stirring; so we came to anchor a little below his ship, thinking to have rowed on board him; but the wind and tide was so strong against us that we could not get up to him; no, though rowed by a boat of the *Prince*'s that came to us to tow us up; at last, however, he brought us within a little way, and then they flung out a rope to us from the *Prince*, and so came on board, but with great trouble and time and patience, it being very cold. We find my Lord newly up in his nightgown, very well. He received us kindly, telling us the state of the fleet; lacking provisions, having no beer at all, nor have had most of them these three weeks or month, and but few days' dry provisions. And endeed, he tells us that he believes no fleet was ever set to sea in so ill condition of provision as this was when it went out last. By and by was called a council of warr on board, when came Sir W. Pen there – and Sir Chr. Mings, Sir Edwd. Spragg, Sir Jos. Jordan, Sir Tho. Teddiman, and Sir Rogr. Cuttance. And so the necessities of the fleet for victuals, clothes, and money was discoursed, but by the discourse there of all but my Lord – that is to say, the counterfeit grave nonsense of Sir W. Pen and the poor mean

discourse of the rest, methinks I see how the government and management of the greatest business of the three nations is committed to very ordinary heads, saving my Lord; and in effect, is only upon him, who is able to do what he please with them, they not having the meanest degree of reason to be able to oppose anything that he says. And so I fear it is ordered but like all the rest of the King's public affayres. The council being up, they most of them went away, only Sir W. Penn, who stayed to dine there, and did so; but the wind being high, the ship (though the motion of it was hardly discernible to the eye) did make me sick, so as I could not eat anything almost. After dinner Cocke did pray me to help him to 500*l* of W. How, who is Deputy-Treasurer, wherein my Lord Bruncker and I am to be concerned; and I did ask it my Lord, and he did consent to have us furnished with 500*l*, and I did get it paid to Sir Roger Cuttance and Mr. Pierce in part for above 1000*l*-worth of goods, Mace, Nuttmeggs, Cynamon, and Cloves. And he tells us we may hope to get 500*l* by it – which God send. Great spoil, I hear, there hath been of the two East India ships, and that yet they will come in to the King very rich – so that I hope this journy will be worth 100*l* to me.[1] After having paid this money, we took leave of my Lord, and so to our Yacht again, having seen many of my friends there. Among others, I hear that W. Howe will grow very rich by this last business and grows very proud and insolent by it – but it is what I ever expected. I hear by everybody how much my poor Lord of Sandwich was concerned for me during my silence awhile, lest I had been dead of the plague in this sickly time.

No sooner come into the Yacht, though overjoyed with the good work we have done today, but I was overcome with seasickness, so that I begun to spew soundly – and so continued a good while – till at last I went into the Cabbin, and shutting my eys, my trouble did cease, that I fell asleep; which continued till we came into Chatham River, where the water was smooth, and then I rose and was very well. And the tide coming to be against us, we did land before we came to Chatham and walked a mile – having very good discourse by the way – it being dark and it beginning to rain just as we got

---

1. Two Dutch E. Indiamen (the *Phoenix* and the *Slot van Honingen*) had been captured by Sandwich. Most imprudently he had allowed his officers and seamen to take some of the goods before they were judged to be prize in the prize court. He came under heavy criticism and in December 1665 was sent off to Spain as ambassador in consequence. Pepys very wisely soon sold the goods he now purchased.

thither. At Comissioner Petts we did eat and drink very well, and very merry we were. And about 10 at night, it being moonshine and very cold, we set out, his coach carrying us, and so all night travelled to Greenwich – we sometimes sleeping a little, and then talking and laughing by the way; and with much pleasure, but that it was very horrible cold, that I was afeared of an ague. A pretty passage was that the coach stood of a sudden, and the coachman came down, and the horses stirring, he cried "Hold!" which waked me; and the coach[man] standing at the boot to [do] something or other, and crying "Hold!", I did wake of a sudden; and not knowing who he was nor thinking of the coachman, between sleeping and waking I did take up the heart to take him by the shoulder, thinking verily he had been a thief. But when I waked, I found my cowardly heart to discover a fear within me, and that I should never have done it if I had been awake.

22.   Up betimes, and to the office, meaning to have entered my last five or six days' journall, but was called away by my Lord Bruncker and Sir J. Mennes; and to Blackewall, there to look after the storehouses, in order to the laying of goods out of the East India ships when they shall be unloaden. That being done, we into Johnsons house and were much made of – eating and drinking. But here it is observable what he tells us; that digging his late Docke, he did 12-foot under ground find perfect trees over-Covered with earth – nut-trees, with the branches and the very nuts upon them – some of whose nuts he showed us – their shells black with age and their Kernell, upon opening, decayed; but their shell perfectly hard as ever. And an Ewe tree he showed us (upon which he says the very Ivy was taken up whole about it), which upon cutting with an addes, we found to be rather harder then the living tree usually is – they say very much; but I do not know how hard a yew-tree naturally is.

23.   Up, and to my Lord Sandwich – who did advise alone with me how far he might trust Capt. Cocke in the business of the prize goods – my Lord telling me that he hath taken into his hands 2 or 3000l value of them. It being a good way, he says, to get money, and afterward to get the King's allowance thereof – it being easier, he observes, to keep money when got of the King, then to get it when it is too late. I advised him not to trust Cocke too far. And did thereupon offer him ready money for a thousand pound or two,

which he listens to and doth agree to – which is great joy to me, hoping thereby to get something. Thence by coaches to Lambeth, his Lordshipp and all our office, and Mr. Eveling, to the Duke of Albemarle – where after the compliment with my Lord, very kind, we sat down to consult of the disposing and supporting of the fleet with victuals and money, and for the sick men and prisoners. And I did propose the taking out of some goods out of the prizes, to the value of 10000*l*; which was accorded to, and an order drawn up and signed by the Duke and my Lord, done in the best manner I can and referred to my Lord Brouncker and Sir J. Mennes. But what inconveniences may arise from it I do not yet see, but fear there may be many. Here we dined, and I did hear my Lord Craven whisper (as he is mightily possessed with a good opinion of me) much to my advantage, which my good Lord did second; and anon my Lord Craven did speak publicly of me to the Duke, in the hearing of all the rest, and the Duke did say something of the like advantage to me; I believe, not much to the satisfaction of my brethren – but I was mightily joyed at it. Thence took leave, leaving my Lord Sandwich to go visit the Bishop of Canterbury, and I and Sir W. Batten down to the tower, where he went further by water, and I home; and among other things, took out all my gold to carry along with me tonight with Capt. Cocke down to the fleet – being 180*l* and more – hoping to lay out that and a great deal more to good advantage. Thence down to Greenwich to the office, and there wrote several letters; and so to my Lord Sandwich and mighty merry, and he mighty kind to me in the face of all, saying much in my favour; and after supper I took leave and with Capt. Cocke set out in the Yacht about 10 a-clock at night. And after some discourse and drinking a little – my mind full of what we are going about, and jealous of Cocke's out-doing me – so to sleep upon beds brought by Cocke on board, mighty handsome, and never slept better then upon this bed upon the floor in the Cabbin.

24.  *Lords day*. Waked, and up and drank and then to discourse. And then, being about Grayes and a very calme curious morning – we took our wherry, and to the Fishermen and bought a great deal of fine fish – and to Gravesend to Whites and had part of it dressed. And in the meantime, we to walk about a mile from the town, and so back again. And there, after breakfast, one of our watermen told us he had heard of a bargain of Cloves for us. And we went to a blind alehouse at the further end of the town, to a couple of

wretched, dirty seamen, who, poor wretches, had got together about 37 *lb* of Cloves and 10 *lb* of Nuttmeggs. And we bought them of them – the first at 5*s.*-6*d.* per *lb.*, and the latter at 4*s.* – and paid them in gold; but Lord, to see how silly these men are in the selling of it, and easily to be persuaded almost to anything – offering a bag to us, to pass as 20 *lb* of cloves which upon weighing proved 25 *lb.* But it would never have been allowed by my conscience to have wronged the poor wretches, who told us how dangerously they had got some and dearly paid for the rest of these goods. By and by to dinner about 3 a-clock. And then I in the cabin to writing down my journall for these last seven days, to my great content – it having pleased God that in this sad time of the plague, everything else hath conspired to my happiness and pleasure, more for these last three months then in all my life before in so little time. God long preserve it, and make me thankful for it. After finishing my Journall, then to discourse and to read, and then to supper and to bed, my mind not being at full ease, having not fully satisfied myself how Capt. Cocke will deal with me as to the share of the profits.

25. Found ourselfs come to the fleet; and so aboard the *Prince*, and there, after a good while in discourse, we did agree a bargain of 5000*l* with Sir Rog. Cuttance for my Lord Sandwich, for silk, cinnamon, nutmegs and Indico. And I was near signing to an undertaking for the payment of the whole sum, but I did by chance escape it, having since, upon second thoughts, great cause to be glad of it, reflecting upon the craft and not good condition, it may be, of Capt. Cocke. I could get no trifles for my wife. Anon to dinner, and thence in great haste to make a short visit to Sir W. Pen, where I found them, and his lady and daughter and many commanders at dinner – among others, Sir G. Askue, of whom, whatever the matter is, the world is silent altogether. But a very pretty dinner there was; and after dinner Sir W. Penn made a bargain with Cocke for ten bales of Silke at 16*s.* per *lb* – which, as Cocke says, will be a good pennorth. And so away to the *Prince*, and presently comes my Lord on board from Greenwich, with whom, after a little discourse about his trusting of Cocke, we parted and to our Yacht; but it being calme, we, to make haste, took our Wherry toward Chatham; but it growing dark, we were put to great difficultys, our simple yet confident waterman not knowing a step of the way; and we found ourselfs to go backward and forward, which, in that dark night and a wild place, did vex us mightily. At

last we got a fisherboy by chance and took him into the boat; and being an odd kind of boy, did vex us too, for he would not answer us aloud when we spoke to him; but did carry us safe thither, though with a mistake or two, but I wonder they were not more. In our way I was [surprised], and so we were all, at the strange nature of the Sea water in a dark night; that it seemed like fire upon every stroke of the Oare – and they say is a sign of Winde. We went to the Crowne Inne at Rochester, and there to supper and made ourselfs merry with our poor fisherboy, who told us he had not been in a bed in the whole seven year since he came to prentice, and hath two or three year more to serve. After eating something, we in our clothes to bed.

26.   Up by 5 a-clock and got post-horses and so set out for Greenwich, calling and drinking at Dartford. Being come to Greenwich, and shifting myself, I to the office; from whence by and by my Lord Bruncker and Sir Jo. Minnes set out toward Erith to take charge of the two East India Shipps which I had a hand in contriving for the King's service, and may do myself a good office too thereby. I to dinner with Mr. Waight to his father-in-law's in Greenwich – one of the most silly, harmless, prating old men that ever I heard in my life. Thence to the office; and after some letters, down to Woolwich, where I have not lain with my wife these eight days I think, or more.[1] After supper, and telling her my mind about my trouble in what I have done as to buying of these goods – we to bed.

27.   Up, and saw and admired my wife's picture of Our Saviour, now finished, which is very pretty. So by water to Greenwich to Mr. Evelins, where much company, and thence in his coach with him to the Duke of Albemarle by Lambeth, who was in a mighty pleasant humour. There the Duke tells us that the Dutch do stay abroad, and our fleet must go out again, or to be ready to do so. Here we got several things ordered as we desired, for the relief of the prisoners and sick and wounded men. Here I saw this week's Bill of Mortality, wherein, blessed be God, there is above 1800 decrease, being the first considerable decrease we have had. Back again the same way, and had most excellent discourse of Mr. Eveling touching all manner of learning; wherein I find him a very

---

1. For his movements, see above, p. 503, n.

fine gentleman, and perticularly of Paynting, in which he tells me the beautiful Mrs. Middleton is rare, and his own wife doth brave things. He brought me to the office, whither comes unexpectedly Capt. Cocke, who hath brought one parcel of our goods by waggons. And at first resolved to have lodged them at our office; but then the thoughts of its being the King's house altered our resolution, and so put them at his friend's, Mr. Glanvill's, and there they are safe: would the rest of them were so too. In discourse we came to mention my profit, and he offers me 500*l* profit clear, and I demand 600*l* for my certain profit. We part tonight, and I lie there at Mr. Glanvill's house, there being none there but a maydservant and a young man.

30.   Up, and to the office, where busy all the morning; and at noon with Sir W. Batten to Coll. Cleggat to dinner, being invited – where a very pretty dinner to my full content, and very merry. The great burden we have upon us at this time at the office is the providing for prisoners and sick men that are recovered, they lying before our office doors all night and all day, poor wretches. Having been on shore, the Captains won't receive them on board, and other ships we have not to put them on, nor money to pay them off or provide for them. God remove this difficulty. This made us fallowed all the way to this gentleman's house, and there are waited for our coming out after dinner. Thence, mighty merry and much pleased with the dinner and company, and they with me, I parted; and there was set upon by the poor wretches, whom I did give words and some little money to; and the poor people went away like lambs, and in good earnest are not to be censured if their necessities drive them to bad Courses of stealing or the like, while they lack wherewith to live. Thence to the office, and there wrote a letter or two and despatched a little business; and then to Capt. Cocke's, where I find Mr. Temple, the fat blade, Sir Rob. Viner's chief man, and we three, and two companions of his, in the evening by agreement took ship in the *Bezan*, and the tide carried us no further then Woolwich, about 8 at night. And so I on shore to my wife and so to sleep with a good deal of content.

   And saving only this night, and a day or two about the same business about a month or six weeks ago, I do end this month with the greatest content, and may say that these last three months, for joy, health and profit, have been much the greatest that ever I received in all my life in any twelve months almost in my life –

having nothing upon me but the consideration of the sickliness of the season during this great plague to mortify mee. For all which, the Lord God be praised.

# –✸OCTOBER✸–

1.   *Lords day*. Called up about 4 of the clock, and so dressed myself; and so on board the *Bezan*, and there finding all my company asleep, I would not wake them; but it beginning to be break of day, I did stay upon the Decke walking and then into the Maisters Cabbin and there leaned and slept a little; and so at last was wakened by Capt. Cockes calling of me, and so I turned out, and then to chat and talk and laugh, and mighty merry. We spent most of the morning talking, and reading of *The Seige of Rhodes*, which is certainly (the more I read it the more I think so) the best poem that ever was wrote. We breakfasted betimes and came to the fleet about 2 of the clock in the afternoon, having a fine day and a fine winde. My Lord received us mighty kindly; and after discourse with us in general, left us to our business, and he to his officers, having called a council of Warr. We in the meantime settling of papers with Mr. Pierce and everybody else, and by and by with Capt. Cuttance. Anon called down to my Lord, and there with him till supper, talking and discourse. Among other things, to my great joy he did assure me that he had wrote to the King and Duke about these prize goods, and told me that they did approve of what he had done and that he would own what he had done, and would have me to tell all the world so; and did under his hand give Cocke and me his Certificate of our bargains, and giving us full power of disposal of what we have so bought. This doth ease my mind of all my fear, and makes my heart lighter by 100*lb* then it was before. He did discourse to us of the Dutch fleet being abroad, 85 of them still, and are now at the Texell he believes, in expectation of our Eastland ships coming home with masts and hemp, and our loaden Hambrough ships going to Hambrough. He discoursed against them that would have us yield to no conditions but conquest over the Dutch, and seems to believe that the Dutch will call for the protection of the King of France and come under his power – which were to be wished they might be brought to do under ours, by fair means; and to that end would have all Dutchmen and families that

would come hither and settled, to be declared Denizens. And my Lord did whisper to me alone, that things here must break in pieces, nobody minding anything, but every man his own business of profit or pleasure, and the King some little designs of his own; and that certainly the Kingdom could not stand in this condition long – which I fear and believe is very true. So to supper, and there my Lord the kindest man to me before all the table, talking of me to my advantage, and with tenderness too, that it overjoyed me. So after supper Capt. Cocke and I and Temple on board the *Bezan*, and there to Cards for a while, and then to read again in *Rhodes* and so to sleep. But Lord, the mirth which it caused to me to be waked in the night by their Snoaring round about me – I did laugh till I was ready to burst, and waked one of the two companions of Temple, who could not a good while tell where he was, that he heard one laugh so, till he recollected himself and I told him what it was at; and so to sleep again, they still Snoaring.

2. We having sailed all night (and I do wonder how they in the dark could find the way), we got by morning to Gillingham; and thence all walked to Chatham, and there with Comissioner Pett viewed the Yard; and among other things, a Teame of four horses came close by us, he being with me, drawing a piece of timber that I am confident one man would easily have carried upon his back; I made the horses be taken away and a man or two take the timber away with their hands. This the Comissioner did see, but said nothing; but I think had cause to be ashamed of. We walked, he and I and Cocke, to the Hill house, where we find Sir Wm. Pen in bed, and there much talk and much dissembling of kindness from him; but he is a false rogue and I shall not trust him. But my being there did procure his consent to have his silk carried away before the money received, which he would not have done for Cocke I am sure. Thence to Rochester; walked to the Crowne, and while dinner was getting ready, I did there walk to visit the old Castle ruines, which hath been a noble place; and there going up, I did upon the stairs overtake three pretty maids or women and took them up with me, and I did besarlas muchas vezes et tocar leur mains and necks, to my great pleasure: but Lord, to see what a dreadful thing it is to look down præcipices, for it did fright me mightily and hinder me of much pleasure which I would have made to myself in the company of these three if it had not been for that. The place hath been very noble, and great and strong in former ages. So to walk up and down

537

the Cathedrall, and thence to the Crowne, whither Mr. Fowler, the Mayor of the towne, was come in his gowne, and is a very Reverend Magistrate. After I had eat a bit, not staying to eat with them, I went away; and so took horses and to Gravesend, and there stayed not, but got a boat (the sickness being very much in the Towne still) and so called on board my Lord Bruncker and Sir Jo. Minnes, on board one of the East Indiamen at Erith, and there do find them full of envious complaints for the pillageing of the ships. But I did pacify them and discoursed about making money of some of the goods, and do hope to be the better by it honestly. So took leave (Madam Williams being here also with my Lord) and about 8 a-clock got to Woolwich; and there supped and mighty pleasant with my wife, who is, for aught I see, all friends with her maids; and so in great joy and content to bed.

5. Lay long in bed, talking; among other things, talking of my sister Pall, and my wife of herself is very willing that I should give her 400*l* to her portion – and would have her married as soon as we could; but this great sickness time doth make it unfit to send for her up. I abroad to the office, and thence to the Duke of Albemarle, all my way reading a book of Mr. Evelins translating, and sending me as a present, about directions of gathering a Library, but the book is above my reach, but his epistle to my Lord Chancellor is a very fine piece. When I came to the Duke, it was about the victuallers business, to put it into other hands, or more hands – which I do advise in, but I hope to do myself a jobb of work in it. So I walked through Westminster to my old house, the Swan, and there did pass some time with Sarah; and so down by water to Deptford and there to my Valentine's; round about and next door on every side is the plague, but I did not value it but there did what I would con ella; and so away to Mr. Evelings to discourse of our confounded business of prisoners and sick and wounded seamen, wherein he and we are so much put out of order. And here he showed me his gardens, which are, for variety of Evergreens and hedge of Holly, the finest things I ever saw in my life. Thence in his coach to Greenwich, and there to my office, all the way having fine discourse of Trees and the nature of vegetables. And so to write letters I very late, to Sir W. Coventry, of great concernment; and so to my last night's lodging,[1] but my wife is gone home to Woolwich. The Bill, blessed be

1. At Greenwich.

God, is less this week by 740 of what it was the last week. Being come to my lodging, I got something to eat, having eat little all the day, and so to bed – having this night renewed my promises of observing my vowes as I used to do, for I find that since I left them off, my minde is run a'wool-gathering and neglected my business.

7.   Up, and to the office along with Mr. Childe, whom I sent for to discourse about the victualling business; who will not come into partenership (no more will Capt. Beckford) but I do find him a mighty understanding man, and one I will keep a knowledge of. Did business, though not much, at the office, because of the horrible Crowd and lamentable moan of the poor seamen that lie starving in the streets for lack of money – which doth trouble and perplex me to the heart. And more at noon, when we were to go through them; for then a whole hundred of them fallowed us – some cursing, some swearing, and some praying to us. And that that made me more troubled, was a letter come this noon from the Duke of Albemarle, signifying the Duch to be in sight, with 80 sail, yesterday morning off of Soldbay, coming right into the bay; God knows what they will and may do to us, we having no force abroad able to oppose them, but to be sacrifized to them. Here came Sir Wm. Rider to me, whom I sent for about the victualling business also; but he neither will not come into partenership, but desires to be of the Commission, if there be one. Thence back the back way to my office, where very late, very busy – but most of all when at night comes two waggons from Rochester with more goods from Capt. Cocke; and in housing them at Mr. Tookers lodgings, comes two of the Custome house to seize them, and did seize them, but I showed them my Transire. However, after some heat and angry words, we locked them up, and sealed up the key and did give it to the constable to keep till Monday – and so parted. But Lord, to think how the poor constable came to me in the dark, going home: "Sir," says he, "I have the Key, and if you would have me do any service for you, send for me betimes tomorrow morning and I will do what you would have me." Whether the fellow doth this out of kindness or knavery, I cannot tell, but it is pretty to observe. Talking with him in the highway, comes close by the bearers with a dead corps of the plague; but Lord, to see what custom is, that I am come almost to think nothing of it. So to my lodging, and there with Mr. Hater and Will ending a busines of the

state of the last six months' charge of the Navy, which we bring to 1000000*l* and above – I think we do not enlarge much in it, if anything. So to bed.

8. *Lords day.* Up, and after being trimmed, to the office, whither I, upon a letter from the Duke of Albemarle to me to order as many ships forth out of the River as I can presently, to joyne to meet the Duch, had ordered all the Captains of the ships in the River to come to me. I did some business with them, and so to Capt. Cockes to dinner – he being in the country, but here his brother Salomon was, and for guests, myself, Sir G. Smith, and a very fine lady, one Mrs. Penington – and two more Gentlemen. But, both [before] and after dinner, most excellent witty discourse with this lady, who is a very fine witty lady, one of the best I ever heard speak – and indifferent handsome. There after dinner an hour or two, and so to the office, where ended my business with the Captains; and I think of 22 ships, we shall make shift to get out seven (God help us – men being sick – or provisions lacking); and so to write letters to Sir Ph. Warwicke, Sir W. Coventry, and Sir G. Carteret to Court, about the last six months' accounts, and sent away by an express tonight.

11. Up, and so in my chamber stayed all the morning, doing something toward my Tanger accounts for the stating of them; and also comes up my landlady, Mrs. Clerke, to make an agreement for the time to come; and I, for the having room enough, and to keep out strangers and to have a place to retreat to for my wife if the sickness should come to Woolwich, am contented to pay dear; so, for three rooms and a dining-room, and for linen and bread and beer and butter at nights and mornings, I am to give her 5*l*–10*s*. per month – and I wrote, and we signed to an agreement. By and by comes Cocke, and so he and I (having eat something at his house) by water to Erith; and there we met Mr. Seamour, one of the Comissioners for Prizes, and a Parliament Man, and he was mighty high and had now seized our goods on their behalf – and he mighty imperiously would have all forfeited and I know not what. It growing late, and I having something to do at home, took my leave alone, leaving Cocke there for all night; and so, against tide and in the dark and very cold weather, to Woolwich, where we had appointed to keep the night merrily; and so, by Capt. Cockes coach, had brought a very pretty child (a daughter of one Mrs. Tookers, next door to my lodging), and so she and a daughter and

kinsman of Mr. Petts made up a fine company at my lodgings at Woolwich, where my wife and Mercer and Mrs. Barbara danced, and mighty merry we were, but especially at Mercer's dancing a Jigg, which she does the best I ever did see, having the most natural way of it and keeps time the most perfectly I ever did see. This night is kept, in lieu of yesterday, for my wedding-day of Ten Yeares[1] – for which God be praised – being now in an extreme good condition of health and estate and honour, and a way of getting more money – though at this hour under some discomposure, rather then dammage, about some prize goods that I have bought of the Fleete in partenership with Capt. Cocke – and for the discourse about the world concerning my Lord Sandwich, that he hath done a thing so bad; and indeed it must needs have been a very rash act. And the rather, because of a parliament now newly met to give money and will have some account of what hath already been spent – besides the precedent for a General to take what prizes he pleases – and the giving a pretence to take away much more then he entended, and all will lie upon him. And not giving to all the Commanders, as well as the Flags, he displeases all them – and offends even some of them, thinking others to be better served then themselfs. And lastly, puts himself out of a power of begging anything again a great while of the King. Having danced my people as long as I saw fit to sit up, I to bed, and left them to do what they would. I forgot that we had W. Hewer there and Tom – and Golding, my barber at Greenwich, for our fiddler, to whom I did give x*s*.

12.    Called up before day, and so I dressed myself and down, it being horrid cold, by water to my Lord Bruncker's ship, who advised me to do so, and it was civilly to show me what the King had commanded about the prize goods, to examine most severely all that had been done in the taking out any, with or without order, without respect to my Lord Sandwich at all – and that he had been doing of it, and find him examining one man. And I do find that extreme ill use was made of my Lord's order, for they did toss and tumble and spoil and break things in hold, to a great loss and shame, to come at the fine goods, and did take a man that knew where the fine goods were – and did this over and over again for many days – Sir W. Berkely being the chief hand that did it; but others did the

_____

1. See above, p. 159 (10 October) & n.

like at other times. And they did say in doing it, that my Lord Sandwichs back was broad enough to bear it. Having learned as much as I could, which was that the King and Duke are very severe in this point, whatever order they before had given my Lord in approbation of what he had done, and that all will come out, and the King see by the entries at the Custome house what all doth amount to that had been taken. And so I took leave and by water, very cold, and to Woolwich – where it was now noon; and so I stayed dinner and talking part of the afternoon; and then by coach, Capt. Cocke, to Greenwich, taking the young lady home. And so to Cocke, and he tells me that he hath cajolled with Seymour, who will be our friend; but that above all, Seymour tells him that my Lord Duke did show him today an order from Court for having all respect paid to the Earle of Sandwich, and what goods had been delivered by his order – which doth overjoy us; and that tomorrow our goods shall be weighed and he doubts not, possession tomorrow or next day. Being overjoyed at this, I to write my letters, and at it very late. Good news this week that there are about 600 less dead of the plague then the last. So home to bed.

13.    This day the Duke tells me that there is no news heard of the Dutch, what they do or where they are; but believes that they are all gone home – for none of our Spyes can give us any tidings of them.

15.    *Lords day*. Up, and while stayed for the barber, tried to compose a duo of Counterpoint; and I think it will do very well, it being by Mr. Berchensha's rule. By and by, by appointment comes Mr. Povy's coach, and, more then I expected, him himself to fetch me to Brainford; so he and I immediately set out, having drunk a draught of Mull'd Sacke, and so rode most nobly in his most pretty and best-contrived Charriott in the world, with many new conveniences, his never having, till now in a day or two, not yet finished – our discourse upon Tanger business – want of money – and then of public miscarriages – nobody minding the public, but everybody himself and his lusts. Anon we came to his house and there I eat a bit, and so with fresh horses, his noble fine horses (the best confessedly in England, the King having none such), he sent me to Sir Rob. Viner's, whom I met coming just from church; and so after having spent half an hour almost looking upon the horses with some gentlemen that were in company – he and I into his garden to discourse of money, but none is to be had – he confessing

himself in great straits, and I believe it. Having his answer, and that I could not get better, we fell to public talk and to think how the fleet and seamen will be paid; which he protests he doth not think it possible to compass, as the world is now; no money got by trade, nor the persons that have it by them in the City to be come at. The Parliament, it seems, have voted the King 1250000*l* at 50000*l* per month tax for the war – and voted to assist the King against the Duch and all that shall adhere to them – and thanks to be given him for his care of the Duke of Yorke – which last is a very popular vote on the Dukes behalf. He tells me how the taxes of the last assessment, which should have been in good part gathered, are not yet laid, and that even in part of the City of London – and that the Chimny money comes almost to nothing – nor anything else looked after. Having done this, I parted, my mind not eased by any money, but only that I had done my part to the King's service. And so in a very pleasant evening, back to Mr. Povys and there supped. And after supper to talk and to sing, his man Dutton's wife singing very prettily (a mighty fat woman), and I wrote out one song from her and pricked the Tune, being very pretty. But I did never hear one sing with so much pleasure to herself as this lady doth, relishing it to her very heart – which was mighty pleasant.

16. Upon the Exchange, which is very empty, God knows, and but mean people there. The news for certain, that the Duch are come with their fleet before Margett, and some men were endeavouring to come on shore when the post came away – perhaps to steal some sheep. But Lord, how Colvill talks of the business of public Revenue like a madman, and yet I doubt all true; that nobody minds it, but that the King and Kingdom must speedily be undone – and rails at my Lord about the Prizes, but I think knows not my relation to him. Here I endeavoured to satisfy all I could people about bills of exchange from Tanger; but it is only with good words, for money I have not, nor can get. God knows what will become of all the King's matters in a little time, for he runs in debt every day, and nothing to pay them looked after. Thence I walked to the Tower. But Lord, how empty the streets are, and melancholy, so many poor sick people in the streets, full of sores, and so many sad stories overheard as I walk, everybody talking of this dead, and that man sick, and so many in this place, and so many in that. And they tell me that in Westminster there is never a physitian, and but one apothecary left, all being dead – but that there are great

hopes of a great decrease this week: God send it. Much talk there is of the Chancellors speech, and the King's, at the Parliaments meeting, which are very well liked. And that we shall certainly, by their speeches, fall out with France at this time, together with the Dutch – which will find us work. Late at the office, entering my Journall for eight days past, the greatness of my business hindering me of late to put it down daily; but I have done it now very true and perticularly, and hereafter will, I hope, be able to fall into my old way of doing it daily. So to my lodging, and there had a good pullet to my supper; and so to bed, it being very cold again, God be thanked for it.[1]

19. My business of the victualling goes on as I would have it; and now my head is full how to make some profit of it to myself or people. To that end, when I came home, I wrote a letter to Mr. Coventry, offering myself to be the Surveyor-Generall, and am apt to think he will assist me in it; but I do not set my heart much on it, though it would be a good help. So back to my office, and there till past one before I could get all these letters and papers copied out, which vexed me. But so sent them away without hopes of saving the post, and so to my lodging to bed.

23. Up, and after doing some business, I down by water, calling to see my wife, with whom very merry for ten minutes; and so to Erith, where my Lord Brouncker and I kept the office and despatched some business by appointment on the *Bizan*. Among other things, about the slopsellers who have trusted us so long; they are not able, nor can be expected to trust us further – and I fear this winter the fleet will be undone by that perticular. Thence on board the East India ship, where his Lordshipp had provided a great dinner, and thither comes by and by Sir Jo. Minnes, and before him Sir W. Warren – and anon a Perspective-glass maker, of whom we every one bought a pocket-glass. But I am troubled with the much talk and conceitedness of Mrs. Williams and her impudence, in case she be not married to my Lord. They are getting themselfs ready to deliver the goods all out to the East India Company, who are to have the goods in their possession, and advance two-thirds of the moderate value thereof and sell them as well as they can, and the King to give them 6 per cent for the use of the money they shall so

1. The plague decreased in cold weather.

advance. By this means, the Company will not suffer by the King's goods bringing down the price of their own.

25. Up, and to my Lord Sandwiches, where several commanders of whom I took the state of all their ships, and of all could find not above four capable of going out – the truth is, the want of victuals being the whole overthrow of this year, both at sea and now at the Noure here and Portsmouth, where all the fleet lies. By and by comes down my Lord, and then he and I an hour together alone upon private discourse. He tells me that Mr. Coventry and he are not reconcilable, but declared enemies. He tells me, as very private, that there are great factions at the Court between the King's party and the Duke of Yorkes, and that the King (which is a strange difficulty) doth favour my Lord in opposition to the Duke's party. That Prince Rupert and he are all possible friends in the world. That Coventry hath aggravated this business of the prizes, though never so great plundering in the world as while the Duke and he were at sea. And in Sir Jo. Lawsons time he could take and pillage and then sink a whole ship in the Streights, and Coventry say nothing to it. That my Lord Arlington is his fast friend. That my Lord Chancellor doth begin to be cold to him, because of his seeing him and Arlington so great. That nothing at Court is minded but faction and pleasure, and nothing intended of general good to the Kingdom by anybody heartily, so that he believes, with me, in a little time confusion will certainly come over all the nation. He told me how a design was carried on a while ago for the Duke of Yorke to raise an army in the North, and to be General of it, and all this without the knowledge or advice of the Duke of Albemarle; which when he came to know, he was so vexed, they were fain to let it fall to content him. That his maching with the family of Sir G. Carteret doth make the difference greater between Coventry and him, they being enemies. After dinner my Lord by a Ketch down to Erith, where the *Bezan* was – it blowing these last two days, and now both night and day very hard Southwardly – so that it hath certainly drove the Duch off the coast.

26. Up, and to the office; and thither comes Sir Jer. Smith and Sir Chr. Mings to see me, being just come from Portsmouth and going down to the fleet. Here I sat and talked with them a good while, and then parted, only Sir Chr. Mings and I together by water to the Tower. And I find him a very witty well-spoken fellow, and

mighty free to tell his parentage, being a shoemaker's son, to whom
he is now going. And I to the Change – where I hear how the French
have taken two and sunk one of our Merchantmen in the Streights
and carried the ships to Toulon – so that there is no expectation but
we must fall out with them. The Change pretty full, and the town
begins to be lively again – though the streets very empty and most
shops shut. So back again I, and took boat and called for Sir Chr.
Mings at St. Katharines, who was fallowed with some ordinary
friends, of which he says he is proud; and so down to Greenwich,
the wind furious high, and we with our sail up till I made it be taken
down. I took him, it being 3 a-clock, to my lodgings, and did give
him a good dinner and so parted, he being pretty close to me as to
any business of the fleet, knowing me to be a servant of my Lord
Sandwiches. He gone, I to the office till night; and then they come
and tell me my wife is come to town, so I to her, vexed at her
coming; but it was upon innocent business, and so I was pleased and
made her stay, Capt. Ferrers and his lady being yet there. And so I
left them to dance, and I to the office till past 9 at night; and so to
them and there saw them dance very prettily, the Captain and his
wife, my wife, and Mrs. Barbary and Mercer, and my landlady's
daughter; and then little Mrs. Fr. Tooker and her mother, a pretty
woman, come to see my wife. Anon to supper, and then to dance
again (Golding being our fidler, who plays very well and all tunes)
till past 12 at night, and then we broke up and everyone to bed.

27.    Up, and after some pleasant discourse with my wife, I out,
leaving her and Mrs. Ferrers there; and I to Capt. Cocke's, there to
do some business; and then away with Cocke in his coach through
Kent street, a miserable, wretched, poor place, people sitting sick
and muffled up with plasters at every four or five door. So to the
Change, and thence I by water to the Duke of Albemarle; and there
much company, but I stayed and dined, and he makes mighty much
of me; and here he tells us the Dutch are gone, and have lost above
160 cables and anchors through the last foul weather. Here he
proposed to me from Mr. Coventry (as I had desired of Mr.
Coventry) that I should be Surveyor-Generall of the victualling
business, which I accepted. But endeed, the terms in which Mr.
Coventry proposes it for me are the most obliging that ever I could
expect from any man, and more – it saying me to be the fittest man
in England, and that he is sure, if I will undertake it, I will perform it
– and that it will be also a very desirable thing that I might have this

encouragement, my encouragement in the Navy alone being in no wise proportionable to my pains or deserts. This, added to the letter I had three days since from Mr. Southerne, signifying that the Duke of Yorke had in his master's absence opened my letter and commanded him to tell me that he did approve of my being the Surveyor-general, doth make me joyful beyond myself, that I cannot express it; to see that as I do take pains, so God blesses me and hath sent me masters that do observe that I take pains.

29.   *Lords day.* Up, and being ready, set out with Capt. Cocke in his coach toward Erith, Mr. Deane riding along with us – where we dined and were very merry. After dinner we fell to discourse about the Dutch, Cocke undertaking to prove that they were able to wage war with us three year together – which, though it may be true, yet, not being satisfied with his arguments, my Lord and I did oppose the strength of his arguments, which brought us to a great heat – he being a conceited man but of no Logique in his head at all, which made my Lord and I mirth. Anon we parted and back again, we hardly having a word all the way, he being so vexed at our not yielding to his persuasion. I was set down at Woolwich town's-end and walked through the town in the dark, it being now night. But in the street did overtake and almost run upon two women, crying and carrying a man's Coffin between them: I suppose the husband of one of them, which methinks is a sad thing.

31.   Up, and to the office, where Sir W. Batten met me and did tell me that Capt. Cockes black was dead of the plague – which I had heard of before but took no notice. By and by Capt. Cocke came to the office, and Sir W. Batten and I did send to him that he would either forbear the office or forbear going to his own office. However, meeting yesterday the Searchers with their rods in their hands coming from his house, I did overhear them say that the fellow did not die of the plague. But he had I know been ill a good while, and I am told that his boy Jacke is also ill. At noon home to dinner, and then to the office again, leaving Mr. Hill, if he can, to get Mrs. Coleman at night. About 9 at night I came home, and there find Mrs. Pierce come, and little Franke Tooker and Mr. Hill and other people, a great many, dancing. Anon comes Mrs. Coleman, with her husband and Laneare. The dancing ended, and to sing, which Mrs. Coleman doth very finely, though her voice is decayed as to strength; but mighty sweet, though saft – and a pleasant jolly

woman, and in mighty good humour was tonight. Among other things, Laneare did at the request of Mr. Hill bring two or three the finest prints for my wife to see that ever I did see in all my life. But for singing, among other things, we got Mrs. Coleman to sing part of the Opera; but above all, her counterfeiting of Capt. Cooke's part, in his reproaching his men with Cowardize, Base Slaves &c., she doth it most excellently: at it till past midnight, and then broke up and to bed. Hill and I together again – and being very sleepy, we had little discourse as we had the other night.

Thus we end the month merrily; and the more, for that after some fears that the plague would have encreased again this week, I hear for certain that there is above 400 [decrease] – the whole number being 1388; and of them, of the plague, 1031. Want of money in the Navy puts everything out of order. Men grow mutinous. And nobody here to mind the business of the Navy but myself. At least, Sir W. Batten for the few days he hath been here doth nothing. I in great hopes of my place of Surveyor-Generall of the Victualling, which will bring me 300*l* per annum.

## –✣ NOVEMBER ✣–

1.   Lay very long in bed, discoursing with Mr. Hill of most things of a man's life, and how little merit doth prevail in the world, but only favour – and that for myself, chance without merit brought me in, and that diligence only keeps me so, and will, living as I do among so many lazy people, that the diligent man becomes necessary, that they cannot do anything without him. And so told him of my late business of the victualling and what cares I am in to keep myself, having to do with people of so different factions at Court, and yet must be fair with them all – which was very pleasant discourse for me to tell, as well, as he seemed to take it, for him to hear. At last up, and it being a very foul day for rain and a hideous wind, yet having promised I would go, by water to Erith – and bearing sail, was in danger of oversetting – but made them take down their sail; and so, cold and wet, got thither as they had ended their dinner. How[ever], I dined well. And after dinner, all on shore, my Lord Brouncker with us, to Mrs. Williams's lodgings, and Sir W. Batten, Sir Edmd. Pooly and others; and there, it being my Lord's birthday, had everyone a greene riband tied in our hats,

very foolishly, and methinks mighty disgracefully for my Lord to have his folly so open to all the world with this woman. But by and by Sir W. Batten and I took coach, and home to Boremans; and so going home by the backside, I saw Capt. Cocke lighting out of his coach (he having been at Erith also with her, but not on board), and so he would come along with me home to my lodging; and there sat and supped and talked with us, but we were angry a little a while about our message to him the other day, about bidding him keep from the office or his own office because of his black dying. I owned it and the reason of it, and would have been glad he had been out of the house, but I could not bid him go; and so supped, and after much other talk of the sad condition and state of the King's matters, we broke up, and my wife and I to bed. This night, coming with Sir W. Batten into Greenwich, we called upon Coll. Clegatt, who tells us for certain that the King of Denmarke hath declared to stand for the King of England; but since, I hear it is wholly false.

2.    Up, left my wife, and to the office; and there to my great content Sir W. Warren came to me to settle the business of the Tanger boates, wherein I shall get above 100*l*, besides a 100*l* which he gives me in the paying for them out of his own purse. He gone, I home to my lodgings to dinner; and there comes Capt. Wager, newly returned from the Streights, who puts me in great fears for our last ships that went to Tanger with provisions, that they will be taken. A brave stout fellow this Captain is, and I think very honest. To the office again after dinner, and there late, writing letters. And then about 8 at night set out from my office, and fitting myself at my lodging, entended to have gone this night in a ketch down to the fleet. But calling in my way at Sir Jo. Minnes's, who is coming up from Erith about something about the prizes – they persuaded me not to go till the morning, it being a horrible dark and a windy night. So I back to my lodgings, and to bed.

3.    Was called up about 4 a-clock, and in the dark by lanthorn took boat, and to the ketch and set sail – sleeping a little in the Cabbin till day; and then up, and fell to reading of Mr. Eveling's book about Paynting, which is a very pretty book. Carrying good victuals, and Tom with me, I to breakfast about 9 a-clock, and then to read again, and came to the fleet about 12 – where found my Lord (the *Prince* being gone in) on board the *Royall James*, Sir Tho. Allen commander; and with my Lord an hour alone, discoursing, which

was my chief and only errand, about what was advisable for his Lordshipp to do in this state of things, himself being under the Duke of York and Mr. Coventrys envy and a great many more – and likely never to do anything honourably but he shall be envied, and the honour taken as much as can be from it. His absence lessens his interest at Court – and which is worst, we never able to set out a fleet fit for him to command; or if out, to keep them out, or fit them to do any great thing; or if that were so, yet nobody at home minds him or his condition when he is abroad; and lastly, the whole affairs of state looking as if they would all on a sudden break in pieces, and then what a sad thing it would be for him to be out of the way. We after this talked of some other little things, and so to dinner, where my Lord infinitely kind to me; and after dinner I rose and left him with some Commanders at the table, taking tobacco; and I took the *Bezan* back with me, and with a brave gale and tide reached up that night to the Hope, taking great pleasure in learning the seamen's manner of singing when they sound the depths. And then to supper and to sleep, which I did most excellently all night, it being a horrible foul night for wind and rain.

4.    They sailed from midnight, and came to Greenwich about 5 a-clock in the morning – I, however, lay till about 7 or 8; and so to my office – my head a little akeing, partly for want of natural rest – partly having so much business to do today, and partly from the news I hear, that one of the little boys at my lodging is not well, and they suspect that it may be the plague. Sir W. Batten and myself at the office all the morning. At noon with him to dinner at Boreman's, where Mr. Seymour with us – who is a most conceited fellow, and not over-much in him. Here Sir W. Batten told us (which I had not heard before) that the last sitting-day his cloak was taken from Mingo, going home to dinner, and that he was beaten by the seamen, and swears he will come to Greenwich but no more to the office (till he can sit safe); after dinner, I to the office and there very late. And much troubled to have 100 seamen all the afternoon there, swearing below and cursing us and breaking the glass windows; and swear they will pull the house down on Tuseday next. I sent word of this to Court, but nothing will help it but money and a rope. Late at night I to Mr. Glanvill's, there to lie for a night or two, and to bed.

5. *Lords day.* Up, and after being trimmed, by boate to the Cockepitt, where I heard the Duke of Albemarle's chaplain make a simple sermon. Among other things, reproaching the imperfection of humane learning, he cried – "All our physicians can't tell what an ague is, and all our Arithmetique is not able to number the days of a man" – which, God knows, is not the fault of arithmetique, but that our understandings reach not that thing. To dinner, where a great deal of silly discourse. But the worst is, I hear that the plague encreases much at Lambeth, St. Martins, and Westminster, and fear it will all over the City. Thence I to the Swan, there thinking to have seen Sarah, but she was at church; and so by water to Deptford, and there made a visit to Mr. Evelings, who, among other things, showed me most excellent painting in little – in distemper, Indian Incke – water colours – graveing; and above all, the whole secret of Mezzo Tinto and the manner of it, which is very pretty, and good things done with it. He read to me very much also of his discourse he hath been many years and now is about, about Guardenage; which will be a most noble and pleasant piece. He read me part of a play or two of his making, very good, but not as he conceits them, I think, to be. He showed me his *Hortus hyemalis*; leaves laid up in a book of several plants, kept dry, which preserve Colour however, and look very finely, better than any herball. In fine, a most excellent person he is, and must be allowed a little for a little conceitedness; but he may well be so, being a man so much above others. He read me, though with too much gusto, some little poems of his own, that were not transcendent, yet one or two very pretty Epigrams: among others, of a lady looking in at a grate and being pecked at by an Eagle that was there. Here comes in in the middle of our discourse, Capt. Cocke, as drunk as a dog, but could stand and talk and laugh. He did so joy himself in a brave woman that he had been with all the afternoon, and who should it be but my Lady Robinson. But very troublesome he is with his noise and talk and laughing, though very pleasant. With him in his coach to Mr. Glanvills, where he sat with Mrs. Penington and myself a good while, talking of this fine woman again, and then went away. Then the lady and I to very serious discourse; and among other things, of what a bonny lass my Lady Robinson is, who is reported to be kind to the prisoners, and hath said to Sir G. Smith, who is her great Chrony: "Look, there is a pretty man; I could be contented to break a commandment with him" – and such loose

expressions she will have often. After an hour's talk, we to bed – the lady mightily troubled about a little pretty bitch she hath, which is very sick and will eat nothing. And the jest was, I could hear her in her chamber bemoaning the bitch; and by and by taking her to bed with her, the bitch pissed and shit abed, and she was fain to rise and had coals out of my chamber to dry the bed again. This night, I had a letter that Sir G. Carteret would be in town tomorrow, which did much surprize me.

7. Spent the evening till midnight talking with Mrs. Penington, who is a very discreet, understanding lady; and very pretty discourse we had, and great variety. And she tells me, with great sorrow, her bitch is dead this morning – died in her bed. So broke up, and to bed.

10. Up, and enter all my Journall since the 28th of October, having every day's passage well in my head, though it troubles me to remember it; and what I was forced to, being kept from my lodging, where my books and papers are, for several days. So to my office – where, till 2 or 3 a-clock, busy before I could go to my lodging to dinner. Then did it, and to my office again. In the evening news is brought me my wife is come; so I to her, and with her spent the evening, but with no great pleasure, I being vexed about her putting away of Mary in my absence; but yet I took no notice of it at all – but fell into other discourse; and she told me, having herself been this day at my house at London (which was boldly done) to see Mary have her things, that Mr. Harrington our neighbour, and East Country merchant, is dead at Epsum of the plague. And that another neighbour of ours, Mr. Hallworthy, a very able* man, is also dead, by a fall in the country from his horse, his foot hanging in the stirrup and his brains beat out. Here we sat talking; and after supper, to bed.

12. *Lords day.* Up, and invited by Capt. Cocke to dinner. So after being ready, I went to him, and there he and I and Mr. Yard (one of the Guiny Company) dined together, and very merry. Thence back by water to Capt. Cockes, and there he and I spent a great deal of the evening, as we had done of the day, reading and discoursing over part of Mr. Stillingfleete's *Origines Sacræ*, wherein many things are very good – and some frivolous.

13.   Up, and to my office, where busy all the morning; and at noon to Capt. Cockes to dinner as we had appointed, in order to settle our business of accounts. But here came in an Alderman, a merchant, a very merry man, and we dined; and he being gone – after dinner Cocke and I walked into the garden and there, after a little discourse, he did undertake under his hand to secure me in 500*l* profit for my share of the profit of what we bought of the prize goods; we agreed upon the terms, which were easier on my side then I expected; and so, with extraordinary inward joy, we part till the evening. So I to the office, and among other business, prepared a deed for him to sign and seal to me about our agreement, which at night I got him to come and sign and seal. And so he and I to Glanvills, and there he and I sat talking and playing with Mrs. Penington, whom we found undressed in her smock and petticoats by the fireside; and there we drank and laughed, and she willingly suffered me to put my hand in her bosom very wantonly, and keep it there long – which methought was very strange, and I looked upon myself as a man mightily deceived in a lady, for I could not have thought she could have suffered it, by her former discourse with me – so modest she seemed, and I know not what. We stayed here late; and so home, after he and I had walked till past midnight, a bright moonshine, clear, cool night, before his door by the water; and so I home after one of the clock.

14.   Called up by break of day by Capt. Cocke by agreement, and he and I in his coach through Kent Streete (a sad place through the plague, people sitting sick and with plasters about them in the street, begging) to Viners and Colvills about money business; and so to my house there and took 300*l*, in order to the carrying it down to my Lord Sandwich, in part of the money I am to pay for Capt. Cocke by our agreement. So I took it down, and down went to Greenwich to my office, and there sat busy till noon; and so home to dinner, and thence to the office again, and by and by to the Duke of Albemarles by water, late – where I find he had remembered that I had appointed to come to him this day about money, which I excused not doing sooner. But I see, a dull fellow as he is, doth sometimes remember what another thinks he minded not. My business was about getting money of the East India Company. But Lord, to see how the Duke himself magnifies himself in what he had done with that Company, and my Lord Craven, what the King could have done without my Lord Duke; and a deal of stir, but most

mightily, what a brave fellow I am. Back by water, it raining hard, and so to the office and stopped my going, as I entended, to the Buoy of the Noure; and great reason I had to rejoice at it, for it proved the night of as great a Storme as was almost ever remembered. Late at the office, and so home to bed. This day, calling at Mr. Rawlinson's to know how all did there, I hear that my pretty grocer's wife, Mrs. Beversham, over the way there, her husband is lately dead of the plague at Bow, which I am sorry for, for fear of losing her neighbourhood.

15.  Up, and all the morning at the office busy; and at noon to the Kings head Taverne, where all the Trinity house dined today to choose a new Maister in the room of Hurlestone that is dead. And Capt. Crispe is chosen. But Lord, to see how Sir W. Batten governs all and tramples upon Hurlstone; but I am confident that company will grow the worse for that man's death, for now Batten, and in him a lazy, corrupt, doting rogue, will have all the sway there. After dinner, who comes in but my Lady Batten and a troop of a dozen women almost; and expected, as I found afterward, to be made mighty much of, but nobody minded them. But the best Jest was, that when they saw themselfs not regarded, they would go away; and it was horrible foul weather, and my Lady Batten walking through the dirty lane with new spick-and-span white shoes, she dropped one of her Galloshes in the dirt, where it stuck, and she forced to go home without one – at which she was horrible vexed, and I led her. And after vexing her a little more in mirth, I parted, and to Glanvills, where I knew Sir Jo. Robinson, Sir G. Smith and Capt. Cocke were gone. And there, with the company of Mrs. Penington (whose father I hear was one of the Court of Justice, and died prisoner, of the stone, in the Towre), I made them against their resolutions to stay from hour to hour till it was almost midnight, and a furious dark and rainy and windy stormy night; and which was best, I, with drinking small beer, made them all drunk drinking wine, at which Sir Jo. Robinson made great sport. But they being gone, the lady and I very civilly sat an hour by the fireside observing the Folly of this Robinson, that makes it his work to praise himself and all he says and doth – like a heavy-headed coxcomb. The plague, blessed be God, is decreased near 400; making the whole this week but 1300 and odd – for which the Lord be praised.

16–17. Up, and fitted myself for my Journy down to the Fleete; and sending my money and boy down by water to Eriffe, I borrowed a horse of Mr. Boreman's son, and after having sat an hour laughing with my Lady Batten and Mrs. Turner and eat and drank with them, I took horse and rode to Eriffe; where after making a little visit to Madam Williams, who did give me information of W. Hows having bought eight bags of precious stones, taken from about the Dutch Viceadmirall's neck, of which there were eight Dyamonds, which cost him 4000*l* sterling in India and hoped to have made 12000*l* here for them – and that this is told by one that sold him one of the bags, which hath nothing but rubys in it, which he hath for 35*s*. – and that it will be proved he hath made 125*l* of one stone that he bought. This she desired, and I resolved, I would give my Lord Sandwich notice of. So I on board my Lord Bruncker, and there he and Sir Edmd. Pooly carried me down into the Hold of the India Shipp, and there did show me the greatest wealth lie in confusion that a man can see in the world – pepper scatter[ed] through every chink, you trod upon it; and in cloves and nutmegs, I walked above the knees – whole rooms full – and silk in bales, and boxes of Copperplate, one of which I saw opened. Having seen this, which was as noble a sight as ever I saw in my life, I away on board the other ship in despair, to get the pleasure-boat of the gentlemen there to carry me to the fleet. They came, Mr. Ashburnham and Coll. Wyndham – but pleading the King's business, they did presently agree I should have it. So I presently on board and got under sail, and had a good bedd by the shift of Wyndhams; and so sailed all night and got down to Quinbrough water, where all the great ships are now come; and there on board my Lord, and was soon received with great content. And after some little discourse, he and I on board Sir W. Pen and there held a council of Warr about many wants of the fleet, but chiefly how to get Slopps and victuals for the fleet now going out to convoy our Hambrough Ships, that have been so long detained, for four or five months, for want of Convoy; which we did accomodate one way or other, and so after much chatt, Sir W. Penn did give us a very good and neat dinner, neater I think then ever I did see at his own house at home in my life, and so was the other I eat with him. After dinner, much talk; and among other things, he and I about his money for his prize goods, wherein I did give him a cool answer but so as we did not disagree in words much; and so let that fall, and so fallowed my Lord Sandwich, who was gone a little before me on board the *Royall James*. And there spent an hour, my Lord playing upon the Gittarr, which he now commends above all Musique in the world, because it is bass enough for a single voice, and is so portable, and manageable without much trouble. As an infinite secret, my Lord tells me the factions are high between the King and the Duke, and all the Court are in an uproare with their loose amours – the Duke of York being in love desperately with Mrs. Stewart. Nay, that the Duchesse herself is fallen in love with her new Maister of the Horse, one Harry Sidny, and another Harry Savill – so that God knows what will be the end of it. And that the Duke is not so obsequious as he used to be, but very high of late – and would be glad to be in the head of an army as generall; and that it is said that he doth propose to go and command under the King of Spayne in Flanders. That his amours to Mrs. Stewart are told the King – so that all is like to be nought among them. After he had given thanks to me for my kind visit and good counsel, on which he seems to set much by, I left him; and so away to my *Bezan* againe – and there to read in a pretty French book, *La Nouvelle Allegorique*, upon the strife between Rhetorique and its enemies – very pleasant. So after supper to sleep; and sailed all night, and came to Erith before break of day.

18.    About 9 of the clock I went on shore there (calling by the way only to look upon my Lord Brouncker), and so hired an ill-favoured hoss and away to Greenwich to my lodgings, where I hear how rude the Souldiers have been in my absence, swearing what they would do with me – which troubled me; but however, after eating a bit, I to the office and there very late writing letters, and so home and to bed.

21.    Up, and to the office, where all the morning doing business. And at noon home to dinner, and quickly back again to the office, where very busy all the evening; and late, sent a long discourse to Mr. Coventry by his desire, about the regulateing of the method of our payment of bills in the Navy – which will be very good; though it may be he did ayme principally at striking at Sir G. Carteret. So, weary, but pleased with this business being over, I home to supper and to bed.

22.    Up, and by water to the Duke of Albemarle and there did some little business – but most to show myself, and mightily I am

yet in his and Lord Cravens books; and thence to the Swan and there drank, and so down to the bridge, and so to the Change, where spoke with many people and about a great deal of business, which kept me late. I heard this day that Mr. Harrington is not dead of the plague as we believed; at which I was very glad – but most of all to hear that the plague is come very low; that is, the whole under 1000 and the plague 600 and odd – and great hopes of a further decrease, because of this day's being a very exceeding hard frost – and continues freezing. This day the first of the *Oxford Gazettes* came out, which is very pretty, full of news, and no folly in it – wrote by Williamson. From the Change, which is pretty full again, I to my house and there took some things, and so by water to my lodging at Greenwich and dined; and then to the office a while and at night home to my lodgings, and took T. Willson and T. Hater with me and there spent the evening till midnight, discoursing and settling of our Victualling business, that thereby I might draw up instructions for the Surveyours, and that we might be doing something to earne our money. This done, I late to bed. Among other things, it pleased me to have it demonstrated that a purser without professed cheating is a professed loser, twice as much as he gets.

23. Up betimes, and so being trimmed, I to get papers ready against Sir H. Cholmly come to me by appointment, he being newly come over from Tanger. He did by and by come, and we settled all matters about his money; and he is a most satisfied man in me, and doth declare his resolution to give me 200*l* per annum. It continuing to be a great frost (which gives us hope for a perfect cure of the plague), he and I to walk in the park, and there discoursed with grief of the calamity of the times; how the King's service is performed, and how Tanger is governed by a man, who, though honourable, yet doth mind his ways of getting, and little else compared,[1] which will never make the place flourish. I brought him home and had a good dinner for him; and there come by chance Capt. Cuttance – who tells me how for a Quarrell (which endeed my Lord the other night told me), Capt. Ferrers, having cut all over the back of another of my Lord's servants, is parted from my Lord. I sent for little Mrs. Fr. Tooker; and after they were gone, I sat dallying with her an hour, doing what I would with my hand about

---

1. Lord Belasyse.

her – and a very pretty creature it is. So in the evening parted, and I to the office, where late writing letters; and at my lodging later, writing for the last twelve days my Journall, and so to bed. Great expectation what mischief more the French will do us – for we must fall out. We in extraordinary lack of money and everything else to go to sea the next year. My Lord Sandwich is gone from the Fleete yesterday toward Oxford.

24. After dinner, Capt. Cocke and I about some business; and then with my other barrel of oysters home to Greenwich, sent them by water to Mrs. Penington, while he and I landed and visited Mr. Eveling – where most excellent discourse with him; among other things, he showed me a Lieger of a Treasurer of the Navy, his great-grandfather, just 100 years old; which I seemed mighty fond of, and he did present me with it; which I take as a great rarity, and he hopes to find me more, older then it. He also showed us several letters of the old Lord of Liecesters in Queen Elizabeth's time – under the very handwriting of Queen Elizabeth and Queen Mary Queen of Scotts and others, very venerable names. But Lord, how poorly methinks they wrote in those days, and on what plain uncut paper. Thence, Cocke having sent for his coach, we to Mrs. Penington, and there sat and talked and eat our oysters with great pleasure; and so home to my lodging late, and to bed.

30. Up, and at the office all the morning. At noon comes Sir Tho. Allen and I made him dine with me, and very friendly he is; and a good man I think, but one that professes he loves to get and to save. He dined with my wife and me and Mrs. Barbary, whom my wife brings along with her from Woolwich for as long as she stays here. In the afternoon to the office, and there very late writing letters; and then home, my wife and people sitting up for me, and after supper, to bed. Great joy we have this week in the weekly Bill, it being come to 544 in all, and but 333 of the plague – so that we are encouraged to get to London as soon as we can. And my father writes as great news of joy to them, that he saw Yorkes waggon go again this week to London, and was full of passengers – and tells me that my aunt Bell hath been dead of the plague these seven weeks.

14. Whitehall Palace and St James's Park in the time of Charles II. Ascribed traditionally to Hendrick Danckerts, but possibly by Jacob Knyff.

15. Whitehall Palace, by Leonard Knyff, c.1694. The Banqueting House is in the centre; behind is St James's Park with its ornamental canal, and to the right St James's Palace.

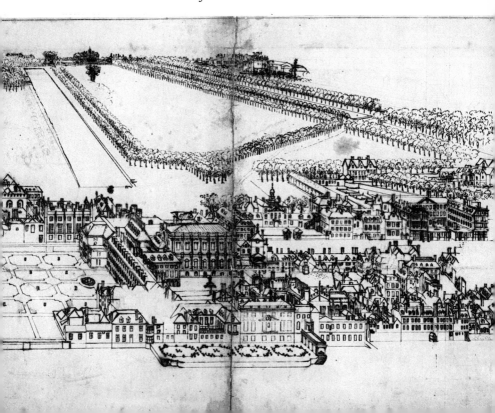

16. Cheapside, by St Mary-le-Bow, c.1680

17. Old St Paul's, by W. Hollar, 1658

...lament House — the Hall — the Abby

WHollar fecit, 1647

8. Westminster from the river, by W. Hollar, 1644

9. The Royal Exchange, by W. Hollar, 1644

BYRSA LONDINENSIS.
vulgo
The Royall Exchange of London

20. London Bridge, by C. de Jongh, c.1639

21. The Tower, by W. Hollar, c.1637–43

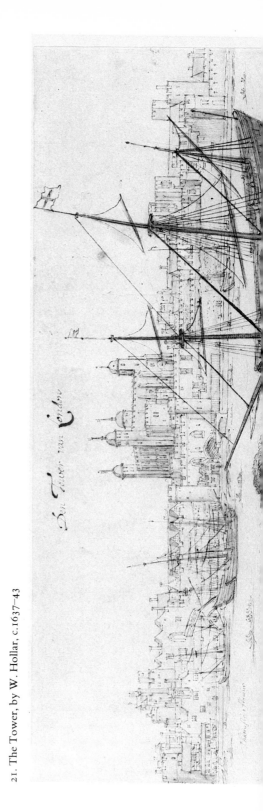

Der Tower von London

# -❖DECEMBER❖-

1. This morning to the office, full of resolution to spend the whole day at business. And there, among other things, I did agree with Poynter to be my clerk for my Victualling business. And so I all alone all the day long, shut up in my little closet at my office, drawing up instructions which I should long since have done for my Surveyors of the Ports – Sir W. Coventry desiring much to have them, and he might well have expected them long since. After dinner to it again; and at night had long discourse with Gibbson, who is for Yarmouth, who makes me understand so much of the victualling business and the pursers trade, that I am shamed I should go about the concerning myself in a business which I understand so very very little of, and made me distrust all I had been doing today. So I did lay it by till tomorrow morning, to think of it fresh. And so home, by promise to my wife to have mirth there; so we have our neighbours, little Mis Tooker and Mrs. Daniels, to dance; and after supper I to bed and left them merry below, which they did not part from till 2 or 3 in the morning.

2. Up, and discoursing with my wife, who is resolved to go to London for good and all this day, we did agree upon giving Mr. Sheldon 10*l*, and Mrs. Barb. two pieces. And so I left her to go down thither to fetch away the rest of the things and pay him the money; and so I to the office, where very busy, setting Mr. Poynter to write out my last night's work; which pleases me this day, but yet it is pretty to reflect how much I am out of countenance with what I had done up[on] Gibsons discourse with me, for fear I should have done it sillily. But Poynter likes them, and Mr. Hater also; but yet I am afeared lest they should do it out of flattery, so conscious I am of my ignorance.

4. Several people to me about business; among others, Capt. Taylor, intended Storekeeper for Harwich, whom I did give some assistance in his despatch – by lending him money. So out, and by water to London, and to the Change and up and down about several businesses. And after the observing (God forgive me) one or two of my neighbour hermosa mohers come to town, which did please me very well, home to my house at the office, where my wife had got a dinner for me. And it was a joyful thing for us to meet here – for which God be praised. Here was her brother, come to see her and

speak with me about business – it seems my recommending of him hath not only obtained presently being admitted into the Duke of Albemarle's guard and present pay – but also, by the Dukes and Sir Ph. Howards directions, to be put as a right-hand man, and other marks of special respect; at which I am very glad, partly for him, and partly to see that I am reckoned something in my recommendations – but wish he may carry himself that I may receive no disgrace by him. Upon the Change today, Colvill tells me from Oxford that the King in person hath justified my Lord Sandwich to the highest degree – and is right in his favour to the uttermost. So late by water home, taking a barrel of oysters with me; and at Greenwich went and sat with Madam Penington, con laquelle je faisais almost whatever je voudrais – con mi mano, sino tocar la chose même; and I was very near it, and made her undress her head and set dishevelled all night, sporting till two in the morning; and so away to my lodging, almost cloyed with this dalliance, and so to bed. Over-fasting all the morning hath filled me mightily with wind, and nothing else hath done it, that I fear a fit of the Cholique.

6.   Up betimes, it being Fast day, and by water to the Duke of Albemarle, who came to town from Oxford last night. He is mighty brisk, and very kind to me and asks my advice principally in everything. He surprizes me with the news that my Lord Sandwich goes Embassador to Spayne speedily – though I know not whence this arises, yet I am heartily glad of it. He did give me several directions what to do; and so I home by water again, and to church a little, thinking to have met Mrs. Pierce in order to our meeting at night. But she not there, I home – and dined; and comes presently by appointment my wife. I spent the afternoon upon a song of Solyman's words to Roxolana that I have set; and so with my wife walked, and Mercer, to Mrs. Pierces, where Capt. Rolt and Mrs. Knipp, Mr. Coleman and his wife, and Laneare, Mrs. Worship, and her singing daughter met; and by and by unexpectedly comes Mr. Pierce from Oxford. Here the best company for Musique I ever was in in my life, and wish I could live and die in it, both for music and the face of Mrs. Pierce and my wife and Knipp, who is pretty enough, but the most excellent mad-hum[ou]rd thing; and sings the noblest that ever I heard in my life, and Rolt with her, some things together most excellently – I spent the night in an ecstasy almost; and having invited them to my house a day or two hence, we broke up – Pierce having told me that he is told how the King

hath done my Lord Sandwich all the right imaginable, by showing him his countenance before all the world on every occasion, to remove thoughts of discontent – and that he is to go Embassador; and that the Duke of Yorke is made Generall of all forces by land and sea, and the Duke of Albemarle Lieutenant-Generall; whether the two latter alterations be so true or no, he knows not, but he is told so – but my Lord is in full favour with the King. So all home and to bed.

9. Called up betimes by my Lord Brouncker, who is come to town from his long Water worke at Erith last night – to go with him to the Duke of Albemarle, which by his coach I did – our discourse upon the ill posture of the times through lack of money. At the Dukes did some business, and I believe he was not pleased to see all the Duke's discourse and applications to me and everybodys else. Discoursed also with Sir G. Carteret about office business, but no money in view. Here my Lord and I stayed and dined, the Vice-Chamberlain taking his leave. At table, the Duchesse, a damned ill-looked woman, complaining of her Lord's going to sea the next year, said these cursed words – "If my Lord had been a coward he had gone to sea no more it may be; then he might have been excused and made an Embassador" (meaning my Lord Sandwich); this made me mad, and I believe she perceived my countenance change, and blushed herself very much. I was in hopes others had not minded it; but my Lord Bruncker, after we were come away, took notice of the words to me with displeasure. Thence after dinner away by water, calling and taking leave of Sir G. Carteret, whom we found going through at Whitehall; and so over to Lambeth and took coach and home; and so to the office, where late writing letters; and then home to Mr. Hill and sang, among other things, my song of *Beauty [retire]*, which he likes; only, excepts against two notes in the bass, but likes the whole very well. So, late to bed.

10. *Lords day*. Lay long talking, Hill and I, with great pleasure, and then up; and being ready, walked to Cocke's for some news, but heard none; only, they would have us stay their dinner, and sent for my wife, who came, and very merry we were – there being Sir Edm. Pooly and Mr. Eveling. Before we had dined comes Mr. Andrews, whom we had sent for to Bow, and so after dinner, home; and there we sang some things, but not with much pleasure, Mr. Andrews being in so great haste to go home, his wife looking

every hour to be brought to bed. He gone, Mr. Hill and I continued our Musique, one thing after another, late till supper; and so to bed with great pleasure.

15. Up, and spent all the morning with my Surveyors of the Ports for the victualling, and there read to them what instructions I had provided for them, and discoursed largely much of our business and the business of the pursers. I left them to dine with my people, and I to my Lord Brunckers, where I met with a great good dinner. There till almost night, and so away toward the office and in my way met with Sir James Bunch, and after asking what news, he cried (I know [not] whether in earnest or jest): "Aye," says he, "this is the time for you," says he, "that were for Oliver heretofore; you are full of imployment, and we poor Cavaliers sit still and can get nothing" – which was a pretty reproach, I thought, but answered nothing to it, for fear of making it worse. So away, and I to see Mrs. Penington; but company being to come to her, I stayed not, but to the office a little; and so home, and after supper to bed.

21. At the office all the morning. At noon all of us dined at Capt. Cockes at a good chine of beef and other good meat, but being all frost-bitten, was most of it unroast; but very merry, and a good dish of fowl we dressed ourselfs. Mr. Eveling there, in very good humour. All the afternoon till night, pleasant, and then I took my leave of them and to the office, where I wrote my letters, and away home, my head full of business and some trouble for my letting my accounts go so far; but I have made an oath this night for the drinking no wine, &c., on such penalties, till I have passed my account and cleared all. Coming home and going to bed, the boy tells me his sister Daniel hath provided me a supper of little birds, killed by her husband; and I made her sup with me, and after supper were alone a great while and I had the pleasure of her lips – she being a pretty woman, and one whom a great belly becomes as well as ever I saw any. She gone, I to bed. This day I was come to by Mrs. Burrows of Westminster, Lieut. Burrows (lately dead) his widow, a most pretty woman, and my old acquaintance. I had a kiss or two of her, and a most modest woman she is.

22. Up betimes, and to my Lord Brouncker to consider the late instructions sent us, of the method of our signing bills hereafter and paying them. By and by, by agreement, comes Sir Jo. Mines and Sir

W. Batten; and then to read them publicly, and consider of putting them in execution. About this all the morning. And it appearing necessary for the Controller to have another clark, I recommend Poynter to him, which he accepts, and I by that means rid of one that I fear would not have been fit for my turn – though he writes very well. At noon comes Mr. Hill to town, and finds me out here and brings Mr. Houbland, who met him here. So I was compelled to leave my Lord and his dinner and company, and with them to the Beare and dined with them and their brothers, of which Hill had his, and the other two of his – and mighty merry and very fine company they are, and I glad to see them. After dinner I forced to take leave of them, by being called upon by Mr. Andrews, I having sent for him; and by a fine glosse did bring him to desire tallies for what orders I have to pay him and his company for Tanger victualls; and I by that means cleared to myself 210l, coming to me upon their two orders, which is also a noble addition to my late profits, which have been very considerable of late; but how great, I know not till I come to cast up my accounts which burdens my mind that it should be so backward, but I am resolved to settle to nothing till I have done it. He gone, I to my Lord Brouncker and there spent the evening, by my desire, in seeing his Lordship open to pieces and make up again his Wach, thereby being taught what I never knew before; and it is a thing very well worth my having seen, and am mightily pleased and satisfied with it. So I sat talking with him till late at night – somewhat vexed at a snappish answer Madam Williams did give me to herself, upon my speaking a free word to her in mirth, calling her a mad Jade. She answered, we were not so well acquainted yet. But I was more [vexed] at a letter from my Lord Duke of Albemarle today, pressing us to continue our meetings for all Christmas, which, though everybody intended not to have done, yet I am concluded in it, who intended nothing else. But I see it is necessary that I do make often visits to my Lord Duke, which nothing shall hinder after I have evened my accounts; and now the River is frozen, I know not how to get to him. Thence to my lodging, making up my Journall for eight or nine days; and so my mind being eased of it, I to supper and to bed. The weather hath been frosty these eight or nine days, and so we hope for an abatement of the plague the next week; or else God have mercy upon us, for the plague will certainly continue the next year if it doth not.

25. *Christmas Day*. To church in the morning, and there saw a wedding in the church, which I have not seen many a day, and the young people so merry one with another; and strange, to see what delight we married people have to see these poor fools decoyed into our condition, every man and wife gazing and smiling at them. Here I saw again my beauty Lethulier. Thence to my Lord Brouncker by invitation, and dined there – and so home to my lodgings to settle myself to look over and settle my papers, both of my accounts private and those of Tanger, which I have let go so long that it were impossible for any soul, had I died, to understand them or ever come to any good end in them. I hope God will never suffer me to come to that disorder again.

26. Up, and to the office, where Sir Jo. Minnes and my Lord Brouncker and I met, to give our directions to the Comanders of all the ships in the River to bring in lists of their ships' companies, with entries, discharges, &c, all the last voyage – where young Seamour, among twenty that stood bare, stood with his hat on, a proud saucy young man. Thence with them to Mr. Cuttles, being invited, and dined nobly and neatly – with a very pretty house, and a fine Turret at top, with windeing stairs, and the finest prospect I know about all Greenwich, save the top of the hill – and yet in some respects better then that. Here I also saw some fine writing-work and Flourishing of Mr. Hore; he, one that I knew long ago, an acquaintance of Mr. Tomson's at Westminster, that is this man's clerk. It is the stories of the several Archbishops of Canterbury, engrossed in vellum to hang up in Canterbury Cathedrall in tables, in lieu of the old ones, which are almost worn out. Thence to the office a while, and so to Capt. Cockes and there talked, and home to look over my papers, and so to bed.

30. Up, and to the office. At noon home to dinner, and all the afternoon to my accounts again; and there find myself, to my great joy, a great deal worth above 4000*l*, for which the Lord be praised – and is principally occasioned by my getting 500*l* of Cocke for my profit in his bargains of prize goods, and from Mr. Gawden's making me a present of 500*l* more when I paid him 8000*l* for Tanger. So to my office to write letters, then to my accounts again, and so to bed, being in great ease of mind.

31. *Lords day*. All the morning in my chamber, writing fair the

state of my Tanger accounts, and so dined at home. In the afternoon to the Duke of Albemarle, and thence back again by water, and so to my chamber to finish the entry of my accounts and to think of the business I am next to do, which is the stating my thoughts and putting in order my collections about the business of Pursers, to see where the fault of our present constitution relating to them lies, and what to propose to mend it. And upon this late, and, with my head full of this business, to bed.

Thus ends this year, to my great joy, in this manner: – I have raised my estate from 1300*l* in this year to 4400*l*. I have got myself greater interest, I think, by my diligence; and my imployments encreased by that of Treasurer for Tanger and Surveyor of the Victuals. It is true we have gone through great melancholy because of the great plague, and I put to great charges by it, by keeping my family long at Woolwich, and myself and another part of my family, my clerks, at my charge at Greenwich, and a maid at London. But I hope the King will give us some satisfaction for that. But now the plague is abated almost to nothing, and I entending to get to London as fast as I can, my family, that is, my wife and maids, having been there these two or three weeks. The Duch war goes on very ill, by reason of lack of money; having none to hope for, all being put into disorder by a new Act that is made as an experiment to bring Credit to the Exchequer, for goods and money to be advanced upon the credit of that Act. I have never lived so merrily (besides that I never got so much) as I have done this plague time, by my Lord Brouncker's and Capt. Cocke's good company, and the acquaintance of Mrs. Knipp, Coleman and her husband, and Mr. Laneare; and great store of dancings we have had at my cost (which I was willing to indulge myself and wife) at my lodgings. The great evil of this year, and the only one endeed, is the fall of my Lord of Sandwich, whose mistake about the Prizes hath undone him, I believe, as to interest at Court; though sent (for a little palliateing it) Imbassador into Spayne, which he is now fitting himself for. But the Duke of Albemarle goes with the Prince to sea this next year, and my Lord very meanly spoken of; and endeed, his miscarriage about the prize goods is not to be excused, to suffer a company of rogues to go away with ten times as much as himself, and the blame of all to be deservedly laid upon him. My whole family hath been well all this while, and all my friends I know of, saving my aunt Bell, who is dead, and some children of my Cosen Sarah's, of the plague. But many of such as I know very well, dead.

Yet to our great joy, the town fills apace, and shops begin to be open again. Pray God continue the plague's decrease – for that keeps the Court away from the place of business, and so all goes to wrack as to public matters, they at this distance not thinking of it.

**1666**

# ⊹ JANUARY ⊹

1. *New yeare's Day.* Called up by 5 a-clock by my order by Mr. Tooker, who wrote, while I dictated to him, my business of the Pursers, and so without eating or drinking till 3 in the afternoon, and then to my great content finished it. So to dinner, Gibson and he and I – and then to Copying it over, Mr. Gibson reading and I writing, and went a good way in it till interrupted by Sir W. Warren's coming, of whom I alway learn something or other, his discourse being very good, and his brains also. He being gone, we to our business again, and wrote more of it fair; and then late to bed.

2. Up by candlelight again, and wrote the greatest part of my business fair; and then to the office, and so home to dinner, and after dinner up and made an end of my fair-writing it. And that being done, set [?my clerks] to entering, while I to my Lord Bruncker's; and there find Sir J. Mennes and all his company, and Mr. Boreman and Mrs. Turner, but above all, my dear Mrs. Knipp, with whom I sang; and in perfect pleasure I was to hear her sing, and especially her little Scotch song of *Barbary Allen.* And to make our mirth the completer, Sir Jo. Minnes was in the highest pitch of mirth, and his Mimicall tricks, that ever I saw; and most excellent pleasant company he is, and the best Mimique that ever I saw, and certainly would have made an excellent Actor, and now would be an excellent teacher of Actors. Thence, it being post-night, against my will took leave; but before I came to my office, longing for more of her company, returned and met them coming home in coaches; so I got into the coach where Mrs. Knipp was, and got her upon my knee (the coach being full) and played with her breasts and sung; and at last set her at her house, and so good-night. So home to my lodgings, and there endeavoured to have finished the examining my paper of Pursers business to have sent away tonight; but I was so sleepy with my late early risings and late goings to bed, that I could not do it, but was forced to go to

bed and leave it to send away tomorrow by an Expresse.

3.     Up, and all the morning till 3 in the afternoon examining and fitting up my pursers' paper, and so sent it away by an express. Then comes my wife, and I set her to get supper ready against I go to the Duke of Albemarle; and back again – and at the Dukes, with great joy, I received the good news of the decrease of the plague this week to 70, and but 253 in all; which is the least Bill hath been known these twenty years in the City – though the want of people in London is it that must make it so low, below the ordinary number for Bills. So home, and find all my good company I had bespoke, as, Coleman and his wife and Laneare, Knipp, and her surly husband. And good music we had, and among other things, Mrs. Coleman sang my words I set of *Beauty retire*, and I think it is a good song and they praise it mightily. Then to dancing and supper, and mighty merry till Mr. Rolt came in, whose pain of the Toothake made him no company and spoilt ours; so he away, and then my wife's teeth fell of akeing, and she to bed; so forced to break up all with a good song, and so to bed.

4.     Up, and to the office – where my Lord Brouncker and I (against Sir W. Batten and Sir J. Mennes and the whole table) for Sir W. Warren in the business of his mast contract, and overcame them and got them to do what I had a mind to; endeed, my Lord being unconcerned in what I aimed at. So home to dinner, where Mr. Sheldon came by invitation from Woolwich; and as merry as I could be, with all my thoughts about me, and my wife still in pain of her teeth. He anon took leave and took Mrs. Barbary his niece home with him, and seems very thankful to me for the 10*l* I did give him for my wife's rent of his house; and I am sure I am beholding to him, for it was a great convenience to me. And then my wife home to London by water, and I to the office till 8 at night; and so to my Lord Brouncker, thinking to have been merry, having appointed a meeting for Sir J. Mennes and his company and Mrs. Knipp again; but whatever hindered I know not, but no company came, which vexed me, because it disappointed me of the glut of mirth I hoped for. However, good discourse with my Lord, and merry with Mrs. Williams's descants upon Sir J. Mennes and Mrs. Turner's not coming; so home and to bed.

5.     I, with my Lord Brouncker and Mrs. Williams, by coach with

four horses to London, to my Lord's house in Covent Guarden. But Lord, what staring to see a nobleman's coach come to town – and porters everywhere bow to us, and such begging of beggars. And a delightful thing it is to see the town full of people again, as now it is, and shops begin to open, though in many places, seven or eight together, and more, all shut; but yet the town is full compared with what it used to be – I mean the City end, for Covent Gu[a]rden and Westminster are yet very empty of people, no Court nor gentry being there. Set Mrs. Williams down at my Lord's house, and he and I to Sir G. Carteret at his chamber at Whitehall, he being come to town last night to stay one day. So my Lord and he and I, much talk about the Act,[1] what credit we find upon it; but no private talk between him and I. So I to the Change, and there met Mr. Povey, newly come to town, and he and I to Sir George Smith's and there dined nobly. He tells me how my Lord Bellases complains for want of money, and of him and me therein; but I value it not, for I know I do all that can be done. We had no time to talk of perticulars, but leave it to another day; and I away to Cornhill to expect my Lord Brouncker's coming back again; and I stayed at my Stationer's house, and by and by comes my Lord and did take me up; and so to Greenwich, and after sitting with them a while at their house, home, thinking to get Mrs. Knipp but could not, she being busy with company; but sent me a pleasant letter, writing herself *Barbary Allen*. I went therefore to Mr. Boreman's for pastime, and there stayed an hour or two, talking with him and reading a discourse about the River of Thames the reason of its being choked up in several places with Shelfes; which is plain, is by the encroachments made upon the River, and running-out of Cawseways into the River at every wood wharfe, which was not heretofore when Westminster hall and Whitehall was built, and Redriffe church, which now are sometimes overflown with water. I had great satisfaction herein; so home, and to my papers for lack of company, but by and by comes little Mrs. Tooker and sat and supped with me, and I kept her very late, talking and making her comb my head; and did what I will with her et tena grande plaisir con ella, tocando sa cosa con mi cosa, and hazendo la cosa par cette moyen. So late to bed.

7. *Lords day*. Up, and being trimmed, I was invited by Capt.

1. The 'Additional Aid' of 1665.

Cocke; so I left my wife, having a mind to some discourse with him, and dined with him. He tells me of new difficulties about his goods, which troubles me and I fear they will be great. He tells me too, what I hear everywhere, how the town talks of my Lord Craven being to come into Sir G. Carteret's place; but sure it cannot be true. But I do fear those two families, his and my Lord Sandwiches, are quite broken – and I must now stand upon my own legs. Thence to my lodging; and considering how I am hindered by company there to do anything among my papers, I did resolve to go away today, rather then stay to no purpose till tomorrow; and so got all my things packed up – and spent half an hour with W. How about his papers of accounts for contingencies and my Lord's accounts, and so took leave of my landlady and daughters, having paid dear for what time I have spent there; but yet, having been quiet and in health, I am very well contented therewith. So with my wife and Mercer took boat, and away home. But in the evening, before I went, comes Mrs. Knipp just to speak with me privately, to excuse her not coming to me yesterday, complaining how like a devil her husband treats her, but will be with us in town a week hence; and so I kissed her and parted. Being come home, my wife and I to look over our house, and consider laying out a little money to hang our bedchamber better then it is; and so resolved to go and buy something tomorrow; and so after supper, with great joy in my heart for my coming once again hither, to bed.

8.   Up, and my wife and I by coach to Bennetts in Paternoster row (few shops there being yet open), and there bought velvett for a coat and Camelott for a cloak for myself. And thence to a place to look over some fine counterfeit damasks to hang my wife's closet, and pitched upon one. And so by coach home again, I calling at the Change; and so home to dinner, and all the afternoon look after my papers at home and my office against tomorrow; and so after supper, and considering the uselessness of laying out so much money upon my wife's closet, but only the chamber – to bed.

9.   Up, and then to the office, where we met first since the plague, which God preserve us in. At noon home to dinner, where Uncle Tho. with me, and in comes Pierce, lately come from Oxford, and Ferrers. After dinner Pierce and I up to my chamber, where he tells me how a great difference hath been between the Duke and Duchesse, he suspecting her to be naught with Mr. Sidny – but

some way or other the matter is made up; but he was banished the Court, and the Duke for many days did not speak to the Duchesse at all. He tells me that my Lord Sandwich is lost there at Court, though the King is perticularly his friend. But people do speak everywhere slightly of him. Which is a sad story to me, but I hope it may be better again. And that Sir G. Carteret is neglected, and hath great enemies at work against him. That matters must needs go bad while all the town and every boy in the street openly cries the King cannot go away till my Lady Castlemayne be ready to come along with him, she being lately brought to bed. And that he visits her and Mrs. Stewart every morning before he eats his breakfast. All this put together makes me very sad; but yet I hope I shall do pretty well among them for all this, by my not meddling with either of their matters. And then comes Mr. Gawden, and he and I talked above-stairs together a good while about his business; and to my great joy, got him to declare that of the 500*l* he did give me the other day, none of it was for my Treasurershipp for Tanger – (I first telling him how matters stood between Povy and I, that he was to have half of whatever was coming to me by that office); and that he will gratify me at two per cent for that when he next receives any money – so there is 80*l* due to me more then I thought of. He gone, I with a glad heart to the office to write my letters; and so home to supper and bed. My wife mighty full of her work she hath today in furnishing her bedchamber.

10.    Up, and by coach to Sir G. Downing, where Mr. Gawden met me by agreement to talk upon the Act. I do find Sir G. Downing to be a mighty talker, more then is true; which I now know to be so, and suspected it before; but for all that, I have good grounds to think it will succeed for goods, and in time for money too; but not presently. Having done with him, I to my Lord Brunckers house in Covent Guarden; and among other things, it was to acquaint him with my paper of pursers; and read it to him and had his good liking of it. Showed him Mr. Coventry's sense of it, which he sent me last post, much to my satisfaction. Thence to the Change, and there hear, to our grief, how the plague is encreased this week from 70 to 89. We have also great fear of our Hambrough fleet, of their meeting the Dutch; as also have certain news that by storms Sir Jer. Smith's fleet is scattered, and three of them come without masts back to Plymouth; which is another very exceeding great disappointment, and if the victualling ships are

miscarried, will tend to the loss of the garrison of Tanger. Thence home; in my way, had the opportunity I longed for, of seeing and saluting Mrs. Stokes, my little goldsmiths wife in Paternoster row; and there bespoke something, a silver chafing-dish for warming plates. And so home to dinner. Found my wife busy about making her hangings for her chamber with the Upholster. So I to the office, and anon to the Duke of Albemarle by coach at night (taking, for saving time, Sir W. Warren with me, talking of our businesses all the way going and coming) and there got his reference of my pursers' paper to the Board, to consider of it before he read it, for he will never understand it I am sure. Here I saw Sir W. Coventry's kind letter to him concerning my paper. And among other of his letters (which I see all, and that is a strange thing, that whatever is writ to this Duke of Albemarle, all the world may see; for this very night he did give me Mr. Coventry's letter to read as soon as it came to his hand, before he had read it himself, and bid me take out of it what concerned the Navy; and many things there was in it which I should not have thought fit for him to have let anybody so suddenly see). But among other things, find him profess himself to the Duke a friend into the enquiring further into the business of Prizes,[1] and advises that it may be public, for the righting the King and satisfying the people and getting the blame to be rightly laid where it should be – which strikes very hard upon my Lord Sandwich – and troubles me to read it. Besides, what vexed me more, I heard the damned Duchesse again say,[2] to twenty gentlemen publicly in the room, that she would have Mountagu sent once more to sea, before he goes his Embassy, that we may see whether he will make amends for his cowardize, and repeated the answer she did give the other day in my hearing to Sir G. Downing – wishing her Lord had been a coward, for then perhaps he might have been made an Embassador and not been sent now to sea. But one good thing she said – she cried mightily out against the having of gentlemen Captains with feathers and ribbands, and wished the King would send her husband to sea with the old plain sea-Captains that he served with formerly, that would make their ships swim with blood, though they could not make legs as captains nowadays can.

12.  By coach to the Duke of Albemarle, where Sir W. Batten and I

1. See above, p. 159 (10 October) & n.
2. cf. above, p. 561 (9 December).

only met. Troubled at my heart to see how things are ordered there
– without consideration or understanding. Thence back by coach,
and called at Wottons my shoemaker, lately come to town, and
bespoke shoes; as also got him to find me a Taylor to make me some
clothes, my own being not yet in Towne, nor Pym, my Lord
Sandwiches tailor. So he helped me to a pretty man, one Mr.
Penny, against St. Dunstan's Church. Thence to the Change, and
there met Mr. Moore, newly come to town, and took him home to
dinner with me; and after dinner to talk – and he and I do conclude
my Lord's case to be very bad, and may be worse if he do not get a
pardon for his doings about the prizes, and his business at Bergen
and other thing[s] done by him at sea, before he goes for Spayne.
Having done discourse with him, and directed him to go with my
advice to my Lord express tomorrow to get his pardon perfected
before his going, because of what I read the other night in Sir W.
Coventry's letters, I to the office and there had an extraordinary
meeting of Sir J. Mennes, Sir W. Batten, Sir W. Penn, and my Lord
Brouncker and I, to hear my paper read about pursers, which they
did all of them, with great good will and great approbation of my
method and pains in all; only Sir W. Penn, who must except against
everything and remedy nothing, did except against my proposal,
for some reasons which I could not understand, I confess, nor my
Lord Brouncker neither. But he did detect, endeed, a failure or two
of mine in my report about the ill condition of the present pursers,
which I did magnify in one or two little things; to which I think he
did with reason except. But at last, with all respect did declare the
best thing he ever heard of this kind; but when Sir W. Batten did
say, "Let us that do know the practical part of the Victualling meet
Sir J. Mennes, Sir W. Penn and I, and see what we can do to mend
all," he was so far from offering or furthering it, that he declined it
and said he must be out of town. So, as I ever knew him, never did
in his life ever attempt to mend anything, but suffer all things to go
on in the way they are, though never so bad, rather then improve
his experience to the King's advantage. So we broke up; however,
they promising to meet to offer something in it of their opinions –
and so we ris; and I and my Lord Brouncker by coach a little way, I
with him for discourse sake – till our coach broke and tumbled me
over him quite down the side of the coach, falling on the ground
about the Stockes. But up again, and thinking it fit to have for my
honour something reported in writing to the Duke in favour of my
pains in this, lest it should be thought to be rejected as Frivolous, I

did move it to my Lord, and he will see it done tomorrow. So we parted; and I to the office, and thence home to my poor wife, who works all day at home like a horse at the making of her hangings for our chamber and the bed. So to supper and to bed.

14. *Lords day*. Long in bed – till raised by my new Taylor, Mr. Penny; comes and brings me my new velvet coat, very handsome but plain; and a day hence will bring me my Camelott cloak. He gone, I close to my papers to set all in order, and to perform my vow to finish my Journall and other things before I kiss any woman more, or drink any wine, which I must be forced to do tomorrow if I go to Greenwich, as I am invited by Mr. Boreman to hear Mrs. Knipp sing. And I would be glad to go, so as we may be merry. At noon eat the second of the two Cygnets Mr. Sheply sent us for a New Year's gift; and presently to my chamber again, and so to work hard all day about my Tanger accounts, which I am going again to make up – as also upon writing a letter to my father about Pall, whom it is time now, I find, to think of disposing of, while God Almighty hath given me something to give with her; and in my letter to my father I do offer to give her 450*l*, to make her own 50*l*, given her by my uncle, up 500*l*. I do also therein propose Mr. Harman the upholster for a husband for her, to whom I have a great love, and did heretofore love his former wife, and a civil man he is, and careful in his way. Besides, I like his trade and place he lives in, being Cornehill. Thus late at work; and so to supper and to bed.

15.   Busy all the morning in my chamber in my old cloth suit, while my usual one is to my tailor's to mend; which I had at noon again, and an answer to a letter I had sent this morning to Mrs. Pierce to go along with my wife and I down to Greenwich tonight, upon an invitation to Mr. Boreman's to be merry, to dance and sing with Mrs. Knipp. Being dressed and having dined, I took coach and to Mrs. Pierce, to her new house in Covent garden, a very fine place and fine house. Took her thence home to my house, and so by water to Boremans by night – where the greatest disappointment that ever I saw in my life: much company – a good supper provided, and all come with expectation of excess of mirth; but all blank through the waywardnesse of Mrs. Knipp, who, though she had appointed the night, could not be got to come – not so much as her husband could get her to come; but, which was a pleasant thing in all my anger – I asking him (while we were in expectation what

answer one of our many messengers would bring) what he thought, whether she would come or no, he answered that for his part he could not so much as think. By and by we all to supper, which the silly maister of the feast commanded; but what with my being out of humour, and the badness of the meat dressed, I did never eat a worse supper in my life. At last, very late and supper done, she came undressed; but it brought me no mirth at all; only, after all being done, without singing, or very little, and no dancing – Pierce and I to bed together; and he and I very merry to find how little and thin clothes they give us to cover us, so that we were fain to lie in our stockings and drawers and lay all our coats and clothes upon the bed. So to sleep.

20.  To the office, where upon Mr. Kinaston's coming to me about some business of Coll. Norwood's, I sent my boy[1] home for some papers; where, he staying longer then I would have him and being vexed at the business and to be kept from my fellows in the office longer then was fit, I became angry and boxed my boy when he came, that I do hurt my Thumb so much, that I was not able to stir all the day after and in great pain. At noon to dinner, and then to the office again late, and so to supper and to bed.

22.  To the Crowne tavern behind the Exchange by appointment, and there met the first meeing of Gresham College since the plague. Dr. Goddard did fill us with talk in defence of his and his fellow-physicians' going out of town in the plague-time; saying that their perticular patients were most gone out of town, and they left at liberty – and a great deal more, &c. But what, among other fine discourse, pleased me most, was Sir G. Ent about Respiration; that it is not to this day known or concluded on among physicians, nor to be done either, how that action is managed by nature or for what use it is. Here late, till poor Dr. Merritt was drunk; and so all home, and I to bed.

24.  *Greate Storme*. By agreement, my Lord Brouncker called me up; and though it was a very foul windy and rainy morning, yet down to the waterside we went, but no boat could go, the storm continued so. So my Lord, to stay till fairer weather, carried me into the Tower to Mr. Hores, and there we stayed talking an hour;

1. Tom Edwards.

but at last we found no boat yet could go, so we to the office, where we met upon an occasion extraordinary, of examining abuses of our clerks in taking money for examining of tickets, but nothing done in it. Thence my Lord and I, the weather being a little fairer, by water to Detford to Sir G. Carteret's house, where W. How met us; and there we opened the chests and saw the poor sorry Rubys which have caused all this ado to the undoing of W. How;[1] though I am not much sorry for it, because of his pride and ill-nature. About 200 of these very small stones and a cod of Muske (which it is strange I was not able to smell) is all we could find. So locked them up again, and my Lord and I, the wind being again very furious, so as we durst not go by water, walked to London quite round the Bridge, no boat being able to Stirre; and Lord, what a dirty walk we had, and so strong the wind, that in the fields we many times could not carry our bodies against it, but was driven backward. We went through Horsydowne, where I never was since a little boy, that I went to enquire after my father, whom we did give over for lost, coming from Holland. It was dangerous to walk the streets, the bricks and tiles falling from the houses, that the whole streets were covered in them – and whole chimneys, nay, whole houses in two or three places, blowed down. But above all, the pales on London bridge on both sides were blown away, so that we were fain to stoop very low, for fear of blowing off of the bridge. We could see no boats in the Thames afloat but what were broke loose and carried through the bridge, it being ebbing water. And the greatest sight of all was, among other parcels of ships driven here and there in clusters together, one was quite overset, and lay with her masts all along in the water and keel above water. So walked home; my Lord away to his house and I to dinner, Mr. Creede being come to town and to dine with me, though now it was 3 a-clock. After dinner, he and I to our accounts; and very troublesome he is and with tricks, which I found plainly and was vexed at.

25. Up, and to the office. At noon home to dinner. So abroad to the Duke of Albemarle and K. Joyces and her husband, with whom I talked a great deal about Pall's business; and told them what portion I would give her, and they do mightily like of it and will

1. Deputy-Treasurer of Sandwich's fleet; he had been examined before the Privy Council on a charge of embezzling the jewels taken as prize from the Dutch E. Indiamen (q.v. above, p. 541 (11 October)).

roceed further in speaking with Harman, who hath already been poke to about it, as from them only; and he is mighty glad of it, but loubts it may be an offence to me if I should know of it; so thinks hat it doth come only from Joyce, which I like the better. So I do pelieve the business will go on, and I desire it were over. I to the office then, where I did much business and set my people to work gainst furnishing me to go to Hampton Court, where the King and Duke will be on Sunday next. It is now certain that the King of France hath publicly declared war against us, and God knows how ittle fit we are for it. At night comes Sir W. Warren, and he and I nto the garden and talked over all our business. He gives me good idvice, not to imbark into trade (as I have had it in my thoughts bout Coll. Norwood) so as to be seen to mind it, for it will do me nurt, and draw my mind off from my business and imbroil my state too soon. So to the office business, and I find him as cunning a nan in all points as ever I met with in my life; and mighty merry we were in the discourse of our own tricks. So about 10 a-clock at night, I home and stayed with him there, talking and laughing at the olly of some of our neighbours of this office, till 2 in the morning; and so to bed.

28. *Lords day*. Being dressed in my velvet coat and plain Cravatt, ook a hackney coach provided ready for me by 8 a-clock; and so to ny Lord Brouncker with all my papers. And there took his coach with four horses and away towards Hampton Court, having a great deal of good discourse with him. At the Wicke found Sir J. Mennes and Sir W. Batten at a lodging provided for us by our Messenger, and there a good dinner ready. After dinner took coach, and to Court, where we find the King and Duke and Lords all in council; so we walked up and down – there being none of the ladies come, and so much the more business I hope will be done. The Council peing up, out comes the King, and I kissed his hand and he grasped ne very kindly by the hand. The Duke also, I kissed his; and he nighty kind, and Sir W. Coventry. After changing a few words with Sir W. Coventry, who assures me of his respect and love to me and his concernment for my health in all this sickness – I went down nto one of the Courts and there met the King and Duke; and the Duke called me to him – and the King came to me of himself and told me: "Mr. Pepys," says he, "I do give you thanks for your good service all this year, and I assure you I am very sensible of it." And the Duke of Yorke did tell me with pleasure that he had read over

my discourse about Pursers and would have it ordered in my way
We took boat and by water to Kingstone; and so to our Lodgeings
where a good supper and merry; only, I sleepy, and therefore afte
supper I slunk away from the rest to bed, and lay very well and slep
soundly – my mind being in a great delirium, between joy for wha
the King and Duke have said to me and Sir W. Coventry – anc
trouble for my Lord Sandwiches concernments and how hard i
will be for me to preserve myself from feeling thereof.

29.     Up, and to Court by coach, where to council before the Duke
of Yorke – the Duke of Albemarle with us. And after Sir W
Coventry had gone over his notes that he had provided with the
Duke of Albemarle, I went over all mine, with good success. Only,
I fear I did once offend the Duke of Albemarle, but I was much
joyed to find the Duke of Yorke so much contending for my
discourse about the pursers against Sir W. Penn, who opposed it
like a fool. My Lord Sandwich came in in the middle of the
business; and, poor man, very melancholy methought, and saic
little at all or to the business, and sat at the lower end, just as he
comes, no room being made for him; only, I did give him my stool,
and another was reached for me. This council done, I walked to and
again up and down the house, discoursing with this and that man.
Among others, took occasion to thank the Duke of Yorke for his
good opinion in general of my service, and perticularly his favour in
conferring on me the victualling business. He told me that he knew
nobody so fit as I for it. And next, he was very glad to find that to
give me for my encouragement – speaking very kindly of me. So to
Sir W. Coventry's to dinner with him, whom I took occasion to
thank for his favour and good thoughts of what little service I did,
desiring he would do the last act of friendship, in telling me of my
faults also. He told me he would [be] sure he would do that also, if
there were any occasion for it. So that, as much as it is possible
under so great a fall of my Lord Sandwich's and difference between
them, I may conclude that I am thoroughly right with Sir W.
Coventry. I dined with him with a great deal of company and much
merry discourse. I was called away before dinner ended, to go to
my company who dined at our lodgings – whither I went with Mr.
Eveling (whom I met) in his coach going that way – but found my
company gone; but my Lord Brouncker left his coach for me, so
Mr. Eveling and I into my Lord's coach and rode together, with
excellent discourse till we came to Clapham – talking of the vanity

and vices of the Court, which makes it a most contemptible thing; and endeed, in all his discourse I find him a most worthy person. Perticularly, he intertained me with discourse of an Infirmery which he hath projected for the sick and wounded seamen against the next year, which I mightily approve of – and will endeavour to promote, it being a worthy thing – and of use and will save money. He set me down at Mr. Gawden's, where nobody yet come home, I having left him and his sons and Creed at Court. So I took a book, and into the gardens and there walked and read till dark – with great pleasure; and then in, and in comes Osborne and he and I to talk, and Mr. Jaggard, who came from London; and great hopes there is of a decrease this week also of the plague. Anon comes in Creed, and after that, Mr. Gauden and his sons – and then they bring in three ladies who were in the house, but I do not know of them; his daughter and two nieces, daughters of Dr. Whistlers – with whom, and Creed, mighty sport at supper, the ladies very pretty – and mirthful. I perceive they know Creeds gut and stomach as well as I, and made as much mirth as I with it at supper. After supper I made the ladies sing, and they have been taught; but Lord, though I was forced to commend them, yet it was the saddest stuff I ever heard. However, we sat up late; and then I, in the best chamber like a prince, to bed – and Creede with me. And being sleepy, talked but little.

30. Lay long, till Mr. Gawden was gone out, being to take a little journy. I took coach and home, finding the town keeping the day solemly, it being the day of the King's Murther; and they being at church, I presently into the church, thinking to see Mrs. Lethulier or Batelier, but did not – and a dull sermon of our young Lecturer to boot. This is the first time I have been in this church since I left London for the plague; and it frighted me indeed to go through the church, more then I thought it could have done, to see so [many] graves lie so high upon the churchyard, where people have been buried of the plague. I was much troubled at it, and do not think to go through it again a good while.

# –❧FEBRUARY❧–

2.   Up betimes, and knowing that my Lord Sandwich is come to town with the King and Duke, I to wait upon him; which I did and find him in very good humour, which I am glad to see with all my heart. Having received his commands and discoursed with some of his people about my Lord's going, and with Sir Rog. Cuttance, who was there and finds himself slighted by Sir W. Coventry, I advised him however to look after imployment, lest it be said that my Lord's friends do forsake the service after he hath made them rich with the prizes. I to London, and there, among other things, did look over some pictures at Cades for my house, and did carry home a Silver Drudger for my cupboard of plate, and did call for my silver chafing-dishes, but they are sent home and the man would not be paid for them, saying that he was paid for them already, and with much ado got him to tell me, by Mr. Wayth; but I would not accept of that, but will send him his money, not knowing any courtesy I have yet done him to deserve it. So home, and with my wife looked over our plate and picked out 40*l* worth I believe, to change for more useful plate, to our great content; and then we shall have a very handsome cupboard of plate. So to dinner, and then to the office, where we had a meeting extraordinary about stating to the Duke the present debts of the Navy for which ready money must be had. And that being done, I to my business, where late; and then home to supper and to bed.

4.   *Lords day.* And my wife and I the first time together at church since the plague, and now only because of Mr. Mills his coming home to preach his first sermon, expecting a great excuse for his leaving the parish before anybody went, and now staying till all are come home; but he made but a very poor and short excuse, and a bad sermon. It was a frost, and had snowed last night, which covered the graves in the churchyard, so I was the less afeared for going through. Here I had the content to see my noble Mrs. Lethulier; and so home to dinner, and all the afternoon at my Journall till supper, it being a long while behindhand. At supper my wife tells me that W. Joyce hath been with her this evening, the first time since the plague – and tells her my aunt James is lately dead of the stone, and what she had hath given to his and his brother's wife and my cousin Sarah. So after supper to work again, and late to bed.

6.  Up, and to the office, where very busy all the morning; we met upon a report to the Duke of Yorke of the debts of the Navy, which we finished by 3 a-clock; and having eat one little bit of meat, I by water before the rest to Whitehall (and they to come after me) because of a committee for Tanger; where I did my business of stating my accounts perfectly well and to good liking, and do not discern but the Duke of Albemarle is my friend in his intentions, notwithstanding my general fears. After that to our Navy business, where my fellow-officers were called in; and did that also very well. And then broke up, and I home by coach, Tooker with me, and stayed in Lumberdstreete at Viners and sent home for the plate which my wife and I had a mind to change, and there changed it.

7.  It being fast-day, I stayed at home all day long to set things to rights in my chamber, by taking out all my books and putting my chamber in the same condition it was before the plague. But in the morning, doing of it and knocking up a nail, I did bruise my left thumb, so as broke a great deal of my flesh off, that it hung by a little. It was a sight frighted my wife – but I put some balsam of Mrs. Turners to it, and though in great pain, yet went on with my business; and did it to my full content, setting everything in order, in hopes now that the worst of our fears are over as to the plague for the next year. Interrupted I was by two or three occasions this day, to my great vexation, having this the only day I have been able to set apart for this work since my coming to town. At night to supper, weary, and to bed – having had the plasterers and joiners also to do some jobbs.

9.  Up, and betimes to Sir Ph. Warwicke, who was glad to see me and very kind. Thence to Coll. Norwood's lodgings, and there set right Houblons business about their ships. Thence to Westminster to the Exchequer about my Tanger business, to get orders for tallies, and so to the Hall, where the first day of the Tearme and the hall very full of people, and much more then was expected, considering the plague that hath been. Thence to the Change, and to the Sun behind it to dinner with the Lieutenant of the Tower and Coll. Norwood and others – where strange pleasure they seem to take in their wine and meat, and discourse of it with the curiosity and joy that methinks was below men of worth. Thence home, and there very much angry with my people till I had put all things in good forwardness about my supper for the Houblons; but that

being done, I was in good humour again, and all things in good order. Anon the five brothers Houblons came, and Mr. Hill, and a very good supper we had, and good company and discourse, with great pleasure. My new plate sets off my cupboard very nobly. Here they were till about 11 at night, with great pleasure; and a fine sight it is to see these five brothers thus loving one to another, and all industrious merchants. Our subject was principally Mr. Hills going for them to Portugall, which was the occasion of this entertainment. They gone, we to bed.

11. *Lords day.* Up, and put on a new black cloth suit to an old coat that I make to be in mourning at Court, where they are all, for the King of Spain. To church I, and at noon dined well; and then by water to Whitehall, carying a Captain of the Tower (who desired his freight thither); there I to the park, and walk two or three turns of the Pall Mall with the company about the King and Duke – the Duke speaking to me a good deal. There met Lord Brouncker and Mr. Coventry and discoursed about the Navy business, and all of us much at a loss that we yet can hear nothing of Sir Jere. Smith's fleet that went away to the Streights the middle of December – through all the storms that we have had since, that have driven back three or four of them, with their masts by the board. Yesterday came out the King's Declaration of war against the French; but with such mild invitations of both them and [the] Duch to come over hither, with a promise of their protection, that everybody wonders at it. Thence home with my Lord Brouncker for discourse sake; and thence by hackney coach home; and so my wife and I mighty pleasant discourse, supped, and to bed – the great wound I had Wednesday last in my thumb having, with once dressing by Mrs. Turners balsam, been perfectly cured, whereas I did not hope to save my nail, whatever else trouble it did give me. My wife and I are much thoughtful nowadays about Pall's coming up, in order to a husband.

12. Up, and very busy to perform an oath in finishing my Journall this morning for seven or eight days past. Then to several people attending upon business; among others, Mr. Grant and the executors of Barlow for the 25*l* due for the quarter before he died; which I scruple to pay, being obliged but to pay every half-year. Then comes Mr. Cæsar, my boy's lute-master, whom I have not seen since the plague before, but he hath been in Westminster all this

while very well – and tells me how, in the heighth of it, how bold people there were to go in sport to one another's burials. And in spite to well people, would breathe in the faces (out of their windows) of well people going by. Then to dinner before the Change, and so to the Change and then to the tavern to talk with Sir Wm. Warren; and so by coach to several places, among others, to my Lord Treasurer's, there to meet my Lord Sandwich, but missed; and met him at Lord Chancellors and there talked with him about his accounts, and then about Sir G. Carteret; and I find by him that Sir G. Carteret hath a worse game to play then my Lord Sandwich, for people are heaving at him. And he cries out of the business of Sir W. Coventry, who strikes at all and doth all. Then to my bookseller's, and then received some books I have new bought; and here late, choosing some more to new bind, having resolved to give myself 10*l* in books. And so home to the office, and then home to supper, where Mr. Hill was, and supped with us, and good discourse; a excellent person he still appears to me. After supper, and he gone, we to bed.

13. Up, and all the morning at the office. At noon to the Change, and thence, after business, dined at the Sheriffes (Hooker), being carried by Mr. Lethulier; where to my heart's content I met his wife, a most beautiful fat woman. But all the house melancholy upon the sickness of a daughter of the house in childbed, Mr. Vaughans lady – so all of them undressed; but however, this lady a very fine woman – I had a salute of her; and after dinner some discourse, the Sheriff and I, about a parcel of tallow I am buying for the office of him, I away home, and there at the office all the afternoon till late at night, and then away home to supper and to bed. Ill news this night, that the plague is encreased this week, and in many places else about the town, and at Chatham and elsewhere. This day, my wife wanting a chambermaid, with much ado got our old little Jane to be found out, who came to see her; and hath lived all this while in one place, but is so well, that we will not desire her removal; but are mighty glad to see the poor wench, who is very well, and doth well.

14. *St. Valentine's day.* This morning called up by Mr. Hill, who my wife thought had been come to be her Valentine, she it seems having drawn him last night, but it proved not; however, calling him up to our bedside, my wife challenged him. I up and made

myself ready, and so with him by coach to my Lord Sandwiches by appointment – to deliver Mr. How's accounts to my Lord. Which done, my Lord did give me hearty and large studied thanks for all my kindnesses to him and care of him and his business. I, after profession of all duty to his Lordshipp, took occasion to bemoan myself that I should fall into such a difficulty about Sir G. Carteret, as not to be for him but I must be against Sir W. Coventry, and therefore desired to be neutrall – which my Lord approved and confessed reasonable, but desired me to befriend him privately. Having done in private with my Lord, I brought Mr. Hill to kiss his hands, to whom my Lord professed great respects upon my score. My Lord being gone, I took Mr. Hill to my Lord Chancellors new house that is building, and went with trouble up to the top of it and there is there the noblest prospect that ever I saw in my life, Greenwich being nothing to it. And in everything is a beautiful house – and most strongly built in every respect – and as if, as it hath, it had the Chancellor for its maister. Thence with him to his painter, Mr. Hales, who is drawing his picture – which will be mighty like him, and pleased me, so that I am resolved presently to have my wife's and mine done by him, he having a very maisterly hand. So with mighty satisfaction to the Change, and thence home; and after dinner abroad, taking Mrs. Mary Batelier with us, who was just come to see my wife; and they set me down at my Lord Treasurer's, and themselfs went with the coach into the fields to take the ayre. I stayed a meeting of the Duke of Yorkes and the officers of the Navy and Ordinance – my Lord Treasurer lying in bed of the gowte. Our business was discourse of the straits of the Navy for want of money; but after long discourse, as much out of order as ordinary people's, we came to no issue, nor any money promised or like to be had, and yet the work must be done. Here I perceive Sir G. Carteret had prepared himself to answer a Choque of Sir W. Coventry, by offering of himself to show all he had paid, and what is unpaid and what moneys and assignments he hath in his hands – which, if he makes good, was the best thing he ever did say in his life – and the best timed, for else it must have fallen very foul on him.

15. Up, and my wife not come home all night. To the office, where sat all the morning. At noon to Starkys, a great cook's in Austin Fryers, invited by Coll. Atkins, and a good dinner for Coll. Norwood and his friends; among others, Sir Edw. Spragg and

others – but ill attendance. Before dined, called on by my wife in a coach; and so I took leave, and there with her and Knipp and Mercer (Mr. Hunt, newly come out of the country, being there also, come to see us) to Mr. Hales the painter's, having set down Mr. Hunt by the way. Here Mr. Hales begun my wife in the posture we saw one of my Lady Peters, like a St. Katharine. While he painted, Knipp and Mercer and I sang; and by and by comes Mrs. Pierce with my name in her bosom for her Valentine, which will cost me money. But strange, how like his very first dead Colouring is, that it did me good to see it, and pleases me mightily – and I believe will be a noble picture. Thence with them all as far as Fleet street and there set Pierce and Knipp down; and we home, I to the office, whither the Houb[l]ons come, telling me of a little new trouble from Norwood about their ship, which troubles me, though without reason. So late home to supper and to bed.

16.  I walked a good while tonight with Mr. Hater in the garden, talking about a husband for my sister and reckoning up all our clerks about us, none of which he thinks fit for her and her portion. At last I thought of young Gawden, and will think of it again.

18.  *Lords day*. Lay long in bed, discoursing with pleasure with my wife; among other things, about Pall's coming up, for she must be here a little to be fashioned. And my wife hath a mind to go down for her – which I am not much against, and so I rose and to my chamber to settle several things. At noon comes my Uncle Wight to dinner, and brings with him Mrs. Wight; sad company to me, nor was I much pleased with it – only, I must show respect to my Uncle. After dinner, they gone and it being a brave day, I walked to Whitehall, where the Queene and ladies are all come; I saw some few of them, but not the Queen nor any of the great beauties. I endeavoured to have seen my Lord Hinchingbrooke, who came to town yesterday, but I could not. Met with Creed, and walked with him a turn or two in the park, but without much content, having now designs of getting money in my head, which allows me not the leisure I used to have with him. Besides, an odde story lately told of him for a great truth, of his endeavouring to lie with a woman at Oxford, and her crying out saved her; and this being publicly known, doth a little make me hate him. Thence took coach, and calling by the way at my bookseller's for a book, writ about twenty years ago in prophecy of this year coming on, 1666, explaining it to

be the mark of the beast. I home and there fell to reading, and then to supper and to bed.

19. At noon by coach to St. Paul's churchyard to my bookseller's and there bespoke a few more books, to bring all I have lately bought to 10*l*. Here I am told for certain, what I have heard once or twice already, of a Jew in town, that in the name of the rest doth offer to give any man 10*l*, to be paid 100*l* if a certain person now in Smirna be within these two years owned by all the princes of the East, and perticularly the Grand Segnor, as the King of the world, in the same manner we do the King of England here, and that this man is the true Messiah. One named a friend of his that had received ten pieces in gold upon this score, and says that the Jew hath disposed of 1100*l* in this manner – which is very strange; and certainly this year of 1666 will be a year of great action, but what the consequence of it will be, God knows. Thence to the Change, and from my stationer's thereabouts carried home by coach two books of Ogilbys, his *Æsop* and *Coronacion*, which fell to my lot at his lottery; cost me 4*l*, besides the binding. So home. I find my wife gone out to Hales her painter's, and I after a little dinner do fallow her, and there do find him at work, and with great content I do see it will be a very rare picture. Left her there, and I to my Lord Treasurer's, where Sir G. Carteret and Sir J. Mennes met me; and before my Lord Treasurer and Duke of Albemarle, the state of our Navy debts was laid open, being very great, and their want of money to answer them openly professed – there being but 1500000*l* to answer a certain expense and debt of 2300000*l*. Thence walked with Fenn down to Whitehall, and there saw the Queene at Cards with many ladies, but none of our beauties were there. But glad I was to see the Queen so well, who looks prettily – and methinks hath more life then before, since it is confessed of all that she miscarryed lately – Dr. Clerke telling me yesterday at Whitehall that he had the membranes and other vessels in his hands which she voided, and were perfect as ever woman's was that bore a child.

20. Up, and to the office – where, among other businesses, Mr. Evelyn's proposition about public Infirmarys was read and agreed on, he being there. And at noon I took him home to dinner, being desirous of keeping my acquaintance with him; and a most excellent-humourd man I still find him, and mighty knowing. After dinner I took him by coach to Whitehall, and there he and I

parted; and I to my Lord Sandwiches, where, coming and bolting into the dining-room, I there found Capt. Ferrer going to christen a child of his, born yesterday, and I came just pat to be a godfather, along with my Lord Hinchingbrooke and Madam Pierce my valentine – which for that reason I was pretty well contented with – though a little vexed to see myself so beset with people to spend my money, as, she for a Valentine, and little Mrs. Tooker, who is come to my house this day from Greenwich, and will cost me 20s., my wife going out with her this afternoon, and now this Christening. Well, by and by the child is brought, and christened Katharine. And I this day on this occasion drank a glass of wine, which I have not professedly done these two years I think – but a little in the time of the sickness. After that done, and gone and kissed the mother in bed – I away to Westminster hall and there hear that Mrs. Lane is come to town. So I stayed loitering up and down, till anon she comes and agreed to meet at Swayns; and there I went anon and she came, but stayed but little, the place not being private. I have not seen her since before the plague. So thence parted, and rencontrai à her last logis, and in that place did hazer what I tena a mind para faire con her. At last she desired to borrow money of me, 5l, and would pawn gold with me for it; which I accepted, and promised in a day or two to supply her. So away home to the office, and thence home. So to bed – a little troubled that I have been at two houses this afternoon with Mrs. Lane that were formerly shut up of the plague.

21. Up, and with Sir J. Mennes to Whitehall by his coach, by the way talking of my brother John, to get a spiritual promotion for him, which I now am to look after, forasmuch as he is shortly to be Maister in Arts, and writes me this week a Latin letter that he is to go into Orders this Lent. There to the Duke's chamber and find our fellows discoursing there on our business; so I was sorry to come late, but no hurt was done thereby. Here the Duke, among other things, did bring out a book, of great antiquity, of some of the customs of the Navy about 100 years since, which he did lend us to read and deliver him back again. Thence I to the Exchequer, and there did strike my tallies for a quarter for Tanger and carried them home with me. And thence to Trinity house, being invited to an Elder Brother's feast. And there met and sat by Mr. Prin and had good discourse about the privileges of Parliament, which he says are few to the Commons' house, and those not examinable by them but only by the House of Lords. Thence with my Lord Bruncker to

Gresham College, the first time after the sickness that I was there, and the second time any met. And hear a good lecture of Mr. Hookes about the trade of Felt making, very pretty. And anon alone with me about art of drawing pictures by Prince Roberts rule and machine, and another of Dr. Wren's; but he says nothing doth like Squares, or, which is the best in the world, like a darke roome – which pleased me mightily. Thence with Povy home to my house, and there late, settling accounts with him – which was very troublesome to me. And he gone, found Mr. Hill below, who sat with me till late talking; and so away, and we to bed.

22. Up, and to the office, where sat all morning; at noon home to dinner, and thence by coach with my wife for ayre, principally for her. I alone stopped at Hales's, and there mightily am pleased with my wife's picture that is begun there – and with Mr. Hill's, though I must [own] I am not more pleased with it, now the face is finished, then I was when I saw the second time of sitting. Thence to my Lord Sandwiches, but he not within, but goes tomorrow. My wife to Mrs. Hunts, who is lately come to town, and grown mighty fat. I called her there, and so home – and late at the office, and so home to supper and bed. We are much troubled that the sickness in general (the town being so full of people) should be [up] by 3, and yet of the perticular disease of the plague, there should be 10 encrease.

23. Up betimes, and out of doors by 6 of the clock and walked (W. How with me) to my Lord Sandwiches, who did lie the last night at his house in Lincolns Inne fields – it being fine walking in the morning, and the streets full of people again. There I stayed, and the house full of people come to take leave of my Lord, who this day goes out of Towne upon his Embassy towards Spayne. And I was glad to find Sir W. Coventry to come, though I know it is only a piece of Courtshipp. I had much discourse with my Lord, he telling me how fully he leaves the King his friend. But we could not make an end of discourse, so I promised to wait upon [him] on Sunday at Cranborne. And took leave, and away thence to Mr. Hales's (with Mr. Hill and two of the Houblons, who came thither to speak with me) and there saw my wife's picture, which pleases me well; but Mr. Hills picture never a whit so well as it did before it was finished, which troubled me – and I begin to doubt the picture of my Lady Peters my wife's takes her posture from, and which is an excellent picture, is not of his making, it is so master-like. I set them down at

the Change, and I home to the office, and at noon dined at home, and to the office again. Anon comes Mrs. Knipp to see my wife, who is gone out; so I fain to entertain her, and took her out by coach to look my wife at Mrs. Pierces and Unthankes, but find her not; so back again, and then my wife comes home, having been buying of things. And at home I spent all the night talking with this baggage and teaching her my song of *Beauty retire,* which she sings and makes go most rarely, and a very fine song it seems to be. She also entertained me with repeating many of her own and others' parts of the playhouse, which she doth most excellently; and tells me the whole practices of the playhouse and players, and is in every respect most excellent company. So I supped, and was merry at home all the evening, and the rather it being my Birthday, 33 years – for which God be praised that I am in so good a condition of health and state and everything else as I am, beyond expectation in all. So she to Mrs. Turner's to lie, and we to bed – mightily pleased to find myself in condition to have these people come about me, and to be able to entertain them and have the pleasure of their qualities, then which no man can have more in this world.

25. *Lords day.* My wife up between 3 and 4 of the clock in the morning to dress herself, and I about 5, and were all ready to take coach, she and I and Mercer a little past 5; but to our trouble, the coach did not come till 6. Then, with our coach of four horses I hire on purpose, and Lashmore to ride by, we through the City, it being clear day, to Branford, and so to Windsor (Capt. Ferrer overtaking us at Kensington, being to go with us) and here drank; and so through, making no stay, to Cranborne about 11 a-clock, and found my Lord and the ladies at a sermon in the house – which being ended, we to them; and all the company glad to see us, and mighty merry to dinner. Here was my Lord, and Lord Hinchingbrooke and Mr. Sidny – Sir Ch. Herbert and Mr. Carteret – my Lady Carteret, my Lady Jemimah, and Lady Slaning. After dinner to talk to and again, and then to walk in the Parke, my Lord and I alone, talking upon these heads – first, he hath left his business of the prizes as well as is possible for him, having cleared himself before the Commissioners by the King's commands, so that nothing or little is to be feared from that point – he goes fully assured, he tells me, of the King's favour. That upon occasion I may know, I desired to know his friends I may trust to. He tells me, but that he is not yet in England but continues this summer in Ireland,

my Lord Orrery is his father almost in affection. He tells me, my Lord of Suffolke – Lord Arlington – Archbishop of Canterbury – Lord Treasurer – Mr. Atturny Mountagu – (Sir Tho. Clifford in the House of Commons), Sir G. Carteret, and some others I cannot presently remember, are friends that I may rely on for him. He tells me my Lord Chancellor seems his very good friend, but doubts that he may not think him as much a servant of the Duke of York's as he would have him; and endeed my Lord tells me he hath lately made it his business to be seen studious of the King's favour, and not of the Duke's, and by the King will stand or fall – for factions there are, as he tells me, and God knows how high they may come. The Duke of Albemarles post is so great, having had the name of bringing in the King, that he is like to stand; or, if it were not for him, God knows in what troubles we might be from some private factions, if an army could be got into another hand, which God forbid. It is believed that though Mr. Coventry be in appearance so great against the Chancellor, yet that there is a good understanding between the Duke[1] and him. He dreads the issue of this year, and fears there will be some very great revolutions* before his coming back again. He doubts it is needful for him to have a pardon for his last year's action,[2] all which he did without commission, and at most but the King's private single word for that of Bergen; but he dares not ask it at this time, lest it should make them think that there is something more in it then yet they know; and if it should be denied, it would be of very ill consequence. He says also, if it should in Parliament be enquired into, the selling of Dunkirke (though the Chancellor was the man that would have it sold to France, saying the King of Spain had no money to give for it), yet he will be found to have been the greatest adviser of it – which he is a little apprehensive may be called upon this Parliament. He told me it would not be necessary for him to tell me his debts, because he thinks I know them so well. The Duke hath for this week or two been very kind to him, more then lately, and so others; which he thinks is a good sign of fair weather again. He says the Archbishop of Canterbury hath been very kind to him, and hath plainly said to him that he and all the world knows the difference between his judgment and brains and the Duke of Albema[r]les – and then calls my Lady Duchess the veriest slut and drudge, and the foulest word

1. The Duke of York.
2. The prize goods affair.

2. The Diary manuscript

3. *(above)* 25 September 1660. 'To the office. . . and went away' (see p. 81)

4. *(below)* 5–8 June 1668. Note-form passage (see p. 921)

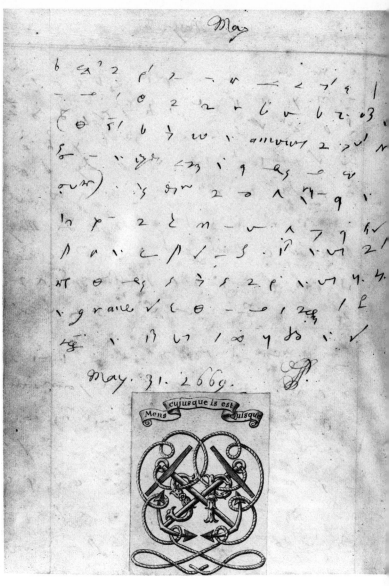

May. 31. 2669.

25. The Diary manuscript: the last page, with Pepys's end bookplate

that can be spoke of a woman almost. My Lord having walked an hour with me talking thus, and going in, and my Lady Carteret not suffering me to go back again tonight, my Lord to walk again with me about some of this and other discourse; and then in a-doors and to talk, he alone with my Lady Carteret, and I with the young ladies and gentlemen, who played on the guittarr and mighty merry, and anon to supper; and then my Lord going away to write, the young gentlemen to flinging cushions and other mad sports. At this late, till towards 12 at night; and then being sleepy, I and my wife in a passage-room to bed, and slept not very well, because of noise.

26.    Called up about 5 in the morning, and my Lord upp and took coach a little after 6, very kindly, of me and the whole company. Then I in, and my wife up and to visit my Lady Slaning in her bed, and there sat three hours, with Lady Jemimah with us, talking and laughing. Here stayed till 9 a-clock almost, and then took coach, with so much love and kindness from my Lady Carteret, Lady Jemimah, and Lady Slaning, that it joys my heart (and when I consider the manner of my going hither, with a coach and four horses, and servants and a woman with us, and coming hither, being so much made of, and used with that state, and then going to Windsor and being shown all that we were there, and had wherewith to give everybody something for their pains, and then going home, and all in fine weather, and no fears nor cares upon me, I do think myself obliged to think myself happy, and do look upon myself at this time in the happiest occasion a man can be; and whereas we take pains in expectation of future comfort and ease, I have taught myself to reflect upon myself at present as happy and enjoy myself in that consideration, and not only please myself with thoughts of future wealth, and forget the pleasures we at present enjoy).

So took coach and to Windsor to the guarter, and thither sent for Dr. Childe – who came to us, and carried us to St. Georges Chapel and there placed us among the Knights' Stalls (and pretty the observation, that no man, but a woman, may sit in a Knight's place where any brasse-plates are set). And hither comes cushions to us, and a young singing-boy to bring us a copy of the Anthemne to be sung. And here, for our sakes, had this anthem and the great service sung extraordinary, only to entertain us. It is a noble place endeed, and good Quire of voices. Great bowing by all the people, the poor Knights perticularly, to the Alter. After prayers, we to see the plate of the Chapel and the Robes of Knights, and a man to show us the banners of the several Knights in being, which hang up over the stalls. And so to other discourse, very pretty, about that Order. Was shown where the late [King] is buried, and King Henry the 8, and my Lady Seymour. This being done, to the King's house and to observe the neatness and contrivance of the house and gates; it is the most Romantique castle that is in the world. But Lord, the prospect that is in the Balcone in the Queen's lodgings, and the Tarrace and walk, are strange things to consider, being the best in the world, sure. Infinitely satisfied, I and my wife with all this; she being in all points mightily pleased too, which added to my pleasure. And so giving a great deal of money to this and that man and woman, we to our tavern and there dined, the Doctor with us; and so took coach and away to Eaton, the Doctor with me. At Eaton I left my wife in the coach, and he and I to the college and there find all mighty fine. The school good, and the custom pretty of boys cutting their names in the shuts of the window when they go to Cambrige; by which many a one hath lived to see himself Provost and Fellow, that had his name in the window standing. To the hall, and there find the boys' verses, *De peste*; it being their custom to make verses at Shrovetide. I read several, and very good they were, and better I think then ever I made when I was a boy – and in rolls as long and longer then the whole hall by much. Here is a picture of Venice hung up, given, and a Monument made of Sir H. Wottons giving it, to the College. Thence to the Porters, in the absence of the Butler, and did drink of the College beer, which is very good, and went into the back fields to see the scholars play. Thence took leave of the Doctor; and so took coach, and finely, but sleepy, away home, and got thither about 8 at night; and after a little at my office, I to bed. And an hour after was waked with my wife's quarrelling with Mercer, at which I was angry, and my wife and I fell out – but with much ado to sleep again, I beginning to practise more temper, and to give her her way.

27. Up, and after a harsh word or two, my wife and I good friends; and so up and to the office, where all the morning. At noon, late to dinner, my wife gone out to Hales's about her picture. And after dinner I after her, and do mightily like her picture and think it will be as good as my Lady Peters's. So home, mightily pleased, and there late at business; and so home and set down my three last days' Journalls, and so to bed – overjoyed to think of the pleasure of

the last Sunday and yesterday, and my ability to bear the charge of those pleasures – and with profit too – by obliging my Lord and reconciling Sir G. Carteret's family.

28.    *Ashwendsday*. Up, and after doing a little business at my office, I walked (it being a most curious dry and cold morning) to Whitehall; and there I went into the parke, and meeting Sir Ph. Warwicke, took a turn with him in the Pell Mell, talking of the melancholy posture of affairs, where everybody is snarling one at another, and all things put together look ominously. This new Act,[1] too, putting us out of a power of raising money – so that he fears as I do, but is fearful of enlarging in that discourse of a whole confusion in everything, and the State and all. We appointed another time to meet to talk of the business of the Navy alone, seriously, and so parted and I to Whitehall; and there we did our business with the Duke of Yorke, and so parted and walked to Westminster hall, where I stayed talking with Mrs. Michell and Howlett long, and her daughter, which is become a mighty pretty woman; and thence, going out of the hall, was called to by Mrs. Martin. So I went to her, and bought two bands and so parted, and by and by met at her chamber and there did what I would; and so away home, and there find Mrs. Knipp and we dined together, she the pleasantest company in the world. After dinner I did give my wife money to lay out on Knipp, 20*s.*, and I abroad to Whitehall to visit Coll. Norwood and then Sir G. Carteret, with whom I have brought myself right again, and he very open to me. Is very melancholy, and matters, I fear, go down with him; but he seems most afeared of a general catastrophe to the whole Kingdom, and thinks, as I fear, that all things will come to nothing. Thence to the Palace yard to the Swan and there stayed till it was dark; and then to Mrs. Lanes and there lent her 5*l*, upon 4*l* 01*s*. in gold – and then did what I would with her; and I perceive she is come to be very bad and offers anything, that it is dangerous to have to do with her; nor will I see any more a good while. Thence by coach home and to the office, where a while; and then betimes to bed, by 10 a-clock, sooner then I have done many a day. And thus ends this month, with my mind full of resolution to apply myself better, from this time forward, to my business then I have done within these six or eight days – visibly to my prejudice, both in quiet of mind and

---

1. The 'Additional Aid'.

setting backward of my business, that I cannot give a good account of it as I ought to do.

# –✣MARCH✣–

1. Up, and to the office and there all the morning sitting; and at noon to dinner with my Lord Brouncker, Sir W. Batten, and Sir W. Penn at the White Horse in Lumbard street – where, God forgive us, good sport with Capt. Cockes having his maid sick of the plague a day or two ago, and sent to the pest-house, where she now is – but he will not say anything but that she is well. But, blessed be God, a good Bill this week we have – being but 237 in all, and 42 of the plague, and of them, but 6 in the City – though my Lord Brouncker says that these 6 are most of them in new parishes, where they were not the last week. Here was with us also Mr. Williamson, who the more I know, the more I honour. Thence I slipped after dinner without notice home, and there close to my business at my office till 12 at night, having with great comfort returned to my business by some fresh vows, in addition to my former and more severe; and a great joy it is to me to see myself in a good disposition to business. So home to supper, and to my journall and to bed.

2. Up, as I have of late resolved, before 7 in the morning, and to the office, where all the morning; among other things, setting my wife and Mercer with much pleasure to work upon the ruling of some paper for the making of books for pursers, which will require a great deal of work, and they will earn a good deal of money by it – the hopes of which makes them work mighty hard. At noon dined, and to the office again; and about 4 a-clock took coach and to my Lord Treasurer's, and thence to Sir Ph. Warwicke's new house by appointment, there to spend an hour in talking; and we were together above an hour, and very good discourse about the state of the King as to money, and perticularly, in that point, of the Navy. He endeavours hard to come to a good understanding of Sir. G. Carteret's accounts. And by his discourse, I find Sir G. Carteret must be brought to it, and he is a madman that he doth not do it of himself, for the King expects the Parliament will call upon him for his promise of giving an account of the money, and he will be ready

for it, which cannot be, I am sure, without Sir G. Carteret's accounts be better understood then they are. Thence by coach, calling at my bookseller's, and carried home 10*l*-worth of books, all I hope I shall buy a great while. There by appointment find Mr. Hill come to sup and take his last leave of me;[1] and by and by in comes Mr. James Houbland to bear us company, a man I love mightily, and will not lose his acquaintance. He told me in my eare this night what he and his brothers have resolved to give me, which is 200*l* for helping them out with two or three ships – a good sum, and that which I did believe they would give me, and I did expect little less. Here we talked, and very good company till late, and then took leave of one another; and endeed I am heartily sorry for Mr. Hill's leaving us – for he is a very worthy gentleman, as most I know – God give him a good voyage and success in his business. Thus we parted, and my wife and I to bed, heavy for the loss of our friend.

4. *Lords day*. And all day at my Tanger and private accounts, having neglected them since Christmas; which I hope I shall never do again, for I find the inconvenience of it, it being ten times the labour to remember and settle things; but I thank God I did it at last, and brought them all fine and right; and I am, I think, by all appears to me (and I am sure I cannot be 10*l* wrong), worth above 4600*l*; for which the Lord be praised, being the biggest sum I ever was worth yet.

6. Up betimes, and did much business before office-time. Then to the office and there till noon, and so home to dinner, and to the office again till night. In the evening, being at Sir W. Batten's, stepped in (for I have not used to go thither a great while); I find my Lord Bruncker and Mrs. Williams, and they would of their own accord, though I had never obliged them (nor my wife neither) with one visit for many of theirs, go see my house and my wife; which I showed them, and made them welcome with wine and China oranges (now a great rarity since the war; none to be had), there being also Capt. Cocke and Mrs. Turner, who had never been in my house since I came to the office before, and Mrs. Carcasse, wife of Mr. Carcasse's. My house happened to be mighty clean and did me great honour, and they mightily pleased with it. They gone, I to the office and did some business; and then home to supper and to

1. He was about to go to Portugal as the Houblons' agent.

bed, my mind troubled through a doubtfulness of my having incurred Sir W. Coventry's displeasure by not having waited on him since his coming to town, which is a mighty fault and that I can bear the fears of the bad effects of till I have been with him, which shall be tomorrow, God willing. So to bed.

7. Up betimes and to St. James's, thinking Mr. Coventry had lain there, but he doth not, but at Whitehall; so thither I went, and had as good a time as heart could wish; and after an hour in his chamber about public business, he and I walked up; and the Duke being gone abroad, we walked an hour in the Matted Gallery, he of himself beginning to discourse of the unhappy differences between him and my Lord of Sandwich, and from the beginning to the end did run through all passages wherein my Lord hath at any time gathered any dissatisfaction, and cleared himself to me most honourably; and in truth, I do believe he doth as he says. And when I said I was jealous of myself, that having now come to such an income as I am by his favour, I should not be found to do as much service as might deserve it, he did assure me he thinks it not too much for me, but thinks I deserve it as much as any man in England. All this discourse did cheer my heart, and sets me right again, after a good deal of melancholy, out of fears of his disinclination to me upon the differences with my Lord Sandwich and Sir G. Carteret; but I am satisfied thoroughly, and so went away quite another man, and by the grace of God will never lose it again by my folly in not visiting and writing to him as I used heretofore to do. Thence by coach to the Temple; and home and to writing and hear my boy play on the lute, and a turn with my wife pleasantly in the garden by moonshine, my heart being in great peace. And so home to supper and to bed. The King and Duke are to go tomorrow to Audly end in order to the seeing and buying of it of my Lord Suffolke.

8. Up betimes and to the office, where all the morning – sitting; and did discover three or four fresh instances of Sir W. Pen's old cheating dissembling tricks – he being as false a fellow as ever was born. Thence with Sir W. Batten and Lord Brouncker to the White horse in Lumberd street, to dine with Capt. Cocke upon perticular business of Canvas to buy for the King. And here by chance I saw the mistress of the house I have heard much of; and a very pretty woman she is endeed – and her husband the simplest-looked fellow and old that ever I saw. After dinner I took coach and away to

Hales's, where my wife is sitting; and endeed, her face and neck, which are now finished, do so please me, that I am not myself almost, nor was not all the night after, in writing of my letters, in consideration of the fine picture that I shall be maister of. Thence home and to the office, where very late, and so home to supper and to bed.

9. Up, and being ready, to the Cockepitt – to make a visit to the Duke of Albemarle; and to my great joy find him the same man to me that heretofore, which I was in great doubt of through my negligence in not visiting of him a great while; and having now set all to rights there, I am in mighty ease in my mind, and I think shall never suffer matters to run so far backward again, as I have done of late with reference to my neglecting him and Sir W. Coventry. Thence by water down to Deptford, where I met my Lord Brouncker and Sir W. Batten by agreement, and to measuring Mr. Castles new third-rate ship, which is to be called the *Defyance*. And here I had my end, in saving the King some money and getting myself some experience in knowing how they do measure ships. Thence I left them and walked to Redriffe, and there taking water, was overtaken by them in their boat, and so they would have me in with them to Castle's house, where my Lady Batten and Madame Williams were, and there dined and a deal of doings. I had a good dinner, and counterfeit mirth and pleasure with them, but had but little, thinking how I neglected my business. Anon all home to Sir W. Batten's, and there, Mrs. Knipp coming, we did spend the even[ing] together very merry, she and I singing; and God forgive me, I do still see that my nature is not to be quite conquered, but will esteem pleasure above all things; though, yet in the middle of it, it hath reluctancy after my business, which is neglected by my following my pleasure. However, music and women I cannot but give way to, whatever my business is. They being gone, I to the office a while, and so home to supper and to bed.

10. Up and to the office, and there busy sitting till noon. I find at home Mrs. Pierce and Knipp, come to dine with me. We were mighty merry. And after dinner I carried them and my wife out by coach to the New Exchange, and there I did give my valentine, Mrs. Pierce, a dozen pair of gloves and a pair of silk stockings – and Knipp, for company sake (though my wife had by my consent laid out 20s. upon her the other day), six pair of gloves. Thence to

Hales's to have seen our pictures; but could not get in, he being abroad. And so to the cake-house hard by, and there sat in the coach with great pleasure and eat some fine cakes; and so carried them to Pierces, and away home. It is a mighty fine witty boy, Mrs. pierce's little boy. Thence home and to the office, where late writing letters; and leaving a great deal to do on Monday – I home to supper and to bed. The truth is, I do indulge myself a little the more pleasure, knowing that this is the proper age of my life to do it, and out of my observation that most men that do thrive in the world do forget to take pleasure during the time that they are getting their estate but reserve that till they have got one, and then it is too late for them to enjoy it with any pleasure.

14. To Hales's to see my wife's picture, which I like mighty well; and there had the pleasure to see how suddenly he draws the Heavens, laying a dark ground and then lightening it when and where he will. Thence to walk all alone in the fields behind Grays Inne, making an end of reading over my dear *Faber Fortunæ* of my Lord Bacon's; and thence, it growing dark, took two or three wanton turns about the idle places and lanes about Drury lane, but to no satisfaction, but a great fear of the plague among them; and so anon I walked by invitation to Mrs. Pierce's, where I find much good company; that is to say, Mrs. Pierce, my wife, Mrs. Worship and her daughter, and Harris the player and Knipp, and my wife and Mercer, and Mrs. Barbary Shelden, who is come this day to spend a week with my wife. And here, with music, we danced and sung and supped, and then to sing and dance till past one in the morning. And much mirth with Sir Anthony Apsly and one Coll. Sidny, who lodge in the house – and above all, they are mightily taken with Mrs. Knipp. Hence, weary and sleepy, we broke up, and I and my company home well by coach and to bed.

15. Lay till it was full time to rise, it being 8 a-clock, and so to the office and there sat till almost 3 a-clock, and then to dinner; and after dinner (my wife and Mercer and Mrs. Barbary being gone to Hales's before), I and my Cosen Anth. Joyce, who came on purpose to dinner with me. And he and I to discourse of our proposition of marriage between Pall and Harman. And upon discourse, he and I to Harman's house, and took him to a tavern hard by and we to discourse of our business, and I offered 500*l*. And he declares most ingenuously that his trade is not to be trusted on – that he however

needs no money, but would have her money bestowed on her – which I like well, he saying that he would adventure 2 or 300*l* with her. I like him as a most good-natured and discreet man, and I believe very cunning.* We came to this conclusion, for us to meet one another the next week, and then we hope to come to some end, for I did declare myself well satisfied with the mach. Thence to Hales, where I met my wife and people, and do find the picture, above all things, a most pretty picture and mighty like my wife – and I asked him his price: he says 14*l*; and the truth is, I think he doth deserve it. Thence toward London and home, and I to the office, where I did much, and betimes to bed, having had of late so little sleep, and there slept till 7 this morning.

17. Up, and to finish my Journall, which I had not sense enough the last night to make an end of – and thence to the office, where very busy all the morning. At noon home to dinner, and presently with my wife out to Hales's, where I am still infinitely pleased with my wife's picture. I paid him 14*l* for it, and 25*s*. for the frame, and I think it not a whit too dear for so good a picture. It is not yet quite finished and dry, so as to be fit to bring home yet. This day I begun to sit, and he will make me, I think, a very fine picture. He promises it shall be as good as my wife's, and I sit to have it full of shadows, and do almost break my neck looking over my shoulder to make the posture for him to work by. Thence home and to the office; and so home, having a great cold, and so my wife and Mrs. Barbary have very great ones – we are at a loss how we all come by it together. So to bed, drinking butter-ale. This day my W. Hewers comes from Portsmouth – and gives me an instance of another piece of knaveries of Sir W. Penn, who wrote to Comissioner Middleton that it was my negligence the other day he was not acquainted, as the Board directed, with our clerks coming down to the pay. But I need no new arguments to teach me that he is a false rogue to me, and all the world besides.

19. Up betimes, and upon a meeting extraordinary at the office most of the morning, with Lord Brouncker, Sir W. Coventry, Sir W. Penn – upon the business of the accounts – where, now we have got almost as much as we would have, we begin to lay all on the Controller – and I fear he will be run down with it, for he is every day less and less capable of doing business. Thence with my Lord Brouncker [and] Sir W. Coventry to the ticket office to see in what

little order things are there; and there it is a shame to see how the King is served. Thence to the Chamberlain of London and satisfy ourselfs more perticularly how much credit we have there, which proves very little. Thence to Sir Rob. Long's [in his] absence – about much the same business, but have not the satisfaction we would have there neither. So Sir W. Coventry parted, and my Lord and I to Mrs. Williams's and there I saw her closet, where endeed a great many fine things there are – but the woman I hate. Here we dined, and Sir J. Minnes came to us – and after dinner we walked to the King's playhouse, all in dirt, they being altering of the Stage to make it wider – but God knows when they will begin to act again. But my business here was to see the inside of the Stage and all the tiring roomes and Machines; and endeed it was a sight worthy seeing. But to see their clothes and the various sorts, and what a mixture of things there was, here a wooden leg, there a ruff, here a hobby-horse, there a Crowne, would make a man split himself to see with laughing – and perticularly Lacys wardrobe, and Shotrell's. But then again, to think how fine they show on the stage by candlelight, and how poor things they are to look now too nearhand, is not pleasant at all. The Machines are fine, and the paintings very pretty.

20. Up, and to the office, where busy all the morning. At noon dined in haste, and so my wife, Mrs. Barbary, Mercer, and I by coach to Hales, where I find my wife's picture now perfectly finished in all respects, and a beautiful picture it is, as almost I ever saw. I sat again, and had a great deal done; but whatever the matter is, I do not fancy that it hath the ayre of my face, though it will be a very fine picture. Thence home and to my business, being postnight; and so home to supper and to bed.

23. Up, and going out of my dressing-room when ready to go downstairs, I spied little Mrs. Tooker, my pretty little girl, which it seems did come yesterday to our house to stay a little while with us, but I did not know of it till now. I was glad of her coming, she being a very pretty child and now grown almost a woman. I out by 6 a-clock by appointment to Hales's, where we fell to my picture presently very hard, and it comes on a very fine picture – and very merry, pleasant discourse we had all the morning while he was painting. Anon comes my wife, and Mercer and little Tooker. And having done with me, we all to a picture drawer's hard by, Hales

carrying me to see some lanskip of a man's doing – but I do not [like] any of them, save only a piece of fruit, which endeed was very fine. Thence I to Westminster to the Chequer about a little business, and then to the Swan and there sent for a bit of meat and dined, and after dinner had opportunity of being pleased with Sarah; and so away to Westminster hall, and there Mrs. Michell tells me with great joy how little Betty Howlet is married to her young son Michell; which is a pretty odd thing, that he should so soon succeed in that match to his elder brother, that died of the plague – and to the house and trade entended for him. And more, they say that the girle hath heretofore said that she did love this little one more then the other brother that was entended her all along. I am glad of this match, and more that they are likely to live near me in Thames street – where I may see Betty now and then, whom I from a girl did use to call my second wife,[1] and mighty pretty she is. Thence by coach to Anthony Joyce to receive Harman's answer; which did trouble me to receive, for he now demands 800*l*, whereas he never made exception at the portion, but accepted of 500*l* – this I do not like; but however, I cannot much blame the man, if he thinks he can get more of another then of me. So home, and hard to my business at the office, where much business; and so home to supper and to bed.

24.    After dinner I to Whitehall to a committee for Tanger, where the Duke of York was – and I acquitted myself well in what I had to do. After the committee up, I had occasion to fallow the Duke into his lodgings into a chamber where the Duchesse was sitting to have her picture drawn by Lilly, who was there at work. But I was well pleased to see that there was nothing near so much resemblance of her face in his work, which is now the second, if not the third time, as there was of my wife's at the very first time. Nor do I think at last it can be like, the lines not being in proportion to those of her face. So home and to the office, where late; and so to bed.

25.    *Lady day and Sunday.* Up, and to my chamber, in my gown all the morning, about settling my papers there. At noon to dinner, where my wife's brother, whom I sent for to offer making him a muster-master and send to sea; which the poor man likes well of and will go, and it will be a good preferment to him – only

1. This suggests that Pepys's Elizabeth was known as Betty.

hazardous. I hope he will prove a good discreet man. After dinner, to my papers and Tanger accounts again till supper, and after supper, again to them; but by my mixing them, I know not how, my private and public accounts, it makes me mad to see how hard it is to bring them to be understood; and my head is confounded, that though I did swear to sit up till one a-clock upon them, yet I fear it will be to no purpose, for I cannot understand what I do or have been doing of them today.

29. All the morning hard at the office. At noon dined, and then out to Lumbard street to look after the getting in of some money that is lodged there of mine in Viner's hands, I having no mind to have it lie there longer. So back again and to the office, where, and at home, about public and private business and accounts till past 12 at night, and so to bed. This day poor Jane,[1] my old little Jane, came to us again, to my wife's and my great content; and we hope to take mighty pleasure in her, she having all the marks and qualities of a good and loving and honest servant – she coming by force away from the other place where she hath lived ever since she went from us, and at our desire – her late mistress having used all the stratagems she could to keep her.

30. To Hales's and there sat till almost quite dark upon working my gowne, which I hired to be drawn [in] – an Indian gown, and I do see all the reason to expect a most excellent picture of it. Thus home, and to my private accounts in my chamber till past one in the morning; and so to bed – with my head full of thoughts for my evening of all my accounts tomorrow, the latter end of the month; in which God give me good issue, for I never was in such a confusion in my life, and that in great sums.

31. All the morning at the office busy. At noon to dinner, and thence to the office and did my business there as soon as I could, and then home and to my accounts, where very late at them. But Lord, what a deal of do I have to understand any part of them. And in short, do what I could, I could not come to an understanding of them; but after I had thoroughly wearied myself, I was forced to go to bed and leave them, much against my will, and vow too; but I hope God will forgive me in it, for I have sat up these four nights till

1. Jane Birch.

past 12 at night to master them, but cannot. Thus ends this month – with my head and mind mightily full and disquiet because of my accounts, which I have let go too long and confounded my public with my private, that I cannot come to any liquidating of them. However, I do see that I must be grown richer then I was by a good deal the last month. Busy also I am in thoughts for a husband for my sister; and to that end, my wife and I have determined that she shall presently go into the country to my father and mother, and consider of a proffer made them for her in the country; which, if she likes, shall go forward.

# –❧ APRILL ❧–

1. *Lords day*. Up and abroad, and by coach to Charing cross to wait on Sir Ph. Howard – whom I found in bed, and he doth receive me very civilly. My request was about suffering my wife's brother to go to sea, and to save his pay in the Duke's guards – which, after a little difficulty, he did with great respect agree to. I find him a very fine-spoken gentleman, and one of great parts – and very courteous. Much pleased with this visit, I to Whitehall, where I met Sir G. Downing; and to discourse with him an hour about the Exchequer payments upon the late act, and informed myself of him thoroughly in my safety in lending 2000*l* to Sir W. Warren upon an order of his upon the Exchequer for 2602*l* – and I do purpose to do it. Thence, meeting Dr. Allen the physician, he and I and another walked in the park, a most pleasant warm day, and to the Queen's chapel – where I do not so dislike the music. Here I saw on a post an invitation to all good Catholics to pray for the soul of such a one, departed this life.

6. Up mighty betimes, upon my wife's going this day toward Brampton. I could not go to the coach with her, but W. Hewers did, and hath leave from me to go the whole day's journey with her. All the morning upon business at the office, and at noon dined; and Mrs. Hunt coming, lent her 5*l* on her occasions, and so carried her to axe yard end at Westminster and there left her – a good and understanding woman, and her husband, I perceive, thrives mightily in his business of the Excise. Thence to Mr. Hales, and there sat and my picture almost finished; which, by the word of Mr.

and Mrs. Pierce (who came in accidentally), is mighty like, and I am sure I am mightily pleased, both in the thing and the posture. Thence with them home a little, and so to Whitehall and there met by agreement with Sir St. Fox and Mr. Ashburnham, and discoursed the business of our Excize tallies – the former being Treasurer of the guards, and the other Cofferer of the King's household – I benefited much by their discourse. We came to no great conclusion upon our discourse; but parted, and I home, where all things methinks melancholy in the absence of my wife. This day great news of the Swedes declaring for us against the Dutch; and so far as that, I believe it.[1] After a little supper, to bed.

7. Lay pretty long today, lying alone and thinking on several businesses. So up to the office, and there till noon; thence with my Lord Brouncker home by coach to Mrs. Williams's, where Bab Allen[2] and Dr. Charleton dined. Bab and I sang, and were mighty merry as we could be there, where the rest of the company did not overplease. Thence took her by coach to Hales's, and there find Mrs. Pierce and her boy and Mary. She had done sitting the first time, and endeed her face is mighty like, at first dash. Thence took them to the cake-house, and there called in the coach for cakes, and drank; and thence I carried them to my Lord Chancellors new house to show them that, and all mightily pleased; thence set each down at home, and so I home to the office – where about 10 of the clock W. Hewers comes to me, to tell me that he left my wife well this morning at Bugden (which was great riding), and brings me a letter from her. She is very well got thither, of which I am heartily glad. After writing several letters, I home to supper and to bed. The Parliament, of which I was afeared of their calling us of the Navy to an account of the expense of money and stores, and wherein we were so little ready to give them a good answer. The Bishop of Munster, everybody says, is coming to peace with the Dutch, we having not supplied him with the monies promised him.

8. Up, and was in great trouble how to get a passage to Whitehall, it raining – and no coach to be had. So I walked to the Old Swan and there got a scull. To the Duke of Yorke, where we all met to hear the debate between Sir Tho. Allen and Mr. Wayth – the former

1. It was however untrue.
2. Mrs. Knepp.

complaining of the latter's ill-usage of him at the late pay of his ship – but a very sorry poor occasion he had for it. The Duke did determine it with great judgment, chiding both, but encouraging Wayth to continue to be a check to all Captains in anything to the King's right. And endeed I never did see the Duke do anything more in order, nor with more judgment, then he did pass the verdict in this business. The Court full this morning of the news of Tom Cheffins's death, the King's closet-keeper. He was well last night as ever, playing at tables in the House – and not very ill this morning, 6 a-clock; yet dead before 7 – they think of an impostume in his breast. But it looks fearfully among people nowadays, the plague, as we hear, increasing everywhere again. To the Chapel, but could not get in to hear well. But I had the pleasure once in my life to see an Ar[ch]bishop (this was of Yorke) in a pulpit. Then at a loss how to get home to dinner, having promised to carry Mrs. Hunt thither. At last got my Lord Hinchingbrooke's coach, he staying at Court; and so took her up in axe yard, and home and dined – and good discourse of the old matters of the Protector[1] and his family, she having a relation to them. The Protector lives in France; spends about 500*l* per annum. Thence carried her home again; and then to Court, and walked over to St. James's chapel, thinking to have heard a Jesuite preach but came too late. So got a hackney, and home and there to business. At night had Mercer comb my head; and so to supper, sing a psalm, and to bed.

9. Up betimes, and with my Joyner begun the making of the window in my boy's chamber bigger, purposing it shall be a room to eat and for have Musique in. To the office, where a meeting upon extraordinary business. At noon to the Change about more, and then home with Creed and dined, and then with him to the Committee of Tanger, where I got two or three things done I had a mind too – of convenience to me. Thence by coach to Mrs. Pierces, and with her and Knipp and Mrs. Pierce's boy and girl abroad, thinking to have been merry at Chelsey; but being come almost to the house by coach near the waterside, a house alone, I think the Swan – a gentleman walking by called to us to tell us that the house was shut up of the sickness. So we with great affright turned back, being holden to the gentleman, and went away (I for my part in great disorder) for Kensington; and there I spent about 30*s.* upon

1. Richard Cromwell.

the jades with great pleasure – and we sang finely, and stayed till about 8 at night, the night coming on apace; and so set them down at Pierce's, and so away home – where a while with Sir W. Warren about business, and then to bed.

13. Up, being called up by my wife's brother, for whom I have got a commission from the Duke of Yorke for muster-master of one of the Divisions of which Harman is Rereadmirall, of which I am glad as well as he. After I had acquainted him with it and discoursed a little of it, I went forth and took him with me by coach to the Duke of Albemarle; who being not up, I took a walk with Balty into the park, and to the Queen's chapel, it being Goodfriday; where people were all upon their knees, very silent – but it seems no Masse this day. So back, and waited on the Duke and received some commands of his; and so by coach to Mr. Hales's – where it is pretty strange to see that his second doing, I mean the second time of her sitting, is less like Mrs. Pierce then the first – and yet I am confident will be most like her, for he is so curious that I do not see how it is possible for him to mistake. Here, he and I presently resolved of going to Whitehall, to spend an hour in the galleries there among the pictures; and we did so to my extraordinary satisfaction, he showing me the difference in the painting; and when I come more and more to distinguish and observe the workmanship, I do not find so many good things as I thought there was – but yet great difference between the works of some and others – and while my head and judgment was full of these, I would go back again to his house to see his pictures. And endeed, though I think at first sight some difference doth open, yet very inconsiderably; but that I may judge his to be very good pictures. Here we fell into discourse of my picture, and I am for his putting out the Lanskipp, though he says it is very well done; yet I do judge it will be best without it, and so it shall be put out – and be made a plain sky, like my wife[s] picture, which will be very noble.

15. *Easter day.* Up, and by water to Westminster to the Swan to lay down my cloak, and there found Sarah alone; with whom after I had stayed awhile, I to Whitehall chapel; and there coming late, could hear nothing of the Bishop of London's sermon; so walked into the park to the Queen's chapel and there heard a good deal of their mass and some of their Musique, which is not so contemptible, I think, as our people would make it, it pleasing me very well –

and indeed, better then the Anthemne I heard afterward at Whitehall at my coming back. I stayed till the King went down to receive the Sacrament; and stood in his Closett with a great many others and there saw him receive it – which I did never see the manner of before. But do see very little difference between the degree of the ceremonies used by our people in the administration thereof and that in the Roman church, saving that methought our chapel was not so fine, nor the manner of doing it so glorious, as it was in the Queenes chapel. Thence walked to Mr. Pierce's and there dined, I alone with him and her and their children. Very good company, and good discourse, they being able to tell me all the businesses of the Court – the Amours and the mad doings that are there – how for certain, Mrs. Steward doth do everything now with the King that a mistress should do – and that the King hath many bastard children that are known and owned, besides the Duke of Monmouth. After a great deal of this discourse – I walked thence into the park, with her little boy James with me, who is the wittiest boy, and the best company in the world. And so back again through Whitehall both coming and going. And people did generally take him to be my boy – and some would ask me.

17. Up and to the office, where all the morning. At noon dined at home, my brother Balty with me, who is fitting himself to go to sea. So I after dinner to my accounts, and did proceed a good way in settling them; and thence to the office, where all the afternoon late writing my letters and doing business. But Lord, what a conflict I had with myself, my heart tempting me a thousand times to go abroad about some pleasure or other, notwithstanding the weather foul. However, I reproached myself with my weakness in yielding so much my judgment to my sense, and prevailed with difficulty; and did not budge, but stayed within and to my great content did a great deal of business; and so home to supper and to bed. This day I am told that Mall Davis, the pretty girl that sang and danced so well at the Duke's house, is dead.

18. And by coach with Sir W. Batten and Sir Tho. Allen to Whitehall: and there, after attending the Duke as usual, and there concluding of many things preparative to the Prince and the Generalls going to sea on Monday next – Sir W. Batten and Sir Tho. Allen and I to Mr. Lillys the painter's, and there saw the heads, some finished and all begun, of the Flaggmen in the late great fight

with the Duke of Yorke against the Dutch. The Duke of York hath
them done to hang in his chamber, and very finely they are done
endeed. There is the Prince's – Sir G. Askues, Sir Tho. Teddiman's
– Sir Chr. Mings, Sir Joseph Jordan, Sir Wm. Barkely, Sir Tho.
Allen, and Captain Harman's, as also the Duke of Albemarles – and
will be my Lord Sandwiche's, Sir W. Pen's, and Sir Jerem. Smiths.
Being very well satisfied with this sight, and other good pictures
hanging in the house, we parted; and I left them, and [to] pass away
a little time went to the printed picture-seller's in the way thence to
the Exchange; and there did see great plenty of fine prints but did
not buy any, only a print of an old pillar in Rome, made for a Navall
Triumph, which for the antiquity of the shape of ships I buy an
keep. Thence to the Exchange, that is, the New Exchange, and
looked over some play-books, and entend to get all the late new
plays. So to Westminster and there at the Swan got a bit of meat and
dined alone, and so away toward King's street; and spying out of
my coach Jane that lived heretofore at Jervas my barber's, I went a
little further, and stopped and went on foot back and overtook her
taking water at Westminster bridge and spoke to her; and she telling
me whither she was going, I over the water and met her at
Lambeth, and there drank with her, she telling me how he that was
so long her servant did prove to be a married man, though her
maister told me (which she denies) that he had lain with her several
times at his house. There left her, sin hazer alguna cosa con ella; and
so away by boat to the Change and took coach and to Mr. Hales,
where he would have persuaded me to have had the landskip stand
in my picture; but I like it not and will have it otherwise, which I
perceive he doth not like so well – however, is so civil as to say it
shall be altered. Thence away to Mrs. Pierces, who was not at
home, but gone to my house to visit me with Mrs. Knipp. I
therefore took up the little girl Betty and my maid Mary that now
lives there. And to my house, where they had been but were gone;
so in our way back again, met them coming back again to my house
in Cornehill, and there stopped, laughing at our pretty misfortunes;
and so I carried them to Fish street and there treated them with
prawns and lobsters; and it beginning to grow dark, we away; but
the jest is, our horses would not draw us up the Hill, but we were
fain to light and stay till the coachman had made them draw down
to the bottom of the hill, thereby warming their legs; and then they
came up cheerfully enough, and we got up and I carried them home;
and coming home, called at my paper ruler's and there found black*

Nan, which pleases me mightily; and having saluted her again and again, away home and to bed – apres ayant tocado les mamelles de Mercer, que eran ouverts, con grand plaisir. So to bed. In all my riding in the coach, and intervals, my mind hath been full these three weeks of setting to music *It is decreed* &c..

19.  Lay long in bed; so to the office, where all the morning. At noon dined with Sir W. Warren at the Pope's head. So back to the office, and there met with the Comissioners of the Ordnance, where Sir W. Pen, being almost drunk, vexed me, and the more because Mr. Chichly observed it with me – and it was a disparagement to the office. They gone, I to my office. Anon comes home my wife from Brampton – not looked for till Saturday; which will hinder me of a little pleasure, but I am glad of her coming. She tells me Palls business with Ensum is like to go on; but I must give, and she consents to it, another 100*l*. She says she doubts my father is in want of money, for rents come in mighty slowly. My mother grows very impatient and troublesome, and my father mighty infirm, through his old distemper – which all together makes me mighty thoughtful. Having heard all this, and bid her welcome, I to the office, where late; and so home, and after a little more talk with my wife, she to bed and I after her.

20.  Up, and after an hour or two's talk with my poor wife, who gives me more and more content every day then other, I abroad by coach to Westminster; and there met with Mrs. Martin, and she and I over the water to Stangate; and after a walk in the fields, to the King's head and there spent an hour or two with pleasure with her, and eat a tansy and so parted. And I to the New Exchange, there to get a list of all the modern plays – which I entend to collect and to have them bound up together. Thence to Mr. Hales; and there, though against his perticular mind, I had my landskip done out, and only a heaven made in the room of it; which though it doth not please me thoroughly now it is done, yet it will do better then as it was before.

21.  Up betimes and to the office, there to prepare some things against the afternoon, for discourse about the business of the pursers and settling the pursers' matters of the fleet according to my proposition. By and by the office sat; and they being up, I continued at the office to finish my matters against the meeting before the

Duke this afternoon; so home about 3 to clap a bit of meat in my mouth, and so away with Sir W. Batten to Whitehall – and there to the Duke; but he being to go abroad to take the ayre, he dismissed us presently – without doing anything till tomorrow morning. So my Lord Brouncker and I down to walk in the garden, it being a mighty hot and pleasant day; and there was the King, who, among others, talked to us a little; and among other pretty things, he swore merrily that he believed the Ketch that Sir W. Batten bought the last year at Colchester was of his own getting, it was so thick to its length. Another pleasant thing he said of Chr. Pett, commending him that he will not alter his moulds of his ships upon any man's advice ("as", says he, "Comissioner Taylor, I fear, doth of his *New London*, that he makes it differ, in hopes of mending the *Old London*, built by him): for," says he, "he finds that God hath put him into the right, and so will keep in it while he is in. And," says the King, "I am sure it must be God put him in, for no art of his own ever could have done it" – for it seems he cannot give a good account of what he doth as an Artist.

23.     Walked to Westminster hall; and after a little stay there, I took coach and away home, in my way asking in two or three places the worth of pearl – I being now come to the time that I have long ago promised my wife a necklace.

27.     Up (taking Balty with me, who lay at my house last [night] in order to his going away today to sea with the pursers of the *Henery*, whom I appointed to call him). Abroad to many several places about several businesses: to my Lord Treasurer's, Westminster, and I know not where. At noon to the Change a little, and then bespoke some maps to hang in my new Roome (my boy's room), which will be very pretty. Home to dinner; and after dinner to the hanging up of maps and other things for the fitting of the room, and now it will certainly be one of the handsomest and most useful rooms in my house – so that what with this room and the room on my leads, my house is half as good again as it was. All this afternoon about this, till I was so weary, and it was late, I could do no more, but finished the room; so I did not get out to the office all the day long. At night spent a good deal of time with my wife and Mercer, teaching them a song; and so after supper, to bed.

28.     I very busy all the afternon till night – among other things,

writing a letter to my brother John, the first I have done since my being angry with him; and that so sharp a one too, that I was sorry almost to send it when I had wrote it; but it is preparative to my being kind to him, and sending for him up hither when he hath passed his degree of Maister in Arts. So home to supper and to bed.

29. *Lords day*. Up and to church, where Mr. Mills; a lazy, simple sermon upon the Devil's having no right to anything in this world. So home to dinner; and after dinner I and my boy down by water to Redriffe; and thence walked to Mr. Evelin's, where I walked in his garden till he came from church, with great pleasure reading Ridlys discourse all my way going and coming, upon the Civill and Ecclesiastical Law. He being come home, he and I walked together in the garden with mighty pleasure, he being a very ingenious man, and the more I know him, the more I love him. His chief business with me was to propose having my Cosen Tho. Pepys in Commission of the Peace; which I do not know what to say to till I speak with him, but should be glad of it – and will put him upon it. Thence walked back again, reading; and so took water and home, where I find my Uncle and Aunt Wight and supped with them upon my leads with mighty pleasure and mirth. And they being gone, I mighty weary to bed, after having my hair of my head cut shorter, even close to my skull, for coolness, it being mighty hot weather.

30. Up, and being ready to finish my journalls for four days past – to the office, where busy all the morning. At noon dined alone, my wife gone abroad to conclude about her necklace of pearl. I after dinner to even all my accounts of this month; and, bless God, I find myself, notwithstanding great expenses of late – *viz*., 80*l* now to pay for a necklace – near 40*l* for a set of chairs and couch – near 40*l* for my three pictures – yet I do gather, and am now worth 5200*l*. My wife comes home by and by, and hath pitched upon a necklace with three rows, which is a very good one, and 80*l* is the price. In the evening with my [wife] and Mercer by coach to take the ayre as far as Bow, and eat and drank in the coach by the way, and with much pleasure and pleased with my company: at night home and up to the leads; but were, contrary to expectation, driven down again with a stink, by Sir W. Pen's emptying of a shitten pot in their house of office close by; which doth trouble me, for fear it do hereafter annoy me. So down to sing a little, and then to bed. So ends this month, with great layings-out – good health and gettings, and

advanced well in the whole of my estate; for which God make me thankful.


# –✣MAY✣–

1. Up, and all the morning at the office. At noon my Cosen Tho. Pepys did come to me to consult about the business of his being a Justice of the Peace, which he is much against; and among other reasons, tells me as a confidence that he is not free to exercise punishment according to the act against Quakers and other people, for religion. Nor doth he understand Latin, and so is not capable of the place as formerly, now all warrants do run in Latin. Not is he in Kent, though he be of Deptford parish, his house standing in Surry. However, I did bring him to encline toward it if he be pressed to take it. I do think it may be some repute to me to have my kinsman in commission there – especially if he behave himself to content in the country. He gone, and my wife gone abroad, I out also, to and fro to see and be seen; among others, to find out in Thames street where Betty Howlett is come to live, being married to Mrs. Michells son – which I did about the Old Swan, but did not think fit to go thither or see them. Thence by water to Redriffe, reading a new French book my Lord Brouncker did give me today, *L'histoire amoureuse des Gaules*, being a pretty Libell against the amours of the Court of France. I walked up and down Deptford yard, where I had not been since I came from living at Greenwich – which is some months. There I met with Mr. Castle and was forced against my will to have his company back with me. So we walked and drank at the Halfway house, and so to his house, where I drank a cup of Syder; and so home – where I find Mr. Norbury, newly come to town, come to see us. After he gone, my wife tells me the ill News that our Su is sick, and gone to bed with great pain in her head and back – which troubles us all. However, we to bed, expecting what tomorrow would produce. She hath, we conceive, wrought a little too much, having neither maid nor girl to help her.

2. Up, and find the girl better, which we are glad of. I with Sir W. Batten to Whitehall by coach. There attended the Duke as usual. Thence with Capt. Cocke, whom I met there, to London to my office to consult about serving him in getting him some money, he

being already tired of his slavery to my Lord Brouncker and the charge it costs him, and gets no manner of courtesy from him for it. He gone, I home to dinner. Find the girl yet better, so no fear of being forced to send her out of doors as we intended.

3. Up, and all the morning at the office. At noon home, and contrary to my expectation find my little girl Su worse then she was, which troubled me; and the more to see my wife minding her painting, and not thinking of her house business (this being the first day of her beginning the second time to paint). This together made me froward, that I was angry with my wife and would not have Browne[1] to think to dine at my table with me always, being desirous to have my house to myself, without a stranger and Mechanique to be privy to all my concernments. Upon this my wife and I had a little disagreement, but it ended by and by. And then to send up and down for a nurse to take the girle home, and would have given anything; I offered to the only one that we could get 20s. per week, and we to find clothes and bedding and physic. And would have given 30s. as demanded, but desired an hour or two's time. So I away by water to Westminster and there sent for the girl's mother to Westminster hall to me; she came, and undertakes to get her daughter a lodging and nurse at next door to her, though she dare not, for the parish sake (whose sexton her husband is), to [take] her into her own house. Thence home, calling at my bookseller's and other trifling places, three or four, and so home. And in the evening the mother came, and with a nurse she hath got, who demanded, and I did agree at, xs. per week to take her. And so she away – and my house mighty uncouth, having so few in it, and we shall want a servant or two by it. And the truth is, my heart was a little sad all the afternoon, and jealous of myself. But she went, and we all glad of it. And so a little to the office; and so to home to supper and to bed.

4. Had a great fray with my wife again about Brown's coming to teach her to paint and sitting with me at table, which I will not yield to. I do thoroughly believe she means no hurt in it, but very angry we were; and I resolved all into my having my will done without disputing, be the reason what it will – and so I will have it. After dinner abroad again, and to the New Exchange about play-books –

---

1. Her drawing master.

and to Whitehall, thinking to have met Sir G. Carteret, but failed. So to the Swan at Westminster, and there spent quarter of an hour with Jane and thence away home. This evening, being weary of my late idle courses and the little good I shall do the King or myself in the office, I bound myself to very strict rules till Whitsunday next.

5. At the office all the morning. After dinner, upon a letter from the fleet from Sir W. Coventry, I did do a great deal of work for the sending away of the victuallers that are in the River &c. – too much to remember. Till 10 at night busy about letters and other necessary matters of the office. About 11, I home, it being a fine moonshine; and so my wife and Mercer came into the garden, and my business being done, we sang till about 12 at night with mighty pleasure to ourselfs and neighbours, by their Casements opening. And so home to supper and to bed.

7. Up betimes to set my victualling papers in order against Sir W. Coventry comes – which endeed makes me very melancholy, being conscious that I am much to seek in giving good answer to his queries about the victualling businesses. At the office mighty busy, and brought myself into a pretty plausible condition before Sir W. Coventry came, and did give him a pretty tolerable account of everything; and went with him unto the Victualling Office, where we sat and examined his businesses and state of the victualling of the fleet; which made me in my heart blush that I could say no more to it then I did or could – but I trust in God I shall never be in that condition again. We parted, and I with pretty good grace; and so home to dinner, where my wife troubled more and more with her swollen cheek. So to dinner, my sister-in-law with us, who I find more and more a witty woman. And then I to my Lord Treasurer's and the Exchequer about my Tanger businesses. And with mighty content passed by all things and persons, without so much as desiring any stay or loss of time with them, being by strong vow obliged on no occasion to stay abroad but my public offices. So home again, where I find Mrs. Pierce and Mrs. Ferrers come to see my wife. I stayed a little with them, being full of business; and so to the office, where busy till late at night; and so, weary – and a little conscious of my failures today, yet proud that the day is over without more observation on Sir W. Coventry's part; and so to bed and to sleep soundly.

8.   Up and to the office all the morning. At noon dined at home – my wife's cheek bad still. After dinner to the office again; and thither comes Mr. Downing the Anchor-smith, who had given me 50 pieces in gold the last month to speak for him to Sir W. Coventry for his being smith at Deptford. But after I had got it granted him, he finds himself not fit to go on with it, so lets it fall – so hath no benefit of my motion; I therefore in honour and conscience took him home, and though much to my grief, did yet willingly and forcibly force him to take it again, the poor man having no mind to have it. However, I made him take it, and away he went; and I glad I had given him so much cause to speak well of me. So to my office again late; and then home to supper to a good lobster with my wife; and then a little to my office again; and so to bed.

9.   Up by 5 a-clock, which I have not a long time done, and down the river by water to Deptford; among other things, to examine the state of Ironworke, in order to the doing something with reference to Downing that may induce him to return me the 50 pieces. Walked back again, reading of my civil law book. And so home and by coach to Whitehall, where we did our usual business before the Duke – and heard the Duke commend Deane's ship, the *Rupert*, before the *Defyance*, built lately by Castle, in hearing of Sir W. Batten, which pleased me mightily. Thence by water to Westminster and there looked after my Tanger Order; and so by coach to Mrs. Pierces, thinking to have gone to Hales's; but she was not ready, so away home and to dinner. So away to my Lord Treasurer's; and thence to Pierces, where I find Knipp and I took them to Hales's to see our pictures finished; which are very pretty, but I like not hers half so well as I thought at first, it being not so like, nor so well painted as I expected or as mine and my wife's are. Thence with them to Cornehill to call and choose a chimney-piece for Pierce's closet; and so home, where my wife in mighty pain, and mightily vexed at my being abroad with these women – and when they were gone, called them "whores" and I know not what; which vexed me, having been so innocent with them. So I with them to Mrs. Turner's and there sat with them a while; anon my wife sends for me; I come, and what was it but to scold at me, and she would go abroad to take the ayre presently, that she would. So I left my company and went with her to Bow, but was vexed and spoke not one word to her all the way, going nor coming – or being come home; but went up straight to bed. Half an hour after (she in the

coach leaning on me, as being desirous to be friends), she comes up, mighty sick with a fit of the Cholique and in mighty pain, and calls for me out of the bed; I rose and held her; she prays me to forgive her, and in mighty pain we put her to bed – where the pain ceased by and by; and so had some sparagus to our beds-side for supper, and very kindly afterward to sleep, and good friends in the morning.

10.    So up and to the office, where all the morning. At noon home to dinner, and there busy all the afternoon till past 6 a-clock; and then abroad with my wife by coach – who is now at great ease, her cheek being broke inward. We took with us Mrs. Turner, who was come to visit my wife, just as we were going out. A great deal of tittle-tattle discourse to little purpose; I finding her (though in other things a very discreet woman) as very a gossip, speaking of her neighbours, as anybody. Going out toward Hackny by coach for the ayre, the silly coachman carries us to Shorditch, which was so pleasant a piece of simplicity in him and us, that made us mighty merry. So back again late, it being wonderous hot all the day [and] night, and it lightening exceedingly all the way we went and came, but without Thunder. Coming home, we called at a little alehouse and had an eele pie, of which my wife eat part, and brought home the rest. So being come home, we to supper and so to bed. This day came our new cookmaid Mary, commended by Mrs. Batters.

12.    Up to the office very betimes to draw up a letter for the Duke of Yorke, relating to him the badness of our condition in this office for want of money. That being in good time done, we met at the office and there sat all the morning. At noon home, where I find my wife troubled still at my checking her last night in the coach in her long stories out of *Grand Cyrus*, which she would tell, though nothing to the purpose nor in any good manner. This she took unkindly, and I think I was to blame indeed – but she doth find, with reason, that in the company of Pierce – Knipp – or other women that I love, I do not value her, or mind her as I ought. However, very good friends by and by, and to dinner, and after dinner up to the putting our dining-room in order, which will be clean again anon, but not as it is to be, because of the pictures, which are not come home. To the office and did much business; in the evening to Westminster and Whitehall about business, and among other things, met Sir G. Downing on Whitehall bridge and there walked half an hour, talking of the success of the late new act; and

endeed it is very much that that hath stood really in the room of 800000*l* now since Christmas, being itself but 1250000*l*. And so I do really take it to be a very considerable thing done by him, for the beginning, end, and every part of it is to be imputed to him. So home by water, and there hard, till 12 at night, at work, finishing the great letter to the Duke of York against tomorrow morning; and so home to bed. This day came home again my girle Susan, her sickness proving an ague, and she had a fit as soon almost as she came home. The fleet is not yet gone from the Nore. The plague encreases in many places, and is 53 this week with us.

14.  Comes betimes a letter from Sir W. Coventry that he and Sir G. Carteret are ordered presently down to the fleet. I up, and saw Sir W. Penn gone also after them; and so I, finding it a leisure day, fell to making clean my closet in my office, which I did to my content, and set up my Platts again – being much taken also with Griffin's maid that did clean it – being a pretty maid. I left her at it and toward Westminster, myself with my wife, by coach; and meeting, took up Mr. Lovett the varnisher with us – who is a pleasant-speaking and humoured man, so my wife much taken with him, and a good deal of work I believe I shall procure him. I left my wife at the New Exchange, and myself to the Exchequer to look after my Tanger tallies; and there met Sir G. Downing, who showed me his present practice, now begun this day, to paste up upon the Exchequer door a note of what Orders upon the new Act are paid and now in paying. And my Lord of Oxford coming by also, took him and showed him his whole method of keeping his books, and everything of it, which endeed is very pretty; and at this day, there is assigned upon the Act 804000*l*. Thence at the New Exchange took up my wife again, and so home to dinner. After dinner to my office again to set things in order. In the evening, out with my wife and my aunt Wight to take the ayre, and happened to have a pleasant race between our Hackny coach and a gentleman's. At Bow we eat and drank, and so back again, it being very coole in the evening. Having set home my aunt and come home, I fell to examine my wife's kitchen book, and find 20*s*. mistake, which made me mighty angry, and great differences between us. And so in that difference, to bed.

17.  To the office, where all the morning, with fresh occasions of vexing at myself for my late neglect of business, by which I cannot

appear half so useful as I used to do. Home at noon to dinner, and then to my office again, where I could not hold my eyes open for an hour, but I drowsed (so little sensible I apprehend my soul is of my necessity of minding business). But I anon wakened and minded my business, and did a very great deal with very great pleasure; and so home at night to supper and to bed – mightily pleased with myself for the business that I have done, and convinced that if I would but keep constantly to do the same, I might have leisure enough and yet do all my business; and by the grace of God, so I will. So to bed.

19. Up, and to the office all the morning. At noon took Mr. Deane (lately come to town) home with me to dinner; and there, after giving him some reprimendes and good advice about his deportment in the place where by my interest he is at Harwich, and then declaring my resolution of being his friend still – we did then fall to discourse about his ship *Rupert*, built by him there; which succeeds so well, as he hath got great honour by it, and I some by recommending him – the King, Duke, and everybody saying it is the best ship that was ever built. And then he fell to explain to me his manner of casting the draught of water which a ship will draw beforehand – which is a secret the King and all admire in him; and he is the first that hath come to any certainty beforehand of foretelling the draught of water of a ship before she be launched.

23. Up by 5 a-clock, and to my chamber, setting several matters in order. So out toward Whitehall, calling in my way on my Lord Bellaces – where I came to his bedside and did give me a full and long account of his matters how he left them at Tanger. Declares himself fully satisfied with my care. Seems cunningly to argue for encreasing the number of men there. Told me the whole story of his gains by the Turky prizes, which he owns he hath got about 5000*l* by. Promised me the same profits Povy was to have had. And in fine, I find him a pretty subtle man; and so I left him and to Whitehall before the Duke and did our usual business, and eased my mind of two or three things of weight that lay upon me about Lanyon's salary, which I have got to be 150*l* per annum. Thence to Westminster to look after getting some little for some great tallies, but shall find trouble in it. Thence homeward, and met with Sir Ph. Warwicke and spoke about this, in which he is scrupulous. After that, to talk of the wants of the Navy; he lays all the fault now upon

the new act, and owns his own folly in thinking once so well of it as to give way to others' endeavours about it. And is grieved at heart to see what pass things are like to come to. Thence to the Excize Office to the Commissioners to get a meeting between them and myself and others about our concernments in the Excise for Tanger. And so to the Change a while, and thence home with Creed and find my wife at dinner with Mr. Cooke, who is going down to Hinchingbrooke; after dinner Creed and I and wife and Mercer out by coach, leaving them at the New Exchange, while I to Whitehall and there stayed at Sir G. Carteret's chamber till the Council rose; and then he and I, by agreement this morning, went forth in his coach by Tiburne to the park – discoursing of the state of the Navy as to money, and the state of the Kingdom too; how ill able to raise more. And of our office, as to the condition of the officers – he giving me caution as to myself, that there are those that are my enemies too, as well as his; and by name, my Lord Bruncker, who hath said some odd speeches against me. So that he advises me to stand on my guard – which I shall do; and unless my too-much addiction to pleasure undo me, will be hard enough for any of them. We rode to and again in the park a good while; and at last home and set me down at Charing cross; and thence I to Mrs. Pierce's to take up my wife and Mercer – where I find her new picture by Hales doth not please her, nor me endeed, it making no show nor is very like nor no good painting. Home to supper and to bed – having my right eye sore and full of humour of late, I think by my late change of my brewer and having of 8s. beere.

25.     Up betimes, and to my chamber to do business, where the greatest part of the morning. Then out to the Change to speak with Capt. [Cocke], who tells me my silver plates are ready for me, and shall be sent me speedily. And proposes another proposition of serving us with a thousand tons of hemp, and tells me it shall bring me 500l if the bargain go forward – which is a good word. Thence I to Sir G. Carteret, who is at the pay of the tickets with Sir J. Mennes this day; and here sat with them a while, the first time I ever was there. And thence to dinner with him – a good dinner. Here came a Gentleman over from France, arrived here this day, Mr. Browne of St. Mellos – who, among other things, tells me the meaning of the setting out of dogs every night out of the town walls, which are said to secure the city; but it is not so, but only to secure the Anchors, cables, and ships that lie dry, which might otherwise in the night be

liable to be robbed. And these dogs are set out every night and called together in every morning by a man with a horne, and they go in very orderly.

27. *Lords day*. Rose betimes, and to my office till church-time to write two copies of my Will fair, bearing date this day. Wherein I have given my sister Pall 500*l* – my father, for his own and my mother's support, 2000*l* – to my wife, the rest of my estate; but to have 2500*l* secured to her though, by deducting out of what I have given my father and my sister. I despatched all before church-time, and then home and to church, my wife with me. Thence home to dinner, whither came my uncle Wight and aunt and uncle Norbury – and Mr. Sheply. A good dinner, and very merry. After dinner we broke up, and I by water to Westminster to Mrs. Martin's and there sat with her and her husband and Mrs. Burrows, the pretty, an hour or two; then to the Swan a while; and so home by water, and with my wife by and by, by water as low as Greenwich for ayre only; and so back again home to supper and to bed with great pleasure.

29. *King's Birth and Restauracion day*. Waked with the ringing of the bells all over the town. So up before 5 a-clock, and to the office, where we met; and I all the morning with great trouble upon my spirit to think how I should come off in the afternoon when Sir W. Coventry did go to the Victualling Office to see the state of matters there. And methought, by his doing of it without speaking to me, and only with Sir W. Penn, it must be of design to find my negligence. However, at noon I did, upon a small invitation of Sir W. Pen's go and dine with Sir W. Coventry at his office, where great good cheer – and many pleasant stories of Sir W. Coventry, but I had no pleasure in them. However, I had last night and this morning made myself a little able to report how matters were – and did readily go with them after dinner to the Victualling Office; and there beyond belief did acquit myself very well, to full content. Being broke up there, I with a merry heart home to my office; and thither my wife comes to me to tell me that if I would see the handsomest woman in England, I shall come home presently; and who should it be but the pretty lady of our parish that did heretofore sit on the other side of our church over against our gallery, that is since married. She, with Mrs. Anne Jones, one of this parish that dances finely, did come to see her this afternoon. And so I home, and there found Creed also come to me; so there I spent most of the

afternoon with them; and endeed, she is a pretty black woman – her name, Mrs. Horesely. But Lord, to see how my nature could not refrain from the temptation, but I must invite them to go to Foxhall to Spring Garden, though I had freshly received minutes of a great deal of extraordinary business. However, I could not help it; but sent them before with Creed, and I did some of my business, and so after them and find them there in an Arbour; and had met with Mrs. Pierce and some company with her. So here I spent 20s. upon them, and were pretty merry. Among other things, had a fellow that imitated all manner of birds and dogs and hogs with his voice, which was mighty pleasant. Stayed here till night; then set Mrs. Pierce in at the New Exchange, and ourselfs took coach and so set Mrs. Horsly home, and then home ourselfs, but with great trouble in the streets by bonefires, it being the King's birthday and day of restoration; but Lord, to see the difference, how many there was on the other side, and so few our, the City side of Temple, would make one wonder the difference between the temper of one sort of people and the other – and the difference among all, between what they do now, and what it was the night when Monke came into the City[1] – such a night as that I never think to see again, not think it can be. After I came home, I was till one in the morning with Capt. Cocke drawing up a contract with him, intended to be offered to the Duke tomorrow – which if it proceeds, he promises me 500l.

30. Up, and to my office, there to settle some businesses in order to our waiting on the Duke today. That done, to Whitehall to Sir W. Coventry's chamber, where I find the Duke gone out with the King today on hunting. So after some discourse with him, I by water to Westminster and there drew a draught of an order for my Lord Treasurer to sign, for my having some little tallies made me in lieu of two great ones of 2000l each, to enable me to pay small sums therewith. I showed it to Sir R. Long and had his approbation, and so to Sir Ph. Warwicke's and did give it him to get signed. So home to my office, and there did business. By and by, towards noon, word is brought me that my father and sister are come – I expected them today, but not so soon. I to them, and am heartily glad to see them, especially my father, who, poor man, looks very well, and hath rode up this journey on horseback very well – only, his eyesight and hearing is very bad. I stayed and dined with them, my

1. On 11 February 1660.

wife being gone by coach to Barnitt with W. Hewer and Mercer to meet them, and they did come Ware way.

31. Waked very betimes in the morning by extraordinary Thunder and rain, which did keep me sleeping and waking till very late; and it being a holiday, and my eye very sore, and myself having had very little sleep for a good while till 9 a-clock – and so up, and so saw all my family up, and my father and sister (who is a pretty good-bodied woman and not over-thicke, as I thought she would have been; but full of Freckles and not handsome in face); and so I out by water among the ships, and to Deptford and Blackewall about business; and so home and to dinner with my father and sister and family, mighty pleasant all of us – and among other things, with a Sparrow that our Mercer hath brought up now for three weeks, which is so tame, that [it] flies up and down and upon the table and eats and pecks, and doth everything so pleasantly, that we are mightily pleased with it. To my accounts and settled them clear; but to my grief, find myself poorer then I was the last by near 20*l* – by reason of my being forced to return 50*l* to Downing the smith which he had presented me with. However, I am well contented, finding myself yet to be worth 5200*l*.

Thus ends this month, with my mind oppressed by my defect in my duty of the victualling, which lies upon me as a burden till I get myself into a better posture therein, and hinders me and casts down my courage in everything else that belongs to me – and the jealousy I have of Sir W. Coventry's being displeased with me about it. But I hope in a little time to remedy all. As to public business: by late tidings of the French Fleete being come to Rochell (how true, though, I know not), our fleet is Divided; Prince Rupert being gone with about 30 ships to the Westward; as is conceived, to meet the French, to hinder their coming to join with the Duch. My Lord Duke of Albemarle lies in the Downes with the rest, and intends presently to sail to the Gunfleete.

# ⁓⁂JUNE⁂⁓

2. Up, and to the office, where certain news is brought us of a letter come to the King this morning from the Duke of Albemarle, dated yesterday at 11 a-clock as they were sailing to the Gunfleet,

that they were in sight of the Duch Fleete and were fitting themselfs to fight them – so that they are, ere this, certainly engaged; besides, several do averr they heard the guns all yesterday in the afternoon. This put us at the board into a Tosse. Presently comes orders for our sending away to the fleet a recruite of 200 soldiers. So I rose from the table, and to the Victualling Office and thence upon the river among several vessels, to consider of the sending them away; and lastly down to Greenwich and there appointed two Yachts to be ready for them – and did order the soldiers to march to Blackewall. Having set all things in order against the next Flood, I went on shore with Capt. Erwin at Greenwich and into the parke and there we could hear the guns from the Fleete most plainly. Thence he and I to the King's head and there bespoke a dish of steaks for our dinner about 4 a-clock. While that was doing, we walked to the waterside, and there seeing the King and Duke come down in their barge to Greenwich house, I to them and did give them an account what I was doing. They went up to the park to hear the guns of the fleet go off. All our hopes now is that Prince Rupert with his fleet is coming back and will be with the fleet this noon – a message being sent to him to that purpose on Wednesday last. And a return is come from him this morning, that he did intend to sail from St. Ellens point about 4 in the afternoon on Wednesday, which was yesterday; which gives us great hopes, the wind being very fair, that he is with them this noon; and the fresh going-off of the guns makes us believe the same. After dinner, having nothing else to do till flood, I went and saw Mrs. Daniel – to whom I did not tell that the fleets were engaged, because of her husband, who is in the *Royal Charles*. Very pleasant with her half an hour, and so away, and down to Blackewall and there saw the soldiers (who were by this time gotten most of them drunk) shipped off. But Lord, to see how the poor fellows kissed their wifes and sweethearts in that simple manner at their going off, and shouted and let off their guns, was strange sport. Having put the soldiers on board, I home and wrote what I had to write by the post; and so home to supper and to bed, it being late.

3.   *Lords day. Whitsunday.* Up and by water to Whitehall; and there met with Mr. Coventry, who tells me the only news from the fleet is brought by Capt. Elliott of the *Portland*, which, by being run on board by the *Guernsey*, was disabled from staying abroad – so is coming in to Albrough. That he saw one of the Duch great ships

blown up, and three on fire. That they begun to fight on Friday. And at his coming into port, could make another ship of the King's coming in, which he judged to be the *Rupert*. That he knows of no other hurt to our ships. With this good news, I home by water again, and to church in the sermon time and with great joy told it my fellows in the pew. So home after church-time to dinner. And after dinner my father, wife, sister, and Mercer by water to Woolwich, while I walked by land and saw the Exchange as full of people, and hath been all this noon, as of any other day, only for news. A letter is also come this afternoon from Harman in the *Henery* (which is she was taken by Elliott for the *Rupert*), that being fallen into the body of the Duch fleet, he made his way through them, was set on by three fireships, one after another – got two of them off and disabled the third – was set on fire himself; upon which many of his men leaped into the sea and perished; among others, the Parson first – hath lost above 100 men and a good many wounded (God knows what is become of Balty); and at last quenched his own fire and got to Albrough – being, as all say, the greatest hazard that ever any ship scaped, and as bravely managed by him. The mast of the third fireship fell into their ship on Fire and hurt Harman's leg, which makes him lame now, but not dangerous. I to Sir G. Carteret, who told me there hath been great bad management in all this; that the King's orders that went on Friday for calling back the Prince, was sent but by the ordinary post on Wednesdy, and came to the Prince his hands but on Friday. And then instead of sailing presently, he stays till 4 in the evening; and that which is worst of all – the *Hampshire*, laden with merchants money come from the Streights, set out with or but just before the fleet and was in the Downes by 5 of the clock yesterday morning – and the Prince with his fleet came over to Dover but at 10 of the clock at night. This is hard to [be] answered, if it be true. This puts great astonishment into the King and Duke and Court, everybody being out of countenance. So meeting Creed, he and I by coach to Hide parke alone to talk of these things, and do bless God that my Lord Sandwich was not here at this time – to be concerned in a business like to be so misfortunate. It was a pleasant thing to consider how fearful I was of being seen with Creed all this afternoon, for fear of people's thinking that by our relation to my Lord Sandwich we should be making ill constructions of the Prince's failure. But God knows, I am heartily sorry, for the sake of the whole nation; though if it were not for that, it would not be amisse to have these high blades find some check to their presumption – and their disparaging of so good men. Thence set him down in Common Guarden, and so home by the Change; which is full of people still, and all talk highly of the failure of the Prince in not making more haste after his instructions did come, and of our managements herein, not giving it sooner and with more care and oftener thence. After supper, to bed.

4.    Up, and with Sir Jo. Minnes and Sir W. Pen to Whitehall in the latter's coach – where when we came, we find the Duke at St. James's, whither he is lately gone to lodge. So walking through the park, we saw hundreds of people listening at the Gravell pits, and to and again in the park to hear the guns. And I saw a letter, dated last night, from Strowd, Governor of Dover Castle, which says that the Prince came thither the night before with his fleet. But that for the guns which we writ that we heard, it is only a mistake for Thunder; and so far as to yesterday, it is a miraculous thing that we all Friday and Saturday and yesterday did hear everywhere most plainly the guns go off, and yet at Deale and Dover, to last night, they did not hear one word of a fight, nor think they heard one gun. This, added to what I have set down before the other day about the *Katharine*, makes room for a great dispute in Philosophy: how we should hear it and not they, the same wind that brought it to us being the same that should bring it to them. But so it is. After Wayting upon the Duke, Sir W. Penn (who was commanded to go to rights by water down to Harwich to despatch away all the ships he can) and I home, drinking two bottles of Cocke ale in the street, in his new fine coach, and so home – where no sooner come, but news is brought me of a couple of men come to speak with me from the fleet. So I down, and who should it be but Mr. Daniel, all muffled up, and his face as black as the chimney and covered with dirt, pitch and tar, and powder, and muffled with dirty clouts and his right eye stopped with Okum. He is come last night at 5 a-clock from the fleet, with a comrade of his that hath endangered another eye. They were set on shore at Harwich this morning at 2 a-clock in a ketch, with about twenty more wounded men from the *Royal Charles*. They being able to ride, took post about 3 this morning and was here between 11 and 12. I went presently into the coach with them, and carried them to Sumersett house stairs and there took water (all the world gazing upon us and concluding it to be news from the fleet; and everybody's face appeared expecting of news) to the Privy stairs

and left them at Mr. Coventry's lodging (he, though, not being there); and so I into the park to the King, and told him my Lord Generall was well the last night at 5 o'clock, and the Prince come with his fleet and joyned with his about 7. The King was mightily pleased with this news and so took me by the hand and talked a little of it – I giving him the best account I could; and then he bid me fetch the two seamen to him – he walking into the house. So I went and fetched the seamen into the Vane-room to him, and there he heard the whole account.

### The Fight[1]

How we found the Duch fleet at anchor on Friday, half-seas-over, between Dunkirke and Oastend, and made them let slip their Anchors – they about 90, and we less then 60. We fought them and put them to the run, till they met with about 16 sail of fresh ships and so bore up again. The fight continued till night, and then again the next morning from 5 till 7 at night – and so too, yesterday morning they begun again, and continued till about 4 a-clock – they chasing us for the most part of Saturday and yesterday; we fleeing from them. The Duke himself, then those people, were put into the ketch, and by and by spied the Prince's fleet coming – upon which, De Ruyter called a little council (being in chase at this time of us); and thereupon their fleet divided into two squadrons, 40 in one and about 30 in the other (the fleet being at first about 90, but by one accident or other supposed to be lessened to about 70); the bigger to fallow the Duke, the less to meet the Prince. But the Prince came up with the Generalls fleet, and the Dutch came together again and bore toward their own coast – and we with them. And now, what the consequence of this day will be, that we [hear] them fighting, we know not. The Duke was forced to come to Anchor on Friday, having lost his sails and rigging. No perticular person spoken of to be hurt but Sir W. Clerke, who hath lost his leg, and bore it bravely. The Duke himself had a little hurt in his thigh, but signified little. The King did pull out of his pocket about twenty pieces in gold, and did give it Daniel for himself and his companion. And so parted, mightily pleased with the account he did give him of the fight and the success it ended with – of the Prince's coming – though it seems the Duke did give way again and again. The King did give order for care to be had of Mr. Daniel and his companion; and so we parted

1. The Four Days Battle, 1–4 June.

from him, and then met the Duke and gave him the same account; and so broke up, and I left them going to the surgeon's; and I myself by water to the Change, and to several people did give account of the business; and so home about 4 a-clock to dinner and was fallowed by several people home, to be told the news, and good news it is.

Fresh letters are come from Harwich – where the *Glocester*, Capt. Clerke, is come in. And says that on Sunday night, upon coming in of the Prince, the Duch did fly. But all this day they have been fighting; therefore, they did face again, to be sure. Capt. Bacon of the *Bristoll* is killed. They cry up Jenings of the *Ruby* and Saunders of the *Sweepstakes*. They condemn mightily Sir Tho. Teddiman for a Coward, but with what reason, time must show. Having heard all this, Creed and I walked into the park till 9 or 10 at night, it being fine moonshine – discoursing of the unhappiness of our fleet. What it would have been if the Prince had not come in. How much the Duke hath failed of what he was so presumptuous of. How little we deserve of God Almighty to give us better fortune. How much this excuse[s] all that was imputed to my Lord Sandwich; and how much more he is a man fit to be trusted with all these matters then these that now command, who act by nor with any advice, but rashly and without any order. How bad we are at intelligence, that should give the Prince no sooner notice of anything, but let him come to Dover without notice of any fight, or where the fleet were, or anything else; nor give the Duke any notice that he might depend upon the Prince's reserve. And lastly, of how good use all may be to check our pride and presumption in adventuring upon hazards upon unequal force, against a people that can fight, it seems now, as well as we, and that will not be discouraged by any losses, but that they will rise again. Thence by water home, and to supper (my father, wife, and sister having been at Islington today at Pitts's) and to bed.

6.    By water to St. James's. There we all met and did our business as usual with the Duke; thence after the Duke into the park, walking through to Whitehall; and there everybody listening for guns, but none heard; and every creature is now overjoyed and conclude, upon very good grounds, that the Duch are beaten, because we have heard no guns nor no news of our fleet. By and by, walking a little further, Sir Ph. Frowde did meet the Duke with an express to Sir W. Coventry (who was by) from Capt. Taylor, the Storekeeper

at Harwich; being the narration of Capt. Hayward of the *Dunkirke*; who gives a very serious account how upon Monday the two fleets [were] fighting all day till 7 at night, and then the whole fleet of Duch did betake themselfs to a very plain flight and never looked back again. That Sir Chr. Mings is wounded in the leg. That the Generall is well. That it is conceived reasonably that of all the Dutch fleet, which, with what recruits they had, came to 100 sail, there is not above 50 got home – and of them, few, if any, of their flags. And that little Capt. Bell in one of the fireships did at the end of the day fire a ship of 70 guns. We were all so overtaken with this good news that the Duke ran with it to the King, who was gone to chapel; and there all the Court was in a hubbub, being rejoiced over head and ears in this good news. Away go I by coach to the New Exchange and there did spread this good news a little, though I find it had broken out before. And so home to our own church, it being the common fast-day; and it was just before sermon, but Lord, how all the people in the church stared upon me to see me whisper to Sir Jo. Minnes and my Lady Pen. Anon I saw people stirring and whispering below, and by and by comes up the Sexton from my Lady Ford to tell me the news (which I had brought), being now sent into the church by Sir W. Batten – in writing, and handed from pew to pew. But that which pleased me as much as the news, was to have the fair Mrs. Middleton at our church, who indeed is a very beautiful lady. Here after sermon comes to our office 40 people almost, of all sorts and qualities, to hear the news; which I took great delight to tell them.

7. Up betimes, and to my office about business (Sir W. Coventry having sent me word that he is gone down to the fleet to see how matters stand, and to be back again speedily), and with the same expectation of congratulating ourselfs with the victory that I had yesterday. But my Lord Brouncker and Sir T. Harvey, that came from Court, tell me quite contrary news, which astonishes me. That is to say, that we are beaten – lost many ships and good commanders – have not taken one ship of the enemy's, and so can only report ourselfs a victory; nor is it certain that we were left maisters of the field. But above all, that the *Prince* run on shore upon the Galoper, and there stuck – was endeavoured to be fetched off by the Duch but could not, and so they burned her – and Sir G. Ascue is taken prisoner and carried into Holland. This news doth much trouble me, and the thoughts of the ill consequences of it, and the

pride and presumption that brought us to it. I do find great reason to think we are beaten in every respect, and that we are the losers. The *Prince* upon the Galloper, where both the *Royall Charles* and *Royall Katharine*, had come twice aground, but got off. The *Essex* carried into Holland. The *Swiftsure* misseing (Sir Wm. Barkely) ever since the beginning of the fight. Captains Bacon, Tearne, Wood, Mootham, Whitty, and Coppin Slayne. The Duke of Albemarle writes that he never fought with worse officers in his life, not above 20 of them behaving themselfs like men. Sir Wm. Clerke lost his leg, and in two days died. The *Loyall George, Seven Oakes,* and *Swiftsure* are still missing, having never, as the Generall writes himself, engaged with them.

8.   To the Exchequer about some Tanger businesses; and then home, where to my very great joy I find Balty come home without any hurt, after the utmost imaginable danger he hath gone through in the *Henery*, being upon the Quarter-deck with Harman all the time; and for which service Harman, I heard this day, commended most seriously, and most eminently by the Duke of Yorke.

10.   *Lords day*. Pierce the surgeon tells me how the Duke of York is wholly given up to his new mistress, my Lady Denham, going at noonday, with all his gentlemen with him, to visit her in Scotland yard – she declaring she will not be his mistress, as Mrs. Price, to go up and down the privy stairs, but will be owned publicly; and so she is. Mr. Brouncker it seems was the pimp to bring it about, and my Lady Castlemayne, who designs thereby to fortify herself by the Duke – there being a falling-out the other day between King and her. On this occasion the Queene, in ordinary talk before the ladies in her drawing-room, did say to my Lady Castlemayne that she feared the King did take cold by staying so late abroad at her house. She answered, before them all, that he did not stay so late abroad with her, for he went betimes thence (though he doth not before 1, 2, or 3 in the morning), but must stay somewhere else. The King then coming in, and overhearing, did whisper in the eare aside and told her she was a bold impertinent woman, and bid her be gone out of the Court and not come again till he sent for her – which she did presently; and went to a lodging in the Pell mell and kept there two or three days, and then sent to the King to know whether she might send for her things away out of her house; the King sent to her, she must first come and view them; and so she came, and the King went

to her and all friends again. He tells me she did in her anger say she would be even with the King, and print his letters to her. So putting all together, we are, and are like to be, in a sad condition. We are endeavouring to raise money by borrowing it on the City; but I do not think the City will lend a farthing.

Sir G. Carteret tells me, as I hear from everybody else, that the management in the late fight was bad from top to bottom. That several have said this would not have been, if my Lord Sandwich had had the ordering of it. Nay, he tells me that certainly, had my Lord Sandwich had the misfortune to have done as they have done, the King could not have saved him. There is, too, nothing but discontent among the officers; and all the old experienced men are slighted. He tells me, to my question (but as a great secret), that the dividing of the fleet[1] did proceed first from a proposition from the fleet, though agreed to hence. But he confesses it arose from want of due intelligence – which he confesses we do want. He doth, however, call the fight on Sunday a very honourable retreat, and that the Duke of Albemarle did do well in it, and could have been well if he had done it sooner, rather than venture the loss of the fleet and crown, as he must have done if the Prince had not come.

11.    Comes Sir Jo. Bankes to see me, and tell me that coming up from Rochester, he overtook above 3 or 400 seamen, and he believes every day they come flocking from the fleet in like numbers; which is a sad neglect there, when it will be impossible to get others and we have little reason to think these will return presently again.

12.    To Whitehall in hopes of a meeting of Tanger, but it could not be obtained. Walking here in the galleries, I find the Ladies of Honour dressed in their riding garbs, with coats and doublets with deep skirts, just for all the world like men, and buttoned their doublets up the breast, with perriwigs and with hats; so that, only for a long petticoat dragging under their men's coats, nobody could take them for women in any point whatever – which was an odde sight, and a sight did not please me. It was Mrs. Wells and another fine lady that I saw thus.

13.    With Balty to Hales's by coach (it being the seventh day from

---

1. Rupert's squadron had been sent westwards on receipt of false intelligence that a French fleet was sailing up-Channel.

my making my last oaths, and by them I am at liberty to dispense with any of my oaths every seventh day, after I had for the six days before-going performed all my vows). Here I find my father's picture begun; and so much to my content, that it joys my very heart to think that I should have his picture so well done – who, besides that he is my father, and a man that loves me and hath ever done so – is also at this day one of the most careful and innocent men in the world. Thence with mighty content homeward; and in my way, at the Stockes, did buy a couple of lobsters, and so home to dinner. Where I find my wife and father had dined, and were going out to Hales's to sit there. So Balty and I alone to dinner; and in the middle of my grace, praying for a blessing upon (these his good creatures), my mind fell upon my Lobsters – upon which I cried, "Cuds zookes!" And Balty looked upon me like a man at a loss what I meant, thinking at first that I meant only that I had said the grace after meat, instead of that before meat; but then I cried, "What is become of my lobsters?", whereupon he run out of doors to overtake the coach, but could not, and so came back again, and mighty merry at dinner to think of my Surprize. After dinner to the Excize office by appointment, thence home, and put off Balty; and so (being invited) to Sir Chr. Mings's Funerall, but find them gone to church. However, I into the church (which is a fair large church, and a great Chappell), and there heard the service and stayed till they buried him, and then out. And there met with Sir W. Coventry (who was there out of great generosity, and no person of quality there but he) and went with him into his Coach; and being in it with him, there happened this extraordinary case – one of the most Romantique that ever I heard of in my life, and could not have believed but that I did see it – which was this.

About a Dozen able, lusty, proper men came to the coach-side with tears in their eyes, and one of them, that spoke for the rest, begun and says to Sir W. Coventry – "We are here a Dozen of us that have long known and loved and served our dead commander, Sir Chr. Mings, and have now done the last office of laying him in the ground. We would be glad we had any other to offer after him, and in revenge of him – all we have is our lives. If you will please to get his Royal Highness to give us a Fireshipp among us all, here is a Dozen of us, out of all which choose you one to be commander, and the rest of us, whoever he is, will serve him, and, if possible, do that that shall show our memory of our dead commander and our revenge." Sir W. Coventry was herewith much moved (as well as I, who could hardly abstain from weeping) and took their names; and so parted, telling me that he would move his Royal Highness as in a thing very extraordinary, and so we parted. The truth is, Sir Chr. Mings was a very stout man, and a man of great parts and most excellent tongue among ordinary men; and as Sir W. Coventry says, could have been the most useful man in the world at such a pinch of time as this. He was come into great renowne here at home, and more abroad, in the West Indys. He had brought his family into a way of being great. But dying at this time, his memory and name (his father being always, and at this day, a Shoomaker, and his mother a Hoymans daughter, of which he was used frequently to boast) will be quite forgot in a few months, as if he had never been, nor any of his name be the better by it – he having not had time to coll[ect] any estate; but is dead poor rather then rich. So we left the church and crowd, and I home (being set down on Tower hill) and there did a little business, and then in the evening went down by water to Deptford, it being very late. And there I stayed out as much time as I could and then took boat again homeward. But the officers being gone in, returned and walked to Mrs. Bagwell's house; and there (it being by this time pretty dark and past 10 a-clock) went into her house and did what I would. So away to the waterside and sent for a pint of sack, and so home, drank what I would and gave the waterman the rest, and so adieu. Home about 12 at night, and so to bed – finding most of my people gone to bed. In my way home I called on a fisherman and bought three Eeles, which cost me 3s.

17. *Lords day*. My father and I walked to Grayse Inn fields and there spent an hour or two, walking and talking of several businesses. First, as to his estate, he told me it produced about 80*l* per annum. But then there goes 30*l* per annum taxes and other things, certain charge – which I do promise to make good, as far as this 30*l* – at which the poor man was overjoyed and wept. As to Pall, he tells me he is mightily satisfied with Ensum; and so I promised to give her 500*l* presently, and to oblige myself to 100*l* more on the birth of her first child, he insuring her in 10*l* per annum for every 100*l*. And in the meantime, till she doth marry, I promise to allow her 10*l* per annum. Then as to John, I tell him I will promise him nothing, but will supply him as so much lent him – I declaring that I am not pleased with him yet. And that when his degree is over, I will send for him up hither, and if he be good for

anything, doubt not to get him preferment. This discourse ended to the joy of my father, and no less to me, to see that I am able to do this; we return to Joyces and there, wanting a coach to carry us home, I walked out as far as the New Exchange to find one, but could not. So down to the Milke-house and drank three glasses of whey, and then up into the Strand again, and there met with a coach. And so to Joyces and took up my father, wife, sister, and Mercer, and to Islington, where we drank, and then our Tour by Hackny home – where, after a little business at my office and then talk with my Lady and Pegg Pen in the garden, I home and to bed – being very weary.

18.    Up betimes, and in my chamber most of the morning, setting things to right there, my Journall and accounts with my father and brother. Then to the office a little, and so to Lumberd street to borrow a little money upon a tally, but cannot. Thence to Exchequer, and there after much wrangling got consent that I should have a great tally broken into little ones. Thence to Hales's to see how my father's picture goes on, which pleases me mighty well, though I find again, as I did in Mrs. Pierces, that a picture may have more of likeness in the first or second working then it shall have when finished; though this is very well, and to my full content; but so it is. And contrarily, mine was not so like at the first, second, or third sitting as it was afterward. Thence to my Lord Bellasyse by invitation, and there dined with him and his lady and daughter; and at dinner there played to us a young boy lately come from France, where he had been learning a year or two on the viallin, and plays finely. But impartially, I do not find any goodness in their ayres (though very good) beyond ours, when played by the same hand; I observed in several of Baptiste's (the present great composer) and our Bannisters. But it was pretty to see how passionately my Lord's daughter loves music, the most that ever I saw creature in my life.

19.    At my business till late at night; then with my wife into the garden, and there sang with Mercer – whom I feel myself beginning to love too much, by handling of her breasts in a morning when she dresses me, they being the finest that ever I saw in my life; that is the truth of it. So home, and to supper with beans and bacon, and to bed.

20.    Up, but in some pain of the Collique – hav[ing] of late taken

too much cold by washing my feet and going in a thin silk waistcoat, without any other coat over it, and open-breasted. But I hope it will go over. I did this morning (my father being to go away tomorrow) give my father some money to buy him a horse, and for other things, to himself and my mother and sister, among them, 20*l* – besides undertaking to pay for other things for them to about 3*l* – which the poor man takes with infinite kindness, and I do not think I can bestow it better. At home all the evening doing business, and at night in the garden (it having been these three or four days mighty hot weather) singing in the evening; and then home to supper and to bed.

23. My father and sister very betimes took their leave; and my wife, with all possible kindness, went with them to the Coach – I being mightily pleased with their company thus long, and my father with his being here; and it rejoices my heart that I am in condition to do anything to comfort him, and could, were it not for my mother, have been contented he should have stayed alway here with me – he is such innocent company. In the evening down to Tower wharfe, thinking to go by water; but could not get watermen, they being now so scarce by reason of the great press. So to the Custome house; and there with great threats got a couple to carry me down to Deptford, all the way reading *Pompey the Great* (a play translated from French by several noble persons; among other, my Lord Buckehurst); but to me is but a mean play, and the words and sense not very extraordinary. From Deptford I walked to Redriffe, and was in my way overtaken by Bagwell, lately come from sea in the *Providence*; who did give me an account of several perticulars in the late fight, and how his ship was deserted basely by the *Yorke*, Capt. Swanly, commander. So I home; and there, after writing my letters, home to supper and to bed – fully resolved to rise betimes and go down the River tomorrow morning, being vexed this night to find none of the officers in the yard at 7 at night, nor anybody concerned, as if it were a Dutch warr.

24. *Sunday. Midsummer Day.* Up, but, being weary the last night, not so soon as I intended. Then being dressed, I down by water to Deptford and there did a great deal of business, being in a mighty hurry – Sir W. Coventry writing to me that there was some thoughts that the Duch fleet were out or coming out. Business being done, in providing for the carrying down of some provisions

to the fleet, I away back home. And after dinner, by water to Whitehall and there waited, till the Council rose, in the boarden gallery. By and by the Council rises, and Sir W. Coventry comes out and he and I went aside and discoursed of much business of the Navy; and afterwards took his coach and to Hide parke, he and I alone. There we had much talk. First, he started a discourse of a talk he hears about the town, which, says he, is a very bad one, and fit to be suppressed if we knew how: which is the comparing of the success of the last year with that of this, saying that that was good and that bad. Then to discourse of himself, saying that he heard that he was under the lash of people's discourse about the Princes not having notice of the Dutch being out and for him to come back again, nor the Duke of Albemarle notice that the Prince was sent for back again. To which, he told me very perticularly how careful he was, the very same night that it was to resolve to send for the Prince back, to cause orders to be writ; and waked the Duke,[1] who was then in bed, to sign them; and that they went by express that very night, being the Wednesdy night before the Fight, which begun on the Friday; and that, for sending them by the post express and not by gentlemen on purpose, he made a sport of it, and said, "I knew none to send it with but would at least have lost more time in fitting themselfs out then any diligence of theirs beyond that that the ordinary post would have recovered." I told him that this was not so much the towne talk as the reason of dividing the Fleete. To this, he told me he ought not to say much; but did assure me in general, that the proposition did first come from the Fleete; and the resolution not being prosecuted with orders so soon as the Generall[2] thought fit, the Generall did send Sir Edwd. Spragge up on purpose for them; and that there was nothing in the whole business which was not done with the full consent and advice of the Duke of Albemarle. He tells me, as to the business of Intelligence, the want whereof the world did complain much of, that for that it was not his business, and as he was therefore to have no share in the blame, so he would not meddle to lay it anywhere else. He doth not disowne but that the dividing of the fleet, upon the presumptions that was then had (which I suppose was the French fleet being come this way), was a good resolution.

1. The Duke of York.
2. Albemarle.

26.    Up, and to the office betimes, and there all the morning – very busy to get out the fleet, the Dutch being now for certain out, and we shall not, we think, be much behindhand with them. At noon to the Change about business, and so home to dinner, and after dinner to the setting my Journall to rights; and so to the office again – where all the afternoon full of business, and there till night, that my eyes were sore, that I could not write no longer. Then into the garden; then my wife and Mercer, and my Lady Pen and her daughter with us. And here we sang in the dark very finely half an hour, and so home to supper and to bed. This afternoon, after a long drowth, we had a good shoure of rain, but it will not signify much if no more come. This day, in the morning came Mr. Chichly to Sir W. Coventry to tell him the ill-successe of the guns made for the *Loyall London*; which is, that in the trial, every one of the great guns, the whole Cannon of seven (as I take it), broke to pieces – which is a strange mishap, and that which will give more occasion to people's discourse of the King's business being done ill.

27.    Up, and to my office awhile. Then down the River a little way to see vessels ready for the carrying down of 400 land-soldiers to the fleet. Then back to the office for my papers, and so to St. James's, where we did our usual attendance on the Duke. I did this afternoon visit my Lord Bellasses – who professes all imaginable satisfaction in me. He spoke dissatisfiedly with Creed, which I was pleased well enough with. My Lord is going down to his Guarrison to Hull, by the King's command to put it in order, for fear of an invasion – which course I perceive is taken upon the sea-coasts round; for we have a real apprehension of the King of France's invading us.

29.    To Whitehall; and thence, the Council being up, walked to St. James's and there had much discourse with Sir W. Coventry at his chamber – who I find quite weary of the war. Decries our having any war at all, or himself to have been any occasion of it. That he hopes this will make us shy of any war hereafter, or to prepare better for it. Believes that one overthrow on the Duch side would make them desire peace, and that one on ours will make us willing to accept of one. Tells me that Comissioner Pett is fallen infinitely under the displeasure of the Prince and Duke of Albemarle, not giving them satisfaction in the getting out of the fleet; and that that complaint, he believes, is come to the King. Thence home, and to the office – where I met with a letter from Dover which tells me

(and it did come by express) that news is brought over by a gentleman from Callice that the Duch fleet, 130 sail, are come upon the French coast – and that the country is bringing in Pickeaxes and Shovells and wheelbarrows into Callice. That there are 6000 men, armed with head, back, and breast (Frenchmen), ready to go on board the Duch fleet, and will be fallowed by 12000 more. That they pretend they are to come to Dover. And that thereupon the Governor of Dover Castle is getting the victuallers' provision out of the town into the castle, to secure it – but I do think this is a ridiculous conceit. But a little time will show. At night, home to supper and to bed.

30.   Up and to the office; and mightily troubled all this morning with going to my Lord Mayor (Sir Tho. Bludworth, a silly man I think) and other places about getting shipped some men that they have these two last nights pressed in the City out of houses – the persons wholly unfit for sea, and many of them people of very good fashion – which is a shame to think of; and carried to Bridewell they are, yet without being impressed with money legally, as they ought to be. But to see how the King's business is done, my Lord Mayor himself did scruple, at this time of extremity, to do this thing, because he had not money to pay the prest money to the men – he told me so himself; nor to take up boats to carry them down through bridge to the ships I have prepared to carry them down in. Insomuch that I was forced to promise to be his paymaister; and he did send his City Remembrancer afterward to the office, and at the table, in the face of the officers, I did there out of my own purse disburse 15*l* to pay for their pressing and diet last night and this morning – which is a thing worth record of my Lord Mayor. Busy about this all the morning. At noon dined, and then to the office again, and all the afternoon, till 12 at night, full of this business and others. And among those others, about the getting of men pressed by our officers of the fleet into the service, even our own men that [are] at the office and the boats that carries us – so that it is now become impossible to have so much as a letter carried from place to place, or any message done for us. Nay, out of victualling ships full loaden to go down to the fleet, and out of vessels of the Officers of the Ordinance, they press men; so that for want of discipline in this respect, I do fear all will be undone. Vexed with these things, but eased in mind by my ridding of a great deal of business from the office, I late home to supper and to bed. But before I was in bed,

while I was undressing myself, our new ugly maid Luce had like to have broke her neck in the dark, going down our upper stairs; but (which I was glad of) the poor girl did only bruise her head. But at first did lie on the ground groaning, and drawing her breath like one a-dying.

This month I end in much hurry of business, but in much more trouble in mind to think what will become of public businesses, having so many enemies abroad, and neither force – nor money at all – and but little Courage for ourselfs. It being really true that the spirits of our seamen, and commanders too, are really broke by the last defeat with the Duch; and this is not my conjecture only, but the real and serious thoughts of Sir G. Carteret and Sir W. Coventry, whom I have at distinct times hear[d] the same thing come from, with a great deal of grief and trouble. But lastly, I am providing against a foul day, to get as much money into my hands as I can, at least out of the public hands, that so, if a turn (which I fear) do come, I may have a little to trust to. I pray God give me good success in my choice how to dispose of what little I have, that I may not take it out of public hands and put it into worse.

# –❊JULY❊–

1. *Sunday*. Up betimes and to the office, receiving letters, two or three one after another, from Sir W. Coventry, and sent as many to him – being full of variety of business and hurry; but among the chiefest, is the getting of these pressed men out of the City down the River to the fleet. While I was hard at it, comes Sir W. Pen to town, which I little expected, having invited my Lady and her daughter Pegg to dine with me today – which at noon they did, and Sir W. Penn with them, and pretty merry we were. And though I do not love him, yet I find it necessary to keep in with him – his good service at Sherenesse in getting out the fleet being much taken notice of, and reported to the King and Duke even from the Prince and Duke of Albemarle themselfs, and made the most of to me and them by Sir W. Coventry. Therefore, I think it discretion, great and necessary discretion, to keep in with him. After dinner to the office again, where busy; and then down to Deptford to the yard, thinking to have seen Bagwell's wife, whose husband is gone yesterday back to the fleet; but I did not see her, so missed what I

went for; and so back and to the Tower several times about the business of the pressed men, and late at it, till 12 at night, shipping of them. But Lord, how some poor women did cry, and in my life I never did see such natural expression of passion as I did here – in some women's bewailing themselfs, and running to every parcel of men that were brought, one after another, to look for their husbands, and wept over every vessel that went off, thinking they might be there, and looking after the ship as far as ever they could by moonlight – that it grieved me to the heart to hear them. Besides, to see poor patient labouring men and housekeepers, leaving poor wifes and families, taken up on a sudden by strangers, was very hard; and that without press-money, but forced against all law to be gone. It is a great tyranny. Having done this, I to the Lieutenant of the Tower and bade him good-night, and so away home and to bed.

4. Up, and visited very betimes by Mr. Sheply, who is come to town upon business from Hinchingbrooke, where he left all well. I out, and walked along with him as far as Fleetestreete, it being a fast-day, the usual fast for the plague, and few coaches to be had. Thanks be to God, the plague is as I hear encreased but two this week. But in the country in several places it rages mightily, and perticularly in Colchester, where it hath long been, and is believed will quite depopulate the place. To St. James's, and there did our usual business with the Duke, all of us. Among other things, discoursing about the places where to build ten great ships, the King and Council have resolved on none to be under third-rates; but it is impossible to do it – unless we have more money towards the doing it then yet we have in any view. But however, the show must be made to the world. Thence home and dined; and then to the office, where busy all day. And in the evening Sir W. Pen came to me, and we walked together and talked of the late fight. I find him very plain that the whole conduct of the late fight was ill, and that that of truth's all, and he tells me that it is not he, but two-thirds of the commanders of the whole fleet have told him so – they all saying that they durst not oppose it at the council of war, for fear of being called Cowards, though it was wholly against their judgment to fight that day with that disproportion of force; and then we not being able to use one gun of our lower tire, which was a greater disproportion then the other. Besides, we might very well have stayed in the Downs without fighting, or anywhere else, till the

Prince could have come up to them – or at least till the weather was fair, that we might have the benefit of our whole force in the ships that we had. He says three things must [be] remedied, or else we shall be undone, by this fleet.

1.  That we must fight in a line, whereas we fight promiscuously, to our utter and demonstrable ruine – the Duch fighting otherwise – and we, whenever we beat them.
2.  We must not desert ships of our own in distress as we did, for that makes a captain desperate, and will fling away his ship when there is no hopes left him of succour.
3.  That ships, when they are a little shattered, must not take the liberty to come in of themselfs; but refit themselfs the best they can, and stay out – many of our ships coming in with very small disablings.

He told me that our very commanders, nay, our very flag-officers, do stand in need of exercizing among themselfs and discoursing the business of commanding a fleet – he telling me that even one of our flagmen in the fleet did not know which Tacke lost the wind or which kept it in the last engagement. He says it was pure dismaying and fear that made them all run upon the Galloper, not having their wits about them; and that it was a miracle they were not all lost. He much inveighs upon my discoursing of Sir John Lawson's saying heretofore, that 60 sail would do as much as 100. And says that he was a man of no counsel at all, but had got the confidence to say as the gallants did, and did propose to himself to make himself great by them, and saying as they did; but was no man of judgment in his business, but had been out in the greatest points that have come before them. And then in the business of Forecastles, which he did oppose, all the world sees now the use of them for shelter of men. He did talk very rationally to me, insomuch that I took more pleasure this night in hearing him discourse then I ever did in my life in anything that he said. He gone, I to the office again; and so after some business, home to supper and to bed.

6.  Up, and after doing some business at my office, abroad to Lumbardstreete, about the getting of a good sum of money; thence home, in preparation for my having some good sum in my hands, for fear of a trouble in the State, that I may not have all I have in the world out of my hands and so be left a beggar. Having put that in a way, I home to the office; and so to the Tower about shipping of

some more pressed men – and that done, away to Broadstreete to Sir G. Carteret, who is at a pay of Tickets all alone. And I believe not less then 1000 people in the streets. But it is a pretty thing to observe, that both there and everywhere else a man shall see many women nowadays of mean sort in the streets, but no men; men being so afeared of the press. I dined with Sir G. Carteret; and after dinner had much discourse about our public business, and he doth seem to fear every day more and more what I do, which is a general confusion in the State. Plainly answering me to the question, Who is it that the weight of the Warr depends? that it is only Sir W. Coventry. Thence to Lumberdstreete, and received 2000*l* and carried it home – whereof, 1000*l* in gold, the greatest quantity, not only that I ever had of gold, but that ever I saw together. Thence down to the Old Swan, calling at Michells, he not being within; and there I did steal a kiss or two of her, and staying a little longer, he came in, and her father, whom I carried to Westminster, my business being thither; and so back again home, and very busy all the evening; at night, a song in the garden and to bed.

10. Up, and to the office, where busy all the morning sitting. At noon home to dinner, and then to the office, the yard being very full of women (I believe above 300) coming to get money for their husbands and friends that are prisoners in Holland; and they lay clamouring and swearing, and cursing us, that my wife and I were afeared to send a venison-pasty that we have for supper tonight to the cook's to be baked, for fear of their offering violence to it – but it went, and no hurt done. Then I took an opportunity, when they were all gone into the foreyard, and slipped into the office and there busy all the afternoon. But by and by the women got into the garden, and came all to my closet window and there tormented me; and I confess, their cries were so sad for money, and laying down the condition of their families and their husbands, and what they have done and suffered for the King, and how ill they are used by us, and how well the Duch are used here by the allowance of their masters, and what their husbands are offered to serve the Duch abroad, that I do most heartily pity them, and was ready to cry to hear them – but cannot help them; however, when the rest was gone, I did call one to me, that I heard complain only and pity her husband, and did give her some money; and she blessed me and went away.

14. Up betimes to the office, to write fair a laborious letter I wrote, as from the Board, to the Duke of York, laying out our want of money again. That being done, I down to Thames Streete and there agreed for four or five Tons of Corke to send this day to the fleet, being a new device to make Barrecados with, instead of Junke. By this means I came to see and kiss Mr. Hill's young wife; and a blithe young woman she is. So to the office, and at noon home to dinner; and then sent for young Michell and imployed him all the afternoon about weighing and shipping off of the Corke – having by this means an opportunity of getting him 30 or 40s. Having set him a-doing, I home and to the office very late, very busy, and did endeed despatch much business; and so to supper and to bed – after a song in the garden – which, and after dinner, is now the greatest pleasure I take, and endeed doth please me mightily. To bed, after washing my legs and feet with warm water in my Kitchin. This evening I had Davila brought home to me, and I find it a most excellent history as ever I read.

15. *Lords day.* Up, and to church, where our lecturer made a sorry silly sermon upon the great point of proving the truth of the Christian religion. Home, and had a good dinner, expecting Mr. Hunt, but there comes only young Michell and his wife – whom my wife concurs with me to be a pretty woman, and with her husband, is a pretty innocent couple. Mighty pleasant we were, and I mightily pleased in her company and to find my wife so well pleased with them also. After dinner he and I walked to Whitehall, not being able to get a coach – he to the Abbey and I to Whitehall; but met with nobody to discourse with, having no great mind to be found idling there and be asked questions of the fleet; so walked only through to the park, and there, it being mighty hot, and I weary, lay down by the Canaille upon the grasse and slept a while, and was thinking of a Lampoone which hath run in my head this week, to make upon the late fight at sea and the miscarriages there – but other businesses put it out of my head. Having lain there a while, I then to the Abbey and there called Michell; and so walked in great pain, having new shoos on, as far as Fleet street; and there got a coach, and so in some little ease home – and there drank a great deal of small beer. And so took up my wife and Betty Michell and her husband, and away into the fields to take the ayre – as far as beyond Hackny, and so back again. In our way drinking a great deale of Milke, which I drank to take away my Heartburne,

wherewith I have been of late mightily troubled. But all the way home I did break abundance of wind behind – which did presage no good, but a great deal of cold gotten. So home and supped; and away went Michell and his wife – of whom I stole two or three salutes. And so to bed, in some pain and in fear of more – which accordingly I met with, for I was in mighty pain all night long, of the Winde griping of my belly and making of me shit often, and vomit too – which is a thing not usual with me. But this I impute to the milk that I drank, after so much beer. But the cold, to my washing my feet the night before.

18.    Up in good ease, and so by coach to St. James's after my fellows, and there did our business, which is mostly every day to complain of want of money – and that only will undo us in a little time. Here, among other things, before us all, the Duke of York did say that now at length he is come to a sure knowledge that the Duch did lose in the late engagements 29 captains and 13 ships – upon which, Sir W. Coventry did publicly move that if his Royal Highness had this of a certainty, it would be of use to send this down to the fleet, and to cause it to be spread about the fleet for the recovering of the spirits of the officers and seamen – who are under great dejectedness for want of knowing that they did do anything against the enemy, notwithstanding all that they did to us – which though it be true, yet methought was one of the most dishonour-able motions to our countrymen that ever was made – and is worth remembering. Thence with Sir W. Pen home, calling at Lillys to have a time appointed when to be drawn among the other Commanders of Flags the last year's fight. And so full of work Lilly is, that he was fain to take his table-book out to see how his time is appointed; and appointed six days hence for him to come, between 7 and 8 in the morning. Thence with him home; and there by appointment I find Dr. Fuller, now Bishop of Limbricke in Ireland – whom I knew in his low condition at Twittenham. I had also, by his desire, Sir W. Penn, and with him his lady and daughter. And had a good dinner, and find the Bishopp the same good man as ever; and in a word, kind to us, and methinks one of the comeliest and most becoming Pr[e]lates in all respects that ever I saw in my life. During dinner comes an acquaintance of his, Sir Thomas Littleton – whom I knew not while he was in my house, but liked his discourse. And afterward by Sir W. Penn do come to know that he is one of the greatest speakers in the House of Commons, and the

usual Second to the great Vaughan. So was sorry I did observe him no more and gain more of his acquaintance. After dinner, they being gone, and I mightily pleased with my guests – I down the River to Greenwich about business; and thence walked to Woolwich, reading *The Rivall Ladys* all the way, and find it a most pleasant and fine-writ play. At Woolwige saw Mr. Shelden, it being late, and there eat and drank, being kindly used by him and Bab; and so by water to Depford, it being 10 a-clock before I got to Depford, and dark – and there to Bagwell's. And having stayed there a while, away home; and after supper to bed. The Duke of York said this day, that by letters from the Generalls[1], they would sail with the fleet this day or tomorrow.

21. Up, and to the office, where all the morning sitting. At noon walked in the garden with Comissioner Pett (newly come to town), who tells me how infinite the disorders are among the commanders and all officers of the fleet – no discipline – nothing but swearing and cursing, and everybody doing what they please; and the Generalls, understanding no better, suffer it, to the reproaching of this Board or whoever it will be. He himself hath been challenged twice to the field, or something as good, by Sir Edwd. Spragg and Captain Seamour; he tells me the captains carry, for all the late orders, what men they please. Demand and consume what provisions they please. So that he fears, and I do no less, that God Almighty can[not] bless us while we keep in this disorder that we are in. He observing to me too, that there is no man of counsel or advice in the fleet; and the truth is, the gentlemen Captains will undo us, for they are not to be kept in order, their friends about the King and Duke and their own houses is so free, that it is not for any person but the Duke himself to have any command over them. He gone, I to dinner, and then to the office, where busy all the afternoon.

22. *Lords day*. Up, and to my chamber and there till noon, mighty busy setting money matters and other things of mighty moment to rights, to the great content of my mind, I finding that accounts but a little let go can never be put in order by strangers, for I cannot without much difficulty do it myself. After dinner to them again till about 4 a-clock, and then walked to Whitehall, where saw nobody almost, but walked up and down with Hugh May, who is a very

---

1. Rupert and Albemarle.

ingenious man – among other things, discoursing of the present fashion of gardens, to make them plain – that we have the best walks of Gravell in the world – France having none, nor Italy; and our green of our bowling-alleys is better then any they have. So our business here being ayre, this is the best way, only with a little mixture of Statues or pots, which may be handsome, and so filled with another pot of such or such, a flower or greene, as the season of the year will bear. And then for Flowers, they are best seen in a little plat by themselfs; besides, their borders spoil the walks of any other garden. And then for fruit, the best way is to have Walls built Circularly, one within another, to the South, on purpose for fruit, and leaving the walking-garden only for that use. Thence walked through the house, where most people mighty hush, and methinks melancholy, I saw not a smiling face through the whole Court.

23. Up and to my chamber, doing several things there of moment. And then comes Simpson the Joyner, and he and I with great pains contriving presses to put my books up in; they now growing numerous, and lying one upon another on my chairs, I lose the use, to avoid the trouble of removing them when I would open a book.

28. Up and to the office, where no more news of the fleet then was yesterday. Here we sat. And at noon to dinner to the Popes head, where my Lord Brouncker (and his mistress dined) and Comissioner Pett, Dr. Charleton, and myself entertained with a venison pasty by Sir W. Warren. Here, very pretty discourse of Dr. Charleton concerning Nature's fashioning every creature's teeth according to the food she intends them. And that man's, it is plain, was not for flesh, but for fruit. And that he can at any time tell the food of a beast unknown, by the teeth. My Lord Brouncker made one or two objections to it; that creatures find their food proper for their teeth, rather then that the teeth was fitted for the food. But the Doctor, I think, did well observe that creatures do naturally, and from the first, before they have had experience to try, do love such a food rather then another. And that all children love fruit, and none brought to flesh but against their wills at first. Thence with my Lord to his Coach-house, and there put in six horses into his coach and he and I alone to Highgate – all the way, going and coming, I learning of him the principles of Optickes, and what it is that makes an object seem less or bigger. And how much distance doth lessen

an object. And that it is not the eye at all, or any rule in optiques, that can tell distance; but it is only an act of reason, comparing of one mark with another. Which did both please and inform me mightily. Being come thither, we went to my Lord Lauderdale's house to speak with him about getting a man at Lieth to join with one we imploy to buy some prize goods for the King. We find [him] and his lady and some Scotch people at supper – pretty odd company; though my Lord Brouncker tells me my Lord Lauderdale is a man of mighty good reason and judgment. But at supper there played one of their servants upon the viallin, some Scotch tunes only – several – and the best of their country, as they seemed to esteem them by their praising and admiring them; but Lord, the strangest ayre that ever I heard in my life, and all of one cast. But strange to hear my Lord Lauderdale say himself, that he had rather hear a Catt mew then the best Musique in the world – and the better the music, the more sick it makes him. And that of all instruments, he hates the Lute most; and next to that, the Baggpipe. Thence back with my Lord to his house; all the way good discourse, informing of myself about optiques still; and there left him, and by a hackney home; and after writing three or four letters, home to supper and to bed.

29. *Lords day*. Up and all the morning in my chamber, making up my accounts in my book with my father and brother, and stating them. Towards noon, before sermon was done at church, comes news by a letter to Sir W. Batten (to my hand) of the late fight[1] – which I sent to his house, he at church: but Lord, with what impatience I stayed till sermon was done, to know the issue of the fight, with a thousand hopes and fears and thoughts about the consequences of either. At last sermon is done and he came home, and the bells immediately rung as soon as the church was done; but coming to Sir W. Batten to know the news, his letter said nothing of it – but all the town is full of a victory. By and by, a letter from Sir W. Coventry tells me that we have the victory. Beat them into the Weelings. Had taken two of their great ships, but by the orders of the Generals they are burned – this being methought but a poor result after the fighting of two so great fleets; and four days having no tidings of them, I was still impatient – but could know no more; so away home to dinner, where Mr. Spong and Reeves dined with

1. The Battle of St James's Day, 25 July.

me by invitation. After dinner to our business of my Microscope, to be shown some of the observables of that; and then down to my office to look in a dark room with my glasses and Tube, and most excellently things appeared indeed, beyond imagination. This was our work all the afternoon, trying the several glasses and several objects; among others, one of my plats, where the lines appeared so very plain, that it is not possible to think how plain it was done. Thence, satisfied exceedingly with all this, we home, and to discourse many pretty things; and so stayed out the afternoon till it begun to be dark and then they away, and I to Sir W. Batten, where the Lieutenant of the Tower was, and Sir J. Mennes; and the news, I fear, is no more [nor] less then what I had heard before. Only, that our Blue Squadron, it seems, was pursued the most of the time, having more ships, a great many, then its number allotted to her share. Young Seamour is killed, the only captain slain. The *Resolution* burned; but, as they say, most of her [men] and commander saved. This is all; only, we keep the sea; which denotes a victory, or at least that we are not beaten. But no great matters to brag on, God knows. So home to supper and to bed.

## –✣AUGUST✣–

5. *Lords day*. Up, and down to the old Swan; and there called Betty Michell and her husband and had two or three long salutes from her out of sight of su marido, which pleased me mightily. And so carried them by water to Westminster; and I to St. James's and there had a meeting before the Duke of York, complaining of want of money; but nothing done to any purpose, for want we shall; so that now our advices to him signify nothing. Here Sir W. Coventry did acquaint the Duke of York how the world doth discourse of the ill method of our books, and that we would consider how to answer any enquiry which shall be made after our practice therein – which will, I think, concern the Controller most. But I shall make it a memento to myself. Thence walked to the parish church to have one look upon Betty Michell; and so away homeward by water, and landed to go to the church, where I believe Mrs. Horsly goes, by Merchant-Taylor hall. And there I find in the pulpit Elborough, my old schoolfellow and a simple rogue; and yet I find preaching a very good sermon, and in as right a parson-like manner, and in

good manner too, as I have heard anybody; and the church very full
– which is a surprizing consideration. But I did not see her. So
home, and had a good dinner; and after dinner, with my wife and
Mercer and Jane by water all the afternoon up as high as
Moreclacke, with great pleasure, and a fine day – reading over the
second part of *The Siege of Rhodes* with great delight. We landed and
walked at Barne elmes; and then at the neat houses I landed and
bought a Millon (and we did also land and eat and drink at
Wandsworth); and so to the Old Swan, and there walked home – it
being a mighty fine evening, cool evening; and there being come,
my wife and I spent an hour in the garden, talking of our living in
the country when I shall be turned out of the office, as I fear the
Parliament may find faults enough with the office to remove us all.
And I am joyed to think in how good a condition I am to retire
thither, and have wherewith very well to subsist. Thence home and
to bed.

6.    Up and to the office a while. And then by water to my Lady
Mountagu's at Westminster and there visited my Lord Hinchingbrooke, newly come from Hinchingbrooke; and find him a
mighty sober gentleman – to my great content. Thence to Sir Ph.
Warwickes and my Lord Treasurer's, but failed in my business. So
home, and in Fanchurch street met with Mr. Battersby; says he,
"Do you see Dan Rawlinson's door shut up?" (which I did, and
wondered); "Why," says he, "after all the sickness, and himself
spending all the last year in the country – one of his men is now dead
of the plague, and his wife and one of his maids sick, and himself
shut up;" which troubles me mightily. So home, and there do hear
also from Mrs. Sarah Daniel that Greenwich is at this time much
worse then ever it was, and Deptford too; and she told us that they
believed all the town would leave the town and come to London;
which is now the receptacle of all the people from all infected places.
God preserve us. So by and by to dinner; and after dinner in comes
Mrs. Knepp; and I being at the office, went home to her, and there I
sat and talked with her, it being the first time of her being here since
her being brought to bed. I very pleasant with her, but perceive my
wife hath no great pleasure in her being here, she not being pleased
with my kindness here to her. However, we talked and sang, and
were very pleasant. By and by comes Mr. Pierce and his wife, the
first time she also hath been here since her lying-in (both having
been brought to bed of boys, and both of them dead). And here we

talked and were pleasant; only, my wife in a chagrin humour, she not being pleased with my kindness to either of them. But by this means we had little pleasure in their visit; however, Knipp and I sang, and then I offered them to carry them home and to take my wife with me, but she would not go: so I with them, leaving my wife in a very ill humour, and very slighting to them, which vexed me. However, I would not be removed from my civility to them, but sent for a coach and went with them; and in our way, Knipp saying that she came out of doors without a dinner to us, I took them to old Fishstreete, to the very house and room where I kept my wedding-dinner, where I never was since; and there I did give them a jole of Salmon and what else was to be had.

7.   Up and to the office, where we sat all the morning; and home to dinner, and then to the office again, being pretty good friends with my wife again, no angry words passing. In the evening comes Mr. Reeves with a 12-foote glasse; and so I left the office and home, where I met Mr. Batelier with my wife, in order to their going tomorrow by agreement to Bow to see a dancing meeting. But Lord, to see how soon I could conceive evil fears and thought concerning them. So Reeves and I and they up to the top of the house, and there we endeavoured to see the moon and Saturne and Jupiter; but the heaven proved cloudy, and so we lost our labour, having taken pains to get things together in order to the managing of our long glass. So down to supper and then to bed, Reeves lying at my house; but good discourse I had from him in his own trade concerning glasses. And so all of us late to bed. I receive fresh intelligence that Deptford and Greenwich are now afresh exceedingly afflicted with the sickness, more then ever.

8.   Up, and with Reeves walk as far as the Temple, doing some business in my way, at my bookseller's and elsewhere; and there parted, and I took coach (having first discoursed with Mr. Hooke a little, whom we met in the street, about the nature of Sounds, and he did make me understand the nature of Musicall sounds made by Strings, mighty prettily; and told me that having come to a certain Number of Vibracions proper to make any tone, he is able to tell how many strokes a fly makes with her wings (those flies that hum in their flying) by the note that it answers to in Musique during their flying. That, I suppose, is a little too much raffined; but his discourse in general of sound was mighty fine). There I left them,

and myself by coach to St. James's, where we attended with the rest of my fellows on the Duke, whom I found with two or three patches upon his nose and about his right eye, which came from being struck with the bow of a tree the other day in his hunting; and it is a wonder it did not strike out his eye. After we had done our business with him, which is now but little, the want of money being such as leaves us little to do but to answer complaints of the want thereof, and nothing to offer to the Duke – the representing of our wants of money being now become uselesse – I into the park, and there I met with Mrs. Burroughs by appointment, and did agree (after discoursing upon some business of hers) for her to meet me at the New Exchange; while I by coach to my Lord Treasurer's, and then called at the New Exchange, and thence carried her by water to parliament stayres, and I to the Exchequer about my Tanger Quarters tallies; and that done, I took coach and to the west door of the abby, where she came to me; and I with her by coach to Lissen greene, where we were last, and stayed an hour or two before dinner could be got for us, I in the meantime having much pleasure with her, but all honest. And by and by dinner came up, and then to my sport again, but still honest; and then took coach, and up and down in the country toward Acton, and then toward Chelsy, and so to Westminster, and there set her down where I took her up, with mighty pleasure in her company; and so I by coach home, and thence to Bow with all the haste I could, to my Lady Pooly's, where my wife was with Mr. Batelier and his sisters; and there I found a noble Supper, and everything exceeding pleasant; and their mother, Mrs. Batelier, a fine woman (but mighty passionate upon sudden news brought her of the loss of a dog, borrowed of the Duke of Albemarle's son to lime a bitch of hers that is very pretty; but the dog was by and by found, and so all well again); their company mighty innocent and pleasant, we having never been here before.

About 10 a-clock we rose from table, and sang a song, and so home in two coaches (W. Batelier and his sister Mary and my wife and I in one, and Mercer alone in the other); and after being examined at Allgate whether we were husbands and wifes, home. And being there come and sent away W. Batelier and his sister, I find Reeves there, it being a mighty fine bright night; and so upon my leads, though very sleepy, till one in the morning, looking on the moon and Jupiter with this 12-foot glass, and another of 6-foot that he hath brought with him tonight, and the sights mighty pleasant. And one of the glasses I will buy, it being very usefull. So to bed, mighty sleepy, but with much pleasure – Reeves lying at my house again; and mighty proud I am (and ought to be thankful to God Almighty) that I am able to have a spare bed for my friends.

12. *Lords day*. Up and to my chamber, where busy all the morning; and my thoughts very much upon the manner of my removal of my closet things the next week into my present Musique-room, if I find I can spare or get money to furnish it. By and by comes Reeves by appointment, but did not bring the glasses and things I expected for our discourse and my information today, but we have agreed on it for next Sunday. By and by in comes Betty Michell and her husband; and so to dinner, I mightily pleased with their company. We passed the whole day talking with them, but without any pleasure but only her being there. In the evening all parted, and I and my wife up to her closet to consider how to order that the next summer, if we live to it. And then down to my chamber at night to examine her kitchen accounts; and there I took occasion to fall out with her, for buying of a laced handkercher and pinner without my leave; though the thing is not much, yet I would not permit her begin to do so, lest worse should fallow; from this we begin both to be angry very much, and so continued till bed, and did not sleep friends.

13. Up, without being friends with my wife, nor great enemies, being both quiet and silent. So out to Colvills; but he not being come to town yet, I to Paul's churchyard to treat with a bookbinder to come and gild the backs of all my books to make them handsome, to stand up in my new presses when they come.

14. *Thankesgiving day*. Up, and comes Mr. Foly and his man with a box of great variety of Carpenters and Joyners tooles which I had bespoke, to me, which please me mightily, but I will have more. Then I abroad down to the Old Swan, and there I called and kissed Betty Michell and would have got her to go with me to Westminster, but I find her a little colder then she used to be methought, which did a little molest me. So I away, not pleased, and to Whitehall, to the chapel, and heard a piece of the Dean of Westminsters sermon and a special good Anthemne before the king after sermon. And then home by coach with Capt. Cocke – who is in pain about his Hemp, of which he says he hath bought great

quantities, and would gladly be upon good terms with us for it – wherein I promise to assist him. So we light at the Change, where after a small turn or two, taking no pleasure nowadays to be there, because of answering questions that would be asked there which I cannot answer. So home and dined. And after dinner with my wife and Mercer to the Beare garden, where I have not been I think of many years, and saw some good sport of the bull's tossing of the dogs – one into the very boxes. But it is a very rude and nasty pleasure. We had a great many hectors in the same box with us (and one, very fine, went into the pit and played his dog for a wager, which was a strange sport for a gentleman), where they drank wine, and drank Mercer's health first, which I pledged with my hat off. And who should be in the house but Mr. Pierce the surgeon, who saw us and spoke to us.

Thence home, well enough satisfied however with the variety of this afternoon's exercise; and so I to my chamber, till in the evening our company came to supper we had invited to a venison pasty – Mr. Batelier and his sister Mary, Mrs. Mercer – her daughter Anne, Mr. Le Brun, and W. Hewers. And so we supped, and very merry. And then about 9 a-clock, to Mrs. Mercers gate, where the fire and boys expected us and her son had provided abundance of Serpents and rockets; and there mighty merry (my Lady Pen and Pegg going thither with us and Nan Wright) till about 12 at night, flinging our fireworks and burning one another and the people over the way. And at last, our businesses being most spent – we into Mrs. Mercers, and there mighty merry, smutting one another with Candlegresse and soot, till most of us were like devils; and that being done, then we broke up and to my house, and there I made them drink; and upstairs we went, and then fell into dancing (W. Batelier dancing well) and dressing, him and I and one Mr. Banister (who with his wife came over also with us) like women; and Mercer put on a suit of Toms, like a boy, and mighty mirth we had, and Mercer danced a Jigg, and Nan Wright and my wife and Pegg Pen put on periwigs. Thus we spent till 3 or 4 in the morning, mighty merry; and then parted and to bed.

15.    Mighty sleepy; slept till past 8 of the clock, and was called up by a letter from Sir W. Coventry; which, among other things, tells me how we have burned 160 ships of the enemy within the Fly. I up, and with all possible haste, and in pain for fear of coming late, it being our day of attending the Duke of York, to St. James's, where

they are full of the perticulars – how they are generally good merchant ships, some of them laden, and supposed rich ships. We spent five fireships upon them. We landed on the Schelling (Sir Ph. Howard with some men, and Holmes I think with others, about 1000 in all), and burned a town – and so came away. By and by the Duke of York with his books showed us the very place and manner – and that it was not our design or expectation to have done this, but only to have landed on the Fly and burned some of their stores; but being come in, we spied these ships, and with our longboats one by one fired them, our ships running all aground, it being so shoal water. We were led to this by, it seems, a Renegado Captain of the Hollanders, who found himself ill-used by De Ruyter for his good service, and so came over to us; and hath done us good service, so that now we trust him, and he himself did go on this expedition. The service is very great – and our joys as great for it. All is, it will make the Duke of Albemarle in repute again I doubt – though there be nothing of his in this. But Lord, to see what success doth, whether with or without reason, and making a man seem wise, notwithstanding never so late demonstration of the profoundest folly in the world. Thence to the Exchequer, but did nothing, they being all gone from their offices; and so to the Old Exchange, where the town full of this good news; but I did not stay to tell or hear any, but home, my head akeing and drowzy, and to dinner; and then lay down upon the couch, thinking to get a little rest, but could not. So down the River, reading *The Adventures of five houres*, which the more I read the more I admire. So down below Greenwich; but the wind and tide being against us, I back again to Deptford and did a little business there, and thence walked to Redriffe, and so home – and to the office a while; in the evening comes W. Batelier and his sister and my wife and fair Mrs. Turner into the garden, and there we walked; and then with my Lady Pen and Pegg in a-doors, and eat and were merry; and so pretty late broke up and to bed – the guns of the Tower going off, and there being bonefires also in the street for this late good Successe.

16. Up, having slept well; and after entering my journall, to the office – where all the morning; but of late Sir W. Coventry hath not come to us, he being discouraged from the little we have to do but to answer the clamours of people for money. At noon home, and there dined with me my Lady Pen only, and W. Hewer, at a haunch of venison boiled – where pretty merry. Only, my wife vexed me a

little about demanding money to go with my Lady Pen to the Exchange to lay out. I to the office, where all the afternoon very busy and doing much business. But here I had a most eminent experience of the evil of being behindhand in business; I was the most backward to begin anything, and would fain have framed to myself an occasion of going abroad, and should I doubt have done it – but some business coming in, one after another, kept me there, and I fell to the ridding away of a great deal of business; and when my hand was in it, was so pleasing a sight to [see] my papers disposed of, and letters answered which troubled my book and table, that I could have continued there with delight all night long; and did, till called away by my Lady Pen and Pegg and my wife to their house to eat with them; and there I went, and exceeding merry, there being Nan Wright, now Mrs. Markeham, and sits at table with my Lady. So mighty merry, home and to bed.

17.   With Capt. Erwin, discoursing about the East Indys, where he hath often been. And among other things, he tells me how the King of Syam seldom goes out without 30 or 40000 people with him, and not a word spoke nor a hum or cough in the whole company to be heard. He tells me the punishment frequently there for malefactors is cutting off the Crowne of their head, which they do very dexterously, leaving their brains bare, which kills them presently. He told me, what I remember he hath once done heretofore – that everybody is to lie flat down at the coming by of the King, and nobody to look upon him, upon pain of death. And that he and his fellows, being strangers, were invited to see the sport of taking of a wild Eliphant. And they did only kneel and look toward the King. Their Druggerman did desire them to fall down, for otherwise he should suffer for their contempt of the King. The sport being ended, a messenger comes from the King, which the Druggerman thought had been to have taken away his life. But it was to enquire how the strangers liked the sport. The Druggerman answered that they did cry it up to be the best that ever they saw, and that they never heard of any prince so great in everything as this King. The messenger being gone back, Erwin and his company asked their Druggerman what he had said, which he told them. "But why," say they, "would you say that without our leave, it being not true?" "It is no matter for that," says he, "I must have said it, or have been hanged, for our King doth not live by meat nor drink, but by having great lyes told him."

19. *Lords day*. Up, and to my chamber, and there begun to draw out fair and methodically my accounts of Tanger in order to show them to the Lords. But by and by comes by agreement Mr. Reeves, and after him Mr. Spong; and all day with them, both before and after dinner till 10 a-clock at night, upon Opticke enquiries – he bringing me a frame with closes on, to see how the Rays of light do cut one another, and in a dark room with smoake, which is very pretty. He did also bring a lantern, with pictures in glass to make strange things appear on a wall, very pretty. We did also at night see Jupiter and his girdle and Satellites very fine with my 12-foot glass, but could not Saturne, he being very dark. Spong and I also had several fine discourses upon the globes this afternoon, perticularly why the fixed stars do not rise and set at the same hour all the year long, which he could not demonstrate, nor I neither, the reason of. So it being late, after supper they away home. But it vexed me to understand no more from Reeves and his glasses touching the nature and reason of the several refractions of the several figured glasses, he understanding the acting part but not one bit the theory, nor can make anybody understand it – which is a strange dullness methinks.

20. Up and to Deptford by water, reading *Othello, Moore of Venice*, which I ever heretofore esteemed a mighty good play; but having so lately read *The Adventures of five hours*, it seems a mean thing. Walked back, and so home and then down to the old Swan and drank at B. Michells; and so to Westminster to the Exchequer about my quarter's tallies; and so to Lumberdstreete to choose stuff to hang my new intended closet, and have chosen purple. So home to dinner, and all the afternoon, till almost midnight, upon my Tanger accounts, getting Tom Willson to help me in writing as I read, and at night W. Hewers; and find myself most happy in the keeping of all my accounts, for that after all the changings and turnings necessary in such an account, I find myself right to a farding, in an account of 127000*l*. This afternoon I visited Sir J. Mennes, who, poor man, is much impaired by these few days sickness; and I fear endeed it will kill him.

21. Late at the office; and then home and there find Mr. Batelier and his sister Mary, and we sat chatting a great while, talking of Wiches and Spirits; and he told me of his own knowledge, being with some others at Bourdeaux, making a bargain with another

man at a taverne for some Claretts, they did hire a fellow to thunder (which he had the art of doing upon a deale board) and to rain and hail; that is, make the noise of – so as did give them a pretence of undervaluing their Merchants wines, by saying this thunder would spoil and turn them – which was so reasonable to the Merchant that he did abate two *pistolls* per Ton for the wine, in belief of that – whereas, going out, there was no such thing. This Batelier did see and was the cause of, to his profit, as is above said. By and by broke up, and to bed.

22. Up and by coach with 100*l* to the Exchequer to pay fees there. There left it, and I to St. James's and there with the Duke of York. I had opportunity of much talk with Sir W. Penn today (he being newly come from the fleet); and he doth much undervalue the honour that is given to the conduct of the late business of Holmes in burning the ships and town, saying it was a great thing endeed, and of great profit to us, in being of great loss to the enemy; but that it was wholly a business of chance, and no conduct imployed in it. I find Sir W. Penn doth hold up his head at this time higher then ever he did in his life. I perceive he doth look after Sir J. Mennes's place if he dies; and though I love him not, nor do desire to have him in, yet I do think him the ablest man in England for it. To the Chequer, and there received my tallies and paid my fees in good order. And so home, and there find Mrs. Knipp and my wife going to dinner. She tells me my song of *Beauty Retire* is mightily cried up – which I am not a little proud of; and do think I have done *It is Decreed* better, but I have not finished it. My Closet is doing by Upholsters, which I am pleased with, but fear my purple will be too sad for that melancholy room. After dinner and doing something at the office, I with my wife, Knepp, and Mercer by coach to Moorefields and there saw *Polichinelle*, which pleases me mightily; and here I saw our Mary, our last chambermaid, who is gone from Mrs. Pierce's it seems. Then carried Knipp home, calling at the Cocke alehouse at the door and drank. And so home and there find Reeves; and so up to look upon the Starrs, and do like my glass very well and did even with him for it, and a little perspective and the Lanthorne that shows tricks – all together costing me 9*l* 5*s*. So to bed, he lying at our house.

24. Up, and despatched several businesses at home in the morning; and then comes Sympson to set up my other new Presse

for my books; and so he and I fell in to the Furnishing of my new closet, and taking out the things out of my old. I kept him with me all day, and he dined with me; and so all the afternoon, till it was quite dark – hanging things; that is, my maps and picture[s] – and Draughts – and setting up my books, and as much as we could do – to my most extraordinary satisfaction; so that I think it will be as noble a closet as any man hath, and light enough; though endeed, it would be better to have had a little more light. He gone, my wife and I to talk – and sup; and then to setting right my Tanger accounts and enter my Journall; and then to bed, with great content in my day's work. This afternoon came Mrs. Barbary Shelden, now Mrs. Wood, to see my wife. I was so busy, I would not see her. But she came, it seems, mighty rich in rings and fine clothes, and like a lady; and says she is matched mighty well – at which I am very glad, but wonder at her good fortune and the folly of her husband – and vexed at myself for not paying her the respect of seeing her. But I will come out of her debt another time.

26.   *Lords day.* Up betimes, and to the finishing the setting things in order in my new closet out of my old; which I did thoroughly by the time sermon was done at church – to my exceeding joy; only, I was a little disturbed with news my Lord Bruncker brought me, that we are to attend the King at Whitehall this afternoon, and that it is about a complaint from the Generals[1] against us. Sir W. Penn dined by invitation with me, his Lady and daughter being gone into the country. We very merry. After dinner we parted, and I to my office, whither I sent for Mr. Lewes and instructed myself fully in the business of the victualling, to enable me to answer in that matter; and then Sir W. Penn and I by coach to Whitehall and there stayed till the King and Cabinet was met in the green Chamber, and then were called in; and there the King begun with me, to hear how the victualls of the fleet stood; I did in long discourse tell him and the rest (the Duke of York, Lord Chancellor, Lord Treasurer, both the Secretarys, Sir G. Carteret, and Sir W. Coventry) how it stood; wherein they seemed satisfied, but press mightily for more supplies; and the letter of the Generals, which was read, did lay their not going, or too soon returning from the Duch coast, this next bout, to the want of victuals. Then they proceeded to the enquiry after the fireships; and did all very superficially – and without any

1. See above, p. 644 (18 July) & n.

severity at all. But however, I was in pain, after we came out, to know how I had done – and hear, well enough. But however, it shall be a caution to me to prepare myself against a day of inquisition.

28. Up, and in my new closet a good while, doing business. Then called on by Mrs. Martin and Burroughs of Westminster, about business of the former's husband – which done, I to the office, where we sat all the morning. At noon I with my wife and Mercer to Philpott lane, a great cook's shop, to the wedding of Mr. Longracke our Purveyor, a good sober civil man, and hath married a sober serious mayde. Here I met much ordinary company, going thither at his great request – but there was Mr. Madden and his lady, a fine noble pretty lady – and he a fine gentleman seems to be. We four were most together; but the whole company was very simple and innocent. A good dinner, and what was best, good Musique. After dinner the young women went to dance – among others, Mr. Chr. Pett his daughter, who is a very pretty modest girl – I am mightily taken with her. And that being done, about 5 a-clock home, very well pleased with the afternoon's work. And so we broke up mighty civilly, the bride and bridegroom going to Greenwich (they keeping their dinner here only for my sake) to lie; and we home – where I to the office. And anon am on a sudden called to meet Sir W. Coventry and Sir W. Penn at the Victualling Office, which did put me out of order to be so surprized. But I went, and there Sir W. Coventry did read me a letter from the Generalls to the King, a most scurvy letter, reflecting most upon Sir W. Coventry, and then upon me for my accounts (not that they are not true, but that we do not consider the expense of the fleet), and then of the whole office in neglecting them and the King's service; and this in very plain and sharp and menacing terms. I did give a good account of matters, according to our computation of the expense of the fleet. I find Sir W. Coventry willing enough to accept of anything to confront the Generals. But a great supply must be made, and shall be, in grace of God; but however, our accounts here will be found the true ones. Having done here, and much work set me, I with greater content home then I thought I should have done; and so to the office awhile, and then home and a while in my new closet, which delights me every day more and more. And so late to bed.

29. To St James's, and there Sir W. Coventry took Sir W. Penn

and me apart and read to us his answer to the Generalls letter to the King that he read last night; wherein he is very plain, and states the matter in full defence of himself, and of me with him, which he could not avoid – which is a good comfort to me, that I happen to be involved with him in the same cause. And then speaking of the supplies which have been made to this fleet, more then ever in all kinds to any, even that wherein the Duke of York himself was – "Well," says he, "if this will not do, I will say, as Sir J. Falstaffe did to the Prince – 'Tell your father, that if he do not like this, let him kill the next Piercy himself.'" And so we broke up, and to the Duke and there did our usual business.

## ⟶✛SEPTEMBER✛⟵

2. *Lords day*. Some of our maids sitting up late last night to get things ready against our feast today, Jane called us up, about 3 in the morning, to tell us of a great fire they saw in the City. So I rose, and slipped on my nightgown and went to her window, and thought it to be on the back side of Markelane at the furthest; but being unused to such fires as fallowed, I thought it far enough off, and so went to bed again and to sleep. About 7 rose again to dress myself, and there looked out at the window and saw the fire not so much as it was, and further off. So to my closet to set things to rights after yesterday's cleaning. By and by Jane comes and tells me that she hears that above 300 houses have been burned down tonight by the fire we saw, and that it was now burning down all Fishstreet by London Bridge. So I made myself ready presently, and walked to the Tower and there got up upon one of the high places, Sir J. Robinsons little son going up with me; and there I did see the houses at that end of the bridge all on fire, and an infinite great fire on this and the other side the end of the bridge – which, among other people, did trouble me for poor little Michell and our Sarah on the Bridge. So down, with my heart full of trouble, to the Lieutenant of the Tower, who tells me that it begun this morning in the King's bakers house in Pudding lane, and that it hath burned down St. Magnes Church and most part of Fishstreete already. So I down to the waterside and there got a boat and through the bridge, and there saw a lamentable fire. Poor Michells house, as far as the Old Swan, already burned that way and the fire running further, that in a very

little time it got as far as the Stillyard while I was there. Everybody endeavouring to remove their goods, and flinging into the River or bringing them into lighters that lay off. Poor people staying in their houses as long as till the very fire touched them, and then running into boats or clambering from one pair of stair by the waterside to another. And among other things, the poor pigeons I perceive were loath to leave their houses, but hovered about the windows and balconies till they were some of them burned, their wings, and fell down.

Having stayed, and in an hour's time seen the fire rage every way, and nobody to my sight endeavouring to quench it, but to remove their goods and leave all to the fire; and having seen it get as far as the Steeleyard, and the wind mighty high and driving it into the city, and everything, after so long a drougth, proving combustible, even the very stones of churches, and among other things, the poor steeple by which pretty Mrs. [Horsley] lives, and whereof my old schoolfellow Elborough is parson, taken fire in the very top and there burned till it fall down – I to Whitehall with a gentleman with me who desired to go off from the Tower to see the fire in my boat – to Whitehall, and there up to the King's closet in the chapel, where people came about me and I did give them an account dismayed them all; and word was carried in to the King, so I was called for and did tell the King and Duke of York what I saw, and that unless his Majesty did command houses to be pulled down, nothing could stop the fire. They seemed much troubled, and the King commanded me to go to my Lord Mayor from him and command him to spare no houses but to pull down before the fire every way. The Duke of York bid me tell him that if he would have any more soldiers, he shall; and so did my Lord Arlington afterward, as a great secret. Here meeting with Capt. Cocke, I in his coach, which he lent me, and Creed with me, to Pauls; and there walked along Watling street as well as I could, every creature coming away loaden with goods to save – and here and there sick people carried away in beds. Extraordinary good goods carried in carts and on backs. At last met my Lord Mayor in Canning Streete, like a man spent, with a handkercher about his neck. To the King's message, he cried like a fainting woman, "Lord, what can I do? I am spent! People will not obey me. I have been pull[ing] down houses. But the fire overtakes us faster then we can do it." That he needed no more soldiers; and that for himself, he must go and refresh himself, having been up all night. So he left me, and I him, and walked home

– seeing people all almost distracted and no manner of means used to quench the fire. The houses too, so very thick thereabouts, and full of matter for burning, as pitch and tar, in Thames street – and warehouses of oyle and wines and Brandy and other things. Here I saw Mr. Isaccke Houblon, that handsome man – prettily dressed and dirty at his door at Dowgate, receiving some of his brothers things whose houses were on fire; and as he says, have been removed twice already, and he doubts (as it soon proved) that they must be in a little time removed from his house also – which was a sad consideration. And to see the churches all filling with goods, by people who themselfs should have been quietly there at this time. By this time it was about 12 a-clock, and so home and there find my guests, which was Mr. Wood and his wife, Barbary Shelden, and also Mr. Moone – she mighty fine, and her husband, for aught I see, a likely man. But Mr. Moones design and mine, which was to look over my closet and please him with the sight thereof, which he hath long desired, was wholly disappointed, for we were in great trouble and disturbance at this fire, not knowing what to think of it. However, we had an extraordinary good dinner, and as merry as at this time we could be. While at dinner, Mrs. Batelier came to enquire after Mr. Woolfe and Stanes (who it seems are related to them), whose houses in Fishstreet are all burned, and they in a sad condition. She would not stay in the fright.

As soon as dined, I and Moone away and walked through the City, the streets full of nothing but people and horses and carts loaden with goods, ready to run over one another, and removing goods from one burned house to another – they now removing out of Canning street (which received goods in the morning) into Lumbard Streete and further; and among others, I now saw my little goldsmith Stokes receiving some friend's goods, whose house itself was burned the day after. We parted at Pauls, he home and I to Pauls Wharf, where I had appointed a boat to attend me; and took in Mr. Carcasse and his brother, whom I met in the street, and carried them below and above bridge, to and again, to see the fire, which was now got further, both below and above, and no likelihood of stopping it. Met with the King and Duke of York in their Barge, and with them to Queen Hith and there called Sir Rd. Browne to them. Their order was only to pull down houses apace, and so below bridge at the waterside; but little was or could be done, the fire coming upon them so fast. Good hopes there was of stopping it at the Three Cranes above, and at Buttolphs Wharf below bridge, if care be used; but the wind carries it into the City, so as we know not by the waterside what it doth there. River full of lighter[s] and boats taking in goods, and good goods swimming in the water; and only, I observed that hardly one lighter or boat in three that had goods of a house in, but there was a pair of virginalls in it. Having seen as much as I could now, I away to Whitehall by appointment, and there walked to St. James's Park, and there met my wife and Creed and Wood and his wife and walked to my boat, and there upon the water again, and to the fire up and down, it still increasing and the wind great. So near the fire as we could for smoke; and all over the Thames, with one's face in the wind you were almost burned with a shower of Firedrops – this is very true – so as houses were burned by these drops and flakes of fire, three or four, nay five or six houses, one from another. When we could endure no more upon the water, we to a little alehouse on the Bankside over against the Three Cranes, and there stayed till it was dark almost and saw the fire grow; and as it grow darker, appeared more and more, and in Corners and upon steeples and between churches and houses, as far as we could see up the hill of the City, in a most horrid malicious bloody flame, not like the fine flame of an ordinary fire. Barbary and her husband away before us. We stayed till, it being darkish, we saw the fire as only one entire arch of fire from this to the other side of the bridge, and in a bow up the hill, for an arch of above a mile long. It made me weep to see it. The churches, houses, and all on fire and flaming at once, and a horrid noise the flames made, and the cracking of houses at their ruine.

So home with a sad heart, and there find everybody discoursing and lamenting the fire; and poor Tom Hater came with some few of his goods saved out of his house, which is burned upon Fish street hill. I invited him to lie at my house, and did receive his goods: but was deceived in his lying there, the noise coming every moment of the growth of the Fire, so as we were forced to begin to pack up our own goods and prepare for their removal. And did by Mooneshine (it being brave, dry, and moonshine and warm weather) carry much of my goods into the garden, and Mr. Hater and I did remove my money and Iron chests into my cellar – as thinking that the safest place. And got my bags of gold into my office ready to carry away, and my chief papers of accounts also there, and my tallies into a box by themselfs. So great was our fear, as Sir W. Batten had carts come out of the country to fetch away his goods this night. We did put Mr. Hater, poor man, to bed a little; but he got but very little rest, so much noise being in my house, taking down of goods.

3.    About 4 a-clock in the morning, my Lady Batten sent me a cart to carry away all my money and plate and best things to Sir W. Riders at Bednall greene; which I did, riding myself in my nightgown in the Cart; and Lord, to see how the streets and the highways are crowded with people, running and riding and getting of carts at any rate to fetch away thing[s]. I find Sir W. Rider tired with being called up all night and receiving things from several friends. His house full of goods – and much of Sir W. Batten and Sir W. Penn's. I am eased at my heart to have my treasure so well secured. Then home with much ado to find a way. Nor any sleep all this night to me nor my poor wife. But then, and all this day, she and I and all my people labouring to get away the rest of our things, and did get Mr. Tooker to get me a lighter to take them in, and we did carry them (myself some) over Tower hill, which was by this time full of people's goods, bringing their goods thither. And down to the lighter, which lay at the next quay above the Tower dock. And there was my neighbour's wife, Mrs. [Buckworth], with her pretty child and some few of her things, which I did willingly give way to be saved with mine. But there was no passing with anything through the postern, the crowd was so great. The Duke of York came this day by the office and spoke to us, and did ride with his guard up and down the City to keep all quiet (he being now General, and having the care of all). This day, Mercer being not at home, but against her mistress order gone to her mother's, and my wife going thither to speak with W. Hewer, met her there and was angry; and her mother saying that she was not a prentice girl, to ask leave every time she goes abroad, my wife with good reason was angry, and when she came home, bid her be gone again. And so she went away, which troubled me; but yet less then it would, because of the condition we are in fear of coming into in a little time, of being less able to keep one in her quality. At night, lay down a little upon a quilt of W. Hewer in the office (all my own things being packed up or gone); and after me, my poor wife did the like – we having fed upon the remains of yesterday's dinner, having no fire nor dishes, nor any opportunity of dressing anything.

4.    Up by break of day to get away the remainder of my things, which I did by a lighter at the Iron gate; and my hands so few, that it was the afternoon before we could get them all away. Sir W. Penn

and I to Tower street, and there met the fire Burning three or four doors beyond Mr. Howells; whose goods, poor man (his trayes and dishes, Shovells &c., were flung all along Tower street in the kennels, and people working therewith from one end to the other), the fire coming on in that narrow street, on both sides, with infinite fury. Sir W. Batten, not knowing how to remove his wind,* did dig a pit in the garden and laid it in there; and I took the opportunity of laying all the papers of my office that I could not otherwise dispose of. And in the evening Sir W. Penn and I did dig another and put our wine in it, and I my parmazan cheese as well as my wine and some other things. The Duke of York was at the office this day at Sir W. Penn's, but I happened not to be within. This afternoon, sitting melancholy with Sir W. Penn in our garden and thinking of the certain burning of this office without extraordinary means, I did propose for the sending up of all our workmen from Woolwich and Deptford yards (none whereof yet appeared), and to write to Sir W. Coventry to have the Duke of York's permission to pull down houses rather then lose this office, which would much hinder the King's business. So Sir W. Penn he went down this night, in order to the sending them up tomorrow morning; and I wrote to Sir W. Coventry about the business, but received no answer.

This night Mrs. Turner (who, poor woman, was removing her goods all this day – good goods, into the garden, and knew not how to dispose of them) – and her husband supped with my wife and I at night in the office, upon a shoulder of mutton from the cook's, without any napkin or anything, in a sad manner but were merry. Only, now and then walking into the garden and saw how horridly the sky looks, all on a fire in the night, was enough to put us out of our wits; and endeed it was extremely dreadfull – for it looks just as if it was at us, and the whole heaven on fire. I after supper walked in the dark down to Tower street, and there saw it all on fire at the Trinity house on that side and the Dolphin tavern on this side, which was very near us – and the fire with extraordinary vehemence. Now begins the practice of blowing up of houses in Tower street, those next the Tower, which at first did frighten people more then anything; but it stop[ped] the fire where it was done – it bringing down the houses to the ground in the same places they stood, and then it was easy to quench what little fire was in it, though it kindled nothing almost. W. Hewer this day went to see how his mother did, and comes late home, but telling us how he hath been forced to remove her to Islington, her house in pye

Corner being burned. So that it is got so far that way and all the Old Bayly, and was running down to Fleetestreet. And Pauls is burned, and all Cheapside. I wrote to my father this night; but the post-house being burned, the letter could not go.

5. I lay down in the office again upon W. Hewer's quilt, being mighty weary and sore in my feet with going till I was hardly able to stand. About 2 in the morning my wife calls me up and tells of new Cryes of "Fyre!" – it being come to Barkeing Church, which is the bottom of our lane. I up; and finding it so, resolved presently to take her away; and did, and took my gold (which was about 2350*l*), W. Hewer, and Jane down by Poundy's boat to Woolwich. But Lord, what a sad sight it was by moonlight to see the whole City almost on fire – that you might see it plain at Woolwich, as if you were by it. There when I came, I find the gates shut, but no guard kept at all; which troubled me, because of discourses now begun that there is plot in it and that the French had done it. I got the gates open, and to Mr. Shelden's, where I locked up my gold and charged my wife and W. Hewer never to leave the room without one of them in it night nor day. So back again, by the way seeing my goods well in the lighters at Deptford and watched well by people. Home, and whereas I expected to have seen our house on fire, it being now about 7 a-clock, it was not. But to the Fyre, and there find greater hopes then I expected; for my confidence of finding our office on fire was such, that I durst not ask anybody how it was with us, till I came and saw it not burned. But going to the fire, I find, by the blowing up of houses and the great help given by the workmen out of the King's yards, sent up by Sir W. Penn, there is a good stop given to it, as well at Marke lane end as ours – it having only burned the Dyall of Barkeing Church, and part of the porch, and was there quenched. I up to the top of Barkeing steeple, and there saw the saddest sight of desolation that I ever saw. Everywhere great fires. Oyle cellars and brimstone and other things burning. I became afeared to stay there long; and therefore down again as fast as I could, the fire being spread as far as I could see it, and to Sir W. Penn's and there eat a piece of cold meat, having eaten nothing since Sunday but the remains of Sunday's dinner.

Here I met with Mr. Young and Whistler; and having removed all my things, and received good hopes that the fire at our end is stopped, they and I walked into the town and find Fanchurch street, Gracious street, and Lumbard street all in dust. The Exchange a sad sight, nothing standing there of all the statues or pillars but Sir Tho. Gresham's picture in the corner. Walked into Moorefields (our feet ready to burn, walking through the town among the hot coles) and find that full of people, and poor wretches carrying their goods there, and everybody keeping his goods together by themselfs (and a great blessing it is to them that it is fair weather for them to keep abroad night and day); drank there, and paid twopence for a plain penny loaf. Thence homeward, having passed through Cheapside and Newgate market, all burned – and seen Anthony Joyces house in fire. And took up (which I keep by me) a piece of glass of Mercer's chapel in the street, where much more was, so melted and buckled with the heat of the fire, like parchment. I also did see a poor Catt taken out of a hole in the chimney joyning to the wall of the Exchange, with the hair all burned off the body and yet alive. So home at night, and find there good hopes of saving our office – but great endeavours of watching all night and having men ready; and so we lodged them in the office, and had drink and bread and cheese for them. And I lay down and slept a good night about midnight – though when I rose, I hear that there had been a great alarme of French and Duch being risen – which proved nothing. But it is a strange thing to see how long this time did look since Sunday, having been alway full of variety of actions, and little sleep, that it looked like a week or more. And I had forgot almost the day of the week.

6. Up about 5 a-clock, and there met Mr. Gawden at the gate of the office (I entending to go out, as I used every now and then to do, to see how the fire is) to call our men to Bishoppsgate, where no fire had yet been near, and there is now one broke out – which did give great grounds to people, and to me too, to think that there is some kind of plott in this (on which many by this time have been taken, and it hath been dangerous for any stranger to walk in the streets); but I went with the men and we did put it out in a little time, so that that was well again. It was pretty to see how hard the women did work in the cannells sweeping of water; but then they would scold for drink and be as drunk as devils. I saw good Butts of sugar broke open in the street, and people go and take handfuls out and put into beer and drink it. And now all being pretty well, I took boat and over to Southwarke, and took boat on the other side the bridge and so to Westminster, thinking to Shift myself, being all in dirt from top to bottom. But could not there find any place to buy a Shirt or

pair of gloves, Westminster hall being full of people's goods – those in Westminster having removed all their goods, and the Exchequer money put into vessels to carry to Nonsuch. But to the Swan, and there was trimmed. And then to Whitehall, but saw nobody, and so home. A sad sight to see how the River looks – no houses nor church near it to the Temple – where it stopped. At home did go with Sir W. Batten and our neighbour Knightly (who, with one more, was the only man of any fashion left in all the neighbourhood hereabouts, they all removing their goods and leaving their houses to the mercy of the fire) to Sir R. Ford's, and there dined, in an earthen platter a fried breast of mutton, a great many of us. But very merry; and endeed as good a meal, though as ugly a one, as ever I had in my life. Thence down to Deptford, and there with great satisfaction landed all my goods at Sir G. Carteret's, safe, and nothing missed I could see, or hurt. This being done to my great content, I home; and to Sir W. Batten's and there with Sir R. Ford, Mr. Knightly, and one Withers, a professed lying rogue, supped well; and mighty merry and our fears over. From them to the office and there slept, with the office full of labourers, who talked and slept and walked all night long there. But strange it was to see Cloathworkers hall on fire these three days and nights in one body of Flame – it being the cellar, full of Oyle.

7.    Up by 5 a-clock and, blessed be God, find all well, and by water to Paul's wharfe. Walked thence and saw all the town burned, and a miserable sight of Pauls church, with all the roofs fallen and the body of the Quire fallen into St Fayths – Paul's school also – Ludgate – Fleet street – my father's house, and the church, and a good part of the Temple the like. So to Creeds lodging near the New Exchange, and there find him laid down upon a bed – the house all unfurnished, there being fears of the fire's coming to them. There borrowed a shirt of him – and washed. To Sir W. Coventry at St. James's, who lay without Curtains, having removed all his goods – as the King at Whitehall and everybody had done and was doing. He hopes we shall have no public distractions upon this fire, which is what everybody fears – because of the talk of the French having a hand in it. And it is a proper time for discontents – but all men's minds are full of care to protect themselfs and save their goods. The Militia is in armes everywhere. Our Fleetes, he tells me, have been in sight of one another, and most unhappily by Fowle weather were parted, to our great loss, as in

reason they do conclude – the Duch being come out only to make a show and please their people; but in very bad condition as to stores, victuals, and men. They are at Bullen, and our fleet come to St. Ellens. We have got nothing, but have lost one ship, but he knows not what.

Thence to the Swan and there drank; and so home and find all well. My Lord Brouncker at Sir W. Batten's, and tells us the Generall is sent for up to come to advise with the King about business at this juncture, and to keep all quiet – which is great honour to him, but I am sure is but a piece of dissimulation. So home and did give order for my house to be made clean; and then down to Woolwich and there find all well. Dined, and Mrs. Markeham came to see my wife. So I up again, and calling at Deptford for some things of W. Hewer, he being with me; and then home and spent the evening with Sir R. Ford, Mr. Knightly, and Sir W. Penn at Sir W. Batten's. This day our Merchants first met at Gresham College, which by proclamation is to be their Exchange. Strange to hear what is bid for houses all up and down here – a friend of Sir W. Riders having 150*l* for what he used to let for 40*l* per annum. Much dispute where the Custome house shall be; thereby the growth of the City again to be foreseen. My Lord Treasurer, they say, and others, would have it at the other end of the town. I home late to Sir W. Penn, who did give me a bed – but without curtains or hangings, all being down. So here I went the first time into a naked bed, only my drawers on – and did sleep pretty well; but still, both sleeping and waking, had a fear of fire in my heart, that I took little rest. People do all the world over cry out of the simplicity of my Lord Mayor in general, and more perticularly in this business of the fire, laying it all upon him. A proclamation is come out for markets to be kept at Leadenhall and Mile end greene and several other places about the town, and Tower hill, and all churches to be set open to receive poor people.

8. Up, and with Sir W. Batten and Sir W. Penn by water to Whitehall, and they to St. James's. I stopped with Sir G. Carteret, to desire him to go with us and to enquire after money. But the first he cannot do, and the other as little, or says, "When can we get any, or what shall we do for it?" He, it seems, is imployed in the correspondence between the City and the King every day, in settling of things. I find him full of trouble to think how things will go. I left him, and to St. James's, where we met first at Sir W.

Coventry's chamber and there did what business we can without any books. Our discourse, as everything else, was confused. The fleet is at Portsmouth, there staying a wind to carry them to the Downes or toward Bullen, where they say the Duch fleete is gone and stays. We concluded upon private meetings for a while, not having any money to satisfy any people that may come to us. I bought two eeles upon the Thames, cost me 6s. Thence with Sir W. Batten to the Cockpit, whither the Duke of Albemarle is come. It seems the King holds him so necessary at this time, that he hath sent for him and will keep him here. Endeed, his interest in the City, being acquainted, and his care in keeping things quiet, is reckoned that wherein he will be very serviceable. We to him. He is courted in appearance by everybody. He very kind to us. I perceive he lays by all business of the fleet at present and minds the City, and is now hastening to Gresham College to discourse with the Aldermen. Sir W. Batten and I home (where met by my Brother John, come to town to see how things are with us). And then presently he with me to Gresham College – where infinite of people; partly through novelty to see the new place, and partly to find out and hear what is become one man of another. I met with many people undone, and more that have extraordinary great losses. People speaking their thoughts variously about the beginning of the fire and the rebuilding of the City. Then to Sir W. Batten and took my brother with me, and there dined with a great company of neighbours, and much good discourse; among others, of the low spirits of some rich men in the City, in sparing any encouragement to the poor people that wrought for the saving their houses. Among others, Ald. Starling, a very rich man, without children, the fire at next door to him in our Lane – after our men had saved his house, did give 2s. 6d. among 30 of them, and did quarrel with some that would remove the rubbish out of the way of the fire, saying that they came to steal. Sir W. Coventry told me of another this morning in Holborne, which he showed the King – that when it was offered to stop the fire near his house for such a reward, that came but to 2s. 6d. a man among the neighbours, he would give but 18d. Thence to Bednall green by coach, my brother with me, and saw all well there and fetched away my Journall-book to enter for five days past. To the office, and late writing letters; and then to Sir W. Penn, my brother lying with me, and Sir W. Penn gone down to rest himself at Woolwich. But I was much frighted, and kept awake in my bed, by some noise I heard a great while below-stairs and the boys not coming up to me when I knocked. It was by their discovery of people stealing of some neighbours' wine that lay in vessels in the street. So to sleep. And all well all night.

9. *Sunday*. Up, and was trimmed, and sent my brother to Woolwich to my wife to dine with her. I to church, where our parson made a melancholy but good sermon – and many, and most, in the church cried, especially the women. The church mighty full, but few of fashion, and most strangers. I walked to Bednall green; and there dined well, but a bad venison pasty, at Sir W. Rider's. Good people they are, and good discourse. And his daughter Middleton, a fine woman and discreet. Thence home, and to church again, and there preached Deane Harding; but methinks a bad poor sermon, though proper for the time – nor eloquent, in saying at this time that the City is reduced from a large Folio to a Decimo tertio. So to my office, there to write down my journall and take leave of my brother, whom I sent back this afternoon, though rainy – which it hath not done a good while before. But I had no room nor convenience for him here till my house is fitted; but I was very kind to him, and do take very well of him his journey. I did give him 40s. for his pocket; and so he being gone, and it presently rayning, I was troubled for him, though it is good for the Fyre. Anon to Sir W. Penn to bed, and made my boy Tom to read me asleep.

13. Up, and down to Tower wharfe; and there with Balty and labourers from Deptford did get my goods housed well at home. So down to Deptford again to fetch the rest, and there eat a bit of dinner at the Globe, with the maister of the *Bezan* with me, while the labourers went to dinner. Here I hear that this poor town doth bury still of the plague seven or eight in a day. So to Sir G. Carteret's to work; and there did, to my great content, ship off into the *Bezan* all the rest of my goods, saving my pictures and fine things, that I will bring home in wherrys when my house is fit to receive them. And so home and unloaden them by carts and hands before night, to my exceeding satisfaction; and so after supper to bed in my house, the first time I have lain there; and lay with my wife in my old closet upon the ground, and Balty and his wife in the best chamber, upon the ground also.

14. Up, and to work, having Carpenters come to help in setting

up bedsteads and hangings; and at that trade my people and I all the morning, till pressed by public business to leave them, against my will, in the afternoon; and yet I was troubled in being at home, to see all my goods lie up and down the house in a bad condition, and strange workmen going to and fro might take what they would almost. All the afternoon busy; and Sir W. Coventry came to me, and found me, as God would have it, in my office, and people about me setting my papers to rights; and there discoursed about getting an account ready against the Parliament, and thereby did create me infinite of business, and to be done on a sudden, which troubled me; but however, he being gone, I about it late to good purpose; and so home, having this day also got my wine out of the ground again and set it in my cellar; but with great pain to keep the port[er]s that carried it in from observing the money-chests there. So to bed as last night; only, my wife and I upon a bedstead with curtains in that which was Mercer's chamber, and Balty and his wife (who are here and do us good service) where we lay last night.

15.    All morning at the office, Harman being come, to my great satisfaction, to put up my beds and hangings; so I am at rest, and fallowed my business all day. Dined with Sir W. Batten. Mighty busy about this account, and while my people were busy, myself wrote near 30 letters and orders with my own hand. At it till 11 at night; and it is strange to see how clear my head was, being eased of all the matter of all those letters; whereas one would think that I should have been dozed – I never did observe so much of myself in my life. In the evening there comes to me Capt. Cocke, and walked a good while in the garden; he says he hath computed that the rents of houses lost this fire in the City comes to 600000l per annum. That this will make the Parliament more quiet then otherwise they would have been and give the King a more ready supply. That the supply must be by excise, as it is in holland. That the Parliament will see it necessary to carry on the war. That the late storm hindered our beating the Duch fleet, who were gone out only to satisfy the people, having no business to do but to avoid us. That the French, as late in the year as it is, are coming. That the Duch are really in bad condition, but that this unhappiness of ours doth give them heart. That, certainly, never so great a loss as this was borne so well by citizens in the world as this; he believing that not one merchant upon the Change will break upon it. That he doth not apprehend there will be any disturbances in estate upon it, for that

all men are busy in looking after their own business, to save themselfs. He gone, I to finish my letters; and home to bed and find, to my infinite joy, many rooms clean, and myself and wife lie in our own chamber again. But much terrified in the nights nowadays, with dreams of fire and falling down of houses.

17. Up betimes, and shaved myself after a week's growth; but Lord, how ugly I was yesterday and how fine today. By water, seeing the City all the way, a sad sight endeed, much fire being still in – to Sir W. Coventry, and there read over my collection of the perticulars of the excess of charge created by a war – with good content. Sir W. Coventry was in great pain lest the French fleet should be passed by our fleet – who had notice of them on Saturday, and were preparing to go meet them; but their minds altered, and judged them merchantmen, when the same day, the *Success*, Capt. Ball, made their whole fleet, and came to Brightemson and thence at 5 a-clock afternoon, Saturday, wrote Sir W. Coventry news thereof. So that we do much fear our missing them. Here came in and talked with him, Sir Tho. Clifford, who appears a very fine gentleman, and much set by at Court for his activity in going to sea, and stoutness everywhere and stirring up and down. Thence by coach over the ruines, down Fleete streete and Cheapside to Broad street to Sir G. Carteret, where Sir W. Batten (and Sir J. Mennes, whom I had not seen a long time before, being his first coming abroad) and Lord Brouncker passing his accounts. Thence home a little to look after my people at work, and back to Sir G. Carteret to dinner; and thence, after some discourse with him upon our public accounts, I back home, and all the day with Harman and his people finishing the hangings and beds in my house; and the hangings will be as good as ever, and perticularly in my new closet. They gone, and I weary, my wife and I, and Balty and his wife, who came hither today to help us, to a barrel of oysters I sent from the River today, and so to bed.

18. Strange, with what freedom and quantity I pissed this night, which I know not what to impute to but my oysters – unless the coldness of the night should cause it, for it was a sad rainy and tempestuous night. As soon as up, I begun to have some pain in my blather and belly as usual, which made me go to dinner betimes to fill my belly; and that did ease me, so as I did my business in the afternoon, in forwarding the settling of my house, very well.

Betimes to bed, my wife also being all this day ill in the same manner. Troubled at my wife's hair coming off so much. This day the Parliament met, and adjourned till Friday, when the King will be with them.

21. With great pleasure very late, new setting all my books; and now I am in as good condition as I desire to be in all wordly respects, the Lord of heaven make me thankful and continue me therein. So to bed. This day I had new stairs of main timber put to my cellar going into the yard.

22. To my closet and had it new washed, and now my house is so clean as I never saw it, or any other house in my life, and everything in as good condition as ever before the fire; but with I believe about 20*l* cost one way or other, besides about 20*l* charge in removing my goods; and do not find that I have lost anything but two little pictures of shipping and sea, and a little gold frame for one of my sea-cards. My glazier, endeed, is so full of work that I cannot get him to come to perfect my house. In the afternoon I paid for the two lighters that carried my goods to Deptford, and they cost me 8*l*.

23. *Sunday*. Up, and after being trimmed, all the morning at the office, with my people about me, till about one a-clock; and then home, and my people with me, and Mr. Wayth; and eat a bit of victuals in my old closet, now my little dining-room, which makes a pretty room; and my house being so clean makes me mightily pleased, but only I do lack Mercer or somebody in the house to sing with. As soon as eat a bit, Mr. Wayth and I by water to Whitehall, and there at Sir G. Carteret's lodgings Sir W. Coventry met, and we did debate the whole business of our account to the Parliament – where it appears to us that the charge of the war, from September 1 1664 to this Michaelmas, will have been but 3200000*l*, and we have paid in that time somewhat about 2200000*l*; so that we owe above 900000*l*: but our method of accounting, though it cannot I believe be far wide from the mark, yet will not abide a strict examination if the Parliament should be troublesome. Here happened a pretty question of Sir W. Coventry, whether this account of ours will not put my Lord Treasurer to a difficulty to tell what is become of all the money the Parliament hath given in this time for the war, which hath amounted to about 4000000*l* – which nobody there could answer; but I perceive they did doubt what his answer could be.

Having done, and taken from Sir W. Coventry the minutes of a letter to my Lord Treasurer, Wayth and I back again to the office. And thence back down to the water with my wife, and landed him in Southworke, and my wife and I for pleasure to Foxhall, and there eat and drank, and so back home; and I to my office till midnight, drawing the letter we are to send with our account to my Lord Treasurer; and that being done to my mind, I home to bed.

26. By Mr. Dugdale I hear the great loss of books in St. Pauls churchyard, and at their hall[1] also – which they value at about 150000*l*; some booksellers being wholly undone; and among others, they say, my poor Kirton. And Mr. Crumlum, all his books and household stuff burned; they trusting to St. Fayths, and the roof of the church falling, broke the Arch down into the lower church, and so all the goods burned – a very great loss. His father hath lost above 1000*l* in books – one book newly-printed, a discourse it seems of Courts.

27. A very furious blowing night all the night, and my mind still mightily perplexed with dreams and burning the rest of the town – and waking in much pain for the fleet. Up, and with my wife by coach as far as the Temple; and there she to the mercer's and I to look out Penny, my tailor, to speak for a cloak and cassock for my brother, who is coming to town and I will have him in a canonical dress – that he may be the fitter to go abroad with me.

28. Lay long in bed, and am come to agreement with my wife to have Mercer again, on condition she may learn this winter two months to dance, and she promises me she will endeavour to learn to sing; and all this I am willing enough to. So up, and by and by the glazier comes to finish the windows of my house, which pleases me, and the bookbinder to gild the backs of my books. I got the glass of my book-presses to be done presently, which did mightily content me. And to setting my study in a little better order; and so to my office to my people busy about our Parliament accounts; and so to dinner – and then at them again close. At night comes Sir W. Penn, and he and I a turn in the garden, and he broke to me a proposition of his and my joining in a design of fetching timber and deals from Scotland by the help of Mr. Pett upon the place; which

---

1. The booksellers': sc. Stationers' Hall.

while London is building, will yield good money. I approve it. We judged a third man, that is knowing, is necessary; and concluded on Sir W. Warren, and sent for him to come to us tomorrow morning.

30. *Lords day.* Up and to church, where I have not been a good while; and there the church infinitely thronged with strangers since the fire came into our parish; but not one handsome face in all of them, as if endeed there was a curse, as Bishopp Fuller heretofore said, upon our parish. Here I saw Mercer come into the church; which I had a mind to, but she avoided looking up – which vexed me. A pretty good sermon; and then home, and comes Balty and dined with us – a good dinner; and then to have my hair cut against winter close to my head, and then to church again. A sorry sermon, and away home. W. Penn and I to walk, to talk about several businesses; and then home, and my wife and I to read in Fullers *Church History*, and so to supper and to bed.

   This month ends with my mind full of business and concernment how this office will speed with the Parliament, which begins to be mighty severe in the examining our accounts and the expense of the Navy this war.

# ❧OCTOBER❧

2. Up, and am sent for to Sir G. Carteret; and to him, and there he tells me how our lists [of the ships and vessels employed in the war] are referred to a sub-committee to consider and examine, and that I am ordered to be there this afternoon. So I away thence to my new bookbinder to see my books gilding in the backs, and then to Westminster hall to the House and spoke with Sir W. Coventry, where he told me I must attend the committee in the afternoon, and received some hints of more work to do. So I away to the Chequer, and thence to an alehouse and found Mr. Falconbrige, and agreed for his kinswoman to come to me. He says she can dress my wife and will do anything we would have her to do, and is of a good spirit – and mighty cheerful. He is much pleased therewith, and so we shall be. So agreed for her coming the next week. So away home, and eat a short dinner, and then with Sir W. Penn to Westminster hall, and do give his boy my book of papers to hold, while he went into the committee chamber in the inner Court of

Wardes and I walked without with Mr. Slingsby of the tower (who was there, and did in walking inform me mightily in several things; among others, that the heightening or lowering of money is only a cheat, and doth good to some perticular men; which, if I can but remember how, I am now by him fully convinced of); anon Sir W. Penn went away, telling me that W. Coventry, that was within, had told him that the fleet is all come in to the buoy of the Nore, and that he must hasten down to them, and so went away. And I into the committee chamber before the committee sat, and there heard Birch discourse highly and understandingly about the Navy business and a proposal made heretofore to farm the Navy. But W. Coventry did abundantly answer him – and is a most excellent person. By and by the committee met, and I walked out; and anon they rose and called me in, and appointed me to attend a committee of them tomorrow at the office to examine our lists. This put me into a mighty fear and trouble, they doing it in a very ill humour methought. So I away, and called on my Lord Brouncker to desire him to be there tomorrow. And so home, having taken up my wife at Unthankes – full of trouble in mind to think what I shall be obliged to answer, that am neither fully fit, nor in any measure concerned to take the shame and trouble of this office upon me; but only from the inability and folly of the Controller occasions it. When come home, I to Sir W. Penn to his boy for my book, and there find he hath it not, but delivered it to the doorkeeper of the committee for me. This, added to my former disquiet, made me stark mad, considering all the nakedness of the office lay open in papers within those Covers. I could not tell in the world what to do, but was mad on all sides; and that which made me worse, Capt. Cocke was there, and he did so swear and curse at the boy that told me. So Cocke, Griffin, and the boy with me – they to find out the housekeeper of the Parliament, Hughes, while I to Sir W. Coventry, but could hear nothing of it there; but coming to our Rendezvous at the Swan tavern in King street, I find they have found the housekeeper, and the book simply locked up in the Court. So I stayed and drank, and rewarded the doorkeeper and away home, my heart lighter by all this; but to bed very sad notwithstanding, in fear of what will happen tomorrow upon their coming.

3. Waked betimes, mightily troubled in mind, and in the most true trouble that I ever was in my life, saving in that business last

year of the East India prizes. So up, and with Mr. Hayter and W. Hewer and Gibson to consider of our business and books and papers necessary for this examination; and by and by, by 8 a-clock, comes Birch the first, with the list and books of accounts delivered in. He calls me to work, and there he and I begin; when by and by comes Garraway, the first time I ever saw him, and Sir W. Thomson and Mr. Boscawen. They to it, and I did make shift to answer them better then I expected. Sir W. Batten, Lord Brouncker, W. Penn came in, but presently went out; and J. Mennes came in, and said two or three words from the purpose but to do hurt; and so away he went also – and left me all the morning with them alone, to stand or fall. At noon W. Batten comes to them to invite them (though fast-day) to dinner – which they did, and good company they were, but especially Garraway. Here I have news brought me of my father's com[ing] to town, and I presently to him. Glad to see him, poor man, he being come unexpected to see us and the City. I could not stay with him, but after dinner to work again, only the committee and I, till dark night; and by that time they cast up all the lists and found out what the medium of men was borne all the war, of all sorts – and ended with good peace and much seeming satisfaction; but I find them wise and reserved, and instructed to hit all our blots – as, among others, that we reckon the ships full manned from the beginning. They gone, and my heart eased of a great deal of fear and pain, and reckoning myself to come off with victory, because not overcome in anything or much foiled, I away to Sir W. Coventry's chamber, but he not within; then to Whitehall and there among the ladies, and saw my Lady Castlemaine never looked so ill, nor Mrs. Stewart neither, as in this plain natural dress; I was not pleased with either of them. Away, not finding W. Coventry; and so home, and there find my father and my brother come to town – my father without my expectation; but glad I am to see him. And so to supper with him, and to work again at the office; then home to set up all my Folio books, which are come home gilt on the backs, very handsome to the eye; and then at midnight to bed.

4. Up, and mighty betimes to W. Coventry to give him an account of yesterday's work, which doth give him good content. He did then tell me his speech lately to the House in his own vindication, about the report of his selling of places – he having a small occasion offered him by chance, which he did desire, and took

and did it to his content; and he says to the House's seeming to
approve of it, by their hum. He confessed how long he had done it,
and how he desired to have something else;[1] and since then he had
taken nothing, and challenged all the world. I was glad of this also.
Thence up to the Duke of York by appointment, with fellow-
officers, to complain, but to no purpose, of want of money; and so
away – I to Sir G. Carteret to his lodging, and there discoursed
much of the want of money and our being designed for destruction.
How the King hath lost his power by submitting himself to this
way of examining his accounts – and is become as a private man. He
says the King is troubled at it, but they talk an entry shall be made
that it is not to be brought into example. That the King must, if they
do not agree presently, make them a courageous speech; which he
says he may do (the City of London being now burned, and himself
master of an army) better then any prince before him – and so I
believe. Thence home about noon and to dinner. After dinner the
bookbinder came, and I sent by him some more books to gild. I to
the office all day, and spent most of it with W. Warren, whom I
have had no discourse with a great while. And when all is done, I do
find him a mighty wise man as any I know, and his counsel as much
to be fallowed. Late with Mr. Hayter, upon comparing the charge
and husbandry of the last Duch war with ours now; and do find
good room to think we have done little worse then they – whereof
good use may and will be made. So home to supper and to bed.

7.    *Lords day.* Up, and after visiting my father in his chamber, to
church, and then home to dinner. Little Michell and his wife came
to dine with us – which they did; and then presently after dinner, I
with Sir J. Mennes to Whitehall, where met by W. Batten and Lord
Brouncker, to attend the King and Duke of York at the Cabinet; but
nobody had determined what to speak of, but only in general to ask
for money – so I was forced immediately to prepare in my mind a
method of discoursing. And anon we were called in to the green
room, where the King, Duke of York, Prince Rupert, Lord
Chancellor, Lord Treasurer, Duke of Albemarle, G. Carteret, W.
Coventry, Morrice. Nobody beginning, I did, and made a current
and, I thought, a good speech, laying open the ill state of the Navy –
by the greatness of the debt – greatness of work to do against next
year – the time and materials it would take – and our incapacity,

---

1. i.e. a salary, which he had enjoyed since September 1664.

through a total want of money. I had no sooner done, but Prince Rupert rose up and told the King in a heat that whatever the gentleman had said, he had brought home his fleet in as good a condition as ever any fleet was brought home – that twenty boats would be as many as the fleet would want – and all the anchors and cables left in the storm might be taken up again. This arose from my saying, among other things we had to do, that the fleet was come in, the greatest fleet that ever his Majesty had yet together, and that in as bad condition as the enemy or weather could put it. And to use Sir W. Penn's words, who is upon the place taking a Survey, he dreads the reports he is to receive from the Surveyors of its defects. I therefore did only answer that I was sorry for his Highness's offence, but that what I said was but the report we received from those entrusted in the fleet to inform us. He muttered, and repeated what he had said; and so after a long silence on all hands, nobody, not so much as the Duke of Albemarle, seconding the Prince, nor taking notice of what he said, we withdrew. I was not a little troubled at this passage; and the more, when speaking with Jacke Fenn about it, he told me that the Prince will now be asking who this Pepys is, and find him to be a creature of my Lord Sandwiches, and therefore this was done only to disparage him. Anon they broke up and Sir W. Coventry came out, so I asked his advice: he told me he had said something to salve it, which was that his Highnesse had, he believed, rightly informed the King that the fleet is in good condition to have stayed out yet longer, and hath fought the enemy; but yet that Mr. Pepys his meaning might be that though in so good condition, if they should come in and lie all the winter, we shall be very loath to send them to sea for another year's service with[out] great repairs. He said it would be no hurt if I went to him and showed him the report himself brought up from the fleet, where every ship, by the commander's report, doth need more or less – and not to mention more of Sir W. Penn for doing him a mischief; so I said I would – but do not think that all this will redound to my hurt, because the truth of what I said will soon appear. Thence, having been informed that after all this pains the King hath found out how to supply us with 5 or 6000*l*, when 100000*l* were at this time but absolutely necessary, and we mentioned 50000*l* – this is every day a greater and greater omen of Ruine – God fit us for it – Sir J. Mennes and I home (it raining) by coach (calling only on Sir G. Carteret at his lodging, who is, I find, troubled at my Lord Treasurer and Sir Ph. Warwick bungling in his accounts); and being come home to supper, with my father, and then all to bed. I made my brother in his Cassocke to say grace this day, but I like his voice so ill, that I begin to be sorry he hath taken this order upon him.

11. *Memorandum.* I had taken my Journall during the fire and the disorders fallowing in loose papers until this very day, and could not get time to enter them in my book till January 18 in the morning, having made my eyes sore by frequent attempts this winter to do it. But now it is done, for which I thank God, and pray never the like occasion may happen.

12. Up, and after taking leave of my poor father, who is setting out this day for Brampton by the Cambrige coach, he having taken a journey to see the city burned and to bring my brother to town – I out by water; and so [by] coach to St. James's, the weather being foul – and there from Sir W. Coventry do hear how the House hath cut us off 150000*l* of our wear and tear – for that which was saved by the King while the fleet lay in harbour in winter. However, he seems pleased, and so am I, that they have abated no more – and do intend to allow of 28000 men for the next year; and this day have appointed to declare the sum they will give the King, and to propose the way of raising it – so that this is likely to be the great day. After done in his chamber, I with him to Westminster hall and there took a few turns, the Hall mighty full of people and the House likely to be very full today about the money business. Thence to Mrs. Martin's lodging and did what I would with her. She is very big, and resolves I must be godfather. Thence away by water with Cropp to Deptford. It was almost night before I got thither, so I only did give direction concerning a press that I have making there, to hold my turning and Joyners tooles that were lately given me, which will be very handsome; and so away back again, it being now dark; and so home, and there find my wife come home and hath brought her new Girle I have helped her to of Mr. Falconbrige's. She is wretched poor and but ordinary favoured, and we fain to lay out seven or eight pound-worth of clothes upon her back, which methinks doth go against my heart, and do not think I can ever esteem her as I could have done another that had come fine and handsome; and which is more, her voice, for want of use, is so Furr'd, that it doth not at present please me; but her manner of singing is such, that I shall, I think, take great pleasure in it. Well,

she is come, and I wish us good fortune in her.

13.  At a committee for Tanger. My Lord Bellasses propositions were read and discoursed of, about reducing the garrison to less charge. And endeed, I am mad in love with my Lord Chancellor, for he doth comprehend and speak as well, and with the greatest easiness and authority, that ever I saw man in my life. I did never observe how much easier a man doth speak, when he knows all the company to be below him, then in him; for though he spoke endeed excellent well, yet his manner and freedom of doing it, as if he played with it and was informing only all the rest of the company, was mighty pretty. He did call again and again upon Mr. Povy for his accounts. I did think fit to make the solemn tender of my accounts that I entended. I said somethink that was liked, touching the want of money and the bad Creditt of our tallies. My Lord Chancellor moved that without any trouble to any of the rest of the Lords, I might alone attend the King when he was with his private council, and open the state of the garrison's want of credit; and all that could be done, should. Most things moved were referred to committees, and so we broke up.

15.  Called up, though a very rainy morning, by Sir H. Cholmly, and he and I most of the morning together, evening of accounts, which I was very glad of. Thence he and I together to Westminster hall – in our way talking of matters and passages of state. The viciousness of the Court. The contempt the King brings himself into thereby. His minding nothing, but doing all things just as his people about him will have it. The Duke of York becoming a slave to this whore Denham – and wholly minds her. That there really was amours between the Duchesse and Sidny. That there is reason to fear that as soon as the Parliament have raised this money, the King will see that he hath got all that he can get, and then make up a peace. He tells me, which I wonder at but that I find it confirmed by Mr. Pierce, whom I met by and by in the Hall, that Sir W. Coventry is of the Caball with the Duke of York and Brouncker, with this Lady Denham, which is a shame and I am sorry for it; and that Sir W. Coventry doth make her visits. But yet I hope it is not so. Pierce tells me that, as little agreement as there is between the Prince and Duke of Albemarle, yet they are likely to go to sea again – for the first will not be trusted alone, and nobody will go with him but this Duke of Albemarle. He tells me much, how all the commanders of

the fleet and officers that are sober men do cry out upon their bad discipline, and the ruine that must fallow it if it continue. But that which I wonder most at, it seems their secretaries have been the most exorbitant in their fees to all sorts of people, that it is not to be believed that they durst do it, so as it is believed they have got 800*l* apiece by the very vacancies in the fleet. He tells me that Lady Castlemayne is concluded to be with child again. And that all the people about the King do make no scruple of saying that the King doth lie with Mrs. Stuart, whom he says is a most excellent-natured lady. This day the King begins to put on his Vest,[1] and I did see several persons of the House of Lords, and Commons too, great courtiers, who are in it – being a long Cassocke close to the body, of black cloth and pinked with white silk under it, and a coat over it, and the legs ruffled with black riband like a pigeon's leg – and upon the whole, I wish the King may keep it, for it is a very fine and handsome garment.

16.   Up, and to the office, where sat to do little business but hear clamours for money. At noon home to dinner, and to the office again, after hearing my brother play a little upon the Lyra viall, which he doth so as to show that he hath a love to Musique and a spirit for it – which I am well pleased with. I all the afternoon at the office, and at night with Sir W. Batten, W. Penn, J. Mennes at W. Penn's lodgings, advising about business and orders fit presently to make about discharging of ships come into the river, and which to pay first, and many things in order thereto. But it vexed me, that it being now past 7 a-clock, and the businesses of great weight and I had done them by 8 a-clock, and sending them to be signed, they were all gone to bed, and Sir W. Penn, though awake, would not, being in bed, have them brought him to sign. This made me quite angry. Late at work at the office, and then home to supper and to bed.

17.   Up, and busy about public and private business all the morning at the office. At noon home to dinner, alone with my brother, with whom I had now the first private talk I have had, and find he hath preached but twice in his life. I did give him some advice to study pronunciation;* but I do fear he will never make a good speaker – nor, I fear, any general good scholar – for I do not

---

1. A new anti-French fashion.

see that he minds Optickes or Mathematics of any sort, nor anything else that I can find – I know not what he may be at divinity and ordinary school-learning. However, he seems sober, and that pleases me. After dinner took him and my wife and Barker (for so is our new woman called, and is yet but a sorry girl) and set them down at Unthankes; and so to Whitehall and there find some of my brethren with the Duke of York; but so few, I put off the meeting.

26.   Up, and all the morning and most of the afternoon within doors, beginning to set my accounts in order from before this Fire, I being behindhand with them ever since. And this day I got most of my tradesmen to bring in their bills, and paid them. Dined at home, and busy again after dinner; and then abroad by water to Westminster hall, where I walked till the evening; and then out, the first time I ever was abroad with Doll Lane, to the Dog tavern, and there drank with her – a bad face, but good-bodied girl. Did nothing but salute and play with her, and talk; and thence away by coach home, and so to do a little more in my accounts, and then to supper and to bed.

29.   Up, and to the office to do business, and thither comes to me Sir Tho. Teddiman, and he and I walked a good while in the garden together, discoursing of the disorder and discipline of the fleet, wherein he told me how bad everything is but was very wary in speaking anything to the dishonour of the Prince or Duke of Albemarle; but doth magnify my Lord Sandwich much before them both for ability to serve the King, and doth heartily wish for him here – for he fears that we shall be undone the next year, but that he will, however, see an end of it. To prevent the necessity of his dining with me, I was forced to pretend occasion of going to Westminster; so away I went, and Mr. Barber the clerk, having a request to make to me to get him into imployment, did walk along with me and by water to Westminster with me – he professing great love to me, and an able clerk he is. When I come thither, I find the new Lord Mayor Bolton a-swearing at the Exchequer with some of the Aldermen and Livery; but Lord, to see how meanely they now look, who upon this day used to be all little lords, is a sad sight and worthy consideration. And everybody did reflect with pity upon the poor City, to which they are now coming to choose and swear their Lord Mayor, compared with what it heretofore was. Thence by coach (having in the Hall bought me a velvet riding cap, cost me

20*s*.) to my Taylors, and there bespoke a plain vest. And so to my goldsmith to bid him look out for some gold for me; and he tells me that Ginnys, which I bought 2000 of not long ago, and cost me but 18½*d*. change, will now cost me 22*d*., and but very few to be had at any price. However, some more I will have, for they are very convenient – and of easy disposal. So home to dinner, and to discourse with my brother upon his translation of my Lord Bacon's *Faber Fortunæ* which I gave him to do; and he hath done it but meanly, I am not pleased with it at all – having done it only literally, but without any life at all. About 5 a-clock I took my wife (who is mighty fine, and with a new fair pair of locks, which vex me, though like a fool I helped her the other night to buy them), and to Mrs. Pierce's; and there staying a little, I away before to Whitehall and into the new playhouse there, the first time I ever was there, and the first play I have seen since before the great plague. By and by Mr. Pierce comes, bringing my wife and his, and Knipp. By and by the King and Queen, Duke and Duchesse, and all the great ladies of the Court; which endeed was a fine sight – but the play, being *Love in a Tubb*, a silly play; and though done by the Duke's people, yet having neither Baterton nor his wife – and the whole thing done ill, and being ill also, I had no manner of pleasure in the play. Besides, the House, though very fine, yet bad for the voice – for hearing. The sight of the ladies, endeed, was exceeding noble; and above all my Lady Castlemayne. The play done by 10 a-clock, I carried them all home; and then home myself and, well satisfied with the sight but not the play, we with great content to bed.

30. Up and to the office, where sat all the morning; and at noon home to dinner, and then to the office again, where late, very busy and despatching much business. Mr. Hater staying most of the afternoon abroad, he came to me, poor man, to make excuse; and it was that he had been looking out for a little house for his family, his wife being much frightened in the country with the discourses about the country of troubles and disorders like to be, and therefore durst not be from him; and therefore he is forced to bring her to town, that they may be together. This is now the general apprehension of all people. Perticulars I do not know, but my own fears are also great, and I do think it time to look out to save something if a storm should come. At night home to supper and singing with my wife, who hath lately begun to learn, and I think will come to do something, though her ear is not good; nor I, I

confess, have patience enough to teach her or hear her sing now and then a note out of tune, and am to blame that I cannot bear with that in her which is fit I should do with her as a learner, and one that I desire much could sing, and so should encourage her. This I was troubled at, for I find that I do put her out of heart and make her fearful to sing before me. So after supper to bed.

31. Out with Sir W. Batten toward Whitehall, being in pain in my cods by being squeezed the other night in a little coach when I carried Pierce and his wife and my people. But I hope I shall be soon well again. And after dinner to my closet, where I spent the whole afternoon till late at evening of all my accounts, public and private; and to my great satisfaction I do find that I do bring my accounts to a very near balance, notwithstanding all the hurries and troubles I have been put to by the late Fire, that I have not been able to even my accounts since July last before. And I bless God, I do find that I am worth more then ever I yet was, which is 6200*l* – for which the holy name of God be praised. And my other accounts, of Tanger, in a very plain and clear condition, that I am not liable to any trouble from them. But in fear great I am, and I perceive the whole City is, of some distractions and disorders among us, which God of his goodness prevent. Late to supper with my wife and brother, and then to bed.

And thus ends the month – with an ill aspect. The business of the Navy standing wholly still. No credit. No goods sold us. Nobody will trust. All we have to do at the office is to hear complaints for want of money. The Duke of York himself, for now three weeks, seems to rest satisfied that we can do nothing without money, and that all must stand still till the King gets money – which the Parliament have been a great while about, but are so dissatisfied with the King's management, and his giving himself up to pleasures, and not minding the calling to account any of his officers – and they observe so much the expense of the war, and yet that after we have made it the most we can, it doth not amount to what they have given the King for the Warr, that they are backward of giving any more. However, 1800000*l* they have voted, but the way of gathering it hath taken up more time then is fit to be now lost. The seamen grow very rude, and everything out of order – commanders having no power over their seamen, but the seamen do what they please. Few stay on board, but all coming running up hither to town; and nobody can with justice blame them, we owing them so much money, and their families must starve if we do not give them money or they procure upon their tickets from some people that will trust them. A great folly is observed by all people, in the King's giving leave to so many merchantmen to go abroad this winter, and some upon voyages where it is impossible they should be back again by the spring; and the rest will be doubtful, but yet we let them go. What the reason of state is, nobody can tell, but all condemn it. The Prince and Duke of Albemarle have got no great credit by this year's service, our losses, both of reputation and ships, having been greater then is thought have ever been suffered in all ages put together before. Great folly in both Houses of Parliament, several persons falling together by the eares; among others, in the House of Lords, the Duke of Buckingham and my Lord Ossory. Such is our case, that everybody fears an invasion the next year; and for my part, I do methinks foresee some great unhappiness coming upon us, and do provide for it by laying by something against a rainy day – dividing what I have and laying it in several places – but with all faithfulness to the King in all respects – my grief only being that the King doth not look after his business himself, and thereby will be undone, both himself and his nations – it being not yet, I believe, too late, if he would apply himself to it, to save all and conquer the Duch; but while he and the Duke of York mind their pleasure as they do, and nothing else, we must be beaten. So late, with my mind in good condition of quiet after the settling all my accounts, and to bed.

## –❖NOVEMBER❖–

2. Up betimes, and with Sir W. Batten to Woolwich, where first we went on board the *Ruby*, [a] French prize, the only ship of war we have taken from any of our enemies this year. It seems a very good ship, but with galleries quite round the Sterne to walk in, as a Balcone, which will be taken down. She had also about 40 good brass guns, but will make little amends to our loss in the *Prince*. Thence to the Ropeyard and the other yards to do several businesses. He, and I also, did buy some apples and pork; by the same token, the Bucher commended it as the best in England for Cloath and Colour – and for his beef, says he, "Look how fat it is; the lean appears only here and there a speck, like Beauty spots."

Having done at Woolwich, we to Depford (it being very cold upon the water) and there did also a little more business; and so home, I reading all the way to make end of *The Bondman* (which the oftener I read, the more I like), and begin *The Duchesse of Malfy*, which seems a good play. At home to dinner, and there came Mr. Pierce, Chyrurgeon, to see me; and after I had eat something, he and I and my wife by coach to Westminster; she set us down at Whitehall and she to her brother's – I up into the House, and among other things walked a good while with the Sergeant Trumpet, who tells me, as I wished, that the King's Italian here is about setting three parts for Trumpets and shall teach some to sound them, and believes they will [be] admirable Musique. I also walked with Sir St. Fox an hour, and good discourse of public business with him – who seems very much satisfied with my discourse, and desired more of my acquaintance. Then comes out the King and Duke of York from the Council, and so I spoke a while to Sir W. Coventry about some office business; and so called my wife and so home; and I to my chamber to do some business, and then to supper and to bed.

4. *Lords day*. Comes my Taylors man in the morning and brings my vest home, and coat to wear with it, and belt and silver-hilted sword. So I rose and dressed myself, and I like myself mightily in it, and so doth my wife. Then being dressed, to church; and after church pulled my Lady Pen and Mrs. Markeham into my house to dinner; and Sir J. Mennes, he got Mrs. Pegg along with him. I had a good dinner for them, and very merry. And after dinner to the waterside, and so, it being very cold, to Whitehall, and was mighty fearful of an ague (my vest being new and thin, and the Coate cut not to meet before upon my breast). Here I waited in the gallery till the Council was up; and among others, did speak with Mr. Cooling, my Lord Chamberlain's secretary – who tells me my Lord-Generall is become mighty low in all people's opinion, and that he hath received several slurs from the King and Duke of York. That people at Court do see the difference between his and the Prince's management and my Lord Sandwiches. That this business which he is put upon, of crying out against the Catholiques and turning them out of all imployment, will undo him when he comes to turn out the officers out of the army – and this is a thing of his own seeking. That he is grown a drunken sot, and drinks with nobody but Troutbecke, whom nobody else will keep company with – of whom he told me this story: That once, the Duke of

Albemarle in his drink taking notice as of a wonder that Nan Hide should ever come to be Duchess of Yorke – "Nay," says Troutbecke, "ne'er wonder at that; for if you will give me another bottle of wine, I will tell you as great, if not greater, a miracle." And what was that but that "Our Dirty Besse" (meaning his Duchesse) should come to be Duchesse of Albemarle. Here we parted, and then by water (landing in Southwarke) home to the Tower; and so home, and there begun to read Potters discourse upon 666, which pleases me mightily; and then broke off, and to supper and to bed.

5.   To my Lord Crews, and there dined and mightily made of, having not, to my shame, been there in eight months before. Here my Lord and Sir Tho. Crew, Mr. John, and Dr. Crew – and two strangers. The best family in the world for goodness and sobriety. Here, beyond my expectation, I met my Lord Hinchingbrooke, who is come to town two days since from Hinchingbrooke, and brought his sister and brother Carteret with him – who are at Sir G. Carteret's. After dinner I and Sir Tho. Crew went aside to discourse of public matters, and do find by him that all the country gentlemen are publicly jealous of the Courtiers in the Parliament, and that they do doubt everything that they propose. And that the true reason why the country-gentleman is for a land Tax and against a general Excize, is because they are fearful that if the latter be granted, they shall never get it down again; whereas the land tax will be but for so much, and when the war ceases there will be no ground got by the Court to keep it up. He doth much cry out upon our accounts, and that all that they have had from the King hath been but Estimates, both from my Lord Treasurer and us, and from all people else – so that the Parliament is weary of it. He says the House would be very glad to get something against Sir G. Carteret, and will not let their enquiries die till they have got something. He doth, from what he hath heard at the Committee for examining the burning of the City, conclude it as a thing certain, that it was done by plot – it being proved by many witnesses that endeavours were made in several places to encrease the fire, and that both in city and country it was bragged by several papists that upon such a day or in such a time we should find the hottest weather that ever was in England, and words of plainer sense.

7.   Up, and with Sir W. Batten to Whitehall, where we attended as usual the Duke of York; and there was, by the folly of Sir W.

Batten, prevented in obtaining a bargain for Capt. Cocke which would, I think, have [been] at this time (during our great want of hemp) both profitable to the King and of good convenience to me. But I matter it not – it being done only by the folly, not any design, of Sir W. Batten. Thence to Westminster hall; and it being fast-day,[1] there was no shops open; but meeting with Doll Lane, did go with her to the Rose tavern and there drank and played with her a good while. She went away, and I stayed a good while after, and was seen going out by one of our neighbours near the office and two of the Hall people that I had no mind to have been seen by; but there was no hurt in it, nor can be alleged from it – therefore I am not solicitous in it; but took coach and called at Faythornes to buy some prints for my wife to draw by this winter; and here did see my Lady Castlemaynes picture, done by him from Lillys, in red chalke and other colours, by which he hath cut it in copper to be printed. The picture in chalke is the finest thing I ever saw in my life I think, and did desire to buy it; but he says he must keep it awhile to correct his Copper plate by, and when that is done, he will sell it me.

By the Duke of York his discourse today in his chamber, they have it at Court, as well as we here, that a fatal day is to be expected shortly, of some great mischiefe in the remainder of this week; whether by the papists, or what, they are not certain. But the day is disputed; some say next Friday, others a day sooner, others later; and I hope all will prove a foolery. But it is observable how everybody's fears are busy at this time.

8.   Mr. Grey did assure me this night that he was told this day by one of the greater Ministers of State in England and one of the King's Cabinet, that we had little left to agree on between the Duch and us towards a peace, but only the place of Treaty – which doth astonish me to hear, but am glad of it, for I fear the consequence of the war. But he says that the King having all the money he is like to have, we shall be sure of a peace in a little time.

9.   Up and to the office, where did a good deal of business. And then at noon to the Exchange and to my little goldsmith's, whose wife is very pretty and modest, that ever I saw any. Upon the Change, where I have seldom of late been, I find all people mightily at a loss what to expect, but confusion and fears in every man's head

1. For the Plague.

and heart. Whether war or peace, all fear the event will be bad. Thence home and with my brother to dinner, my wife being dressing herself against night. After dinner I to my closet all the afternoon, till the porter brought my vest back from the Taylors, and then to dress myself very fine, about 4 or 5 a-clock; and by that time comes Mr. Batelier and Mercer, and away by coach to Mrs. Pierces by appointment, where we find good company – a fair lady, my Lady Prettyman – Mrs. Corbet – Knipp. And for men, Capt. Downing – Mr. Lloyd, Sir W. Coventry's clerk – and one Mr. Tripp, who dances well. After some trifling discourse, we to dancing and very good sport, and mightily pleased I was with the company. After our first bout of dancing, Knipp and I to sing, and Mercer and Capt. Downing (who loves and understands music) would by all means have my song of *Beauty Retire* – which Knipp hath spread abroad, and he extols it above anything he ever heard. And without flattery, I think it is good in its kind. This being done, and going to dance again, comes news that Whitehall was on fire – and presently more perticulars, that the Horse guard was on fire. And so we run up to the garret and find it so, a horrid great fire – and by and by we saw and heard part of it blown up with powder. The ladies begun presently to be afeared – one fell into fits. The whole town in an Alarme. Drums beat and trumpets, and the guards everywhere spread – running up and down in the street. And I begun to have mighty apprehensions how things might be at home, and so was in mighty pain to get home; and that that encreased all is that we are in expectation (from common fame) this night or tomorrow to have a Massacre – by the having so many fires one after another – as that in the City. And at the same time begun in Westminster by the Palace, but put out – and since in Southworke, to the burning down some houses; and now this, doth make all people conclude there is something extraordinary in it, but nobody knows what. By and by comes news that the fire is slackened; so then we were a little cheered up again, and to supper and pretty merry. After supper another dance or two, and then news that the fire is as great as ever, which put us all to our wit's end, and I mightily [eager] to go home; but the coach being gone, and it being about 10 at night and rainy dirty weather, I knew not what to do but to walk out with Mr. Batelier, myself resolving to go home on foot and leave the women there. And so did; but at the Savoy got a coach and came back and took up the women; and so (having by people come from the fire understood that the fire was overcome, and all well) we merrily parted, and home. Stopped by several guards and Constables quite through the town (round the wall as we went), all being in armes. We got well home; and in the way I did con mi mano tocar la jambe de Mercer sa chair. Elle retirait sa jambe modestement, but I did tocar sa peau with my naked hand. And the truth is, la fille hath something that is assez jolie. Being come home, we to Cards till 2 in the morning; and drinking lamb's-wool, to bed.

10.　This is the fatal day that everybody hath discoursed for a long time to be the day that the papists, or I know not who, had designed to commit a Massacre upon; but however, I trust in God we shall rise tomorrow morning as well as ever.

11.　*Lords day.* Up, and to church, myself and wife – where that old dunce Meriton, brother to the known Meriton of St. Martins of Westminster, did make a very good sermon, beyond my expectation. Home to dinner, and we carried in Pegg Pen and there also came to us little Michell and his wife, and dined very pleasantly. Anon to church, my wife and I and Betty Michell, her husband being gone to Westminster. After church, home, and I to my chamber and there did finish the putting time to my song of *It is decreed*. And do please myself at last, and think it will be thought a good song. By and by little Michell comes and takes away his wife home, and my wife and brother and I to my Uncle Wights, where my aunt is grown so ugly, and their entertainment so bad, that I am in pain to be there, nor will go thither again a good while if sent for – for we were sent for tonight; we had not gone else. Woolly's wife a silly woman and not very handsome, but no spirit in her at all – and their discourse mean. And the fear of the troubles of the times hath made them not to bring their plate to town since it was carried out upon the business of the Fire, so that they drink in earth and a wooden can, which I do not like. So home, and my people to bed. I late to finish my song, and then to bed also. And the business of the firing of the City, and the fears we have of new troubles and violences, and the fear of fire among ourselfs, did keep me awake a good while, considering the sad condition I and my family should be in. So at last to sleep.

12.　This afternoon, going toward Westminster, Creed and I did step [in] (the Duke of York being just going away from seeing of it) at Pauls, and in the Convocation house yard did there see the body of Robt. Braybrooke, Bishop of London, that died 1404. He fell down in his tomb out of the great church into St. Fayths this late Fire, and is here seen his Skeleton with the flesh on; but all tough and dry like a spongy dry leather or Touchwood all upon his bones. His head turned aside. A great man in his time, and Lord Chancellor – and now exposed to be handled and derided by some, though admired for its duration by others. Many flocking to see it.

14. To Knipp's lodging, whom I find not ready to go home with me, so I away to do a little business; among others, to call upon Mr. Osborne for my Tanger warrant for the last Quarter, and so to the New Exchange for some things for my wife, and then to Knipp again and there stayed, reading of Wallers verses while she finished her dressing – her husband being by, I had no other pastime. Her lodging very mean, and the condition she lives in; yet makes a show without doors, God bless us. I carried him along with us into the City, and set him down in Bishopsgate street and then home with her. She tells me how Smith of the Duke's house hath killed a man upon a quarrel in play – which makes everybody sorry, he being a good actor, and they say a good man, however this happens. The ladies of the Court do much bemoan him, she says. Here she and we alone at dinner. After dinner, I to teach her my new Recitative of *It is decreed* – of which she learnt a good part; and I do well like it, and believe shall be well pleased when she hath it all, and that it will be found an agreeable thing. Then carried her home, and myself to the Popeshead, where all the Houblons were, and Dr. Croone; and by and by to an exceeding pretty supper – excellent discourse of all sorts; and endeed, are a set of the finest gentlemen that ever I met withal in my life. Here Dr. Croone told me that at the meeting at Gresham College tonight (which it seems they now have every Wednesday again) there was a pretty experiment, of the blood of one Dogg let out (till he died) into the body of another on one side, while all his own run out on the other side. The first died upon the place, and the other very well, and likely to do well. This did give occasion to many pretty wishes, as of the blood of a Quaker to be let into an Archbishop, and such like. But, as Dr. Croone says, may if it takes be of mighty use to man's health, for the amending of bad blood by borrowing from a better body. After supper James Houblon and another brother took me aside, and to talk of some businesses of their own, where I am to serve them, and will. And

then to talk of public matters; and I do find that they, and all merchants else, do give over trade and the nation for lost – nothing being done with care or foresight – no convoys granted, nor anything done to satisfaction. But do think that the Duch and French will master us the next year, do what we can; and so do I, unless God Almighty makes the King to mind his business; which might yet save all. Here we sat talking till past one in the morning, and then home – where my people sat up for me, my wife and all; and so to bed.

15. This [morning] came Mr. Sheply (newly out of the country) to see me; after a little discourse with him, I to the office, where we sat all the morning. And at noon home, and there dined, Sheply with me, and after dinner I did pay him 70l, which he had paid my father for my use in the country. He being gone, I took coach and to Mr. Pierce's, where I find her as fine as possible, and himself going to the Ball at night at Court, it being the Queenes Birthday. And so I carried them in my coach; and having set them into the house, and gotten Mr. Pierce to undertake the carrying in my wife, I to Unthankes, where she appointed to be, and there told her; and back again about business to Whitehall while Pierce went and fetched her and carried her in. I, after I had met with Sir W. Coventry and given him some account of matters, I also to the Ball, and with much ado got up to the Loft, where with much trouble I could see very well. Anon the house grew full, and the candles lit, and the King and Queen and all the ladies set. And it was endeed a glorious sight to see Mrs. Steward in black and white lace – and her head and shoulders dressed with Dyamonds. And the like a great many great ladies more (only, the Queene none); and the King in his rich vest of some rich silk and silver trimming, as the Duke of York and all the dancers were, some of cloth of silver, and others of other sorts, exceeding rich. Presently after the King was come in, he took the Queene, and about fourteen more couple there was, and begun the Bransles. As many of the men as I can remember presently, were: the King – Duke of York – Prince Rupert – Duke of Monmouth – Duke of Buckingham – Lord Douglas – Mr. Hamilton – Coll. Russell – Mr. Griffith – Lord Ossory – Lord Rochester. And of the ladies – the Queene – Duchess of York – Mrs. Steward – Duchess of Monmouth – Lady Essex Howard – Mrs. Temple – Swedes Embassadresse – Lady Arlington – Lord George Barkeley's daughter. And many others I remember not. But all most

excellently dressed, in rich petticoats and gowns and Dyamonds – and pearl. After the Bransles, then to a Corant, and now and then a French Dance; but that so rare that the Corants grew tiresome, that I wished it done. Only, Mrs. Steward danced mighty finely, and many French dances, especially one the King called the New Dance, which was very pretty. But upon the whole matter, the business of the dancing itself was not extraordinary pleasing. But the clothes and sight of the persons was indeed very pleasing, and worth my coming, being never likely to see more gallantry while I live – if I should come twenty times. About 12 at night it broke up, and I to hire a coach with much difficulty; but Pierce had hired a chair for my wife, and so she being gone to his house – he and I (taking up Barker at Unthankes) to his house – whither his wife was come home a good while ago, and gone to bed. So away home with my wife – between displeased at the dull dancing, and satisfied at the clothes and persons (my Lady Castlemayne (without whom all is nothing) being there, very rich, though not dancing); and so after supper, it being very cold, to bed.

17.     Up, and to the office, where all the morning. At noon home to dinner, and in the afternoon shut myself in my chamber, and there till 12 at night finishing my great letter to the Duke of York; which doth lay the ill condition of the Navy so open to him, that it is impossible, if the King and he minds anything of their business, but it will operate upon them to set all matters right, and get money to carry on the war before it be too late, or else lay out for a peace upon any Tearmes. It was a great convenience tonight, that what I had writ fowle in shorthand, I could read to W. Hewer and he take it fair in shorthand so as I can read it tomorrow to Sir W. Coventry, and then come home and he read to me, while I take it in longhand to present – which saves me much time. So to bed.

20.     After church, home, where I met Mr. Gregory who I did then agree with to come to teach my wife to play on the Viall; and he being an able and sober man, I am mighty glad of it. He had dined, therefore went away, and I to dinner; and after dinner by coach to Barkeshire house, and there did get a very great meeting, the Duke of York being there, and much business done, though not in proportion to the greatness of the business, and my Lord Chancellor sleeping and snoring the greater part of the time. Among other things, I declared the state of our Credit as to tallies to raise money

by. And there was an order for payment of 5000*l* to Mr. Gauden, out of which I hope to get something against Christmas. Here we sat late, and here I did hear that there are some troubles like to be in Scottland,[1] there being a discontented party already risen, that hath seized on the Governor of Dumfreeze and imprisoned him. But the story is yet very uncertain, and therefore I set no great weight on it. I home, by Mr. Gauden in his coach; and so with great pleasure to spend the evening at home upon my Lyra Viall, and then to supper and to bed – with mighty peace of mind, and a hearty desire that I had but what I have quietly in the country – but I fear I do at this day see the best that either I, or the rest of our nation, will ever see.

21. Up; with Sir W. Batten to Charing cross, and thence I to wait on Sir Ph. Howard, whom I find dressing himself in his night-gown and Turban like a Turke; but one of the finest persons that ever I saw in my life. He had several gentlemen of his own waiting on him, and one playing finely on the gittarr. He discourses as well as ever I heard man, in few words and handsome. He expressed all kindness to Balty, whom I told how sick he is. He says that before he comes to be mustered again, he must bring certificate of his swearing the oaths of Allegiance and Supremacy and having taken the sacrament according to the rites of the Church of England. This I perceive is imposed on all – and he will be ready to do. I pray God he may have his health again to be able to do it. Being mightily satisfied with his civility, I away to Westminster hall; and there walked with several people, and all the discourse is about some trouble in Scotland I heard of yesterday, but nobody can tell the truth of it. And thence I to the Excize Office about some tallies, and then to the Exchange, where I did much business; and so home to dinner, and then to the office, where busy all the afternoon till night; and then home to supper, and after supper an hour reading to my wife and brother something in Chaucer with great pleasure, and so to bed.

22. Up, and to the office, where we sat all the morning. And my Lord Brouncker did show me Holler's new print of the City, with a pretty representation of that part which is burnt, very fine endeed. And tells me that he was yesterday sworn the King's servant, and that the King hath commanded him to go on with his great map of

---

1. The Pentland Rising; a rebellion of Covenanters in the South-West.

the City which he was upon before the City was burned, like Gombout of Paris; which I am glad of. At noon home to dinner, where my wife and I fell out, I being displeased with her cutting away a lace hankercher so wide about the neck, down to her breasts almost, out of belief, but without reason, that it is the fashion. Here we did give one another the lie too much, but were presently friends; and then I to my office, where very late and did much business; and then home, and there find Mr. Batelier – and did sup and play at Cards awhile. But he tells me the news how the King of France hath, in defiance to the King of England, caused all his footmen to be put into Vests, and that the noblemen of France will do the like; which, if true, is the greatest indignity ever done by one prince to another.[1] So I left my people at Cards, and to my chamber to read, and then to bed. Batelier did bring us some oysters tonight, and some bottles of new French wine of this year, mighty good – but I drank but little. This noon Bagwell's wife was with me at the office, and I did what I would; and at night came Mrs. Burroughs, and appointed to meet upon the next holiday and go abroad together.

25. *Lords day*. Up, and with Sir J. Mennes by coach to Whitehall; and there coming late, I to rights to the chapel – where in my usual place I heard one of the King's chaplains, one Mr. Floyd, preach. He was out two or three times in his prayer, and as many in his sermon; but yet he made a most excellent good sermon, of our duty to imitate the lives and practice of Christ and the saints departed. And did it very handsomely, and excellent style – but was a little over-large in magnifying the graces of the nobility and prelates that we have seen in our memories in the world, whom God hath taken from us. Thence into the Court, and there delivered copies of my report to my Lord Treasurer, to the Duke of York, Sir W. Coventry, and others. And attended there till the Council met, and then was called in and I read my letter. My Lord Treasurer declared that the King had nothing to give till the Parliament did give him some money. So the King did of himself bid me to declare to all that would take our tallies for payment, that he should, as soon as the Parliament's money doth come in, take back their tallies and give them money – which I giving him occasion to repeat to me (it coming from him against the *gré*, I perceive, of my Lord Treasurer),

---

1. cf. above, p. 682 (15 October) & n.

I was content therewith and went home – and glad that I have got so much. Here I saw Mrs. Steward this afternoon, methought the beautifullest creature that ever I saw in my life, more then ever I thought her, as often as I have seen her – and I begin to think doth exceed my Lady Castlemayne, at least now.

28.    Up, and with Sir W. Penn to Whitehall (setting his Lady and daughter down by the way at a mercer's in the Strand, where they are going to lay out some money); and to Whitehall, where, though it blows hard and rains hard, yet the Duke of York is gone a-hunting. We therefore lost our labour, and so back again – and I by hackney coach to several places to get things ready against dinner, and then home and did the like there, to my great satisfaction; and at noon comes my Lord Hinchingbrooke, Sir Tho. Crew, Mr. John Crew, Mr. Carteret, and Brisband. I had six noble dishes for them, dressed by a man-cook, and commended, as endeed they deserved, for exceedingly well done. We eat with great pleasure, and I enjoyed myself in it with reflections upon the pleasures which I at best can expect, yet not to exceed this – eating in silver plates, and all things mighty rich and handsome about me. A great deal of fine discourse, sitting almost till dark at dinner; and then broke up with great pleasure, especially to myself, and they away; only, Mr. Carteret and I to Gresham College, where they meet now weekly again. And here they had good discourse how this late experiment of the dog (which is in perfect good health) may be improved to good uses to men – and other pretty things, and then broke up. Here was Mr. Henery Howard, that will hereafter be Duke of Norfolke, who is admitted this day into the Society; and being a very proud man, and that values himself upon his family, writes his name, as he doth everywhere: *Henery Howard of Norfolke*. Thence home, and there comes my Lady Pen, Pegg, and Mrs. Turner, and played at cards and supped with us, and were pretty merry – and Pegg with me in my closet a good while, and did suffer me a la besar mucho et tocar ses cosas upon her breast – wherein I had great pleasure, and so spent the evening; and then broke up, and I to bed, my mind mightily pleased with this day's entertainment.

30.    Up and with Sir W. Batten to Whitehall, and there we did attend the Duke of York and had much business with him. And pretty to see (it being St. Andrew's day) how some few did wear St. Andrew's Crosse; but most did make a mockery at it, and the

House of Parliament, contrary to practice, did sit also – people having no mind to observe that Scotch saint's day till they hear better news from Scotland. Thence to Westminster hall and the abby, thinking, as I had appointed, to have met Mrs. Burroughs there; but not meeting her, I home and just overtook my Cosen Rogr. Pepys, Mrs. Turner, Dike, and Joyce Norton, coming by invitation to dine with me – these ladies I have not seen since before the plague. Mrs. Turner is come to town to look after her things in her house; but all is lost. She is quite weary of the country, but cannot get her husband to let her live here any more, which troubles her mightily. She was mighty angry with me, that in all this time I never writ to her; which I do think and take to myself as a fault, and which I have promised to mend. Here I had a noble and costly dinner for them, dressed by a man cooke, as that the other day was. And pretty merry we were, as I could be with this company and so great charge. We sat long; and after much talk of the plenty of her country[1] in Fish, but in nothing also that is pleasing, we broke up with great kindness; and when it begun to be dark, we parted, they in one coach home, and I in another to Westminster hall – where by appointment Mrs. Burroughs and I were to meet, but did not, after I had spent the whole evening there. Only, I did go drink at the Swan, and there did meet with Sarah, who is now newly married; and there I did lay the beginnings of a future amor con ella, which in time may come para laisser me hazer alguna cosa con elle. Thence, it being late, away; called at Mrs. Burroughs mother's door, and she came out to me and I did hazer whatever I would con su mano tocando mi cosa; and then parted and home; and after some playing at cards with my wife, we to supper and to bed.

## –❖DECEMBER❖–

1.  Up and to the office, where we sat all the morning. At home to dinner, and then abroad, walking to the Old Swan, and in my way did see a cellar in Tower streete in a very fresh Fire, the late great winds having blown it up; it seemed to be only of Loggwood, that hath kept the fire all this while in it. Going further, I met my late Lord Mayor Bludworth, under whom the City was burned, and

---

1. North Yorkshire.

went with him by water to Whitehall. But Lord, the silly talk that this fellow had – only, how ready he would be to part with all his estate in these difficult times to advance the King's service, and complaining that now (as everybody did lately in the Fire) everybody endeavours to save himself and let the whole perish – but a very weak man he seems to be. I left him at Whitehall, he giving 6d. towards the boat, and I to Westminster hall, where I was again defeated in my expectation of Burroughs – however, I was not much sorry for it; but by coach home in the evening, calling at Faythornes and buying three of my Lady Castlemaynes heads, printed this day; which endeed is, as to the head, I think a very fine picture, and like her. I did this afternoon get Mrs. Michell to let me only have a sight of a pamphlett lately printed, but suppressed and much called after, called *The Catholiques Apology*, lamenting the severity of the Parliament against them – and comparing it with the lenity of other princes to protestants. Giving old and late instances of their Loyalty to their princes, whatever is objected against them. And excusing their disquiets in Queen Elizabeths time, for that it was impossible for them to think her a lawful queen, if Queene Mary, who had been owned as such, were so; one being the daughter of the true, and the other of a false wife – and that of the Gunpowder Treason, by saying that it was only the practice of some of us, if not the King, to trapan some of their religion into it, it never being defended by the generality of their Church, nor endeed known by them. And ends with a large Catalogue in red Letters, of the Catholiques which have lost their lives in the quarrel of the late King and this. The thing is very well writ endeed. So home to my letters, and then to my supper and to bed.

5. Up and by water to Whitehall, where we did much business before the Duke of York; which being done, I away home by water again, and there to my office till noon, busy. At noon home, and Goodgroome dined with us – who teaches my wife to sing. After dinner I did give him my song, *Beauty retire*, which he hath often desired of me; and without flattery, I think is a very good song. He gone, I to the office and there late very busy, doing much business; and then home to supper and talk; and then scold with my wife for not reckoning well the times that her music masters have been with her, but setting down more then I am sure, and did convince her, they had been with her; and in an ill humour of anger with her, to bed.

7. Up and by water to the Exchequer, where I got my tallies finished for the last Quarter for Tanger; and having paid all my fees, I to the Swan, whither I sent for some oysters; and thither comes Mr. Falconbrige and Spicer and many more clerks, and there we eat and drank, and a great deal of their sorry discourse; and so parted, and I by coach home, meeting Balty in the street about Charing cross, walking; which I was glad to see, and spoke to him about his mustering business, I being now to give an account how the several muster-maisters have behaved themselfs; and so home to dinner, where finding the cloth laid, and much crumpled but clean, I grew angry and flung the trenchers about the room, and in a mighty heat I was; so a clean cloth was laid, and my poor wife very patient; and so to dinner, and in comes Mrs. Barbara Shelden, now Mrs. Wood, and dined with us. She mighty fine – and lives, I perceive, mighty happily; which I am glad for her sake, but hate her husband for a blockhead in his choice.[1] So away after dinner, leaving my wife and her, and by water to the Strand and so to the King's playhouse, where two acts were almost done when I came in; and there I sat with my cloak about my face and saw the remainder of *The Mayds Tragedy* – a good play, and well acted, especially by the younger Marshall, which is become a pretty good actor. And is the first play I have seen in either of the houses since before the great plague – they having acted now about fourteen days publicly. But I was in mighty pain lest I should be seen by anybody to be at a play. As soon as done, I home and there to my office awhile; and then home and spent the night evening my Tanger accounts, much to my satisfaction; and then to supper, and mighty good friends with my poor wife, and so to bed.

8. Up and to the office, where we sat all the morning; and at noon home to dinner, and there find Mr. Pierce and his wife and Betty, a pretty girl – who in discourse at table told me of the great Proviso passed the House of Parliament yesterday, which makes the King and Court mad – the King having given order to my Lord Chamberlain to send the playhouses (and bawdy houses) to bid all the Parliament-men that were there to go to the Parliament presently – this is true, it seems – but it was carried against the Court by 30 or 40 voices. It is a Proviso to the Poll Bill, that there shall be a committee of nine persons that shall have the inspection, upon oath

---

1. sc. in her choice of him.

and power of giving oaths, of all the accounts of the money given and spent for this warr. This hath a most sad face, and will breed very ill blood – he tells me brought in by Sir Robt. Howard, who is one of the King's servants, at least hath a great office and hath got, they say, 20000*l* since the King came in. Mr. Pierce did also tell me as a great truth, as being told it by Mr. Cowly, who was by and heard it – that Tom Killigrew should publicly tell the King that his matters were coming into a very ill state, but that yet there was a way to help all – which is, says he, "There is a good honest able man that I could name, that if your Majesty would imploy and command to see all things well executed, all things would soon be mended; and this is one Charles Stuart – who now spends his time in imploying his lips and his prick about the Court, and hath no other imployment. But if you would give him this imployment, he were the fittest man in the world to perform it." This he says is most true. But the King doth not profit by any of this, but lays all aside and remembers nothing, but to his pleasures again – which is a sorrowful consideration.

I saw smoke in the ruines this very day.

9.  *Lords day*. Up, not to church but to my chamber, and there begun to enter into this book my Jou[r]nall of September, which in the Fire time I could not enter here, but in loose papers. At noon dined, and then to my chamber all the afternoon and night, looking over and tearing and burning all the unnecessary letters which I have had upon my File for four or five years backward – which I entend to do quite through all my papers, that I may have nothing by me but what is worth keeping, and fit to be seen if I should miscarry. At this work till midnight, and then to supper and to bed.

12.  Up, and to the office, where some accounts of Mr. Gawdens were examined. But I home most of the morning to even some accounts with Sir H. Cholmly – Mr. Moone – and others, one after another. Sir H. Cholmly did with grief tell me how the Parliament hath been told plainly that the King hath been heard to say that he would dissolve them rather then pass this Bill with the Proviso. But tells me that the Proviso is removed, and now carried that it shall be done by a Bill by itself. He tells me how the King hath lately paid above 30000*l* to clear debts of my Lady Castlemaynes – and that she and her husband are parted for ever, upon good terms, never to trouble one another more. He says that he hears that above 400000*l*

hath gone into the Privy purse since this Warr, and that that hath consumed so much of our money and makes the King and Court so mad to be brought to discover it. He gone, and after him the rest – I to the office; and at noon to the Change, where the very good newes is just come of our four ships from Smyrna come safe without convoy even into the Downes, without seeing any enemy – which is the best, and endeed only considerable good news to our Exchange since the burning of the City; and it is strange to see how it doth cheer up men's hearts. Here I saw shops now come to be in this Exchange. And met little Batelier – who sits here, but at 3*l* per annum, whereas he sat at the other at 100*l* – which he says he believes will prove of as good account to him now, as the other did at that rent. From the Change to Capt. Cockes, and there by agreement dined. And there was Charles Porter – Temple – Fenn – De Busty (whose bad English and pleasant discourses was exceeding good entertainment), Matt Wren – Maj. Cooper, and myself. Mighty merry, and pretty discourse. They talked for certain that now the King doth fallow Mrs. Steward wholly – and my Lady Castlemayne not above once a week. That the Duke of York doth not haunt my Lady Denham so much. That she troubles him with matters of state, being of my Lord Bristoll's faction, and that he avoids. That she is ill still. After dinner I away to the office, where we sat late upon Mr. Gaudens accounts – Sir J. Mennes being gone home sick. I late at the office, and then home to supper and to bed, being mightily troubled with a pain in the small of my back, through cold, or (which I think most true) by straining last night to get open my plate chest. In such pain all night, I could not turn myself in my bed. News this day from Brampton of Mr. Ensum, my sister's sweetheart, being dead – a clowne.

13. This afternoon Sir W. Warren and Mr. Moore, one after another, walked with me in the garden; and they both tell me that my Lord Sandwich is called home. And that he doth grow more and more in esteem everywhere, and is better spoken of – which I am mighty glad – though I know well enough his deserving the same before, and did foresee that it will come to it. In mighty great pain in my back still. But I perceive it changes its place – and doth not trouble me at all in making of water; and that is my joy, so that I believe it is nothing but a strain. And for these three or four days I perceive my overworking of my eyes by Candlelight doth hurt them, as it did the last winter. That by day I am well and do get

them right – but then after candlelight they begin to sore and run – so that I entend to get some green spectacles.

16. *Lords day*. Lay long, talking with my wife in bed. Then up with great content, and to my chamber to set right a picture or two – Lovett having sent me yesterday Santa Clara's head varnished, which is very fine. And now my closet is so full stored and so fine, as I would never desire to have it better. Dined without any strangers with me – which I do not like on Sundays. Then after dinner by water to Westminster to see Mrs. Martin, whom I found up in her chamber and ready to go abroad. I sat there with her and her husband and others a pretty while; and then away to Whitehall and there walked up and down to the Queen's side, and there saw my dear Lady Castlemayne, who continues admirable methinks – and I do not hear but that the King is the same to her still as ever. Anon to chapel, by the King's closet, and heard a very good Anthemne. Then with Lord Brouncker to Sir W. Coventry's chamber, and there we sat with him and talked. He is weary of anything to do, he says, in the Navy. He tells us this Committee of Accounts[1] will enquire sharply into our office; and (speaking of Sir J. Mennes) he says he will not bear anybody's faults but his own. He discoursed as bad of Sir W. Batten almost. And cries out upon the discipline of the fleet, which is lost. And that there is not, in any of the fourth-rates, and under, scarce left one Sea Comander, but all young gentlemen. And which troubles him, he hears that the gentlemen do give out that in two or three years a Tarpawlin shall not dare to look after being better then a Boatswain – which he is troubled at, and with good reason. So we parted, and I with Lord Brouncker to Sir P. Neale's chamber, and there sat and talked awhile – Sir Edwd. Walker being there, and telling us how he hath lost many fine Rowles of antiquity in Heraldry by the late fire, but hath saved the most of his papers. Here was also Dr. Wallis, the famous scholar and mathematician; but he promises little. Left them, and in the dark and cold home by water; and so to supper and to read, and so to bed – my eyes being better today – and I cannot impute it to anything but my being much in the dark tonight, for I plainly find that it is only excess of light that makes my eyes sore.

17. Up, and several people to speak with me. Then comes Mr.

1. See above, pp. 700–01.

Cæsar, and then Goodgroome, and what with one and the other, nothing but Musique with me this morning, to my great content; and the more to see that God Almighty hath put me into condition to bear the charge of all this. So out to the Change I, and did a little business; and then home, where they two musicians and Mr. Cooke came to see me – and Mercer, to go along with my wife this afternoon to a play. To dinner, and then our company all broke up, and I to my chamber to do several things – among other things, to write a letter to my Lord Sandwich, it being one of the burdens upon my mind that I have not writ to him since he went into Spain. But now I do intend to give him a brief account of our whole year's action since he went, which will make amends. My wife well home in the evening from the play; which I was glad of, it being cold and dark, and she having her necklace of pearl on, and none but Mercer with her. Spent the evening in fitting my books, to have the number set upon each in order to my having an Alphabet of my whole, which will be of great ease to me. After supper, to bed.

19. Up and by water to Whitehall, and there with the Duke of York did our usual business. But nothing but complaints of want of money, with[out] success, and Sir W. Coventry's complaint of the defects of our office (endeed Sir J. Mennes's), without any amendment. And he tells us so plainly of the committee of Parliament's resolution to enquire home into all our managements, that it makes me resolve to be wary and to do all things betimes to be ready for them. Thence, going away, met Mr. Hingston the Organist (my old acquaintance) in the Court, and I took him to the Dogg tavern and got him to set me a bass to my *It is decreed*, which I think will go well; but he commends the song, not knowing the words, but says the ayre is good, and believes the words are plainly expressed. He is of my mind, against having of eighths unnecessarily in composition. This did all please me mightily. Then to talk of the King's family: he says many of the Musique are ready to starve, they being five years behindhand for their wages. Nay, Evens, the famous man upon the Harp, having not his equal in the world, did the other day die for mere want, and was fain to be buried at the almes of the parish – and carried to his grave in the dark of night, without one Linke, but that Mr. Hingston met it by chance and did give 12*d*. to buy two or three links. He says all must come to ruin at this rate, and I believe him. Thence home, and upon Tower hill saw about 3 or 400 seamen get together; and one,

standing upon a pile of bricks, made his sign with his handkercher upon his stick, and called all the rest to him, and several shouts they gave. This made me afeared, so I got home as fast as I could – and hearing of no present hurt, did go to Sir Robt. Viners about my plate again; and coming home, do hear of 1000 seamen said in the streets to be in armes. So in great fear home, expecting to find a tumult about our house, and was doubtful of my riches there – but I thank God, I found all well. But by and by Sir W. Batten and Sir R. Ford do tell me that the seamen have been at some prisons to release some seamen, and that the Duke of Albemarle is in armes, and all the Guards at the other end of the town; and the Duke of Albemarle is gone with some forces to Wapping to quell the seamen – which is a thing of infinite disgrace to us. I sat long, talking with them. And among other things, Sir R. Ford did make me understand how the House of Commons is a beast not to be understood – it being impossible to know beforehand the success almost of any small plain thing – there being so many to think and speak to any business, and they of so uncertain minds and interests and passions. He did tell me and so did Sir W. Batten, how Sir Allen Brodericke and Sir Allen Apsly did come drunk the other day into the House, and did both speak for half an hour together, and could not be either laughed or pulled or bid to sit down and hold their peace – to the great contempt of the King's servants and cause – which I am aggrieved at with all my heart. We were full in discourse of the sad state of our times. And the horrid shame brought on the King's service by the just clamours of the poor seamen. And that we must be undone in a little time. Home, full of trouble on these considerations. And among other things, I to my chamber and there to ticket a good part of my books, in order to the Numbring of them – for my easy finding them to read, as I have occasion. So to supper and to bed – with my heart full of trouble.

24. Up, and to the office, where Lord Brouncker, J. Mennes, W. Penn, and myself met; and there I did use my notes I took on Saturday night about tickets, and did come to a good settlement in that business of that office, if it be kept to – this morning being a meeting on purpose. At noon, to prevent my Lord Brouncker's dining here, I walked as if upon business with him (it being frost and dry) as far as Paul's, and so back again through the City by Yildhall, observing the ruines thereabouts, till I did truly lose myself; and so home to dinner. I do truly find that I have

overwrought my eyes, so that now they are become weak and apt to be tired, and all excess of light makes them sore, so that now, to the candlelight I am forced to sit by, adding the Snow upon the ground all day, my eyes are very bad, and will be worse if not helped; so my Lord Brouncker doth advise me, as a certain cure, to use Greene Spectacles, which I will do. So to dinner, where Mercer with us, and very merry. After dinner, she goes and fetches a little son of Mr. Buckeworths, the whitest-haired and of the most spirit that ever I saw in my life – for discourse of all kind, and so ready and to the purpose, not above four year old. Thence to Sir Robt. Viners and there paid for the plate I have bought, to the value of 94*l*, with the 100*l* Capt. Cocke did give me to that purpose, and received the rest in money. I this evening did buy me a pair of green spectacles, to see whether they will help my eyes or no. So to the Change, and went to the Upper Change, which is almost as good as the old one; only shops are but on one side. Then home to the office and did business till my eyes begun to be bad; and so home to supper (my people busy making mince pies) and so to bed. No news yet of our Gottenburgh fleet; which makes [me] have some fears, it being of mighty concernment to have our supply of masts safe. I met with Mr. Cade tonight, my stationer, and he tells me that he hears for certain that the Queene-Mother is about and hath near finished a peace with France; which, as a Presbyterian, he doth not like, but seems to fear it will be a means to introduce Popery.

25. *Christmas day*. Lay pretty long in bed. And then rise, leaving my wife desirous to sleep, having sat up till 4 this morning seeing her maids make mince pies. I to church, where our parson Mills made a good sermon. Then home, and dined well on some good ribbs of beef roasted and mince pies; only my wife, brother, and Barker, and plenty of good wine of my own; and my heart full of true joy and thanks to God Almighty for the goodness of my condition at this day. After dinner I begun to teach my wife and Barker my song, *It is decreed* – which pleases me mightily, as now I have Mr. Hinxton's bass. Then out, and walked alone on foot to Temple, it being a fine frost, thinking to have seen a play all alone; but there missing of any Bills, concluded there was none; and so back home, and there with my brother, reducing the names of all my books to an Alphabet, which kept us till 7 or 8 at night; and then to supper, W. Hewer with us, and pretty merry; and then to my chamber to enter this day's journal only, and then to bed.

27.   Up, and called up by the King's Trumpets, which cost me 10s. So to the office, where we sat all the morning. At noon, by invitation, my wife (who had not been there these ten months I think) and I to meet, all our families, at Sir W. Batten's at dinner; where neither a great dinner for so much company, nor anything good or handsome. In middle of dinner I rose, and my wife, and by coach to the King's playhouse; and meeting Creed, took him up, and there saw *The Scornfull Lady* well acted, Doll Common doing Abigail most excellently, and Knipp the Widow very well (and will be an excellent actor I think); in other parts, the play not so well done as used to be by the old actors. Anon to Whitehall by coach, thinking to have seen a play there tonight – but found it a mistake; so back again, and missed our coach, who was gone, thinking to come time enough three hours hence; and we could not blame him. So forced to get another coach, and all three home to my house; and there to Sir W. Batten's to eat a bit of cold chine of beef, and then stayed and talked; and then home, and sat and talked a little by the fire's side with wife and Creed; and so to bed, my left eye being very sore. No business, public nor private, minded all these two days.

28.   To the Duke's house, and there saw *Mackbeth* most excellently acted, and a most excellent play for variety. I had sent for my wife to meet me there, who did come. And after the play done, I out so soon to meet her at the other door, that I left my cloak in the playhouse; and while I returned to get it, she was gone out and missed me, and with W. Hewer away home. I, not sorry for it much, did go to Whitehall and got my Lord Bellasses to get me into the playhouse; and there, after all staying above an hour for the players (the King and all waiting, which was absurd), saw *Henry the 5th* – well done by the Dukes people, and in most excellent habit, all new vests, being put on but this night. But I sat so high and far off, that I missed most of the words; and sat with a wind coming into my back and neck, which did much trouble me. The play continued till 12 at night; and then up, and a most horrid cold night it was, and frosty – and moonshine. But the worst is, I had left my cloak at Sir G. Carteret's; and they being abed, I was forced to go home without it. So by chance got a coach, and to the Golden Lion tavern in the Strand and there drank some mulled sack; and so home – where find my poor wife staying for me. And then to bed – mighty cold.

31. Rising this day with a full design to mind nothing else but to make up my accounts for the year past, I did take money and walk forth to several places in the town, as far as the New Exchange, to pay all my debts, it being still a very great frost and good walking. I stayed at the Fleece tavern in Covent garden, while my boy Tom went to W. Joyces to pay what I owed for candles there. Thence to the New Exchange to clear my wife's score; and so going back again, I met Doll Lane (Mrs. Martin's sister) with another young woman of the Hall, one Scott, and took them to the Half-Moon tavern and there drank some burned wine with them, without more pleasure; and so away home by coach, and there to dinner and then to my accounts, wherein at last I find them clear and right; but to my great discontent, do find that my gettings this year have been 573*l* less then my last – it being this year in all, but 2986*l*; whereas the last I got 3560*l*. And then again, my spendings this year have exceeded my spendings the last, by 644 – my whole spendings last year being but 509*l*; whereas this year it appears I have spent 1154*l* which is a sum not fit to be said that ever I should spend in one year, before I am maister of a better estate then I am. Yet, blessed be God, and I pray God make me thankful for it, I do find myself worth in money, all good, above 6200*l*; which is above 1800*l* more than I was the last year. This, I trust in God, will make me thankful for what I have, and careful to make up by care next year what by my negligence and prodigality I have lost and spent this year. The doing of this and entering it fair, with the sorting of all my expenses to see how and in what points I have exceeded, did make it late work, till my eyes became very sore and ill; and then did give over, and supper and to bed.

Thus ends this year of public wonder and mischief to this nation – and therefore generally wished by all people to have an end. Myself and family well, having four maids and one clerk, Tom, in my house; and my brother now with me, to spend time in order to his preferment. Our healths all well; only, my eyes, with overworking them, are sore as soon as candlelight comes to them, and not else. Public matters in a most sad condition. Seamen discouraged for want of pay, and are become not to be governed. Nor, as matters are now, can any fleet go out next year. Our enemies, French and Duch, great, and grow more, by our poverty. The Parliament backward in raising, because jealous of the spending, of the money. The City less and less likely to be built again, everybody settling elsewhere, and nobody encouraged to trade. A sad, vicious, negligent Court, and all sober men there fearful of the ruin of the whole Kingdom this next year – from which, good God deliver us. One thing I reckon remarkable in my own condition is that I am come to abound in good plate, so as at all entertainments to be served wholly with silver plates, having two dozen and a half.

## -⁂JANUARY⁂-

2. Up I, and walked to Whitehall to attend the Duke of York as usual. My wife up, and with Mrs. Pen to walk in the fields to frost-bite* themselfs. I find the Court full of great apprehensions of the French, who have certainly shipped landsmen, great numbers, at Brest; and most of our people here guess his design for Ireland. We have orders to send all the ships we can possible to the Downes. God have mercy on us, for we can send forth no ships without men; nor will men go without money, every day bringing us news of new mutinies among the seamen – so that our condition is like to be very miserable. Thence to Westminster hall and there met all the Houblons, who do laugh at this discourse of the French and say they are verily of opinion it is nothing but to send to their plantations in the West Indys, and that we at Court do blow up a design of invading us only to make the Parliament make more haste in the money matters – and perhaps it may be so, but I do not believe we have any such plots in our heads. After them, I with several people; among others, Mr. George Mountagu, whom I have not seen long. He mighty kind. He tells me all is like to go ill, the King displeasing the House of Commons by evading their Bill for examining accounts, and putting it into a commission. This doth not please them. He tells me he finds the enmity almost over for my Lord Sandwich, and that now all is upon the Vice chamberlaine, who bears up well and stands upon his vindication – which he seems to like well, and the others do construe well also. So to the Rose tavern, while Doll Lane came to me and we did biber a good deal de vino, et jo did give ella 12 solidos para comprar ella some gans for a new ano's gift. I did tocar et no mas su cosa, but in fit time and place jo creo que je pouvais faire whatever I would con ella. Thence to the Hall again and with Sir W. Pen by coach to the Temple, and there light and eat at an ordinary by; and then alone to the King's House and there saw *The Custome of the Country*, the second time of its being acted, wherein Knipp does the Widow

well; but of all the plays that ever I did see, the worst, having neither plot, language, nor anything in the earth that is acceptable. Only, Knipp sings a little song admirably. But fully the worst play that ever I saw or I believe shall see. So away home, much displeased for the loss of so much time, and disobliging my wife by being there without her; and so by link walked home, it being mighty cold but dry; yet bad walking because very slippery with the frost and treading. Home and to my chamber to set down my journal; and then to thinking upon establishing my Vows against the next year. And so to supper and to bed.

4.   Up; and seeing things put in order for a dinner at my house today, I to the office awhile; and about noon home, and there saw all things in good order. Anon comes our company – my Lord Brouncker – Sir W. Penn, his Lady, and Peg and her servant, Mr. Lowder – my Lady Batten – Sir W. Batten being forced to dine at Sir R. Ford's, being invited – Mr. Turner and his wife. Here I had good room for ten, and no more would my table have held well had Sir J. Mennes (who was fallen lame) and his sister and niece and Sir W. Batten come, which was a great content to me to be without them. I did make them all gaze to see themselfs served so nobly in plate; and a neat dinner endeed, though but of seven dishes. Mighty merry I was and made them all – and they mightily pleased. My Lord Brouncker went away after dinner to the Ticket Office, the rest stayed; only my Lady Batten home, her ague-fit coming on her at table. The rest merry, and to cards and then to sing and talk; and at night to sup and then to cards; and last of all, to have a flagon of Ale and apples, drunk out of a wood Cupp as a Christmas draught, made all merry; and they full of admiration at my plate, perticularly my flagons (which endeed are noble); and so late home, all with great mirth and satisfaction to them as I thought, and to myself to see all I have and do so much out-do, for neatness and plenty, anything done by any of them. They gone, I to bed much pleased. And do observe Mr. Lowder to be a pretty gentleman – and I think too good for Peg. And by the way, Peg Penn seems mightily to be kind to me, and I believe by her father's advice, who is also himself so – but I believe not a little troubled to see my plenty; and was much troubled to hear the song I sung – *The new Droll* – it touching him home. So to bed.

7.   Lay long in bed. Then up and to the office, where busy all the

morning. At noon (my wife being gone to Westminster) I with my Lord Brouncker by coach as far as the Temple – in the way, he telling me that my Lady Denham is at last dead. Some suspect her poisoned, but it will be best known when her body is opened; which will be today, she dying yesterday morning. The Duke of York is troubled for her; but hath declared he will never have another public mistress again – which I shall be glad of, and would the King would do the like. He tells me how the Parliament is grown so jealous of the King's being unfayre to them in the business of the Bill for examining accounts – Irish Bill, and the business of the papists, that they will not pass that business for money till they see themselfs secure that those Bills will pass, which they observe the Court to keep off till all the Bills come together, that the King may accept what he pleases and what he pleases to reject – which will undo all our business, and the kingdom too. He tells me how Mr. Henery Howard of Norfolke hath given our Royall Society all his grandfather's Library; which is a noble gift they value at 1000*l*. And gives them accommodation to meet in at his house – Arundell house, they being now disturbed at Gresham College. Thence, lighting at the Temple, to the ordinary hard by and eat a bit of meat; and then by coach to fetch my wife from her b[r]other's, and thence to the Duke's house and saw *Macbeth*; which though I saw it lately, yet appears a most excellent play in all respects, but especially in divertisement, though it be a deep tragedy; which is a strange perfection in a tragedy, it being most proper here and suitable. So home to write over fair my vows for this year, and then to supper and to bed – in great peace of mind, having now done it and brought myself into order again and a resolution of keeping it – and having entered my Journall to this night. So to bed, my eyes failing me with writing.

10. Up, and at the office all the morning. At noon home; and there being business to do in the afternoon, took my Lord Brouncker home with me, who dined with me – his discourse and mine about the bad performances of the Controller's and Surveyor's places by the hands they are now in, and the shame to the service, and loss the King suffers by it. Then after dinner to the office, where we and some of the chief of Trinity house met to examine the occasion of the loss of the *Prince Royall*, the maister and Mates being examined – which I took and keep. And so broke up, and I to my letters by the post; and so home and to supper with my

mind at pretty good ease, being entered upon minding my business; and so to bed.

11.  Up, being troubled at my being found abed a-days by all sorts of people – I having got a trick of sitting up later then I need, never supping, or very seldom, before 12 at night. Then to the office; there busy all the morning; and among other things, comes Sir W. Warren and talked with me a good while; whose discourse I love, he being a very wise man and full of good counsel, and his own practices for wisdom much to be observed. And among other things, he tells me how he is fallen in with my Lord Brouncker, who hath promised him most perticular inward friendship, and yet not to appear at the board to do so. And he told me how my Lord Brouncker should take notice of the two flagons he saw at my house at dinner at my late feast, and merrily (yet I know enviously) said I could not come honestly by them. This I am glad to hear, though vexed to see his ignoble soul. But I shall beware of him; and yet it is fit he should see I am no mean fellow but can live in the world and have something. At noon home to dinner; and then to the office with my people and very busy, and did despatch to my great satisfaction abundance of business, and do resolve by the grace of God to stick to it till I have cleared my hand of most things wherein I am in arrear in public and private matters. At night home to supper and to bed. This day, ill news of my father's being very ill of his old grief, the Rupture, which troubles me.

16.  Up, and by coach to Whitehall – and there to the Duke of York as usual. Here Sir W. Coventry came to me aside in the Duke's chamber, to tell that he had not answered part of a late letter of mine, because *littera Scripta manet* – about his leaving the office – he tells me because he finds that his business at Court will not permit him to attend it; and then he confesses that he seldom of late could come from it with satisfaction, and there[fore] would not take the King's money for nothing. I professed my sorrow for it, and prayed the continuance of his favour; which he promised. I do believe he hath done like a very wise man in reference to himself; but I doubt it will prove ill for the King and for the office. Prince Rupert, I hear today, is very ill – yesterday given over, but better today. This day before the Duke of York, the business of the Mustermaisters was reported, and Balty found the best of the whole number, so as the Duke enquired who he was and whether

he was a stranger by his two names, both strange. And offered that he and one more, who hath done the next best, should have not only their own, but part of the others' salary; but that, I having said he was my brother-in-law, did stop; but they two are ordered their pay, which I am glad of, and some of the rest will lose their pay and others be laid by the heels. I was very glad of this being ended so well. Then with the Duke of York to the King to receive his commands for stopping the sale this day of some prize goods at the Prize Office, goods fit for the Navy, and received the King's commands and carried them to the Lords' House to my Lord Ashly, who was angry much thereat; and I am sorry it fell to me to carry that order, but I cannot help it; so against his will, he signed a note I writ to the Commissioners of Prizes, which I carried and delivered to Kingdom at their new office in Aldergate Streete. Thence a little to the Exchange, where it was hot that the Prince was dead, but I did rectify it. So home to dinner and found Balty, told him the good news, and then after dinner away; I presently to Whitehall and did give the Duke of York a memorial of the salt business against the Council. And did wait all the Council for answer – walking a good while with Sir St. Fox; who, among other things, told me his whole mystery in the business of the interest he pays as Treasurer for the Army. They give him 12*d.* per cent quite through the Army, with condition to be paid weekly. This he undertakes upon his own private credit, and to be paid by the King at the end of every four months. If the King pay him not at the end of the four months, then for all the time he stays longer, my Lord Treasurer by agreement allows him 8 per cent per annum for the forebearance – so that in fine, he hath about twelve per cent from the King and the Army for fifteen or sixteen months' interest – out of which he gains soundly, his expense being about 130000*l* per annum – and hath no trouble in it compared (as I told him) to the trouble I must have to bring in an account of interest. I was, however, glad of being thus enlightened. And so away to the council door, and there got in and hear a piece of a cause heard before the King, about a ship deserted by her fellows (who were bound mutually to defend each other) in their way to Virginy and taken by the enemy – but it was but meanly pleaded.

This day I observe still in many places the smoking remains of the late fire. The ways mighty bad and dirty. This night Sir R. Ford told me how this day at Christ Church Hospital they have given a living of 200*l* per annum to Mr. Sanchy, my old acquaintance;

which I wonder at, he commending him mightily; but am glad of it. He tells me too, how the famous Stillingfleete was a Bluecoat boy. The children at this day are provided for in the country by the House, which I am glad also to hear.

18. Up, and most of the morning finishing my entry of my Journall during the late fire out of loose papers into this book, which did please me mightily when done, I writing till my eyes were almost blind therewith to make end of it. Then all the rest of the morning, and after a mouthful of dinner, all the afternoon in my closet till night, sorting all my papers which have lain unsorted for all the time we were at Greenwich during the plague. Which did please me also – I drawing on to put my office into a good posture, though much is behind.

20. *Lords day*. I to church, and there beyond expectation find our seat and all the church crammed by twice as many people as used to be; and to my great joy find Mr. Frampton in the pulpit. So to my great joy I hear him preach, and I think the best sermon, for goodness – oratory – without affectation or study – that ever I heard in my life. The truth is, he preaches the most like an Apostle that ever I heard man. And was much the best time that ever I spent in my life at church. His text, *Ecclesiastes* 11, verse 8th – the words – "But if a man live many years and rejoice in them all, yet let him remember the days of darkness, which shall be many. All that cometh is vanity." He done, I home; and there Michell and his wife and we dined, and mighty merry; I mightily taken, more and more, with her. After dinner, I with my brother away by water to Whitehall and there walked in the park. And a little to my Lord Chancellors, where the King and Cabinet met, and there met Mr. Brisband, with whom good discourse; to Whitehall towards night, and there he did lend me the *Third Advice to a paynter*, a bitter Satyr upon the service of the Duke of Albemarle the last year. I took it home with me and will copy it, having the former – being also mightily pleased with it. So after reading it, I to Sir W. Penn to discourse a little with him, and so home to supper and to bed.

22. Up, and there came to me Darnell the Fidler, one of the Duke's house, and brought me a set of lessons, all three parts. I heard them play[ed] to the Duke of York this Christmas at his lodgings, and bid him get me them. I did give him a Crowne for

them – and did enquire after the music of *The Siege of Rhodes*, which he tells me he can get me, which I am mighty glad of. So to the office, where among other things I read the Council's order about my Lord Brouncker and W. Penn to be assistants to the Controller – which quietly went down, with Sir J. Mennes, poor man, seeming a little as if he would be thought to have desired it, but yet apparently to his discontent. And I fear, as the order runs, it will hardly do much good. At noon to dinner; and there comes a letter from Mrs. Pierce, telling me she will come and dine with us on Thursday next with some of the players, Knipp, &c., which I was glad of but my wife vexed, which vexed me but I seemed merry, but know not how to order the matter whether they shall come or no. After dinner to the office and there late; doing much business; and so home to supper and to bed.

23.    Up, and with Sir W. Batten and W. Penn to Whitehall, and there to the Duke of York and did our usual business. Having done there, I to St. James's to see the Organ Mrs. Turner told me of the other night, of my late Lord Aubigny's; and I took my Lord Brouncker with me, he being acquainted with my present lord Almoner, Mr. Howard, brother of the Duke of Norfolke. So he and I thither and did see the Organ; but I do not like it, it being but a bawble, with a virginall joining to it – so I shall not meddle with it. Here we sat and talked with him a good while, and he seems a good-natured gentleman. Here I observed the Deske which he hath to remove, and is fastened to one of the armes of his Chayre. I do also observe the counterfeit windows there was in the form of Doores, with Looking glasses instead of windows, which makes the room seem both bigger and lighter I think; and I have some thoughts to have the like in one of my rooms. He discoursed much of the goodness of the Musique in Rome, but could not tell me how long Musique had been in any perfection in that Church – which I would be glad to know. He speaks much of the great buildings that this Pope (whom in mirth to us he calls Antichrist) hath done in his time. Having done with this discourse, we away; and my Lord and I walking into the parke back again, I did observe the new buildings; and my Lord seeing I had a desire to see them, they being the place for the priests and Friers, he took me back to my Lord Almner and he took us quite through the whole house and chapel and the new Monastery, showing me most excellent pieces in Waxworke – a crucifix given by a Pope to Mary Queene of Scotts, where a piece of

the Cross is – two bits set in the manner of a cross in the foot of the crucifix. Several fine pictures, but especially very good prints of holy pictures. I saw the Dortoire and the Cells of the priests, and we went into one – a very pretty little room, very clean, hung with pictures – set with books. The priest was in his Cell – with his hair-cloths to his skin, bare-legged, with a Sandall only on, and his little bed without sheets, and no feather bed; but yet I thought saft enough. His Cord about his middle. But in so good company, living with[out] care, I thought it a very good life. A pretty Library they have, and I was in the Refectoire, where every man his napkin – knife – cup of earth – and basin of the same – and a place for one to sit and read while the rest are at meals. And into the Kitchin I went, where a good neck of Mutton at the fire – and other victuals boiling – I do not think they feed very hard. Their windows looking all into a fine garden and the park. And mighty pretty rooms all. I wished myself one of the Capuchins – having seen what we could here, and all with mighty pleasure. So away with the Almoner in his coach, talking merrily about the difference in our religions, to Whitehall and there we left him.

To the New Exchange, there to take up my wife and Mercer, and to Temple Barr to my ordinary and had a dish of meat for them, they having not dined; and thence to the King's House and there saw *The Humerous Lieutenant* – a silly play, I think – only the spirit in it, that grows very Tall and then sinks again to nothing, having two heads treading upon one, and then Knipps singing, did please us. Here, in a box above, we spied Mrs. Pierce; and going out, they called us, and so we stayed for them and Knipp took us all in and brought to us Nelly, a most pretty woman, who acted the great part, Cœlia, today very fine, and did it pretty well; I kissed her and so did my wife, and a mighty pretty soul she is. We also saw Mrs. Hall, which is my little Roman-nose black girl that is mighty pretty: she is usually called Betty. Knipp made us stay in a box and see the dancing preparatory to tomorrow for *The Goblins*, a play of Suckelings not acted these 25 years, which was pretty; and so away thence, pleased with this sight also, and especially kissing of Nell; we away, Mr. Pierce and I on foot to his house, the women by coach. In our way we find the Guards of Horse in the street, and hear the occasion to be news that the Seamen are in a mutiny, which put me into a great fright; so away with my wife and Mercer home, preparing against tomorrow night to have Mrs. Pierce and Knipp and a great deal more company to dance. And when I came home, hear of no disturbance there of the seamen, but that one of them being arrested today, others do go and rescue him. So to the office a little, and then home to supper and to my chamber a while, and then to bed.

24. Up, and to the office, full of thoughts how to order the business of our merry meeting tonight. So to the office, where busy all the morning. At noon home to dinner and presently to the office to despatch my business betimes; and also we sat all the afternoon to examine the loss of the *Bredagh*, which was done by as plain negligence as ever ship was. We being rose and I ending my letters and getting the office swept and a good fire made and abundance of candles lighted, I home, where most of my company come of this end of the town – Mercer and her sister – Mr. Batelier and Pendleton – (my Ladies Pen and Pegg and Mr. Lowder; but they did not stay long, and I believe it was by Sir W. Penn's order, for they had a great mind to have stayed) and also Captain Rolt; and anon, at about 7 or 8 a-clock comes Mr. Harris of the Duke's playhouse and brings Mrs. Pierce with him, and also one dressed like a country maid, with a straw hatt on, which at first I could not tell who it was, though I expected Knipp – but it was she, coming off the stage just as she acted this day in *The Goblins* – a merry jade. Now my house is full, and four fiddlers that play well. Harris I first took to my closet, and I find him a very curious and understanding person in all pictures and other things – and a man of fine conversation. And so is Rolt. So away with all my company down to the office, and there fell to dancing and continued at [it] an hour or two – there coming Mrs. Anne Jones, a merchant's daughter hard by, who dances well. And all in mighty good humour; and danced with great pleasure, and then sung, and then danced, and then sung many things of three voices, both Harris and Rolt singing their parts excellently. Among other things, Harris sung his Irish song, the strangest in itself and the prettiest sung by him that ever I heard. Then to supper in the office, a cold good supper and wondrous merry. After supper to dancing again and singing, and so continued till almost 3 in the morning and then with extraordinary pleasure broke up; only, towards morning Knipp fell a little ill, and so my wife home with her to put her to bed, and we continued dancing – and singing; and among other things, our Mercer unexpectedly did happen to sing an Italian song I knew not, of which they two sung the other two parts too, that did almost ravish me and made me in love with her

more then ever with her singing. As late as it was, yet Rolt and
Harris would go home tonight, and walked it, though I had a bed
for them; and it proved dark, and a misly night – and very windy.
The company being all gone to their homes, I up with Mrs. Pierce
to Knipp, who was in bed; and we waked her and there I handled
her breasts and did baiser la and sing a song, lying by her on the
bed; and then left my wife to see Mrs. Pierce in bed with her in our
best chamber, and so to bed myself – my mind mightily satisfied
with all this evening's work, and thinking it to be one of the
merriest enjoyments I must look for in the world, and did content
myself therefore with the thoughts of it, and so to bed. Only, the
Musique did not please me, they not being contented with less
then 30*s*.

26.    Up, and at the office sat all the morning – where among other
things, I did the first unkind [thing] that ever I did design to Sir W.
Warren. But I did it now to some purpose, to make him sensible
how little any friendship shall avail him if he wants mine. I perceive
he doth nowadays court much my Lord Brouncker's favour, who
never did any man much courtesy at the Board, nor ever will be able
– at least, so much as myself. Besides, my Lord would do him a
kindness in concurrence with me; but he would have the danger of
the thing to be done lie upon me, if there be any danger in it (in
drawing up a letter to Sir W. Warren's advantage); which I do not
like, nor will endure. I was, I confess, very angry, and will venture
the loss of Sir W. Warren's kindnesses rather then he shall have any
man's friendship in greater esteem then mine.

30.    *Fast day for the King's death.* I all the morning at my chamber,
making up my month's accounts; which I did before dinner to my
thorough content, and find myself but a small gainer this month,
having no manner of profits but just my salary. But blessed be God
that I am able to save out of that, living as I do. So to dinner. Then to
my chamber all the afternoon; and in the evening my wife and I and
Mercer and Barker to little Michells, walked, with some neats'
tongues and cake and wine; and there sat with the little Couple with
great pleasure, and talked and eat and drank and saw their little
house, which is very pretty – and I much pleased therewith; and so
walked home about 8 at night, it being a little Mooneshine and fair
weather; and so into the garden and with Mercer sang till my wife
put me in mind of its being a fast day, and so I was sorry for it and

stopped; and home to Cards a while, and had opportunity para besar Mercer several times, and so to bed.

## FEBRUARY

1. Up, and to the office, where I was all the morning doing business. At noon home to dinner; and after dinner down by water, though it was a thick misty and raining day, and walked to Deptford from Redriffe and there to Bagwells by appointment – where the moher erat within expecting mi venida. And did sensa alguna difficulty monter los degres and lie, comme jo desired it, upon lo lectum; and there I did la cosa con much voluptas. By and by su marido came in, and there, without any notice taken by him, we discoursed of our business of getting him the new ship building by Mr. Deane, which I shall do for him.

2. Up, and to the office. This day I hear that Prince Rupert is to be trepanned – God give good issue to it. Sir W. Penn looks upon me and I on him, and speak about business together at the table well enough, but no friendship or intimacy, nor do I desire to have any. At noon dined well, and my brother and I to write over once more with my own hand my Catalogue of books, while he reads to me. After something of that done, and dined, I to the office, where all the afternoon till night busy. At night, having done all my office matters, I home, and my brother and I to go on with my Catalogue, and so to supper. This night comes home my new Silver Snuffe dish which I do give myself for my closet; which is all I purpose to bestow in plate of myself or shall need many a day, if I can keep what I have. So to bed. I am very well pleased this night with reading a poem I brought home with me last night from Westminster hall, of Driden's upon the present war – a very good poem.

5. This morning, before I went to the office there came to me Mr. Young and Whistler, Flaggmakers, and with mighty earnestness did present me with and press me to take a box, wherein I could not guess there was less then 100*l* in gold. But I do wholly refuse it, and did not at last take it – the truth is, not thinking them safe men to receive such a gratuity from nor knowing any considerable courtesy that ever I did do them – but desirous to keep myself free

from their reports and to have it in my power to say I had refused their offer.

7. Lay long with pleasure with my wife; and then up and to the office, where all the morning; then home to dinner, and before dinner I went into my green dining room; and there talking with my brother upon matters relating to his Journy to Brampton tomorrow and giving him good counsel about spending that time which he shall stay in the country with my father, I looking another way, I heard him fall down, and turned my head and he was fallen down all along upon the ground, dead – which did put me into a great fright; and to see my brotherly love, I did presently lift him up from [the] ground, he being as pale as death. And being upon his legs, he did presently come to himself, and said he had something come into his stomach, very hot; he knew not what it was, nor ever had such a fit before. I never was so frighted but once, when my wife was ill at Ware upon the road. And I did continue trembling a good while, and ready to weep to see him, he continuing mighty pale all dinner, and melancholy, that I was loath to let him take his journey tomorrow. But begun to be pretty well; and after dinner my wife and Barker fell to singing, which pleased me pretty well, my wife taking mighty pains and pride that she shall come to trill; and endeed, I think she will. So to the office and there all the afternoon late doing business; and then home and find my brother pretty well. So to write a letter to my Lady Sandwich for him to carry, I having not writ to her a great while. Then to supper and so to bed. I did this night give him 20s. for books and as much for his pocket, and 15s. to carry him down. And so to bed. Poor fellow, he is so melancholy and withal, my wife says, harmless, that I begin to love him, and would be loath he should not do well.

8. This morning my brother John came up to my bedside and took his leave of us, going this day to Brampton. He gone, I up and to the office, where we sat upon the Victualler's accounts all the morning. At noon Lord Brouncker, W. Batten, W. Penn and myself to the Sun in Leadenhall street to dinner, where an exceeding good dinner and good discourse. At dinner we talked much of Cromwell, all saying he was a brave fellow and did owe his Crowne he got to himself as much as any man that ever got one.

10. *Lords day.* Up and with my wife to church, where Mr. Mills

made an unnecessary sermon upon Originall Sin, neither understood by himself nor the people. Home, where Michell and his
wife, and also there came Mr. Carter, my old acquaintance of
Magdalen College, who hath not been here of many years. He hath
spent his time in the North with the Bishop of Carlisle much. He is
grown a very comely person and of good discourse, and one that I
like very much. We had much talk of all our old acquaintance of the
College, concerning their various fortunes; wherein, to my joy, I
met not with any that have sped better then myself.

12.　Up, and to the office, where we sat all the morning – with
several things (among others) discoursed relating to our two new
Assistant-Controllers; but especially Sir W. Penn, who is mighty
troublesome in it. At noon home to dinner, and then to the office
again and there did much business; and by and by comes Mr.
Moore, who in discourse did almost convince me that it is necessary
for my Lord Sandwich to come home and take his command at Sea
this year, for that a peace is like to be. Many considerations he did
give me hereupon which were very good, both in reference to the
public and his private condition. By and by with my Lord
Brouncker by coach to his house, there to hear some Italian
Musique; and here we met Tom Killigrew, Sir Rob. Murray, and
the Italian Seignor Baptista – who hath composed a play in Italian
for the Opera which T. Killigrew doth intend to have up; and here
he did sing one of the acts. Himself is the poet as well as the
Musician, which is very much; and did sing the whole from the
words without any Musique pricked, and played all along upon a
Harpsicon most admirably; and the composition most excellent.
The words I did not understand, and so know not how they are
fitted; but believe very well, and all in the Recitativo very fine. But I
perceive there is a proper accent in every country's discourse; and
that doth reach in their setting of notes to words, which therefore
cannot be natural to anybody else but them; so that I am not so
much smitten with it as it may be I should be if I were acquainted
with their accent. But the whole composition is certainly most
excellent; and the poetry, T. Killigrew and Sir R. Murray, who
understood the words, did say was excellent. I confess I was
mightily pleased with the music. He pretends not to voice, though
it be good but not excellent. This done, T. Killigrew and I to talk;
and he tells me how the Audience at his House is not above half so
much as it used to be before the late fire. That Knipp is like to make

the best actor that ever came upon the stage, she understanding so well. That they are going to give her 30*l* a year more. That the stage is now by his pains a thousand times better and more glorious then ever heretofore.[1] Now, wax-candles, and many of them; then, not above 3*lb*. of tallow. Now, all things civil, no rudeness anywhere; then, as in a bear-garden. Then, two or three fiddlers; now, nine or ten of the best. Then, nothing but rushes upon the ground and everything else mean; and now, all otherwise. Then, the Queen seldom and the King never would come; now, not the King only for state, but all civil people do think they may come as well as any. He tells me that he hath gone several times, eight or ten times he tells me, hence to Rome to hear good music; so much he loves it, though he never did sing or play a note. That he hath ever endeavoured, in the last King's time and in this, to introduce good Musique; but he never could do it, there never having been any music here better then ballads. "No", [he] says "*Hermitt poore* and *Chivy chase* was all the music we had – and yet no ordinary Fidlers get so much money as ours do here, which speaks our rudeness still." That he hath gathered nine Italians from several Courts in Christendome to come to make a consort for the King, which he doth give 200*l* a year apiece to, but badly paid, and do come in the room of keeping four ridiculous Gundilows – he having got the King to put them away and lay out the money this way. And endeed, I do commend him for it, for I think it is a very noble undertaking. He doth entend to have some times of the year these Operas to be performed at the two present Theatres, since he is defeated in what he intended in Moore Fields on purpose of it. And he tells me plainly that the Citty Audience was as good as the Court – but now they are most gone.

Having done our discourse, we all took coaches (my Lord's and T. Killigrew's) and to Mrs. Knepp's chamber, where this Italian is to teach her to sing her part. And so we all thither, and there she did sing an Italian song or two very fine, while he played the bass upon a Harpsicon there; and exceedingly taken I am with her singing, and believe she will do miracles at that and acting. Her little girl is mighty pretty and witty. After being there an hour, and I mightily pleased with this evening's work, we all parted; and I took coach and home, where late at my office and then home to enter my last three days' Journal; and so to supper and to bed – troubled at

1. sc. before the Civil War.

nothing but that these pleasures do hinder me in my business, and the more by reason of our being to dine abroad tomorrow, and then Saturdy next is appointed to meet again at my Lord Brouncker's lodgings and there to have the whole Quire of Italians. But then I do consider that this is all the pleasure I live for in the world, and the greatest I can ever expect in the best of my life; and one thing more, that by hearing this man tonight, and I think Capt. Cooke tomorrow and the Quire of Italians on Saturday, I shall be truly able to distinguish which of them pleases me truly best, which I do much desire to know and have good reason and fresh occasion of judging.

14.   After dinner by coach to my Lord Chancellor's, and there a meeting – the Duke of York – the Duke of Albemarle – and several other Lords of the Commission of Tanger; and there I did present a state of my accounts, and managed them well; and my Lord Chancellor did say, though he was in other things in an ill humour, that no man in England was of more method nor made himself better understood then myself. Thence away by coach with Sir H. Cholmly and Fitzgerald and Creed, setting down the two latter at the New Exchange; and H. Cholmly and I to the Temple and there walked in the dark in the walks, talking of news; and he surprizes me with the certain news that the King did last night in council declare his being in Treaty with the Dutch. God therefore give a good end to it, for I doubt it; and yet do much more doubt the issue of our continuing the war, for we are in no wise fit for it. And yet it troubles me to think what Sir H. Cholmly says, that he believes they will not give us any reparation for what we have suffered by the warr, nor put us into any better condition then what we were in before the war, for that will be shameful for us. Thence parted with him and home through the dark over the ruins by coach, with my sword drawn, to my office, where despatched some business; and so home to my chamber and to supper and to bed. This morning came up to my wife's bedside, I being up dressing myself, little Will Mercer to be her Valentine; and brought her name writ upon blue paper in gold letters, done by himself, very pretty – and we were both well pleased with it. But I am also this year my wife's Valentine, and it will cost me 5*l* – but that I must have laid out if we had not been Valentines. So to bed.

16.   To my Lord Bruncker's, and there was Sir Rob. Murray, whom I never understood so well as now by this opportunity of discourse; he is a most excellent man of reason and learning, and understands the doctrine of Musique and everything else I could discourse of very finely. Here came Mr. Hooke, Sir George Ent, Dr. Wren, and many others; and by and by the music, that is to say, Seignor Vincentio, who is the maister Composer, and six more, whereof two Eunuches (so tall, that Sir T. Harvy said well that he believes they did grow large by being gelt, as our Oxen do) and one woman, very well dressed and handsome enough but would not be kissed, as Mr. Killigrew, who brought the company in, did acquaint us. They sent two Harpsicons before; and by and by, after tuning them, they begun; and I confess, very good music they made; that is, the composition exceeding good, but yet not at all more pleasing to me then what I have heard in English by Mrs. Knipp, Capt. Cooke and others. Nor do I dote on the Eunuchs; they sing endeed pretty high and have a mellow kind of sound, but yet I have been as well satisfied with several women's voices, and men also, as Crispe of the Wardrobe. The woman sung well, but that which distinguishes all is this: that in singing, the words are to be considered and how they are fitted with notes, and then the common accent of the country is to be known and understood by the hearer, or he will never be a good judge of the vocall music of another country. So that I was not taken with this at all, neither understanding the first nor by practice reconciled to the latter, so that their motions and risings and fallings, though it may be pleasing to an Italian or one that understands that tongue, yet to me it did not; but do from my heart believe that I could set words in English, and make music of them, more agreeable to any Englishman's eare (the most judicious) then any Italian music set for the voice and performed before the same man, unless he be acquainted with the Italian accent of speech. The composition as to the Musique part was exceeding good, and their justness in keeping time by practice much before any that we have, unless it be a good band of practised fiddlers.

So away; here being Capt. Cocke, with him stole away, leaving them at it, in his coach; and to Mrs. Pierces, where I took up my wife and there find that Mrs. Pierce's little girl is my Valentine, she having drawn me – which I was not sorry for, it easing me of something more that I must have given to others. But here I do first observe the fashion of drawing of Motto's as well as names; so that

Pierce, who drew my wife, did draw also a motto, and this girl drew another for me. What mine was I have forgot; but my wife's was (*Most virtuous and most fair*); which, as it may be used, or an Anagram made upon each name, might be very pretty. Thence with Cocke and my wife; set him at home, and then we home. To the office and there did a little business, troubled that I have so much been hindered by matters of pleasure from my business; but I shall recover it I hope in a little time. So home and to supper, not at all smitten with the music tonight, which I did expect should have been so extraordinary, Tom Killigrew crying it up, and so all the world, above all things in the world; and so to bed.

17. *Lords day.* Up, and called at Michell's and took him and his wife and carried them to Westminster, I landing at Whitehall and having no pleasure in the way con ella; and so to the Duke's, where we all met and had a hot encounter before the Duke of York about the business of our payments at the Ticket Office; where we urged that we had nothing to do to be troubled with the pay, having examined the tickets. Besides, we are neglected, having not money sent us in time. But to see the baseness of my brethren, not a man almost put in a word but Sir W. Coventry, though at the office like very devils in this point. But I did plainly declare that without money no fleet could be expected, and desired the Duke of York to take notice of [it] and notice was taken of it – but I doubt will do no good. But I desire to remember it as a most prodigious thing that to this day my Lord Treasurer hath not consulted counsel (which Sir W. Coventry and I and others do think is necessary) about the late Pole act, enough to put the same into such order as that anybody dare lend money upon it, though we have from this office under our hands related the necessity thereof to the Duke of York. Nor was like to be determined in, for aught I see, a good while, had not Sir W. Coventry plainly said that he did believe it would be a better work for the King then going to church this morning, to send for the Atturny Generall to meet at the Lord Treasurer's this afternoon and to bring the thing to an issue, saying that himself, were he going to the Sacrament, would not think he should offend God to leave it and go to the ending this work, so much it is of moment to the King and Kingdom. Hereupon the Duke of York said he would presently speak to the King, and cause it to be done this afternoon. Having done here, we broke up, having done nothing almost though, for all this; and by and by I met Sir G. Carteret, and he is

stark mad at what hath passed this morning, and I believe is heartily vexed with me. I said little, but I am sure the King will suffer if some better care be not taken then he takes to look after this business of money. So parted, and I by water home and to dinner, W. Hewer with us; a good dinner and very merry, my wife and I; and after dinner, to my chamber to fit something against the Council anon; and that being done, away to Whitehall by water and thence to my Lord Chancellors, where I met with and had much pretty discourse with one of the Progers's that knows me. And it was pretty to hear him tell me of his own accord, as a matter of no shame, that in Spain he had a pretty woman his mistress; whom, when money grew scarce with him, he was forced to leave, and afterward heard how she and her husband lived well, she being kept by an old Fryer who used her as his whore; but this, says he, is better then as our Ministers do, who have wifes that lay up their estates and do no good nor relieve any poor; no, not our greatest prelates – and I think he is in the right for my part.

Stayed till the Council was up, and attended the King and Duke of York round the park and was asked several Questions by both; but I was in pain lest they should ask me what I could not answer; as the Duke of York did the value of the hull of the *St. Patricke*, lately lost; which I told him I could not presently answer – though I might have easily furnished myself to answer all those Questions. They stood a good while to see the ganders and geese tread one another in the water, the goose being all the while kept for a great while quite under water, which was new to me; but they did make mighty sport at it, saying (as the King did often), "Now you shall see a marriage between this and that" – which did not please me. They gone by coach to my Lord Treasurer's, as the Duke of York told me, to settle the business of money for the Navy; I walked into the Court to and again till night, and then met Coll. Reames and he and I walked together a great while, complaining of the ill-management of things, whereof he is as full as I am. We run over many persons and things, and see nothing done like men like to do well while the King minds his pleasures so much. We did bemoan it that nobody would or had authority enough with the King to tell him how all things go to wrack and will be lost. Then he and I parted, and I to Westminster to the Swan, and there stayed till Michell and his wife came. Old Michell and his wife came to see me, and there we drank and laughed a little; and then the young ones and I took boat, it being fine moonshine. I did to my trouble see all the way that ella did get as close a su marido as ella could, and turn her manos away quando yo did endeavour take one de los – so that I had no pleasure at all con ella ce night. When we landed, I did take occasion to send him back a the bateau while I did get un baiser or two, and would have taken la by la hand; but ella did turn away, and quando I said "Shall I not tocar te?" answered "Yo no love touching", in a slight modo. I seemed not to take notice of it, but parted kindly et su marido did andar with me almost a mi casa, and there parted; and so I home, troubled at this; but I think I shall make good use of it and mind my business more. This evening, going to the Queen's side to see the ladies, I did find the Queene, the Duchess of York, and another or two at Cards, with the room full of great ladies and men – which I was amazed at to see on a Sunday, having not believed it; but contrarily, flatly denied the same a little while since to my Cosen Roger Pepys. I did this day, going by water, read the Answer to the *Apology for Papists*, which did like me mightily, it being a thing as well writ as I think most things that ever I read in my life, and glad I am that I read it.

18.    Up, and to my bookbinders and there mightily pleased to see some papers of the account we did give the Parliament of the expense of the Navy, sewed together; which I could not have conceived before how prettily it was done. Then by coach to the Exchequer about some tallies; and thence back again home, by the way meeting Mr. Weaver of Huntington, and did discourse our business of law together; which did ease my mind, for I was afeared I have omitted the doing what I in prudence ought to have done. So home and to dinner; and after dinner to the office, where yo had Mrs. Burrows all sola a my closet, and did there besar and tocar su mamelles as much as yo quisere hasta a hazer me hazer, but ella would not suffer that yo should poner mi mano abaxo ses jupes, which yo endeavoured. Thence away, and with my wife by coach to the Duke of York's playhouse, expecting a new play; so stayed not no more then other people, but to the King's to *The Mayds Tragedy*; but vexed all the while with two talking ladies and Sir Ch. Sidly, yet pleased to hear their discourse, he being a stranger; and one of the ladies would, and did, sit with her mask on all the play; and being exceeding witty as ever I heard woman, did talk most pleasantly with him; but was, I believe, a virtuous woman and of quality. He would fain know who she was, but she would not tell. Yet did give him many pleasant hints of her knowledge of him, by

that means setting his brains at work to find out who she was; and did give him leave to use all means to find out who she was but pulling off her mask. He was mighty witty; and she also making sport with him very inoffensively, that a more pleasant rencontre I never heard. But by that means lost the pleasure of the play wholly, to which now and then Sir Ch. Sidlys exceptions against both words and pronouncing was very pretty. So home and to the office; did much business; then home to supper and to bed.

19. Up, and to the office, where all the morning doing little business, our want of money being so infinite great. At noon home, and there find old Mr. Michell and Howlett come to desire mine and my wife's company to dinner to their son's; and so away by coach with them, it being Betty's wedding-day a year – as also Shrove tuseday. Here I made myself mighty merry, the two old women being there also; and a mighty pretty dinner we had in this little house, to my exceeding great content and my wife's, and my heart pleased to see Betty. But I have not been so merry a very great while as with them, everything pleasing me there as much as among so mean company I could be pleased. After dinner I fell to read the Acts about the building of the City again; and endeed, the laws seem to be very good, and I pray God I may live to see it built in that manner. Anon, with much content home, walking with my wife and her woman; and there to my office, where late doing much business; and then home to supper and to bed. This morning I hear that our discourse of peace is all in the dirt, for the Dutch do not like of the place;[1] or at least, the French will not agree to it; so that I do wonder what we shall do, for carry on the war we cannot. I long to hear the truth of it tomorrow at Court.

23. This day I am by the blessing of God 34 years old – in very good health and mind's content, and in condition of estate much beyond whatever my friends could expect of a child of theirs this day 34 year. The Lord's name be praised and may I be ever thankful for it. Up betimes to the office, in order to my letter to the Duke of York tomorrow. And then the office met and spent the greatest part about this letter. At noon home to dinner and then to the office again, very close at it all day till midnight, making an end and writing fair this great letter and other things, to my full content – it

1. The Hague.

abundantly providing for the vindication of this office, whatever the success* be of our wants of money.

24. *Lords day*. Up, and with W. Batten by coach; he set me down at my Lord Brouncker's; and I with my Lord, by and by when ready, to Whitehall. And by and by up to the Duke of York and there presented our great letter and other papers; and among the rest, my report of the victualling, which is good I think, and will continue my pretence to the place, which I am still afeared Sir W. Coventry's imployment may extinguish. We have discharged ourselfs in this letter fully from blame in the bad success of the Navy if money do not come soon to us – and so my heart is at pretty good rest in this point. Having done here, Sir W. Batten and I home by coach; and though the sermon at our church was begun, yet he would light and go home and eat a slice of roast beef off of the spit, and did; and then he and I to church in the middle of the sermon. After sermon home and alone with my wife dined. In the afternoon away to Whitehall by water, and took a turn or two in the park and then back to Whitehall; and there meeting my Lord Arlington, he, by I know not what kindness, offered to carry me along with him to my Lord Treasurer's, whither I told him I was going. I believe he had a mind to discourse of some Navy business; but Sir Tho. Clifford coming into the coach to us, we were prevented; which I was sorry for, for I had a mind to begin an acquaintance with him. He speaks well and hath pretty slight superficial parts, I believe. He in our going talked much of the plain habit of the Spaniards; how the King and lords themselfs wear but a cloak of Colchester bayze, and the ladies mantles, in cold weather, of white flannel. And that the endeavours frequently of setting up the manufacture of making these stuffs there have only been prevented by the Inquisition – the English and Duchmen that have been sent for to work being taken with a Psalm-book or Testament, and so clapped up and the house pulled down by the Inquisitors, and the greatest lord in Spain dare not say a word against it – if the word "Inquisition" be but mentioned. At my Lord Treasurers light and parted with them, they going into Council, and I walked with Capt. Cocke, who did tell me that the Duch are in very great straits, so as to be said to be not able to set out their fleet this year.

By and by comes Sir Robt. Viner and Lord Mayor to ask the King's direction about measuring out the streets according to the new Act for building of the City, wherein the King is to be pleased.

But he says that the way proposed in Parliament by Coll. Birch would have been the best, to have chosen some persons in trust and sold the whole ground, and let it be sold again by them with preference to the old owner; which would have certainly caused the City to be built where these trustees pleased; whereas now, great differences will be and the streets built by fits, and not entire till all differences be decided. This, as he tells it, I think would have been the best way. I enquired about the Frenchman[1] that was said to fire the City, and was hanged for it by his own confession that he was hired for it by a Frenchman of Roane, and that he did with a stick reach in a Fireball in at a window of the house – whereas the maister of the house, who is the King's Baker, and his son and daughter do all swear there was no such window – and that the fire did not begin thereabouts. Asking Sir R. Viner what he thought was the cause of the fire, he tells me that the Baker, son and his daughter did all swear again and again that their Oven was drawn by 10 a-clock at night. That having occasion to light a candle about 12, there was not so much fire in the bakehouse as to light a match for a candle, so as they were fain to go into another place to light it. That about 2 in the morning they felt themselfs almost choked with smoke; and rising, did find the fire coming upstairs – so they rose to save themselfs; but that at that time the bavins were not on fire in the yard. So that they are, as they swear, in absolute ignorance how this fire should come – which is a strange thing, that so horrid an effect should have so mean and uncertain a beginning. By and by called in to the King and Cabinet and there had a few insipid words about money for Tanger, but to no purpose. Thence away, walked to my boat at Whitehall, and so home and to supper; and so to my Journall and to bed.

This night, going through bridge by water, my waterman told me how the mistress of the Beare tavern at the bridge foot did lately fling herself into the Thames and drownded herself; which did trouble me the more when they tell me it was she that did live at the White Horse tavern in Lumbard street; which was a most beautiful woman, as most I have seen. It seems hath had long melancholy upon her, and hath endeavoured to make away with herself often.

25. Lay long in bed, talking with pleasure with my poor wife how

1. Robert Hubert, hanged in October 1666.

she used to make coal fires and wash my foul clothes with her own
hand for me, poor wretch, in our little room at my Lord
Sandwiches; for which I ought for ever to love and admire her, and
do, and persuade myself she would do the same thing again if God
should reduce us to it. So up, and by coach abroad to the Duke of
Albemarle's about sending soldiers down to some ships; and so
home, calling at a belt-makers to mend my belt, and so home and to
dinner, where pleasant with my wife; and then to the office, where
mighty busy all the day, saving going forth to the Change to pay for
some things and on other occasions; and at my goldsmith's did
observe the King's new Medall, where in little there is Mrs.
Stewards face, as well done as ever I saw anything in my whole life I
think – and a pretty thing it is that he should choose her face to
represent Britannia by. So at the office late very busy, and much
business with great joy despatched; and so home to supper and to
bed.

27.    Up by candlelight about 6 a-clock, it being bitter cold weather
again after all our warm weather, and by water down to Woolwich
ropeyard (I being this day at a leisure, the King and Duke of York
being gone down to Sherenesse this morning to lay out the design
for a fortification there to the River Medway, and so we do not
attend the Duke of York as we should otherwise have done); and
then to the Dockyard to enquire of the state of things; and went into
Mr. Pett's and there, beyond expectation, he did present me with a
Japan cane with a silver head, and his wife sent me by him a ring
with a Woolwich stone, now much in request; which I accepted, the
value not being great and knowing that I had done them courtesies,
which he did own in very high terms; and then, at my asking, did
give me an old draft of an ancient-built ship, given him by his
father, of the *Beare* in Queen Elizabeths time. This did much please
me, it being a thing I much desired to have, to show the difference
in the built of ships now and heretofore. Being much taken with
this kindness – away to Blackwall and Deptford to satisfy myself
there about the King's business; and then walked to Redriffe and so
home about noon; there find Mr. Hunt, newly come out of the
country, who tells me the country is much impoverished by the
greatness of taxes. The Farmers do break every day almost, and
1000*l* a year became not worth 500*l*. He dined with us, and we had
good discourse of the generall ill state of things; and by the way he
told me some ridiculous pieces of thrift of Sir G. Downing's, who is

their countryman – in inviting some poor people at Christmas last, to charm the country people's mouths; but did give them nothing but beef porridge, pudding, and pork, and nothing said all dinner, but only his mother would say, "It's good broth, son." He would answer, "Yes, it is good broth." Then his lady confirm all and say, "Yes, very good broth." By and by she would begin and say, "Good pork;" "Yes," says the mother, "good pork." Then he cries, "Yes, very good pork." And so they said of all things; to which nobody made any answer, they going there not out of love or esteem of them, but to eat his victuals, knowing him to be a niggardly fellow – and with this he is jeered now all over the country. After dinner with my wife by coach abroad, and set Mr. Hunt down at the Temple and her at her brother's. And I to Whitehall to meet W. Coventry, but found him not. But met Mr. Cooling, who tells me of my Lord Duke of Buckingham's being sent for last night by a Serjeant-at-armes to the Tower for treasonable practices; and that the King is infinitely angry with him and declared him no longer one of his Council – I know not the reason of it, or occasion. To Westminster hall and there paid what I owed for books; and so by coach took up my wife to the Exchange and there bought things for Mr. Pierces little daughter, my Valentine; and so to their house, where we find Knipp, who also challengeth me for her valentine. She looks well, sang well, and very merry we were for half an hour. Tells me Harris is well again, having been very ill. And so we home and I to the office. So late home and to bed.

28.　Up, and there comes to me Drumbleby with a flagelette made to suit with my former, and brings me one Greeting, a master to teach my wife. I agree by the whole with him, to teach her to take out any lesson of herself for 4*l.* She was not ready to begin today, but doth tomorrow. So I to the office, where my Lord Brouncker and I only, all the morning, and did business. At noon to the Exchange and to Sir Rob. Viner's about settling my accounts there. So back home and to dinner, where Mr. Holliard dined with us – and pleasant company he is. I love his company and he secures me against ever having the stone again. He gives it me as his opinion that the City will never be built again together as is expected while any restraint is laid upon them. He hath been a great loser, and would be a builder again; but he says he knows not what restrictions there will be, so as it is unsafe for him to begin. He gone, I to the office and there busy till night, doing much business; then home and to my accounts; wherein, beyond expectation, I succeeded so well as to settle them very clear and plain, though by borrowing of monies this month to pay D. Gawden and chopping and changing with my Tanger money, they were become somewhat intricate. And blessed be God, upon the evening my accounts, I do appear 6800*l* creditor. This done, I to supper about 12 at night, and so to bed – the weather for three or four days being come to be exceeding cold again, as any time this year. I did within these six days see smoke still remaining of the late fire in the City; and it is strange to think how to this very day I cannot sleep a-night without great terrors of fire; and this very night could not sleep till almost 2 in the morning through thoughts of fire. Thus this month is ended with great content of mind to me – thriving in my estate, and my matters in my offices going pretty well as to myself. This afternoon Mr. Gawden was with me, and tells me more then I knew before: that he hath orders to get all the victuals he can to Plymouth and the Western ports and other outports, and some to Scotland; so that we do entend to keep but a flying fleet this year; which it may be may preserve us a year longer, but the end of it must be ruin. Sir J. Mennes this night tells me that he hears for certain that ballads are made of us in Holland for begging of a peace; which I expected, but am vexed at. So ends this month, with nothing of weight upon my mind but for my father and mother, who are both ill and have been so for some weeks – whom God help, but I do fear my poor father will hardly be ever thoroughly well again.

## –⁜MARCH⁜–

1. In the street in Mark lane do observe (it being St. Davids' day) the picture of a man dressed like a Welchman, hanging by the neck upon one of the poles that stand out at the top of one of the merchants' houses, in full proportion and very handsomely done – which is one of the oddest sights I have seen a good while, for it was so like a man that one would have thought it was endeed a man. Being returned home, I find Greeting the flagelette-master come and teaching my wife; and I do think my wife will take pleasure in it, and it will be easy for her and pleasant – so I, as I am well contented with the charge it will occasion me. So to the office till

dinner, busy; and then home to dinner, and before dinner making my wife to sing; poor wretch, her ear is so bad that it made me angry, till the poor wretch cried to see me so vexed at her, that I think I shall not discourage her so much again but will endeavour to make her understand sounds and do her good that way, for she hath a great mind to learn, only to please me; and therefore I am mighty unjust to her in discouraging her so much. But we were good friends, and to dinner; and had she not been ill with those and that it were not Friday (on which in Lent there are no plays), I had carried her to a play. But she not being fit to go abroad, I to the office; where all the afternoon close, examining the collection of my papers of the accounts of the Navy since this war to my great content; and so at night home to talk and sing with my wife; and then to supper and so to bed with great pleasure.

2. After dinner with my wife to the King's house, to see *The Mayden Queene*, a new play of Dryden's mightily commended for the regularity of it and the strain and wit; and the truth is, there is a comical part done by Nell, which is Florimell, that I never can hope ever to see the like done again by man or woman. The King and Duke of York was at the play; but so great performance of a comical part was never, I believe, in the world before as Nell doth this, both as a mad girle and then, most and best of all, when she comes in like a young gallant; and hath the motions and carriage of a spark the most that ever I saw any man have. It makes me, I confess, admire her. Thence home and to the office, where busy a while; and then home to read the lives of Henry the 5th and 6th, very fine, in Speede; and so to bed.

3. Lay long, merrily talking with my wife; and then up and to church, where a dull sermon of Mr. Mills touching Originall Sin; and then home and there find little Michell and his wife, whom I love mightily. Mightily contented I was in their company, for I love her much; and so after dinner I left them and by water from the Old Swan to Whitehall; where walking in the galleries, I in the first place met Mr. Pierce, who tells me the story of the death of Tom Woodall the surgeon, killed in a drunken quarrel, and how the Duke of York hath a mind to get him one of his places in St. Tho. Hospitall. They do also tell me that news is this day come to the King that the King of France is come with his army to the frontiers of Flanders, demanding leave to pass through their country

towards Poland, but is denied; and thereupon, that he is gone into the country: how true this is, I dare not believe till I hear more.[1] From them I walked into the park, it being a fine but very cold day, and there took two or three turns the length of the Pell Mell. And there I met Serjeant Barcroft, who was sent for the Duke of Buckingham to have brought him prisoner to the Towre. He came to town this day; and brings word that being overtaken and outridd by the Duchess of Buckingham, within a few miles of the Duke's house of Westthorp he believes, she got thither about a quarter of an hour before him and so had time to consider – so that when he came, the doors were kept shut against him. The next day, coming with officers of the neighbour market-town to force open the doors, they were open for him, but the Duke of Buckingham gone; so he took horse presently, and heard upon the road that the Duke of Buckingham was gone before him for London; so that he believes he is this day also come to town before him – but no news is yet heard of him. This is all he brings. Thence to my Lord Chancellor; and there meeting Sir H. Cholmly, he and I walked in my Lord's garden and talked, among other things, of the treaty; and he says there will certainly be a peace, but I cannot believe it. He tells me that the Duke of Buckingham his crimes, as far as he knows, is his being of a Caball with some discontented persons of the late House of Commons, and opposing the desires of the King in all his matters in the House – and endeavouring to become popular – and advising how the Commons' House should proceed, and how he would order the House of Lords – and that he hath been endeavouring to have the King's nativity calculated; which was done, and the fellow now in the Tower about it – which itself hath heretofore, as he says, been held treason, and people died for it – but by the Statute of Treasons, in Queen Mary's times and since, it hath been left out. He tells me that this silly Lord hath provoked, by his ill-carriage, the Duke of York, my lord Chancellor, and all the great persons, and therefore most likely will die. He tells me too, many practices of treachery against this King; as betraying him in Scotland and giving Oliver an account of the King's private councils; which the King knows very well and yet hath pardoned him. Here I passed away a little time more, talking with him and Creed, whom I met there; and so away, Creed walking with me to Whitehall; and there I took water, and staying at Michells to drink, I

1. It was untrue.

home and there to read very good things in Fullers *Church History* and *Worthies*, and so to supper; and after supper had much good discourse with W. Hewers, who supped with us, about the Ticket Office and the knaveries and extortions every day used there. So parted with him, and then to bed.

4. Up, and with Sir J. Mennes and W. Batten by barge to Deptford by 8 in the morning, where to the King's yard a little to look after business there, and then to a private storehouse to look upon some cordage of Sir W. Batten's; and there being a hole formerly made for a drain for Tarr to run into, wherein the barrel stood still full of stinking water, Sir W. Batten did fall with one leg into it; which might have been very bad to him, by breaking a leg or other hurt, but thanks be to God he only sprained his foot a little. So after his shifting his stocking at a strong-water shop close by, we took barge again and so to Woolwich, where our business was chiefly to look upon the ballast-wharf there, which is offered us for the King's use to hire. But we do not think it worth the laying-out much money upon, unless we could buy the fee-simple of it; which cannot be sold us, so we wholly flung it off. So to the Dockyard and there stayed a while, talking about business of the yard, and thence to the Ropeyard; and so to the White Hart and there dined, and Capt. Cocke with us, who we find at the Ropeyard; and very merry at dinner, and many pretty tales of Sir J. Mennes, which I have entered in my tale book. But by this time Sir W. Batten was come to be in much pain in his foot, so as he was forced to be carried down in a chair to the barge again; and so away to Deptford, and there I a little in the yard; and then to Bagwells, where I find his wife washing, and I did hazer todo que jo voudrais con her; and then sent for her husband and discoursed of his going to Harwich this week to his charge of the new ship building there which I have got him – and so away, walked to Redriffe and there took boat and away home, upon Tower hill, near the Ticket Office, meeting with my old acquaintance Mr. Chaplin the cheesemonger; and there fell to talk of news and he tells me that for certain the King of France is denied passage with his army through Flanders – and that he hears the Dutch do stand upon high terms with us, and will have a promise of not being obliged to strike the flag to us before they will treat with us, and other high things which I am ashamed of and do hope will never be yielded to. That they do make all imaginable preparations, but that he believes they will be in mighty want of

men. That the King of France doth court us mightily. He tells me too, that our Lord Treasurer is going to lay down, and that my Lord Arlington is to be Lord Treasurer; but I believe nothing of it – for he is not yet of an estate visible enough to have that charge I suppose upon him. So being parted from him, I home to the office; and after having done business there, I home to supper; and there mighty pleased with my wife's beginning on the Flagelette, believing that she will come to [play] very well thereon. So to bed. This day in the barge I took Berchensha's translation of Alsted his *Templum*; but the most ridiculous book, as he hath translated it, that ever I saw in my life; I declaring that I understood not three lines together, from one end of the book to the other.

6. Up, and with W. Penn to Whitehall by coach. Here the Duke of York did acquaint us (and the King did the like also, afterward coming in) with his resolution of altering the manner of the war this year; that is, that we shall keep what fleet we have abroad in several squadrons; so that now all is come out, but we are to keep it as close as we can, without hindering the work that is to be done in preparation to this. Great preparations there are to fortify Sheernesse and the yard at Portsmouth, and forces are drawing down to both those places, and elsewhere by the seaside; so that we have some fear of an invasion, and the Duke of York himself did declare his expectation of the enemy's blocking us up here in the River, and therefore directed that we should send away all the ships that we have to fit out hence. Sir W. Penn told me, going with me this morning to Whitehall, that for certain the Duke of Buckingham is brought into the Tower, and that he hath had an hour's private conference with the King before he was sent thither. To Westminster hall; there bought some newsbooks and, as everywhere else, hear everybody complain of the dearness of coals, being at 4*l* per chaldron; the weather too being become most bitter cold, the King saying today that it was the coldest day he ever knew in England.

12. At noon home and there find Mr. Goodgroome, whose teaching of my wife, only by singing over and over again to her and letting her sing with him, not by herself, to correct her faults, I do not like at all but was angry at it; but have this content, that I do think she will come to sing pretty well and to trill in time, which pleases me well. He dined with us; and then to the office, where we had a silly meeting to little purpose and then broke up; and I to my

office and busy late to good purpose; and so home to supper and to bed. This day a poor seaman, almost starved for want of food, lay in our yard a-dying; I sent him half-a-crown – and we ordered his ticket to be paid.

14.    Up, and with W. Batten and W. Penn to my Lord Treasurer's, where we met with my Lord Brouncker an hour before the King came, and had time to talk a little of our business. Then came much company; among others, Sir H. Cholmly, who tells me that undoubtedly my Lord Bellasses will go no more as Governor to Tanger, and that he doth put in fair for it and believes he shall have it; and proposes how it may conduce to his account and mine in the business of money. Here we fell into talk with Sir St. Fox; and among other things, of the Spanish manner of walking when three are together; and showed me how, which was pretty, to prevent differences. By and by comes the King and Duke of York, and presently the officers of the Ordinance were called – my Lord Barkely, Sir Jo. Duncomb, and Mr. Chichly – then we, my Lord Brouncker, W. Batten, W. Penn, and myself, where we find only the King and the Duke of York and my Lord Treasurer and Sir G. Carteret; where I only did speak, laying down the state of our wants; which the King and Duke of York seemed very well pleased with, and we did get what we asked, 500000*l*, assigned upon the Eleven Months Tax: but that is not so much ready money, or what will raise 40000*l* per week, which we desired and the business will want. Yet are we fain to come away answered; when God knows it will undo the King's business to have matters of this moment put off in this manner. The King did prevent my offering anything by and by as Treasurer for Tanger, telling me that he had ordered us 30000*l* on the same tax; but that is not what we would have to bring our payments to come within a year. So we gone out, in went others – *viz.*, one after another, Sir St. Fox for the army – Capt. Cocke for sick and wounded – Mr. Ashburnham for the household. Thence W. Batten, W. Penn and I back again, I mightily pleased with what I had said and done and the success thereof. But it being a fine clear day, I did *en gayeté de Cœur* propose going to Bow for ayre sake and dine there; which they imbraced, and so W. Batten and I (setting W. Penn down at Mark lane end) straight to Bow to the Queen's Head and there bespoke our dinner, carrying meat with us from London; and anon comes W. Penn with my wife and Lady Batten, and then Mr. Lowder with his mother and wife. While W.

Batten and I were alone, we had much friendly discourse, though I will never trust him far. They being come, we to Oysters and so to talk; very pleasant I was all day; and anon to dinner, and we made very good company. Here till the evening, so as it was dark almost before we got home (back again in the same method I think we went); and spent the night talking at Sir W. Batten's; only, a little at my office to look over the Victualler's contract and draw up some arguments for him to plead for his charges in transportation of goods beyond the ports which the letter of one article in his contract doth lay upon him. This done, I home to supper and to bed – troubled a little at my fear that my Lord Brouncker should tell Sir W. Coventry of our neglecting the office this afternoon to look after our pleasures; but nothing will fall upon me alone about this.

15. Up, and pleased at Tom's teaching of Barker something to sing a third part to a song, which will please me mightily. So I to the office all the morning, and at noon to the Change, where I do hear that letters this day come to Court do tell us that we are likely not to agree, the Dutch demanding high terms and the King of France the like, in a most braveing manner. The merchants do give themselfs over for lost, no man knowing what to do, whether to sell or buy, not knowing whether peace or war to expect; and I am told that could that be now known, a man might get 20000*l* in a week's time – by buying up of goods in case there should be war. Thence home and dined well; and then with my wife, set her at Unthankes and I to Sir G. Carteret, where talked with the ladies a while; and my Lady Carteret talks nothing but sorrow and afflictions coming on us; and endeed, I do fear the same. So away, and met Dr. Fuller, Bishop of Limricke, and walked an hour with him in the Court, talking of news only; and he doth think that matters will be bad with us. Then to Westminster hall and then spent an hour or two walking up and down, thinking para aver got out Doll Lane, sed yo no could do it, having no opportunity de hazer le, ainsi lost the todo afternoon; and so away and called my wife and home, where a little at the office and then home to my closet to enter my Journalls, and so to supper and to bed.

16. Up, and to the office, where all the morning. At noon home to dinner; and then to the office again in the afternoon and there all day, very busy till night; and then having done much business, home to supper, and so to bed. This afternoon came home Sir J.

Mennes, who hath been down, but to little purpose, to pay the ships below at the Nore. This evening, having done my letters, I did write out the heads of what I had prepared to speak to the King the other day at my Lord Treasurer's, which I do think convenient to keep by me for future use. The weather is now grown warm again, after much cold weather; and it is observable that within these eight days I did see smoke remaining, coming out of some cellars, from the late great Fire, now above six months since. There was this day at the office (as he is most days) Sir W. Warren; against whom I did manifestly plead, and heartily too, God forgive me – but the reason is because I do find that he doth now wholly rely almost upon my Lord Brouncker.

17. *Lords day*. Up betimes with my wife, and by coach with Sir W. Penn and Sir Tho. Allen to Whitehall; there my wife and I the first time that ever we went to my Lady Jemimah's chamber at Sir Edw. Carteret's lodgings. I confess I have been much to blame and much ashamed of our not visiting her sooner, but better now then never. Here we took her before she was up, which I was sorry for, so only saw her and away to chapel, leaving further visit till after sermon. I put my wife into the pew below in the chapel; but it was pretty to see (myself being but in a plain band, and every way else ordinary) how the verger took me for her man I think; and I was fain to tell him she was a kinswoman of my Lord Sandwiches, he saying that none under Knight Baronets ladies are to go into that pew. So she being there, I to the Duke of York's lodging, where in his dressing-chamber he talking of his Journy tomorrow or next day to Harwich – to prepare some fortifications there; so that we are wholly upon the defensive part this year; only, we have some expectations that we may by our squadrons annoy them in their trade by the North of Scotland and to the Westward. That done, I to walk in the parke, where to the Queenes chapel and there heard a Fryer preach, with his Cord about his middle, in Portuguez – something I could understand, showing that God did respect the meek and humble as well as the high and rich. He was full of action; but very decent and good I thought, and his manner of delivery very good. I went back to Whitehall, and there up to the closet and spoke with several people till sermon was ended, which was preached by the Bishop of Hereford, an old good man, that they say made an excellent sermon. He was by birth a Catholique and a great gallant, having 1500*l* per annum patrimony, and is a Knight-

Barronet – was turned from his persuasion by the late Archbishop Laud. He and the Bishop of Exeter, Dr. Ward, are the two Bishops that the King doth say he cannot have bad sermons from. Here I met with Sir H. Cholmly, who tells me that undoubtedly my Lord Bellasses doth go no more to Tanger, and that he doth believe he doth stand in a likely way to go Governor – though he says, and showed me, a young silly Lord (one Lord Allington) who hath offered a great sum of money to go; and will put hard for it, he having a fine lady and a great man would be glad to have him out of the way.

18. Up betimes, and to the office to write fair my paper for D. Gawden against anon; and then to other business, where all the morning. D. Gawden by and by comes, and I did read over and give him the paper, which I think I have much obliged him in. A little before noon comes my old good friend Mr. Rd. Cumberland to see me, being newly come to town, whom I have not seen almost, if not quite, these seven years – in his plain country-parson dress. I could not spend much time with him, but prayed him come with his brother, who was with him, to dine with me today; which he did do and I had a great deal of his good company; and a most excellent person he is as any I know, and one that I am sorry should be lost and buried in a little country town, and would be glad to remove him thence; and the truth is, if he would accept of my sister's fortune, I should give 100*l* more with him then to a man able to settle her four times as much as I fear he is able to do. And I will think of it, and a way how to move it, he having in discourse said he was not against marrying, nor yet engaged. I showed him my closet, and did give him some very good music, Mr. Cæsar being here upon his Lute. They gone, I to the office, where all the afternoon very busy. Anon Sir W. Penn came and talked with me in the garden; and tells me that for certain the Duke of Richmond is to marry Mrs. Stewart, he having this day brought in an account of his estate and debts to the King on that account. At night home to supper and so to bed. My father's letter this day doth tell me of his own continued illness, and that my mother grows so much worse that he fears she cannot long continue – which troubles me much. This day Mr. Cæsar told me a pretty experiment of his, of Angling with a Minikin, a gut-string varnished over, which keeps it from swelling and is beyond any hair for strength and smallness – the secret I like mightily.

20.   With Sir W. Batten and J. Mennes to our church to the vestry
to be assessed by the late Pole bill, where I am rated at an Esquire;
and for my office, all will come to about 50*l* – but not more then I
expected, nor so much by a great deal as I ought to be for all my
offices – so shall be glad to escape so. Thence by water again to
Whitehall, and there up into the House and do hear that news is
come now that the enemy doth incline again to a peace; but could
hear no perticulars, so do not believe it. Thence to Westminster
hall, and there saw Betty Michell and bought a pair of gloves of her,
she being fain to keep shop there, her mother being sick and father
gathering of the tax. I aime her de todo mi corazon. Thence, my
mind wandering all this day upon mauvais amours which yo be
merry for. So home by water again, where I find my wife gone
abroad; so I to Sir W. Batten to dinner, and had a good dinner of
Ling and herring pie, very good meat – best of that kind that ever I
had – thus having dined, I by coach to the Temple and there did buy
a little book or two; and it is strange how Rycaut's discourse of
Turky, which before the fire I was asked but 8*s.* for, there being all
but 22 or thereabouts burnt, I did now offer 20*s.*, and he demands
50*s.*; and I think I shall give it him, though it be only as a monument
of the Fire. So home to the office a little, where I met with a sad
letter from my brother, who tells me my mother is declared by the
Doctors to be past recovery and that my father is also very ill every
hour; so that I fear we shall see a sudden change there – God fit them
and us for it. So to Sir W. Penn's, where my wife was, and supped
with a little, but yet little, mirth and a bad nasty supper; which
makes me not love that family, they do all things so meanly, to
make a little bad show upon their backs. Thence home and to bed,
very much troubled about my father's and my mother's illness.

22.   Up and by coach to Sir Ph. Warwicke about business for
Tanger, about money. And then to Sir St. Fox to give him account
of a little service I have done him about money coming to him from
our office; and then to Lovetts and saw a few baubling things of
their doing, which are very pretty; but the quality of the people,
living only by shifts, doth not please me, that it makes me I do no
more care for them, nor shall have more acquaintance with them
after I have got my Lady Castlemaine's picture home. So to
Whitehall, where the King at chapel; and I would not stay, but to
Westminster to Herbert's and there, he being not well, I sent for a
quart of claret and burnt it and drank, and had a besado or three or

four of Sarah, whom yo trouvais aqui; and so by coach to Sir Rob. Viner's about my accounts with him; and so to the Change, where I hear for certain that we are going on with our treaty of peace, and that we are to treat at Bredah. But this our condescension people do think will undo us – and I do much fear it. So home to dinner, where my wife having dressed herself in a silly dress, of a blue petticoat uppermost and a white satin waistcoat and white hood (though I think she did it because her gown is gone to the tailor's) did, together with my being hungry (which always makes me peevish), make me angry. But when my belly was full, was friends again, and dined and then by water down to Greenwich and thence walked to Woolwich, all the way reading Playfords *Introduction to Musique*, wherein are some things very pretty. At Woolwich I did much business, taking an account of the state of the ships there under hand; thence to Blackewall and did the like for two ships we have repairing there; and then to Deptford and did the like there; and so home, Capt. Perriman with me from Deptford, telling me many perticulars how the King's business is ill ordered; and indeed so they are, God knows. So home and to the office, where did business; and so home to my chamber, and then to supper and to bed.

23. At the office all the morning, where Sir W. Penn came, being returned from Chatham from considering the means of fortifying the River Medway, by a chain at the stakes and ships laid there, with guns to keep the enemy from coming up to burn our ships – all our care now being [to] fortify ourselfs against their invading us. At noon home to dinner, and then to the office all the afternoon again – where Mr. Moore came, who tells me that there is now no doubt made of a peace being agreed on, the King having declared this week in council that they would treat at Bredagh. He gone, I to my office, where busy late; and so to supper and to bed – vexed with our maid Luce, our cook-maid, who is a good drudging servant in everything else and pleases us, but that she will be drunk, and hath been so last night and all this day, that she could not make clean the house – my fear is only fire.

25. *Lady day*. To the King's playhouse, and by and by comes Mr. Lowder and his wife and mine and into a box forsooth, neither of them being dressed, which I was almost ashamed of – Sir W. Penn and I in the pit; and here saw *The Mayden Queene* again; which endeed, the more I see the more I like; and is an excellent play, and

so done by Nell her merry part, as cannot be better done in Nature I think. Thence home, and there I find letters from my brother which tell me that yesterday, when he wrote, my mother did rattle in the throat, so as they did expect every moment her death, which though I have a good while expected, did much surprize me; yet was obliged to sup at Sir W. Penn's, and my wife; and there counterfeited some little mirth, but my heart was sad; and so home after supper and to bed, and much troubled in my sleep with dreams of my being crying by my mother's bedside, laying my head over hers and crying, she almost dead and dying, and so waked; but which is strange, methought she had hair on her face, and not the same kind of face as my mother really has; but yet did not consider that, but did weep over her as my mother – whose soul God have mercy of.

26. Up, with a sad heart in reference to my mother, of whose death I do undoubtedly expect to hear the next post, if not of my father's also, who, by his pain as well as his grief for her, is very ill. But on my own behalf, I have cause to be joyful this day, as being my usual feast-day for my being cut of the stone this day nine years; and through God's blessing am at this day and have long been in as good condition of health as ever I was in my life, or any man in England is, God make me thankful for it. But the condition I am in in reference to my mother makes it unfit for me to keep my usual feast, unless it should please God to send her well (which I despair wholly of); and then I will make amends for it by observing another day in its room.

27. To Whitehall; and our business with the Duke of York being done, W. Penn and I towards the Exchequer and in our way met Sir G. Downing going to chapel; but we stopped, and he would go with us back to the Exchequer and showed us in his office his chests full, and ground and shelves full of money, and says that there is 50000*l* at this day in his office of people's money; who may demand it this day and might have had it away several weeks ago upon the late Act[1] but do rather choose to have it continue there then to put it into the Banquier's hands; and I must confess it is more then I should have believed had I not seen it, and more then ever I could have expected would have arisen for this new act in so short a time;

1. sc. on the credit of the Eleven Months Tax.

and if it do so now already, what would it do if the money was
collected upon the Act and returned into the Exchequer so timelily
as it ought to be. But it comes into my mind here to observe what I
have heard from Sir Jo. Bankes (though I cannot fully conceive the
reason of it): that it will be impossible to make the Exchequer ever a
true bank to all intents, unless the Exchequer stood nearer the
Exchange, where merchants might with ease, while they are going
about their business, at all hours and without trouble or loss of
time, have their satisfaction; which they cannot have now with[out]
much trouble and loss of half a day, and no certainty of having the
offices open. By this, he means a bank for common practice and use
of merchants, and therein I do agree with him. Being parted from
Sir W. Penn and G. Downing, I to Westminster hall and there met
Balty, whom I had sent for; and there did break the business of my
getting him the place of going again as Muster-maister with
Harman this voyage to the West Indys; which endeed I do owe to
Sir W. Penn. He is mighty glad of it and earnest to fit himself for it;
but I do find, poor man, that he is troubled how to dispose of his
wife, and apparently it is out of fear of her and his honour, and I
believe he hath received some cause of this his jealousy and care.
And I do pity him in it, and will endeavour to find out some way to
do it for him. Having put him in a way of preparing himself for the
voyage, I did go to the Swan; and there sent for Jervas my old
periwig-maker and he did bring me a periwig; but it was full of nits,
so as I was troubled to see it (it being his old fault) and did send him
to make it clean; and in the meantime, having stayed for him a good
while, did go away by water and to the Castle Taverne by Exeter
house and there met W. Batten, W. Penn and several others; among
the rest, Sir Ellis Layton, who doth apply himself to discourse with
me; and I think by his discourse, out of his opinion of my interest in
Sir W. Coventry. The man I find a wonderful witty, ready man for
sudden answers and little tales and sayings very extraordinary
witty; but in the bottom, I doubt he is not so. Yet he pretends to
have studied men; and the truth is, in several that I do know he did
give me a very inward account of them.

So I home, and there up to my wife in our chamber; and there
received from my brother the news of my mother's dying on
Monday, about 5 or 6 a-clock in the afternoon, and that the last time
she spoke of her children was on Friday last, and her last words was,
"God bless my poor Sam!" The reading thereof did set me a-
weeping heartily; and so, weeping to myself a while and my wife

also to herself – I then spoke to my wife, recollecting myself, and endeed having some thoughts how much better, both for her and us, it is then it might have been had she outlived my father and me or my happy present condition in the world, she being helpless, I was the sooner at ease in my mind; and then found it necessary to go abroad with my wife to look after the providing mourning to send into the country, some tomorrow and more against Sundy, for my family, being resolved to put myself and wife, and Barker and Jane, W. Hewers and Tom, in mourning; and my two under-maids, to give them hoods and scarfs and gloves. So to my tailor's and up and down; and then home and to my office a little; and then to supper and to bed – my heart sad and afflicted, though my judgment at ease.

29.   [With Balty] to my shoemaker's, cutler's, tailor's, and up and down about my mourning; and in my going do observe the great streets in the City are marked out with piles drove into the ground; and if ever it be built in that form, with so fair streets, it will be a noble sight. So to the Council chamber, but stayed not there; but to a periwig-maker's of his acquaintance and there bought two periwigs, mighty fine; endeed, too fine I thought for me; but he persuaded me, and I did buy them, 4*l* 10*s*. the two. Then to the Exchange and bought gloves, and so to the Bull head taverne, whither he brought my French Gun and one True Locke the famous gunsmith, that is a mighty ingenious man, and he did take my gun in pieces and made me understand the secrets thereof; and upon the whole, doth find it a very good piece of work and truly wrought, but for certain not a thing to be used much with safety; and he doth find that this very gun was never yet shot off. I was mightily satisfied with it and him and the sight of so much curiosity of this kind. Here he brought also a haberdasher at my desire, and I bought a hat of him. And so away and called my wife from his house; and so home and to read, and then to supper and to bed.

31.   *Lords day*. Up; and my tailor's boy brings my mourning clothes home, and my wife's, hers and Barker's; but they go not to church this morning. I to church, and with my mourning, very handsome, and new periwig make a great show. After church, home to dinner, and there came Betty Michell and her husband; I do and shall love her; but, poor wretch, she is now almost ready to lie down. After dinner, Balty (who dined also with us) and I with Sir J.

Mennes in his coach to Whitehall, but did nothing; but by water to Strand bridge and thence walked to my Lord Treasurer's, where the King, Duke of York, and the Caball, and much company without; and a fine day. Anon comes out from the Caball my Lord Hollis and Mr. H. Coventry, who it is conceived have received their instructions from the King this day; they being to begin their journey towards their treaty at Bredagh speedily, their passes being come. Here I saw Lady Northumberland and her daughter-in-law (my Lord Treasurer's daughter), my Lady Piercy, a beautiful lady endeed. So away back by water; and left Balty at Whitehall, and I to Mrs. Martin and there haze todo which yo would hazer con her; and so by coach home and there to my chamber; and then to supper and bed – having not had time to make up my accounts of this month at this very day, but will in a day or two and pay my forfeit for not doing it, though business hath most hindered me. The month shuts up, only with great desires of peace in all of us, and a belief that we shall have a peace in most people, if a peace can be had on any terms, for there is a necessity of it; for we cannot go on with the war, and our maisters are afeared to come to depend upon the good will of the Parliament any more as I do hear.

# –❧APRILL❧–

2. Up and to the office, where all the morning sitting; and much trouble, but little business done for want of money, which makes me mighty melancholy. At noon home to dinner, and Mr. Deane with me; who hath promised me a very fine draught of the *Rupert*, which he will make purposely for me with great perfection; which he will make one of the beautifullest things that ever was seen of that kind in the world – she being a ship that will deserve it. Then to the office, where all the afternoon very busy; and in the evening, weary home; and there to sing, but vexed with the unreadiness of the girl's voice to learn the latter part of my song,[1] though I confess it is very hard half-notes. So to supper and to bed.

3. Up and with Sir W. Batten to Whitehall to Sir W. Coventry's chamber, and there did receive the Duke's order for Balty's

---

1. *It is decreed.*

receiving of the contingent money to be paymaister of it; and it pleases me the more for that it is but 1500*l*, which will be but a little sum for to try his ability and honesty in the disposing of – and so I am the willinger to trust him and pass my word for him therein. By and by up to the Duke of York, where our usual business; and among other things, I read two most dismal letters of the straits we are in (from Coll. Middleton and Comissioner Taylor) that ever were writ in the world, so as the Duke of York would have them to show the King. And to every demand of money, whereof we proposed many and very pressing ones, Sir G. Carteret could make no answer but "No money", which I confess made me almost ready to cry for sorrow and vexation; but that which was the most considerable was when Sir G. Carteret did say that he had no fond to raise money on; and being asked by Sir W. Coventry whether the Eleven Months Tax was not a fond, and he answered no – that the banquiers would not lend money upon it. Thence to the chapel, and there by chance hear that Dr. Crew is to preach; and so into the Organ loft, where I met Mr. Carteret and my Lady Jemimah and Sir Tho. Crew's two daughters, and Dr. Childe played – and Dr. Crew did make a very pretty, neat, sober, honest sermon; and delivered it very readily, decently, and gravely, beyond his years – so as I was exceedingly taken with it, and I believe the whole chapel – he being but young; but his manner of his delivery I do like exceedingly. His text was, "But first seeke the kingdom of God and all these things shall be added unto you." Thence with my Lady to Sir G. Carteret's lodgings, and so up into the house and there do hear that the Dutch letters are come and say that the Dutch have ordered a passe to be sent for our Commissioners; and that it is now upon the way, coming with a Trumpeter, blinded as is usual. But I perceive everybody begins to doubt the success of the treaty, all their hopes being only that if it can be had on any terms, the Chancellor will have it; for he dare not come before a Parliament, nor a great many more of the Courtiers, and the King himself doth declare he doth not desire it, nor entend it but on a strait – which God defend him from. Here I hear how the King is not so well pleased of this marriage between the Duke of Richmond and Mrs. Stewart as is talked; and that he by a wilde did fetch her to the Beare at the Bridge foot, where a coach was ready, and they are stole away into Kent without the King's leave; and that the King hath said he will never see her more, but people do think that it is only a trick. This day I saw Prince Rupert abroad in the Vane Roome, pretty well as he used to be, and looks as well; only, something appears to be under his periwig on the crown of his head.

4. Up; and going down, found Jervas the barber with a periwig which I had the other day cheapened at Westminster; but it being full of nits, as heretofore his work used to be, I did now refuse it, having bought elsewhere. So to the office till noon, busy; and then (which I think I have not done three times in my life) left the board upon occasion of a letter from Sir W. Coventry; and meeting Balty at my house, I took him with me by water, and to the Duke of Albemarle to give him an account of that business; which was the shipping off of some soldiers for the manning of the few ships now going out with Harman to the West Indies; which is a sad consideration, that at the very beginning of the year, and few ships abroad, we should be in such want of men; but they do hide themselfs and swear they will not go to be killed and have no pay. I find the Duke of Albemarle at dinner with sorry company, some of his officers of the Army – dirty dishes and a nasty wife at table – and bad meat; of which I made but an ill dinner. Pretty, to hear how she talked against Capt. Du Tel, the Frenchman that the Prince and her husband put out last year; and how, says she, the Duke of York hath made for his good services his cup-bearer; yet fired more shot into the Prince's ship, and others of the King's ships, then of the enemy.[1] And the Duke of Albemarle did confirm it, and that somebody in the fight did cry out that a little Dutchman by his ship did plague him more then any other; upon which they were going to order him to be sunk, when they looked and found it was Du Tell, who, as the Duke of Albemarle says, had killed several men in several of our ships. He said, but for his interest which he knew he had at Court, he had hanged him at the yard's arm without staying for a Court Martiall. My Lady Duchesse, among other things, discoursed of the wisdom of dividing the fleet; which the Generall said nothing to, though he knows well that it come from themselfs in the fleet and was brought up hither by Sir Edw. Spragge. One at the table told an odd passage in this late plague: that at Petersfield (I think he said) one side of the street had every house almost infected through the town; and the other, not one shut up. Dinner being done, I brought Balty to the Duke of Albemarle to kiss his hands and thank him for his kindness the last year to him and take leave of him. And

---

1. In the Four Days Battle.

then Balty and I to walk in the park; and out of pity to his father, told him what I had in my thoughts to do for him about the money – that is, to make him Deputy-Treasurer of the fleet, which I have done by getting Sir G. Carteret's consent and an order from the Duke of York for 1500*l* to be paid to him. He promises the whole profit to be paid to my wife, for to be disposed on as she sees fit for her father and mother's relief. So, mightily pleased with our walk, it being mighty pleasant weather, I back to Sir G. Carteret's and there he had newly dined; and talked and find that he doth give everything over for lost, declaring no money to be raised. I made him merry with telling him how many land-Admiralls we are to have this year – Allen at Plymouth, Holmes at Portsmouth, Spragg for Medway, Teddyman at Dover, Smith to the North, and Harman to the South. Mightily pleased I am with his family; and my Lady Carteret was on the bed today, having been let blood, and tells me of my Lady Jem's being big-bellied.

Thence with him to Lord Treasurer's, and there walked during Council-sitting with Sir St. Fox, talking of the sad condition of the King's purse, and affairs thereby – and how sad the King's life must be, to pass by his officers every hour that are four years behindhand unpaid. Here I spoke with Sir W. Coventry, who tells me plainly that to all future complaints of lack of money he will answer but with a shrugg of his shoulder; which methought did come to my heart, to see him to begin to abandon the King's affairs and let them sink or swim, so he do his own part; which I confess I believe he doth, beyond any officer the King hath; but unless he do endeavour to make others do theirs, nothing will be done. The consideration hereof did make me go away very sad; and so home by coach and there took up my wife and Mercer (who had been today at Whitehall to the Maundy, it being Maundy Thursday; but the King did not wash the poor people's feet himself, but the Bishop of London did it for him; but I did not see it) and with them took up Mrs. Anne Jones at her mother's door; and so to take the ayre to Hackny, where good neat's tongue and things to eat and drink, and very merry, the weather being mighty pleasant; and here I was told that at their church they have a fair pair of Organs, which plays while the people sing; which I am mighty glad of, wishing the like at our church at London, and would give 50*l* towards it. So, very pleasant and hugging of Mercer in our going home, we home; and there I to the office to do a little business, and so to supper at home and to bed.

5. In the street met with Mr. Sanchy, my old acquaintance at Cambrige, reckoned a great minister here in the City, and by Sir Rd. Ford perticularly, which I wonder at, for methinks in his talk he is but a mean man. I set him down in Holburne, and I to the Old Exchange and there to Sir Rob. Viners and made up my accounts there to my great content; but I find they do not keep them so regularly as to be able to do it easily and truly and readily. So to the Change, and there met with Mr. James Hubland; and no hopes, as he sees, of peace, whatever we pretend; but we shall be abused by the King of France. This morning came to me the Collectors for my Pole mony; for which I paid for my title as Esquire and place of Clerk of Acts, and my head and wife's, and servants' and their wages, 40*l* 17*s*. 00*d*. And though this be a great deal, yet it is a shame I should pay no more; that is, that I should not be assessed for my pay, as in the Victualling business and Tanger, and for my money, which of my own accord I had determined to charge myself with 1000*l* money, till coming to the Vestry and seeing nobody of our ablest merchants, as Sir Andrew Rickard, to do it, I thought it not decent for me to do it; nor would it be thought wisdom to do it unnecessarily, but vainglory.

6. Up, and betimes in the morning down to the Tower wharfe, there to attend the shipping of soldiers to go down to man some ships going out; and pretty to see how merrily some and most go and how sad others, the leave they take of their friends, and the tears that some wifes and others' wenches shed to part with them: a pretty mixture. So to the office, having stayed as long as I could, and there sat all the morning; and then home at noon to dinner; and then abroad, Balty with me, and to Whitehall by water to Sir G. Carteret about Balty's 1500*l* contingent money for the fleet to the West Indys; and so away with him to the Exchange and mercers and drapers, up and down, to pay all my scores occasioned by this mourning for my mother – and emptied a 50*l* bag; and it was a joy to me to see that I am able to part with such a sum without much inconvenience – at least, without any trouble of mind. So [to] Capt. Cocke's to meet Fenn to talk about this money for Balty; and there Cocke tells me that he is confident there will be a peace, whatever terms be asked us; and he confides that it will take, because the French and Dutch will be jealous one of another which shall give the best terms, lest the other should make the peace with us alone, to the ruin of the third – which is our best defence, this jealousy, for

aught I at present see. So home and there very late, very busy; and
then home to supper and to bed – the people having got their house
very clean against Mondy dinner.

8.   Up; and having dressed myself, and to the office a little and out,
and expecting to have seen the pretty daughter of the Ship tavern at
the hither end of Billiter lane (whom I never yet have opportunity
to speak to), I in there to drink my morning draught of a half pint of
Rhenish wine, but a mi dolor ella and their family are going away
thence and a new man come to the house. So I away to the Temple
to my new bookseller's, and there I did agree for Rycaut's late
history of the Turkish Policy, which costs me 55s.; whereas it was
sold plain before the late fire for 8s., and bound and coloured as this
is for 20 – for I have bought it finely bound and truly coloured, all
the figures; of which there was but six books done so, whereof the
King and the Duke of York and Duke of Monmouth and Lord
Arlington had four – the 5th was sold, and I have bought the 6th. So
to enquire out Mrs. Knepp's new lodging, but could not; but do
hear of her at the Playhouse, where she was practising, and I sent for
her out by a porter, and the jade came to me all undressed, so cannot
go home to my house to dinner as I had invited her; which I was not
much troubled at, because I think there is a distance between her
and Mrs. Pierce, and so our company would not be so pleasant. So I
home and there find all things in good readiness for a good dinner;
and here unexpectedly I find little Mis Tooker, whom my wife
loves not from the report of her being already naught; however, I
do show her countenance, and by and by come my guests, Dr.
Clerke and his wife, and Mrs. Worshipp and her daughter, and then
Mr. Pierce and his wife and boy, and Betty, and then I sent for
Mercer; so that we had, with my wife and I, twelve at table; and
very good and pleasant company, and a most neat and excellent,
but dear dinner; but Lord, to see with what envy they looked upon
all my fine plate was pleasant, for I made the best show I could, to
let them understand me and my condition, to take down the pride
of Mrs. Clerke, who thinks herself very great. We sat long, and
very merry and all things agreable; and after dinner went out by
coaches, thinking to have seen a play, but came too late to both
houses and then they had thoughts of going abroad somewhere; but
I thought all the charge ought to be mine, and therefore I
endeavoured to part the company, and so ordered it to set them all
down at Mr. Pierces; and there my wife and I and Mercer left them

in good humour, and we three to the King's house and saw the latter end of *The Surprizall*; wherein was no great matter I thought, by what I saw. Thence away to *Polichenelli*,[1] and there had three times more sport then at the play; and so home and there, the first night we have been this year, in the garden late, we three and our Barker singing very well; and then home to supper; and so broke up and to bed, mightily pleased with this day's pleasure.

11. At noon, I to the Change and there hear by Mr. Hublon that letters are come that the Dutch have stopped the fitting of their great ships and the coming out of a fleet of theirs of 50 sail that was ready to come out; but I doubt the truth of it yet. Thence to Sir G. Carteret by his invitation to his office, where my Lady was, and dined with him and very merry, and good people they are when pleased as any I know. After dinner, I to Whitehall, thinking there to have seen the Duchesse of Newcastle's coming this night to Court to make a visit to the Queen, the King having been with her yesterday to make her a visit since her coming to town. The whole story of this Lady is a romance, and all she doth is romantic. Her footmen in velvet coats, and herself in an antique* dress, as they say; and was the other day at her own play, *The Humourous Lovers*; the most ridiculous thing that ever was wrote, but yet she and her Lord mightily pleased with it, and she at the end made her respect to the players from her box and did give them thanks. There is as much expectation of her coming to Court, that so [many] people may come to see her, as if it were the Queen of Sweden. But I lost my labour, for she did not come this night.

12. Up; and when ready, I to my office to do a little business; and coming homeward again, saw my door and hatch open, left so by Luce our cookmaid; which so vexed me, that I did give her a kick in our entry and offered a blow ᷧt her, and was seen doing so by Sir W. Penn's footboy, which did vex me to the heart because I know he will be telling their family of it, though I did put on presently a very pleasant face to the boy and spoke kindly to him as one without passion, so as it may be he might not think I was angry; but yet I was troubled at it. I close at my office all the afternoon, getting off of hand my papers, which by the late holidays and my laziness were

1. A puppet-play (probably in Moorfields), from which the modern Punch and Judy show is descended.

grown too many upon my hands, to my great trouble; and therefore at it as late as my eyes would give me leave; and then by water down to Redriffe, meaning to meet my wife, who is gone with Mercer, Barker, and the boy (it being most sweet weather) to walk; and I did meet with them and walked back, and then by the time we got home it was dark, and we stayed singing in the garden till supper was ready, and there with great pleasure. But I tried my girls, Mercer and Barker singly, one after another, a single song, *At dead low Ebb*, &c.; and I do clearly find that as to manner of singing, the latter doth much the better, the other thinking herself, as I do myself, above taking pains for a manner of singing, contenting ourselfs with the judgment and goodness of eare. So to supper, and then parted and to bed.

14.    *Lords day*. Up, and to read a little in my new History of Turky; and so with my wife to church, and then home to dinner, where is little Michell and my pretty Betty and also Mercer; and very merry, a good dinner of roast beef. After dinner, I away to take water at the Tower; and thence to Westminster, where Mrs. Martin was not at home; so to Whitehall and there walked up and down; and among other things, visited Sir G. Carteret, and much talk with him; who is discontented, as he hath reason, to see how things are like to come all to naught. And it is very much that this resolution of having of country-Admirals should not come to his eares till I told it him the other day, so that I doubt who manages things. From him to Margaret Church, and there spied Martin and home with her, who had those, so could have ninguno placer; but fell out to see her expensefulness, having bought Turkey work chairs &c; by and by away home, and there took out my wife and the two Mercers and two of ur maids, Barker and Jane, and over the water to the Jamaica house, where I never was before; and there the girls did run for wagers over the bowling-green. And there with much pleasure, spent little, and so home; and they home, and I read with satisfaction in my book of Turky and so to bed.

15.    Lay long in bed – and by and by called up by Sir H. Chumbly, who tells me that my Lord Middleton is for certain chosen Governor of Tanger; a man of moderate understanding, not covetous, but a soldier of fortune and poor. But by and by comes Dr. Childe by appointment, and sat with me all the morning, making me Bases and inward parts to several songs that I desired of

him – to my great content. Then dined and then abroad by coach, and I set him down at Hatton Guarden and I to the King's house by chance, where a new play; so full as I never saw it, I forced to stand all the while close to the very door, till I took cold, and many people went away for want of room. The King and Queen and Duke of York and Duchesse there and all the Court, and Sir W. Coventry. The play called *The Change of Crownes*, a play of Ned Howard's, the best that I ever saw at that House, being a great play and serious; only, Lacy did act the country gentleman come up to Court, who doth abuse the Court with all the imaginable wit and plainness, about selling of places and doing everything for money. The play took very much. Thence I to my new bookseller's and there bought Hookers *Policy*, the new edition, and Dugdale's history of the Inns of Court, of which there was but a few saved out of the Fire – and Playfords new ketch-book, that hath a great many new fooleries in it. Then home; a little at the office, and then to supper and to bed, mightily pleased with the new play.

18. To the office, where the news is strong that not only the Dutch cannot set out a fleet this year, but that the French will not; and that he hath given that answer to the Dutch Imbassador, saying that he is for the King of England's having an honourable peace – which, if true, is the best news we have heard a good while. At the office all the morning; and there pleased with the little pretty Deptford woman I have wished for long, and she hath occasion given her to come again to me. After office, I to the Change a little and then home and to dinner; and then by coach with my wife to the Duke of York's House and there saw *The Wits,* a play I formerly loved and is now corrected and enlarged – but though I like the acting, yet I find not much in the play now. The Duke of York and W. Coventry gone to Portsmouth makes me thus to go [to] plays. So home; and to the office a little and then home, where I find Goodgroome and he and I did sing several things over and tried two or three three-parts in Playford's new book, my wife pleasing me in singing her part of the things she knew; which is a comfort to my very heart. So he being gone, we to supper and to bed.

19. Up, and to the office all the morning, doing a great deal of business. At noon to dinner betimes; and then my wife and I by coach to the Duke's House, calling at Lovetts, where I find my Lady Castlemaynes picture not yet done, which has lain so many months

there; which vexes me, but I mean not to trouble them more after this is done. So to the playhouse, where not much company come, which I impute to the heat of the weather, it being very hot. Here we saw *Macbeth*, which though I have seen it often, yet is it one of the best plays for a stage, and variety of dancing and music, that ever I saw. So being very much pleased, thence home by coach with young Goodyer and his own sister, who offered us to go in their coach – a good-natured youth I believe he is, but I fear will mind his pleasures too much; she is pretty, and a modest, brown girl. Set us down; so my wife and I into the garden, a fine moonshine evening, and there talking; and among other things, she tells me that she finds by W. Hewer that my people do observe my minding my pleasure more then usual; which I confess and am ashamed of, and so from this day take upon me to leave it till Whit-Sunday. While we were setting there in the garden, comes Mrs. Turner to advise about her son, the Captain; which I did give her the best advice I could, to look out for some land imployment for him – a peace being at hand, when few ships will be imployed, and very many, and those old Captains, to be provided for – which she thanked me for. Then to other talk: and among the rest, about Sir W. Penn's being to buy Wansted house of Sir Rt. Brookes, but hath put him off again; and left him the other day to pay for a dinner at a tavern, which she says our parish[ioner] Mrs. Hollworthy talks of. And I dare be hanged if ever he could mean to buy that great house,[1] that knows not how to furnish one that is not the tenth part so big. Thence I to my chamber to write a little; and then to bed, having got a mighty cold in my right eare and side of my throat, and in much trouble with it almost all the night.

21. *Lords day.* Up, and John, a hackney coachman whom of late I have much used, as being formerly Sir W. Penn's coachman, coming to me by my direction to see whether I would use him today or no, I took him to our back gate to look upon the ground which is to be let there, where I have a mind to buy enough to build a coach-house and stable; for I have had it much in my thoughts lately that it is not too much for me now, in degree or cost, to keep a coach; but contrarily, that I am almost ashamed to be seen in a hackney; and therefore, if I can have the conveniency, I will secure the ground at least till peace comes, that I do receive encouragement

1. He did not buy it.

to keep a coach or else that I may part with the ground again. The place I like very well, being close by my own house, and so resolve to go about it. And so home and with my wife to church; and then to dinner, Mercer with us, with design to go to Hackney to church in the afternoon. So after dinner she and I sung *Scio Moro*, which is one of the best pieces of music to my thinking that ever I did hear in my life; then took coach and to Hackny church, where very full; and found much difficulty to get pews, I offering the sexton money and he could not help me – so my wife and Mercer ventured into a pew, and I into another. A knight and his lady very civil to me when they came, and the like to my wife in hers, being Sir George Viner's; and his lady rich in Jewells, but most in beauty; almost the finest woman that ever I saw. That which we went chiefly to see was the young ladies of the schools, whereof there is great store, very pretty; and also the organ, which is handsome and tunes the psalm and plays with the people; which is mighty pretty and makes me mighty earnest to have a pair at our church, I having almost a mind to give them a pair if they would settle a maintenance on them for it – I am mightily taken with them. So church done, we to coach and away to Kingsland and Islington and there eat and drank at the old house; and so back, it raining a little; which is mighty welcome, it having not rained in many weeks, so that they say it makes the fields just now mighty sweet; so with great pleasure home by night. Set Mercer down, and I to my chamber and there read a great deal in Rycaut's Turks book with great pleasure, and so eat and to bed – my sore throat still troubling me, but not so much. This night I do come to full resolution of diligence for a good while, and I hope God will give me the grace and wisdom to perform it.

22.    Capt. Cocke tells me how the King was vexed the other day for having no paper laid him at the Council table as was usual; and that Sir Rd. Browne did tell his Majesty he would call the person whose work it was to provide it – who being come, did tell His Majesty that he was but a poor man, and was out 4 or 500*l* for it, which was as much as he is worth; and that he cannot provide it any longer without money, having not received a penny since the King's coming in. So the King spoke to my Lord Chamberlaine; and many such Mementos the King doth nowadays meet withal, enough to make an ingenuous [man] mad. I to Deptford, and there scolded with a master for his ship's not being gone. And so home to the office and did business till my eyes are sore again; and so home

to sing and then to bed, my eyes failing me mightily.

24. By coach to Sir Jo. Duncomb's lodging in the Pell Mell; and there awhile sat and discoursed; and I find him that he is a very proper man for business, being very resolute and proud and industrious. He told me what reformation they had made in the office of the Ordnance, taking away Legg's fees. Have got an order that no Treasurer after him shall ever sit at the Board, and it is a good one – that no maister of the Ordinance here shall ever sell a place. He tells me they have not paid any encrease of price for anything during this war, but in most have paid less. And at this day have greater stores then they know where to lay, if there should be peace, and then ever was any time this war. That they pay every man in course, and have notice of the disposal of every farding. Every man that they owe money to hath his share of every sum they receive. Never borrowed all this war but 30000*l* by the King's express command, but do usually stay until their assignments become payable in their own course; which is the whole mystery, that they have had assignments for a fifth part of whatever was assigned to the Navy. They have power of putting out and in of all officers. Are beginning upon a building that will cost them 12000*l*. That they out of their stock of tallies have been forced to help the Treasurer of the Navy at this great pinch. Then to talk of news: that he thinks the want of money hath undone the King, for the Parliament will never give the King more money without calling all people to account; nor, as he believes, will ever make war again but they will manage it themselfs. He says that he believes but four men (such as he could name) would do the business of both offices, his and ours; and if ever the war were to do again, it should be so he believes. He told me to my face that I was a very good Clerk, and did understand the business and do it very well, and that he would never desire a better. He doth believe that the Parliament, if ever they meet, will offer some alterations to the King, and will turn some of us out. And I protest I think he is in the right, that either they or the King will be advised to some regulation; and therefore I ought to beware – as it is easy for me to keep myself up if I will.

26. Up, and by coach with W. Batten and W. Penn to Whitehall and there saw the Duke of Albemarle, who is not well and doth grow crazy.* And then I took a turn with Mr. Eveling, with whom walked two hours, till almost one of the clock – talking of the

badness of the Government, where nothing but wickedness, and wicked men and women command the King. That it is not in his nature to gainsay anything that relates to his pleasures. That much of it arises from the sickliness of our Ministers of State, who cannot be about him as the idle companions are, and therefore give way to the young rogues; and then from the negligence of the Clergy, that a Bishop shall never be seen about him, as the King of France hath always. He tells me mighty stories of the King of France, how great a prince he is. He hath made a Code to shorten the law. He hath put out all the ancient commanders of castles that were become hereditary. He hath made all the Fryers subject to the Bishops, which before were only subject to Rome and so were hardly the King's subjects. And that none shall become religious* but at such an age – which he thinks will in few years ruin the pope and bring France into a patriarchate. He confirmed to me the business of the want of paper at the Council table the other day, which I have observed – Wooly being to have found it, and did, being called, tell the King to his face the reason of it. And Mr. Eveling tells me that several of the menial servants of the Court lack bread, that have not received a farding wages since the King's coming in. He tells me the King of France hath his Maistresses, but laughs at the foolery of our King, that makes his bastards princes, and loses his revenue upon them – and makes his mistresses his maisters. And the King of France did never grant Lavaliere anything to bestow on others; and gives a little subsistence, but no more, to his bastards.

By and by we discoursed of Sir Tho. Clifford, whom I took for a very rich and learned man, and of the great family of that name. He tells me he is only a man of about seven-score pound a year – of little learning, more then the law of a Justice of Peace, which he knows well – a parson's son, got to be Burges in a little borough in the West and there fell into the acquaintance of my Lord Arlington, whose creature he is and never from him. A man of virtue, and comely and good parts enough; and hath come into his place with a great grace, though with a great skip over the heads of a great many, as Chichly and Dunkum and some Lords that did expect it. By the way he tells me that of all the great men of England, there is none that endeavours more to raise those that he takes into favour then my Lord Arlington; and that on that score, he is much more to be made one's patron then my Lord Chancellor, who never did nor will do anything but for money. After having this long discourse, we parted about one of the clock; and in the way met my Lady

Newcastle, going with her coaches and footmen all in velvet; herself (whom I never saw before) as I have heard her often described (for all the town talk is nowadays of her extravagancies), with her velvet cap, her hair about her ears, many black patches because of pimples about her mouth, naked necked, without anything about it, and a black juste-au-corps; she seemed to me a very comely woman – but I hope to see more of her on May day. My mind is mightily of late upon a coach.

28. *Lords day*. Lay long, my pain in my back being still great, though not so great as it was. However, up and to church, where a lazy sermon; and then home and to dinner, my wife and I alone, and Barker. After dinner by water, the day being mighty pleasant and the tide serving finely – I up (reading in Boyles book of Colours) as high as Barne Elmes; and there took one turn alone and then back to Putny church, where I saw the girls of the schools, few of which pretty. And there I came into a pew and met with little James Pierce; which I was much pleased at, the little rogue being very glad to see me – his maister, Reader to the church. Here was a good sermon and much company, but I sleepy and a little out of order for my hat falling down through a hole underneath the pulpit; which however, after sermon, by a stick and the help of the clerk, I got up again. And then walked out of the church with the boy, and then left him, promising him to get him a play another time. And so by water, the tide being with me again, down to Deptford; and there I walked down the yard, Shish and Cox with me, and discoursed about cleaning of the wet Docke; and heard (which I had before) how when the Docke was made, a ship of near 500 Tons was there found, a ship supposed of Queen Elizabeth's time and well wrought, with a great deal of stone shot in her of 18-inch Diameter, which was shot then in use; and aferward meeting with Capt. Perriman and Mr. Castle at Halfway Tree, they tell me of stone shot of 36-inches Diameter which they shot out of mortar pieces. Thence walked to Halfway Tree, and there stopped and talk with Mr. Castle and Capt. Perriman, and so to Redriffe and took boat again; and so home, and there to write down my Journall, and so to supper and to read, and so to bed – mightily pleased with my reading Boyles book of Colours today; only, troubled that some part of it, endeed the greatest part, I am not able to understand for want of study.

My wife this night troubled at my leaving her alone so much and keeping her within doors; which endeed I do not well nor wisely in.

29. Up, being visited very early by Creed, newly come from Hinchingbrooke; who went thither without my knowledge, and I believe only to save being taxed to the Poll Bill. By and by to Whitehall to Sir G. Carteret to dinner, where very good company and discourse; and I think it my part to keep in there now more then ordinary, because of the probability of my Lord's coming soon home. Our commissioners for the treaty set out this morning betimes down the River. Here I hear that the Duke of Cambrige, the Duke of York's son, is very sick – and my Lord Treasurer very bad of the stone, and hath been so some days. After dinner, Sir G. Carteret and I alone in his closet an hour or more, talking of my Lord Sandwiches coming home; which, the peace being likely to be made here, he expects, both for my Lord's sake and his own (whose interest he wants) it will be best for him to be at home. He says, if my Lord were here, he were the fittest man to be Lord Treasurer of any man in England. And he thinks it might be compassed, for he confesses that the King's matters do suffer through the inability of this man, who is likely to die; and he will propound him to the King – it will remove him from his place at sea, and the King will have a good place to bestow. He says to me that he could wish, when my Lord comes, that he would think fit to forbear playing, as a thing below him and which will lessen him as it doth my Lord St. Albans, in the King's esteem. And as a great secret, tells me that he hath made a match for my Lord Hinchingbrooke, to a daughter of my Lord Burlington's; where there is great alliance, 10000*l* portion, a civil family, and relation to my Lord Chancellor, whose son hath married one of the daughters; and that my Lord Chancellor doth take it with very great kindness, so that he doth hold himself obliged by it. My Lord Sandwich hath referred it to my Lord Crew, Sir G. Carteret, and Mr. Mountagu to end it – my Lord Hinchingbrooke and the lady know nothing yet of it. It will, I think, be very happy. Very glad of this discourse, I away, mightily pleased with the confidence I have in this family; and so away, took up my wife, who was at her mother's, and so home; where I settled to my chamber about my accounts, both Tanger and private, and up at it till 12 at night with good success, when news is brought me that there is a great fire in Southworke; so we up to the leads, and then I and the boy down to the end of our lane and there saw it, it

seeming pretty great but nothing to the fire of London, that it made me think little of it. We could at that distance see an engine play; that is, the water go out, it being moonlight. By and by it began to slacken, and then I home and to bed.

30. Up, and Mr. Madden came to speak with me; whom my people not knowing, have made to wait long without doors, which vexed me. Then comes Sir Jo. Winter to discourse with me about the Forest of Deane and then about my Lord Treasurer; and asking me whether, as he had heard, I had not been cut of the stone, I took him to my closet and there showed it him; of which he took the dimensions and had some discourse of it, and I believe will show my Lord Treasurer it. Thence to the office, where we sat all the morning, but little to do; and then to the Change, where for certain I hear, and the newsbook declares, a peace between France and Portugal. Met here with Mr. Pierce, and he tells me the Duke of Cambrige is very ill and full of spots about his body, that Dr. Frazier knows not what to think of it. Then home and to dinner, and then to the office, where all the afternoon; we met about Sir W. Warren's business and accounts, wherein I do rather oppone then forward him; but not in declared terms, for I will not be at enmity with him. But I will not have him find any friendship so good as mine.[1] By and by rose, and by water to Whitehall, and then called my wife at Unthankes; and so home and to my chamber to my accounts, and finished them to my heart's wish and admiration, they being very great and intricate, being let alone for two months; but I brought them together all naturally, within a few shillings; but to my sorrow, the pole Mony I paid this month, and mourning, have made me 80*l* a worse man then at my last balance, so that I am worth now but 6700*l*; which is yet an infinite mercy to me – for which God make me thankful. So late to supper, with a glad heart for the evening of my accounts so well, and so to bed.

## –✤MAY✤–

1. Up, it being a fine day; and after doing a little business in my chamber, I left my wife to go abroad with W. Hewer and his mother in a hackney coach incognit to the park, while I abroad to

1. He refers to Warren's alliance with Brouncker: see above, p. 719 (26 January).

the Excize Office first, and there met the Cofferer and Sir St. Fox about our money matters there, wherein we agreed; and so to discourse of my Lord Treasurer, who is a little better then he was of the stone, having rested a little this night. I there did acquaint them with my knowledge of that disease, which I believe will be told my Lord Treasurer. Thence to Westminster, in the way meeting many milkmaids with their garlands upon their pails, dancing with a fiddler before them, and saw pretty Nelly standing at her lodgings door in Drury lane in her smock-sleeves and bodice, looking upon one – she seemed a mighty pretty creature. To the Hall and there walked a while, it being term; and thence home to the Rose and there had Doll Lane vener para me; but it was in a lugar mighty ouvert, so as we no poda hazer algo; so parted and then met again at the Swan, where for la misma reason we no pode hazer, but put off to recontrar anon, which I only used as a put-off; and so parted and to my Lord Crew's, where I found them at dinner; and among others, Mrs. Bocket, which I have not seen a long time, and two little dirty children, and she as idle a prating, impertinent woman as ever she was. After dinner my Lord took me alone, walked with me, giving me an account of the meeting of the Commissioners for Accounts, whereof he is one. My Lord tells me he doth believe this Commission will do more hurt then good; it may undo some accounts if these men shall think fit, but it can never clear an accountant, for he must come into the Exchequer for all this. Besides, it is a kind of Inquisition that hath seldom, if ever, been granted in England; and [he] believes it will never besides give any satisfaction to the people or Parliament, but be looked upon as a forced, packed business of the King, especially if these Parliament men that are of it shall not concur with them – which he doubts they will not – and therefore wishes much that the King would lay hold of this fit occasion, and let the Commission fall. Then to talk of my Lord Sandwich, whom my Lord Crew hath a great desire might get to be Lord Treasurer if the present Lord should die, as it's believed he will in a little time – and thinks he can have no competitor but my Lord Arlington, who it is given out desires [it]. But my Lord thinks it is not so, for that the being Secretary doth keep him a great[er] interest with the King then the other would do – at least, doth believe that if my Lord would surrender him his Wardrobe place, it would be a temptation to Arlington to assist my Lord in getting the Treasurer['s]. I did object to my Lord that it would be no place of content nor safety, nor honour for my Lord – the State being so indigent as it is and the [King] so irregular, and those about him, that my Lord must be forced to part with anything to answer his warrants; and that therefore I do believe the King had rather have a man that may be one of his vicious cabal, then a sober man that will mind the public, that so they may sit at cards and dispose of the revenue of the kingdom. This my Lord was moved at, and said he did not indeed know how to answer it.

Thence away to the King's playhouse by agreement; met Sir W. Penn and saw *Love in a Maze*; but a sorry play, only Lacy's clowne's* part, which he did most admirably endeed. Thence Sir W. Penn and I in his coach, Tiburne way, into the park; where a horrid dust and number of coaches, without pleasure or order. That which we and almost all went for was to see my Lady Newcastle; which we could not, she being fallowed and crowded upon by coaches all the way she went, that nobody could come near her; only, I could see she was in a large black coach, adorned with silver instead of gold, and so with the curtains and everything black and white, and herself in her cap; but other parts I could not make. But that which I did see and wonder at, with reason, was to find Pegg Penn in a new coach, with only her husband's pretty sister with her, both patched and very fine, and in much the finest coach in the park and I think that ever I did see, one or other, for neatness and richness in gold and everything that is noble – my Lady Castlemaine, the King, my Lord St. Albans, nor Mr. Germin have so neat a coach that ever I saw – and Lord, to have them have this, and nothing else that is correspondent, is to me one of the most ridiculous sights that ever I did see, though her present dress was well enough; but to live in the condition they do at home, and be abroad in this coach, astonishes me. When we had spent half an hour in the park, we went out again, weary of the dust and despairing of seeing my Lady Newcastle; and so back the same way and to St. Jones's, thinking to have met my Lady Newcastle before she got home; but we staying by the way to drink, she got home a little before us, so we lost our labours; and then home, where we find the two young ladies come home and their patches off (I suppose Sir W. Penn doth not allow of them in his sight) and going out of town tonight, though late, to Walthamstow. So to talk a little at Sir W. Batten's, and then home to supper, where I find Mrs. Hewer and her son, who have been abroad with my wife in the park; and so after supper to read and then to bed. Sir W. Penn did give me an account this afternoon of his design of buying Sir Rob. Brookes's fine house at Wanstead, which I so wondered at; and did give him reasons against it, which he allowed of and told me that he did intend to pull down that house and build a less, and that he should get 1500*l* by the old house, and I know not what fooleries; but I will never believe he ever intended to buy it for my part, though he troubled Mr. Gawden to go and look upon it and advise him in it.

4.   Up and to the office, where sat all the morning. Among other things, a great conflict I had with Sir W. Warren, he bringing a letter to the Board, flatly in words charging them with their delays in passing his accounts, which have been with them these two years – part of which I said was not true, and the other undecent. The whole Board was concerned to take notice of it, as well as myself, but none of them had the honour to do it, but suffered me to do it alone; only Sir W. Batten, which did what he did out of common spite to him. So I writ in the margin of the letter, "Returned as untrue," and by consent of the Board did give it him again – and so parted. After dinner, to the office again and there late all the afternoon, doing much business; and with great content, home and to supper and to bed.

5.   *Lords day.* Up; and going down to the waterside, I met Sir Jo. Robinson, and so with him by coach to Whitehall – still a vain, prating, boasting man as ever I know, as if the whole City and Kingdom had all its work done by him. He tells me he hath now got a street ordered to be continued, 40 feet broad, from Paul's through Cannon street to the Tower, which will be very fine. He, and others this day where I was in the afternoon, doth tell me of at least six or eight fires within these few days, and continually stories of fires; and real fires there have been in one place or other almost ever since the late great fire, as if there was a fate over people for fire. I walked over the park to Sir W. Coventry; among other things, to tell him what I hear of people's being forced to sell their bills before September for 35 and 40 per cent loss; and which is worst, that there are some Courtiers that have made a knot to buy them, in hopes of some ways to get money of the King to pay them – which Sir W. Coventry is amazed at, and says we are a people made up for destruction; and will do what he can to prevent all this, by getting the King to provide wherewith to pay them. We talked of Tanger, of which he is ashamed; also that it should put the King to this charge for no good in the world, and now a man going over that is a

good Souldier but a debauched man,[1] which that place needs not to have. And so used these words: "That this place was to the King as my Lord Carnarvan says of Wood; that it is an Excrescence of the earth provided by God for the payment of debts." Thence away to Sir G. Carteret, whom I find taking physic; I stayed talking with him but a little, and so home to church and heard a dull sermon; and most of the best women of our parish gone into the country, or at least not at church. So home and find my boy not there, nor was at church; which vexed me, and when he came home I enquired; he tells me he went to see his mother; I sent him back to her to send me some token that he was with her; so there came a man with him back of good fashion; he says he saw him with her; which pacified me, but I did soundly threaten him before him. And so to dinner, and then had a little scolding with my wife for not being fine enough to go to the christening today; which she excused by being ill, as she was endeed, and cried; but I was in an ill humour, and ashamed endeed that she should not go dressed. However, friends by and by, and we went by water to Michell's; and there his little house full of his father and mothers and the kindred, hardly any else, and mighty merry in this innocent company; and Betty mighty pretty in bed, but her head akeing, not very merry; but the company mighty merry, and I with them; and so the child was christened, my wife, his father, and her mother the witnesses, and the child's name Elizabeth. So we had gloves and wine and wafers, very pretty, and talked and tattled; and so we away by water and up with the tide, she and I and Barker, as high as Barne Elmes, it being a fine evening; and back again to pass the bridge at standing-water between 9 and 10 at night; and then home and to supper, and then to bed with much pleasure. This day Sir W. Coventry tells me the Dutch fleet hath shot some shot, 4 or 500, into Burnt Iland in the Frith, but without any hurt; and so are gone.

6.   Up; and angry with my maids for letting in watermen and I know not who, anybody that they are acquainted with, into the kitchen to talk and prate with them, which I will not endure. Then out and by coach to my Lord Treasurer's, who continues still very ill. Then to Sir Ph. Warwicke's house and there did a little business about my Tanger tallies; and so to Westminster hall and there to the Exchequer to consult about some way of getting our poor creditors

1. The Earl of Middleton.

of the Navy (who served in their goods before the last session of Parliament) paid out of the Eleven Months Tax, which seems to relate only for goods to be then served in – and I think I have found out a way to bring them into the act; which if it doth, I shall think a good service done.

9. To St. James's and there found Sir W. Coventry alone in his chamber, and sat and talked with him more then I have done a great while, of several things – of the Navy, how our debts and wants do unfit us for doing anything. He tells me he hears stories of Commissioner Pett of selling Timber to the Navy under other names; which I told him I believe is true, and did give him an instance. He told me also how his clerk Floyd he hath put away for his common idlenesse and ill company; and perticularly, that yesterday he was found not able to come to attend him, by being run into the arme in a squable, though he pretends it was done in the street by strangers, at 9 at night by the Maypole in the Strand. Sir W. Coventry did write to me this morning to recommend him another; which I could find my heart to do W. Hewers for his good, but do believe he will not part with me, nor have I any mind to let him go. I would my brother were fit for it; I would adventure him there. He insists upon an unmarried man – that can write well – and hath French enough to transcribe it only from a copy, and may write shorthand if it may be. Thence with him to my Lord Chancellors at Clarendon house to a Committee for Tanger, where several things spoke of and proceeded on; and perticularly sending Commissioners[1] thither before the new Governor goes, which I think will signify as much good as everything else that hath been done about the place; which is, none at all. Mightily pleased with the nobleness of this house and the brave furniture and pictures, which endeed is very noble. And being broke up, I with Sir G. Carteret in his coach into Hyde park to discourse of things, and spent an hour in this manner with great pleasure; telling me all his concernments, and how he is gone through with the purchase for my Lady Jemimah and her husband. How the Treasury is like to come into the hands of a committee; but that not that, nor anything else, will do our business, unless the King himself will mind his business; and how his servants do execute their parts. He doth fear an utter ruin in the state, and that in a little time, if the King do not

1. To reorganise the garrison.

mind his business soon. That the King is very kind to him and to my Lord Sandwich; and that he doubts not but at his coming home, which he expects about Michaelmas, he will be very well received. But it is pretty strange how he begun again the business of the intention of a marriage of my Lord Hinchingbrooke to a daughter of my Lord Burlington's to my Lord Chancellor; which he now tells me as a great secret, when he told it me the last Sunday but one. But it may be the poor man hath forgot, and I do believe he doth make it a secret, he telling me that he hath not told it to any but myself, and this day to his daughter my Lady Jemimah – who looks to lie down about two months hence. After all this discourse, we turned back and to Whitehall, where we parted; and I took up my wife at Unthankes and so home; and in our street, at the Three Tuns tavern door, find a great hubbub, and what was [it] but two brothers have fallen out and one killed the other; and who should they be but the two Fieldings, one whereof, Bazill, was page to my Lady Sandwich; and he hath killed the other, himself being very drunk, and so is sent to Newgate. I to the office and did as much business as my eyes would let me, and so home to supper and to bed.

11. Up; and being called on by Mr. Commander, he and I out to the ground behind Sir W. Penn's, where I am resolved to take a lease of some of it for a stable and coach, and so to keep a coach, unless some change come before I can do it; for I do see it is a greater charge to me now in hackneys and I am a little dishonoured by going in them. We spoke with him that hath the letting it, and I do believe, when I can tell how much it will be fit for me to have, we shall go near to agree. So home, and there find my door open, which makes me very angry with Nell and do think to put her away for it; though it doth so go against me to part with a servant, that it troubles me more than anything in the world. So to the office, where all the morning. At noon home to dinner, where Mr. Goodgroome and Creed, and I have great hopes that my wife will come to sing to my mind. After dinner, my wife and Creed and I being entered a hackney coach to go to the other end of the town, we espied The[oph]. Turner coming in her coach to see us – which we were surprized at; and so light and took her and another young lady home, and there sat and talked with The[oph]., she being lately come out of the North after two or three years absence – she is come to put out her sister and brothers to school at Putny. After a little

talk, I over Tower hill with them to a lady's they go to visit; and so away with my wife, whose being dressed this day in fair hair did make me so mad, that I spoke not one word to her in our going, though I was ready to burst with anger. So to Whitehall to the Committee of Tanger, where they were discoursing about laws for the civil government of that place; but so dull and so little to purpose, that I fell to slumber; which the fear of being seen by Sir W. Coventry did trouble me much afterwards, but I hope he did not. After that broke up, Creed and I into the park and walked, a most pleasant evening; and so took coach and took up my wife, and in my way home discovered my trouble to my wife for her white locks, swearing by God several times (which I pray God forgive me for) and bending my fist, that I would not endure it. She, poor wretch, was surprized with it, and made me no answer all the way home. But there we parted, and I to the office late; and then home, and without supper to bed, vexed.

12. *Lords day.* Up, and to my chamber to settle some accounts there; and by and by down comes my wife to me in her nightgown; and we begun calmly, that upon having money to lace her gown for second mourning, she would promise to wear white locks no more in my sight; which I, like a severe fool, thinking not enough, begun to except against and made her fly out to very high terms, and cry; and in her heat told me of keeping company with Mrs. Knipp, saying that if I would promise never to see her more (of whom she hath more reason to suspect then I had heretofore of Pembleton), she would never wear white locks more. This vexed me, but I restrained myself from saying anything; but do think never to see this woman; at least, to have her here more. But by and by I did give her money to buy lace, and she promised to wear no more white locks while I lived; and so all very good friends as ever, and I to my business and she to dress herself. Against noon we had a coach ready for us; and she and I to Whitehall, where I went to see whether Sir G. Carteret was at dinner or no, our design being to make a visit there, and I found them sat down, which troubled me, for I would not then go up; but back to the coach to my wife, and she and I homeward again; and in our way bethought ourselfs of going alone, she and I, to a French house to dinner, and so enquired out Monsieur Robins my periwig-maker, who keeps an ordinary, and in an ugly street in Covent garden did find him at the door, and so we in; and in a moment almost have the table covered, and clean

glasses, and all in the French manner, and a mess of potage first and then a couple of pigeons *a l'esteuvé*, and then a piece of *bœuf-a-la-mode*, all exceeding well seasoned and to our great liking; at least, it would have been anywhere else but in this bad street and in a periwig-maker's house; but to see the pleasant and ready attendance that we had, and all things so desirous to please and ingenious in the people, did take me mightily – our dinner cost us 6s.; and so my wife and I away and by coach to Islington, it being a fine day, and thence to Sir G. Whitmore's house, where we light and walked over the fields to Kingsland and back again, a walk I think I have not taken these twenty years but puts me in mind of my boy's time, when I boarded at Kingsland and used to shoot with my bow and arrows in these fields. A very pretty place it is – and little did any of my friends think I should come to walk in these fields in this condition and state that I am. Then took coach again and home through Shoreditch; and at home my wife finds Barker to have been abroad, and telling her so many lies about it, that she struck her, and the wench said she would not stay with her; so I examined the wench, and found her in so many lies myself, that I was glad to be rid of her, and so resolved of having her go away tomorrow.

16.   To my office, where busy; and anon, at 7 at night, I and my wife and Sir W. Penn in his coach to Unthanke's, my wife's tailor's, for her to speak one word; and then we to my Lord Treasurer's, where I find the porter crying, and suspected it was that my Lord is dead; and, poor Lord, we did find that he was dead just now; and the crying of that fellow did so trouble me, that considering that I was not likely to trouble him any more, nor have occasion to give any more anything, I did give him 3s.; but it may be, poor man, he hath lost a considerable hope by the death of this Lord, whose house will be no more frequented as before – and perhaps I may never come thither again about any business. There is a good man gone; and I pray God that the Treasury may not be worse managed by the hand or hands it shall now be put into; though, for certain, the slowness (though he was of great integrity) of this man, and remissness, have gone as far to undo the nation as anything else that hath happened; and yet if I knew all the difficulties that he hath lain under, and his instrument Sir Ph. Warwick, I might be brought to another mind. Thence, we to Islington to the old house and there eat and drank; and then, it being late and a pleasant evening, we home; and there to my chamber and to bed.

18. Up and all morning at the office, and then to dinner; and after dinner to the office to dictate some letters, and then with my wife down to Sir W. Turner's to visit The[oph].; but she being abroad, we back again home; and then I to the office, finished my letters, and then to walk an hour in the garden talking with my wife, whose growth in music doth begin to please me mightily; and by and by home and there find our Luce drunk, and when her mistress told her of it, would be gone; and so put up some of her things and did go away of her accord, nobody pressing her to it; and the truth is, though she be the dirtiest and homeliest servant that ever I kept, yet I was sorry to have her go, partly through my love to my servants and partly because she was a very drudging, working wench; only, she would be drunk.

19. *Lords day.* Up, and to my chamber to set some papers in order; and then to church, where my old acquaintance, that dull fellow Meriton, made a good sermon; and hath a strange knack of a grave, serious delivery, which is very agreeable. After church, to Whitehall and there find Sir G. Carteret just sat down to dinner; and I dined with them as I entended, and good company, the best people and family in the world I think. Here was great talk of the good end that my Lord Treasurer made; closing his own eyes and setting his mouth, and bidding Adieu with the greatest content and freedom in the world; and is said to die with the cleanest hands that ever any Lord Treasurer did. After dinner, Sir G. Carteret and I alone; and there among other discourse, he did declare that he would be content to part with his place of Treasurer of the Navy upon good terms. I did propose my Lord Bellasses as a man likely to buy it; which he listened to, and I did fully concur and promote his design of parting with it, for though I would have my father live, I would not have him die Treasurer of the Navy, because of the accounts which must be uncleared at his death; besides many other circumstances making it advisable for him to let it go. I took leave of him, and directly by water home; and there to read the Life of Mr. Hooker, which pleases me as much as anything I have read a great while; and by and by comes Mr. How to see us, and after him a little, Mr. Sheply, and so we all to talk; and Mercer being there, we some of us to sing and so to supper; a great deal of silly talk; among other things, W. How told us how the barristers and students of Grays Inne rose in rebellion against the Benchers the other day; who outlawed them, and a great deal of do but now they

are at peace again. They being gone, I to my book again and made an end of Mr. Hooker's Life, and so to bed.

20.    Up betimes; and comes my Flagelette man and set me a new tune, which I played presently and shall in a month do as much as I desire at it. He being [gone], I to several businesses in my chamber; and then by coach to the Commissioners of Excise, and so to Westminster hall and there spoke with several persons I had to do with. Having done my business, I then homeward and overtook Mr. Comander; so took him into a coach with me, and he and I into Lincoln's Inne Fields, there to look upon the coach-houses to see what ground is necessary for coach-house and horses, because of that that I am going about to do; and having satisfied myself in this, he and I home and he dined with me all alone, my wife being unfit to be seen: and so after dinner, he and I to Mr. Hides to look upon the ground again behind our house, and concluded upon his going along with us tomorrow to see some stables, he thinking that we demand more room then is necessary. So away home; and then I, it being a broken day and had power by my vows, did walk abroad; first through the Minorys (the first time I have been over the Hill to the postern-gate and seen that place since the houses were pulled down about that side of the Tower since the fire) to find where my young Mercer with my pretty little woman to his wife lives, who lived in Lumbard street – and I did espy them, but took no notice now of them but may do hereafter. Thence down to the Old Swan and there saw Betty Michell, whom I have not seen since her christening. But Lord, how pretty she is, and looks so well as ever I saw her; and her child (which I am fain to seem very fond of) is pretty also I think, and will be. Thence by water to Westminster hall and there walked a while, talking at random with Sir Wm. Doyly; and so away to Mrs. Martin's lodging, who was gone before expecting me; and there yo haze what yo vellem cum her, and drank; and so by coach home (but I have forgot that I did in the morning go to the Swan; and there tumbling of la little fille, son uncle did trouver her cum su neckcloth off, which I was ashamed of, but made no great matter of it but let it pass with a laugh) and there spent the evening with my wife at our Flagelettes; and so to supper, and after a little reading, to bed. My wife still troubled with her cold. I find it everywhere now to be a thing doubted whether we shall have peace or no; and the captain of one of our ships that went with the Embassadors doth say that the seamen of Holland, to

his hearing, did defy us, and called us English dogs and cried out against peace; and that the great people there do oppose peace, though he says the common people do wish it.

21.   Up and to the office, where sat all the morning. At noon dined at home with my wife, and find a new girle, a good big girl, come to us, got by Payne to be our girl; and his daughter Nell we make our cook. This wench's name is Mary – and seems a good likely maid. After dinner, I with Mr. Comander amd Mr. Hide's brother to Lincoln's Inne Fields, and there viewed several coach-houses and satisfied ourselfs now fully in it. And then there parted, leaving the rest to future discourse between us. Thence, I home; but Lord, how it went against my heart to go away from the very door of the Duke's playhouse, and my Lady Castlemayns coach and many great coaches there to see *The Siege of Rhodes*; I was very near making a forfeit, but I did command myself; and so home to my office and there did much business to my good content, much better then going to a play; and then home to my wife, who is not well with her cold, and sat and read [a] piece of *Grand Cyrus* in English by her; and then to my chamber and to supper, and so to bed. This evening, after I came from the office, Mrs. Turner came to see my wife and me and sit and talk with us; and so my wife not being well and going to bed, Mrs. Turner and I sat up till 12 at night talking alone in my chamber, and most of our discourse was of our neighbours. As to my Lord Brouncker, she says how Mrs. Griffin, our housekeeper's wife, hath it from his maid, that comes to her house often, that they are very poor; that the other day Mrs. Williams was fain to send a jewell to pawn. That they have a most lewd and nasty family here in the office; but Mrs. Turner doth tell me that my Lord hath put the King to infinite charge since his coming thither, in alterations; and perticularly, that Mr. Harper at Deptford did himself tell her that my Lord hath had of Foly the ironmonger 50*l*-worth in locks and keys for his house, and that it is from the fineness of them, having some of 4 and 5*l* a lock, such as is in ladies closets; that he hath several of these. That Mrs. Griffin doth say that he doth not keep Mrs. Williams now for love, but need, he having another whore that he keeps in Covent garden. That they do owe money everywhere, almost for everything; even Mrs. Shipman for her butter and cheese about 3*l*, and after many demands cannot get it.

Then we fall to talk of Sir W. Penn and his family and rise. She says that he was a pitiful [fellow] when she first knew them. That his lady was one of the sorriest, dirty women that ever she saw. That his rise hath been his giving of large Bribes, wherein (and she agrees with my opinion and knowledge before therein) he is very profuse. That long ago endeed, he would drink the King's health privately with Mr. Turner; but that when he saw it fit to turn Roundhead, and was offered by Mr. Turner to drink the King's health, he answered no, he was changed, and now he that would make him drink the King's health, or any health but the Protectors and the State's (or to that purpose), he would be the first man should sheath his sword in his guts. That at the King's coming in, he did send for her husband and told him what a great man Sir W. Coventry was like to be; and that he having all the records in his hands of the Navy, if he would transcribe what was of most present use of the practice of the Navy, and give them him to give Sir W. Coventry from him, it would undoubtedly do his business of getting him a Principal Officer's place. That he was the last war a most devilish plunderer, and that got him his estate which he hath in Ireland, and nothing else; and that he hath always been a very liberal man in his bribes. That upon his coming into this part of the Controller's business wherein he is, he did send for T. Willson and told him how against his knowledge he was put in, and had so little wit as to say to him, "This will make the pot boyle, will it not, Mr. Willson? will it not make the pot boil?" and doth offer him to come in and do his business for him, and he would reward him. Upon the whole, she told me stories enough to confirm me that he is the most false fellow that ever was born of woman, and that so she thinks and knows him to be.

22. Up and by water to Whitehall to Sir G. Carteret, who tells me now for certain how the Commission for the Treasury is disposed of: *viz.*, to Duke of Albemarle, Lord Ashly, Sir W. Coventry, Sir Jo. Duncum, and Sir Tho. Clifford; at which he says all the whole Court is disturbed, it having been once concluded otherwise, but all of a sudden the King's choice was changed, and these are to be the men; the first of which is only for a puppet to give honour to the rest. He doth presage that these men will make it their business to find faults in the management of the late Lord Treasurer and in discouraging the banquiers; but I am (whatever I in compliance do say to him) of another mind, and my heart is very glad of it; for I do expect they will do much good, and that it is the happiest thing that

hath appeared to me for the good of the nation since the King came in. Thence to St. James's and up to the Duke of York; and there in his chamber Sir W. Coventry did of himself take notice of this business of the Treasury, wherein he is in the Commission, and desired that I would be thinking of anything fit for him to be acquainted with for the lessening of charge and bettering of our credit; and what our expense hath been since the King's coming home, which he believes will be one of the first things they shall enquire into – which I promised him; and from time to time, which he desires, give him an account of what I can think of worthy his knowledge. So into the Duke of York's closet; and there, among other things, Sir W. Coventry did take notice of what he told me the other day, about a report of Comissioner Pett's dealing for timber in the Navy and selling it to us in other names; and besides his own proof did produce a paper I had given him this morning about it, in the case of Widow Murford and Morecocke – which was so handled, that the Duke of York grew very angry, and commanded us presently to fall into the examination of it, saying that he would [not] trust a man for his sake that lifts up the whites of his eyes. And it was declared that if he be found to have done so, he should be reckoned unfit to serve the Navy. And I do believe he will be turned out; and it was methought, a worthy saying of W. Coventry to the Duke of York – "Sir," says he, "I do not make this complaint out of any disrespect to Comissioner Pett, but because I do love to do these things fairly and openly."

And so home; and by and by comes my poor father, much better then I expected, being at ease by fits, according as his truss sits, and another time in as much pain. I am mighty glad to see him come well to town. So to dinner, where Creed comes. After dinner, my wife and father abroad; and Creed and I also by water, and parted at the Temple stairs; where I landed and to the King's house, where I did give 18*d*. and saw the two last acts of *The Goblins*, a play I could not make anything of by those two acts; but here Knipp spied me out of the tiring-room and came to the pit door: and I out to her and kissed her, she only coming to see me, being in a country-dress, she and others having it seemed had a country-dance in the play, but she no other part; so we parted, and I into the pit again till it was done. The house full, but I had no mind to be seen; but thence to my cutler's and two or three other places on small errands; and so home, where my father and wife come home; and pretty well, my father, who to supper and betimes to bed at his country hours.

26.  *Lords day*. Up sooner then usual on Sundays, and to walk, it
being exceeding hot all night (so as this night I begin to leave off my
waistcoat this year) and this morning; and so to walk in the garden
till toward church time, when my wife and I to church; where
several strangers of good condition came to our pew, where the
pew was full. At noon dined at home, where little Michell came,
and his wife, who continues mighty pretty. After dinner, I by water
alone to Westminster, where not finding Mrs. Martin within, did
go toward the parish church and in the way did overtake her, who
resolved to go into the church with her that she was going with
(Mrs. Hargrave, the little crooked woman, the vintner's wife of the
Dog) and then go out again; and so I to the church; and seeing her
return, did go to go out again myself, but met with Mr. Howlett,
who offering me a pew in the gallery, I had no excuse but up with
him I must go, and there, much against my will, stayed out the
whole church in pain, while she expected me at home; but I did
entertain myself with my perspective glass up and down the
church, by which I had the greatest pleasure of seeing and gazing a
great many very fine women; and what with that and sleeping, I
passed away the time till sermon was done; and then to Mrs. Martin
and there stayed with her an hour or two, and there did what jo
would with her. And after having been here so long, I away to my
boat, and up with it as far as Barne Elmes, reading of Mr. Eveling's
late new book against Solitude, in which I do not find much excess
of good matter, though it be pretty for a by-discourse. I walked the
length of the Elmes, and with great pleasure saw some gallant ladies
and people, come with their bottles and basket[s] and chairs and
forms[s] to sup under the trees by the waterside, which was mighty
pleasant. I to boat again and to my book; and having done that, I
took another book, Mr. Boyles of Colours, and there read where I
left, finding many fine things worthy observation. And so landed at
the Old Swan and so home, where I find my poor father newly
come out of an unexpected fit of his pain, that they feared he would
have died. They had sent for me to Whitehall and all up and down,
and for Mr. Holliard also, who did come. But W. Hewers being
here did I think do the business, in getting my father's bowel, that
was fallen down, into his body again. But above all things, the poor
man's patience under it, and his good heart and humour as soon as
he was out of it, did so work upon me, that my heart was sad to
think of his condition; but do hope that a way will be found by a
steele truss to relieve him. By and by to supper, all our discourse

about Brampton, and my intentions to build there if I could be free of my engagement to my Uncle Tho. and his son, that they may not have what I have built, against my will, to them, whether I will or no, in case of my and my brothers being without heirs males – which is the true reason why I am against laying out money upon that place, together with my fear of some inconvenience by being so near Hinchingbrooke; being obliged to be a servant to that family, and subject to what expenses they shall cost me, and to have all that I shall buy or do esteemed as got by the death of my Uncle; when endeed, what I have from him is not worth naming. After supper, I to read and then to bed.

27.    Up, and there comes Greeting my Flagelette-maister and I practised with him. There came also Richardson the bookbinder with one of Ogilby's Bible's in quires for me to see and buy, it being Mr. Cade's my stationer's; but it is like to be so big, that I shall not use it, it being too great to stir up and down without much trouble, which I shall not like nor do intend it for. So by water to Whitehall and there found Sir G. Carteret at home; and talked with him a while and find that the new Commissioners of the Treasury did meet this morning. So I to find out Sir W. Coventry, but missed; only, I do hear that they have chosen Sir G. Downing for their Secretary; and I think in my conscience they have done a great thing in it – for he is a busy active man, and values himself upon having of things do well under his hand; so that I am mightily pleased in their choice. So home; and there to sing with my wife before dinner, and then to dinner; and then abroad by [water] and stopped at the Bear-garden stairs, there to see a Prize fought; but the house so full, there was no getting in there; so forced to [go] through an alehouse into the pit where the bears are baited, and upon a stool did see them fight, which they did very furiously, a butcher and a waterman. The former had the better all along, till by and by the latter dropped his sword out of his hand, and the butcher, whether not seeing his sword dropped or I know not, but did give him a cut over the wrist, so as he was disabled to fight any longer. But Lord, to see how in a minute the whole stage was full of watermen to revenge the foul play, and the butchers to defend their fellow, though most blamed him; and there they all fell to it, to knocking down and cutting many of each side. It was pleasant to see, but that I stood in the pit and feared that in the tumult I might get some hurt. At last the rabble broke up, and so I away to Whitehall; and so to St. James's,

but found not Sir W. Coventry; so into the park and took a turn or two, it being a most sweet day; and so by water home, and with my father and wife walked in the garden, and then anon to supper and to bed.

28. After dinner, my wife away down with Jane and W. Hewer to Woolwich in order to a little ayre, and to lie there tonight and so to gather May dew tomorrow morning, which Mrs. Turner hath taught her as the only thing in the world to wash her face with, and I am contented with it. Presently comes Creed, and he and I by water to Foxhall and there walked in Spring garden; a great deal of company, and the weather and garden pleasant; that it is very pleasant and cheap going thither, for a man may go to spend what he will, or nothing, all as one – but to hear the nightingale and other birds, and here fiddles and there a harp, and here a jews trump, and here laughing, and there fine people walking, is mighty divertising. Among others, there were two pretty women alone, that walked a great while; which [being] discovered by some idle gentlemen, they would needs take them up; but to see the poor ladies, how they were put to it to run from them, and they after them; and sometimes the ladies put themselfs along with other company, then the others drew back; at last, the ladies did get off out of the house and took boat and away. I was troubled to see them abused so; and could have found my heart, as little desire of fighting as I have, to have protected the ladies. So by water; set Creed down at Whitehall, and I to Old Swan and so home. My father gone to bed and wife abroad at Woolwich, I to Sir W. Penn, where he and his Lady and Pegg, and pretty Mrs. Lowther, her sister-in-law, at supper; where I sat and talked, and Sir W. Penn, half drunk, did talk like a fool and vex his wife, that I was half pleased and half vexed to see so much folly and rudeness from him; and so late home to bed.

29. Up and by coach to St. James's, where by and by up to the Duke of York; where among other things, our Parson Mills having the offer of another benefice by Sir Rob. Brookes, who was his pupil, he by my Lord Barkely's [desire] – is made one of the Duke's chaplains; which qualifies him for two livings. But to see how slightly such things are done; the Duke of York only taking my Lord Barkely's word upon saying that we, the Officers of the Navy, do say he is a good man and minister of our parish; and the Duke of York admits him to kiss his hand but speaks not one word

779

to him, but so a warrant will be drawn from the Duke of York to qualify him, and there's an end of it. Thence home, and there settle to some accounts of mine in my chamber, all the morning till dinner. My wife comes home from Woolwich but did not dine with me, going to dress herself against night to go to Mrs. Pierces to be merry, where we are to have Knipp and Harris and other good people. I at my accounts all the afternoon, being a little lost in them as to reckonings of interest. Anon comes down my wife, dress[ed] in her second mourning, with her black moyre waistcoat and short petticoat, laced with silver lace so basely that I could not endure to see her, and with laced lining, which is too soon; so that I was horrid angry and went out of doors to the office, and there stayed and would not go to our intended meeting, which vexed me to the blood; and my wife sent twice or thrice to me to direct her any way to dress her but to put on her cloth gown, which she would not venture, which made me mad; and so in the evening to my chamber, vexed, and to my accounts, which I ended to my great content, and did make amends for the loss of our mirth this night by getting this done, which otherwise I fear I should not have done a good while else. So to bed.

30.     Up, and to the office, where all the morning. At noon dined at home; being, without any words, friends with my wife, though last night I was very angry, and do think I did give her as much cause to be angry with me. After dinner I walked to Arundell house, the way very dusty (the day of meeting of the Society[1] being changed from Wednesday to Thursday; which I knew not before because the Wednesday is a Council day and several of the Council are of the Society, and would come but for their attending the King at Council); where I find much company, endeed very much company, in expectation of the Duchesse of Newcastle, who had desired to be invited to the Society, and was, after much debate pro and con, it seems many being against it, and we do believe the town will be full of ballets of it. Anon comes the Duchesse, with her women attending her; among others, that Ferrabosco of whom so much talk is, that her lady would bid her show her face and kill the gallants. She is endeed black and hath good black little eyes, but otherwise but a very ordinary woman I do think; but they say sings well. The Duchesse hath been a good comely woman; but her dress

1. The Royal Society.

so antic and her deportment so unordinary, that I do not like her at all, nor did I hear her say anything that was worth hearing, but that she was full of admiration, all admiration. Several fine experiments were shown her of Colours, Loadstones, Microscope, and of liquors: among others, of one that did while she was there turn a piece of roasted mutton into pure blood – which was very rare – here was Mr. Moore of Cambrige, whom I had not seen before, and I was glad to see him – as also a very pretty black boy that run up and down the room, somebody's child in Arundell house. After they had shown her many experiments, and she cried still she was "full of admiration," she departed, being led out and in by several Lords that were there; among others, Lord George Barkely and the Earl of Carlisle and a very pretty young man, the Duke of Somersett. She gone, I by coach home and there busy at my letters till night; and then with my wife in the evening, singing with her in the garden with great pleasure. And so home to supper and to bed.

## ⚜JUNE⚜

2.  *Lords day.* Up betimes, and down to [my] chamber, without trimming myself or putting on clean linen, thinking only to keep to my chamber to do business today; but when I came there, I find that without being shaved I am not fully awake nor ready to settle to business, and so was fain to go up again and dress myself; which I did, and so down to my chamber and fell roundly to business, and did to my satisfaction by dinner go far in the drawing up a state of my accounts of Tanger for the new Lords Comissioners. So to dinner, and then to my business again all the afternoon close, when Creed came to visit me; but I did put him off, and to my business; till anon I did make an end and wrote it fair, with a letter to the Lords to accompany my account; which I think will be so much satisfaction, and so soon done (their order for my doing it being dated but May. 30), as they will not find from any hand else. Being weary and almost blind with writing and reading so much today, I took boat at the Old Swan, and there up the River all alone, as high as Puttny almost; and then back again, all the way reading and finishing Mr. Boyle's book of Colours, which is so Chymicall that I can understand but little of it, but understand enough to see that he is a most excellent man.

So back and home, and there to supper and so to bed.

3. Up; and by coach to St. James's and with Sir W. Coventry a great while, talking about several businesses – but especially about accounts and how backward our Treasurer is in giving them satisfaction; and the truth is, I do doubt he cannot do better. But it is strange to see, that being conscious of our doing little at this day nor for some time past in our office, for want of money, I do hang my head to him and cannot be so free with him as I used to be, nor can be free with him, though of all men I think I have the least cause to be so, having taken so much more pains (while I could do anything) then the rest of my fellows. Parted with him; and so going through the park, met Mr. Mills our parson, whom I went back with to bring him to W. Coventry to give him the form of a Qualificacion for the Duke of York to sign to, to enable him to have two livings; which was a service I did, but much against my will, for a lazy, fat priest. Thence to Westminster hall and there walked a turn or two with Sir Wm. Doyly, who did lay a wager with me the Treasurer-ship would be in one hand (notwithstanding this present Commission) before Christmas; on which we did lay a pole of ling, a brace of carps, and a pottle of wine, and Sir W. Penn and Mr. Scowen to be at the eating of them. Thence down by water to Deptford, it being Trinity Monday, when the Maister is chosen. And there finding them all at church, and thinking they dined as usual at Stepny, I turned back, having a good book in my hand (the Life of Cardinal Wolsey, wrote by his own servant), and to Ratcliffe; and so walked to Stepny and spent my time in the churchyard looking over the gravestones, expecting when the company would come; but finding no company stirring, I sent to the house to see, and it seems they dine not there, but at Deptford; so I back again to Deptford and there find them just sat down; and so I down with them and we had a good dinner of plain meat, and a good company at our Table; among others, my good Mr. Evelyn, with whom after dinner I stepped aside and talked upon the present posture of our affairs; which is, that the Dutch are known to be abroad with 80 sail of ships of war and 20 fireships and the French come into the Channell with 20 sail of men-of-war and 5 fireships, while we have not a ship at sea to do them any hurt with, but are calling in all we can, while our Imbassadors are treating at Bredah and the Duch look upon them as come to beg peace, and use them accordingly. And all this through the negligence of our Prince; who

hath power, if he would, to maister all these with the money and men that he hath had the command of, and may now have if he would mind his business. But for [aught] we see, the Kingdom is likely to be lost, as well as the reputation of it is, for ever – notwithstanding so much reputation got and preserved by a Rebell that went before him.

This discourse of ours ended with sorrowful reflections upon our condition, and so broke up; and Creed and I got out of the room and away by water to Whitehall, and there he and I waited in the Treasury chamber. By and by, I upon desire was called in and delivered in my report of my accounts: present, Lord Ashly, Clifford, and Duncomb; who being busy, did not read it but committed it to Sir G. Downing, and so I was dismissed. But Lord, to see how Duncomb doth take upon him is an eysore, though I think he deserves great honour; but only, the suddenness of his rise and his pride. But I do like the way of these Lords, that they admit nobody to use many words; nor do they spend many words themselfs, but in great state do hear what they see necessary, and say little themselfs but bid withdraw. Thence Creed and I by water up to Foxhall; and over against it stopped, thinking to see some cock-fighting, but it was just being done; and therefore back again to the other side and to Spring garden and there eat and drank a little; and then to walk up and down the garden, reflecting upon the bad management of things now compared with what it was in the late rebellious times, when men, some for fear and some for religion, minded their business; which none now do, by being void of both. Much talk of this and other kinds, very pleasant; and so when it was almost night, we home, setting him in at Whitehall, I to [the] Old Swan; and thence home, where to supper and then to read a little; and so to bed.

4.    Up and to the office; and there busy all the morning putting in order the answering the great letter sent to the office by the new Commissioners of the Treasury, who demand an account from the King's coming in to this day; which we shall do in the best manner we can. At noon home to dinner; and to the office all the afternoon, where I despatched much business to my great content; and then home in the evening, and there to sing and pipe with my wife; and that being done, she fell all of a sudden to discourse about her clothes and my humours in not suffering her to wear them as she pleases, and grew to high words between us. But I fell to read a

book (Boyle's *Hydrostatickes*) aloud in my chamber and let her talk till she was tired, and vexed that I would not hear her; and so become friends and to bed together, the first night after four or five that she hath lain from me by reason of a great cold she had got.

6. Up, and to the office all the morning, where (which he hath not done a great while) Sir G. Carteret came to advise with us for the disposing of 10000*l*, which is the first sum the new Lords Treasurers have provided us; but unless we have more, this will not enable us to cut off any of the growing charge, which they seem to give it us for and expect we should discharge several ships quite off with it. So home and with my father and wife to Sir W. Penn's to dinner, which they invited us to out of their respect to my father, as a stranger; though I know them as false as the devil himself, and that it is only that they think it fit to oblige me; wherein I am a happy man, that all of my fellow-officers are desirous of my friendship. Here as merry as in so false a place and where I must dissemble my hatred, I could be. And after dinner, my father and wife to a play and I to my office; and there busy all the afternoon till late at night; and then my wife and I sang a song or two in the garden, and so home to supper and to bed.

8. Up and to the office, where all the news this morning is that the Duch are come with a fleet of 80 sail to Harwich, and that guns were heard plain by Sir W. Rider's people at Bednall Greene all yesterday noon. So to the office we all, and sat all the morning; and then home to dinner – where our dinner, a ham of French Bacon boiled with pigeons – an excellent dish. Here dined with us only W. Hewers and his mother. After dinner to the office again, where busy till night; and then home and to read a little and then to bed. The news is confirmed that the Dutch are off of Harwich, but had done nothing last night. The King hath sent down my Lord of Oxford to raise the country there; and all the Westerne Barges are taken up to make a bridge over river about the Hope, for horse to cross the river if there be occasion.

10. Up; and news brought us that the Dutch are come up as high as the Nore. W. Batten, W. Penn and I to St. James, where the Duke of York gone this morning betimes to send away some men down to Chatham. So we three to Whitehall and met Sir W. Coventry, who presses all the possible for fireships; so we three to the office

presently, and thither comes Sir Fr. Hollis, who is to command them all in some exploits he is to do with them on the enemy in the river. So we all down to Deptford and pitch upon ships and set men at work; but Lord, to see how backwardly things move at this pinch, notwithstanding that by the enemy's being now come up as high as almost the Hope, Sir J. Mennes (who was gone down to pay some ships there) hath sent up the money; and so we are possessed of money to [do] what we will with. Here I eat a bit; and then in the afternoon took boat and down to Greenwich, where I find the stairs full of people, there being a great Riding there today for a man, the constable of the town, whose wife beat him. Here I was with much ado fain to press two watermen to make me a galley; and so to Woolwich to give order for the despatch of a ship I have taken under my care to see despatched; and orders being so given, I, under pretence to fetch up the ship, which lay at Grays (the *Golden hand*), did do that in my way; and went down to Gravesend, where I find the Duke of Albemarle just come, with a great many idle lords and gentlemen with their pistols and fooleries, and the Bulworke not able to have stood half an hour had they come up; but the Dutch are fallen down from the Hope and Shell haven as low as the Sheernesse, and we do plainly at this time hear the guns play. Yet I do not find the Duke of Albemarle entends to go thither, but stays here tonight and hath (though the Dutch are gone) ordered our frigates to be brought in a line between the two block-houses[1] – which I took then to be a ridiculous thing. So I away into the town and took a Captain or two of our ships (who did give me an account of the proceedings of the Dutch fleet in the river) to the tavern and there we eat and drank; and I find the town had removed most of their goods out of the town, for fear of the Duch coming up to them; and Sir Jo. Griffen [told me] that last night there was not twelve men to be got in the town to defend it – which the master of the house tells me is not true; but that the men of the town did entend to stay, though they did endeed, and so had he (at the Ship), removed their goods. Thence went off to an Ostend man-of-war, just now come up, who met the Dutch fleet, who took three ships that he came convoying hither from him – says they are as low as the Nore or thereabouts. So I homeward, as long as it was light reading Mr. Boyles book of *Hydrostatickes*, which is a most excellent book as ever I read; and I will take much pains to

1. At Gravesend.

understand him through if I can, the doctrine being very useful. When it grew too dark to read, I lay down and took a nap, it being a most excellent fine evening; and about one a-clock got home, and after having wrote to Sir W. Coventry an account of what I had done and seen (which is entered in my letter-book), I to bed.

11.    Up, and more letters still from Sir W. Coventry about more fireships; and so W. Batten and I to the office, where Brouncker came to us; who is just now going to Chatham upon a desire of Commissioner Pett's, who is in a very fearful stink for fear of the Dutch, and desires help for God and King and kingdom's sake. So Brouncker goes down, and Sir J. Mennes also, from Gravesend. This morning Pett writes us word that Sherenesse is lost last night, after two or three hours' dispute – the enemy hath possessed himself of the place; which is very sad and puts us into great fears of Chatham. Sir W. Batten and I down by water to Deptford, and there Sir W. Penn and we did consider of several matters relating to the despatch of the Fireshipps; and so W. Batten and I home again – and there to dinner, my wife and father having dined. And after dinner, by W. Hewer's lucky advice, went to Mr. Fenn and did get him to pay me above 400*l* of my Wages, and W. Hewer received it for me and brought it home this night. Then home and there to our business, hiring some fireships and receiving every hour almost letters from Sir W. Coventry, calling for more Fireshipps – and an order from Council to enable us to take any man's ships; and Sir W. Coventry in his letter to us says he doth not doubt but at this time (under an Invasion, as he owns it to be) the King may by law take any man's goods. At this business late, and then home, where a great deal of serious talk with my wife about the sad state we are in, and especially from the beating-up of drums this night for the trainbands, upon pain of death to appear in arms tomorrow morning, with bullet and powder and money to supply themselfs with victuals for a fortnight – which, considering the soldiers drawn out to Chatham and elsewhere, looks as if they had a design to ruin the City and give it up to be undone – which I hear makes the sober citizens to think very sadly of things. So to bed after supper, ill in my mind.

12.    Up very betimes to our business at the office, there hiring of more fireships; and at it close all the morning. At noon home, and Sir W. Penn dined with us. By and by, after dinner, my wife out by

coach to see her mother; and I in another (being afeared at this busy time to be seen with a woman in a coach, as if I were idle) toward The[oph]. Turners; but met Sir W. Coventry's boy, and there in his letter find that the Dutch had made no motion since their taking Sherenesse; and the Duke of Albemarle writes that all is safe as to the great ships against any assault – the boom and Chaine[1] being so fortified; which put my heart into great joy. When I came to Sir W. Coventry's chamber, I find him abroad; but his clerk Powell doth tell me that ill news is come to Court of the Dutch breaking the Chaine at Chatham, which struck me to the heart, and to Whitehall to hear the truth of it; and there, going up the park stairs, I did hear some lackeys speaking of sad news come to Court, saying that hardly anybody in the court but doth look as if they cried; and would not go into the house for fear of being seen, but slunk out and got into a coach, and to The[oph]. Turner to Sir W. Turner's, where I met Roger Pepys, newly come out of the country (he and I talked aside a little, he offering a match for Pall, one Barnes, of whom we shall talk more the next time; his father married a Pepys). In discourse, he told me further that his grandfather, my great grandfather, had 800*l* per annum in Queen Elizabeth's time in the very town of Cottenham – and that we did certainly come out of Scotland with the Abbot of Crowland. More talk I had, and shall have more with him, but my mind is so sad and head full of all this ill news, that I cannot now set it down.

A short visit here, my wife coming to me, and took leave of The[oph].; and so home, where all our hearts do now ake; for the news is true, that the Dutch have broke the Chain and burned our ships, and perticularly the *Royall Charles*; other perticulars I know not, but most sad to be sure. And the truth is, I do fear so much that the whole kingdom is undone, that I do this night resolve to study with my father and wife what to do with the little that I have in money by me, for I give all the rest that I have in the King's hands for Tanger for lost. So God help us, and God knows what disorders we may fall into and whether any violence on this office, or perhaps some severity on our persons, as being reckoned by the silly people, or perhaps may by policy of State be thought fit to be condemned by the King and Duke of York, and so put to trouble; though God knows I have in my own person done my full duty, I am sure. So having with much ado finished my business at the office, I home to

---

1. Across the channel of the Medway.

consider with my father and wife of things; and then to supper and
to bed with a heavy heart. The manner of my advising this night
with my father was: I took him and my wife up to her chamber, and
shut the door and there told them the sad state of the times; how we
are like to be all undone – that I do fear some violence will be offered
to this office, where all I have in the world is. And resolved upon
sending it away – sometimes into the country, sometimes my father
to lie in town and have the gold with him at Sarah Giles's, and with
that resolution went to bed – full of fear and fright; hardly slept all
night.

13.   No sooner up but hear the sad news confirmed, of the *Royall
Charles* being taken by them and now in fitting by them (which Pett
should have carried up higher by our several orders, and deserves
therefore to be hanged for not doing it) and burning several others,
and that another fleet is come up into the Hope; upon which news
the King and Duke of York have been below since 4 a-clock in the
morning, to command the sinking of ships at Barking Creeke and
other places, to stop their coming up higher; which put me into
such fear that I presently resolved of my father's and wife's going
into the country; and at two hours' warning they did go by the
coach this day – with about 1300*l* in gold in their night-bag; pray
God give them good passage and good care to hide it when they
come home, but my heart is full of fear. They gone, I continued in
frights and fear what to do with the rest. W. Hewer hath been at the
banquiers and hath got 500*l* out of Backewell's hands of his own
money; but they are so called upon that they will be all broke,
hundreds coming to them for money – and their answer is, "It is
payable at twenty days; when the days are out, we will pay you;"
and those that are not so, they make tell over their money, and
make their bags false on purpose to give cause to retell it and so
spend time; I cannot have my 200 pieces of gold again for silver, all
being bought up last night that were to be had – and sold for 24 and
25*s*. a-piece. So I must keep the silver by me, which sometimes I
think to fling into the house of office – and then again, know not
how I shall come by it if we be made to leave the office. Every
minute some[one] or other calls for this order or that order; and so I
forced to be at the office most of the day about the fireships which
are to be suddenly fitted out; and it's a most strange thing that we
hear nothing from any of my Brethren at Chatham; so that we are
wholly in the dark, various being the reports of what is done there –

insomuch, that I sent Mr. Clapham express thither to see how matters go. I did about noon resolve to send Mr. Gibson away after my wife with another 1000 pieces, under colour of an express to Sir Jer. Smith, who is, as I hear, with some ships at Newcastle; which I did really send to him, and may possibly prove of good use to the King; for it is possible, in the hurry of business that they may not think of it at Court, and the charge of express is not considerable to the King. So though I entend Gibson no further then to Hunt-ington, yet I direct him to send the packet forward.

My business the most of the afternoon is listening to everybody that comes to the office, what news, which is variously related, some better, some worse, but nothing certain. The King and Duke of York up and down all the day here and there; some time on Tower hill, where the City Militia was; where the King did make a speech to them that they should venture themselfs no further then he would himself. I also sent (my mind being in pain) Saunders after my wife and father, to overtake them at their night's lodging to see how matters go with them. In the evening I sent for my cousin Sarah and her husband; who came and I did deliver them my chest of writings about Brampton, and my brother Tom's papers and my Journalls, which I value much – and did send my two silver flagons to Kate Joyce's: that so, being scattered what I have, something might be saved. I have also made a girdle, by which with some trouble I do carry about me 300*l* in gold about my body, that I may not be without something in case I should be surprized; for I think, in any nation but ours, people that appear (for we are not endeed so) so faulty as we would have their throats cut. In the evening comes Mr. Pelling and several others to the office, and tell me that never were people so dejected as they are in the City all over at this day, and do talk most loudly, even treason; as, that we are bought and sold, that we are betrayed by the papists and others about the King – cry out that the Office of the Ordinance hath been so backward as no powder to have been at Chatham nor Upner Castle till such a time, and the carriages all broken – that Legg is a papist – that Upner, the old good castle built by Queen Elizabeth, should be lately slighted – that the ships at Chatham should not be carried up higher. They look upon us as lost; and remove their families and rich goods in the City and do think verily that the French, being come down with his army to Dunkirke, it is to invade us – and that we shall be invaded. Mr. Clerke the solicitor comes to me about business, and tells me that he hears that the King hath chosen Mr.

Pierpoint and Vaughan of the West privy councillors – that my Lord Chancellor was affronted in the Hall this day by people telling him of his Dunkirke house – and that there are Regiments ordered to be got together, whereof to be commanders my Lord Fairfax, Ingolsby, Bethell, Norton, and Birch and other presbyterians; and that Dr. Bates will have liberty to preach. Now whether this be true or not, I know not; but do think that nothing but this will unite us together. Late at night comes Mr. Hudson the cooper, my neighbour, and tells me that he came from Chatham this evening at 5 a-clock and saw this afternoon the *Royall James, Oake,* and *London* burnt by the enemy with their fireships; that two or three men-of-war came up with them, and made no more of Upner castle's shooting then of a fly – that these ships lay below Upner Castle (but therein I conceive he is in an error) – that the Dutch are fitting out the *Royall Charles* – that we shot so far as from the yard thither, so that the shot did no good, for the bullets grazed on the water – that Upner played hard with their guns at first, but slowly afterward, either from the men being beat off or their powder spent. But we hear that the fleet in the Hope is not come up any higher the last flood. And Sir W. Batten tells me that ships are provided to sink in the River about Woolwich, that will prevent their coming up higher if they should attempt it. I made my will also this day, and did give all I had equally between my father and wife – and left copies of it in each of Mr. Hater and W. Hewer's hands, who both witnessed the will; and so to supper and then to bed; and slept pretty well, but yet often waking.

14.    A man of Mr. Gawden's came from Chatham last night and saw the three ships burnt, they lying all dry, and boats going from the men-of-war and fire them. But that that he tells me of worst consequence is that he himself (I think he said) did hear many Englishmen on board the Dutch ships, speaking to one another in English, and that they did cry and say, "We did heretofore fight for tickets; now we fight for Dollers!" and did ask how such and such a one did, and would commend themself to them – which is a sad consideration. And several seamen came this morning to me to tell me that if I would get their tickets paid, they would go and do all they could against the Dutch; but otherwise they would not venture being killed and lose all they have already fought for – so that I was forced to try what I could do to get them paid. And endeed, the hearts as well as affections of the seamen are turned away; and in the

open streets in wapping, and up and down, the wifes have cried publicly, "This comes of your not paying our husbands; and now your work is undone, or done by hands that understand it not;" and Sir W. Batten told me that he was himself affronted with a woman in language of this kind himself on tower hill publicly yesterday; and we are fain to bear it – and to keep one at the office-door to let no idle people in, for fear of firing of the office and doing us mischief. The City is troubled at their [trainbands] being put upon duty: summoned one hour and discharged two hours after and then again summoned two hours after that, to their great charge as well as trouble; and Pelling the pothecary tells me the world says all over that less charge then what the kingdom is put to, of one kind or other, by this business, would have set out all our great ships. It is said they did in open streets yesterday, at Westminster, cry, "A Parliament! a Parliament!"; and do believe it will cost blood to answer for these miscarriages. We do not hear that the Duch are come to Gravesend, which is a wonder; but a wonderful thing it is that to this day we have not one word yet from Brouncker or P. Pett or J. Mennes of anything at Chatham; the people that come hither to hear how things go make me ashamed to be found unable to answer them, for I am left alone here at the office; and the truth is, I am glad my station is to be here – near my own home and out of danger, yet in a place of doing the King good service.

I have this morning good news from Gibson; three letters, from three several stages, that he was safe last night as far as Royston at between 9 and 10 at night. The dismay that is upon us all in the business of the kingdom and Navy at this day, is not to be expressed otherwise then by the condition the citizens were in when the City was on fire, nobody knowing which way to turn themselfs, while everything concurred to greaten the fire; as here, the easterly gale and spring-tides, for coming up both rivers and enabling them to break the chain. D. Gawden did tell me yesterday that the day before at the Council, they were ready to fall together by the ears at the council-table, arraigning one another of being guilty of the counsel that brought us into this misery, by laying up all the great ships. Mr. Hater tells me at noon that some rude people have been, as he hears, at my Lord Chancellor's, where they have cut down the trees before his house and broke his windows; and a Gibbet either set up before or painted upon his gate, and these words writ – "Three sights to be seen; Dunkirke, Tanger, and a barren Queen." It gives great matter of talk that it is said there is at this hour in the

Exchequer as much money as is ready to break down the floor. This arises, I believe, from Sir G. Downing's late talk of the greatness of the sum lying there of people's money that they would not fetch away, which he showed me and a great many others. Most people that I speak with are in doubt how we shall do to secure our seamen from running over to the Duch; which is a sad but very true consideration at this day. At noon am told that my Lord Duke of Albemarle is made Lord High Constable; the meaning whereof at this time I know not, nor whether it be true or no. Dined, and Mr. Hater and W. Hewer with me; where they do speak very sorrowfully of the posture of the times, and how people do cry out in the streets of their being bought and sold; and both they and everybody that come to me do tell me that people make nothing of talking treason in the streets openly: as, that we are bought and sold and governed by Papists and that we are betrayed by people about the King and shall be delivered up to the French, and I know not what. At dinner we discoursed of Tom-of-the-Wood, a fellow that lives like a Hermit near Woolwich, who as they say (and Mr. Bodham, they tell me, affirms that he was by at the Justice's when some did accuse him there for it) [did] foretell the burning of the City, now says that a greater desolation is at hand. Thence we read and laughed at Lillys prophecies this month – in his almanac this year. So to the office after dinner; and thither comes Mr. Pierce, who tells me his condition: how he cannot get his money (about 500*l*, which he says is a very great part of what he hath for his family and children) out of Viner's hand – and endeed, it is to be feared that this will wholly undo the banquiers. He says he knows nothing of the late affronts to my Lord Chancellors house as is said, nor hears of the Duke of Albemarle's being made High Constable; but says that they are in great distraction at Whitehall – and that everywhere people do speak high against Sir W. Coventry; but he agrees with me that he is the best Minister of State the King hath, and so from my heart I believe.

At night came home Sir W. Batten and Sir W. Penn, who only can tell me that they have placed guns at Woolwich and Deptford and sunk some ships below Woolwich and Blackwall, and are in hopes that they will stop the enemy's coming up. But strange our confusion; that among them that are sunk they have gone and sunk without consideration the *Franckin*, one of the King's ships, with stores to a very considerable value, that hath been long loaden for supply of the ships and the new ship at Bristoll, and much wanted there – and nobody will own that they directed it, but do lay it on Sir W. Rider; they speak also of another ship, loaden to the value of 80000*l*, sunk with the goods in her, or at least was mighily contended for by him, and a foreign ship that had the faith of the nation for her security; this Sir R. Ford tells us. And it is too plain a truth, that both here and at Chatham the ships that we have sunk have many, and the first of them, been ships completely fitted for fireships at great charge. But most strange, the backwardness and disorder of all people, especially the King's people in pay, to do any work (Sir W. Penn tells me), all crying out for money. And it was so at Chatham, that this night comes an order from Sir W. Coventry to stop the pay of the wages of that Yard, the Duke of Albemarle having related that not above three of 1100 in pay there did attend to do any work there. This evening, having sent a messenger to Chatham on purpose, we have received a dull letter from my Lord Brouncker and P. Pett how matters have gone there this week; but not so much, or so perticular as we knew it by common talk before, and as true. I doubt they will be found to have been but slow men in this business; and they say the Duke of Albemarle did tell my Lord Brouncker to his face that his discharging of the great ships there was the cause of all this; and I am told that it is become common talk against my Lord Brouncker, but in that he is to be justified, for he did it by verball order from Sir W. Coventry, and with good intent; and was to good purpose, whatever the success* be, for the men would have but spent the King so much the more in wages, and yet not attended on board to have done the King any service. And this morning also, some of the *Cambriges* men came up from Portsmouth by order from Sir Fre. Hollis, who boasted to us the other day that he had sent for 50, and would be hanged if 100 did not come up, that would do as much as twice the number of other men: I say some of them, instead of being at work at Deptford where they were intended, do come to the office this morning to demand the payment of their tickets, for otherwise they would, they said, do no more work; and are, as I understand from everybody that have do with them, the most debauched, damning, swearing rogues that ever were in the Navy, just like their profane commander. So to W. Batten's to sit and talk a little; and then home to my flagelette, my heart being at pretty good ease by a letter from my wife, brought by Saunders, that my father and wife got well last night to their Inne and out again this morning, and Gibson's being got safe to Caxton at 12 last night. So to supper, and then to bed. No news today of any motion of the enemy, either upwards towards Chatham or this way.

15. All the morning at the office. No news more then last night; only, Purser Tyler comes and tells me that he being at all the passages in this business at Chatham, he says there have been horrible miscarriages, such as we shall shortly hear of. That the want of boats hath undone us; and it is commonly said, and Sir J. Mennes under his hand tells us, that they were imployed by the men of the Yard to carry away their goods; and I hear that Comissioner Pett will be found the first man that begun to remove; he is much spoken against – and Brouncker is complained of and reproached for discharging the men of the great ships heretofore. At noon Mr. Hater dined with me, and tells me he believes that it will hardly be the want of money alone that will excuse to the Parliament the neglect of not setting out a fleet, it having never been [harbour-] bound in our greatest straits; but how[ever] unlikely that it appeared, yet when it was gone about, the State or King did compass it; and there is something in it. In like manner, all the afternoon busy, vexed to see how slowly things go on for want of money. At night comes (unexpectedly so soon) Mr. Gibson, who left my wife well and all got down well with them, but not with himself, who (which I was afeared of and cannot blame him, but must myself be wiser against another time) had one of his bags broke through his breeches. And some pieces dropped out, not many (he thinks but two, for he light and took them up, and went back and could find no more); but I am not able to tell how many, which troubles me; but the joy of having the greatest part safe there makes me bear with it, so as not to afflict myself for it. This afternoon, poor Betty Michell, whom I love, sent to tell my wife her child was dying; which I am troubled for, poor girl. At night home and to my flagelette; played with pleasure, but with a heavy heart; only, it pleased me to think how it may please God I may live to spend my time in the country with plainness and pleasure, though but with little glory. So to supper and to bed.

18. To the office; and by and by word was brought me that Comissioner Pett is brought to the Tower and there laid up close prisoner – which puts me into a fright, lest they may do the same with us as they do with him. This puts me upon hastening what I am doing with my people, and collecting out of my papers our

defence. Myself got Fist, Sir W. Batten's clerk, and busy with him writing letters late; and then home to supper and to read myself asleep, after piping; and so to bed.

19.    Up and to the office, where all the morning busy with Fist again, beginning early to overtake my business in my letters, which for a post or two have by the late and present troubles been interrupted. At noon comes Sir W. Batten and W. Penn, and we to W. Penn's house and there discoursed of business an hour; and by and by comes an order from Sir R. Browne, commanding me this afternoon to attend the Council board with all my books and papers touching the Medway. I was ready [to fear] some mischief to myself, though that that appears most reasonable is that it is to inform them about Comissioner Pett. I eat a little bit in haste at W. Batten's without much comfort, being fearful, though I show it not; and to my office and did get up some papers and find out the most material letters and orders in our books. And so took coach and to the Council chamber lobby, where I met Mr. Eveling, who doth miserably decry our follies that brings all this misery upon us. While we were discoursing over our public misfortunes, I am called in to a large committee of the Council: present, the Duke of Albemarle, Anglesy, Arlington, Ashly, Carteret, Duncomb, Coventry, Ingram, Clifford, Lauderdale, Morice, Manchester, Craven, Carlisle, Bridgewater; and after Sir W. Coventry's telling them what orders his Royal Highness had made for the safety of the Medway, I told them to great full content what we had done, and showed them our letters. Then was P. Pett call[ed] in with the Lieutenant of the Tower. He is in his old clothes, and looked most sillily. His charge was chiefly the not carrying up of the great ships, and the using of the boats in carrying away his goods; in which he answered very sillily – though his faults to me seem only great omissions. Lord Arlington and Coventry very severe against him; the former saying that if he was not guilty, the world would think them all guilty. The latter urged that there must be some fault, and that the Admiral must be found to have done his part. He said he used never a boat till they were all gone but one – and that was to carry away things of great value, and those were his models of ships; which when the Council, some of them, had said they wished that the Dutch had had them instead of the King's ships, he answered he did believe the Dutch would have made more advantage of the models then of the ships, and the King have had

greater loss thereby. This they all laughed at. After having heard him for an hour or more, they bid him withdraw, I all this while showing him no respect, but rather against him; for which God forgive me, for I mean no hurt to him, but only find that these Lords are upon their own purgation, and it is necessary I should be so in behalf of the office. He being gone, they caused Sir Rd. Browne to read over his minutes; and then my Lord Arlington moved that they might be put into my hands to put into form, I being more acquainted with such business; and they were so.

So I away back with my books and papers; and when I got into the Court, it was pretty to see how people gazed upon me – that I thought myself obliged to salute people and to smile, lest they should think I was a prisoner too; but afterward I found the most did take me to be there to bear evidence against P. Pett. But my fear was such, at my going in, of the success of the day, that at my going in I did think fit to give T. Hater (whom I took with me to wait the event) my closet-key and directions where to find 500*l* and more in silver and gold, and my tallies, to remove in case of any misfortune to me. I got home; and I and my wife to talk; who did give me so bad an account of her and my father's method in burying of our gold, that made me mad – and she herself is not pleased with it, she believing that my sister knows of it. My father and she did it on Sunday when they were gone to church, in open daylight in the midst of the garden, where for aught they knew, many eyes might see them; which put me into such trouble, that I was almost mad about it, and presently cast about how to have it back again to secure it here, the times being a little better now; at least, at Whitehall they seem as if they were – but one way or other, I am resolved to free them from the place if I can get them. Such was my trouble at this, that I fell out with my wife; that though new come to town, I did not sup with her nor speak to her tonight, but to bed and sleep.

21.    Sir H. Cholmly came to me this day, and tells me the Court is as mad as ever and that the night the Duch burned our ships, the King did sup with my Lady Castlemayne at the Duchess of Monmouth, and there were all mad in hunting of a poor moth. All the Court afeared of a Parliament; but he thinks nothing can save us but the King's giving up all to a Parliament.

22.    In the evening came Capts. Hart and Hayword, and in talk

they told me about the taking of *Royall Charles*; that nothing but carelessness lost the ship, for they might have saved her the very tide that the Duch came up, if they would have but used means and had had but boats, and that the want of boats plainly lost all the other ships. That the Duch did take her with a boat of nine Men, who found not a man on board her (and her laying so near them was a main temptation to them to come on); and presently a man went up and struck her flag and Jacke, and a trumpeter sounded upon her "Joan's placket is torn." That they did carry her down at a time, both for tides and wind, when the best pilot in Chatham would not have undertaken it, they heeling her on one side to make her draw little water, and so carried her away safe. They being gone, by and by comes Sir W. Pen home, and he and I together talking. He tells me that it is most manifest that one great thing making it impossible for us to have set out a fleet this year (if we could have done it for money or stores) was the liberty given the beginning of the year for the setting out of merchantmen, which did take up, as is said, above 10 if not 15000 seamen (and this the other day Capt. Cocke tells me appears in the council-books; that is, the number of seamen required to man the merchant ships that had passes to go abroad); by and by, my wife being here, they sat down and eat a bit of their nasty victuals, and so parted and we to bed.

24. Up, and to the office, where much business upon me by the coming of people of all sorts about the despatch of one business or other of the fireships or other ships to be set out now. This morning Greeting came, and I with him at my flagelette. At noon dined at home with my wife alone; and then in the afternoon, all the day at my office – troubled a little at a letter from my father which tells me of an idle companion, one Coleman, who went down with him and my wife in the coach and came up again with my wife, a pensioner of the King's Guard and one that my wife, endeed, made the feast for on Saturday last, though he did not come; but if he knows nothing of our money, I will prevent any other inconvenience. In the evening comes Mr. Povy about business, and he and I to walk in the garden an hour or two and to talk of State matters; he tells me his opinion that it is out of possibility for us to escape being undone, there being nothing in our power to do that is necessary for the saving us – a lazy prince – no council – no money; no reputation at home or abroad. He says that to this day the King doth fallow the women as much as ever he did. That the Duke of York hath not got

Mrs. Middleton, as I was told the other day; but says that he wants not her, for he hath others and hath alway had, and that he hath known them brought through the Matted Gallery at Whitehall into his closet. Nay, he hath come out of his wife's bed and gone to others laid in bed for him. That Mr. Brouncker is not the only pimp, but that the whole family is of the same strain, and will do anything to please him. That, besides the death of the two princes lately, the family is in horrible disorder by being in debt, by spending above 60000*l* per annum when he hath not 40000*l*. That the Duchesse is not only the proudest woman in the world, but the most expenseful; and that the Duke of York's marriage with her hath undone the kingdom by making the Chancellor so great above reach, who otherwise would have been but an ordinary man, to have been dealt with by other people, and he would have been careful of managing things well, for fear of being called to account; whereas now, he is secure and hath let things run to wrack, as they now appear.

He tells me that the other day, upon this ill news of the Duch being upon us, Whitehall was shut up and the Council called and sat close (and by the way he doth assure me, from the mouth of some privy councillors, that at this day the Privy council in general doth know no more what the state of the kingdom as to peace and war is then he or I, nor knows who manages it nor upon whom it depends); and there my Lord Chancellor did make a speech to them, saying that they knew well that he was no friend to the war from the beginning, and therefore had concerned himself little in, nor could say much to it; and a great deal of that kind, to discharge himself of the fault of the war – upon which, my Lord Anglesy rose up and told his Majesty that he thought their coming now together was not to enquire who was or was not the cause of the war, but to enquire what was or could be done in the business of making a peace, and in whose hands that was and where it was stopped or forwarded; and went on very highly to have all made open to them: he tells me, speaking of the horrid effeminacy of the King, that the King hath taken ten times more care and pains making friends between my Lady Castlemayne and Mrs. Steward when they have fallen out, then ever he did to save his kingdom. That the King is at this day every night in Hyde park with the Duke of Monmouth or with my Lady Castlemaine. Having done all this discourse and concluded the Kingdom in a desperate condition, we parted; and I to my wife, with whom was Mercer and Betty Michell; we sat in the garden together a while, it being night; and then Mercer and I a song or two, and then in (the Michells home), my wife, Mercer and I, to supper; and then parted and to bed.

27.     Wakened this morning about 3 a-clock by Mr. Griffin, with a letter from Sir W. Coventry to W. Penn (which W. Penn sent me to see) that the Dutch are come up to the Nore again, and he knows not whether further or no – and would have, therefore, several things done: ships sunk, and I know not what; which Sir W. Penn (who it seems is very ill this night, or would be thought so) hath directed Griffin to carry to the Trinity house; so he went away with the letter, and I tried and with much ado did get a little sleep more; and so up about 6 a-clock, full of thought what to do with the little money I have left, and my plate, wishing with all my heart that that was all secured. So to the office, where much business all the morning, and the more by my Brethren being all out of the way; Sir W. Penn this night taken so ill, cannot stir – W. Batten ill at Walthamstow – Sir J. Mennes the like at Chatham; and my Lord Brouncker there also upon business – horrible trouble with the backwardness of the merchants to let us have their ships, and seamen's running away and not to be got or kept without money. It is worth turning to our letters this day to Sir W. Coventry about these matters. At noon to dinner, having a haunch of venison boiled, and all my clerks at dinner with me; and mightily taken with Mr. Gibson's discourse of the faults of this war in its management compared [with] that in the last war, which I will get him to put into writing. Thence after dinner to the office again, and there I saw the proclamations come out this day, for the Parliament to meet the 25th of next month; for which God be praised – and another to invite seamen to bring in their complaints of their being ill-used in the getting their tickets and money – there being a committee of the Council appointed to receive their complaints. Pierce tells me that all the town doth cry out of our office for a pack of fools and knaves, but says that everybody speaks either well, or at least the best, of me, which is my great comfort and I do think I do deserve it and shall show I have; but yet do think, and he also, that the Parliament will send us all going; and I shall be well contented with it, God knows. News this tide, that about 80 sail of Duch, great and small, were seen coming up the River this morning; and this tide, some of them to the upper end of the Hope.

28.   They do tell me that the Duke of Buckingham hath surren-
dered himself to Secretary Morrice and is going to the Tower. Mr.
Fenn at the table says that he hath been taken by the Wach two or
three times of late at unseasonable hours, but so disguised that they
could not know him (and when I came home by and by, Mr.
Lowther tells me that the Duke of Buckingham doth dine publicly
this day at Wadlow's at the Sun tavern and is mighty merry, and
sent word to the Lieutenant of the Tower that he would come to
him as soon as he had dined). Now, how sad a thing it is when we
come to make sport of proclaiming men traitors and banishing
them, and putting them out of their offices and Privy Council, and
of sending to and going to the Tower: God have mercy on us. At
table, my Lady and Sir Phill. Carteret have great and good
discourse of the greatness of the present King of France; what great
things he hath done, that a man may pass at any hour in the night all
over that wild city, with a purse in his hand and no danger. That
there is not a beggar to be seen in it, nor dirt lying in it. That he hath
married two of Colberts daughters to two of the greatest princes of
France, and given them portions. Bought the greatest Dukedome
in France and given it to Colbert, and ne'er a prince in France dare
whisper against it; whereas here, our King cannot do any such thing
but everybody's mouth is open against him for it, and the man that
hath the favour also. But then they did enlarge upon the slavery of
the people: that they are taxed more then the real estates they have;
nay, it is an ordinary thing for people to desire to give the King all
their land that they have, and themselfs become only their tenants
and pay him rent to the full value for it, so they may have but their
earnings. After dinner Sir G. Carteret came in, and I to him and my
Lady and there he did tell me that the business was done between
him and my Lord Anglesy: that himself is to have the other's place
of Deputy Treasurer of Ireland (which is a place of honour and great
profit, being far better (I know not by what reason but a reason
there is) then the Treasurer's, my Lord of Corke's) and to give the
other his of Treasurer of the Navy. That the King, at his earnest
entreaty, did with much unwillingness, but with owning of great
obligations to him for his faithful and long service to him and his
father; and therefore was willing to grant his desire.

Having done this discourse with Sir G. Carteret and signified my
great satisfaction in it, which they seem to look upon as something,
I went away; and by coach home and there find my wife making of
Tea, a drink which Mr. Pelling the pothecary tells her is good for

her for her cold and defluxions. We hear that the Dutch are gone
down again; and thanks be to God, the trouble they give us this
second time is not very considerable.

29.    Up, having had many ugly dreams tonight – of my father and
my sister and mother's coming to us and meeting my wife and me
at the gate of the office going out – they all in laced suits, and come,
they told me, to be with me this May day. My mother told me she
lacked a pair of gloves, and I remembered a pair of my wife's in my
chamber and resolved she should have them. But then recollected
how my mother came to be here when I was in mourning for her;
and so thinking it to be a mistake in our thinking her all this while
dead, I did contrive that it should be said to any that enquired, that it
was my mother-in-law, my wife's mother, that was dead and we in
mourning for. This dream troubled me and I waked.

# ✳ JULY ✳

2.    Up, and put on my new silk Camelott suit, made of my cloak,
and suit now made into a vest. So to the office, where W. Penn and
myself and Sir T. Harvy met, the first time we have had a meeting
since the coming of the Dutch upon the coast. Our only business
(for we have little else to do, nobody being willing to trust us for
anything) was to speak with the owners of six merchantmen which
we have been taking up this fortmight, and are yet in no readiness,
they not fitting their ships without money advanced to them, we
owing them for what their ships have earned the last year. This day
I am told that poor Tooker is dead, a very painful poor man as ever I
knew.

3.    Up, and within most of the morning, my tailor's boy coming
to alter something in my new suit I put on yesterday. Then to the
office and did business, and then (my wife being a little ill of those in
the bed) I to Sir W. Batten's and dined, and there comes in Sir Rd.
Ford and tells us how he hath been at the Session's house, and there
it is plain that there is a combination of rogues in the town that do
make it their business to set houses on fire, and that one house they
did set on fire in Aldersgate street last Easter, and that this is proved
by two young men, whom one of them debauched by degrees to

steal their father's plate and clothes, and at last to be of their company, and they had their places to take up what goods were flung into the streets out of the windows when the houses were on fire; and this is like to be proved to a great number of rogues, whereof five are already found, and some found guilty this day. Then by water to Whitehall (calling at Michells in my way, but the rogue would not invite me in, I having a mind para ver his wife); and there to the Council chamber to deliver a letter to their Lordships about the state of the six merchantmen which we have been so long fitting out. When I came, the King and the whole tableful of Lords were hearing of a pitiful cause of a complaint of an old man, with a great gray beard, against his son, for not allowing himself something to live on; and at last came to the ordering the son to allow his father 10*l* a year. This cause lasted them near two hours; which methinks, at this time to be the work of the Council board of England, is a scandalous thing, and methought Sir W. Coventry to me did own as much. Here I find all the news is the enemy's landing 3000 men near Harwich, and attacquing Langner-fort and being beat off thence with our great guns, killing some of their men and they leaving their lathers behind them; but we had no Horse in the way on Suffolke side, otherwise we might have galled their Foot. The Duke of York is gone down thither this day, while the Generall sat sleeping this afternoon at the Council table. The news so much talked of this Exchange, of a peace, I find by Sir Rd. Browne arises from a letter the Swedes agent hath received from Bredah, and showed at Court today, that they are come very near it, but I do not find anybody here relying on it. This cause being over, the Trinity house men, whom I did not expect to meet, were called in; and there Sir W. Pen made a formal speech in answer to a Question of the King's, whether the lying of the sunk ships in the River would spoil the River; but Lord, how gingerly he answered it, and with a deal of do, that he did not know whether it would be safe as to the enemy to have them taken up, but that doubtless it would be better for the River to have them taken up. Methought the Council found them answer like fools, and it ended in bidding them think more of it and bring their answer in writing.

Thence I to Westminster hall and there hear how they talk against the present management of things, and against Sir W. Coventry for his bringing in of new commanders and casting out the old seamen; which I did endeavour to rectify Mr. Michell and them in, letting them know that he hath opposed it all his life, the most of any man in England. After a deal of this bibble babble, I to Mrs. Martins and there she was gone in before; but when I came, contrary to my expectation, I find her all in trouble, and what was it for but that I have got her with child, for those do not venir upon her as they should have done; and is in exceeding grief, and swears that the child is mine; which I do not believe, but yet do comfort her that either it can[not] be so; or if it be, that I will take care to send for her husband, though I do hardly see how I can be sure of that, the ship being at sea and as far as Scotland; but however, I must do it, and shall find some way or other of doing it, though it doth trouble me not a little.

6. Up and to the office, where some of us sat busy all the morning. At noon home to dinner, whither Creed came to dine with us and brings the first word I hear of the news of a peace, the King having letters come to him this noon, signifying that it is concluded on. The news was so good and sudden, that I went with great joy to W. Batten and then to W. Penn to tell it them; and so home to dinner, mighty merry and light at my heart only on this ground, that a continuing of the war must undo us, and so, though peace may do the like, if we do not make good use of it to reform ourselfs and get up money, yet there is an opportunity for us to save ourselfs – at least, for my own perticular, we shall continue well till I can get my money into my hands, and then I will shift for myself. After dinner away, leaving Creed there, by coach to Westminster, where to the Swan and drank; and then to the Hall and there talked a little, with great joy of the peace; and then to Mrs. Martins, where I met with the good news que esta no es con child, she having de estos upon her – the fear of which, which she did give me the other day, had troubled me much. My joy in this made me send for wine, and thither came her sister and Mrs. Cragg and I stayed a good while there. But here happened the best instance of a woman's falseness in the world; that her sister Doll, who went for a bottle of wine, did come home all blubbering and swearing against one Capt. Vandena, a Dutchman of the Rhenish winehouse, that pulled her into a stable by the Dog tavern and there did tumble her and toss her; calling him all the rogues and toads in the world, when she knows that ella hath suffered me to do anything with her a hundred times.

7. *Lords day*. Up; and to my chamber, there to settle some papers;

and thither comes Mr. Moore to me and talked till church-time of the news of the times about the peace, and the bad consequences of it if it be not improved to good purpose of fitting ourselfs for another war. He tells me he hears that the discontented Parliament-men are fearful that the next sitting the King will put for a general Excize, by which to raise him money, and then to fling off the Parliament, and raise a land-army and keep them all down like slaves; and it is gotten among them that Bab. May, the Privy Purse, hath been heard to say that 300*l* a year is enough for any country gentleman; which makes them mad, and they do talk of 6 or 800000*l* gone into the Privy Purse this war, when in King James's time it arose but to 5000*l* and in King Charles's but 10000*l* in a year. He tells me that a goldsmith in town told him, that being with some plate with my Lady Castlemaine lately, she directed her woman (the great beauty), "Willson," says she, "make a note for this and for that to the Privy purse for money." Busy till noon and then home to dinner and Mr. Moore come and dined with us, and much more discourse at and after dinner of the same kind; and then he gone, I to my office, busy till the evening; and then with my wife and Jane over to Halfway house, a very good walk, and there drank; and in the cool of the evening back again, and sang with pleasure upon the water and were mightily pleased in hearing a boat full of spaniards sing; and so home to supper and to bed. Jane of late mighty fine, by reason of a laced whiske her mistress hath given her, which makes her a very gracefull servant. But above all, my wife and I were the most surprized in the beauty of a plain girle which we met in the little lane going from Redriffe stairs into the fields, one of the prettiest faces that we think we ever saw in our lives.

8.   Up and to my chamber; and by and by comes Greeting, and to my flagelette with him with a pretty deal of pleasure; and then to the office, where W. Batten, W. Penn and I met about putting men to work for the weighing of the ships in the River sunk. Then home again and there heard Mr. Cæsar play some very good things on the lute, together with myself on the viall and Greeting on the viallin. Then with my wife abroad by coach, she to her tailor's, I to Westminster to Burges about my Tanger business; and thence to Whitehall, where I spoke with Sir John Nicholas, who tells me that Mr. Coventry is come from Bredah as was expected; but I perceive the certainty of peace is blown over. So called on my wife and met

Creed by the way, and they two and I to Charing cross, there to see the great Boy and Girle that are lately come out of Ireland; the latter, eight, the former four years old, of most prodigious bigness for their age. I tried to weigh them in my arms, and find them twice as heavy as people almost twice their age; and yet I am apt to believe they are very young – their father a little sorry fellow, and their mother an old Irish woman. They have had four children of this bigness and four of ordinary growth, whereof two of each are dead. If (as my Lord Ormond certifies) it be true that they are no older, it is very monstrous. So home and to dinner with my wife, and to pipe. And then I to the office, where busy all the afternoon till the evening; and then with my wife by coach abroad to Bow and Stratford, it being so dusty weather, that there was little pleasure in it; and so home and to walk in the garden, and thither comes Pelling to us to talk; and so in and to supper, and then to bed – all the world being, as I hear, very much damped that their hopes of peace is become uncertain again.

9.   Up pretty betimes and to the office, where busy till office time; and then we sat, but nothing to do but receive clamours about money. This day my Lord Anglesy, our new Treasurer, came the first time to the Board, and there sat with us till noon; and I do perceive he is a very notable man and understanding, and will do things regular and understand them himself, not trust Fenn as Sir G. Carteret did, and will solicit soundly for money; which I do fear was Sir G. Carteret's fault, that he did not do that enough, considering the age we live in, that nothing will do but by solicitation – though never so good for the King or Kingdom; and a bad business well solicited shall for peace sake speed, when a good one shall not. But I do confess I do think it a very bold act of him to take upon him the place of Treasurer of the Navy at this time; but when I consider that a regular accountant* never ought to fear anything, nor have reason, I then do cease to wonder. At noon home to dinner and to play on the flagelette with my wife; and then to the office, where very busy, close at my office till late at night; at night walked and sang with my wife in the garden, and so home to supper and to bed. This evening news comes for certain that the Dutch are with their fleet before Dover, and that it is expected they will attempt something there. The business of the peace is quite dashed again, so as now it is doubtful whether the King will condescend to what the Dutch demand, it being so near the

Parliament, it being a thing that will, it may be, recommend him to them when they shall find that the not having of a peace lies on his side, by denying some of their demands.

11. Up betimes and to my office, and there busy till the office (which was only Sir T. Harvy and myself) met; and did little business and then broke up. He tells me that the Council last night did sit close, to determine of the King's answer about the peace; and that though he doth not certainly know, yet by all discourse yesterday, he doth believe it is peace; and that the King had said it should be peace and had bidden Ald. Backewell to declare upon the Change.

12. After dinner to St. James's, but missed Sir W. Coventry; and so home and there find my wife in a dogged humour for my not dining at home, and I did give her a pull by the nose and some ill words, which she provoked me to by something she spoke, that we fell extraordinarily out; insomuch, that I going to the office to avoid further anger, she fallowed me in a devilish manner thither, and with much ado I got her into the garden out of hearing, to prevent shame; and so home, and by degrees I found it necessary to calme her, and did; and then to the office, where pretty late, and then to walk with her in the garden, and so to supper and pretty good friends; and so to bed – with my mind very quiet.

13. Up pretty betimes, it being mighty hot weather and I lying this night (which I have not done I believe since a boy; I am sure not since before I had the stone before) with only a rugg and sheet upon me. To my chamber, and my wife up to do something and by chance we fell out again; but I to the office, and there we did at the board much business, though the most was the dividing of 5000*l* (which the Lords Comissioners have with great difficulty found upon our letter to them this week that would have required 50000*l*) among a great many occasions. After rising, my Lord Anglesy, this being the second time of his being with us, did take me aside and asked me where I lived, because he would be glad to have some discourse with me. This I liked well enough, and told him I would wait upon him, which I will do; and so all broke up, and I home to dinner, where Mr. Pierce dined with us; who tells us what troubles me, that my Lord Buckhurst hath got Nell away from the King's House, lies with her, and gives her 100*l* a year, so as she hath sent

her parts to the House and will act no more. And yesterday Sir Tho. Crew told me that Lacy lies a-dying of the pox, and yet hath his whore by him; whom he will have to look on, he says, though he can do no more; nor would receive any ghostly advice from a Bishop, an old acquaintance of his that went to see him. He says there is a strangeness between the King and my Lady Castlemayne, as I was told yesterday.

14. *Lords day.* Up, and my wife, a little before 4, and to make us ready; and by and by Mrs. Turner came to us by agreement, and she and I stayed talking below while my wife dressed herself; which vexed me that she was so long about it, keeping us till past 5 a-clock before she was ready. She ready, and taking some bottles of wine and beer and some cold Fowle with us into the Coach, we took coach and four horses which I had provided last night, and so away – a very fine day; and so towards Epsum, talking all the way pleasantly. The country very fine; only, the way very dusty. We got to Epsum by 8 a-clock to the Well, where much company; and there we light and I drank the water; they did not, but do go about and walk a little among the women, but I did drink four pints and had some very good stools by it. Here I met with divers of our town; among others, with several of the tradesmen of our office, but did talk but little with them, it growing hot in the sun; and so we took coach again and to the Towne to the King's Head, where our coachman carried us; and there had an ill room for us to go into, but the best in the house that was not taken up; here we called for drink and bespoke dinner. And hear that my Lord Buckhurst and Nelly is lodged at the next house, and Sir Ch. Sidly with them, and keep a merry house. Poor girl, I pity her; but more the loss of her at the King's House. W. Hewers rode with us, and I left him and the women, and myself walked to church, where few people (contrary to what I expected) and none I knew but all the Houblons brothers; and them after sermon I did salute and walk with towards my Inne, which was in their way to their lodgings. They came last night to see their elder brother, who stays here at the waters, and away tomorrow. James did tell me that I was the only happy man of the Navy; of whom, he says, during all this freedom the people have taken of speaking treason, he hath not heard one bad word of me – which is a great joy to me, for I hear the same of others; but do know that I have deserved as well as most. We parted, to meet anon; and I to my women into a better room, which the people of the

house borrowed for us; and there to dinner, a good dinner, and were merry; and Pendleton came to us, who happened to be in the house, and there talked and were merry.

After dinner, he gone, we all lay down after dinner (the day being wonderful hot) to sleep, and each of us took a good nap and then rose; and Tom Willson came to see me and sat and talked an hour, and I perceive he hath been much acquainted with Dr. Fuller (Tom) and Dr. Pierson and several of the great Cavalier parsons during the late troubles; and I was glad to hear him talk of them, which he did very ingeniously, and very much of Dr. Fullers art of memory, which he did tell me several instances of. By and by he parted, and we took coach and to take the ayre, there being a fine breeze abroad; and I went and carried them to the Well and there filled some bottles of water to carry home with me. Here W. Hewer's horse broke loose, and we had the sport to see him taken again. Then I carried them to see my Cosen Pepys's house; and light and walked round about it, and they like it (as endeed it deserves) very well, and is a pretty place; and then I walked them to the wood hard by and there got them in in the thickets, till they had lost themselfs and I could not find the way into any of the walks in the wood, which endeed are very pleasant if I could have found them. At last got out of the wood again; and I, by leaping down the little bank coming out of the wood, did sprain my right foot, which brought me great present pain; but presently, with walking, it went away for the present, and so the women and W. Hewer and I walked upon the Downes, where a flock of sheep was, and the most pleasant and innocent sight that ever I saw in my life; we find a shepheard and his little boy reading, far from any houses or sight of people, the Bible to him. So I made the boy read to me, which he did with the forced Tone that children do usually read, that was mighty pretty; and then I did give him something and went to the father and talked with him; and I find he had been a servant in my Cosen Pepys's house, and told me what was become of their old servants. He did content himself mightily in my liking his boy's reading and did bless God for him, the most like one of the old Patriarchs that ever I saw in my life, and it brought those thoughts of the old age of the world in my mind for two or three days after. We took notice of his woolen knit stockings of two colours mixed, and of his shoes shod with Iron shoes, both at the toe and heels, and with great nails in the soles of his feet, which was mighty pretty; and taking notice of them, "Why," says the poor man, "the Downes, you see, are full of stones, and we are fain to shoe ourselfs thus; and these," says he, "will make the stones fly till they sing before me." I did give the poor man something, for which he was mighty thankful, and I tried to cast stones with his Horne Crooke. He values his dog mightily, that would turn a sheep any way which he would have him when he goes to fold them. Told me there was about 18 Scoare sheep in his flock, and that he hath 4s. a week the year round for keeping of them. So we parted thence, with mighty pleasure in the discourse we had with this poor man; and Mrs. Turner, in the common fields here, did gather one of the prettiest nosegays that ever I saw in my life.

So to our coach, and through Mr. Minnes's wood and looked upon Mr. Eveling's house; and so over the common and through Epsum towne to our Inne, in the way stopping a poor woman with her milk-pail and in one of my gilt Tumblers did drink our bellyfuls of milk, better then any Creame; and so to our Inne and there had a dish of creame, but it was sour and so had no pleasure in it; and so paid our reckoning and took coach, it being about 7 at night, and passed and saw the people walking with their wifes and children to take the ayre; and we set out for home, the sun by and by going down, and we in the cool of the evening all the way with much pleasure home, talking and pleasing ourselfs with the pleasure of this day's work; and Mrs. Turner mightily pleased with my resolution, which I tell her is never to keep a country-house, but to keep a coach and with my wife on the Saturday to go sometimes for a day to this place and then quite to another place; and there is more variety, and as little charge and no trouble, as there is in a country-house. Anon it grew dark, and as it grew dark we had pleasure to see several Glow wormes, which was mighty pretty. But my foot begins more and more to pain me; which Mrs. Turner, by keeping her warm hand upon it, did much ease; but so that when we came home, which was just at 11 at night, I was not able to walk from the lane's end to my house without being helped, which did trouble me; and therefore to bed presently; but thanks be to God, found that I had not been missed nor any business happened in my absence; so to bed and there had a cere-cloth laid to my foot; and lay alone, but in great pain all night long.

21. *Lords day.* Up betimes, and all the morning [in my chamber]; and then to dinner with my wife alone, and then all the afternoon in like manner in my chamber, making up my Tanger accounts and

drawing a letter, which I have done at last to my full content, to present to the Lords Commissioners for Tanger tomorrow. And about 7 at night, when finished my letter and weary, I and my wife and Mercer up by water to Barne elmes, where we walked by Mooneshine; and called at Lambeth and drank, and had cold meat in the boat, and did eat and sang, and down home by almost 12 at night, very fine and pleasant; only, could not sing ordinary songs with that freedom that otherwise I would. Here Mercer tells me that the pretty maid of the Ship tavern I spoke of yesterday is married there, which I am glad of. So having spent this night with much serious pleasure, to consider that I am in a condition to fling away an angell in such a refreshment to myself and family, we home and to bed, leaving Mercer by the way at her own door.

22. Up, and with Sir W. Batten and J. Mennes to St. James's, where the first time I have been there since the enemy's being with us. Where little business but lack of money, which now is so professed by Sir W. Coventry as nothing is more, and the King's whole business owned to be at a stand for want of it. So up to my Lord Chancellors, where was a Committee of Tanger in my Lord's Roome where he is to hear causes, where all the Judges' pictures hang up very fine. Here I read my letter to them, which was well received and they did fall seriously to discourse the want of money and other perticulars, and to some pretty good purpose. But to see how Sir W. Coventry did oppose both my Lord Chancellor and the Duke of York himself, about the order of the Commissioners of the Treasury to me for not paying of Pensions, and with so much reason and eloquence, so natural, was admirable – and another thing, about his pressing for the reduction of the charge of Tanger, which they would have put off to another time; "But," says [he], "the King suffers so much by the putting off of the consideration of reductions of charge, that he is undone; and therefore I do pray you, Sir," (to his Royal Highness) "that when anything offers of that kind, you will not let it scape you." I perceive they do all profess their expectation of a peace, and that suddenly; and do advise of things accordingly – and do all speak of it (and expressly I remember the Duke of Albemarle) saying that they hoped for it.

23. Up betimes and to the office, doing something towards our great account to [the] Lords Commissioners of the Treasury; and anon the office sat, and all the morning doing business. At noon

home to dinner and then close to my business all the afternoon.

24.   I to my office, and there hard at work all the morning, to my
great content, abstracting the contract Booke in into my abstract
book; which I have by reason of the war omitted for above two
years, but now am endeavouring to have all my books ready and
perfect against the Parliament comes, that upon examination I may
be in condition to value myself upon my perfect doing of my own
duty. At noon home to dinner, where my wife mighty musty, but I
took no notice of it; but after dinner to the office, and there with
Mr. Harper did another good piece of work about my late
collection of the accounts of the Navy presented to the Parliament
at their last session, which was left unfinished and now I have done
it, which sets my mind at my ease. And so having tired myself, I
took a pair of oares about 5 a-clock, which I made a gally at Redriffe; and so with very much pleasure down to Gravesend, all the
way with extraordinary content reading of Boyl's *Hydrostatickes*;
which the more I read and understand, the more I admire as a most
excellent piece of philosophy.

25.   Up, and to the office, where we sat all the morning. At noon
home to dinner and there sang with much pleasure with my wife;
and so to the office again and busy all the afternoon. At night, Sir
W. Batten, W. Penn and myself and Sir R. Ford did meet in the
garden. I demanded of Sir R. Ford and the rest what passed today at
the meeting of the Parliament – who told me, that contrary to all
expectation by the King that there would be but a thin meeting,
there met above 300 this first day, and all the discontented party;
and endeed, the whole House seems to be no other almost. The
Speaker told them, as soon as they were sat, that he was ordered by
the King to let them know he was hindered by some important
business to come to them and speak to them as he intended; and
therefore ordered him to move that they would adjourn themselfs
till Monday next (it being very plain to all the House that he expects
to hear by that time of the sealing of the peace, which by letters, it
seems from my Lord Hollis, was to be sealed the last Sunday); but
before they would come to the Question whether they would
adjourne, Sir Tho. Tomkins steps up and tells them that all the
country is grieved at this new-raised standing army, and that they
thought themselfs safe enough in their Traynbands, and that
therefore he desired the King might be moved to disband them.

Then rises Garraway and seconds him; only, with this explanation (which he said he believed the other meant): that as soon as peace should be concluded, they might be disbanded. Then rose Sir W. Coventry and told them that he did approve of what the last gentleman said; but also that at the same time he did no more then what, he durst be bold to say, he knew to be the King's mind, that as soon as peace was concluded, he would do of himself. Then rose Sir Tho. Littleton and did give several reasons, from the uncertainty of their meeting again but to adjourne (in case news comes of the peace being ended before Monday next), and the possibility of the King's having some about him that may endeavour to alter his own, and the good part of his Council's, advice for the keeping up of the land army; and therefore it was fit that they did present it to the King as their desire, that as soon as peace was concluded, the land army might be laid down, and that this their request might be carried to the King by them of their House that were privy councillors; which was put to the vote, and carried *nemine contradicente*. So after this vote passed, they adjourned; but it is plain what the effects of this Parliament will be if they be suffered to sit, that they will fall foul upon the faults of the government; and I pray God they may be permitted to do it, for nothing else I fear will save the King and Kingdom then the doing it betimes. They gone, I to walk with my wife in the garden, and then home to supper and to bed.

27. Up and to the office, where I hear that Sir John Coventry is come over from Bredagh[1] (a nephew I think of Sir W. Coventry's); but what message he brings I know not. This morning, news is come that Sir Jos. Jordan is come from Harwich with 16 fireships and 4 other little ships-of-war; and did attempt to do some execution upon the enemy, but did it without discretion as most do say, so as that they have been able to do no good, but have lost 4 of their fireships. They attempted, it seems, when the wind was too strong, that our grapplings would not hold; others say we came to leeward of them, but all condemn it as a foolish management. They are come to Sir Edwd. Spragg about Lee, and the Duch are below at the Noure. At the office all the morning; and at noon to the Change, where I met Fenn and he tells me that Sir Jo. Coventry doth bring the confirmation of the peace; but I do not find the

1. Where the peace treaty was being negotiated.

Change at all glad of it, but rather the worse, they looking upon it as a peace made only to preserve the King for a time in his lusts and ease, and to sacrifice trade and his kingdoms only to his own pleasures; so that the hearts of merchants are quite down. He told me that Sir G. Carteret was at this end of the town; so I went to visit him in Broad street, and there he and I together. He tells me, as to news, that the peace is now confirmed and all that over. He says it was a very unhappy motion in the House the other day about the land army; for whether the King hath a mind of his own to do the thing desired or no, his doing it will be looked upon as a thing done only in fear of the Parliament. He says that the Duke of York is suspected to be the great man that is for raising of this army and bringing things to be commanded by an army; but he believes that he is wronged, and says that he doth know that he is wronged therein. He doth say that the Court is in a way to ruin all for their pleasures; and says that he himself hath once taken the liberty to tell the King the necessity of having at least a show of religion in the government, and sobriety; and that it was that that did set up and keep up Oliver, though he was the greatest rogue in the world. And that it is so fixed in the nature of the common Englishman, that it will not out of him. He tells me that while all should be labouring to settle the Kingdom, they are at Court all in factions, some for and others against my Lord Chancellor, and another for and against another man; and the King adheres to no man, but this day delivers himself up to this and the next to that, to the ruin of himself and business. That he is at the command of any woman like a slave, though he be the best man to the Queene in the world, with so much respect and never lies a night from her; but yet cannot command himself in the presence of a woman he likes. Having had this discourse, I parted and home to dinner, and thence to the office all the afternoon to my great content, very busy. It raining this day all day to our great joy, it having not rained I think this month before, so as the ground was everywhere as burned and dry as could be – and no travelling in the road or streets in London for dust. At night, late home to supper and to bed.

28. *Lords day.* Up, and to my chamber, where all the morning close, to draw up a letter to Sir W. Coventry upon this tidings of peace, taking occasion (before I am forced to it) to resign up to his Royal Highness my place of the Victualling and to recommend myself to him by promise of doing my utmost to improve this

peace in the best manner we may, to save the Kingdom from ruin. By noon I had done this to my good content; and then with my wife all alone to dinner, and so to my chamber all the afternoon to write my letter fair; and sent it away, and then to talk with my wife and read, and so by daylight (the only time I think I have done it this year) to supper; and then to my chamber to read, and so to bed – my mind very much eased after what I have done today.

29. To Westminster hall, where the Hall full of people to see the issue of the day, the King being to come to speak to the House today. One thing extraordinary was this day, a man, a Quaker, came naked through the Hall, only very civilly tied about the privities to avoid scandal, and with a chafing-dish of fire and brimstone burning upon his head did pass through the Hall, crying, "Repent! Repent!" I up to the Painted Chamber, thinking to have got in to have heard the King's speech, but upon second thoughts did not think it would be worth the crowd, and so went down again into the Hall and there walked with several; among others, my Lord Rutherford, who is come out of Scotland, and I hope I may get some advantage by it in reference to the business of the interest of the great sum of money I paid him long since without interest – but I did not now move him in it; but presently comes down the House of Commons, the King having made them a very short and no pleasing speech to them at all, not at all giving them thanks for their readiness to come up to town at this busy time; but told them that he did think he should have had occasion for them, but had none and therefore did dismiss them to look after their own occasions till October; and that he did wonder any should offer to bring in a suspicion that he intended to rule by an army or otherwise then by the laws of the land, which he promised them he would not; and so bade them go home and settle the minds of the country in that perticular; and only added that he hath had made a peace, which he did believe they would find reasonable and a good peace, but did give them none of the perticulars thereof. Thus, they are dismissed again, to their general great distaste, I believe the greatest that ever Parliament was, to see themselfs so fooled and the nation in certain condition of ruin, while the King, they see, is only governed by his lust and women and rogues about him. They do all give up the kingdom for lost that I speak of, and do hear what the King says, how he and the Duke of York do do what they can to get up an army, that they may need no more Parliaments. And how my Lady

Castlemayne hath, before the late breach between her and the King, said to the King that he must rule by an Army or all would be lost. The kingdom never in so troubled a condition in this world as now; nobody pleased with the peace, and yet nobody daring to wish for the continuance of the war, it being plain that nothing doth nor can thrive under us. Here I saw old good Mr. Vaughan and several of the great men of the Commons, and some of them old men, that are come 200 mile and more to attend this session of Parliament, and been at great charge and disappointments in their other private business; and now all to no purpose, neither to serve their country, content themselfs, nor receive any thanks from the King. It is verily expected by many of them that the King will continue the prorogacion in October, so as, if it be possible, never to have Parliament more. But among other things, they told me of the strange bold sermon of Dr. Creeton yesterday before the King; how he preach against the sins of the Court, and perticularly against adultery, over and over instancing how for that single sin in David, the whole nation was undone.

30. Up and to the office, where we sat busy all the morning. At noon home to dinner, where Daniel and his wife with us, come to see whether I could get him any imployment. But I am so far from it, that I have trouble upon my mind how to dispose of Mr. Gibson and one or two more I am concerned for in the victualling business, which are to be now discharged. After dinner by coach to Whitehall. Having done my business, I to Creeds chamber and thence out to Whitehall with him, in our way meeting with Mr. Cooling, my Lord Chamberlaines secretary, on horseback, who stopped to speak to us; and he proved very drunk and did talk and would have talked all night with us, I not being able to break loose from him, he holding me so by the hand. But Lord, to see his present humour; how he swears at every word and talks of the King and my Lady Castleman in the plainest words in the world. And from him I gather that the story I learned yesterday is true – that the King hath declared that he did not get the child of which she is conceived at this time, he having not as he says lain with her this half year; but she told him – "God damn me, but you shall own it!" It seems he is jealous of Jermin and she loves him, so that the thoughts of his marrying of my Lady Falmouth puts her into fits of the mother. And he, it seems, hath lain with her from time to time continually, for a good while; and once, as this Cooling says, the

King had like to have taken him a-bed with her, but that he was fain to creep under the bed into her closet. And so he talked very lewdly. And then took notice of my kindness to him on shipboard seven years ago, when the King was coming over, and how much he was obliged to me; but says, "Pray look upon this acknowledgement of a kindness in me to be a miracle; for," says [he], "it is against the law at Court for a man that borrows money of me, even to buy his place with, to own it the next Sunday." And then told us his horse was a Bribe, and his boots a bribe; and told us he was made up of bribes, as a Oxford scholar is set out with other men's goods when he goes out of town, and that he makes every sort of tradesmen to bribe him; and invited me home to his house to taste of his bribe-wine. I never heard so much vanity from a man in my life. So being now weary of him, we parted, and I took coach and carried Creed to the Temple, there set him down, and to my office, where busy late till my eyes begun to ake; and then home to supper: a pullet, with good sauce, to my liking; and then to play on the flagelette with my wife, which she now does very prettily, and so to bed.

# –✣AUGUST✣–

4. *Lords day*. Busy at my office from morning till night in writing with my own hand fair our large general account of the expense and debt of the Navy – which lasted me till night to do, that I was almost blind; and Mr. Gibson with me all day long, and dined with me; and excellent discourse I had with him, he understanding all the business of the Navy most admirably. To walk a little with my wife at night in the garden, it being very hot weather again, and so to supper and to bed.

9. Up, and betimes with Sir H. Cholmly upon some accounts of Tanger; and then he and I to Westminster to Mr. Burges and then walked in the Hall. And he and I talked, and he doth really declare that he expects that of necessity this Kingdom will fall back again to a commonwealth; and other wise men are of the same mind, this family doing all that silly men can do to make themselfs unable to support their Kingdom – minding their lust and their pleasure, and making their government so chargeable, that people do well remember better things were done, and better managed and with

much less charge, under a commonwealth then they have been by this King.

10. At the office all the morning, and at noon home to dinner, where I sang and piped with my wife with great pleasure, and did hire a coach to carry us to Barnet tomorrow. After dinner, I to the office and there wrote as long as my eyes would give me leave, and then abroad and to the New Exchange to the bookseller's there, where I hear of several new books coming out – Mr. Pratts history of the Royal Society and Mrs. Phillips's poems. Sir Jo. Denhams poems are going to be all printed together; and among others, some new things, and among them he showed me a copy of verses of his upon Sir Jo. Minnes's going heretofore to Bulloigne to eat a pig. Cowly, he tells me, is dead, who it seems was a mighty civil, serious man, which I did not know before. Several good plays are also likely to be abroad soon – as, *Mustapha* and *Henry the 5th*. Here having stayed and divertized myself a good while, I home again and to finish my letters by the post; and so home, and betimes to bed with my wife because of rising betimes tomorrow.

11. *Lords day*. Up by 4 a-clock and ready with Mrs. Turner to take coach before 5; which we did, and set on our Journy and got to the Wells at Barnett by 7 a-clock, and there found many people a-drinking; but the morning is a very cold morning, so as we were very cold all the way in the coach. Here we met Joseph Batelier and I talked with him, and here was W. Hewers also and his uncle Steventon. So after drink[ing] three glasses, and the women nothing, we back by coach to Barnett, where to the Red Lyon; where we light and went up into the Great Room and there drank and eat some of the best cheese-cakes that ever I eat in my life; and so took coach again, and W. Hewers on horseback with us, and so to Hatfield to the inn next my Lord Salsbury's house, and there we rested ourselfs and drank and bespoke dinner; and so to church, it being just church-time, and there we find my Lord and my Lady Sands and several fine ladies of the family and a great many handsome faces and gentile persons more in the church, and did hear a most excellent good sermon, which pleased me mightily; and very devout, it being upon the signs of saving grace where it is in a man; and one sign, which held him all this day, was that where that grace was, there is also the grace of prayer; which he did handle very finely. In this church lies the former Lord Salsbury, Cecill, buried in

a noble tomb. So the church being done, we to our inn and there dined very well and mighty merry; and as soon as had dined, we walked out into the park, through the fine walk of trees and to the vineyard, and there showed them that; which is in good order, and endeed a place of great delight; which together with our fine walk through the park, was of as much pleasure as could be desired in the world for country pleasure, and good ayre. Being come back, and weary with the walk, for as I made it it was pretty long, being come back to our Inne, there the women had pleasure in putting on some straw hats, which are much worn in this country; and did become them mightily, but especially my wife. So after resting a while, we took coach again and back to Barnett, where W. Hewers took us into his lodging, which is very handsome, and there did treat us very highly with cheesecakes, cream, tarts, and other good things; and then walked into the garden, which was pretty, and there filled my pockets full of Filberts, and so with much pleasure (among other things, I met in this house with a printed book of the life of O. Cromwell, to his honour as a soldier and politician, though as a rebell, the first of that kind that ever I saw, and it is well done) took coach again; and got home with great content, just at day shutting in; and so as soon as home, eat a little, and then to bed with exceeding great content at our day's work.

12. My wife waked betimes to call up her people to washing, and so to bed again; whom I then hugged, it being cold now in the mornings, and then did la otra cosa con her, which I had not done con ella for these tres meses past, which I do believe is a great matter towards the making her of late so indifferent towards me, and with good reason; but now she had much pleasure, and so to sleep again. Up by and by, and I with Mr. Gawden by coach to St. James's, where we find the Duke gone a-hunting with the King but found Sir W. Coventry within; with whom we discoursed, and he did largely discourse with us about our speedy falling upon considering of retrenchments in the expense of the Navy; which I will put forward as much as I can. So having done there, I to Westminster to Burges and then walked to the New Exchange; and there to my bookseller's there and did buy Scotts discourse of Witches, and do hear Mr. Cowly mightily lamented his death by Dr. Ward the Bishop of [Exeter] and Dr. Bates, who were standing there – as the best poet of our nation, and as good a man. Thence I to the printsellers over against the Exchange towards Covent garden, and there

bought a few more prints of Cittys and so home with them; and my wife and maids being gone over the water to the Whitsters with their clothes, this being the first time of her trying this way of washing her linen, I dined at Sir W. Batten's; and after dinner, all alone to the King's playhouse, and there did happen to sit just before Mrs. Pierce and Mrs. Knepp, who pulled me by the hair, and so I addressed myself to them and talked to them all the intervalls of the play, and did give them fruit. The play is *Breneralt*, which I do find but little in for my part.

16.    Up, and at the office all the morning; and so at noon to dinner. And after dinner, my wife and I to the Duke's playhouse, where we saw the new play acted yesterday. *The Feign Innocence or Sir Martin Marr-all*, a play made by my Lord Duke of Newcastle, but as everybody says corrected by Dryden. It is the most entire piece of Mirth, a complete Farce from one end to the other, that certainly was ever writ. I never laughed so in all my life; I laughed till my head [ached] all the evening and night with my laughing, and at very good wit therein, not fooling. The house full, and in all things of mighty content to me. Thence to the New Exchange with my wife, where at my bookseller's I saw the *History of the Royall Society*, which I believe is a fine book and I have bespoke one in quires. So home, and I to the office a little; and so to my chamber and read the history of 88 in Speede, in order to my seeing the play thereof acted tomorrow at the King's House. So to supper, in some pain by the sudden change of the weather cold and my drinking of cold drink; which I must I fear begin to leave off, though I shall try it as long as I can without much pain. But I find myself to be full of wind, and my anus to be knit together, as it is always with cold. Everybody wonders that we have no news from Bredah of the ratification of the peace, and do suspect that there is some stop in it. So to bed.

17.    Up and all the morning at the office, where we sat. At noon home to dinner; and presently my wife and I and Sir W. Penn to the King's playhouse, where the house extraordinary full; and there was the King and Duke of York to see the new play, *Queen Elizabeths Troubles, and the History of Eighty-Eight*. I confess I have sucked in so much of the sad story of Queen Elizabeth from my cradle, that I was ready to weep for her sometimes. But the play is the most ridiculous that sure ever came upon stage, and endeed is merely a show; only, shows the true garbe of the queens in those

days, just as we see Queen Mary and Queen Elizabeth painted – but the play is merely a puppet-play acted by living puppets. Neither the design nor language better; and one stands by and tells us the meaning of things. Only, I was pleased to see Knipp dance among the milkmaids, and to hear her sing a song to Queen Elizabeth – and to see her come out in her nightgowne, with no locks on, but her bare face and hair only tied up in a knot behind; which is the comeliest dress that ever I saw her in to her advantage. Thence home and went as far as Mile end with Sir W. Penn, whose coach took him up there for his country-house; and after having drunk there at the Rose and Crowne, a good house for Ald. Bides Ale, we parted; and we home, and there I finished my letters and then home to supper and to bed.

18. *Lords day*. Up; and being ready, walked up and down into the streets to Creed Church to see it how it is, but I find no alteration there, as they say there was, for my Lord Mayor and Aldermen to come to sermon as they do every Sunday, as they did formerly to Paul's. Walk back home and to our own church, where a dull sermon and our church empty of the best sort of people, they being at their country-houses; and so home, and there dined with me Mr. Turner and his daughter Betty. We had a good haunch of venison, powdered and boiled, and a good dinner and merry. After dinner comes Mr. Pelling the pothecary, whom I had sent for to dine with me, but he was engaged. After sitting an hour to talk, we broke up, all leaving Pelling to talk with my wife, and I walked toward Whitehall; but being weary, turned into St. Dunstan's church, where I hear an able sermon of the Minister of the place. And stood by a pretty, modest maid, whom I did labour to take by the hand and body; but she would not, but got further and further from me, and at last I could perceive her to take pins out of her pocket to prick me if I should touch her again; which seeing, I did forbear, and was glad I did espy her design. And then I fell to gaze upon another pretty maid in a pew close to me, and she on me; and I did go about to take her by the hand, which she suffered a little and then withdrew. So the sermon ended and the church broke up, and my amours ended also; and so took coach and home, and there took up my wife and to Islington with her, our old road; but before we got to Islington, between that and Kingsland, there happened an odd adventure; one of our coach-horses fell sick of the staggers, so as he was ready to fall down. The coachman was fain to light and hold

him up and cut his tongue to make him bleed, and his tail – the horse continued shakeing every part of him, as if he had been in an ague a good while, and his blood settled in his tongue, and the coachman thought and believed he would presently drop down dead. Then he blew some tobacco in his nose; upon which the horse sneezed, and by and by grows well and draws us the rest of the way as well as ever he did; which was one of the strangest things of a horse I ever observed – but he says it is usual. It is the staggers. Stayed and eat and drank at Islington at the old house, and so home and to my chamber to read; and then to supper and to bed.

20.     Up, and to my chamber to set down my journall for the last three days; and then to the office – where busy all the morning. At noon home to dinner and then with my wife abroad; set her down at the Exchange and I to St. James's, where find Sir W. Coventry alone and fell to discourse of retrenchments; and thereon he tells how he hath already propounded to the Lord's committee of the Council how he would have the Treasurer of the Navy a less man, that might not sit at the Board but be subject to the Board. He would have two Controllers to do his work, and two Surveyors, whereof one of each to take it by turns to reside at Portsmouth and Chatham, by a kind of Rotation. He would have but only one Clerk of the Acts. He doth tell me he hath propounded how the charge of the Navy in peace shall come within 200000*l*, by keeping out 24 ships in summer and 10 in winter. And several other perticulars we went over of retrenchment; and I find I must provide some things to offer, that I may be found studious to lessen the King's charge.

24.     *St. Bartholomew's day*. This morning was proclaimed the peace between us and the States of the United Provinces, and also of the King of France and Denmarke, and in the afternoon the proclamations were printed and came out. And at night the bells rung, but no bonfires that I hear of anywhere, partly from the dearness of firing but principally from the little content most people have in the peace. All the morning at the office. At noon dined, and Creed with me, at home. After dinner, we to a play and there saw *The Cardinall* at the King's House, wherewith I am mightily pleased; but above all with Becke Marshall. But it is pretty to observe how I look up and down for and did espy Knepp; but durst not own it to my wife that I saw her, for fear of angering her, who doth not like my kindness to her – and so I was forced not to take notice of her. And so

homeward, leaving Creed at the Temple: and my belly now full
with Plays, that I do entend to bind myself to see no more till
Michaelmas. So with my wife to Mile end and there drank of Bides
ale, and so home; most of our discourse about our keeping a coach
the next year, which pleases my wife mightily; and if I continue as
able as now, it will save us money. This day came a letter from the
Duke of York to the Board, to invite us, which is as much as to
fright us, into the lending the King money; which is a poor thing
and most dishonourable – and shows in what a case we are at the end
of the war to our neighbours. And the King doth now declare
publicly to give 10 per cent to all lenders; which makes some think
that the Dutch themselfs will send over money and lend it upon our
public faith, the Act of Parliament.[1] So home and to my office;
wrote a little and then home to supper and to bed.

26.    Up; and Greeting came and I reckoned with him for his
teaching of my wife and me upon the Flagielette to this day, and
so paid him off, having as much as he can teach us. Then to the
office, where we sat upon a perticular business all the morning,
and my Lord Anglesey with us; who, and my Lord Brouncker, do
bring us news how my Lord Chancellors seal is to be taken away
from him today. The thing is so great and sudden to me, that it
put me into a very great admiration what should be the meaning
of it; and they do not own that they know what it should be. But
this is certain: that the King did resolve it on Saturday, and did
yesterday send the Duke of Albemarle (the only man fit for those
works) to him for his purse; to which the Chancellor answered
that he received it from the King, and would deliver it to the
King's own hand, and so civilly returned the Duke of Albemarle
without it; and this morning my Lord Chancellor is to be with the
King, to come to an end in that business. And it is said that the
King doth say that he will have the Parliament meet, and that it
will prevent much trouble by having of him out of their envy, by
his place being taken away – for that all their envy will be at him.
It is said also that my Lord Chancellor answers that he desires he
may be brought to his trial if he have done anything to lose his
office; and that he will be willing, and is most desirous, to lose that
and his head both together. Upon what terms they parted nobody
knows; but the Chancellor looked sad, he says.

1. The Eleven Months Tax.

27.   This day Mr. Pierce the surgeon was with me; and tells me how this business of my Lord Chancellors was certainly designed in my Lady Castlemaine's chamber, and that when he went from the King on Monday morning, she was in bed (though about 12 a-clock) and ran out in her smock into her Aviary looking into Whitehall garden, and thither her woman brought her her night-gown, and stood joying herself at the old man's going away. And several of the gallants of Whitehall (of which there was many staying to see the Chancellor return) did talk to her in her Bird cage; among others, Blanckford, telling her she was the Bird of paradise.

31.   At the office all the morning – where by Sir W. Penn I do hear that the Seal was fetched away to the King yesterday from the Lord Chancellor, by Secretary Morrice – which puts me into a great horror, to have it done after so much debate and confidence that it would not be done at last. When we rose I took a turn with Lord Brouncker in the garden, and he tells me that he hath of late discoursed about this business with Sir W. Coventry, who he finds is the great man in the doing this business of the Chancellors, and that he doth persevere in it, though against the Duke of York's opinion. After having wrote my letters at the office in the afternoon, I in the evening to Whitehall to see how matters go; and there I met with Mr. Ball of the Excise Office and he tells me that the Seal is delivered to Sir Orlando Bridgeman, the man of the whole nation that is the best spoken of and will please most people; and therefore I am mighty glad of it. He was then at my Lord Arlington's, whither I went, expecting to see him come out; but stayed so long, and Sir W. Coventry coming thither, whom I had not a mind should see me there idle upon a post-night, I went home without seeing him; but he is there with his Seal in his hand. So I home; took up my wife, whom I left at Unthankes, and so home; and after signing my letters, to bed. This day, being dissatisfied with my wife's learning so few songs of Goodgroome, I did come to a new bargain with him, to teach her songs at so much, *viz.*, 10s. a song; which he accepts of and will teach her.

## –❧SEPTEMBER❧–

1. *Lords day.* Up, and betimes by water from the Tower; and called at the Old Swan for a glass of strong water and sent word to have little Michell and his wife come and dine with us today; and so, taking in a gentleman and his lady that wanted a boat, I to Westminster, setting them on shore at Charing cross; I to Mrs. Martin's, where I had two pair of cuffs which I bespoke, and there did sit and talk with her and no mas, ella having aquellos upon her; and here I did see her little girl my god-daughter, which will be pretty. And there having stayed a little, I away to Creeds chamber; and when he was ready, away to Whitehall, where I met with several people and had my fill of talk. So home by water to dinner, where comes Pelling and young Michell and his wife, whom I have not seen a great while, poor girl. And then comes Mr. How, and all dined with me very merry; and spent all the afternoon, Pelling, How, I and my boy, sing[ing] of Locke's Response to the Ten Commandments, which he hath set very finely, and was a good while since sung before the King and spoilt in the performance – which occasioned his printing them for his vindication, and are excellent good. They parted, in the evening my wife and I to walk in the garden; and there scolded a little, I being doubtful that she had received a couple of fine pinners (one of point-de-Gesne), which I find she hath from some[one] or other of a present; but on the contrary, I find she hath bought them for me to pay for them, without my knowledge. This doth displease me much; but yet doth so much please me better then if she had received them the other way, that I was not much angry, but fell to other discourse; and so to my chamber, and got her to read to me for saving of my eyes; and then having got a great cold, I know not how, I to bed and lay ill at ease all the night.

2. This day is kept in the City as a public fast for the fire this day twelve months. But I was not at church, being commanded with the rest to attend the Duke of York; and therefore with Sir J. Mennes to St. James's, where we had much business before the Duke of York; and observed all things to be very kind between the Duke of York and W. Coventry, which did mightily joy me. When we had done, Sir W. Coventry called me down with him to his chamber and there told me that he is leaving the Duke of York's service, which I was amazed at; but he tells me that it is not with the

least unkindness on the Duke of York's side, though he expects (and I told him he was in the right) it will be interpreted otherwise, because done just at this time. "But," says he, "I did desire it a good while since, and the Duke of York did with much entreaty grant it, desiring that I would say nothing of it, and that he might have time and liberty to choose his successor without being importuned for others whom he should not like" – and that he hath chosen Mr. Wren; which I am glad of, he being a very ingenious man, and so W. Coventry says of him, though he knows him little; but perticularly commends him for the book he writ in answer to Harrington's *Oceana*, which for that reason I intend to buy. He tells me the true reason is that he being a man not willing to undertake more business then he can go through, and being desirous to have his whole time to spend upon the business of the Treasury and a little for his own ease, he did desire this of the Duke of York. He assures me that the kindness with which he goes away from the Duke of York is one of the greatest joys that ever he had in the world. I used some freedom with him, telling him how the world hath discourse of his having offended the Duke of York about the late business of the Chancellor; he doth not deny it, but says that perhaps the Duke of York might have some reason for it, he opposing him in a thing wherein he was so earnest; but tells me that notwithstanding all that, the Duke of York doth not now, nor can blame him – but that the Duke of York knows that he did first speak of it to the Duke of York, before he spoke to any mortal creature besides, which was fair dealing. I did then desire to know what was the great matter that grounded his desire of the Chancellor's removal; he told me many things not fit to be spoken, and yet not anything of his being unfaithful to the King; but, *instar omnium*, he told me that while he was so great at the Council board and in the administration of matters, there was no room for anybody to propose any remedy to what was amiss or to compass anything, though never so good for the Kingdom, unless approved of by the Chancellor, he managing all things with that greatness which now will be removed, that the King may have the benefit of others' advice.

To Whitehall, where I met with many people; and among other things Mr. May showed me the King's new buildings, in order to their having of some old sails for the closing of the windows this winter. I dined with Sir G. Carteret, with whom dined Mr. Jack Ashburnham and Dr. Creeton (who I observe to be a most good man and humble). In discourse at dinner concerning the change of men's humours and fashions touching meats, Mr. Ashburnham told us that he remembers since the only fruit in request, and eaten by the King and Queen at table as the best fruit, was the Katharine payre, though they knew at that time other fruits of France and our own country. After dinner comes in Mr. Townsend; and there I was witness of a horrid rateing, which Mr. Ashburnham, as one of the Grooms of the King's Bedchamber, did give him for want of linen for the King's person; which he swore was not to be endured, and that the King would not endure it, and that the King his father would have hanged his wardrobe-man should he have been served so; the King having at this day no handkerchers and but three bands to his neck, he swore. Mr. Townsend answered want of money and the owing of the linendraper 5000*l*; and that he hath of late got many rich things made, beds and sheets and saddles, and all without money, and he can go no further; but still this old man (endeed, like an old loving servant) did cry out for the King's person to be neglected. But when he was gone, Townsend told me that it is the grooms taking away the King's linen at the Quarter's end, as their Fees, which makes this great want: for whether the King can get it or no, they will run away at the Quarter's end with what he hath had, let the King get more as he can. From him I went to see a great match at tennis between Prince Rupert and one Capt. Cooke against Bab. May and the elder Chichly, where the King was and Court, and it seems are the best players at tennis in the nation. But this puts me in mind of what I observed in the morning; that the King, playing at tennis, had a Steeleyard carried to him, and I was told it was to weigh him after he had done playing; and at noon Mr. Ashburnham told me that it is only the King's curiosity, which he usually hath, of weighing himself before and after his play, to see how much he loses in weight by playing; and this day he lost 4½ lb. Thence home and took my wife out to Mile end green and there drank; and so home, having a very fine evening. Then home, and I to Sir W. Batten and W. Penn and there discoursed of Sir W. Coventry's leaving the Duke of York and Mr. Wren's succeeding him; they told me both seriously, that they had long cut me out for Secretary to the Duke of York if ever W. Coventry left him; which, agreeing with what I have heard from other hands heretofore, doth make me not only think that something of that kind hath been thought on, but doth comfort me to see that the world hath such an esteem of my qualities as to think me fit for any such thing – though

I am glad with all my heart that I am not so, for it would never please me to be forced to the attendance that that would require, and leave my wife and family to themselfs, as I must do in such a case; thinking myself now in the best place that ever man was in to please his own mind in, and therefore I will take care to preserve it. So to bed, my cold remaining, though not so much, upon me.

4. By coach to Whitehall to the Council chamber; and there met with Sir W. Coventry going in, who took me aside and told me that he was just come from delivering up his seal and papers to Mr. Wren; and told me he must now take his leave of me as a naval man, but that he shall always bear respect to his friends there, and perticularly to myself, with great kindness, which I returned to him with thanks; and so with much kindness parted, and he into the Council. I met with Sir Sam. Moreland, who showed me two orders upon the Exchequer, one of 600*l* and another of 400*l*, for money assigned to him, which he would have me lend him money upon and he would allow 12 per cent. I would not meddle with them, though they are very good; and would, had I not so much money out already on public credit. But I see by this, his condition will always be bad. I stayed and heard Ald. Barker's case of his being abused by the Council of Ireland touching his lands there. All I observed there is the silliness of the King, playing with his dog all the while, or his codpiece, and not minding the business, and what he said was mighty weak; but my Lord Keeper I observe to be a mighty able man. The business broke off without any end to it, and so I home and thence with my wife and W. Hewer to Bartholomew fayre and there saw *Polichinelli* (where we saw Mrs. Clerke and all her crew); and so to a private house and sent for a side of pig and eat it at an acquaintance of W. Hewer's, where there was some learned physique and Chymical Bookes; and among others, a natural Herball, very fine. Here we stayed not; but to the Duke of York's playhouse and there see *Mustapha*, which the more I see, the more I like; and is a most admirable poem – and bravely acted; only, both Batterton and Harris could not contain from laughing in the midst of a most serious part, from the ridiculous mistake of one of the men upon the stage – which I did not like. Thence home, where Batelier and his sister Mary came to us and sat and talked; and so they gone, we to supper and to bed.

11. Mr. Moore discoursed with me of public matters; the sum of

which is that he doth doubt that there is more at the bottom then the removal of the Chancellor; that is, he doth verily believe that the King doth resolve to declare the Duke of Monmouth legitimate – and that we shall soon see it. This I do not think the Duke of York will endure without blows; but his poverty, and being lessened by having the Chancellor fallen and W. Coventry gone from him, will disable him from being able to do anything almost, he being himself almost lost in the esteem of people; and will be more and more, unless my Lord Chancellor (who is already begun to be pitied by some people, and to be better thought of then was expected) doth recover himself in Parliament. He would seem to fear that this difference about the Crowne (if there be nothing else) will undo us.

13. To the office and there despatched business till 10 a-clock, and then with Sir W. Batten and my wife and Mrs. Turner to Walthamstow by hackney coach to Mrs. Shipman's to dinner, where Sir W. Penn and my Lady and Mrs. Lowther (the latter of which hath got a sore nose, given her I believe from her husband, which made me I could not look upon her with any pleasure); and here a very good and plentiful wholesome dinner and above all thing, such plenty of milke-meats (she keeping a great dairy) and so good as I never met with. Afternoon proved very foul weather, the morning fair. We stayed talking till evening, and then home and there to my flagelette with my wife; and so to bed without any supper, my belly being full and dinner not digested. It vexed me to hear how Sir W. Penn, who came alone from London, being to send his coachman for his wife and daughter and bidding his coachman in much anger to go for them (he being vexed, like a rogue, to do anything to please his wife), his coachman Tom was heard to say, "A pox of God rot her! Can she [not] walk hither?" These words do so mad me, that I could find in my heart to give him or my Lady notice of them.

15. *Lords day*. Up to my chamber, there to set some papers to rights. By and by to church, where I stood in continual fear of Mrs. Markham's coming to church and offering to come into our pew; to prevent which, as soon as ever I heard the great door open, I did step back and clapped my breech to our pew door, that she might be forced to shove me to come in; but as God would have it, she did not come. Mr. Mills preached; and after sermon, by invitation he

and his wife came to dine with me (which is the first time they have been in my house I think these five years), I thinking it not amiss, because of their acquaintance in our country, to show them some respect. Mr. Turner and his wife and their son the Captain dined with me, and I had a very good dinner for them – and very merry; and after dinner he was forced to go, though it rained, to Stepny to preach. We also to church, and then home, and there comes Mr. Pelling with two men by promise, one Wallington and Piggott; the former whereof, being a very little fellow, did sing a most excellent bass, and yet a poor fellow, a working goldsmith, that goes without gloves to his hands. Here we sung several good things, but I am more and more confirmed that singing with many voices is not singing, but a sort of Instrumentall music, the sense of the words being lost by not being heard, and especially as they set them with Fuges of words, one after another; whereas singing properly, I think, should be but with one or two voices at most, and that counterpoint. They supped with me; and so broke up, and then my wife and I to my chamber, where through the badness of my eyes she was forced to read to me, which she doth very well; and was Mr. Boyle's discourse upon the Style of the Scripture, which is a very fine piece. And so to bed.

19. Up, and all the morning at the office. At noon home to dinner, W. Hewer and I and my wife, when comes my Cosen Kate Joyce and an aunt of ours, Lettice, formerly Hanes and now Howlett, come to town to see her friends, and also Sarah Kite, with her little boy in her armes, a very pretty little boy. The child I like very well, and could wish it my own. My wife, being all unready, did not appear. I made as much of them as I could such ordinary company; and yet my heart was glad to see them, though their condition was a little below my present state to be familiar with. She tells me how the Lifeguard, which we thought a little while since was sent down into the country about some insurrection, was sent to Winchcombe to spoil the Tobacco there, which it seems the people there do plant contrary to law and have always done, and still been under force and danger of having it spoiled; as it hath been oftentimes, and yet they will continue to plant it. The place, she says, is a miserable poor place. They gone, I to the office, where all the afternoon very busy; and at night, when my Eyes were weary of the light, I and my wife to walk in the garden, and then home to supper and pipe and then to bed.

22. *Lords day*. At my chamber all the morning, making up some accounts to my great content. At noon comes Mr. Sheres, whom I find a good engenious man, but doth talk a little too much of his travels. He left my Lord Sandwich well, but in pain to be at home for want of money, which comes very hardly. Most of the afternoon talking of Spain and informing him against his return how things are here. And so spent most of the afternoon, and then he parted. And then to my chamber busy, till my eyes were almost blind with writing and reading and I was fain to get the boy to come and write for me. And then to supper, and Pelling come to me at supper and then to sing a Psalm with him; and so parted and to bed – after my wife had read something to me (to save my eyes) in a good book. This night I did even my accounts of the house, which I have (to my great shame) omitted now above two months or more; and therefore am content to take my wife's and maids' accounts as they give them, being not able to correct them, which vexes me; but the fault being my own, contrary to my wife's frequent desires, I cannot find fault; but am resolved never to let them come to that pass again. The truth is, I have indulged myself more to pleasure for these last two months then ever I did in my life before since I came to be a person concerned in business – and I doubt when I come to make up my accounts, I shall find it so by the expense.

27. Up and to the office, where very busy all the morning. While I was busy at the office, my wife sends for me to come to home, and what was it but to see the pretty girl[1] which she is taking to wait upon her; and though she seems not altogether so great a beauty as she had before told me, yet endeed she is mighty pretty; and so pretty, that I find I shall be too much pleased with it, and therefore could be contented as to my judgment, though not to my passion, that she might not come, lest I may be found too much minding her, to the discontent of my wife. She is to come next week. She seems by her discourse to be grave beyond her bigness and age, and exceeding well-bred as to her deportment, having been a scholar in a school at Bow these seven or eight year. To the office again, my [thoughts] running on this pretty girl; and there till noon, when Creed and Sheres come and dined with me; and we had a great deal of pretty discourse of the ceremoniousness of the Spaniards – whose ceremonies are so many and so known, that he tells me, upon all

1. Deborah Willet.

occasions of joy or sorrow in a grandee's family, my Lord Embassador is fain to send one with an *en hora buena* (if it be upon a marriage or birth of a child) or a *pesa me*, if it be upon the death of a child or so. And these ceremonies are so set, and the words of the compliment, that he hath been sent from my Lord when he hath done no more then send in word to the grandee that one was there from the Embassador; and he knowing what was his errand, that hath been enough, and he hath never spoken with him. Nay, several grandees, having been to marry a daughter, have wrote letters to my Lord to give him notice and out of the greatness of his wisdom to desire his advice, though people he never saw; and then my Lord, he answers by commending the greatness of his discretion in making so good an alliance &c., so ends. He says that it is so far from dishonour to a man to give private revenge for an affront, that the contrary is a disgrace; they holding that he that receives an affront is not fit to appear in the sight of the world till he hath revenged himself; and therefore, that a gentleman there that receives an affront oftentimes never appears again in the world till he hath by some private way or other revenged himself; and that on this account, several have fallowed their enemy privately to the Indys, thence to Italy, thence to France and back again, watching for an opportunity to be revenged. He says my Lord was fain to keep a letter from the Duke of York to the Queen of Spain a great while in his hands before he could think fit to deliver it, till he had learnt whether the Queen would receive it, it being directed to his "Cosen." He says that many ladies in Spain, after they are found to be with child, do never stir out of their beds or chambers till they are brought to bed – so ceremonious they are in that point also. He tells of their wooing by serenades at the window, and that their friends do alway make the match; but yet that they have opportunities to meet at Masse at church, and there they make love. That the Court there hath no dancings, nor visits at night to see the King or Queene, but is always just like a Cloyster, nobody stirring in it. That my Lord Sandwich wears a beard now, turned up in the Spanish manner. But that which pleases me most endeed, is that the peace which he hath made with Spain[1] is now printed here, and is acknowledged by all the merchants to be the best peace that ever England had with them; and it appears that the King thinks it so, for this is printed before the Ratification is gone over; whereas that

1. A commercial treaty which proved to be to the advantage of both nations.

with France and Holland was not in a good while after, till Copys came over of it in English out of Holland and France, that it was a reproach not to have it printed here. This I am mighty glad of; and is the first and only piece of good news, or thing fit to be owned, that this nation hath done several years.

After dinner, I to the office; and they gone and anon, comes Pelling, and he and I to Greys Inne fields, thinking to have heard Mrs. Knight sing at her lodgings by a friend's means of his; but we came too late, so must try another time. So lost our labour, and I by coach home and there to my chamber and did a great deal of good business about my Tanger accounts; and so with pleasure discoursing with my wife of our Journy shortly to Brampton, and of this little girle, which endeed runs in my head and pleases me mightily, though I dare not own it; and so to supper and to bed.

29.   *Lords day*. Up, and put off first my summer's silk suit and put on a cloth one. Then to church and so home to dinner, my wife and I alone to a good dinner. All the afternoon talking in my chamber with my wife about my keeping a coach the next year, and doing something to my house which will cost money – that is, furnish our best chamber with tapestry – and other rooms with pictures. In the evening read [a] good book, my wife to me; and I did even my kitchen accounts. Then to supper, and so to bed.

# —✢OCTOBER✢—

1.   All the morning busy at the office. Pleased mightily with my girl that we have got to wait on my wife. At noon dined with Sir G. Carteret and the rest of our officers at his house in Broad street, they being there upon his accounts. After dinner took coach and to my wife, who was gone before into the Strand, there to buy a nightgowne; where I found her in a shop with her pretty girl, and having bought it, away home; and I thence to Sir G. Carteret's again, and so took coach alone, it now being almost night, to Whitehall and there in the Boarded gallery did hear the music with which the King is presented this night by Monsieur Grebus, the master of his music – both instrumental (I think 24 violins) and vocall, an English song upon peace; but God forgive me, I was never so little pleased with a consort of music in my life – the

manner of setting of words and repeating them out of order, and that with a number of voices, makes me sick, the whole design of vocall music being lost by it. Here was a great press of people, but I did not see many pleased with it; only, the instrumental music he had brought by practice to play very just. So thence late, in the dark round by the Wall home by coach; and there to sing and sup with my wife and look upon our pretty girl, and so to bed.

3. Up; and going out of doors, I understand that Sir W. Batten is gone to bed on a sudden again this morning, being struck very ill. And I confess I have observed him for these last two months to look very ill and to look worse and worse. I to St. James's (though it be a sitting day) to the Duke of York about [the] Tanger Committee, which met this morning; and he came to us, and the charter for the city of Tanger was read and the form of the Court Merchant.

4. To my Lord Crews and there did stay with him an hour discoursing about the ill state of my Lord Sandwich, that he can neither be got to be called home nor money got to maintain him there, which will ruin his family: and the truth is, he doth almost deserve it, for by all relation he hath in a little more then a year and a half spent 20000*l* of the King's money and the best part of 10000*l* of his own; which is a most prodigious expense, more then ever Embassadors spent there and more then these Commissioners of the Treasury will or do allow; and they demand an account before they will give him any more money; which puts all his friends to a loss what to answer – but more money we must get him, or to be called home. So home, and there to see Sir W. Batten, who fell sick yesterday morning. He is asleep and so I could not see him; but in an hour after, word is brought me that he is so ill, that it is believed he cannot live till tomorrow; which troubles me and my wife mightily, partly out of kindness, he being a good neighbour, and partly because of the money he owes me. So home and to supper and to bed.

5. Up, and to the office and there all the morning, none but my Lord Anglesy and myself. But much surprized with the news of the death of Sir W. Batten, who died this morning, having been but two days sick. Sir W. Penn and I did despatch a letter this morning to Sir W. Coventry to recommend Coll. Middleton, who we think a most honest and understanding man, and fit for that place. At

noon home, and by coach to Temple bar to a India shop and there bought a gown and Shash, which cost me 26s. And so [my wife] and Willett away to the Change, and I to my Lord Crew and there met my Lord Hinchingbrooke and Lady Jemimah, and there dined with them and my Lord – where pretty merry. And after dinner, my Lord Crew and Hinchingbrooke and myself went aside to discourse about my Lord Sandwiches business, which is in a very ill state for want of money; and so parted, and I to my tailors and there took up my wife and Willet, who stayed there for me, and to the Duke of York's playhouse; but the House so full, it being a new play *The Coffee House*, that we could not get in, and so to the King's House; and there going in, met with Knipp and she took us up into the Tireing-rooms and to the women's Shift, where Nell was dressing herself and was all unready; and is very pretty, prettier then I thought; and so walked all up and down the House above, and then below into the Scene-room, and there sat down and she gave us fruit; and here I read the Qu's to Knepp while she answered me, through all her part of *Flora's Figarys*, which was acted today. But Lord, to see how they were both painted would make a man mad – and did make me loath them – and what base company of men comes among them, and how lewdly they talk – and how poor the men are in clothes, and yet what a show they make on the stage by candlelight, is very observable. But to see how Nell cursed for having so few people in the pit was pretty, the other House carrying away all the people at the new play, and is said nowadays to have generally most company, as being better players. By and by into the pit and there saw the play; which is pretty good, but my belly was full of what I had seen in the House; and so after the play done, away home and there to the writing my letters; and so home to supper and to bed.

6. *Lords day*. Up, and dressed myself and so walked out with the boy to Smithfield to Cow lane to Lincolnes, and there spoke with him and agree upon the hour tomorrow to set out toward Brampton; but vexed that he is not likely to go himself, but sends another for him. Here I took a hackney coach, and to Whitehall and there met Sir W. Coventry and discoursed with him; and then with my Lord Brouncker and many others to end my matters, in order to my going into the country tomorrow for five or six days, which I have not been for now above three years.

7.    Up betimes, and did do several things towards the settling all matters, both of house and office, in order for my journey this day; and did leave my chief care, and the key of my closet, with Mr. Hater, with direction what papers to secure in case of fire or other accident; and so about 9 a-clock, I and my wife and Willett set out in a coach I have hired, with four horses, and W. Hewer and Murford rode by us on horseback; and so, my wife and she in their morning gowns, very handsome and pretty and to my great liking, we set out; and so out at Allgate and so to the Greenman and so on to Enfield, in our way seeing Mr. Louther and his lady in a coach going to Walthamstow, and he told us that he would overtake us at night, he being to go that way. So we to Enfield and there bayted, it being but a foul, bad day; and there Louther and Mr. Burford, an acquaintance of his, did overtake us, and there drank and eat together; and by and by we parted, we going before them; and very merry, my wife and girl and [I], talking and telling tales and singing; and before night did come to Bishop stafford, where Louther and his friend did meet us again and carried us to the Raynedeere, where Mrs. Aynsworth (who lived heretofore at Cambrige and whom I knew better then they think for, doth live – it was the woman that, among other things, was great with my Cosen Barmston of Cottenham, and did use to sing to him and did teach me *Full forty times over*, a very lewd song) doth live, a woman they are well acquainted with, and is here what she was at Cambrige, and all the goodfellows of the country come hither. Louther and his friend stayed and drank and then went further this night, but here we stayed and supped and lodged. But as soon as they were gone and my supper getting ready, I fell to write my letter to my Lord Sandwich, which I could not finish before my coming from London; so did finish it to my good content, and a good letter, telling him the present state of all matters; and did get a man to promise to carry it tomorrow morning to be there at my house by noon, and I paid him well for it. So that being done and my mind at ease, we to supper and so to bed, my wife and I in one bed and the girl in another in the same room. And lay very well, but there was so much tearing company in the house, that we could not see my landlady, so I had no opportunity of renewing my old acquaintance with her. But here we slept very well.

8.    Up pretty betimes, though not so soon as we entended, by reason of Murford's not rising and then not knowing how to open

our door; which, and some other pleasant simplicities of the fellow, did give occasion to us to call him Sir Martin Marr-all;[1] and W. Hewers being his helper and counsellor, we did call him all this journey, Mr. Warner, which did give us good occasion of mirth now and then. At last rose, and up and broke our fast, and then took coach and away; and at Newport did call on Mr. Louther, and he and his friend and the maister of the house, their friend where they were (a gentleman), did presently get a-horseback and overtook us, and went with us to Audly end and did go along with us all over the house and garden; and mighty merry we were. The house endeed doth appear very fine, but not so fine as it hath heretofore to me. Perticularly, the ceilings are not so good as I alway took them to be, being nothing so well wrought as my Lord Chancellors are; and though the figure of the house without be very extraordinary good, yet the stayrecase is exceeding poor; and a great many pictures, and not one good one in the house but one of Harry the 8th done by Holben; and not one good suit of hangings in all the house, but all most ancient things, such as I would not give the hanging-up of in my house; and the other furniture, beds and other things, accordingly. Only, the gallery is good; and above all things, the cellars, where we went down and drank of much good liquor, and endeed the cellars are fine; and here my wife and I did sing to my great content, and then to the garden and there eat many grapes, and took some with us; and so away thence, exceeding well satisfied, though not to that degree that by my old esteem of the house I ought and did expect to have done – the situation of it not pleasing me. Here we parted with Louther and his friends, and away to Cambrige, it being foul, rainy weather; and there did take up at the Rose, for the sake of Mrs. Dorothy Drawwater, the vintener's daughter, which is mentioned in the play of *Sir Martin Marr-all*. Here we had a good chamber and bespoke a good supper; and then I took my wife and W. Hewer and Willett (it holding up a little) and showed them Trinity College and St. Johns Library, and went to King's College chapel to see the outside of it only, and so to our Inne; and with much pleasure did this, they walking in their pretty morning gowns, very handsome, and I proud to find myself in condition to do this; and so home to our lodging, and there by and by to supper with much good sport, talking with the drawers concerning matters of the town and persons whom I remember;

1. From the character in Dryden's play of that name.

and so after supper to cards and then to bed, lying, I in one bed and my wife and girl in another in the same room; and very merry we talking together and mightily pleased both of us with the girl.

9.   Up, and got ready and eat our breakfast and then took coach; and the poor, as they did yesterday, did stand at the coach to have something given them, as they do to all great persons, and I did give them something; and the town musique did also come and play; but Lord, what sad music they made – however, I was pleased with them, being all of us in very good humour; and so set forth and through the town, and observed at our College of Magdalen the posts new-painted, and understand that the Vice-Chancellor is there this year. And so away for Huntington, mightily pleased all along the road to remember old stories; and came to Brampton at about noon and there find my father and sister and brother all well; and here laid up our things, and up and down to see the garden with my father, and the house, and do altogether find it very pretty – especially the little parlour and the summer-houses in the garden. Only, the wall doth want greens upon it and the house is too low-roofed; but that is only because of my coming from a house with higher ceilings; but altogether is very pretty and I bless God that I am like to have such a pretty place to retire to. And I did walk with my father without doors and do find a very convenient way of laying out money there in building, which will make a very good seat; and the place deserves it, I think, very well. Mr. Sheply stayed with us and supped, and full of good country discourse; and when supper done, took his leave and we all to bed – my wife and I in the high bed in our chamber, and Willet in the trundle-bed, which she desired to lie in, by us.

10–11.   Waked in the morning with great pain I, of the Collique, by cold taken yesterday, I believe with going up and down in my shirt; but with rubbing my belly, keeping of it warm, I did at last come to some ease, and rose; and up to walk up and down the garden with my father, to talk of all our concernments – about a husband for my sister, whereof there is at present no appearance. But we must endeavour to find her one now, for she grows old and ugly. Then for my brother; and resolve he shall stay here this winter, and then I will either send him to Cambridge for a year, till I get him some church promotion, or send him to sea as a chaplain – where he may study and earn his living. By this time it was almost noon, and then my father and I and wife and Willett abroad by coach round the Towne of Brampton to observe any other place as good as ours, and find none; and so back with great pleasure and thence went all of us, my sister and brother and W. Hewer, to dinner to Hinchingbrooke, where we had a good plain country dinner, but most kindly used; and here dined the Minister of Brampton and his wife, who is reported a very good, but poor man. Here I spent alone with my Lady, after dinner, the most of the afternoon; and anon the two Twins[1] were sent for from Schoole at Mr. Taylors to come to see me; and I took them into the garden and there in one of the Summer-houses did examine them; and do find them so well advanced in their learning, that I was amazed at it, they repeating a whole Ode without book out of Horace, and did give me a very good account of anything almost, and did make me very readily very good Latin and did give me good account of their Greek grammer, beyond all possible expectation; and so grave and manly as I never saw, I confess, nor could have believed – so that they will be fit to go on to Cambridge in two years at most. They are but little, but very like one another; and well-looked children. Then in to my Lady again, and stayed till it was almost night again; and then took leave for a great while again, but with extraordinary kindness from my Lady, who looks upon me like one of her own family and interest.

So thence, my wife and people [by] the highway, and I walked over the park with Mr. Sheply and through the grove, which is mighty pretty as is imaginable; and so over their drawbridge to Nun's Bridge and so to my father's, and there sat and drank and talked a little and then parted; and he being gone, and what company there was, my father and I with a dark lantern, it being now night, into the guarden with my wife and there went about our great work to dig up my gold. But Lord, what a tosse I was for some time in, that they could not justly tell where it was, that I begun heartily to sweat and be angry that they should not agree better upon the place, and at last to fear that it was gone; but by and by, poking with a spit, we found it, and then begun with a spudd to lift up the ground; but good God, to see how sillily they did it, not half a foot under ground and in the sight of the world from a hundred places if anybody by accident were near-hand, and within sight of a neighbour's window and their hearing also, being close

1. Oliver and John, Sandwich's twelve-year old sons.

by; only, my father says that he saw them all gone to church before he begun the work when he laid the money, but that doth not excuse it to me; but I was out of my wits almost, and the more from that upon my lifting up the earth with the spud, I did discern that I scattered the pieces of gold round about the ground among the grass and loose earth; and taking up the Iron head-pieces wherein they were put, I perceive the earth was got among the gold and wet, so that the bags were all rotten, all the notes, that I could not tell what in the world to say to it, not knowing how to judge what was wanting or what had been lost by Gibson in his coming down; which, all put together, did make me mad; and at last was forced to take up the head-pieces, dirt and all, and as many of the scattered pieces as I could with the dirt discern by the candlelight, and carry them up into my brother's chamber and there lock them up till I had eat a little supper; and then all people going to bed, W. Hewer and I did all alone, with several pales of water and basins, at last wash the dirt off of the pieces and parted the pieces and the dirt, and then begun to tell; and by a note which I had of the value of the whole (in my pocket) do find that there was short above 100 pieces, which did make me mad; and considering that the neighbour's house was so near, that we could not suppose we could speak one to another in the garden at the place where the gold lay (especially by my father being deaf) but they must know what we had been doing on, I feared that they might in the night come and gather some pieces and prevent us the next morning; so W. Hewer and I out again about midnight (for it was now grown so late) and there by candlelight did make shift to gather 45 pieces more – and so in and to cleanse them, and by this time it was past 2 in the morning; and so to bed, with my mind pretty quiet to think that I have recovered so many.

And then to bed, and I lay in the trundle-bed, the girl being gone to bed to my wife. And there lay in some disquiet all night, telling of the clock till it was daylight; and then rose and called W. Hewer, and he and I, with pails and a Sive, did lock ourselfs into the garden and there gather all the earth about the place into pails, and then Sive those pails in one of the summer-houses (just as they do for Dyamonds in other parts of the world); and there to our great content did with much trouble by 9 a-clock, and by that time we emptied several pails and could not find one, we did make the last night's 45 up 79; so that we are come to about 20 or 30 of what I think the true number should be, and perhaps within less; and of them I may reasonably think that Mr. Gibson might lose some, so that I am pretty well satisfied that my loss is not great and do bless God that it is so well; and do leave my father to make a second examination of the dirt – which he promises he will do; and poor man, is mightily troubled for this accident. But I declared myself very well satisfied, and so endeed I am and my mind at rest in it, it being but an accident which is unusual; and so gives me some kind of content to remember how painful it is sometimes to keep money, as well as to get it, and how doubtful I was how to keep it all night and how to secure it to London. And so got all my gold put up in bags; and so having the last night wrote to my Lady Sandwich to lend me John Bowles to go along with me my Journy, not telling her the reason, but it was only to secure my gold, we to breakfast; and then about 10 a-clock took coach, my wife and I, and Willett and W. Hewer, and Murford and Bowles (whom my Lady lent me), and my brother John on horseback; and with these four I thought myself pretty safe. But before we went out, the Huntington music came to me and played, and it was better then that of Cambridge. Here I took leave of my father, and did give my sister 20*s*. She cried at my going; but whether it was at her unwillingness for my going or any unkindness of my wife's or no, I know not; but God forgive me, I take her to be so cunning and ill-natured that I have no great love for her; but only, is my sister and must be provided for. My gold, I put into a basket and set under one of the seats; and so my work every quarter of an hour was to look to see whether all was well, and did ride in great fear all the day; but it was a pleasant day and good company, and I mightily contented. Mr. Sheply saw me beyond St. Neotts and there parted, and we straight to Stevenage, through Baldock lanes, which are already very bad. And at Stevenage we came well before night, and all safe; and there with great care I got the gold up to the chamber, my wife carrying one bag and the girl another and W. Hewer the rest in the basket, and set it all under a bed in our chamber; and then sat down to talk and were very pleasant, satisfying myself, among other things from Jo. Bowles, in some terms of Hunting and about deere, bucks, and does; and so anon to supper, and very merry we were and a good supper; and after supper to bed. Brecocke alive still, and the best Host I know almost.

12.     Up, and eat our breakfast and set out about 9 a-clock; and so to Barnett, where we stayed and baited (the weather very good all day and yesterday) and by 5 a-clock got home, where I find all well; and

did bring my gold, to my heart's content, very safe home, having not this day carried it in a basket but in our hands: the girl took care of one and my wife another bag, and I the rest – I being afeared of the bottom of the coach, lest it should break; and therefore was at more ease in my mind then I was yesterday. At home do find that Sir W. Batten's buriall was today; carried from hence with a hundred or two of coaches to Walthamstow and there buried.

15. Up, and to the office; where Sir W. Penn being ill of the gout, we all of us met there in his parlour and did the business of the office, our greatest business now being to manage the pay of the ships in order and with speed, to satisfy the Commissioners of the Treasury. This morning my brother set out for Brampton again, and is gone. At noon home to dinner; and thence my wife and I and Willett to the Duke of York's House, where after long stay the King and Duke of York came, and there saw *The Coffee house*, the most ridiculous, insipid play that ever I saw in my life – and glad we were that Baterton had no part in it. But here, before the play begin, my wife begin to complain to me of Willetts confidence in sitting cheek by jowl by us; which was a poor thing, but I perceive she is already jealous of my kindness to her, so that I begin to fear this girl is not likely to stay long with us. The play done, we home by coach, it being moonlight; and got well home, and I to my chamber to settle some papers, and so to supper and to bed.

16. Up, and at home most of the morning with Sir H. Cholmly about some accounts of his; and for news, he tells me that the Commons and Lords have concurred, and delivered the King their thanks, among other things, for his removal of the Chancellor – who took their thanks very well; and among other things, promised them (in these words) "never in any degree to entertain the Chancellor [in] any imployment again."

17. Up; and being sent for by my Lady Batten, I to her and there she found fault with my not seeing her since her being a widow; which I excused as well as I could, though it is a fault, but it is my nature not to be forward in visits. But here she told me her condition (which is good enough, being sole executrix, to the disappointment of all her husband's children). And here do see what creatures widows are in weeping for their husbands, and then presently leaving off; but I cannot wonder at it, the cares of the

world taking place of all other passions. Thence to the office – where all the morning busy; and at noon home to dinner, where Mr. John Andrews and his wife came and dined with me, and pretty merry we were; only, I out of humour the greatest part of the dinner, by reason that my people had forgot to get wine ready (I having none in my house, which I cannot say now these almost three years I think, without having two or three sorts), by which we were fain to stay a great while while some could be fetched. When it came, I begun to be merry, and merry we were; but it was an odd, strange thing to observe of Mr. Andrews what a fancy he hath to raw meat, that he eats it with no pleasure unless the blood run about his chops; which it did now, by a leg of mutton that was not above half-boiled; but it seems, at home all his meat is dressed so, and beef and all, and eats it so at nights also. This afternoon my Lord Anglesy tells us that the House of Commons have this morning run into the enquiry in many things; as, the sale of Dunkirke, the dividing of the fleet the last year, the business of the prizes with my Lord Sandwich, and many other things; so that now they begin to fall close upon it and God knows what will be the end of it, but a committee they have chosen to inquire into the miscarriages of the Warr.

18. To several places to buy a hat and books and neckcloths, and several errands I did before I got home; and among others, bought me two new pair of spectacles of Turlington, who it seems is famous for them. And his daughter, he being out of the way, doth advise me to very young sights,[1] as that that will help me most; and promises me great ease from them, and I will try them.

20. *Lords day*. Up, and put on my new Tunique of velvett, which is very plain, but good. This morning is brought to me an order for the presenting the committee of Parliament tomorrow with a list of the commanders and ships' names of all the fleets set out since the war, and perticularly of those ships which were divided from the fleet with Prince Rupert;[2] which gives me occasion to see that they are busy after that business – and I am glad of it. So I alone to church and then home, and there Mr. Deane comes and dines with me by appointment; and both at and after dinner, he and I spent all the day

1. Lenses suitable for young people with short sight.
2. In the Four Days Battle, June 1666.

till it was dark in discourse of business of the Navy and the ground of the many miscarriages; wherein he doth inform me in many more then I knew, and I had desired him to put them in writing; and many endeed they are, and good ones. And also we discoursed of the business of shipping, and he hath promised me a Draught of the ship he is now building – wherein I am mightily pleased. This afternoon comes to me Capt. O Bryan, about a ship that the King hath given him, and he and I talk of the Parliament and he tells me that the business of the Duke of York's slackening sail in the first fight, at the beginning of the war,[1] is brought into Question, and Sir W. Pen and Captain Cox is to appear tomorrow about it. And is thought will at last be laid upon Mr. Brouncker's bringing orders from the Duke of York (which the Duke of York doth not own) to Capt. Cox to do it; but it seems they do resent this very highly, and are mad in going through all businesses where they can lay any fault. I am glad to hear that in the world I am as kindly spoke of as anybody; for, for aught I see, there is bloody work like to be, Sir W. Coventry having been forced to produce a letter in Parliament wherein the Duke of Albemarle did from Sherenesse write in what good posture all things were at Chatham, and that the Chain was so well placed that he feared no attempts of the enemy. So that, among other things, I see everybody is upon his own defence, and spares not to blame another to defend himself; and the same course I shall take. But God knows where it will end.

21.    After dinner, I away to Westminster, and up to the Parliament house and there did wait with great patience, till 7 at night, to be called in to the Committee, who sat all this afternoon examining the business of Chatham; and at last was called in and told that the list they expected from us Mr. Wren had promised them, and only bade me to bring all my fellow-officers thither to attend them tomorrow afternoon – Sir Rob. Brookes in the chair; methinks a sorry fellow to be there, because a young man, and yet he seems to speak very well.

22.    Slept but ill all the last part of the night, for fear of this day's success in Parliament; therefore up, and all of us all the morning close, till almost 2 a-clock, collecting all we had to say and had done from the beginning touching the safety of the River Medway and

1. The Battle of Lowestoft, June 1665.

Chatham; and having done this and put it into order, we away, I not having time to eat my dinner; and so all in my Lord Brouncker's coach (that is to say, Brouncker, W. Penn, T. Harvy, and myself), talking of the other great matter with which they charge us, that is, of discharging men by ticket, in order to our defence in case that should be asked. We came to the Parliament door; and there, after a little waiting till the Committee was sat, we were, the House being very full, called in (Sir W. Penn went in and sat as a Member; and my Lord Brouncker would not at first go in, expecting to have a chair set for him; but after a few words I had occasion to mention him, and so he was called in, but without any more chair or respect paid him then myself); and so Brouncker and T. Harvy and I were there to answer, and I had a chair brought for me to lean my books upon; and so did give them such an account, in a series, of the whole business that had passed the office touching the matter, and so answered all Questions given me about it, that I did not perceive but they were fully satisfied with me and the business as to our Office; and then Comissioner Pett (who was by at all my discourse, and this held till within an hour after candlelight, for I had candles brought in to read my papers by) was to answer for himself, we having lodged all matters with him for execution. But Lord, what a tumultuous thing this committee is, for all the reputation they have of a great council, is a strange consideration; there being as impertinent Questions, and as disorderly proposed, as any man could make. But Comissioner Pett, of all men living, did make the weakest defence for himself; nothing to the purpose nor to satisfaction nor certain, but sometimes one thing and sometimes another, sometimes for himself and sometimes against him; and his greatest failure was (that I observed) from his not considering whether the Question propounded was his part to answer to or no, and the thing to be done was his work to do – the want of which distinction will overthrow him; for he concerns himself in giving an account of the disposal of the boats, which he had no reason at all to do, or take any blame upon him for them. None of my Brethren said anything but myself; only two or three silly words my Lord Brouncker gave, in answer to one Question about the number of men there in the King's yard at that time. At last the House dismissed us, and shortly after did adjourne the debate till Friday next; and my Cosen Pepys did come out and joy me in my acquitting myself so well, and so did several others, and my fellow-officers all very briske to see themselfs so well acquitted – which makes me a little proud, but yet not secure but we may yet meet with a back-blow which we see not. So, with our hearts very light, Sir W. Penn and I in his coach home, it being now near 8 a-clock; and so to the office and did a little business by the post, and so home, hungry, and eat a good supper and so, with my mind well at ease, to bed – my wife not very well of those.

23. This day it was moved in the House that a day might be appointed to bring in an Impeachment against the Chancellor, but it was decried as being irreguler; but that if there was ground for complaint, it might be brought to the committee for miscarriages, and if they thought good, to present it to the House; and so it was carried.

30. All the morning, till past noon, preparing over again our report this afternoon to the committee of Parliament about Tickets, and then home to eat a bit. And then with Sir W. Penn to Whitehall, where we did a very little business with the Duke of York at our usual meeting. Thence to the Parliament house, where after the Committee was sat, I was called in; and the first thing was upon the complaint of a dirty slut that was there, about a ticket which she had lost and had applied herself to me for another. I did give them a short and satisfactory answer to that; and so they sent her away, and were ashamed of their foolery in giving occasion to 500 seamen and seamen's wifes to come before them, as there was this afternoon. But then they fell to the business of tickets; and I did give them the best answer I could, but had not scope to do it in that methodical manner which I had prepared myself for; but they did ask a great many broken rude questions about it, and were mighty hot whether my Lord Brouncker had any order to discharge whole ships by ticket; and because my answer was with distinction and not direct, I did perceive they were not so fully satisfied therewith as I could wish they were: so my Lord Brouncker was called in, and they could fasten nothing on him that I could see, nor endeed was there any proper matter for blame. But Lord, to see that we should be brought to justify ourselfs in a thing of necessity and profit to the King, and of no profit or convenience to us, but the contrary.

31. I to Westminster, and there at the lobby do hear by Comissioner Pett to my great amazement that he is in worse condition then before, by the coming in of the Duke of Albemarle's

and Prince Rupert's narratives[1] this day; wherein the former doth most severely lay matters upon him, so as the House this day have I think ordered him to the Tower again. I did then go down, and there met with Coll. Reemes and Cosen Rogr. Pepys; and there they do tell me how the Duke of Albemarle and the Prince have lay blame on a great many; and perticularly on our office in general, and perticularly for want of provisions, wherein I shall come to be questioned again in that business myself; which doth trouble me.

# –✳NOVEMBER✳–

2.   Up, and to the office, where busy all the morning. At noon home; and after dinner, my wife and Willett and I to the King's House and there saw *Henry the Fourth*; and contrary to expectation, was pleased in nothing more then in Cartwright's speaking of Falstaffe's speech about *What is Honour?* The house full of Parliament-men, it being holiday with them. And it was observable how a gentleman of good habitt, sitting just before us eating of some fruit, in the midst of the play did drop down as dead, being choked; but with much ado, Orange Mall did thrust her finger down his throat and brought him to life again. After the play, we home and I busy at the office late; and then home to supper and to bed.

4.   Sir H. Cholmly and I to the Excise Office to see what tallies are paying; and thence back to the Old Exchange, by the way talking of news, and he owning Sir W. Coventry in his opinion to be one of the worthiest men in the nation – as I do really think he is. He tells me he doth think really that they will cut off my Lord Chancellor's head, the Chancellor at this day showing as much pride as is possible to those few that venture their fortunes by coming to see him; and that the Duke of York is troubled much, knowing that those that fling down the Chancellor cannot stop there, but will do something to him to prevent his having it in his power hereafter to revenge himself and father-in-law upon them. And this, Sir H. Cholmly fears, may be by divorcing the Queen and getting another, or declaring the Duke of Monmouth legitimate – which

1. Reports presented to the Commons' committee on the miscarriages of the war.

God forbid. He tells me he doth verily believe that there will come in an Impeachment of high treason against my Lord of Ormond; among other things, for ordering the quartering of soldiers in Ireland on free quarter, which it seems is high treason in that country and was one of the things that lost the Lord Strafford his head.

7. Up, and at the office hard all the morning; and at noon resolve with Sir W. Penn to go see *The Tempest*, an old play of Shakespeares, acted here the first day. And so my wife and girl and W. Hewer by themselfs, and Sir W. Penn and I afterward by ourselfs, and forced to sit in the side Balcone over against the Musique-room at the Dukes House, close by my Lady Dorsett and a great many great ones: the house mighty full, the King and Court there, and the most innocent play that ever I saw, and a curious piece of Musique in an Echo of half-sentences, the Echo repeating the former half while the man goes on to the latter, which is mighty pretty. The play no great wit; but yet good, above ordinary plays. Thence home with W. Penn, and there all mightily pleased with the play; and so to supper and to bed, after having done at the office.

11. Up, and to Simpson at work in my office; and thence with Sir G. Carteret (who came to talk with me) to Broad streete, where great crowding of people for money, at which he blessed himself. Thence with him and Lord Brouncker to Capt. Cockes (he out of doors) and there drunk their morning draught; and thence G. Carteret and I toward the Temple in coach together, and there he did tell me how the King doth all he can in the world to overthrow my Lord Chancellor, and that notice is taken of every man about the King that is not seen to promote the ruine of the Chancellor; and that this being another great day in his business, he dares not but be there. He tells me that as soon as Secretary Morrice brought the great Seale from my Lord Chancellor, Babb. May fell upon his knees and ketched the King about the legs and joyed him, and said that this was the first time that ever he could call him King of England, being freed this great man – which was a most ridiculous saying.

15. To Westminster, and there I walked with several and do hear that there is to be a conference between the two Houses today; so I stayed, and it was only to tell the Commons that the Lords cannot

agree to the confining or sequestering of the Earle of Clarendon from Parliament, forasmuch as they do not specify any perticular crime which they lay upon him and call treason. This the House did receive, and so parted; at which, I hear the Commons are like to grow very high, and will insist upon their privileges and the Lords will on theirs – though the Duke of Buckingham, Bristoll and others have been very high in the House of Lords to have had him committed. This is likely to breed ill blood. Thence I away home (calling at my Mercer and tailor's) and there find, as I expected, Mr. Cæsar and little Pellam Humphrys, lately returned from France and is an absolute Monsieur, as full of form and confidence and vanity, and disparages everything and everybody's skill but his own. The truth is, everybody says he is very able; but to hear how he laughs at all the King's music here, as Blagrave and others, that they cannot keep time nor tune nor understand anything, and that Grebus the Frenchman, the King's Master of the Musique, how he understands nothing nor can play on any instrument and so cannot compose, and that he will give him a lift out of his place, and that he and the King are mighty great, and that he hath already spoke to the King of Grebus, would make a man piss. I had a good dinner for them, as a venison pasty and some fowl, and after dinner we did play, he on the Theorbo, Mr. Cæsar on his French lute, and I on the viol, but made but mean music; nor do I see that this Frenchman doth so much wonders on the Theorbo, but without question he is a good musician; but his vanity doth offend me. They gone towards night, I to the office awhile, and then home and to my chamber, where busy; till by and by comes Mr. Moore, and he stayed and supped and talked with me about many things. By and by I got him to read part of my Lord Cooke's chapter of Treason, which is mighty well worth reading and doth inform me in many things; and for aught I see, it is useful now to know what these crimes are. And then to supper; and after supper he went away, and so I got the girl to comb my head and then to bed – my eyes bad.

18.    Up, and all the morning at my office till 3 after noon with Mr. Hater, about perfecting my little pocket market-book of the office, till my eyes were ready to fall out of my head. And then home to dinner, glad that I had done so much; and so abroad to Whitehall to Commissioners of the Treasury and there did a little business with them; and so home, leaving multitude of solicitors at their door, of one sort or other, complaining for want of such despatch as they

had in my Lord Treasurer's time; when I believe more business was despatched, but it was in his manner, to the King's wrong. Thence took up my wife, whom I had left at her tailor's, and home; and there to save my eyes, got my wife at home to read again, as last night, in the same book, till W. Batelier came and spent the evening talking with us, and supped with us, and so to bed.

20. Up, and all the morning at my office shut up with Mr. Gibson, I walking and he reading to me the order-books of the office from the beginning of the Warr, for preventing the Parliament's having them in their hands before I have looked them over and seen the utmost that can be said against us from any of our orders – and to my great content, all the morning I found none. So at noon home to dinner with my clerks – who have of late dined frequently with me, and I do purpose to have them so still, by that means I having opportunity to talk with them about business, and I love their company very well. All the morning Mr. Hater and the boy did shut up themselfs at my house, doing something towards the finishing the abstract-book of our contracts for my pocket, which I shall now want very much. After dinner I stayed at home all the afternoon, and Gibson with me, and he and I shut up till about 10 at night; we went through all our orders and towards the end I do meet with two or three orders for our discharging of two or three little vessels by ticket without money, which doth plunge me; but however, I have the advantage by this means to study an answer – and to prepare a defence, at least for myself.

21. Up, and to the office, where all the morning; and at noon home, where my wife not very well, but is to go to Mr. Mills's child's christening, where she is godmother, Sir J. Mennes and Sir R. Brookes her companions. I left her after dinner (my clerks dining with me) to go with Sir J. Mennes, and I to the office, where did much business till after candlelight; and then, my eyes beginning to fail me, I out and took coach and to Arundell house, where the meeting of Gresham College was broke up; but there meeting Creed, I with him to the tavern in St. Clements churchyard, where was Deane Wilkins, Dr. Whistler, Dr. Floyd, a divine, admitted, I perceive, this day, and other brave men. Among the rest, they discourse of a man that is a little frantic (that hath been a kind of minister, Dr. Wilkins saying that he hath read for him in his church) that is poor and a debauched man, that the College have hired for

20*s*. to have some of the blood of a Sheep let into his body; and it is to be done on Saturday next. They purpose to let in about twelve ounces, which they compute is what will be let in in a minutes time by a watch. They differ in the opinion they have of the effects of it; some think that it may have a good effect upon him as a frantic man, by cooling his blood; others, that it will not have any effect at all. But the man is a healthy man, and by this means will be able to give an account what alteration, if any, he doth find in himself, and so may be usefull. On this occasion Dr. Whistler told a pretty story related by Muffett, a good author, of Dr. Cayus that built Key's College: that being very old and lived only at that time upon woman's milk, he, while he fed upon the milk of a angry fretful woman, was so himself; and then being advised to take of a good-natured patient woman, he did become so, beyond the common temper of his age. Thus much nutriment, they observed, might do. Their discourse was very fine; and if I should be put out of my office, I do take great content in the liberty I shall be at of frequenting these gentlemen's companies.

29.     Waked about 7 a-clock this morning with a noise I supposed I heard near our chamber, of knocking, which by and by increased, and I more awake, could distinguish it better; I then waked my wife and both of us wondered at it, and lay so a great while, while that encreased; and at last heard it plainer, knocking as if it were breaking down a window for people to get out – and then removing of stools and chairs, and plainly by and by going up and down our stairs. We lay both of us afeared; yet I would have rose, but my wife would not let me; besides, I could not do it without making noise; and we did both conclude that thiefs were in the house, but wondered what our people did, whom we thought either killed or afeared as we were. Thus we lay till the clock struck 8, and high day. At last I removed my gown and slippers safely to the other side of the bed over my wife, and there safely rose and put on my gown and breeches, and then with a firebrand in my hand safely opened the door, and saw nor heard anything. Then (with fear, I confess) went to the maid's chamber-door, and all quiet and safe. Called Jane up, and went down safely and opened my chamber, where all well. Then more freely about, and to the kitchen, where the cook-maid up and all safe. So up again, and when Jane came and we demanded whether she heard no noise, she said, "Yes, and was afeared," but rose with the other maid and found nothing, but heard a noise in the

great stack of chimneys that goes from Sir J. Mennes's through our house; and so we sent, and their chimneys have been swept this morning, and the noise was that and nothing else. It is one of the most extraordinary accidents in my life, and gives ground to think of Don Quixot's adventures how people may be surprized – and the more from an accident last night, that our young gibb-cat did leap down our stairs from top to bottom at two leaps and frighted us, that we could not tell well whether it was the cat or a spirit, and do sometimes think this morning that the house might be haunted. Glad to have this so well over, and endeed really glad in my mind, for I was much afeared. I dressed myself, and to the office both forenoon and afternoon, mighty hard putting papers and things in order to my extraordinary satisfaction, and consulting my clerks in many things, who are infinite helps to my memory and reasons of things. And so, being weary and my eyes akeing, having over-wrought them today reading so much shorthand, I home and there to supper, it being late, and to bed.

30. Up and to the office, where all the morning, and then by coach to Arundell house to the elections of Officers for the next year; where I was near being chosen of the Council, but am glad I was not, for I could not have attended; though above all things, I could wish it, and do take it as a mighty respect to have been named there. The company great and elections long; and then to Cary house, a house now of entertainment, next my Lord Ashly's; and there, where I have heretofore heard Common-Prayer in the time of Dr. Mossum, we after two hours' stay, sitting at the table with our napkins open, had our dinners brought; but badly done. But here was good company, I choosing to sit next Dr. Wilkins, Sir George Ent, and others whom I value. And there talked of several things; among others, Dr. Wilkins, talking of the universall speech, of which he hath a book coming out, did first inform me how man was certainly made for society, he being of all creatures the least armed for defence; and of all creatures in the world, the young ones are not able to do anything to help themselfs, nor can find the dug without being put to it, but would die if the mother did not help it. And he says were it not for speech, man would be a very mean creature. Much of this good discourse we had. But here above all, I was pleased to see the person who had his blood taken out. He speaks well, and did this day give the Society a relation thereof in Latin, saying that he finds himself much better since, and as a new

man. But he is cracked a little in his head, though he speaks very reasonably and very well. He had but 20*s*. for his suffering it, and is to have the same again tried upon him – the first sound man that ever had it tried on him in England, and but one that we hear of in France, which was a porter hired by the virtuosi. Here all the afternoon till within night. Then I took coach and to the Exchange, where I was to meet my wife, but she was gone home; and so I to Westminster hall and there took a turn or two; but meeting nobody to discourse with, returned to Cary house and there stayed a little and saw a pretty deception of the sight, by a glass with water poured into it, with a stick standing up with three balls of wax upon it, one distant from the other – how these balls did seem double and disappear one after another, mighty pretty.

# –❧DECEMBER❧–

3.   At noon home to dinner and busy all the afternoon; and at night home and there met W. Batelier, who tells me the first great news, that my Lord Chancellor is fled this day. By and by to Sir W. Penn's, where I hear the whole, that my Lord Chancellor is gone and left a paper behind him for the House of Lords, telling them the reason of his retiring, complaining of a design for his ruin. But the paper I must get; only, the thing at present is great and will put the King and Commons to some new counsels certainly. So home to supper and to bed.

6.   My Lord Anglesy told me how my Lord Northampton brought in a Bill into the House of Lords yesterday, under the name of *A Bill for the honour and privilege of the House, and mercy to my Lord Clarendon* – which he told me he opposed, saying that he was a man accused of treason by the House of Commons, and mercy was not proper for him, having not been tried yet, and so no mercy needful for him. However, the Duke of Buckingham did, and others, desire the Bill might be read; and it was for banishing my Lord Clarendon from all his Majesty's dominions and that it should be treason to have him found in any of them. The thing is only a thing of vanity and to insult over him; which is mighty poor I think, and so doth everybody else. By and by home with Sir J. Mennes, who tells me that my Lord Clarendon did go away in a Custom-house boat and is

now at Callis; upon [whom], I confess, nothing seems to hang more heavy then his leaving of this unfortunate paper behind him, that hath angered both Houses and hath I think reconciled them in that which otherwise would have broke them in pieces; so that I do hence, and from Sir W. Coventry's late example and doctrine to me, learn that on these sorts of occasions there is nothing like silence – it being seldom any wrong to a man to say nothing, but for the most part it is to say anything. This day, in coming home, Sir J. Mennes told me a pretty story of Sir Lewes Dives, whom I saw this morning speaking with him; that having escaped once out of prison through a house of office, and another time in woman's apparel and leaping over a broad canal, a soldier in roguery put his hand towards her belly, and swore, says he, "This is a strong Jade, but I never felt a cunt with a handle to it before." He told me also a story of my Lord Cottington: who wanting a son, entended to make his Nephew his heir, a country boy, but did alter his mind upon the boy's being persuaded by another young heir (in roguery) to Crow like a cock at my Lord's table, much company being there and the boy having a great trick at doing that perfectly – my Lord bade them take away that fool from the table, and so gave over the thoughts of making him his heir from this piece of folly. To the office, where Capt Cocke came to me; and among other discourse, tells me that he is told that an impeachment against Sir W. Coventry will be brought in very soon.

7.    All the morning at the office, and at noon home to dinner with my clerks. And while we were at dinner comes Willett's aunt to see her and my wife. She is a very fine widow and pretty handsome, but extraordinary well-carriaged and speaks very handsomely and with extraordinary understanding, so as I spent the whole after-noon in her company with my wife, she understanding all the things of note touching plays and fashions and Court and everything, and speaks rarely, which pleases me mightily, and seems to love her niece very well, and was so glad (which was pretty odde) to see that since she came hither her breasts begin to swell, she being afeared before that she would have none – which was a pretty kind of content she gave herself. She tells us that *Catelin* is likely to be soon acted; which I am glad to hear – but it is at the King's House. But the King's House is at present, and hath for some days been, silenced upon some difference [between] Heart and Moone. She being gone, I to the office and there late doing

business; and so home to supper and to bed. Somebody told me this day that they hear that Thompson with the wooden leg, and Wildman the Fifth-Monarchy man (a great creature of the Duke of Buckinghams) are in nomination to be commissioners,[1] among other, upon the Bill of Accounts.

19. Up, and to the office, where Comissioner Middleton first took place at the Board as Surveyor of the Navy; and endeed I think will be an excellent officer I am sure, much beyond what his predecessor was. At noon, to avoid being forced to invite him to dinner, it being his first day and nobody inviting him, I did go to the Change with Sir W. Penn in his coach, who first went to Guildhall, whither I went with him – he to speak with Sheriffe Gawden, I only for company; and did here look up and down this place, where I have not been before since the fire, and I saw the City are going apace on in the rebuilding of Guildhall. Thence to the Change, where I stayed very little; and so away home to dinner and there find my wife mightily out of order with her teeth. At the office all the afternoon, and at night by coach to Westminster to the Hall, where I met nobody walking, and do find that this evening the King by Message (which he never did before) hath passed several bills; among others, that for the accounts and for banishing my Lord Chancellor, and hath adjourned the House to February; at which I am glad, hoping in this time to get leisure to state my Tanger accounts and to prepare better for the Parliament's enquiries.

21. At the office all the morning, and at noon home to dinner with my clerks and Creed; who among other things, all alone after dinner, talking of the times, he tells me that the Nonconformists are mighty high and their meetings frequented and connived at; and they do expect to have their day now soon, for my Lord of Buckingham is a declared friend to them, and even to the Quakers, who had very good words the other day from the King himself; and which is more, the Archbishop of Canterbury is called no more to the Caball (nor, by the way, Sir W. Coventry; which I am sorry for, the Caball at present being, as he says, the King and Duke of Buckingham and Lord Keeper, Albemarle and Privy Seale), the Bishops differing from the King in the late business in the House of

1. The Brooke House committee which now conducted a severe enquiry and reported in October 1669.

Lords[1] having caused this and what is like to fallow, for everybody is encouraged nowadays to speak and even to print (as I have one of them) as bad things against them as ever in the year 1640; which is a strange change. He gone, I to the office, where busy till late at night; and then home to sit with my wife, who is a little better and her cheek asswaged. I read to her out of the *History of Algiers*, which is mighty pretty reading – and did discourse alone about my sister Pall's match which is now on foot with one Jackson, another nephew of Mr. Phillips's, to whom the former[2] hath left his estate. And so to supper and then to bed.

22. *Lords day.* Up, and my wife, poor wretch, still in pain; and then to dress myself and down to my chamber to settle some papers; and thither came to me Willet with an errand from her mistress, and this time I first did give her a little kiss, she being a very pretty-humoured girl, and so one that I do love mightily. Thence to my office and there did a little business; and so to church – where a dull sermon; and then home and there to dinner, and Cosen Kate Joyce came and dined with me and Mr. Holliard; but by chance, I offering occasion to him to discourse of the church of Rome, Lord, how he run on to discourse with the greatest vehemence and importunity in the world, as the only thing in the world that he is full of – and it was good sport to me to see him so earnest on so little occasion. She came to see us and to tell me that her husband is going to build his house again, and would borrow of me 300*l*; which I shall upon good security be willing to do, and so told her, being willing to have some money out of my hands upon good security. After dinner, up to my wife again, and who is in great pain still with her tooth and cheek; and there, they gone, I spent the most of the afternoon and night reading and talking to bear her company, and so to supper and to bed.

24. Up, and all the morning at the office; and at noon with my clerks to dinner and then to the office again, busy at the office till 6 at night; and then by coach to St. James's, it being now about 6 at night, my design being to see the Ceremonys, this night being the Eve of Christmas, at the Queen's Chapel, But it being not begun, I to Westminster hall and there stayed and walked; and then to the

1. Clarendon's impeachment.
2. Her former suitor, Robert Ensum (d. 1666).

Swan and there drank and talked, and did besar a little Frank; and so to Whitehall and sent my coach round, and I through the park to chapel, where I got in up almost to the rail and with a great deal of patience, stayed from 9 at night to 2 in the morning in a very great Crowd; and there expected, but found nothing extraordinary, there being nothing but a high Masse. The Queen was there and some ladies. But Lord, what an odde thing it was for me to be in a crowd of people, here a footman, there a beggar, here a fine lady, there a zealous poor papist, and here a Protestant, two or three together, come to see the show. I was afeared of my pocket being picked very much. Their music very good endeed, but their service I confess too frivolous, that there can be no zeal go along with it; and I do find by them themselfs, that they do run over their beads with one hand, and point and play and talk and make signs with the other, in the midst of their Messe. But all things very rich and beautiful. And I see the papists had the wit, most of them, to bring cushions to kneel on; which I wanted, and was mightily troubled to kneel. All being done, and I sorry for my coming, missing of what I expected; which was to have had a child borne and dressed there and a great deal of do, but we broke up and nothing like it done; and there I left people receiving the sacrament, and the Queen gone, and ladies; only my [Lady] Castlemayne, who looks prettily in her night-clothes. And so took my coach, which waited, and away through Covent garden to set down two gentlemen and a lady, who came thither to see also and did make mighty mirth in their talk of the folly of this religion; and so I stopped, having set them down, and drank some burnt wine at the Rose tavern door, while the constables came and two or three Bell-men went by, it being a fine light moonshine morning; and so home round the City and stopped and dropped money at five or six places, which I was the willinger to do, it being Christmas day; and so home and there find wife in bed, and Jane and the maids making pyes, and so I to bed and slept well.

28. Up, and to the office, where busy all the morning. At noon home, and there to dinner with my clerks and Mr. Pelling, and had a very good dinner; among others, a haunch of venison boiled, and merry we were. And I rose soon from dinner, and with my wife and girl to The King's House and there saw *The Mad Couple*, which is but an ordinary play; but only, Nells and Hearts mad parts are most excellently done, but especially hers; which makes it a miracle to me

to think how ill she doth any serious part, as the other day, just like a fool or changeling; and in a mad part, doth beyond all imitation almost. Many fine faces here today. It pleased us mightily to see the natural affection of a poor woman, the mother of one of the children brought on the stage – the child crying, she by force got upon the stage, and took up her child and carried it away off of the stage from Hart. Thence home, and there to the office late and then home to supper and to bed.

30.    Up before day and by coach to Westminster; and there first to Sir H. Cholmly, and there I did to my great content deliver him up his little several papers for sums of money paid him, and took his regular receipts upon his orders, wherein I am safe. Thence to Whitehall and there to visit Sir G. Carteret, and there was with him a great while and my Lady and they seem in very good humour; but by and by Sir G. Carteret and I all alone, and there we did talk of the ruinous condition we are in. That the Duke of Buckingham doth rule all now; and the Duke of York comes endeed to the Caball but signifies little there. That this new faction doth not endure, nor the King, Sir W. Coventry; but yet that he is so usefull that they cannot be without him, but that he is not now called to the Caball. That my Lord of Buckingham, Bristoll, and Arlington do seem to agree in these things; but that they do not in their hearts trust one another, but do drive several ways, all of them. In short, he doth bless himself that he is no more concerned in matters now and the hopes he hath of being at liberty, when his accounts are over, to retire into the country. That he doth give over the Kingdom for wholly lost. So after some other little discourse, I away; and meeting Mr. Cooling, I with him by coach to the Wardrobe, where I never was since the Fire, in Hatton garden, but did not light; and he tells me he fears that my Lord Sandwich will suffer much by Mr. Townsends' being untrue to him, he being now unable to give the Commis-sioners of the Treasury an account of his money received, by many thousands of pounds – which I am troubled for. This day I did carry money out and paid several debts; among others, my tailor, and shoemaker, and draper, Sir W. Turner, who begun to talk of the commission of accounts, wherein he is one; but though they are the greatest people that ever were in the nation as to power, and like to be our judges, yet I did never speak one word to him of desiring favour or bidding him joy in it; but did answer him to what he said, and do resolve to stand and fall by my silent preparing to answer

whatever can be laid to me; and that will be my best proceeding I think. This day I got a little rent in my new fine Camlett cloak with the latch of Sir G. Carteret's door; but it is darned up at my tailor's, that it will be no great blemish to it; but it troubled me.

31.   Thus ends the year, with great happiness to myself and family as to health and good condition in the world, blessed be God for it; only, with great trouble to my mind in reference to the public, there being little hopes left but that the whole nation must in a very little time be lost, either by troubles at home, the Parliament being dissatisfied and the King led into unsettled counsels by some about him, himself considering little – and divisions growing between the King and Duke of York; or else by foreign invasion, to which we must submit, if any at this bad point of time should come upon us; which the King of France is well able to do. These thoughts, and some cares upon me concerning my standing in this office when the committee of Parliament shall come to examine our Navy matters, which they will now shortly do. I pray God they may do the Kingdom service therein, as they will have sufficient opportunity of doing it.

# 1668

## ✣JANUARY✣

1. Up, and all the morning in my chamber making up some accounts against this beginning of the new year; and so about noon abroad with my wife, who was to dine with W. Hewer and Willet at Mrs. Pierce's; but I had no mind to be with them, for I do clearly find that my wife is troubled at my friendship with her and Knepp, and so dined with my Lord Crew, with whom was Mr. Browne, Clerk of the House of Lords, and Mr. John Crew. Here was mighty good discourse, as there is alway; and among other things, my Lord Crew did turn to a place in the *Life of Sir Ph. Sidny*, wrote by Sir Fulke Grevill, which doth foretell the present condition of this nation in relation to the Dutch, to the very degree of a prophecy; and is so remarkable that I am resolved to buy one of them, it being quite through a good discourse. Thence I after dinner to the Duke of York's playhouse, and there saw *Sir Martin Marrall*, which I have seen so often; and yet am mightily pleased with it and think it mighty witty, and the fullest of proper matter for mirth that ever was writ. And I do clearly see that they do improve in their acting of it. Here a mighty company of citizens, prentices and others; and it makes me observe that when I begin first to be able to bestow a play on myself, I do not remember that I saw so many by half of the ordinary prentices and mean people in the pit, at 2*s.*–6*d.* apiece, as now; I going for several years no higher then the 12*d.*, and then the 18*d.* places, and though I strained hard to go in then when I did – so much the vanity and prodigality of the age is to be observed in this perticular. Thence I to Whitehall, and there walked up and down the House a while.

By and by I met with Mr. Brisban; and having it in my mind this Christmas to (do what I never can remember that I did) go to see the manner of the gaming at the Groome porter's (I having in my coming from the playhouse stepped into the two Temple halls, and there saw the dirty prentices and idle people playing – wherein I was mistaken in thinking to have seen gentlemen of quality playing

there, as I think it was when I was a little child, that one of my
father's servants, John Bassum I think, carried me in his armes
thither), I did tell him of it and he did lead me thither; where after
staying an hour, they begin to play at about 8 at night – where to see
how differently one man took his losing from another, one cursing
and swearing, and another only muttering and grumbling to
himself, a third without any appearing discontent at all – to see how
the dice will run good luck in one hand for half an hour together –
and another have no good luck at all. To see how easily here, where
they play nothing but guinnys, 100*l* is won or lost. To see two or
three gentlemen come in there drunk, and putting their stock of
gold together – one 22 pieces, the second 4, and the third 5 pieces;
and these to play one with another, and forget how much each of
them brought, but he that brought the 22 think that he brought no
more then the rest. To see the different humours of gamesters to
change their luck when it is bad – how ceremonious they are as to
call for new dice – to shift their places – to alter their manner of
throwing; and that with great industry, as if there was anything in
it. To see how some gamesters, that have no money now to spend
as formerly, do come and sit and look on; as among others, Sir
Lewes Dives, who was here and hath been a great gamester in his
time. To hear their cursing and damning to no purpose; as one man,
being to throw a seven if he could and failing to do it after a great
many throws, cried he would be damned if ever he flung seven
more while he lived, his despair of throwing it being so great, while
others did it as their luck served, almost every throw. To see how
persons of the best quality do here sit down and play with people of
any, though meaner; and to see how people in ordinary clothes shall
come hither and play away 100, or 2 or 300 guinnys, without any
kind of difficulty. And lastly, to see the formality of the Groome
porter, who is their judge of all disputes in play and all quarrels that
may arise therein; and how his under-officers are there to observe
true play at each table and to give new dice, is a consideration I
never could have thought had been in the world, had I not now seen
it. And mighty glad I am that I did see it; and it may be will find
another evening, before Christmas be over, to see it again; when I
may stay later, for their heat of play begins not till about 11 or 12 a-
clock; which did give me another pretty observation, of a man that
did win mighty fast when I was there: I think he won 100*l* at single
pieces in a little time; while all the rest envied him his good fortune,
he cursed it, saying, "A pox on it that it should come so earely upon

me! For this fortune two hours hence would be worth something to me; but then, God damn me, I shall have no such luck." This kind of profane, mad entertainment they give themselfs. And so I having enough for once, refusing to venture, though Brisband pressed me hard and tempted me with saying that no man was ever known to lose the first time, the Devil being too cunning to discourage a gamester; and he offered me also to lend me ten pieces to venture, but I did refuse and so went away – and took coach and home about 9 or 10 at night.

6. *Twelfe day.* Up, leaving my wife to get her ready and the maids to get a supper ready against night for our company; and I by coach to Whitehall and there up and down the House; and among others, met with Mr. Pierce, by whom I find (as I was afeared from the folly of my wife) that he understood that he and his wife was to dine at my house today, whereas it was to sup; and therefore I having done my business at Court, did go home to dinner, and there find Mr. Harris by the like mistake come to dine with me. However, we did get a pretty dinner ready for him; and there he and I to discourse of many things, and I do find him a very excellent person, such as in my whole [life] I do not know another better qualified for converse, whether in things of his own trade or of other kinds, a man of great understanding and observation, and very agreeable in the manner of his discourse, and civil as far as is possible. I was mightily pleased with his company; and after dinner did take coach with him and my wife and girl to go to a play and to carry him thither to his own house. But I light by the way to return home, thinking to have spoke with Mrs. Bagwell, who I did see today in our entry, come from Harwich, whom I have not seen these twelve months I think and more, and voudrais haver hazer algo with her, sed she was gone; and so I took coach, and away to my wife at the Duke of York's House in the pit; and so left her, and to Mrs. Pierce and took her and her cousin Corbet, Knipp, and little James, and brought them to the Duke's House; and the House being full, was forced to carry them to a box, which did cost me 20s. besides oranges; which troubled me – though their company did please me.

Thence, after the play, stayed till Harris was undressed (there being Acted *The Tempest*) and so he withal, all by coaches home, where we find my house with good fires and candles ready, and our office the like, and the two Mercers, and Betty Turner, Pendleton, and W. Batelier; and so with much pleasure we into the house and there fell to dancing, having extraordinary music, two violins and a bass viallin and Theorbo (four hands), the Duke of Buckingham's Musique, the best in Towne, sent me by Greeting; and there we set in to dancing. By and by to my house to a very good supper, and mighty merry and good music playing; and after supper to dancing and singing till about 12 at night; and then we had a good sack-posset for them and an excellent Cake, cost me near 20s. of our Jane's making, which was cut into twenty pieces, there being by this time so many of our company by the coming in of young Goodyer and some others of our neighbours, young men that could dance, hearing of our dancing; and anon comes in Mrs. Turner the mother and brings with her Mrs. Hollworthy, which pleased me mightily; and so to dancing again and singing with extraordinary great pleasure, till about 2 in the morning; and then broke up, and Mrs. Pierce and her family and Harris and Knip by coach home, as late as it was; and they gone, I took Mrs. Turner and Hollworthy home to my house and there gave them wine and sweetmeats; but I find Mrs. Hollworthy but a mean woman, I think, for understanding; only, a little conceited and proud and talking, but nothing extraordinary in person or discourse or understanding. However, I mightily pleased with her being there, I having long longed for to know her; and they being gone, I paid the fiddler 3*l* among the four, and so away to bed, weary and mightily pleased; and have the happiness to reflect upon it as I do sometimes on other things, as going to a play or the like, to be the greatest real comforts that I am to expect in the world, and that it is that that we do really labour in the hopes of; and so I do really enjoy myself, and understand that if I do not do it now, I shall not hereafter, it may be, be able to pay for it or have health to take pleasure in it, and so fool myself with vain expectation of pleasure and go without it.

8. Up; and it being dirty, I by coach (which I was forced to go to the Change for) to Whitehall, and there did deliver the Duke of York a Memoriall for the Council about the case of Tanger's want of money, and I was called in and there my paper was read; I did not think fit to say much, but left them to make what use they pleased of my paper; and so went out and waited without all the morning, and at noon hear that there is something ordered towards our help; and so I away by coach home, taking up Mr. Prin at the Court gate (it raining) and setting him down at the Temple. And by the way did ask him about the manner of holding of Parliaments, and whether

the number of Knights and Burges's were alway the same; and he
says that the latter were not, but that for aught he can find, they
were sent up at the discretion, at first, of the Sheriffes, to whom the
writs are sent to send up generally the Burges's and Cittizens of
their county; and he doth find that heretofore, that Parliament-men
being paid by the country,\* several Burroughs have complained of
the Sheriffes putting them to the charge of sending up Burges's;
which is a very extraordinary thing to me that knew not this but
thought that the number had been known, and always the same.
Thence home to the office, and so with my Lord Brouncker and his
mistress, Williams, to Capt. Cocke's to dinner, where was Temple
and Mr. Porter – and a very good dinner, and merry. Thence with
Lord Brouncker to Whitehall to [the] Commissioners of Treasury,
at their sending for us to discourse about the paying of tickets; and
so away, and I by coach to the Change and there took up my wife
and Mercer and the girl by agreement; and so home, and there with
Mercer to teach her more of *It is decreed*, and to sing other songs and
talk all the evening; and so after supper, I to even my Journall since
Saturday last, and so to bed.

10.    This day I received a letter from my father and another from
my Cosen Roger Pepys, who have had a view of Jackson's
evidences of his estate and do mightily like of the man and his
condition and estate, and do advise me to accept of the match for
my sister and to finish it as soon as I can; and he doth it so as I confess
I am contented to have it done, and so give her her portion; and so I
shall be eased of one care how to provide for her. And do in many
respects think that it may be a match proper enough to have her
married there, and to one that may look after my concernments if
my father should die and I continue where I am. And there[fore] I
am well pleased with it. And so to bed.

11.    Lay some time talking with my wife in bed about Pall's
business, and she doth conclude to have her married here and to be
merry at it; and to have W. Hewer and Batelier, and Mercer and
Willet bridemen and bridemaids, and to be very merry; and so I am
glad of it and do resolve to let it be done as soon as I can. So up and
to the office, where all the morning busy; and thence home to
dinner, and from dinner with Mercer (who dined with us) and wife
and Deb to the King's House, there to see *The Wildgoose chase*,
which I never saw but have long longed to see, it being a famous

play; but as it was yesterday, I do find that where I expect most I find least satisfaction, for in this play I met with nothing extraordinary at all, but very dull inventions and designs. Knipp came and sat by us, and her talk pleased me a little, she telling me how Mis Davis is for certain going away from the Duke's House, the King being in love with her; and a house is taken for her and furnishing and she hath a ring given her already, worth 600*l*. That the King did send several times for Nelly, and she was with him, but what he did she knows not; this was a good while ago, and she says that the King first spoiled Mrs. Weaver – which is very mean methinks in a prince, and I am sorry for it – and can hope for no good to the State from having a prince so devoted to his pleasure. She told me also of a play shortly coming upon the stage of Sir Ch. Sidly's, which she thinks will be called *The Wandring Ladys*, a comedy that she thinks will be most pleasant; and also another play, called *The Duke of Lerma*; besides *Catelin*, which she thinks, for want of the clothes which the King promised them, will not be acted for a good while. Thence home, and there to the office and did some business; and so with my wife for half an hour walking by moonlight and, it being cold frosty weather, walking in the garden; and then home to supper, and so by the fireside to have my head combed, as I do now often do, by Deb, whom I love should be fiddling about me; and so to bed.

12. *Lords day*. Up and to dress myself, and then called in to my wife's chamber, and there she without any occasion fell to discourse of my father's coming to live with us when my sister marries. She declared if he came, she would not live with me but would shame me all over the City and Court; which I made slight of, and so we fell very foul; and I do find she doth keep very bad remembrances of my former unkindnesses to her, and doth mightily complain of her want of money and liberty; which I will rather hear and bear the complaint of then grant the contrary, and so we had very hot work a great while; but at last I did declare as I intend, that my father shall not come and that he doth not desire and intend it; and so we parted with pretty good quiet, and so away I; and being ready, went to church, where first I saw Ald. Backewell and his lady come to our church, they living in Mark lane; and I could find my heart to invite her to sit with us – she being a fine lady. I came in while they were singing the 119 Psalm, while the Sexton was gathering to his box, to which I did give 5*s*. And so after sermon home, my wife, Deb,

and I all alone, and very kind, full of good discourse; and after dinner, I to my chamber, ordering my Tanger accounts to give to the Auditor in a day or two, which should have been long ago with him. At them to my great content all the afternoon till supper and after supper (with my wife, W. Hewer and Deb, pretty merry) till 12 at night, and then to bed.

13.   Up, and Mr. Gibbs comes to me and I give him instructions about the writing fair my Tanger accounts against tomorrow. So I abroad with Sir W. Penn to Whitehall, and there did with the rest attend the Duke of York, where nothing extraordinary; only I perceive there is nothing yet declared for the next year what fleet shall be abroad. Thence homeward by coach and stopped at Martins my bookseller, where I saw the French book which I did think to have had for my wife to translate, called *L'escholle de Filles*, but when I came to look into it, it is the most bawdy, lewd book that ever I saw, rather worse then *putana errante* – so that I was ashamed of reading in it; and so away home, and there to the Change to discourse with Sir H. Cholmly and so home to dinner; and in the evening, having done some business, I with my wife and girl out, and left them at Unthankes while I to Whitehall to the Treasury chamber for an order for Tanger; and so back, took up my wife, and home, and there busy about my Tanger accounts against tomorrow, which I do get ready in good condition; and so with great content to bed.

16.   Up, after talking with my wife with pleasure about her learning on the Flag[el]ette a month or two again this winter, and all the rest of the year her painting, which I do love. And so to the office, where sat all the morning. At noon home to dinner with my gang of clerks, in whose society I am mightily pleased, and mightily with Mr. Gibsons talking; he telling me so many good stories relating to the Warr and practices of commanders, which I will find a time to recollect; and he will be an admirable help to my writing a history of the Navy, if ever I do. So to the office, where busy all the afternoon and evening, and then home. My work this night with my clerks till midnight at the office was to examine my list of ships I am making for myself, and their dimensions, and to see how it agrees or differs from other lists; and I do find so great a difference between them all, that I am at a loss which to take; and therefore think mine to be as much depended upon as any I can

make out of them all. So little care there hath been to this day to know or keep any history of the Navy.

17. Up, and by coach to Whitehall to attend the Council there; and here I met, first by Mr. Castle the shipwright whom I met there, and then from the whole House, all the discourse of the Duell yesterday between the Duke of Buckingham, Holmes, and one Jenkins on one side, and my Lord of Shrewsbury, Sir Jo. Talbot, and one Bernard Howard, on the other side; and all about my Lady Shrewsbury, who is a whore and is at this time, and hath for a great while been, a whore to the Duke of Buckingham; and so her husband challenged him, and they met yesterday in a close near Barne Elmes and there fought; and my Lord Shrewsbury is run through the body from the right breast through the shoulder, and Sir J. Talbot all along up one of his arms, and Jenkins killed upon the place, and the rest all in a little measure wounded. This will make the world think that the King hath good councillors about him, when the Duke of Buckingham, the greatest man about him, is a fellow of no more sobriety then to fight about a whore.

20. Up, and all the morning at the office very busy; and at noon by coach to Westminster to the Chequer about a warrant for Tanger money. In my way, both coming and going, I did stop at Drumbleby's the pipe-maker, there to advise about the making of a flagelette to go low and saft; and he doth show me a way which doth do, and also a fashion of having two pipes of the same note fastened together, so as I can play on one and then echo it upon the other; which is mighty pretty. So to my Lord Crew's to dinner, where we hear all the good news of our making a league now with Holland against the French power coming over them or us, which is the first good act that hath been done a great while, and done secretly and with great seeming wisdom; and is certainly good for us at this time, while we are in no condition to resist the French if he should come over hither; and then a little time of peace will give us time to lay up something; which these Commissioners of the Treasury are doing, and the world doth begin to see that they will do the King's work for him if he will let them. Here dined Mr. Case the Minister, who, Lord, doth talk just as I remember he used to preach; and did tell a pretty story of a religious lady, the Queen of Navarre; and my Lord also a good story of Mr. Newman, the minister in New England who wrote the Concordance, of his foretelling his death

and preaching his funeral sermon, and did at last bid the Angells do their office, and died. It seems there is great presumption that there will be a Toleration granted; so that the presbyters do hold up their heads, but they will hardly trust the King or the Parliament where to yield to them – though most of the sober party be for some kind of allowance to be given them.

21. Up, and while at the office comes news from Kate Joyce that if I would see her hus[band] alive, I must come presently; so after the office was up, I to him, and W. Hewer with me, and find him in his sick bed (I never was at their house, this Inne, before), very sensible in discourse and thankful for my kindnesses to him; but his breath rattled in his throate and they did lay pigeons to his feet while I was in the house; and all despair of him, and with good reason. But the sorrow is that it seems on Thursday last he went sober and quiet out of doors in the morning to Islington, and behind one of the Inns, the White Lion, did fling himself into a pond – was spied by a poor woman and got out by some people binding up Hay in a barn there, and set on his head and got to life; and known by a woman coming that way, and so his wife and friends sent for. He confessed his doing the thing, being led by the Devil; and doth declare his reason to be his trouble that he found in having forgot to serve God as he ought since he came to this new imployment; and I believe that, and the sense of his great loss by the fire, did bring him to it, and so everybody concludes. He stayed there all that night, and came home by coach next morning; and there grew sick, and worse and worse to this day. I stayed a while among the friends that were there; and they being now in fear that the goods and estate would be seized on, though he lived all this while, because of his endeavour-ing to drown himself,[1] my cousin did endeavour to remove what she could of plate out of the house, and desired me to take [her] flagons; which I was glad of, and did take them away with me, in great fear all the way of being seized; though there was no reason for it, he not being dead; but yet so fearful I was. So home and there eat my dinner, and busy all the afternoon, and troubled at this business. In the evening, with Sir D. Gawden to Guildhall to advise with the Towne Clerke about the practice of the City and nation in this case, and he thinks it cannot be found Selfe-murder; but if it be, it will fall, all the estate, to the King. So we parted, and I to my cousin's

1. Until 1870 the property of suicides was forfeit to the Crown.

again; where I no sooner came but news was brought down from his chamber that he was departed. So at their entreaty I presently took coach and to Whitehall, and there find W. Coventry and he carried me to the King, the Duke of York being with him, and there told my story which I had told him; and the King without more ado granted that if it was found [self-murder] the estate should be to the widow and children. I presently to each Secretary's office and there left Caveats, and so away back again to my cousin's – leaving a Chimny on fire at Whitehall in the King's closet, but no danger. And so when I came thither, I found her all in sorrow, but she and the rest mightily pleased with my doing this for them; and endeed, it was a very great courtesy, for people are looking out for the estate, and the Coroner will be sent to and a jury called to examine his death. This being well done, to my and their great joy, I home and there to my office; and so to supper and to bed.

23. At the office all the morning and at noon find the Bishop of Lincolne come to dine with us; and after him comes Mr. Brisban, and there mighty good company; but the Bishop a very extraordinary good-natured man and one that is mightily pleased, as well as I am, that I live so near Bugden, the seat of his Bishopricke, where he is like to reside; and endeed I am glad of it. In discourse, we think ourselfs safe for this year by this league with Holland, which pleases everybody, and they say vexes France; insomuch that De lestrade the French Imbassador in Holland, when he heard it, told the States that he would have them not forget that his Maister is in the head of 100000 men, and is but 28 years old – which was a great speech. The Bishop tells me he thinks that the great business of Toleration will not, notwithstanding this talk, be carried this Parliament; nor for the King's taking away the Deanes and Chapters' lands to supply his wants, they signifying little to him – if he had them for his present service. He gone, I mightily pleased with his kindness, I to the office, where busy till night; and then to Mrs. Turners, where my wife and Deb and I and Batelier spent that night and supped and played at Cards, and very merry; and so I home to bed. She is either a very prodigal woman or richer then she would be thought, by her buying of the best things and laying out much money in new-fashioned pewter; and among other things, a new-fashion case for a pair of Snuffers, which is very pretty, but I could never have guessed what it was for had I not seen the snuffers in it.

31. Up and by coach, with W. Griffin with me and our contract-books, to Durham Yard to the Commissioners for Accounts – the first time I ever was there; and staying a while before I was admitted to them, I did observe a great many people attending about complaints of seamen concerning tickets; and among others, Mr. Carcasse and Mr. Martin my purser. And I observe a fellow, one Collins, is there, who is imployed by these Commissioners perticularly to hold an office in Bishopsgate street, or somewhere thereabouts, to receive complaints of all people about tickets – and I believe he will have work enough. Presently I was called in, where I found the whole number of Commissioners, and was there received with great respect and kindness and did give them great satisfaction, making it my endeavour to inform them what it was they were to expect from me and what was the duty of other people, this being my only way to preserve myself after all my pains and trouble. They did ask many questions and demand other books of me; which I did give them very ready and acceptable answers to; and upon the whole, I observe they do go about their business like men resolved to go through with it, and in a very good method, like men of understanding. They have Mr. Jessop their secretary; and it is pretty to see that they are fain to find out an old-fashion man of Cromwell's to do their business for them, as well as the Parliament to pitch upon such for the most part in the list of people that were brought into the House for Commissioners. I went away with giving and receiving great satisfaction; and so away to Whitehall to the Commissioners of Treasury – where waiting some time, I met there with Coll. Birch and he and I fell into discourse, and I did give him thanks for his kindness to me in the Parliament-house, both before my face and behind my back; he told me he knew me to be a man of the old way for taking pains, and did always endeavour to do me right and prevent anything that was moved that might tend to my injury – which I was obliged to him for, and thanked him. Thence to talk of other things and the want of money and he told me of the general want of money in the country; that land sold for nothing, and the many pennyworths he knew of lands and houses upon them with good titles in his country, at 16 years' purchase. "And," says he, "though I am in debt, yet I have a mind to one, and that is a Bishop's lease;" "But," said I, "will you choose such a lease before any other?" – "Yes," says he plainly, "because I know they cannot stand, and then it will fall into the King's hands, and I in possession shall have an advantage by it – and," says he, "I know

they must fall, and they are now near it, taking all the ways they can to undo themselfs and showing us the way;" and thereupon told me a story of the present quarrel between the Bishop and Deane of Coventry and Lichfield; the former of which did excommunicate the latter and caused his excommunication to be read in the church while he was there; and after it was read, the Deane made the service be gone through with, though himself, an excommunicate, was present (which is contrary to the Canon), and said he would justify the Quire therein against the Bishop; and so they are at law in the Arches about it – which is a very pretty story. He tells me that the King is for Toleration, though the Bishops be against it; and that he doth not doubt but it will be carried in Parliament but that he fears some will stand for the tolerating of papists with the rest; and that he knows not what to say to, but rather thinks that the sober party will be without it rather then have it upon those terms – and I do believe so. Here we broke off, and I home to dinner; and after dinner set down my wife and Deb at the Change, and I to make a visit to Mr. Godolphin at his lodgings; who is come late from Spain from my Lord Sandwich, and did the other day, meeting me in Whitehall, compliment me mightily; and so I did offer him this visit, but missed him. And so back and took up my wife and set her at Mrs. Turner's, and I to my bookbinder's and there till late at night, binding up my second part of my Tanger accounts; and I all the while observing his working and his manner of gilding books with great pleasure; and so home and there busy late, and then to bed.

## –✲FEBRUARY✲–

2. *Lords day.* Wife took physic this day. I all day at home, and all the morning setting my books in order in my presses for the fallowing year, their number being much encreased since the last, so as I am fain to lay by several books to make room for better, being resolved to keep no more then just my presses will contain. At noon to dinner, my wife coming down to me; and a very good dinner we had, of a powdered leg of pork and a loin of lamb roasted – and with much content, she and I and Deb. After dinner, my head combed an hour together, and then to work again – and at it, doing many things towards the setting my accounts and papers in order;

and so in the evening, Mr. Pelling supping with us, to supper and so to bed.

5.    Up, and I to Capt. Cockes, where he and I did discourse of our business that we are to go about to the Comissioners of Accounts, about our prizes.[1] And having resolved to conceal nothing but confess the truth, the truth being likely to do us most good, we parted; and I to Whitehall, where missing of the Commissioners of the Treasury, I to the Commissioners of Accounts, where I was forced to stay two hours I believe before I was called in; and when came in, did take an oath to declare the truth to what they should ask me (which is a great power, I doubt more then the Act doth, or as some say can, give them: to force a man to swear against himself); and so they fell to enquire about the business of prize goods, wherein I did answer them as well as I could answer them, to everything the just truth, keeping myself to that. I do perceive at last that that they did lay most like a fault to me was that I did buy goods upon my Lord Sandwiches declaring that it was with the King's allowance, and my believing it without seeing the King's allowance – which is a thing I will own, and doubt not to justify myself in. They were inquisitive into the meanest perticulars, and had had great information; but I think that it can do me no hurt, at the worst more then to make me refund, if it must be known, what profit I did make of my agreement with Capt. Cocke. And yet though this be all, yet I do find so poor a spirit within me, that it makes me almost out of my wits, and puts me to so much pain that I cannot think of anything, nor do anything but vex and fret and imagine myself undone – so that I am ashamed of myself to myself, and do fear what would become of me if any real affliction should come upon me.

6.    Up and to the office, where all the morning; and among other things, Sir H. Cholmly comes to me about a little business and there tells me how the Parliament (which is to meet again today) are likely to fall heavy on the business of the Duke of Buckingham's pardon;[2] and I shall be glad of it. And that the King hath put out of the Court the two Hides, my Lord Chancellor's two sons, and also the Bishops of Rochester and Winchester, the latter of which should

1. The prize goods taken from the Dutch E. Indiamen in 1665; see above, p. 530 & n.
2. For the duel with Shrewsbury.

have preached before him yesterday, being Ashwendsdy; and had his sermon ready, but was put by – which is great news.

7.  Up, and to the office to the getting of my books in order to carry to the Commissioners of Accounts this morning. This being done, I away, first to Westminster hall and there met my Cosen Rogr. Pepys by his desire (the first time I have seen him since his coming to town, the Parliament meeting yesterday and adjurned to Monday next); and here he tells me that Mr. Jackson, my sister's servant, is come to town. Thence I to the Comissioners of Accounts and there presented my books, and was made to sit down and used with much respect, otherwise then the other day when I came to them as a Criminall about the business of the prizes. I sat here with them a great while, while my books were inventoried; and here do hear from them by discourse that they are like to undo the Treasurer's instruments of the Navy by making it a rule that they shall repay all money paid to wrong parties; which is a thing not to be supported by these poor creatures, the Treasurer's instruments; as it is also hard for seamen to be ruined by their paying money to whom they please. I know not what will be the issue of it. I find these gentlemen to sit all day and only eat a bit of bread at noon and a glass of wine; and are resolved to go through their business with great severity and method. Thence I about 2 a-clock to Westminster hall by appointment, and there met my cousin Roger again and Mr. Jackson, who is a plain young man, handsome enough for her; one of no education nor discourse, but of few words, and one altogether that I think will please me well enough. My cousin hath got me to give the od sixth, 100*l*, presently, which I intended to keep to the birth of the first child: and let it go, I shall be eased of that care; and so after little talk we parted, resolving to dine all together at my house tomorrow. So there parted, my mind pretty well satisfied with this plain fellow for my sister, though I shall I see have no pleasure nor content in him, as if he had been a man of breeding and parts like Cumberland.

8.  Up and to the office, where sat all day; and at noon home and there find Cosen Roger and Jackson by appointment come to dine with me, and Creed – and very merry; only, Jackson hath few words, and like him never the worse for it. We had a great deal of good discourse at table; and after dinner we four men took coach, and they set me down at the Old Exchange and they home, having

discoursed nothing today with cousin or Jackson about our business. I to Capt. Cocke's and there discoursed over our business of prizes; and I think I shall go near to state the matter so as to secure myself without wrong to him, doing nor saying anything but the very truth. Thence away to the Strand to my bookseller's, and there stayed an hour and bought that idle, roguish book, *L'escholle des Filles*; which I have bought in plain binding (avoiding the buying of it better bound) because I resolve, as soon as I have read it, to burn it, that it may not stand in the list of books, nor among them, to disgrace them if it should be found. Thence home, and busy late at the office; and then home to supper and to bed. My wife well pleased with my sister's match, and designing how to be merry at their marriage. And I am well at ease in my mind to think that that care will be over.

9. *Lords day*. Up, and at my chamber all the morning and the office, doing business and also reading a little of *L'escolle des Filles*, which is a mighty lewd book, but yet not amiss for a sober man once to read over to inform himself in the villainy of the world. At noon home to dinner, where by appointment Mr. Pelling came, and with him three friends: Wallington that sings the good bass, and one Rogers, and a gentleman, a young man, his name Tempest, who sings very well endeed and understands anything in the world at first sight. After dinner, we into our dining-room and there to singing all the afternoon (by the way, I must remember that Pegg Pen was brought to bed yesterday of a girl; and among other things, if I have not already set it down, that hardly ever was remembered such a season for the smallpox as these last two months have been, people being seen all up and down the streets, newly come out after the smallpox): but though they sang fine things, yet I must confess that I did take no pleasure in it, or very little, because I understood not the words; and with the rests that the words are set, there is no sense nor understanding in them, though they be English – which makes us weary of singing in that manner, it being but a worse sort of instrumental music. We sang till almost night, and drank my good store of wine; and then they parted and I to my chamber, where I did read through *L'escholle des Filles*; and after I had done it, I burned it, that it might not be among my books to my shame; and so at night to supper and then to bed.

10. Up, and by coach to Westminster and there made a visit to

Mr. Godolphin at his chamber; and I do find him a very pretty and able person, a man of very fine parts and infinite zeal to my Lord Sandwich, and one that says he is, he believes, as wise and able a person as any prince in the world hath. He tells me that he meets with unmannerly usage by Sir Robt. Southwell in Portugall, who would sign with him in his negotiations there, being a forward young man, but that my Lord maister[ed] him in that point, it being ruled for my Lord here at a hearing of a committee of the Council. He says that if my Lord can compass a peace between Spain and Portugall, and hath the doing of it and the honour himself, it will be a thing of more honour then ever any man hath, and of as much advantage. Thence to Westminster hall, where the Hall mighty full; and among other things, the House begins to sit today, and the King came. But before the King's coming, the House of Commons met; and upon information given them of a Bill intended to be brought in, as common report said, for Comprehension, they did mightily and generally inveigh against it, and did vote that the King should be desired by the House, and the message delivered by the Privy counsellors of the House, that the laws against breakers of the Act of Uniformity should be put in execution. And it was moved in the House that if any people had a mind to bring any new laws into the House about religion, they might come as a proposer of new laws did in Athens, with ropes about their necks. By and by the King comes to the Lords' House and there tells them of his league with Holland – and the necessity of a fleet, and his debts and therefore want of money; and his desire that they would think of some way to bring in all his protestant subjects to a right understanding and peace one with another, meaning the Bill of Comprehension. The Commons coming to their House, it was moved that the vote passed this morning might be suspended, because of the King's speech, till the House was full and called over two days hence; but it was denied, so furious they are against this Bill; and thereby a great blow either given to the King and presbyters; or, which is the rather of the two, to the House itself, by denying a thing desired by the King and so much desired by much the greater part of the nation. Whatever the consequence be, if the King be a man of any stomach and heat, all do believe that he will resent this vote. Thence with Creed home to my house to dinner, where I met with Mr. Jackson and find my wife angry with Deb, which vexes me. After dinner by coach away to Westminster, taking up a friend of Mr. Jacksons, a young lawyer; and parting with Creed at Whitehall, they and I to Westminster hall; and there met Roger Pepys and with him to his chamber and there read over and agreed upon the deed of Settlement to our minds: my sister to have 600*l* presently and she to be joyntured in 60*l* per annum – wherein I am very well satisfied.

11. At the office all the morning, where comes a damned summons to attend the Committee of Miscarriges today; which makes me mad that I should by my place become the hackney of this Office, in perpetual trouble and vexation, that need it least. At noon home to dinner, where little pleasure, my head being split almost with the variety of troubles upon me at this time and cares. And after dinner by coach to Westminster hall and sent my wife and Deb to see *Mustapha* acted. Here I brought a book to the Committee, and do find them, and perticularly Sir Tho. Clerges, mighty hot in the business of tickets; which makes me mad, to see them bite at the stone and not at the hand that flings it. And here my Lord Bruncker unnecessarily orders it that he is called in, to give opportunity to present his report of the state of that business of paying by ticket; which I do not think will do him any right, though he was made believe that it did operate mightily, and that Sir Fresh. Hollis did make a mighty harangue and to much purpose in his defence; but I believe no such effects of it, for going in afterward I did hear them speak with prejudice of it, and that his pleading of the Admirall's warrant for it now was only an evasion, if not an aspersion upon the Admirall, and therefore they would not admit of this his report, but go on with their report as they had resolved before. The orders they sent for this day was the first order that I have yet met with about this business, and was of my own single hand warranting; but I do think it will do me no harm, and therefore do not much trouble myself with it – more then to see how much trouble I am brought to who have best deported myself in all the King's business. Thence with Lord Brouncker and set him down at Bowstreete, and so to the Duke of York's playhouse and there saw the last Act for nothing; where I never saw such good acting of any creature as Smith's part of Zanger; and I do also, though it was excellently acted by [blank], do yet want Betterton mightily. Thence to the Temple to Porter's chamber, where Cocke met me; and after a stay there some time, they two and I to Pemerton's chamber and there did read over the act of calling people to account and did discourse all our business of the prizes;

and upon the whole, he doth make it plainly appear that there is no avoiding to give these Commissioners satisfaction in everything they will ask; and that there is fear lest they may find reason to make us refund for all the extraordinary profit made by those bargains; and doth make me resolve rather to declare plainly and once for all the truth of the whole and what my profit hath been, then be forced at last to do it and in the meantime live in pain – as I must always do. And with this resolution on my part, I departed with some more satisfaction of mind, though with less hopes of profit then I expected. This morning, my wife in bed told me the story of our Tom and Jane; how the rogue did first demand her consent to love and marry him and then, with pretence of displeasing me, did slight her; but both he and she have confessed the matter to her, and she hath charged him to go on with his love to her and be true to her, and so I think the business will go on; which, for my love to her because she is in love with him, I am pleased with, but otherwise I think she will have no good bargain of it; at least, if I should not do well in my place. But if I do stand, I do entend to give her 5o*l* in money and do them all the good I can in my way.

12.   Up and to my office, where all the morning drawing up my Narrative of my proceedings and concernments in the buying of Prize goods, which I am to present to the Committee for Accounts. At noon home to dinner, where Mr. Jackson dined with me; and after dinner I (calling at the Excise Office, and setting my wife and Deb at her tailor's) did with Mr. Jackson go to find my Cosen Rog. Pepys, which I did in the Parliament-house, where I met him and Sir Tho. Crew and Mr. George Mountagu, who are mighty busy how to save my Lord's name from being in the report for anything which the Committee is commanded to report to the House of the Miscarriages of the late war. I find they drive furiously still in the business of Tickets, which is nonsense in itself and cannot come to anything. Thence with Cosen Rogr. to his lodgings and there sealed the writings with Jackson about my sister's marriage.

14.   *Valentine's day.* Up, being called up by Mercer, who came to be my Valentine; and so I rose, and my wife, and were merry a little, I staying to talk; and did give her a Guinny in gold for her Valentine's gift. There comes also my Cosen Rogr. Pepys betimes, and comes to my wife for her to be his Valentine, whose Valentine I was also, by agreement to be so to her every year; and this year I

find it is likely to cost 4 or 5*l* in a ring for her which she desires.

15. Up betimes, and with Capt. Cocke by coach to the Temple to his Counsel again about the prize goods, in order to the drawing up his answer to them; where little done but a confirmation that our best interest is for him to tell the whole truth; and so parted, and I home to the office, where all the morning. And at noon home to dinner; and after dinner, all the afternoon and evening till midnight almost, and till I had tired my own backe and my wife's and Deb's, in titleing of my books for the present year and in setting them in order; which is now done to my very good satisfaction, though not altogether so completely as I think they were last year, when my mind was more at leisure to mind it. So about midnight to bed, where my wife taking some physic overnight it wrought with her; and those coming upon her with great gripes, she was in mighty pain all night long; yet God forgive me, I did find that I was more desirous to take my rest then to ease her; but there was nothing I could do to do her any good with.

16. *Lords day.* Up and to my chamber, where all the morning making a Catalogue of my books; which did find me work, but with great pleasure, my chamber and books being now set in very good order and my chamber washed and cleaned, which it had not been in some months before – my business and trouble having been so much. At noon Mr. Hollier put in and dined with my wife and me, who was a little better today. His company very good; his story of his love and fortune, which hath been very good and very bad in the world, well worth hearing. Much discourse also about the bad state of the church, and how the clergy are come to be men of no worth in the world – and, as the world doth now generally discourse, they must be reformed; and I believe the Hierarchy will in a little time be shaken, whether they will or no – the King being offended with them and set upon it as I hear. He gone, after dinner to have my head combed; and then to my chamber and read most of the evening till pretty late, when, my wife not being well, I did lie below stairs in our great chamber, where I slept well.

17. Up and to the office, where all the morning till noon getting some things more ready against the afternoon for the Committee of Accounts – which did give me great trouble, to see how I am forced to dance after them in one place and to answer committees of

Parliament in another. At noon thence toward the committee; but meeting with Sir W. Warren in Fleet street, he and I to the ordinary by Temple bar and there dined together, and to talk, where he doth seem to be very high now in defiance of the Board: now he says that the worst is come upon him, to have his accounts brought to the Committee of Accounts, and he doth reflect upon my late coldness to him; but upon the whole, I do find that he is still a cunning fellow, and will find it necessary to be fair to me; and what hath passed between us of kindness, to hold his tongue – which doth please me very well. Thence to the Committee, where I did deliver the several things they expected from me with great respect and show of satisfaction, and my mind thereby eased of some care. But thence I to Westminster hall and there spent till late at night, walking to and again with many people; and there in general I hear of the great high words that was in the House on Saturdy last, upon the first part of the Committee's Report about the dividing of the fleet;[1] wherein some would have the counsels of the King to be declared, and the reasons of them and who did give them; where Sir W. Coventry lay open to them the consequences of doing that, that the King would never have any honest and wise men ever to be of his Council. They did here in the House talk boldly of the King's bad counsellors, and how they must be all turned out, and many of them, and better, brought in; and the proceedings of the Long Parliament in the beginning of the war were called to memory. And the King's bad intelligence was mentioned, wherein they were bitter against my Lord Arlington; saying, among other things, that whatever Morrices was, who declared he had but 750*l* a year allowed him for intelligence, the King paid too dear for my Lord Arlington's in giving him 10000*l* and a Barony for it. Some mutterings I did hear of a design of dissolveing the Parliament, but I think there is no ground for it yet, though Oliver would have dissolved them for half the trouble and contempt these have put upon the King and his councils. The dividing of the fleet, however, is I hear voted a miscarriage, and the not building a fortification at Sherenesse; and I have reason every hour to expect that they will vote the like of our paying men off by ticket; and what the consequence of that will be I know not, but am put thereby into great trouble of mind. I did spend a little time at the Swan, and there did kiss the maid Sarah. At night home, and there up to my wife,

---

1. In the Four Days Battle, June 1666: see above, p. 630 (10 June) & n.

who is still ill, and supped with her, my mind mighty full of trouble for the office and my concernments therein; and so to supper and talking with W. Hewer in her chamber about business of the office, wherein he doth well understand himself and our case, and it doth me advantage to talk with him and the rest of my people. I to bed below, as I did last night.

18. Up by break of day, and walked down to the Old Swan, where I find little Michell building, his Booth being taken down and a foundation laid for a new house, so that that street is like to be a very fine place. I drank, but did not see Betty. And so to Charing cross stairs, and thence walked to Sir W. Coventry and talked with him; who tells me how he hath been prosecuted, and how he is yet well come off in the business of the dividing of the fleet and the sending of the letter. He expects next to be troubled about the business of bad officers in the fleet, wherein he will bid them name whom they call bad and he will justify himself – having never disposed of any but by the Admiral's liking. And he is able to give an account of all them, how they came recommended, and more will be found to have been placed by the Prince and Duke of Albemarle then by the Duke of York during the war. And as a no bad instance of the badness of officers, he and I did look over the list of commanders, and found that we could presently recollect 37 commanders that have been killed in actuall service this war. Thence walked over St. James's park to Whitehall; and thence to Westminster hall and there walked all the morning and did speak with several Parliament-men; among others, Birch, who is very kind to me and calls me, with great respect and kindness, a man of business, and he thinks honest; and so, long will stand by me and every such man to the death. Here I did get a copy of the report itself, about our paying off men by tickets; and am mightily glad to see it now, knowing the state of our case and what we have to answer to, and the more for that the House is like to be kept by other business today and tomorrow; so that against Thursdy I shall be able to draw up some defence to put into some members' hands to inform them; and I think we may [make] a very good one, and therefore my mind is mightily at ease about it.

19. Up, and to the office, where all the morning drawing up an answer to the Report of the Committee for Miscarriages to the Parliament, touching our paying men by tickets – which I did do in

a very good manner I think. Dined with my clerks at home, where much good discourse of our business of the Navy and the troubles now upon us, more then we expected. After dinner, my wife out with Deb to buy some things against my sister's wedding[1] and I to the office to write fair my business I did in the morning; and in the evening to Whitehall, where I find Sir W. Coventry all alone a great while with the Duke of York in the King's drawing-room, they two talking together all alone, which did mightily please me; then I did get W. Coventry (the Duke of York being gone) aside, and there read over my paper; which he liked and corrected, and tells me it will be hard to escape, though the thing be never so fair, to have it voted a miscarriage; but did advise me and my Lord Brouncker, who coming by did join with us, to prepare some members in it; which we shall do.

24. Up, and to my office, where most of the morning entering my Journall for the three days past. Thence about noon with my wife to the New Exchange, by the way stopping at my bookseller's and there leaving my Kircher's *Musurgia* to be bound, and did buy *L'illustre Bassa* in four volumes for my wife. Thence to the Exchange and left her; while meeting Dr. Gibbons there, he and I to see an Organ at the Deane of Westminster's lodgings at the Abby, the Bishop of Rochester's, where he lives like a great prelate, his lodgings being very good, though at present under great disgrace at Court, being put by his Clerk of the Closet's place. I saw his lady, of whom the *Terrae filius* of Oxford was once so merry – and two children, whereof one very pretty little boy like him, so fat and black. Here I saw the organ; but it is too big for my house and the fashion doth not please me enough, and therefore will not have it. Thence to the Change back again leaving him, and took my wife and Deb home and there to dinner alone; and after dinner I took them to the Nursery, where none of us ever was before; where the house is better and the Musique better then we looked for, and the acting not much worse, because I expected as bad as could: and I was not much mistaken, for it was so. However, I was pleased well to see it once, it being worth a man's seeing to discover the different ability and understanding of people, and the different growths of people's abilities by practice. Their play was a bad one, called *Jeronimo is Mad Again* – a tragedy. Here was some good company by

1. She was married to John Jackson at Brampton on 27 February.

us who did make mighty sport at the folly of their Acting, which I could not neither refrain from sometimes, though I was sorry for it. So away thence home, where to the office to do business a while, and then home to supper and to read, and then to bed. I was prettily served this day at the playhouse door; where giving six shillings into the fellow's hand for us three, the fellow by legerdemain did convey one away, and with so much grace face me down that I did give him but five, that though I knew the contrary, yet I was overpowered by his so grave and serious demanding the other shilling that I could not deny him, but was forced by myself to give it him. After I came home this evening comes a letter to me from Capt. Allin, formerly Clerk of the Ropeyard at Chatham and whom I was kind to in those days, who in recompense of my favour to him then doth give me notice that he hears of an accusation likely to be exhibited against me, of my receiving 50*l* of Mason the timber merchant, and that his wife hath spoke it. I am mightily beholden to Capt. Allin for this, though the thing is to the best of my memory utterly false, and I do believe it to be wholly so; but yet it troubles me to have my name mentioned in this business, and more to consider how I may be liable to be accused where I have endeed taken presents, and therefore puts me upon an enquiry into my actings in this kind and prepare against a day of accusation.

26. Up, and by water to Charin cross stairs, and thence to W. Coventry to discourse concerning the state of matters in the Navy, where he perticularly acquainted me again with the trouble he is like to meet with about the selling of places, all carried on by Sir Fr. Hollis; but he seems not to value it, being able to justify it to be lawful and constant practice, and never by him used in the least degree since he upon his own motion did obtain a salary of 500*l* in lieu thereof. Thence to the Treasury chamber about a little business and so home by coach; and in my way did meet W. How going to the Commissioners of Accounts; I stopped and spoke to him, and he seems well resolved what to answer them, but he will find them very strict and not easily put off. So home and there to dinner; and after dinner comes W. How to tell me how he sped; who says he was used civilly and not so many questions asked as he expected, but yet I do perceive enough to show that they do entend to know the bottom of things and where to lay the great weight of the disposal of these East India goods, and that they entend plainly to do upon my Lord Sandwich.

27. All the morning at the office, and at noon home to dinner; and thence with my wife and Deb to the King's House to see *Virgin Martyr*, the first time it hath been acted a great while, and is mighty pleasant; not that the play is worth much, but it is finely Acted by Becke Marshall; but that which did please me beyond anything in the whole world was the wind-musique when the Angell comes down, which is so sweet that it ravished me; and endeed, in a word, did wrap up my soul so that it made me really sick, just as I have formerly been when in love with my wife; that neither then, nor all the evening going home and at home, I was able to think of anything, but remained all night transported, so as I could not believe that ever any music hath that real command over the soul of a man as this did upon me; and makes me resolve to practise wind-music and to make my wife do the like.

28. Up and to the office, where all the morning doing business; and after dinner with Sir W. Penn to Whitehall, where we and the rest of us presented a great letter of the state of our want of money to his Royal Highness. I did also present a demand of mine for consideration for my travelling charges of coach and boat hire during the war – which though his Royal Highness and the company did all like of, yet contrary to my expectation I find him so jealous now of doing anything extraordinary, that he desired the gentlemen that they would consider it and report their minds in it to him. This did unsettle my mind a great while, not expecting this stop: but however, I shall do as well I know, though it causes me a little stop. But that that troubles me most is that while we were thus together with the Duke of York, comes in Mr. Wren from the House, where he tells us another storm hath been all this day almost against the Officers of the Navy upon this complaint: that though they have made good rules for payment of tickets, yet they have not observed them themselfs; which was driven so high as to have it urged that we should presently be put out of our places – and so they have at last ordered that we be heard at the bar of the House upon this business on Thursdy next.

# ⚜MARCH⚜

1. *Lords day*. Up very betimes and by coach to Sir W. Coventry, and there, largely carrying with me all my notes and papers, did run over our whole defence in the business of Tickets, in order to the answering the House on Thursday next; and I do think, unless they be set without reason to ruin us, we shall make a good defence. I find him in great anxiety, though he will not discover it, in the business of the proceedings of Parliament; and would as little as is possible have his name mentioned in our discourses to them; and perticularly the business of selling places is now upon his hand to defend himself in – wherein I did help him in his defence about the Flaggmaker's place which is named in the House. We did here do the like about the complaint of want of victuals in the fleet in the year 1666, which will lie upon me to defend also; so that my head is full of care and weariness in my imployment. Thence home; and there, my mind being a little lightened by my morning's work in the arguments I have now laid together in better method for our defence to the Parliament, I to talk with my wife; and in lieu of a Coach this year, I have got my wife to be contented with her closet being made up this summer and going into the country this summer for a month or two to my father's, and there Mercer and Deb and Jane shall go with them; which [I] the rather do for the entertaining my wife, and preventing of fallings-out between her and my father or Deb – which uses to be the fate of her going into the country.

4–5. Up betimes and with Sir W. Penn in his coach to Whitehall, there to wait upon the Duke of York and the Commissioners of the Treasury, W. Coventry and Sir Jo. Duncombe – who do declare that they cannot find the money we demand; and we, that less then what we demand will not set out the fleet intended; and so broke up with no other conclusion then that they would let us have what they could get, and we would improve that as well as we could. So God bless us and prepare us against the consequences of these matters. Thence, it being a cold wet day, I home with Sir J. Mennes in his coach, and called by the way at my bookseller's and took home with me Kercher's *Musica,* very well bound. But I had no comfort to look upon them, but as soon as I came home fell to my work at the office, shutting the doors that we, I and my clerks, might not be interrupted; and so, only with room for a little dinner, we very busy all the day till night, that the officers met for me to give them the heads of what I intended to say; which I did, with great discontent to see them all rely on me that have no reason at all to trouble myself about it, nor have any thanks from them for my labour; but contrarily, Brouncker looked mighty dogged, as thinking that I did not intend to do it so as to save him. This troubled me so much, as together with the shortness of the time, and muchness of the business, did let me be at it till but about 10 at night; and then, quite weary and dull and vexed, I could go no further, but resolved to leave the rest to tomorrow morning; and so in full discontent and weariness did give over and went home, with[out] supper vexed and sickish, to bed – and there slept about three hours; but then waked, and never in so much trouble in all my life of mind, thinking of the task I have upon me, and upon what dissatisfactory grounds, and what the issue of it may be to me. With these thoughts I lay troubling myself till 6 a-clock, restless, and at last getting my wife to talk to me to comfort me; which she at last did, and made me resolve to quit my hands of this office and endure the trouble [of] it no longer then till I can clear myself of it. So, with great trouble but yet with some ease from this discourse with my wife, I up and to my office, whither came my clerks; and so I did huddle up the best I could some more notes for my discourse today; and by 9 a-clock was ready and did go down to the Old Swan, and there by boat, with T. Hater and W. Hewer with me, to Wesminster, where I found myself come time enough and my Brethren all ready. But I full of thoughts and trouble touching the issue of this day; and to comfort myself did go to the Dogg and drink half a pint of mulled sack, and in the Hall did drink a dram of brandy at Mrs. Howletts, and with the warmth of this did find myself in better order as to courage, truly.

So we all up to the Lobby; and between 11 and 12 a-clock were called in, with the Mace before us, into the House; where a mighty full House, and we stood at the Barr – *viz.*, Brouncker, Sir J. Mennes, Sir T. Harvey and myself – W. Penn being in the House as a Member. I perceive the whole House was full, and full of expectation of our defence what it would be, and with great præjudice. After the Speaker had told us the dissatisfaction of the House, and read the report of the Committee, I begin our defence most acceptably and smoothly, and continued at it without any hesitation or losse but with full scope and all my reason free about me, as if it had been at my own table, from that time till past 3 in the afternoon; and so ended without any interruption from the Speaker, but we withdrew. And there all my fellow-officers, and all the world that was within hearing, did congratulate me and cry up my speech as the best thing they ever heard, and my fellow-officers overjoyed in it. We were called in again by and by to answer only one question, touching our paying tickets to ticket-mongers – and so out; and we were in hopes to have had a vote this day in our favour, and so the generality of the House was; but my speech being so long, many had gone out to dinner and come in again half drunk, and then there are two or three that are professed enemies to us and everybody else; among others, Sir T. Littleton, Sir Tho. Lee, Mr. Wiles (the coxcomb whom I saw heretofore at the cockfighting) and a few others; I saw these did rise up and speak against the coming to a vote now, the House not being full, by reason of several being at dinner but most because that the House was to attend the King this afternoon about the business of Religion (wherein they pray him to put in force all the laws against nonconformists and papists); and this prevented it, so that they put it off to tomorrow come sennit. However, it is plain we have got great ground; and everybody says I have got the most honour that any could have had opportunity of getting. And so, with our hearts mightily overjoyed at this success, we all to dinner to Lord Brouncker; that is to say, myself, T. Harvey, and W. Penn, and there dined; and thence with Sir Anth. Morgan, who is an acquaintance of Brouncker's, a very wise man, we after dinner to the King's House and there saw part of *The Discontented Colonell* – but could take no great pleasure in it because of our coming in the middle of it. After the play, home with W. Penn and there to my wife, whom W. Hewer had told of my success; and she overjoyed, and I also as to my perticular. And after talking awhile, I betimes to bed, having had no quiet rest a good while.

6. Up betimes, and with Sir D. Gawden to Sir W. Coventry's chamber, where the first word he said to me was, "Goodmorrow Mr. Pepys, that must be Speaker of the Parliament-house" – and did protest I had got honour for ever in Parliament. He said that his brother, that sat by him, admires me; and another gentleman said that I could not get less than 1000*l* a year if I would put on a gown and plead at the Chancery bar. But what pleases me most, he tells me that the Sollicitor generall did protest that he thought I spoke the best of any man in England. After several talks with him alone

touching his own businesses, he carried me to Whitehall and there parted; and I to the Duke of York's lodging and find him going to the parke, it being a very fine morning; and I after him, and as soon as he saw me, he told me with great satisfaction that I had converted a great many yesterday, and did with great praise of me go on with the discourse with me. And by and by overtaking the King, the King and Duke of York came to me both, and he said, "Mr. Pepys, I am very glad of your success yesterday;" and fell to talk of my well speaking; and many of the Lords there, my Lord Berkely did cry me up for what they had heard of it; and others, Parliament[-men] there about the King, did say that they never heard such a speech in their lives delivered in that manner. Progers of the Bedchamber swore to me afterward before Brouncker in the afternoon, that he did tell the King that he thought I might teach the Sollicitor generall. Everybody that saw me almost came to me, as Joseph Williamson and others, with such eulogy as cannot be expressed. From thence I went to Westminster hall, where I met Mr. G. Mountagu; who came to me and kissed me, and told me that he had often heretofore kissed my hands, but now he would kiss my lips, protesting that I was another Cicero, and said all the world said the same of me. Mr. Ashburnham, and every creature I met there of the Parliament or that knew anything of the Parliament's actings, did salute me with this honour – Mr. Godolphin, Mr. Sands, who swore he would go twenty mile at any time to hear the like again, and that he never saw so many sit four hours together to hear any man in his life as there did to hear me. Mr. Chichly, Sir J. Duncom, and everybody doth say that the Kingdom will ring of my ability, and that I have done myself right for my whole life; and so Capt. Cocke, and other of my friends, say that no man had ever such opportunity of making his abilities known. And, that I may cite all at once, Mr. Lieutenant of the Tower did tell me that Mr. Vaughan did protest to him, and that in his hearing it, said so to the Duke of Albemarle and afterward to W. Coventry, that he had sat 26 years in Parliament and never heard such a speech there before – for which the Lord God make me thankful, and that I may make use of it not to pride and vainglory, but that now I have this esteem, I may do nothing that may lessen it.

12. Up, and to the office, where all the morning. At noon home; and after dinner with wife and Deb, carried them to Unthankes; and I to Westminster hall, expecting our being with the Committee this

afternoon about Victualling business, but once more waited in vain. So after a turn or two with Lord Brouncker, I took my wife up and left her at the Change, while I to Gresham College, there to show myself, and was there greeted by Dr. Wilkins, Whistler, and others, as the patron of the Navy Office and one that got great fame by my late speech to the Parliament. Here I saw a great trial of the goodness of a burning-glass, made of a new figure, not Sphæricall (by one Smithys, I think they call him), that did burn a glove of my Lord Brouncker's from the heat of a very little fire – which a burning-glass of the old form, very much bigger, could not do – which was mighty pretty. Here I heard Sir Rob. Southwell give an account of some things committed to him by the Society at his going to Portugall, which he did deliver in a mighty handsome manner. Thence went away home, and there at my office as long as my eyes would endure; and then home to supper and to talk with Mr. Pelling, who tells me what a fame I have in the City for my late performance; and upon the whole, I bless God for it, I think I have, if I can keep it, done myself a great deal of repute. So by and by to bed.

13.   Up betimes to my office, where to fit myself to attending the Parliament again; not to make any more speeches, which while my fame is good I will avoid for fear of losing of it, but only to anwer to what objections shall be made against us. Thence walked to the Old Swan and drank at Michell's, whose house is going up apace; here I saw Betty, but could not besar la; and so to Westminster, there to the Hall, where up to my Cosen Rogr. Pepys at the Parliament door, and there he took me aside and told me how he was taken up by one of the House yesterday for moving for going on with the King's supply of money without regard to the keeping pace therewith with the looking into miscarriages, and was told by this man privately that it arose because that he had a kinsman concerned therein and therefore he would prefer the safety of his kinsman to the good of the nation. And that there was great things against us, and against me, for all my fine discourse the other day. But I did bid him be at no pain for me, for I knew of nothing but what I was very well prepared to answer; and so I think I am, and therefore was not at all disquieted by this. Thence, he to the House and I to the Hall, where my Lord Brouncker and the rest waiting till noon and not called for by the House, they being upon the business of money again; and at noon, all of us to Chatelin, the French house in Covent

garden, to dinner, Brouncker, J. Mennes, W. Penn, T. Harvey, and myself; and there had a dinner cost us 8*s*. 6*d*. apiece, a damned base dinner, which did not please us at all – so that I am not fond of this house at all, but do rather choose the Beare. After dinner, to Whitehall to the Duke of York and there did our usual business, complaining of our standing still in every respect for want of money; but no remedy propounded, but so I must still be.

Thence with our company to the King's playhouse, where I left them; and I, my head being full of tomorrow's dinner, I to my Lord Crews, there to invite Sir Tho. Crew; and there met with my Lord Hinchingbrooke and his Lady, the first time I spoke to her. I saluted her, and she mighty civil; and with my Lady Jem do all resolve to be very merry tomorrow at my house. My Lady Hinchingbrooke I cannot say is a beauty, nor ugly; but is altogether a comely lady enough, and seems very good-humoured, and I mighty glad of this occasion of seeing her before tomorrow. Thence home; and there find one laying of my napkins against tomorrow in figures of all sorts, which is mighty pretty; and it seems it is his trade and gets much money by it, and doth now and then furnish tables with plate and linen for a feast at so much – which is mighty pretty – and a trade I could not have thought of. I find my wife upon the bed, not very well, her breast being broke out with heate; which troubles her, but I hope it will be for her good. Thence I to Mrs. Turner and did get her to go along with me to the French pewterers, and there did buy some new pewter against tomorrow. And thence to Whitehall to have got a cook of her acquaintance, the best in England as she says. But after we have with much ado found him, he could not come; nor was Mr. Gentleman in town, whom next I would have had; nor would Mrs. Stone let her man Lewis come, whom this man recommended to me; so that I was at a mighty loss what in the world to do for a Cooke, Philips being out of town. Therefore, after staying here at Westminster a great while, we back to London and there to Phillips's and his man directed us to Mr. Levetts, who could not come; and he sent to two more, and they could not; so that at last, Levett, as a great kindness, did resolve he would leave his business and come himself, which set me in great ease in my mind; and so home, and there with my wife and people setting all things in order against tomorrow, having seen Mrs. Turner at home; and so late to bed.

14. Up very betimes, and with Jane to Levetts, there to conclude

upon our dinner; and thence to the pewterers to buy a pewter Sestorne, which I have ever hitherto been without. And so up and down upon several occasions to set matters in order. And that being done, I out of doors to Westminster hall and there met my Lord Brouncker, who tells me that our business is put off till Monday, and so I was mighty glad that I was eased of my attendance here and of any occasion that might put me out of humour, as it is likely if we had been called before the Parliament. Therefore, after having spoke with Mr. Godolphin and Cosen Roger, I away home and there do find everything in mighty good order; only, my wife not dressed, which troubles me. Anon comes my company, *viz.*, my Lord Hinchingbrooke and his Lady, Sir Ph. Carteret and his Lady, Godolphin and my Cosen Roger, and Creed, and mighty merry; and by and by to dinner, which was very good and plentiful (I should have said, and Mr. George Mountagu, who came at a very little warning, which was exceeding kind of him): and there among other things, my Lord had Sir Samuel Morland's late invention for casting up sums of ol os. od.; which is very pretty, but not very useful. Most of our discourse was of my Lord Sandwich and his family, as being all of us of that family; and with extraordinary pleasure all the afternoon thus together, eating and looking over my closet: and my Lady Hinchingbrooke I find a very sweet-natured and well-disposed lady, a lover of books and pictures and of good understanding. About 5 a-clock they went, and then my wife and I abroad by coach into Moorefields, only for a little ayre; and so home again, staying nowhere, and then up to her chamber, there to talk with pleasure of this day's passages, and so to bed.

15. *Lords day*. To Whitehall and there walked with this man and that man till chapel done and the King dined; and then Sir Tho. Clifford the Controller took me with him to dinner to his lodgings, where my Lord Arlington and a great deal of good and great company – where I very civilly used by them – and had a most excellent dinner. And good discourse of Spain, Mr. Godolphin being there – perticularly of the removal of the bodies of all the dead Kings of Spain that could be got together, and brought to the Pantheon at the Escuriall (when it was finished) and there placed before the Alter, there to lie for ever. And there was a sermon made to them upon this text, *Arida ossa, audite verbum dei* – a most eloquent sermon as they say who say they have read it. After dinner, away thence; and I to Mrs. Martin's and there spent the afternoon and did hazer con

ella; and here was her sister and Mrs. Burrows; and so in the evening got a coach and home, and there find Mr. Pelling and W. Hewer, and there talked and supped (Pelling being gone); and mightily pleased with a picture that W. Hewer brought hither of several things painted upon a deal Board, which board is so well painted that in my whole life I never was so pleased or surprized with any picture, and so troubled that so good pictures should be painted upon a piece of bad deale; even after I knew that it was not board, but only the picture of a board, I could not remove my fancy. After supper to bed, being very sleepy and, I bless God, my mind at very good present rest.

19. Up, and betimes to the Old Swan and by water to Whitehall; and thence to W. Coventry, where stayed but a little to talk with him and thence by water back again, it being a mighty fine, clear Spring morning. Back to the Old Swan and drank at Michells, whose house goes up apace, but I could not see Betty; and thence walked all along Thames street, which I have not done since it was burned, as far as Billings gate and there do see a brave street likely to be, many brave houses being built, and of them a great many by Mr. Jaggard. But the raising of the street will make it mighty fine. So to the office, where busy all the morning. At noon home to dinner; and thence to the office, very busy till 5 a-clock; and then to ease my eyes I took my wife out and Deb to the Change, and there bought them some things; and so home again and to the office, ended my letters, and so home to read a little more in last night's book[1] with much sport, it being a foolish book. And so to supper and to bed.

20. Up betimes and to my office, where we had a meeting extraordinary to consider of several things; among others, the sum of money fit to be demanded ready money to enable us to set out 27 ships, everybody being now in pain for a fleet and everybody endeavouring to excuse themselfs for the not setting out of one, and our true excuse is lack of money. At it all the morning; and so at noon home to dinner with my clerks, my wife and Deb being busy at work above in her chamber, getting things ready and fine for her

---

1. The Duchess of Newcastle's *Life of the thrice noble, high and puissant Prince, William Cavendish, Duke . . . of Newcastle, written by the thrice noble illustrious and excellent Princess . . . his wife* (1667).

going into the country a week or two hence. I away by coach to
Whitehall, where we met to wait on the Duke of York; and as soon
as prayers were done, it being Good Friday, he came to us and we
did a little business and presented him with our demand of money,
and so broke up; and I thence by coach to Kate Joyces, being
desirous and in pain to speak with her about the business that I
received a letter yesterday, but had no opportunity of speaking with
her about it, company being with her; so I only invited her to come
and dine with me on Sunday next; and so away home, and for
saving my eyes, at my chamber all the evening, pricking down
some things and trying some conclusions upon my viall, in order to
the inventing of a better theory of Musique then hath yet been
abroad; and I think verily I shall do it. So to supper with my wife,
who is in very good humour with her working, and so am I; and so
to bed.

22.    *Easter day*. I up and walked to the Temple; and there got a
coach to Whitehall, where spoke with several people, and find
by all that Pen is to go to sea this year with this fleet. And they
excuse the Prince's going by saying that it is not a command great
enough for him. Here I met with Brisban; and after hearing the
service at the King's chapel, where I heard the Bishop of Norwich,
Dr. Reynolds the old presbyterian, begin a very plain sermon, he
and I to the Queen's chapel and there did hear the Italians sing; and
endeed, their music did appear most admirable to me, beyond
anything of ours – I was never so well satisfied in my life with it. So
back to Whitehall, and there met Mr. Pierce and adjousted together
how we should spend tomorrow together. And so by coach, I
home to dinner, where Kate Joyce was, as I invited her; and had a
good dinner, only she and us; and after dinner, she and I alone to
talk about her business as I designed; and I find her very discreet, and
assures me she neither doth nor will incline to the doing anything
towards marriage without my advice, and did tell me that she had
many offers, and that Harman and his friends would fain have her
but he is poor and hath poor friends, and so it will not be advisable.
But that there is another, a Tobacconist, one Holinshed, whom she
speaks well of to be a plain, sober man and in good condition, that
offers her very well; and submits to me my examining and
inquiring after it – if I see good – which I do like of it, for it will be
best for her to marry I think as soon as she can; at least, to be rid of
this house – for the trade will not agree with a young widow that is

a little handsome; at least, ordinary people think her so. Being well satisfied with her answer, she anon went away; and I to my closet to make a few more experiments of my notions in Musique; and so then my wife and I to walk in the garden, and then home to supper and to bed.

23. Up, and after discoursing with my wife about many things touching this day's dinner, I abroad; and first to the tavern to pay what I owe there, but missed of seeing the mistress of the house. And there bespoke wine for dinner; and so away thence and to Bishopsgate street, thinking to have found a Harpsicon-maker that used to live there before the fire, but he is gone; and I have a mind forthwith to have a little Harpsicon made me – to confirm and help me in my music notions, which my head is nowadays full of, and I do believe will come to something that is very good. Thence to Whitehall, expecting to have heard the Bishop of Lincolne, my friend, preach, for so I understood he would do yesterday, but was mistaken; and therefore away presently back again and there find everything in good order against dinner; and at noon come Mr. Pierce and she, and Mrs. Manuel the Jew's wife, and Mrs. Corbett, and Mrs. Pierce's boy and girl. But we are defeated of Knepp by her being forced to act today, and also of Harris; which did trouble me, they being my chief guests. However, I had an extraordinary good dinner, and the better because dressed by my own servants – and were mighty merry; and here was Mr. Pelling, by chance came and dined with me. And after sitting long at dinner, I had a barge ready at Tower wharfe to take us in; and so we went, all of us, up as high as Barne elmes, a very fine day, and all the way sang; and Mrs. Manuel sings very finely and is a mighty discreet, sober-carriaged woman, that both my wife and I are mightily taken with her; and sings well, and without importunity or the contrary. At Barne Elms we walked round; and then to the barge again and had much merry talk and good singing; and came before it was [dark] back to the New Exchange stairs, and there landed and walked up to Mrs. Pierce's, where we sat awhile and then up to their dining-room; and so having a violin and theorbo, did fall to dance, here being also Mr. Floyd come thither, and by and by Mr. Harris. But there being so few of us that could dance, and my wife not being very well, we had not much pleasure in the dancing (there was Knepp also, by which with much pleasure we did sing a little); and so about 10 a-clock I took coach with my wife and Deb, and so home and there to bed.

24.   Up pretty betimes; and so there comes to me Mr. Shish to desire my appearing for him to succeed Mr. Chr. Pett, lately dead, in his place of Maister-Shipwright of Deptford and Woolwich; which I do resolve to promote when I can. So by and by to Whitehall and there to the Duke of York's chamber, where I understand it is already resolved by the King and Duke of York that Shish shall have the place. From the Duke's chamber, Sir W. Coventry and I to walk in the Matted Gallery; and there, among other things, he tells me of the wicked design that now is at last contriving against him, to get a petition presented from people, that the money they have paid to W. Coventry for their places may be repaid them back. And that this is set on by Temple and Hollis of the Parliament and among other mean people in it, by Capt. Tatnell. And he prays me that I will use some effectual way to sift Tatnell what he doth, and who puts him on on this business; which I do undertake, and will do with all my skill for his service – being troubled that he is still under this difficulty. Thence up and down Westminster, by Mrs. Burroughes her mother's shop, thinking to have seen her, but could not; and therefore back to Whitehall, where great talk of the tumult at the other end of the town about Moorefields among the prentices, taking the liberty of these holidays to pull down bawdy houses. And Lord, to see the apprehensions which this did give to all people at Court, that presently order was given for all the soldiers, horse and foot, to be in armes; and forthwith alarmes were beat by drum and trumpet through Westminster, and all to their colours and to horse, as if the French were coming into the town. So Creed, whom I met here, and I to Lincolnes Inn fields, thinking to have gone into the fields to have seen the prentices; but here we found these fields full of soldiers all in a body, and my Lord Craven commanding of them, and riding up and down to give orders like a madman. And some young men we saw brought by soldiers to the guard at Whitehall, and overheard others that stood by say that it was only for pulling down of bawdy houses. And none of the bystanders finding fault with them, but rather of the soldiers for hindering them. And we heard a Justice of Peace this morning say to the King that he had been endeavouring to suppress this tumult, but could not; and that imprisoning some in the new prison at Clerkenwell, the rest did come and break open the prison and release them. And that they do give out that they are for pulling down of bawdy houses, which is one of the great grievances of the nation. To which the King made a

very poor, cold, insipid answer: "Why, why do they go to them, then?", and that was all, and had no mind to go on with the discourse.

Mr. Creed and I to dinner to my Lord Crew, where little discourse, and there being none but us at the table and my Lord and my Lady Jemimah. And so after dinner away, Creed and I, to Whitehall, expecting a committee of Tanger, but came too late. So I to attend the Council, and by and by were called in with Lord Brouncker and Sir W. Penn to advise how to pay away a little money to most advantage to the men of the yards, to make them despatch the ships going out; and there I did make a little speech, which was well liked. And after all, it was found most satisfactory to the men and best for the King's despatch, that what money we had should be paid weekly to the men for their week's work, until a greater sum could be got to pay them their arreares and then discharge them. But Lord, to see what shifts and what cares and thoughts there was imployed in this matter, how to do the King's work and please the men and stop clamours, would make a man think the King should not eat a bit of good meat till he hath got money to pay the men – but I do not see the least print of care or thoughts in him about it all. Having done here, I out and there met Sir Fr. Hollis, who doth still tell me that above all things in the world he wishes he had my tongue in his mouth; meaning, since my speech in Parliament. He took Lord Brouncker and me down to the guards, he and his company being upon the guards today; and there he did, in a handsome room to that purpose, make us drink, and did call for his Bagpiper; which, with pipes of ebony tipped with silver, he did play beyond anything of that kind that ever I heard in my life. And with great pains he must have obtained it, but with pains that the instrument doth not deserve at all; for at the best, it is mighty barbarous music. So home, and there to my chamber to prick out my song, *It is decreed*, intending to have it ready to give Mr. Harris on Thursdy when we meet for him to sing, believing that he will do it more right then a woman that sings better, unless it were Knipp – which I cannot have opportunity to teach it to.

25. The Duke of York and all with him this morning were full of the talk of the prentices, who are not yet down, though the Guards and militia of the town have been in arms all this night and the night before; and the prentices have made fools of them, sometimes by running from them and flinging stones at them. Some blood hath

been spilt, but a great many houses pulled down; and among others, the Duke of York was mighty merry at that of Damaris Page's, the great bawd of the seamen. And the Duke of York complained merrily that he hath lost two tenants by their houses being pulled down, who paid him for their wine licences 15*l* a year. But here it was said how these idle fellows have had the confidence so say that they did ill in contenting themselfs in pulling down the little bawdy houses and did not go and pull down the great bawdy house at Whitehall. And some of them have the last night had a word among them, and it was "Reformation and Reducement!" This doth make the courtiers ill at ease to see this spirit among people, though they think this matter will not come to much; but it speaks people's mind. And then they do say that there are men of understanding among them, that have been of Cromwell's army; but how true that is I know not.

26. Up betimes to the office, where by and by my Lord Brouncker and I met and made an end of our business betimes; so I away with him to Mrs. Williams's and there dined, and thence I alone to the Duke of York's House to see the new play called *The Man is the Maister*, where the house was, it being not above one a-clock, very full; but my wife and Deb being there before with Mrs. Pierce and Corbett and Betty Turner, whom my wife carried with her, they made me room; and there I sat, it costing me 8*s.* upon them in oranges, at 6*d.* apiece. By and by the King came and we sat just under him, so that I durst not turn my back all the play. The play is a translation out of French, and the plot Spanish; but not anything extraordinary at all in it, though translated by Sir W. Davenant; and so I found the King and his company did think meanly of it, though there was here and there something pretty; but the most of the mirth was sorry, poor stuffe, of eating of sack-posset and slabbering themselfs, and mirth fit for Clownes. The prologue but poor; and the epilogue, little in it but the extraordi-nariness of it, it being sung by Harris and another in the form of a ballet. Thence by agreement, we all of us to the Blue Balls hard by, whither Mr. Pierce also goes with us, who met us at the play; and anon comes Manuel and his wife and Knipp and Harris, who brings with him Mr. Banester, the great maister of Musique. And after much difficulty in getting of Musique, we to dancing and then to a supper of some French dishes (which yet did not please me) and then to dance and sing; and mighty merry we were till about 11 or

12 at night, with mighty great content in all my company; and I did, as I love to do, enjoy myself in my pleasure, as being the heighth of what we take pains for and can hope for in this world – and therefore to be enjoyed while we are young and capable of these joys. My wife extraordinary fine today in her Flower tabby suit, bought a year and more ago, before my mother's death put her into mourning, and so not worn till this day – and everybody in love with it; and endeed, she is very fine and handsome in it. I having paid the reckoning, which came to almost 4*l*, we parted: my company and Wm. Batelier, who was also with us, home in a coach round by the Wall, where we met so many stops by the Waches that it cost us much time and some trouble, and more money to every watch to them to drink – this being encreased by the trouble the prentices did lately give the City, so that the militia and watches are very strict at this time; and we had like to have met with a stop for all night at the Constables watch at Mooregate, by a pragmatical Constable. But we came well home at about 2 in the morning, and so to bed.

27. Up and walked to the waterside, and thence to Whitehall to the Duke of York's chamber; where he being ready, he went to a Committee of Tanger, where I first understand that my Lord Sandwich is in his coming back from Spayne, to step over thither to see in what condition the place is – which I am glad of, hoping that he will be able to do some good there for the good of the place – which is so much out of order. Thence to walk a little in Westminster hall, where the Parliament I find sitting, but spoke with nobody to let me know what they are doing, nor did I enquire. Thence to the Swan and drank, and did besar Frank; and so down by water back again and to the Exchange a turn or two, only to show myself; and then home to dinner, where my wife and I had a small squabble; but I first this day tried the effect of my silence and not provoking her when she is in an ill humour, and do find it very good, for it prevents its coming to that heighth on both sides, which used to exceed what was fit between us. So she became calm by and by, and fond; and so took coach, and she to the mercer's to buy some lace, while I to Whitehall but did nothing; but then to Westminster hall and took a turn, and so to Mrs. Martins and there did sit a little and talk and drink and did hazer con her; and so took coach and called my wife at Unthankes, and so up and down to the Nursery, where they did not act; then to the New Cockepitt and

there missed, and then to Hide parke, where many coaches, but the Dust so great that it was troublesome; and so by night home, where to my chamber and finished my pricking out of my song for Mr. Harris (*It is decreed*); and so a little supper, being very sleepy and weary since last night, and so by 10 a-clock to bed – and slept well all night. This day at noon comes Mr. Pelling to me and shows me the stone cut lately out of Sir Tho. Adam's (the old comely Alderman) body, which is very large endeed, bigger I think then my fist, and weighs above 25 ounces – and which is very miraculous, never in all his life had any fit of it, but lived to a great age without pain, and died at last of something else, without any sense of this in all his life.

29. *Lords day.* Up, and I to church, where I have not been these many weeks before; and there did first find a strange Reader, who could not find in the service-book the place for churching of women, but was fain to change books with the Clerke. And then a stranger preached, a seeming able man; but said in his pulpit that God did a greater work in raising of a oake-tree from an akehorne than a man's body raising it at the last day from his dust (showing the possibility of the Resurrection); which was methought a strange saying. At home to dinner, whither comes and dines with me W. How, and by invitation Mr. Harris and Mr. Banister, most extraordinary company both, the latter for music of all sorts, the former for everything. Here we sang, and Banister played on the Theorbo. And afterward Banister played on his flagelette and I had very good discourse with him about music, so confirming some of my new notions about music that it puts me upon a resolution to go on and make a Scheme and Theory of music not yet ever made in the world. Harris doth so commend my wife's picture of Mr. Hales's, that I will have him draw Harris's head; and he hath also persuaded me to have Cooper draw my wife's; which though it cost 30*l*, yet I will have done.

30. Up betimes and so to my office, there to do business – till about 10 a-clock; and then out with my wife and Deb and W. Hewers by coach to Common garden Coffee-house, where by appointment I was to meet Harris; which I did, and also Mr. Cooper the great painter and Mr. Hales; and thence presently to Mr. Cooper's house to see some of his work; which is all in little, but so excellent, as though I must confess I do think the colouring of

the flesh to be a little forced, yet the painting is so extraordinary, as I do never expect to see the like again. Here I did see Mrs. Stewards picture as when a young maid, and now again done just before her having the smallpox; and it would make a man weep to see what she was then, and what she is like to be, by people's discourse, now. Here I saw my Lord Generalls picture, and my Lord Arlington and Ashlys, and several others; but among the rest, one Swinfen, that was Secretary to my Lord Manchester, Lord Chamberlain (with Cooling), done so admirably as I never saw anything; but the misery was, this fellow died in debt and never paid Cooper for his picture; but it being seized on by his creditors among his other goods after his death, Cooper himself says that he did buy it, and gave 25*l* out of his purse for it, for what he was to have had but 30*l*.

31. Up pretty betimes and to the office, where we sat all the morning; and at noon I home to dinner, where my Uncle Tho. dined with me, as he doth every quarter, and I paid him his pension;[1] and also comes Mr. Hollier, a little fuddled and so did talk nothing but Latin and laugh, that it was very good sport to see a sober man in such a humour, though he was not drunk to scandal. At dinner comes a summons for this office to attend a committee of Parliament this afternoon with Sir D. Gawden, which I accordingly did, with my papers relating to the sending of victuals to Sir Jo. Harman's fleet; and there, Sir R. Brookes in the chair, we did give them a full account. Having given them good satisfaction, I away thence up and down, wandering a little to see whether I could get Mrs. Burroughs out, but ella being in the shop ego did speak con her, but she could not then go foras. And so I took coach, and away to Unthankes and there took up my wife and Deb and to the parke; where being in a Hackny and they undressed, I was ashamed to go into the Tour, but went round the park; and so with pleasure home, where Mr. Pelling came and sat and talked with us; and he being gone, I called Deb to take pen, ink, and paper and write down what things came into my head for my wife to do, in order to her going into the country; and the girl writing not so well as she would do, cried, and her mistress construed it to be sullenness and so was angry, and I seemed angry with her too; but going to bed, she undressed me, and there I did give her good advice and beso la, ella weeping still; and yo did

---

1. An annuity payable under his brother Robert Pepys's will.

take her, the first time in my life, sobra mi genu and did poner mi mano sub her jupes and toca su thigh, which did hazer me great pleasure; and so did no more, but besando-la went to my bed.

# ⚜APRILL⚜

1.  Up and to dress myself; and called, as I use, Deb to brush me and dress me and there I did again as I did the last night con mi mano, but would have tocado su thing; but ella endeavoured to prevent me con much modesty by putting su hand there about, which I was well pleased with and would not do too much, and so con great kindness dismissed la; and I to my office, where busy till noon, and then out to bespeak some things against my wife's going into the country tomorrow. And so home to dinner, my wife and I alone, she being mighty busy getting her things ready for her journey. I all the afternoon with her looking after things on the same account, and then in the afternoon out and all alone to the King's House; and there sat in an upper box to hide myself and saw *The Blacke prince*, a very good play, but only the fancy; most of it the same as in the rest of my Lord Orery's plays – but the dance very stately. But it was pretty to see, how coming after dinner and no company with me to talk to, and at a play that I had seen and went to now not for curiosity but only idleness, I did fall asleep the former part of the play but afterward did mind it and like it very well. Thence called at my bookseller's and took Mr. Boyles book of Formes, newly imprinted, and sent my brother my old one. So home, and there to my chamber, till anon comes Mr. Turner and his wife and daughter and Pelling to sup with us and talk of my wife's journey tomorrow, her daughter going with my wife; and after supper to talk with her husband about the office and his place, which by Sir J. Mennes's age and inability is very uncomfortable to him, as well as without profit or certainty what he shall do when Sir J. Mennes [dies]; which is a sad condition for a man that hath lived so long in the office as Mr. Turner hath done; but he aymes, and I advise him to it, to look for Mr. Ackworth's place in case he should be removed. His wife afterward did take me into my closet and give me a cellar of waters of her own distilling for my father, to be carried down with my wife and her daughter tomorrow; which was very handsome. So broke up and to bed.

2. Up, after much pleasant talk with my wife and upon some alterations I will make in my house in her absence, and I do intend to lay out some money thereon. So she and I up, and she got her ready to be gone; and by and by comes Betty Turner and her mother and W. Batelier, and they and Deb, to whom I did give 10s. this morning to oblige her to please her mistress (and yo did besar her mucho) and also Jane; and so in two coaches set out about 8 a-clock toward the carrier, there for to take coach for my father's (that is to say, my wife and Betty Turner, Deb and Jane); but I meeting my Lord Anglesy going to the office, was forced to light in Cheapside, and there took my leave of them (not besando Deb, which yo had a great mind to); left them to go to their coach, and I to the office, where all the morning busy. And so at noon with my other clerks (W. Hewer being a day's journey with my wife) to dinner. Thence with Lord Brouncker to the Royall Society, where they were just done; but there I was forced to subscribe to the building of a College, and did give 40l. And several others did subscribe, some greater and some less sums; but several I saw hang off, and I doubt it will spoil the Society – for it breeds faction and ill will, and becomes burdensome to some that cannot or would not do it. Here to my great content I did try the use of the Otacousticon, which was only a great glass bottle broke at the bottom, putting the neck to my eare; and there I did plainly hear the dashing of the oares of the boats in the Thames to Arundell gallery window; which without it I could not in the least do, and may I believe be improved to a great heighth – which I was mighty glad of. Thence with Lord Brouncker and several of them to the King's Head tavern by Chancery lane, and there did drink and eat and talk; and above the rest, I did desire of Mr. Hooke and my Lord an account of the reason of Concords and Discords in music – which they say is from the æquality of the vibrations; but I am not satisfied in it, but will at my leisure think of it more and see how far that doth go to explain it.

4. Up betimes, and by coach towards Whitehall; and took Aldgate street in my way and there called upon one Hayward that makes virginalls, and did there like of a little Espinettes and will have him finish them for me; for I had a mind to a small Harpsicon, but this takes up less room and will do my business as to finding out of Chords – and I am very well pleased that I have found it. Thence to Whitehall; and after long waiting did get a small running Committee of Tanger, where I stayed but little; and little done but

the correcting two or three egregious faults in the Charter for Tanger, after it had so long lain before the Council and been passed there and drawn up by the Atturny general, so slightly are all things in this age done.

5. *Lords day.* Up, and to my chamber and there to the writing fair some of my late music notions; and so to church, where I have not been a good while. And thence home, and dined at home with W. Hewers with me; and after dinner, he and I a great deal of good talk touching this office: how it is spoilt by having so many persons in it, and so much work that is not made the work of any one man but of all, and so is never done; and that the best way to have it well done were to have the whole trust in one (as myself) to set whom I pleased to work in the several businesses of the Office, and me to be accountable for the whole; and that would do it, as I would find instruments. But this is not to be compassed; but something I am resolved to do about Sir J. Mennes before it be long. Then to my chamber again, to my music, and so to church; and then home, and thither comes Capt. Silas Taylor to me, the Storekeeper of Harwich; where much talk, and most of it against Capt. Deane, whom I do believe to be a high, proud fellow; but he is an active man, and able in his way, and so I love him. He gone, I to my music again and to read a little and to sing with Mr. Pelling, who came to see me and so spent the evening; and then to supper and to bed. I hear that eight of the ringleaders in the late tumults of the prentices at Easter are condemned to die.

6. Meeting Creed, he and I to the new Cockepitt by the King's gate, and there saw the manner of it and the mixed rabble of people that came thither; and saw two battles of cocks, wherein is no great sport, but only to consider how these creatures without any provocation do fight and kill one another – and aim only at one another's heads, and by their good wills not leave till one of them be killed. And thence to the park in a hackney coach, so would not go into the Tour, but round about the park and to the [Lodge], and there at the door eat and drank; whither came my Lady Kerneagy, of whom Creed tells me more perticularly: how her Lord, finding her and the Duke of York at the King's first coming in too kind, did get it out of her that he did dishonour him; and so he bid her continue to let him, and himself went to the foulest whore he could find, that he might get the pox; and did, and did give his wife it on

purpose, that she (and he persuaded and threatened her that she should) might give it the Duke of York; which she did, and he did give it the Duchesse; and since, all her children are thus sickly and infirm – which is the most pernicious and foul piece of revenge that ever I heard of. And he at this day owns it with great glory, and looks upon the Duke of York and the world with great content in the ampleness of his revenge. Thence (where the place was now by the last night's rain very pleasant, and no dust) to Whitehall and set Creed down, and I home and to my chamber; there about my music notions again, wherein I take delight and find great satisfaction in them; and so after a little supper, to bed. This day in the afternoon, stepping with the Duke of York into St. James's park, it rained and I was forced to lend the Duke of York my cloak, which he wore through the park.

23. Up and to the office, where all the morning. And at noon comes Knepp and Mrs. Pierce and her daughter, and one Mrs. Foster, and dined with me – and mighty merry; and after dinner carried them to the Tower and showed them all to be seen there; and among other things, the Crown and Scepters and rich plate, which I myself never saw before and endeed is noble – and I mightily pleased with it. Thence by water to the Temple, and there to the Cocke alehouse and drank and eat a lobster and sang, and mighty merry. So, almost night, I carried Mrs. Pierce home, and then Knipp and I to the Temple again and took boat, it being darkish, and to Foxhall, it being now night and a bonfire burning at Lambeth for the King's Coronacion day. And there she and I drank; and yo did tocar her corps all over and besar sans fin her, but did not offer algo mas; and so back and led her home, it being now 10 at night, and so got a link; and walking towards home, just at my entrance into the ruines at St. Dunstan's, I was met by two rogues with clubs, who came towards us; so I went back and walked home quite round by the Wall and got well home; and to bed, weary but pleased at my day's pleasure – but yet displeased at my expense and time I lose.

26. *Lords day.* Lay long, and then up and to church; and so home, where there came and dined with me Harris, Rolt, and Bannester, and one Bland, that sings well also; and very merry at dinner; and after dinner, to sing all the afternoon. But when all was done, I did begin to think that the pleasure of these people was not worth so

often charge and cost to me as it hath occasioned me. They being gone, I and Balty walked as far as Charing cross, and there got a coach and to Hales's the painter, thinking to have found Harris sitting there for his picture which is drawing for me. But he and all this day's company, and Hales, were got to the Crown tavern at next door; and thither I to them and stayed a minute (leaving Capt. Grant telling pretty stories of people that have killed themselfs or been accessory to it, in revenge to other people and to mischief other people); and thence with Hales to his house and there did see his beginning of Harris's picture, which I think will be pretty like, and he promises a very good picture. Thence with Balty away, and got a coach and to Hide Parke, and there up and down and did drink some milk at the Lodge; and so home and to bed.

28. Up betimes and to Sir W. Coventry's by water, but lost my labour; so through the park to Whitehall, and thence to my Lord Crews to advise again with him about my Lord Sandwich; and so to the office, where till noon; and then I by coach to Westminster hall, and there do understand that the business of religion and the act against Conventicles have so taken them up all this morning, and doth still, that my Lord Sandwiches business is not like to come on today; which I am heartily glad of. This law against Conventicles is very severe; but Creed, whom I met here, doth tell me that it being moved that Papists meetings might be included, the House was divided upon it and it was carried in the negative; which will give great disgust to the people I doubt. Thence with Creed to Hercules Pillars by the Temple again, and there dined, he and I all alone; and thence to the King's House and there did see *Love in a maze*; wherein very good mirth of Lacy the clown and Wintersell the country-knight, his maister. Thence to the New Exchange to pay a debt of my wife's there, and so home; and there to the office and walk in the garden in the dark to ease my eyes; and so home to supper and to bed.

30. Up, and at the office all the morning. At noon Sir J. Mennes and I to the Dolphin tavern, there to meet our neighbours, all of the Parish, this being procession-day,[1] to dine – and did; and much very good discourse, they being most of them very able merchants, as any in the City – Sir Andr. Rickard, Mr. Vandeputt, Sir Jo. Fredricke, Harrington, and others. They talked with Mr. Mills

1. Ascension Day, when the parish bounds were beaten.

about the meaning of this day and the other good uses of it; and how heretofore, and yet in several places, they do whip a boy at every place they stop at in their procession. Thence I to the Duke of York's playhouse and there saw *The Tempest*, which still pleases me mightily. And thence to the New Exchange, and then home; and in the way stopped to talk with Mr. Brisband, who gives me an account of the rough usage Sir G. Carteret and his counsel had the other day before the Commissioners of Accounts, and what I do believe we shall all of us have, in a greater degree then any we have had yet with them, before their three years are out; which are not yet begun, nor God knows when they will, this being like to be no session of Parliament when they now rise. So home, and there took up Mrs. Turner and carried her to Mile end and drank; and so back, talking, and so home and to bed, I being mighty cold, this being a mighty cold day, and I had left off my waistcoat three or four days. This evening, coming home in the dark, I saw and spoke to our Nell, Pain's daughter, and had I not been very cold, I should have taken her to Tower-hill para talk together et tocar her.

Thus ends this month: my wife in the country. Myself full of pleasure and expense; and some trouble for my friends, my Lord Sandwich by the Parliament, and more for my eyes, which are daily worse and worse, that I dare not write or read almost anything. The Parliament going in a few days to rise. Myself, so long without accounting now, for seven or eight months I think or more, that I know not what condition almost I am in as to getting or spending for all that time – which troubles me, but I will soon do it. The kingdom in an ill state through poverty. A fleet going out, and no money to maintain it or set it out. Seamen yet unpaid, and mutinous when pressed to go out again. Our office able to do little, nobody trusting us nor we desiring any to trust us, and yet have not money to [do] anything but only what perticularly belongs to this fleet going out, and that but lamely too. The Parliament several months upon an act for 300000*l*, but cannot or will not agree upon it – but do keep it back, in spite of the King's desires to hasten it, till they can obtain what they have a mind, in revenge upon some men for the late ill managements; and he is forced to submit to what they please, knowing that without it he shall have no money; and they as well, that if they give the money, the King will suffer them to do little more. And then the business of religion doth disquiet everybody, the Parliament being vehement against the nonconformists, while the King seems to be willing to countenance them:

so we are all poor and in pieces, God help us; while the peace is like to go on between Spain and France, and then the French may be apprehended able to attack us. So God help us.

## –❧MAY❧–

2. Up, and at the office all the morning. At noon with Lord Brouncker in his coach as far as the Temple, and there light and to Hercules Pillars and there dined; and thence to the Duke of York's playhouse at a little past 12, to get a good place in the pit against the new play; and there setting a poor man to keep my place, I out and spent an hour at Martin's my bookseller's; and so back again, where I find the house quite full; but I had my place, and by and by the King comes and the Duke of York; and then the play begins, called *The Sullen lovers or The Impertinents*, having many good humours in it; but the play tedious and no design at all in it. But a little boy, for a farce, doth dance Polichinelli the best that ever anything was done in the world by all men's report – most pleased with that, beyond anything in the world, and much beyond all the play. Thence to the King's House to see Knipp, but the play done; and so I took a hackney alone, and to the park and there spend the evening, and to the Lodge and drank new milk; and so home to the office, ended my letters and, to spare my eyes, home and played on my pipes; and so to bed.

5. Up, and all the morning at the office. At noon home to dinner, and Creed with me; and after dinner, he and I to the Duke of York's playhouse; and there coming late, he and I up to the Balcony-box, where we find my Lady Castlemayne and several great ladies and there we sat with them. And I saw *The Impertinents* once more, now three times, and the three only days it hath been acted; and to see the folly how the house doth this day cry up the play more then yesterday; and I for that reason like it, I find, the better too. By Sir Positive At all, I understand, is meant Sir Rob. Howard. My Lady pretty well pleased with it; but here I sat close to her fine woman, Willson, who endeed is very handsome, but they say with child by the King. I asked, and she told me this was the first time her Lady had seen it, I having a mind to say something to her. One thing of familiarity I observed in my Lady Castlemayne; she called to one of

her women, another that sat by this, for a little patch off of her face, and put it into her mouth and wetted it and so clapped it upon her own by the side of her mouth, I suppose she feeling a pimple rising there. Thence with Creed to Westminster hall and there met with Cosen Roger, who tells me of the great conference this day between the Lords and Commons about the business of the East India Company – as being one of the weightiest conferences that hath been, and managed as weightily; I am heartily sorry I was not there, it being upon a mighty point of the privileges of the subjects of England in regard to the authority of the House of Lords and their being condemned by them as the supreme court; which they say ought not to be but by appeal from other courts. And he tells me that the Commons had much the better of them in reason and history there quoted, and believes the Lords will let it fall. Thence to walk in the Hall; and there hear that Mrs. Martin's child, my god-daughter, is dead. And so by water to the Old Swan; and thence home and there a little at Sir W. Penn's; and so to bed.

7. Up, and to the office, where all the morning. At noon home to dinner, and thither I sent for Mercer to dine with me; and after dinner, she and I called Mrs. Turner and I carried them to the Duke of York's House and there saw *The Man's the Maister*, which proves, upon my seeing it again, a very good play. Thence called Knepp from the King's House; where going in for her, the play being done, I did see Becke Marshall come dressed off of the stage, and looks mighty fine and pretty, and noble – and also Nell in her boy's clothes, mighty pretty; but Lord, their confidence, and how many men do hover about them as soon as they come off of the stage, and how confident they in their talk. Here I did kiss the pretty woman newly come, called Pegg, that was Sir Ch. Sidly's mistress – a mighty pretty woman, and seems, but is not, modest.* Here took up Knepp into our coach and all of us with her to her lodging, and thither comes Bannester with a song of hers that he hath set in Sir Ch. Sidly's play for her, which is I think but very meanly set; but this he did before us, teach her; and it being but a slight, silly, short ayre, she learnt it presently. But I did here get him to prick me down the notes of the Echo in *The Tempest*, which pleases me mightily. And here was also Haynes, the incomparable dancer of the King's house, and a seeming civil man and sings pretty well. And they gone, we abroad to Marrowbone and there walked in the garden, the first time I ever there, and a pretty place it is; and here

we eat and drank and stayed till 9 at night; and so home by moonshine, I all the way having mi mano abaxo la jupe de Knepp con much placer and freedom; but endeavouring afterward to tocar her con mi cosa, ella did strive against that, but yet I do not think that she did find much fault with it, but I was a little moved at my offering it and not having it. And so set Mrs. Knepp at her lodging, and so the rest and I home, talking with a great deal of pleasure, and so home to bed.

10. *Lords day*. Up, and to my office, there to do business till church time, when Mr. Sheply, lately come to town, came to see me; and we had some discourse of all matters, and perticularly of my Lord Sandwiches concernments; and here he did by the by, as he would seem, tell me that my Lady had it in her thoughts, if she had occasion, to borrow 100*l* of me – which I did not declare any opposition to, though I doubt it will be so much lost; but however, I will not deny my Lady if she ask it, whatever comes of it, though it be lost; but shall be glad that it is no bigger sum. And yet it vexes me though, and the more because it brings into my head some apprehensions what trouble I may hereafter be brought to when my Lord comes home, if he should ask me to come into bonds with him, as [I] fear he will have occasions to take up money. But I hope I shall have the wit to deny it. He being gone, I to church and so home; and there comes W. Hewer and Balty, and by and by I sent for Mercer to come and dine with me – and pretty merry. And after dinner I fell to teach her *Canite Jehovæ*, which she did a great part presently. And so she away, and I to church, and from church home with my Lady Pen; and after being there an hour or so talking, I took her and Mrs. Lowther, and old Mrs. Whistler her mother-in-law, by water with great pleasure as far as Chelsy; and so back to Spring garden at Foxhall and there walked and eat and drank; and so to water again and set down the old woman at home at Durham yard; and it raining all the way, it troubles us; but however, my cloak kept us all dry; and so home, and at the Tower wharf there we did send for a pair of old shoes for Mrs. Lowther, and there I did pull the others off and put them on, and did endeavour para tocar su thigh but ella had drawers on, but yo did besar la and tocar sus mamelles, ella being poco shy but doth speak con mighty kindness to me that she would desire me por su marido if it were to be done. Here stayed a little at Sir W. Penn's, who was gone to bed, it being about 11 at night; and so I home to bed.

11. Up, and to my office, where alone all the morning. About noon comes to me my cousin Sarah and my aunt Licett, newly come out of Gloucestershire, good woman, and come to see me; I took them home and made them drink, but they would not stay dinner, I being alone. But here they tell me that they hear that this day Kate Joyce was to be married to a man called Hollinshed, whom she endeed did once tell me of and desired me to enquire after him. But whatever she said of his being rich, I do fear, by her doing this without my advice, it is not as it ought to be; but as she brews, let her bake. They being gone, I to dinner with Balty and his wife, who is come to town today from Deptford to see us. And after dinner, I out and took a coach and called Mercer, and she and I to the Duke of York's playhouse and there saw *The Tempest*; and between two acts, I went out to Mr. Harris and got him to repeat to me the words of the Echo, while I writ them down, having tried in the play to have wrote them; but when I had done it, having done it without looking upon my paper, I find I could not read the blacklead – but now I have got the words clear; and in going in thither, had the pleasure to see the Actors in their several dresses, especially the seamen and monster, which were very droll. So into the play again. But there happened one thing which vexed me; which is, that the orange-woman did come in the pit and challenge me for twelve oranges which she delivered by my order at a late play at night, to give to some ladies in a box, which was wholly untrue, but yet she swore it to be true; but however, I did deny it and did not pay her, but for quiet did buy 4*s*. worth of oranges of her – at 6*d*. a piece. Here I saw first my Lord Ormond since his coming from Ireland, which is now about eight days. After the play done, I took Mercer by water to Spring garden and there with great pleasure walked and eat and drank and sang, making people come about us to hear us, and two little children of one of our neighbours that happened to be there did come into our Arbour and we made them dance prettily. So by water, with great pleasure down to the Bridge, and there landed and took water again on the other side; and so to the Tower, and I saw her home, and myself home to my chamber and by and by to bed.

13. Up and by water to Whitehall, and so to Sir H. Cholmlys, who not being up, I made a short visit to Sir W. Coventry, and he and I through the park to Whitehall; and thence I back into the park and there met Sir H. Cholmly, and he and I to Sir St. Fox's; where we met and considered the business of the Excize, how far it is

charged in reference to the payment of the Guards and Tanger. Thence he and I walked to Westminster hall and there took a turn, it being holiday; and so back again, and I to the Mercers and my tailor's about a stuff suit that I am going to make; and thence at noon to Hercules Pillars and there dined alone. And so to Whitehall, some of us, attended the Duke of York as usual and so to attend the Council about the business of Hemskirke's project of building a ship that shall [sail] two foot for one of any other ship – which the Council did agree to be put in practice, the King to give him, if it proves good, 5000*l* in hand and 15000*l* more in seven years – which, for my part, I think a piece of folly for them to meddle with, because the secret cannot be long kept. So thence after Council, having drunk some of the King's wine and water with Mr. Chevins, my Lord Brouncker, and some others; I by water to the Old Swan and there to Michells and did see her and drink there; but he being there, yo no puede besar la. And so back again by water to Spring garden all alone, and walked a little; and so back again home and there a little to my viall; and so to bed, Mrs. Turner having sat and supped with me. This morning, I hear that last night Sir Tho. Teddiman, poor man, did die by a thrush in his mouth – a good man, and stout and able, and much lamented; though people do make a little mirth and say, as I believe it did in good part, that the business of the Parliament did break his heart, or at least put him into this fever and disorder that caused his death.

14. Up and to the office, where we sat all the morning; and at noon home to dinner with my people; but did not stay to dine out with them, but rose and straight by water to the Temple, and so to Penny's my tailor; where by and by, by agreement comes Mercer and she to my great content brings Mrs. Gayet, and I carried them to the King's House; but coming too soon, we out again to the Rose tavern and there I did give them a tankard of cool drink, the weather being very hot; and then into the playhouse again and there saw *The Country Captain*, a very dull play that did give us no content; and besides, little company there, which made it very unpleasing. Thence to the waterside at Strand bridge, and so up by water and to Foxhall, where we walked a great while, and pleased mightily with the pleasure thereof and the company there; and then in and eat and drank, and then out again and walked; and it beginning to be dark, we to a Corner and sang, that everybody got about us to hear us; and so home, where I saw them both at their doors; and full of the

content of this afternoon's pleasure, I home and to walk in the garden a little, and so home to bed.

15. Up, and betimes to Whitehall and there met with Sir H. Cholmly at Sir St. Fox's; and there was also the Cofferer, and we did there consider about our money and the condition of the Excize; and after much dispute, agreed upon a state thereof and the manner of our future course of payments. Thence to the Duke of York and there did a little Navy business as we used to do; and so to a Committee for Tanger, where God knows how, my Lord Bellasses accounts passed, understood by nobody but my Lord Ashly, who I believe was mad to let them go as he pleased. But here Sir H. Cholmly had his propositions read, about a greater price for his work of the Mole, or to do it upon account; which being read, he was bid to withdraw; but Lord, to see how unlucky a man may be by chance; for taking an unfortunate minute when they were almost tired with other business, the Duke of York did find fault with it, and that made all the rest, that I believe he had better have given a great deal and had it had nothing said to it today; whereas, I have seen other things more extravagant pass at first hearing without any difficulty. Thence I to my Lord Brouncker's at Mrs. Williams's and there dined, and she did show me her closet; which I was sorry to see, for fear of her expecting something from me; and here she took notice of my wife's not once coming to see her; which I am glad of, for she shall not – a prating, vain, idle woman. Thence with Lord Brouncker to Loriners hall by Mooregate (a hall [I] never heard of before) to Sir Tho. Teddiman's burial – where most people belonging to the sea were; and here we had rings, and here I do hear that some of the last words that he said was: that he had a very good King, God bless him, but that the Parliament had very ill rewarded him for all the service he had endeavoured to do them and his country – so that for certain, this did go far towards his death. But Lord, to see among the young commanders and Tho. Killigrew and others that came, how unlike a burial this was, Obrian taking out some ballets out of his pocket, which I read and the rest came about me to hear; and there very merry we were all, they being new ballets. By and by the Corps went, and I with my Lord Brouncker and Dr. Clerke and Mr. Pierce as far as the foot of London bridge; and there we struck off into Thames street, the rest going to Redriffe, where he is to be buried. And we light at the Temple and there parted; and I to the King's House and there saw the last act of

*The Committee*, thinking to have seen Knepp there, but she did not act. And so to my bookseller's and there carried home some books; among others, Dr. Wilkins's *Reall Character*. And thence to Mrs. Turner's, and there went and sat and she showed me her house from top to bottom, which I had not seen before – very handsome. And here supped; and so home and got Mercer, and she and I in the garden singing till 10 at night; and so home to a little supper, and then parted with great content and I to bed. The Duchess of Monmouth's hip is I hear now set again, after much pain. I am told also that the Countesse of Shrewsbery is brought home by the Duke of Buckingham to his house; where his Duchess saying that it was not for her and the other to live together in a house, he answered, "Why, Madam, I did think so; and therefore have ordered your coach to be ready to carry you to your father's;" which was a devilish speech, but they say true; and my Lady Shrewsbry is there it seems.

16. Up; and to the office, where we sat all the morning. And at noon home with my people to dinner; and thence to the office all the afternoon, till, my eyes weary, I did go forth by coach to the King's playhouse and there saw the best part of *The Sea Voyage*, where Knepp I saw do her part of sorrow very well. I afterward to her house, but she did not come presently home; and here yo did besar her ancilla, which is so mighty belle. And I to my tailor's, and to buy me a belt for my new suit against tomorrow. And so home and there to my office, and afterward late walking in the garden; and so home to supper and to bed, after Nell's cutting of my hair close, the weather being very hot.

17. *Lords day*. Up, and put on my new stuff suit with a shoulder-belt, according to the new fashion, and the hands of my vest and tunic laced with silk lace of the colour of my suit. And so, very handsome, to church, where a dull sermon of a stranger. And so home and there I find W. How and a younger brother of his come to dine with me; and there comes Mercer and brings with her Mrs. Gayet, which pleased me mightily, and here was also W. Hewers; and mighty merry and after dinner to sing psalms; but Lord, to hear what an excellent Base this younger brother of W. How's sings, even to my astonishment and mighty pleasant. By and by Gayet goes away, being a Catholique, to her devotions, and Mercer to church, but we continued an hour or two singing, and so parted;

and I to Sir W. Penn's, and there sent for a hackney coach and he and she and I out to take the ayre. We went to Stepny and there stopped at the Trinity house, he to talk with the servants there against tomorrow, which is a great day for the choice of a new Maister. And thence to Mile end and there eat and drank; and so home, and I supped with them; that is, eat some butter and radishes, which is my excuse for not eating of any other of their victuals, which I hate because of their sluttery. And so home and made my boy read to me part of Dr. Wilkins's new book of the *Real Character*, and so to bed.

18.    Up and to my office, where most of the morning doing business and seeing my window-frames new painted; and then I out by coach to my Lord Bellasses at his new house by my late Lord Treasurer's; and there met him and Mr. Sherwin, Auditor Beale, and Creed about my Lord's accounts; and here my Lord showed me his new house, which endeed is mighty noble; and good pictures, endeed not one bad one in it. Thence to my tailor's, and there did find Mercer come with Mrs. Horsfield and Gayet according to my desire; and there I took them up, it being almost 12 a-clock or little more, and carried them to the King's playhouse, where the doors were not then open; but presently they did open, and we in and find many people already come in by private ways into the pit, it being the first day of Sir Charles Sidly's new play, so long expected, *The Mulbery guarden*; of whom, being so reputed a wit, all the world doth expect great matters. I having sat here a while and eat nothing today, did slip out, getting a boy to keep my place; and to the Rose tavern and there got half a breast of mutton off of the spit and dined all alone; and so to the play again, where the King and Queen by and by came, and all the Court, and the house infinitely full. But the play when it came, though there was here and there a pretty saying, and that not very many neither, yet the whole of the play had nothing extraordinary in it at all, neither of language nor design; insomuch that the King I did not see laugh nor pleased the whole play from the beginning to the end, nor the company; insomuch that I have not been less pleased at a new play in my life I think. And which made it the worse was that there never was worse music played; that is, worse things composed; which made me and Capt. Rolt, who happened to sit near me, mad. So away thence, very little satisfied with the play, but pleased with my company: I carried them to Kensington to the Grotto, and there we sang to my great content; only, vexed in going in to see a son of Sir Heneage Finche's

beating of a poor little dog to death, letting it lie in so much pain that made me mad to see it; till by and by, the servants of the house chiding of their young maister, one of them came with a thong and killed the dog outright presently. Thence to Westminster Palace and there took boat and to Foxhall, where we walked and eat and drank and sang, and very merry; but I find Mrs. Horsfield one of the veriest citizen's wifes in the world, so full of little silly talk, and now and then a little sillily bawdy, that I believe if you had her sola, a man might hazer algo with her. So back by water to Westminster Palace and there got a coach who carried us as far as the Minorys, and there something of the traces broke, and we forced to light and walked to Mrs. Horsfields house, it being a long and bad way, and dark; and having there put her in a-doors, her husband being in bed, we left her; and so back to our coach, where the coachman had put it in order, but could not find his whip in the dark a great while, which made us stay long; at last, getting a neighbour to hold a candle out of their window, Mercer found it, and so away; we home at almost 12 at night; and setting them both at their homes, I home and to bed.

19.    Up, and called on by Mr. Pierce, who tells me that after all this ado Ward is come to town, and hath appeared to the Commissioners of Accounts and given such answers as he thinks will do everybody right and let the world see that their great expectations and jealousies have been vain in this matter of the prizes. The Commissioners were mighty inquisitive whether he was not instructed by letters or otherwise from hence from my Lord Sandwiches friends what to say and do, and perticularly from me – which he did wholly deny, as it was true, I not knowing the man that I know of. He tells me also that for certain Mr. Vaughan is made Lord Chief Justice; which I am glad of. He tells me too, that since my Lord of Ormond's coming over, the King begins to be mightily reclaimed, and sups every night with great pleasure with the Queene; and yet it seems he is mighty hot upon the Duchess of Richmond; insomuch that upon Sunday was sennit, at night, after he had ordered his guards and coach to be ready to carry him to the park, he did on a sudden take a pair of oars or sculler, and all alone, or but one with him, go to Somerset house and there, the garden-door not being open, himself clamber over the walls to make a visit to her where she is; which is a horrid shame. He gone, I to the office, where we sat all the morning. Sir W. Pen, sick of the gout, comes

not out. After dinner at home, to Whitehall, it being a very rainy day. And there a Committee for Tanger, where I was mightily pleased to see Sir W. Coventry fall upon my Lord Bellasses's business of the 3*d.* in every piece of eight, which he would get to himself, making the King pay 4*s.*–9*d.* while he puts them off for 4*s.*–6*d.* – so that Sir W. Coventry continues still the same man for the King's good. But here Creed did vex me with saying that I ought first to have my account passed by the Commissioners of Tanger before in the Exchequer. Thence, W. Coventry and I in the Matted Gallery to talk; and there he did talk very well to me about the way to save the credit of the Officers of the Navy, and their places too, by making use of this intervall of Parliament to be found to be mending of matters in the Navy, and that nothing but this will do it; and gives an instance in themselfs of the Treasury, whereof himself and Sir Jo. Duncome all the world knows have enemies, and my Lord Ashly a man obnoxious to most, and Sir Tho. Clifford one that, as a man suddenly rising and a creature of my Lord Arlington's, hath enemies enough (none of them being otherwise but the Duke of Albemarle); yet with all this fault, they hear nothing of the business of the Treasury, but all well spoken of there. He is for the removal of Sir J. Mennes, thinking that thereby the world will see a greater change in the hands then now they do. And I will endeavour it, and endeavour to do some good in the office also. So home by coach and to the office, where ended my letters and then home; and there got Balty to read to me out of Sorbiere's observations in his voyage into England; and then to bed.

20. Up and with Coll. Middleton in a new coach he hath made him, very handsome, to Whitehall; where the Duke of York having removed his lodgings for this year to St. James's, we walked thither and there find the Duke of York coming to Whitehall; and so back to the Council chamber, where the Committee of the Navy sat, and here we discoursed several things; but Lord, like fools, so as it was a shame to see things of this importance managed by a Council that understand nothing of them. And among other things, one was about this building of a ship with Hemskirkes secret, to sail a third faster than any other ship; but he hath got Prince Rupart on his side, and by that means I believe will get his conditions made better then he would otherwise, or ought endeed. Having done there, I met with Sir Rd. Browne and he took me to dinner with him to a new tavern above Charing cross, where some Clients of his did give him

a good dinner, and good company; among others, one Bovy, a solicitor* and lawyer and merchant all together, who hath travelled very much, did talk some things well, but only he is a Sir Positive; but the talk of their travels over the Alps very fine. Thence walked to the King's playhouse and there saw *The Mulbery-Garden* again; and cannot be reconciled to it, but only do find here and there an independent sentence of wit, and that is all. Here met with Creed and took him to Hales's, and there saw the beginnings of Harris's head which he draws for me and which I do not yet like. So he and I down to the New Exchange and there cheapened ribbands for my wife, and so down to the Wheyhouse and drank some and eat some curds, which did by and by make my belly ake mightily. So he and I to Whitehall and walked over the park to the Mulbery garden, where I never was before; and find it a very silly place, worse then Spring garden, and but little company and those a rascally, whoring, roguing sort of people; only, a wilderness here is that is somewhat pretty, but rude. Did not stay to drink, but walked an hour, and so away to Charing cross and there took coach and away home – in my way going into Bishopsgate street to bespeak places for myself and boy to go to Cambridge in the coach this week, and so to Brampton to see my wife. So home and to supper and to bed.

23.    Up by 4 a-clock; and getting my things ready and recommending the care of my house to W. Hewer, I with the boy Tom, whom I take with me, to the Bull in Bishopsgate street and there about 6 took coach, he and I and a gentleman and his man – there being another coach also, with as many more I think in it. And so away to Bishops Stafford, and there dine and changed horses and coach at Mrs. Aynsworth's; but I took no knowledge of her.[1] Here this gentleman and I to dinner, and in comes Capt. Foster, an acquaintance of his, he that doth belong to my Lord Anglesy, who had been at the late horse-races at Newmarket, where the King now is; and says that they had fair weather there yesterday, though we here, and at London, had nothing but rain, insomuch that the ways are mighty full of water, so as hardly to be passed. Here I hear Mrs. Aynsworth is going to live at London; but I believe will be mistaken in it, for it will be found better for her to be chief where she is then to have little to do at London, there being many finer then she there. After dinner, away again and came to Cambridge, after much bad

---

1. cf. above, p. 835 (7 October).

way, about 9 at night; and there at the Rose I met my father's horses, with a man staying for me; but it is so late, and the waters so deep, that I durst not go tonight; but after supper to bed and lay very ill by reason of some drunken scholars making a noise all night, and vexed for fear that the horses should not be taken up from grass time enough for the morning.

24. *Lords day*. I up at between 2 and 3 in the morning; and calling up my boy and father's boy, we set out by 3 a-clock, it being high day; and so through the waters with very good success, though very deep almost all the way, and got to Brampton about [blank], where most of them in bed; and so I weary up to my wife's chamber, whom I find in bed and pretended a little not well, and endeed she hath those upon her, but fell to talk and mightily pleased both of us; and up got the rest, Betty Turner and Willet and Jane, all whom I was glad to see, and very merry; and got me ready in my new stuff clothes that I sent down before me; and so my wife and they got ready too, while I to my father, poor man, and walked with him up and down the house, it raining a little – and the waters all over Portholme and the meadows – so as no pleasure abroad. Here I saw my brothers and sister Jackson, she growing fat, and since being married, I think looks comelier then before. But a mighty pert woman she is, and I think proud, he keeping her mighty handsome, and they say mighty fond – and are going shortly to live at Ellington of themselfs, and will keep malting and grazing of cattle. At noon comes Mr. Phillips and dines with us, and a pretty odd-humoured man he seems to be – but good withal, but of mighty great methods in his eating and drinking, and will not kiss a woman since his wife's death. After dinner, my Lady Sandwich sending to see whether I was come, I presently took horse and find her and her family at chapel; and thither I went in to them and sat out the sermon, where I heard Jervas Fullwood, now their chaplain, preach a very good and seraphic kind of sermon, too good for an ordinary congregation. After sermon, I with my Lady and my Lady Hinchingbrooke and Paulina and Lord Hinchingbrooke to the dining-room, saluting none of them, and there sat and talked an hour or two, with great pleasure and satisfaction, to my Lady about my Lord's matters; but I think not with that satisfaction to her or me that otherwise would, she knowing that she did design to borrow, and I remaining all the while in fear of being asked to lend her some money, as I was afterward (when I had

taken leave of her) by Mr. Sheply, 100*l*; which I will not deny my Lady, and am willing to be found when my Lord comes home to have done something of that kind for them. And so he riding to Brampton and supping there with me, he did desire it of me from my Lady; and I promised it, though much against my will, for I fear it is as good as lost. After supper, where very merry, we to bed, myself very weary, and to sleep all night.

25. Waked betimes, and lay long hazendo doz vezes con mi moher con grando pleasure to me and ella; and there fell to talking, and by and by rose, it being the first fair day, and yet not quite fair, that we have had some time; and so up and to walk with my father again in the garden, consulting what to do with him and this house when Pall and her husband goes away; and I think it will be to let it and he go live with her, though I am against letting the house for any long time – because of having it to retire to ourselfs. So I do entend to think more of it before I resolve. By and by comes Mr. Cooke to see me, and so spent the morning; and he gone by and by, at noon to dinner, where Mr. Sheply came and we merry, all being in good humour between my wife and her people about her; and after dinner took horse, I promising to fetch her away about fourteen days hence. And so calling all of us, we men on horseback and the women and my father, at Goody Gorum's and there in a frolic drinking, I took leave, there going with me and my boy, my two brothers, and one Browne, whom they call in mirth "Collonell", for our guide, and also Mr. Sheply to the end of Huntington, and another gentleman who accidentally came thither, one Mr. Castle; and I made them drink at the Chequer, where I observed the same Tapster, Tom, that was there when I was a little boy; and so at the end of the town, took leave of Sheply and the other gentleman, and so we away and got well to Cambridge about 7 to the Rose, the waters not being now so high as before. And here lighting, I took my boy and two brothers and walked to Magdalen College; and there into the Butterys as a stranger and there drank my bellyfull of their beer, which pleased me as the best I ever drank; and hear by the butler's man, who was son to Goody Mulliner over against the College that we used to buy stewed prunes of, concerning the College and persons in it; and find very few, only Mr. Hollins and Peachell I think, that were of my time. But I was mightily pleased to come in this condition to see and ask; and thence, giving the fellow something, away; walked to Chesterton to see our old walk; and

there into the church, the bells ringing, and saw the place I used to sit in; and so to the ferry, and ferried over to the other side and walked with great pleasure, the river being mighty high by Barnwell Abbey; and so by Jesus College to the town, and so to our quarters and to supper; and then to bed, being very weary and sleepy, and mightily pleased with this night's walk.

26.    Up by 4 a-clock; and by the time we were ready and had eat, we were called to the coach; where about 6 a-clock we set out, there being a man and two women of one company, ordinary people, and one lady alone that is tolerable handsome, but mighty well spoken, whom I took great pleasure in talking to, and did get her to read aloud in a book she was reading in the coach, being the King's Meditations; and then the boy and I to sing, and so about noon came to Bishop's Stafford, to another house then what we were at the other day, and better used; and here I paid for the reckoning 11*s*., we dining all together and pretty merry. And then set out again, sleeping most part of the way, and got to Bishopsgate street before 8 a-clock, the waters being now most of them down, and we avoiding the bad way in the Forrest by a privy way which brought us to Hodsden, and so to Tibalds that road – which was mighty pleasant. So home, where we find all well, and Brother Balty and his wife looking to the house, she mighty fine in a new gold-laced juste-au-corps. I shifted myself, and so to see Mrs. Turner; and Mercer appearing over the way, called her in and sat and talked; and then home to my house by and by and there supped and talked mighty merry; and then broke up and to bed – being a little vexed at what W. Hewers tells me Sir Jo. Shaw did this day in my absence say at the Board, complaining of my doing of him injury and the board permitting it; whereas they had more reason to except against his attributing that to me alone which I could not do but with their consent and direction, it being to very good service to the King, and what I shall be proud [to] have imputed to me alone. The King, I hear, came to town last night.

29.    To Sir G. Carteret's to dinner, with much good company, it being the King's birthday and many healths drunk; and here I did receive another letter from my Lord Sandwich; which troubles me, to see how I have neglected him, in not writing, or but once, all this time of his being abroad. And I see he takes notice, but yet gently, of it, that it puts me to great trouble and I know not how to get out

of it, having no good excuse, and too late now to mend, he being
coming home. Thence home, whither by agreement by and by
comes Mercer and Gayett, and two gentlemen with them, Mr.
Montouth and Pelham, the former a swaggering young handsome
gentleman – the latter a sober citizen merchant; both sing, but the
latter with great skill; the other, no skill but a good voice and a good
basse – but used to sing only tavern tunes; and so I spent all this
evening till 11 at night singing with them, till I tired of them
because of the swaggering fellow with the basse, though the girl
Mercer did mightily commend him before to me. This night yo had
agreed para andar at Deptford, there para haber lain con the moher
de Bagwell, but this company did hinder me.

30.    Up, and put on a new summer black bombazin suit, and so to
the office; and being come now to an agreement with my barber to
keep my perriwigs in good order at 20s. a year, I am like to go very
spruce, more then I used to do. All the morning at the office; and at
noon home to dinner, and so to the King's playhouse and there saw
*Philaster*; where it is pretty to see how I could remember almost all
along, ever since I was a boy, Arethusa's part which I was to have
acted at Sir Rob. Cooke's; and it was very pleasant to me, but more
to think what a ridiculous thing it would have been for me to have
acted a beautiful woman. Thence to Mrs. Pierces, and there saw
Knepp also, and were merry; and here saw my little Lady Kath.
Mountagu, come to town about her eyes, which are sore, and they
think the King's Evil, poor pretty lady. Here I was freed from a fear
that Knepp was angry or might take advantage; did parlar the esto
that yo did the otra day quand yo was con her in ponendo her mano
upon mi cosa – but I saw no such thing; but as pleased as ever, and I
believe she can bear with any such thing. Thence to the New
Exchange, and there met Harris and Rolt and one Richards, a tailor
and great company-keeper; and with these over to Foxhall and
there fell into the company of Harry Killigrew, a rogue, newly
come back out of France but still in disgrace at our Court, and
young Newport and others, as very rogues as any in the town, who
were ready to take hold of every woman that came by them. And so
to supper in an arbor; but Lord, their mad bawdy talk did make my
heart ake. And here I first understood by their talk the meaning of
the company that lately were called "Ballers", Harris telling how it
was by a meeting of some young blades, where he was among
them, and my Lady Bennet and her ladies, and there dancing naked,

and all the roguish things in the world. But Lord, what loose cursed company was this that I was in tonight; though full of wit and worth a man's being in for once, to know the nature of it and their manner of talk and lives. Thence set Rolt and some of [them] at the New Exchange, and so I home; and my business being done at the office, I to bed.

–❧JUNE❧–

1. Up, and with Sir J. Mennes to Westminster; and in the hall there I met with Harris and Rolt and carried them to the Rhenish winehouse, where I have not been in a morning, nor any tavern I think, these seven years and more. Here I did get the words of a song of Harris that I wanted. Here was also Mr. Young and Whistler by chance met us and drank with us. Thence home and to prepare business against the afternoon; and did walk an hour in the garden with Sir W. Warren, who doth tell me of the great difficulty he is under in the business of his accounts with the Commissioners of Parliament, and I fear some inconveniences and troubles may be occasioned thereby to me. So to dinner, and then with Sir J. Mennes to Whitehall; and there attended the Lords of the Treasury and also a committee of Council with the Duke of York about the charge of this year's fleet; and thence I to Westminster, and to Mrs. Martins and did hazer what yo would con her, and did aussi tocar la thigh de su landlady. And thence all alone to Foxhall and walked, and saw young Newport and two more rogues of the town seize on two ladies, who walked with them an hour with their masks on, perhaps civil ladies; and there I left them, and so home and thence to Mr. Mills's, where I never was before, and here find (whom I endeed saw go in, and that did make me go thither) Mrs. Halworthy and Mrs. Andrews; and here supped and extraordinary merry till one in the morning, Mr. Andrews coming to us: and mightily pleased with this night's company and mirth, I home to bed. Mrs. Turner too was with us.

4. Up, and to the office, where all the morning. And at noon home to dinner, where Mr. Clerke the solicitor dined with me and my clerks. After dinner I carried and set him down at the Temple, he observing to me how St. Sepulchers church steeple is repaired

already a good deal, and the Fleet bridge is contracted for by the City to begin to be built this summer; which doth please me mightily. I to Whitehall and walked through the park for a little ayre; and so back to the Council chamber to the Committee of the Navy, about the business of fitting the present fleet suitable to the money given; which as the King orders it and by what appears, will be very little, and so as I perceive the Duke of York will have nothing to command, nor can intend to go abroad. But it is pretty to see how careful these great men are to do everything so as they may answer it to the Parliament.

*The entries from 5–17 June are written in note form on sheets of paper inserted into the volume, where ten pages are left blank for the finished version which Pepys never composed. A few changes have been made in this version of the notes: the dates of the entries are given in the form Pepys normally used in the finished diary; where words are repeated they are omitted although they have not been struck through, and the money sums have been abbreviated. A draft letter has also been omitted.*

5. *Friday.*   At Barnet, for milk, 6d. On the highway, to menders of the highway, 6d. Dinner at Stevenage, 5s. 6d.

6. *Saturday.*   Spent at Huntington with Bowles and Appleyard and Shepley, 2s.

7. *Sunday.*   My father, for money lent, and horse-hire, £1 11s.

8. *Monday.*   Father's servants (father having in the garden told me bad stories of my wife's ill words), 14s.; one that helped at the horses, 1s.; menders of the highway, 2s. Pleasant country to Bedfd., where, while they stay, I rode through the town; and a good country-town; and there, drinking, we on to Newport; and there light, and I and W. Hewer to the church, and there give the boy 1s. So to Buckingh., a good old town. Here I to see the church, which very good, and the leads, and a school in it. Did give the sexton's boy 1s. A fair bridge here, with many arches. Vexed at my people's making me lose so much time. Reckoning, 13s. 4d. Mighty pleased with the pleasure of the ground all the day. At night to Newpt. Pagnell; and there a good pleasant country-town, but few people in it. A very fair – and like a cathedral – church; and I saw the leads, and a vault that goes far under ground, and here lay with

Betty Turner's sparrow. The town, and so most of this country, well watered. Lay here well, and rose next day by 4 a'clock. Few people in the town. And so away. Reckoning for supper 9s. 6d.; poor, 6d. Mischance to the coach, but no time lost.

9. *Tuesdy.* When come to Oxfd., a very sweet place, paid our guide, 1l 2s. 6d.; barber, 2s. 6d.; book, Stonheng, 4s. To dinner, and then out with my wife and people and landlord; and to him that showed us the schools and library, 10s.; and to him that showed us All Souls College, and Chichly's pictures, 5s. So to see Christ Church with my wife, I seeing several others very fine alone, with W. Hewer, before dinner, and did give the boy that went with me 1s. Strawberries, 1s. 2d. Dinner and servants, 1l 0s. 6d. After came home from the schools, I out with the landlord to Brazen Nose College to the butteries, and in the cellar find the hand of the child of Hales. Butler, 2s. Thence with coach and people to Physic Garden, 1s. So to Friar Bacons study: I up and saw it, and give the man 1s. Bottle of sack for landlord, 2s. Oxford mighty fine place; and well seated, and cheap entertainment. At night come to Abington, where had been a fair of custard, and met many people and scholars going home; and there did get some pretty good music, and sang and danced till supper: 5s.

10. *W.* Up, and walked to the Hospitall: very large and fine; and pictures of founders, and the history of the Hospitall; and is said to be worth 700l per annum; and that Mr. Foly was here lately to see how their lands were settled. And here, in old English, the story of the occasion of it, and a Rebus at the bottom. So did give the poor, which they would not take but in their box, 2s. 6d. So to the inn, and paid the reckoning and servants, 13s. So forth towards Hungerford, led this good way by our landlord, one Heart, a old but very civil and well-spoken man, more than I ever heard of that quality. He gone, we forward; and I vexed at my peoples not minding the way. So came to Hungerford, where very good trouts, eels, and crayfish dinner. A bad mean town. At dinner there, 12s. Thence set out with a guide, who saw us to [Black Heath], and then left us, 3s. 6d. So all over the Plain by the sight of the steeple, the plain high and low, to Salsbury, by night; but before came to the town, I saw a great fortification, and there light, and to it and in it; and find it prodigious, so as to fright me to be in it all alone at that time of night, it being dark. I understand it since to be that that is

called Old Sarum. Came to the town, George Inne, where lay in silk bed; and very good diet. To supper; then to bed.

11. *Thursday.* And up, and W. H[ewer] and I up and down the town, and find it a very brave place with river go through every street; and a most capacious market-place. The city great, I think greater then Oxford. But the minster most admirable; as big, I think, and handsomer than Westmr., and a most large close about it, and houses for the officers thereof, and a fine palace for the Bp. So to my lodging back, and took out my wife and people to shew them the town and church; but they being at prayers, could not be shown the Quire. A very good Organ; and I looked in, and saw the Bp., my friend Dr. Ward. Thence to the Inne; and there not being able to hire coach-horses, and not willing to use our own, we got saddle-horses, very dear. Boy that went to look for them, 6d. So the three women behind W. H[ewer], Murfd., and our guide, and I single to Stonehege, over the plain and some prodigious great hills, even to fright us. Came thither, and find them as prodigious as any tales I ever heard of them, and worth going this journey to see. God knows what their use was. They are hard to tell, but yet may be told. Give the shepherd woman, for leading our horses, 4d. So back to Wilton, my Lord Pembr's house, which we could not see, he being just coming to town; but the situation I do not like, nor the house promise much, it being in a low but rich valley. So back home; and there being light, we to the church, and there find them at prayers again, so could not see the quire; but I sent the women home, and I did go in, and saw very many fine tombs, and among the rest some very ancient, of the Montagus. So home to dinner; and, that being done, paid the reckoning, which was so exorbitant, and perticularly in rate of my horses, and 7s. 6d. for bread and beer, that I was mad, and resolve to trouble the mistress about it, and get something for the poor. And came away in that humour: 2l 5s. 6d. Servants, 1s. 6d.; poor, 1s.; guide to the stones, 2s.; poor woman in the street, 1s.; ribbands, 9d.; washwoman, 1s.; seamstress for W. H[ewer], 3s.; lent W. Hewer, 2s. Thence about 6 a'clock, and with a guide went over the smooth plain endeed till night; and then by a happy mistake, and that looked like an adventure, we were carried out of our way to a town where we would lie, since we could not go so far as we would. And there with great difficulty came about 10 at night to a little inn, where we were fain to go into a room where a pedlar was in bed, and made him rise; and there wife and I lay, and

in a truckle-bed Betty Turner and Willet. But good beds, and the master of the house a sober, understanding man, and I had pl[?easant] discourse with him about this country matters, as Wool and Corne and other things. And he also merry, and made us mighty merry at supper, about manning the new ship, at Bristol, with none but men whose wifes do master them; and it seems it is become in reproach to some men of estate that are such hereabouts, that this is become common talk. By and by to bed, glad of this mistake, because, it seems, had we gone on as we pretended, we could not have passed with our coach, and must have lain on the plain all night. This day from Salsb. I wrote by the post my excuse for not coming home, which I hope will do, for I am resolved to see the Bath, and, it may be, Bristol.

12. *Friday*.    Up, finding our beds good, but we lousy; which made us merry. We set out, the reckoning and servants coming to 9*s.* 6*d.*; my guide thither, 2*s.*; coachman, advanced, 10*s.* So rode a very good way, led to my great content by our landlord to Phillip's Norton, with great pleasure, being now come into Somersetshire; where my wife and Deb mightily joyed thereat, I commending the country, as endeed it deserves. And the first town we came to was Brekington where, we stopping for something for the horses, we called two or three little boys to us, and pleased ourselfs with their manner of speech, and did make one of them kiss Deb, and another say the Lord's Prayer (hallowed be thy Kingdom come). At Ph. Norton I walked to the church, and there saw a very ancient tomb of some Kt. Templar, I think;[1] and here saw the tombstone whereon there were only two heads cut, which, the story goes, and credibly, were two sisters, called the Fair Maids of Foscott, that had two bodies upward and one below, and there lie buried. Here is also a very fine ring of six bells, and chimes mighty tuneable. Having dined very well, 10*s.*, we come before night to the Bath; where I presently stepped out with my landlord, and saw the baths, with people in them. They are not so large as I expected, but yet pleasant; and the town most of stone, and clean, though the streets generally narrow. I home, and being weary, went to bed without supper; the rest supping.

13. *Sat.*    Up at 4 a'clock, being by appointment called up to the

---

1. In fact an unidentified lawyer, c.1460.

Cross Bath, where we were carried one after one another, myself, and wife, and Betty Turner, Willett, and W. H[ewer]. And by and by, though we designed to have done before company came, much company came; very fine ladies; and the manner pretty enough, only methinks it cannot be clean to go so many bodies together in to the same water. Good conversation among them that are acquainted here, and stay together. Strange to see how hot the water is; and in some places, though this is the most temperate bath, the springs so hot as the feet not able to endure. But strange to see when women and men herein, that live all the season in these waters, that cannot but be parboiled, and look like the creatures of the Bath. Carried back, wrapped in a sheet, and in a chair, home; and there one after another thus carried (I staying above two hours in the water), home to bed, sweating for an hour; and by and by, comes music to play to me, extraordinary good as ever I heard at London almost, or anywhere: 5s. Up, to go to Bristol, about 11 a'clock, and paying my landlord that was our guide from Chiltren, 10s., and the Sergt. of the bath, 10s., and the man that carried us in chairs, 3s. 6d. Set out towards Bristow, and come thither (in a coach hired to spare our own horses); the way bad, but country good, about two a'clock, where set down at the Horse Shoe, and there, being trimmed by a very handsome fellow, 2s., walked with my wife and people through the city, which is in every respect another London, that one can hardly know it, to stand in the country, no more then that. No carts, it standing generally on vaults, only dog-carts. So to the Three Cranes Tavern I was directed; but, when I come in, the master told me that he had newly given over selling of wine, it seems, grown rich; and so went to the Sun; and there Deb going with W. H[ewer] and Betty Turner to see her uncle, and leaving my wife with the mistress of the house, I to see the key, which is a most large and noble place; and to see the new ship building by Bailey, neither he nor Furzer being in town. It will be a fine ship. Spoke with the foreman, and did give the boys that kept the cabin 2s. Walked back to the Sun, where I find Deb come back, and with her, her uncle, a sober merchant, very good company, and so like one of our sober, wealthy, London merchants, as pleased me mightily. Here we dined, and much good talk with him, 7s. 6d: a messenger to Sir Jo. Knight, who was not at home, 6d. Then walked with him and my wife and company round the key, and to the ship; and he shewed me the Custom House, and made me understand many things of the place, and led us through Marsh street, where our girl was born. But, Lord! the joy that was among the old poor people of the place, to see Mrs. Willet's daughter, it seems her mother being a brave woman and mightily beloved. And so brought us a back way by surprize to his house, where a substantial good house, and well furnished; and did give us good entertainment of strawberries, a whole venison pasty, cold, and plenty of brave wine, and above all Bristoll milk; where comes in another poor woman, who, hearing that Deb was here, did come running hither, and with her eyes so full of tears, and heart so full of joy, that she could not speak when she come in, that it made me weep too: I protest that I was not able to speak to her (which I would have done) to have diverted her tears. His wife a good woman, and so sober and substantial as I was never more pleased anywhere. Servant maid, 2*s.* So thence took leave, and he with us through the city, where in walking I find the city pay him great respect, and he the like to the meanest, which pleased me mightily. He shewed us the place where the merchants meet here, and fine cross yet standing, like Cheapside. And so to the Horse Shoe, where paying the reckoning, 2*s.* 6*d.* We back, and by moonshine to the Bath again, about ten a'clock: bad way; and giving the coachman 1*s.*, went all of us to bed.

14. S.  Up, and walked up and down the town, and saw a pretty good market place, and many good streets, and very fair stone houses. And so to the great church, and there saw Bp. Montagu's tomb; and, when placed, did there see many brave people come, and, among other, two men brought in, in litters, and set down in the chancel to hear: but I did not know one face. Here a good Organ; but a vain, pragmatic fellow preached a ridiculous affected sermon, that made me angry, and some gent. that sat next me and sang well. So home, walking round the walls of the city, which are good, and the battlemts. all whole. The sexton of the church, 1*s.* So home to dinner, and after dinner comes Mr. Butts again to see me, and he and I to church, where the same idle fellow preached; and I slept most of the sermon. Thence home, and took my wife out and the girls, and come to this church again, to see it, and look over the monuments, where, among others, Dr. Venner and Pelling, and a lady of Sr. W. Waller's; he lying with his face broken. So to the fields a little and walked, and then home and had my head looked [at], and so to supper, and then comes my landlord to me, a sober understanding man, and did give me a good account of the antiquity of this town and Wells; and of two heads, on two pillars,

in Wells church. But he a catholic. So he gone, I to bed.

15. *Monday.*    Up, and with Mr. Butts to look into the Baths, and find the King and Queen's full of a mixed sort, of good and bad, and the Cross only almost for the gentry. So home and did the like with my wife, and did pay my guides, two women, 5*s*.; one man, 2*s*. 6*d*.; poor 6*d*.; woman to lay my foot-cloth, 1*s*. So to our Inne, and there eat and paid reckoning, 1*l* 8*s*. 6*d*.; servants, 3*s*.; poor, 1*s*.; lent the coachman, 10*s*. Before I took coach, I went to make a boy dive in the King's bath, 1*s*. I paid also for my coach and a horse to Bristol, 1*l* 1*s*. 6*d*. Took coach, and away, without any of the company of the other stage-coaches that go out of this town to-day; and rode all day with some trouble, for fear of being out of our way, over the downes, where the life of the shepherds is, in fair weather only, pretty. In the afternoon came to Abebury, where, seeing great stones like those of Stonage standing up, I stepped, and took a countryman of that town, and he carried me and shewed me a place trenched in, like Old Sarum almost, with great stones pitched in it, some bigger than those at Stonage in figure, to my great admiration: and he told me that most people of learning, coming by, do come and view them, and that the King did so: and that the Mount cast hard by is called Selbury, from one King Seale buried there, as tradition says. I did give this man 1*s*. So took coach again, (seeing one place with great high stones pitched round, which, I believe, was once some particular building, in some measure like that of Stonag). But, about a mile on, it was prodigious to see how full the downes are of great stones; and all along the valleys, stones of considerable bigness, most of them growing certainly out of the ground so thick as to cover the ground, which makes me think the less of the wonder of Stonage, for hence they might undoubtedly supply themselves with stones, as well as those at Abebery. In my way did give to the poor and menders of the highway 3*s*. Before night come to Marlborough, and lay at the Hart; a good house, and a pretty fair town for a street or two; and what is most singular is their houses on one side having their penthouses supported with pillars, which makes it a good walk. My wife pleased with all, this evening reading of *Mustapha* to me till supper, and then to supper, and had music whose innocence pleased me, and I did give them 3*s*. So to bed and lay well all night, and long, so as all the five coaches that come this day from Bath, as well as we, were gone out of the town before us.

16. *Tuesday.* So paying the reckoning, 14s. 4d., and servants, 2s., poor 1s., set out; and overtook one coach and kept a while company with it till one of our horses losing a shoe, we stopped and drank and spent 1s. So on, and passing through a good part of this county of Wiltshire, saw good house of Alex. Popham's, and another of my Lord Craven's, I think in Barkeshire. We came to Newbery, and there dined, which cost me, and musick, which a song of the old Courtier of Q. Eliz, and how he was changed upon the coming in of the King, did please me mightily, and I did cause W. H[ewer] to write it out, 3s. 6d. Then comes the reckoning, forced to change gold, 8s. 7d.; servants and poor, 1s. 6d. So out, and lost our way, which made me vexed, but come into it again; and in the evening betimes came to Reding, and there heard my wife read more of Mustapha. Then to supper, and then I to walk about the town, which is a very great one, I think bigger than Salsbury: a river runs through it in seven branches, and unite in one, in one part of the town, and runs into the Thames a half-mile off. One odd sign of The Broad Face. W. H[ewer] troubled with the headake we had none of his company last night, nor all this day nor night to talk. Then to my inn, and so to bed.

17. *Wedn.* Rose, and paying the reckoning, 12s. 6d.; servants and poor, 2s. 6d.; music, the worst we have had, coming to our chamber-door, but calling us by wrong names, we gave him nothing. So set out with one coach in company, and through Mydenhead, which I never saw before, to Colebrooke by noon; the way mighty good; and there dined, and fitted ourselves a little to go through London anon. Somewhat out of humour all day, reflecting on my wife's neglect of things and impertinent humour got by this liberty of being from me, which she is never to be trusted with; for she is a fool. Thence pleasant way to London, before night, and find all very well, to great content; and there to talk with my wife, and saw Sr. W. P[enn], who is well again. Hear of the ill news by the great fire at Berbedos. By and by home, and there with my people to supper, all in pretty good humour, though I find my wife hath something in her gizzard, that only waits an opportunity of being provoked to bring up; but I will not, for my content sake, give it. So I to bed, glad to find all so well here, and slept well.

18–19. Up betimes and to the office, there to set my papers in order and books, my office having been new-whited and windows

made clean. And so to sit, where all the morning; and did receive a
hint or two from my Lord Anglesy, as if he thought much of my
taking the ayre as I have done – but I care not a turd. But whatever
the matter is, I think he hath some ill-will to me, or at least an
opinion that I am more the servant of the Board then I am. At noon
home to dinner, where my wife still in a melancholy fusty humour,
and crying; and doth not tell me plainly what it is, but I by little
words find that she hath heard of my going to plays and carrying
people abroad every day in her absence; and that I cannot help, but
the storm will break out, I know, in a little time. After dinner,
carried her by coach to St. James's, where she sat in the coach till I to
my Lady Peterborough; who tells me, among other things, her
Lord's good words to the Duke of York lately about my Lord
Sandwich, and that the Duke of York is kind to my Lord Sandwich
– which I am glad to hear. My business here was about her Lord's
pension from Tanger. Here met with Povy, who tells me how hard
Creed is upon him, though he did give him, about six months since
I think he said, 50 pieces in gold. And one thing there is in his
accounts that I fear may touch me; but I shall help it, I hope. So, my
wife not speaking a word going nor coming, nor willing to go to a
play, though a new one, I to the office and did much business. At
night home, where supped Mr. Turner and his wife, and Betty and
Mercer and Pelling, as merry as the ill melancholy humour that my
wife was in would let us; which vexed me, but I took no notice of it,
thinking that will be the best way, and let it wear away itself.

   After supper, parted and to bed; and my wife troubled all night,
and about one a-clock goes out of the bed to the girl's bed; which
did trouble me, she crying and sobbing, without telling the cause.
By and by comes back to me, and still crying; I then rose and would
have sat up all night, but she would have me come to bed again.
And being pretty well pacified, we to sleep; when between 2 and 3
in the morning, we were waked with my maids crying out, "Fire!
Fire! in Marke lane!" so I rose and looked out, and it was dreadful;
and strange apprehensions in me, and us all, of being presently
burnt: so we all rose, and my care presently was to secure my gold
and plate and papers, and could quickly have done it, but I went
forth to see where it was, and the whole town was presently in the
streets; and I found it in a new-built house that stood alone in
Minchin lane, over against the Clothworkers hall – which burned
furiously, the house not yet quite finished. And the benefit of brick
was well seen, for it burnt all inward and fell down within itself – so

no fear of doing more hurt; so homeward and stopped at Mr. Mills, where he and she at the door, and Mrs. Turner and Betty and Mrs. Hollworthy; and there I stayed and talked, and up to the church leads and saw the fire, which spent and spent itself, till all fear over; I home, and there we to bed again and slept pretty well. And about 9 rose; and then my wife fell into her blubbering again and at length had a request to make to me, which was that she might go into France and live there out of trouble: and then all came out, that I loved pleasure and denied her any, and a deal of do; and I find that there have been great fallings-out between my father and her, whom for ever hereafter I must keep asunder, for they cannot possibly agree. And I said nothing; but with very mild words and few suffered her humour to spend, till we begin to be very quiet and I think all will be over, and friends; and so I to the office, where all the morning doing business. Yesterday I heard how my Lord Ashly is like to die, having some imposthume in his breast, that he hath been fain to be cut into the body. At noon home to dinner; and thence by coach to Whitehall, where we attended the Duke of York in his closet upon our usual business. And thence out and did see many of the Knights of the Guarter with the King and Duke of York, going into the Privy-chamber to elect the Elector of Saxony into the Order; who I did hear the Duke of York say was a good drinker; I know not upon what score this compliment is done him. Thence with W. Penn, who is in great pain of the gowte, by coach round by Hoborn home, he being at every kennel full of pain. There home; and by and by comes in my wife and Deb, who have been at the King's House today, thinking to spy me there; and saw the new play, *Evening Love* (of Dryden's); which though the world commends, she likes not. So to supper and talk, and all in good humour; and then to bed – where I slept not well, from my apprehensions of some trouble about some business of Mr. Povy's he told me of the other day.

21. *Lords day.* Up, and to church; and home and dined with my wife and Deb alone, but merry and in good humour; which is, when all is done, the greatest felicity of all. And after dinner, she to read in the *Illustr. Bassa.* And so to church, I alone, and thence to see Sir W. Penn, who is ill again; and then home – and there get my wife to read to me till supper, and then to bed.

23. Up, and all the morning at the office. At noon home to dinner;

and so to the office again all the afternoon, and then to Westminster to Dr. Turberville about my eyes; whom I met with, and he did discourse I thought learnedly about them, and takes time, before he did prescribe me anything, to think of it. So I away with my wife and Deb, whom I left at Unthankes; and so to Hercules Pillars, and there we three supped on cold powdered beef; and thence home and in the garden walked a good while with Deane, talking well of the Navy miscarriages and faults. So home to bed.

27.   At the office all the morning; at noon dined at home; and then my wife and Deb and I to the King's playhouse and saw *The Indian Queene*; but do not dote up[on] Nan Marshall's acting therein as the world talks of her excellence therein. Thence with my wife to buy some linen, 13*l* worth, for sheets, &c., at the new shop over against the New Exchange, come out of London since the fire; who says his and other tradesmen's retail trade is so great here, and better then it was in London, that they believe they shall not return, nor the City be ever so great for retail as heretofore. So home and to my business and supper, and to bed.

29.   Called up by my Lady Peterborough's servant about some business of hers, and so to the office. Thence by and by with Sir J. Mennes toward St. James's; and I stop at Dr. Turbervilles and there did receive a direction for some physic, and also a glass of something to drop into my eyes; who gives me hopes that I may do well. Thence to St. James's and thence to Whitehall, where find the Duke of York in the Council chamber, where the Officers of the Navy were called in about Navy business, about calling in of more ships; the King of France having, as the Duke of York says, ordered his fleet to come in, notwithstanding what he had lately ordered for their staying abroad. Thence to the Chapel, it being St. Peter's day, and did hear an Anthem of Silas Taylors making – a dull old-fashion thing of six and seven parts that nobody could understand; and the Duke of York, when he came out, told me that he was a better store-keeper then Anthem-maker – and that was bad enough too. (This morning, Mr. May showed me the King's new buildings at Whitehall, very fine; and among other things, his ceilings and his houses of office.) So home to dinner, and then with my wife to the King's playhouse: *The Mulbery Garden*, which she had not seen. And so by coach to Islington and round by Hackney home with much pleasure. And to supper and bed.

30. Up and at the office all the morning. Then home to dinner, where a stinking leg of mutton – the weather being very wet and hot to keep meat in. Then to the office again all the afternoon; we met about the Victualler's new contract. And so up, and to walk all the evening with my wife and Mrs. Turner in the garden till supper, about 11 at night; and so after supper parted and to bed – my eyes bad but not worse; only, weary with working. But however, I very melancholy under the fear of my eyes being spoilt and not to be recovered; for I am come that I am not able to read out a small letter, and yet my sight good, for the little while I can read, as ever they were I think.

## –✷JULY✷–

3. Betimes to the office, my head full of business. Then by coach to Commissioners of Accounts at Brooke house, the first time I ever there. And there Sir W. Turner in the chair; and present, Lord Halifax, Thomson, Gregory, Dunster, and Osborne. I long with them, and see them hot set on this matter; but I did give them proper and safe answers. Halifax, I perceive, was industrious on my side, on behalf of his uncle Coventry, it being the business of Sir W. Warren – vexed only at their denial of a copy of what I set my hand to and swore. Here till almost 2 a-clock; and then home to dinner and set down presently what I had done and said this day; and so abroad by water, I to Eagle Court in the Strand and there to a alehouse; met Mr. Pierce the surgeon and Dr. Clerke, Waldron, Turberville my physician for the eyes, and Lowre, to dissect several Eyes of sheep and oxen, with great pleasure – and to my great information; but strange that this Turberville should be so great a man, and yet to this day had seen no eyes dissected, or but once, but desired this Dr. Lowre to give him the opportunity to see him dissect some. Thence to Unthankes to my wife and carried her home, and there walked in the garden; and so to supper and to bed.

4. Up, and to see Sir W. Coventry and give him account of my doings yesterday; which he well liked of, and was told thereof by my Lord Halifax before. But I do perceive he is much concerned for this business – gives me advice to write a smart letter to the Duke of York about the want of money in the Navy, and desire him to

communicate it to the Commissioners of the Treasury; for he tells me he hath hot work sometimes to contend with the rest for the Navy, they being all concerned for some other part of the King's expense, which they would prefer to this of the Navy. He showed me his closet, with his round table for him to sit in the middle, very convenient. And I borrowed several books of him to collect things out of of the Navy which I have not. And so home and there busy sitting all the morning; and at noon dined, and then all the afternoon busy till night; and then to Mile end with my wife and girl, and there eat and drank a Jole of salmon at the Rose and Crown, our old house; and so home to bed.

5. *Lords day*. About 4 in the morning took four pills of Dr. Turberville's prescribing for my eyes, and they wrought pretty well most of the morning, and I did get my wife to spend the morning reading of Wilkins's *Real Character*. At noon comes W. How and Pelling, and young Michell and his wife, and dined with us. And most of the afternoon talking; and then at night, my wife to read again and to supper and to bed.

8. Betimes by water to Sir W. Coventry and there discoursed of several things; and I find him much concerned in the present enquiries now on foot of the Commissioners of Accounts, though he reckons himself and the rest very safe; but vexed to see us liable to these troubles in things wherein we have laboured to do best. Thence, he being to go out of town tomorrow to drink Banbury waters – I to the Duke of York to attend him about business of the Office; and find him mighty free to me, and how he is concerned to mend things in the Navy himself, and not leave it to other people. So home to dinner; and then with my wife to Coopers and there saw her sit; and he doth do extraordinary things endeed. So to Whitehall; and there by and by the Duke of York comes to the Robe Chamber and spent with us three hours till night, in hearing the business of the Maisters-Attendants of Chatham and the Store-keeper of Woolwich; and resolves to displace them all, so hot he is of giving proofs of his justice at this time – that it is their great fate now, to come to be questioned at such a time as this. Thence I to Unthankes and took my wife and Deb home – and to supper and bed.

13. Up, and to my office; and thence by water to Whitehall to attend the Council, but did not; and so home to dinner; and so out

with my wife and Deb and W. Hewer towards Coopers; but I light and walked to Ducke lane, and there to the bookseller's at the Bible, whose moher yo have a mind to, but ella no era dentro; but I did there look upon and buy some books, and made way for coming again to the man; which pleases me. Thence to Reeves's and there saw some, and bespoke a little, perspective – and was mightily pleased with seeing objects in a dark room. And so to Coopers and spent the afternoon with them; and it will be an excellent picture. Thence my people all by water to Deptford to see Balty, while I to buy my Espinette which I did now agree for; and did at Hawards meet with Mr. Thacker and hear him play on the Harpsicon, so as I never heard man before I think. So home, it being almost night, and there find in the garden Pelling, who hath brought Tempest, Wallington, and Pelham to sing; and there had most excellent music, late in the dark, with great pleasure. Made them drink and eat; and so with much pleasure to bed, but above all with little Wallington. This morning I was let blood, and did bleed about 14 ounces, towards curing my eyes.

15. Up, and all the morning busy at the office to my great content, tending to the settling of papers there, that I may have the more rest in winter for my eyes by how much I do the more in the settling of all things in the summer by daylight. At noon home to dinner, where is brought home the Espinette I bought the other day of Haward; costs me 5*l.* So to St. James's, where did our ordinary business with the Duke of York. And so to Unthankes to my wife, and with her and Deb to visit Mrs. Pierce, whom I do not now so much affect since she paints. But stayed here a while, and understood from her how my Lady Duchess of Monmouth is still lame, and likely alway to be so – which is a sad chance for a young [lady] to get, only by trying of tricks in dancing. So home, and there Capt. Deane came and spent the evening with me, to draw some finishing lines on his fine draft of the *Resolution*, the best ship, by all report, in the world. And so to bed. Wonderful hot all day and night, and this the first night that I remember in my life that ever I could lie with only a sheet and one rug; so much I am now stronger then ever I remember myself to be, at least since before I had the stone.

16. Up, and to the office, where Yeabsly and Lanyon came to town and to speak with me about a matter wherein they are accused

of cheating the King before the Lords-Commissioners of Tanger; and I doubt it true, but I have no hand [in] it; but will serve them what I can. All the morning at the office; and at noon dined at home, and then to the office again, where we met to finish the draft of the Victualler's contract; and so I by water with my Lord Brouncker to Arundell house to the Royal Society, and there saw an experiment of a dog's being tied through the back about the spinal Artery, and thereby made void of all motion; and the artery being loosened again, the dog recovers. Thence to Coopers and saw his advance on my wife's picture, which will be endeed very fine. So with her to the Change to buy some things, and here I first bought of the seamstress next my bookseller's, where the pretty young girl is that will be a great beauty. So home, and to supper with my wife in the garden, it being these two days excessive hot. And so to bed.

18. At the office all the morning. At noon dined at home, and Creed with me, who I do really begin to hate, and do use him with some reservedness. Here was also my old acquaintance Will Swan to see me, who continues a factious fanatic still; and I do use him civilly, in expectation that those fellows may grow great again. Thence to the office, and then with my wife to the Change and Unthankes, after having been at Coopers and sat there for her picture; which will be a noble picture, but yet I think not so like as Hales's is. So home and to my office, and then to walk in the garden, and home to supper and to bed. Creed told me this day how when the King was at my Lord Cornwallis, when he went last to Newmarket, that being there on a Sunday, the Duke of Buckingham did in the afternoon, to please the King, make a bawdy sermon to him out of the Canticles. And that my Lord Cornwallis did endeavour to get the King a whore, and that must be a pretty girl, the daughter of the parson of the place; but that she did get away, and leaped off of some place and killed herself– which if true, is very sad.[1]

24. Up, and by water to St. James (having by the way shown Symson Sir W. Coventry's chimny-pieces, in order to the making me one); and there, after the Duke of York was ready, he called me to his closet, and there I did long and largely show him the weakness of our office, and did give him advice to call us to account for our duties; which he did take mighty well, and desired me to

---

1. The story has not been traced elsewhere.

draw up what I would have him write to the office. I did lay open the whole failings of the office, and how it was his duty to find them and to find fault with them, as Admiral, especially at this time – which he agreed to – and seemed much to rely on what I said. Thence to Whitehall and there waited to attend the Council, but was not called in; and so home, and after dinner back with Sir J. Mennes by coach, and there attended, all of us, the Duke of York, and had the hearing of Mr. Pett's business, the maister-shipwright at Chatham; and I believe he will be put out. But here Commissioner Middleton did, among others, show his good-nature and easiness to the Maisters-Attendants by mitigating their faults, so as I believe they will come in again. So home and to supper and to bed, the Duke of York staying with us till almost night.

29.   Busy all the morning at the office. So home to dinner, where Mercer; and there comes Mr. Swan, my old acquaintance, and dines with me, and tells me for a certainty that Creed is to marry Betty Pickering and that the thing is concluded; which I wonder at – and am vexed for. So he gone, I with my wife and two girls to the King's House and saw *The Mad Couple*, a mean play altogether; and thence to Hyde park, where but few coaches; and so to the New Exchange and thence by water home with much pleasure; and then to sing in the garden, and so home to bed, my eyes for these four days being my trouble, and my heart thereby mighty sad.

31.   Up, and at my office all the morning. About noon, with Mr. Ashburnham to the new Excise Office; and there discoursed about our business and I made him admire my drawing a thing presently in shorthand; but God knows, I have paid dear for it in my eyes. Home and to dinner; and then my wife and Deb and I with Sir J. Mennes to Whitehall, she going thence to New Exchange; and the Duke of York not being in the way, J. Mennes and I to her and took them two to the King's House to see the first day of Lacy's *Monsieur Ragou*, now new-acted. The King and Court all there, and mighty merry: a Farce. Thence, Sir J. Mennes giving us like a gentleman his coach, hearing we had some business, we to the park, and so home; little pleasure there, there being little company. But mightily taken with a little chariot that we saw in the street, and which we are resolved to have ours like it. So home to walk in the garden a little, and then to bed. The month ends mighty sadly with me, my eyes being now past all use almost; and I am mighty hot upon trying the

late printed experiment of paper Tubes.

## ⊰AUGUST⊱

11.  Up, and by water to Sir W. Coventry to visit him, whom I find yet troubled at the Commissioners of Accounts about this business of Sir W. Warren; which is a ridiculous thing – and can come to nothing but contempt. And thence to Westminster hall, where the Parliament met enough to adjourne, which they did, to the 10th of November next; and so I by water home to the office, and so to dinner; and thence at the office all the afternoon till night, being mightily pleased with a little trial I have made of the use of a Tube spectacall of paper, tried with my right eye. This day, I hear that to the great joy of the nonconformists, the time is out of the Act against them, so that they may meet; and they have declared that they will have a morning lecture up again, which is pretty strange; and they are connived at by the King everywhere I hear, in city and country. So to visit W. Penn, who is yet ill; and then home, where W. Batelier and Mrs. Turner came and sat and supped with us; and so they gone, we to bed. This afternoon, my wife and Mercer and Deb went with Pelling to see the Gipsys at Lambeth and have their fortunes told; but what they did, I did not enquire.

13.  Up, and Greeting comes and there he and I tried some things of Mr. Lockes for two flagelettes, to my great content; and this day my wife begins again to learn of him, for I have a great mind for her to be able to play a part with me. Thence I to the office, where all the morning; and then to dinner, where W. How dined with me, who tells me for certain that Creed is like to speed in his match with Mrs. Betty Pickering. Here dined with me also Mr. Hollier, who is mighty vain in his pretence to talk Latin. So to the office again all the afternoon till night, very busy; and so with much content home at night, and made my wife sing and play on the flagelette to me till I slept with great pleasure in bed.

16.  *Lords day.* All the morning at my office with W. Hewer, there drawing up my report to the Duke of York, as I have promised, about the faults of this office, hoping therein to have opportunity of

doing myself [some good]. At noon to dinner; and again with him, to work all the afternoon till night, till I was weary and had despatched a good deal of business. And so to bed, after hearing my wife read a little.

19.   Up betimes; and all day and afternoon, without going out, busy upon my great letter to the Duke of York, which goes on to my content. W. Hewer and Gibson I imploy with me in it. This week my people wash over the water, and so I little company at home. In the evening, being busy above, a great cry I hear, and go down; and what should it be but Jane, in a fit of direct raveing which lasted half-an-hour; beyond four or five of our strength to keep her down. And when all came to all, a fit of jealousy about Tom, with whom she is in love. So at night, I and my wife and W. Hewer called them to us, and there I did examine all the thing, and them in league. She in love, and he hath got her to promise him to marry, and he is now cold in it – so that I must rid my hands of them. Which troubles me, and the more because my head is now busy upon other greater things. I am vexed also to be told by W. Hewer that he is summoned to Commissioners of Accounts about receiving a present of 30*l* from Mr. Mason the timber merchant – though there be no harm in it that will appear on his part – he having done them several lawful kindnesses and never demanded anything, as they themselfs have this day declared to the Commissioners, they being forced up by the discovery of somebody that they in confidence had once told it to. So to supper, vexed and my head full of care; and so to bed.

22.   Up betimes, at it again with great content, and so to office I, where all the morning; and did fall out with W. Penn about his slight performance of his office; and so home to dinner, fully satisfied that this office must sink or the whole service be undone. To the office all the afternoon again; and then home to supper and to bed, my mind being pretty well at ease, my great letter being now finished to my full content; and I thank God I have opportunity of doing it, though I know it will set the office and me by the ears for ever. This morning Capt. Cocke comes and tells me that he is now assured that it is true what he told me the other day, that our whole office will be turned out, only me; which, whether he says true or no, I know not nor am much concerned, though I should be better contented to have it thus then otherwise. This afternoon, after I was

weary in my business of the office, I went forth to the Change, thinking to have spoken with Capt. Cocke, but he was not within. So I home, and took London bridge in my way, walking down Fish street and Gracious street to see how very fine a descent they have now made down the hill, that it is become very easy and pleasant. And going through Leadenhall, it being market-day, I did see a woman ketched that had stolen a shoulder of mutton off of a butcher's stall, and carrying it wrapped up in a cloth in a basket. The jade was surprized, and did not deny it; and the woman so silly that took it as to let her go, only taking the meat.

23. *Lords day*. Up betimes, my head busy on my great letter, and I did first hang up my new map of Paris in my green room – and changed others in other places. Then to Capt. Cocke's, thinking to have talked more of what he told me yesterday, but he was not within; so back to church and heard a good sermon of Mr. Gifford's at our church, upon "Seek ye first the Kingdom of Heaven and its righteousness, and all these things shall be added to you." A very excellent and persuasive, good and moral sermon; showed like a wise man that righteousness is a surer moral way of being rich then sin and villainy. Then home to dinner, where Mr. Pelling, who brought us a hare, which we had at dinner, and W. How. After dinner to the office, Mr. Gibson and I, to examine my letter to the Duke of York; which to my great joy, I did very well by my paper tube, without pain to my eyes. And I do mightily like what I have therein done; [and] did, according to the Duke of York's order, make haste to St. James'; and about 4 a-clock got thither, and there the Duke of York was ready to expect me, and did hear it all over with extraordinary content and did give me many and hearty thanks, and in words the most expressive tell me his sense of my good endeavours, and that he would have a care of me on all occasions, and did with much inwardness tell me what was doing, suitable almost to what Capt. Cocke tells me, of design to make alterations in the Navy; and is most open to me in them, and with utmost confidence desires my further advice on all occasions. And he resolves to have my letter transcribed and sent forthwith to the office. So, with as much satisfaction as I could possibly or did hope for, and obligation on the Duke of York's side professed to me, I away into the park, and there met Mr. Pierce and his wife and sister and brother and little boy, and with them to Mullbery garden and spent 18s. on them; and there left them, she being again with child,

and by it, the least pretty that ever I saw her; and so I away and got a coach and home; and there with [my] wife and W. Hewers talking all the evening, my mind running on the business of the office, to see what more I can do to the rendering myself acceptable and useful to all and to the King: we to supper and to bed.

25.    Up, and by water to St. James's and there with Mr. Wren did discourse about my great letter; which the Duke of York hath given him and he hath set it to be transcribed by Billup his man, whom, as he tells me, he can most confide in for secrecy. And is much pleased with it, and earnest to have it with us; and he and I are like to be much together in the considering how to reform the Office, and that by the Duke of York's command. Thence I, mightily pleased with this success, away to the office, where all the morning, my head full of this business; and it is pretty how Lord Brouncker this day did tell me how he hears that a design is on foot to remove us out of the office, and proposes that we two do agree to draw up a form of a new constitution of the office, there to provide remedies for the evils we are now under, that so we may be beforehand with the world – which I agreed to, saying nothing of my design. And the truth is, he is the best man of them all, and I would be glad, next myself, to save him; for as he deserves best, so I doubt he needs his place most. So home to dinner at noon, and all the afternoon busy at the office till night; and then, with my mind full of businesses now in my head, I to supper and to bed.

26–27.    Up, and to the office, where all the morning almost, busy about business against the afternoon; and we met a little, to sign two or three things at the Board of moment. And thence at noon home to dinner, and so away to Whitehall by water, in my way to the Old Swan finding a great many people gathered together in Cannon street about a man that was working in the ruins, and the ground did sink under him, and he sunk in and was forced to be dug out again, but without hurt. Thence to Whitehall; and it is strange to see with what speed the people imployed do pull down Paul's steeple – and with what ease. It is said that it and the Quire are to be taken down this year, and another church begun in the room thereof the next. At Whitehall we met at the Treasury chamber, and there before the Lords did debate our draft of the victualling contract with the several bidders for it – which were Sir D. Gawden – Mr. Child and his fellows, and Mr. Dorrington and his – a poor variety in a business of this value. There till after candle-lighting, and so home by coach with Sir D. Gawden, who by the way tells me how the City doth go on in several things toward the building of the public places; which I am glad to hear, and gives hope that in a few years it will be a glorious place. But we met with several stops and new troubles in the way in the streets, so as makes it bad to travel in the dark now through the City. So I to Mr. Bateliers by appointment, where I find my wife and Deb and Mercer – Mrs. Pierce and her husband, son and daughter; and Knipp and Harris; and W. Batelier and his sister Mary and cousin Gumbleton, a good-humoured, fat young gentleman, son to the Jeweller, that dances well. And here danced all night long, with a noble supper; and about 2 in the morning, the table spread again for a noble breakfast, beyond all moderation, that put me out of countenance – so much and so good. Mrs. Pierce and her people went home betimes, she being big with child; but Knipp and the rest stayed till almost 3 in the morning, and then broke up and Knipp home with us; and I to bed and rose about 6 – mightily pleased with this night's mirth; and away by water to St. James's and there with Mr. Wren did correct his copy of my letter; which the Duke of York hath signed in my very words, without alteration of a syllable.

And so, pleased therewith, I to my Lord Brouncker, who I find within, but hath business and so comes not to the office today; and so I by water to the office, where we sat all the morning; and just as the Board rises, comes the Duke of York's letter; which I knowing, and the Board not being full and desiring rather to have the Duke of York deliver himself to us, I suppressed it for this day, my heart beginning to falsify in this business – as being doubtful of the trouble it may give me by provoking them; but however, I am resolved to go through it, and it is too late to help it now. At noon to dinner to Capt. Cocke's, where I met with Mr. Wren, my going being to tell him what I have done; which he likes – and to confer with Cocke about our office; who tells me that he is confident the design of removing our officers doth hold, but that he is sure that I am safe enough – which pleases me; though I do not much show it to him, but as a thing indifferent. So away home, and there met at Sir Rd. Ford's with the Duke of York's Commissioners about our prizes, with whom we shall have some trouble before we make an end with them. And thence, staying a little with them, I with my wife and W. Batelier and Deb; carried them to Bartholomew fayre, where we saw the dancing of the ropes and nothing else, it being late; and so back home to supper and to bed – after having done at my office.

## –✣SEPTEMBER✣–

3.   Up, and to the office, where busy till it was time to go to the Commissioners of Accounts – which I did about noon, and there was received with all possible respect, their business being only to explain the meaning of one of their late demands to us, which we had not answered in our answer to them; and this being done, away with great content, my mind being troubled before; and so to the Exchequer and several places, calling on several businesses, and perticularly my bookseller's, among others, for Hobbs's *Leviathan,* which is now mightily called for; and what was heretofore sold for 8s. I now give 24s. at the second hand, and is sold for 30s., it being a book the Bishops will not let be printed again. And so home to dinner, and then to the office all the afternoon; and towards the evening, by water to the Commissioners of the Treasury; and presently back again and there met a little with W. Penn, and so W. Penn and Lord Brouncker and I at the lodging of the latter to read over our new drafts of the victualler's contract; and so broke up, and home to supper and to bed.

4.   Up, and met at the office all the morning; and at noon, my wife and Deb and Mercer and W. Hewer to the Fair, and there at the old house did eat a pig, and was pretty merry; but saw no sights, my wife having a mind to see the play, *Bartholomew fayre* with puppets; which we did, and it is an excellent play; the more I see it, the more I love the wit of it; only, the business of abusing the puritans begins to grow stale, and of no use, they being the people that at last will be found the wisest. And here Knipp came to us and sat with us, and thence took coach in two coaches; and losing one another, my wife and Knipp and I to Hercules Pillars and there supped, and I did take from her both the words and notes of her song of the Larke, which pleases me mightily. And so set her at home, and away we home, where our company came home before us. This night, Knipp tells us that there is a Spanish woman, lately come over, that pretends to sing as well as Mrs. Knight; both of which I must endeavour to hear. So after supper, to bed.

6.   *Lords day*. Up betimes and got myself ready to go by water; and about 9 a-clock took boat with Hen. Russell to Gravesend, coming thither about one, where at the Ship I dined; and thither came to me Mr. Hosier, whom I went to speak with about several businesses of work that he is doing, and I would have him do, of writing work for me. And I did go with him to his lodging and there did see his wife, a pretty tolerable woman, and do find him upon an extraordinary good work of designing a method of keeping our storekeepers' accounts in the Navy. Here I should have met with Mr. Willson, but he is sick and could not come from Chatham to me. So having done with Hosier, I took boat again the beginning of the flood, and came home by 9 at night – with much pleasure, it being a fine day. Going down I spent reading of the *Five Sermons of Five Several Styles*; worth comparing one with another, but I do think when all is done, that contrary to the design of the book, the Presbyterian style and the Independent are the best of the five for sermons to be preached in; this I do by the best of my present judgment think. And coming back I spent reading the book of warrants of our office in the first Dutch war, and do find that my letters and warrants and method will be found another-gate's business than this that the world so much adores – and I am glad for my own sake to find it so. My boy was with me, and read to me all day, and we sang a while together; and so home to supper a little, and so to bed.

8.   Up and by water to Whitehall and to St. James's, there to talk a little with Mr. Wren about the private business we are upon in the office, where he tells me he finds that they all suspect me to be the author of the great letter; which I value not – being satisfied that it is the best thing I could ever do for myself. And so after some discourse of this kind more, I back to the office, where all the morning; and after dinner, to it again all the afternoon and very late; and then home to supper, where met W. Batelier and B. Turner; and after some talk with them, and supper, we to bed. This day, I received so earnest an invitation again from Roger Pepys to come to Sturbridge Fair, that I resolve to let my wife go, which she shall do the next week; and so to bed. This day I received two letters from the Duke of Richmond about his Yacht, which is newly taken into the King's service, and I am glad of it, hoping hereby to oblige him and to have occasions of seeing his noble Duchess, which I adore.

9. Up, and to the office; and thence to the Duke of Richmond's lodgings by his desire, by letter yesterday. I found him at his lodgings in the little building in the Bouling-green at Whitehall, that that was begun to be built by Capt. Rolt. They are fine rooms. I did hope to see his Lady, the beautiful Mrs. Stuart; but she, I hear, is in the country. His business was about his Yacht, and seems a mighty good-natured man, and did presently write me a warrant for a Doe from Cobham when the season comes, bucks season being past. I shall make much of this acquaintance, that I may live to see his Lady near. Thence to Westminster to Sir R. Long's office; and going, met Mr. George Mountagu, who talked and complimented me mightily; and long discourse I had with him – who, for news, tells me for certain that Trevor doth come to be Secretary at Michaelmas and that Morris goes out, and he believes without any compensation. He tells me that now Buckingham does rule all; and the other day, in the King's Journy he is now in, at Bagshot and that way, he caused Prince Rupert's horses to be turned out of an Inne, and caused his own to be kept there; which the Prince complained of to the King, and the Duke of York seconded the complaint but the King did over-rule it for Buckingham; by which there are high displeasures among them – and Buckingham and Arlington rule all. Thence by water home and to dinner; and after dinner by water again to Whitehall, where Brouncker, W. Penn and I attended the Commissioners of the Treasury about the victualling contract – where high words between Sir Tho. Clifford and us, and myself more perticularly, who told him that something that he said was told him about this business was a flat untruth. However, we went on to our business in the examination of the draft, and so parted, and I vexed at what happened. And Brouncker, W. Penn and I home in a hackney coach – and I all the night so vexed, that I did not sleep almost all night; which shows how unfit I am for trouble. So after a little supper, vexed and spending a little time melancholy in making a base to the Lark's song, I to bed.

13. *Lords day.* The like all this morning and afternoon, and finished it to my mind. So about 4 a-clock walked to the Temple, and there by coach to St. James's and met, to my wish, the Duke of York and Mr. Wren; and understand the Duke of York hath received answers from Brouncker, W. Penn and J. Mennes; and as soon as he saw me, he bid Mr. Wren read them over with me. So having no opportunity of talk with the Duke of York, and Mr.

Wren some business to do, he puts them into my hand like an idle companion, to take home with me before himself had read them; which doth give me great opportunity of altering my answer, if there was cause. So took a hackney and home; and after supper made my wife to read them all over, wherein she is mighty useful to me. And I find them all evasions, and in many things false, and in few to the full purpose. Little said reflective on me, though W. Penn and J. Mennes do mean me in one or two places, and J. Mennes a little more plainly would lead the Duke of York to question the exactness of my keeping my records – but all to no purpose. My mind is mightily pleased by this, if I can but get them to have a copy taken of them for my future use; but I must return them tomorrow. So to bed.

15. Up mighty betimes, my wife and people, Mercer lying here all night, by 3 a-clock and I about 5; and they before and I after them to the Coach in Bishopsgate street; which was not ready to set out, so took wife and Mercer, Deb and W. Hewer (who all set out this day for Cambridge to Cosen Rogr. Pepys's to see Sturbridge fayre) and I showed them the Exchange, which is very finely and carried on with good despatch.

16. To the office, and thence to St. James's to the Duke of York – walking it to the Temple; and in my way observe that the Stockes are now pulled quite down, and it will make the coming into Cornhill and Lumber street mighty noble. I stopped too at Paul's, and there did go into St. Fayth's church and also into the body of the west part of the church, and do see a hideous sight, of the walls of the church ready to fall, that I was in fear as long as I was in it. And here I saw the great vaults underneath the body of the church. No hurt, I hear, is done yet, since their going to pull down the church and steeple; but one man, on Monday this week, fell from the top to a piece of the roof of the east end that stands next the steeple, and there broke himself all to pieces. It is pretty here, to see how the last church was but a case brought over the old church; for you may see the very old pillars standing whole within the wall of this. When I came to St. James's, I find the Duke of York gone with the King to see the muster of the Guards in Hyde Park; and their colonel, the Duke of Monmouth, to take his command this day of the King's Life-Guard, by surrender of my Lord Gerard's. So I took a hackney coach and saw it all; and endeed, it was mighty noble and their

firing mighty fine, and the Duke of Monmouth in mighty rich clothes; but the well-ordering of the men I understand not.

23.    At my office busy all the morning. At noon comes Mr. Eveling to me about some business with the office, and there in discourse tells me of his loss, to the value of 500*l*, which he hath met with in a late attempt of making of Bricks upon an adventure with others, by which he presumed to have got a great deal of money – so that I see the most ingenious men may sometimes be mistaken. So to the Change a little, and then home to dinner; and then by water to Whitehall to attend the Commissioners of the Treasury with Ald. Backwell about 10000*l* he is to lend us for Tanger. And then up to a committee of the Council, where was the Duke of York; and they did give us, the Officers of the Navy, the proposals of the several bidders for the victualling of the Navy, for us to give them our answer to which is the best, and whether it be better to victual by commission or contract – and to bring them our answer by Friday afternoon – which is a great deal of work. So thence back with Sir J. Mennes home, and came after us Sir W. Penn and Lord Brouncker, and we fell to the business; and I late when they were gone, to digest something of it; and so to supper and to bed.

26.    Could sleep but little last night for my concernment in this business of the victualling for Sir D. Gawden. So up in the morning and he comes to me, and there I did tell him all and give him my advice; and so he away, and I to the office, where we met and did a little business; and I left them, and by water to attend the Council, which I did all the morning, but was not called in; but the Council meets again in the afternoon on purpose about it. So I at noon to Westminster hall and there stayed a little, and at the Swan also, thinking to have got Doll Lane thither, but ella did not understand my signs; and so I away and walked to Charing cross, and there into the great new ordinary by my Lord Mulgrave's, being led thither by Mr. Beale, one of Oliver's and now of the King's Guards; and he sat with me while I had two grilled pigeons, very handsome, and good meat; and there he and I talked of our old acquaintance, W. Clerke and others, being a very civil man; and so walked to Westminster and there parted, and I to the Swan again but did nothing; and so to Whitehall and there attended the King and Council, who met and heard our answer; I present and then withdrew, and they spent two hours at least afterwards about it,

and at last rose; and to my great content, the Duke of York at coming out told me that it was carried for D. Gawden.

27. *Lords day.* To the Queen's Chapel and there heard some good singing; and so to Whitehall and saw the King and Queen at dinner; and thence with Sir St. Fox to dinner, and the Cofferer with us, and there mighty kind usage – and good discourse. Thence, spent all the afternoon walking in the park; and then in the evening at Court, on the Queen's side, and there met Mr. Godolphin, who tells me that the news is true we heard yesterday, of my Lord Sandwiches being come to Mounts bay in Cornwall; and so I heard this afternoon at Mrs. Pierce's, whom I went to make a short visit to. This night, in the Queen's drawing-room, my Lord Brouncker told me the difference that is now between the three Imbassadors here, the Venetian, French, and Spaniard, the third not being willing to make a visit to the first, because he would not receive him at the door.

28. I by coach towards the King's playhouse; and meeting W. How, took him with me and there saw *The Citty Match*, a play not acted these 30 years, and but a silly play. The King and Court there. The house mighty full. So I to Whitehall, and there all the evening on the Queen's side; and it being a most summerlike day and a fine warm evening, the Italians came in a barge under the leads before the Queen's drawing-room, and so the Queen and ladies went out and heard it for almost an hour; and it was endeed very good together but yet there was but one voice that alone did appear considerable, and that was Seignor Joanni. This done, by and by they went in; and here I saw Mr. Sidny Mountagu kiss the Queen's hand; who was mighty kind to him – and the ladies looked mightily on him, and the King came by and by and did talk to him. So I away by coach with Ald. Backewell home, who is mighty kind to me, more then ordinary, in his expressions. But I do hear this day what troubles me: that Sir W. Coventry is quite out of play. So home to read and sup; and to bed.

*Here the diary breaks off until 11 October, twelve pages being left blank for entries that were presumably never made. No rough notes survive, but from other sources we know that Pepys made two journeys at this time – one to Hampshire to meet Sandwich on his return from Spain, and the other to East Anglia, in the course of which he brought his wife back to London on 10 October.*

## ❧OCTOBER❧

15.    Up and all the morning at the office, and at home at dinner; where after dinner, my wife and I and Deb out by coach to the Upholster's in Long lane, Ald. Reeves, and then to Ald. Crow's, to see variety of Hangings; and were mightily pleased therewith and spent the whole afternoon thereupon; and at last, I think we shall pitch upon the best suit of Apostles, where three pieces for my room will come to almost 8o*l*. So home and to my office, and then home to supper and to bed.

17.    Up and to the office, where all the morning sitting; and at noon home to dinner and to the office all the afternoon; and then late home and there with much pleasure getting Mr. Gibbs, that writes well, to write the name upon my new draft of the *Resolution*; and so set it up and altered the situation of some of my pictures in my closet, to my extraordinary content, and at it with much pleasure till almost 12 at night. Mr. Moore and Seamour were with me this afternoon, who tell me that my Lord Sandwich was received mighty kindly by the King, and is in exceeding great esteem with him and the rest about him; but I doubt it will be hard for him to please both King and Duke of York; which I shall be sorry for. Mr. Moore tells me the sad condition my Lord is in in his estate and debts and the way he now lives in, so high, and so many vain servants about him, that he must be ruined if he doth not take up; which by the grace of God, I will put him upon when I come to see him.

20.    Up and to the office all the morning; and then home to dinner, having this day a new girle come to us in the room of Nell, who is lately, about four days since, gone away, being grown lazy and proud. This girl to stay only till we have a boy, which I intend to keep when I have a coach; which I am now about. At this time, my wife and I mighty busy laying out money in dressing up our best chamber and thinking of a coach and coachman and horses &c., and the more because of Creed's being now married to Mrs. Pickering; a thing I could never have expected, but it is done about seven or ten days since – as I hear out of the country. At noon home to dinner, and my wife and Harman and girl abroad to buy things; and I walked out to several places to pay debts, and among other things to look out for a coach; and saw many, and did light on one, for

which I bid 50*l*, which doth please me mightily – and I believe I shall have it. So to my tailor's and the New Exchange, and so by coach home; and there, having this day bought the *Queene of Arragon* play, I did get my wife and W. Batelier to read it over this night by 11 a-clock, and so to bed.

21.　Lay pretty long, talking with content with my wife about our coach and things; and so to the office, where Sir D. Gawden was to do something in his accounts. At noon to dinner to Mr. Batelier's, his mother coming this day a' house-warming to him, and several friends of his, to which he invited us. Here mighty merry, and his mother the same; I heretofore took her for a gentlewoman, and understanding. I rose from table before the rest, because under an obligation to go to my Lord Brouncker's, where to meet several gentlemen of the Royal Society to go and make a visit to the French Embassador Colbert at Leicester house, he having endeavoured to make one or two to my Lord Brouncker, as our President, but he was not within. But I came too late, they being gone before; but I fallowed to Leicester house, but they are gone in and up before me; and so I away to the New Exchange and there stayed for my wife; and she come, we to cow lane and there I showed her the coach which I pitch on, and she is out of herself for joy almost; but the man not within, so did nothing more towards an agreement; but to Mr. Crow's about a bed, to have his advice; and so home and there had my wife to read to me, and so to supper and to bed. *Memorandum*: that from Crows, we went back to Charing cross and there left my people at their tailor's while I to my Lord Sandwiches lodgings, who came to town the last night and is come thither to lie – and met with him within; and among others, my new Cosen Creed, who looks mighty soberly; and he and I salute one another with mighty gravity, till we came to a little more freedom of talk about it. But here I hear that Sir Gilb. Pickering is lately dead, about three days since, which makes some sorrow there; though not much, because of his being long expected to die, having been in a Lethargy long. So waited on my Lord to Court, and there stayed and saw the ladies awhile; and thence to my wife and took them up; and so home and to supper and bed.

24.　This morning comes to me the coachmaker, and agreed with me for 53*l*, and stand to the courtesy for what more I should give him upon the finishing of it. He is likely also to fit me with a coachman. There comes also to me Mr. Shotgrave, the Operator of our Royal Society, to show me his method of making the Tubes for Eyes, which are clouterly done, so that mine are better; but I have well informed myself in several things from him and so am glad of speaking with him.

25. *Lords day*. Up, and discoursing with my wife about our house and many new things we are doing of; and so to church I, and there find Jack Fen come, and his wife, a pretty black woman; I never saw her before, nor took notice of her now. So home and to dinner; and after dinner, all the afternoon got my wife and boy to read to me. And at night W. Batelier comes and sups with us; and after supper, to have my head combed by Deb, which occasioned the greatest sorrow to me that ever I knew in this world; for my wife, coming up suddenly, did find me imbracing the girl con my hand sub su coats; and endeed, I was with my main in her cunny. I was at a wonderful loss upon it, and the girl also; and I endeavoured to put it off, but my wife was struck mute and grew angry, and as her voice came to her, grew quite out of order; and I do say little, but to bed; and my wife said little also, but could not sleep all night; but about 2 in the morning waked me and cried, and fell to tell me as a great secret that she was a Roman Catholique and had received the Holy Sacrament; which troubled me but I took no notice of it, but she went on from one thing to another, till at last it appeared plainly her trouble was at what she saw; but yet I did not know how much she saw and therefore said nothing to her. But after her much crying and reproaching me with inconstancy and preferring a sorry girl before her, I did give her no provocations but did promise all fair usage to her, and love, and foreswore any hurt that I did with her – till at last she seemed to be at ease again; and so toward morning, a little sleep; and so I, with some little repose and rest, rose, and 26 up and by water to Whitehall, but with my mind mightily troubled for the poor girl, whom I fear I have undone by this, my [wife] telling me that she would turn her out of door. However, I was obliged to attend the Duke of York, thinking to have had a meeing of Tanger today, but had not; but he did take me and Mr. Wren into his closet, and there did press me to prepare what I had to say upon the answers of my fellow-officers to his great letter; which I promised to do against his coming to town again the next week; and so to other discourse, finding plainly that he is in trouble and apprehensions of the reformers, and would be found to do what he

can towards reforming himself.

And so thence to my Lord Sandwich; where after long stay, he being in talk with others privately, I to him; and there he taking physic and keeping his chamber, I had an hour's talk with him about the ill posture of things at this time, while the King gives countenance to Sir Ch. Sidly and Lord Buckhurst, telling him their late story of running up and down the streets a little while since all night, and their being beaten and clapped up all the night by the constable, who is since chid and imprisoned for his pains. He tells me that he thinks his matters do stand well with the King – and hopes to have despatch to his mind; but I doubt it, and do see that he doth fear it too. He told me my Lady Carteret's trouble about my writing of that letter of the Duke of York's lately to the office; which I did not own, but declared to be of no injury to G. Carteret, and that I would write a letter to him to satisfy him therein. But this I am in pain how to do without doing myself wrong, and the end I had, of preparing a justification to myself hereafter, when the faults of the Navy come to be found out. However, I will do it in the best manner I can. Thence by coach home and to dinner, finding my wife mightily discontented and the girl sad, and no words from my wife to her. So after dinner, they out with me about two or three things; and so home again, I all the evening busy and my wife full of trouble in her looks; and anon to bed – where about midnight, she wakes me and there falls foul on me again, affirming that she saw me hug and kiss the girl; the latter I denied, and truly; the other I confessed and no more. And upon her pressing me, did offer to give her under my hand that I would never see Mrs. Pierce more, nor Knepp, but did promise her perticular demonstrations of my true love to her, owning some indiscretion in what I did, but that there was no harm in it. She at last on these promises was quiet, and very

27   kind we were, and so to sleep; and in the morning up, but with my mind troubled for the poor girl, with whom I could not get opportunity to speak; but to the office, my mind mighty full of sorrow for her, where all the morning, and to dinner with my people and to the office all the afternoon; and so at night home and there busy to get some things ready against tomorrow's meeting of Tanger; and that being done and my clerks gone, my wife did towards bedtime begin to be in a mighty rage from some new matter that she had got in her head, and did most part of the night in bed rant at me in most high terms, of threats of publishing my shame; and when I offered to rise, would have rose too, and caused

a candle to be lit, to burn by her all night in the chimney while she ranted; while [I], that knew myself to have given some grounds for it, did make it my business to appease her all I could possibly, and by good words and fair promises did make her very quiet; and so rested all night and rose with perfect good peace, being heartily afflicted for this folly of mine that did occasion it; but was forced to be silent about the girl, which I have no mind to part with, but much less that the poor girl should be undone by my folly. So

28 up, with mighty kindness from my wife and a thorough peace; and being up, did by a note advise the girl what I had done and owned, which note I was in pain for till she told me that she had burned it.

So by coach with Mr. Gibson to Chancery lane, and there made oath before a Maister of Chancery to my Tanger account of Fees; and so to Whitehall, where by and by a Committee met; my Lord Sandwich there, but his report was not received, it being late; but only a little business done, about the supplying the place with victuals; but I did get, to my great content, my account allowed of Fees, with great applause by my Lord Ashly and Sir W. Penn. Thence home, calling at one or two places, and there about our workmen, who are at work upon my wife's closet and other parts of my house, that we are all in dirt. So after dinner, with Mr. Gibson all the afternoon in my closet; and at night to supper and to bed, my wife and I at good peace, but yet some little grudgeings of trouble in her, and more in me, about the poor girl.

29. At the office all the morning, where Mr. Wren first tells us of the order from the King, come last night to the Duke of York, for signifying his pleasure to the Sollicitor generall for drawing up a commission for suspending of my Lord Anglesy and putting in Sir Tho. Littleton and Sir Tho. Osborne (the former a creature of Arlington's, and the latter of the Duke of Buckingham's) during the suspension. The Duke of York was forced to obey, and did grant it, he being to go to Newmarket this day with the King, and so the King pressed for it. But Mr. Wren doth own that the Duke of York is the most wounded in this in the world, for it is done and concluded without his privity, after his appearing for him – and that it is plain that they do ayme to bring the Admiralty into commission too, and lessen the Duke of York. This doth put strange apprehensions into all our Board; only, I think I am the least troubled at it, for I care not at all for it – but my Lord Brouncker and

Pen do seem to think much of it. So home to dinner, full of this news; and after dinner to the office, and so home all the afternoon to do business towards my drawing up an account for the Duke of York of the answers of this office to his late great letter, and late at it; and so to bed, with great peace from my wife and quiet, I bless God.

30.     Up betimes, and Mr. Povy comes to even accounts with me; which we did, and then fell to other talk; he tells me, in short, how the King is made a child of by Buckingham and Arlington, to the lessening of the Duke of York, whom they cannot suffer to be great, for fear of my Lord Chancellors return; which therefore they make the King violent against. That he believes it is impossible these two great men can hold together long – or at least that the ambition of the former is so great that he will endeavour to master all, and bring into play as many as he can. That Anglesy will not lose his place easily, but will contend in law with whoever comes to execute it. That the Duke of York, in all things but in his codpiece, is led by the nose by his wife. That he doth believe that these present great men will break in time, and that W. Coventry will be a great man again; for he doth labour to have nothing to do in matters of the State, and is so useful to the side that he is on, that he will stand, though at present he is quite out of play. This done, he and I to talk of my coach, and I got him to go see it; where he finds most infinite fault with it, both as to being out of fashion and heavy; with so good reason, that I am mightily glad of his having corrected me in it; and so I do resolve to have one of his build, and with his advice, both in coach and horses, he being the fittest man in the world for it. And so he carried me home and said the same to my wife. So I to the office and he away; and at noon I home to dinner and all the afternoon late, with Gibson at my chamber late, about my present great business; only, a little in the afternoon at the office about Sir D. Gawden's accounts; and so to bed and slept heartily; my wife and I at good peace, but my heart troubled and her mind not at ease I perceive, she against and I for the girl; to whom I have not said anything these three days – but resolve to be mighty strange in appearance to her. This night, W. Batelier came and took his leave of us, he setting out for France to-morrow.

31.     So ends this month, with some quiet to my mind, though not perfect, after the greatest falling out with my poor wife, and through my folly with the girl, that ever I had; and I have reason to

be sorry and ashamed of it – and more, to be troubled for the poor girl's sake; whom I fear I shall by this means prove the ruin of – though I shall think myself concerned both to love and be a friend to her. This day, Rogr. Pepys and his son Talbot, newly come to town, came and dined with me, and mighty glad I am to see them.

# –⚜NOVEMBER⚜–

1.   *Lords day.* Up, and with W. Hewers at my chamber all this morning, going further in my great business for the Duke of York; and so at noon to dinner, and then W. Hewer to write fair what he had writ, and my wife to read to me all the afternoon; till anon Mr. Gibson came, and he and I to perfect it to my full mind. And so to supper and to bed – my mind yet at disquiet that I cannot be informed how poor Deb stands with her mistress, but I fear she will put her away; and the truth is, though it be much against my mind and to my trouble, yet I think it will be fit that she be gone, for my wife's peace and mine; for she cannot but be offended at the sight of her, my wife having conceived this jealousy of me with reason. And therefore, for that, and other reasons of expense, it will be best for me to let her go – but I shall love and pity her. This noon Mr. Povy sent his Coach for my wife and I to see; which we like mightily, and will endeavour to have him get us just such another.

2.   Up, and a cold morning, by water through bridge without a cloak; and there to Mr. Wren at his chamber at Whitehall, the first time of his coming thither this year, the Duchess coming thither tonight. And there he and I did read over my paper that I have with so much labour drawn up about the several answers of the Officers of this office to the Duke of York's reflections, and did debate a little what advice to give the Duke of York when he comes to town upon it. Here came in Lord Anglesy, and I perceive he makes nothing of this order for his suspension, resolving to contend and to bring it to the Council on Wednesday when the King is come to town tomorrow. And Mr. Wren doth join with him mightily in it, and doth look upon the Duke of York as concerned more in it then he. So I to visit Creed at his chamber, but his wife not come thither yet; nor doth he tell me where she is, though she be in town at Stepny, at Atkins's. So to Mr. Povy's to talk about a coach, but there I find my

Lord Sandwich and Peterborough and Hinchingbrooke, Ch. Herbert and Sidny Mountagu; and there I was stopped, and dined mighty nobly at a little table, with one little dish at a time upon it – but mighty merry; I was glad to see it, but sorry, methought, to see my Lord hath so little reason to be merry, and yet glad for his sake to have him cheerful. After dinner, up, and looked up and down the house, and so to the cellar and thence I slipped away without taking leave; and so to a few places about business; and among others, to my bookseller's in Duck lane; and so home, where the house still full of dirt by painters and others, and will not be clean a good while. This day I went by Mr. Povy's direction to a coachmaker near him for a coach just like his, but it was sold this very morning.

3. Up and all the morning at the office. At noon to dinner; and then to the office and there busy till 12 at night, without much pain to my eyes; but I did not use them to read or write, and so did hold out very well. So home, and there to supper; and I observed my wife to eye my eyes whether I did ever look upon Deb; which I could not but do now and then (and to my grief did see the poor wretch look on me and see me look on her, and then let drop a tear or two; which doth make my heart relent at this minute that I am writing this, with great trouble of mind, for she is endeed my sacrifice, poor girl); and my wife did tell me in bed, by the by, of my looking on other people, and that the only way is to put things out of sight; and this I know she means by Deb, for she tells me that her aunt was here on Monday and she did tell her of her desire of parting with Deb; but in such kind terms on both sides, that my wife is mightily taken with her. I see it will be, and it is but necessary; and therefore, though it cannot but grieve me, yet I must bring my mind to give way to it.

4. Up, and by coach to Whitehall; and there I find the King and Duke of York come the last night, and everybody's mouth full of my Lord Anglesy's suspension being sealed; which it was, it seems, yesterday; so that he is prevented in his remedy at the Council; and it seems the two new Treasurers did kiss the King's hand this morning, brought in by my Lord Arlington. They walked up and down together the Court this day, and several people joyed them. But I avoided it, that I might not be seen to look either way. This day also, I hear that my Lord Ormond is to be declared in Council no more Deputy-Governor of Ireland, his commission being

expired, and the King is prevailed with to take it out of his hands; which people do mightily admire, saying that he is the greatest subject of any prince in Christendome, and hath more acres of land then any – and hath done more for his prince then ever any yet did. But all will not do; he must down it seems – the Duke of Buckingham carrying all before him. But that that troubles me most, is that they begin to talk that the Duke of York's regiment is ordered to be disbanded; and more, that undoubtedly his Admiralcy will fallow; which doth shake me mightily, and I fear will have ill consequences in the nation, for these counsels are very mad. The Duke of York doth, by all men's report, carry himself wonderful submissive to the King, in the most humble manner in the world; but yet it seems nothing must be spared that tends to the keeping out of the Chancellor, and that is the reason of all this. The great discourse now is that the Parliament shall be dissolved, and another called which shall give the King the Deane and Chapters lands; and that will put him out of debt. And it is said that Buckingham doth knownly meet daily with Wildman and other Commonwealthsmen; and that when he is with them, he makes the King believe that he is with his wenches. But that that pleases me most, is that several do tell me that Pen is to be removed; and others, that he hath resigned his place; and perticularly, Spragge tells me for certain that he hath resigned it and is become a partener with Gawden in the victualling – in which I think he hath done a very cunning thing, but I am sure I am glad of it, and it will be well for the King – to have him out of this office. When I came home tonight, I find Deb not come home, and do doubt whether she be not quite gone or no; but my wife is silent to me in it, and I to her, but fell to other discourse; and endeed am well satisfied that my house will never be at peace between my wife and I unless I let her go, though it grieves me to the heart. My wife and I spent much time this evening talking of our being put out of the office and my going to live at Deptford at her brother's till I can clear my accounts and rid my hands of the town – which will take me a year or more; and I do think it will be best for me to do so, in order to our living cheap and out of sight.

5.   Up, and Willet came home in the morning; and God forgive
me, I could not conceal my content thereat, by smiling, and my
wife observed it; but I said nothing, nor she, but away to the office.
Presently, up by water to Whitehall, and there all of us to wait on
the Duke of York; which we did, having little to do. And then I up
and down the House, till by and by the Duke of York (who had bid
me stay) did come to his closet again, and there did call in me and
Mr. Wren; and there my paper that I have lately taken pains to draw
up was read, and the Duke of York pleased therewith; and we did all
along conclude upon answers to my mind for the Board, and that
that, if put in execution, will do the King's business. But I do now
more and more perceive the Duke of York's trouble, and that he
doth lie under great weight of mind from the Duke of Buckingham's carrying things against him; and perticularly when I
advised that he would use his interest that a seaman might come
into the room of W. Penn, who is now declared to be gone from us
to that of the Victualling, and did show how the office would now
be left without one seaman in it but the Surveyor and the
Controller, who is so old as to be able to do nothing. He told me
plainly that I knew his mind well enough as to seamen, but that it
must be as others will. To the Treasurer's, Sir Tho. Clifford, where
I did go and eat some oysters. Thence with Mr. Povy spent all the
afternoon going up and down among the coachmakers in Cow
lane, and did see several, and at last did pitch upon a little Chariott,
whose body was framed but not Covered, at the widow's that made
Mr. Lowther's fine coach. And we are mightily pleased with it, it
being light, and will be very gent and sober – to be covered with
leather, but yet will hold four. Being much satisfied with this, I
carried him to Whitehall; and so by coach home, where give my
wife a good account of my day's work; and so to the office and there
late, and so to bed.

6.[1]   Up, and presently my wife up with me, which she professedly
now doth every day to dress me, that I may not see Willett; and doth
eye me whether I cast my eye upon her or no. And doth keep me
from going into the room where she is among the Upholsters at

---

1. Pepys here transposes the entries for the 5th and 6th – 'my mind being now so
troubled', he adds after the latter entry, 'that it is no wonder that I fall into this
mistake more then ever I did in my life before'. He later confuses his accounts of the
afternoons' events of the 11th and 12th.

work in our blue chamber. At the office all the morning; and so to dinner, my wife with me, but so as I durst not look upon the girl; though God knows, notwithstanding all my protestations, I could not keep my mind from desiring it. After dinner to the office again and there did some business; and then by coach to see Roger Pepys at his lodgings next door to Arundell house, a barber's. And there I did see a book which my Lord Sandwich hath promised one to me of – a description of the Escuriall in Spain; which I have a great desire to have, though I took it for a finer book when he promised it me. With him to see my Cosen Turner and The[oph]., and there sat and talked, they being newly come out of the country; and here pretty merry, and with The[oph]. to show her a coach at Mr. Povy's man's, she being in want of one; and so back again with her and then home by coach, with my mind troubled and finding no content, my wife still troubled, nor can be at peace while the girl is there; which I am troubled at on the other side. We passed the evening together, and then to bed and slept ill, she being troubled and troubling me in the night with talk and complaint upon the old business.

7. Up, and at the office all the morning; and so to it again after dinner and there busy late, choosing to imploy myself rather then go home to trouble with my wife, whom, however, I am forced to comply with; and endeed I do pity her, as having cause enough for her grief. So to bed, and there slept ill because of my wife.

8. *Lords day*. Up, and at my chamber all the morning, setting papers to rights with my boy. And so to dinner at noon, the girl with us; but my wife troubled thereat to see her, and doth tell me so; which troubles me, for I love the girl. At my chamber again to work all the afternoon till night, when Pelling comes, who wonders to find my wife so dull and melancholy; but God knows, she hath too much cause. However, as pleasant as we can, we supped together; and so made the boy read to me, the poor girl not appearing at supper, but hides herself in her chamber – so that I could wish in that respect that she was out of the house, for our peace is broke to all of us while she is here. And so to bed – where my wife mighty unquiet all night, so as my bed is become burdensome to me.

9. Up, and I did, by a little note which I flung to Deb, advise her

that I did continue to deny that ever I kissed her, and so she might govern herself. The truth [is], that I did adventure upon God's pardoning me this lie, knowing how heavy a thing it would be for me to be the ruin of the poor girl; and next, knowing that if my wife should know all, it were impossible ever for her to be at peace with me again – and so our whole lives would be uncomfortable. The girl read, and as I bid her, returned me the note, flinging it to me in passing by. And so I abroad by [coach] to Whitehall, and there to the Duke of Yorke's to wait on him.

10.    Up, and my wife still every day as ill as she is all night; will rise to see me out doors, telling me plainly that she dares not let me see the girl; and so I out to the office, where all the morning; and so home to dinner, where I find my wife mightily troubled again, more then ever, and she tells me that it is from her examining the girl and getting a confession now from her of all, even to the very *tocando su* thing with my hand – which doth mightily trouble me, as not being able to foresee the consequences of it as to our future peace together. So my wife would not go down to dinner, but I would dine in her chamber with her; and there, after mollifying her as much as I could, we were pretty quiet and eat; and by and by comes Mr. Hollier, and dines there by himself after we had dined. And he being gone, we to talk again, and she to be troubled, reproaching me with my unkindness and perjury, I having denied my ever kissing her – as also with all her old kindnesses to me, and my ill-using of her from the beginning, and the many temptations she hath refused out of faithfulness to me; whereof several she was perticular in, and especially from my Lord Sandwich by the sollicitation of Capt. Ferrer; and then afterward, the courtship of my Lord Hinchingbrooke, even to the trouble of his Lady. All which I did acknowledge and was troubled for, and wept; and at last pretty good friends again, and so I to my office and there late, and so home to supper with her; and so to bed, where after half-an-hour's slumber, she wakes me and cries out that she should never sleep more, and so kept raving till past midnight, that made me cry and weep heartily all the while for her, and troubled for what she reproached me with as before; and at last, with new vows, and perticularly that I would myself bid the girl be gone and show my dislike to her – which I shall endeavour to perform, but with much trouble. And so, this appeasing her, we to sleep as well as we could till morning.

12.   Up, and [my wife] with me as heretofore; and so I to the office, where all the morning; and at noon to dinner, and Mr. Wayth, who being at my office about business, I took him with me to talk and understand his matters. And so having dined, we parted, and I to my wife and to sit with her a little; and then called her and Willet to my chamber, and there did with tears in my eyes, which I could not help, discharge her and advise her to be gone as soon as she could, and never to see me or let me see her more while she was in the house; which she took with tears too, but I believe understands me to be her friend; and I am apt to believe, by what my wife hath of late told me, is a Cunning girl, if not a slut.

13.   All the evening with my wife, who tells me that Deb hath been abroad today, and is come home and says she hath got a place to go to, so as she will be gone tomorrow morning. This troubled me; and the truth is, I have a great mind for to have the maidenhead of this girl, which I should not doubt to have if yo could get time para be con her – but she will be gone and I know not whither. Before we went to bed, my wife told me she would not have me to see her or give her her wages; and so I did give my wife 10*l* for her year and half-a-quarter's wages, which she went into her chamber and paid her; and so to bed, and there, blessed be God, we did sleep well and with peace, which I had not done in now almost twenty nights together. This afternoon I went to my coachmaker and Crows, and there saw things go on to my great content.

14.   Up, and had a mighty mind to have seen or given a note to Deb or to have given her a little money; to which purpose I wrapped up 40*s.* in a paper, thinking to give her; but my wife rose presently, and would not let me be out of her sight; and went down before me into the kitchen, and came up and told me that she was in the kitchen, and therefore would have me go round the other way; which she repeating, and I vexed at it, answered her a little angrily; upon which she instantly flew out into a rage, calling me dog and rogue, and that I had a rotten heart; all which, knowing that I deserved it, I bore with; and word being brought presently up that she was gone away by coach with her things, my wife was friends; and so all quiet, and I to the office with my heart sad, and find that I cannot forget the girl, and vexed I know not where to look for her – and more troubled to see how my wife is by this means likely for

ever to have her hand over me, that I shall for ever be a slave to her; that is to say, only in matters of pleasure, but in other things she will make her business, I know, to please me and to keep me right to her – which I will labour to be endeed, for she deserves it of me, though it will be I fear a little time before I shall be able to wear Deb out of my mind. At the office all the morning, and merry at noon at dinner; and after dinner to the office, where all the afternoon and doing much business late; my mind being free of all troubles, I thank God, but only for my thoughts of this girl, which hang after her. And so at night home to supper, and there did sleep with great content with my wife. I must here remember that I have lain with my moher as a husband more times since this falling-out then in I believe twelve months before – and with more pleasure to her then I think in all the time of our marriage before.

16. Up, and by water to Whitehall, and there at the Robe-chamber at a Committee for Tanger; where some of us, my Lord Sandwich, Sir W. Coventry, and myself, with another or two, met to debate the business of the Molle and there draw up reasons for the King's taking of it into his own hands and managing of it upon accounts with Sir H. Cholmly. This being done, I away to Holborne about Whetstones park, where I never was in my life before, where I understand by my wife's discourse that Deb is gone; which doth trouble me mightily, that the poor girl should be in a desperate condition forced to go thereabouts; and there, not hearing of any such man as Allbon, with whom my wife said she now was, I to the Strand and there, by sending of Drumbleby's boy, my flagelette-maker, to Eagle court, where my wife also by discourse lately let fall that he did lately live, I found that this Dr. Allbon is a kind of a poor broken fellow that dare not show his head nor be known where he is gone; but to Lincoln's Inn fields I went, to Mr. Povy's, but missed him; and so hearing only that this Allbon is gone to Fleet street, I did only call at Martins my bookseller's, and there bought *Cassandra* and some other French books for my wife's closet; and so home, having eat nothing but two pennorth of Oysters, opened for me by a woman in the Strand while the boy went to and again to inform me about this man; and therefore home and to dinner, and so all the afternoon at the office and there late, busy; and so home to supper and, pretty pleasant with my wife, to bed – and rested pretty well.

17. Up, and to the office all the morning, where the new Treasurers came their second time; and before they sat down, did discourse with the Board, and perticularly my Lord Brouncker, about their place which they challenge, as hav[ing] been heretofore due and given to their predecessor; which at last my Lord did own it hath been given him only out of courtesy to his quality, and that he did not take it as of right at the Board; so they for the present sat down and did give him the place, but I think with an intent to have the Duke of York's directions about it. My wife and maids busy now to make clean the house above stairs, the Upholsters having done there in her closet and the blue room; and are mighty pretty. At my office all the afternoon and at night, busy; and so home to my wife, and pretty pleasant and at mighty ease in my mind, being in hopes to find Deb, and without trouble or the knowledge of my wife. So to supper at night, and to bed.

18. Lay long in bed, talking with my wife, she being unwilling to have me go abroad, being and declaring herself jealous of my going out, for fear of my going to Deb; which I do deny – for which God forgive me, for I was no sooner out about noon but I did go by coach directly to Somerset house and there enquired among the porters there for Dr. Allbun; and the first I spoke with told me he knew him, and that he was newly gone into Lincoln's Inn fields, but whither he could not tell me, but that one of his fellows, not then in the way, did carry a chest of drawers thither with him, and that when he comes he would ask him. This put me in some hopes; and I to Whitehall and thence to Mr. Povy's, but he at dinner; and therefore I away and walked up and down the Strand between the two turnstiles, hoping to see her out of a window; and then imployed a porter, one Osbeston, to find out this Doctors lodgings thereabouts; who by appointment comes to me to Hercules pillars, where I dined alone, but tells me that he cannot find out any such but will enquire further. Thence back to Whitehall to the Treasury a while, and thence to the Strand; and towards night did meet with the porter that carried the chest of drawers with this Doctor, but he would not tell me where he lived, being his good maister he told me; but if I would have a message to him, he would deliver it. At last, I told him my business was not with him, but a little gent[le]woman, one Mrs. Willet, that is with him; and sent him to see how she did, from her friend in London, and no other token. He goes while I walk in Somerset house – walk there in the Court; at

last he comes back and tells me she is well, and that I may see her if I will – but no more. So I could not be commanded by my reason, but I must go this very night; and so by coach, it being now dark, I to her, close by my tailor's; and there she came into the coach to me, and yo did besar her and tocar her thing, but ella was against it and laboured with much earnestness, such as I believed to be real; and yet at last yo did make her tener mi cosa in her mano, while mi mano was sobra her pectus, and so did hazer with grand delight. I did nevertheless give her the best counsel I could, to have a care of her honour and to fear God and suffer no man para haver to do con her – as yo have done – which she promised. Yo did give her 20s. and directions para laisser sealed in paper at any time the name of the place of her being, at Herringman's my bookseller in the Change – by which I might go para her. And so bid her good-night, with much content to my mind and resolution to look after her no more till I heard from her. And so home, and there told my wife a fair tale, God knows, how I spent the whole day; with which the poor wretch was satisfied, or at least seemed so; and so to supper and to bed, she having been mighty busy all day in getting of her house in order against tomorrow, to hang up our new hangings and furnishing our best chamber.

19.   Up, and at the office all the morning, with my heart full of joy to think in what a safe condition all my matters now stand between my wife and Deb and me; and at noon, running upstairs to see the upholsters, who are at work upon hanging my best room and setting up my new bed, I find my wife sitting sad in the dining-room; which inquiring into the reason of, she begun to call me all the false, rotten-hearted rogues in the world, letting me understand that I was with Deb yesterday; which, thinking impossible for her ever to understand, I did a while deny; but at last did, for the ease of my mind and hers, and for ever to discharge my heart of this wicked business, I did confess all; and above-stairs in our bed-chamber there, I did endure the sorrow of her threats and vows and curses all the afternoon. And which was worst, she swore by all that was good that she would slit the nose of this girl, and be gone herself this very night from me; and did there demand 3 or 400*l* of me to buy my peace, that she might be gone without making any noise, or else protested that she would make all the world know of it. So, with most perfect confusion of face and heart, and sorrow and shame, in the greatest agony in the world, I did pass this afternoon, fearing

that it will never have an end; but at last I did call for W. Hewers, who I was forced to make privy now to all; and the poor fellow did cry like a child [and] obtained what I could not, that she would be pacified, upon condition that I would agree it under my hand never to see or speak to Deb while I live, as I did before of Pierce and Knepp; and which I did also, God knows, promise for Deb too, but I have the confidence to deny it, to the perjuring of myself. So before it was late, there was, beyond my hopes as well as desert, a tolerable peace; and so to supper, and pretty kind words, and to bed, and there yo did hazer con ella to her content; and so with some rest spent the night in bed, being most absolutely resolved, if ever I can maister this bout, never to give her occasion while I live of more trouble of this or any other kind, there being no curse in the world so great as this of the difference between myself and her; and therefore I do by the grace of God promise never to offend her more, and did this night begin to pray to God upon my knees alone in my chamber; which God knows I cannot yet do heartily, but I hope God will give me the grace more and more every day to fear Him, and to be true to my poor wife. This night the Upholsters did finish the hanging of my best chamber, but my sorrow and trouble is so great about this business, that put me out of all joy in looking upon it or minding how it was.

20.    This morning up, with mighty kind words between my poor wife and I; and so to Whitehall by water, W. Hewer with me, who is to go with me everywhere until my wife be in condition to go out along with me herself; for she doth plainly declare that she dares not trust me out alone, and therefore made it a piece of our league that I should alway take somebody with me, or her herself; which I am mighty willing to, being, by the grace of God resolved never to do her wrong more. We landed at the Temple, and there I did bid him call at my Cosen Roger Pepys's lodgings, and I stayed in the street for him; and so took water again at the Strand stairs and so to Whitehall, in my way I telling him plainly and truly my resolutions, if I can get over this evil, never to give new occasion for it. He is, I think, so honest and true a servant to us both, and one that loves us, that I was not much troubled at his being privy to all this, but rejoiced in my heart that I had him to assist in the making us friends; which he did do truly and heartily, and with good success – for I did get him to go to Deb to tell her that I had told my wife all of my being with her the other night, that so, if my wife should send, she

might not make the business worse by denying it. While I was at
Whitehall with the Duke of York doing our ordinary business with
him, here being also the first time the new Treasurers, W. Hewer
did go to her and come back again; and so I took him into St.
James's park, and there he did tell me he had been with her and
found what I said about my manner of being with her true, and had
given her advice as I desired. I did there enter into more talk about
my wife and myself, and he did give me great assurance of several
perticular cases to which my wife had from time to time made him
privy of her loyalty and truth to me after many and great
temptations, and I believe them truly. I did also discourse the
unfitness to my leaving of my imployment now in many respects,
to go into the country as my wife desires – but that I would labour
fit myself for it; which he thoroughly understands, and doth agree
with me in it; and so, hoping to get over this trouble, we about our
business to Westminster hall to meet Roger Pepys; which I did, and
did there discourse of the business of lending him 500*l* to answer
some occasions of his, which I believe to be safe enough; and so
took leave of him and away by coach home, calling on my coachmaker by the way, where I like my little coach mightily. But when I
came home, hoping for a further degree of peace and quiet, I find
my wife upon her bed in a horrible rage afresh, calling me all the
bitter names; and rising, did fall to revile me in the bitterest manner
in the world, and could not refrain to strike me and pull my hair;
which I resolved to bear with, and had good reason to bear it. So I
by silence and weeping did prevail with her a little to be quiet, and
she would not eat her dinner without me; but yet by and by into a
raging fit she fell again worse then before, that she would slit the
girl's nose; and at last W. Hewer came in and came up, who did
allay her fury, I flinging myself in a sad desperate condition upon
the bed in the blue room, and there lay while they spoke together;
and at last it came to this, that if I would call Deb "whore" under
my hand, and write to her that I hated her and would never see her
more, she would believe me and trust me – which I did agree to;
only, as to the name of "whore" I would have excused, and
therefore wrote to her sparing that word; which my wife thereupon
tore it, and would not be satisfied till, W. Hewer winking upon me,
I did write so, with the name of a whore, as that I did fear she might
too probably have been prevailed upon to have been a whore by her
carriage to me, and therefore, as such, I did resolve never to see her
more. This pleased my wife, and she gives it W. Hewer to carry to

her, with a sharp message from her. So from that minute my wife begun to be kind to me, and we to kiss and be friends, and so continued all the evening and fell to talk of other matters with great comfort, and after supper to bed.

This evening comes Mr. Billup to me to read over Mr. Wren's alterations of my draft of a letter for the Duke of York to sign, to the Board; which I like mighty well, they being not considerable, only in mollifying some hard terms which I had thought fit to put in. From this to other discourse; I do find that the Duke of York and his servant Mr. Wren do look upon this service of mine as a very seasonable service to the Duke of York, as that which he will have to show to his enemies in his own justification of his care of the King's business. And I am sure I am heartily glad of it – both for the King's sake and the Duke of York's, and my own also – for if I continue, my work, by this means, will be the less, and my share in the blame also. He being gone, I to my wife again and so spent the evening with very great joy, and the night also, with good sleep and rest, my wife only troubled in her rest, but less then usual – for which the God of Heaven be praised. I did this night promise to my wife never to go to bed without calling upon God upon my knees by prayer; and I begun this night, and hope I shall never forget to do the like all my life – for I do find that it is much the best for my soul and body to live pleasing to God and my poor wife – and will ease me of much care, as well as much expense.

21. Up, with great joy to my wife and me, and to the office, where W. Hewer did most honestly bring me back that part of my letter under my hand to Deb wherein I called her "whore", assuring me that he did not show it her – and that he did only give her to understand that wherein I did declare my desire never to see her, and did give her the best Christian counsel he could; which was mighty well done of him. But by the grace of God, though I love the poor girl and wish her well, as having gone too far toward the undoing her, yet I will never enquire after or think of her more – my peace being certainly to do right to my wife.

22. *Lords day*. My wife and I lay long, with mighty content, and so rose, and she spent the whole day making herself clean, after four or five weeks being in continued dirt. And I knocking up nails and making little settlements in my house, till noon; and then eat a bit of meat in the kitchen, I all alone, and so to the office to set down my

Journall, for some days leaving it imperfect, the matter being mighty grievous to me and my mind from the nature of it. And so in to solace myself with my wife, whom I got to read to me, and so W. Hewer and the boy; and so after supper, to bed. This day, my boy's Livery is come home, the first I ever had of Greene lined with red; and it likes me well enough.

23. Up, and called upon by W. How, who went with W. Hewers with me by water to the Temple. His business was to have my advice about a place he is going to buy – the Clerk of the Patent's place – which I understand not, and so could say little to him – but fell to other talk; and setting him in at the Temple, we to Whitehall, and there I to visit Lord Sandwich, who is now so reserved, or moped rather, I think with his own business, that he bids welcome to no man, I think, to his satisfaction. However, I bear with it, being willing to give him as little trouble as I can and to receive as little from him, wishing only that I had my money in my purse that I have lent him – but however, I show no discontent at all. So to Whitehall, where a Committee of Tanger expected, but none met. I met with Mr. Povy, who I discoursed with about public business. Thence with W. Hewers (who goes up and down with me like a jaylour, but yet with great love and to my great good liking, it being my desire above all things to please my wife therein). I took up my wife and boy at Unthanks, and from thence to Hercules Pillars and there dined; and thence to our Upholsters about some things more to buy, and so to see our coach, and so to the looking-glass man's by the New Exchange, and so to buy a picture for our blue-chamber chimney, and so home; and there I made my boy to read to me most of the night, to get through the *Life of the Archbishop of Canterbury*. At supper comes Mary Battelier, and with us all the evening prettily talking, and very innocent company she is; and she gone, we with much content to bed and to sleep, with mighty rest all night.

28. Up, and all the morning at the office; where, while I was sitting, one comes and tells me that my Coach is come – so I was forced to go out; and to Sir Rd. Ford's, where I spoke to him, and he is very willing to have it brought in and stand there; and so I ordered it, to my great content, it being mighty pretty; only, the horses do not please me, and therefore resolve to have better. At noon home to dinner; and so to the office again all the afternoon and did a great

deal of business; and so home to supper and to bed, with my mind at pretty good ease, having this day presented to the Board the Duke of York's letter; which I perceive troubled Sir W. Penn, he declaring himself meant in the part that concerned excuse by sickness; but I do not care, but am mightily glad that it is done, and now I shall begin to be at pretty good ease in the office.

29. *Lords day*. Lay long in bed with pleasure [with my wife], with whom I have now a great deal of content; and my mind is in other things also mightily more at ease, and I do mind my business better then ever and am more at peace; and trust in God I shall ever be so, though I cannot yet get my mind off from thinking now and then of Deb. But I do, ever since my promise a while since to my wife, pray to God by myself in my chamber every night, and will endeavour to get my wife to do the like with me ere long; but am in much fear of what she hath lately frighted me with about her being a Catholique – and dare not therefore move her to go to church, for fear she should deny me. But this morning, of her own accord, she spoke of going to church the next Sunday; which pleases me mightily. This morning my coachman's clothes comes home, and I like my livery mightily; and so I all the morning at my chamber, and dined with my wife and got her to read to me in the afternoon, till Sir W. Warren by appointment comes to me, who spent two hours or three with me about his accounts of Gottenbrough; which are so confounded, that I doubt they will hardly ever pass without my doing something; which he desires of me, and which, partly from fear and partly from unwillingness to wrong the King and partly from its being of no profit to me, I am backward to give way to, though the poor man doth endeed deserve to be rid of this trouble that he hath lain so long under from the negligence of this Board. We afterward fell into other talk; and he tells me, as soon as he saw my coach yesterday, he wished that the owner might not contract envy by it; but I told him it was now manifestly for my profit to keep a coach, and that after imployments like mine for eight years, it were hard if I could not be justly thought to be able to do that. He gone, my wife and I to supper; and so she to read and made an end of the *Life of Archbishop Laud*, which is worth reading as informing a man plainly in the posture of the Church, and how the things of it were managed with the same self-interest and design that every other thing is, and have succeeded accordingly. So to bed.

30. Thus ended this month with very good content, that hath been the most sad to my heart and the most expenseful to my purse on things of pleasure, having furnished my wife's closet and the best chamber, and a coach and horses, that ever I yet knew in the world; and doth put me into the greatest condition of outward state that ever I was in, or hoped ever to be, or desired – and this at a time when we do daily expect great changes in this office and by all reports, we must all of us turn out. But my eyes are come to that condition that I am not able to work; and therefore, that, and my wife's desire, makes me have no manner of trouble in my thoughts about it – so God do his will in it.

# –✳DECEMBER✳–

2. Up and at the office all the morning upon some accounts of Sir D. Gawden; and at noon abroad with W. Hewer, thinking to have found Mr. Wren at Capt. Cox, to have spoke something to him about doing a favour for Will's Uncle Stevenson, but missed him; and so back home and abroad with my wife, the first time that ever I rode in my own coach; which doth make my heart rejoice and praise God, and pray him to bless it to me and continue it. So she and I to the King's playhouse, and there sat to avoid seeing of Knepp in a box above, where Mrs. Williams happened to be; and there saw *The Usurper*, a pretty good play in all but what is designed to resemble Cromwell and Hugh Peters, which is mighty silly. The play done, we to Whitehall; where [my] wife stayed, while I up to the Duchesses and Queenes side to speak with the Duke of York; and here saw all the ladies and heard the silly discourse of the King with his people about him, telling a story of my Lord of Rochester's having of his clothes stole while he was with a wench, and his gold all gone but his clothes found afterward, stuffed into a feather-bed by the wench that stole them.

5. Up, after a little talk with my wife which troubled me, she being ever since our late difference mighty watchful of sleep and dreams, and will not be persuaded but I do dream of Deb, and doth tell me that I speak in my dream and that this night I did cry "Huzzy!" and it must be she – and now and then I start otherwise then I used to do, she says; which I know not, for I do not know that

I dream of her more then usual, though I cannot deny that my thoughts waking do run now and then, against my will and judgment, upon her, for that only is wanting to undo me, being now in every other thing as to my mind most happy – and may still be so but for my own fault, if I be ketched loving anybody but my wife again. So up and to the office; and at noon to dinner and thence to office, where late, mighty busy and despatching much business, settling papers in my own office; and so home to supper and to bed. No news stirring but that my Lord of Ormond is likely to go to Ireland again, which doth show that the Duke of Buckingham doth not rule all so absolutely – and that, however, we shall speedily have more changes in the Navy. And it is certain that the non-conformists do now preach openly in houses in many places, and among others, the house that was heretofore Sir G. Carteret's in Leadenhall street, and have ready access to the King. And now the great dispute is whether this Parliament or another; and my great design, if I continue in the Navy, is to get myself to be a Parliament-man.

6. *Lords day.* Up, and with my wife to church; which pleases me mightily, I being full of fear that she would never go to church again after she had declared to me that she was a Roman Catholique. But though I do verily think she fears God, and is truly and sincerely virtuous, yet I do see she is not so strictly so a Catholique as not to go to church with me; which pleases me mightily. Here Mills made a lazy sermon upon Moses's meekenesse; and so home, and my wife and I alone to dinner; and then she to read a little book concerning Speech in general, a translation late out of French, a most excellent piece as ever I read, proving a soul in man and all the ways and secrets by which Nature teaches speech in man – which doth please me most infinitely to read. By and by my wife to church, and I to my office to complete my journall for the last three days; and so home to my chamber to settle some papers, and so to spend the evening with my wife and W. Hewer, talking over the business of the office, and perticularly my own office, how I will make it; and it will become in a little time an office of ease, and not slavery, as it hath for so many years been. So to supper and to bed.

7. This afternoon, passing through Queen's street, I saw pass by our coach on foot, Deb; which God forgive me, did put me into some new thoughts of her and for her, but durst not show them;

and I think my wife did not see her, but I did get my thoughts free of her as soon as I could.

12. This day was brought home my pair of black coach-horses, the first I ever was maister of; they cost me 50*l*, and are a fine pair.

14. Up and by water to Whitehall to a Committee of Tanger; where, among other things, a silly account of a falling-out between Norwood at Tanger and Mr. Bland the Mayor, who is fled to Cales. His complaint is ill-worded; and the other's defence, the most ridiculous that ever I saw – and so everybody else that was there thought it. But never did I see so great an instance of the use of grammar and knowledge how to tell a man's tale as this day, Bland having spoiled his business by ill-telling it; who had work to have made himself notorious by his mastering Norwood his enemy, if he had known how to have used. Thence calling Smith the Auditors clerk at the Temple, I by the Exchange home and there looked over my Tanger accounts with him; and so to dinner, and then set him down again by a hackney, my coachman being this day about breaking of my horses to the coach, they having never yet drawn.

19. Up, and to the office, where all the morning; and at noon, eating very little dinner, my wife and I by hackney to the King's playhouse and there, the pit being full, sat in a box above and saw *Catelin's Conspiracy* – yesterday being the first day – a play of much good sense and words to read, but that doth appear the worst upon the stage, I mean the least divertising, that ever I saw any, though most fine in clothes and a fine Scene of the Senate and of a fight, that ever I saw in my life – but the play is only to be read. And therefore home with no pleasure at all, but only in sitting next to Betty Hall, that did belong to this House and was Sir Ph. Howard's mistress; a mighty pretty wench, though my wife will not think so, and I dare neither commend nor be seen to look upon her or any other now, for fear of offending her. So, our own coach coming for us, home and to end letters; and so home, my wife to read to me out of *The Siege of Rhodes*; and so to supper and to bed.

20. *Lords day*. Up and with my wife to church, and then home; and there found W. Joyce come to dine with me, as troublesome a talking coxcomb as ever he was – and yet once in a year I like him well enough. In the afternoon, my wife and W. Hewer and I to

Whitehall, where they set me down and stayed till I had been with the Duke of York, with the rest of us of the office, and did a little business; and then the Duke of York in good humour did fall to tell us many fine stories of the wars in Flanders, and how the Spaniards are the [best] disciplined foot in the world – will refuse no extraordinary service if commanded, but scorn to be paid for it, as in other countries, though at the same time they will beg in the streets. Not a soldier will carry you a cloak-bag for money for the world, though he will beg a penny, and will do the thing if commanded by his commander. That in the citadel of Antwerp, a soldier hath not a liberty of begging till he hath served three years. They will cry out against their King and commanders and generals, none like them in the world, and yet will not hear a stranger say a word of them but he will cut his throat. That upon a time, some of the commanders of their army exclaiming against their generals, and perticularly the Marquis de Caranene, the confessor of the Marquis coming by and hearing them, he stops and gravely tells them that the three great trades of the world are, the Lawyer[s], who govern the world – the Churchmen, who enjoy the world – and a sort of fools whom they call Souldiers, who make it their work to defend the world. He told us too, that Turein being now become a Catholique, he is likely to get over the head of Colbert, their interests being contrary; the latter to promote Trade and the sea (which, says the Duke of York, is that that we have most cause to fear); and Turin to imploy the King and his forces by land, to encrease his conquests. Thence to the coach to my wife and so home; and there with W. Hewer to my office to do some business, and so set down my journall for four or five days; and then home to supper and read a little, and to bed. W. Hewer tells me today that he hears that the King of France hath declared in print that he doth intend this next summer to forbid his commanders to strike to us, but that both we and the Dutch shall strike to him. And that he hath made his captains swear it already, that they will observe it – which is a great thing if he doth it, as I know nothing to hinder him.

21. My own coach carrying me and my boy Tom, who goes with me in the room of W. Hewer who could not, and I dare not go alone, to the Temple and there set me down – the first time my fine horses ever carried me, and I am mighty proud of them; and there took a hackney and to Whitehall, where a Committee of Tanger, but little to do; and so away home, calling at the Exchange and

buying several little things; and so home and there dined with my wife and people; and then she and W. Hewer and I by appointment out with our coach, but the old horses, not daring yet to use them too much, but only to enter them – and to the Temple, there to call Talbt. Pepys; and took him up, and first went into Holborne and there saw the woman that is to be seen with a Beard; she is a little plain woman, a Dane, her name, Ursula Dyan, about forty years old, her voice like a little girl's, with a beard as much as any man I ever saw, as black almost, and grizzly. They offered [to] show my wife further satisfaction if she desired it, refusing it to men that desired it there – but there is no doubt but by her voice she is a woman. It begun to grow at about seven years old – and was shaved not above seven months ago, and is now so big as any man almost that ever I saw, I say, bushy and thick. It was a strange sight to me, I confess, and what pleased me mightily. Thence to the Duke's playhouse and saw *Mackbeth*; the King and Court there, and we sat just under them and my Lady Castlemayne, and close to the woman that comes into the pit, a kind of a loose gossip, that pretends to be like her, and is so something. And my wife, by my troth, appeared I think as pretty as any of them, I never thought so much before; and so did Talbot and W. Hewer, as they said, I heard, to one another. The King and Duke of York minded me, and smiled upon me at the handsome woman near me: but it vexed me to see Mall Davis, in the box over his and my Lady Castlemaynes head, look down upon the King and he up to her; and so did my Lady Castlemayne once, to see who it was; but when she saw her, she blushed like fire; which troubled me. The play done, took leave of Tall. who goes into the country this Christmas; and so we home, and there I work at the office late; and so home to supper and to bed.

24. A cold day. Up and to the office, where all the morning alone at the office, nobody meeting, being the Eve of Christmas. At noon home to dinner and then to the office, busy all the afternoon, and at night home to supper; and it being now very cold, and in hopes of a frost, I begin this night to put on a Wastecoate, it being the first winter in my whole memory that ever I stayed till this day before I did so. So to bed, in mighty good humour with my wife, but sad in one thing, and that is for my poor eyes.

25. *Christmas day.* Up, and continued on my waistcoat, the first day this winter. And I to church, where Ald. Backewell coming in

late, I beckoned to his lady to come up to us; who did, with another lady; and after sermon I led her down through the church to her husband and coach – a noble, fine woman, and a good one – and one my wife shall be acquainted with. So home and to dinner alone with my wife, who, poor wretch, sat undressed all day till 10 at night, altering and lacing of a black petticoat – while I by her, making the boy read to me the life of Julius Caesar and Des Cartes book of music – the latter of which I understand not, nor think he did well that writ it, though a most learned man. Then after supper made the boy play upon his lute, which I have not done twice before sence he came to me; and so, my mind in mighty content, we to bed.

27. *Lords day.* Walked to Whitehall and there saw the King at chapel; but stayed not to hear anything, but went to walk in the park with W. Hewer, who was with me; and there, among others, met with Sir G. Downing and walked with him an hour, talking of business and how the late war was managed, there being nobody to take care of it; and telling how when he was in Holland, he had so good spies, that he hath had the keys taken out of De Witts pocket when he was a-bed, and his closet opened and papers brought to him and left in his hands for an [hour], and carried back and laid in the place again and the keys put into his pocket again. He says he hath alway had their most private debates that have been, but between two or three of the chief of them, brought to him in an hour after, and an hour after that hath sent word thereof to the King – but nobody here regarded them. But he tells me the sad news that he is out of all expectations that ever the debts of the Navy will be paid, if the Parliament doth not enable the King to do it by money; all they can hope for to do out of the King's revenue being but to keep our wheels a-going on present services, and, if they can, to cut off the growing Interest – which is a sad story, and grieves me to the heart. So home, my coach coming for me, and there find Balty and Mr. How, who dined with me; and there my wife and I fell out a little about the foulness of the linen of the table, but were friends presently; but she cried, poor heart, which I was troubled for, though I did not give her one hard word.

28. Up, called up by drums and trumpets; these things and boxes having cost me much money this Christmas already, and will do more. My wife down by water to see her mother, and I with W. Hewers all day together in my closet, making some advance in the

settling of my accounts, which have been so long unevened that it troubles me how to set them right, having not the use of my eyes to help me. My wife at night home, and tells me how much her mother prays for me and is troubled for my eyes; and I am glad to have friendship with them, and believe they are truly glad to see their daughter come to live so well as she doth. So spent the night in talking, and so to supper and to bed.

29. Up, and at the office all the morning; and at noon to dinner, and there by a pleasant mistake find my uncle and aunt Wight, and three more of their company, come to dine with me today, thinking that they had been invited; which they were not, but yet we did give them a pretty good dinner, and mighty merry at the mistake. They sat most of the afternoon with us, and then parted; and my wife and I out, thinking to have gone to a play, but it was too far begun; and so to the Change, and there she and I bought several things; and so home, with much pleasure talking, and then to reading; and so to supper and to bed.

31. Blessed be God, the year ends, after some late very great sorrow with my wife by my folly; yet ends, I say, with great mutual peace and content – and likely to last so by my care, who am resolved to enjoy the sweet of it which I now possess, by never giving her like cause of trouble. My greatest trouble is now from the backwardness of my accounts, which I have not seen the bottom of now near these two years, so that I know not in what condition I am in the world; but by the grace of God, as fast as my eyes will give me leave, I will do it.

# ⊱JANUARY⊰

1.   Up, and presented from Capt. Beckford with a noble silver warming-pan, which I am doubtful whether to take or no. Up, and with W. Hewer to the New Exchange, and there he and I to the cabinet-shops to look out, and did agree for a Cabinett to give my wife for a New-year's gift; and I did buy one, cost me 11*l*, which is very pretty, of Walnutt tree, and will come home tomorrow. So back to the Old Exchange and there met my uncle Wight; and there walked and met with the Houblons and talked with them, gentlemen whom I honour mightily. And so to my uncles and met my wife, and there, with W. Hewer, we dined with his family and had a very good dinner, and pretty merry; and after dinner my wife and I with our coach to the King's playhouse and there in a box saw *The Mayden Queene.* Knepp looked upon us, but I durst not show her any countenance and, as well as I could carry myself, I found my wife uneasy there, poor wretch. Therefore I shall avoid that House as much as I can. So back to my aunts and there supped and talked, and stayed pretty late, it being dry and moonshine; and so walked home, and to bed in very good humour.

3.   *Lords day.* Up, and busy all the morning, getting rooms and dinner ready for my guests; which were my uncle and aunt Wight and two of their cousins, and an old woman and Mr. Mills and his wife; and a good dinner and all our plate out, and mighty fine and merry. Dinner done, I out with W. Hewer and Mr. Spong, who by accident came to dine with me, and good talk with him, to Whitehall by coach and there left him, and I with my Brethren to attend the Duke of York. So home and to supper and read; and there my wife and I treating about coming to an allowance to my wife for clothes, and there I, out of my natural backwardness, did hang off; which vexed her and did occasion some discontented talk in bed when we went to bed – and also in the morning; but I did recover all in the morning.

4.   Lay long talking with my wife, and did of my own accord come to an allowance of her of 30*l* a year for all expenses, clothes and everything; which she was mightily pleased with, it being more then ever she asked or expected; and so rose with much content, and up and with W. Hewer to Whitehall, there to speak with Mr. Wren; which I did, about several things of the office entered in my memorandum-books; and so about noon, going homeward with W. Hewer, he and I went in and saw the great tall woman that is to be seen, which is but twenty-one years old and I do easily stand under her arms.

7.   Up and to the office, where busy all the morning; and then at noon home to dinner; and thence, my wife and I to the King's playhouse and there saw *The Island princesse*, the first time I ever saw it; and it is a pretty good play, many good things being in it – and a good scene of a town on fire. We sat in an upper box, and that jade Nell came and sat in the next box, a bold merry slut, who lay laughing there upon people, and with a comrade of hers of the Duke's House that came in to see the play. Thence home and to the office to do some business; and so home to supper and to bed.

9.   Up, and at the office all the morning; and at noon my Lord Brouncker, Mr. Wren, Jos. Williamson, and Capt. Cocke dined with me. And being newly sat down, comes in, by an invitation of Williamson's, the Lieutenant of the Tower – and he brings in with him young Mr. Whore, whose father, of the Tower, I know. And here I had a neat dinner, and all in so good manner and fashion and with so good company and everything to my mind, as I never had more in my life – the company being to my heart's content, and they all well pleased. So continued looking over my books and closet till the evening, and so I to the office and did a good deal of business; and so home to supper and to bed, with my mind mightily pleased with this day's management, as one of the days of my life of fullest content.

10.   *Lords day*. Accidentally, talking of our maids before we rose, I said a little word that did give occasion to my wife to fall out, and she did most vexatiously almost all the morning, but ended most perfect good friends; but the thoughts of the unquiet which her ripping up of old faults will give me did make me melancholy all day long. So about noon, past 12, we rose; and to dinner and then to

977

read and talk, my wife and I alone, after Balty was gone, who came to dine with us; and then in the evening comes Pelling to sit and talk with us, and so to supper and pretty merry discourse; only, my mind a little vexed at the morning's work, but yet without any appearance; so after supper, to bed.

11. Up and with W. Hewer, my guard, to Whitehall, where no Committee of Tanger met; so up and down the House talking with this and that man; and so home, calling at the New Exchange for a book or two to send to Mr. Sheply; and thence home, and thence to the Change and there did a little business; and so walked home to dinner and then abroad with my wife to King's playhouse and there saw *The Joviall Crew*, but ill acted to what it was heretofore in Clun's time and when Lacy could dance. Thence to the New Exchange to buy some things; and among others, my wife did give me my pair of gloves, which by contract she is to give me in her 30*l* a year. Here Mrs. Smith tells us of the great murder thereabouts on Saturday last, of one Capt. Brombrige by one Symons, both of her acquaintance, and hectors that were at play and in drink; the former is killed, and is kinsman to my Lord of Ormond; which made him speak of it with so much passion, as I overheard him this morning, but could not make anything of it till now. But would they would kill more of them. So home; and there at home all the evening, and made Tom to prick down some little conceits and notions of mine in Musique, which doth mightily encourage me to spend some more thoughts about it; for I fancy, upon good reason, that I am in the right way of unfolding the mystery of this matter better then ever yet.

12. This evening I observed my wife mighty dull; and I myself was not mighty fond, because of some hard words she did give me at noon, out of a jealousy at my being abroad this morning; when, God knows, it was upon the business of the office unexpectedly; but I to bed, not thinking but she would come after me; but waking by and by out of slumber, which I usually fall into presently after my coming into the bed, I found she did not prepare to come to bed, but got fresh candles and more wood for her fire, it being mighty cold too. At this being troubled, I after a while prayed her to come to bed, all my people being gone to bed; so after an hour or two, she silent, and I now and then praying her to come to bed, she fell out into a fury, that I was a rogue and false to her; but yet I could

perceive that she was to seek what to say; only, she invented, I believe, a business that I was seen in a hackney coach with the glasses up with Deb, but could not tell the time, nor was sure I was he. I did, as I might truly, deny it, and was mightily troubled; but all would not serve. At last, about one a-clock, she came to my side of the bed and drow my curtaine open, and with the tongs, red hot at the ends, made as if she did design to pinch me with them; at which in dismay I rose up, and with a few words she laid them down and did by little and little, very sillily, let all the discourse fall; and about 2, but with much seeming difficulty, came to bed and there lay well all night, and long in bed talking together with much pleasure; it being, I know, nothing but her doubt of my going out yesterday without telling her of my going which did vex her, poor wretch, last night: and I cannot blame her jealousy, though it doth vex me to the heart.

17. *Lords day*. To church myself, after seeing everything fitted for dinner. And so after church, home; and thither comes Mrs. Batelier and her two daughters to dinner to us, and W. Hewer and his mother, and Mr. Spong. We were very civilly merry, and Mrs. Battelier a very discreet woman, but mighty fond in the stories she tells of her son Will. After dinner, Mr. Spong and I to my closet, there to try my instrument Paralellogramm, which doth mighty well, to my full content; but only a little stiff, as being new. Thence, taking leave of my guests, he and I and W. Hewer to Whitehall; and there parting with Spong, a man that I mightily love for his plainness and ingenuity – I into the Court, and there up and down and spoke with my Lord Bellasses and Peterbrough about the business now in dispute, about my deputing a Treasurer to pay the garrison at Tanger; which I would avoid and not be accountable, and they will serve me therein. Here I met Hugh May, and he brings me to the knowledge of Sir Harry Capell, a Member of Parliament and brother of my Lord of Essex, who hath a great value it seems for me; and they appoint a day to come and dine with me and see my books and papers of the office; which I shall be glad to show them and have opportunity to satisfy them therein. Here, all the discourse is that now the King is of opinion to have the Parliament called, notwithstanding his late resolutions for the proroguing them; so unstable are his counsels, and those about him. So staying late talking in the Queen's side, I away with W. Hewer home; and there to read and talk with my wife, and so to bed.

21.  Up and walked to the Temple, it being frosty; and there took coach, my boy Tom with me, and so to Whitehall to [a] Committee of Tanger; where they met by and by and till twelve at noon upon business; among others, mine, where my desire about being eased of appointing and standing accountable for a Treasurer there was well accepted, and they will think of some other way. Thence in my own coach home, where I find Madam Turner, Dike, and The[oph]. – and had a good dinner for them, and merry; and so carried them to the Duke of York's House (all but Dyke, who went away on other business) and there saw *The Tempest*; but it is but ill done, by Gosnell in lieu of Mall Davis. Thence set them at home, and my wife and I to the Change; and so home, where my wife mighty dogged; and vexed to see it, being mightily troubled of late at her being out of humour, for fear of her discovering any new matter of offence against me; though I am conscious of none, but do hate to be unquiet at home. So late up, silent and not supping, but hearing her utter some words of discontent to me with silence; and so to bed weeping to myself for grief – which she discerning, came to bed and mighty kind; and so, with great joy on both sides, to sleep.

22.  Up and with W. Hewer to Whitehall, and there attended the Duke of York; and thence to the Exchange, in the way calling at several places on occasions relating to my feast tomorrow, on which my mind is now set – as, how to get a new looking-glass for my dining-room, and some pewter and good wine against tomorrow. And so home, where I had the looking-glass set up; cost me 6*l* 7*s*. 6*d*. And here at the Change I met with Mr. Dancre, the famous lanskip painter – with whom I was on Wednesdy; and he took measure of my panels in my dining-room, where in the four I intend to have the four houses of the King – Whitehall, Hampton court, Greenwich – and Windsor. He gone, I to dinner with my people, and so to my office to despatch a little business; and then home to look after things against tomorrow. And among other things, was mightily pleased with the fellow that came to lay the cloth and fold the napkins – which I like so well, as that I am resolved to give him 40*s*. to teach my wife to do it. So to supper, with much kindness between me and my wife, which nowadays is all my care; and so to bed.

23. Up, and again to look after the setting things right against dinner, which I did to very good content; and so to the office, where all the morning till noon, when word brought me to the Board that my Lord Sandwich was come; so I presently rose, leaving the Board ready to rise, and there I found my Lord Sandwich, Peterburgh, and Sir Ch. Herberd; and presently after them come my Lord Hinchingbrooke, Mr. Sidny, and Sir Wm. Godolphin; and after greeting them, and some time spent in talk, dinner was brought up, one dish after another, but a dish at a time; but all so good, but above all things, the variety of wines, and excellent of their kind, I had for them, and all in so good order, that they were mightily pleased, and myself full of content at it; and endeed it was, of a dinner of about six or eight dishes, as noble as any man need to have I think – at least, all was done in the noblest manner that ever I had any, and I have rarely seen in my life better anywhere else – even at the Court. After dinner, my Lords to cards, and the rest of us sitting about them and talking, and looking on my books and pictures and my wife's drawings, which they commend mightily; and mighty merry all day long, with exceeding great content, and so till 7 at night; and so took their leaves, it being dark and foul weather. Thus was this entertainment over, the best of its kind, and the fullest of honour and content to me that ever I had in my life, and shall not easily have so good again. The truth is, I have some fear that I am run behindhand in the world for these last two years, since I have not, or for some time could not, look after my accounts; which doth a little allay my pleasure, but I do trust in God I am pretty well yet, and resolve in a very little time to look into my accounts and see how they stand. So to my wife's chamber, and there supped and got her cut my hair and look my shirt, for I have itched mightily these six or seven days; and when all came to all, she finds that I am louzy, having found in my head and body above 20 lice, little and great; which I wonder at, being more then I have had I believe almost these 20 years. I did think I might have got them from the little boy, but they did presently look him, and found none – so how they came, I know not; but presently did shift myself, and so shall be rid of them, and cut my hayre close to my head. And so, with much content to bed.

24. *Lords day*. To my Lord Keepers at Essex house, where I never was before since I saw my old Lord Essex lie in state when he was dead – a large but ugly house. Here all the Officers of the Navy

attended, and by and by were called in to the King and Cabinet, where my Lord, who was ill, did lie upon the bed, as my old Lord Treasurer or Chancellor heretofore used to. And the business was to know in what time all the King's ships might be repaired fit for service; the Surveyor answered, "In two years and not sooner." I did give them hopes that with supplies of money suitable, we might have them all fit for sea some part of the summer after this. Then they demanded in what time we could set out 40 ships: it was answered, as they might be chosen of the newest and most ready, we could, with money, get 40 ready against May. The King seemed mighty full that we should have money to do all that we desired, and satisfied that without it nothing could be done; and so, without determining anything, we were dismissed; and I doubt all will end in some little fleet this year, and those of hired merchantmen; which would endeed be cheaper to the King, and have many conveniences attending it, more then to fit out the King's own. And this I perceive is designed, springing from Sir W. Coventry's counsel; and the King and most of the Lords, I perceive, full of it, to get the King's fleet all at once in condition for service.

25. Up and to the Committee of Tanger, where little done. And thence I home by my own coach, and busy after dinner at my office, all the afternoon till late at night, that my eyes were tired. So home, and my wife showed me many excellent prints of Nantueil's and others, which W. Batelier hath at my desire brought me out of France of the King's and Colberts and others, most excellent, to my great content. But he hath also brought over a great many gloves perfumed, of several sorts; but all too big by half for her, and yet she will have two or three dozen of them, which vexed me and made me angry; so she at last, to please me, did come to take what alone I thought fit; which pleased me. So after a little supper, to bed – my eyes being very bad.

26. Up and to the office, where busy sitting all the morning. Then to the office again, and then to Whitehall, leaving my wife at Unthankes; and I to the Secretary's chamber, where I was by perticular order this day summoned to attend, as I find Sir D. Gawden also was, and here was the King and the Cabinet met; and being called in among the rest, I find my Lord Privy Seale, whom I never before knew to be in so much play as to be of the Cabinet. The business is that the Algerins have broke the peace with us, by taking

out some Spaniards and goods out of an English ship which had the Duke of York's pass – of which advice came this day; and the King is resolved to stop Sir Tho. Allen's fleet from coming home till he hath amends made him for this affront, and therefore sent for us to advise about victuals to be sent to the fleet, and some more ships – wherein I answered them to what they demanded of me, which was but some few mean things; but I see that on all these occasions they seem to rely most upon me. And so this being done, I took coach and took up my wife, and straight home and there late at the office busy; and then home, and there I find W. Batelier hath also sent the books which I bade him bring me out of France; among others, *L'estat de France, Marnix,* &c., to my great content; and so I was well pleased with them and shall take a time to look them over, as also one or two printed music-books of songs; but my eyes are now too much out of tune to look upon them with any pleasure. Therefore, to supper and to bed.

28. Up and to the office, where all the [morning], also after dinner, and there late, despatching much business; and then home to supper and with my wife, and to get her to read to me. And here I did find that Mr. Sheres hath, beyond his promise, not only got me a candlestick made me, after a form he remembers to have seen in Spain, for keeping the light from one's eyes, but hath got it done in silver, very neat, and designs to give it me in thanks for my paying him his 100*l* in money for his service at Tanger which was ordered him. But I do intend to force him to make me [pay] for it. But I yet, without his direction, cannot tell how it is to be made use of. So after a little reading, to bed.

31. *Lords day.* Lay long, talking with pleasure, and so up, and I to church and there did hear the Doctor that is lately turned Divine, I have forgot his name, I met him a while since at Sir D. Gawden's at dinner – Dr. Waterhouse; he preaches in devout manner of way, not elegant nor very persuasive, but seems to mean well and that he would preach holily, and was mighty passionate against people that make a scoff of religion. And the truth is, I did observe Mrs. Hallworthy smile often, and many others of the parish, who I perceive have known him and were in mighty expectation of hearing him preach, but could not forbear smiling; and she perticularly upon me, and I on her. So home to dinner; and before dinner, to my office to set down my journal for this week, and then

home to dinner – and after dinner, to get my wife and boy, one after another, to read to me – and so spent the afternoon and the evening; and so after supper, to bed. And thus ended this month, with many different days of sadness and mirth, from differences between me and my wife, from her remembrance of my late unkindness to her with Willet, she not being able to forget it, but now and then hath her passionate remembrance of it, as often as prompted to it by any occasion; but this night we are at present very kind. And so ends this month.

# –✣FEBRUARY✣–

1. Up and by water from the Tower to Whitehall, the first time that I have gone to that end of the town by water for two or three months I think, since I kept a coach – which God send propitious to me – but it is a very great convenience. I went to a Committee of Tanger, but it did not meet; and so I meeting Mr. Povy, he and I away to Dancres to speak something touching the pictures I am getting him to make for me. And thence he carried me to Mr. Streeters the famous history-painter over the way, whom I have often heard of but did never see him before; and there I found him and Dr. Wren and several virtuosos looking upon the paintings which he is making for the new Theatre at Oxford; and endeed, they look as they would be very fine, and the rest thinks better then those of Rubens in the Banqueting-house at Whitehall, but I do not so fully think so – but they will certainly be very noble, and I am mightily pleased to have the fortune to see this man and his work, which is very famous – and he a very civil little man and lame, but lives very handsomely. So thence to my Lord Bellasses and met him within; my business only to see a chimney-piece of Dancre's doing in distemper with egg to keep off the glaring of the light, which I must have done for my room; and endeed it is pretty, but I must confess I do not think it is not altogether so beautiful as the oyle pictures; but I will have some of one and some of another. Thence set him down at Little Turnstile, and so I home; and there eat a little dinner, and away with my wife by coach to the King's playhouse, thinking to have seen *The Heyresse*, first acted on Saturday last; but when we came thither, we find no play there – Kinaston, that did act a part therein in abuse to Sir Charles Sidly, being last night

exceedingly dry-beaten with sticks by two or three that assaulted him – so as he is mightily bruised, and forced to keep his bed. So we to the Duke of York's playhouse, and there saw *Shee Would if She Could.* And so home and to my office to business, and then to supper and to bed.

[3.] So up, and to the office till noon and then home to a little dinner; and thither again till night, mighty busy, to my great content doing a great deal of business; and so home to supper and to bed – I finding this day that I may be able to do a great deal of business by dictateing, if I do not read myself or write, without spoiling my eyes, I being very well in my eyes after a great day's work.

4. Up and at the office all the morning. At noon, home with my people to dinner; and then after dinner comes Mr. Spong to see me, and brings me my parrallogram in better order then before, and two or three drafts of the port of Brest, to my great content: and I did call Mr. Gibson to take notice of it, who is very much pleased therewith. And it seems this is not, as Mr. Sheres would the other day have persuaded me, the same as a Protractor – which doth so much the more make me value it; but of itself it is a most useful instrument. Thence out with my wife and him, and carried him to a instrument-maker's shop in Chancery lane that was once a prentice of Greatorex's, but the master was not within; and there he showed me a paralellogram in brass, which I like so well that I will buy, and therefore bid it be made clean and fit for me. And so to my cousin Turner's and there just spoke with The[oph]., the mother not being at home; and so to the New Exchange and thence home to my letters; and so home to supper and to bed.

6. Up and to the office, where all the morning, and thence after to dinner to the King's playhouse and there in an upper box (where came in Coll. Poynton and Doll Stacy, who is very fine, and by her wedding ring I suppose he hath married her at last) did see *The Moore of Venice*, but ill acted in most parts; Moone (which did a little surprize me) not acting Iago's part by much so well as Clun used to do, nor another Hart's, which was Cassio's; nor endeed Burt doing the Moor's so well as I once thought he did. Thence home, and just at Holburne Conduit the bolt broke that holds the fore-wheels to the perch, and so the horses went away with them and left the

coachman and us; but being near our coach-makers, and we staying in a little ironmonger's shop, we were presently supplied with another; and so home and there to my letters at the office, and so to supper and to bed.

7. *Lords day.* My wife mighty peevish in the morning about my lying unquietly a-nights, and she will have it that it is a late practice, from my evil thoughts in my dreams; and I do often find that in my dreams she doth lay her hand upon my cockerel to observe what she can. And mightily she is troubled about it, but all blew over; and I up and to church, and so home to dinner, where she in a worse fit, which lasted all afternoon, and shut herself up in her closet; and I mightily grieved and vexed, and could not get her to tell me what ayled her, or to let me into her closet; but at last she did, where I found her crying on the ground, and I could not please her; but I did at last find that she did plainly expound it to me: it was that she did believe me false to her with Jane, and did rip up three or four most silly circumstances, of her not rising till I came out of my chamber and her letting me thereby see her dressing herself, and that I must needs go into her chamber and was naught with her; which was so silly, and so far from truth, that I could not be troubled at it, though I could not wonder at her being troubled, if she had these thoughts. And therefore she would lie from me, and caused sheets to be put on in the blue room and would have Jane to lie with her, lest I should come to her.

10. Up, and with my wife and W. Hewer; she set us down at Whitehall, where the Duke of York was gone a-hunting; and so after I had done a little business there, I to my wife, and with her to the Plasterer's at Charing cross that casts heads and bodies in plaster, and there I had my whole face done; but I was vexed first to be forced to daub all my face over with Pomatum, but it was pretty to feel how saft and easily it is done on the face, and by and by, by degrees, how hard it becomes, that you cannot break it, and sits so close that you cannot pull it off, and yet so easy that it is as soft as a pillow, so safe is everything where many parts of the body do bear alike. Thus was the mold made; but when it came off, there was little pleasure in it as it looks in the mold, nor any resemblance whatever there will be in the figure when I come to see it cast off – which I am to call for a day or two hence; which I shall long to see. Thence to Hercules Pillars, and there my wife and W. Hewer and I

dined. So to Whitehall, where I stayed till the Duke of York came from hunting, which he did by and by; and when dressed, did come out to dinner, and there I waited; and he did tell me that tomorrow was to be the great day that the business of the Navy would be discoursed of before the King and his Caball; and that he must stand on his guard and did design to have had me in readiness by, but upon second thoughts did think it better to let it alone. But they are now upon entering into the Æconimicall part of the Navy. Here he dined, and did mightily magnify his Sawce which he did then eat with everything, and said it was the best universal sauce in the world – it being taught him by the Spanish Imbassador – made of some parsley and a dry toast, beat in a mortar together with vinegar, salt, and a little pepper. He eats it with flesh or fowl or fish. And then he did now mightily commend some new sort of wine lately found out, called Navarr wine; which I tasted, and is I think good wine; but I did like better the notion of the Sawce and by and by did taste it, and liked it mightily. After dinner I did what I went for, which was to get his consent that Balty might hold his muster-maister's place by deputy, in his new imployment which I design for him about the Storekeeper's accounts; which the Duke of York did grant me, and I was mighty glad of it. Thence to the office, and there very busy and did much business till late at night; and so home to supper, and with great pleasure to bed.

12. Up and my wife with me to Whitehall, and Tom, and there she sets us down; and there to wait on the Duke of York, with the rest of us, at the Robes; where the Duke of York did tell us that the King would have us prepare a draft of the present Administracion of the Navy, and what it was in the late times – in order to his being able to distinguish between the good and the bad; which I shall do, but to do it well will give me a great deal of trouble. Here we showed him Sir J. Mennes's propositions about balancing store-keepers accounts; and I did show him Hosiers, which did please him mightily, and he will have it showed the Council and King anon, to be put in practice.

14. *Lords day*. Up and by coach to Sir W. Coventry; and there, he taking physic, I with him all the morning, full of very good discourse of the Navy and public matters, to my great content; wherein I find him doubtful that all will be bad; and for his part, he tells me he takes no more care for anything more then in the

Treasury; and that that being done, he goes to cards and other delights, as plays, and in summer time to Bowles; but here he did show me two or three old books of the Navy of my Lord Northumberland's times, which he hath taken many good notes out of for justifying the Duke of York and us in many things wherein perhaps precedent will be necessary to produce – which did give me great content.

15.  To the Plasterers and there saw the figure of my face taken from the Mold; and it is most admirably like, and I will have another made before I take it away; and therefore I away and to the Temple, and thence to my cousin Turner's; where, having the last night been told by her that she had drawn me for her Valentine, I did this day call at the New Exchange and bought her a pair of green silk stockings and garters and shoe-strings, and two pair of Jessimy-gloves, all coming to about 28s. – and did give them her this noon. At the Change, I did at my bookseller's shop accidentally fall into talk with Sir Sam. Tuke about Trees and Mr. Evelings garden; and I do find him, I think, a little conceited, but a man of very fine discourse as any I ever heard almost – which I was mighty glad of. I dined at my cousin Turner's, and after dinner took up my cousin Turner, and to my cousin Roger's lodgings and there find him pretty well again, and his wife mighty kind and merry and did make mighty much of us; and I believe he is married to a very good woman. Here was also Bab and Betty,[1] who have not their clothes yet, and therefore cannot go out; otherwise I would have had them abroad tomorrow; but the poor girls mighty kind to us, and we must show them kindness also.

16.  Up and to the office, where all the morning, my head full of business of the office now at once on my hand; and so at noon home to dinner, where I find some things of W. Batelier's come out of France; among which, some clothes for my wife, wherein she is likely to lead me to the expense of so much money as vexed me; but I seemed so, more then I at this time was, only to prevent her taking too much – and she was mighty calm under it. But I was mightily pleased with another picture of the King of France's head, of Nantueil's, bigger then the other which he brought over, that

1. Roger Pepys's daughters by a previous marriage, now on a visit to London. They stayed with the diarist.

pleases me infinitely. And so to the office, where busy all the afternoon, though my eyes mighty bad with the light of the candles last night; which was so great as to make my eyes sore all this day, and doth teach me, by a manifest experiment, that it is only too much light that doth make my eyes sore. Nevertheless, with the help of my Tube, and being desirous of easing my mind of five or six days Journall, I did adventure to write it down from ever since this day sennit, and I think without hurting my eyes any more then they were before; which was very much. And so home to supper and to bed.

17. Going to Whitehall I had pleasant *rancontre* of a lady in mourning, that by the little light I had seemed handsome; I passing by her, I did observe she looked back again and again upon me, I suffering her to go before, and it being now duske. I observed she went into the little passage towards the privy water-gate, and I fallowed but missed her; but coming back again, I observed she returned and went to go out of the Court. I fallowed her, and took occasion in the new passage now built, where the walke is to be, to take her by the hand to lead her through; which she willingly accepted, and I led her to the great gate and there left her, she telling me of her own accord that she was going as far as Charing cross; but my boy was at the gate, and so yo durst not go out con her – which vexed me; and my mind (God forgive me) did run après her todo the night, though I have reason to thank God, and so I do now, that I was not tempted to go further.

19. Up, and after seeing the girls, who lodged in our bed with their Mayd Martha (who hath been their father's maid these twenty years and more), I with Lord Brouncker to Whitehall, where all of us waited on the Duke of York; and after our usual business done, W. Hewer and I to look my wife at the Black Lion, Mercer's, but she is gone home; and so I home and there dined, and W. Battelier and W. Hewer with us; and all the afternoon I at the office while the young people went to see Bedlam; and at night home to them to supper, and pretty merry; only, troubled with a great cold at this time – and my eyes very bad, ever since Monday night last that the light of the candles spoiled me. So to bed. This morning, among other things, talking with Sir W. Coventry, I did propose to him my putting in to serve in Parliament, if there should, as the world begins to expect, be a new one chose. He likes it mightily, both for

the King's and service's sake, and the Duke of York's, and will propound it to the Duke of York. And I confess, if there be one, I would be glad to be in.

20. Up, and all the morning at the office, and then home to dinner; and after dinner, out with my wife and my two girls to the Duke of York's House and there saw *The Gratefull Servant*, a pretty good play, and which I have forgot that ever I did see. And thence with them to Mrs. Gotiers, the Queen's tire-woman's, for a pair of locks for my wife (she is a oldish French woman, but with a pretty hand as most I have seen); and so home and to supper, W. Battelier and W. Hewer with us; and so my cold being great, and the greater by my having left my coat at my tailor's tonight and come home in a thinner that I borrowed there, I went to bed before them, and slept pretty well.

21. *Lords day*. Up, and with my wife and two girls to church, they very fine; and so home, where comes my Cosen Roger and his wife (I having sent for them) to dine with us, and there comes in by chance also Mr. Sheply, who is come to town with my Lady Paulina, who is desperately sick and is gone to Chelsy to the old house where my Lord himself was once sick – where I doubt my Lord means to visit her, more for young Mrs. Beck's sake then for hers. Here we dined with W. Battelier and W. Hewer with us (these two girls making it necessary that they be always with us, for I am not company light enough to be always merry with them); and so sat talking all the afternoon, and then Sheply went away first, and then to my cousin Roger and his wife; and so I to my office to write down my journall, and so home to my chamber to do a little business there, my papers being in mighty disorder and likely so to continue while these girls are with us. In the evening comes W. Batelier and his sisters and supped and talked with us, and so spent the evening, myself being somewhat out of order because of my eyes, which have never been well since last Sundy's reading at Sir W. Coventry's chamber. And so after supper to bed.

23. Up, and to the office, where all the morning. And then home and put a mouthful of victuals in my mouth; and by a hackney coach fallowed my wife and girls, who are gone by 11 a-clock, thinking to have seen a new play at the Duke of York's House; but I do find them staying at my tailor's, the play not being today, and

therefore I now took them to Westminster Abbey and there did show them all the tombs very finely, having one with us alone (there being other company this day to see the tombs, it being Shrove Tuesday); and here we did see, by perticular favour, the body of Queen Katherine of Valois, and had her upper part of her body in my hands. And I did kiss her mouth, reflecting upon it that I did kiss a Queen, and that this was my birthday, 36 years old, that I did first kiss a Queen. Thence to the Duke of York's playhouse, and there finding the play begun, we homeward to the glass-house and there showed my cousins the making of glass, and had several things made with great content; and among others, I had one or two singing-glasses made, which make an echo to the voice, the first that ever I saw; but so thin that the very breath broke one or two of them. So home, and thence to Mr. Batelier's, where we supped, and had a good supper; and here was Mr. Gumbleton, and after supper some fiddles and so to dance; but my eyes were so out of order that I had little pleasure this night at all, though I was glad to see the rest merry. And so about midnight home and to bed.

24.    Lay long in bed, both being sleepy and my eyes bad, and myself having a great cold, so as I was hardly able to speak; but however, by and by up and to the office; and at noon home with my people to dinner; and then I to the office again and there till the evening, doing of much business; and at night my wife sends for me to W. Hewer's lodging, where I find two most [fine] chambers of his, so finely furnished and all so rich and neat, that I was mightily pleased with him and them; and here only my wife and I and the two girls, and had a mighty neat dish of custards and tarts, and good drink and talk; and so away home to bed, with infinite content at this his treat, for it was mighty pretty and everything mighty rich.

25.    All the morning at the office; at noon home and eat a bit myself, and then fallowed my wife and girls to the Duke of York's House and there before one, but the house infinite full; where by and by the King and Court comes, it being a new play, or an old one new-vamp[ed] by Shadwell, called *The Royall Shepheardesse*; but the silliest for words and design, and everything, that ever I saw in my whole life – there being nothing in the world pleasing in it but a good martiall dance of pikemen, where Harris and another do handle their pikes in a dance to admiration – but never less satisfied with a play in my life. Thence to the office I, and did a little business;

and so home to supper with my girls, and pretty merry; only my eyes, which continue very bad, and my cold, that I cannot speak at all, do trouble me.

27. Up and at the office all the morning, where I could speak but a little. At noon home to dinner, and all the afternoon till night busy at the office again, where forced to speak low and dictate. But that that troubles me most is my eyes, which are still mighty bad, night and day. And so home at night to talk and sup with my cousins; and so all of us in mighty good humour to bed.

# –❊MARCH❊–

1. Up and to Whitehall to the Committee of Tanger, but it did not meet. But here I do hear first that my Lady Paulina Montagu did die yesterday; at which I went to my Lord's lodgings, but he is shut up with sorrow and so not to be spoken with; and therefore I returned and to Westminster hall, where I have not been I think in some months; and here the Hall was very full, the King having, by commission to some Lords, this day prorogued the Parliament till the 19th of October next; at which I am glad, hoping to have time to go over to France this year. But I was most of all surprised this morning by my Lord Bellasses, who by appointment met me at Auditor Wood's at the Temple and tells me of a Duell designed between the Duke of Buckingham and my Lord Halifax or Sir W. Coventry – the challenge being carried by Harry Savill, but prevented by my Lord Arlington and the King told of it. And this was all the discourse at Court this day. But I meeting Sir W. Coventry in the Duke of York's chamber, he would not own it to me, but told me that he was a man of too much peace to meddle with fighting; and so it rested.

2. Up and at the office till noon, when home; and there I find my company come – *viz*, Madam Turner, Dike, The[oph]. and Betty Turner, and Mr. Bellwood, formerly their father's clerk but now set up for himself, a conceited silly fellow but one they make mightily of – my Cosen Roger Pepys and his wife and two daughters. And I had a noble dinner for them as I almost ever had, and mighty merry; and perticularly, myself pleased with looking

on Betty Turner – who is might pretty. After dinner we fell one to one talk, and another to another, and looking over my house and closet and things, and The[oph]. Turner to write a letter to a lady in the country, in which I did now and then put in half a dozen words, and sometimes five or six lines, and then she as much, and made up a long and good letter, she being mighty witty really, though troublesome-humoured with it. And thus till night, that our music came and the office ready, and candles; and also W. Batelier and his sister Susan came, and also Will How and two gentlemen more, strangers, which at my request yesterday he did bring to dance, called Mr. Ireton and Mr. Starkey; we fell to dancing and continued, only with intermission for a good supper, till 2 in the morning, the music being Greeting and another most excellent violin and Theorbo, the best in town; and so, with mighty mirth and pleased with their dancing of Jiggs afterward, several of them, and among others Betty Turner, who did it mighty prettily; and lastly, W. Batelier's blackmore and blackmore-maid, and then to a country-dance again; and so broke up with extraordinary pleasure, as being one of the days and nights of my life spent with the greatest content, and that which I can but hope to repeat again a few times in my whole life. This done, we parted, the strangers home, and I did lodge my cousin Pepys and his wife in our blue chamber – my cousin Turner, her sister, and The[oph]. in our best chamber – Babb, Betty, and Betty Turner in our own chamber; and myself and my wife in the maid's bed, which is very good – our maids in the coachman's bed – the coachman with the boy in his settle-bed; and Tom where he uses to lie; and so I did to my great content lodge at once in my house, with great ease, fifteen, and eight of them strangers of quality. My wife this day put on first her French gown, called a *Sac*, which becomes her very well, brought her over by W. Batelier.

4.  Up, and a while at the office; but thinking to have Mr. Povy's business today at the Committee for Tanger, I left the Board and away to Whitehall; where in the first court I did meet Sir Jere. Smith, who did tell me that Sir W. Coventry was just now sent to the tower about the business of his challenging the Duke of Buckingham, and so was also Harry Savill to the Gate-house – which, as a gentleman and of the Duke of York's bed-chamber, I heard afterward that the Duke of York is mightily incensed at, and doth appear very high to the King that he might not be sent thither,

but to the Tower – this being done only in contempt to him. This news of Sir W. Coventry did strike me to the heart; and with reason, for by this and my Lord of Ormond's business, I do doubt that the Duke of Buckingham will be so fleshed, that he will not stop at anything but be forced to do anything now, as thinking it not safe to end here; and Sir W. Coventry being gone, the King will have never a good counsellor, nor the Duke of York any sure friend to stick to him – nor any good many will be left to advise what is good. So meeting with my Lord Bellasses, he told me the perticulars of this matter; that it arises about a quarrel which Sir W. Coventry had with the Duke of Buckingham about a design between him and Sir Rob. Howard to bring him into a play at the King's House. Being very much troubled at this, I away by coach homeward, and directly to the Tower, where I find him in one Mr. Bennet's house, in the Bricke tower – where I find him busy with my Lord Halifax and his brother; so I would not stay to interrupt them, but only to give him comfort and offer my service to him; and so I parted, with great content that I had so earlily seen him there; and so going out, did meet Sir Jer. Smith going to meet me, who had newly been with Sir W. Coventry; and so he and I by water to Redriffe, and so walked to Deptford, where I have not been I think these twelve months; and there to the Treasurer's house, where the Duke of York is, and his Duchesse; and there we find them at dinner in the great room, unhung, and there was with them my Lady Duchess of Monmouth, the Countess of Falmouth, Castlemayne, Henrietta Hide my Lady Hinchingbrooke's sister, and my Lady Peterbrough. And after dinner, Sir Jer. Smith and I were invited down to dinner with some of the Maids of Honour; *viz.*, Mrs. Ogle, Blake, and Howard (which did me good to have the honour to dine with and look on); and the Mother of the Maids, and Mrs. Howard, the mother of the Maid of Honour of that name, and the Duke's housekeeper here. Here was also Monsieur Blancfort, Sir Rd. Powell, Coll. Villers, Sir Jona. Trelany, and others. And here drank most excellent and great variety and plenty of wines, more then I have drank at once these seven years, but yet did me no great hurt. Having dined and very merry, and understanding by Blancfort how angry the Duke of York was about their offering to send Savill to the Gate-house among the rogues and talking of others as their enemies – they parted; and so we up, and there I did find the Duke of York and Duchess with all the great ladies, sitting upon a carpet on the ground, there being no chairs, playing at "I love my love with an A because he is so and so; and I hate him with an A because of this and that;" and some of them, but perticularly the Duchess herself and my Lady Castlemaine, were very witty. This done, they took barge, and I with Sir J. Smith to Capt. Cox's and there to talk, and left them and other company to drink while I slunk out to Bagwells and there saw her and her mother and our late maid Nell, who cried for joy to see me; but I had no time for pleasure there nor could stay; but after drinking, I back to the yard, having a month's mind *para* have had a bout with Nell – which I believe I could have had – and may another time. So to Cox's and thence walked with Sir J. Smith back to Redriffe, and so by water home; and there my wife mighty angry for my absence and fell mightily out; but not being certain of anything, but think[s] only that Pierce or Knepp were there, and did ask me, and I perceive the boy, many questions, but I did answer her; and so after much ado, did go to bed and lie quiet all night; but had another bout with me in the morning, but I did make shift to quiet her; but yet she was not fully satisfied, poor wretch, in her mind, and thinks much at my taking so much pleasure from her; which endeed is a fault, though I did not design or foresee it when I went.

6. Up and to the office, where all the morning. Only before the office, I stepped to Sir W. Coventry at the Tower and there had a great deal of discourse with him – among others, of the King's putting him out of the Council yesterday – with which he is well contented, as with what else they can strip him of – he telling me, and so hath long, that he is weary and surfeited of business. But he joins with me in his fears that all will go to naught as matters are now managed. He told me the matter of the play that was intended for his abuse – wherein they foolishly and sillily bring in two tables like that which he hath made, with a round hole in the middle, in his closet, to turn himself in; and he is to be in one of them as maister, and Sir J. Duncomb in the other as his man or imitator – and their discourse in those tables, about the disposing of their books and papers, very foolish. But that that he is offended with, is his being made so contemptible, as that any should dare to make a gentleman a subject for the mirth of the world; and that therefore he had told Tom Killigrew that he should tell his actors, whoever they were, that did offer at anything like representing him, that he would not complain to my Lord Chamberlain, which was too weak, nor get him beaten, as Sir Ch. Sidly is said to do, but that he would cause his

nose to be cut. This day, my wife made it appear to me that my late entertainment this week cost me above 12*l*, a expense which I am almost ashamed of, though it is but once in a great while, and is the end for which in the most part we live, to have such a merry day once or twice in a man's life.

7. *Lords day*. Up and to the office, busy till church time; and then to church, where a dull sermon; and so home to dinner all alone with my wife, and then to even my journall to this day; and then to the Tower to see Sir W. Coventry, who had H. Jermin and a great many more with him, and more, while I was there, came in; so that I do hear that there was not less then 60 coaches there yesterday and the other day – which I hear also, that there is a great exception taken at by the King and the Duke of Buckingham, but it cannot be helped.

9. Up, and to the tower and there find Sir W. Coventry alone, writing down his journall, which he tells me he now keeps of the material things; [upon] which I told him, and he is the only man that I ever told it to I think, that I have kept it most strictly these eight or ten years; and I am sorry almost that I told it him – it not being necessary, nor may be convenient to have it known. Here he showed me the petition he had sent to the King by my Lord Keeper; which was not to desire any admittance to imployment, but submitting himself therein humbly to his Majesty; but prayed the removal of his displeasure and that he might be set free. But by this discourse he was pleased to take occasion to show me and read to me his account, which he hath kept by him under his own hand, of all his discourse and the King's answers to him upon the great business of my Lord Clarendon. And really, I was mighty proud to be privy to this great transaction, it giving me great conviction of the noble nature and ends of Sir W. Coventry in it, and considerations in general of the consequences of great men's actions, and the uncertainty of their estates, and other very serious considerations.

11. Up and to Sir W. Coventry to the Tower, where I walked and talked with him an hour alone, from one good thing to another; who tells me that he hears that the Commission is gone down to the King with a blank to fill for his place in the Treasury; and he believes it will be filled with one of our Treasurers of the Navy, but which

he knows not, but he believes it will be Osborne. We walked down to the Stone Walk, which is called, it seems, "My Lord of Northumberland's Walk," being paved by some of that title that was prisoner there; and at the end of it there is a piece of Iron upon the wall with his armes upon it, and holes to put in a peg for every turn that they make upon that walk. So away to the office, where busy all morning, and so to dinner; and so very busy all the afternoon at my office late, and then home, tired, to supper, with content with my wife; and so to bed – she pleasing me, though I dare not own it, that she hath hired a chambermaid; but she, after many commendations, told me that she had one great fault, and that was that she was very handsome; at which I made nothing, but let her go on; but many times tonight she took occasion to discourse of her handsomeness and the danger she was in by taking her, and that she did doubt yet whether it would be fit for her to take her. But I did assure her of my resolutions to having nothing to do with her maids, but in myself I was glad to have the content to have a handsome one to look on.

13. Up and to the Tower to see Sir W. Coventry, and with him talking of business of the Navy all alone an hour, he taking physic. And so away to the office, where all the morning; and then home to dinner with my people and so to the office again. And there all the afternoon till night, when comes by mistake my cousin Turner and her two daughters (which loves such freaks) to eat some anchoves and ham of bacon with me, by mistake instead of noon at dinner, when I expected them; but however, I had done my business before they came and so was in good humour enough to be with them; and so home to them to supper, and pretty merry – being pleased to see Betty Turner, which hath something mighty pretty. But that which put me in good humour, both at noon and night, is the fancy that I am this day made a Captain of one of the King's ships. Mr. Wren having this day sent me the Duke of York's commission to be Captain of the *Jerzy*, in order to my being of a Court Martiall for examining the loss of the *Defyance*, and other things – which doth give me occasion of much mirth, and may be of some use to me; at least, I shall get a little money by it for the time I have it, it being designed that I must really be a Captain to be able to sit in this Court. They stayed till about 8 at night, and then away; and my wife to read to me, and then to bed in mighty good humour, but for my eyes.

14.   *Lords day.* Before I went from my office this night, I did tell Tom my resolution not to keep him after Jane was gone, but shall do well by him – which pleases him; and I think he will presently marry her and go away out of my house with her.

15.   Up, and by water with W. Hewer to the Temple; and thence to the Chapel of Rolles, where I made enquiry for several Rolles and was soon informed in the manner of it; and so spent the whole morning with W. Hewer, he taking little notes in shorthand, while I hired a clerk there to read to me about twelve or more several rolls which I did call for: and it was great pleasure to me to see the method wherein their Rolles are kept; that when the Master of the Office, one Mr. Case, doth call for them (who is a man that I have heretofore known by coming to my Lord Sandwiches) he did most readily turn to them. At noon they shut up, and W. Hewer and I did walk to the Cocke at the end of Suffolke street, where I never was, a great ordinary, mightily cried up, and there bespoke a pullet; which while dressing, he and I walked into St. James's park, and thence back and dined very handsome, with a good Soup and a pullet, for 4*s.*–6*d.* the whole. Thence back to the Rolles and did a little more business; and so by water from Whitehall, thither I went to speak with Mr. Williamson (that if he hath any papers relating to the Navy, I might see them, which he promises me); and so by water home, with great content for what I have this day found, having got almost as much as I desire of the history of the Navy from 1618 to 1642, when the King and Parliament fell out. So home, and did get my wife to read, and so to supper and to bed.

16.   Up and to the office, after having visited Sir W. Coventry at the Tower and walked with him upon the Stone Walk alone, till other company came to him, and had very good discourse with him. At noon home, where my wife and Jane gone abroad, and Tom, in order to their buying of things for their wedding; which, upon my discourse the last night, is now resolved to be done upon the 26 of this month, the day of my solemnity for my cutting of the stone, when my Cosen Turner must be with us. My wife therefore not at dinner; and in comes to me Mr. Evelin of Deptford, a worthy good man, and dined with me, but a bad dinner; who is grieved for, and speaks openly to me his thoughts of the times and our ruin approaching, and all by the folly of the King.

18.   Up, and to see Sir W. Coventry, and walked with him a good
while in the Stone Walk; and brave discourse about my Lord
Chancellor and his ill managements – and mistakes – and several
things of the Navy; and thence to the office, where we sat all the
morning; and so home to dinner, where my wife mighty finely
dressed, by a maid that she hath taken and is to come to her when
Jane goes, and the same she the other day told me of to be so
handsome. I therefore longed to see her, but did not till after dinner,
that my wife and I going by coach, she went with us to Holburne,
where we set her down. She is a mighty proper maid and pretty
comely, but so-so – but hath a most pleasing tone of a voice and
speaks handsomely, but hath most great hands, and I believe ugly,
but very well dressed in good clothes; and the maid I believe will
please me well enough. So my wife and I to Hide park, the first time
we were there this year, or ever in our own coach – where with
mighty pride rode up and down; and many coaches there, and I
thought our horses and coach as pretty as any there, and observed
so to be by others. Here stayed till night, and so home and to the
office, where busy late; and so home to supper and to bed with great
content, but much business in my head of the office, which troubles
me.

20.   Up and to the Tower to W. Coventry, and there walked with
him alone on the Stone Walk till company came to him; and there
about the business of the Navy discoursed with him, and about my
Lord Chancellor and Treasurer; that they were against the war at
first – declaring, as wise men and statesmen at first to the King, that
they thought it fit to have a war with them at some time or other,
but that it ought not to be till we found the Crowns of Spain and
France together by the eares; the want of which did ruin our Warr.
But then he told me, that a great deal before the Warr, my Lord
Chancellor did speak of a Warr with some heat, as a thing to be
desired, and did it upon a belief that he could with his speeches
make the Parliament give what money he pleased, and do what he
would or would make the King desire; but he found himself soon
deceived of that, the Parliament having a long time before his
removal been cloyed with his speeches and good words – and were
come to hate him. Sir W. Coventry did tell me it, as the wisest thing
that ever was said to the King by any statesman of his time, and it
was by my Lord Treasurer that is dead, whom I find he takes for a
very great statesman; that when the King did show himself forward

for passing the Act of Indemnity, he did advise the King that he would hold his hand in doing it, till he had got his power restored that had been diminished by the late times, and his revenue settled in such a manner as he might depend on himself, without resting upon Parliaments, and then pass it. But my Lord Chancellor, who thought he could have the command of Parliaments for ever, because for the King's sake they were awhile willing to grant all the King desire[d], did press for its being done; and so it was, and the King from that time able to do nothing with the Parliament almost. Thence to the office, where sat all the forenoon; and then home to dinner and so to the office, where late busy; and so home, mightily pleased with the news brought me tonight, that the King and the Duke of York are come back this afternoon to town, and no sooner come but a Warrant was sent to the Tower for the releasing Sir W. Coventry.

21. Met with Mr. May, who tells me the story of his being put by Sir John Denham's place (of Surveyor of the King's Works, who it seems is lately dead) by the unkindness of the Duke of Buckingham, who hath brought in Dr. Wren – though he tells me he hath been his servant for twenty years together, in all his wants and dangers, saving him from want of bread by his care and management, and with a promise of having his help in his advancement, and an engagement under his hand for 1000*l* not yet paid; and yet the Duke of Buckingham is so ungrateful as to put him by – which is an ill thing – though Dr. Wren is a worthy man. But he tells me that the King is kind to him, and hath promised him a pension of 300*l* a year out of the Works, which will be of more content to him then the place, which under their present wants of money is a place that disobliges most people, being not able to do what they desire to their lodgings.

23. Up and to my office to do a little business there; and so my things being all ready, I took coach with Commissioner Middleton, Capt. Tinker and Mr. Huchinson, a hackney coach, and over the bridge, and so out towards Chatham; and dined at Dartford, where we stayed an hour or two, it being a cold day; and so on and got to Chatham just at night, with very good discourse by the way; but mostly of matters or religion, wherein Huchinson his vein lies. After supper we fell to talk of spirits and apparitions, whereupon many pretty perticular stories were told, so as to make me almost

afeared to lie alone, but for shame I could not help it; and so to bed, and being sleepy, fell soon to rest and so rested well.

24. Up and walked about in the garden, and I find that Mrs. Tooker hath not any of her daughters here as I expected. And so walked to the yard, leaving Middleton at the pay; and there I only walked up and down the yard, and then to the Hill house and there did give order for the coach to be made ready and got Mr. Gibson, whom I carried with me, to go with me and Mr. Coney the surgeon towards Maydston, which I had a mighty mind to see; and took occasion in my way, at St. Margetts, to pretend to call to see Capt. Allen, to see whether Mrs. Jowles his daughter was there; and there his wife came to the door, he being at London, and through a window I spied Jowles, but took no notice of her; but made excuse till night, and then promised to come and see Mrs. Allen again; and so away, it being a mighty cold and windy, but clear day, and had the pleasure of seeing the Medway running, winding up and down mightily, and a very fine country; and I went a little way out of the way to have visited Sir Jo. Bankes, but he at London; but here I had a sight of his seat and house, the outside, which is an old abbey just like Hinchingbrooke, and as good at least, and mighty finely placed by the river; and he keeps the grounds about it, and walls and the house, very handsome – I was mightily pleased with the sight of it. Thence to Maydstone, which I had a mighty mind to see, having never been there; and walked all up and down the town, and up to the top of the steeple and had a noble view, and then down again and in the town did see an old man beating of Flax, and did step into the barn and give him money and saw that piece of husbandry, which I never saw, and it is very pretty. In the street also, I did buy and send to our Inne, the Bell, a dish of fresh fish; and so having walked all round the town, and find it very pretty as most towns I ever saw, though not very big, and people of good fashion in it, we to our Inne to dinner, and had a good dinner; and after dinner a barber came to me and there trimmed me, that I might be clean against night to go to Mrs. Allen; and so staying till about 4 a-clock, we set out, I alone in the coach going and coming; and in our way back, I light out of the way to see a Saxon monument, as they say, of a king; which is three stones staying upright and a great round one lying on them, of great bigness, although not so big as those on Salsbury-plain, but certainly it is a thing of great antiquity, and I mightily glad to see it; it is near to Alesford, where Sir Jo. Bankes

lives. So homeward and stopped again at Capt. Allen's and there light, and sent the coach and Gibson home and I and Cony stayed; and there comes to us Mrs. Jowles, who is a very fine proper lady as most I know, and well dressed. Here was also a gentleman, one Maj. Manly, and his wife, neighbours; and here we stayed and drank and talked, and set Cony and him to play while Mrs. Jowles and I to talk, and there had all our old stories up; and there I had the liberty to salute her often and pull off her glove, where her hand mighty moist; and she mighty free in kindness to me, and yo do not at all doubt but I might have had todo that yo would have desired de ella had I had time to have carried her to Cobham; as she, upon my proposing it, was willing to go, for ella is a whore, that is certain, but a very brave and comely one. Here was a pretty cousin of hers came in to supper also, of a great fortune, daughter-in-law to this Manly; mighty pretty, but had now such a cold, she could not speak.

Here mightily pleased with Mrs. Jowles, and did get her to the street-door in the dark, and there toca su breasts and besar her without any force, and creo that I might have hecho algo else; but it was not time nor place. Here stayed till almost 12 at night; and then with a lanthorn from thence walked over the fields, as dark as pitch, and mighty cold and snow, to Chatham, and Mr. Cony with great kindness with me; and there all in bed before I came home, and so I presently to bed.

25. Up, and by and by, about 8 a-clock, comes Rere-Adm. Kempthorne and seven captains more by the Duke of York's order, as we expected, to hold the Court Martiall about the loss of the *Defyance*; and so presently, we by boat to the *Charles*, which lies over against Upnor Castle, and there we fell to the business; and there I did manage the business, the Duke of York having by special order directed them to take the assistance of Commissioner Middleton and me, forasmuch as there might be need of advice in what relates to the government of the ship in Harbour; and so I did lay the law open to them, and rattle the Maister-Attendants out of their wits almost, and I made the trial last till 7 at night, not eating a bit all the day; only, when we had done examination and I given my thoughts that the neglect of the gunner of the ship was as great as I thought any neglect could be, which might by the law deserve death, but Commissioner Middleton did declare that he was against giving the sentence of death, we withdrew, as not being of the

Court, and so left them to do what they pleased; and while they were debating it, the bosun of the ship did bring us out of the Kettle a piece of hot salt beef and some brown bread and brandy; and there we did make a little meal, but so good as I never would desire to eat better meat while I live – only, I would have cleaner dishes. By and by they had done, and called us down from the quarter-deck; and there we find they do sentence that the gunner of the *Defyance* should stand upon the *Charles* three hours, with his fault writ upon his breast and with a halter about his neck, and be made uncapable of any office. The truth is, the man doth seem, and is I believe, a good man; but his neglect, in trusting a girle to carry fire into his cabin, is not to be pardoned. This being done, we took boat and home; and there a good supper was ready for us, which should have been our dinner. The Captains, desirous to be at London, went away presently for Gravesend, to get thither by this night's tide. And so we to supper, it having been a great snowy and mighty cold foul day; and so after supper, to bed.

27.   Up, and did a little business, Middleton and I; then after drinking a little buttered ale, he and Hutchinson and I took coach, and exceeding merry in talk, to Dartford, Middleton finding stories of his own life at Berbados and up and down, at Venice and elsewhere, that are mighty pretty and worth hearing; and he is a strange good-companion and droll upon the road, more then ever I could have thought to have been in him. Here we dined and met Capt. Allen of Rochester, who dined with us and so went on his journey homeward. And we by and by took coach again, and got home about 6 at night, it being all morning as cold, snowy, windy, and rainy day as any in the whole winter past, but pretty clear in the afternoon. I find all well, but my wife abroad with Jane, who was married yesterday; and I to the office busy, till by and by my wife comes home; so home and there hear how merry they were yesterday; and I glad at it, they being married it seems very handsomely, at Islington, and dined at the old house and lay in our blue chamber, with much company and wonderful merry. The[oph]. Turner and Mary Battalier bridemaids, and Talb. Pepys and W. Hewers bridemen. Anon to supper and to bed, my head a little troubled with the muchness of business I have upon me at present. So to bed.

29.   Up and by water to Whitehall, and there to the Duke of York

to show myself after my journey to Chatham, but did no business today with him. Only, after gone from him, I to Sir T. Clifford's and there, after an hour's waiting, he being alone in his closet, I did speak with him and fell to talk of the business of the Navy; and giving me good words, did fall foule of the constitution, and did then discover his thoughts that Sir J. Mennes was too old, and so was Coll. Middleton, and that my Lord Brouncker did mind his mathematics too much. I did not give much encouragement to that of finding fault with my fellow-officers, but did stand up for the constitution, and did say that what faults there was in our office would be found not to arise from the constitution, but from the failures of the officers in whose hands it was. This he did seem to give good ear to. But did give me of myself very good words; which pleased me well, though I shall not build upon them anything.

31. Up and by water to W. Coventry, there to talk with him about business of the Navy, and received from him direction what to advise the Duke of York at this time; which was, to submit and give way to the King's naming a man or two that the people about him have a mind should be brought into the Navy, and perhaps that may stop their fury in running further against the whole – and this he believes will do it. After much discourse with him, I walked out with him into St. James's park; where being afeared to be seen with him (he having not leave yet to kiss the King's hand, but notice taken, as I hear, of all that go to him) I did take the pretence of my attending [the] Tanger Committee to take my leave; though to serve him, I should I think stick at nothing. At the Committee this morning, my Lord Middleton declares at last his being ready to go as soon as ever money can be made ready to pay the garrison. And so I have orders to get money, but how soon I know not. Thence home and there find Mr. Sheres, for whom I find my moher of late to talk with mighty kindness; and perticularly, he hath shown himself to be a poet, and that she doth mightily value him for. He did not stay to dine with us; but we to dinner, and then in the afternoon, my wife being very well dressed by her new maid, we abroad to make a visit to Mrs. Pickering; but she abroad again, and so we never yet saw her. Thence to Dancre's and there saw our pictures which are in doing, and I did choose a view of Rome instead of Hampton Court – and mightily pleased I shall be in them. Here was Sir Ch. Cotterell and his son, bespeaking something;

both ingenious men I hear. Thence my wife and I to the park, and pretty store of company, and so home with great content: and so ends the month – my mind in pretty good content for all things but the designs on foot to bring alterations in the Office; which troubles me.

# –✤APRILL✤–

2. Up and by water to Whitehall, and there with the Office attended the Duke of York, and stayed in Whitehall till about noon; and so with W. Hewer to the Cock, and there he and I dined alone with great content, he reading to me, for my memory sake, my late collections of the history of the Navy, that I might represent the same by and by to the Duke of York; and so after dinner he and I to Whitehall and there to the Duke of York's lodgings, whither he by and by, by his appointment, came; and alone with him an hour in his closet, telling him mine and W. Coventry's advice touching the present posture of the Navy, as the Duke of Buckingham and the rest do now labour to make changes therein; and that it were best for him to suffer the King to be satisfied with the bringing in of a man or two which they desire. I did also give the Duke of York a short account of the history of the Navy, as to our Office, wherewith he was very well satisfied; but I do find that he is pretty stiff against their bringing in of men against his mind, as the Treasurers were, and perticularly against Child's coming in, because he is a merchant. This night I did bring home from the King's potticary's in Whitehall, by Mr. Cooling's direction, a water that he says did him mighty good for his eyes; I pray God it may do me good, but by his description, his disease was the same as mine, and this doth encourage me to use it.

5. To the Mullberry garden, where Sheres is to treat us with a Spanish *Oleo* by a cook of his acquaintance that is there, that was with my Lord in Spain. And without any other company, he did do it, and mighty nobly; and the *Oleo* was endeed a very noble dish, such as I never saw better, or any more of. This, and the discourse he did give us of Spain, and description of the Escuriall, was a fine treat. So we left other things that would keep till night for a collation – and with much content took coach again and went five

or six miles towards Branford: the Prince of Tuscany, who comes into England only to spend money and see our country, comes into the town today, and is much expected; and we met him, but the coach passing by apace, we could not see much of him, but he seems a very jolly and good comely man. By the way we overtook Capt. Ferrers upon his fine Spanish horse; and he is a fine horse endeed, but not so good, I think, as I have seen some. He did ride by us most of the way, and with us to the park and there he left us, where we passed the evening; and meeting The[oph]. Turner, Talbt., W. Batelier and his sister in coach, we anon took them with us to the Mullberry garden; and there, after a walk, to supper upon what was left at noon, and very good; only, Mr. Sheres being taken suddenly ill for a while did spoil our mirth; but by and by was well again, and we mighty merry. And so broke up, and left him at Charing cross; and so calling only at my cousin Turner's, away home, mightily pleased with that day's work: and this day came another new mayd for a middle-maid, but her name I know not yet – and for a cook-maid, we have ever since Bridget went used a blackmoore of Mr. Batelier's (Doll), who dresses our meat mighty well, and we mightily pleased with her. So by and by to bed.

11. *Lords day. Easter day.* Up, and to church, where Ald. Backewell's wife and mother and boy and another gentlewoman did come and sit in our pew – but no women of our own there, and so there was room enough. Our parson made a dull sermon; and so home to dinner, and after dinner my wife and I out by coach, and Balty with us, to Loton the landskip-drawer, a Dutchman living in St. James's market, but there saw no good pictures; but by accident he did direct us to a painter that was then in the house with him, a Dutchman newly come over, one Everelst, who took us to his lodging close by and did show us a little flower pott of his doing, the finest thing that ever I saw in my life – the drops of Dew hanging on the leaves, so as I was forced again and again to put my finger to it to feel whether my eyes were deceived or no. He doth ask 70*l* for it; I had the vanity to bid him 20*l* – but a better picture I never saw in my whole life, and it is worth going twenty miles to see. Thence, leaving Balty there, I took my wife to St. James's and there carried her to the Queen's Chapel, the first time I ever did it – and heard excellent music. Thence to the park, my wife and I; and here Sir W. Coventry did first see me and my wife in a coach of our own, and so did also this night the Duke of York, who did eye my wife

mightily. But I begin to doubt that my being so much seen in my own coach at this time may be observed to my prejudice – but I must venture it now. So home; and by night home and so to my office and there set down my journal, with the help of my left eye through my tube, for fourteen days past; which is so much, as I hope shall not run in arrear again, but the badness of my eyes doth force me to it. So home to supper and to bed.

13.  Sent for W. Hewer and he and I by water to Whitehall to look, among other things, Mr. May, to unbespeak his dining with me tomorrow. But here, being with him in the Courtyard, as God would have it I spied Deb. which made my heart and head to work; and I presently could not refrain, but sent W. Hewer away to look for Mr. Wren (W. Hewer, I perceive, did see her, but whether he did see me see her I know not, or suspect my sending him away I know not) but my heart could not hinder me. And I run after her and two women and a man, more ordinary people, and she in her old clothes; and after hunting a little, find them in the lobby of the Chapel below-stairs; and there I observed she endeavoured to avoid me, but I did speak to her and she to me, and did get her para docere me ou she demeures now. And did charge her para say nothing of me that I had vu elle – which she did promise; and so, with my heart full of surprize and disorder, I away; and meeting with Sir H. Cholmley, walked into the park with him and back again, looking to see if I could spy her again in the park, but I could not. And so back to Whitehall, and then back to the park with Mr. May, but could see her no more; and so with W. Hewer, who I doubt by my countenance might see some disorder in me, we home by water; and there I find Talb. Pepys and Mrs. Turner, and Betty too, come to invite us to dinner on Thursday; and after drinking, I saw them to the waterside, and so back home through Crutched Friars, and there saw Mary Mercer and put off my hat to her on the other side the way; but it being a little darkish, she did not, I think, know me well. And so to my office to put my papers in order, they having been removed for my closet to be made clean; and so home to my wife, who is come home from Deptford. But, God forgive me, I hardly know how to put on confidence enough to speak as innocent, having had this passage today with Deb, though only, God knows, by accident. But my great pain is lest God Almighty shall suffer me to find out this girl, whom endeed I love, and with a bad amour; but I will pray to God to give me grace to forbear it. So

home to supper, where very sparing in my discourse, not giving occasion of any enquiry where I have been today, or what I have done; and so, without any trouble tonight more then my fear, we to bed.

15. Up and to the office; and thence, before the office sat, to the Excise Office with W. Hewer, but found some occasion to go another way to the Temple upon business; and I, by Deb's direction, did know whither in Jewen street to direct my hackney coachman, while I stayed in the coach in Aldgate street, to go thither first to enquire whether Mrs. Hunt her aunt was in town, who brought me word she was not; I thought this was as much as I could do at once, and therefore went away, troubled though that I could do no more; but to the office I must go, and did, and there all the morning; but coming thither, I find Bagwell's wife, who did give me a little note into my hand, wherein I find her para invite me para meet her in Moorfields this noon, where I might speak with her; and so after the office was up, my wife being gone before by invitation to my cousin Turner's to dine, I to that place; and there, after walking up and down by the windmills, I did find her and talk with her; but it being holiday and the place full of people, we parted, leaving further discourse and doing to another time: thence I away and through Jewen street, my mind, God knows, running that way, but stopped not; but going down Holburn hill by the Conduit, I did see Deb on foot going up the hill; I saw her, and she me, but she made no stop, but seemed unwilling to speak to me; so I away on, but then stopped and light and after her, and overtook her at the end of Hosier lane in Smithfield; and without standing in the street, desired her to fallow me, and I led her into a little blind alehouse within the walls; and there she and I alone fell to talk and besar la and tocar su mamelles, but she mighty coy, and I hope modest; but however, though with great force, did hazer ella con su hand para tocar mi thing, but ella was in great pain para be brought para it. I did give her in a paper 20*s.*, and we did agree para meet again in the Hall at Westminster on Monday next; and so, giving me great hopes by her carriage that she continues modest and honest, we did there part, she going home and I to Mrs. Turner's; but when I came back to the place where I left my coach, it was gone, I having stayed too long, which did trouble me to abuse a poor fellow so; but taking another coach, I did direct him to find out the fellow and send him to me.

17.   Up and to the office, where all the morning. At noon home to dinner, and there find Mr. Pierce the surgeon, and he dined with us; and there hearing that *The Alchymist* was acted, we did go and took him with us, at the King's House; and is still a good play, it having not been acted for two or three years before; but I do miss Clun for the Doctor – but more, my eyes will not let me enjoy the pleasure I used to have in a play. Thence with my wife in hackney to Sir W. Coventry's; who being gone to the park, we drove after him; and there met him coming out and fallowed him home, and there sent my wife to Unthankes while I spent an hour with him, reading over first my draft of the Administracion of the Navy, which he doth like very well. And so fell to talk of other things; and among the rest, of the story of his late disgrace, and how basely and in a mean manner the Duke of Buckingham hath proceeded against him, not like a man of honour. He tells me that the King will not give other answer about his coming to kiss his hands then "not yett". But he says that this that he desires, of kissing the King's hand, is only to show to the world that he is not a discontent, and not in any desire to come again into play; though I do perceive that he speaks this with less earnestness then heretofore; and this, it may [be], is from what he told me lately, that the King is offended at what is talked: that he hath declared himself desirous not to have to do with any imployment more. But he doth tell me that the leisure he hath yet had doth not at all begin to be burdensome to him, he knowing how to spend his time with content to him; and that he hopes shortly to contract his expense, so as that he shall not be under any straits in that respect neither – and so seems to be in very good condition of content. Thence I away over the park, it being now night, to Whitehall, and there in the Duchess's chamber to find the Duke of York; and upon my offer to speak with him, he did come to me; and withdrew to his closet and there did hear and approve my paper of the Administration of the Navy; only, did bid me alter these words, "upon the rupture between the late King and the Parliament," to these, "the beginning of the late Rebellion;" giving it me as but reason to show that it was with the Rebellion that the Navy was put by out of its old good course into that of a Commission.

18.   *Lords day.* Up, and all morning till 2 a-clock at my office with Gibson and Tom, about drawing up fair my discourse of the Administracion of the Navy. And then Mr. Spong being come to dine with me, I in to dinner and then out to my office again to

examine the fair draft; and so borrowing Sir J. Mennes's coach, he going with Commissioner Middleton, I to Whitehall, where we all met and did sign it; and then to my Lord Arlington's, where the King and Duke of York and Prince Rupert, as also Ormond and the two Secretaries, with my Lord Ashly and Sir T. Clifford, was; and there, by and by being called in, Mr. Williamson did read over our paper, which was in a letter to the Duke of York, bound up in a book with the Duke of York's book of Instructions. He read it well; and after read, we were bid to withdraw, nothing being at all said to it. And by and by we were called in again, and nothing said to that business but another begun, about the state of this year's Action and our wants of money, as I had stated the same lately to our Treasurers – which I was bid, and did largely and with great content, open; and having so done, we all withdrew and left them to debate our supply of money; after which, being called in and referred to attend on the Lords of the Treasury, we all departed; and I only stayed in the House till the Council rose, and then to the Duke of York, who in the Duchess's chamber came to me and told me that the book was there left with my Lord Arlington, for any of the Lords to view that had a mind, and to prepare and present to the King what they had to say in writing to any part of it; which is all we can desire, and so that rested. The Duke of York then went to other talk; and by and by comes the Prince of Tuscany to visit him and the Duchess, and I find that he doth still remain Incognito, and so intends to do all the time he stays here – for avoiding trouble to the King and himself, and expense also to both. Thence I to Whitehall gate, thinking to have found Sir. J. Mennes's coach staying for me; but not being there, and this being the first day of rain we have had many a day, the streets being as dusty as in summer, I forced to walk to my cousin Turner's, and there find my wife newly gone home, which vexed me; and so I having kissed and taken leave of Betty, who goes to Putny to school tomorrow, I walked through the rain to the Temple and there with much ado got a coach; and so home and there to supper, and Pelling comes to us; and after much talk we parted and to bed.

19.    Up, and with Tom (whom, with his wife, I and my wife had this morning taken occasion to tell that I did intend to give him 40*l* for himself and 20*l* to his wife toward their setting out in the world, and that my wife would give her 20*l* more, that so she might have as much to begin with as he) by coach to Whitehall; and there having

set him work in the robe-chamber to write something for me, I to Westminster hall and there walked from 10 a-clock to past 12, expecting to have met Deb; but whether she had been there before, and missing me went away, or is prevented in coming and hath no mind to come to me (the last whereof, as being most pleasing, as showing most modesty, I should be most glad of) I know not; but she not then appearing, I being tired with walking went home.

20. Up and to the office, and my wife abroad with Mary Batelier with our own coach, but borrowed Sir J. Mennes's coachman, that so our own might stay at home to attend at dinner, our family being mightily disordered by our little boy's falling sick the last night, and we fear it will prove the smallpox. At noon comes my guest, Mr. Hugh May, and with him Sir Henry Capell, my old Lord Capells son, and Mr. Packer; and I had a pretty dinner for them, and both before and after dinner had excellent discourse, and showed them my closet and my office and the method of it, to their great content; and more extraordinary manly discourse, and opportunity of showing myself and learning from others, I have not in ordinary discourse had in my life – they being all persons of worth; but especially Sir H. Capell, whose being a Parliament[-man] and hearing my discourse in the Parliament-house hath, as May tells me, given him a long desire to know and discourse with me. In the afternoon we walked to the old Artillery ground near the Spitalfields, where I never was before; but now, by Capt. Deanes invitation, did go to see his new gun tryed, this being the place where the officers of the Ordnance do try all their great guns; and when we came, did find that the trial had been made, and they going away with extraordinary report of the proof of his gun, which, from the shortness and bigness, they do call "*punchinello*". But I desired Coll. Legg to stay and give us a sight of her performance, which he did; and there, in short, against a gun more then as long and as heavy again, and charged with as much powder again, she carried the same bullet as strong to the mark, and nearer and above the mark at a point-blank then theirs, and is more easily managed and recoyls no more then that – which is a thing so extraordinary, as to be admired for the happiness of his invention, and to the great regret of the old gunners and officers of the Ordinance that were there; only, Coll. Legg did do her much right in his report of her. And so having seen this great and first experiment, we all parted, I seeing my guests into a hackney coach,

and myself, with Capt. Deane, taking a hackney, did go out toward Bow and went as far as Stratford, and all the way talking of this invention, and he offering me a third of the profit of the invention; which, for aught I know or do at present think, may prove matter considerable to us; for either the King will give him a reward for it, if he keeps it to himself, or he will give us a patent to make our profit of it; and no doubt but it will be of profit to merchantmen and others, to have guns of the same force at half the charge. This was our talk; and then to talk of other things of the Navy in general; and among other things, he did tell me that he doth hear how the Duke of Buckingham hath a spite at me, which I knew before but value it not; and he tells me that Sir T. Allen is not my friend; but for all this I am not much troubled, for I know myself so useful, that, as I believe, they will not part with me; so I thank [God], my condition is such that I can retire and be able to live with comfort, though not with abundance. Thus we spent the evening with extraordinary good discourse, to my great content; and so home to the office and there did some business; and then home, where my wife doth come home, and I vexed at her staying out so late; but she tells me that she hath been at home with M. Batelier a good while, so I made nothing of it – but to supper and to bed.

21.    After dinner, by water to Whitehall, where the Duke of York did meet our Office and went with us to the Lord Commissioners of the Treasury; and there we did go over all the business of the state I had drawn up, of this year's action and expense; which I did do to their satisfaction, and convincing them of the necessity of providing more money, if possible, for us. Thence, the Duke of York being gone, I did there stay walking with Sir H. Cholmly in the Court, talking of news; where he told me that now the great design of the Duke of Buckingham is to prevent the meeting, since he cannot bring about with the King the dissolving, of this Parliament, that the King may not need it; and therefore my Lord St. Albans is hourly expected, with great offers of a million of money, to buy our breach with the Dutch; and this they do think may tempt the King to take the money, and thereby be out of a necessity of calling the Parliament again – which these people dare not suffer to meet again. But this he doubts, and so do I, that it will be to the ruin of the nation if we fall out with Holland. This we were discoursing, when my boy comes to tell me that his mistress was at the gate with the coach; whither I went and there find my wife and the whole

company; so she and Mrs. Turner and The[oph]. and Talbot in mine, and Joyce, W. Batelier, and I in a hackney to Hyde park, where I was ashamed to be seen; but mightily pleased, though troubled with a drunken coachman that did not remember, when we came to light, where it was he took us up; but said at Hammersmith, and thither he was carrying of us when we came first out of the Park. So I carried them all to Hercules Pillars and there did treat them; and so about 10 at night parted, and my wife and I and W. Batelier home; and he gone, we to bed.

24. Up and to the office, where all the morning; and at noon home to dinner, Mr. Sheres dining with us by agreement, and my wife, which troubled me, mighty careful to have a handsome dinner for him. But yet I see no reason to be troubled at it, he being a very civil and worthy man I think; but only, it doth seem to imply some little neglect of me. After dinner to the King's House and there saw *The Generall* revived, a good play, that pleases me well; and thence, our coach coming for us, we parted and home, and I busy late at the office and then home to supper and to bed – well pleased tonight to have Lead the vizard-maker bring me home my vizard with a Tube fastened to it, which I think will do my business, at least in a great measure, for the easing of my eyes.

28. Up, and was called upon by Sir H. Cholmly to discourse about some accounts of his of Tanger; and then to other talk, and I find by him that it is brought almost to effect, the late endeavours of the Duke of York and Duchess, the Queen Mother, and my Lord St. Albans, together [with] some of the contrary faction, my Lord Arlington, that for a sum of money we shall enter into a league with the King of France;[1] wherein he says my Lord Chancellor is also concerned, and he believes that in the doing hereof, it is meant that he shall come in again, and that this sum of money will so help the King as that he will not need the Parliament; and that in that regard, it will be forwarded by the Duke of Buckingham and his faction, who dread the Parliament; but hereby, we must leave the Dutch, and that I doubt will undo us, and Sir H. Cholmly says he finds W. Coventry to think the like. My Lady Castlemayne is instrumental in this matter and, he says, never more great with the King then she is now. But this is a thing that will make the Parliament and

1. These negotiations led to the secret treaty of Dover, May 1670.

Kingdom mad, and will turn to our ruine – for with this money the King shall wanton away his time in pleasures, and think nothing of the main till it be too late. He gone, I to the office, where busy till noon; and then home to dinner, where M. Batelier dined with us, and pretty merry; and so I to the office again. This morning, Mr. Sheres sent me, in two volumes, Mariana his history of Spaine in Spanish, an excellent book and I am much obliged for it to him.

30. Up and by coach to the coachmaker's, and there I do find a great many ladies sitting in the body of a coach that must be ended by tomorrow; they were my Lady Marquess of Winchester, Bellasses, and other great ladies, eating of bread and butter and drinking ale. I to my coach, which is silvered over, but no varnish yet laid on; so I put it in a way of doing, and myself about other business; and perticularly to see Sir W. Coventry, with whom I talked a good while to my great content; and so to other places, among others, to my tailor's and then to the belt-maker's, where my belt cost me 55s., of the colour of my new suit; and here, understanding that the mistress of the house, an oldish woman in a hat, hath some water good for the eyes, she did dress me, making my eyes smart most horribly, and did give me a little glass of it, which I will use and hope it will do me good. So to the Cutler's and there did give Tom, who was with me all day, a sword, cost me 12s., and a belt of my owne – and set my own silver-hilt sword a-gilding against tomorrow. This morning I did visit Mr. Oldenburgh and did see the instrument for perspective made by Dr. Wren, of which I have one making by Browne; and the sight of this doth please me mightily. At noon, my wife came to me at my tailor's; and I sent her home, and myself and Tom dined at Hercules pillers; and so about our business again, and perticularly to Lillys the varnisher about my prints, whereof some are pasted upon the boards, and to my full content. Thence to the frame-maker's, one Norris in Long Acre – who showed me several forms of frames to choose by; which was pretty, in little bits of mouldings to choose by. This done, I to my coachmaker's, and there vexed to see nothing yet done to my coach at 3 in the afternoon; but I set it in doing, and stood by it till 8 at night and saw the painter varnish it; which is pretty, to see how every doing it over doth make it more and more yellow. And it dries as fast in the sun as it can be laid on almost. And most coaches are nowadays done so, and it is very pretty when laid on well – and not too pale, as some are, even to

show the silver. Here I did make the workmen drink, and saw my coach cleaned and oyled; and staying among poor people there in the ally, did hear them call their fat child "punch"; which pleased me mightily, that word being become a word of common use for all that is thick and short. At night home, and there find my wife hath been making herself clean against tomorrow. And late as it was, I did send my coachman and horses to fetch home the coach tonight. And so we to supper, myself most weary with walking and standing so much to see all things fine against tomorrow; and so to bed – God give a blessing to it.

# –❊MAY❊–

1. Up betimes, called up by my tailor, and there first put on a summer suit this year – but it was not my fine one of flowered tabby vest and coloured camelott tunic, because it was too fine with the gold lace at the hands, that I was afeared to be seen in it – but put on the stuff-suit I made the last year, which is now repaired; and so did go to the office in it and sat all the morning, the day looking as if it would be fowle. At noon home to dinner, and there find my wife extraordinary fine with her flowered tabby gown that she made two years ago, now laced exceeding pretty, and endeed was fine all over – and mighty earnest to go, though the day was very lowering, and she would have me put on my fine suit, which I did; and so anon we went alone through the town with our new Liverys of serge, and the horses' manes and tails tied with red ribbon and the standards thus gilt with varnish and all clean, and green raynes, that people did mightily look upon us; and the truth is, I did not see any coach more pretty, or more gay, then ours all the day. But we set out out of humour; I because Betty, whom I expected, was not come to go with us; and my wife, that I would sit on the same seat with her, which she liked not, being so fine; and then expected to meet Sheres, which we did in the Pell Mell, and against my will I was forced to take him into the coach, but was sullen all day almost, and little complaisant; the day also being unpleasing, though the park full of coaches; but dusty and windy and cold, and now and then a little dribbling rain; and what made it worst, there were so many hackney coaches as spoiled the sight of the gentlemen's, and so we had little pleasure. But here was W. Batelier and his sister in a

borrowed coach by themselfs, and I took them and we to the Lodge, and at the door did give them a sullabub and other things, cost me 12*s*., and pretty merry; and so back to the coaches and there till the evening; and then home, leaving Mr. Sheres at St. James's gate, where he took leave of us for altogether, he being this night to set out for Portsmouth post, in his way to Tanger – which troubled my wife mightily, who is mighty, though not I think too fond of him. But she was out of humour all the evening, and I vexed at her for it; and she did not rest almost all the night, so as in the night I was forced to take her and hug her to put her to rest. So home, and after a little supper, to bed.

4. Up and to the office; and then my wife being gone with the coach to see her mother at Deptford, I, before the office sat, went to the Excise Office; and thence, being alone, stepped into Duck lane and thence tried to have sent a porter to Deb's, but durst not trust him. And therefore, having bought a book to satisfy the bookseller for my stay there, a 12*d*. book, *Andronicus* of Tom Fuller, I took coach; and at the end of Jewen street next Red cross street, I sent the coachman to her lodging, and understand she is gone to Greenwich to one Marys's, a tanner's; at which I was glad, hoping to have opportunity to find her out there. And so, in great fear of being seen, I to the office and there all morning. Dined at home; and presently after dinner comes home my wife, who I believe was jealous of my spending the day; and I had very good fortune in being at home, for if Deb had been to have been found, it is forty to one but I had been abroad – God forgive me. So the afternoon at the office; and at night walked with my wife in the garden, and my Lord Brouncker with us, who is newly come to W. Pen's lodgings. And by and by comes Mr. Hooke, and my Lord and he and I into my Lord's lodging and there discoursed of many fine things in philosophy, to my great content; and so home to supper and to bed.

5. Up, and thought to have gone with Lord Brouncker to Mr. Hooke's this morning betimes; but my Lord is taken ill of the gowte, and says his new lodgings have infected him, he having never had any symptoms of it till now. So walked to Gresham College to tell Hooke that my Lord could not come; and so left word, he being abroad; and I to St. James's and thence with the Duke of York to Whitehall, where the Board waited on him all the morning; and so at noon with Sir Tho. Allen and Sir Ed. Scott and

Lord Carlingford to the Spanish Embassadors, where I dined the
first time – the *Oleo* not so good as Shere's. There was at the table,
himself and a Spanish Countess, a good, comely, and witty lady –
three fathers – and us. Discourse good and pleasant; and here was an
Oxford scholar in a Doctor's of Laws gowne, where the Embassador lay when the Court was there, to salute him from the college
before his return to Spain. This man, though a gentle sort of
scholar, yet sat like a fool for want of French or Spanish; but only
Latin, which he spoke like a Englishman to one of the fathers. And
by and by, he and I to talk and the company very merry at my
defending Cambridge against Oxford: and I made much use of my
French and Spanish here, to my great content. But the dinner not
extraordinary at all, either for quantity or quality. Thence home,
where my wife ill of those upon the maid's bed, and troubled at my
being abroad. So I to the office, and there till night; and then to her,
and she read to me the *Epistle* of *Cassandra*, which is very good
endeed, and the better to her because recommended by Sheres. So
to supper, and I to bed.

6.   Up and by coach to W. Coventry's; but he gone out, I by water
back to the office and there all the morning; then to dinner and then
the office again; and anon with my wife by coach to take the ayre, it
being a noble day, as far as the greene Man, mightily pleased with
our journey and our condition of doing it in our own coach; and so
home and to walk in the garden; and so to supper and to bed, my
eyes being bad with writing my journall, part of it, tonight.

8.   Up, and to the office and there comes Lead to me; and at last my
vizards are done, and glasses got to put in and out as I will; and I
think I have brought it to the utmost, both for easiness of using and
benefit, that I can; and so I paid him 15s. for what he hath done now
last in the finishing them, and they, I hope, will do me a great deal of
ease. At the office all the morning; and this day the first time did
alter my side of the table, after above eight years sitting on that next
the fire. But now I am not able to bear the light of the windows in
my eyes, I do go there; and I did sit with much more content then I
had done on the other side for a great while, and in winter the fire
will not trouble my back. At noon home to dinner; and after dinner,
all the afternoon within with Mr. Hater, Gibson, and W. Hewer,
reading over and drawing up new things in the instructions of
commanders; which will be good, and I hope to get them

confirmed by the Duke of York, though I perceive nothing will effectually perfect them but to look over the whole body of the instructions of all the officers of a ship, and make them all perfect together. This being done, comes my bookseller and brings me home, bound, my collection of papers about my Addresse to the Duke of York in August; which makes me glad, it being that which shall do me more right many years hence then perhaps all I ever did in my life – and therefore I do, both for my own and the King's sake, value it much. By and by also comes Browne the Mathematical-instrument maker, and brings me home my instrument for Perspective, made according to the description of Dr. Wren's in the late *Transactions*, and he hath made it, I think, very well; and that that I believe will do the thing, and therein give me great content, but that I fear all the contents that must be received by my eyes are almost lost. So to the office and there late at business, and then home to supper and to bed.

10. Troubled, about 3 in the morning, with my wife's calling her maid up, and rising herself, to go with her coach abroad to gather May-dew[1] – which she did; and I troubled for it, for fear of any hurt, going abroad so betimes, happening to her. But I to sleep again, and she came home about 6 and to bed again, all well. And I up, and with Mr. Gibson by coach to St. James and thence to Whitehall, where the Duke of York met the office and there discoursed of several things, perticularly the instructions to commanders of ships. Thence walked, my boy Jacke with me, to my Lord Crew, whom I have not seen since he was sick, which is eight months ago I think – and there dined with him. He is mightily broke. A stranger, a country gentleman, was with him, and he pleased with my discourse accidentally about the decay of gentlemen's families in the country, telling us that the old rule was that a family might remain 50 miles from London 100 year, 100 mile off from London 200 years, and so, farther or nearer London, more or less years. He also told us that he hath heard his father say that in his time it was so rare for a country gentleman to come to London, that when he did come, he used to make his will before he set out. Thence walked a little with Creed, who tells me he hears how fine my horses and coach are, and advises me to avoid being noted for it; which I was vexed to hear taken notice of, it being what I feared;

---

1. Used as a cosmetic.

and Povy told me of my gold-lace sleeves in the park yesterday, which vexed me also, so as to resolve never to appear in Court with it, but presently to have it taken off, as it is fit I should. And so to my wife at Unthankes, and coach, and called at my tailor's to that purpose; and so home, and after a walk in the garden, home to supper and to bed.

12. Up and to Westminster hall, where the term is; and this is the first day of my being there, and here by chance met Rogr. Pepys, come to town the last night. I glad to see him. After some talk with him and others, and among others, Sir Ch. Herberd and Sidny Mountagu, the latter of whom is to set out tomorrow toward Flanders and Italy, I invited them to dine with me tomorrow; and so to Mrs. Martin's lodging, who come to town last night, and there yo did hazer her, she having been a month, I think, at Portsmouth with her husband, newly come home from the Streights. But Lord, how silly the woman talks of her great entertainment there, and how all the gentry came to visit her, and that she believes her husband is worth 6 or 700*l*; which nevertheless I am glad of, but I doubt they will spend it as fast. Thence home; and after dinner, my wife and I to the Duke of York's playhouse, and there in the side balcone over against the music, did hear, but not see, a new play, the first day acted, *The Roman Virgin*, an old play and but ordinary I thought; but the trouble of my eyes with the light of the candles did almost kill me. Thence to my Lord Sandwiches, and there have a promise from Sidny to come and dine with me tomorrow; and so my wife and I home in our coach, and there find my Brother John, as I looked for, come to town from Ellington; where, among other things, he tells me the first news that my sister is with child and far gone; which I know not whether it did more trouble or please me, having no great care for my friends to have children, though I love other people's. So, glad to see him, we to supper and so to bed.

13. Up and to the office, where all the morning, it being a rainy foul day. But at noon comes my Lord Hinchingbrooke and Sidny and Sir Ch. Herberd and Rogr. Pepys, and dined with me; and had a good dinner, and very merry, and with us all the afternoon, it being a farewell to Sidny; and so in the evening, they away and I to my business at the office; and so to supper and talk with my brother, and so to bed.

14. Up, and to St. James's to the Duke of York and thence to Whitehall, where we met about office business; and then at noon to dinner with Mr. Wren to Lambeth, with the Archbishop of Canterbury; the first time I was ever there, and I have long longed for it – where a noble house, and well furnished with good pictures and furniture, and noble attendance in good order, and a great deal of company, though an ordinary day, and exceeding great cheer, nowhere better, or so much that ever I think I saw for an ordinary table. And the Bishop mighty kind to me, perticularly desiring my company another time, when less company there. Most of the company gone, and I going, I heard by a gentleman of a sermon that was to be there; and so I stayed to hear it, thinking it serious, till by and by the gentleman told me it was a mockery by one Cornet Bolton, a very gentleman-like man, that behind a chair did pray and preach like a presbyter-Scot that ever I heard in my life, with all the possible imitation in grimaces and voice – and his text about the hanging up their harps upon the willows – and a serious good sermon too, exclaiming against Bishops and crying up of my good Lord Eglington – till it made us all burst; but I did wonder to have the Bishop make himself at this time to make himself sport with things of this kind, but I perceive it was shown him as a rarity. And he took care to have the room-door shut, but there was about twenty gentlemen there – and myself infinitely pleased with the novelty. So over to Whitehall to a little Committee of Tanger; and thence walking in the Gallery, I met Sir Tho. Osborne, who to my great content did of his own accord fall into discourse with me, with so much professions of value and respect, placing the whole virtue of the office of the Navy upon me, and that for the Controller's place, no man in England was fit for it but me when Sir J. Mennes, as he says it is necessary, is removed – but then, knows not what to do for a man in my place; and in discourse, though I have no mind to the other, did bring in Tom Hater to be the fittest man in the world for it – which he took good notice of. But in the whole, I was mightily pleased, reckoning myself now 50 per cent securer in my place then I did before think myself to be. Thence to Unthankes and there find my wife, but not dressed; which vexed me, because of going to the park, it being a most pleasant day after yesterday's rain, which lays all the dust, and most people going out thither, which vexed me. So home, sullen; but then my wife and I by water, with my brother, as high as Fulham, talking and singing and playing the rogue with the western bargemen about the women

of Woolwich, which mads them. And so back home to supper and
to bed.

16. *Lords day.* My wife and I at church, our pew filled (which
vexed me at her confidence) with Mrs. Backwell and six more that
she brought with her. Dined at home, and W. Batelier with us, and
I all the afternoon drawing up a foul draft of my petition to the
Duke of York about my eyes, for leave to spend three or four
months out of the office, drawing it so as to give occasion to a
voyage abroad; which I did to my pretty good liking. And then
with my wife to Hyde park, where a good deal of company, and
good weather; and so home to supper and to bed.

19. With my coach to St. James, and there, finding the Duke of
York gone to muster his men in Hyde park, I alone with my boy
thither; and there saw more, walking out of my coach as other
gentlemen did, of a soldier's trade then ever I did in my life – the
men being mighty fine, and their commanders, perticularly the
Duke of Monmouth; but methought their trade but very easy, as to
the mustering of their men, and the men but indifferently ready to
perform what was commanded in the handling their arms. Here
news was first talked of Harry Killigrews' being wounded in nine
places last night by footmen in the highway, going from the park in
a hackney coach toward Hammersmith to his house at Turnam
greene – they being supposed to be my Lady Shrewsbury's men –
she being by in her coach with six horses. Upon an old grudge, of
his saying openly that he had lain with her. Thence by and by to
Whitehall, and there I waited upon the King and Queen all dinner-
time in the Queen's lodgings, she being in her white pinner and
apern, like a woman with child; and she seemed handsomer, plain
so, then dressed. And by and by, dinner done, I out and to walk in
the Gallery for the Duke of York's coming out; and there meeting
Mr. May, he took me down about 4 a-clock to Mr. Chevins's
lodgings, and all alone did get me a dish of cold chickens and good
wine, and I dined like a prince, being before very hungry and
empty. By and by the Duke of York comes, and readily took me to
his closet and received my petition, and discoursed it about my eyes
and pitied me, and with much kindness did give me his consent to
be absent, and approved of my proposition to go into Holland to
observe things there of the Navy, but would first ask the King's
leave; which he anon did, and did tell me that the King would be

"a good maister to me" (these were his words about my eyes) and doth like of my going into Holland, but doth advise that nobody should know of my going thither – but pretend that I did go into the country somewhither – which I liked well. Glad of this, I home; and thence took out my wife and to Mr. Holliards about a swelling in her cheek, but he not at home; and so round by Islington and eat and drink; and so home and after supper, to bed.

24.  To Whitehall, and there all the morning, and thence home; and giving order for some business, and setting my brother to making a catalogue of my books, I back again to W. Hewer to Whitehall, where I attended the Duke of York and was by him led to the King, who expressed great sense of my misfortune in my eyes, and concernment for their recovery; and accordingly signified not only his assent to my desire therein, but commanded me to give them rest this summer, according to my late petition to the Duke of York. W. Hewer and I dined alone at the Swan, and thence, having thus waited on the King, spent till 4 a-clock in St. James's park, when I met my wife at Unthankes and so home.

29.  *The King's birth day.* To Whitehall, where all very gay; and perticularly, the Prince of Tuscany very fine, and is the first day of his appearing out of morning since he came. I heard the Bishop of Peterborough preach, but dully; but a good anthem of Pelham's. Home to dinner, and then with my wife to Hyde park, where all the evening great store of company, and great preparations by the Prince of Tuscany to celebrate the night with fireworks for the King's birthday; and so home.

30.  *Whitsunday.* By water to Whitehall, and thence to Sir W. Coventry, where all the morning by his bedside, he being indisposed; our discourse was upon the notes I had lately prepared for commanders' instructions; but concluded that nothing will render them effectual without an amendment in the choice of them, that they be seamen, and not gentlemen above the command of the Admiral by the greatness of their relations at Court. Thence to Whitehall and dined alone with Mr. Chevins his sister; whither by and by came in Mr. Progers and Sir Tho. Allen, and by and by fine Mrs. Wells, who is a great beauty and there I had my full gaze upon her, to my great content, she being a woman of pretty conversation. Thence to the Duke of York, who, with the officers of the

Navy, made a good entrance on my draft of my new instructions to commanders, as well as expressing his general [views] of a reformation among them, as liking of my humble offers towards it. Thence, being called by my wife, Mr. Gibson and we to the park, whence the rain sent us suddenly home.

31. [Up] very betimes, and so continued all the morning, with W. Hewer, upon examining and stating my accounts, in order to the fitting myself to go abroad beyond sea, which the ill condition of my eyes, and my neglect for a year or two, hath kept me behindhand in, and so as to render it very difficult now, and troublesome to my mind to do it; but I this day made a satisfactory entrance therein. Dined at home, and in the afternoon by water to Whitehall, calling by the way at Michell's, where I have not been many a day till just the other day; and now I met her mother there and knew her husband to be out of town. And here yo did besar ella, but have not opportunity para hazer mas with her as I would have offered if yo had had it. And thence had another meeting with the Duke of York at Whitehall with the Duke of York on yesterday's work, and made a good advance; and so being called by my wife, we to the park, Mary Batelier, a Duch gentleman, a friend of hers, being with us. Thence to the World's end, a drinking-house by the park, and there merry; and so home late.

And thus ends all that I doubt I shall ever be able to do with my own eyes in the keeping of my journall, I being not able to do it any longer, having done now so long as to undo my eyes almost every time that I take a pen in my hand; and therefore, whatever comes of it, I must forbear; and therefore resolve from this time forward to have it kept by my people in longhand, and must therefore be contented to set down no more then is fit for them and all the world to know; or if there be anything (which cannot be much, now my amours to Deb are past, and my eyes hindering me in almost all other pleasures), I must endeavour to keep a margin in my book open, to add here and there a note in shorthand with my own hand. And so I betake myself that course which [is] almost as much as to see myself go into my grave – for which, and all the discomforts that will accompany my being blind, the good God prepare me.

May. 31. 1669. S.P.[1]

1. The initials are formed into a monogram: see plate 25.

# –❧POSTSCRIPT❧–

Pepys never kept another diary comparable in scale and character with this, although his eyes quickly recovered from the worst effects of the strain which had led him to end it. He later composed other journals, which were for the most part not personal diaries but memoranda arranged in diary form and written out by clerks. But in July 1683 when he was sent to Tangier as secretary of the Commission which supervised the evacuation of the colony, the occasion called for a descriptive diary. He wrote it in shorthand and it covers the voyage there and back, his time in Tangier, and a trip he took in mid-winter to S.W. Spain. It has passages that are reminiscent of his diary keeping at its best. But it suffers from its shortness and from the limitations of its purpose: he does not attempt in its pages to lay bare his life. What readers of Pepys must regret is that he did not resume his great diary in the 1670s and '80s. His version of those critical years, which included the Popish Plot and Glorious Revolution of 1688 (in both of which he was closely involved), told in diary form and in Pepysian detail by one who knew James II so well, would have been an historical source of incomparable value. It must rank as one of the most interesting books never written.

# ⤖FURTHER READING[1]⤖

Of the commentaries on the diary the most comprehensive is vol. X of the complete edition edited by myself and Professor William Matthews – the *Companion*, 1983 – which has essays by various authors on persons, places and subjects. The most succinct is a work written for the general reader by J. R. Tanner, a pioneer scholar to whom all students of Pepys are indebted, *Mr Pepys* (1925), which summarises the subject matter of the diary in chapters entitled 'Books', 'The Household' and so on, and has excellent short accounts of his life before and after the diary period. C. S. Emden's *Pepys Himself* (Oxford, 1963) and Percival Hunt's *Pepys in the Diary* (Pittsburgh, 1959) are also useful. The latter succeeds in preserving something of the charm of the original. H. B. Wheatley's *Samuel Pepys and World he Lived in* (1880) and the concluding volume of his edition of the diary (*Pepysiana*, 1899), like W. H. Whitear, *More Pepysiana* (1927), have information mostly of an antiquarian sort. So have the two volumes of *Occasional Papers . . . of the Samuel Pepys Club* (priv. prtd, 1917, 1925). Special aspects are dealt with in H. C. Levis, *Extracts from the Diaries and Correspondence of John Evelyn and Samuel Pepys relating to Engraving* (1915); Helen McAfee, *Pepys on the Restoration Stage* (New Haven, 1916); A. G. Matthews, *Mr Pepys and Nonconformity* (1954); J. H. Wilson, *The Private Life of Mr Pepys* (1960) and M. H. Nicolson, *Pepys' Diary and the New Science* (Charlottesville; 1965). The diary's evidence necessarily plays a large part in W. G. Bell's *The Great Fire* (1923) and the same author's *The Great Plague* (rev. ed., 1951). Pepys's shorthand may be studied in the modern reprint of the manual from which he learned the system – Thomas Shelton's *A Tutor to Tachygraphy, or Short-writing* (for a modern reprint, see above, p. xiv, n. 2).

1. The place of publication is London unless otherwise stated.

Apart from the diary and his letters the most important of Pepys's writings which have been printed are three: his Tangier diary, in *The Tangier Papers of Samuel Pepys*, transcribed, edited and collated with the transcription by William Matthews by Edwin Chappell (Navy Records Society, 1935): his *Memoires relating to the Royal Navy* (1690, cf. pp. xxx–xxxi above) reprinted at Oxford in 1906 in the Tudor and Stuart Library and edited by J. R. Tanner; and his *Naval Minutes* (ed. Tanner, Navy Records Society, 1926), a commonplace book of notes he kept in the 1680s and '90s, mostly reflecting on the nation's neglect of its navy. Six of the pamphlets he wrote in 1698–9 in his attempt to reform Christ's Hospital have been reproduced in facsimile (Rudolf Kirk, ed., *Mr Pepys upon the State of Christ-Hospital*, Philadelphia, 1939). His transcription of Charles II's oral account of his escape after the Battle of Worcester has been edited by William Matthews (*Charles II's Escape from Worcester*, 1966).

A substantial number of Pepys's letters are available in print. He preserved much of his official and private correspondence in four letter-books inherited by his nephew Jackson, who himself added some that were among his own papers. A small selection from the letter-books was printed in the nineteenth-century editions of the diary by Braybrooke and by Bright. The letter-books have now been published much more fully by J. R. Tanner in *Private Correspondence and Miscellaneous Papers of Samuel Pepys, 1679–1703* (2 vols, 1926) and *Further Correspondence of Samuel Pepys 1662–79* (1929). A few of the miscellaneous papers and all the shorthand letters were omitted by Tanner. The latter were printed by Edwin Chappell in *Shorthand Letters of Samuel Pepys* (Cambridge, 1933). Other letters survive in manuscript, principally in the Rawlinson collection in the Bodleian Library. A handful of these were printed by Braybrooke and by Bright in their editions of the diary; a larger selection (together with a selection from the Tanner volumes) was published and edited by R. G. Howarth in his *Letters and the Second Diary of Samuel Pepys* (1933). (The second diary is the Tangier diary which Howarth printed from John Smith's defective text of 1841.) Two other selections have appeared – H. T. Heath's edition of *The Letters of Samuel Pepys and his Family Circle* (Oxford, 1955, repr. Westport, Conn., 1979) and some of his correspondence with Evelyn in C. Marburg, *Mr Pepys and Mr Evelyn* (Philadelphia, 1935).

Of biographies of Pepys, that by Sir Arthur Bryant is the fullest, though it goes no further than 1689 (3 vols, 1933–8 and later issues, Cambridge and London: *Samuel Pepys*, vol. I, *The Man in the Making*; vol. II, *The Years of Peril*; vol. III, *The Saviour of the Navy*). Its strong points derive from the author's gift for vivid narrative. Richard Ollard's *Pepys, a Biography* (1974; also in paperback 1978 and, Oxford, 1984), elegantly written, is far and away the best single-volume life and is superior to Bryant as a character study. Edwin Chappell's *Eight Generations of the Pepys Family, 1500–1800* (1926) presents the genealogical information in an ingenious and accessible form. Pepys's patron Sandwich is well served by the sound and ample biography by F. R. Harris (2 vols, 1912).

The political background is best studied in David Ogg, *England in the Reign of Charles II* (vol. I, 2nd ed., Oxford, 1955); J. R. Jones, *Country and Court, 1658–1714* (1981), and John Miller, *James II, a Study in Kingship* (Hove, 1977). Debate on the character and political behaviour of Charles II continues; the latest defence is by Antonia Fraser (*King Charles II*, 1979) and the latest attack by Richard Ollard (*The Image of the King: Charles I and Charles II*, 1979). J. R. Tanner's *Samuel Pepys and the Royal Navy* (Cambridge, 1920), covers Pepys's career as an administrator. It is admirably supplemented by N. A. M. Rodger, *The Admiralty* (Lavenham, 1979); J. P. W. Ehrman, *The Navy in the Wars of William III* (Cambridge, 1958), which casts a great deal of light on the Pepys period, and Michael Lewis, *England's Sea-Officers* (1939). For the Second Dutch War, see A. W. Tedder, *The Navy of the Restoration* (Cambridge, 1916); C. H. Wilson, *Profit and Power: A study of England and the Dutch Wars* (1957); Richard Ollard, *Man of War: Sir Robert Holmes and the Restoration Navy* (1969) and P. G. Rogers, *The Dutch in the Medway* (1970). The ships of the line are described, with illustrations, in F. Fox, *Great Ships: The Battle-fleet of Charles II* (1980). There are three diaries that give vivid pictures of life at sea: by a seaman, Edward Barlow (*Barlow's Journals*, ed. B. Lubbock, 2 vols, 1934); a naval surgeon, James Yonge (*Journal*, ed. F. N. L. Poynter, 1963), and a naval chaplain, Henry Teonge (*Diary, 1675–1679*, ed. G. E. Manwaring, The Broadway Travellers, 1927). The Tangier episode is dealt with in E. M. G. Routh, *Tangier, an Outpost of Empire, 1661–84* (1912).

A list of diaries roughly contemporary with that of Pepys (embellished with a sprightly introduction) is to be found in William Matthews's standard bibliography: *British Diaries [1442–1942]* (Univ. Cal. Press and Cambridge, 1950). They are, principally, those of John Evelyn (the definitive edition is by E. S. De Beer, Oxford, 6 vols, 1955; he also published it in slightly reduced form in one volume in the Oxford Standard Authors series in 1959); Robert Hooke (ed. H. W. Robinson and W. Adams, 1935); Ralph Josselin (the definitive edition is by A. Macfarlane, 1976, who has written an interesting commentary, from the point of view of a social anthropologist, in *The Family Life of Ralph Josselin*, Cambridge, 1970); Roger Lowe (ed. W. L. Sachse, 1938); John Locke (*Locke's Travels in France 1675–1679*, ed. J. Lough, Cambridge, 1953); Anthony à Wood (*Life and Times*, 5 vols, ed. A. Clark, Oxford Historical Society, 1891–1900) and Celia Fiennes (*Journeys*, ed. C. Morris, 1947; illust. ed. 1982). Of slighter interest are those of Thomas Rugge, annalist of events in London (*Diurnal*, ed. W. L. Sachse, Camden Society, 1961), and Elias Ashmole the astrologer (ed. R. T. Gunther, Old Ashmolean Reprints, 1927). There are summaries of many sixteenth- and seventeenth-century diaries, and some observations on diary keeping in general, in A. Ponsonby, *English Diaries* (1923) and *More English Diaries* (1927).

# —✤GLOSSARY✤—

This list consists of words and phrases, mostly obsolete, which the reader may find it difficult to understand. It does not include obsolete forms whose meaning is sufficiently clear without explanation – e.g. jangle (quarrel) or bedaggled (bedraggled). Where a word is used by Pepys in several senses the different meanings are separated by semicolons. No note is made of the modern meaning where a word is used in both obsolete and modern senses, nor are all the spellings recorded. Old forms of place names – Gracious (Gracechurch) Street, Cales (Cadiz) etc. – are to be found not here but in the Index. A few foreign words and phrases are included, but there is no attempt to translate titles of books and songs, or Pepys's macaronic language.

The definitions in many cases owe much to those given by Dr Richard Luckett in the Large Glossary which he compiled for the *Companion* volume of the full edition of the diary.

ABLE: wealthy
ACCENT: accentuation
ACCOUNTANT: official responsible for expenditure
ACTOR: male or female performer
ADMIRAL SHIP: flagship carrying a.
ADMIRE, ADMIRATION: wonder
AGUE: malarial fever
ALPHABET: index
AMUSED: bemused
ANABAPTISTS: Baptists and other extreme Noncomformists
ANGEL: gold coin worth c. 10s.
ANNOY: molest, hurt
ANOTHER GATE'S BUSINESS: different altogether
APPOSITION DAY: public examination at St Paul's School

BAGGAGE: woman (in affectionate sense)
BAILEY (BAYLY): bailiff

BALK: beam of timber
BALLET: ballad
BAND: neckband
BASS: bass viol
BATTELL: cockfight
BAVIN: bundle of kindling wood
BAYS: baize, light woollen cloth
BEARD: moustache
BEAVER: fur hat
BEWPERS: fabric used for flags
BILL: legal warrant; b. of exchange; b. of mortality (weekly list of burials issued by Parish Clerks' Company)
BIRD'S EYE: spotted fabric
BLACK: dark-haired
BLACKAMORE: a black (m. or f.)
BLADE: gallant
BLIND: obscure, out of the way
BOWPOTT: flower pot
BRANSLE: ceremonious round dance
BREACH: bay; harbour

BREAK THOUGHTS: disclose
BRIG(ANTINE): small vessel equipped for sailing and rowing
BRISTOL MILK: sweet sherry
BROTHER: brother-in-law; colleague
BULLET: cannon ball
BUSSE: heavily built N. Sea fishing vessel
BUTT: cask
BUTTERED ALE: a. with butter, sugar and cinnamon
BY-BOOK: notebook

CABAL: inner group of ministers; faction
CALL: call on/for
CAMELOT: strong ribbed woollen cloth
CAMPAGNIA (It.): campaign
CANAILLE, KENNEL: sewer; ornamental canal
CANCRE: ulcer
CANONS: boot hose tops
CARESSE: make much of
CAST: calculate
CATAPLASM: poultice

CAUDLE: hot thin gruel with wine or ale

CERECLOTH: medicated plaster

CHAGRIN (Fr.): disquieted

CHANGELING: idiot

CHAPTER: usually of Bible

CHARACTER: code, cipher

CHARIOT: light four-wheeled carriage

CHEAPEN: ask the price of

CHEST: the Chatham Chest, pension fund for seamen

CHIMNEY-MONEY: hearth tax

CHIMNEY-PIECE: picture over fireplace

CHINA ORANGE: sweet o.

CHOQUE: choke, obstruction

CHOUSE: to swindle

CHYRURGEON: surgeon

CINQUE PORTS: p. on S.E. coast (Hastings, Sandwich, Dover, Romney and Hythe) originally providing men and services for navy in return for privileges

CLAP: gonorrhoea

CLAP UP: imprison

CLERK OF THE CHEQUE: principal clerical officer of dockyard

CLOSE: shutter

CLOSET: small or private room

CLOUTERLY: clumsily

CLOWN: clodhopper

CLUB: share of expenses

CLYSTER, GLISTER: enema

COACH: captain's state-room in large ship

COD: testicle; small bag

CODPIECE: bagged appen-dage in front of breeches

COLLIER: coal ship

COLLY-FEAST: feast of cullies (friends) at which each pays his share

COMMONS: allowance of food

COMPREHENSION: church union (among Protes-tants)

CONSUMPTION: any wasting disease. *Also* consumptive

CONVENTICLE: meeting of Protestant Nonconform-ists for worship

COOLE: cowl

COPPY, COPYHOLD: tenure of manorial land by copy of customs of manor

COQUIN (Fr.): knave

CORANT(O): French/Italian dance involving running or gliding step

COXON: coxswain

CRAZY: infirm

CROP: crop-eared

CRUSADO: Portuguese coin worth 3s.

CUDDY: cabin in large ship in which officers took meals

CUNNING: knowledgeable

CURIOUS: discriminating; fine, delicate

DEAD COLOUR: preparatory layer of colour in painting

DEALS: sawn timber for decks etc.

DEDIMUS: writ empowering Justice of the Peace

DEFLUXION: discharge of humours

DEFYANCE (Fr.): mistrust

DELICATE: pleasant

DEPUTACION: appointment of deputy

DIALECT: jargon

DISPENSE: outgoings

DOCKET: abstract of letters patent

DOG: to follow

DOGGED: surly

DORTOIRE (Fr.): monastic dormitory

DOXY: whore, mistress

DRAM: timber from Drammen, Norway

DRAUGHT: drawing

DRAW: to draft; (of liquids) extract, cause to flow

DRAW IN SPECIES: to focus image

DRAWER: tapster

DROLL: a wag

DRUDGER: dredger, container for sweetmeats etc.

DRUGGERMAN: dragoman

DUCKET: ducat; foreign gold coin worth 9s.

EARTH: earthenware

EASILY AND EASILY: more and more slowly

EFFEMINACY: love of women

EN HORA BUENA (Span.): expression of con-gratulation

ESPINETTE: spinet; plucked keyboard instrument with strings running at 45° to keyboard

ESTABLISHMENT: number of men, officers, ships etc. in fleet

EUPHROE (shipbuilding): uphroe, deadeye, long piece of wood (with holes) supporting lines

FACTORY: trading station

FALL: to go bankrupt

FALLOW: to court

FAMILY: household (including servants)

FANATIC: extreme Nonconformist

FANFARROON: braggart

FARTHINGALE: hooped skirt or petticoat

FAT: vat

FATHER: senior official under whom clerks served

FELLET (OF TREES): a cutting

FERRANDIN, FARANDINE (Fr.): cloth of silk mixed with wool or hair

FIDDLE: usually violin

FINE: payment for lease

FIREBALL: used for kindling

FIRESHIP: ship filled with combustibles used to ram enemy

FLAG, FLAGMAN: flag officer

FLAGEOLET (Fr.): whistle-flute

FLESHED: relentless

FLOWER: beautiful girl

FLUX: to induce (by mercury) discharge of bodily secretions (esp. saliva) for cure of pox

FOND (Fr.): fund

FOY, FOY-DINNER: departure gift or feast

FRENCH BACON: b. cured with brine and saltpetre

FROST-BITE: to invigorate by exposure to cold

FUMBLER: an unperforming husband

GALL: to harass

# Glossary

GALLEY: large open rowing boat

GENIUS: inborn character

GHOSTLY: spiritual

GILDER, GUILDER: Dutch money of account worth 2s.

GITTAR, GUITTAR (Span.): instrument with five (rather than the modern six) double courses of gut strings

GITTERNE: small member of guitar family with four double courses of gut strings

GLASS: telescope

GLEEKE: three-handed card game

GLISTER: see Clyster

GLOSSE, BY A FINE: by a plausible pretext

GOOD WORD: good news

GOSSIP: to act as godparent

GREEN GOOSE: young g.

GREENS: plants, creepers

GRIEF: bodily pain

GROOM: male servant, attendant

GRUDGING: a 'touch' of an illness

GUARDA MI SPADA! (Span.): Beware of my sword!

GUESTHOUSE (Du. *gasthuis*): almshouse

HABIT: dress

HALF-SHIRT: short s.

HAND-TO-FIST: with a will

HARSLET: pork offal

HAUNT: pay court to (amorous)

HEAD-PIECE: helmet

HECTOR: boaster, swashbuckler

HOG-HIGH: pig-headedly

HOGSHEAD: half a butt

HOLLAND: a variety of linen

HOT-HOUSE: bath-house

HOUSE: royal household; H. of Parliament

HOUSE OF OFFICE: latrine

HUEGO (*juego*) de Toros (Span.): bullfight

HUMOUR: mood; character; bodily fluid

HUSBAND: one who gets good/bad value for money; steward

HUSBANDRY: economy

HYPOCRAS: sweet spiced wine

IMPERTINENT: irrelevant

IMPOSTUME: abscess

INDIAN GOWN: undress g. of rich material

INSTAR OMNIUM (Lat.): typical of them all

INSTITUCIONS: instructions

INSTRUMENT: agent; clerk

JACK: spit

JACKANAPES COAT: sailor's short jacket (monkey jacket)

JADE: woman (in affectionate sense)

JAMAICA BRAWN: b. made from wild pig of J.

JAPAN: lacquer

JAPAN GOWN: Japanese silk g.

JOLE (of fish): cut consisting of head and shoulders

JUSTE-AU-CORPS (Fr.): close fitting knee-length coat

KEEP: housekeep, live, stay

KENNEL: see Canaille

KETCH: sailing vesssel with two masts; round song (catch)

KNEES: angle-shaped timbers

KNOT: clique

LACE: braid made with gold- or silver-thread

LAISSER ALLER LES FEMMES (Fr.): let women alone

LAMB'S WOOL: hot spiced ale with roasted apples

LAVER: basin of fountain

LEADS: flat space on roof, sometimes boarded over

LEAN: lie down

LESSON: piece of music

LETTER OF MART: l. of marque (official licence to fit out vessel to attack hostile shipping)

LINES (of ship): designer's drawings

LOAD (of timber): 50 cu. ft

LOCK: artificial tress of hair

LUTE: plucked instrument with six courses of strings and peg-box at right-angle to neck

LYRA-VIOL: small bass viol with 'lyra' or 'harp-way' tuning

MACHINE: device for creating spectacular stage effect

MAD: whimsical

MADAME (prefix): used of widows and elderly ladies

MAIN: strong, bulky

MA(I)STER: expert, professional

MAKE (of cocks): match

MANAGED-HORSE (Fr.): h. trained in riding school

MASTY: burly

MEAT: food

MECHANIQUE: one having manual occupation

MEDIUM. mean, average

MILK-MEAT: dairy produce

MILLON: water-melon (*Citrullus vulgaris*): cf. Musk melon

MIS (prefix): used of young maids

MISLING, MISLY: drizzling

MISTRESS (prefix): used of young unmarried women as well as of married w.

MITHRYDATE: sleeping draught

MODERN: recent

MODEST: virtuous

MOHER (Span. *mujer*): woman, wife

MOLD: mole, breakwater

MOLEST: annoy

MOND: orb (royal jewel)

MONTH'S MIND, TO HAVE A: to have a great desire

MORNING DRAUGHT: drink (sometimes with snack) at mid-morning

MOULD (shipbuilding): full-scale wooden pattern of ship set out on mould-loft floor

MUM: strong spiced ale imported from Germany

MUSIC: band, choir

MUSK MELON: ordinary m. (*Cucumis Melo*)

MUSTY: peevish

MYSTERY: craft; art; trade

NAKED BED, TO GO TO ONE'S: to go to bed without nightclothes

NATIVITY: horoscope

NAVY: Navy Office

NAVY OFFICERS: officials of Navy Office

NEAT: ox

NIGHTGOWN: dressing gown

NOISE: band of musical instruments

NORTHDOWN ALE: Margate ale

NULLA PUELLA NEGAT (Lat.): no girl ever refuses

NURSERY: training school for actors

OARS: *see* Pair of oars

OF COURSE: as usual

OFFICERS: *see* Navy

OLEO (Span.): stew

OLIM, HERI, HODI, CRAS NESCIO CUJUS (Lat.): once upon a time; yesterday; today; tomorrow I know not whose

OMBRE (Span.): three-handed card game

ONLY: main, mainly

OPEN: to explain

OPERA: spectacular entertainment involving painted scenery and stage machinery

OPINIASTREMENT (Fr.): obstinately

ORA (Lat.): brim of pot or basin

ORDINARY: eating place serving fixed-price meals

OTACOUSTICON: ear trumpet

OYER AND TERMINER (Law Fr.): commission (issued to a judge) to hear and determine

PACQUET-BOAT: mail-boat

PAIR OF OARS: large river-boat rowed by two men each with two oars. cf. Scull

PAIR (of organs): a single instrument consisting of several parts

PASSION: feeling, mood

PASSIONATE: pathetic; provoking compassion

PATTEN: overshoe (wooden sole mounted on iron, with leather strap)

PENDANCES: ear-rings

PENDANTS: ship's flags

PERSPECTIVE GLASS: telescope or binoculars

PERUQUES: artificial curls

PESA ME (*pésame*, Span.): expression of sympathy

PHILOSOPHY: natural science

PHYSIC: laxative, purge

PIECE: gold coin worth c. 20s.

PINNER: fill-in above décolletage; coif

PIPKIN: earthenware pot with handle

PLACKET: petticoat

PLEASANT: comic

PLAT: chart, map; level; flower-plot

PLATERY: craft of making metal plate

POINT-DE-GESNE (Fr.): Genoa lace

POLICY: cunning

POOR WRETCH: poor dear

POSSET: spiced hot milk with wine or beer

POWDERED: salted

PRAGMATIC: interfering, conceited

PRESENT, PRESENTLY: immediate, immediately

PRESS: cupboard, bookcase; impressment

PRESS-BED: bed folding into p.

PRETEND: to allege

PRICK: to write out music

PRINCE: ruler

PRISE, PRIZE: price, worth

PRONUNCIATION: elocution, delivery

PUNCH: short thick man or boy

PURL: hot beer mixed with bitter herbs

PUSS: ill-favoured woman

RAKE-SHAMED: disreputable

RA(E)NCONTRE (Fr.): encounter

RARE: fine, splendid

RECEIVER: receptacle

RECEPI (Lat.): receipt

RECRUITE: reinforcement

REFORMADO: naval/military officer serving without commission

RELIGIOUS: monk, nun

RIDING: satirical procession in mockery of shrewish

wife

RIGHT-HAND MAN: soldier on whom drill man-oeuvre turns

ROMANCE: tale

ROMANTIQUE: having characteristics of tale

RUB: check, stop

RUNNING (of committee): temporary

SACK: white wine from Spain or Canaries

SASSE (Du.): lock

SCALE (of music): gamut, hexachordal system predating major/minor key system

SCHOOL: to scold

SCOTOSCOPE: portable spyglass for seeing objects in dark room

SCRIVENER: copyist, sometimes equivalent of modern notary or solicitor

SCULL: small river-boat rowed by single waterman using pair of oars. cf. Pair of oars.

SEEM: pretend (make it s.)

SET UP ONE'S REST: to make one's whole aim

SHAG: worsted or silk cloth with velvet nap on one side

SIT: to hold meeting

SKIMMER: flat pan with perforated base

SLOPS: seamen's ready-made clothes

SLUG: rough metal projectile, bullet

SOLICITOR: agent; one who solicits business

SOUND: fish-bladder

SPECIES: *see* Draw in s.

SPIKET: spigot, faucet, tap

SPINET: *see* Espinette

S.P.Q.R. (Lat.): *Senatus Populusque Romanus* (the Senate and people of Rome), official formula and motto used under Roman Republic

SPUDD: spade

SPY: spy-ship, ship used for reconnaissance

STAY: to keep waiting

STIRRED (of beer in cask): disturbed, perturbed

STOUT: courageous

STUFF: usually woollen fabric

SUCCESS: eventuality (good or bad)

SURRENDER (legal): deed yielding up tenancy of copyhold estate

SYMPHONY: instrumental introduction or interlude in vocal composition

TABBY: ribbed silk

TABLES: backgammon

TAILLE, TALLE: figure, shape

TALLY: wooden stick used by Exchequer in account-ing, in two matching parts for security, and notched to show value

TANSY: sweetened egg pudding with flavouring

TARPAULIN: sea-bred captain, as opposed to gentleman captain

TELL: count, reckon

TENNIS: real (royal) tennis, played indoors

TENT (Span.): red wine

TERCE: measure of wine (42 gallons)

TERMS: menstrual periods

THEORBO: large lute with two heads used for accompanying

THOSE: menstrual periods

THRUSH: inflammation of throat and mouth

TICKET: seaman's pay-ticket

TIRE: tier, gun-deck

TIRING ROOM (theat.):

dressing room

TONGUE: reputation, fame

TOSSE: fright, confusion

TOUR: turn

TOUR, THE: coach parade of *beau monde* in Hyde Park

TRANSIRE (Law Lat.): warrant allowing goods through customs

TRAPAN: to perform brain surgery

TREAD (of birds): copulate

TREBLE: t. viol

TRIANGLE: triangular virginals

TRILL(O): rhythmical repetition of one note

TRIM: shave

TRIPOS: licensed jester at Cambridge degree ceremony

TRUCKLE/TRUNDLE BED: low bed on castors kept under main bed

UMBLES: entrails of deer

UNCOUTH: unfamiliar

UNTRUSS: undo breeches, defecate

USE: usury, interest

USE (V.): to be accustomed

USE UPON USE: compound interest

VAUNT: sell

VIOL: flat-backed fretted bowed instrument with six gut strings, held between knees and bowed with underhand grip; surpassed in

popularity by violin from 1670s

VIRGINALS: small oblong plucked instrument in which the strings run at right-angles to keyboard

VIRTUOSO: man of wide learning

VIRTUOSOS, COLLEGE OF: Royal Society

WAISTCLOTH (ship's): cloth hung between quarter-deck and forecastle as decoration or camouflage

WAISTCOAT: male under-garment sometimes partly exposed through doublet

WAIT: to serve turn of duty as official

WATCH: clock

WEEKLY BILL: *see* Bill

WELCH HARP: h. with straight pillar and flat soundboard

WHERRY: small river boat for passengers

WHISK: woman's stiffened neckerchief

WILDE: wile

WIND: wine

WIND LIKE A CHICKEN: to wind round one's little finger

WIPE: sarcasm, insult

YARD: penis

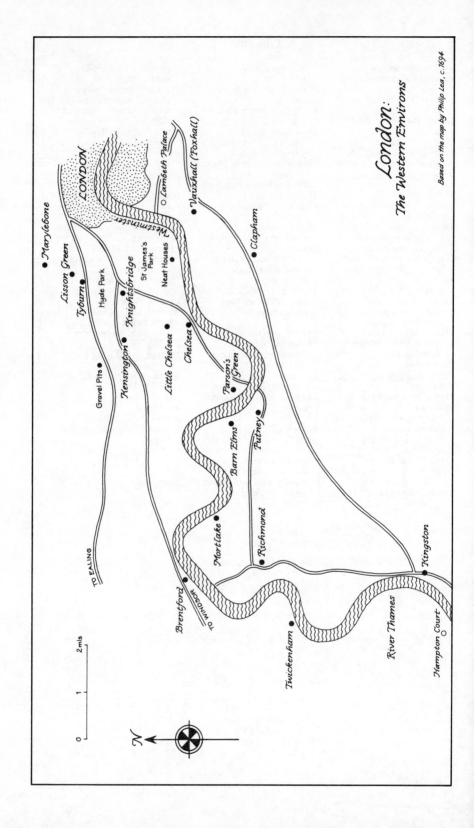

London:
The Western Environs

Based on the map by Philip Lea, c.1694

LONDON

Marylebone

Lisson Green

Tyburn

Hyde Park

Knightsbridge

Kensington

Gravel Pits

Little Chelsea

Chelsea

St James's Park

Neat Houses

Westminster

Lambeth Palace

Vauxhall (Foxhall)

Clapham

Parson's Green

Putney

Barn Elms

Mortlake

Richmond

Brentford

TO WINDSOR

TO EALING

Twickenham

River Thames

Hampton Court

Kingston

N

0    1    2 mls

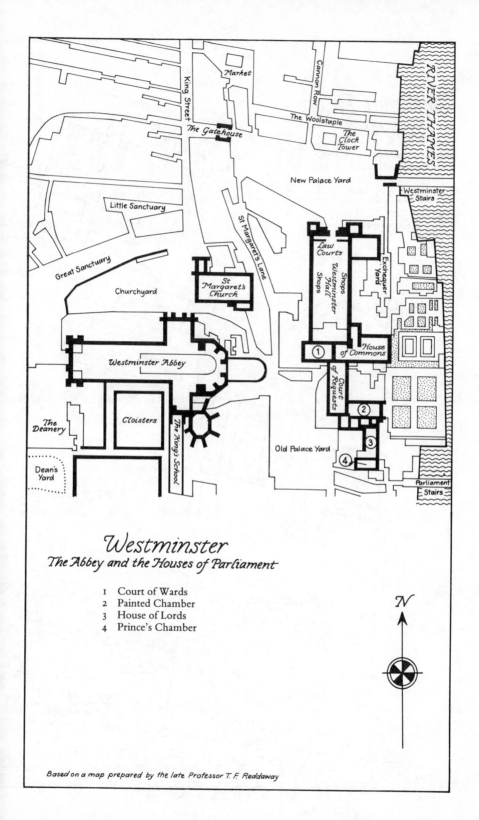

# Westminster
## The Abbey and the Houses of Parliament

1   Court of Wards
2   Painted Chamber
3   House of Lords
4   Prince's Chamber

N

Based on a map prepared by the late Professor T. F. Reddaway

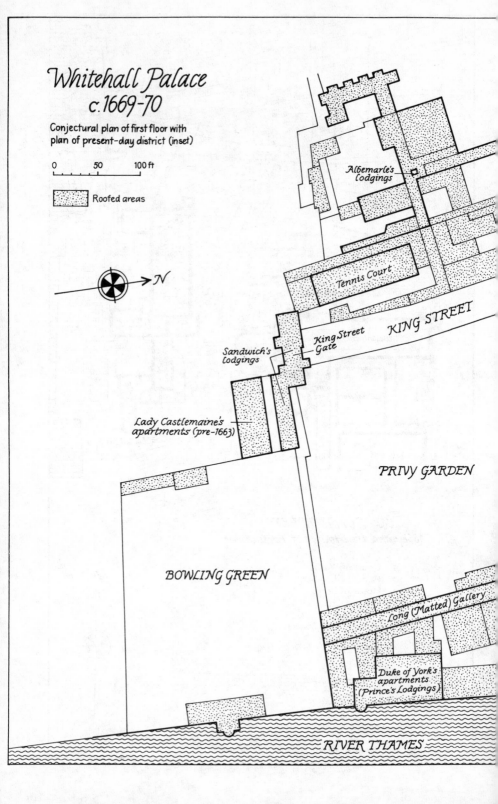

# Whitehall Palace
## c.1669-70

Conjectural plan of first floor with
plan of present-day district (inset)

0     50     100 ft

Roofed areas

N

Albemarle's
lodgings

Tennis Court

King Street
Gate

KING STREET

Sandwich's
lodgings

Lady Castlemaine's
apartments (pre-1663)

PRIVY GARDEN

BOWLING GREEN

Long (Matted) Gallery

Duke of York's
apartments
(Prince's Lodgings)

RIVER THAMES

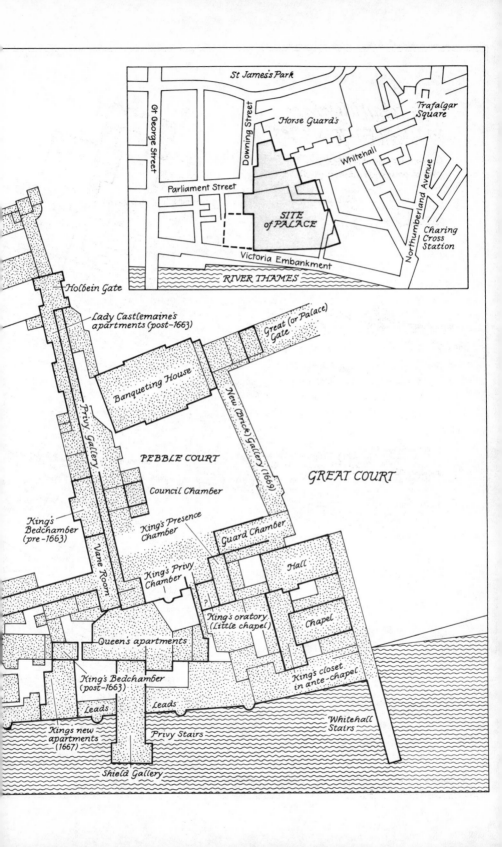

St James's Park

Gt George Street

Downing Street

Horse Guards

Trafalgar Square

Whitehall

Parliament Street

SITE of PALACE

Northumberland Avenue

Charing Cross Station

Victoria Embankment

RIVER THAMES

Holbein Gate

Lady Castlemaine's apartments (post-1663)

Great (or Palace) Gate

Banqueting House

New (Brick) Gallery (1669)

Privy Gallery

PEBBLE COURT

GREAT COURT

Council Chamber

King's Bedchamber (pre-1663)

King's Presence Chamber

Vane Room

Guard Chamber

Hall

King's Privy Chamber

?

King's oratory (little chapel)

Chapel

Queen's apartments

King's Bedchamber (post-1663)

King's closet in ante-chapel

Leads

Leads

Whitehall Stairs

Kings new apartments (1667)

Privy Stairs

Shield Gallery

TO HAMPSTEAD

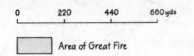

# London
## in the sixteen-sixties

Western half (omitting most minor streets & alleys)

0      220      440     660 yds

Area of Great Fire

Tyburn Gibbet

TO OXFORD

Burlington House

Clarendon House

Piccadilly

Berkeley House

St James's Fields (being develope

Berkshire House

TO KNIGHTSBRIDGE AND KENSINGTON

St James's Palace

The Mall

St James's Pa

Canal

Goring House

TO CHELSEA

Petty Fran

| | |
|---|---|
| 1 | St Martin-in-the-Fields |
| 2 | The Cockpit |
| 3 | Axe Yard |
| 4 | Holbein Gate |
| 5 | King St Gate |
| 6 | Westminster Hall |
| 7 | St Margaret's Church |
| 8 | The Gatehouse |
| 9 | The King's Playhouse, Drury Lane |
| 10 | The New Exchange |
| 11 | The Maypole |
| 12 | St Clement Danes Church |
| 13 | Clare Market |
| 14 | The Duke's Playhouse, Lincoln's Inn Fields |
| 15 | Temple Bar |
| 16 | St Dunstan-in-the-West |
| 17 | The Rolls Chapel |
| 18 | St Andrew's Church, Holborn |

Based on a map prepared by the late Professor T. F. Reddaway

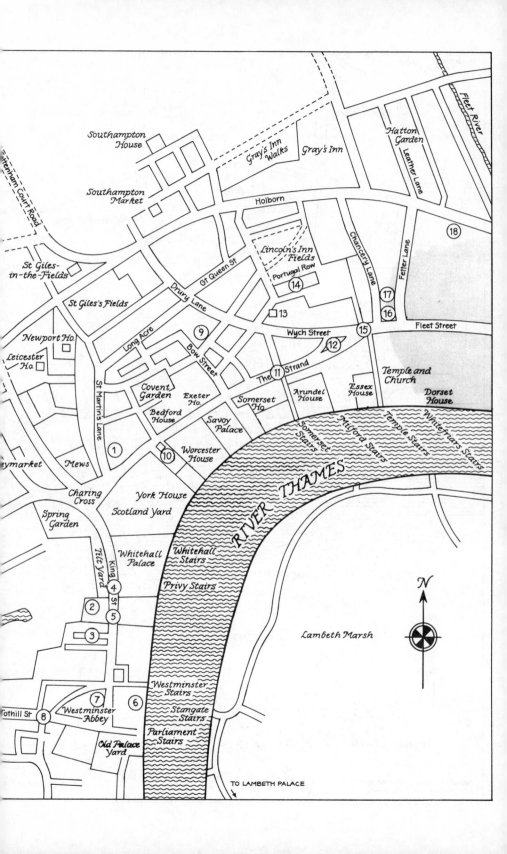

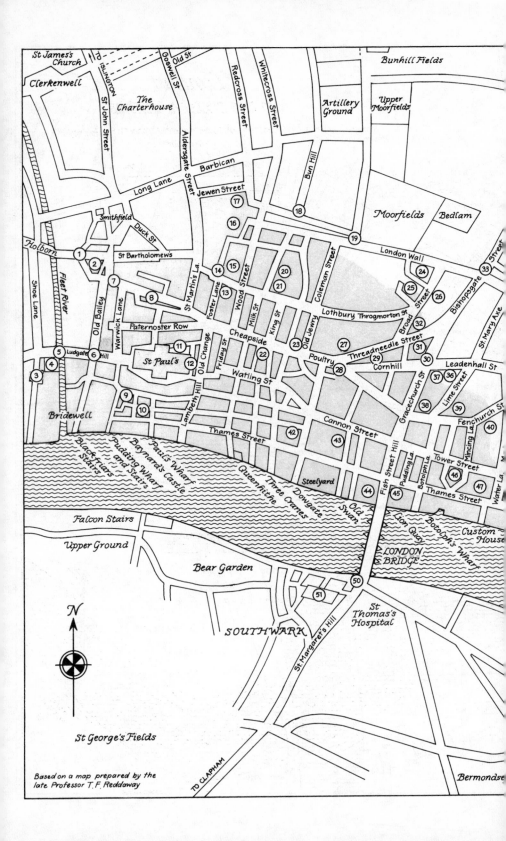

# London
## in the sixteen-sixties
### Eastern half (omitting most minor streets & alleys)

0     220     440     660 yds

Area of Great Fire

| | | | |
|---|---|---|---|
| 1 | Holborn Conduit | 27 | Post Office, 1666 |
| 2 | St Sepulchre's Church | 28 | Stocks Market |
| 3 | SALISBURY COURT | 29 | Royal Exchange |
| 4 | ST BRIDE'S CHURCH | 30 | Cornhill Conduit |
| 5 | Strand Bridge | 31 | Merchant Taylors' Hall |
| 6 | Ludgate | 32 | French Church |
| 7 | Newgate | 33 | Bishopsgate |
| 8 | Newgate Market | 34 | Aldgate |
| 9 | The Wardrobe | 35 | St Katherine Cree |
| 10 | Doctors' Commons | 36 | E. India House |
| 11 | St Paul's Churchyard | 37 | Leadenhall Market |
| 12 | St Paul's School | 38 | St Dionis Backchurch |
| 13 | Goldsmiths' Hall | 39 | The Mitre, Fenchurch St |
| 14 | Aldersgate | 40 | Clothworkers' Hall |
| 15 | Haberdashers' Hall | 41 | ST OLAVE'S, HART ST |
| 16 | Barber-Surgeons' Hall | 42 | Skinners' Hall, Dowgate St |
| 17 | St Giles, Cripplegate | 43 | St Lawrence Poultney |
| 18 | Cripplegate | 44 | Fishmongers' Hall |
| 19 | Moorgate | 45 | St Magnus's Church |
| 20 | Guildhall | 46 | St Dunstan-in-the-East |
| 21 | St Lawrence Jewry | 47 | Trinity House |
| 22 | St Mary-le-Bow | 48 | All Hallows, Barking |
| 23 | Mercers' Hall | 49 | NAVY OFFICE |
| 24 | NAVY TREASURY | 50 | The Bear at the Bridge Foot |
| 25 | Dutch Church, Austin Friars | 51 | St Mary Overie |
| 26 | Gresham College | | (now Southwark Cathedral) |

Artillery Yard

Petticoat Lane

TO MILE END

Whitechapel

34

Minories

Goodman's Fields

Victualling Office and Yards

he Tower

East Smithfield

Ratcliff Highway

Irongate Stairs

Pasture Grounds

TO RATCLIFF & LIMEHOUSE

RIVER THAMES

Wapping

sleydown

TO DEPTFORD & WOOLWICH

Rotherhithe

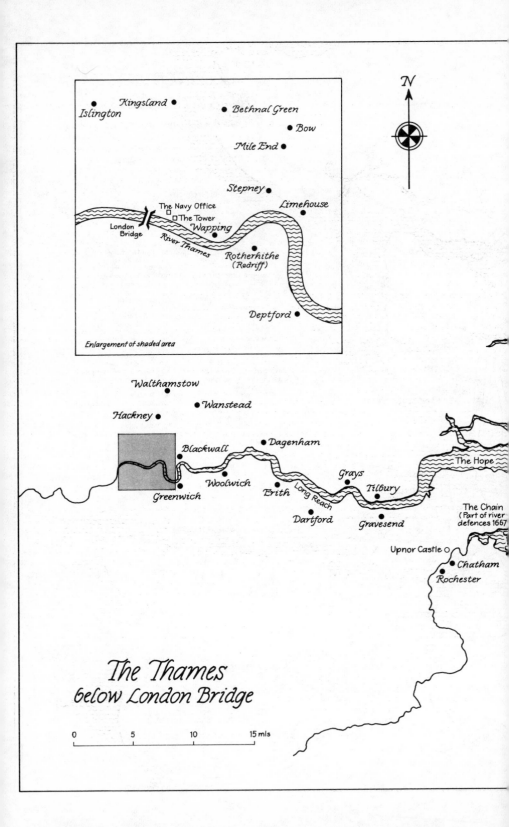

The Thames
below London Bridge

0    5    10    15 mls

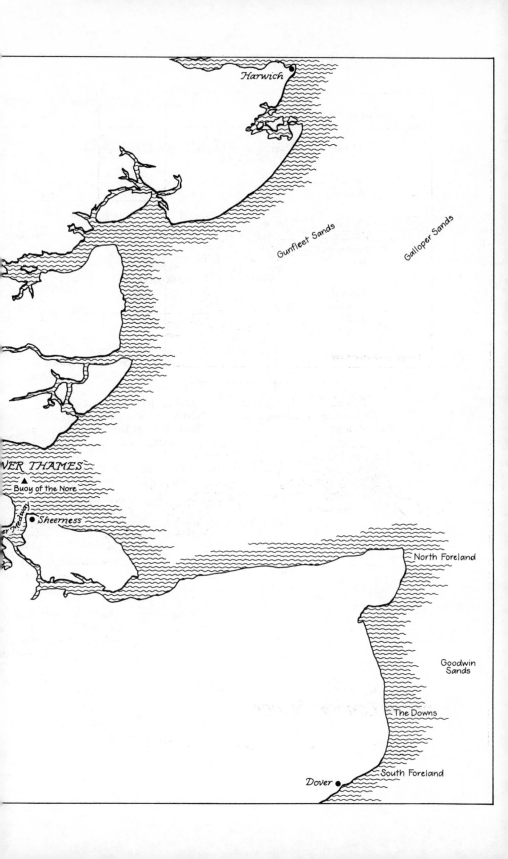

# THE PEPYS FAMILY c.1519-1723

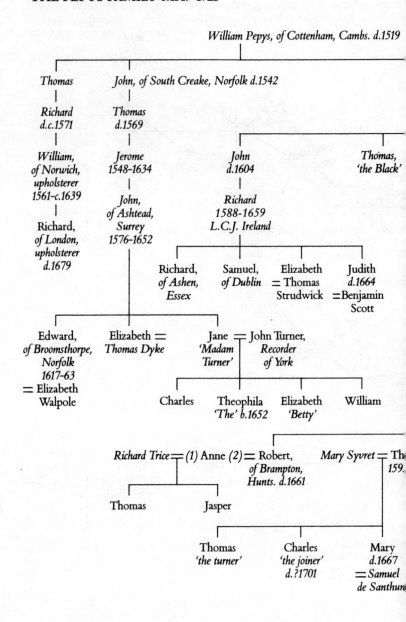

William Pepys, of Cottenham, Cambs. d.1519

Thomas

John, of South Creake, Norfolk d.1542

Richard
d.c.1571

Thomas
d.1569

William,
of Norwich,
upholsterer
1561-c.1639

Jerome
1548-1634

John
d.1604

Thomas,
'the Black'

Richard,
of London,
upholsterer
d.1679

John,
of Ashtead,
Surrey
1576-1652

Richard
1588-1659
L.C.J. Ireland

Richard,
of Ashen,
Essex

Samuel,
of Dublin

Elizabeth
= Thomas
Strudwick

Judith
d.1664
=Benjamin
Scott

Edward,
of Broomsthorpe,
Norfolk
1617-63
= Elizabeth
Walpole

Elizabeth =
Thomas Dyke

Jane = John Turner,
'Madam    Recorder
Turner'     of York

Charles

Theophila
'The' b.1652

Elizabeth
'Betty'

William

Richard Trice = (1) Anne (2) = Robert,
of Brampton,
Hunts. d.1661

Mary Syvret = Th
159.

Thomas

Jasper

Thomas
'the turner'

Charles
'the joiner'
d.?1701

Mary
d.1667
= Samuel
de Santhun

Based on E. Chappell, *Eight Generations of the Pepys Family 1500-1800* (Blackheath, London, 1936). All names except those in italic are those of persons alive in the diary period. Some members of the family, of minor importance in the diary, are omitted, either from lack of information or lack of space.

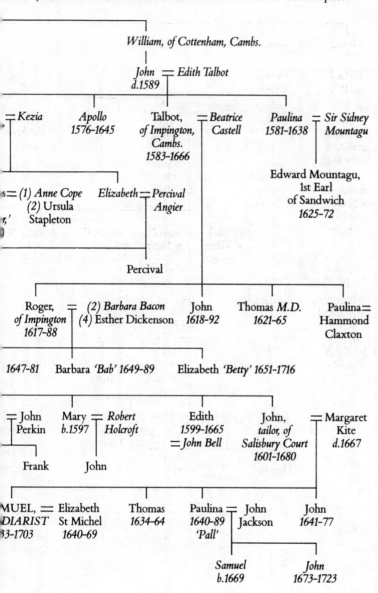

# RELATIVES AND CONNECTIONS BY MARRIAGE OF THE PARENTS OF THE DIARIST

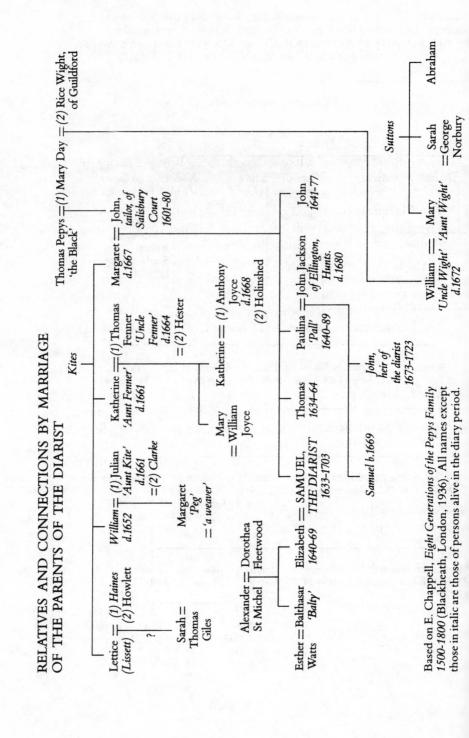

Based on E. Chappell, *Eight Generations of the Pepys Family 1500–1800* (Blackheath, London, 1936). All names except those in italic are those of persons alive in the diary period.

# ILLUSTRATION ACKNOWLEDGEMENTS

The publishers would like to thank the following for permission to reproduce illustrations:

The Marquess of Bath, Longleat House (plate 6)
The Trustee of the Will of the late Earl of Berkeley (plate 14); photograph: Courtauld Institute of Art
The Trustees of the British Museum (plates 15, 19 and 21)
The Greater London Council as Trustees of the Iveagh Bequest, Kenwood (plate 18)
The Guildhall Library, London (plate 17)
The Master and Fellows of Magdalene College, Cambridge (plates 2, 16, 22, 23, 24 and 25)
Mr P. Malet de Carteret (plate 5)
The Mansell Collection (plate 20)
Victor Montagu Esq. (plate 10)
The National Maritime Museum, London (plates 7, 8, 9 and 13); plates 7 and 13 are from the Greenwich Hospital Collection
The National Portrait Gallery, London (plates 1 and 3)
Lord Sackville (plate 11); the portrait comes from the collection at Knole; photograph: Courtauld Institute of Art

Plates 4 and 12 come from private collections.

# ❖INDEX❖

# —❧INDEX❧—

The index is intended both as a guide to the text (though necessarily selective) and as a means of conveying information which might otherwise have been given in footnotes. Its general design and many of its conventions are based on the index to the complete edition. *Pepys* himself is understood to be the subject of the whole diary. A small number of references have been gathered under his name, covering events before the diary period. Other references to him are distributed throughout the index, signalled by the initial P; *Elizabeth Pepys* (EP) is similarly treated, the references under her name being restricted to principal events and activities. *London* is the almost permanent venue of the events described, and references under that heading are confined to civic affairs. Otherwise *persons and places* are given in the commonest of forms used in the text here printed (with modern or received forms given in square brackets) save where it is convenient or logical to give the modern forms followed by any textual variant enclosed in round brackets. *Peers* and holders of courtesy titles appear under their titles; titles and offices held are limited to the diary era, except in a few cases of well-known persons best remembered by titles or offices held after 1669 (which information is added in square brackets). *Bishops* are to be found under the names of their sees unless at some point Pepys mentions them by surname. *Books, plays and musical compositions* are indexed under the names of their authors and composers where these are given by Pepys or if more than one work is mentioned; otherwise by title as printed in italic in the text (representing longhand in the MS.); or else under the subject matter if Pepys offers neither author/composer nor title.

It remains for me to thank the Editor and his wife for their help at many points in my work.

C.S. Knighton

# Index

# Index

# Index

# Index

# Index

# Index

# Index

# Index

# Index

Creed Church [St Katherine Cree]: 820

Creighton (Creeton, Critton), Dr Robert, chaplain to the King, Dean of Wells 1660–70 [Bishop 1670–2]: 184, 370, 815, 825–6

Crew, John Crew, 1st Baron Crew of Stene 1661, Councillor of State Feb.-May 1660; Sandwich's father-in-law: political: 18–19, 37, 764; personal: 510, 762, 1018; P visits/dines with: 171, 243, 308, 401, 416, 504–5, 688, 833, 834, 859, 866, 894, 903; P visits house, Lincoln's Inn Fields (where Sandwich lodged): 2, 5, 10, 20, 23, 25, 26, 29, 55, 56, 58, 71, 76, 82, 105, 177, 193, 253, 294; wife: 171, 405; sons: Sir Thomas (Kt 1660) [2nd Baron 1679]: 30, 49, 58, 71, 163, 193, 275, 308, 688, 697, 807, 876, 888; his children: 193, 749; John: 30, 688, 697, 859; his servant: 23; Dr Nathaniel, Fellow [later Rector] of Lincoln College, Oxford: 688, 749

Crisp, Diana: 72, 77, 79, 80, 81; brother Laud, of the Wardrobe: 215, 725 (children of P's neighbour, Axe Yard)

Crisp, Sir Nicholas, merchant, W. African trade: 175, 179, 223

Crofts, Mr see Monmouth

Cromleholme (Cromlom, Crumlum), Samuel, High Master of St Paul's School 1657–72: 14, 168, 256, 349, 475–6, 674

Cromwell, Oliver, Lord Protector 1653–8: death: 180; exhumation: 100, 115, 117; coinage: 262; government recalled: 423, 433, 447, 481–2, 721, 783, 813; biography [?anon., The Perfect Politician, 1660]: 818; children: Frances: 433; Mary, Lady Fauconberg: 286; Richard, Lord Protector 1658–9: 23&n., 24, 26&n., 432

Crowe, Ald. William, upholsterer, St Bartholomew's: 88, 948, 949, 960

Crowland, Lincs., Benedictine Abbey, P's ancestral links with: 787

Cumberland, Richard, P's contemporary at school and Magdalene, [Bishop of Peterborough 1691–1718]: 742, 872

Custom House: new site for: 668; officers of: 223, 313, 539; boat: 852

Cutler, Ald. Sir John, Bt, merchant: 299, 318

Cutler, William, merchant and naval victualler, Austin Friars and Hackney: 205, 312, 326, 352, 353, 381, 418, 427, 448

Cuttance, Capt. Sir Roger (Kt 1665), naval commander, Flag Captain to Sandwich 1660–5: 17, 31, 32, 33, 35–8 passim, 42, 52, 74, 86, 87, 104, 114, 529, 533, 536, 557, 580; Tangier commissioner: 230, 238, 311

Cutter of Colemanstreete: see Cowley, A.

Dagenham (Dagnams), Essex: 527; P/EP visit: 503–5, 506, 508, 509–12

Dancing/dances: P/EP learn: 269, 271, 273, 274, 276, 278, 281; attend/participate: 81, 125, 127, 300–1, 482, 541, 546, 547, 598, 649, 652, 658, 690, 717, 718, 862, 892, 895, 922, 991, 993; P discusses: 484; morris: 270; stage: 757, 776, 820, 899, 905, 991; at court: 245–6, 354, 693–4, 919

Danckerts (Dancre), Hendrick, painter: pictures by: 980, 984, 1004

Daniel, Richard, Clerk of the Victualling Office: 79, 429

Daniel, Samuel, naval officer: 562, 623, 625, 815; wife, dau. of P's Greenwich landlady Mrs Clerke (q.v.): ?546, 559, 562, 570, 623, ?648, 815

Daniel, Samuel, The collection of the historie of England (1612–18): 417

Dartford, Kent, P visits: 117, 534, 1000, 1003

Davenant, Sir William, poet, dramatist, manager of the King's Company 1660–8: opera: The Siege of Rhodes: 143, 164, 196, 774; P reads (1663 edn): 536–7, 648, 971; has excerpts sung: 548; seeks score: 716; plays: Love and honour: 161; The man's the master: 895, 906; The wits: 756; for adaptations see Fletcher; Shakespeare

Davies, John, Storekeeper, Deptford: 111, 205, 211, 220, 229, 277

Davila, Enrico Caterino, Storia della guerre civile di Francia, trs. William Aylesbury (1647): 642

Davis, John, clerk to Lord Berkeley of Stratton (q.v.): 93, 102, 110, 115; wife: 90&n., 115; son Jack, Navy Office clerk: ?93, 115

Davis, Mary (Mall), actress (Duke's Company): 607, 864, 980

Day, John, Leverington, Cambs., P's gt-uncle by marriage: 309, 310

Deal, Kent: 38, 43, 406; fleet off: 34, 625

Dean, Forest of, Glos.: 181, 218

Deane, Capt. Anthony, shipwright; Assistant, Woolwich 1660; Master Shipwright, Harwich 1664, Portsmouth 1668: 264, 283, 299–300, 312, 379, 384, 387, 414, 437, 547, 615, 618, 720, 748, 842–3, 901, 934, 1011–12

Debussy (De Busty), Lawrence, merchant: 526, 702

De Cretz: Emmanuel de Critz, Serjeant-Painter to the King: 58

Deering [Dering], Sir Edward, Bt: 481

De Lestrade: Godefroy, Comte d'Estrades, French ambassador to England: 157; to the United Provinces: 868

Delft, Netherlands, P visits: 46–7

1061

# Index

1062

# Index

# Index

# Index

at Great Yarmouth 1665–7: P admires/ values: 559, 799, 815, 816; assists P officially: 567, 677, 849; 938, 939, 952, 953, 954, 1009, 1017; private errands/ journeys &c.: 789, 791, 793, 794, 839, 1001, 1002, 1023

Glanville, William, barrister, Greenwich, Evelyn's brother-in-law: 535, 550, 551, 554

Gloucester, Henry, Duke of, youngest brother of Charles II: 48, 49, 50, 77, 78, 79

Goddard, Jonathan, F.R.S., Professor of Physic, Gresham College from 1653, inventor of Goddard's drops: 469, 575

Godolphin, Sir William (Kt 1668), secretary to Sandwich's Spanish embassy 1667–8: 870, 873–4, 886, 889, 947, 981

Gold, Sir Nicholas, 1st Bt 1660, M.P., merchant: 5, 338; widow: 338, 397–8

Goldsmiths' Hall, Foster Lane: 493

Gomboust, Jacques, map of Paris (1652): 696

Goodgroome, John, composer, singing-master, royal musician in ordinary: 142, 158, 203, 245, 699, 704, 738, 756, 769, 823

Goods, John, servant to Sandwich: 37, 43, 48, 51, 115

Goring House (on site of present Buckingham Palace): 62

Gosnell, ?Winifred, briefly companion to EP: 234, 235, 237, 239, 240, 241; later actress (Duke's Company): 281, 424, 980

Göteborg (Gottenburg(h)), Sweden, shipping from: 407, 420

Gotier: ?Jacques Gaultier, lutenist and singer, formerly of the King's Musick: 295

*Grand Cyrus: see* Scudéri

Graunt, Capt. John, F.R.S., draper, trainband officer, pioneer demographer: 299, 300, 342, 431, 582, 903; his *Natural and political observations . . . upon the bills of mortality* (1662): 186

Graveley, Cambs., dispute over Robert P's land: 152, 154&n., 155

Gravesend, Kent, P visits: 55, 126, 517, 532–3, 538, 785, 811, 943

Gray (Grey), Thomas, merchant (R. Africa Company), member of the Fishery Corporation: 421, 434, 440

Gray's Inn: student rebellion: 772–3

Grays, Essex: 532, 785

'Great, good and just' *see* Wilson, J.

Greatorex, Ralph, scientific instrument-maker, Strand: 5, 89, 113, 138, 202, 277–8, 302, 316; apprentice: 985

Grebus [Grabu], Luis, French composer, Master of the King's Musick 1666–74: 832, 848

Greenwich, Kent: P visits: 189, 217, 264, 277, 344, 379, 382, 396, 399, 493, 620, 623; visits palace (rebuilt 1662–c.70)/ park (privately): 190, 205, 209, 395; (officially): 507, 623; castle (converted into observatory 1675–6): 190; painting: 980; Navy Office removed to during Plague: 503n., 517, 518, 520, 521, 523, 525, 538; P lodges at: 540, 570

Greeting, Thomas, flageolet teacher, player in the King's Musick and Chapel Royal: 733, 734, 773, 778, 797, 804, 822, 862, 937, 993

Gregory, John, of the Exchequer, from 1660 of the Secretary of State's office: 19, 932

Gresham, Sir Thomas (d. 1579): statue: 666

Gresham College, Old Broad St/ Bishopsgate (est. 1596 as civic academy) 668, 669; as premises of Royal Society *see that heading*

Greville, Sir Fulke (1st Baron Brooke), *Life of . . . Sir Philip Sidney* (1652): 859

Griffith (Griffin), William, doorkeeper, Navy Office: 96, 799; wife: 774; child: 393–4; maid: 209, 617

Grove, Capt. Edward, River Agent for Navy Board and Tangier Committee: 260, 265, 265–6, 270–1, 279, 498; wife: 349

Guildhall: 121, 122, 207, 315, 867; rebuilding: 854

Guinea: 101, 149; conflict with Dutch in: 374, 377, 379, 411, 415, 417–18, 422, 427, 428, 448, 454, 471, 472

Guinea Company *see* Royal Africa Company

Gunfleet, the: shoal off Essex coast: 489, 622

Gunning, Peter, prominent Anglican officiant during Commonwealth, [Bishop of Chichester 1669, of Ely 1675–84]: 1–2, 4, 10, 13, 17, 18, 24

Gunpowder Plot Day, observance: 92, 440

Guns (P): 110, 747

'Guyland': 'Abd Allāh al-Ghailān, Moroccan warlord: 220

Gwyn, Nell, orange-girl, actress (King's Company), the King's mistress from c.1669, ancestress of Dukes of St Albans: P admires: 480&n., 764, 834, 977; kisses: 717; her performances: 717, 735, 744–5, 834, 856–7, 906; off stage: 807; King's interest: 864

Gyles [Giles], Sarah, (b. Kite), P's cousin: 423, 789, 829; children: 565, 829

Haberdashers' Hall, Staining Lane/Maiden Lane: 493

Hacket, John, Bishop of Coventry and

1066

# Index

Lichfield: 195, 870
Hackney, Mdx: P/EP visit: 381, 393, 404, 480, 616, 633, 642, 751, 758, 905, 931
Hague, The: 76, 729&n.; P visits: 43–7
Hairdressing *see* Dress
Hale, Lancs., John Middleton of, wrestler (d. 1623): 922
Halifax, George Savile, 1st Viscount, [1st Marquess of, 1682], statesman: 932, 992, 994
Hall, Betty, actress (King's Company): 717, 971
Hall, – , husband of Anne P, Worcs.: 62
Hallworthy *see* Hollworthy
Hamburg, trade with: 327, 493, 536, 555, 571
Hamilton, – , courtier: ?one of six sons of Sir George Hamilton of Dunalong: 56; (the same): 693
Hammersmith, Mdx: 1013, 1021
Hampton Court, Mdx, royal palace, largely built by Wolsey and Henry VIII: 115, 202, 216, 221, 508; court at: 197, 199, 200, 210, 577; P/EP visit: 195, 577; P orders/rejects painting at: 980, 1004
Hampton Wick, Mdx: P's lodgings: 577–8
Hardy, Nathaniel, Dean of Rochester 1660–70: 46, 78–9, 670
Harman, Rear-Adm. Sir John (Kt 1665): 497, 606, 608, 624, 629, 746, 750, 751, 898
Harman, Philip, upholsterer, Cornhill: 417, 423, 574, 598–9, 601, 671, 672, 891, 948; wife Mary (b. Bromfield, d. 1665, distant relative of P): 301, 410, 423, 424, 496
Harper, Thomas, Storekeeper, Deptford: 774, 811
Harrington, Sir James, M.P.: 522
Harrington, James, republican author: 5, 6, 7
Harrington, William, St Olave's parish, East Country merchant; Navy contractor: 330–1, 349, 552, 557, 903
Harris, Henry, actor (Duke's Company): performances: 415, 424, 447, 827, 895, 991; social: 349, 718–19, 733, 780, 861, 862, 892, 894, 897, 902–3, 908, 915, 919, 920, 941
Harris, John, sailmaker to the Navy from 1660: 125, 251
Harrison, Maj.–Gen. Thomas, regicide: 85, 86
Hart, Charles, leading actor of King's Company: 853, 856, 985
Hartlib, Samuel, jun., minor civil servant: 66
Harvey [Hervey], Sir Thomas, Navy Commissioner 1665–8: 628, 725, 801, 806, 844, 884, 888
Harwich, Essex: lighthouse: 439, 459;

fortifications: 741; naval activity off: 481, 484, 494, 627, 784; Dutch landing nr: 802
Haslerig [Heselrige], Sir Arthur, Bt, republican politician: 15, 16
Hatfield, Herts.: P/EP visit: House, (mainly Eliz.), seat of 2nd Earl of Salisbury: 146; church: 434, 817–18
Hatton Garden: 756, 857
Havre de Grace [Le Havre]: 117
Hawley, John, P's colleague in the Exchequer, later in service of Bishop of London: 2–3, 5, 13, 16, 17, 25, 29, 58, 260, 344, 429, 435
Hayls, John, portrait painter: paints P/EP: 584–609 passim, 615, 619, 897, 935; P's father: 630–1, 633; also: 903, 915
Haynes, Joseph, actor (King's Company): 906
Hayter, Thomas, clerk in the Navy Office [and P's successor as Clerk of the Acts 1673–7; Secretary to the Admiralty 1679–80; Comptroller 1680–3]: appointed P's clerk: 60; official work: 73, 98, 99, 100, 127, 190, 202, 203, 539, 557, 559, 677, 678, 848, 849, 884; P recommends as his successor: 1020; unofficial work for P: 662, 790, 796, 835; private/social: 27, 73, 78, 98, 99, 585, 791–2, 794; arrested for conventicling: 273, 274, 281; house burnt: 662, 684
Hayward, Charles, virginals-maker, Aldgate St: 900, 934
Hayward, Edward, assistant to Surveyor of the Navy: 220
Hayward, Capt. John, naval officer: 69, 628, 796–7
Heart *see* Hart
Hempson, William, Clerk of the Survey, Chatham: 126, 127, 382–3
Hemskirke [Heemskerck], Capt. Laurens van (Kt 1669), renegade Dutch naval officer: 653, 909, 914
Henchman, Humphrey, Bishop of Salisbury 1660–3, of London 1663–75: 84, 358, 484, 606, 751
*Henery the 5th, Henry the 5th: see* Orrery
Henrietta, Princess, youngest sister of Charles II, m. (1660) Duc d'Anjou [later Orléans], brother of Louis XIV: 77, 97
Henrietta Maria, Queen-Mother, dau. of Henri IV of France, widow of Charles I: appearance: 97; portrait: 525; return to England: 84&n., 90, 91; subsequent travels to/from France: 107, 114, 214, 500; secret diplomacy: 1013; her court/ household: 97, 223, 247, 272, 354, 464; public appearances: 96, 245; rumour of re-marriage: 96, 245; also: 195, 223, 826
Henry VIII, King of England 1509–47:

1067

# Index

## Index

# Index

# Index

# Index

# Index

# Index

468, 583, 724, 726, 877; P fears her
becoming Catholic: 369, 417, 950, 968,
970; her parents: 196, 460; ashamed of:
284; P's concern for: 351, 751, 975;
brother *see* St Michel
Pepys, John (gt-grandfather), of
Cottenham and Impington, Cambs.
(d. 1589): 787
Pepys, John (father); tailor, Salisbury
Court; retired 1661 to Brampton house,
Hunts., inherited from his brother
Robert (q.v.): character: 631, 777; as
tailor: 26, 54, 80, 84, 141, 142; visits/
dines with P/EP during last years in
London: 2, 8, 20, 27, 28, 65, 73, 93, 98,
107, 116, 128, 138, 199; wedding
anniversary: 86–7; family affairs: 112;
Brampton inheritance: 26, 142–5
passim, 148&n., 149, 151, 200, 271, 272;
income/affairs there: 609, 632, 633,
777–8; P/EP visit: 433, 837–40, 916;
return visits to London: 621, 624, 627,
632–4, 776, 784, 788; to see Fire ruins:
677–80; P sends gold away with: 788,
789, 796; recovers: 838–9; may return to
live with P/EP: 864; P's affection for:
377, 621, 631, 634, 677, 776; advice to P
on his going to sea: 26–7; advises on/
approves P's domestic arrangements: 82,
98, 155; P seeks place for in Wardrobe:
64, 120, 138; P may have to support in
retirement: 247, 272, 411; P sends gifts
to: 250, 353, 421, 449, 450; financial
advice/assistance: 620, 632, 634; P's
bequest to: 790; his relations with other
children: 9, 21–2, 83, 94, 135, 147, 369,
370, 377, 633, 721, 837, 917; and with
other family: 424; with EP: 4, 93, 149,
226, 609, 921, 930; health: 135, 309, 368,
378, 609, 621, 713, 734, 742, 743, 745,
776, 777, 839; visit to Holland (1656):
576; old house destroyed in Fire: 667;
portrait: 631; wife *see* Margaret
Pepys, John (younger brother); ineffectual
cleric; [Clerk of Trinity House 1670–7;
Joint-Clerk of the Acts (with Hayter)
1673–7]: at St Paul's School: 4, 6, 13, 14;
at Cambridge: 9, 19, 20, 21, 22, 78, 302,
305, 336, 611, 632; ill feeling with EP:
306; quarrel with P: 368, 369, 433, 611,
632; visits P: 669, 677; at Brampton:
721, 838, 916, 917; P to support/
patronise in clerical career: 632, 674,
680, 682–3, 837; original legatee of P's
books: 29; helps catalogue them: 706,
1022
Pepys, John (cousin), of Ashtead, Surr.,
lawyer; secretary to Lord Chief Justice
Coke (d. 1652): house: 297, 808;
daughters *see* Dyke; Turner, Jane
Pepys, Dr John (cousin), lawyer, Fellow of

Trinity Hall, Cambridge: 145
Pepys, Margaret (mother: b. Kite): social:
4, 65, 81, 125; religion: 24–5&n.;
improvidence: 147–8; visits Brampton:
148, 489; moves there: 151; P concerned
over her life there: 413; visits: 433;
supports: 620; she seeks reconciliation
between P and brother John: 433; return
visit to London: 489, 490, 493, 499;
quarrels with EP: 226, 609; P finds her
increasingly 'simple': 148, 489; illness:
73, 74, 98, 100, 734, 742, 743; P dreams
of: 745; death: 746–7
Pepys, Nan *see* Anne
Pepys, Paulina (sister) *see* Jackson
Pepys, Richard (cousin), of Ashen, Essex:
81
Pepys, Robert (uncle), of Brampton,
Hunts.: P's expectations of: 23&n., 26,
54, 144; illness/death: 26, 104, 142, 143,
144; legacy: 147–8; P handles estate: 145,
185, 270, 271, 309, 346, 453; wife Anne:
illness: 104, 108, 112, 123, 144; sends for
P's father: 142; troublesome: 144, 145,
146, 453
Pepys, Roger (cousin) Recorder of
Cambridge 1660–79; M.P. Cambridge
borough 1661–79: P seeks legal advice
from: 256; as M.P.: 844; political news
from: 280, 289, 846, 887; family news/
history/business: 280, 787, 863, 872,
875, 876; social: 12, 266, 287, 889, 943,
945, 954, 958, 990, 992–3, 988, 1019;
EP's valentine: 293; P sends gift to: 293;
daughters Bab and Betty: 988&n.,
989–92 passim; son *see* Talbot; (fourth)
wife Esther: 988, 990, 992–3
Pepys, Samuel (the diarist): recollections of
childhood: 136, 296, 334, 381, 860, 917;
schooldays: 91, 113; theatre: 919;
Cambridge: 21, 188, 917–18; early
passions: 165; 296; political talk: 65, 91;
wedding: 159&n., 252, 659; separation
from EP: 159&n., 251; privations of
early married life: 732; voyage to Baltic:
156&n.; destroys adolescent books and
papers: 346, 457; operation for stone: 1,
32
Pepys, Samuel (cousin), of Ireland, cleric:
164
Pepys, Talbot (cousin), s. of Roger (q.v.),
student, Middle Temple: 954, 973, 1003,
1006, 1007, 1013
Pepys, Talbot (gt-uncle), of Impington,
Cambs., Recorder of Cambridge
1624–60, M.P. Cambridge borough
1625: 145&n., 154
Pepys, Thomas (brother), succeeded to
father's tailoring business 1661:
childhood recalled: 381; quarrels with
parents: 83, 135; P's concern for his

1079

# Index

marrying: 170, 171; as tailor: 57, 60,
105, 147, 151, 171, 186, 305, 306, 336,
363, 370; P visits: 226, 305; reluctant to
lend to: 305, 306; gives old clothes
to:125; social: 6, 10, 24, 72, 107, 116,
159, 168, 169, 268, 282, 333; theatre:
109; illness/death: 346, 362–8 passim;
leaves personal/financial disorder: 363,
364, 370, 374, 411
Pepys, Thomas (uncle), elder brother of
P's father; of St Alphage's parish:
dispute over Brampton inheritance:
145&n., 155, 179, 247; settlement: 262,
292, 309, 411, 435, 778, 898&n.; social:
312, 343; son Thomas: carpenter: sends
P tools: 89; dispute over Brampton
inheritance: 155, 256, 309, 310; child's
christening: 490
Pepys, Thomas (cousin) ('the Executor'),
of St Martin-in-the-Fields; magistrate
and government commissioner during
Commonwealth; from 1663 living in
Surrey: P seeks legal advice from: 179;
loan to Sandwich: 351–2; proposed as
J.P.: 611, 612; social: 4, 16, 107; (second)
wife: 107–8, 121
Perkin, John, Parson Drove, Cambs., P's
uncle: 309
Perriman, Capt. John, River Agent to the
Navy Board: 744, 761
Peter, Hugh, Independent divine and
eccentric preacher: 77, 85, 184
Peterborough, Joseph Henshaw, Bishop
of: 1022
Peterborough, Henry Mordaunt, 2nd Earl
of, Governor of Tangier 1661–2;
connoisseur and genealogist: 220, 230,
241, 476, 955, 979, 981; accounts: 353,
356, 358, 371, 378, 382, 385, 393;
pension: 266, 929; wife: 929, 931, 944
Petersfield, Hants.: P at: 191, 192; plague:
750
Petre, Elizabeth Petre, Lady, widow of 4th
Baron, portrait: 585, 588, 592
Pett, Christopher, s. of the Commissioner,
Master-Shipwright, Deptford and
Woolwich 1660–8: 213, 344, 373, 387,
435, 436, 610, 732, 893; daughter: 658
Pett, Peter, F.R.S., Navy Commissioner,
Chatham 1648–60, 1660–7; Master-
Shipwright, Chatham 1664–7: 60, 65,
211, 274, 318, 488, 516–17, 537;
challenged to duel: 644; corruption
alleged: 768, 776; criticised for
unpreparedness of fleet: 636; fears Dutch
attack: 786; blamed for Medway
disaster: 788, 793, 794, 795, 844, 845–6;
as shipbuilder: 93, 119, 129; critical of
others: 345, 361; Chatham Chest: 239;
social: 47, 111, 218, 481, 531, 645; visits
P: 208; accompanies him to Lely's

studio: 229; to Barber-Surgeons' lecture:
261; drinks chocolate with: 445
Pett, Phineas (Capt. Pett), [Kt 1680],
cousin of the Commissioner, Assistant-
Shipwright, Chatham 1660; Master-
Shipwright 1661–80: 73, 127, 674, 936
Pett, Phineas, cousin of the Commissioner;
shipwright, Limehouse: 373
Petty, Sir William (Kt 1661), a founder of
the Royal Society; political economist,
scientist and inventor: as T. Barlow's
agent: 59, 467; P's regard for: 345;
discourse with: 5, 342, 373, 477–8;
experimental double-keeled vessels: 299,
300, 344, 345, 346–7, 468, 469, 477;
mocked by the King: 346–7
*Philaster see* Beaumont and Fletcher
Philip IV, King of Spain 1621–55: 582, 590
Philips, Katherine, *Poems* (1667): 817
Phillips, Lewis, lawyer, Brampton and
Huntingdon: 146, 855, 916
Phillip's Norton [Norton St Philip], Som.:
P at: 924
Pickering, Edward (Ned): in Sandwich's
service: 47, 80; news of Sandwich's
liaison: 307, 325, 397; court news: 347;
social: 150, 255; mistress, later wife,
Dorothy Wilde: 347, 1004; father Sir
Gilbert, Lord Chamberlain to
Cromwell: 949; mother (b. Mountagu):
89; brother John: 36, 37
Pictures (paintings/prints/drawings): P
buys prints: 61, 608, 818–19; keeps in
folder: 173; French prints given to: 982,
988–9; buys/hangs pictures: 97, 171,
616, 657, 703, 967; for EP: 335, 689;
losses after Fire: 673; orders landscapes
by Danckerts: 980, 1004; his pictures/
EP's drawings admired by visitors: 981;
tastes: admires miniatures by Cooper
(q.v.): 987–8; murals by Streeter: 984;
portraits of naval commanders by Lely
(q.v.): 607–8; of Queen Mother by Van
Dyke: 525; of Henry VIII by Holbein:
22, 836; of Lady Castlemaine by
Faithorne (after Lely): 689, 699; Royal
Collection, Hampton Court: 195;
fascinated by trompes: 83, 890, 1006;
observations on perspective: 254; on
stages of portrait composition: 633; on
shading: 601; dislikes landscapes: 601;
has landscape removed from own
portrait by Hayls (q.v.): 606; alterations
to EP's by Savill: 170
Pierce *see* Pearse
Piercy [Percy], Elizabeth, Lady Percy,
dau.-in-law of 10th Earl of
Northumberland (q.v.): 748
Pierrepont (Pierpont), William, politician:
789–90
Pierson [Pearson], John, Master of Trinity

# Index

1081

# Index

# Index

taunts with threat of conversion: 950, 970

Reynolds [Renalds], Edward, Bishop of Norwich 1661–72: 37, 891

Richardson, William, bookbinder: 651, 675, 678, 728, 778, 870, 1018

Richmond, Frances Teresa Stuart (b. Stuart), Duchess of, Maid of Honour to the Queen from 1663; Lady of the Bedchamber from 1667: appearance: 372, 677, 898; as Britannia (on Breda medal): 732; court: 257–8, 492, 693; loved by the King: 258, 284, 319, 350, 571, 607, 702, 913; by the Duke of York: 556; marries (1667) Charles Stuart, 3rd Duke of Richmond and 6th of Lennox: 742, 749; P hopes business with him may lead to meeting her: 943–4

Richmond, Surr.: 213, 294; P at: 195

Rickard [Riccard], Ald. Sir Andrew, leading Levant and E. India merchant, St Olave's parish: 465, 752, 903

Rider, Sir William (Kt 1661), Baltic merchant and Navy contractor: business with Navy Board: 205, 211, 352, 381; Tangier Committee: 230, 238, 342, 371, 378, 382; Trinity House: 175, 179, 369, 491; blamed for sinking ships: 793; social: 5, 355, 448; stories of Genoa: 173, 290; fine house at Bethnal Green: 290; P sends valuables to during Fire: 663, 670, 671

Ridley, Sir Thomas, *A view of the civile and ecclesiastical law* (3rd edn 1662): 611, 615

Riga, Latvia (Sweden): 201

Riots/disorders/affrays: 98, 157, 275, 372, 409, 550, 704–5, 772, 778, 791–2, 893–6 passim, 1021; P fears for EP's safety: 1018

Robartes, John Robartes, 2nd Baron [1st Earl of Radnor 1679], Lord Privy Seal 1661–73: 152&n., 164, 168; criticised: 360; political influence: 854, 982

Robbery/burglary/street crime: 103, 225, 320, 669–70, 801–2, 939; P/EP victims: 146, 255, 310; P fears: 201, 225, 396, 399, 404, 432, 466, 531, 671, 704, 705, 724, 850, 856, 902; police measures against: 308, 691, 856, 896

Robert, Prince *see* Rupert

Robinson, Ald. Sir John, 1st Bt, M.P.; Lieutenant of the Tower 1660–79: 122, 202, 261, 313, 358–9, 440, 647, 659, 800, 977; P's contempt for: 263–4, 342, 554, 581, 766, 795; wife: 358, 551

Rochell [La Rochelle]: 622

Rochester, John Warner, Bishop of: 84; *see also* Dolben

Rochester, John Wilmot, 2nd Earl of, courtier and poet: 492, 693, 969

Rochester, Kent: 539, 630; P visits: 126, 534, 537–8

Roder [Rothe], Johannes, Kt 1660 for services to Charles II in exile; millenarian evangelist: 62

Rolls Chapel *see* Chancery

Rolt, Capt. Edward, Cromwellian soldier; Gentleman of the Bedchamber to the Lord Protector: 141, 560, 568, 718, 902, 912, 919, 920, 944

Roman Catholics: excluded from office/ penal laws: 290, 687, 712, 885; prominent in Tangier: 241; Duke of York's friendship towards: 120; blamed for disasters: 688, 789, 792; services: 225, 355, 603, 605, 606–7, 741, 856; religious: 605, 717, 741; Petrine claims refuted in (Anglican) sermon: 10

Rome: 511; buildings of Pope Alexander VII: 716; music: 716, 723; P buys views of: 608, 1004; his Spanish guidebook: Girolamo Franzini, *Las cosas maravillosas della sancta ciudad de Roma* (1651): 14

Rosinus, Johannes, *Antiquitatum romanorum* (1583): 78

Rosamond [Clifford], mistress of Henry II (d.? 1176): 370

Rota Club: 5&n., 6, 7, 8, 19

Rotyer [Roettier], John, medallist, chief engraver to the Mint 1661–98: 262; Breda medal: 732

'Roxalana': Hester Davenport, actress (Duke's Company), known by name of her part in Davenant's *Siege of Rhodes*: 196, 238

Royal Africa Company (est. under Elizabeth I; new charters 1662, 1672; its premises at this time African House, off Broad St): 83, 334, 342, 353, 434

Royal Exchange, the ('the Change', 'Exchange', 'Old Exchange'), Threadneedle St/Cornhill (opened 1571, the first bourse in England, owned by City Corporation and Mercers' Company; rebuilt after Fire by Edward Jerman): cartoon hung: 14; statue of Charles I: 29, 32; war proclaimed: 474; empty during Plague: 505, 515–16, 519, 526, 543; fills up again: 546; destroyed in Fire: 665–6; removed to Gresham College 668; rebuilding: 702, 706, 945; P becomes well known at: 207; official business: 185, 326, 417, 418, 420, 480; private affairs: 190, 452; P/EP shop at: 97, 252, 304, 402, 480, 490, 497

Royal Fishery *see* Fishery

Royal Society, the (the club of 'virtuosi', receiving royal charters 1662, 1663; premises at Gresham College until 1666, thereafter Arundel House: vacates London during Plague: 575, 588;

1083

# Index

# Index

# Index

walks: 219, 724; damaged in Fire: 667
Temple Bar: 493
Templer, Benjamin, Rector of Ashley,
Northants.: 177
Teviot, Andrew Rutherford, 1st Baron,
1st Earl of 1663; Roman Catholic
soldier, Governor of Tangier 1663–4;
appointment: 241, 254; accounts/plans
for mole: 311, 390; beats off attack: 295;
killed in action: 390, 390–1, 396; praised:
392; criticised: 464
Texel, island/channel, Netherlands: 489,
495, 536
Thames, River: floods: 30, 30–1, 329, 569;
frozen: 563; fatalities: 188, 731; tides:
396&n., 530, 653; storm: 575–6; P's
boatman loses way: 533–4; boat race:
134
*The adventures of five houres*: see Tuke
*The Alchymist*: see Jonson
Theatre: among P's greatest pleasures: 862;
(for his abstention from see Vows);
recalls acting as a boy: 919; views on
tragedy: 76, 77, 249; opera planned: 722;
improvements since Charles I's time:
723&n.; public performances prohibited
during Commonwealth: 109n.; P sees
women on stage for first time: 108; all-
female cast: 430; lower orders in good
seats: 112, 839; P dislikes crowds: 249;
spat on by pretty lady: 114; theatres
closed in Lent: 186, 361, 735; re-open
after Plague: 700; audiences down after
Fire: 722; P fears to be seen: 700, 776,
899; overcrowding: 756, 776, 819, 834,
847, 912, 971; hailstorm: 390; cold: 707,
756; full of M.P.'s: 846; orange girl:
cheats P: 908; revives choked patron:
846; P slips out to sup: 912; eyes strained
by candlelight: 1019; actors: vain: 120;
bad: 182, 238; hissed: 144; forget lines:
410; mere 'puppets': 819–20; good:
856–7, 859; costume: 362–3, 600, 707,
908, 971; King's House: at Vere St: 96;
moves to Drury Lane: 272; P goes
backstage: 600; Duke's House: at
Salisbury Court: 163; moves to Lincoln's
Inn Fields: 143–4, 182; Whitehall: poor
acoustics: 684; King/court attend: 129,
143, 238, 684, 819, 847, 895, 905, 912;
King kept waiting: 707; his interest in
theatre: 707
*The Bondman*: by Philip Massinger: 122,
123, 163, 410; (publ. 1638): 136, 687
*The Cardinall*: see Shirley
*The Catholique apology*: see Castlemaine
*The Changeling*: by Thomas Middleton and
William Rowley: 120
*The Citty Match*: see Mayne
*The coffee house [Tarugo's Wiles, or]*: by Sir
Thomas St Serfe: 834, 841

*The Committee*: see Howard, Sir R.
*The Country Captain*: see Newcastle
*The Custome of the Country*: see Fletcher
*The Discontented Colonell*: see Suckling
*The Duke of Lerma*: see Howard, Sir R.
*The Duchesse of Malfy*: see Webster
*The fruitlesse precaution*: by Paul Scarron
(trs. 1657): 87
*The Generall*: see Orrery
*The Goblins*: see Suckling
*The Gratefull Servant*: see Shirley
*The Heyresse*: see Newcastle
*The Humorous (Humorsome) Lieutenant*: see
Fletcher
*The Indian Queen(e)*: see Dryden
*The Island princesse*: see Fletcher
*The jovial crew, or The merry beggars*: by
Richard Brome: 150, 978
*The lost lady*: by Sir William Berkeley: 112,
114
*The Mad Couple [All Mistaken, or]*: by
James Howard: 856, 936
*The Mayden Queene*: see Dryden
*The Mayd in the mill*: see Fletcher
*The Mayds Tragedy*: see Beaumont and
Fletcher
*The Moore of Venice*: see Shakespeare
*The Mulbery Garden*: see Sedley
*The parson's dreame* [recte *wedding*]: see
Killigrew, T.
*The Rivall Ladys*: see Dryden
*The Rivalls*: see Fletcher
*The Roman Virgin*: see Webster
Thesaurus [Tesauro], Emanuele,
*Patriarchae, Sive Christi servatoris
genealogia* (1657): 114
*The Scornfull Lady*: see Beaumont and
Fletcher
*The Sea Voyage*: see Fletcher
*The Siege of Rhodes*: see Davenant
*The Silent Woman*: see Jonson
*The Spanish Curate*: see Fletcher
*The Sullen lovers*: see Shadwell
*The Surprizall*: see Howard, Sir R.
*The tamer tamed*: see Fletcher
*The Traytor*: see Shirley
*The Usurper*: see Howard, Edward
*The Valiant Cidd*: see Corneille
*The Villaine*: see Porter, T.
*The Wildgoose chase*: see Fletcher
*Third Advice to a paynter*: MS.,? by Andrew
Marvell (1667): 715
Thomson, Col. George, M.P., Admiralty
and Navy Commissioner during the
Commonwealth; on Brooke House
Committee 1668: 854, 932; brother Sir
William, M.P.: 677
Thornborough (Thornbury), Gilbert,
Gentleman of the Wine Cellar: 132;
?wife and sisters: 158
Thurloe, John, Secretary of State during

1090

# Index

Commonweath: 310

Tibalds [Theobalds] Palace, Cheshunt, Herts.: 918

Tiburne [Tyburn], gallows: 115

Tiviott *see* Teviot

Tobacco: grown illegally: 829; taken by naval commanders: 550; by P, against Plague: 494; given to horse: 820-1

Tomkins, Sir Thomas, M.P. Weobley, Herefs.: 811

Tomson, ?Richard, printseller: 564

Tooker, Frances, Greenwich: 540, 546, 547, 557, 559, 569, 600, 753

Tooker, John, River Agent to the Navy Board: 396, 480, 539, 567, 581, 801; ?widow: 1001

Tower of London: Dunkirk money stored in: 236; salutes from: 322, 653; P visits: chapel: 358; Crown Jewels: 902; menagerie: 193; to dine with Lieutenant, Sir J. Robinson (q.v.): 358, 440; to view Fire: 659; to visit Coventry: 994, 995, 996, 997, 999

Townshend, Thomas, Joint-Clerk of the Great Wardrobe and deputy to Sandwich: 120, 138, 416, 826, 857; social: 58, 89, 147, 154, 195, 244; dresses absent-mindedly: 126

Treasury, Commissioners of the (1667): appointment: 768, 775-6, 778, 782, 848-9, 914, 996-7; P's business with: (Navy): 848, 863, 883, 940, 944, 1012; (Tangier): 781, 783; (Sandwich's embassy): 833

Trelawny, Sir Jonathan, Comptroller to the Duke of York 1668-74: 994

Treswell, Col. Daniel, Surveyor-General of Woods south of Trent: 172

Trevor, Sir John (Kt 1668), Secretary of State 1668-72: 944, 1010

Trice, Thomas, lawyer, Brampton, stepson of Robert P: dispute over inheritance: 144&n., 145-6, 153, 166, 278; agreement: 453; also: 432, 433

Trinity House, Deptford (originally a seamen's guild; from 1514 a corporation responsible for pilotage, navigation and (from 1566) lights; re-established 1660): business: almshouse: 375; dock: 175, 179; lighthouses: 439; ships lost: 712, 799; buildings in Water Lane destroyed in the Fire: 664; P sworn younger brother: 179; attends feasts: 232, 587; ordinary dinners: 175, 202, 369, 430, 469; elections: 198, 287, 491, 554, 782, 912

Tripoli, peace with (1662): 236, 238

Troutbeck, John, Surgeon to the King from 1660: 687

Trump [Tromp], Adm. Martin Harpertszoon van (d. 1653): 46

Trump [Tromp], Cornelis van, Dutch naval commander: falsely reported killed: 495

Tuke, Sir Samuel, dramatist: 988; his *The adventures of five hours*: 251, (publ. 1663): 653, 655

Tunbridge Wells, Kent, (then becoming fashionable): 303

Tunis, peace with: 236, 238

Turberville, Dr Daubigny, leading oculist of the day: 931, 932

Turenne (Turin), Henri de la Tour d'Auvergne, Vicomte, Marshal of France: 972

Turkey/Turks *see* Algiers; Ottoman Empire; Tangier; Tunis; history: *see* Rycaut

Turkey Company *see* Levant

Turlington, John, spectacle maker, Cornhill: 842

Turner, Jane ('Madam Turner'), P's cousin: 12, 13, 121, 125, 126, 127, 187, 266, 345-6, 363-8 passim, 371, 379, 698, 958, 1013; P's valentine: 988; attends stone feast: 32, 998; husband John, Recorder of York 1662-85: 115, 698, 988; daughters: Betty: 992-3, 997, 1007, 1010, 1015; Theophila ('The'): 2, 12, 80, 121, 125, 187, 266, 364, 366, 371, 379, 488, 769, 772, 787, 958, 980, 985, 992, 997, 1003, 1006, 1013

Turner [Turnour], Sir Edward, Speaker of the House of Commons 1661-73: 298, 342

Turner, John, chaplain to Sandwich and Rector of Eynesbury, Hunts.: 144, ?357

Turner, Thomas, Clerk-General of the Navy Office c. 1646-60; Purveyor of Petty Provisions 1660-8; clerk to the Comptroller 1661-8; Storekeeper, Deptford 1668-?80: hopes for Clerkship of the Acts: 57, 59; business: 73, 123, 178, 201, 341; official lodgings: 87, 205, 293; political views: 775; lends P naval MSS: 215, 373; social: 175, 664, 711, 820, 829, 899, 929; wife: 293, 581, 582, 664, 757, 774, 779, 809, 868, 888, 899, 911, 929; daughter Betty: 820, 861, 895, 900, 916, 929-30, 943; tours with P/EP: 923-6 passim; her sparrow: 922

Turner, Ald. Sir William, draper, Lord Mayor 1668-9; brother-in-law of Jane (q.v.): 772, 787, 857, 932

Turnham Green, Mdx: 1021

Tuscany, Cosimo III (de'Medici), Grand Duke of: 1006, 1010, 1022

Twelfth Night: customs: 4, 109, 460, 861-2; P finds Shakespeare's play irrelevant: 250

Twickenham (Twittenham), Mdx, School: 643

1091